Principles of Conservation Biology

Second Edition

Principles of Conservation Biology

Second Edition

Gary K. Meffe
Department of Wildlife Ecology and Conservation,
University of Florida

C. Ronald Carroll
Institute of Ecology, University of Georgia

and Contributors

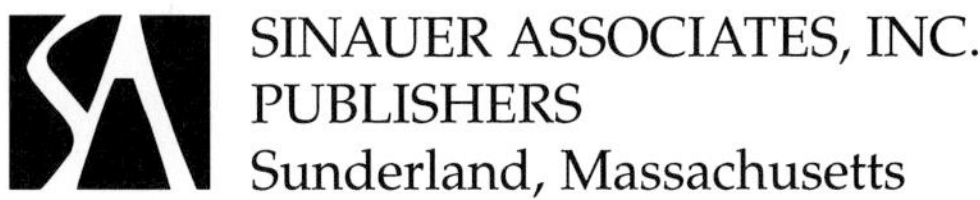
SINAUER ASSOCIATES, INC.
PUBLISHERS
Sunderland, Massachusetts

THE COVER
An undeveloped expanse of the Gulf Coast of Florida, U.S.A. This area, a mixture of freshwater, terrestrial, and marine systems, is representative of large, coastal landscapes where ecosystem management is being implemented on broad temporal and spatial scales. Coastal areas such as the Florida Everglades and the Chesapeake Bay are heavily influenced by human activities and are a focus of new ecosystem management approaches that seek to protect and restore the ecological composition, structure, and function of these complex systems while satisfying human demands for resources. Note the naturally heterogeneous, fragmented, and dynamic (i.e., tidally influenced) nature of this landscape. Photograph © Stephen Krasemann/Tony Stone Images.

PRINCIPLES OF CONSERVATION BIOLOGY, SECOND EDITION
 For information or to order, address: Sinauer Associates, Inc., P. O. Box 407, Sunderland, Massachusetts, 01375-0407, U.S.A. FAX: 413-549-1118.
Internet: publish@sinauer.com; http://www.sinauer.com

Library of Congress Cataloging-in-Publication Data
Meffe, Gary K.
Principles of conservation biology / Gary K. Meffe, C. Ronald Carroll and contributors. —2nd ed.
p. cm.
Includes bibliographical references (p.) and index.
ISBN 0-87893-521-5 (hardcover)
1. Conservation biology. I. Carroll, C. Ronald (Carl Ronald), 1941- . II. Title.
QH75.M386 1997
333.95'16—dc21 97–8018
CIP

 Printed in U.S.A. on recycled paper, 50% pre-consumer/10% post-consumer waste.

6 5

To the students of conservation biology, in whose collective hands the future of biodiversity rests, and to the pioneers of the field, upon whose shoulders we stand.

Contents in Brief

Contents

12. Management to Meet Conservation Goals: Applications 385

C. Ronald Carroll and Gary K. Meffe

13. Conservation Management Case Studies 419

Contributing Chapter Authors

J. Baird Callicott, Department of Philosophy and Religion Studies, University of North Texas

Tim W. Clark, School of Forestry and Environmental Studies, Yale University, and Northern Rockies Conservation Cooperative

Blair Csuti, College of Forestry, University of Idaho

John B. Dunning, Department of Forestry and Natural Resources, Purdue University

James A. MacMahon, College of Science, Utah State University

Norman Myers, Meadlington, Oxford, Great Britain

Richard B. Norgaard, Energy and Resources Group, University of California, Berkeley

Reed F. Noss, Corvallis, Oregon

Gordon H. Orians, Department of Zoology, University of Washington

Stuart L. Pimm, Department of Zoology, University of Tennessee, Knoxville

H. Ronald Pulliam, Institute of Ecology, University of Georgia

Stephen Viederman, Jesse Smith Noyes Foundation, New York

Preface to the Second Edition

Conservation biology is a dynamic and rapidly developing discipline. Since publication of the first edition in 1994, the field of conservation biology has become more involved in complex environmental policy issues, and ecosystem management has become a central focus. There has been a continuing infusion of sociology, economics, policy sciences, and other humanistic disciplines, which has bolstered and expanded the field. In writing *Principles of Conservation Biology*, our aim was to provide students and practitioners with as broad and diverse a "snapshot" of the field as any textbook could hope to convey. By all accounts, the first edition was a success. It was praised in critical reviews and we received many positive comments from students and faculty, as well as from practitioners in various natural resource management agencies. To build on the first edition's success, we sought to follow the physician's maxim: "first, do no harm." Thus, we retained the basic structure and approach of that effort while updating material and enhancing coverage throughout.

We made several major modifications for this edition. First, the two management chapters now focus on ecosystem management—a topic that was just emerging as we wrote the first edition. In fact, ecosystem management serves as the unofficial theme of this book: we feel that its broad-scale and inclusive approach toward a healthy human–land relationship is our best hope for a liveable planet. Second, we added a new chapter on becoming more practical and effective in the policy process. This chapter discusses the challenges of and possibilities for transposing conservation biologists' scientific information into useful social policy. Third, some two dozen new essays and several new case studies were added (and others removed) to continue to provide fresh, relevant perspectives. These viewpoints from "front-line" practitioners help to bring the field alive and illustrate the many frustrations, successes, and failures that are inherent in the field (for, as always, conservation biology is not for the faint-hearted). Finally, we have increased coverage of the marine environment. Although marine systems collectively represent more than 70% of the earth's surface, they remain badly underrepresented in the conservation literature.

As before, we and our publisher will donate one-third of our royalties to three prominent conservation organizations. We expressed hope in the first edition that this would become the norm for conservation publishing, and we have been gratified to see several of our colleagues make similar arrangements. We have always found this field to be disproportionately populated by good and decent people, and that is perhaps the greatest stimulus for us to forge ahead in difficult times. We thank these colleagues and friends for their integrity and generosity.

Acknowledgments

No book is completed without the support and assistance of many, and we had more than our share of both. First, our respective institutions continue to make it possible for us to pursue such time-consuming work. Second, we wish to again thank the many people who assisted with and are listed in the first edition acknowledgments; their efforts continue to be appreciated and are evidenced in the second edition. Third, we gratefully acknowledge the extraordinary people at Sinauer Associates who once again made publishing a delight. Andy Sinauer, Maggie Haddad, Christopher Small, Carole Cotten, Marie Scavotto, Dean Scudder, and others behind the scenes continue to practice their craft with admirable skill and the highest degree of professionalism. Norma Roche's copyediting skills are unparalleled, and we appreciate her many biological as well as editorial insights. Project Editor Kerry Falvey put her entire heart and soul into this book and probably deserves coauthorship. Her care for detail and her precision improved the final product in immeasurable ways. Finally, former California Fish and Game biologist Phil Pister continues to inspire multiple generations by showing that it is possible to retain one's principles within largely unsupportive bureaucracies and make significant contributions to posterity. His example is to be emulated.

G.K.M.: Several people, institutions, and events influenced my present understanding of and appreciation for the developing field of ecosystem management. The U.S. Fish and Wildlife Service's National Conservation Training Center developed a training course for ecosystem management, of which I am honored to be a part, and I am deeply indebted to my co-instructors—Richard L. Knight, Larry A. Nielsen, and Dennis A. Schenborn—for sharing their wisdom, expertise, and friendship, and to June McIlwain, course leader, for bringing and keeping us together. Discussions with C. S. Holling and Rebecca R. Sharitz helped to mold my understanding of ecosystem management, as did my work on a conservation handbook for the U.S. Department of Defense; I thank my co-authors, Michele Leslie and Jeffrey L. Hardesty of The Nature Conservancy, for sharing their expertise and practical experiences. My past and present interactions with the U.S. Forest Service, U.S. Bureau of Land Management, and National Park Service continue to hone my perceptions of natural resource management in a complex world. My parents, Mary and the late Edward Meffe, provided the moral foundation of values, fairness, and simple decency that must be at the center of true conservation; there is no greater gift. Most importantly, neither this edition nor its predecessor would have been completed were it not for the efforts of my wife, advisor, and best friend, Nancy Meffe. She continues to challenge me to greater professional heights, deeper personal satisfaction, and inner peace in a turbulent world, for all of which I am forever indebted.

C.R.C.: I want to express my admiration and deep respect for the many small, grass roots conservation organizations that are playing powerful roles despite being chronically underfunded and overworked. They are truly "keystone organizations." To the growing millions of individuals, in rich and poor countries, who live their commitment to good environmental stewardship, I can only say that future generations will owe them a great deal. At a personal level, I want to thank my mentor, Dan Janzen, for helping me recognize the important parts of ecology and evolution and for showing all of us how academics can use their talents to conserve biodiversity in the "real world." At an even more personal level, I want to express my great gratitude to my wife, Carol Hoffman, both for her support and for her knack of asking the most insightful questions; to my children for revealing their wonderous view of nature; and to my parents for encouraging me to explore and for indulging my interests in very noncharismatic species.

March, 1997

Preface to the First Edition

The field of conservation biology is a new, rapidly growing, and swiftly changing endeavor, a product of the calamitous decline of biodiversity formally recognized by the scientific community in the 1970s. The field grew in the 1980s from an amalgam of disciplines but until the fall of 1993 no textbook existed to guide its new practitioners. This is the second textbook in the field, and the first at a more advanced level.

The two primary authors initially undertook this project several years ago on their own, but soon realized that two people cannot comprehensively and fairly represent the broad interests of conservation biology without input from others. If conservation biology is the study and protection of biological diversity, then diversity in its presentation is surely appropriate. Thus, after a period of retrenchment, the project moved forward with a new concept: to recruit the best minds available in the field to strengthen certain topics and provide insight in areas for which we lacked expertise. In addition to recruiting authors for nine chapters (see the Brief Contents that precedes this Preface), we also invited a number of individuals to provide 11 case studies based on their experiences in conservation, and we asked more than 50 people to write essays on pertinent topics. If there is strength in diversity, then you have it in front of you.

The book proceeds in four parts. Part I introduces the philosophical, ethical, and biological framework upon which all conservation must be built. A strong ethical standard is a prerequisite for success in any venture, and lack of ethical direction is a root cause of many of the problems we face in conservation today. We paraphrase conservation biologist and ethicist Phil Pister, who has said that training people in any field without also providing an ethical foundation is like launching missiles without guidance systems. They will certainly take off and do *something,* but we really do not know what. The discussion on ethics is followed by an exploration of definitions and roles of species and populations in conservation, which also has strong bearing on legal aspects of protection. Part I finishes with two chapters that define biodiversity and its local and global patterns, causes, and dynamics, and focuses on patterns and causes of biodiversity losses.

Part II presents two chapters on the population level. First, the genetic basis of conservation is examined, including discussion of the importance and losses of genetic diversity, and management approaches to its conservation. We then discuss demographic processes of populations, emphasizing mechanisms of population regulation, dynamics of populations, and the importance of linking the population and landscape levels in conservation.

Part III focuses on system-wide issues. The implications of species interactions and community influences on conservation are discussed by examining the keystone species concept, mutualistic interactions, and the effects of invasive species on communities. We then move to a dominant global problem in conservation, habitat fragmentation, exploring various concepts of fragmentation and its effects on biota. This sets the stage for a discussion of the design of nature reserves, a major challenge in conservation biology.

The eight chapters in Part IV build on the foundation of the previous parts, and address practical applications and human concerns in conservation. First, two chapters on the theory and practice of management ask why management is necessary, explain different types and levels of management, and discuss management priorities and external threats to management plans. This is followed by a series of management case studies written by individuals experienced in management issues ranging from working with endangered species to managing conservation units. We then explore one particular management approach, habitat restoration and mitigation of habitat loss. Although it is not a substitute for protection of natural areas, restoration ecology can potentially reclaim some degraded and destroyed areas and make them ecologically valuable again. Conservation biology is then melded with economics and politics in the next chapter. If the political and economic arenas are not modified to recognize long-term problems associated with biodiversity losses and global environmental change, then even the best biological knowledge will have little effect.

One of the greatest potentials for progress in conservation is within the political and economic realms. The way this can happen is to understand how policy is developed and how science influences that process. The next chapter deals with these topics, setting the groundwork for a series of case studies on sustainable development by people who have been in the thick of such projects. Sustainable development is considered by many to be the best hope for both conservation of biodiversity and a reasonable standard of living for much of the world. Others fear it is an excuse for continued global exploitation. Finally, we look at future prospects and directions of conservation biology, and address some of the most pressing problems and possible solutions.

We emphasize that this book is incomplete, in the sense that no single work can possibly cover all relevant aspects of conservation biology. The field is nearly limitless in scope, and the serious student must pursue literature far beyond the materials covered here. In particular, we highly recommend regular reading of the journal *Conservation Biology* for cutting-edge reports in the field. Conservation biology literature is growing rapidly, and numerous outstanding works are available; many of these are listed at the ends of each chapter, as suggestions for further reading. Each chapter also includes a series of discussion questions, which we hope will be the basis for a participatory classroom exercise. Many of the questions have no easy answer, but reflect real world problems that conservation biologists must grapple with daily. It is never too soon to be exposed to these practical and difficult issues.

We encourage teachers and students alike to respond with comments that might improve future editions of the text. You are the users of this material, and you must tell us what you like and dislike about it.

Finally, a message about *commitment.* Conservation requires more than good intentions, scientific insight, and wishful thinking: it requires money. Consequently, one-third of royalties from this textbook will be donated by the authors and the publisher to two major conservation organizations plus the Organization for Tropical Studies, in hopes of turning student book costs into actual conservation gains. We challenge other authors and publishers in ecological and conservation fields to also give something back to the systems about which they write. It will make a tangible difference if that commitment becomes the norm of conservation publishing.

1994

I

Introductory Concepts

1

What Is Conservation Biology?

When the last individual of a race of living things breathes no more, another heaven and another earth must pass before such a one can be again.

William Beebe

Environmental Problems and Human Population Growth

The natural world is a far different place now than it was 10,000 years ago, or even 100 years ago. Every natural ecosystem on the planet has been altered by humanity, some to the point of collapse. Vast numbers of species have gone prematurely extinct, natural hydrologic and chemical cycles have been disrupted, billions of tons of topsoil have been lost, genetic diversity has eroded, and the very climate of the planet may have been disrupted. What is the cause of such vast environmental change? Very simply, the cumulative effects of 5.7 billion people (Figure 1.1), a number growing by 95 million each year (260,000 per day), have stressed the many ecological support systems of the planet, possibly beyond their powers of resilience. As a consequence, biological diversity (**biodiversity**, for short), the grand result of evolutionary processes and events tracing back several billion years, is itself at stake and rapidly declining. One of the many species suffering the consequences of ecological destruction is *Homo sapiens*, the perpetrator of it all.

The seeming inevitability of human population growth outstripping our planet's resources can easily lead to a feeling of helplessness and apathy in the face of so much destruction. However, there are three points that should provide reason for optimism. First, some countries have significantly lowered their population growth rates, and have done so in a short period of time. Examples include Costa Rica, Cuba, Mexico, Venezuela, and Thailand. Some, such as Hungary and West Germany, have even had periods of negative growth in the past few decades.

Second, the destruction of biodiversity today is due not so much to numbers of people per se, but to where they live and what they consume. In developing countries the expansion of highly commercialized agriculture and forestry has displaced the rural poor into city slums or onto steep hillsides and other ecologically fragile areas. In the industrialized world, the wealthy con-

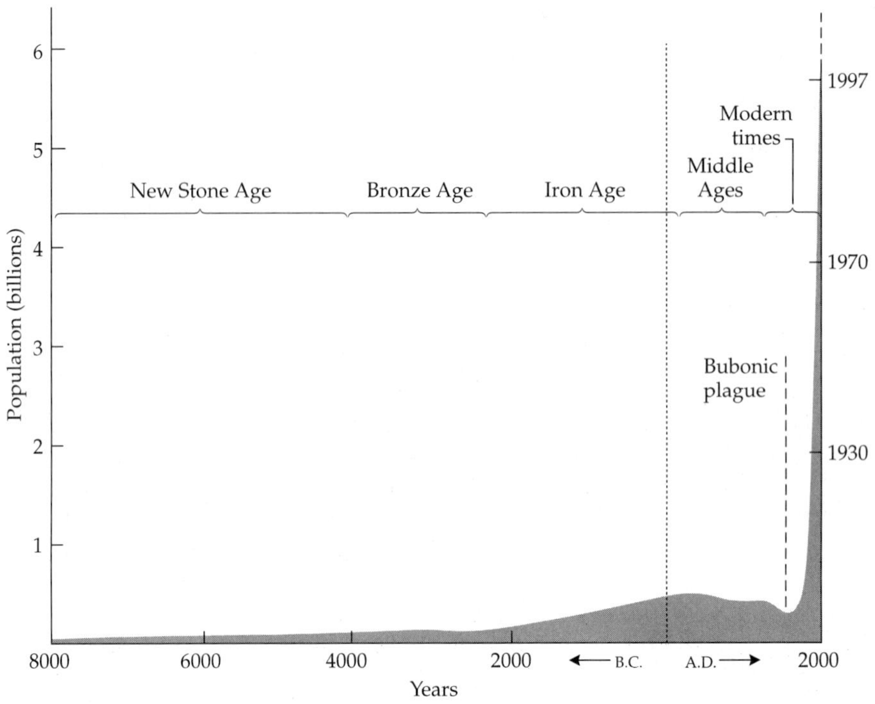

Figure 1.1 Estimated global human population size from the last Ice Age to the present, illustrating the exponential nature of human population growth since the Industrial Revolution. Note that the human population took hundreds of thousands of years to reach 2 billion, but then more than doubled in 40 years. (Modified from various sources.)

sume a disproportionate share of the global resources. These patterns are reversible.

Third—and this is the key—birth rates are high where family survival depends on being successful in an unskilled and uneducated labor pool; that is, where there are strong economic incentives for large families. The corollary is that education and the appropriate kinds of economic development can greatly reduce population growth rates.

The many ways that human population growth rates can be humanely reduced have several features in common: gender equity, access to education, equitable distribution of rural income, and rural economies based on something other than simple exploitation of natural resources. The take-home message is that we must think broadly about conservation. The **stewardship** of natural biodiversity requires that a strong link be forged between conservation biology and environmentally **sustainable development**.

The field of **conservation biology** is a response by the scientific community to the biodiversity crisis. It is a new, synthetic field that applies the principles of ecology, biogeography, population genetics, economics, sociology, anthropology, philosophy, and other theoretically based disciplines to the maintenance of biological diversity throughout the world. It is new in that it is a product of the 1980s, although its roots go back centuries. It is synthetic in that it unites traditionally academic disciplines such as population biology and genetics with the applied traditions of game and forest management and allied fields. It is most of all challenging and imperative, in that it is motivated by human-caused global changes that have resulted in the greatest episode of mass extinction since the loss of the dinosaurs, 65 million years ago.

Environmentally, we are at the most critical point in the history of humanity, and the current population of students and professionals has a unique place in that history: of the hundreds of thousands of human generations that ever existed, no previous generation has had to respond to possible annihilation by humans of a large percentage of the species diversity on the planet.

Unless humanity acts quickly and in a significant way, the next generation will not have this opportunity. We are "it," and conservation biology is, in every sense of the word, a "crisis discipline" (Soulé 1985, and discussed below). One of the major developments needed in conservation is a shift from a reactive analysis of each crisis to a proactive science that permits us to anticipate developing crises and to prepare scientifically grounded contingency plans.

Many would ask, "What's so new about conservation biology? People have been doing conservation for decades, even centuries." This is true, but the "new" conservation biology differs in at least three ways. First, it now includes, and has been partially led by, major contributions from theoretically oriented academicians, whose ecological and genetic models are being applied to real-world situations. The unfortunate and false dichotomy of "pure" and "applied" research is finally breaking down, as the academic researcher and the resource manager have joined intellects, professional experience, and perspectives to address local to global conservation problems.

Second, much of traditional conservation was rooted in an economic, **utilitarian** philosophy whose primary motivation was to maintain high yields of selected species for harvest. Nature was seen as providing benefits to people, mostly from Western nations, through highly visible, selected components such as deer, trout, minerals, or timber, and was managed for maximization of a single or a few species, a small subset of the huge diversity of nature. The "new" conservation biology views all of nature's diversity as important and having inherent value. With this perspective, management has been redirected toward stewardship of the world's biodiversity and natural ecosystems, rather than toward single species. Four detailed perspectives on the "new" conservation biology are offered in essays in this chapter from academic (Stanley A. Temple), government agency (Hal Salwasser), nongovernmental organization, or NGO (Kathryn S. Fuller), and private landowner (Bill McDonald) viewpoints.

ESSAY 1A

An Academic Perspective

The Role of the University in Conservation Biology

Stanley A. Temple, University of Wisconsin

Conservation biology was largely conceived in academia, and academic scientists have continued to play a major role in guiding its development. The generally recognized vision for conservation biology features at least four characteristics that have encouraged an academic bias: a focus on biological diversity, an expectation of scientific rigor, a focus on multidisciplinary and interdisciplinary approaches, and innovative practical measures for dealing with the biodiversity crisis. Because conservation biology focuses on understanding and conserving biodiversity, rather than on selected utilitarian species, academic prevalence in the field seems inevitable. The scope of biodiversity topics is so broad that no other institution outside of academia encompasses a wide enough range of specialists to cover the territory. Only in universities does one find such a broad array of geneticists, population biologists, ecologists, social scientists, philosophers, resource economists, and other disciplinarians who share an interest in and concern for biodiversity.

In contrast, government conservation agencies and private conservation groups tend to harbor a narrower range of specialists among their ranks, and the collective diversity of their interests may be too limited to provide expertise in all aspects of conservation biology. Conservation agencies have typically targeted specific categories of biological resources for attention (forests, fisheries, wildlife, rangeland) rather than biodiversity. Even the network of subjects that these government bureaus collectively cover leaves enormous gaps because they may provide minimal attention to elements of the biota that are "non-resources." Conservation organizations also specialize, though recently some have expanded their missions to encompass biodiversity. Still, their collective staffs are far smaller and more narrowly focused than academic departments.

Conservation biology has always regarded itself as a field in which the usual criteria of scientific rigor should be imposed. Search for new generalizations from theoretical models that explain widespread patterns, use of the scientific method to test hypotheses generated from these models, and publication of findings in peer-reviewed journals where they can be critically evaluated by the scientific community are important traits of academic science. The credibility that attends this approach has allowed conservation biologists to gain a general level of respect within the scientific community that previously had not been extended to many scientists who worked in conservation fields.

How rigorous has conservation biology proven to be? The report card is mixed. Although the field emerged with a body of useful theory already in hand (such as the equilibrium theory of island biogeography and its various manifestations), there have been few new theoretical contributions, in contrast to many tests and validations of existing models. This has led some scientists to question whether conservation biology, as a synthetic field, has actually generated any principles of its own or instead just borrows extensively from other disciplines.

Conservation biology aims to encourage collaborative work among specialists from many disciplines who share an interest in biodiversity. Ideally, these collaborations result in interdisciplinary problem-solving, and most recognized centers of excellence in conservation biology have tried to foster an interdisciplinary approach. An academic bias again results because universities are the home of many of the potential collaborating disciplines.

When incorporating conservation biology into the academic bureaucracy, most institutions have opted to create new administrative units in conservation biology rather than to introduce biodiversity as a conspicuous issue in many existing units. Because these units include individuals from a broad array of disciplines, one of the consequences of this approach will be a new generation of conservation biologists who are trained as broadly versed generalists, rather than as disciplinary specialists, who can think and work well in an interdisciplinary mode. This situation contrasts sharply with the training of the first generation of leaders in the field, who had no specific training in conservation biology but typically focused on a particular aspect of conservation. Although the next generation of conservation biologists may be well equipped to promote more interdisciplinary work, their educational backgrounds may also reduce the likelihood of new scientific breakthroughs.

Conservation biology stresses the importance of generating new scientifically sound approaches to solving the complex web of problems that have created the biodiversity crisis. Producing innovations is a central mission of university scientists, whereas applying such research is often the challenge for nonacademic scientists. Often self-described as a mission-oriented, crisis-driven group, conservation biologists in academia have a heavy responsibility to make their research applicable and to venture forth from the Ivory Tower environment and make their findings available to the decision makers and managers who will actually implement strategies for preserving biodiversity in the real world.

Relations between academics and practitioners can be awkward, and there were early hints of disharmony in conservation biology. The new breed of conservation scientists in academia was initially perceived by some in the conservation establishment as arrogant, out-of-touch, and unwilling to work cooperatively with practitioners. Whether justified or not, this initial reaction hampered progress, and there are still old-guard conservationists who are threatened by the ascendancy of conservation biology and remain antagonistic to it. There are also some academics who do remain arrogant and out of touch. This unfortunate divisiveness may be one of the most serious handicaps associated with conservation biology's academic roots, and one that all conservation biologists should try hard to dispel. Fortunately, the barriers are crumbling and their dissolution should be encouraged by all parties.

The urgent and lofty goals of conservation biology can be achieved only if all members of the conservation community work together on biodiversity issues. As a university scientist who has been closely involved with conservation biology, I have fluctuated between enthusiasm for, and concern over, the academic bias in the field. Despite occasional apprehension, I continue to believe that conservation biology's development and ongoing evolution have been well served by its academic roots. Working closely with colleagues in conservation agencies and organizations, academic scientists will continue to have a vital role to play in preserving biological diversity.

The "new" conservation biologist recognizes that diverse and functioning ecosystems are critical not only to maintenance of the few species we harvest, but also to perpetuation of the nearly limitless variety of life forms of which we know little or nothing. The conservationist realizes that intact and functioning ecosystems are also important as life-support systems for the planet, and are critical to our own continued survival and well-being as a species (Odum 1989; Daily 1997).

Third, conservation biology fully recognizes and embraces the contributions that need to be made by nonbiologists to conservation of biodiversity. In particular, the social sciences, economics, and political science may ultimately have more influence on real advances or losses in conservation than the biological sciences. Unless major changes can be made in the way that humanity does business with the natural world, and in humanity's destructive patterns of population growth and resource consumption, it would appear that much of our biological knowledge of conservation will be rendered useless under the sheer weight of the human presence.

A goal of conservation biology is to understand natural ecological systems well enough to maintain their diversity in the face of an exploding human population that has fragmented, simplified, homogenized, and destroyed many ecosystems to the point that contemporary species extinction rates are estimated to be 1000 to 10,000 times higher than the normal **background extinction rate** expected in the absence of human influences (Wilson 1989). Thus, conservation biology tries to provide the basis for intelligent and informed management of highly disrupted ecosystems.

In 1965, the ecologist G. Evelyn Hutchinson described the natural world as an "ecological theater" serving as a stage for an "evolutionary play." Perhaps no better metaphor sums up the mission of conservation biology: *to retain the actors in that evolutionary play and the ecological stage on which it is performed.* Conservation biology strives to maintain the diversity of genes, populations, species, habitats, ecosystems, and landscapes, and the processes normally carried out by them, such as natural selection, biogeochemical cycling, photosynthesis, energy transfer, and hydrologic cycles. It is a dynamic play, with players and action on many different spatial and temporal scales, with old actors disappearing and new ones arriving. But the play ultimately comes down to one thing: dynamic evolutionary processes in a changing ecological background. Conservation biology attempts to keep those normal evolutionary processes working within a functioning ecological setting.

A Brief History of Conservation Biology

The global effort to conserve and protect the natural environment is a recent phenomenon, though efforts to conserve economically important natural resources have a long history. Although we may think of environmental destruction as a product of recent times—and certainly the scale of contemporary destruction is unprecedented—significant environmental degradation has always accompanied humankind. Humans may have been responsible for the extinction of most of the large mammal fauna of North America, which occurred shortly after human colonization from Asia about 11,000 years ago (Martin and Klein 1984). According to what has been termed the "blitzkrieg" hypothesis (Martin 1973), mastodons, camels, tapirs, glyptodonts, giant ground sloths, and many other species may have been hunted to extinction shortly after human colonization of the continent.

In the classical Greek period, Aristotle commented on the widespread destruction of forests in the Baltic region. At the same time in southern Asia, forests were felled to meet the growing need for timber to build trading ships to serve expanding mercantile centers such as Constantinople (now Istanbul). The barren landscapes that we associate with much of Turkey, Syria, Iraq, and Iran are unnatural deserts resulting from massive exploitation of fragile woodlands. Indeed, this part of Asia had been known in earlier times as the "land of perpetual shade." The Mediterranean region of Italy and Greece was likewise heavily wooded before human settlement.

Diamond (1992) argues that virtually wherever humans have settled, environmental destruction has been the rule; he and others (e.g., Redford 1992) largely debunk the notion of the "noble savage," primitive but wise peoples who had great concern for natural resources. Many, if not most, societies have had some lasting, destructive impact on the natural world. However, some societies have certainly minimized their environmental influences and lived in a more sustainable fashion than most.

In the humid tropics, early agrarian societies dealt with declining resources by moving when yields began to drop and local game became scarce, an option no longer available in today's crowded world. Some of these shifting cultivators practiced, and some still practice, forms of conservation management. In many tropical regions, complex tree gardens helped stabilize land use

Figure 1.2 Highly diverse agro forestry systems, such as the Dammar system from Indonesia, can be found in many tropical regions. This photograph shows a similar agroforestry system from southeastern Mexico. It is known locally as a "huerto," or tree-garden. These traditional agroforestry systems of mixed, cultivated perennials may be structurally similar to old, second-growth natural forests and contain nearly as many tree species on a per-hectare basis. (Photograph by C. R. Carroll.)

(see Carroll 1990 for examples), and some shifting cultivators practiced a kind of management of natural succession. Today, in "Dammar" agroforestry in Sumatra, for example, natural forest plots are converted over a period of 10–20 years into complex modified forests based primarily on dammar (*Shorea javanica*), a tree that is tapped for resins, and other economically important native trees (Mary and Michon 1987). The plots are structurally similar to natural successional plots and probably help support regional biodiversity. Although we may think of conservation management as a modern Western notion, there are many such examples of management of natural resources to be found in other cultures (Figure 1.2).

We would be remiss if we failed to point out the fragility of these traditional systems in the modern, interconnected global marketplace. To continue with the Dammar example, the practice is disappearing for two unexpected reasons. First, the establishment of Burkit National Park appropriated a major portion of Dammar forestry land and put severe constraints on the use of the remaining land. In particular, the long fallow period needed became increasingly difficult to accommodate. Second, a growing urban market created great demand for rice and, to a lesser extent, coffee and cloves. In response to these two factors, Dammar agroforestry has been replaced largely by dryland rice and coffee cultivation.

In Europe, conservation efforts were mainly devoted to private game management and maintenance of royal preserves and private manor lands. Until the 18th and 19th centuries, little notice was given to problems of the **commons**, the public lands. As a consequence, exploitation of these common-use resources led to the deforestation of most of Europe by the early 18th century. This occurred even earlier in Great Britain, where many of the native forests were destroyed by the 12th century (McKibben 1989); the demand for charcoal to supply home heating and industrial needs led to virtual elimination of the remaining public forests by the late 18th century. Similarly, in Asia, conservation efforts were game-oriented and largely restricted to the private lands of the privileged. An artist's early rendition of a forest and pastoral scene in China, juxtaposed against a later photograph of the same place, which depicted an eroded and barren landscape, is said to have been the telling argument made to

President Theodore Roosevelt's administration by forester Gifford Pinchot in his successful campaign to establish the U.S. Forest Service in 1905.

Conservation in the United States

Conservation in the continental United States has had a somewhat unusual history. Europeans colonizing America found a landscape that, by comparison

ESSAY 1B

A Government Agency Perspective

Conservation Biology and the Management of Natural Resources

Hal Salwasser, University of Montana (formerly U.S. Forest Service)

In the closing decades of the 19th century, the concept of conservation was developed and promoted as an ethical relationship between people, land, and resources. It meant wise use of lands and resources so as not to destroy their capacity to serve future generations. Its champions were men such as William Hornaday, Theodore Roosevelt, George Bird Grinnell, and Gifford Pinchot. They were sportsmen, lovers of the outdoors, and political activists, the progressive thinkers of their time. The result of their zeal was the start of national conservation laws, government agencies to manage lands and resources in the public trust, and the great systems of national parks, forests, wildlife refuges, and public lands that now encompass about one-third of the land area of the United States.

The ideals of conservation can be traced back to Henry David Thoreau, George Perkins Marsh, and landscape artists of the mid-1800s. The philosophical roots go even further back to Native American beliefs and ancient cultures from other lands. What is significant about the period of the late 1800s in the United States is that the philosophy, ideals, and action to conserve natural resources came together in a set of government policies, public institutions, and social commitment.

Yet almost immediately, the conservation movement diverged along pragmatic utilitarian and romantic preservationist lines, a split in perspectives that to some extent continues to this day. Natural resource disciplines such as forestry, range management, wildlife management, and fisheries, along with their respective government agencies, arose from the utilitarian roots. Wilderness advocacy and its public agents arose from the preservationist roots. Eventually, The Nature Conservancy, a nongovernmental conservation organization, emerged from the scientific discipline of ecology. The field of endeavor now called Conservation Biology shares common roots with these contemporary resource disciplines and their government agencies. It also shares with them a wide array of aims and methods.

One example of the common roots and shared aims of conservation biology and natural resource management comes from the opening sentence of the first article in the first issue of the first volume of the *Journal of Wildlife Management*: "In the new field of conservation biology, few life history phenomena have occasioned more comment than the heavy percentages of nest failures for many species of birds thus far studied" (Errington and Hamerstrom 1937). The discipline described is now known as Wildlife Management. From the start it recognized conservation biology as its scientific basis. As an aside, nest failures of birds are still a perplexing subject of both old and new traditions in conservation biology.

Some 40 years after Errington and Hamerstrom published their article, a new discipline was forming under the title of Conservation Biology. It confused a lot of people in government agencies and academia who thought all along that they were conservation biologists. But there must have been a need or the new field would not have emerged. The need was to compensate for a weakness in applied conservation disciplines that focused most of their attention on the continued productivity of already common or productive plants and animals. Conservation Biology has its current focus on population viability of all native plant and animal species, many of them uncommon, and on biological diversity in general. Beyond counterbalancing the weakness in applied conservation disciplines, however, Conservation Biology has more in common with traditional conservation fields than it has differences with them.

For those intent on finding differences between the values and aims of Conservation Biology and Wildlife Management, a review of the preface in that 1937 issue of the *Journal of Wildlife Management* might be useful. The officers of The Wildlife Society stated their policy in unequivocal terms:

> Management along sound biological lines means management according to the needs and capacities of the animals concerned, as related to the environmental complex in which they are managed. It does not include the sacrifice of any species for the benefit of others, though it may entail the reduction of competing forms where research shows this is necessary. It consists largely of enrichment of environment so that there shall be maximum production of the entire wildlife complex adapted to the managed areas. Wildlife management is not restricted to game management, though game management is recognized as an important branch of wildlife management. It embraces the practical ecology of all vertebrates and their plant and animal associates. While emphasis may be placed on species of special economic importance, wildlife management along sound biological lines is also part of the greater movement for conservation of our entire native fauna and flora. (Bennitt et al. 1937)

This statement, if extended to fisheries, forestry, recreation, and range management, would put conservation biology squarely in a role as the foundation science for resource management and the agencies that carry it out.

While conservation biology is not entirely new, Conservation Biology is. As an organized discipline, it is about 15 years old. But still it is not exactly clear what role the discipline will play in resource management and government programs. These are the perspectives of one who had a hand in the birthing of Conservation Biology out of a need to implement federal policies to better protect biological diversity and out of a desire to obtain a broader set of concepts, theories, and methods than traditional conservation disciplines had provided.

First, let's retreat to the dictionary for some help. For most speakers of the English language, *conservation* means the care and protection of resources so as to prevent loss or waste. It includes actions that government agencies call preservation, restoration, enhancement, recycling, extending useful life, and sustained-yield management. *Biology* is the body of scientific knowledge and methods that deals with the origin, history, physical characteristics, life processes, and habits of plants and animals. Thus a "common-folks" definition for conservation biology would be the application of biology to the care and protection of plants and animals to prevent their loss or waste. This is a broad field for conservation biology, certainly broader than a focus on just the scarce elements of a flora and fauna.

This broad view of conservation biology is consistent with how I suspect Errington, Hamerstrom, and probably Aldo Leopold might have seen it: the basic biological sciences that underpin the applied conservation fields of forestry, wildlife management, fisheries, nature protection, and so on. These basic sciences would include genetics, physiology, population biology, natural history, and ecology. Because conservation entails more than biology, other sciences or disciplines are necessary complements to Conservation Biology, such as economics, geography, history, sociology, and philosophy.

The issue now facing Conservation Biology is this: will it become the foundation of biological sciences that supports conservation of plant and animal diversity and productivity? Or will it become another subspecialty that focuses on preservation of the scarcer parts and processes of biological diversity? Both would be legitimate outcomes. Both are needed. But the latter would leave it to another synthetic field to form the foundation needed by all the subdisciplines of biological conservation.

The polarized rhetoric swirling around Conservation Biology's role in issues such as endangered species, old-growth forests, landscape fragmentation, and biological diversity during the latter decades of the 20th century seems to indicate that Conservation Biology is destined for the rank of a new subspecialty. I hope this is not the case.

Conservation Biology sits on the horns of a dilemma. It can become the foundation of biological sciences that serves the broad spectrum of conservation in both public and private sectors. Or, it can become a special part of the framework of biological conservation, that part dealing with rare elements and processes. There are significant implications to how the practitioners of Conservation Biology decide to resolve this dilemma. The choice still exists, but it won't for much longer. I would like to see Conservation Biology become a foundation of biological sciences for conservation rather than just a subdiscipline for preservation of the rare elements of diversity. I would like to see it embrace the full spectrum of aims and methods in biological conservation, from preservation of natural systems and their diversity to sustainable management to produce the natural resources upon which all human life depends. But regardless of how the field evolves, the world of biological management programs is better off because Conservation Biology came into being in the 1980s. We needed the new perspectives and methods it brought to conservation, and they will continue to be useful for a long time to come.

---

with a highly exploited Europe, must have seemed pristine. Aboriginal peoples had exploited natural resources and driven some species to extinction, but their low population densities and lack of technologies for widespread devastation prevented wholesale destruction. American Indians apparently made extensive use of fire to manage lands for both agriculture and game. Some historians argue that Atlantic coastal lands cleared by Indians became important colonization sites for European settlers and helped them survive their first winters (Russell 1976).

During the colonial period, North American forests were extensively exploited for lumber, ship masts, naval stores (gum and turpentine), and charcoal for heating. Huge tracts were cleared for agriculture. Demand for forest products in Europe and domestic demand by a rapidly growing population were eagerly met by exploiting the seemingly endless forests. Later, forests were again called upon to provide lumber for vast railroad networks and building construction as the nation expanded westward. In coastal areas, salt marshes were harvested for salt hay (*Spartina*) to feed cattle before the opening of the prairies to grain farming.

The value of forests as an economic resource was not the only philosophical perspective held by the colonists, however. Religious attitudes of some groups, especially the Puritans, held that the forest was the abode of the devil. This is perhaps not an unfamiliar attitude even today, for many children's stories place witches, trolls, and goblins in deep, dark forests, and many otherwise reasonable adults are more frightened in a remote forest than in the heart of a large city with high murder rates.

Thus, the forests were beset by increasing economic demands and were perceived to be endless and vaguely evil—hardly a nourishing environment for conservation. Conservation did, of course, develop in North America, but it required several centuries after initial European colonization to become firmly established. Perhaps it was necessary first to develop a significant population whose livelihood was not intimately tied to forest exploitation.

American conservation efforts can be traced to three philosophical movements, two of the 19th century and one of the 20th (Callicott 1990). The **Romantic-Transcendental Conservation Ethic** derived from the writings of Ralph Waldo Emerson and Henry David Thoreau in the East, and John Muir in the West. Emerson and Thoreau were the first prominent North American writers to argue, in the mid-1800s, that nature has uses other than human economic gain. Specifically, they spoke of nature in a quasi-religious sense, as a temple in which to commune with and appreciate the works of God. Nature was seen as a place to cleanse and refresh the human soul, away from the tarnishings of civilization. This was the philosophical and aesthetic position that Muir took as he argued for a national movement to preserve nature in its wild and pristine state, and condemned its destruction for material and economic gain. John Muir's movement flourishes today in the form of many citizen conservation groups; his direct organizational legacy is the Sierra Club.

This noneconomic view was countered by the so-called **Resource Conservation Ethic**, made popular by the forester Gifford Pinchot at the turn of the 20th century. His was an approach to nature based in the popular utilitarian philosophy of John Stuart Mill and his followers. Pinchot saw only "natural resources" in nature, and adopted the motto, "the greatest good of the greatest number for the longest time" (Pinchot 1947). Nature, to Pinchot, was an assortment of components that were either useful, useless, or noxious to people. Note the **anthropocentric** valuing of nature, not because it is part of "God's design" (as per the Romantic-Transcendentalists), but because natural resources feed the economic machine and contribute to the material quality of life. Pinchot (1947) once stated that "the first great fact about conservation is that it stands for development."

Pinchot's approach to conservation stressed equity—a fair distribution of resources among consumers, both present and future—and efficiency, or lack of waste. This led to adoption of the **multiple use concept** for the nation's lands and waters, which is the current mandate of the U.S. Forest Service and Bureau of Land Management. Under multiple use, many different uses of the land are attempted simultaneously, such as logging, grazing, wilderness preservation, recreation, and watershed protection. Because a market economy may or may not be efficient and has little to do with equity, governmental regulation or outright public ownership of resources was deemed necessary to develop and enforce conservation policy. An insightful perspective on multiple-use conflicts based on personal experience is offered by Edwin P. Pister in Essay 1C.

These two movements thus created a schism, with the Preservationists (Muir, Emerson, Thoreau) advocating pure wilderness and a spiritual appreciation for nature, and the Conservationists (Pinchot) adopting a resource-based, utilitarian view of the world. A third movement, born of the 20th century, emerged with the development of evolutionary ecology. This **Evolutionary-Ecological Land Ethic** was developed by Aldo Leopold in his classic essays, published shortly after his death as *A Sand County Almanac* (1949), and in other writings. Leopold was educated in the Pinchot tradition of resource-based conservation, but later saw it as inadequate and scientifically inaccurate. The development of ecology and evolution as scholarly disciplines conclusively demonstrated that nature was not a simple collection of independent parts, some useful and others to be discarded, but a complicated and integrated sys-

ESSAY 1C
Agency Multiple-Use Conflicts

Edwin P. Pister, Bishop, California

Having conducted my 38-year career within the philosophical and practical insulation of an essentially unilateral California Department of Fish and Game, dichotomies inherent within federal land and resource management departments and their constituent agencies have intrigued and perplexed me. Early on I had naively assumed that such agencies, and the personnel staffing them, were all focused toward a common and righteous goal, and essentially comprised a team directed toward the long-term benefit of the natural resource (and, therefore, the people). I was sadly mistaken! The infighting and budgetary battles within "the system," largely directed by politically driven economic considerations and pushed by Administration priorities in Washington, D.C., were astounding.

My first significant encounter with bureaucratic dichotomies involved five agencies within the U.S. Department of the Interior in the early days of an effort to save the Devils Hole pupfish (*Cyprinodon diabolis*) in a remote portion of the Nevada desert. Devil's Hole (see Figure 5.2) is a disjunct portion of Death Valley National Monument, administered by the National Park Service, with the endangered fish primarily a responsibility of the U.S. Fish and Wildlife Service. Causing the fish's endangerment was deep well pumping on federal land administered by the Bureau of Land Management under lease to private farming interests, encouraged strongly by the Bureau of Reclamation, which was actively involved in drilling exploratory wells to allow more pumping. A fifth agency of Interior, the U.S. Geological Survey, was monitoring the venture, with its hydrologists confirming our worst fears that if the pumping were allowed to continue unabated, virtually every spring in the biological wonderland of Ash Meadows (Nye County, Nevada), along with its highly endemic biota, would be severely affected and ultimately destroyed (Deacon and Williams 1991). It was only after a strong threat of legal action that Secretary of the Interior Walter Hickel called together a Washington-level task force representing all involved agencies, and progress was made to save the fish.

Often we are not so fortunate. Devil's Hole and Ash Meadows were the subject of dramatic events that came and went rather quickly, with the fish ultimately receiving protection by a unanimous decision of the U.S. Supreme Court. Much more cumbersome and damaging to the nation's biodiversity are chronic problems resulting from multiple-use management on public lands throughout the western United States, primarily for extractive activities such as timber harvest, mining, livestock grazing, and energy development. A representative situation, which began for me in 1965 and persists to this day, involves the Inyo National Forest and a series of livestock grazing permits within the Golden Trout Wilderness of the southern Sierra Nevada.

During the 1860s, the meadows of the Kern River Plateau, 2500–3000 m in elevation and underlain by recently formed and very fragile granitic soils, were viewed by livestock operators as a source of quick wealth. Eyewitness accounts during the latter part of the 19th century told of invasions of hundreds of thousands of sheep and cattle that quickly removed the meadow grasses and began watershed degradation that has never fully healed (King 1935). Attempts by fish and wildlife biologists to effect significant reductions in livestock numbers were countered politically by the livestock operators, supported by a Forest Service range lobby eager to retain a budgetary status quo. When the Golden Trout Wilderness was created under the Endangered American Wilderness Act of 1978, Western congressmen made retention of the grazing leases part of the price to be paid to achieve "wilderness" status. Consequently, a wilderness dedicated to California's state fish continually and needlessly suffers severe habitat degradation and riparian damage. Major eroded areas are widespread, riparian growth and undercut banks are virtually nonexistent, the best campsites near water have been reduced to dust bins fouled with cow manure, and one cannot drink safely from the South Fork Kern River (the evolutionary habitat of the golden trout, *Oncorhynchus aguabonita*) without prior filtering or boiling. The habitat change thus effected brought the added ecological problem of favoring an invasion of brown trout (*Salmo trutta*) which, in the early 1970s, nearly succeeded in extirpating the endemic goldens.

Other rare life forms have been similarly affected. A very rare species of sand verbena, *Abronia alpina*, exists on only a few acres of the Plateau and must be fenced by the Forest Service to protect it from cattle. Only recently has some progress been made toward rectifying these problems, utilizing an ecosystem-wide approach involving major adjustments in the cattle operation, fencing of riparian areas, erection of fish barriers, eradication of brown trout, and very costly repair of headcuts and eroded areas (USDA Forest Service 1982a,b).

To make the situation even less acceptable, cattle operations on public lands are often subsidized by taxpayers. The costs of supporting such programs are several times greater than revenues derived from lease fees, and monetary returns to the Forest Service are so minimal that many readers could (and would, if permitted) easily pay them out of their own pockets. Resource abuse under multiple-use management is not restricted to livestock operations. Perhaps even more flagrant is energy development in key recreation areas.

The Inyo National Forest constitutes perhaps the most heavily used (and therefore most important) recreation area in the United States. Located but a half day's drive away for more than 20 million people in metropolitan southern California, the Inyo presently supports more recreational use than Yellowstone, Grand Canyon, and Glacier National Parks combined. Yet, while geothermal features comprise major tourist attractions in Yellowstone, energy projects encouraged by multiple-use management have tapped the Inyo National Forest's geothermal resources (already very popular with tourists), which are gradually and inexorably being reduced, first to subsurface levels and eventually to nothing.

As Ellis (1975) points out in a classic paper describing geothermal development in New Zealand, "After major well production, the hot springs of Wairakei Geyser Valley and Broadlands no longer discharge, and what were once tourist attractions are now gray holes in the ground." When these fears were emphasized to federal decision makers during the environmental review process, they were almost totally ignored, and the plants were built, with accompanying press fanfare from Bureau of Land Management bureaucrats about how multiple-use management was playing a major role in freeing the nation from reliance upon foreign oil! (BLM administers all geothermal leases on federal lands). Absolutely no mention was made of the negative impacts. Probably nothing is more intransigent than bureaucracy at the policymaking level that takes comfort in the status quo.

At this writing, predictions are indeed proving to be accurate. We are already experiencing "gray holes in the ground," a major trout hatchery operated on geothermally heated water since the 1930s is currently running at less than half capacity because of reduced flows and altered water temperatures, and the lawyers are sharpening their pencils. However, successful legal action would be but a hollow victory. It is unlikely that the geothermal resource will recover within several lifetimes. Considering the limited life expectancy of geothermal projects (30 years at best), even the most loyal, "system-dedicated" federal land manager would now find it difficult to defend such irresponsible development as achieving "the greatest good of the greatest number for the longest time." The underlying (but arguable) utilitarian principle of multiple-use management is a concept that badly needs to be redefined in light of modern ecological thought and understanding (Callicott 1989).

Similar threats are posed by hydroelectric development on the streams that form the basis and backbone of the roadside recreational resource. All this, of course, is simply because multiple-use management is expected, encouraged, and budgeted for on Forest Service and BLM lands, and valuable and irreplaceable resources located thereon are not afforded the protection required by law within the boundaries of a national park. Long-term destruction of publicly owned recreational resources is routinely sanctioned to accommodate private business interests.

What I have pointed out above constitutes only the most obvious of problems created by the monster frequently produced by a combination of politics and multiple-use mandates. To livestock and energy development can be added other extractive uses such as mining and timber harvest. Even though local Forest Service and BLM officials may oppose particularly flagrant projects, they are required to fulfill the congressional mandates that direct their agencies, mandates that may be significantly skewed during pre-project evaluation and planning. Value judgments and resultant employee zeal basic to constructive change are seldom manifested and lie far outside of the training (or career aspirations) of most federal land managers. Many are keenly aware of the case involving John Mumma, Regional Forester from Missoula, Montana, who was fired from his job for refusing to implement timber harvest quotas assigned to him because doing so would have required violation of federal law (Wilkinson 1992).

The public can benefit in the long run from multiple-use management, but much too often politics and blind bureaucracy take precedence over the long-term public interest. It is not multiple use per se that works against the public interest, but questionable management priorities that allow certain favored uses to proceed to the detriment of the overall resource. Williams and Rinne (1992) propose a solution to this long-standing problem by suggesting management for biodiversity within a broader, ecosystem management approach, a concept that offers much hope for federal land managers and, more importantly, the publicly owned resources under their stewardship.

---

tem of interdependent processes and components, something like a fine Swiss watch. There are really only a few parts of a watch that appear to be of direct utility to its owner, namely, the hour, second, and minute hands (back when watches had hands). However, proper functioning of those parts depends on dozens of unseen components that must all function well and together. Leopold saw ecosystems in this context, and this is the context in which modern ecology first developed. This **equilibrium** view was subsequently replaced by a dynamic, **nonequilibrium** ecological perspective, discussed below. Nevertheless, the Leopold land ethic remains as the philosophical foundation for conservation biology.

Although the Evolutionary-Ecological view of the world, updated by the nonequilibrium perspective, is the most biologically sensible and comprehensive approach to conservation, much of modern conservation is based on various mixtures of these three philosophies. The Resource Conservation Ethic of the late 19th century is still a dominant paradigm followed by public resource agencies such as the U.S. Forest Service, under which U.S. forest tracts are seen as economic resources to be managed for multiple human use

(Figure 1.3). The Romantic-Transcendental Conservation Ethic, though more typically without the overt religious rationale of its early proponents, is the basis for activism by many private conservation organizations throughout the world, whose goals are to save natural areas in a pristine state for their inherent value. This difference has resulted in repeated confrontations among so-called "special interest groups."

Leopold's Evolutionary-Ecological Land Ethic is the best informed and most firmly grounded of any approach to nature and should serve as the philosophical basis for most decisions affecting biodiversity. It is the only system that can provide even moderately useful predictions about our effects on the natural world, but it is still only part of the total decision-making process; the economic, spiritual, and social needs of people must also be met. It is curious that management decisions concerning natural areas can be made without recourse to evolutionary ecology, yet this still routinely happens in many resource agencies (such policy issues are thoroughly discussed in Chapter 17). Similarly, it would be a fruitless, counterproductive, and ethically suspect exercise to base comprehensive land use decisions solely on evolutionary ecology without regard to the people who will be affected.

Most natural areas today are remnant patches of formerly contiguous habitats in landscapes dominated by human economic endeavors (Figure 1.4). The biological activity within any one of these natural areas is strongly dependent on what happens outside its boundaries. Any long-term security for a natural area will come about only when it is accepted as an integral and contributing part of broader economic and development planning. Just as the Evolutionary-Ecological Land Ethic grew out of traditional disciplines to meet the emerging crises in biodiversity, so too are the traditional disciplines of resource economics and anthropology giving rise to new interdisciplinary views, sometimes called "ecological economics" and "ecological anthropology," views that stress long-term environmental sustainability.

Modern Conservation Biology: A Synthesis

The time is ripe to replace both the extreme preservationist and the exploitative utilitarian philosophies of the 19th century with a balanced approach that looks to an ethic of stewardship for philosophical guidance, and to a melding of natural and social sciences for theory and practice. This new context is necessary for conservation biology to flourish and make contributions to a sustainable biosphere.

Figure 1.3 The deeply rooted multiple-use paradigm of the U.S. Forest Service is reflected in the irony of this sign in Aiken County, South Carolina, and the virtually clear-cut forest in the background. The Resource Conservation Ethic that has dominated most public resource agencies demands that forests and other natural areas be treated as economic resources to be managed for human gain. True "protection" for biodiversity often is not an option. (Photograph by G. K. Meffe.)

Figure 1.4 An example of a mixed natural and human landscape in South Carolina. This aerial photograph shows patches of natural areas of various sizes interspersed with human-dominated activities such as agriculture and housing. (Photograph courtesy of Savannah River Ecology Laboratory.)

By the 1960s and 1970s, it was becoming painfully obvious to many ecologists that prime ecosystems throughout the world, including their favorite study sites, were disappearing rapidly. Biodiversity, the outcome of millions of years of the evolutionary process, was being carelessly discarded, and, in some cases, willfully destroyed. Previous conservation efforts, while focusing on important components of nature such as large vertebrates, soils, or water, still had not embraced the intricacies of complex ecosystem function and the importance of all the "minor," less charismatic, biotic components such as insects, nematodes, fungi, and bacteria. It was time to change this attitude.

Early attempts at moving in this direction included Raymond Dasmann's *Environmental Conservation* (1959) and David Ehrenfeld's *Biological Conservation* (1970). These books helped to lay the groundwork for today's conservation biology by melding good evolutionary ecology with human resource conservation, and by providing a vision of where modern conservation should go.

In 1980, Michael Soulé and Bruce Wilcox published a seminal work entitled *Conservation Biology: An Evolutionary-Ecological Perspective*, in which they presented conservation in this new light. This was quickly followed by Frankel and Soulé's (1981) *Conservation and Evolution*, another attempt to draw attention to evolution as a basis for conservation decisions. The lesson was further driven home in 1983 with Schonewald-Cox et al.'s *Genetics and Conservation: A Reference for Managing Wild Animal and Plant Populations*, which specifically addressed the short- and long-term genetic (and thus evolutionary) health of managed populations. Shortly thereafter, in 1985, the Society for Conservation Biology was formed, a large membership rapidly grew, and a new journal, *Conservation Biology* (Figure 1.5), was developed to complement existing journals such as *Biological Conservation* and *The Journal of Wildlife Management*. Thus, in little more than a decade, the thrust and outlook of international conservation had dramatically changed, and it continues to change as conservation science matures.

Students of conservation biology today should be excited to know that they are still "getting in on the ground floor." The science of conservation is still developing and needs many bright minds to determine its future direc-

Figure 1.5 The first issue of the journal *Conservation Biology*, published in May 1987. (Photograph courtesy of E. P. Pister.)

tions. Anyone who thinks that much of the science has already been done, and that there is little room left for contributions, does not yet understand the many challenges of conservation biology; hopefully, the following chapters will set that record straight.

Guiding Principles for Conservation Biology

Three principles or themes that serve as working paradigms for conservation biology will appear repeatedly throughout this book (Table 1.1). A **paradigm** is "the world view shared by a scientific discipline or community" (Kuhn 1972), or "the family of theories that undergird a discipline" (Pickett et al. 1992). A paradigm underlies, in a very basic way, the approach taken to a discipline, and guides the practitioners of that discipline. We believe that these three principles are so basic to conservation practice that they should permeate all aspects of conservation efforts and should be a presence in any endeavor in the field.

Principle 1: Evolutionary Change. The population geneticist Theodosius Dobzhansky once said, "Nothing in biology makes sense except in the light of evolution." Evolution is indeed the single principle that unites all of biology; it is the common tie across all areas of biological thought. Evolution is the only reasonable mechanism able to explain the patterns of biodiversity that we see in the world today; it offers a historical perspective on the dynamics of life. The processes of evolutionary change are the "ground rules" for how the living world operates.

Conservationists would do well to recall repeatedly Hutchinson's metaphor, "the ecological theater and the evolutionary play," discussed above. Answers to biological conservation problems must be developed within an evolutionary framework; to do otherwise would be to fight natural laws (Meffe 1993), a foolish approach that could eventually destroy the endeavor.

The genetic composition of most populations is likely to change over time, whether due to drift in small populations, immigration from other populations, or natural selection (discussed in Chapter 6). From the perspective of conservation biology, the goal is not to stop genetic (and thus evolutionary) change, not to try and conserve the status quo, but rather to ensure that populations may continue to respond to environmental change in an adaptive manner.

Principle 2: Dynamic Ecology. The ecological world, the "theater" of evolution, is a dynamic, largely nonequilibrial world. The classic paradigm in ecology for many years was the "equilibrium paradigm," the idea that ecological systems are in equilibrium, with a definable stable point such as a "climax community." This paradigm implies closed systems with self-regulating struc-

Table 1.1
Three Guiding Principles of Conservation Biology

Principle 1:	Evolution is the basic axiom that unites all of biology. (The evolutionary play.)
Principle 2:	The ecological world is dynamic and largely nonequilibrial. (The ecological theater.)
Principle 3:	The human presence must be included in conservation planning. (Humans are part of the play.)

ture and function, and embraces the popular "balance of nature" concept. Conservation under this paradigm would be relatively easy: simply select pieces of nature for protection, leave them undisturbed, and they will retain their species composition and function indefinitely and in balance. Would that it were so simple!

The past several decades of ecological research have taught us that nature is dynamic (Pickett et al. 1992). The old "balance of nature" concept may be aesthetically pleasing, but it is inaccurate and misleading; ecosystems or populations or gene frequencies may appear constant and balanced on some temporal and spatial scales, but other scales soon reveal their dynamic character. This principle applies to ecological structure, such as the number of species in a community, as well to as evolutionary structure, such as the characteristics of a particular species. Conservation actions based on a static view of ecology or evolution will misrepresent nature and be less effective than those based on a more dynamic perspective.

The contemporary dominant paradigm in ecology (Botkin 1990) recognizes that ecological systems are generally not in dynamic equilibrium, at least not indefinitely, and have no stable point. Regulation of ecological structure and function is often not internally generated; external processes, in the form of

ESSAY 1D

A Nongovernmental Organization Perspective

The Role of Science in Defining Conservation Priorities for Nongovernmental Organizations

Kathryn S. Fuller, World Wildlife Fund

The proposition that science should play a key role in setting conservation priorities seems self-evident: after all, where would conservation *be* without ecology? Isn't science the foundation of the environmental movement?

Science indeed lies at the heart of conservation, but the relationship is complex. Understanding how science contributes to conservation requires us to reexamine our notions of both endeavors, to reconcile ecology with disciplines that would once have seemed completely alien to it.

A crucial part of that process has been the emergence of conservation biology. As might be expected, this effort to conserve biological diversity by wedding the disciplines of ecology, genetics, and practical wildlife management has prompted dissent, some of it from wildlife managers who have worked for years without benefit—or, many of them would argue, *need*—of scientific oversight. It is clear that conservationists need to build more bridges between these managers and the scientists now entering the field, simply because both sides have much to learn from each other.

Some dissenters claim that conservation biology is simply the latest in a series of gimmicky cross-disciplines, aimed at dazzling foundations with gaudy new academic packages. Nothing could be further from the truth. Conservation biology is here to stay because it looks at long-standing fieldwork through the prisms of new theoretical frameworks, and thus creates a synergy of enormous potential power. The proper question is not whether conservation biology is just a passing fad, but rather, what do we *do* with this new hybrid? How do we tap its potential?

There are two answers to this question. First, science no longer exclusively sets the boundaries of conservation. This is due in part to the uniquely multidisciplinary nature of modern conservation, which is the product of years of evolving philosophy and practice. My own organization, World Wildlife Fund (WWF), is a useful case study in this evolution. When we began in 1961, we concentrated our efforts on individual species, animals like the Arabian oryx, the rhinoceros, and the giant panda, our organization's symbol. We emphasized scientific research and hands-on fieldwork.

Achieving genuine long-term conservation, however, requires a broader approach. Initially, that meant looking not just at species but at their habitats. That, in turn, led us toward the humans who interact with those habitats and the connection between human poverty and resource destruction. Now, every day, WWF addresses itself to what is perhaps conservation's bitterest irony: some of the world's poorest people struggle to survive alongside the world's greatest natural treasures. Beyond the borders of parks live people desperate for cropland and firewood. Adjacent to herds of wildlife in Africa are villagers without an adequate source of protein. And around the world is a vastly increasing new category of refugees, fleeing not tyrants but a deteriorating environment.

Clearly, unless we can help ease the economic burdens that drive people to overexploit their natural resources, we can never hope to arrest the environmental degradation of the developing world. So WWF seeks ways to marry the preservation of biological diversity with environmentally sound economic development.

This transition from "pure" conservation to one that integrates conservation and development means we can no longer closet ourselves behind laboratory doors. We must delve into areas unfamiliar to conservationists, such as anthropology, sociology, economics, and political science. And, recognizing that the best-designed projects will fail without ongoing funding, we must take on the role of conservation financiers, brokering debt-for-nature swaps and creating new financial mechanisms to leverage our limited resources into lasting change.

Given all this, it might be easy to go on and say that science has less of a claim on today's conservation agenda, fighting for attention as it is with the fields of economics and politics. But that would be a mistake. Because the second answer to the question of science's role in conservation is this: science is more critical than ever. If we posit ourselves as architects, then science is the foundation of our edifice, the base from which we use various tools—sustainable development, conservation finance—to structure something strong and enduring.

In a way, science is not just foundation but continuing illumination, telling us where we need to go and how to get there. How, for instance, do we help people in the developing world improve their quality of life in sustainable ways unless we give them viable models of development? This is where science plays a role. Already, we are seeing exciting and promising new sustainable-use techniques at work in our tropical forests: harvesting of non-timber products like fruits, seeds, medicinal plants, and wild game; agroforestry methods that combine traditional crops with multiple-purpose trees; restoration ecology and watershed protection.

Science can and must contribute to the fruitful mélange of ideas currently circulating in the field. Without science's help, we cannot hope to tackle the truly forbidding problems facing our planet today—problems that in fact were first identified by scientists: global warming, ozone depletion, fragmentation and degradation of habitat, and perhaps foremost of all, the loss of biological diversity.

We can only guess at the number of species on this planet. Some estimates put the number at 50 million or more, but with millions still to be identified, most of this is highly educated guesswork. What we do know is that we are losing species at an almost unimaginable rate. The renowned biologist E. O. Wilson says we are on the brink of a catastrophic extinction of species—of a kind unseen since the demise of dinosaurs 65 million years ago.

When confronted with mass extinctions on this scale, the inevitable temptation is to throw up one's hands and ask, "Where to begin?" Again, this is where science comes in. Science can tell us where to begin our path, and equally important, it can help correct our path while we forge it. Science also provides the kind of foresight that every conservation organization desperately needs—the ability to look ten, twenty years in the future and figure out where we need to be.

Of course, setting conservation priorities for our planet will never be simple or straightforward. As a start, we know that most of today's mass extinctions are taking place in the tropical forests, which contain at least half of all earth's species and are being depleted faster than any other ecological community. Tropical forests are in fact the crucible of modern conservation. Knowing this only takes us so far, however, since it still leaves us with billions of acres of forest to somehow incorporate into our planning. But scientists at WWF and elsewhere are working to identify key natural areas featuring exceptional concentrations of endemic species and facing exceptional degrees of threat. By concentrating efforts in those areas where the needs and the potential payoffs are greatest, conservationists can respond in a more informed and systematic way to the challenge of preserving biodiversity.

Science can be a partner in that effort, anchoring the economic and political exigencies of modern conservation in intellectual bedrock. Conservation biology can rise to the moment, expanding its temporal and spatial reach to fully incorporate today's conservation challenges. Although foundations and endowments encourage scientists to think in small and discrete terms, the problems confronting us are so massive that scientists must scale their thinking accordingly. The need for solid science to inform decisive action by nongovernmental organizations and other groups has never been so great.

---

natural disturbances such as fires, floods, droughts, storms, earth movement, and outbreaks of diseases or parasites, are frequently of overriding importance. Indeed, we now know that biodiversity in ecosystems as different as prairies, temperate and tropical forests, and the intertidal zone is maintained by nonequilibrial processes (Figure 1.6). Ecosystems consist of patches and mosaics of habitat types, not of uniform and clearly categorized communities.

It is important to understand that our emphasis on nonequilibrial processes does not imply that species interactions are ephemeral or unpredictable, and therefore unimportant. Communities are not chaotic assemblages of species; they do have structure. Embedded within all communities are clusters of species that have strong interactions, and in many cases, these interactions have a long evolutionary legacy. Nevertheless, this does not mean that community structure is invariant and that species composition does not change at some scale of space and time. Change at some scale is a universal feature of ecological communities.

Figure 1.6 Nonequilibrial processes play a major role in most ecosystems. Surface disturbances by bison create openings or "wallows" in prairies (A). Hurricanes and other storms open gaps in both temperate (B) and tropical (C) forests. Wave action (D) and tidal changes on rocky shorelines open up disturbance patches. (A, photograph courtesy of Jerry Wolfe; B, Congaree Swamp, South Carolina after Hurricane Hugo, 1989, by Rebecca Sharitz; C, lower montane forest in Costa Rica, by C. R. Carroll; D, coral rock in the Dominican Republic, Caribbean Sea, by Michael C. Newman.)

Conservation within this paradigm focuses on dynamic processes and physical contexts. An important research goal for conservation biologists is to understand how the interplay between nonequilibrial processes and the hierarchy of species interactions determines community structure and biodiversity. Ecosystems are open systems with fluxes of species, materials, and energy, and must be understood in the context of their surroundings. A further implication is that nature reserves cannot be treated in isolation, but must be part of larger conservation plans whose design recognizes and accounts for spatial and temporal change. This principle is further developed by Petraitis et al. (1989), Botkin (1990), Pickett et al. (1992) and Pickett and Ostfeld (1995).

Principle 3: The Human Presence. Humans are and will continue to be a part of both natural and degraded ecological systems, and their presence must be included in conservation planning. Conservation efforts that attempt to wall off nature and safeguard it from humans will ultimately fail. As discussed under principle 2, ecosystems are open to the exchange of materials and species, and to the flux of energy. Because nature reserves are typically surrounded by lands and waters intensively used by humans, it is impossible to isolate reserves completely from these outside influences. There is simply no way to "protect" nature from human influences, and those influences must be taken into account in planning efforts. Indeed, isolating reserves carries its own liability in terms of increased extinction probabilities and gene losses for many species.

On the positive side, there are benefits to be gained by explicitly integrating humans into the equation for conservation. First, people who have been longtime residents in the region of a reserve often know a great deal about local natural history. This "indigenous knowledge" can be useful in developing reserve management plans (see Essay 11B), and local residents can play important roles on reserve staffs as, for example, guards and environmental educators. Second, reserves should be "user-friendly" in order to build public support. Two ways to achieve this are by allowing limited public access to those portions of the reserve with established nature trails, and by bringing ecological knowledge about the reserve into formal and informal educational programs. Most people take pride in their natural heritage, and a critical mission for all conservation ecologists is to build upon that pride through public education. If people do not perceive that the reserve has any value to them, they will not support it.

Finally, native human cultures are a historical part of the ecological landscape and have an ethical right to the areas where they live. Aboriginal and tribal peoples from alpine to tropical regions have existed for millennia in their local systems, and to displace them in the name of conservation is simply unethical. Furthermore, they themselves add other types of diversity—cultural and linguistic diversity—which the earth is rapidly losing. The loss of indigenous human cultures and languages is as large a problem as is the loss of other levels of biological diversity. What's more, some of these cultures have developed sustainable methods of existence that can serve as models for modern sustainable development.

We must equally recognize that indigenous cultures have the right to control their destiny. We would be hopelessly naive to imagine that indigenous cultures can remain unchanged and unaffected by outside influences. What we can do is understand their internal systems of values and their knowledge of local natural resources, and then try to work with them toward the twin goals of conservation of biodiversity and sustainable economic development.

We must also incorporate problems of modern cultures into conservation, for they will have the largest influences on resource use. Many conservationists feel that the only realistic path to conservation in the long term is to ensure a reasonable standard of living for all people. Of course, this requires greater equity among peoples, with less disparity between the "haves" and the "have-nots." Achieving equity will involve convincing some to accept lower standards of living so that others may climb out of desperate poverty, with the result that all will have a lesser impact on biodiversity. This will not be an easy task. It will also involve attention to a number of other issues, such as birth control, revised concepts of land ownership and use, education, health care, empowerment of women, and so forth.

Some Postulates of Conservation Biology

Of course, the foundation of conservation biology is much broader than these three principles. For example, Michael Soulé, a cofounder of the Society for Conservation Biology, listed four postulates, and their corollaries, that characterize value statements relevant to conservation biology (Soulé 1985). Like the principles listed above, these postulates help to define the ethical and philosophical foundations of the field. Soulé's first postulate is that *diversity of organisms is good.* Humans seem to inherently enjoy diversity of life forms (called **biophilia** by E. O. Wilson [1984]), and seem to understand that natural diversity is good for our well-being and that of nature. A corollary of this postulate is that untimely extinction (that is, extinction caused by human activities) is bad. His second postulate, *ecological complexity is good*, is an extension of the first, and "expresses a preference for nature over artifice, for wilderness over gardens." It also carries the corollary that simplification of ecosystems by humans is bad. The third postulate, *evolution is good*, has already been discussed above, and carries the corollary that interference with evolutionary patterns is bad. The final postulate is that *biotic diversity has intrinsic value*, regardless of its utilitarian value. This postulate recognizes inherent value in nonhuman life, regardless of its utility to humans, and carries the corollary that destruction of diversity by humans is bad. This is perhaps the most fundamental motivation for conservation of biodiversity.

ESSAY 1E

A Private Landowner's Perspective

Conservation Biology and the Rural Landowner

Bill McDonald, Malpai Borderlands Group

To this rural private landowner, who also leases public land for livestock grazing, the emerging discipline of conservation biology embodies both my greatest hope for the future and my worst fear. Hope—that the best scientific minds will work with the best managerial minds to help us to come to grips with the fallout from the remarkable changes of this past century, and to chart a sustainable course to the future. Fear—that a tendency to use big government, in the mistaken belief that government alone can tackle massive issues such as biodiversity loss, will add conservation biology to the growing list of buzzwords abhorred by many rural landowners, and thus make it an impediment to the very effort it represents.

The complexity of our ecosystems, on whatever scale you wish to define the term, simply defies our complete comprehension. Yet, as human beings, we are the only species with the intellectual capacity to recognize the consequences of our collective actions and consciously attempt change for the better. As the dominant species on earth, we must strive to do better; it is both our responsibility and our hope for survival. It is not easy work. A popular way to attempt to effect such positive change is through governmental edict. In some very clear-cut cases (direct pollution of waters, for instance), this can be a successful approach. In more complex situations, however, this approach results in partial success at best, and often in complete failure. This is particularly true when those who will be most directly affected by the "chosen course of action" are not involved in determining and implementing that course. I am involved in a different approach.

The Malpai Borderlands is a million-acre region in southeastern Arizona and southwestern New Mexico. It contains open space, mountains, and valleys, and its use by people is almost exclusively for cattle grazing. My family has maintained our ranch here for 90 years. Of the families who live here, many, like mine, are descended from the area's original homesteaders. The region is home to many species of plants and animals, some considered rare and/or endangered.

The Malpai Borderlands Group is composed of area landowners, scientists, and other stakeholders, the latter defined as anyone who has an interest in the future of the place and is willing to work to make it happen. At our invitation, federal and state land agency personnel are included in our effort; federal and state land makes up 47% of the land ownership.

The Goal Statement of our group reads as follows:

> Our goal is to restore and maintain the natural processes that create and protect a healthy, unfragmented landscape to support a diverse, flourishing community of human, plant and animal life in our Borderlands Region.
>
> Together, we will accomplish this goal by working to encourage ranching and other traditional livelihoods that will sustain the open space nature of our lands for generations to come.

Early on, we identified two major threats to the natural diversity and health of our landscape. First is the historical suppression of fire, which is leading to a landscape dominated by woody shrub species at the expense of grasses. Second is the threat of development—a distant threat at the moment, which is the best time to address it. Both are also threats to the future of ranching livelihoods, which require both open space and healthy grasses.

While acknowledging that mistakes have been made in the past, and that much remains to be learned about the effects of grazing on semiarid grasslands, we believe that ranching livelihoods, which depend directly on the open space resource for their survival, are the best hope for the future sustainability of that resource.

To date, after just three years of existence, our group has some impressive results to show for our efforts, not the least of which is improved coordination and communication between government agencies and private landowners and between the different agencies themselves. We have completed the first prescribed burn in the history of the area. The burn plan involved a wilderness study area, two states, four private landowners, five different government agencies in both states, coordination with Mexico, and adherence to the regulations of the National Environmental Policy Act and the National Antiquities Act. While the burn itself was successful, the effort to make it happen was exhausting. We have now embarked on a search for a less bureaucratic way to bring the beneficial effects of fire to the landscape.

Our group has supported a cattle ranching family in their efforts to protect a population of Chiricahuan leopard frogs (*Rana chiracahuaensis*) that reside in stock tanks on their ranch. This project has blossomed into a joint effort with the state wildlife department that will result in improved habitat for the frog and an enhanced cattle operation for the ranchers.

We have begun a unique program of grassbanking, in which ranchers gain access to grass on another ranch in exchange for conservation action of value equal to the value of the grass. For the initial users of the grassbank, this has meant conveyance of conservation easements to the Malpai Borderlands Group, which will result in the private lands on those ranches never being subdivided.

A number of other actions have been taken or facilitated by the group that, while perhaps not as dramatic, have nudged the land a little closer to a long-lasting, healthy, sustainable future. Most important of all, we are working together, creating as we go a structure of support for actions that promote the biological diversity of our area and the long-term sustainability of our ranching livelihoods.

This grassroots alternative to traditional land management approaches is based on the voluntary actions of individuals. Our approach does not, and will never, involve coercion or the force of law. Our approach has been embraced by government agencies, politicians from both parties, and most of the news media. It is not, however, without its critics. Some of the landowners remain suspicious of an effort that welcomes the involvement of government agency personnel and other stakeholders, particularly The Nature Conservancy. There are also those in the environmental community who simply do not believe that cattle grazing and healthy semiarid grasslands can coexist. We find ourselves between these two poles, in what we call the "radical center." We believe that our approach is the one that brings results.

Where does conservation biology fit into such an effort? The role of conservation biology should be informational, certainly. Sound scientific information is crucial to helping us to understand what actions will be beneficial to biological diversity, and to analyze the effects of actions already taken. Equally important, conservation biology's role must be supportive. It is important to champion those efforts that are showing results.

Will the results come fast enough? Conservation biology has been called a crisis science, which certainly suggests an urgency for its application. The question of how fast, however, becomes irrelevant when we are still struggling for something that works at all. The idea that you can artificially speed up a process and then inflict that approach upon all the relevant habitats of the world will ensure failure by changing the very dynamics that made the process initially successful. The continued failure of grand schemes is the real threat to the future diversity of the planet, not the pace or scope of the truly successful efforts. As our effort in the Malpai Borderlands shows, it takes time and hard work to build the trusting relationships necessary to achieve real success. And it takes time and hard work to maintain them. This crisis does not call for a few broad strokes, but for millions of little ones.

These postulates can be, and have been, debated, as can any philosophical position, which, by definition, cannot be founded on an entirely objective, scientific basis. Nevertheless, they are explicitly or implicitly accepted by many, both in and out of the conservation profession. Aspects of these arguments will be further pursued in the next chapter.

Some Characteristics of Conservation Biology

Conservation biology has some unusual characteristics not associated with many other sciences. These result partly from the daunting nature of the problem of how to preserve the evolutionary potential and ecological viability of a vast array of biodiversity. Some of the uniqueness of conservation biology also stems from basic conflicts between the complexity, dynamics, and interrelatedness of natural systems and humankind's propensity to try to control, simplify, and conquer those systems.

A Crisis Discipline

Soulé (1985) labeled conservation biology a "crisis discipline," with a relationship to the larger field of biology analogous to surgery's relationship to physiology, or that of war to political science (or, we suppose, AIDS to epidemiology). In such crisis disciplines, action often must be taken without complete knowledge, because waiting to collect the necessary data could mean inaction that would destroy the effort at hand. Such immediate action requires working with available information with the best intuition and creativity one can muster, while tolerating a great deal of uncertainty. This, of course, runs counter to the way that scientists are trained, but nonetheless is necessary given the practical matters at hand. These problems are discussed further in Chapters 16 and 17.

Conservation biologists are often asked for advice and input by government and private agencies regarding such issues as design of nature reserves, potential effects of introduced species, propagation of rare and endangered species, or ecological effects of development. These issues are usually politically and economically charged, and decisions cannot wait for detailed studies that take months or even years. The "expert" is expected to provide quick, clear, and unambiguous answers (which is, of course, generally impossible), and is looked upon askance if such answers are not there, or seem contrary to short-term economic gain. This is a major challenge for conservation biologists, who must walk a fine line between strict scientific credibility, and thus conservatism and possible inaction, versus taking action and providing advice based on general and perhaps incomplete knowledge, thereby risking their scientific reputations.

A Multidisciplinary Science

No single field of study prepares one to be a conservation biologist, and the field does not focus on input from any single area of expertise. It is an eclectic, broad discipline, to which contributions are needed from fields as different as molecular genetics, biogeography, philosophy, landscape ecology, policy development, sociology, population biology, and anthropology. This multidisciplinary nature is diagrammed in Figure 1.7, which shows how the overlapping fields of natural and social sciences contribute to the special interdisciplinary identity of conservation biology.

This conceptualization of conservation biology has several important features. First is the melding of the formerly "pure" fields of population biology and ecology with the "applied" fields that encompass natural resource management. The historical distinction between these disciplines is beginning to blur, and practitioners in these areas are working together toward common goals. Second is the need for a strong philosophical foundation and input from the social sciences. Because the need for conservation in the first place is the direct result of human intervention in natural systems, an understanding of humanistic viewpoints is vital for reducing present and future confrontations between human expansion and the natural world. Finally, conservation biol-

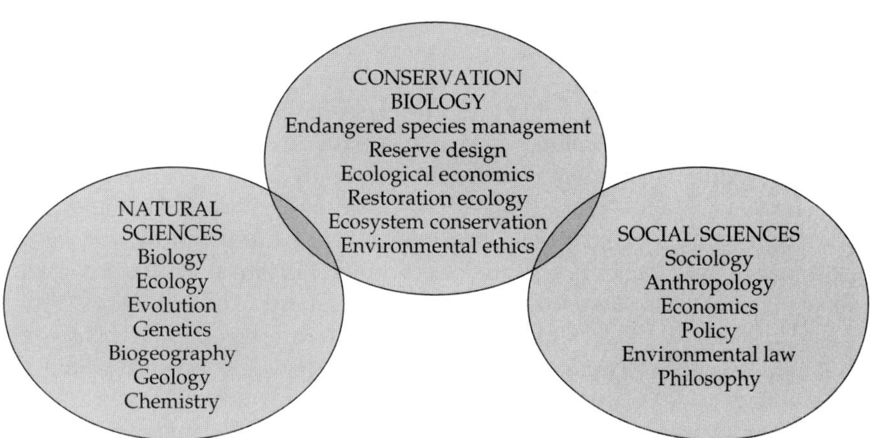

Figure 1.7 The interdisciplinary nature of conservation biology merges many traditional fields of natural and social sciences. The list of relevant subdisciplines and interactions shown is not meant to be exhaustive.

ogy is a holistic field because conservation involves entire ecosystems, and multidisciplinary approaches and cooperation among disparate groups will be the most successful approach.

A strong cross-disciplinary perspective is desirable and necessary for success in conservation. A conference held in 1989 that included several global resource agencies outlined their collective vision of the training necessary for their future conservation employees (Jacobson 1990). The interests of these agencies were less in narrow, disciplinary skills than in "real-world" problem-solving abilities. These included "(1) cross-disciplinary breadth as well as disciplinary depth; (2) field experience; (3) language and communications skills; and (4) leadership skills, especially a mix of diplomacy and humility" (Jacobson 1990). Cannon et al. (1996) also indicated the strong need for development of human interaction skills in conservation biologists. A broad, liberal education and an ability to communicate across disciplines, combined with strength within a specialized area, is probably an ideal combination for achieving success and making real contributions in conservation biology.

An Inexact Science

Ecological systems are complex, often unique, and currently unpredictable beyond limited generalities. The public, and even other scientists, often do not appreciate this and cannot understand why ecologists are such uncertain folks who hedge their bets and will not provide a simple answer to an environmental problem. The reason is, of course, that there usually *is* no simple answer. Ecological systems are complex, their dynamics are expressed in probabilities, **stochastic** influences may be strong, and many significant processes are nonlinear. *Uncertainty is inherently part of ecology and conservation, and probabilistic, rather than prescriptive, answers to problems are the norm.*

Thus, the conservation biologist often faces a credibility gap, not because he or she is incompetent, or because the field is poorly developed, but because even the simplest of ecosystems is far more complicated than the most complex of human inventions, and most people have not the slightest notion that this is the case. This gap can easily be exploited by representatives of special interest groups, such as lawyers, engineers, and developers, all of whom are used to dealing with concrete situations that can be easily quantified and a "bottom line" extracted. There is never an easy bottom line in ecology, and we can only hope to educate others to that fact, rather than be forced to develop meaningless and dangerous answers that have no basis in reality. The conservation biologist must think "probabilistically" and understand the nature of scientific uncertainty. Consequently, conservationists should include safety margins in the design of management and recovery strategies, as does an engineer in the design of a bridge or an aircraft.

A Value-Laden Science

Science is supposed to be value-free. It is presumably completely objective and free from such human frailties as opinions, goals, and desires. Because science is done by humans, however, it is never value-free, but is influenced by the experiences and goals of the scientists, although they often will not admit that. "Too many teachers, managers, and researchers are trapped by the Western positivist image of science as value-free; . . . Biologists must realize that science, like everything else, is shot through with values. Sorting out the norms behind positions is the initial step of critical thinking" (Grumbine 1992). This recognition of value-laden science has been called "post-modern science" and is discussed in depth in Chapter 16 and Essay 19A.

Unlike many other areas of science, conservation biology is "mission-oriented" (Soulé 1986); its goal clearly is to conserve natural ecosystems and biological processes, and there is nothing value-free about it. However, the methodology used to obtain information and put it to use must be good, objective science; if not, all credibility will quickly be lost. Nevertheless, conservation biologists should not delude themselves into thinking that their science is value-neutral. Its values are clearly defined: natural systems and biological diversity are good and should be conserved.

The question of values and advocacy in conservation science has been debated recently in conservation journals and within various scientific societies (Barry and Oelschlaeger 1996 and associated responses; Meffe 1996). Whether and how conservation scientists should become involved in policy development is a major issue; the emerging consensus seems to be that scientists have a clear responsibility to society to lend their knowledge and expertise to the value-laden goal of biodiversity preservation, but that good, objective science must serve as the foundation for reaching that goal. Objectivity in how science is conducted cannot be compromised to reach predetermined goals, for then all scientific credibility is lost.

A Science with an Evolutionary Time Scale

In contrast to traditional resource management, whose currency includes maximum sustained yields, economic feasibility, and immediate public satisfaction with a product, the currency of conservation biology is long-term viability of ecosystems and preservation of biodiversity *in perpetuity*. A conservation biology program is successful not when more deer are harvested this year, or even when more natural areas are protected, but when a system retains the diversity of its structure and function over long periods, and when the processes of evolutionary adaptation and ecological change are permitted to continue. If there is a common thread running throughout conservation biology, it is the recognition that evolution is *the* central concept in biology, and has played and should continue to play *the* central role in nature.

A Science of Eternal Vigilance

The price of ecosystem protection is eternal vigilance. Even "protected" areas may be destroyed in the future if they contain resources that are deemed desirable enough by powerful groups or individuals. A case in point is the United States' Arctic National Wildlife Refuge, an area set aside for its ecological significance, but repeatedly under pressure to be opened up for oil extraction as world political affairs affect the price and availability of oil. What appears secure today may well be exploited tomorrow for transitory resource use, and the conservation biologist must continually be protective of natural areas and must stay on top of policy developments that affect conservation. Natural ecosystems can easily be destroyed, but they cannot be created, and at best can be only partially restored.

A Final Word

Throughout this book you may find cases of seeming opposites or contradictions in our messages. It may seem that at one point we advise letting natural processes occur and at another suggest interventionist management. We will recognize nonequilibrial processes in general, but then discuss deterministic processes that can reach equilibrium in particular cases. This is not done to confuse you. Ecological systems are complex, and their situations are often unique. What makes sense in one system or circumstance will be inapplicable in another. Idiosyncrasies abound, as do conflicting demands. Conservation scenarios need to be defined and pursued individually, and not be part of an automatic, "cookbook" approach.

Conservation biology is not easy, but it is not hopelessly complicated either, and much research and application remains to be done. Above all, it can provide exciting and unparalleled career opportunities for students interested in solving real-world problems. The world's biodiversity desperately needs bright, energetic, and imaginative students who feel they can make a difference. And they certainly can, and must.

Summary

Exponential human population growth in the last few centuries has affected the natural world to the extent that massive alteration of habitats and associated biological changes threaten the existence of millions of species and basic ecosystem processes. The field of conservation biology developed over the last 20 years as a response of the scientific community to this crisis. The "new" conservation biology differs from traditional resource conservation in being motivated not by utilitarian, single-species issues, but by the need for conservation of entire systems and all their biological components and processes.

Conservation practices have a varied history around the world, but generally have focused on human use of resources. In the United States, two value systems dominated resource conservation early in the 20th century. The Romantic-Transcendental Conservation Ethic of Emerson, Thoreau, and Muir recognized that nature has inherent value and should not simply be used for human gain. The Resource Conservation Ethic of Pinchot was based on a utilitarian philosophy of the greatest good for the greatest number of people; many resource agencies in the United States and elsewhere follow this view. Aldo Leopold's Evolutionary-Ecological Land Ethic developed later, and is the most biologically relevant perspective, recognizing the importance of ecological and evolutionary processes in producing and controlling the natural resources we use. Much of modern conservation biology has grown from and is guided by Leopold's land ethic.

Three overriding principles should guide all of conservation biology. First, evolution is the basis for understanding all of biology, and should be a central focus of conservation action. Second, ecological systems are dynamic and nonequilibrial, and therefore change must be a part of conservation. Finally, humans are a part of the natural world and must be included in conservation concerns.

Conservation biology has some unusual characteristics not always found in other sciences. It is a crisis discipline that requires multidisciplinary approaches. It is an inexact science that operates on an evolutionary time scale. It is a value-laden science that requires long-term vigilance to succeed. It also requires of its practitioners innovation, flexibility, multiple talents, and an understanding of the idiosyncrasies of ecological systems, but offers outstanding career challenges and rewards.

Suggestions for Further Reading

Gore, A., Jr. 1992. *Earth in the Balance: Ecology and the Human Spirit.* Penguin Books, New York. A stunningly good grasp of global environmental crises is shown by the Vice President of the United States. A better account of biodiversity problems and potential solutions written by a nonscientist cannot be found.

Grumbine, R. E. 1992. *Ghost Bears: Exploring the Biodiversity Crisis.* Island Press, Washington, D.C. An outstanding summary of the biodiversity crisis written in the context of old-growth forests of the Pacific Northwest, and encompassing ethics, law, environmental policy, and activism. A very broad, "real-world" perspective of the challenges facing biodiversity conservation.

Soulé, M. E. (ed.). 1986. *Conservation Biology: The Science of Scarcity and Diversity.* Sinauer Associates, Sunderland, MA. Already a classic, this book laid much of the groundwork for the science of conservation biology. It contains 25 chapters written by scientists who helped define modern conservation biology.

Western, D. and M. Pearl (eds.). 1989. *Conservation for the Twenty-First Century.* Oxford University Press, New York. An outstanding follow-up to the Soulé text that presents a broader perspective of conservation. In addition to biological issues, it includes much information on management of parklands, global issues, human value systems, and planning and legislation in conservation.

Wilson, E. O. 1992. *The Diversity of Life.* Belknap Press of Harvard University Press, Cambridge, MA. This is an excellent overview of the biodiversity crisis, in easily understood terms, spanning the gene to the ecosystem. It also covers basic concepts such as evolutionary change, extinction, and speciation, all described in an engaging style.

In addition, two good introductory textbooks and a more applied text offer broad overviews of conservation biology. These are, respectively, *Fundamentals of Conservation Biology*, by Malcolm L. Hunter, Jr. (1996, Blackwell Science), *Essentials of Conservation Biology*, by Richard B. Primack (1993, Sinauer Associates), and *Saving Nature's Legacy. Protecting and Restoring Biodiversity*, by Reed F. Noss and Allen Y. Cooperrider (1994, Island Press).

2

Conservation Values and Ethics

It is inconceivable to me that an ethical relation to land can exist without love, respect, and admiration for land, and a high regard for its value. By value, I of course mean something far broader than mere economic value; I mean value in the philosophical sense.

Aldo Leopold, 1949

The Value of Biodiversity

Conservation biologists often treat the value of biodiversity as a given. To many laypeople, however, the value of biodiversity may not be so obvious. Because conservation efforts require broad public support, the conservation biologist should be able to articulate fully the value of biodiversity. Why should we care about—that is, value—biodiversity?

Environmental philosophers customarily divide value into two main types, expressed by alternative pairs of terms: **instrumental** or **utilitarian** as opposed to **intrinsic** or **inherent**. Instrumental or utilitarian value is the value that something has as a means to another's ends. Intrinsic or inherent value is the value that something has as an end in itself. The intrinsic value of human beings is rarely contested. The intrinsic value of nonhuman natural entities and nature as a whole has been the subject of much controversy. Perhaps because the suggestion that nonhuman natural entities and nature may also have intrinsic value is so new and controversial, some prominent conservationists (e.g., Myers 1983) have preferred to provide a purely utilitarian rationale for conserving biodiversity. The view that biodiversity has value only as a means to human ends is called **anthropocentric** (human-centered). On the other hand, the view that biodiversity is valuable simply because it exists, independently of its use to human beings, is called **biocentric**.

Instrumental Value

The anthropocentric instrumental (or utilitarian) value of biodiversity may be divided into three basic categories—goods, services, and information. The

Table 2.1
Four Categories of the Instrumental Value of Biodiversity

Category	Examples
Goods	Food, fuel, fiber, medicine
Services	Pollination, recycling, nitrogen fixation, homeostatic regulation
Information	Genetic engineering, applied biology, pure science
Psycho-spiritual	Aesthetic beauty, religious awe, scientific knowledge

psycho-spiritual value of biodiversity is possibly a fourth kind of anthropocentric utilitarian value (Table 2.1).

First, goods. Human beings eat, heat with, build with, and otherwise consume many other living beings. But only a small fraction of all life-forms have been investigated for their utility as food, fuel, fiber, and other commodities. Many potential food plants and animals may await discovery. And many of these might be grown on a horticultural or agricultural scale, as well as harvested in the wild, adding variety at least to the human diet, and possibly even saving us from starvation if conventional crops fail due to incurable plant diseases or uncontrollable pests (Vietmeyer 1986a, b). Fast-growing trees—useful for fuelwood or making charcoal, or useful for pulp or timber—may still be undiscovered in tropical forests. New organic pesticides may be manufactured from yet to be screened or discovered plants (Plotkin 1988). The medicinal potential of hitherto undiscovered and/or unassayed plants and animals seems to be the most popular and persuasive rationale of this type for preserving biodiversity. Vincristine, extracted from the Madagascar periwinkle, is the drug of choice for the treatment of childhood leukemia (Farnsworth 1988). Discovered in the late 1950s, it is the most often cited example of a recent and dramatic cure for cancer manufactured from a species found in a place where the native biota is now threatened with wholesale destruction. Doubtless many other hitherto unscreened, perhaps even undiscovered, species might turn out to have equally important medical uses—if we can save them.

The degree to which conservationists rely on the argument that potential medicines may be lost if we allow species extinction to grind on is revealing. It reflects the reverence and esteem with which medicines are held in contemporary Western culture—a culture, it would seem, of hypochondriacs. Spare no expense or inconvenience to save them, if unexplored ecosystems may harbor undiscovered cures for our diseases! According to Meadows (1990), "some ecologists are so tired of this line of reasoning that they refer wearily to the 'Madagascar periwinkle argument.' . . . [Those] ecologists hate the argument because it is both arrogant and trivial. It assumes that the Earth's millions of species are here to serve the economic purposes of just one species. And even if you buy that idea, it misses the larger and more valuable ways that nature serves us."

Which brings us to the second point, services. Often overlooked by people who identify themselves first and foremost as "consumers" are the services performed by other species working diligently in the complexly orchestrated economy of nature (Meadows 1990). Green plants replenish the oxygen in the atmosphere and remove carbon dioxide. Certain kinds of insects, birds, and bats pollinate flowering plants, including many agricultural species, and are being lost at a frightening rate (Buchmann and Nabhan 1996). Fungal and microbial life-forms in the soil decompose dead organic material and play a key role in recycling plant nutrients. Rhizobial bacteria turn atmospheric nitrogen into usable nitrate fertilizer for plants. If the **Gaia hypothesis** (Lovelock 1988) is correct, the Earth's temperature and the salinity of its oceans are organically regulated. The human economy is no more than a small subsystem of the economy of nature and would abruptly collapse if major environmental service sectors of the larger natural economy were to be disrupted.

Third, information. The mindless destruction of species "uncared for and unknown"—in the words of Darwin's contemporary and codiscoverer of evolution by natural selection, Alfred Russel Wallace (1863)—has been compared to setting fire to sections of a vast library and burning books that no one has read. Each is a storehouse of information. Desirable characteristics encoded in isolatable genes and transferable, by means of gene splicing, to edible or medical resources, may be "burned up" with the "volume" in which they could once be found. Genetic information, in other words, is a potential economic good. Such information also has another utility, more difficult to express. Meadows (1990), however, captures it nicely:

> Biodiversity contains the accumulated wisdom of nature and the key to its future. If you ever wanted to destroy a society, you would burn its libraries and kill its intellectuals. You would destroy its knowledge. Nature's knowledge is contained in the DNA within living cells. The variety of genetic information is the driving engine of evolution, the immune system for life, the source of adaptability.

Some 1.5 million species have been formally named and described (see Chapter 4). Based upon the most conservative recent estimates of the total number of the planet's species—between five and ten million—that means that only 15–30%, at most, are known to science (Gaston 1991). Based upon more liberal recent estimates of the total—30 million or more—the number known to science could represent less than 5% (Erwin 1988). Imagine the loss to science if, as Raven (1988) predicts, 25% of the world's life-forms, due to the destruction of much of their moist tropical habitat, become extinct in the coming quarter-century, before they can even be scientifically named and described.

The vast majority of these threatened species are not vascular plants or vertebrate animals; they are insects (Wilson 1985b). The reason that Erwin (1988) suspects that there may be so many species of invertebrates is that so many may be endemic or host-specific. Most of these unknown insects at risk of extinction would probably prove to be useless as human food or medicine—either as whole organisms, as sources of chemical extracts, or as sources of gene fragments—nor would many be likely to play a vital role in the functioning of regional ecosystems (Ehrenfeld 1988). Though it may be difficult to so callously view such a tragedy, we may account their loss, nevertheless, in purely utilitarian terms—as a significant loss of a potential nonmaterial human good, namely, pure human knowledge of the biota.

Fourth, psycho-spiritual resources. Aldo Leopold (1953) hoped that, through science, people would acquire "a refined taste in natural objects." A beetle, however tiny and ordinary as beetles go, is as potentially beautiful as any work of fine art. And natural variety—a rich and diverse biota—is something Soulé (1985) thinks nearly everyone prefers to monotony. Wilson (1984) finds a special wonder, awe, and mystery in nature—which he calls "biophilia," and which for him seems almost to lie at the foundations of a religion of natural history. To be moved by the beauty of organisms and whole, healthy ecosystems, to experience a sense of wonder and awe in the face of nature's inexhaustible marvels is to become a better person, according to Norton (1987).

If from the point of view of the value of information—genetic and otherwise—the mindless destruction of biodiversity is like book burning, then from the point of view of natural aesthetics and religion, it is like vandalizing an art gallery or desecrating a church. There has been little doubt expressed that the value of pure scientific knowledge is anthropocentric, and the aesthetic and spiritual value of nature is often understood to be a highfalutin kind of utilitarian value. Ehrenfeld (1976) thinks that aesthetic and spiritual rationales for the conservation of biodiversity are "still rooted in the homocentric, humanistic worldview that is responsible for bringing the natural world, including us, to its present condition." Nevertheless, the beauty and sanctity of nature has sometimes been accounted an intrinsic, not an instrumental, value. According to Sagoff (1980), for example, "we enjoy an object because it is valuable; we do not value it merely because we enjoy it. . . . Esthetic experience is a perception, as it were, of a certain kind of worth."

Intrinsic Value

Unlike instrumental value, intrinsic value is not divisible into categories. Discussion of intrinsic value has focused on two other issues: the sorts of things that may possess intrinsic value, and whether intrinsic value exists objectively or is subjectively conferred.

In response to mounting concern about human destruction of nonhuman life, some contemporary philosophers have broken with Western religious and philosophical tradition and attributed intrinsic value, by whatever name, to the following: robustly conscious animals (Regan 1983); **sentient** animals (Warnock 1971); all living things (Taylor 1986); species (Callicott 1986; Rolston 1988; Johnson 1991); biotic communities (Callicott 1989); ecosystems (Rolston 1988; Johnson 1991); and evolutionary processes (Rolston 1988). Leopold (1949, 1953) attributed "value in the philosophical sense"—by which he could mean only what philosophers call "intrinsic value"—to "land," defined as "all of the things on, over, or in the earth" (Callicott 1987a). Soulé (1985) categorically asserts that "biotic diversity has intrinsic value", and Ehrenfeld (1988) categorically asserts that "value is an intrinsic part of diversity."

Environmental philosophers who claim that intrinsic value exists objectively in human beings and other organisms reason as follows. In contrast to a machine, such as a car or a vacuum cleaner, an organism is "autopoietic"—self-organizing and self-directed (Fox 1990). A car is manufactured; in other words, it does not grow up, orchestrated by its own DNA. And a car's purposes—to transport people and to confer status on its owner—are imposed on it from a source outside itself. Machines do not have their own goals or purposes, as organisms do—neither consciously chosen goals nor genetically determined goals. What are an organism's self-set goals? They may be many and complex. For us human beings they may include anything from winning an Olympic gold medal to watching as much television as possible. All organisms, however, strive (usually unconsciously and in an evolutionary sense) to achieve certain basic predetermined goals—to grow, to reach maturity, to reproduce (Taylor 1986).

Thus, interests may be intelligibly attributed to organisms, but not to machines. Having ample sunlight, water, and rich soil is in an oak tree's interest, though the oak tree may not be actively interested in these things, just as eating fresh vegetables may be in a child's interest, though the child may be actively interested only in junk food. One may counter that, by parity of reasoning, getting regular oil changes is in a car's interest, but because a car's ends or purposes are not its own, being well-maintained is not in its own interest, but in the interest of its user, whose purposes it serves exclusively. Another way of saying that ever striving and often thriving organisms have interests is to say that they have a good of their own. But *good* is just an older, simpler word meaning pretty much the same thing as *value*. Hence to acknowledge that organisms have interests—have goods of their own—is to acknowledge that they have what philosophers call *intrinsic value*.

Intrinsic and instrumental value are not mutually exclusive; many things may be valued both for their utility and for themselves. Employers, for example, may value their employees in both ways. Similarly, intrinsically valuing biodiversity does not preclude appreciating the various ways in which it is instrumentally valuable.

Norton (1991) argues that some environmental philosophers and conservation biologists, by claiming that biodiversity has intrinsic value (or is intrinsically valuable), have actually done more harm than good for the cause of conservation. Why? Because the intrinsic value issue divides conservationists into two mutually suspicious factions—anthropocentrists and biocentrists. The latter dismiss the former as "shallow resourcists;" and the former think that the latter have gone off the deep end (Norton 1991). If biodiversity is valuable because it ensures the continuation of ecological services, represents a pool of potential resources, satisfies us aesthetically, inspires us religiously, and makes better people out of us, the practical upshot is the same as if we attribute intrinsic value to it: we should conserve it. Instrumentally valuing biodiversity and intrinsically valuing it "converge" on identical conservation policies, in Norton's view (Figure 2.1); thus, we don't really need to appeal to the intrinsic value of biodiversity to ground conservation policy. Hence, Norton argues, the controversial and divisive proposition that biodiversity has intrinsic value should be abandoned. A wide and long anthropocentrism, he thinks, is an adequate value package for conservation biology.

Attributing intrinsic value to biodiversity, however, makes a practical difference in one fundamental way that Norton seems not to have considered. If biodiversity's intrinsic value were as widely recognized as is the intrinsic value of human beings, would it make much difference? All forms of natural resource exploitation that might put it at risk would not be absolutely prohibited, as intrinsic value easily can be ignored. After all, recognizing the intrinsic value of human beings does not absolutely prohibit putting people at risk when the benefits to the general welfare (or "aggregate utility") of doing so are sufficiently great. For example, in 1990, soldiers from the United States and other industrial nations were sent into combat, and some were killed or wounded, not to protect themselves and their fellow citizens from imminent annihilation, but to secure supplies of Middle Eastern petroleum and to achieve geopolitical goals.

Rather, if the intrinsic value of biodiversity were widely recognized, then sufficient justification would have to be offered for putting it at risk—just as we demand sufficient justification for putting soldiers at risk by sending them

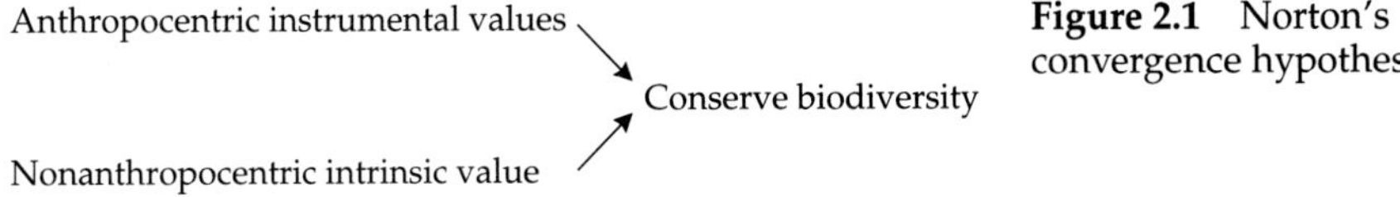

Figure 2.1 Norton's convergence hypothesis.

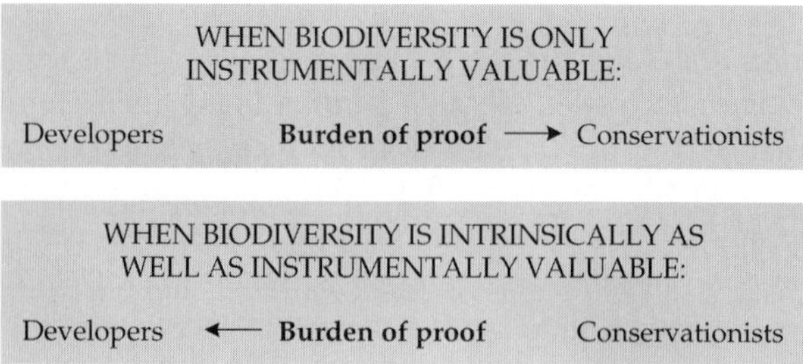

Figure 2.2 Burden of proof according to instrumental and intrinsic value systems.

to war. The practical difference that attributing intrinsic value to biodiversity makes is to shift the burden of proof from conservationists who are trying to protect it to those whose actions might jeopardize it (Figure 2.2). Fox (1993) puts this point clearly and forcefully:

> Recognizing the intrinsic value of the nonhuman world has a dramatic effect upon the framework of environmental debate and decision-making. If the nonhuman world is only considered to be instrumentally valuable then people are permitted to use and otherwise interfere with any aspect of it for whatever reasons they wish. If anyone objects to such interference then, within this framework of reference, the onus is clearly on the person who objects to justify why it is more useful to humans to leave that aspect of the world alone. If, however, the nonhuman world is considered to be intrinsically valuable then the onus shifts to the person who wants to interfere with it to justify why they should be allowed to do so.

Monetizing the Value of Biodiversity

Monetizing the value of biodiversity is a technical task for economists. Here we discuss only the basic ways of putting a dollar value on biodiversity and the philosophical issues raised by the prospect of doing so. It might seem that only the instrumental value of biodiversity is subject to expression in monetary terms. Some environmental economists, accordingly, explicitly endorse a strict anthropocentrism (Randall 1986). However, as we shall see, even the intrinsic value of biodiversity can be taken into account in an economic assessment of conservation goals.

Some endangered species have a market price: notoriously, elephants for their tusks; rhinoceroses for their horns; baleen whales for their meat, bone, and oil; and Bengal tigers for their pelts. In some cases—the blue and sperm whales, for example—their monetary value is the only reason the species are threatened with extinction. In other cases—the Bengal tiger and the mountain gorilla, for example—habitat destruction is also a factor in their endangerment. Myers (1981), however, suggests that taking advantage of their monetary value may be the key to conserving many species. An alternative perspective is provided by Holmes Rolston in Essay 2A.

According to modern economic theory, what is necessary for transforming a species' market price from a conservation liability into a conservation asset is to take it out of a condition that economists call a "commons" and "enclose" it. *Enclosing* here does not mean literally building a fence around a species population; it means, rather, assigning rights to cull it. A wild species that has a market value is subject to overharvesting when property rights to it cannot be legitimately asserted and enforced. This leads to the **tragedy of the commons** (Hardin 1968), discussed in Chapter 19. If a resource can be owned (either privately or publicly) and property rights to it can be enforced, then the species

ESSAY 2A
Our Duties to Endangered Species

Holmes Rolston III, Colorado State University

Few persons doubt that we have obligations *concerning* endangered species, because persons are helped or hurt by the condition of their environment, which includes a wealth of wild species, currently under alarming threat of extinction. Whether humans have duties directly *to* endangered species is a deeper question, important in both ethics and conservation biology, in both practice and theory. Many believe that we do. The U.N. *World Charter for Nature* states, "Every form of life is unique, warranting respect regardless of its worth to man." The *Biodiversity Convention* affirms "the intrinsic value of biological diversity." Both documents are signed by well over a hundred nations. A rationale that centers on species' worth to persons is anthropocentric; a rationale that includes their intrinsic and ecosystem values is naturalistic.

Many endangered species have no resource value, nor are they particularly important for the usual humanistic reasons: scientific study, recreation, ecosystem stability, and so on. Is there any reason to save such "worthless" species? A well-developed environmental ethics argues that species are good in their own right, whether or not they are "good for" anything. The duties-to-persons-only line of argument leaves deeper reasons untouched; such justification is not fully moral and is fundamentally exploitive and self-serving on the part of humans, even if subtly so. Ethics has never been very convincing when pleaded as enlightened self-interest (that one ought always to do what is in one's intelligent self-interest).

An account of duties to species makes claims at two levels: one is about facts (a scientific issue, about species); the other is about values (an ethical issue, involving duties). Sometimes, species can seem simply made up, since taxonomists regularly revise species designations and routinely put after a species the name of the "author" who, they say, "erected" the taxon. If a species is only a category or class, boundary lines may be arbitrarily drawn, and the species is nothing more than a convenient grouping of its members, an artifact of taxonomists. No one proposes duties to genera, families, orders, or phyla; biologists concede that these do not exist in nature.

On a more realistic account, a biological species is a living historical form, propagated in individual organisms, that flows dynamically over generations. A species is a coherent, ongoing, dynamic lineage expressed in organisms, encoded in gene flow. In this sense, species are objectively there—found, not made, by taxonomists. Species are real historical entities, interbreeding populations. By contrast, families, orders, and genera are not levels at which biological reproduction takes place. Far from being arbitrary, species are the real survival units.

This claim—that there are specific forms of life historically maintained over time—does not seem fictional, but rather is as certain as anything else we believe about the empirical world, even though at times scientists revise the theories and taxa with which they map these forms. Species are not so much like lines of latitude and longitude as like mountains and rivers, phenomena objectively there to be mapped. The edges of such natural kinds will sometimes be fuzzy, and to some extent discretionary (see Chapter 3). One species will slide into another over evolutionary time. But it does not follow from the fact that speciation is sometimes in progress that species are merely made up, rather than found as evolutionary lines.

At the level of values and duties, an environmental ethics finds that such species are good kinds, and that humans ought not, without overriding justification, to cause their extinction. A consideration of species offers a biologically based counterexample to the focus on individuals typically sentient and usually persons—so characteristic of Western ethics. In an evolutionary ecosystem, it is not mere individuality that counts. The individual represents, or re-presents anew, a species in each subsequent generation. It is a token of an entity, and the entity is more important than the token. Though species are not moral agents, a biological identity—a kind of value—is here defended. The dignity resides in the dynamic form; the individual inherits this, exemplifies it, and passes it on. The possession of a biological identity reasserted genetically over time is as characteristic of the species as of the individual. Respecting that identity generates duties to species.

The species is a bigger event than the individual, although species are always exemplified in individuals. Biological conservation goes on at this level too, and, really, this level is the more appropriate one for moral concern, a more comprehensive survival unit than the organism. When an individual dies, another one replaces it. Tracking its environment over time, the species is conserved and modified. With extinction, this stops. Extinction shuts down the generative processes in a kind of superkilling. It kills forms (species) beyond individuals. It kills collectively, not just distributively. To kill a particular plant is to stop a life of a few years or decades, while other lives of such kind continue unabated; to eliminate a particular species is to shut down a story of many millennia, and leave no future possibilities.

Because a species lacks moral agency, reflective self-awareness, sentience, or organic individuality, some hold that species-level processes cannot count morally. But each ongoing species represents a form of life, and these forms are, on the whole, good kinds. Such speciation has achieved all the planetary richness of life. All ethicists say that in *Homo sapiens* one species has appeared that not only exists but ought to exist. A naturalistic ethic refuses to say this exclusively of one late-coming, highly developed form, but extends this duty more broadly to the other species—though not with equal intensity over them all, in view of varied levels of development.

The wrong that humans are doing, or allowing to happen through carelessness, is stopping the historical gene flow in which the vitality of life lies. A shutdown of the life stream is the most destructive event possible. Humans ought not to play the role of murderers. The duty to species can be overridden, for example, with pests or disease organisms. But a *prima facie* duty stands nevertheless. What is wrong with human-caused extinction is not just the loss of human resources, but the loss of biotic sources. The question is not: What is this rare plant or animal good for? But: What good is here? Not: Is this species good for my kind, *Homo sapiens?* But: Is *Rhododendron chapmanii* a good of its kind, a good kind? To care about a plant or animal species is to be quite nonanthropocentric and objective about botanical and zoological processes that take place independently of human preferences.

Increasingly, we humans have a vital role in whether these stories continue. The duties that such power generates no longer attach simply to individuals or persons, but are emerging duties to specific forms of life. The species line is the more fundamental living system, the whole, of which individual organisms are the essential parts. The species too has its integrity, its individuality, and it is more important to protect this than to protect individual integrity. The appropriate survival unit is the appropriate level of moral concern.

A species is what it is, inseparable from the environmental niche into which it fits. Particular species may not be essential in the sense that the ecosystem can survive the loss of individual species without adverse effect. But habitats are essential to species, and an endangered species typically means an endangered habitat. Integrity of the species fits into integrity of the ecosystem. Endangered species conservation must be ecosystem-oriented. It is not preservation of *species* that we wish, but the preservation of *species in the system*. It is not merely *what* they are, but *where* they are that we must value correctly.

It might seem that for humans to terminate species now and again is quite natural. Species go extinct all the time. But there are important theoretical and practical differences between natural and anthropogenic extinctions. In natural extinction, a species dies when it has become unfit in its habitat, and other species appear in its place. Such extinction is normal turnover. Though harmful to a species, extinction in nature is seldom an evil in the system. It is rather the key to tomorrow. The species is employed in, but abandoned to, the larger historical evolution of life. By contrast, artificial extinction shuts down tomorrow because it shuts down speciation. One opens doors, the other closes them. Humans generate and regenerate nothing; they only dead-end these lines. Relevant differences make the two as morally distinct as death by natural causes is from murder.

On the scale of evolutionary time, humans appear late and suddenly. Even more lately and suddenly they increase the extinction rate dramatically. What is offensive in such conduct is not merely senseless loss of resources, but the maelstrom of killing and insensitivity to forms of life. What is required is not prudence, but principled responsibility to the biospheric earth. Only the human species contains moral agents, but conscience ought not be used to exempt every other form of life from consideration, with the resulting paradox that the sole moral species acts only in its collective self-interest toward all the rest.

---

will be conserved, so the theory goes, because the owner will not be tempted to "kill the goose that lays the golden egg."

Or will he, she, or it? Other factors, such as species' reproductive rates and growth rates in relationship to interest rates, discount rates, and so on, confound this simple picture. As Haneman (1988) points out, "the interest rate level, the nature of the net benefit function and its movement over time, and the dynamics of the resource's natural growth process combine to determine the optimal intertemporal path of exploitation . . . Other things being equal, the higher the interest rate at which future consequences are discounted, the more it is optimal to deplete the resource now."

The blue whale is a case in point. The International Whaling Commission effectively encloses whale populations, despite occasional poaching, by allotting species harvest quotas to whaling nations (Forcan 1979). Clark (1973) concludes, however, that it would be more profitable to hunt blue whales to complete extinction and invest the proceeds in some other industry than to wait for the species population to recover and harvest blue whales at sustainable levels indefinitely. Clark does not recommend this course of action. On the contrary, his point is that market forces alone cannot always be made to further conservation goals.

The idea of conserving economically exploitable threatened species by enclosing and sustainably harvesting them may work well enough in conserving species with relatively high reproductive and growth rates (such as ungulates), but may not work at all well in conserving species that have relatively low reproductive and growth rates (such as whales). Hence, enlisting the market in the cause of conservation must be done very carefully on a case-by-case basis.

Potential goods—new foods, fuels, medicines, and the like—have no market price, obviously, because they remain unknown or undeveloped. To destroy species willy-nilly, however, before they can be discovered and examined for their resource potential is to eliminate the chance that a desirable commodity will become available in the future. Hence, biodiversity may be assigned an "option price," defined as "the amount people would be willing to pay in advance to guarantee an option for future use" (Raven et al. 1992). The option price of any given undiscovered or unassayed species may be very small because the chance that a given species will prove to be useful is also probably very small (Ehrenfeld 1988). But added together, the option prices of the million or more species currently threatened with wholesale extinction might be quite formidable.

The market confers a dollar value on biodiversity in other ways than the price of the actual and potential goods that nature provides. People pay fees to visit national parks, for example, and to hike in wilderness areas. Such fees—no less than the price of vincristine or of wildebeest steaks—express the value of a bit of biodiversity in money. But often, because user fees are usually low, the true monetary value of the psycho-spiritual "resource" is underexpressed by those fees alone. Subsidies provided from local, state, and federal tax revenues might also be factored in when assessing the monetary value of a psycho-spiritual resource. The money people spend—for such things as gasoline, food, lodging, and camping equipment—to get to a particular spot and visit it may be credited to the resource by employing the "travel cost method" (Peterson and Randall 1984; see also Case Study 3 in Chapter 18). "Contingent valuation," in which people are polled and asked what they would be willing to pay for the opportunity to enjoy a certain experience—say, to hear wolves howling in Yellowstone National Park in the United States—is also used to calculate the dollar value of psycho-spiritual resources (Peterson and Randall 1984).

Even economists now recognize—and of course attempt to monetize—the "existence value" of biodiversity (Randall 1988). Some people take a modicum of satisfaction in just knowing that biodiversity is being protected even if they have no intention of consuming exotic meats or personally enjoying a wilderness experience. Existence value has a price; one way to ascertain it would be to calculate the amount of money sedentary people actually contribute to conservation organizations, such as The Nature Conservancy or the Rainforest Action Network. Further, economists now also recognize "bequest value"—the amount people would be willing to pay to assure that future generations of *Homo sapiens* will inherit a biologically diverse world (Raven et al. 1992).

Monetizing the value of the often free or underpriced recreational, aesthetic, intellectual, and spiritual utility of nature is more often attempted than monetizing the value of the services that the economy of nature provides to the human economy. In part this may simply reflect the level of ecological literacy among economists, who may be growing adept at "shadow pricing" (as contingent valuation is sometimes called) psycho-spiritual resources. As occasional ecotourists and consumers of outdoor recreation, they can readily understand these resources, but the nuances of pollination, nutrient cycling, and the like may remain a mystery to them. Their neglecting to quantify the value of the service sector of the economy of nature may also reflect the fact that so far, most vital services performed for us free of charge by other species are not scarce, and economists calculate prices only for those things that are (but see Buchmann and Nabhan 1996).

Meadows (1990) hints at one way of monetizing natural services: "How would you like the job," she asks, "of pollinating trillions of apple blossoms some sunny afternoon in May? It's conceivable maybe that you could invent a machine to do it, but inconceivable that the machine could work as elegantly and cheaply as the honey bee, much less make honey on the side." The value of nature's service economy could be monetized by calculating the cost of replacing natural services with artificial ones. Put in terms of scarcity and options, what would be the cost of employing human labor or machines to pollinate plants, if—because of present economic practices, such as excessive use of insecticides—in the future pollinating organisms were to become vanishingly scarce?

Ehrenfeld (1988) notes, however, that, just as many species have little potential value as goods, many species are likely to have little importance in the service sector of the economy of nature: "The species whose members are the fewest in number, the rarest, the most narrowly distributed—in short, the ones most likely to become extinct—are obviously the ones least likely to be missed by the biosphere. Many of these species were never common or ecologically influential; by no stretch of the imagination can we make them out to be vital cogs in the ecological machine."

Some philosophers and conservation biologists strenuously object to the penchant of economists for reducing all value to monetary terms (Sagoff 1988; Ehrenfeld 1988). Some things have a price, others have a dignity. And, as a familiar matter of fact, we have attempted to exclude certain things from the market that we believe have a dignity—things, in other words, to which we attribute intrinsic value. Indeed, one possible motive for claiming that biodiversity has intrinsic value (or is intrinsically valuable) is to exclude it from economic valuation, and thus to put it beyond the vagaries of the market. We have, for example, attempted to take human beings off the market by outlawing slavery, and attempted to take sex off the market by outlawing prostitution. Why not take intrinsically valuable biodiversity off the market by outlawing environmentally destructive human activities?

Sagoff (1988) argues that we have two parallel and mutually incommensurable systems for determining the value of things: the market and its surrogates on the one hand, and the ballot box on the other. As private individuals, most of us would refuse to sell our parents, spouses, or children—at any price. And as citizens united into polities, we may refuse to trade biodiversity for any "benefit" projected in a benefit-cost analysis. Indeed, the United States Endangered Species Act of 1973 is a splendid example of a political decision to take biodiversity off the market.

Economists counter that we must often make hard choices between such things as the need to bring arable land into production and protecting the habitat of endangered species (Randall 1986). While we may like to believe, piously and innocently, that intrinsically valuable people are literally priceless, the value of a human life is not uncommonly monetized. The dollar value of a human life, for example, might be reflected by the amount that an automobile insurance company pays a beneficiary when a customer kills another person in an accident, or by the maximum amount that an industry is willing to pay (or is required by law to pay) to protect the health and safety of its employees. Similarly, recognizing the intrinsic value of biodiversity does not imply that it cannot be priced. The only way we can make informed choices is to express the entire spectrum of natural values, from "goods" and "services" to "existence," in comparable terms: dollars.

The Endangered Species Act was amended in 1978 to create a high-level interagency committee, the so-called "God Squad," which could allow a project that put a listed species in jeopardy of extinction to go forward if its economic benefits were deemed sufficiently great. This legislation affirms that we do indeed have two incommensurable systems of determining value—one economic and the other political. It also affirms the original political decision to exempt biodiversity from being routinely monetized and traded off for greater economic benefits. But it acknowledges that politically and economically determined values often clash in the real world. And it provides that when the opportunity cost of conserving biodiversity exceeds an unspecified threshold, the God Squad can allow economic considerations to override the general will of the citizens of the United States, democratically expressed through their Congressional representatives, that the nation's extant native species be conserved, period.

Bishop (1978) formalizes the reasoning behind the God Squad amendment to the U.S. Endangered Species Act. He advocates the safe minimum standard (SMS) approach, an alternative to the practice of aggregating everything from the market price to the shadow price of biodiversity, plugging it into a benefit-cost analysis (BCA), and choosing the economically most efficient course of action (Figure 2.3). Instead, the SMS assumes that biodiversity has incalculable value and should be conserved unless the cost of doing so is prohibitively high. As Randall (1988) explains,

> Whereas the . . . BCA approach starts each case with a clean slate and painstakingly builds from the ground up a body of evidence about the benefits and costs of preservation, the SMS approach starts with a presumption that the maintenance of the SMS for any species is a positive good. The empirical economic question is, "Can we afford it?" Or, more technically, "How high are the opportunity costs of satisfying the SMS?" The SMS decision rule is to maintain the SMS unless the opportunity costs of doing so are intolerably high. In other words, the SMS approach asks, how much will we lose in other domains of human concern by achieving the safe minimum standard of biodiversity? The burden of proof is assigned to the case against maintaining the SMS.

As noted earlier in this chapter, the practical effect of recognizing the intrinsic value of something is not to make it inviolable, but to shift the burden of proof, the onus of justification, onto those whose actions would adversely affect it. Because the safe minimum standard approach to monetizing the value of biodiversity shifts the burden of proof from conservationists to developers, it tacitly acknowledges, and incorporates into economic appraisal, biodiversity's intrinsic value.

Conservation Ethics

According to Leopold (1949), ethics, biologically understood, constitutes "a limitation on freedom of action." Ethics, in other words, constrains self-serving behavior in deference to some other good (Table 2.2).

Anthropocentrism

In the Western religious and philosophical tradition, only human beings are worthy of ethical consideration. All other things are regarded as mere means to human ends. Indeed, anthropocentrism seems to be set out in no uncertain terms at the beginning of the Bible. Man alone is created in the image of God, is given dominion over the earth and all the other creatures, and, finally, is

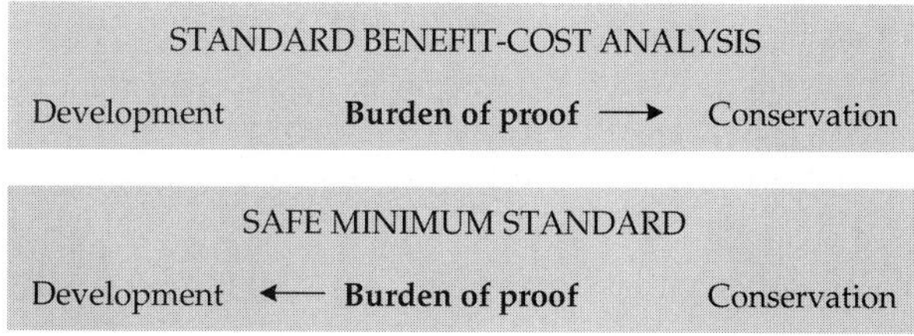

Figure 2.3 Burden of proof according to the standard BCA and the SMS approaches.

Table 2.2
A Comparison of Western Environmental Ethics

Value	Anthropocentrism	Judeo-Christian Stewardship Ethic	Biocentrism	Ecocentrism
Intrinsic value	Human beings	Species/creation as a whole	Individual organisms	Species, ecosystems, biosphere
The value of nature	Instrumental	Holistic–intrinsic	Individualistic–intrinsic	Holistic–intrinsic
"Man's" place in nature	Lord and master	Caretaker	One among equals	Plain member and citizen

commanded to subdue the whole creation. White (1967) claimed that because Jews and Christians believed, for many centuries, that it was not only their God-given right, but their positive religious duty, to dominate all other forms of life, science and an eventually aggressive, environmentally destructive technology developed uniquely in Western civilization.

As Norton (1991) has shown, an effective conservation ethic can be constructed on the basis of traditional Western anthropocentrism. Ecology has revealed a world that is far more systemically integrated than the biblical authors could have imagined, and subduing nature has untoward ecological consequences. An anthropocentric conservation ethic would require individuals, corporations, and other interest groups to fairly consider how their actions that directly affect the natural environment indirectly affect other human beings. Logging tropical forests, for example, may make fine hardwoods available to wealthy consumers, turn a handsome profit for timber companies, employ workers, and earn foreign exchange for debt-ridden countries. But it may also deprive indigenous peoples of their homes and traditional means of subsistence, and people everywhere of undiscovered resources, valuable ecosystem services, aesthetic experiences, and scientific knowledge. And, unchecked, logging may leave future generations of human beings a depauperate world (intergenerational inequity). Thus, logging and other environmentally destructive types of resource development may be judged unethical without any fundamental change in the framework of traditional Western moral thought.

The Judeo-Christian Stewardship Conservation Ethic

Stung by the allegation that the Judeo-Christian worldview was ultimately responsible for bringing about the contemporary environmental crisis, some environmentally concerned Christians and Jews challenged White's (1967) interpretation of biblical environmental attitudes and values (Barr 1972). After all, God pronounced everything that He created during the five days before He created human beings to be "good." Thus, God appears to have conferred intrinsic value on every kind of creature, not just on humanity. Indeed, the text suggests that God intended His creation to be replete and teeming with life:

> And God said, Let the waters bring forth abundantly the moving creature that hath life, and fowl that may fly above the earth in the open firmament of heaven. And God created great whales, and every living creature that moveth, which the waters brought forth abundantly, after their kind, and every winged fowl after his kind: and God saw that it was good. And God blessed them, saying, Be fruitful and multiply, and fill the waters in the seas, and let fowl multiply in the earth. (Genesis 1:20–22)

Further, "dominion" is an ambiguous notion. Just what does it mean for "man" to have dominion over nature? White (1967) argues that, in the past at least, Jews and Christians took it to mean that people should exercise a despotic reign over nature. Later in Genesis, however, God put Adam (who may represent all human beings) in the Garden of Eden (which may represent all of nature) "to dress it and to keep it" (Genesis 2:15). Our "dominion," this suggests, should be that of a responsible caretaker—a *steward*—rather than a tyrant. But what about "man" alone being created in the image of God? That could be taken to confer unique responsibilities, not unique privileges, on human beings. As God cares for humanity, so we who are created in the image of God must care for the earth.

The Judeo-Christian Stewardship Environmental Ethic is elegant and powerful. It also exquisitely matches the ethical requirements of conservation biology (Baker 1996). The Judeo-Christian Stewardship Environmental Ethic confers objective, intrinsic value on nature in the clearest and most unambiguous of ways—by divine decree. But intrinsic value devolves upon species, not individual specimens. For it is clear that during His several acts of creation God is creating species, "kinds," not individual animals and plants—whales, in other words, not specifically the one that swallowed Jonah or the one named Moby Dick. Thus, it is species, not individual specimens, that God pronounces good. Hence, human beings may freely use other living things as long as we do not endanger their species—as long, in other words, as we do not compromise the diversity of the creation. As Ehrenfeld (1988) points out, the Judeo-Christian Stewardship Environmental Ethic makes human beings directly accountable to God for conserving biodiversity: "Diversity is God's property, and we, who bear the relationship to it of strangers and sojourners, have no right to destroy it."

Traditional Non-Western Environmental Ethics

Christianity is a world religion, but so are Islam and Buddhism. Other major religious traditions, such as Hinduism and Confucianism, while more regionally restricted, nevertheless claim millions of devotees. Ordinary people are powerfully motivated to do things that can be justified in terms of their religious beliefs. Therefore, to distill environmental ethics from the world's living religions is extremely important for global conservation. The well-documented effort of Jewish and Christian conservationists to formulate the Judeo-Christian Stewardship Environmental Ethic in biblical terms suggests an important new line of inquiry: How can effective conservation ethics be formulated in terms of other sacred texts? Callicott (1994) offers a comprehensive survey. To provide even a synopsis of that study would be impossible here; however, a few abstracts of traditional non-Western conservation ethics may be suggestive.

Muslims believe that Islam was founded, in the seventh century A.D., by Allah (God) communicating to humanity through the Arabian prophet Mohammed, who regarded himself as part of the same prophetic tradition as Moses and Jesus. Therefore, because the Hebrew Bible and the New Testament are earlier divine revelations underlying distinctly Muslim belief, the basic Islamic worldview has much in common with the basic Judeo-Christian worldview. In particular, Islam teaches that human beings have a privileged place in nature, and, going further in this regard than Judaism and Christianity, that all other natural beings were created to serve humanity. Hence, there has been a strong tendency among Muslims to take a purely instrumental approach to the human-nature relationship. As to the conservation of biodiversity, the Arabian oryx was nearly hunted to extinction by oil-rich sheikhs armed with military assault rifles in the cradle of Islam. But callous indifference to the rest of creation is no longer sanctioned religiously in the Islamic world.

Islam does not distinguish between religious and secular law. Hence, new conservation regulations in Islamic states must be grounded in the Koran, Mohammed's book of divine revelations. In the early 1980s, a group of Saudi scholars scoured the Koran for environmentally relevant passages and drafted *The Islamic Principles for the Conservation of the Natural Environment*. While reaffirming "a relationship of utilization, development, and subjugation for man's benefit and the fulfillment of his interests," this landmark document also clearly articulates an Islamic version of stewardship: "he [man] is only a manager of the earth and not a proprietor, a beneficiary not a disposer or ordainer" (Kadr et al. 1983). The Saudi scholars also emphasize a just distribution of "natural resources," not only among members of the present generation, but among members of future generations. And, as Norton (1991) has argued, conservation goals are well served when future human beings are accorded a moral status equal to that of those currently living. The Saudi scholars have even found passages in the Koran that are vaguely ecological; for example, God "produced therein all kinds of things in due balance" (Kadr et al. 1983).

Ralph Waldo Emerson and Henry David Thoreau, thinkers at the fountainhead of North American conservation philosophy (discussed in Chapter 1), were influenced by the subtle philosophical doctrines of Hinduism, a major religion in India. Hindu thought also inspired Arne Naess's (1989) contemporary "Deep Ecology" conservation philosophy. Hindus believe that at the core of all phenomena there is one and only one Reality or Being. God, in other words, is not a supreme Being among other lesser and subordinate beings, as in the Judeo-Christian-Islamic tradition. Rather, all beings are a manifestation of the one essential Being—called *Brahman*. And all plurality, all difference, is illusory, or at best only apparent.

Such a view would not seem to be a promising point of departure for the conservation of biological diversity, because the actual existence of diversity, biological or otherwise, seems to be denied. Yet in the Hindu concept of *Brahman*, Naess (1989) finds an analogue to the way ecological relationships unite organisms into a systemic whole. However that may be, Hinduism unambiguously invites human beings to identify with other forms of life, for all life-forms share the same essence. Believing that one's own inner self, *atman*, is identical, as an expression of *Brahman*, with the selves of all other creatures leads to compassion for them. The suffering of one life-form is the suffering of all others; to harm other beings is to harm oneself. As a matter of fact, this way of thinking has inspired and helped to motivate one of the most persistent and successful conservation movements in the world, the Chipko movement, which has managed to rescue many of India's Himalayan forests from commercial exploitation (Guha 1989; Shiva 1989).

Jainism is a religion of relatively few adherents, but a religion of great influence in India. Jains believe that every living thing is inhabited by an immaterial soul, no less pure and immortal than the human soul. Bad deeds in past lives, however, have crusted these souls over with *karma*-matter. *Ahimsa* (non-injury of all living things) and asceticism (eschewing all forms of physical pleasure) are parallel paths that will eventually free the soul from future rebirth in the material realm. Hence, Jains take great care to avoid harming other forms of life and to resist the fleeting pleasure of material consumption. Extreme practitioners refuse to eat any but leftover food prepared for others, and carefully strain their water to avoid ingesting any waterborne organisms—not for the sake of their own health, but to avoid inadvertently killing other living beings. Less extreme practitioners are strict vegetarians and own few material possessions. The Jains are bidding for global leadership in environmental ethics. Their low-on-the-food-chain and low-level-of-consumption lifestyle is held up as a model of ecological right livelihood (Chappel 1990). And the author of the *Jain Declaration on Nature* claims that the central Jain moral precept of *ahimsa* "is nothing but environmentalism" (Singhvi n.d.).

Though now virtually extinct in its native India, Buddhism has flourished for many hundreds of years elsewhere in Asia. Its founder, Siddhartha Gautama, first followed the path of meditation to experience the oneness of *Atman-Brahman*, and then the path of extreme asceticism in order to free his soul from his body—all to little effect. Then he realized that his frustration, including his spiritual frustration, was the result of desire. Not by obtaining what one desires—which only leads one to desire something more—but by stilling desire itself can one achieve enlightenment and liberation. Further, desire distorts one's perceptions, exaggerating the importance of some things and diminishing the importance of others. When one overcomes desire, one can appreciate each thing for what it is.

When the Buddha realized all this, he was filled with a sense of joy, and he radiated loving-kindness toward the world around him. He shared his enlightenment with others, and formulated a code of moral conduct for his followers. Many Buddhists believe that all living beings are in the same predicament: we are driven by desire to a life of continuous frustration, and all can be liberated if all can attain enlightenment. Thus Buddhists can regard other living beings as companions on the path to Buddhahood and *nirvana*.

Buddhists, no less than Jains and Christians, are assuming a leadership role in the global conservation movement. Perhaps most notably, the Dalai Lama of Tibet is the foremost conservationist among world religious leaders. In 1985, the Buddhist Perception of Nature Project was launched to extract and collate the many environmentally relevant passages from Buddhist scriptures and secondary literature. Thus, the relevance of Buddhism to contemporary conservation concerns could be demonstrated, and the level of conservation consciousness and conscience in Buddhist monasteries, schools, colleges, and other institutions could be raised (Davies 1987). Bodhi (n.d.) provides a succinct summary of Buddhist environmental ethics: "With its philosophic insight into the interconnectedness and thoroughgoing interdependence of all conditioned things, with its thesis that happiness is to be found through the restraint of desire, with its goal of enlightenment through renunciation and contemplation and its ethic of noninjury and boundless loving-kindness for all beings, Buddhism provides all the essential elements for a relationship to the natural world characterized by respect, care, and compassion."

One-fourth of the world's population is Chinese. Fortunately, traditional Chinese thought provides excellent conceptual resources for a conservation ethic. The Chinese word *tao* means *way* or *road*. The Taoists believe that there is a *Tao*, a Way, of nature. That is, natural processes occur not only in an orderly but also in a harmonious fashion. Human beings can discern the *Tao*, the natural well-orchestrated flow of things. And human activities can either be well adapted to the *Tao*, or they can buck it. In the former case, human goals are accomplished with ease and grace and without disturbing the natural environment; but in the latter they are accomplished, if at all, with difficulty and at the price of considerable disruption of neighboring social and natural systems. Capital-intensive Western technology,—such as nuclear power plants and industrial agriculture,—is very "un-Taoist" in esprit and motif.

Modern conservationists find in Taoism an ancient analogue of today's countermovement toward appropriate technology and sustainable development. The great Mississippi Valley flood of 1993 is a case in point. The river system was not managed in accordance with the *Tao*. Thus, levees and flood walls only exacerbated the big flood when it finally came. Better to locate cities and towns outside the floodplain and allow the mighty Mississippi River occasionally to overflow. The rich alluvial soils in the river's floodplains could be farmed in dryer years, but no permanent structures should be located there. That way, the floodwaters could periodically spread over the land, enriching the soil and replenishing wetlands for wildlife, and the human dwellings on higher ground could remain safe and secure. Perhaps the officers of the U.S. Corps of Engineers should study Taoism. We can only hope that their counterparts in China will abandon newfangled Maoism for old-fashioned Taoism before trying to contain, rather than cooperate with, the Yangtze River.

The other ancient Chinese religious worldview is Confucianism. To most people, Asian and Western alike, Confucianism connotes conservatism, adherence to custom and social forms, filial piety, and resignation to feudal inequality. Hence, it seems to hold little promise as an intellectual soil in which to cultivate a conservation ethic. Ames (1992), however, contradicts the received view: "There is a common ground shared by the teachings of classical Confucianism and Taoism . . . Both express a 'this-worldly' concern for the concrete details of immediate experience rather than . . . grand abstractions and ideals. Both acknowledge the uniqueness, importance, and primacy of particular persons and their contributions to the world, while at the same time expressing the ecological interrelatedness and interdependence of this person with his context."

From a Confucian point of view, a person is not a separate immortal soul temporarily residing in a physical body; a person is, rather, the unique center of a network of relationships. Because his or her identity is constituted by these relationships, the destruction of one's social and environmental context is equivalent to self-destruction. Biocide, in other words, is tantamount to suicide.

In the West, because individuals are not ordinarily conceived to be robustly related to and dependent upon their context—not only for their existence but for their very identity—it is possible to imagine that they can remain themselves and be "better off" at the expense of both their social and natural environments. But from a Confucian point of view, it is impossible to abstract persons from their contexts. Thus, if *context* is expanded from its classic social to its current environmental connotation, Confucianism offers a very firm foundation upon which to build a contemporary Chinese conservation ethic.

The tenets and conservation implications of these various non-Western religions are summarized in Table 2.3. Essay 2B by Susan Bratton further explores the role of religion in conservation.

Biocentrism

Before the advent of environmental ethics, moral philosophers in the Western tradition granted moral standing to human beings and human beings alone, not by appeal to a mystical property, such as the image of God, but by appeal to observable traits, such as rationality or linguistic ability. Because only people, they argued, can reason or speak, only people are worthy of ethical treatment. In the 18th century, Immanuel Kant (1959), for example, argued that human beings are intrinsically valuable ends because we are rational, while animals (and other forms of life) are only instrumentally valuable means because they are not. Contemporary environmental philosophers have attempted to con-

Table 2.3
A Comparison of Traditional Non-Western Conservation Ethics

Characteristic	Islam	Hinduism	Jainism	Buddhism	Taoism	Confucianism
Source of value in nature	External; *Allah* (God)	Internal; *Atman-Brahman*	Internal; soul (*jiva*)	Internal; Buddha-nature	Emergent; the *Tao* (Way)	Emergent; relational
Human attitude toward nature	Respect for creation is respect for Creator	Identification; self-realization	*Ahimsa* (noninjury)	Loving-kindness; solidarity	Harmony; cooperation	Interrelated; interdependent
Conservation practice	Conserve resources for future generations	Conserve trees and other beings that manifest *Atman-Brahman*	Low on the food chain; low level of consumption	Still desires; reduce consumption; contemplate nature	Adapt human economy to nature's economy	Conserve nature to preserve human society

struct a nonanthropocentric environmental ethic without appeal to mystical religious concepts, such as God, the *Tao,* or the universal Buddha-nature. Some have done so by arguing that reason and linguistic ability are inappropriate qualifications for moral standing, and that other observable traits are more appropriate.

Singer (1975) and Regan (1983) exposed classic Western anthropocentric ethics to the following dilemma: if the qualification for ethical standing—or "criterion for moral considerability" as it is more technically called—is pitched high enough to exclude nonhuman beings, then it will exclude as well those human beings who also fail to measure up. Human infants, the severely retarded, and the profoundly senile are not rational. If, following Kant, we make rationality the criterion of moral considerability, then these human "marginal cases" may be treated just as we treat nonhuman beings who fail to meet it. They may become, for example, unwilling subjects of painful medical tests and experiments; they may be hunted for sport; or they may be made into dog

ESSAY 2B

Monks, Temples, and Trees
The Spirit of Diversity

Susan P. Bratton, University of North Texas

A Buddhist monk bends over and carefully waters a small seedling in the temple garden. Others of its kind are nearby. Older, taller trees shade the sanctuary paths with their fan-shaped leaves, and produce a crop of edible nuts each year. The monk looks at the little ginkgo and reflects that he never has seen one growing on its own in the surrounding mountains. Only in the temple gardens and their environs has the ginkgo survived, at least in his region of China.

From a venerable lineage, datable to the lower Jurassic, *Ginkgo biloba* is the only known remaining species of an entire division of vascular plants, the Ginkgophyta. Often called a "living fossil," the modern shade tree is little different from the ginkgos of the early Cretaceous period. *Ginkgo* is also a taxon that may or may not exist in the wild. One of the largest "seminatural" populations, at Tian Mu Shan, is near the Kaishan temple, and thus may have been under partial human protection, if not management, for centuries. Over the last several thousand years, Buddhist monks have probably slowly replaced the ginkgo's natural dispersal agents, such as leopard cats (*Felis bengalensis*) and helped preserve the species for posterity (del Tredici et al. 1992).

Our contemporary technocratic and scientifically oriented society often mistakenly considers religion to be either uninterested or uninformed when it comes to protection and management of the natural world. We also assume that if religion is interested, it is the more "primitive" religions and those that practice magic that attempt to relate to or manipulate wild nature, while the great religions of the world—particularly the "peoples of the book," Judaism, Christianity, and Islam—are too theological and otherworldly to concern themselves with the various small pieces that make up the cosmos. The truth is, religious values have often helped to protect natural diversity, and religion remains one of the most important wellsprings of human concern for other species. E. O. Wilson has suggested that science alone cannot protect biodiversity; other cultural values must be called on as well.

Science attempts to understand the world through objective comparison. The various elements in the environment become "other," or differentiated from the scientist, who makes a conscious effort to distance herself from the phenomena she is observing. Religion, in contrast, establishes relationship or identification with the "other." The shaman becomes an intermediary with nature and links the village with the surrounding forests and their creatures; the Buddhist monk works in the temple garden and increases his spiritual understanding of the cosmos as a whole; the Hebrew psalmist sees the glory of God in the diversity of the wild and praises divine wisdom for placing the stork in the cedars and for maintaining both birds and forests with water gushing from mountain springs. Religion has a freedom of symbolic and aesthetic expression inappropriate to science. Religion can speak with nature, science can only speak about it.

Religion forwards the preservation of natural diversity in several different ways. The first is by providing ethical and social models for living respectfully with nature. For most cultures, religion is a primary means of defining right and wrong. The Koyukon of Alaska, for example, do not separate the natural and the spiritual world, and explain the spiritual power residing in nature through Distant Time stories about the evolution of the cosmos. Since nature has spiritual power, it commands respect and is included in the religious code of morality and etiquette. The Koyukon avoid waste in food harvest and take only what they can use from their fragile far-northern lands. They do not kill female waterfowl preparing to nest, nor do they take young animals. They fear retribution in the form of bad luck if they violate taboos or are disrespectful of the animals they hunt, so their husbandry of natural resources is tightly tied to an animist worldview (Nelson 1983). Other religions with very different notions of the otherworldly may have rather similar rules. The Hebrew scriptures, with their one transcendent God, forbid removal of a mother bird from her nest.

Secondly, religion often provides direct protection for wild and cultivated plants and animals. Many cultures have holy places, including mountains, that humans may approach only for religious purposes, if at all. Rivers or forests may be sacred environs, where wildlife and vegetation are not to be disturbed. Sites are sometimes set aside specifically to protect taxa that have medicinal value or are utilized in religious ritual. Taboos or special religious significance can prevent the killing of individual wildlife species. Buddhism, one of the most abstract and philosophical of all religions, has protected numerous organisms, from ginkgos to cranes to monkeys, resident on the grounds of its temples. Some early Christian monks would not allow the native oak forests to be cleared from around their monasteries. St. Francis of Assisi instructed his followers to leave the borders of a cultivated garden unweeded to provide space for wildflowers, so that the blossoms, in their beauty, could praise the creator God. Even our contemporary wilderness areas in the United States are, among other purposes, supposed to preserve and protect "spiritual values."

Lastly, religion ties the nonhuman residents of the cosmos to the divine or to the overall meaning of human existence. This gives the biota a value that science alone cannot provide. The saffron-robed initiate caring for the temple landscape sees each individual creature as beautiful in itself and beautiful in its interrelationship with its neighbors. The trees, the small clump of flowers, the rock and the sand, become more than xylem and chloroplasts, or feldspar and quartz. For the dedicated practitioner, the sanctity of the environment is an inspiration and a blessing. The spiritual realization of the Buddhist, in turn, blesses the environment (14th Dalai Lama 1992). In early and medieval Christianity, where love and compassion were key values and holiness was fervently pursued, the monks and desert ascetics often cared for wildlife, healing animals with injuries and even rescuing them from hunters. The early Christians thought animals could recognize the pure of heart, and that even wild lions and wolves would show affection for the great saints.

The religious myths and stories that teach us about the importance of other species are often so basic that we, in our human-dominated, industrial world, miss the critical message. Take, for example, the tale of Noah's ark. Noah did not save the animals just to be nice. Noah saved the animals because humans need the animals—all the animals, not just the domestic and the edible. Also, in the Genesis original, it is God who instructs Noah to build the ark. The great God of Israel wanted the animals rescued, and put Noah to a great deal of trouble during a very damp climatic period to accomplish this. God had created the animals in wondrous diversity and in marvelous order, and had blessed them as both good and beautiful well before the Garden of Eden was an official mailing address. When the animals march onto the ark according to their kinds, it is divine organization that is being honored, and when Noah saves them all, not just a few, it is the glory of divine handiwork that is being preserved (Bratton 1993). Modern conservation biology can perhaps take a lesson from this.

---

food. No one would want that to happen. To avoid it, Singer (1975) and Regan (1983) argue, we must lower the criterion for moral considerability. But if it is pitched low enough to include the human marginal cases, then it will also include a number of nonhuman animals. Singer (1975) follows Kant's 18th-century contemporary, Jeremy Bentham, and argues that sentience, the capacity to experience pleasure and pain, ought to be the criterion for ethical standing.

Goodpaster (1978) first took the step from animal liberation to biocentric (literally "life-centered") environmental ethics. From a biological point of view, sentience, he argued, evolved not as an end in itself, but as a means to animals' survival. Hence if there is something morally relevant about sentience, how much more morally relevant is that which sentience evolved to serve—namely, life. Moreover, all living things, as explained earlier in this chapter, have a good of their own, and therefore have interests. That fact too, according to Goodpaster (1978), ought to entitle all living things to ethical standing.

Defining a more extreme view, Taylor (1986) argues that all living things are of equal "inherent worth" (Figure 2.4). Apart from the ethically problematic and practically impossible task of according equal moral consideration to each and every living thing, Taylor's pure and extreme biocentrism has little relevance to conservation biology—which, once more, is not concerned with the fate of specimens, but of species, ecosystems, and evolutionary processes.

As modified by Rolston (1988), however, biocentrism may address the concerns of conservation biologists and hence may represent a viable conservation ethic. Rolston agrees with Taylor that all living things have intrinsic value (or inherent worth) and thus should enjoy moral standing. But he does not agree that all living things are equal. To the baseline intrinsic value that organisms possess by virtue of having interests and a good of their own, Rolston adds a value "bonus," as we might think of it, for being sentient, and he adds an additional value bonus for being rational and self-conscious. Hence, sentient animals have more intrinsic value than insentient plants, and human beings have more intrinsic value than sentient animals (Figure 2.4). Rolston's biocentrism thus better accords with our intuitive sense of a value hierarchy than does Taylor's, because in Rolston's version, the life of a human being is more valuable than that of a white-tailed deer, and that of a deer is more valuable than that of a jack pine. And, as noted earlier in this chapter, Rolston also provides intrinsic value, or something similar to it—a value "dividend" as we might think of it—for species, ecosystems, and their evolutionary processes. He argues, therefore, that we have a moral duty to preserve them as well. The development of biocentric and ecocentric philosophies in a historical framework is further explored in Essay 2C by Roderick Nash.

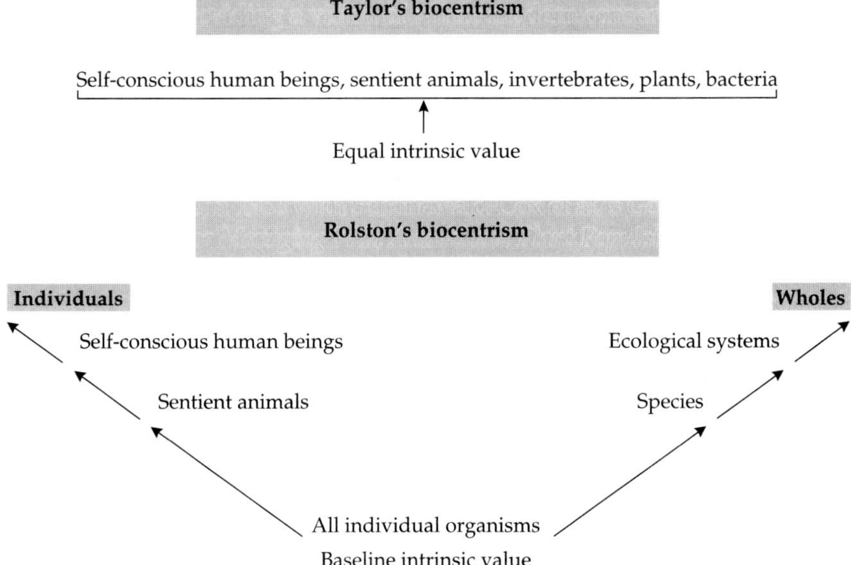

Figure 2.4 Taylor's biocentrism, in which all individual organisms have equal intrinsic value, and Rolston's, in which the baseline intrinsic value at the level of individual organisms is augmented by sentience and self-consciousness; that is, organisms incur increasing intrinsic value for sentience and self-consciousness. Rolston also provides a parallel valuation scheme for "wholes": species and ecosystems.

ESSAY 2C

An American Perspective

Discovering Radical Environmentalism in Our Own Cultural Backyard

From Natural Rights to the Rights of Nature

Roderick Frazier Nash, University of California at Santa Barbara

The search for philosophical foundations for ecocentrism and radical environmentalism have led to ancient Asian religions, pre-Christian Druidic rituals, and Native American cosmologies. Much can be learned—and certainly much inspiration gained—from these attempts to relate humans to nature respectfully and responsibly. But are these belief systems the most promising platform for environmental reform—indeed, paradigm change—in the modern American context?

The problem is that mainstream Americans cannot easily think like Indians, Druids, or Taoists; for better or for worse, we march to the beat of a different cultural drummer. But we do have one powerful ideal with which to change paradigms. It is as American as apple pie, and it could provide the motivation to save the planet and us along with it.

Natural rights liberalism is the most potent concept in the history of American thought. It was present before the American experiment, in 1215, when a handful of English nobles presented a Magna Carta to their king, challenging the exclusivity of the royal definition of rights. The message was straightforward: we are members of this society and we want rights too. By 1776, England's American colonies had expanded the meaning of natural rights considerably. Now "all men" were thought to be endowed with them, and the colonists felt strongly enough about them to fight a war for independence.

Granted that the Jeffersonian sense of "men" was severely limited. Red men, black men, and female men were not yet regarded as full members of the moral community. But the spirit of 1776 was extremely volatile. One of its most dramatic extensions resulted in a huge paradigm change: the abolition of slavery. Beginning in the 1830s, a handful of "radical" American reformers determined to extend basic American natural rights ideals to blacks. The campaign struck one of the most sensitive chords in the American mind: the rights of an oppressed minority to liberation. By 1865 the moral circle had widened and all slaves were legally free.

Today we see in the environmental movement remarkable growth of another "radical" idea: nature has rights that humans should respect. **Deep ecology** calls for the liberation of land and nonhuman life from ownership and abuse. There are appeals for the end of *earth* slavery. Echoing the Abolitionists' cry, "No Compromise with Slave Holders!," Earth First! proclaims, "No Compromise in Defense of Mother Earth!" The Boston Tea Party of 1773 and John Brown's 1859 raid on Harper's Ferry, Virginia, on behalf of slaves inspire environmental radicals. The arresting implication of this parallel is that the slavery issue was not educated or legislated away; it took a civil war and cost a million lives. Will the implementation of environmental ethics also involve conflict?

It is important to acknowledge that the extension of ethics to include nature is not even a simple *conceptual* task. Colonists and slaves, after all, were human; Spotted Owls and wild rivers are not. Classic natural rights are individual-oriented: *every* human has them. This spells trouble in the human relationship to nature. Are we to refrain from *any* impact on our environment? Can we never kill *anything* to eat? Few rational people think so; clearly there must be differences in moral behavior. But for increasing numbers of people it does make sense to say that all the species that share the planet with us have rights to exist and pursue their lives in their own way. Some feel that ecosystem processes have intrinsic value and a claim to freedom from the tyranny often imposed by human civilization.

Already we have legislation such as the Endangered Species Act of 1973, which gives legal protection to nonhuman existence rights. We also have national park and wilderness acts, which protect nonliving things and ecological processes. From this starting point, it is plausible that American morality can once again expand. This time we could move from natural rights to the rights of nature.

Ecocentrism

For sound philosophical as well as temperamental reasons, those conservation biologists with nonanthropocentric sympathies have gravitated to the Aldo Leopold Land Ethic in their search for a fitting conservation ethic. Leopold was himself a conservation biologist; indeed, he was, perhaps, the prototype of the breed (Meine 1992). Further, the Leopold Land Ethic is not based on religious beliefs, nor is it an extension of the ethical paradigm of classic Western moral philosophy. It is grounded, rather, in evolutionary and ecological biology. Hence, most nonanthropocentric conservation biologists, irrespective of their religious or cultural background, find the Leopold Land Ethic intellectually congenial.

In *The Descent of Man*, Darwin tackled the problem of the evolutionary origins and development of ethics. How could "limitations on freedom of action" possibly have arisen through natural selection, given the universal "struggle for existence" (Leopold 1949)? In a nutshell, Darwin (1904) answered as follows: social organization enhances the survival and reproductive efficiency of many kinds of organisms. Among mammals, parental and filial affections, having spilled over to other close kin, bound individuals into small social units such as packs, troops, and bands. When one mammal—*Homo sapiens*—acquired the capacity for reflection and speech, behaviors that were conducive to social integrity and stability were dubbed "good" and those that were antisocial were dubbed "bad." Or, as Darwin (1904) wrote, "No tribe could hold together if murder, robbery, treachery, &c., were common; consequently such crimes within the limits of the same tribe, 'are branded with everlasting infamy.'" Once originated, ethics developed apace with the growth and development of society. According to Darwin (1904),

> As man advances in civilization, and small tribes are united into larger communities, the simplest reason would tell each individual that he ought to extend his social instincts and sympathies to all the members of the same nation though personally unknown to him. This point being once reached, there is only an artificial barrier to prevent his sympathies extending to the men of all nations and races.

Here, at the end of the 20th century, we have finally reached the point that Darwin could only envision in the middle of the 19th: a universal ethic of human rights. But, also during the 20th century, ecology discovered (actually rediscovered, because many tribal peoples seem to have represented their natural environments in analogous terms) that human beings are not only members of various human communities—from the familial clan to the family of man—but members of a "biotic community" as well.

From Darwin we learn that "All ethics so far evolved rest upon a single premise: that the individual is a member of a community of interdependent parts" (Leopold 1949); and from Leopold, that ecology now "simply enlarges the boundaries of the community to include soils, waters, plants, and animals, or collectively: the land." If whenever a new community came to be recognized in the past, "the simplest reason would tell each individual that he ought to extend his social instincts and sympathies," Leopold argues, then the same "simplest reason" ought to kick in again, now that ecology informs us that we are members of a biotic community.

Though it has been altogether forgotten in Western moral philosophy over the last 200 years, human ethics has always had a strong holistic aspect. That is, human beings have felt that they had duties and obligations to their communities as such, as well as to individual members of those communities. About this Darwin (1904) was emphatic: "actions are regarded by savages, and were probably so regarded by primeval man, as good or bad, solely as they obviously affect the tribe, not that of the species, nor that of the individual member of the tribe. This agrees well with the belief that the so-called moral sense is aboriginally derived from the social instincts, for both relate at first exclusively to the community."

Influenced by Darwin, Leopold also gave his land ethic a decided holistic cast: "In short, a land ethic," he writes, "changes the role of *Homo sapiens* from conqueror of the land community to plain member and citizen of it. It implies respect for his fellow-members and also respect for the community as such" (Leopold 1949). Indeed, by the time Leopold came to write the summary moral maxim, or "golden rule," of the land ethic, he seems to have forgotten about "fellow-members" altogether and only mentions the "community as such": *"A thing is right when it tends to preserve the integrity, stability, and beauty of the biotic community. It is wrong when it tends otherwise."*

Staunch apologists for the rugged individualism characteristic of Western moral philosophy during the last two centuries have charged that the land ethic leads to "environmental fascism"—the subordination of the rights of individuals, including human individuals, to the good of the whole (Regan 1983; Aiken 1984). They have a point where nonhuman animals are concerned. The land ethic would permit—nay, even require—killing animals, such as feral goats or rabbits, that pose a threat to populations of endangered floral species or to the general health and integrity of biotic communities. But Leopold, following Darwin, represented the land ethic as an ethical "accretion"—that is, an addition to, not a substitute for, our long-standing human-to-human ethics.

That human beings have recently become members of national and international communities does not mean that we are no longer members of more ancient and more narrowly circumscribed social groups, such as extended families, or that we are relieved of all the moral duties and responsibilities that attend our active family, clan, and civic affiliations (Figure 2.5). Similarly, because we now realize that we are also members of a biotic community does not mean that we are relieved of all the moral duties and responsibilities that attend our membership in the full spectrum of human communities.

This defense of the Leopold land ethic against the charge that it promotes environmental fascism leads to the charge that it is a "paper tiger," an ecocentric environmental ethic without "teeth." For if we must fully acknowledge all our ancient and modern human duties and obligations as well as our more recently discovered environmental ones, how can we ever justify sacrificing human interests to conserve nonhuman species and ecosystems?

Fortunately, not all human-environment conflicts are life and death issues. We rarely face a choice between killing human beings and conserving biodiversity. Rather, most choices are between human lifestyles and biodiversity. For example, Japanese and other consumers of whale meat are not asked to lay down their lives to save the whales, only to change their dietary preferences. To save forests, we do not have to commit suicide; we can save them

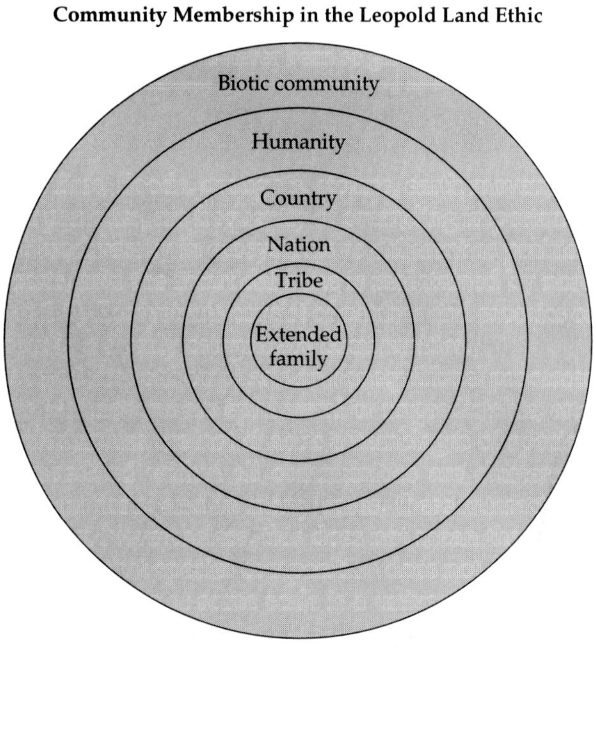

Figure 2.5 The various communities to which human beings belong, and how these communities are hierarchically ordered in the Leopold Land Ethic. The smallest and most intimate community is the family; the largest is the multispecies biotic community. In general, duties and obligations related to the communities at or closer to the center historically have taken precedence over those at or closer to the perimeter. But we must also consider the gravity, or weight, of duties and obligations to these communities, as well as their proximity, when they come into conflict with one another.

Community Membership in the Leopold Land Ethic

Biotic community
Humanity
Country
Nation
Tribe
Extended family

simply by using less lumber and paper, and by recycling what cellulose we must extract. All human interests are not equal. We should be prepared to override less important human interests for the sake of the vital interests of other forms of life, and for ecological health and integrity.

Leopold penned the land ethic at mid-century. Ecological science then represented nature as tending toward a static equilibrium, and portrayed disturbance and perturbation—especially that caused by *Homo sapiens*—as abnormal and destructive (Odum 1953). In light of recent doubts about the very existence of "biotic communities" that persist as such through time (Brubaker 1988), in view of the shift in contemporary ecology to a more dynamic paradigm (Botkin 1990), and in recognition of the incorporation of natural disturbance into theories of patch- and landscape-scale ecological dynamics (Pickett and White 1985), we might wonder whether the Leopoldian Land Ethic has become obsolete. Has the paradigm shift from "the balance of nature" to "the flux of nature" in ecology invalidated the land ethic? No, but recent developments in ecology may require revising the land ethic.

Leopold was aware of and sensitive to natural change. He knew that conservation must aim at a moving target. How can we conserve a biota that is dynamic, ever-changing, when the very words *conserve* and *preserve*—especially when linked to *integrity* and *stability*—connote stasis? The key to solving this conundrum is the concept of temporal and spatial **scale.** A review of Leopold's "The Land Ethic" reveals that he had the key, though he may not have realized just how multiscalar change in nature actually is.

In "The Land Ethic," Leopold (1949) writes, "Evolutionary changes . . . are usually slow and local. Man's invention of tools has enabled him to make changes of unprecedented violence, rapidity, and scope." As noted, Leopold was keenly aware that nature is dynamic, but, under the sway of mid-century equilibrium ecology, he conceived of natural change primarily in evolutionary, not in ecological, terms. Nevertheless, scale is equally relevant when consideration of ecological change is added to that of evolutionary change; that is, when normal climatic oscillations and patch dynamics are added to normal rates of extinction, hybridization, and speciation.

Homo sapiens is a part of nature, "a plain member and citizen" of the "land-community," as Leopold (1949) put it. Hence, anthropogenic (human-caused) changes imposed on nature are no less natural than any other. But, because *Homo sapiens* is a moral species, capable of ethical deliberation and conscious choice, and because our evolutionary kinship and biotic community membership add a land ethic to our familiar social ethics, anthropogenic changes may be land-ethically evaluated. But by what norm? The norm of appropriate scale.

Temporal and spatial scale in combination are the key to the evaluation of direct human ecological impacts. Long before *Homo sapiens* evolved, violent disturbances regularly occurred in nature (Pickett and White 1985), and they still do, quite independently of human agency. Volcanoes bury the biota of whole mountains with lava and ash. Tornadoes rip through forests, leveling trees. Hurricanes erode beaches. Wildfires sweep through forests and savannas. Rivers drown floodplains. Droughts dry up lakes and streams. Why, then, are analogous anthropogenic disturbances—clear-cuts, beach developments, hydroelectric impoundments, and the like—environmentally unethical? As such, they are not; it is a question of scale. In general, frequent, intense disturbances, such as tornadoes, occur at small, widely distributed spatial scales; spatially broader disturbances, such as droughts, occur infrequently. And most disturbances, at whatever level of intensity and scale, are stochastic (random) and chaotic (unpredictable). The problem with anthropogenic perturbations—such as industrial forestry and agriculture, exurban development, drift net fishing, and such—is that they are far more frequent, widespread, and regularly occurring than are nonanthropogenic perturbations; they are well out of the normal spatial and temporal range of disturbances experienced by ecosystems over evolutionary time (Holling and Meffe 1996).

Pickett and Ostfeld (1995)—proponents of the new natural disturbance/patch dynamics paradigm in ecology—agree that appropriate scale is the operative norm for ethically appraising anthropogenic ecological perturbations. They note that

> the flux of nature is a dangerous metaphor. The metaphor and the underlying ecological paradigm may suggest to the thoughtless and greedy that because flux is a fundamental part of the natural world, any human-caused flux is justifiable. Such an inference is wrong because the flux in the natural world has severe limits. . . . Two characteristics of human-induced flux would suggest that it would be excessive: fast rate and large spatial extent.

Among the abnormally frequent and widespread anthropogenic perturbations that Leopold himself censures in "The Land Ethic" are the continent-wide elimination of large predators from biotic communities in North America, the ubiquitous substitution of domestic species for wild ones, the ecological homogenization of the planet resulting from the "world-wide pooling of faunas and floras," and the ubiquitous "polluting of waters or obstructing them with dams."

The summary moral maxim of the land ethic, then, must be updated in light of developments in ecology over the past quarter-century. Leopold acknowledged the existence and significance of natural environmental change, but seems to have thought of it primarily on a very slow evolutionary time scale. Even so, he thereby incorporates the concept of inherent environmental change and the crucial norm of scale into the land ethic. In light of more recent developments in ecology, we can add norms of scale for both climatic and ecological dynamics to the land ethic. Although one hesitates to edit Leopold's elegant prose, we attempt to formulate a contemporary summary moral maxim for the land ethic with the following:

> A thing is right when it tends to disturb the biotic community only at normal spatial and temporal scales. It is wrong when it tends otherwise.

Summary

Conservation biology is driven by the *value* of biodiversity. But why should people value biodiversity? Philosophers have distinguished two basic types of value, instrumental and intrinsic. Biodiversity is instrumentally valuable for the *goods* (e.g., actual and potential food, medicine, fiber, and fuel), *services* (e.g., pollination, nutrient recycling, oxygen production), *information* (e.g., practical scientific knowledge, a genetic library), and *psycho-spiritual satisfaction* (e.g., natural beauty, religious awe, pure scientific knowledge) that it provides for intrinsically valuable human beings. Biodiversity may also be intrinsically valuable—valuable, that is, as an end in itself, as well as a means to human well-being. Like ourselves, other forms of life are self-organizing beings with goods of their own. And we human beings are capable of valuing other beings for their own sakes, as well as for what they do for us.

In order to compare its value with the value of other things, economists have attempted to *monetize* both the instrumental and intrinsic value of biodiversity. Philosophers have also based *conservation ethics* on the value of biodiversity. If biodiversity is only instrumentally valuable to human beings, its destruction by one person in pursuit of personal gain may be harmful to another person—in which case the destruction of biodiversity may be immoral. If biodiversity also has intrinsic value, its destruction may be doubly immoral.

The Bible recognizes the intrinsic value of nonhuman species (God declared them to be "good"). Accordingly, contemporary Jewish and Christian theologians have formulated a Judeo-Christian Stewardship Conservation Ethic. Many other world religions are also developing distinct conservation ethics based on their scriptures and traditions. The Aldo Leopold Land Ethic is not based on any religion, but on contemporary evolutionary and ecological biology. From an evolutionary perspective, human beings are kin to all other forms of life, and from an ecological perspective, human beings are "plain members and citizens" of the "biotic community." According to Leopold, these general scientific facts generate ethical obligations to our "fellow voyagers in the odyssey of evolution," to "fellow-members of the biotic community," and to that "community as such." Though ecology now acknowledges the normalcy of change and disturbance in nature, the Leopold Land Ethic, appropriately revised in light of these recent developments in science, remains the guiding environmental ethic for conservation biology.

Questions for Discussion

1. Should conservation biologists explain the value of biodiversity to the general public in purely instrumental (or utilitarian) terms, or should they also offer reasons for thinking that biodiversity has intrinsic (or inherent) value?
2. How should a conservation biologist trying to save a small endangered plant species, such as Furbish's lousewort, respond to the question, "What good is it?"
3. Suppose that a developer wants to build a dog track outside Houston, Texas, in the last remaining habitat of the Houston toad. If nonhuman species have only instrumental value, should the toad's habitat be saved? If nonhuman species have intrinsic value, could any development proposal that usurped the toad's habitat be morally justified?
4. Would the existence of a legal international market in ivory help or hurt efforts to conserve African elephants?
5. Should conservation biologists campaign to take biodiversity off the market and say, in effect, "Not for sale at any price," or should we try to show that the dollar value of biodiversity exceeds the dollar value of the lumber, electricity, beef, or what-have-you, whose production contributes to the erosion of biodiversity?
6. How does the understanding of human nature and the place of human beings in nature set out in Genesis in the Bible compare with the understanding of human nature and the place of human beings in nature forthcoming from science?
7. Suppose that a population of weedy sentient animals—say, feral goats—is threatening the survival of a plant species endemic to an island. What ethical concerns should a conservation biologist take into account before proposing a course of action?
8. If, in Rolston's biocentrism, the life of a white-tailed deer is more intrinsically valuable than that of a jack pine, would it also follow that the life of

a gray squirrel is more intrinsically valuable than that of a thousand-year-old redwood tree? Is the life of a human being more intrinsically valuable than that of a thousand-year-old redwood tree? Why?

9. Suppose that your brother is a logger or millworker in the Pacific Northwest. As a conservation biologist, should you support a moratorium on all logging of old-growth forests in the region, or do family obligations require you to be more concerned about your brother's lifestyle and livelihood?

10. If indigenous peoples have lived on and significantly affected all continents except Antarctica for at least 10,000 years, are wilderness areas devoid of human residents "artificial?"

11. Suppose that, to your claim that the current episode of abrupt, massive species extinction is immoral, someone replied, "Ninety-nine percent of all species that ever existed on earth are now extinct. Why, then, should we be concerned about rendering more of them extinct?" How would you respond?

12. Suppose that, to your claim that clear-cutting the last remaining old-growth Douglas fir forests of the Pacific Northwest is immoral, someone replied, "Douglas fir is not the climax forest in the region—western hemlock is—and Douglas fir forests are found there because the forest succession in the region is periodically reset by catastrophic fires. Why, then, should we be concerned about imitating the effects of fires by clear-cutting?" Formulate an answer based on melding an ethical argument and scientific reasoning.

Suggestions for Further Reading

Callicott, J. B. (ed.). 1987. *Companion to A Sand County Almanac*. University of Wisconsin Press, Madison. Essays by biographers, historians, literary critics, scientists, and philosophers sketch Leopold's life and the natural history of Wisconsin's sand counties. They analyze his classic work on conservation values and ethics, interpret his land ethic, and trace its impact on conservation policy and practice.

Callicott, J. B. 1994. *Earth's Insights: A Multicultural Survey of Ecological Ethics*. University of California Press, Berkeley. Global conservation efforts can succeed only if they are consistent with and motivated by the deepest beliefs of people all over the world. Sketched in this book are conservation values and ethics grounded in Judaism, Christianity, Islam, Hinduism, Buddhism, Taoism, Confucianism, and in the worldviews of selected Pacific, North American, African, and Australian indigenous peoples.

Kellert, S. R. 1996. *The Value of Life: Biological Diversity and Human Society*. Island Press, Washington, D.C. Kellert identifies the biologically based, but culturally variable, value of biodiversity. Kellert's study incorporates extensive empirical information, based on sociological research, about the value various peoples find in nature.

Krutilla, J. and A. Fisher. 1985. *The Economics of Natural Environments: Studies in the Valuation of Commodity and Amenity Resources*. Revised ed. Resources for the Future, Washington, D.C. This volume provides a straightforward account of methods of monetizing the values of natural environments used by neoclassical economists.

Leopold, A. 1949. *A Sand County Almanac and Sketches Here and There*. Oxford University Press, New York. Leopold is often called a "prophet" because he was a quarter-century ahead of his time in formulating a nonanthropocentric conservation philosophy and environmental ethic. This slender volume of essays is often called "the Bible of the contemporary conservation movement," and is a "must read" for any serious student of conservation.

Norton, B. G. 1991. *Toward Unity Among Environmentalists*. Oxford University Press, New York. The "convergence hypothesis"—the idea that the full spectrum of instrumental and intrinsic values of nature converge on the same environmental policies—is here set out and championed.

Rolston, H. III. 1988. *Environmental Ethics: Duties to and Values in the Natural World*. Temple University Press, Philadelphia. The dean of the new field of environmental ethics provides a sustained defense of the objective intrinsic value of nature from which he derives our duties and obligations to conserve biodiversity.

Sagoff, M. 1988. *The Economy of the Earth: Philosophy, Law, and the Environment*. Cambridge University Press, Cambridge. Sagoff's collected essays provide a critique of the methods used by neoclassical economists to monetize the values of natural environments. Some value questions, Sagoff argues, belong in the political realm, not the economic realm.

3

The Species in Conservation

In all probability more paper has been consumed on the questions of the nature and definition of the species than any other subject in evolutionary and systematic biology.

E. O. Wiley, 1978

One of the main players in conservation—conceptually, biologically, and legally—is the species. Most people have a conception of an entity called the species, and understand that there is a great deal of global diversity at that level, much of which is being lost; in fact, many mistakenly equate biodiversity with species diversity. Biologists have focused on the species level for centuries, and have developed systems for naming, cataloging, and comparing species. Many of our conservation efforts, from fund-raising to recovery programs to reserve design, dwell on species. Species are the focus of some of the most powerful conservation legislation in the world, including the U.S. Endangered Species Act (ESA) and the Convention on International Trade in Endangered Species (CITES).

Because the species plays such a central role in all of conservation, we will explore the implications of a species focus in this chapter. Conservation biologists should develop an understanding of the species category, the biological importance of variation within species, the vagueness of, and different perspectives on, species concepts, the various ways in which species are viewed, and, especially, an appreciation for the ecological and evolutionary values of species and populations.

One of the clear distinctions we hope to draw is between biological and legal definitions of species. Legislation drives much of the emphasis on the species as a unit of conservation, yet it is often difficult to define species biologically. Even if we can, other levels of biological organization, from populations to landscapes, may be more significant or more practical units of concern in various situations.

Views on Species

To the uninitiated, it may seem a simple thing to define a species; after all, most of us have an intuitive feel for species of animals and plants and can identify and name many species, seemingly with great confidence. The species is far from easy to delineate, however, and in fact many different species definitions and concepts exist among biologists.

Much of the **species problem**—the ambiguity of the species category—stems from the fact that the biological world is a continuum of organization, from atoms and molecules, through cells, organ systems, and individuals, to populations and species, to communities, ecosystems, and landscapes. The cutoff points that separate categories within this continuum are fuzzy, or are determined by the particular needs of a research or policy question. Consider something apparently as clear as an individual organism; surely there should be no ambiguity at that level. Yet, what exactly is an "individual" in a vegetatively reproducing plant that covers a hectare as a population of shrubs sprouting from spreading roots originating from one seed? What is an "individual" in a planarian worm, after it is split down the middle and two living physical entities result? How about a lizard that reproduces asexually, resulting in exact genetic replicas of itself?

Similarly, the species category is often ambiguous. Although definitions vary (see below), we may generally think of species as consisting of naturally occurring groups of individuals that can interbreed and that have a common evolutionary history. The species really represents a level of evolutionary discontinuity, but how discontinuous must two populations or individuals be in order to be of different species? (Note that this concept is equally valid if inverted: the species can represent a level of evolutionary continuity. How *continuous* must two populations or individuals be to be considered the same species?) It is obvious that a Mallard Duck (*Anas platyrhynchos*) is evolutionarily discontinuous with a Downy Woodpecker (*Dendrocopos pubescens*), but what about its relationship to the Mexican Duck (*Anas diazi*), with which it sometimes interbreeds? What about subspecies? How discontinuous are they, and what does their category really mean, biologically and legally? To answer such questions, we need to examine various ways of looking at the problem of defining species.

Typological versus Populational Thinking

There are two major ways in which species have been viewed historically, which are reflections of two major schools of philosophical thought. The **typological view** sees species as categorical entities, distinct and somewhat clearly differentiated (Figure 3.1A). This outlook originated with the typological perspective of the Greek philosopher Plato, who maintained that all physical objects in our world represent an "*eidos*," an eternal and changeless ideal or perfect "type"; any variations about that ideal are merely unfortunate imperfections of the material world.

The typological view was adopted by early biologists, including Linnaeus, the originator of our present system of Latin binomial nomenclature (genus and species), and was largely, although not completely, accepted through the middle of the 19th century. It was manifested in the prevailing view of the time that species are immutable creations of God and occur in a fixed number. This view blended nicely with the "balance of nature" perspective, also popular at the time, that nature was a finely tuned, divinely engineered machine with perfectly fitting and unchanging parts. Early taxonomists therefore viewed individual variation as unimportant and even annoying, and species, subspecies, and races were named as though they were discrete and invariant units. The distinctness and fixity of species are central features of the typological perspective.

The **populational** (or evolutionary) **view**, in contrast, focuses directly on variation within species. This perspective recognizes that a category such as the species comprises a group of individuals that collectively express genetic, morphological, physiological, and behavioral variation, and that this variation is not unimportant and annoying, but is in fact the basis of evolutionary change and adaptation (Figure 3.1B). Within-species variation in the populational view is not seen as an unfortunate deviation from a perfect type, but as the result of genetic differences among, and environmental influences upon, individuals. Ernst Mayr (1959) summarized the typological/populational dichotomy clearly when he said, "For the typologist, the type (*eidos*) is real and the variation an illusion, while for the populationist the type (average) is an abstraction and only the variation is real. No two ways of looking at nature could be more different."

In its classic manifestation, the typological perspective results in a "pattern analysis" of species (Rojas 1992). Species are treated as nonhistorical entities, and their delineations are based on the statistical distribution of measurable characters, with no assumptions made about the historical (evolutionary) processes that caused these patterns. The populational perspective results in a "process analysis" of species, in which observed patterns are seen as the result of historical events and dynamic change—real processes—and causal analyses of patterns are offered. In this perspective, evolutionary events operate at the level of localized populations, which are the functional ecological and evolutionary units.

Virtually all contemporary biologists reject classic typological thinking and accept the populational view of species. They recognize the importance of diversity within species and the potential for genetic, morphological, physiological, or behavioral diversification among populations. They recognize that most measurable characteristics of living things vary to some degree, and that much of the variation is genetically based and of evolutionary importance (Futuyma 1986).

Geographic variation is a common type of variation in most species and is an important part of species concepts. Geographic variation consists of measurable divergence among different populations in characters such as color, body size, protein structure, behavior, egg size, or any other measurable trait. The degree of divergence varies, but is typically greater in geographically more distant populations or those living under very dissimilar ecological conditions (Figure 3.2). Well-marked, consistent differences in a character among populations, such as differences in plumage in birds, scale counts in fish, or color patterns in butterflies, are often the basis for subspecies designations, regardless of their biological importance. Less obvious but perhaps more important differences in other characters relevant to natural selection may go unrecognized and thus unheralded.

Geographic populations that clearly differ in the mean state of a particular character may nevertheless have within-population variation in that character such that some individuals overlap with other populations, which further blurs population variation. In other words, an individual from one population (or subspecies) may resemble more closely the mean of another population (or subspecies) than that of its own. Many degrees of mean character divergence and overlap may thus be found among populations, confusing the picture and making determination of species boundaries difficult.

Geographic variation is an important element in the study of evolutionary processes and the practice of conservation biology because it often reflects local adaptation, and is therefore a first step toward the process of **speciation**,

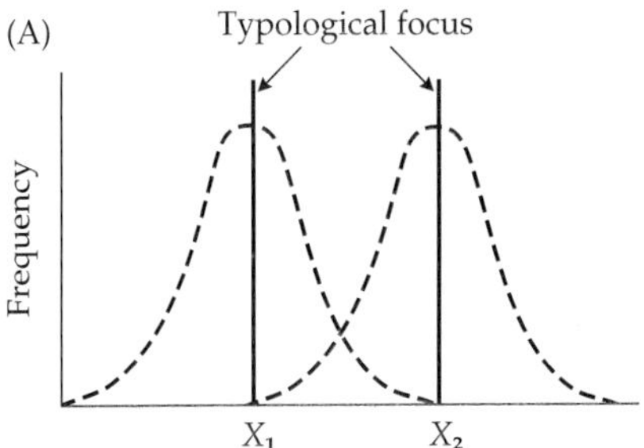

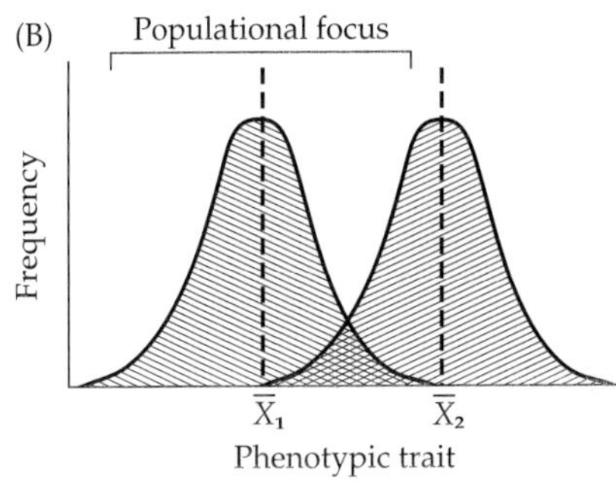

Figure 3.1 Conceptual models of typological and populational species concepts, as illustrated by the distribution of individuals of two species for a given phenotypic trait. (A) In the typological view, the essence of the species is represented by the mode (the "type," X_1 and X_2). Variance around the mean is considered "noise" and therefore unimportant. (B) In the populational view, the essence of the species includes the distribution of the trait, and the mean ($\overline{X}_1$ or $\overline{X}_2$) is simply one statistical descriptor. There is no perfect "type," and species may even grade into one another, with no clear gap. In each figure conceptualization, the perceived reality of the species is represented by a solid line; a dotted line represents the perceived less important aspect.

the development of new species. It is itself a form of biological variation worthy of protection and perpetuation.

Recognition of such biologically relevant variation within the species category raises important conservation questions. For example, how much of within-species variation is (or can be) conserved by species-level protection? How can we decide how much within-species diversity to protect? Is the species the appropriate unit on which to focus? To answer questions such as these, we need to look more closely at various species concepts.

Species Concepts

It should be obvious by now that the nature and definition of species is an area fraught with difficulty, and one that has the potential to bog us down and obstruct our progress toward more pressing questions in conservation. Nevertheless, we must pay heed to species concepts, as they have great bearing on how we approach conservation and what we ultimately conserve. The way species are defined can affect our perceptions of how many species there might be, their importance relative to populations, and their dynamics over time.

Definitions presented in introductory biology textbooks form the first, and perhaps most lasting, impressions most students obtain of the "species" issue, yet these definitions illustrate disparities in use of the term. For example, Campbell (1987) defined a species as "a particular kind of organism, its members possessing similar anatomical characteristics and having the ability to interbreed." Keeton (1972) called a species "the largest unit of population within which effective gene flow occurs or could occur." Kirk (1975) defined a species as "a group of related individuals that are actually or potentially capable of interbreeding; a group of organisms constituting a single gene pool." Each of these definitions has merit, and each has problems, but they collectively indicate that the species is not a universally defined and agreed-upon biological entity.

It is important to realize that species designations are nothing more than testable hypotheses, based upon the best information currently available. Species designations are temporary, and may change when better information becomes available; that is, the hypothesis may be rejected in the future. The main argument over the species question is over how these hypotheses are tested, the type of information used, how it is used, and the philosophical framework chosen.

There are several biological bases upon which species concepts may be developed, such as morphological discontinuity, reproductive isolation, pat-

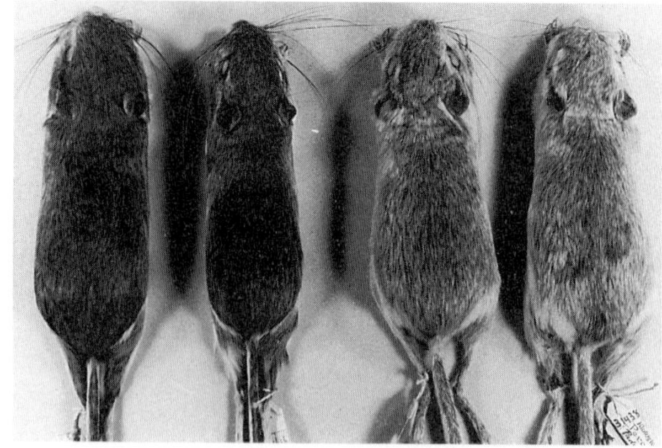

Figure 3.2 Individuals of different populations of the rock pocket mouse (*Perognathus intermedius*), illustrating geographic variation in coat color, presumably a result of different habitats and substrates. The two specimens on the left are from Socorro County, New Mexico, which has darker soils, and the two on the right are from Yuma County, Arizona, which has lighter soils. (Specimens courtesy of the Smithsonian Institution; photograph by G. K. Meffe.)

terns of ancestry and descent, genetic cohesion, and ecological adaptation. In part, these differences arise because the various concepts are sometimes used for different purposes (Endler 1989). Our intent here is not to go into the details and relative merits of the various species concepts, or to settle species issues, but to present some major species concepts as an illustration of the complexity of the topic, and as a preamble to further discussion relative to conservation.

Of the many species concepts in use today, three receive the most attention. The **biological species concept** (**BSC**), or "isolation concept," defines species as "groups of actually or potentially interbreeding populations, which are reproductively isolated from other such groups" (Mayr 1942). Because the essential criterion is reproductive isolation, or conversely, the ability to reproduce and therefore exchange genetic material, this is a genetically based definition. Mayr (1969) explained that, under this concept, a species has three separate "functions": it forms a reproductive community, is an ecological unit, and comprises a genetic unit consisting of a large, intercommunicating gene pool.

Despite modifications to the definition in recent years (Mayr 1982), the BSC has received criticism and has fallen out of favor with some. For one thing, it is often operationally difficult to determine reproductive isolation if the "species" are not **sympatric** (i.e., do not occur together and have the opportunity to interbreed). Reproductive isolation becomes trivial if the two forms live 1000 km apart and never come into contact. So, although defined on the basis of reproductive isolation, in practice species are largely judged on surrogate criteria—morphological measurements; these are assumed to provide evidence of reproductive community versus reproductive isolation, but this correlation is often hard to test (Donoghue 1985). Thus, practically speaking, the BSC is defined by one set of criteria (reproductive isolation), but the practicing taxonomist often finds this difficult to apply and uses another set of criteria (generally, morphology) as evidence for reproductive isolation.

Because its definition is based on reproductive isolation and genetic exchange, the BSC has further limitations. It is inapplicable to asexual species and "chronospecies" (species that are defined by changes through time, such as fossil taxa), and is often difficult to apply to microorganisms and plants, in which natural hybridization and genetic introgression (infiltration of the genes of one species into another) among recognized "species" are common, and where species are found in all stages of divergence (Grant 1957).

The **phylogenetic species concept** (**PSC**), sometimes called the cladistic species concept, is popular today. This concept argues that classification should reflect the branching, or **cladistic**, relationships among species or higher taxa, regardless of their degree of genetic relatedness. The relationships among taxa are described in a **cladogram**, which is an estimate or hypothesis of the true genealogical relationships among them. In the phylogenetic method, a species is defined as "the smallest diagnosable cluster of individual organisms within which there is a parental pattern of ancestry and descent" (Cracraft 1983). The species is an irreducible, or basal, unit distinct from other such units.

The PSC definition is based on the concept of shared derived characters, called **synapomorphies**. If two or more individuals or populations share a derived character (defined as a unique character not found in other, more distantly related groups), then they are assumed to be more closely related than individuals or populations lacking that character. For example (Figure 3.3), all chordates have a dorsal hollow nerve cord and a notochord, which separate chordates from all other animal groups. However, these are common characters within the group (i.e., all chordates have the character) that do nothing to further determine relationships among the chordates, so other characters must be explored. Within the chordates, vertebrates have a true brain, a cranium,

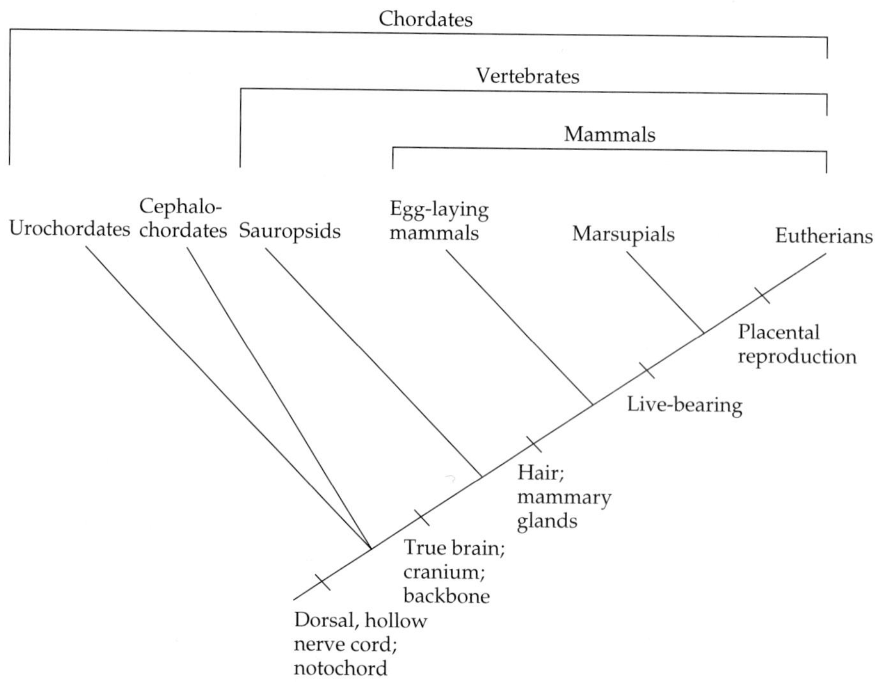

Figure 3.3 A simple cladogram, using some chordates as an example. A series of synapomorphic characters sequentially separates the different chordate groups. A more detailed phylogenetic analysis could separate down to the species level. (Note that, for simplicity, not all vertebrate groups are shown.)

and a backbone, which are unique characters that the other chordates (urochordates and cephalochordates) do not possess. Within the vertebrates, hair and mammary glands are found only in mammals, thus clearly separating them from their closest relatives, the sauropsids (reptiles and birds). Other unique characters, such as livebearing and placental reproduction, further separate the mammals. This sort of analysis, if carried out at finer levels, eventually separates species.

It is important to realize that synapomorphy is a relative term and depends on the particular taxonomic level of interest. For example, the presence of a backbone is a synapomorphy of vertebrates as compared with other chordates; however, within the vertebrates, the presence of a backbone does nothing to further determine relationships among vertebrate taxa, so we must search for other characters that vary within the group. Hair and mammary glands are synapomorphic characters of mammals, and clearly separate them from other vertebrates, but *within* the mammals, they are not synapomorphic (rather, they are **plesiomorphic**), because all mammals have these characters. Other characters, unique to various mammal groups, must be found for further separation of taxa.

The PSC definition is based on the conviction that evolution "results in a hierarchy of **monophyletic** groups . . . and that classifications should reflect genealogical relationships accurately and unambiguously at all levels" (Donoghue 1985). A monophyletic group ". . . is one that contains all and only the descendants of a particular common ancestor [plus the ancestor]. It is a group wherein every member is more closely related (in a strictly genealogical sense) to every other member than to any organisms classified outside the group" (Donoghue 1985). Evidence for monophylies (which define ancestral-descendant relationships) is provided by synapomorphic characters, which may be morphological, genetic, behavioral, biochemical, or any other measurable characteristic of an organism. In the above example, mammals are monophyletic in that they all possess hair and mammary glands; within mammals, eutherians are monophyletic because they all undergo placental reproduction.

Adoption of a phylogenetic species concept would result in the elevation of subspecies to full species in many groups and the recognition of individual populations with even small character differences as species. There are no subspecific designations in a PSC; geographically distinct populations that a BSC proponent would call subspecies would be full species under the PSC, even if the populations interbreed where their ranges meet. Cracraft (1992), for example, applied the phylogenetic species concept to the birds of paradise (family Paradisaeidae) and described 90 species, up from the 40–42 species proposed using the BSC, which also included about 100 subspecies. Such application of the PSC presumably accurately reflects actual evolutionary relationships and pathways.

The **evolutionary species concept** (**ESC**) defines a species as "a single lineage of ancestral descendant populations of organisms which maintains its identity from other such lineages and which has its own evolutionary tendencies and historical fate" (Wiley 1978, modified from Simpson 1961). A species is viewed here as an evolutionary entity with historical, rather than reproductive, ties and is based on phenetic (physical trait) cohesions and discontinuities; in that way it is similar to the phylogenetic species concept. It emphasizes that a species can be held together as a unit of evolution by developmental, genetic, and ecological constraints. Templeton (1989) pointed out several practical problems with the evolutionary species concept: there is no guidance as to which traits are most relevant, and several traits may give contradictory information; there is a problem in judging what constitutes a "common" evolutionary fate; and it is not a mechanistic definition because it deals only with the results of evolutionary cohesion, and not the mechanisms responsible.

A variety of other species concepts have been used, which we will not discuss in detail, but present to illustrate the diversity of approaches to the species problem, as well as the conceptual overlap among them. A modification of the typological approach is the **phenetic** school of taxonomy, based on numerical measurements of individuals and mathematical analysis of morphological discontinuities. The phenetic approach argues that the best classification system is based on the overall pattern of similarity and difference among individuals or groups, based on as many characteristics as possible, regardless of actual ancestral relationships. This concept is rarely used today.

The **ecological species concept** (Van Valen 1976) considers a species to be "a lineage (or a closely related set of lineages) which occupies an adaptive zone minimally different from that of any other lineage in its range and which evolves separately from all other lineages outside its range." An adaptive zone is defined as the resource space plus predators and parasites.

The **recognition species concept** (Paterson 1985) is essentially a corollary of the BSC. It defines a species as a field for gene recombination with reproductive mechanisms facilitating gene exchange; in the BSC, mechanisms that prevent gene exchange among dissimilar individuals are emphasized.

The **cohesion species** is defined by Templeton (1989) as "the most inclusive population of individuals having the potential for phenotypic cohesion through intrinsic cohesion mechanisms." The cohesion concept emphasizes mechanisms (such as gene flow and natural selection) that result in species cohesion, rather than isolation.

Two relevant philosophical perspectives further complicate species concepts. **Nominalists** question the very existence of species as real and natural entities, claiming that only individuals exist and species are artificial mental constructs without objective existence. Charles Darwin was perhaps a nominalist, or at least felt that the species concept had been confused and used in arbitrary ways. He wrote, "I look at the term species as one arbitrarily given, for the sake of convenience, to a set of individuals closely resembling each other, and it does not essentially differ from the term variety which is given to less distinct and more fluctuating forms" (1859).

Although most modern biologists would disagree, there are contemporary adherents to the nominalist view (e.g., Levin 1979), and it is not without its appeal, at least for some groups such as plants. Ehrlich and Holm (1963), for example, wrote, "... the idea of good species.... is a generality without foundation—an artifact of the procedures of taxonomy. These procedures require that distinct clusters be found and assigned to some level in a hierarchy—subspecies, species.... and so on." Ehrlich (1961) stated that, "... *at least at the present level of knowledge*, the prevalence of the clearly defined species is a myth" [italics original].

Contrasted with the nominalist philosophy is the **pluralist** suggestion that species concepts should vary with the taxa under consideration. Thus, Scudder (1974) suggests the existence of paleospecies, sibling species, morphospecies, hybrid species, and a host of other types that arise in different ways or apply to different biological situations.

The particular species concept favored may indeed depend on the particular biota in question. The choice is based less on biological differences than on historical legacies: some species definitions were developed by individuals with expertise in particular taxa, and convention has followed those definitions. For example, the biological species concept was championed by an ornithologist, Ernst Mayr; birds seemed to fit the definition well because so much was known about their individual biologies, and because breeding groups were often clearly delineated. In contrast, plant species provide many examples in which the use of the biological species concept is ambiguous or contradictory. Much more than animals, plants may form fertile hybrids between species, may develop new self-perpetuating varieties through **polyploidy** (multiplication of chromosome numbers), and may form asexual species. The problem of species identification and definition is further developed for freshwater mussels in Essay 3A by James Williams and Margaret Mulvey.

In closing this section on species concepts, we reemphasize that species are not fixed entities. If it were possible to inventory all species in the world every million years or so, each of our time windows would show species going extinct, new species appearing, and the rates of additions and subtrac-

ESSAY 3A

Recognition of Freshwater Mussel Taxa

A Conservation Challenge

James D. Williams, Biological Resources Division, U. S. Geological Survey and Margaret Mulvey, Savannah River Ecology Laboratory

The most diverse freshwater mussel fauna in the world occurs in North America. Currently, 281 species and 16 subspecies belonging to two families, Unionidae and Margaritiferidae, are recognized (Turgeon et al. 1988). They inhabit aquatic systems ranging from small ponds to lakes and from cold upland streams to warm and turbid lowland rivers. The greatest mussel diversity is found in the Tennessee, Cumberland, and Mobile River drainages of the southeastern United States.

Mussels were once a common component of freshwater ecosystems throughout most of the central and eastern United States. The decline of freshwater mussels parallels that of other freshwater organisms that have experienced gradual, but continuous, losses. The earliest threats, during the late 1800s, resulted from excessive commercial harvest of shell for the pearl button industry (Smith 1899). Dams, pollution, and siltation continue to plague mussel populations, but the introduction and spread of nonindigenous mollusks, especially Asiatic clams (*Corbicula fluminea*) and zebra mussels (*Dreissena polymorpha*), have intensified threats. During the past three decades there has been a precipitous decline of mussels both in numbers of individuals and in species diversity. Williams et al. (1993) reported 21 mussel species, 7.1% of the United States fauna, as possibly extinct, 77 species (20.6%) as endangered, and 43 species (14.5%) as threatened. With the present trajectory we will witness the demise of this widespread and diverse fauna during the next 20 years.

Defining Mussel Species: What's in a Name?

Uncertainties in defining and delineating species, discussed in this chapter, are well illustrated with freshwater mussels. Almost all American freshwater mussels were described in an 80-year period between 1820 and 1900, mostly by a single conchologist, Isaac Lea (1827–1874). He was a wealthy individual, and all of his descriptions were accompanied by detailed drawings illustrating variations in shape, thickness, and color that he observed in the shell. Isaac Lea did almost no fieldwork, and specimens on which he based his descriptions were gifts, trades with fellow conchologists, or purchases from collectors. His lack of field experience left him with no concept of the morphological variation that existed in populations of mussels. Like many early naturalists, he had a typological concept of species, which resulted in the description of more than 1000 new "species" of mussels. Of the 297 U.S. taxa recognized today, more than 115 were described by Isaac Lea.

In the early 1900s biologists began to assemble large museum collections of mussels from throughout the central and eastern United States, which provided an opportunity to evaluate variation within and among mussel populations. As they examined the variation exhibited by this new material, researchers were unable to distinguish many of the "species" of mussels described by conchologists during the 1800s. No longer were they seeing distinct morphotypes, but rather parts of a larger, continuously variable morphology. An example of this problem is illustrated by three taxa described by Isaac Lea from the Mobile River drainage (Figure A). Considered alone, these three taxa are separable based on the shape, degree of inflation, and sculpturing of the shell. However, considered with individuals from geographically and ecologically intermediate areas, they were found to morphologically grade into one another. Currently, these forms are treated as a single, highly variable species, *Quadrula asperata*.

To determine the validity of some of the described taxa, research into the factors affecting shell morphology has been undertaken. Earlier in this century, characteristics of the shell, including shape, color, and thickness, were compared among populations of the same species in different environments. Grier (1920) compared the shell morphology of populations of several species from the upper Ohio River and Lake Erie, and found those from Lake Erie to be more inflated and thinner-shelled than those from the Ohio River. Ortmann (1920) compared populations of the same species from small headwater streams and downstream in large river habitats, and found that shells were more inflated (obese), shorter, and less sculptured in riverine habitats than in the smaller headwater streams. In a similar study, Ball (1922) reported that factors other than stream size (discharge) entered into determination of the degree of shell obesity.

Results of these early studies and others (see Eagar 1978; Balla and Walker 1991) suggest that variation in shell morphology reflects the interaction of numerous environmental and genetic factors; thus, shell morphology alone is often insufficient for species identification. Recognition of ecophenotypic variation led to synonymy of many of the older names. In an extreme example, Johnson (1970) listed 102 synonyms for the widespread *Elliptio complanata*. Recent work with *Elliptio* has revisited some of these 102 taxa and argued for their recognition (Davis and Mulvey, 1993); these recent studies incorporate enzyme electrophoresis and multivariate analysis of shell morphology and anatomy. This shifting taxonomy of freshwater mussels reflects both changes in our concept of species, and the application of new methods to problems of species identification.

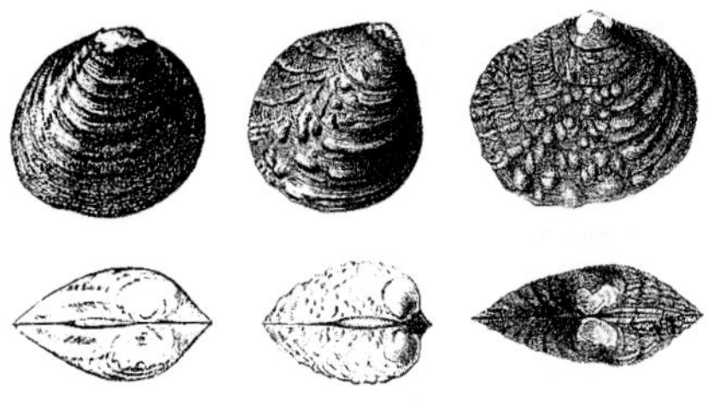

Figure A Three taxa originally described as distinct species, *Unio keineriana* (left), *Unio asperatus* (center), and *Unio cahabensis* (right), and subsequently considered to represent a single species, *Quadrula asperata*. (From Isaac Lee, 1827–1874, Observations of the genus *Unio*. Privately published.)

Although phenotypic variation may confuse the taxonomy of mussel "species," such variation reflects the interaction of environmental and genetic factors and is the basis of evolution and adaptation. We now recognize that delineation of mussel taxa should include shell morphology, soft tissue anatomy, ecology, and genetics. We also recognize that, for most taxa, this will not be easy.

In the task of species conservation we are frequently faced with the question of what to protect. Rarely does one have the opportunity to protect portions of all populations of a species; this necessarily leads to prioritization of populations and geographic areas that need to be protected. In determining priorities for species conservation one should consider the morphological, genetic, ecological, and behavioral variation of the species in question. In the absence of population genetics data for mussels we can turn to the morphological data. For example, in the case of *Quadrula asperata*, conservation efforts should, at a minimum, include the extremes of morphological variation (see Figure A).

Protection of species at the population level, including the full array of morphological and genetic diversity, is essential to the long-term survival of species. This is especially critical in species such as freshwater mussels, where the very nature of species definitions is in question and changes with new information. Saving all the pieces seems a prudent course of action.

tions changing over time. And at every inventory, including today's, we would find species in various stages of formation and decline.

From this omniscient perspective we would see that the ranges of some species are discontinuous, and that comparison of a species in two parts of its range might indicate genetic, morphological, or behavioral differences. When the differences are slight, we may simply say that the species is found in disjunct populations. When the differences are large, we may recognize the beginnings of a new species—an **incipient species**. In a survey of our inventory we might also find a continuum extending from species with highly connected populations to species that are spatially highly fragmented and disjunct. Within the latter group, we would find reason to argue that in some cases the disjunct populations are so different that they should be distinguished as two or more new species. By so doing we would be making a judgment that the species now exists in two or more largely closed gene pools, which now have independent evolutionary pathways. That we see such variation in species formation does not invalidate concepts of species; it only reinforces the fact that the species, whether viewed as a gene pool in various stages of closure or as a diagnosable cluster of individuals with common ancestry, is a unit of continual evolutionary change.

The Species and Conservation

How Do Species Concepts Affect Conservation Efforts?

Adoption of different species concepts could alter the way we define, and thus conserve, species, but would that have any real effect on conservation of biodiversity? We will examine two of the current species concepts in primary use and ask how their perspectives affect species conservation.

The biological species concept has been the reigning species concept for more than half a century, and its use is deeply engrained throughout much of biology; it has resulted in the present estimates of 5 to 30 million species extant today (Wilson 1988a; see also Essay 4B). The BSC has also been adopted de facto in much of conservation with respect to both biological and legal aspects of species protection. The focus of the BSC is on species and subspecies as distinct entities; there is less emphasis on populations and ecological functions within these broader categories, although the Endangered Species Act does recognize endangered or threatened populations of vertebrates.

How would adopting a phylogenetic species concept affect conservation? The PSC would result in more recognized species than at present (McKitrick and Zink 1988) because many currently recognized subspecies or distinct populations would be elevated to species status (Figure 3.4). These new species

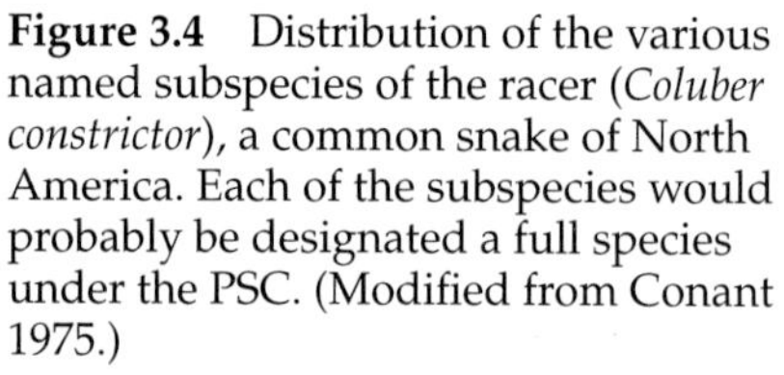

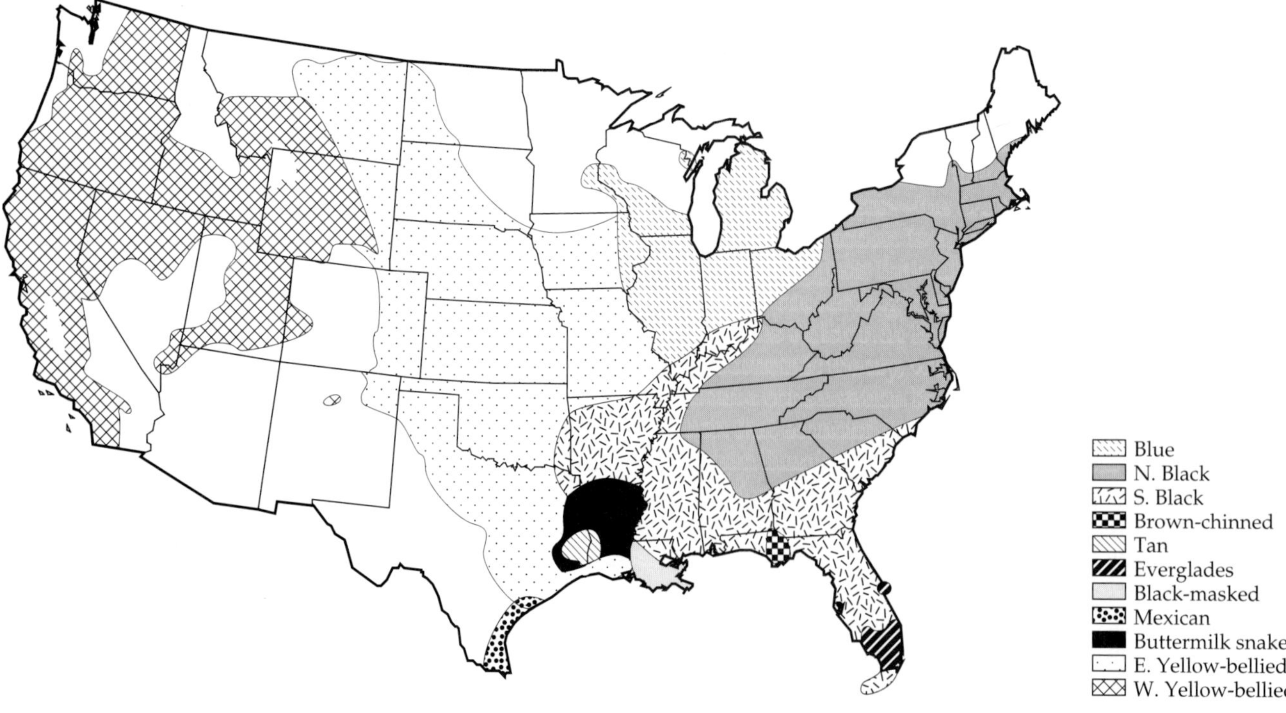

Figure 3.4 Distribution of the various named subspecies of the racer (*Coluber constrictor*), a common snake of North America. Each of the subspecies would probably be designated a full species under the PSC. (Modified from Conant 1975.)

would be distinguished based on genealogical relationships and derived character states, rather than major morphological gaps or genetic isolation. This would better reflect evolutionary history and more appropriately recognize the unique evolutionary pathways traveled. However, the PSC does raise the possibility that any character difference, even a single molecular marker or minor morphological trait unique to a population, could mark that population as a phylogenetic species, begging the question of where one stops in the quest to differentiate forms. Biologically trivial differences among individuals, such as number of facial hairs in primates or variation in striping patterns in zebras, could designate species differences.

Under the PSC, some presently endangered species would undoubtedly be split into several. Populations of species not presently considered endangered because they are widespread and abundant at some localities might attain endangered status as new species if split off under a phylogenetic system. However, single populations or subspecies of vertebrates can already be legally recognized as endangered (U.S. Fish and Wildlife Service 1988) even if the remainder of the species is secure (as in the cases of the southern Bald Eagle, Florida panther, and San Francisco garter snake), so this change would affect only plants and invertebrates.

Although the PSC would result in more species, and perhaps greater recognition of populational diversity (because many populations would be raised to species level), it would not necessarily lead to better conservation of biodiversity. First, a PSC would only change the level of the problem. Instead of being concerned with endangered populations, we would be concerned with those populations newly defined as endangered species. With funding already sorely inadequate for existing endangered species (Campbell 1991), a potential severalfold increase in their number created by a new definition could result in a strong political backlash against their legal protection.

Second, from a biological perspective, the present definition of endangered species places local species recovery efforts within the context of other populations and the species at large; there are strong linkages among populations involved in recovery. If each of those populations became endangered "species," they could be treated in isolation as distinct entities (Figure 3.5). This by itself might increase the chances of local extinction and loss of diversity (see Chapters 6–10).

On the other hand, in order to protect a population of an endangered species in practice, one must essentially prove that loss of that population would jeopardize survival of the species at large. Listing of smaller units, as per the PSC approach, would expedite protection of those populations. Obviously, with respect to conservation actions, there is no species definition that emerges as overtly superior.

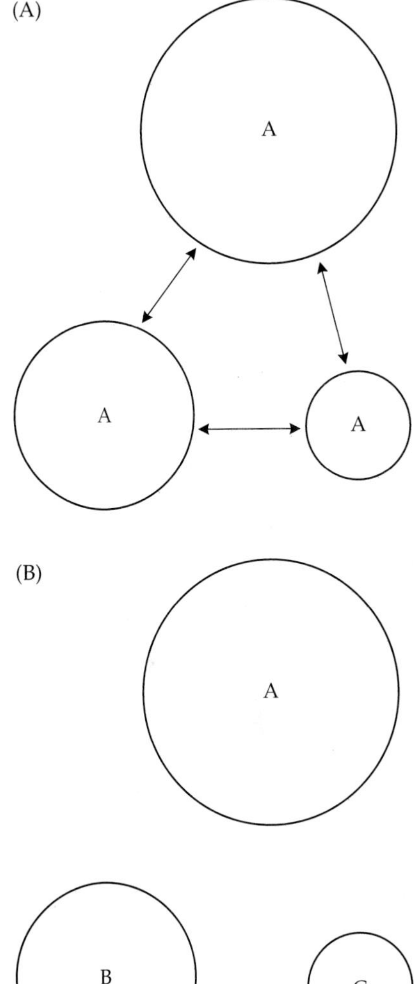

Figure 3.5 Schematic diagram of relationships among endangered entities under two species definitions. (A) The present approach, using the biological species concept. The arrows represent the connection and potential genetic exchange among endangered populations of species A. (B) A modified approach, using the phylogenetic species concept. The three "populations" are now considered species (A, B, C) and are managed in isolation, with no genetic exchange.

Conserve Diversity, Not Latin Binomials

Regardless of the species concept used in conservation, there is need for greater emphasis on the protection of variation within the species category. The critical evolutionary and ecological functional unit is not necessarily the species, but the population. As Williams (1966) stated, the species is "a key taxonomic and evolutionary concept but has no special significance for the study of adaptation. It is not an adapted unit and there are no mechanisms that function for the survival of the species." The local population is where responses to environmental challenges occur, where adaptations arise, and where genetic diversity is maintained and reshuffled each generation.

From a conservation perspective, the species category can provide a false sense of security. The species concept implies that all conspecific populations, by being the same entity, play the same adaptive roles in all environments. This

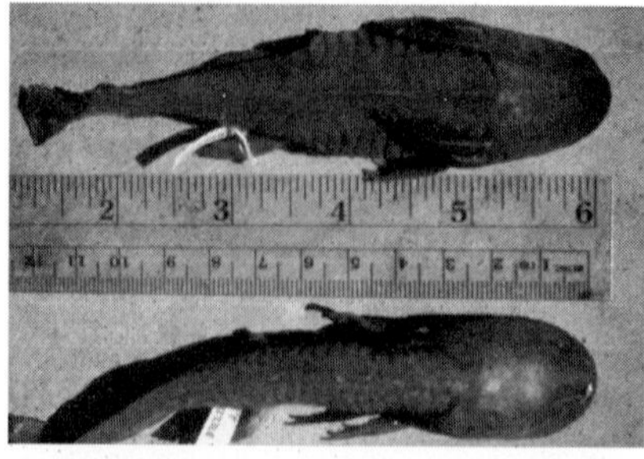
(A)

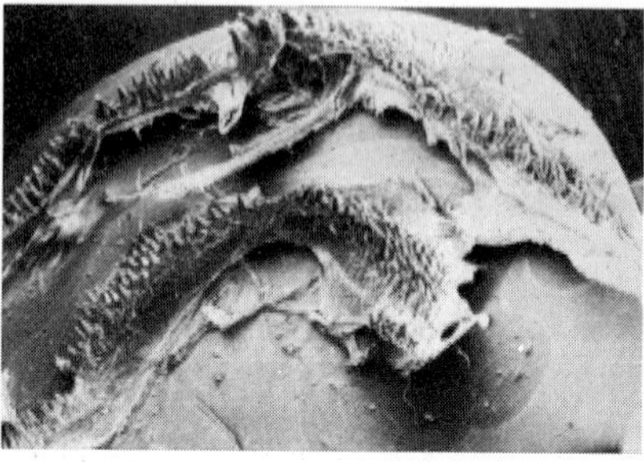
(B)

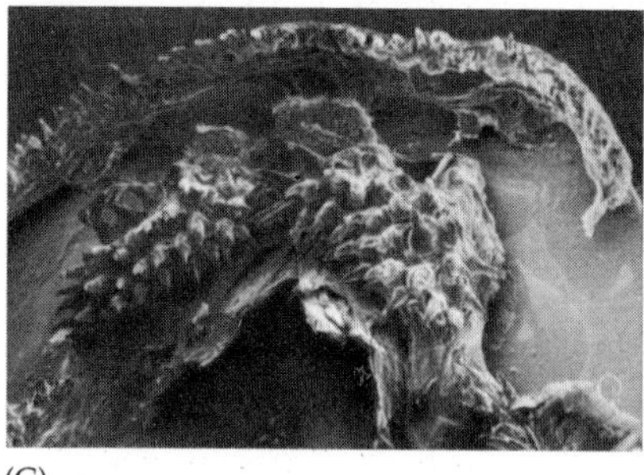
(C)

Figure 3.6 Phenotypic plasticity in *Ambystoma tigrinum*, the tiger salamander. (A) The individual on top is a normal form, that on the bottom is a cannibalistic form (note the broader head) induced by dense larval populations. The electron micrographs show teeth of the normal (B) and cannibalistic (C) form. (Photographs courtesy of James P. Collins.)

is not always the case. A wide-ranging taxon may consist of many genetically isolated or semi-isolated populations that play different functional roles in different systems. For example, some plant populations have evolved different levels of metal tolerance in different habitats (Antonovics et al. 1971), and could not easily be interchanged. Guppies (*Poecilia reticulata*) in Trinidad streams have very different genetically based color patterns, clutch sizes, and offspring sizes depending on whether they occur in streams with or without predaceous fishes (Reznick and Bryga 1987; Reznick et al. 1990). Some plant species have markedly different, genetically based growth forms in low- and high-elevation ecosystems (Clausen et al. 1940). Such genetically based **plasticity** in life history characters is probably a pervasive feature of most organisms (Figure 3.6), but is underappreciated and virtually unexplored in the conservation realm.

Another problem is that the ecological function of each population may be independent of other populations of the species, but this is not recognized when they are all lumped together under one name. If a population of a bee is lost from a river basin due to pesticides, for example, it does no good to the flowers depending on that population for pollination that the "species" still exists elsewhere. The bee was performing a particular role in that particular system and is no longer doing so; unless recolonization from elsewhere can occur, this population extinction is as devastating functionally to that local system as if the entire species were destroyed. *Population persistence within each local system is more important than simple overall species persistence.*

A species approach to conservation also results in an overly optimistic assessment of retention of biodiversity. A species can continue to exist even if many of its populations are destroyed. Those lost populations represent a decline in biodiversity if they contained unique genetic or phenotypic traits, but the species approach tells us that diversity has not been lost because our species count remains unchanged. (Note that the PSC approach to defining species would reduce or eliminate this problem). In fact, we have been losing much more global biodiversity, in the form of populations, than heretofore recognized (Figure 3.7), and the biodiversity problem is far worse than species-level losses would indicate.

A case in point is loss of crop genetic diversity throughout the world (also discussed in Chapters 5 and 6). Many of the original, wild, localized races of domesticated grains or vegetable crops are extinct or exist tenuously in remote areas of the world. The genetic diversity contained in those populations could prove valuable to our modern crops by providing the genetic basis for disease resistance or other traits relevant to agricultural production. In these cases, the species are by no means endangered, but biodiversity in the form of select individual populations has been and is being lost.

Losses of countless populations of even common species have eroded population diversity and variation and have eliminated the diverse roles played by those populations. This issue was addressed by Ehrlich (1986), who pointed out that "... species extinction is only one part of the problem. At least in the temperate zones, it is the smaller part. There the disappearance of parts of species—subspecies, ecotypes, and genetically distinct populations—is much more threatening to the functioning of ecosystems. Numbers of such infraspecific units worldwide are even more difficult to estimate than those of species, but almost certainly there are billions."

Is the Species Category Useful to Conservation?

Is the species category useful to conservation? The answer to this question is an emphatic "yes and no." The species category is useful in that it identifies

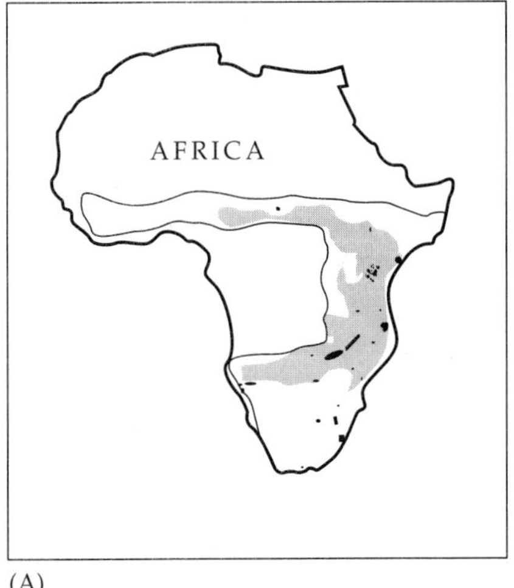

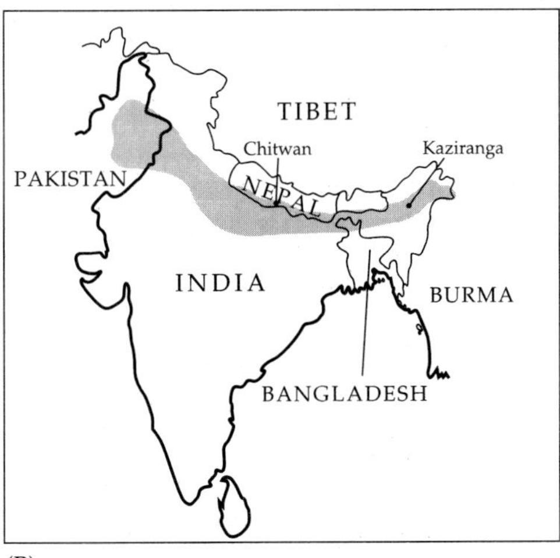

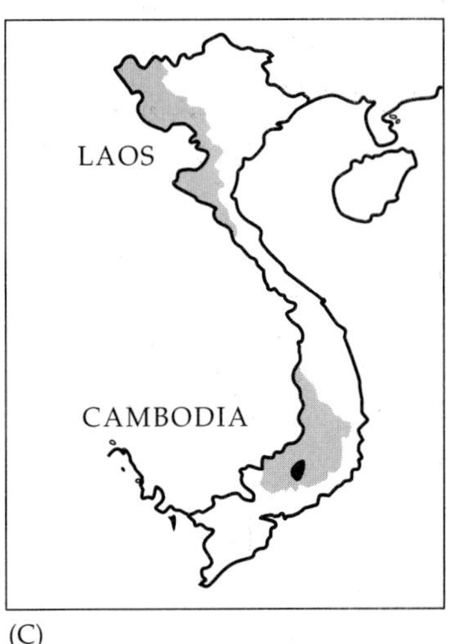

(A) (B) (C)

Figure 3.7 Present and former distributions of three species of rhinoceros, showing loss of populational diversity and retreat to a few refuges. (A) The black rhinoceros (*Diceros bicornis*), showing historical distribution (black outline), distribution in 1900 (shaded area), and distribution in 1987 (black areas). (B) The greater one-horned rhinoceros (*Rhinoceros unicornis*), formerly distributed across the shaded area, is now reduced to two populations at Chitwan and Kaziranga reserves. (C) The Javan rhinoceros (*Rhinoceros sondaicus*), showing historical (shaded) and present (black) distributions. (A, modified from Ashley et al. 1990; B, modified from Dinerstein and McCracken 1990; C, modified from Santiapillai 1992.)

entities for legal attention and facilitates assessment of the problem. We can count species (although we have thus far done a terrible job; see Essay 4B) and determine how individual species are doing over time. There is also public support for species; most people can identify better with the loss of a species than with the loss of a population or erosion of genetic diversity. Even in this context, the species category has different connotations, legally, ecologically, and sociologically, but these can be used to their various advantages when appealing for support for species protection (Box 3A).

BOX 3A
Not All Animals or Plants Are Equal

The category "species" is used and thought about in conservation in a variety of ways, from many biological, political, and socioeconomic perspectives. These perspectives need to be recognized and understood because they appeal to different segments of society and their particular interests, and because a species' "value" to society can vary depending on its role in the world and its relationship to humanity. For example, an ecological or aesthetic argument for protecting a species may have little appeal to a county zoning board, but an economic value for that same species will draw their attention. Similarly, a species' hunting value may be of little interest to a local conservation group, but its vulnerability or ecological role will undoubtedly serve to rally the troops. Six different ways in which species are viewed by society (there may be more), and which you may encounter, are listed below. For each of these ways, we pose one or more questions that would help you to identify species as belonging to that category:

Keystone Species:

- Would major ecological functions of the ecosystem (trophic relationships, community structure, hydrologic flow, succession patterns, disturbance cycles, and so forth) be significantly changed if the species was not present?
- Would other species decline or disappear from the ecosystem if the species was eliminated from it?

Indicator Species:

- Does the species have a highly specific niche or a narrow ecological tolerance?
- Is the species tied to a specific biotic community, successional stage, or substrate?
- Can the species reliably be found under a specific set of circumstances, but not others?

Umbrella Species:

- Does the species require large blocks of relatively natural or unaltered habitat to maintain viable populations?

Flagship (Charismatic) Species:

- Is this a species that people relate to in a positive emotional way ("warm and fuzzy" species; especially interesting or attractive species), and which would elicit a strong protective reaction?

Vulnerable Species:

- Is the species' overall population size small?
- Is the habitat fragmented, or are the individual populations highly isolated, with poor dispersal power?
- Does the species have a narrow or highly specialized niche?
- Is the species especially vulnerable to human activities?

Economically Important Species:

- Is the species harvested for a product (e.g., meat, hides, fat, trophies, pet trade)?
- Does the species' presence and behavior result in economic losses (e.g., to farming or ranching) or economic benefits (e.g., pollination of fruit trees)?

On the other hand, the species, as discussed above, is a conventional breakpoint on a larger biological continuum. The species contains a great deal of hidden diversity in the form of local adaptations and genetic information. A species focus by itself also does not directly address the larger problem of habitat and ecosystem loss, which is the real driving force in extinction (although one part of the U.S. Endangered Species Act does recognize ecosystems and critical habitat). A piecemeal, species-driven approach to conservation draws attention to only one part of the biodiversity crisis; a more comprehensive approach must also be taken.

Taxonomic Problems in Conservation

One improvement that can be made, irrespective of species concept, is better taxonomy and greater recognition of the role of systematics and phylogenetic relationships in conservation (Wilson 1985b; Eldridge 1992; see Essay 3B by Melanie Stiassny). In particular, the broadest possible data set should always

ESSAY 3B
Systematics and Conservation

Melanie L. J. Stiassny, American Museum of Natural History

There is a growing recognition of the vital role that museums and museum-based taxonomic research must play in the biodiversity crisis. Clearly, we need to know what is out there, where it is, how much there is of it, and how endangered it is. Without this very basic information no inventories of threatened areas, endangered species lists, or programs for rational planning are possible. Taxonomic and biogeographic analysis, two major components of systematic biology, also clearly are fundamental elements of conservation biology. However, there is another aspect to systematic biology that has yet to be fully integrated into conservation biology: phylogenetic analysis.

Phylogenetic analysis is essentially concerned with the reconstruction of evolutionary history. By interpreting the distribution of the intrinsic properties of organisms (characters), the composition and interrelationships of lineages are determined and depicted in the form of branching diagrams. Phylogenetic trees portray the genealogical relationships and sequence of historical events uniting taxa, and form the baseline for virtually all comparative evolutionary studies. The potential role of phylogenetics in conservation biology has only begun to be addressed.

Recently a number of different indices encoding notions such as "phylogenetic uniqueness," "higher taxon richness," "taxonomic dispersion," "taxonomic distinctiveness," and "phylogenetic diversity" have been developed to incorporate phylogenetic information into the evaluation of conservation priorities (May 1990; Vane-Wright et al. 1991; Williams et al. 1991; Nixon and Wheeler 1992; Faith 1992; Crozier 1992). The advantage of these measures over simple comparative estimates of species numbers (species richness) is that they incorporate information about genealogical relationships and weighted measures of the phylogenetic uniqueness of the taxa involved. When viewed from this perspective it is clear that not all species contain equivalent information, and there may be strong phylogenetic arguments for conservation prioritization of some taxa over others.

With a well-resolved phylogenetic tree for a group of organisms, many different measures pertinent to conservation issues can be derived. But sadly, for most groups, we are a long way from having such sound phylogenetic data, and lack the trees necessary for analysis. Practically speaking, for some groups this lack of phylogenetic resolution poses little problem; most biologists would agree with a high priority being given to saving, for example, *Sphenodon* (the tuatara), the last surviving member and sister group of the entire Lepidosauria (some 5800 species of worm lizards, snakes, and lizards), or *Latimeria chalumnae* (the coelacanth), a sister group to more than 21,450 species, including all of the tetrapods. The loss of these taxa would be particularly poignant as it would represent the loss of the last living vestige of their lineage. Clearly, if there were hundreds of extant species of *Sphenodon* the issue would be more complex; it is the marked asymmetry in species numbers between sister groups that emerges as a key factor.

A review of current taxonomic literature indicates that many groups exhibit such high-level phylogenetic asymmetry; that is, the basal sister taxon to a diverse and species-rich group has contrastingly low species numbers. Frequently, these basal groups also have extremely restricted geographic distributions, and these two features render them particularly vulnerable to environmental pressures. Numerous examples of this asymmetry occur among teleost fishes. And in freshwater groups, a heterogeneous assemblage representing more than 25% of all extant vertebrates, the association of low species numbers and restricted geographic distribution in basal groups is particularly striking. Phylogenetic data can be used to strengthen arguments for broad regional conservation plans; for example, the eastern coastal forest of Madagascar is recognized as an area harboring a concentration of basal taxa of considerable phylogenetic importance (Figure A). This particular proposal is similar to highlighting an area of extreme species endemism as a priority conservation region, but this need not always be the case (Stiassny 1992).

Basal taxa have importance by virtue of the unique comparative information they contain, which is in a sense complementary to that of the entire membership of their more species-rich sister groups. Perhaps even more important, they are of critical significance when, as is frequently the case, the precise intrarelationships of their sister group are unknown. By virtue of their position, the phylogenetic relevance of basal groups can be appreciated at three levels: (1) character state changes in these taxa can influence hypotheses of relationships among the remaining members of their lineage, regardless of the states observed in more distant outgroups and in more phylogenetically derived taxa; (2) in certain instances knowledge of character states in these basal groups can introduce character conflicts that lead to the proposal of a particular phylogenetic hypothesis; (3) they can sometimes provide the only possible evidence for understanding the evolution of certain character transitions.

A study by Stiassny and DePinna (1994) shows that inclusion of a single species, *Trichogenes longipinnis* (the basal member of the Trichomycteridae,

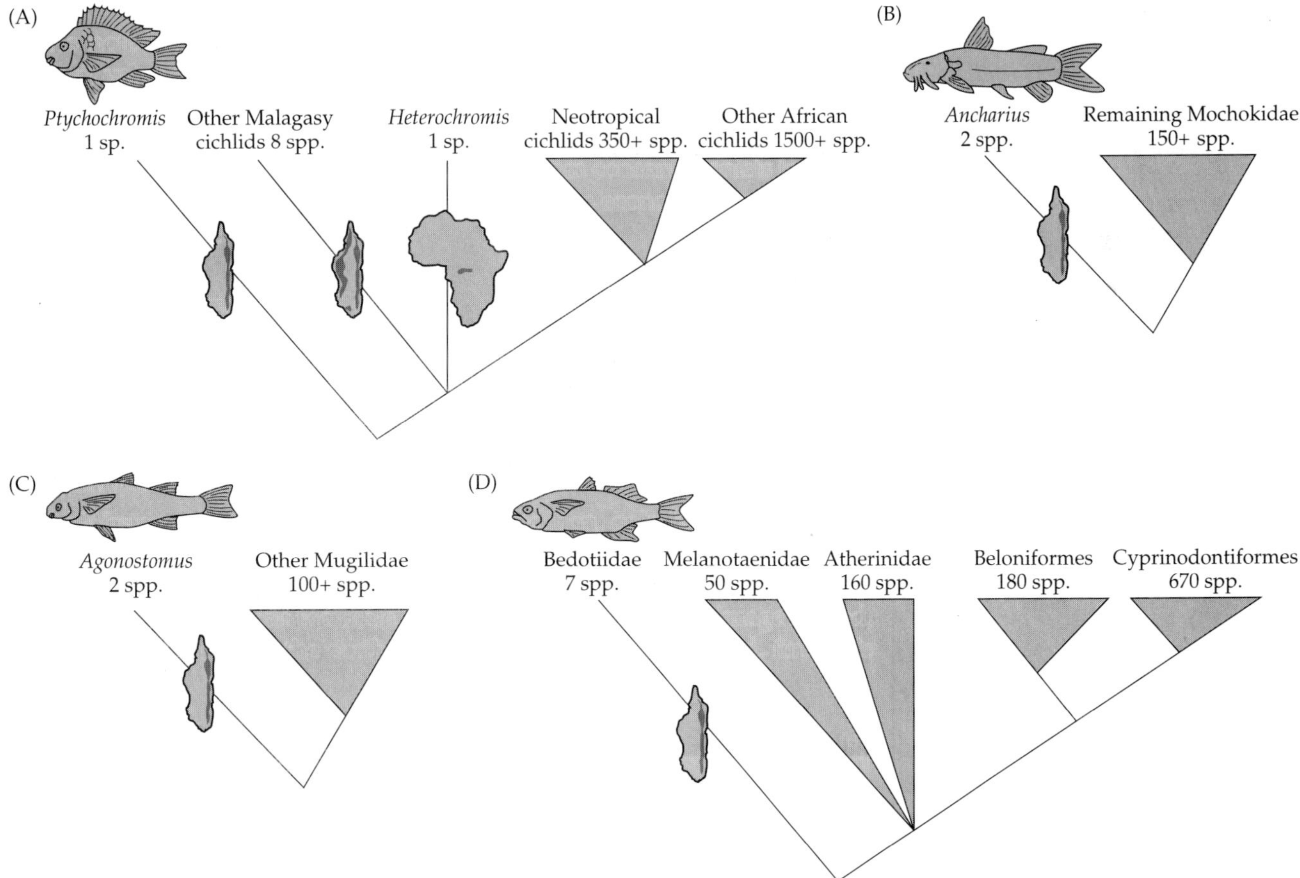

Figure A Phylogenetic relationships of (A) the Cichlidae, (B) the Mochokidae, (C) the Mugilidae, and (D) the Atherinomorpha. Insets indicate geographic distributions of basal taxa restricted to the eastern coastal forests of Madagascar. (Modified from Stiassny and DePinna 1994.)

restricted to a small creek between Rio de Janeiro and São Paulo, and escaping discovery until the early 1980s) in an analysis of relationships among loricarioid catfishes results in a major shift of phylogenetic hypotheses for that large group (Figure B). Not only does the discovery of *T. longipinnis* allow correct resolution of the relationships of a group of well over 1000 species, it enables us to understand the evolution of certain osteological characters within that group. While few conservationists are going to be overly concerned about understanding the evolution of obscure fish bones, what is true for such bones is also true for our understanding of other biological features. The inclusion of *Trichogenes*, a single basal taxon, has a major impact on our understanding of character evolution, and these characters can in turn be of profound importance to the ecology or functional biology of the whole group. Clearly, the loss of this species is not commensurate with the loss of "just another" of the numerous other loricarioid species, and it is phylogenetic analysis that indicates why this is the case.

In the face of a profound crisis of biodiversity, biologists are confronted with the onerous task of allocating conservation priorities. If there were some absolute biological criterion by which to judge the relative value of a given species or community against another, perhaps the problem would not seem so acute, but no such criterion exists. In an ideal world we could argue for saving everything, but our world is far from ideal. The ratchet of extinction clicks faster each day, and our resources seem to diminish in inverse proportion. The potential role of phylogenetic analysis in helping to define and elaborate our understanding of biodiversity and its conservation is only just beginning to be explored, but already promises to be of considerable importance.

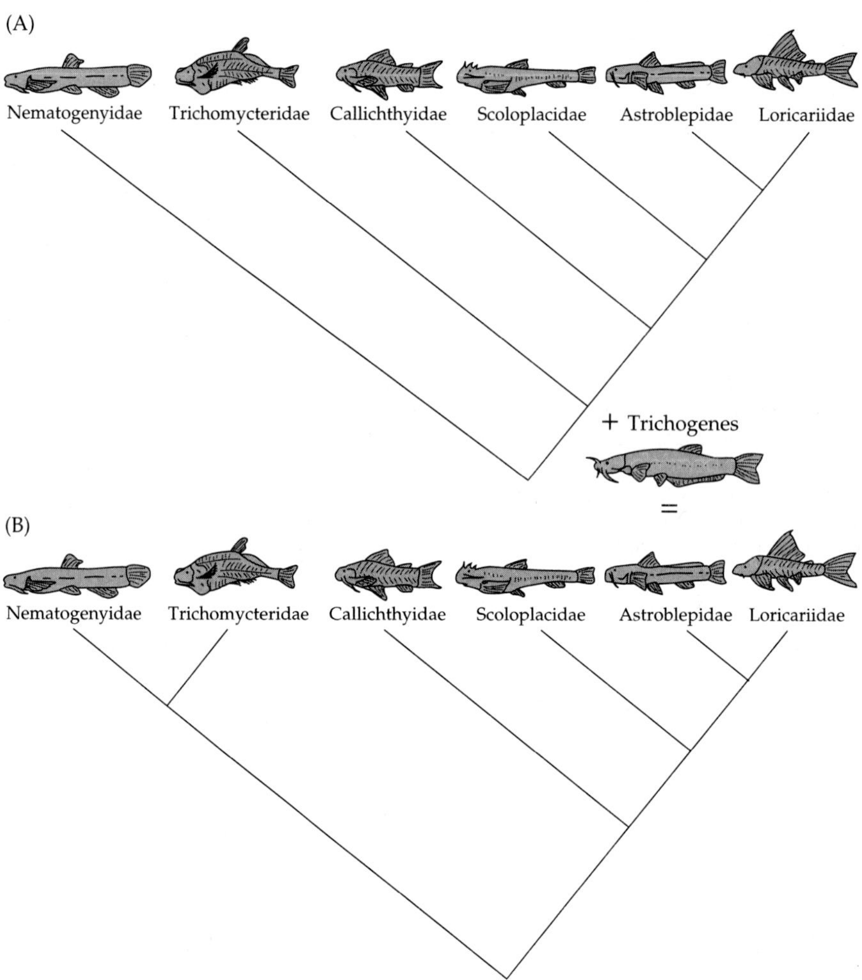

Figure B (A) Traditional view of loricarioid relationships. (B) The single most parsimonious scheme after character distributions in *Trichogenes* are introduced into the matrix. (Modified from Stiassny and DePinna 1994.)

be employed in the designation of species. The recent availability of information from molecular genetics is a case in point. Because the speciation process is ultimately a genetic divergence between populations through time (or conversely, genetic cohesion within a group), genetic data should be considered along with other data sets such as morphology, behavior, and distribution when determining species boundaries. The molecular genetic constitution of biota may sometimes be more conservative than other characters and may more accurately reflect true evolutionary relationships, including divergence (discussed in Essay 3C by John Avise). We encourage inclusion of such data in taxonomic approaches to conservation.

Furthermore, morphology by itself can mislead us due to sexual dimorphism, phenotypic plasticity, or intense selection on particular characters (Avise 1989). In some cases, biologists have described two species only to later

ESSAY 3C

A Rose Is a Rose Is a Rose

John C. Avise, University of Georgia

What's in a name? A "Dusky Seaside Sparrow" by any other name is just as melanistic. Nonetheless, nomenclatural assignments inevitably shape our perceptions of how the biotic world is partitioned, and hence the biological units toward which conservation efforts may be directed. In the case of the Dusky Seaside Sparrow, this dark-plumaged population near Cape Canaveral, Florida, was described in the late 1800s as a species (*Ammodramus nigrescens*) distinct from the other Seaside Sparrows (*Ammodramus maritimus*) common along the Atlantic and Gulf coasts of North America. Although the dusky later was demoted to subspecies status, the nomenclatural legacy stemming from the original taxonomic description prompted continued special focus on this recognized form. Thus, in the late 1960s, when the population crashed due to changing land use practices, the dusky was listed formally as "endangered" by the U.S. Fish and Wildlife Service. Despite last-ditch conservation efforts, the Dusky Seaside Sparrow went extinct in 1987.

The point of relating this sad story involves an unexpected footnote. After the natural death of the last known dusky (in captivity), molecular analyses of DNA isolated from its tissues revealed an exceptionally close genetic relationship to other Atlantic coast Seaside Sparrows, but a deep phylogenetic distinction of all Atlantic coast populations from Gulf of Mexico populations, likely due to the effects of ancient (Pleistocene) population separations (Avise and Nelson 1989). Thus, the traditional taxonomy for the seaside sparrow complex (upon which management efforts were based) apparently had failed to capture the true genetic relationships within the group, in two respects: (1) by giving special emphasis to a presumed biotic partition that proved to be shallow evolutionarily; and (2) by failing to recognize a deeper phylogeographic subdivision between Atlantic and Gulf coast populations. This finding from molecular genetics should not be interpreted as evidence of heartlessness over the loss of the dusky. All population extinctions are regrettable, particularly in this age of accelerated habitat loss. The extinction of the dusky population is to be mourned, but perhaps we can be consoled by the knowledge that it is survived by close genetic relatives elsewhere along the Atlantic coast. Furthermore, the discovery of a deep and previously unrecognized phylogenetic subdivision between Atlantic and Gulf coast forms of the seaside sparrow should be paramount in any conservation plans for the remaining populations.

Many taxonomic assignments in use today were first proposed in the 19th century, often from limited phenotypic information and preliminary assessments of patterns of geographic variation. How adequately these traditional assignments summarize biological diversity remains to be determined, through continued systematic reevaluations to which molecular approaches can contribute. As with the Seaside Sparrows, past errors of phylogenetic commission and omission may be anticipated, at least occasionally. Another example involves pocket gophers in the southeastern United States. An endangered population referable to *"Geomys colonus"* in Camden County, Georgia, first described in 1898, has proven upon molecular reexamination to represent merely a local variant of the widespread *G. pinetis* (Laerm et al. 1982). In these same genetic assays (which involved comparisons of proteins, DNAs, and chromosome karyotypes), a deep but previously unrecognized phylogeographic split was shown to distinguish the pocket gophers of eastern Georgia and peninsular Florida from those to the west.

Inadequate taxonomy also can kill, as exemplified by studies of the tuatara lizards of New Zealand, discussed in this chapter. This complex has been treated as a single species by government and management authorities, despite the fact that molecular (and morphological) appraisals have revealed three distinct groups (Daugherty et al. 1990). Official neglect of this described taxonomic diversity may unwittingly have consigned one form of tuatara (*Sphenodon punctatus reischeki*) to extinction, whereas another form (*S. guentheri*) has survived to this point only by good fortune. As noted by Daugherty et al. (1990), "Taxonomies are not irrelevant abstractions, but the essential foundations of conservation practice."

In other cases, molecular reappraisals of endangered forms may bolster the rationale for special conservation efforts directed toward otherwise suspect taxa. For example, recent molecular appraisals of the endangered Kemp's ridley sea turtle (*Lepidochelys kempi*) showed that this "species" (which had a controversial taxonomic history) does indeed fall outside the range of genetic variability exhibited by assayed samples from its more widespread congener, *L. olivacea* (Bowen et al. 1991).

These examples illustrate but a few of the many ways that molecular genetic methods can contribute to the assessment of biodiversity, and hence to the implementation of conservation programs. Ironically, even as these exciting molecular methods for reexploring the biological world are being developed, the biota to which they might be applied are vanishing at an unprecedented rate through the direct and indirect effects of the human population explosion.

find that they were males and females, or different color or shape morphs, of the same species. In other cases, especially in insects, morphologically similar or indistinguishable individuals have been shown genetically to be different species (Dobzhansky 1970); these are known as **cryptic** or **sibling species**. The

(A)

(B)

Figure 3.8 Two species of tuatara, both adult males. (A) *Sphenodon punctatus* from Stephens Island, New Zealand. (B) *Sphenodon guentheri* from North Brother Island, New Zealand. (Photographs courtesy of Allison Cree.)

mosquito vector of yellow fever, *Aedes aegypti*, is part of such a complex of sibling species. Its affinity for visiting buildings made it an important disease vector, but control programs were ineffective as long as it was not separated from sibling species that had very different foraging behaviors. Once those species differences were recognized, and the behavioral differences understood, control was possible.

Ignorance of genetic relationships, and taxonomic difficulties in general, can hinder conservation efforts. For example, the tuatara (Figure 3.8) is a large, lizardlike animal that is the only surviving representative of an entire order of reptiles (Rhynchocephalia), and occurs only on islands off the coast of New Zealand. Three species were named in the 19th century, one of which is now extinct. One of the remaining species, *Sphenodon guentheri*, was ignored by protective legislation dating back to 1895 because it was morphologically similar to *S. punctatus*, the most abundant species; *S. guentheri* was subsequently reduced to subspecies status. Consequently, *S. guentheri* was not considered unique, most populations were lost, and it now occurs on only one island. Recent genetic data indicate that *S. guentheri* is a distinct species, highly divergent genetically from other populations (Daugherty et al. 1990). Unfortunately, this information comes too late for special efforts to protect any but that single remaining population. New genetic techniques can help in the clarification of such taxonomic difficulties in many other taxa and thereby aid in the identification of critical genetic groupings to guide conservation efforts.

How Will Environmental Degradation Affect Speciation?

Speciation is a term for the various processes by which new species form. The BSC would contend that speciation consists of the development of reproductive (and thus genetic) isolation among populations, which subsequently results in independent evolutionary pathways. The PSC or ESC would argue that speciation consists of cohesion of distinct evolutionary lines, independent of other lines. Regardless of the species concept used, the processes by which speciation occurs may vary among taxa and ecological situations. These processes are most easily discussed in the context of the BSC.

Several models of geographic modes of speciation have been offered. The most widely accepted model is **gradual allopatric speciation** (Figure 3.9A), in which a population is geographically split by a physical barrier (e.g., a mountain range, a river, a lava flow) and the resultant subpopulations diverge genetically or morphologically to the extent that reproduction between them would be impossible if they were reunited (Mayr 1942). Actual reproductive isolation may develop through a variety of isolation mechanisms (Table 3.1). It should be emphasized that reproductive isolation does not cause, but is a result of, divergence.

For populations that diverged because they were isolated completely, there would not be specific selection to reinforce traits that prevent interbreeding. Species formed **allopatrically** become reproductively isolated only as a by-product of the accumulated differences in their genomes and phenotypes. As we said earlier, populations that have been isolated for relatively short periods of time and have therefore diverged only slightly are sometimes called incipient species; they have not gone very far down the path to speciation. If these partially differentiated populations come into secondary contact, they may interbreed in the contact zone, and if their offspring on average have no reproductive disadvantage compared with either parent (are not selected against), much of the distinctness of the populations may be lost through gene exchange. Sometimes such hybrid populations in contact zones can be stable over long periods. Hybrids between two species of the Neotropical butterfly

Table 3.1
Reproductive Isolation Mechanisms Considered in the Biological Species Concept

Premating isolation mechanisms

1. Seasonal and habitat isolation (potential mates do not meet)
2. Behavioral isolation (potential mates meet but do not mate because of behavioral differences)
3. Mechanical isolation (copulation is attempted but transfer of sperm is unsuccessful)

Postmating isolation mechanisms

1. Gametic mortality (sperm transfer occurs but ovum is not fertilized)
2. Zygote mortality (ovum is fertilized but zygote dies)
3. Hybrid inviability (zygote produces an F1 hybrid of reduced viability)
4. Hybrid sterility (F1 hybrid is fully viable but partially or completely sterile or produces deficient F2)

From Mayr 1963.

Heliconius, for example, are thought to have persisted in a narrow contact zone for at least 2000 generations (Turner 1971).

However, when the isolated species have diverged so much that hybrids suffer a reproductive disadvantage, then natural selection may result in the evolution of traits that reinforce reproductive isolation of the species. In the absence of other events, these species will continue to evolve separateness, close their gene pools, and eventually be distinguishable as species.

A variant of the gradual allopatric model is the **founder model** (Mayr 1963), also called **quantum speciation** because it occurs so quickly. In this model (Figure 3.9B), a small and isolated population—perhaps a few colonists on an island, for example—undergoes rapid and substantial genetic change due to random **genetic drift** or homogeneous selective pressures on a small gene pool. Because of the small population size, speciation may be quite rapid.

Other speciation models abound (see Otte and Endler 1989), but it is not critical that we explore them all here. Suffice it to say that speciation is a creative part of biodiversity, and is a dynamic process that may be at work subtly at all times. How might global environmental changes affect speciation processes?

We envision two different scenarios of speciation in light of environmental change. Both are the result of extensive habitat fragmentation, a common process and one that will undoubtedly increase in the foreseeable future (discussed in Chapter 9). Under the first scenario, habitat fragmentation, by increasingly isolating small populations, will offer greater opportunities for local speciation events, according to the quantum speciation model. Recurrent isolation of small populations in small habitats could result in local genetic change, leading to reproductive isolation and rapid speciation events (Figure 3.10).

The second, and much more likely, scenario involves the same physical setting, but a different outcome. Increased habitat fragmentation, although setting the stage for potential speciation, also sets the stage for rapid local extinctions. Extinction probabilities increase greatly in small populations (see Chapters 5, 6, 7, and 9), and extinction often occurs in a matter of years or decades. Because speciation typically takes orders of magnitude longer, it is likely that fragmentation into small populations will favor local extinction rather than

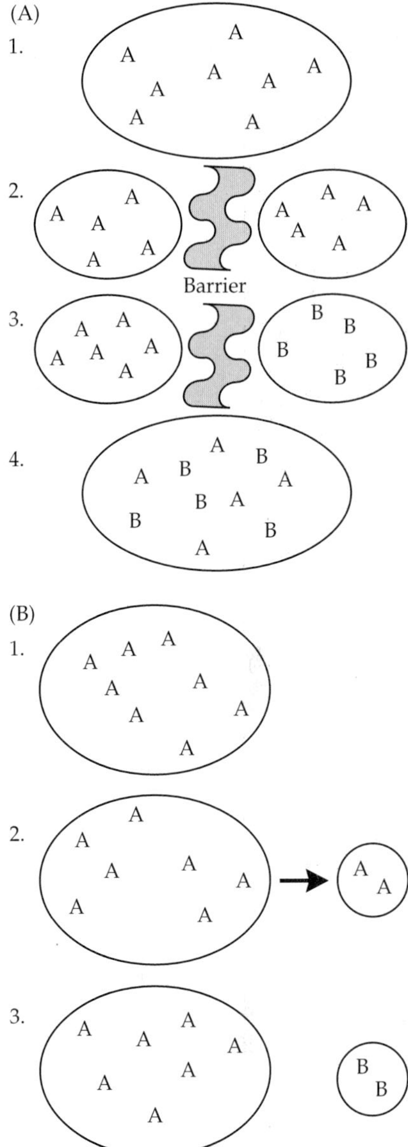

Figure 3.9 (A) Allopatric model of speciation. 1. The original species (A) covers a contiguous range. 2. Upon establishment of a barrier within the range, the species now consists of two isolated populations. 3. One population (now B) diverges in characteristic(s), some of which prevent interbreeding of the two forms. Both populations also could have diverged. 4. If the barrier disappears, the two populations (now species) may again be sympatric but will not interbreed. (B) The founder or quantum model of speciation. 1. The original species in its contiguous range. 2. Some founders form a new colony, isolated from the original range. 3. The colony (now B) diverges in some character(s) and is reproductively isolated from the parent colony.

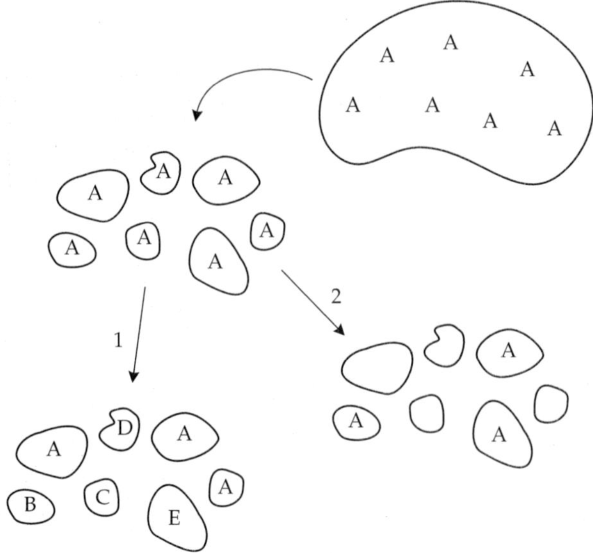

Figure 3.10 Two scenarios of future speciation patterns based on habitat fragmentation. In both scenarios, a formerly contiguous species (A) is split into many small populations in fragmented habitats. In scenario 1, quantum speciation occurs in these habitat fragments, resulting in several new species (B–E). In scenario 2, local extinction occurs more quickly than speciation, and no new species evolve, but several populations go extinct.

local speciation (Figure 3.10). Additionally, the sheer magnitude of loss of biological materials and habitats should also decrease opportunities for speciation. Thus, we speculate that environmental degradation will reduce speciation events, increase extinction events, and result in impoverished biodiversity at the species level.

Species and the Law: The ESA and CITES

We indicated earlier that biological and legal definitions or concepts of species do not necessarily coincide perfectly, and that legal definitions really are more critical because they form the basis for species protection and recovery actions. The U. S. Endangered Species Act of 1973 and the Convention on International Trade in Endangered Species are major biodiversity protection statutes that focus primarily on the species category.

The Endangered Species Act, Public Law 93-205, became effective on December 28, 1973, and is "the most far-reaching wildlife statute ever adopted by any nation" (Reffalt 1991). The stated purpose of the ESA is to "provide a means whereby the ecosystems upon which endangered species and threatened species depend may be conserved, [and] to provide a program for the conservation of such endangered species and threatened species" (USFWS 1988). The ESA thus is ecosystem-oriented in its motivation, but the particular ecosystems protected are determined by which species are deemed to be in danger of extinction. That, in turn, depends in part on how "species" is legally defined.

According to the ESA, "species" is defined to include "any *subspecies* of fish or wildlife or plants, and any *distinct population segment* of any species of vertebrate fish or wildlife which interbreeds when mature" (USFWS 1988; italics added). Under this definition, subspecies of any endangered biota receive legal recognition, as do "distinct populations" of vertebrates. This definition immediately raises two questions. First, what constitutes "distinctness"? A recent National Research Council (NRC) report (Clegg et al. 1995) urged that the concept of an evolutionary unit (EU) be adopted by the ESA to define distinctness. It defined an EU as "a group of organisms that represents a segment of biological diversity that shares evolutionary lineage and contains the potential for a unique evolutionary future. Its uniqueness can be sought in, but is not limited to, attributes of morphology, behavior, physiology, and biochemistry. A basic characteristic of an EU is that it is distinct from other EUs." The difficulties of an objective definition of distinctness will be further addressed in Chapter 6. Second, why offer distinct population segment protection only to vertebrates? The NRC report once again addressed this by stating, "There is no scientific reason (other than lack of knowledge) to exclude any EUs of nonvertebrate animals and plants from coverage under the ESA."

The present ESA definition of distinctness offers protection to endangered and threatened species, and recognizes some degree of within-species diversity in the form of subspecies and selected distinct populations. A species is deemed to be **endangered** if it is "in danger of extinction throughout all or a significant portion of its range." A **threatened** species is one that "is likely to become an endangered species within the foreseeable future throughout all or a significant portion of its range." Both of these terms recognize that the species is the functional unit of concern, and that extinction is the threat to be avoided.

Although it contains no specific reference to genetic diversity, the historical development of the ESA indicates that genetics was in fact a motivation in species protection (Waples 1991). House Resolution 37, a forerunner of the ESA, stated that ". . . it is in the best interests of mankind to minimize the losses of genetic variations. The reason is simple: they are potential resources. They are keys to puzzles which we cannot yet solve, and may provide answers to questions we have not yet learned to ask" (H.R. Rept. 412, 93rd Congress, 1st sess., 1973). However, this astute observation is not overtly reflected in the actual legal statutes.

Is the ESA working to protect biological diversity at the species level? Most certainly it has been effective within the scope of its intentions to conserve species. There have been some clear successes for the ESA (Figure 3.11): the American alligator has recovered to the point of no longer being on the list, the Bald Eagle is increasing in numbers, and Whooping Cranes and black-footed ferrets remain with us in part because of efforts legislated by the ESA (U.S. Department of the Interior 1990). Even among those species that have not recovered, it is likely that many would have been lost some time ago were it not for legal protection and implementation of recovery efforts. Environmental attorney Michael Bean discusses the ESA and new ideas for incentive-based conservation in Essay 3D.

ESSAY 3D
Incentive-Based Approaches to Conservation

Michael J. Bean, Environmental Defense Fund

When the conservation organization Defenders of Wildlife offered a $5000 reward to any private landowner in the northern Rockies on whose land wolves successfully reproduced, it was simply recognizing that sometimes the easiest way to achieve a desired environmental result is through the use of incentives. Defenders knew that the recovery of the wolf in that region, where it is designated an endangered species under the Endangered Species Act of 1973, would require the cooperation of landowners. The area's ranchers had long been among the most vociferous critics and opponents of wolf conservation. They feared that wolves would prey upon their livestock and thereby reduce their livelihoods. That the wolf was legally protected only added to their resentment.

At the same time that Defenders offered its reward fund, it also offered to compensate any rancher who suffered a loss of livestock to wolf depredation. In this manner, it sought to eliminate the principal reason that many area ranchers had long opposed wolf conservation efforts and to create a new reason to support those efforts—the opportunity to benefit economically from wolf recovery. In effect, Defenders recognized that the "stick" of penalties and prohibitions would not suffice to accomplish wolf recovery; in addition, it was necessary to offer the "carrot" of incentives to reward beneficial behavior by private landowners.

Although it is true that incentive-based approaches to endangered species conservation are relatively new, they have a well-established and successful track record in some closely related conservation areas. Two prominent examples are the Conservation Reserve Program and the Wetlands Reserve Program, both initiated by the U.S. Department of Agriculture in 1985. The Conservation Reserve Program's aim is to persuade farmers to take certain environmentally sensitive lands out of crop production and to plant such lands in trees, grasses, or other perennial vegetation. Among the intended benefits of the program are reduced soil erosion and enhanced wildlife habitat. To induce farmers to enroll their land in the program, the government offers 10- or 15-year contracts under which the farmer receives an annual payment in return for managing the land in accordance with program requirements. Farmer response to the program has been enthusiastic. In its first decade, some 36 million acres were enrolled in the Conservation Reserve Program, roughly double the acreage of the entire National Wildlife Refuge system in the lower 48 states. The program is widely credited with reversing the population declines of many grassland birds, species that might have been destined for the endangered species list if their declines had continued.

The object of the Wetlands Reserve Program is to restore wetlands on rural landscapes. The government offers to share the cost of restoring a wetland and to purchase a "conservation easement"—a limited property interest that assures the government that the wetland will not be filled, cropped, or otherwise developed. Like the Conservation Reserve Program, the Wetlands Reserve Program has met with considerable success. It has played a significant part in reducing—and perhaps even reversing—the annual net loss of wetland acreage throughout the United States. It has also contributed to the resurgence of waterfowl populations that only a few years earlier had declined to their lowest levels in recent decades.

The simple fact underlying the success of incentives-based approaches is that, given a choice, most people will do what is in their economic self-interest. If a conservation program can be designed that allows people to further their self-interest by helping the environment, they will do so. For similar reasons, the limits of regulatory approaches are readily apparent. If people believe that regulatory programs require them to act against their own self-interest, a bureaucracy of enforcement officials will be needed to secure compliance. Some who think they can avoid compliance and get away with it will do so. Others will be creative enough to find ways of frustrating the purpose of the law without actually violating it.

In the endangered species conservation context, there are a number of examples of the latter problem. The Endangered Species Act prohibits anyone from killing an endangered animal or from destroying habitat upon which it depends. Nothing in the law, however, compels landowners to create the habitat that endangered species will need in the future. Thus, because tree harvesting is restricted on land occupied by the endangered Red-cockaded Woodpecker, private forestland owners in the Southeast sometimes prematurely harvest timber on land not yet occupied by the bird to prevent the trees from reaching the age most useful to this species. By so doing, they escape possible future restrictions on timber harvest without violating the law. The endangered woodpecker, on the other hand, faces an even bleaker prospect for survival because the habitat that it might have used in the future has been eliminated. Similarly, the woodpecker typically inhabits open pine forests with minimal oak and other hardwood midstory. Historically, these conditions were maintained by regular fires that killed hardwood saplings but left pines unharmed. Without fire or other means of controlling hardwood growth, a pine forest occupied by Red-cockaded Woodpeckers is likely to change over time into a mixed pine and hardwood forest that the birds will abandon; without active management efforts, currently occupied habitat will cease to be occupied. Landowners have a double reason to refrain from such management: management efforts are costly, and refraining from them is likely to eliminate a constraint on timber harvest.

Even if the Endangered Species Act's prohibition against harming rare species were vigilantly enforced and compliance with it were guaranteed, the best it could accomplish would be to preserve the status quo for species that are already in peril of extinction. If species like the Red-cockaded Woodpecker, Kirtland's Warbler, the Karner blue butterfly, Attwater's Prairie Chicken, and others that require active habitat management efforts are to recover, the cooperation of private landowners will be essential. To secure that cooperation, programs that appeal to the self-interest of landowners through incentives will be needed. Incentives-based approaches to conservation are not an alternative to regulatory approaches, but are a valuable and necessary supplement.

However, we must also ask whether the broader category of biodiversity has been well served by legislation centered on species. Species protection carries with it a degree of legislated habitat protection. Indeed, within the language of the ESA, destroying the habitat of an endangered species is legally equivalent to destroying the species itself. The ESA includes provisions to conserve "the ecosystems upon which endangered species and threatened species depend" by designating and listing **critical habitat** when a species is listed. Critical habitat is defined as specific areas within the species' range with physical or biological features either (1) essential to conservation of the species, or (2) which may require special management considerations or protection (USFWS 1988). "Habitat" varies according to species, and could range

(A)

(B)

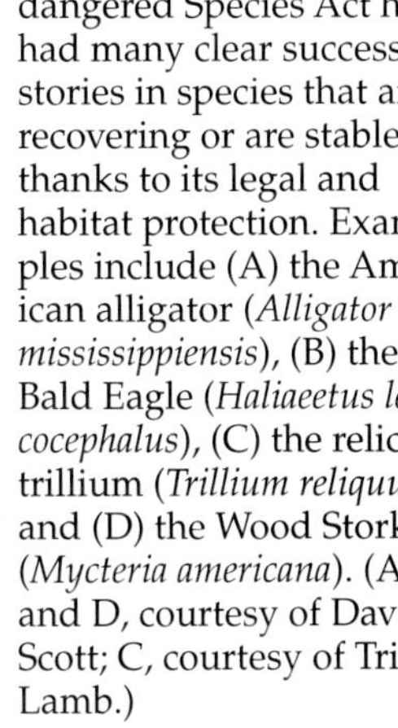
Figure 3.11 The U.S. Endangered Species Act has had many clear success stories in species that are recovering or are stable thanks to its legal and habitat protection. Examples include (A) the American alligator (*Alligator mississippiensis*), (B) the Bald Eagle (*Haliaeetus leucocephalus*), (C) the relict trillium (*Trillium reliquum*), and (D) the Wood Stork (*Mycteria americana*). (A, B, and D, courtesy of David Scott; C, courtesy of Trip Lamb.)

(C)

(D)

from small patches of grassland set in a matrix of housing developments for endangered butterflies, to entire and uninterrupted watersheds for grizzly bears. The ESA, however, provides no systematic, ecosystem-level protection, nor does "critical habitat" refer to more than localized, short-term survival requirements.

At the other end of the diversity spectrum, within-species diversity may be protected by subspecies designations, or by designation of particularly critical individual populations. However, this strategy depends on good taxonomy and on recognition of distinct clusters of variation within the species category. For invertebrates and plants, individual populations are not recognizable for protection, so a subspecific designation must be made in order to protect within-species diversity. Such a designation depends on the particular characters selected by individual taxonomists, and on whether they are "lumpers" or "splitters." Where one taxonomist (a splitter) may assign many subspecific designations to a species, another (a lumper) may be inclined to group geographic variation into a smaller number of subspecies based on stricter criteria. Within-species legal protection by the ESA thus may come down to the choice of a particular taxonomist (Murphy 1991).

One of the criticisms leveled against the ESA by its opponents is that too much protection has been offered in recent years to subspecies and populations, causing undue interference with economic progress. Calls have been made for revision of the ESA to make only full species subject to protection. This view was highlighted by the former U.S. Secretary of the Interior, Manuel Lujan, Jr., in reference to the endangered Mount Graham red squirrel (*Tamiasciurus hudsonicus grahamensis*) of Arizona, when he stated, "Nobody's told me the difference between a red squirrel, a black one or a brown one. Do we have to save every subspecies?" (Sward 1990). In addition to demonstrating a profound ignorance of biodiversity and evolutionary processes on the part of the highest conservation officer in the land, the statement reflects a general public perception that subspecies and populations are not very important. However, a survey of all 492 listings and proposed listings of plants and animals from 1985 to 1991 (Wilcove et al. 1993) indicates that 80% were full species, 18% were subspecies, and only 2% were distinct populations. Obviously, species-level taxonomy is still driving endangered species legislation. The status of the ESA is further discussed in Box 3B.

BOX 3B
U.S. Endangered Species Act Endangered

As of this writing (early 1997), the future of the U.S. Endangered Species Act is in question. Political and economic forces have increasingly fought against the ESA over the last two decades under the impression that it costs too much (it actually costs about $0.25 per year per citizen), prevents development (even though few development projects have been stopped by the ESA), infringes on private property rights (even though the ESA primarily targets activities on public lands), and deals with "useless" plants and animals (even though they are part of the larger fabric of life). Pro- and anti-ESA groups have been battling in the halls of Congress and elsewhere for several years to strengthen or weaken the ESA. An editorial by 11 stellar conservation biologists, all Pew Conservation Scholars, presented 12 points of scientific consensus regarding the value of biodiversity, and thus the need for a strong and effective ESA (Murphy et al. 1994). We briefly summarize those points here:

1. The species extinction rate has increased drastically over the past four centuries, with nearly all extinctions due to human activities.
2. Species losses are irreversible, and lost species cannot be recreated even with our best technologies.
3. Reliable prediction of how many or which species can be removed from ecosystems without causing significant change in function or collapse is impossible.
4. The role of a species in an ecosystem is not proportional to its size, abundance, position in the food web, or charismatic appeal.
5. Because the long-term survival of a species depends on its ability to adapt to changing circumstances, genetic and populational diversity are critical resources and should be protected.
6. We cannot predict which species or subspecies will be critical to long-term species survival, or which genes will prove useful for agriculture, medicine, or industry.
7. The expense, duration, and probability of failure of recovery efforts for imperiled species all increase with delay in protection and recovery actions.
8. Recovery efforts for endangered species have generally been too meager, and their goals too modest.
9. Captive breeding is a useful tool, but is not an effective overall strategy to save rare species. Species must ultimately be saved in their natural habitats.
10. Protection of natural habitats, with intact species assemblages, is the key to species conservation.
11. Imperiled species tend to be concentrated in relatively few areas, or "hot spots," and can thus be protected and recovered in a time- and cost-effective manner.
12. Habitat and species conservation provide economic benefits by preserving natural goods and services. Conservation is often compatible with economic values of land and water and need not cause economic harm.

They then offered four scientifically based recommendations regarding the ESA debate:

1. Listing of species as threatened or endangered under the Endangered Species Act should be expedited to protect vanishing plants and animals while chances of recovery are still high.
   - The listing procedure should not be burdened with further procedural requirements.
   - Greater funding for species listing and recovery should be provided.
   - Agencies should be encouraged to list multiple species from imperiled habitats.
2. Conservation strategies should emphasize the protection and restoration of natural habitats.
   - Priority should be given to the listing of "umbrella species," which would extend protection to other species in the same habitats.
   - Critical habitat designation should be completed quickly, soon after listing, and should be decoupled from economic impact assessment to remain a scientifically based assessment.
3. More effective and timely recovery planning should be encouraged.
   - Strategies to restore species and ecological processes in natural habitats should be emphasized rather than heroic manipulations and artificial, ex situ techniques.
   - Mandated recovery plan deadlines and mandated specific actions will ensure more timely implementation and better recovery.
4. Vertebrates, invertebrates, and plants warrant equal treatment with respect to listing and protection.
   - Authority for listing and conservation of vertebrate populations should be continued and expanded to include invertebrates and plants.
   - Penalties for taking listed plants on public and private lands should be the same as for taking listed animals.

The international CITES treaty also focuses on species as the category of concern, with even less attention paid to within-species diversity. Adopted in March 1973, with at least 126 signatory countries to date (Caughley and Gunn 1996), the goal of CITES is "to regulate the complex wildlife trade by controlling species-specific trade levels on the basis of biological criteria" (Trexler and Kosloff 1991).

The heart of CITES is its three appendices that restrict trade of species that are in need of protection due to various levels of threat (Hemley 1994). Appendix I, containing some 675 species as of 1994 (including all rhinoceroses, sea turtles, great apes, great whales, and most large cats) is the most restrictive list, and includes all species "threatened with extinction which are or may be affected by trade" (CITES, Appendix I). It prohibits all commercial trade in these species, and allows only exceptional noncommercial trade for scientific or zoological purposes, after export and import permits are secured. Appendix II lists species not immediately threatened with extinction but which could become so if trade is not restricted (over 25,000 species, including over 21,000 plants); limited commercial trade in these species is allowed. Appendix III is an optional list that countries can use to protect selected species that might be endangered by trade. Enforcement of the treaty is by individual member countries.

In all cases, species and extinction are the criteria of concern in CITES; subspecies and geographic criteria are not specifically mentioned. Rather, the statute is based on endangered species lists and laws developed in individual countries. Thus, a particular species may be legally captured in and traded from one country, but not another. For example, leopards (*Felis pardus*) may legally be taken from Somalia, but not from Kenya.

The strength of CITES is the "basic principle of strictly limiting international trade in species in genuine need of protection while allowing controlled trade in species that are capable of sustaining some level of exploitation. . . . The treaty's weaknesses lie in its implementation and enforcement mechanisms. Each member state is responsible for enforcing CITES decisions, although the ability and commitment to enforce these decisions varies widely among countries" (Hemley 1994). A complicating factor is the general relationship of trade in wildlife to broader international commerce. For example, major trade agreements such as the General Agreement on Tariffs and Trade (GATT) and the North American Free Trade Agreement (NAFTA) do not distinguish between a product that is produced sustainably and one that is not. Thus, a crocodile skin product made with farm-raised animals is not distinguished from one made from wild animals (Hemley 1994). Lawyer Daniel Rohlf provides a broader legal perspective on biodiversity protection in Essay 3E.

ESSAY 3E
Law and Protection of Biodiversity

Daniel J. Rohlf, Lewis and Clark College

The dictionary defines "law" as both a rule of human conduct and a principle stating something that always works in the same way under the same conditions, such as a "law of nature." The fundamental insights of Muir and Leopold essentially merged these definitions; they argued that instead of acting as if we are above the dictates of the natural world, humans should see themselves as fellow members of the earth's biotic community. But moving legal systems toward this ideal requires far more than simply adding an endangered species act to the statute books or signing an international convention on biodiversity. Providing effective legal protections for biodiversity demands a synthesis of social structure, policy, and regulation. Most important from the standpoint of a conservation biologist, the fuel for this process is an understanding of the biotic community and our place in this community.

Our ability to control our own behavior, even through law, is as yet quite limited. For example, a vast number of stringent environmental laws and treaties are really paper tigers because governments lack the ability or will to enforce them. More significantly, individuals, communities, and even entire countries often have little choice but to ignore laws and treaties. An immediate worldwide agreement to ban clearing of tropical forests, for example, would in reality do little to alter the behavior of exponentially increasing numbers of landless (and hungry) farmers, or of countries scrambling to service huge foreign debts. In sum, no government or treaty can simply legislate biodiversity protection; we must first structure our society so as to make adherence to such protections possible.

In countries with advanced legal systems and a citizenry whose basic needs are consistently met, the structure and degree of legal protections of biodiversity become policy issues. Legislative bodies allocate resources and formulate laws dealing with biodiversity according to their perceptions of costs and benefits, as well as their gauge of public sentiments. The U.S. Endangered Species Act, for example, reflects this deliberative process. In the initial section of the Act, Congress recognized that imperiled species have "esthetic, ecological, educational, historical, recreational, and scientific value to the Nation and its people." However, in funding appropriations, American lawmakers consistently relegate the chronically underfunded endangered species program to a level far below items such as military research. This reflects a policy decision by Congress of the relative social importance of biodiversity protection.

Even assuming policy consensus in placing high priority on conserving biodiversity, however, laws aimed at protecting this resource can successfully achieve their goals only if they are biologically sound in both structure and implementation. In other words, even the most stringent legal protections for biodiversity will fail if they are not written and implemented in a manner consistent with how the physical world works. Two opposite examples illustrate this idea. The U.S. Forest Service's regulation supposedly protecting viable populations of all native species within national forests has proven to be relatively ineffective because the regulation's definition of the term "viable population" is so muddled as to be of little practical use in gauging a target level of habitat protection. On the other hand, unlike many harvest management schemes, the Convention for the Conservation of Antarctic Marine Living Resources explicitly protects ecosystem integrity by restricting harvest of Antarctic marine species to a level that managers determine will produce no adverse effects on the target species or on other species dependent on the target species.

Finally, governments occasionally attempt to manipulate law in order to hide controversial policy decisions behind a veil of science. Former president George Bush, for instance, sought to reverse his pledge to safeguard wetland habitats. To avoid the appearance of breaking a political promise, the Bush administration attempted to eliminate protection for wetlands by restrictively defining the areas considered wetlands. Though the Administration framed its proposal in terms of updating the scientific definition of wetlands, the clear aim was to implement a policy that lifted federal protection on vast areas of important habitat.

It is critical for conservation biologists to understand the process of facilitating, structuring, and implementing legal protection for biodiversity because they have the power to substantially influence this process. They gain this power through generating information about biodiversity and its value to society. It is difficult to overstate the value of such information. Without data demonstrating the importance of maintaining biodiversity, social and policy changes necessary to stem its erosion will not occur. Also, increasing understanding of ecosystems and their constituent elements will enable creation of biologically sound regulatory schemes that effectively protect biodiversity. Information also plays a key role in implementing these regulatory schemes. Many laws that affect biodiversity require resource managers to base their decisions on the best scientific information available, virtually guaranteeing researchers that their data will be used in on-the-ground decision making. Finally, biologists can expose policy decisions masquerading as science.

Conservation biologists' principal challenge, therefore, is to direct their research so as to influence the process of creating and implementing effective legal protections for biodiversity. Doing so requires knowledge of the social, policy, and legal dimensions of this process, as well as careful, unbiased scientific research. With the hemorrhage of biodiversity we currently face, conservation biologists cannot content themselves with merely adding to the general body of scientific knowledge; they must provide knowledge that *counts* in decision-making forums. Such focused research is needed both on overarching questions and on site-specific projects: more empirical information on the importance of biodiversity will encourage policy decisions favoring biodiversity protection, just as more information on the biodiversity impacts of a development proposal will improve managers' ability to gauge whether the project is consistent with the public interest and existing legal standards. In providing this information, conservation biologists play a vital role in bringing human laws closer to natural laws.

If There Are 30 Million Or So Species, Can Conservation Be Based on a Species Approach?

Species will always need to be part of the larger conservation equation. Loss of species diversity is more obvious and quantifiable than, say, loss of genetic or habitat diversity, and the human populace can readily identify with species loss. Even habitat or landscape approaches to conservation ecology (Parts III and IV of this book) depend on understanding species biology. The selection and development of nature reserves, for example (Chapter 10), may rely on knowledge of species–area relationships, the life history requirements of particular species, or the minimum number of individuals of a species necessary to avoid major losses of genetic diversity.

(A)

(B)

(C)

(D)

Figure 3.12 The public often responds positively to "flagship" or "charismatic" endangered species, creating political support for protection of other species and their ecosystems. Typical flagship vertebrates in the United States include (A) the California Condor (*Gymnogyps californianus*), (B) the Florida panther (*Felis concolor*), (C) the black-footed ferret (*Mustela nigripes*), and (D) the grizzly bear (*Ursus horribilis*), shown here eating a potentially endangered species or race of salmon. (A, photograph by Ron Garrison © San Diego Zoo; B, courtesy of Chris Belden; C, Dean Biggins; D, David Scott.)

The focus on species in conservation has largely centered on vertebrates, especially birds and large mammals. They are visible, dominant parts of our natural environments, and, for better or worse, extract more sympathy from the public than do most plants or insects (Kellert 1984). These "flagship" or "charismatic" species (Figure 3.12) draw financial support more easily than do stinging insects or obscure mussels, and by so doing serve to protect habitat and other species under the "umbrella" of their large habitat requirements.

The individual species approach has had tangible successes, some of which were mentioned earlier in this chapter. These successful efforts serve to increase support for conservation programs at all levels. However, the single-species approach can also backfire. The snail darter (*Percina tanasi*), because of its endangered species status, held up construction of the Tellico Dam in Tennessee (Figure 3.13), and the ESA received much criticism and scrutiny as a result. The Northern Spotted Owl (*Strix occidentalis caurina*) is perceived as having negative effects on the timber industry in California, Oregon, and Washington because of its protected status and consequent limitations on logging in its old-growth habitat. In cases such as these, the species may be the legal issue, but the larger biological issue is ecosystem protection. That point is often lost in the struggle, and the public perception is that obscure and "worthless" species are blocking economic progress and hurting people.

Because of such confrontations between single species and economic interests, the species approach, by itself, remains open to attack. The species may be perceived as an enemy of economic development, and can come to be regarded as trivial in comparison with human interests. The larger issues of habitat protection and erosion of biodiversity tend to be lost in the fray; the true focus in these cases should be the habitat and ecosystem of which the species is but one part, and the ecological and evolutionary processes that result in biological diversity and ecological functioning.

Although we argue that species should *always* be a part of the conservation scene, a species-by-species approach will not, *by itself*, make much headway in the big picture. Regardless of whether there are 5 million or 30 million or 100 million species on the planet, and regardless of how "species" is defined, a single-species approach can secure only a minuscule fraction of overall biological diversity. Such security assumes that we even know how many species there are, what they are, and where they are, which of course we do not. We do

(A)

(B)

Figure 3.13 (A) The snail darter (*Percina tanasi*), and (B) Tellico Dam on the Little Tennessee River in Tennessee. This fish was the focal point of a long conflict between enforcement of the U.S. Endangered Species Act and perceived economic progress. The fish's presence blocked the building of the dam until its protection was exempted by the Endangered Species Committee, also known as the "God Squad." (Photographs courtesy of David A. Etnier.)

know that the major concentrations and losses of diversity are among invertebrates, primarily insects, and primarily in the tropics (Wilson 1987, 1992). Much of this diversity is endemic to small regions and is being lost through habitat destruction. Given that we do not know what or where most of these species are, or anything about their natural histories, a species-by-species approach, by itself, is impractical; it must be combined with habitat and ecosystem protection.

That said, a species-oriented conservation agenda would certainly benefit from a more systematic, global approach. Because species are distributed nonrandomly (diversity is concentrated in certain areas), conservation efforts could follow these patterns. For example, 25% of bird species are found in 5% of the world's land area; protection of 14 of 90 studied localities in Thailand would conserve all hawkmoth species in that country; 16% of the land area of South Africa, if properly selected, would protect 95% of the vascular plant species of the region (Georgiadis and Balmford 1992). Such examples indicate that the identification and protection of certain relatively small areas can have disproportionate positive effects on conservation efforts. These "hot spots" of diversity are discussed in great detail in Chapter 5.

A large-scale, ecosystem-level approach has been promoted by any number of conservation ecologists (Grumbine 1994; Gunderson et al. 1995; Sampson and Knopf 1996; Vogt and Gordon 1996; Yaffee et al. 1996), by the U.S. federal government (IEMTF 1995), and even by some politicians (Gore 1992; Scheuer 1993). The ecosystem-level approach affords perhaps the best hope for biodiversity conservation at all biological levels. For example, former U.S. Representative James Scheuer (1993) stated, "We need to become proactive and holistic in our policies and move toward an integrated, multispecies and ecosystem approach to land use and conservation. The issue isn't endangered species per se but endangered ecosystems. Our goal should become the management of ecosystems for the sustainable use of biological resources and the conservation of biodiversity." The NRC review of the ESA (Clegg et al. 1995), although stating that "the ESA is based on sound scientific principles," went on to observe that "the ESA cannot *by itself* prevent all species extinctions, even if it is modified. . . . it is clear that managing ecosystems and landscapes as an addition to the protection of individual species can lead to improved natural-resource management and can help reduce species extinctions."

Summary

The species is a conceptual, biological, and legal focus in conservation, but the species as a biological unit is not a clear and unambiguous entity because species are part of a larger continuum of biological organization. The so-called species problem (i.e., What is a species?) is underlain by two fundamentally different views of species. The typological view sees species as fixed, unchanging entities, within which variation is unimportant. The populational view understands species as highly variable and changing over time, with no clear boundaries, and is the scientifically accepted perspective today. The major modern species concepts include the biological, phylogenetic, and evolutionary; all have advantages and disadvantages. Regardless of the particular concept used, it is important to remember that species are dynamic, changing entities containing a great deal of populational variation that is relevant to conservation efforts. Biological diversity at all levels, rather than Latin binomials, should be the focus of conservation efforts.

The U.S. Endangered Species Act and the Convention on International Trade in Endangered Species are two powerful legislative packages for protection of biological diversity based on species. Although both have been successful, and are critical for the continued protection of species and their habitats, they probably should be supplemented by broader approaches that explicitly protect ecosystems. With anywhere between 5 million and 100 million species on the planet, a species-by-species approach will fall short of the biodiversity protection actually needed to prevent massive extinctions.

Questions for Discussion

1. The predominant view of the world today among biologists is populational. Is it then realistic to even try to delineate all that variation in terms of species, which tends to be a typological concept?
2. Frequently, conflicting information relative to species designations is provided by morphological and genetic data. Should one data set take priority over the other? Can they be reconciled?
3. Programs such as the U.S. Endangered Species Act are chronically underfunded, and much of the limited money available goes toward a few high-profile species such as California Condors, grizzly bears, Florida panthers, and other large birds and mammals, while groups such as fishes, amphibians, reptiles, insects, mollusks, and plants, which represent much more diversity, go underfunded or are ignored. Discuss the biological, political, economic, and legal implications of switching funding toward these "low-profile," but diverse, groups.
4. We do not know the number of species on earth to within even an order of magnitude. Programs have been suggested that would develop species inventories, country by country, throughout the world. Discuss some practical problems that would need to be overcome to make headway in this attempt.
5. Referring back to Question 4, are species inventories necessary for good conservation? Do we really need to know all the details to protect diversity? Discuss how having such information would aid the protection process.
6. We indicated that ecosystem-level legal protection might be a good way to protect diversity of species and ecological processes. Discuss some practical problems and difficulties that would need to be overcome before we could realistically expect an "Endangered Ecosystems Act."

Suggestions for Further Reading

Carroll, C. R., C. Augspurger, A. Dobson, J. Franklin, G. Orians, W. V. Reid, C. R. Tracy, D. Wilcove, and J. Wilson. 1996. Science and reauthorization of the Endangered Species Act: Report of the Ecological Society of America. *Ecol. Applic.* 6:1–11. The Ecological Society of America created a committee to investigate the scientific bases that undergird the Endangered Species Act. This publication resulted from the committee's work, and is an assessment of how well the legislative language is supported by contemporary theory and research in conservation biology. The committee generally found that the Act was based on sound, well-accepted science but also suggested some ways in which the legislation could be improved.

Clark, T. W., R. P. Reading, and A. L. Clarke (eds.). 1994. *Endangered Species Recovery: Finding the Lessons, Improving the Process.* Island Press, Washington, D.C. A critically important collection of papers that examines the lessons of the endangered species experience, including various case studies and theoretical perspectives.

It includes analyses of what goes right and wrong in the process of endangered species management, emphasizing sociological, policy, organizational, and biological aspects.

Clegg, M. and 55 others. 1995. *Science and the Endangered Species Act.* National Academy Press, Washington, D. C. A special committee of the National Research Council was convened to address the Endangered Species Act with respect to scientific aspects of the Act and to consider whether the act is "protecting endangered species and their habitats." The committee generally found a good match between science and the ESA, and this book offers their findings in an extensive and quite readable treatment.

Kohm, K. A. (ed.). 1991. *Balancing on the Brink of Extinction: The Endangered Species Act and Lessons for the Future.* Island Press, Washington, D.C. A collection of papers dealing with various aspects of the U.S. Endangered Species Act, including its history, various perspectives on the Act, legal aspects, and various supplementary approaches to conservation.

Mayr, E. 1976. *Evolution and the Diversity of Life.* Belknap Press of Harvard University Press, Cambridge, MA. A collection of original essays by the person responsible for the biological species concept. Many of these essays deal with speciation, theories of systematics and classification, species concepts, and biogeography.

Otte, D. and J. A. Endler (eds.). 1989. *Speciation and Its Consequences.* Sinauer Associates, Sunderland, MA. Otte and Endler give us an outstanding, contemporary collection of chapters by numerous authors dealing with the complex and controversial topic of biological speciation. Various speciation models and species concepts are presented.

Rohlf, D. J. 1989. *The Endangered Species Act: A Guide to Its Protections and Implementation.* Stanford Environmental Law Society, Stanford, CA. A comprehensive guide to legal aspects of the U.S. Endangered Species Act, written by a lawyer but understandable by scientists and laypeople.

Rojas, M. 1992. The species problem and conservation: What are we protecting? *Conserv. Biol.* 6:170–178. Rojas presents a comprehensive discussion of the species problem in conservation, and of differences between typological and evolutionary (populational) approaches to the species in conservation

4

Global Biodiversity I

Patterns and Processes

The most wonderful mystery of life may well be the means by which it created so much diversity from so little physical matter. The biosphere, all organisms combined, makes up only about one part in ten billion of the earth's mass. It is sparsely distributed through a kilometer-thick layer of soil, water, and air stretched over a half billion square kilometers of surface.

E. O. Wilson, 1992

Biodiversity can refer to a broad spectrum of types and levels of biological variation. Units of biodiversity range from the genetic variability within a species, to the biota of some selected region of the globe, to the number of evolutionary lineages and the degree of distinctness among them, to the great diversity of ecosystems and biomes on earth. There is no one "correct" level at which to measure and analyze biodiversity because different scientific issues and practical problems find their focus at different levels. These various levels of biodiversity are best understood in a hierarchical fashion, an analysis promoted by Reed Noss in Essay 4A.

The Levels of Biodiversity

Genetic Diversity

Genetic variability is the ultimate source of biodiversity at all levels. The number of genes found in organisms ranges over more than three orders of magnitude, although not all of those genes code for products. Even with a small average number of **alleles**, or variant forms, per gene, the possible number of combinations is enormous, much larger than the number of individuals present in any species. This genetic variability is the material upon which the agents of evolution act.

Recent advances in molecular biology have provided the tools needed to measure the amount of genetic variation present in organisms. Measurements of variability within local populations are important for testing theories about the nature of the forces acting on genetic variation that are responsible for evolutionary change. Such knowledge has important practical applications in, for example, designing captive breeding programs for rare species so as to

ESSAY 4A

Hierarchical Indicators for Monitoring Changes in Biodiversity

Reed F. Noss, University of Idaho and Oregon State University

Biodiversity and how to save it is the subject matter of conservation biology. If you have read this far in this book, or even skimmed its pages, two things about biodiversity should be clear: (1) it is complex, and (2) it is always changing. How on earth can a conservation biologist or land manager deal with this mess?

First, we need to make some sense of the complexity of nature. We can dissect the biodiversity concept into meaningful components, and yet retain some idea of how they all fit together, by appealing to hierarchy theory. There are several kinds of hierarchies in nature, including the familiar levels of biological organization (such as genes, populations, species, communities), hierarchies of space and time, and hierarchies of rates. There are also ethical hierarchies; for instance, many people care about the suffering of individual animals, but some also care about the loss of species, ecosystems, and biomes. All of these hierarchies are nested; that is, higher levels enclose lower levels and, to a great extent, constrain their behavior. A tree is part of a forest stand, the stand is part of a landscape, the landscape is part of a physiographic region, and so on. If the physiographic region is inundated by a volcanic flow, everything nested within it also goes.

Biodiversity is not just species diversity. A comprehensive approach to biodiversity conservation must address multiple levels of organization and many different spatial and temporal scales. Most definitions of biodiversity recognize its hierarchical structure, with the genetic, population–species, community–ecosystem, and landscape levels considered most often. Each of these levels can be further divided into compositional, structural, and functional components. Composition includes the genetic constitution of populations, the identity and relative abundances of species in a natural community, and the kinds of habitats and communities distributed across the landscape. Structure includes the sequence of pools and riffles in a stream, downed logs and snags in a forest, and the vertical layering and horizontal patchiness of vegetation. Function includes the climatic, geologic, hydrologic, ecological, and evolutionary processes that generate biodiversity and keep it forever changing.

Change is universal, but some kinds of change threaten biodiversity. Changes in climate, changes in disturbance regime (such as fire suppression, or conversely, increases in ignitions), introductions of novel chemicals into the environment, and species introductions or deletions are all changes likely to degrade native biodiversity. These kinds of changes happen naturally, but often occur faster and are of greater magnitude with human activity. In order to have any chance of protecting biodiversity against the onslaught of these factors, we must have early warning of change; hence the need for monitoring.

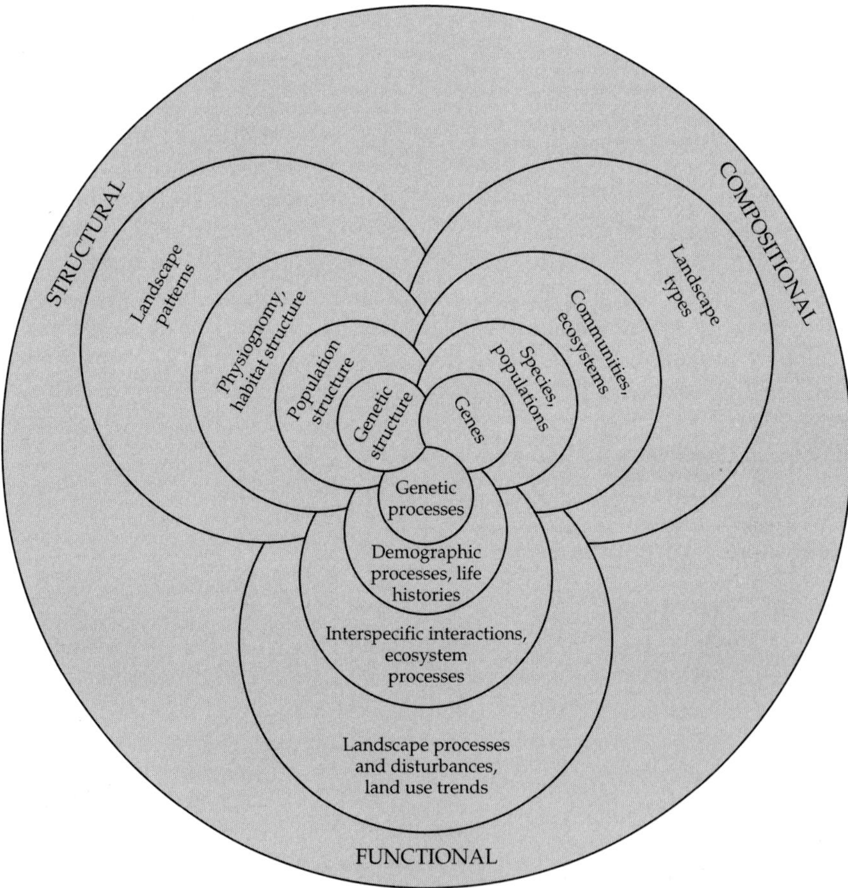

Figure A Compositional, structural, and functional attributes of biodiversity at four levels of organization. (From Noss 1990.)

Because biodiversity is multifaceted and hierarchical, those indicators that we select as targets for monitoring should represent all of this complexity. Otherwise, something might fall through the cracks.

Land managers are familiar with the use of *indicator species,* often selected to represent a suite of species with similar habitat requirements. As a well-known example, the Northern Spotted Owl (*Strix occidentalis caurina*) was selected by managers of national forests in the Pacific Northwest as a surrogate for all other species associated with old-growth forests. However, the use of indicator species has encountered problems, including biased selection criteria, false assumptions about species–habitat relationships, unwarranted extrapolations from one species to others, and flawed design of monitoring programs. But species will continue to be useful as indicators, particularly if we focus on those most sensitive to human activities and those that play pivotal roles in their ecosystems. For example, change in the abundance of woodpeckers may warn us of possible changes in populations of other species that use woodpecker cavities. But we should not carry our extrapolations too far. The idea of one species representing all others that share a similar habitat is not ecologically realistic.

Indicators for monitoring biodiversity must consist of much more than a set of indicator species. Because biodiversity is distributed hierarchically, so too should indicators be. A framework for selecting biodiversity indicators might follow a nested hierarchy of compositional, structural, and functional elements (Figure A). A monitoring program should select a broad range of indicators that correspond to critical management questions, such as: Are populations of rare species being maintained in sizes and distributions that assure long-term demographic and genetic viability? Are the natural structure and species composition of the community being maintained? Is the configuration of the landscape adequate to permit normal movements of organisms? Using the example of a managed forest landscape, some measurable indicators that might help answer such questions are listed in Table A. Only with such a comprehensive approach will conservation biologists be able to track changes in biodiversity and obtain the information they need to preserve it.

Table A
Hierarchical Indicators for Monitoring Biodiversity

GENETIC

Composition
- Allelic diversity
- Presence/absence of rare alleles

Structure
- Heterozygosity
- Phenotypic polymorphism

Function
- Symptoms of inbreeding depression or genetic drift (reduced survivorship or fertility, abnormal sperm, reduced resistance to disease, morphological abnormalities or asymmetries)
- Inbreeding/outbreeding rate
- Rate of genetic interchange between populations (measured by rate of dispersal and subsequent reproduction of migrants)

POPULATION–SPECIES

Composition
- Absolute and relative abundance, density, basal area, cover, importance value for various species

Structure
- Sex ratio, age distribution, and other aspects of population structure for sensitive species, keystone species, and other special interest species
- Distribution and dispersion of special interest species across the region

Function
- Population growth and fluctuation trends of special interest species
- Fertility, fecundity, recruitment rate, survivorship, mortality rate, individual growth rate, and other individual and population health parameters
- Trends in habitat components for special interest species (varies by species)
- Trends in threats to special interest species (depends on life history and sensitivity of species in relation to land use practices and other influences)

COMMUNITY–ECOSYSTEM

Composition
- Identity, relative abundance, frequency, richness, and evenness of species and guilds (in various habitats)
- Diversity of tree ages or sizes in community (stand)
- Ratio of exotic species to native species in community (species richness, cover, and biomass)
- Proportions of endemic, threatened, and endangered species

Structure
- Frequency distribution of seral stages (age classes) for each forest type and across all types
- Average and range of tree ages within defined seral stages
- Ratio of area of natural forest of all ages to area in clear-cuts and plantations
- Abundance and density of snags, downed logs, and other defined structural elements in various size and decay classes
- Spatial dispersion of structural elements and patches
- Foliage density and layering (profiles), and horizontal diversity of foliage profiles in stand
- Canopy density and size, dispersion of canopy openings
- Areal extent of each disturbance event (e.g., fires)

Function
- Frequency, intensity, return interval, or rotation period of fires and other natural and anthropogenic disturbances
- Cycling rates for various key nutrients (e.g., N, P)
- Intensity or severity of disturbance events
- Seasonality or periodicity of disturbances
- Predictability or variability of disturbances
- Human intrusion rates and intensities

LANDSCAPE

Composition
- Identity, distribution, richness, and proportions of patch types (such as forest types and seral stages) across the landscape
- Total amount of late successional forest interior habitat
- Total amount of forest patch perimeter and edge zone

Structure
- Patch size frequency distribution for each seral stage and forest type, and across all stages and types
- Patch size diversity index
- Size frequency distribution of late successional interior forest patches (minus defined edge zone, usually 100–200 m)
- Forest patch perimeter:area ratio
- Edge zone:interior zone ratio
- Fractal dimension
- Patch shape indices
- Patch density
- Fragmentation indices
- Interpatch distance (mean, median, range) for all forest patches and for late successional forest patches
- Juxtaposition measures (percentage of area within a defined distance from patch occupied by different habitat types, length of patch border adjacent to different habitat types)
- Structural contrast (magnitude of difference between adjacent habitats, measured for various structural attributes)
- Road density (mi/mi^2 or km/km^2) for different classes of road and all road classes combined

Function
- Disturbance indicators (see above)
- Rates of nutrient, energy, and biological transfer between different communities and patches in the landscape

reduce the deleterious effects of inbreeding, or determining the best sources of individuals for reestablishing populations in areas from which they have been exterminated. Measurements of the amount of genetic difference among species are important for estimating rates of evolution and for establishing phylogenetic relationships among organisms.

Intraspecific Diversity

Intraspecific diversity has both within-population and between-population genetic components. The nature and extent of such differences is of both theoretical and practical interest. Within populations, the potential rate of evolutionary change is proportional to the amount of available genetic variability. For individuals in those populations, **heterozygosity** is believed to confer **fitness** benefits; conversely, loss of heterozygosity is believed to lead to reductions in fitness. Therefore, the study of within-population genetic variability is a central focus of evolutionary research. Between-population variability is the result primarily of adaptations of populations to local ecological conditions. Locally adapted populations of a widespread species may have particular genes and gene combinations critical for viability in those particular areas. The nature and extent of between-population genetic variation reveals much about the evolutionary history of populations and processes of speciation. The theoretical and practical importance of intraspecific genetic diversity is treated in greater detail in Chapter 6.

Species Richness

The number of species of organisms present in an area—**species richness**—is an important component of biodiversity. If species are weighted by some measure of their importance, such as their abundance, productivity, or size, we speak of **species diversity**. The most frequently used indices of diversity are the Shannon-Wiener index,

$$H' = -\sum p_i \ln(p_i)$$

and the Simpson index,

$$D = \frac{1}{\sum p_i^2}$$

in both of which p_i represents the fractional abundance (or biomass or productivity) of the ith species.

Indices of diversity and species richness are both commonly used in ecological and conservation biology studies because each type gives useful information not provided by the other. Ecologists commonly use diversity measures to compare ecological communities and to assess the adverse effects of pollution and other types of environmental disturbances. Typically, an ecological community subjected to stresses experiences losses of species and increases in abundances—and hence dominance—of a few species. Weighted diversity indices quantify these shifts in relative abundances, and an examination of the nature of the changes often yields clues to their causes. Understanding of causes is essential for the design of management plans that can counteract the changes and restore the systems to their former states.

Conservation biologists usually use unweighted measures of species richness because the many rare species that characterize most biotas are often of greater conservation interest than the more common ones that dominate weighted indices of diversity. In addition, accurate estimates of population densities on geographic scales are seldom available, and species lists are the only type of information that is available for most areas. Therefore, the remainder of this chapter will concentrate upon patterns in numbers of species.

Approximately 1.5 million living and 300,000 fossil species have been described and given scientific names (Table 4.1). Estimates of the actual number of living species vary widely because they are based on incomplete and indirect evidence. Current estimates of the total number of living species range from 10 million to as high as 50 million or more (May 1988; Wilson 1992). In other words, we do not know within an order of magnitude the number of living species. Thus, a large fraction of the species likely to be exterminated during the next century will disappear before they have been named, much

Table 4.1
Numbers of Species Living Today

Kingdom	Phylum (Division)	Number of described species	Estimated number of species	Percent described
Monera	Viruses and bacteria[a]			
Protista		100,000	250,000	40.0
Fungi	Eumycota	80,000	1,500,000	5.3
Plantae	Bryophyta	14,000	30,000	46.7
	Tracheophyta	250,000	500,000	50.0
Animalia	Porifera	5,000		
	Cnidaria	10,000		
	Ctenophora	100		
	Platyhelminthes	25,000		
	Nemertea	900		
	Gastrotricha	500		
	Kinorhyncha	100		
	Priapulida	16		
	Entoprocta	150		
	Nematoda	20,000	1,000,000	2.0
	Rotifera	1,800		
	Annelida	75,000		
	Arthropoda	1,250,000	20,000,000	5.0
	Mollusca	100,000	200,000	50.0
	Sipunculida	250		
	Echiurida	150		
	Pogonophora	145		
	Ectoprocta	5,000		
	Phoronida	70		
	Brachiopoda	350[b]		
	Hemichordata	100		
	Chateognatha	100		
	Echinodermata	7,000		
	Urochordata	1,200		
	Chordata	40,000	50,000	80.0

Data from Andersen 1992; Hawksworth 1991a; Trüper 1992; Vickerman 1992; World Conservation Monitoring Centre 1992.
[a]Numbers for viruses and bacteria are omitted because species limits are poorly defined and essentially unknown in these groups.
[b]26,000 fossil species described

less understood ecologically. Essay 4B, by Peter Raven and E. O. Wilson, explores this problem in more detail.

The immense richness of viruses, bacteria, protists, and unicellular algae is largely uncatalogued today. There are few studies of viruses except for those

---

ESSAY 4B

A 50-Year Plan for Biodiversity Surveys[1]

Peter H. Raven, Missouri Botanical Garden, and
E. O. Wilson, Harvard University

In the wake of the 1992 "Earth Summit" in Rio de Janeiro, it should be evident why biological systematics, hitherto regarded as "little science," is badly in need of growing large—and soon. The roughly 1.5 million species of living organisms known to date are probably fewer than 15% of the actual number, and by some estimates could be fewer than 2%. The Linnaean shortfall reaches from supposedly well known groups to the most obscure, as illustrated by the following examples:

- Eleven of the 80 known living species of cetaceans (whales and porpoises) have been discovered in the 20th century, the most recent in 1991; at least one more undescribed species has been sighted in the eastern Pacific but not yet collected.
- One of the largest shark species, the megamouth, constituting the new family Megaschasmidae, was discovered in 1976 and is now known from five specimens.
- During the past decade, botanists have discovered three new families of flowering plants in Central America and southern Mexico; one, a remarkable relict, is a forest tree, frequent at middle elevations in Costa Rica.
- The most recent new animal phylum, the Cycliophora, was described in 1950.
- The great majority of insects in the canopy of tropical rainforests, possibly in excess of 90% in some groups, remains unknown.
- Although only 69,000 species of fungi have been described thus far, a leading specialist estimates that the world total is 1.5 million or more.
- Although the number of bacterial species recognized by microbiologists is about 4000, the huge majority in existence remain incommunicado, and hence undiscovered, because their culturing requirements are unknown. DNA matching can circumvent this difficulty. Recent studies in Norway indicate the presence of 4000–5000 species in a single gram of beech forest soil and a comparably large but different array in a gram of nearby marine sediment.

Clearly, progress over the past 250 years toward an overall knowledge of the earth's prodigious biodiversity has been very slow. Close attention to this problem might be postponed for the delectation of future generations, except for two compelling circumstances. On the positive side, biodiversity represents a potential source of wealth in the form of new crops, pharmaceuticals, petroleum substitutes, and other products. If used wisely, wild species will also continue to provide essential ecosystem services, from the maintenance of hydrologic cycles to the nitrification of soils. On the negative side, biodiversity is disappearing at a rapid rate, primarily due to habitat destruction. Tropical deforestation alone is reducing species in these biomes by half a percent per year, as estimated by the conservative models of island biogeography. This figure is likely to be boosted many times when the impact of pollution and exotic species is determined and factored in. Coral reefs, the marine equivalent of rainforests in magnitude of diversity, are also in increasing trouble.

There is growing recognition of the need for a crash program to map biodiversity in order to plan its conservation and practical use. With up to a fifth or more of the species of all groups likely to disappear over the next 30 years, as human populations double in the warmer parts of the world, we are clearly faced with a dilemma. But what is the best way to proceed?

Some systematists have urged initiation of a global biodiversity survey, ultimately aimed at full identification and biogeography of all species. Others, noting the shortage of personnel, funds, and above all, time, see the only realistic hope to lie in overall inventories of those groups that are relatively well known now, including flowering plants, vertebrates, butterflies, and a few others. In order to accomplish this second objective as early as possible, it would be necessary to survey transects across broad geographic areas, and to examine a number of carefully selected sites in great detail. A reasonable number of specialists is available to begin this task, and with adequate funding it could be completed in a decade. The results would reveal a great deal about patterns of endemism, including the existence of hot spots, those parts of the world believed to contain the largest numbers of endangered species. They could be applied directly to problems of economic development, land use, science, and conservation. Meanwhile, adequate numbers of specialists could be trained and preparations made to deal with all of the remaining groups of organisms. The aim would be to gain a reasonably accurate idea of the representation of the best-known groups on earth while attempting complete inventories of all the global biota over the course of the next 50 years. As most of the tropical forests of the world are likely to be reduced to less than 10% of their original extent during this half century, adequate planning is of the essence. The results from inventories should be organized in such a way as to apply directly to the development of new crops, sustainable land use, conservation, and the enhancement of allied disciplines of science.

In order to propel systematics into its larger role foreordained by the biodiversity crisis, its practitioners need to formulate an explicitly stated mission with a timetable and cost estimate. In the approach outlined above, the 50-year period could be viewed as a series of successive 10-year plans. As each decade approaches an end, progress to that point could be assessed and new directions for the next decade identified.

Momentum in the enterprise will result in economies of scale. Costs per species will fall as new methods for collecting and distributing specimens are invented and procedures for storing and accessing information approved. Costs are moreover not simply additive when new higher taxa are added, but instead fall off on a per-species basis. For example, entomologists could collect nematodes on the insects they collect, while identifying these hosts for the nematologists—and vice versa. Multiple groups can be collected by mass sampling of entire habitats, and then distributed to systematists specializing in individual taxa.

The results of inventorying, as opposed to the costs, are not just additive but multiplicative. As networks of expertise and monographing grow, ecologists, population biologists, biochemists and others will be drawn into the enterprise. It is also inevitable that genome descriptions similar to those now planned for the human species and *Drosophila* will feed into the data base. Molecular biology is destined to fuse with systematics.

Applied systematics can develop collaterally with basic studies, as is being demonstrated by the organization of the Instituto Nacional de Biodiversidad (INBio) in Costa Rica. Chemical prospecting, the search for new natural products, is readily hooked onto inventories. So is screening for species and gene complexes of special merit in agriculture, forestry, and land reclamation.

Fully 80% of the earth's terrestrial biodiversity is likely to occur in the tropics, where only a few groups of organisms can be described as reasonably well known at present. Aside from the roughly 170,000 flowering plants and 30,000 vertebrates, only about 250,000 species of all groups appear to have been described thus far. With estimates of the remainder ranging from 8 million to 100 million, one can readily appreciate the magnitude of the task at hand, and the fact that the few hundred systematists available are woefully inadequate to complete the task while most of the species are still in existence. We require, in fact, a wholly new approach to this great problem in order to be able to provide even an outline of the nature and occurrence of these species.

Abdus Salam has estimated that some 6% of the world's scientists and engineers live in developing countries, with a rapidly increasing share of 77% of the world's population, 15% of the world's wealth (GDP), and perhaps 20% of the world's use of industrial energy. A net sum amounting to tens of billions of dollars flows annually from these countries to the rich, industrial parts of the world. These relationships must be taken into account if our common objective is to chart the outlines of global biodiversity, use it for humanity's benefit, understand it scientifically, and preserve an intelligently selected sample of it for the future.

We believe that the best strategy for approaching this task is the implementation of national biological surveys throughout the world, conceived like INBio, and set up as management strategies for each nation's biodiversity. Such operations will expedite the increased understanding, efficient use (assisted by biotechnology transfer), and conservation, both in nature and ex situ, of as many organisms as possible. They will allow the people of every nation to see themselves as benefiting from their own biodiversity, while preserving it for their own purposes.

[1]Reprinted with permission and modified from *Science* 1992, 258:1099–1110. Copyright 1992 by the AAAS.

---

that attack people or domesticated plants and animals, and the organisms we study scientifically. How many types attack non-crop plants and insects, for example, is totally unknown, as is the number of marine forms. Similarly, the bacteria and protists that live in soils or attack invertebrates have scarcely been examined. Terrestrial algal species, especially those living on bark and rocks, have been little studied; the existence of some very small marine species, living in interstitial spaces in the ocean floor, was not recognized until 1980. All estimates of the number of species in these groups are crude guesses at best.

About 70,000 species of fungi have been described, but the total number living today almost certainly exceeds 1 million. For example, the 12,000 fungal species described from Britain is about six times the number of native vascular plants described for the same area. If there are, on average, six fungal species for each vascular plant species worldwide (the ratio found in Britain), the number of fungal species would be approximately 1.6 million (Hawksworth 1991). The global ratio could be much higher or lower than the British one, but we have little else upon which to base estimates.

Taxonomists believe that the number of species of nematodes is very large because millions of individuals may be present in a cubic meter of soil or mud; more than 200 species have been reported in samples of just a few cubic centimeters of coastal mud (Poinar 1983). Nonetheless, almost nothing is known about species ranges and rates of species turnover geographically, so global estimates are very uncertain.

Approximately 30,000 species of mites have been described, but, because knowledge of tropical mite faunas is extremely poor, the actual number of living species could easily exceed 1 million. Nearly 1 million species of insects, the world's most species-rich group of organisms, have been described, but this is certainly a small fraction of the total. Most of the insects collected by fogging the canopies of tropical trees, for example, are members of undescribed species (Erwin 1991).

Thus, the earth is a relatively unexplored planet biologically. Not only are most living species still undescribed, but very little is known about the life histories and ecological relations of most of the species that have been named. The rate of description of new species today is higher than it ever has been, but the rate is quite inadequate to accomplish a reasonable inventory prior to the likely extinction of many of the species.

Richness of Higher Taxa

The distinctness of evolving lineages is an important component of biodiversity. The higher taxonomic categories (orders, classes, phyla) of the universally used Linnaean biological classification system provide rough measures of distinctness of lineages. By this measure, marine biodiversity is much higher than terrestrial biodiversity, even though far fewer species of marine organisms than terrestrial organisms have been described. Of the 35 extant phyla of multicellular animals, 34 are marine; 16 of these are exclusively marine, and several others are very poorly represented on land. From this perspective, preservation of marine biodiversity is more important than might be suggested simply by a comparson of the numbers of species in marine and terrestrial environments. Diversity in marine systems is further discussed by Elliott Norse in Essay 4C.

ESSAY 4C

Uncharted Waters

Conserving Marine Biological Diversity

Elliott A. Norse, Marine Conservation Biology Institute

In a movie from my youth, *The Beast from 20,000 Fathoms*, a gigantic marine reptile terrorizing New York is confronted by a courageous, minuscule (and short-lived) policeman firing his service revolver. The clear take-home lesson: It's foolish to take on a big task without commensurate tools.

Maintaining life on our planet is the greatest challenge that humankind faces, yet the resources we devote to it, and the tools at our disposal, are far from adequate. Too few resources are devoted to protecting anything, and the crumbs that do go to conservation are sliced in peculiar ways. For example:

- State fish, wildlife, and natural resource agencies spend far more effort on boosting populations of the species that some people prefer to hook, shoot, or saw than on saving the vast majority of "nongame" animal and plant species that are declining and need help.
- Many more scientist-years, journal articles, and TV programs are devoted to conserving vertebrates than to the more than 99% of species that are not so closely related to us.
- Much of the ongoing research and hands-on conservation work happens in industrialized nations whose biological diversity was relatively modest even before it was further reduced, while there are few conservation biologists and institutions in biotically rich developing nations where wholesale loss is still preventable.

These disparities are reasonably well known. A less appreciated one is the scant conservation effort applied to the realm comprising more than 99% of the biosphere that is permanently inhabited by plants and animals: the sea. Covering more than twice the area of the terrestrial realm in a permanently inhabited layer more than 100 times thicker (average depth: nearly 4,000 meters), the sea is the least protected part of the biosphere. This lack of protection needs to be remedied because estuaries, coastal waters, and the oceans are biologically diverse, vitally important, and seriously threatened (Norse 1993; Butman and Carlton 1995).

The sea's biological diversity is dazzling to anyone familiar with it. Life began in the sea about 3.8 billion years ago. Because our primordial atmosphere had no free oxygen and hence no protective ozone layer, the sun's DNA-disrupting ultraviolet radiation scourged the earth's surface. But, shielded by UV-absorbing seawater, life thrived in the sea, and evolved into far more complex forms after marine cyanobacteria and algae generated substantial amounts of oxygen. The sea was the cradle of every known animal phylum. Many disappeared before land was colonized, but the sea still hosts 34 of the 35 extant animal phyla (all but the Onychophora, which first appeared in the sea but unaccountably left it). Indeed, 16 animal phyla are *exclusively* marine, including echinoderms, lamp shells, and arrow worms. Other algal and animal phyla, such as brown seaweeds and sponges, are almost exclusively marine. The land—where we have focused most of our conservation attention—has proven inhospitable to most multicellular life-forms except fungi, bryophytes, vascular plants, a few invertebrate phyla, and tetrapod vertebrates. Admittedly, the few successful "themes" that colonized land, particularly insects, have evolved into dazzlingly speciose variations, but in a fundamental sense the sea has much higher taxonomic diversity.

Scientists are still discovering phyla—most recently, Cycliophora (Funch and Kristensen 1995)—in the sea. It was only in the 1980s that biologists realized that we had described only a tiny fraction of the land's species because we had previously neglected to look in places such as the canopies of tropical forests. Not surprisingly, even more recent studies (e.g., Grassle and Maciolek 1992) suggest that a comparably tiny fraction of marine species have been described. As on land, many marine species are small things found in places that are difficult for biologists to sample. It is ironic that the increasingly rapid disappearance of life makes cataloguing species such an urgent task at a time when there is ever less money devoted to the task and ever fewer biologists devoting their careers to describing newly discovered life-forms.

Although few recognize this, the sea's ecosystem diversity also exceeds the land's. Like the land, the sea has forests, grasslands, deserts, montane and insular ecosystems, caves, and hot springs, but the sea has three phases—solid, liquid, and gaseous—not just two. The marine ecosystems without terrestrial analogues—the sea–air interface, the underside of pack ice, the water column—are home to life-forms, including pleuston, neuston, plankton, nekton, and filter-feeding substrate dwellers—that are entirely or largely absent on land. Marine ecosystems include those with the highest measured primary production (wave-beaten northeastern Pacific intertidal kelp beds, Leigh et al. 1986), but they also include vast inhabited spaces in which there is no autochthonous primary production, as well as ecosystems based wholly on chemosynthesis, not photosynthesis. But geographic patterns of marine ecosystem diversity have been very poorly described; there are no marine analogues to the Bailey, Küchler, and Udvardy geographic ecosystem classification schemes that are used to determine gaps in protected area coverage on land. In contrast to diversity at ecosystem and species levels, current information suggests that genetically distinct populations are less common within marine species than in terrestrial ones, so genetic diversity might be lower on average. But the sea's biological diversity and its importance far exceed the attention that humans devote to understanding them.

That is unfortunate, because the sea's biological diversity, like the land's, is threatened at all levels. Losses of genetic diversity are largely unquantified and are known mainly from accounts of local population extinction. The fossil record shows that the vast majority of marine species that have ever lived are now extinct, yet very few modern marine species extinctions have been documented. Inattention to marine neoextinctions reflects a peculiar but widespread belief that marine species are somehow "extinction-proof." The first marine invertebrate neoextinctions were reported only recently (Carlton et al. 1991; Carlton 1993); the disappearance of the once abundant eelgrass limpet *Lottia alveus* in the Atlantic was not noticed for six decades after it actually happened. Similarly, no marine invertebrate or seaweed has yet received protection under the U.S. Endangered Species Act. Destruction of marine ecosystems is documented mainly for conspicuous mangrove forests and coral reefs. Yet there is ample reason to believe that documented losses are but a tiny fraction of what has actually disappeared, or will disappear in coming decades. If we want to avoid the loss of the sea's biological diversity, we must have much better ways of detecting alarming trends.

Five fundamental forces jeopardize marine life: (1) there are too many people; (2) we consume too much; (3) our institutions degrade, rather than conserve, biodiversity; (4) we do not have the knowledge we need; and (5) we do not value nature enough. These forces, in turn, drive the five proximate threats to marine biological diversity: (1) overexploitation; (2) physical alteration; (3) pollution; (4) introduction of alien species; and (5) global atmospheric change. Thus, in both ultimate and proximate senses, the list of threats is the same in the sea as on land, although their relative importance differs somewhat. The significance of overexploitation and pollution in the sea, although usually underestimated, has long been recognized, but few people realize the importance of the other three factors. For example, for all the attention to deforestation on land, there has been astoundingly little research on the effects of physical alterations, such as bottom trawling or diversion of riverine flow, on marine species and ecosystems. In 1996, at a Marine Conservation Biology Institute workshop on the effects of bottom trawling on marine ecosystems, benthic ecologists, fisheries biologists, biogeochemists, and geologists from five nations concluded that bottom trawling is a major—often *the* major—cause of physical disturbance over a vast area of the world's continental shelf and slope ecosystems. By crushing, burying, and uncovering benthic organisms, bottom trawling dramatically reduces structural complexity and affects benthic community and ecosystem processes, with important implications for the sustainability of fisheries. It is difficult to imagine the effects of similar terrestrial anthropogenic disturbances, such as clear-cutting, chaining, plowing, and strip-mining, escaping the notice of scientists, decision makers, and the public for so long.

Some principles from terrestrial conservation biology will probably be robust enough to apply to the marine realm. Small populations are in greater jeopardy than large populations, in the sea or on land. As on land, large species with low fecundity are at special risk; endangerment, phyletic distinctness, and ecological importance are useful criteria for establishing priorities for species conservation. Removing guilds such as high-level predators or grazers can profoundly affect organisms at lower trophic levels. Greater structural complexity, providing more kinds of opportunities for feeding and avoiding predation, allows species diversity. Ecosystems are heterogeneous in composition, structure, and function, and certain areas merit special protection, including areas of high diversity, high endemism, or high productivity, spawning areas that serve as sources of recruits, nursery grounds, and migration corridors and stopover points. Unfortunately, an even smaller portion of the sea than the land is protected, and the protection tends to be less stringent. For example, the U.S. National Park system has thus far largely avoided commercial extractive activities such as logging and hunting in its protected areas, but their closest analogues in the sea, U.S. National Marine Sanctuaries, allow commercial exploitation of shellfishes and fishes, even with methods that alter habitats.

Conservation concepts and mechanisms that work effectively on land are not always applicable to the sea without modification because marine and terrestrial species and ecosystems function differently. One major difference is that most marine species (although far from all) have planktonic dispersal stages. Their zoospores or larvae spend hours to months drifting in currents, with the potential of dispersing tens of meters to thousands of kilometers from their parents, dispersal distances that are greater on average than those for terrestrial species. As on land, this strategy probably evolved because it allows individuals to avoid competing with their parents or offspring, but it is facilitated by seawater's buoyancy, which makes currents more important to marine dispersal than winds are on land.

Marine dispersal strategies have major implications for species and ecosystem conservation (e.g., fisheries management and location of marine protected areas). A species may be abundant at a location where recruitment depends on source areas far away, and local reproduction does not recruit new individuals to the population. Allochthonous population sources and sinks are far more important in the sea than on land. But population density can be important as well. Because many marine species (animals as well as plants) are sessile or sedentary and inject their gametes into the water column, the odds against fertilization may become so steep for species whose effective population density drops below some threshold value that the intrinsic rate of natural increase drops instead of increasing (i.e., the Allee effect). Another consequence of long-distance dispersal is that marine species ranges and biogeographic provinces are generally much larger than those on land, often crossing human jurisdictional boundaries.

Spatial structure is also different in the sea. Most organisms in a huge oceanic portion of the marine realm never come into contact with any hard surfaces at all. One conservation consequence is that oceanic species are difficult to maintain and breed ex situ because they are damaged by contact with surfaces such as aquarium walls. Even species that make forays into coastal realms, such as great white sharks, have posed insurmountable challenges to ex situ conservation efforts thus far. Compared with efforts in terrestrial and freshwater realms, ex situ conservation of marine species will be insignificant for the foreseeable future.

Another important spatial factor is that marine ecosystems are most productive and diverse at the edges of the sea, where human population densities, growth, and impact are greatest. This pattern heightens competition between people and seagrasses, amphipods, and shorebirds, which—lacking hands, large brains, metals, fossil fuels, legal rights, and the vote—always fare poorly.

Time scales in the marine realm are different too. For example, the dominant marine primary producers are tiny phytoplankters that can have doubling times of days, rather than large plants with doubling times of months or years. On land, organic materials are produced and decomposed in close proximity; as new leaves age and die, they fall to the ground, are decomposed, and their nutrients made available to roots. In the sea, organic materials are produced mainly in the well-lighted euphotic zone, but decompose in darker, deeper waters, and their nitrogen, phosphorous, and other nutrients do not return to the euphotic zone for centuries. As a consequence, human activities that affect oceanic biogeochemistry commit marine ecosystems to changes that will not become manifest for a long time, by which time it is far too late to remedy anything. Even more than on land, marine conservationists must measure each action by asking, "How will it affect the seventh generation?"

These physicochemical and biological differences between terrestrial and marine realms are compounded by the very different economic, sociological, anthropological, and legal regimes to which humans subject them. For example, the indiscriminate killing of terrestrial apex predators has fallen out of favor in recent decades; having a tiger head on the wall or wearing a snow leopard fur coat is no longer acceptable in many circles. But as more people have become affluent, the fins of sharks and the flesh of giant bluefin tunas and marlins (marine apex predators) are much sought after, even as their numbers have crashed and the price per kilogram has soared. Additionally, the lines humans have drawn on maps to divide the sea are not recognized by dispersing larvae, migrating adults, or current-borne pollutants, which makes interjurisdictional cooperation a precondition for marine conservation. And most of the ocean is not "owned" by anyone, which subjects marine systems to the "tragedy of the commons" (Hardin 1968; see Chapter 19) to a far greater degree than the land. Modern societies have no good models for sustainably managing species and ecosystems with these characteristics. As on land, however, such human considerations usually overshadow oceanographic and biological considerations in marine conservation.

In thinking about the distinctive challenge of conserving marine biodiversity, what surfaces repeatedly is that the greatest difference between terrestrial and marine conservation is that we know so much less about the sea (Murphy and Duffus 1996). Concern about biodiversity loss and marine conservation have only recently converged (Norse 1996), but marine conservation biology lags terrestrial conservation biology by two decades. It lacks recognized leaders, central paradigms, graduate training programs, and significant dedicated funding. Unless this changes, the challenge of protecting marine biological diversity will dwarf the tools available to meet it. We need to know which life history patterns make populations most vulnerable or resilient, how food webs respond to fishing pressure on several of their component species, which areas are most important for replenishing organisms in surrounding areas, and what kinds of legal regimes must be crafted to maintain marine biodiversity. By itself, knowing what is required to protect, sustainably use, and restore marine biodiversity is insufficient, but not knowing is a shameful excuse for continuing to destroy it.

This pernicious lack of information is remediable if marine conservation biology flowers as terrestrial conservation biology did after the first Conference on

Conservation Biology in 1978 and the landmark symposium volume by Soulé and Wilcox (1980). Guided by Michael Soulé, James Carlton, and others, the Marine Conservation Biology Institute organized the first Symposium on Marine Conservation Biology in 1997, and produced a resulting symposium volume. Whether this effort will succeed in generating tools commensurate to the very large task we face, only time will tell.

The preservation of evolutionarily distinct lineages above the level of species is important for a number of reasons. First, the evolutionary potential of life depends upon the distinctness of evolving lineages, not just the number of species. Lineages that have been evolving separately for long periods of time have many unique genes and gene combinations that would be lost if those lineages were to become extinct; closely related species, on the other hand, share nearly all of their alleles. Second, evolutionary lineages are storehouses of information about the history of life. Scientists can read and interpret this information with increasing accuracy using modern molecular methods. Third, the integrated functioning of ecosystems depends, in part, on the variety of species in them. For example, microorganisms have more diverse mechanisms for obtaining energy from the environment, and are able to decompose a wider variety of substances, than can multicellular organisms. Without microorganisms, ecosystems would be unable to provide, at high rates, such goods and services to humankind as absorbing and breaking down pollutants, storing and cycling nutrients, forming soils, and maintaining soil fertility. The numbers and kinds of fuels, construction materials, and medicines we obtain from nature depend upon the evolutionary distinctness of species. Finally, the aesthetic benefits we receive from nature are strongly correlated with the variety of living organisms with which we interact. No matter how many species of beetles there may be, they cannot substitute aesthetically for mammals, fishes, corals, or butterflies.

Ecosystem and Biome Diversity

Terrestrial ecosystems typically have been classified by the dominant plants that determine the structure of those communities. Alexander von Humboldt (1806) classified vegetation on the basis of the shapes of the dominant plants, such as spruce-tree shape or palm shape. In 1874, Augustin-Pyrame de Candolle proposed a classification of plant communities based on life-forms because he believed that life-forms were determined by climate. More complicated schemes of describing life-forms of plants and characterizing plant communities by the relative dominance of plants with different shapes have since been developed (Raunkaier 1934; Dansereau 1957; Halle et al. 1978). Köppen (1884) even used plant life-form distributions to define climates. Holdridge's (1967) widely used life zone system, on the other hand, is based entirely upon climatic variables. This diversity of classification schemes reflects the varied goals of biologists who classify large ecological units.

Although ecological communities clearly grade into one another, recognition of major divisions is useful for ecological discourse. Most textbooks divide the world into **biomes**, the largest ecological units, on the basis of the dominant vegetation. In tropical regions, biomes are divided along precipitation gradients (rainforest, evergreen seasonal forest, dry forest, thorn woodland, desert scrub, and desert) and elevational gradients (rainforest, montane rainforest, cloud forest, elfin woodland, páramo). At temperate latitudes, commonly recognized biomes along a moisture gradient are mesophytic forest, woodland, tallgrass prairie, shortgrass prairie, and desert (Figure 4.1). With increasing latitude, mesophytic forests become conifer-dominated bo-

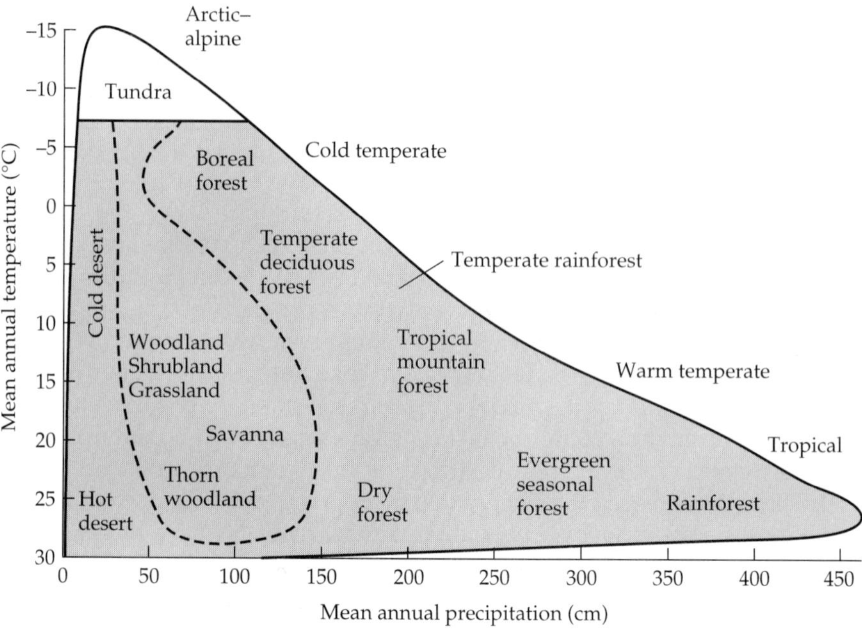

Figure 4.1 Biomes and climate. Distributions of the major biomes are plotted on axes of mean annual temperature and mean annual precipitation. Within the region bounded by the dashed line, factors such as seasonality of drought, fire, and grazing strongly affect which type of vegetation is present. (Modified from Whittaker 1970.)

real forests and eventually tundra. Finer divisions of biomes into ecosystem types use the same kinds of information, but also use data on drainage, soil type, slope, and species composition to identify units. Such classifications, although arbitrary, identify ecological units that are useful for comparative purposes.

Preservation of the variety of the earth's biomes is necessary for preservation of species. Without sufficient quantities of their natural habitats, species become extinct in the wild. Captive propagation can, and does, play a role in keeping species alive for short periods until they can be reintroduced into the wild. But captive propagation is of little ultimate use if there are no suitable sites into which to reintroduce the species. Managing species in zoos and botanical gardens is expensive, and an animal in a cage or a plant in a garden is not a fully functioning member of its species.

Ecosystems can provide the environmental goods and services upon which human life depends only if well-functioning systems are distributed over most of the surface of the earth. This requires a rich variety of ecosystems because the combinations of species that can perform as an integrated ecosystem change with environmental conditions. Deciduous trees cannot adequately replace conifers in boreal environments, nor can conifers function well in the regions dominated by deciduous forests. Finally, the richness of our aesthetic experience depends upon the richness of biomes as well as the richness of species.

Patterns of Species Richness

The earth is not uniform, and neither is the distribution of organisms across its surface. Some important general patterns in the geographic distribution of species richness have been discovered, but much remains unknown, in large part because the inventory of living organisms is so incomplete. Also, the distributions of species are best known for temperate regions, where most taxonomists and ecologists live and work. Tropical regions, where most of the world's species live, are poorly known biologically.

Species Richness over Geologic Time

The fossil record, although very incomplete, provides a rough measure of trends in species richness during the history of life on earth (Table 4.2). Cellular life in the form of bacteria evolved about 3.8 billion years ago (Bya); eukaryotic organisms probably evolved about 2 Bya. About 30 taxa have been described from these early biotas. Although many more species than that must have lived then, species richness was low during the first 2 billion years of the earth's existence. During the late Precambrian, the richer Ediacaran fauna, consisting of strange frond- and disc-shaped soft-bodied animals and some forms that appear to be arthropods and echinoderms, evolved. The first real explosion of biodiversity took place during the early Cambrian period. Some Cambrian species appear to be members of phyla that have not left surviving descendants. As measured by the number of animal phyla, life may have been more diverse during the Cambrian period than at any time since (Gould 1989).

The fossil record for marine invertebrates with hard skeletons is good enough to provide a general picture of the number of evolutionary lineages present at different times in the past. The Cambrian explosion was followed, about 60 million years later, by an extensive radiation of the Paleozoic fauna. After the Permian mass extinction, the modern fauna evolved, and overall species richness has increased steadily throughout the Mesozoic and Cenozoic eras to a maximum today (Figure 4.2). Approximately 40,000 species of marine invertebrates lived in the Paleozoic and Mesozoic eras, a number that

Table 4.2
The Geologic Time Scale

Era	Period	Epoch	Mya[a]
Cenozoic	Quaternary	Recent (Holocene)	0.01
		Pleistocene	2.0
	Tertiary	Pliocene	5.1
		Miocene	24.6
		Oligocene	38.0
		Eocene	54.9
		Paleocene	65.0
Mesozoic	Cretaceous		144
	Jurassic		213
	Triassic		248
Paleozoic	Permian		286
	Carboniferous		360
	Devonian		408
	Silurian		438
	Ordovician		505
	Cambrian		570
Pre-Cambrian	Vendian		670
	Sturtian		800

Modified from Futuyma 1986.
[a]Millions of years from the beginning of the period or epoch to the present.

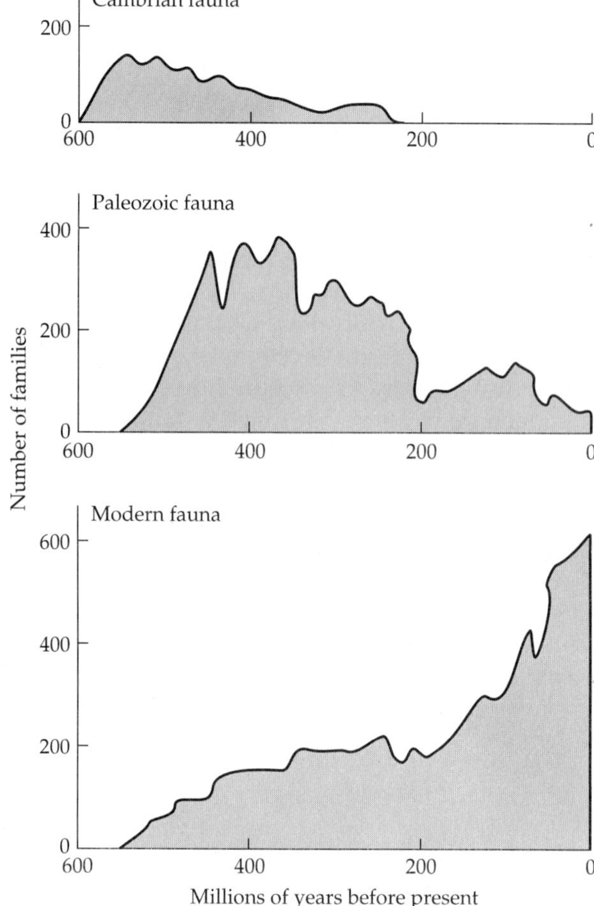

Figure 4.2 The number of families of animals in lineages that arose during the three major evolutionary "explosions," illustrating species richness in the major evolutionary faunas. Important elements of the Cambrian fauna include trilobites, brachiopods, monoplacophorans, and eocrinoids. Important components of the Paleozoic fauna are several lineages of echinoderms, anthozoans, graptolites, ostracods, and cephalopod mollusks. (Modified from Sepkoski 1984.)

increased to about 250,000 in the late Cenozoic era. The fossil record of terrestrial animals is much poorer, especially among such speciose groups as insects. The known fossil record of vertebrates, particularly mammals, is much better, and it indicates that richness, as measured by number of orders, is slightly higher today than earlier in the Cenozoic.

Terrestrial vascular plants appeared in the late Ordovician or early Silurian and increased rapidly during the Devonian, when seed-bearing plants first appeared. Species richness has continued to increase overall, but the number of species of ferns and gymnosperms has decreased, while the number of species of angiosperms has increased dramatically (Figure 4.3).

Local Species Richness

To describe the complex spatial patterns of biodiversity, ecologists and biogeographers have found it useful to divide species richness into four major components: point richness, alpha (α-) richness, beta (β-) richness, and gamma (γ-) richness. **Point richness** refers to the number of species that can be found at a single point in space; **α-richness** refers to the number of species found in a small, homogeneous area; **β-richness** refers to the rate of change in species composition across habitats; and **γ-richness** refers to the rate of change across larger landscape gradients. A high β-richness means that the cumulative number of species recorded increases rapidly as additional areas are censused along some environmental gradient. Species may also drop out rapidly along such gradients, resulting in a high rate of species turnover.

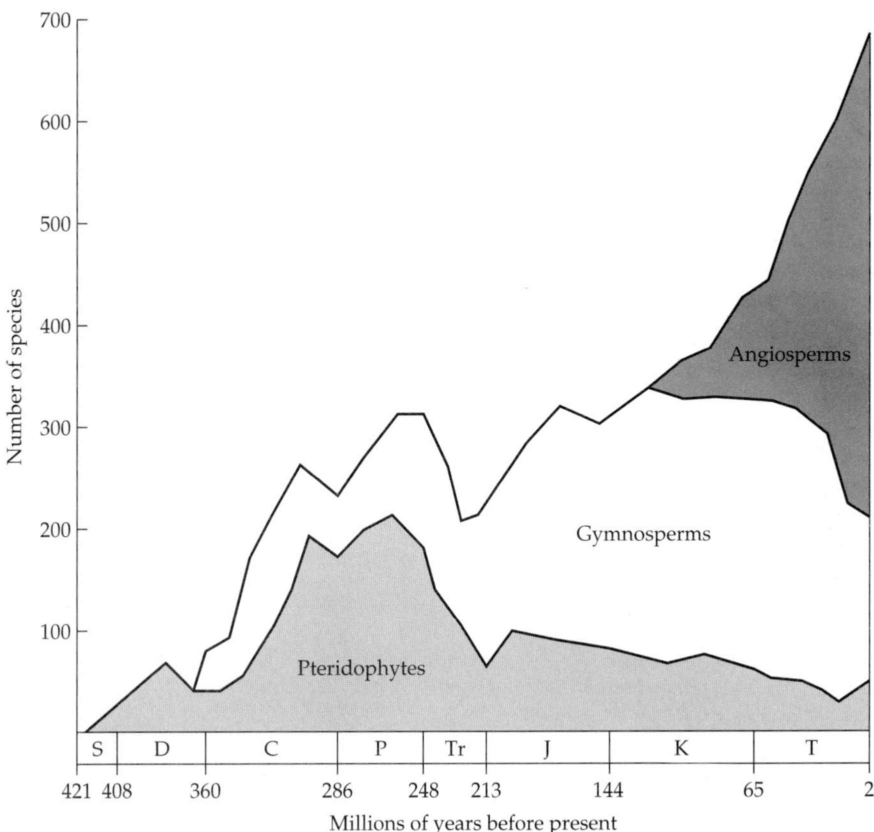

Figure 4.3 Terrestrial plant species richness. Ferns, gymnosperms, and angiosperms have, in turn, dominated the world's flora. (Modified from Signor 1990.)

Alpha-richness is characterized by several widespread patterns that are characteristic of most taxa of organisms. These patterns, which are statistically very different from random patterns, are strongly correlated with physical environmental variables. First, in both marine and terrestrial environments, there are many more species in most higher taxonomic categories in tropical regions than in higher-latitude communities. For example, Arctic waters contain about 100 species of tunicates, 400 species are known from temperate waters, and more than 600 species inhabit tropical seas. The richness of species, genera, and families of bivalve mollusks peaks in tropical regions and declines rapidly with increasing latitude (Figure 4.4). A similar pattern is found among the fauna living on hard substrates (Thorson 1957) and among benthic living and fossil foraminiferans (Buzas and Gibson 1969; Stehli et al. 1969).

On land, the number of ant species found in local regions increases from about 10 at 60° north latitude to as many as 2000 in equatorial regions. Species richness and latitude are also negatively correlated among birds, trees, and mammals (Figure 4.5). However, there are exceptions to these latitudinal patterns; in some orders and families the number of species is greatest at mid- or high latitudes. Examples include marine algae, which reach a maximum richness between latitudes of 20° and 40° (Gaines and Lubchenco 1982), coniferous trees, bees, salamanders, penguins, and waterfowl.

Second, the richness of species in most taxa is positively correlated with habitat structural complexity. Structurally simple habitats, such as the open ocean, grasslands, and cold deserts, generally support fewer species than structurally more complex communities, such as forests and coral reefs. In most terrestrial environments, plants provide the major components of the

Figure 4.4 Latitudinal species richness in bivalve mollusks. Points are average numbers of species (S), genera (G), and families (F). (From Stehli et al. 1969.)

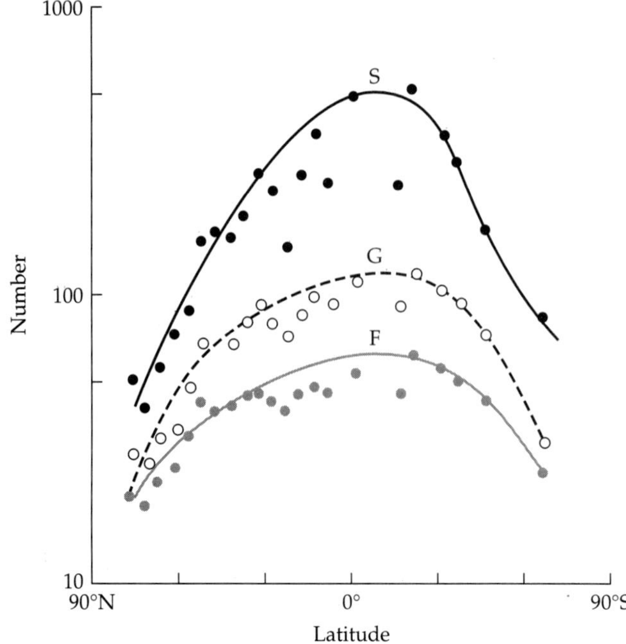

physical structure within which the activities of all other organisms are carried out. Coral reefs create complex structures in tropical marine environments. Structurally complex communities have a greater variety of microclimates, a greater variety of resources, a larger number of ways in which to exploit those resources, and more places in which to find shelter from predators and the physical environment.

Third, in many ecosystems, species richness increases with increasing primary production at low productivity levels, reaches a plateau at moderate levels of production, and then declines at high levels of production (Huston 1994). This phenomenon has been called "the paradox of enrichment" (Rosenzweig 1971) because addition of fertilizer to aquatic and terrestrial plant communities often results in sharp decreases in species richness. Examples of extremely productive ecosystems that are relatively species-poor include salt marshes, seagrass beds, and hot springs. Why the relationship between primary production and species richness is so complex will be discussed later in this chapter.

Primary production is determined largely by temperature, moisture, and soil fertility. The highest terrestrial production is found in regions with high rainfall and year-round warm temperatures. Production drops with elevation

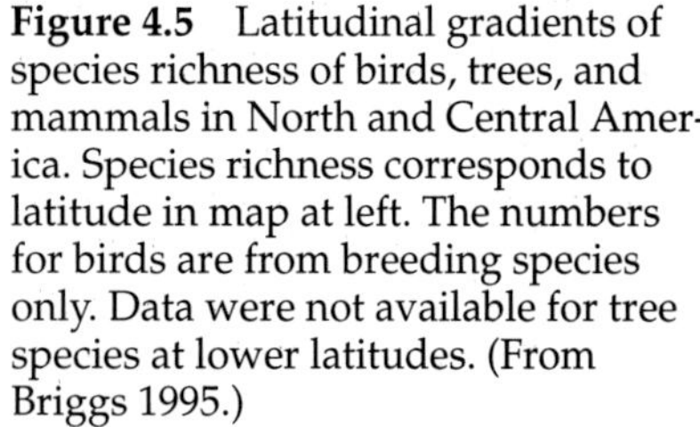

Figure 4.5 Latitudinal gradients of species richness of birds, trees, and mammals in North and Central America. Species richness corresponds to latitude in map at left. The numbers for birds are from breeding species only. Data were not available for tree species at lower latitudes. (From Briggs 1995.)

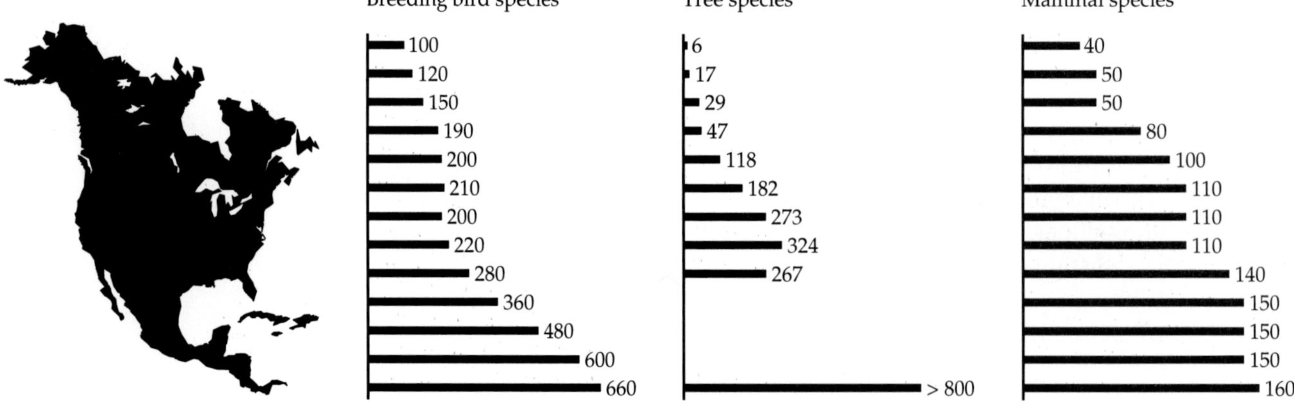

because of lowered temperatures. In many areas of the world, the amount of precipitation determines total production. In arid and semiarid regions, annual production can be predicted fairly accurately from the amount and distribution of precipitation. Marine production in surface waters is limited primarily by nutrient concentrations. Production is highest in coastal regions where nutrient-rich waters upwell, and lowest in the open ocean (Koblentz-Mishke et al. 1970; Bunt 1975). Marine primary production also decreases with depth because light levels attenuate rapidly even in clear water.

Fourth, there is a consistent unimodal relationship between species richness and depth, from the continental shelf to the abyssal plain, for many marine taxa. The maximum richness of most groups is found at depths between 2000 and 4000 meters (Rex 1973, 1983). In contrast, coral species richness peaks at depths between 15 and 30 meters because corals, which obtain much of their energy from photosynthetic algae embedded in their tissues, are confined to the photic zone (Huston 1994).

Fifth, island communities are poorer in species than comparable mainland communities. In general, the number of species found on islands is positively correlated with island size and topographic diversity and negatively correlated with distance from the nearest mainland source of immigrants. Low species richness on islands is attributed to low colonization rates, high extinction rates (because populations are usually small and subject to decimation by local catastrophes and stochastic variation), and the lack of certain resources typically provided by species that are poor dispersers across ocean barriers (MacArthur and Wilson 1967). Also, island communities have experienced extremely high extinction rates during recent centuries, primarily due to anthropogenic introductions of mammalian predators (mammals other than bats disperse poorly across ocean barriers) and mainland diseases.

Regional Turnover of Species Richness

One of the first ecological relationships to be established empirically was the relationship between area and number of species (Arrhenius 1921). This relationship is commonly expressed using a power function of the form

$$S = cA^z$$

where S = the number of species, A = area, and c and z are constants fitted to the data. On a logarithmic scale, this relationship plots as a straight line where c is the y-intercept and z is the slope of the line (Figure 4.6). Analysis of species–area relationships in many groups of organisms reveals that most values of z are between 0.20 and 0.35. For a while, some ecologists argued that the

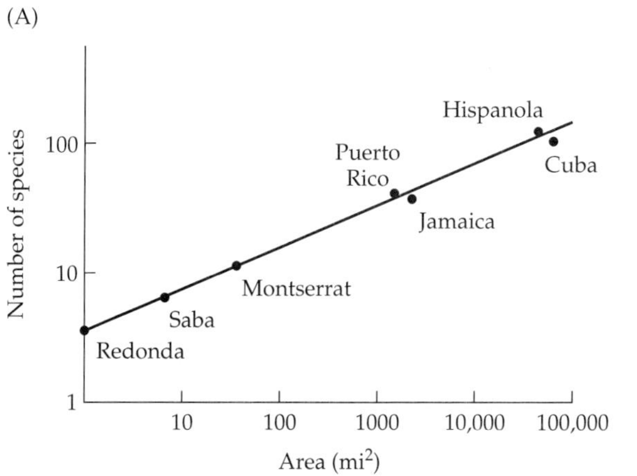

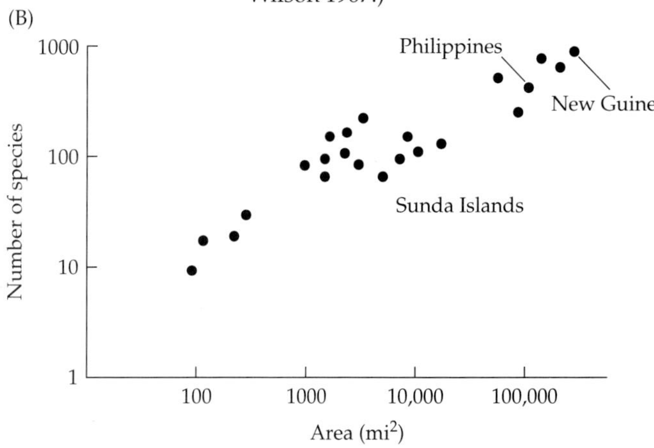

Figure 4.6 Relationship between area and number of species on islands of various sizes. (A) The number of species of amphibians and reptiles found on selected islands in the West Indies. (B) The number of land and freshwater bird species on the Sunda Islands, the Philippines, and New Guinea. These islands are close to the Asian continent, and many were connected to the mainland during glacial periods. Therefore, many of the larger islands are relatively species-rich. (Modified from MacArthur and Wilson 1967.)

narrow range of z values was a simple statistical consequence of the lognormal distribution of species abundances (May 1975), but it became evident that a much wider range of z values is possible even if species abundances are lognormally distributed. The regular relationship between the size of an area and the number of species it supports, which is most readily observed using island data, was a key empirical generalization in the development of the theory of island biogeography (MacArthur and Wilson 1967). This relationship will appear repeatedly throughout this book.

The rate at which the species composition of communities changes across environmental gradients is determined by the sizes of species ranges and the extent to which species are habitat specialists. The ranges of tropical species are more poorly known than the ranges of their temperate counterparts, but on average, terrestrial tropical species appear to have smaller ranges than species of higher latitudes. The altitudinal ranges of species on the slopes of tropical mountains appear to be narrower than ranges on temperate mountains, but this impression may be a statistical artifact of inadequate sampling of rich tropical biotas (Colwell and Hurtt 1994). There is some evidence that tropical species may, on average, be more specialized in their diets than their temperate counterparts, but much more research is needed to establish the degree to which this is true and the dimensions along which the specialization has evolved (Beaver 1979; Marquis and Braker 1994).

For many taxa, local and regional species richness are positively correlated. For example, the number of gall wasp species found locally on any particular species of oak in California is positively correlated with the total number of gall wasp species known to feed on that oak species throughout its entire range (Figure 4.7). Similarly, the more species of birds found on an island, the greater the number of species found in a single habitat on that island (Ricklefs 1987).

Species turnover rates have been extensively studied among birds of Mediterranean-type ecosystems (Cody 1975). Chile, which is isolated from the rest of South America by extremely arid deserts to the north and very high mountains to the east, has both a low number of bird species and a low β-richness; that is, most of the species have ranges that encompass a broad variety of habitat types. Mediterranean-type ecosystems in South Africa and California, by contrast, are not well isolated from the rest of their respective continents, but South Africa is surrounded by much larger semiarid areas than is California. Consequently, both species-accumulation and species-turnover curves are higher in the more arid portions of the Mediterranean habitat gradient from very dry scrub to woodland in Africa than in California or Chile (Figure 4.8).

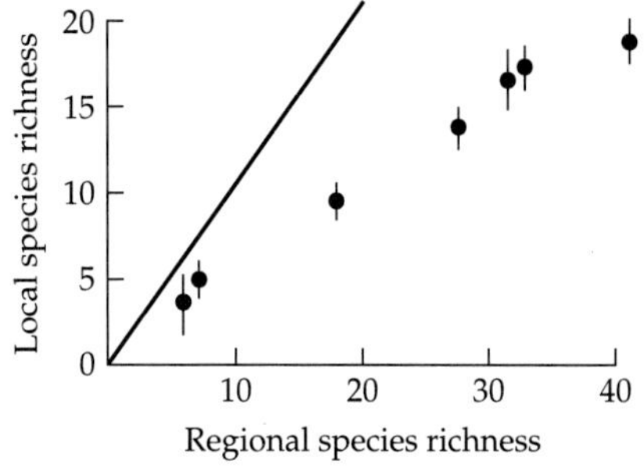

Figure 4.7 Interactions between local and regional species richness. The number of species of cynipid gall wasps found locally on an oak species is strongly correlated with the number of cynipids recorded from throughout the range of that oak species. The solid line connects points at which local and regional richness are equal. (Modified from Ricklefs 1987; data from Cornell 1985.)

A species that is found in a particular region and nowhere else is said to be **endemic** to that region. However, what constitutes a region is ill-defined. All species are, as far as we know, endemic to the earth. At the opposite extreme, some species are restricted to single desert springs (see Figure 5.2), small islands, or isolated mountaintops. Regions with many endemic species are often the result of one or more major events that caused the ranges of many taxa to be fragmented at approximately the same place. Causes of such geographic isolation, commonly called **vicariance**, include continental drift, mountain building, and sea level changes. Following such isolation, many taxa may undergo evolutionary radiations in the same general locality. Vicariance due to continental drift has been extremely important in generating the high degree of endemism found in the biotas of Madagascar, Australia, New Guinea, and New Caledonia. Owing to their isolation, islands often have high proportions of endemic species, but because islands often have relatively impoverished biotas, high endemism often is not associated with high species richness.

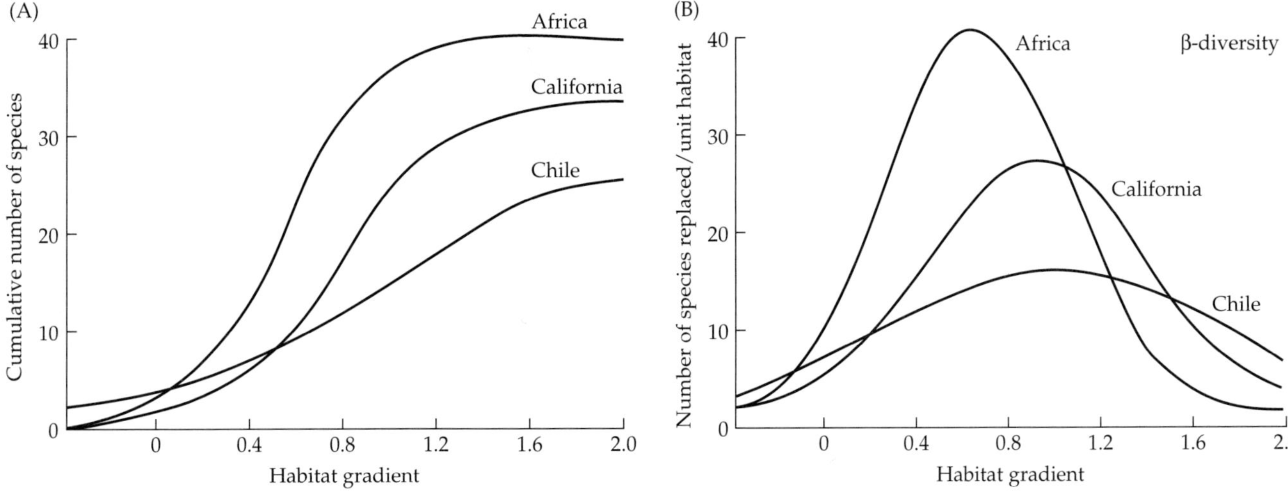

Figure 4.8 Species turnovers along habitat gradients. (A) Species accumulation curves for birds across habitat gradients in Mediterranean vegetation (from dry scrub to woodland) in southern Africa, California, and Chile. (B) The differentials of the curves in (A) give the rate of species turnover across the gradient. (Modified from Cody 1975.)

Biogeographers recognize 18 areas of unusually high endemism worldwide, commonly referred to as **hot spots**. These areas contain about 49,950 endemic plant species, 20% of the world's total, in 746,700 km^2, only 0.5% of the world's land area. They are also rich in endemics in other taxa (Table 4.3). The most important marine hot spot is the island-studded western Pacific Ocean (Figure 4.9), a region of maximum species richness for many taxa (Briggs 1995). The topic of hot spots is explored in greater depth in Chapter 5.

Patterns of endemism differ greatly among taxa (see Table 4.3). Thus, both the Cape region of South Africa and southwestern Australia have extremely high numbers of endemic plant species, but very few endemic mammals or birds (Cowling et al. 1992). These differences arise because plants can speciate

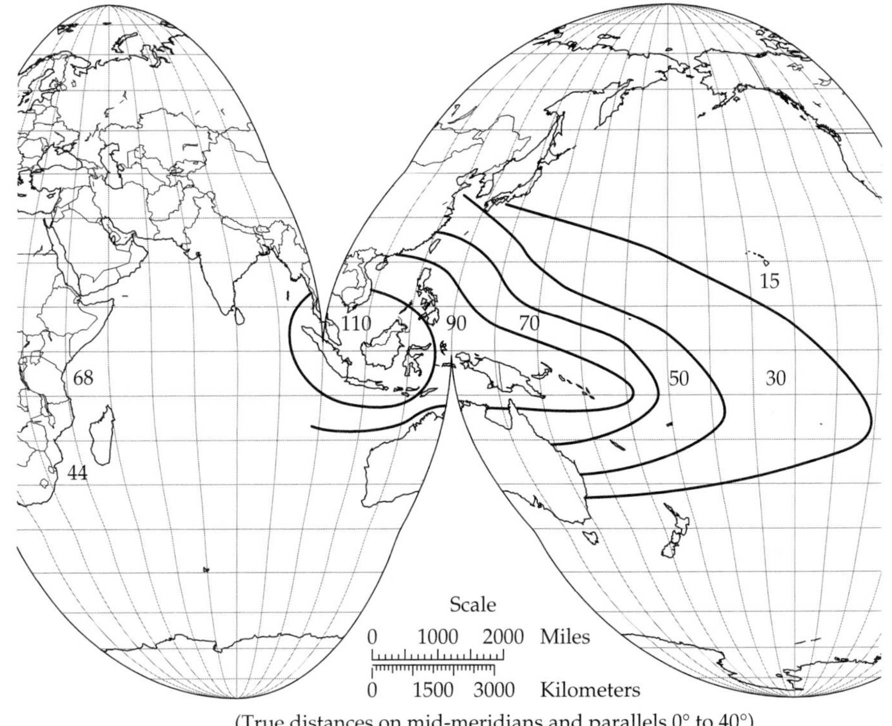

Figure 4.9 The Indo-West Pacific is a marine diversity hot spot. The distribution of species richness for damselfish (Pomacentridae) shown here is typical of many marine taxa in the region. (From Briggs 1995.)

Table 4.3
Numbers of Endemic Species in Some "Hot Spot" Areas

Region	Area (km^2)	Vascular plants	Mammals	Reptiles	Amphibians
Cape region (South Africa)	134,000	6000	16	43	23
Upland western Amazonia	100,000	5000	—	—	ca. 70
Atlantic coastal Brazil	1,000,000	5000	40	92	168
Madagascar	62,000	4900	86	234	142
Philippines	250,000	3700	98	120	41
Northern Borneo	190,000	3500	42	69	47
Eastern Himalayas	340,000	3500	—	20	25
Southwestern Australia	113,000	2830	10	25	22
Western Ecuador	27,000	2500	9	—	—
Colombian Chocó	100,000	2500	8	137	111
Peninsular Malaysia	120,000	2400	4	25	7
California Floristic Province	324,000	2140	15	25	7
Western Ghats (India)	50,000	1600	7	91	84
Central Chile	140,000	1450	—	—	—
New Caledonia	15,000	1400	2	21	0

Data from Myers 1988, 1990; World Conservation and Monitoring Centre 1992.
Note: Original area of rainforest only is given for the tropical regions.

in much smaller areas than vertebrates. Polyploidy, which is a common speciation mechanism among plants but is rare among animals, requires no spatial isolation. However, there are strong correlations of patterns of endemism among mammals, birds, and reptiles, all of which require relatively large areas for allopatric speciation.

An inevitable and important corollary of patterns of species richness is that areas with high α-richness inevitably have many rare species. A tropical wet forest in South America or Southeast Asia, for example, may harbor between 300 and 400 tree species per square kilometer, whereas a temperate forest harbors an order of magnitude fewer. However, the number of individual trees per square kilometer is roughly the same in tropical and temperate forests. It follows that most of the tree species in the tropical forest must be present at very low densities. Many of those species are probably more abundant elsewhere, but some species evidently are present only at low densities throughout their ranges.

What Are the Limits to Species Richness?

The fact that species richness has continued to increase throughout evolutionary time, despite setbacks by mass extinction events, suggests that whatever limits to species richness may exist have not yet been reached on a global scale. Nevertheless, because all regional biotas contain many more species than are found in any single locality or habitat type, there are evidently limits to local species richness in ecological time, whatever may happen over millennia. Therefore, both evolutionary and ecological processes must be considered in analyses of the causes of and limits to species richness.

Evolutionary Limits to Species Richness

Large numbers of new evolutionary lineages have originated three times during the history of life. The first event, known as the Cambrian explosion, took place about half a billion years ago. The second, about 60 million years later, resulted in the Paleozoic fauna. Biodiversity was greatly reduced 300 million years later by the great Permian mass extinction, which was followed by the Triassic explosion that led to our modern biota. Although all three of these explosions resulted in many new species, they were qualitatively very different. Virtually all major groups of living organisms appeared in the Cambrian period, along with some phyla that subsequently became extinct. The Paleozoic and Triassic explosions greatly increased the number of families, genera, and species, but no new phyla of organisms evolved.

The most commonly accepted theory for the differences among these explosions is that, unlike the other two, the Cambrian explosion took place in a world that contained few species of organisms, all of them small. Therefore, the ecological setting was favorable for the evolution of many different life-forms and body plans. Many types of organisms were able to survive initially in this world, but as competition intensified and new types of predators evolved, some forms became extinct. The earth was also relatively poor in species at the times of both of the later explosions, but the existing species included a wide array of body plans and life-forms. They may have preempted the opportunities for the evolution of strikingly new life forms.

Two factors appear to be primarily responsible for the continued rise in species richness over evolutionary time. One is the increasing provinciality that accompanied the breakup of Pangaea and, later, Gondwanaland. At the time of breakup, many species probably had distributions covering much of these huge continental landmasses. Following their separation, evolution on each of the new continents produced many new species that were continental endemics. Much of the Cenozoic era increase in species numbers appears to be due to provincialization. Thus, South America, Africa, and Southeast Asia are all rich in species, but they share few species or genera in common because they have been separated from one another for so many millions of years.

The second major factor contributing to increasing species richness is the increasing number of species within ecological communities. For example, late Cenozoic era marine communities appear to have contained about twice as many species as did earlier communities, primarily because organisms in the later communities were more diverse in their ways of living. In the earlier communities, most organisms lived on or near the surface of bottom sediments. Later, there were many more burrowing forms, species able to move about actively on the surface, and species able to swim in the water column. The number of species living together also increased as a result of finer adaptations to particular environmental conditions and ways of exploiting the environment made possible by minor variations in morphology, physiology, and behavior. A perusal of any museum tray of insect specimens can provide a quick overview of some of the subtle variations in morphology that have contributed so importantly to the richness of insect species.

On land, the richness of vascular plants increased dramatically with the evolution of angiosperms and their complicated interactions with animals during reproduction and dispersal of seeds. The evolution of flight probably also contributed to the great diversity of both insects and birds by allowing better exploitation of the third dimension on land.

More than 99% of the species that have ever lived on earth are extinct. There have been extinctions at all times throughout the history of life, but rates have changed dramatically. Paleontologists distinguish between "normal" or "background" extinction rates and the much higher rates associated with mass extinctions (Sepkoski and Raup 1986). The first of six mass extinctions, at the end of the Cambrian period, destroyed about half of the known animal species. At the end of the Devonian period, 345 million years ago (Mya), about 80% of species became extinct. The catastrophe at the close of the Permian period eliminated about 95% of both marine and terrestrial species. In the oceans, trilobites declined to extinction, and brachiopods almost became extinct. On land, the trees that formed the great coal forests became extinct, as did most lineages of amphibians. At the end of the Triassic period, about 180 Mya, nearly all ammonites and approximately 80% of reptile species vanished, resulting in an overall loss of about 75% of species. At the end of the Cretaceous period, about 65 Mya, about 75% of species became extinct, including dinosaurs, other large reptiles, and most marine lineages. The current mass extinction, promulgated by human expansion over the planet, initially exterminated large mammals and island species, but if current trends continue, organisms of all sizes and lineages will be seriously affected.

Following each of the first five mass extinctions, biodiversity rapidly expanded, and species richness reached its previous value within 1 to 8 million years. Thus, during 90% of geologic history, species richness has not been directly affected by the events that caused mass extinctions. The major effect of these perturbations has been to eliminate some lineages, thereby creating ecological space for other lineages that proliferated following the episodes of mass extinction.

Ecological Limits to Species Richness

A number of ecologically based hypotheses have been proposed to explain patterns of species richness (Pianka 1966). Some, but not all of them, are mutually exclusive, and there is no reason to believe that any one hypothesis can explain all patterns of richness. As mentioned previously, most geographic patterns of species richness are correlated with patterns in the physical environment, which set the stage upon which all biological interactions take place.

Productivity-Stability Hypothesis. The amount of energy available to be divided among individuals and species is positively correlated with primary production. Therefore, the number of viable species should be positively correlated with annual production. Also, a higher proportion of the energy budgets of organisms can be devoted to reproduction if high production is combined with moist tropical conditions so that organisms expend relatively little energy maintaining their temperatures and water balances at appropriate levels (Connell and Orias 1964). The productivity-stability hypothesis is supported by broad correlations between production and species richness along latitudinal and altitudinal gradients. A strong correlation exists between realized annual evapotranspiration, a measure of energy available to plants, and tree species richness in North America (Currie and Paquin 1987). Similarly, there is a strong correlation between plant species richness in Neotropical forests and total annual precipitation, a variable strongly positively correlated with production (Gentry 1988; Clinebell et al. 1995).

However, the relationship between productivity and species richness is more complex than implied by the productivity-stability hypothesis. Many of the world's most productive systems, such as estuaries, sea-grass beds, and

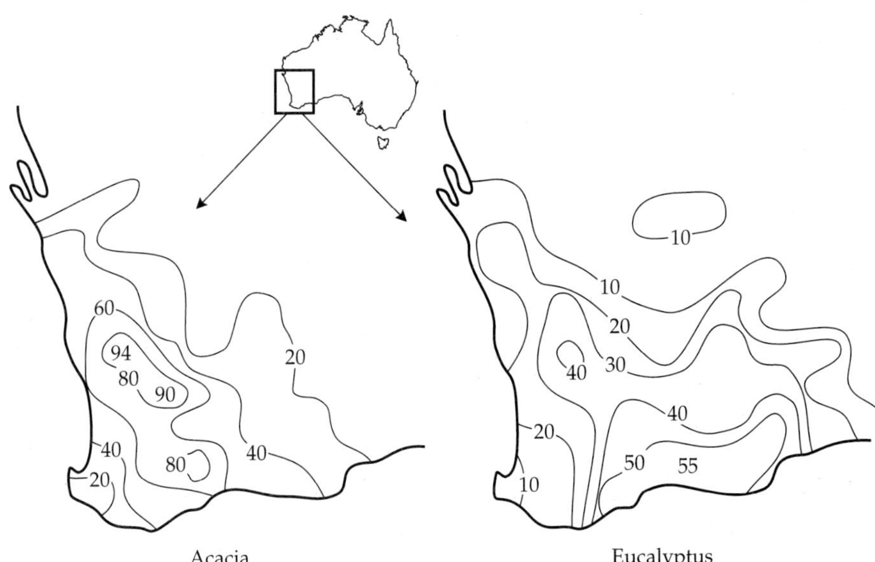

Figure 4.10 Numbers of species of *Eucalyptus* and *Acacia* in southwestern Australia. Notice how many species in these two genera can be found living in close proximity. Similar patterns are found among many other genera of plants in southwestern Australia. (Modified from Lamont et al. 1984.)

hot springs, are species-poor, and, conversely, plant species richness is higher in semiarid regions with nutrient-deficient soils than in similar areas with richer soils. The remarkably rich plant communities of the Cape region of South Africa (fynbos) and the extreme southwestern corner of Australia (Figure 4.10) are found on highly infertile soils (Kruger and Taylor 1979; Bond 1983; Rice and Westoby 1983; Cody 1986; Willis et al. 1996). Nitrogen levels in these soils (Bettenay 1984) are an order of magnitude lower than those in California and Chile (Specht and Moll 1983), which have fewer species.

Some evidence suggests that soil infertility itself is a major contributor to the inverse correlation between soil fertility and plant species richness because it favors the ability to exploit slightly different microhabitats more efficiently (Tilman 1982, 1985; Cowling et al. 1992). Most endemic plants of the Cape region of South Africa are confined to a single soil type (Cowling 1992; Willis et al. 1996). Fynbos vegetation is remarkably variable in leaf morphology (Cody 1986) and growth phenology (Kruger 1981; Cowling 1992); these differences are probably correlated with a corresponding diversity of carbon-fixing strategies. In addition, the low palatability of leaves of plants growing on nutrient-poor soils results in a rapid accumulation of flammable biomass, leading to high frequencies of fires in these summer-dry climates. Frequent fires favor either serotinous (fire-released) seed capsules or rapid burial of seeds. Ants move seeds relatively short distances compared with birds, but they usually bury them. Also, ants pick up and move seeds that offer much smaller rewards than those required to attract birds. Australia, a continent with notoriously poor soils, has the highest proportion of plants with ant-dispersed seeds of any continent (Berg 1975; Westoby et al. 1991) and it has unusually high ant species richness (Anderson 1983; Greenslade and Greenslade 1984). Ant-dispersed seeds are also common in South African fynbos (Milewski and Bond 1982). In combination, these factors could result in very high α-species richness and unusually high β-species richness. Species richness on scales of one hectare is higher in southwestern Australia than it is in the rainforest of Borneo, even though the latter accumulates more species at slightly larger scales (Figure 4.11).

Some highly productive but species-poor systems are distributed as relatively small, fragmented patches whose physical environments differ strikingly from those of the surrounding, more extensive ecosystems. Special ad-

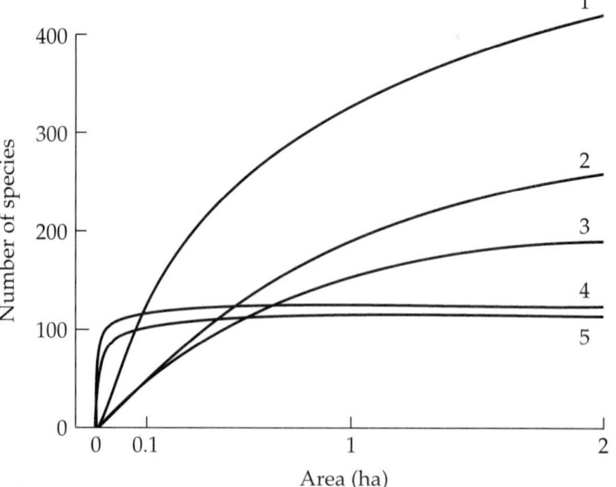

Figure 4.11 Plant species richness in Borneo and in southwestern Australia. Curves 1, 2, and 3 represent trees greater than 10 cm in diameter in mixed forests in Borneo. Curves 4 and 5 are for plots in southwestern Australia. (Modified from Lamont et al. 1984.)

aptations are less likely to evolve in relation to rare than to common habitat types. Evolutionary biologists believe that the combination of major physical environmental differences and isolation of the patches results in fewer species evolving adaptations to these unusual environments. For the same reasons, species adapted to the surrounding environments are unlikely to "spill over" into these rare habitat types. This evolutionary phenomenon is illustrated by the richness of aquatic species as a function of salinity. Both fresh water and seawater are widely distributed, but waters of intermediate salinity and waters that are more saline than the oceans are rare. The species richness of aquatic invertebrates throughout the world parallels this pattern (Figure 4.12).

Structural Hypothesis. Because plants provide the physical structure within which most other organisms live, it is not surprising that species richness in some taxa is correlated with plant community structure. Animal groups that exploit the environment in three dimensions are most sensitive to plant community structure. A positive correlation between foliage height diversity and bird species richness exists in many plant communities on all continents (MacArthur and MacArthur 1961; MacArthur 1964), but the precise details of the relationship differ among continents, between temperate and tropical regions, and between mainlands and islands. Similarly, the species richness of web-building spiders is positively correlated with heterogeneity in the heights of the tips of vegetation to which such spiders attach their webs (Greenstone 1984).

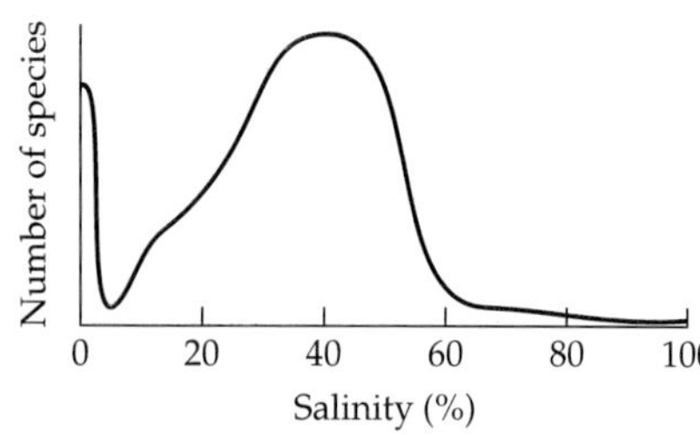

Figure 4.12 Estimated species richness of aquatic invertebrates living in waters of different salinity throughout the world. The two peaks correspond to fresh water (<2%) and seawater (30%–40%). (Modified from Kinne 1971.)

In contrast, there is no consistent relationship between vegetation structure and lizard species richness in hot deserts in North America, Africa, and Australia (Pianka 1986). Pianka compared sites on the three continents with similar vegetation structure. Low, small-leaved shrubs dominated all sites, and the genus *Atriplex* was an important element at all sites. Despite these similarities, the number of lizard species in African deserts averaged twice that in North America, and Australian deserts were about twice as rich as African ones (Table 4.4). The main differences were due to non-lizardlike lizards and nocturnal species. Only one nocturnal lizard was found at the North American sites, whereas there were four nocturnal species at the African and eight at the Australian desert sites. Mammal-like species (the monitors) and wormlike species added to the richness of Australian desert lizard faunas. These differences relate primarily to the long-term evolutionary

Table 4.4
Numbers of Species of Lizards in Three Hot Deserts

	North America		Africa		Australia	
Mode of life	**Mean**	**%**	**Mean**	**%**	**Mean**	**%**
Diurnal	6.3	86	8.2	56	17.0	60
Ground-dwelling	5.4	74	6.3	43	15.4	54
Sit-and-wait	4.4	60	2.4	16	5.3	18
Widely foraging	1.0	14	4.0	27	10.1	36
Arboreal	0.9	12	1.9	13	2.7	9
Nocturnal	1.0	14	5.1	35	10.2	36
Ground-dwelling	1.0	14	3.5	24	7.6	27
Arboreal	0	0	1.6	11	2.7	9
Subterranean	0	0	1.4	10	1.2	4
All ground-dwelling	6.4	88	9.8	67	23.0	78
All arboreal	0.9	12	3.5	24	5.4	18
All lizard species	7.4	100	14.7	100	29.8	100

Data from Pianka 1986.
Note: Semiarboreal species are assigned half to arboreal and half to ground-dwelling categories.

history of deserts on the three continents, not to any differences in today's vegetation (Pianka 1986).

Competition/Predation Hypothesis. Alpha-richness could be reduced by competitive exclusion of some species from ecosystems, but competition could also increase α-richness by favoring finer habitat segregation among species (Rosenzweig 1995). Predation can increase species richness if predators prey preferentially upon competitive dominants, thereby preventing competitive exclusion. A well-known example is the increase in species richness in rocky intertidal communities of the Pacific Coast of North America resulting from selective predation by the sea star *Pisaster ochraceus* on the competitively dominant mussel *Mytilus californianus* (Paine 1974). On the other hand, predation can reduce species richness by preventing vulnerable species from living in an area. Experimental evidence exists for all of these outcomes, but how often and where these forces exert their influence is unknown (Orians and Kunin 1991). Analyses of the literature have reached different conclusions, in part because researchers have used different criteria for including studies in their samples (Connell 1975, 1983; Schoener 1983).

Some researchers have hypothesized that many organisms are held at sufficiently low population densities that competition rarely occurs (Connell 1975). Others have suggested that competition occurs primarily during unusually hard times when resources are scarce, called "competitive crunches" (Wiens 1977). Which of these two scenarios applies depends upon whether low population densities are caused by harsh physical conditions or by scarcity of consumable resources.

Indirect evidence of the role of competition in structuring ecological communities is provided by the fact that when many species coexist within a region, each lives in a smaller number of habitats than in areas where there are fewer species (MacArthur et al. 1966). These relationships are most readily seen in island communities, where those species present often attain higher population densities than they or closely related species attain on the mainland, and often expand into habitats they do not occupy on the mainland (Table 4.5). These processes of density compensation and habitat expansion (or compression) are collectively referred to as **ecological release**.

Predation can serve as a source of disturbance, especially when it acts upon sessile or space-limited prey species that would otherwise dominate available space. Intermediate levels of such disturbance (see Figure 10.3) should result in greater diversity than do either very high or very low levels (Connell 1978; Abugov 1982). Predation should augment species richness where other sources of disturbance are few, but it should reduce species richness where exogenous disturbance is high. Among marine environments, exposed rocky intertidal zones subjected to periodic desiccation, rain-induced osmotic stress, wave shear, and surf-propelled flotsam face higher background disturbance regimes than protected intertidal habitats, benthic mud habitats, or rocky subtidal habitats. Nonetheless, predators have been demonstrated to increase species richness in most studies in the rocky intertidal, in about half of the studies in the rocky subtidal, but only rarely in studies of benthic mud communities.

Stability-Time Hypothesis. The stability-time hypothesis was originally advanced by Sanders (1968), who observed that productive estuaries and continental shelves in most latitudes had fewer species of benthic animals than the cold, dark, unproductive floor of the deep sea. Sanders suggested that the deep sea supported many species because its environments had been highly predictable and stable for millennia. Subsequent research has shown that species richness is actually higher at intermediate depths than in surface waters or in the deep sea. Indeed, the relatively constant levels of temperature, salinity, and oxygen concentration and a low rate of disturbance are now postulated to account for the lower species richness in the deep sea than on the continental shelves (Huston 1994). Food resources are patchily distributed in the deep sea, and the main disturbances are local ones caused by the feeding, burrowing, and mound-building activities of animals (Grassle 1989, 1991). These disturbances probably maintain more species in deep-sea ecosystems than would be present without them.

Ecologists were attracted to the stability-time hypothesis because they were aware that the temperate zones had been subjected to massive distur-

Table 4.5
Relative Abundance and Habitat Distribution of Land Birds on Caribbean Islands and Panama[a]

Locality	Number of species (regional richness)	Average number of species per habitat (local richness)	Habitats per species	Relative abundance per species per habitat	Relative abundance per species per habitat, times number of habitats	Relative abundance of all species together across all habitats
Panama	135	30.2	2.01	2.95	5.93	800
Trinidad	108	28.2	2.35	3.31	7.78	840
Jamaica	56	21.4	3.43	4.97	17.05	955
St. Lucia	33	15.2	4.15	5.77	23.95	790
St. Kitts	20	11.9	5.35	5.88	31.45	629

Data from Cox and Ricklefs 1977.
[a]The table indicates that each habitat in Panama contains more species, but the species are, on average, restricted to fewer habitats than are the island species.

bances during the Pleistocene, but believed that the tropics had been stable for extremely long periods. Therefore, they believed that the tropics might have more species because of the long time over which species could have accumulated, combined with low extinction rates in those stable environments. By comparison, they believed that high-latitude environments, which had undergone a major reshuffling during glacial advances, were still accumulating species following the retreat of the glaciers.

The basic argument was fully stated in 1878 by Alfred Russel Wallace:

> The equatorial zone, in short, exhibits to us the result of a comparatively continuous and unchecked development of organic forms; while in the temperate regions there have been a series of periodical checks and extinctions of a more or less disastrous nature, necessitating the commencement of the work of development in certain lines over and over again. In the one, evolution has a fair chance; in the other, it has had countless difficulties thrown in its way. The equatorial regions are then, as regards their past and present life history, a more ancient world than that represented by the temperate zones, a world in which the laws which have governed the progressive development of life have operated with comparatively little check for countless ages, and have resulted in those wonderful eccentricities of structure, of function, and of instinct—that rich variety of colour, and that nicely balanced harmony of relations which delight and astonish us in the animal productions of all tropical countries.

However, recent evidence shows that tropical regions have not been stable. Well-marked wet and dry seasons are almost universal in the tropics, and precipitation patterns and temperatures changed dramatically with glacial advances at high latitudes. For example, pollen records from Africa reveal that regions that today are wet tropical forests were covered with dry woodland or grassland at the time of the last glaciation (Livingstone 1975; Livingstone and van der Hammen 1978). In South America, equatorial temperatures and rainfall were lower during glacial periods, which favored deciduous forests and savannas over rainforests (Prance 1982; Bush and Colinvaux 1990). Indeed, some authors attribute the extremely high species richness in many groups of forest organisms in South America to rapid speciation in isolated forest fragments during dry glacial periods (Haffer 1969; Simpson and Haffer 1978; Prance 1982). Although these climatic changes repeatedly resulted in habitat shifts in South America, recent phylogenetic analyses indicate that many lineage splits are even more ancient and must have resulted from earlier vicariant events (Bush 1994). Periodic expansions and contractions of forests are believed to account for the diversity of some groups of Australian organisms, such as *Eucalyptus* (Pryor and Johnson 1971) and birds (Keast 1961).

Productivity-Disturbance Hypothesis. The productivity-disturbance hypothesis, which has been developed extensively by Huston (1994), combines elements of several of the previous hypotheses. It assumes that competition eventually results in exclusion of species and that the rate of competitive exclusion is positively correlated with the rate of population growth, which, in turn, is positively correlated with primary productivity. Competitive exclusion is, however, prevented by disturbances that either eliminate competition entirely or reduce it. If the disturbance rate is very low, species richness is low because of competitive exclusion. If the disturbance rate is very high, species richness is also low because populations of many species are unable to recover before the next perturbation arrives. Maximum species richness is predicted to occur when a balance exists between rates of population growth and rates of disturbance. Balances resulting in high species richness are predicted to occur when productivity and disturbance rates are both low, and when they are both high (Figure 4.13). The productivity-disturbance hypothesis is consistent with many species richness patterns in nature, including the peaks in species richness of marine benthic communities and coral reefs at intermediate

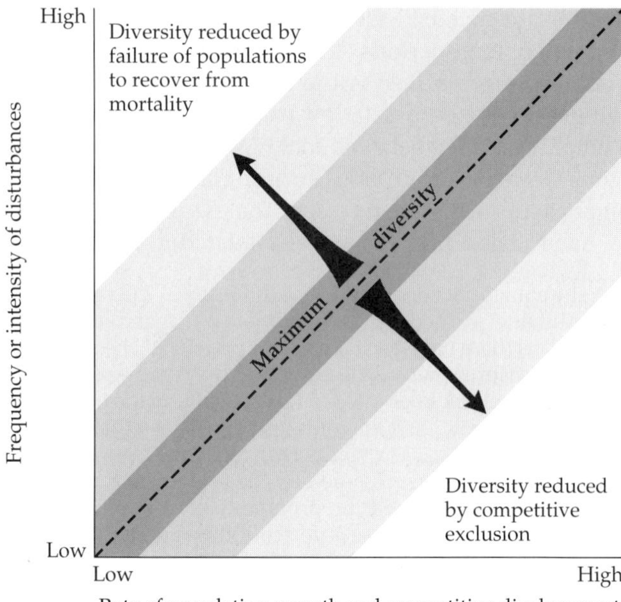

Figure 4.13 Influences of rates of population growth and disturbance on species richness. Maximum diversity is postulated to occur where rates of the two processes are balanced. (From Huston 1994.)

depths, plant species richness in relation to fire frequency, and patterns of endemism (Huston 1994).

The ecological interactions that, in combination with physical environmental factors, appear to determine today's patterns of species richness might set absolute limits to species richness. On the other hand, they might change over time to allow more species to be accommodated. Are there limits to the number of species, limits that can exert major influences on the composition of a given ecological community? Is there a critical limit to overlap in resource use that will prevent more species from being accommodated unless dramatic changes occur in the nature of the available resources? Does the chemical warfare between plants and herbivores set limits on species richness, or does it offer possibilities for more species? Are there limits to the size of mimicry systems, and do mimicry systems allow more species to be accommodated in ecosystems than would be possible without them? Is there reason to believe that the richness-generating interactions between plants and their pollinators and between plants and their seed dispersers have been exhausted? These questions cannot be answered with any assurance today, but research on these and related questions is under way.

The Future of Biodiversity Studies

The incomplete state of our knowledge of the identities, taxonomic relationships, and distributions of the vast majority of the world's organisms means that the primary work of cataloging biodiversity is yet to be done. How this inventory should be carried out is the subject of much debate. Some biologists recommend the initiation of an intense global survey, aimed at the discovery and classification of all species. Others, pointing to the shortage of people, funds, and time, believe that the only realistic hope lies in rapid recognition and preservation of threatened habitats that contain the largest numbers of endemic species. These people give the inventory task a lower immediate priority. Wilson (1992) strongly advocates a mixed strategy that combines global surveys designed to achieve a complete biodiversity inventory in 50 years with immediate attention to hot spots (see Essay 4B). He envisions a three-level strategy. The first level is a Rapid Assessment Program (RAP) that would investigate poorly known ecosystems that might be unidentified hot spots. RAP teams would consist of experts on groups such as flowering plants, reptiles, mammals, birds, fishes, and butterflies that are well enough known to be inventoried quickly and accurately. These taxa would then serve as proxies for the entire biota. (Essay 5C contains a fuller discussion of RAP.)

The next level proposed by Wilson is the BIOTROP approach, patterned after the Neotropical Biological Diversity Program of the University of Kansas and a consortium of other North American universities. The goal of this approach is to establish research stations in areas believed to be major hot spots or to contain multiple hot spots. Inventories and ecological studies would then be carried out across latitudes and elevations in the regions surrounding the stations. The third level, with a time frame of 50 years, would combine the inventories from RAP and BIOTROP with monographic studies of many groups of organisms to provide a more complete picture of global biodiversity and its distribution.

Hot spots are important, but many species would be lost if only hot spots were preserved. Biologists at the World Wildlife Fund have developed a supplementary approach to identify countries where establishing additional reserves should maximize species preservation. They compared countries with respect to the amount of land that is protected and the amount of unprotected land that remains in a more or less natural state. High priority is assigned to establishing additional reserves in countries that have much land already protected and much land remaining in a high-quality state. Countries that have little land already protected but much high-quality land are also high-priority areas for establishing reserves. Countries that have few reserves and little land still available are low-priority countries for conservation efforts.

Whatever approach is taken by society, it will require much more effort than has been invested in biodiversity studies during recent decades. The scope of the untapped wealth residing in biodiversity, as well as the importance of inventorying biodiversity and understanding ecological relationships among species, has been greatly underappreciated. It is doubtful that humans can devise a sustainable future without a more complete knowledge of biodiversity. Even the very notion of biodiversity will be modified as our knowledge grows. For example, Lincoln Brower, in Essay 4D, introduces the concept of an "endangered biological phenomenon," in which a species is likely to sur-

---

ESSAY 4D

A New Paradigm in Biodiversity Conservation

Endangered Biological Phenomena

Lincoln P. Brower, University of Florida

Much of conservation research focuses on describing diminishing species diversity and on understanding the processes that lead species to small populations, and thence to extinction. Here I discuss *endangered biological phenomena,* a recently developed conservation theme (Brower and Malcolm 1991), defined as *a spectacular aspect of the life history of an animal or plant species involving a large number of individuals that is threatened with impoverishment or demise; the species per se need not be in peril, rather, the phenomenon it exhibits is at stake.*

Examples of endangered biological phenomena include the ecological diversity associated with naturally flooding rivers, the vast herds of bison of the North American prairie ecosystems, the synchronous flowering cycles of bamboo in India, the 17- and 13-year cicada emergence events in eastern North America, entire indigenous fish faunas of the African Rift Valley lake ecosystems, and scores of current animal migrations. Instances of the last include seasonal migrations of the African wildebeest and North American caribou, the wet and dry season movements of Costa Rican sphingid moths, the billion individuals of 120 songbird species that migrate from Canada to Neotropical overwintering areas, and the highly disrupted migrations of numerous whale species.

There are two principal biological reasons why animal migrations are endangered by human activities. First, migrant species move through a sequence of ecologically distinct areas, any one of which could become an Achilles' heel. Second, aggregation or bottlenecking of the migrants can occur, making the animals especially vulnerable. The major impact on migratory species is due to accelerating habitat modification throughout the world. Even when problems are recognized, mitigation is difficult because of varying policies and enforcement abilities in the different countries the animals occupy during the different phases of their migration cycles. The extraordinary migration and overwintering behaviors of the monarch butterfly, in both eastern and western North America, well exemplify the concept of endangered phenomena.

The monarch butterfly, *Danaus plexippus*, is a member of the tropical subfamily Danainae, which contains 157 known species. It is alone in its subfamily in having evolved extraordinary spring and fall migrations (Figures A and B) that allow it to exploit the abundant *Asclepias* (milkweed) food supply across the North American continent. Here it has become one of the most abundant butterflies in the world. Remarkably, and in contrast to vertebrate migrations, the monarch's orientation and navigation to its overwintering sites is carried out by descendants three or more generations removed from their migrant forebears. Its fall migration, therefore, is completely inherited, with no opportunity for learned behavior. This pattern, together with the vastness of the migration and overwintering aggregations, constitutes a unique biological phenomenon.

Two migratory populations of the monarch occur in North America. The larger one occurs east of the Rocky Mountains and undoubtedly represents the stock from which the smaller, western North American migration evolved. Both migrations are threatened because the aggregation behavior during winter concentrates the species' gene pool into several tiny and vulnerable geographic areas.

Threats to the Western Population. Monarchs that breed west of the Rocky Mountains migrate in the fall to about 40 known overwintering sites in California. Most of these are within a few hundred meters of the Pacific Ocean, which moderates the winter climate and prevents the butterflies from freezing. Because of the exorbitant value of coastal real estate in California, all overwintering sites on privately owned land are in a tenuous position. Moreover, several of the sites protected in city, county, or state parks are rapidly deteriorating. Four factors contribute to this problem: benign neglect ignores ecological succession and tree senescence, which results in failure of protection against winter winds; trees on unprotected land adjacent to parks are subject to cutting, again leading to wind invasion; human visitors cause soil compaction, erosion, and vegetational deterioration; and there are conflicting policies over native versus exotic plant management.

The people of California are responding to these threats. The city of Pacific Grove managed, by a remarkable 67% vote, to purchase the most famous of all California overwintering habitats, which is now recovering due to extensive citizen involvement. The magnitude of the problem is indicated by the fact that Pacific Grove had to appropriate $1.4 million to buy the 2.5 acre parcel of land. The earlier passage of California Proposition 70 in 1988, which appropriated $2 million to purchase monarch habitat, palls in the face of economic reality. A more creative approach is needed in order to acquire, protect, and manage a substantial number of the coastal overwintering habitats.

Threats to the Eastern Population. The eastern population breeds over a much larger area east of the Rocky Mountains, and is probably at least 10,000 times larger than the western population. Beginning in late August, monarchs migrate to central Mexico, where they overwinter for more than five months in high-altitude fir forests in the Transverse Neovolcanic Belt, about 90 km west of Mexico City (Fig-

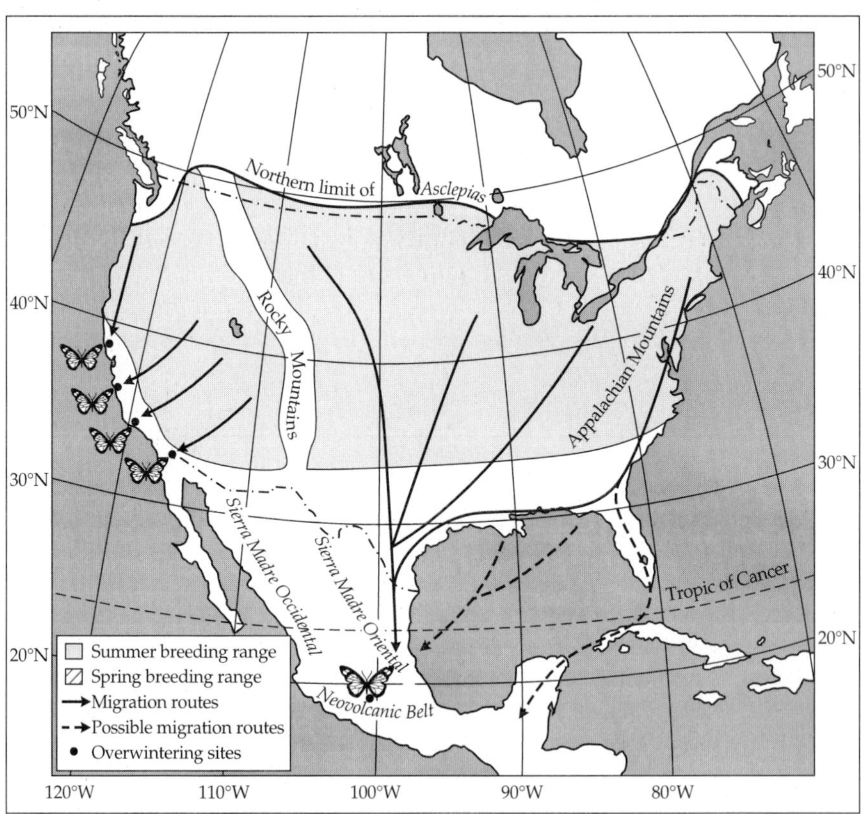

Figure A Fall migrations of the eastern and western populations of the monarch butterfly in North America. (Modified from Brower 1995, with permission of the *Journal of the Lepidopterists' Society*.)

ure A). Here the butterflies coalesce by the tens of millions into dense and stunningly spectacular aggregations that festoon up to 5 ha of forest (Figure C). The butterflies, effectively in cold storage, remain sexually inactive until the approach of the vernal equinox.

Survivors from the Mexican overwintering colonies begin migrating northward late in March to lay their eggs on sprouting milkweed plants (*Asclepias* spp.) along the Gulf Coast (Figure B). These 8-month-old remigrants then die, and their offspring, produced in late April and early May, continue the migration northward to Canada. Over the summer, two or three more generations are produced. Toward the end of August, butterflies of the last summer generation enter reproductive diapause, and the cycle begins anew as these monarchs migrate instinctively southward to the overwintering grounds in Mexico.

To date, about ten overwintering areas have been discovered in the states of Michoacan and Mexico on a few isolated mountain ranges at elevations ranging from 2900 to 3400 m. This elevational band coincides with a summer fog belt and contains boreal-like fir forests that probably are a relict ecosystem from the Pleistocene. The five largest and least disturbed butterfly forests occur in an astoundingly small area of 800 km^2. By clustering on the trees in this cool and moist environment, individual monarchs are able to survive in a state of reproductive inactivity until the resurgence of the North American milkweed flora the following spring.

Because the monarch's specialized overwintering sites are limited to such a small area in Mexico, the eastern North American migratory phenomenon is now threatened with extinction and probably will be destroyed within 15 years if drastic measures are not soon implemented. The following briefly summarizes some of the problems and what must be done to prevent the loss of this endangered phenomenon.

Until recently, human impact on the high-altitude fir forests has been less than that on other forest ecosystems in Mexico. Negative developments over the past 20 years include: (1) increasing commercial harvest of trees, including thinning and clear-cutting; (2) expansion of villages up the mountainsides, which in turn has led to (3) an increased frequency of fires associated with forest clearing for planting corn and oats; (4) legal and illegal removal of logs and firewood; (5) increasing local charcoal manufacturing in pits dug within the fir forest; (6) the setting of fires in the forest to kill and cure young trees for local home construction; (7) the invasion of some areas of the fir ecosystem by forest lepidopteran pests, probably due to stress caused by thinning and deforestation at lower elevations; and, as a result, (8) the spraying of *Bacillus thuringiensis*, an organic pesticide, which has been initiated and considered for widespread use without adequate knowledge of its potential effect on monarchs; (9) heavy ecotourism, which is stressing the infrastructure and generating severe dust precipitation on vegetation along paths through the colonies; and (10), because of the income generated, an increasing demand to open all colonies to tourists.

Barriers to the implementation of conservation practices in Mexico include political and administrative difficulties resulting from the fact that the forests are under the control of numerous

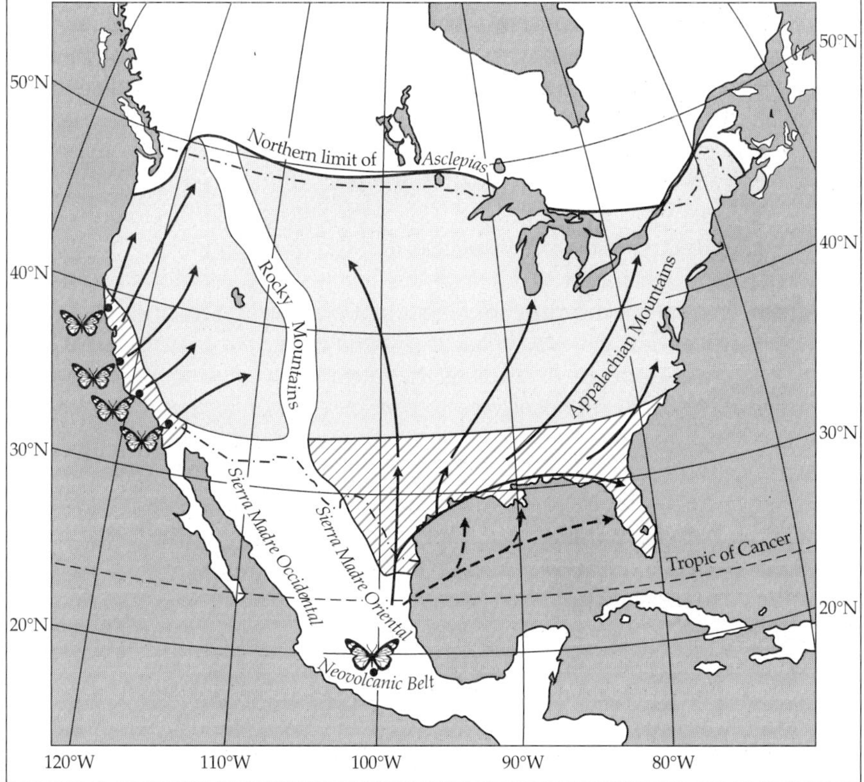

Figure B Spring migrations of the eastern and western populations of the monarch butterfly in North America. (Modified from Brower 1995, with permission of the *Journal of the Lepidopterists' Society*.)

Figure C Dense overwintering clusters of the monarch butterfly on the trunk of an *Abies religiosa* fir tree in the Sierra Chinqua colony, Michoacan, Mexico, on 18 January 1985. (From Calvert and Brower 1986.)

governmental entities. Also, cultural attitudes in Mexico toward land use differ from those in the United States and Canada, and suggestions for purchasing land solely to preserve biodiversity engender hostility. Education on both the world-class aesthetic and the local economic values of the migratory phenomenon is sorely needed in the towns and villages near the butterfly areas. Federal, state, and local governing entities, known as *ejidos*, must cooperate to coordinate major conservation policies that are ecosystem-based and legally enforced. Time is running out.

Because the probability of a species' extinction is inversely proportional to the number of its refuges, prudence argues that all major overwintering mountain areas in Mexico must be preserved. A largely unrecognized benefit of protecting the higher montane slopes that host the fir forests and their monarchs would be the preservation of the hydrologic resources that are economically critical to local towns and villages.

Unlike the Passenger Pigeon or Carolina Parakeet, we will not lose the monarch butterfly as a species, because numerous nonmigratory populations will persist in its tropical range. However, the monarch's spectacular North American migrations will soon be destroyed if extensive overwintering habitat protection and management in Mexico and California are not implemented on a grand scale. The impending fate of this remarkable insect is an omen for the entire world biota, warning us that we must incorporate the concept of endangered biological phenomena into our 21st century plans for conserving biodiversity.

vive, but some spectacular aspect of its life history, such as a mass annual migration, is in jeopardy of disappearing. The mass migrations of springbok in southern Africa have already been eliminated, but the seasonal migrations of vast herds of wildebeest in the Serengeti of Tanzania still exist. The loss of that mass migration would be tragic even though wildebeest would survive in many places.

Once a reasonably complete inventory of the biota of a region, or significant components of it, has been achieved, a monitoring program should be established. Such a program should be designed to detect trends in biodiversity and to identify impending problems to which attention should be directed. Without such a program society cannot know whether its efforts to preserve biodiversity are succeeding, or why and where they are failing.

The relationship between area and species richness has major practical implications for the location, design, and management of parks and reserves established and maintained to preserve biodiversity. There is increasing evidence that even the largest parks and reserves are too small to maintain viable populations of those species with the largest areal requirements (discussed in Chapter 10). Many of the national parks of the United States have already lost their largest mammal species, and the trend continues (Newmark 1987). Therefore, additional studies of the species–area relationship and its causes are essential for informed management of reserves. Meanwhile, existing knowledge of species–area relationships is being used in the establishment of reserves. A notable example is the megareserve system of Costa Rica (see Figure 13.13), which is designed to preserve about 80% of the biodiversity of the country over the long term. Each megareserve includes natural areas and areas managed for economically valuable products. Some of the megareserves also remain the homes of indigenous people who continue to use the environment in their traditional ways. The largest of the Costa Rican megareserves, Talamanca Biosphere Reserve, is a mosaic of more than 500,000 hectares and includes three national or international parks, a large biological reserve, five Indian reservations, and two large forest reserves (Figure 4.14).

Talamanca is part of the UNESCO Man and the Biosphere (MAB) program of worldwide **Biosphere Reserves**. Reserves are nominated by the national MAB committee of the country concerned. The nomination is reviewed by the MAB Bureau, and if accepted, the reserve is formally designated part of the MAB network. Some Biosphere Reserves cross national boundaries and are, therefore, international; such is the case with La Amistad International Park,

Figure 4.14 The mountainous La Amistad International Park is part of the Talamanca Biosphere Reserve of southern Costa Rica and northern Panama. This Biosphere Reserve contains some of the richest biodiversity in all of Central America. At least 263 species of amphibians and reptiles and 400 species of birds have been recorded in the reserve. (Photograph by C. R. Carroll.)

within Talamanca. Biosphere Reserves serve a range of objectives, which include research, monitoring, training, education, and conservation. The "ideal" Biosphere Reserve contains an undisturbed core area surrounded by peripheral zones in which increasing levels of human disturbance are permitted. However, few existing reserves actually have this structure.

On a theoretical level, more biodiversity studies are needed to resolve the many uncertainties surrounding the historical and present-day ecological processes that determine today's patterns of biodiversity. Modern molecular techniques that enable systematists to develop soundly based phylogenies are being combined with biogeographic studies to provide a more complete picture of the history of the distribution of life on earth. Processes operating over ecological time frames are increasingly being studied using manipulative experiments in which restricted areas are defaunated, particular species are removed, or species are introduced. Many "natural experiments" are occurring from which ecological insight may be gained. Among these are volcanic eruptions that eliminate the biotas of islands; the massive inadvertent transport of species around the world by human travel; deliberate introductions for agricultural, aesthetic, or pest-control purposes; and habitat fragmentation by conversion of natural landscapes to ones dominated by highly modified communities that are managed to channel most of their productivity to human uses. Such scenarios provide opportunities to examine the results of manipulations over longer time frames than is possible with investigator-initiated experiments.

Studies of the influence of human activities on species distributions and species richness are adding rapidly to our understanding of the roles of the varied processes that interact to cause the patterns in the distribution of biodiversity on earth that so fascinate us today. This knowledge is also being used to reduce rates of species extinctions and to restore landscapes so that they can continue to support the array of species originally found in them.

Summary

Biodiversity is a term that refers to the variety of living organisms, their genetic diversity, and the types of ecological communities into which they are assembled. The number of species found in an area—species richness—is the measure of biodiversity commonly used in conservation biology, both because accurate information on abundances typically is not available and because rare species are often of great conservation interest. About 1.5 million living and 300,000 fossil species have been described, but estimates of the total number of living species range from 10 million to 50 million or more. Although species richness is higher on land than in the oceans, 34 of the 35 extant animal phyla are marine, and 16 are exclusively marine.

Cellular life in the form of bacteria evolved about 3.8 billion years ago; eukaryotic organisms evolved about 2 billion years ago. The first major explosion of biodiversity took place in the early Cambrian period, and except during times of mass extinctions, the number of species has increased since then. More species are probably alive today than at any other time in the history of life, even though some taxa had more species in the past than they do today. The causes of increasing species richness over evolutionary time include the breakup of the continents and the evolution of more diverse body plans that enabled animals to burrow, swim, and fly.

Several broad patterns characterize the distribution of species today. Among most taxa, more species live in tropical regions than at higher latitudes. Species richness is also positively correlated with structural complexity. Marine species richness peaks at intermediate depths, but is still remarkably high in the deep sea. There is a positive correlation between productivity and species richness at low levels of productivity, but species richness typically declines at higher productivity levels. Some highly productive systems, such as salt marshes, sea-grass beds, and hot springs, are species-poor. Plant species richness is extremely high in some unproductive semiarid regions with poor soils. Island communities are poorer in species than comparable mainland communities at all latitudes.

Areas that have experienced long geographic isolation and which have great topographic relief often support many endemic species. Biogeographers recognize 18 of these "hot spots," which collectively contain about 20% of the world's plant species in only 0.5% of its land area. Some of these areas are also regions of high animal endemism, but others, such as the Cape region of South Africa, and southwestern Australia, are too small to have permitted in situ speciation of most taxa of larger animals.

In addition to productivity and structural complexity, species diversity is influenced by competitive interactions and predation. Formerly it was believed that stability favored high species richness, but more recent evidence strongly suggests that without disturbance, local species richness would be less than it is.

The state of knowledge of the earth's biodiversity is so poor that the primary work of cataloging biodiversity is yet to be done. The resources currently devoted to this task are inadequate, especially given the rate at which species are becoming extinct. Better information on biodiversity, its distribution, and its causes is needed for wise management of the earth's biotic resources.

Questions for Discussion

1. Indices of species diversity that are weighted by abundance, biomass, or productivity have been used frequently by ecologists, but seldom by conservation biologists. For what purposes might conservation biologists wish to use weighted indices instead of simple lists of species?

2. Given that millions of species are yet to be described and named, how should the limited human and financial resources available for taxonomic research be allocated? Should attention be concentrated on poorly known

taxa? Should efforts be directed toward areas threatened with habitat destruction so that species can be collected before they are eliminated? Should major efforts be directed toward obtaining complete "all taxa" surveys of selected areas? How should these decisions be made?

3. The history of life has been punctuated by six episodes during which extinction rates have been very high. If extinction is a normal process, and if life has diversified after each of the previous mass extinctions, why should we be worried about the prospect of high extinction rates during the coming century? How does the current extinction episode differ from previous ones?

4. Many conservation efforts are directed at particular local areas harboring rare species or having high species richness. Why is concentrating only on local problems insufficient as an effective conservation strategy? Why is local species richness dependent, in part, upon regional species richness? How can we find out which processes dominate the interactions between local and regional species richness?

5. For which animal taxa would you expect species richness to be most positively correlated with plant community structure? Mammals? Amphibians? Insects? Why?

6. Evidence gathered by many ecologists suggests that intermediate levels of disturbance often act to increase the number of species found in an area. What are the implications of this finding for investigations in conservation biology and management of reserves?

7. How can biologists determine whether there are limits to the number of species that can be supported in local areas? What type of research could determine whether the global number of species is still increasing (or would be if humans had not intervened)?

Suggestions for Further Reading

Brown, J. H. and A. C. Gibson. 1983. *Biogeography*. C. V. Mosby, St Louis. The best textbook on biogeography. It describes both the history of the distribution of life and the current patterns of distributions of organisms, as well as the theories proposed to account for them.

Heywood, V. H. and R. T. Watson (eds.). 1995. *Global Biodiversity Assessment*. Cambridge University Press, New York. A huge volume from over 1500 scientists around the world with up-to-date information on biodiversity: its magnitude, distribution, losses, human and economic influences, and conservation measures. A gold mine of information.

MacArthur, R. H. and E. O. Wilson. 1967. *The Theory of Island Biogeography*. Princeton University Press, Princeton, NJ. The classic book that launched the modern experimental study of causes of patterns of species richness. It lays out the basic species–area relationships and the patterns of species richness on islands.

Myers, N. 1983. *A Wealth of Wild Species*. Westview Press, Boulder, CO. An engaging account of the ways in which humans benefit from the use and enjoyment of other organisms.

Prance, G. H. (ed.). 1982. *The Biological Model of Diversification in the Tropics*. Columbia University Press, New York. A set of essays that analyzes why the tropics are the home of so much of the earth's biological richness.

World Conservation and Monitoring Centre. 1992. *Global Biodiversity: Status of the Earth's Living Resources*. Chapman & Hall, London. A storehouse of information on biodiversity, intended as a sourcebook of data and analysis rather than a book to be read cover to cover.

5

Global Biodiversity II

Losses and Threats

The worst thing that can happen during the 1980s is not energy depletion, economic collapse, limited nuclear war, or conquest by a totalitarian government. As terrible as these catastrophes would be for us, they can be repaired within a few generations. The one process ongoing in the 1980s that will take millions of years to correct is the loss of genetic and species diversity by the destruction of natural habitats. This is the folly that our descendants are least likely to forgive us.

E. O. Wilson, 1985

In the previous chapter you learned about patterns of biodiversity and some of the processes that result in those patterns. The extent of biodiversity—the tremendous wealth of genetic, species, and ecosystem diversity—should by now be evident. But these biological riches, the information and entities that constitute our biosphere, are individually and collectively in grave danger of major degradation or outright loss. This chapter addresses the patterns and extent of losses of biodiversity as well as the major threats involved.

Losses of Biodiversity

An Overview of Mass Extinctions

Just as all individuals eventually die, all species eventually go extinct. Raup (1991a) estimates that 99.9% of all species that ever lived are now extinct. This is an alarming figure, one that could be interpreted as the dwindling of life on earth, until one places it in the proper context of the immense time span (3.5 billion years) that covers the history of the living earth. On a per year or per century basis, the rate is quite low, even considering the five known periods of mass extinctions that have punctuated life's history (Sepkoski 1982). And, of course, as species have gone extinct, other species have appeared, and the balance of speciation and extinction has resulted in a general increase in living diversity over time. However, there is good evidence that we are in the opening phase of another **mass extinction** of species (Ehrlich and Ehrlich 1981; Wilson, 1989, 1992; Western and Pearl 1989; Club of Earth 1990; Myers 1990a,b; Raven 1990; Soulé 1991a), one that could rival and even surpass in extent any of the great mass extinction episodes of the prehistoric past. This episode is the sole outcome of the activities of humanity.

The evidence for a mass extinction of species is abundant and varied. The earth's stock of species is widely estimated to total a minimum of 10 million (Ehrlich and Ehrlich 1981; Club of Earth 1990; May 1992b; Wilson 1992; Myers 1993; Reaka-Kudla et al. 1996). Some scientists, notably Erwin (1991), argue that the true total could be 30 million, possibly 50 million, and conceivably 100 million (for other views see Stork 1988 and Gaston 1992). Of the conservative number of 10 million species, about 90% are usually considered to be terrestrial (Raven et al. 1993), and of these, some 80%, or 7.2 million, are believed to occur in the tropics (Stevens 1989), with more than two-thirds of them, or roughly 5 million, in tropical forests, ranging from very wet forests to dry forests and thorn scrub (Ricklefs and Schluter 1993). Tropical forests are not only the richest biome biotically, they are also the biome where habitat depletion is occurring fastest—not only outright destruction but also gross degradation and fragmentation, which is resulting in the loss of many ecosystem functions, including food webs. So this biome is the prime locus of mass extinction, and hence the main focus of this chapter.

Several other biomes, however, are also very rich biotically and likewise undergoing depletion. The marine realm, with its estimated 1 million species, has traditionally been viewed as biotically depauperate in comparison with the terrestrial realm. However, recent research suggests that the true species richness on just the ocean floor—mostly mollusks, crustaceans, and polychaete worms—could be as high as 10 million species (Grassle 1991; Grassle et al. 1991; Ray and Grassle 1991; for a different view, proposing half a million species, see May 1992a). There is also a qualitative difference: whereas land habitats feature 11 phyla (only one of which is limited to land), the seas are home to 34 phyla, 16 of which are found nowhere else. A deep sea area no bigger than two tennis courts has been found to contain 798 species representing 14 phyla, a higher-level taxon diversity that could not remotely be matched on land (Grassle and Maciolek 1992; see also Essay 4C).

Figure 5.1 The Nile perch (*Lates niloticus*), an introduced species in Lake Victoria, is responsible for the extinction of numerous endemic species of cichlids. (Photograph courtesy of John N. Rinne.)

Coral reefs are often richer in species per unit area than are tropical forests, and they are undergoing widespread degradation. They cover about 600,000 km^2, or only 0.2%, of the oceans' surface (by comparison, tropical moist forests cover 7.5 million km^2, or 6% of the land surface), yet in this limited expanse they may contain one-third of the oceans' fish species. As many as 93% of coral reefs have already been damaged, and possibly 5–10% destroyed, by human activity; at the present depletion rate 60% could be lost within 20–40 years (Dubinsky 1990; Fujita et al. 1992; Reaka-Kudla et al. 1996). But major habitat losses are not confined to tropical forests or marine systems. Examples of severe losses of other habitat types around the world are listed in Table 5.1.

Freshwater ecosystems feature exceptional concentrations of certain taxa, as well as high rates of endemism, and are rapidly being degraded (Stiassny 1996, 1997). For example, the three main East African Rift Valley lakes (Victoria, Tanganyika, and Malawi) harbor almost 1000 cichlid fish species (about the same number of fishes found in all of North America and Europe combined), the great bulk of them endemic; Lake Victoria has already lost at least 200 of its 300 cichlids, making this the largest vertebrate mass extinction of the modern era (Baskin 1992; Kauffman 1992; Goldschmidt et al. 1993; Lowe-McConnell 1993). Most of this loss is due to the intentional introduction of a single predator species, the Nile perch (Figure 5.1), and an intensive gill net fishery (Stiassny 1996). Many North American freshwater fish species are likewise endangered or are already extinct (Miller et al. 1989; Williams et al. 1989; Minckley and Deacon 1991), and many are at extreme risk due to their highly

Table 5.1
Examples of Major Nonforested Habitat Types, Their Original Extent, and Percentage Remaining

Country or region	Habitat type	Original extent (km^2)	% remaining	Reference
North America	Tallgrass prairie	1,430,000	1	WRI 1991
Sri Lanka	Thorn scrub	19,800	25	MacKinnon and MacKinnon 1986b
United Kingdom	Heathland	1,432	27	Nature Conservancy (UK) 1984
Nigeria	Mangrove	24,440	50	MacKinnon and MacKinnon 1986a
Paraguay	Chaco	320,000	57	Redford et al. 1990
South Africa	Fynbos	75,000	67	Mooney 1988

From Groom and Schumaker 1993.

Figure 5.2 Devil's Hole, Nye County, Nevada, home of the Devils Hole pupfish (*Cyprinodon diabolis*). This deep, water-filled fissure in the rocks encompasses the entire range of this species, and may represent the most restrictive distribution of any vertebrate in the world. (Photograph by G. K. Meffe.)

restricted distributions. The Devils Hole pupfish, for example, has a global habitat totaling a few square meters (Figure 5.2), which is dependent on groundwater stability in a desert that is under constant pressure for development. Other, seemingly more mundane, areas may also be hot spots of aquatic diversity. The state of Alabama, for example, has an extraordinarily high diversity of native gill-breathing snails, mussels, fishes, and turtles (Lydeard and Mayden 1995), many of which are endangered or extinct, and relatively few of which are protected by legislation (Table 5.2).

But let us return to the tropical forests and consider the higher estimates for the global number of species, between 30 million and 100 million. Because many of the additional species are thought to live in tropical moist forests, the true planetary total is not merely a matter of academic speculation. These forests are where habitats are being lost fastest and where the bulk of extinctions is likely occurring. So if the real total is at least 30 million species, potential extinction is much higher than that postulated on a basis of only 10 million species. But for the sake of caution and conservatism, let us accept a total of 10 million species. At least half of these species live in tropical moist forests (see Figure 5.6), even though remaining forests of this type now cover only 6% of earth's land surface, an expanse equivalent to the continental United States.

Table 5.2
Selected Aquatic Species of the State of Alabama

Taxon	No. species	% of North American fauna	% endemic[a]	% of conservation concern[b]	% protected by ESA	No. extinct
Snails	147	43%	77%	44%	<1%	31
Mussels	171	60%	34%	62%	22%	11
Fishes	303	38%	41%	10%	4%	2
Turtles	23	52%	22%	26%	9%	0

Modified from Lydeard and Mayden 1995.
[a]Includes Alabama drainages that originate in or flow to adjacent states.
[b]Includes the categories extinct, endangered, threatened, and special concern.

According to estimates from Myers (1989, 1992a,b), these forests are being destroyed at a rate of at least 150,000 km^2 per year. Globally, rates of loss of forest cover of all types vary greatly by continent (Figure 5.3), but the inarguable trend is toward continual losses. "True" deforestation rates are difficult to pin down, and have been a matter of some controversy (discussed in Box 5A). With regard to tropical forests, controversy surrounds the separate estimates for 1980 deforestation rates worked out by Myers and by the main United Nations agency concerned with tropical forests, the Food and Agriculture Organization (FAO). The FAO (1993) subsequently estimated that deforestation in 1991 was 134,000 km^2—a figure only 11% lower than Myers's estimate.

In addition to outright forest destruction, an equivalent expanse of forest is being disrupted through logging and slash-and-burn conversion to pasture and cropland (Figure 5.4), with resultant degradation and impoverishment of ecosystems and their species' life-support systems. Recent information from the Amazonian region of Brazil, based on satellite data, shows that not only are forests being lost outright, but the remaining forests are highly degraded through edge effects and isolation (concepts discussed in detail in Chapter 9), which greatly increases the total negative effects on biodiversity (Table 5.3).

But in the interests of being cautious and conservative, let us consider only the first form of habitat loss, outright destruction of forests. The current loss of 150,000 km^2 per year represents 2% of remaining forests. The annual rate of loss increased by 89% during the 1980s, and if patterns and trends of forest destruction persist with a similar acceleration in the annual rate, the rate of 2% may double in the near future.

This current annual rate of forest destruction does not mean that 2% of the forests' species are disappearing as well. Many species have wide distributions, sometimes extending across hundreds of thousands of square kilometers. However, many other species have highly restricted ranges, with their entire populations confined to just a few tens of thousands of square kilometers (Gentry 1992), and a large number of cloud forest plants in tropical Latin America are endemic to isolated sites smaller than 10 km^2 (Gentry 1992). In tropical forests of South America, 440 bird species (25% of the total) have ranges of less than 50,000 km^2, in contrast to 8 species (2% of the total) with similarly restricted ranges in the United States and Canada (Terborgh and Winter 1980).

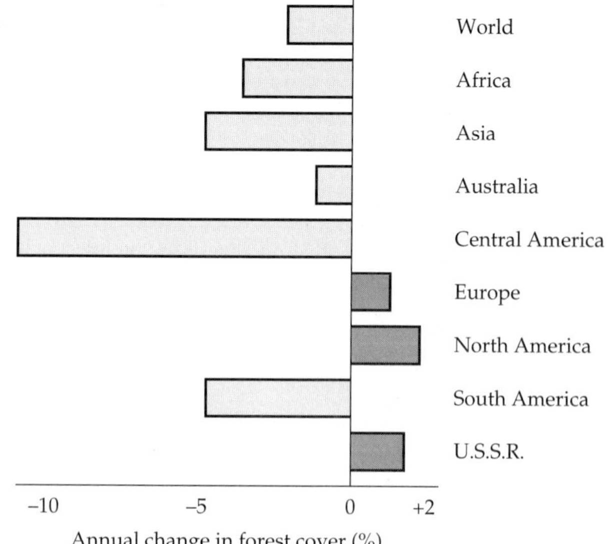

Figure 5.3 Estimates of average annual rates of change in forest cover around the world for the period 1977–1989. Deforestation is estimated as the amount of forest converted to nonforest use. (Modified from WRI 1992.)

BOX 5A
Quantifying Patterns of Deforestation

Martha J. Groom, North Carolina State University

Landscape change is one of the foremost threats to both biodiversity and the sustainability of human development. Although it is clear that the pace of landscape alteration has increased in recent decades, the details of the patterns and processes underlying habitat loss are poorly known. We need detailed information on the effects of landscape change throughout the world in order to interpret how habitat losses may affect biodiversity and human development. Patterns of forest loss are generally better quantified than losses in nonforested habitats, yet data limitations abound here as well. Unfortunately, the comparability among deforestation estimates is often low due to differences in the methods and definitions used by researchers.

Estimates of deforestation rates vary tremendously, both for global and regional totals (Table A) and for single countries (Figure A). There is often profound disagreement over deforestation statistics, largely because they have very real political consequences. Statistics on deforestation are influential in both conservation and development policy, affecting the design of national or multinational agreements to preserve the environment as well as allocation of funding for development programs (Groom and Schumaker 1993). Deforestation estimates may be used to determine the contribution of individual countries to global greenhouse gas emissions under the treaties signed at the 1992 Earth Summit in Rio de Janeiro. Countries may be pressured to reduce forest conversion if the available estimates of deforestation rates are high and their contribution to greenhouse emissions is consequently above an agreed-upon level (Monastersky 1993). Yet, because the data available for evaluating landscape change are so few, it is inevitable that disagreements will occur. Understanding some of the reasons why the statistics vary can help us to interpret them better.

Differences in the definitions and assumptions used in quantifying both the forests' original extent and the amount of forest that has been converted to another land use are the primary reasons deforestation statistics have varied so widely. There are many different types of forest, and different authors may include all or just one or a few types in their calculations. The broadest classification is "closed" versus "open" forest, which refers to whether or not trees cover a sufficiently high proportion of the area to prevent a continuous grass layer from growing. Open forests are more commonly degraded by low levels of human use (such as timber gathering) than closed forests, although closed forests are often more sensitive to less direct forms of degradation, such as edge effects. Some of the earliest data on deforestation did not include gross disruption of forests (FAO 1981), and thus underestimated global forest losses. More recent reports usually include separate estimates for open and closed forests (FAO 1988; Myers 1989). Information on forest losses at this scale is generally used to evaluate conservation needs on a country-by-country basis, or in general circulation models that predict global climate change (Schneider 1993; Esser 1995).

To evaluate whether particular habitats are in critical need of protection, it is necessary to make finer distinctions among habitat types in reports of deforestation and other forms of landscape change (Groom and Schumaker 1993). There are many types of vegetational associations, each of which may harbor characteristic suites of species. To the extent that we can distinguish among different habitat types, we can begin to discover where habitat losses have been concentrated, and thus begin to set our conservation priorities. Table B shows a detailed breakdown of forest losses in three countries. It is clear that some forest types are severely threatened (such as dry deciduous forests in Costa Rica and tropical pine forests in Thailand), while others are relatively intact (such as tropical montane evergreen forests in Thailand and montane rainforests in Costa Rica).

Further, although the modification of forested lands can have large impacts on the extinction rates of forest species, not

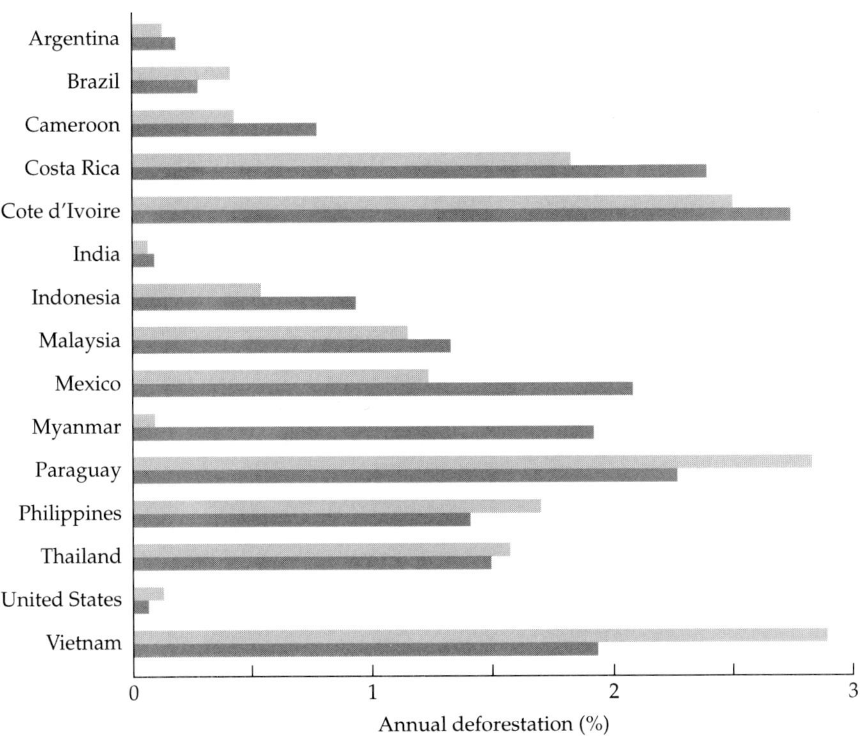

Figure A Two different estimates of annual deforestation rates for 15 countries. Dark bars: data adapted from FAO 1980 and 1990 estimates (WRI 1992: Table 17.1); light bars: data taken from several independent country-based estimates made between 1980 and 1991 (WRI 1992: Table 19.1). Methods used for the latter are not uniform. (From Groom and Schumaker 1993.)

Table A
Tropical Forest Area and Reported Deforestation Rates

Country	Total forest area (km²)	% of world total	1970s: Deforestation rate (km²/yr) (FAO)	Late 1980s: Deforestation rate (km²/yr) (Myers)	Late 1980s: Deforestation rate (km²/yr) (WRI)
Brazil	3,562,800	30.7	13,600	50,000	80,000
Indonesia	1,135,750	9.8	5,500	12,000	9,000
Zaire	1,056,500	9.1	1,700	4,000	1,820
Peru	693,100	6.0	2,450	3,500	2,700
Columbia	464,000	4.0	8,000	6,500	8,200
India	460,440	4.0	1,320	4,000	15,000
Others[a]	4,237,760	37.5	36,330	58,600	48,670
Total	11,610,350	100.0	68,900	138,600	165,400

From Skole and Tucker 1993.
[a]Sixty-seven other countries combined.

all types of modification are tallied in deforestation statistics (Houghton et al. 1991). Most often, land used in commercial forestry is not included in deforestation statistics. From the perspective of biodiversity, however, even low-intensity forestry (such as selective logging) often causes local extinctions (Johns 1985; Myers 1989). Commercial logging may cause smaller changes in geochemical processes than conversion to open pasture or other agricultural uses, but differences from primary forests are still detectable (Jordan 1986), and may be important in global greenhouse gas absorption or in the long-term productivity of such land uses.

Clearly, forestry has negative effects on species, communities, and ecosystems. What is not clear is how large these negative effects are relative to those associated with other changes in land use. There is some agreement that the effects of small-scale or temporary land uses are generally transient (Lovejoy and Shubart 1980), but these uses often lead to more destructive ones (Uhl and Buschbacher 1985), and thus some authors feel they should be monitored (Myers 1989; Groom and Schumaker 1993). Those who choose not to distinguish between primary forest and lands subjected to commercial forestry or shifting cultivation do so either because they believe the differences between these land uses are not large enough to be a primary focus of concern, or because it is too difficult to distinguish between them in satellite images. Because different landscape alterations have different consequences, it is likely that the finer the distinctions we can make, the better we will be able to set conservation priorities or define development policy.

Table B
Habitat Loss by Forest Type in Thailand, Madagascar, and Costa Rica

Forest type	Original extent (km²)	% lost
Thailand		
Lowland rainforest	12,027	84
Tropical semi-evergreen forest	88,799	51
Tropical pine forest	4,222	93
Montane deciduous forest	144,500	77
Tropical montane evergreen forest	9,331	10
Forest over limestone	200	0
Freshwater swamp	1,250	63
Monsoon forest	6,794	79
Mangrove forest	2,223	69
Dry deciduous forest	219,451	81
Total	507,267	74
Madagascar		
Lowland rainforest	80,729	85
Lowland rainforest/grassland	21,875	80
Moist montane forest	45,312	80
Mixed montane forest	3,646	70
Montane forest/secondary grassland	121,354	70
Dry deciduous forest	51,875	85
Dry deciduous forest/grassland	198,875	70
Deciduous thicket	38,125	85
Thicket/secondary grassland	31,250	70
Mangrove forest and swamp	2,170	40
Total	595,211	75
Costa Rica		
Dry deciduous forest	3,733	>99
Lowland moist forest	9,903	>99
Lowland wet forest	11,517	78
Premontane moist forest	3,659	>99
Premontane wet forest	12,005	81
Premontane rainforest	4,341	50
Lower montane moist forest	127	>99
Lower montane wet forest	925	86
Lower montane rainforest	3,576	35
Montane wet forest	38	>99
Montane rainforest	1,165	32
Total	50,990	79

From Groom and Schumaker 1993.

There is much promise for improving our estimates of the patterns of landscape change through the use of satellite imagery (Rey-Benayas and Pope 1995; Figure B). For example, a recent study of Landsat images of the Brazilian Amazon has provided the most accurate estimates to date of the extent of forest loss in that region (Skole and Tucker 1993). Using fairly high resolution images, Skole and Tucker have not only quantified deforestation, but have estimated the amount of area that may be affected by edge influences or isolation (see Table 5.3). Currently, there are plans by NASA and the FAO to analyze large numbers of satellite images from across the tropics to obtain more accurate data on the status of tropical forests (Monastersky 1993).

Although satellite imagery presents the most promising avenue for estimating and monitoring landscape change in a consistent and relatively detailed manner (see Figure B), it is important to keep in mind the limitations of satellite data. First, the images themselves and the facilities needed to interpret them are expensive (each image can cost as much as $4000, although costs may go down; Roughgarden et al. 1991). Second, not all land uses can be distinguished, particularly different types of low-intensity forestry, and secondary versus primary forest. Until extensive field verification of the actual vegetation is made, the number of habitat types that can be distiguished will be limited. Third, the satellite data cannot tell us anything about the effects of the changes we see—that is, losses of species and disruption of ecosystem processes are invisible to a satellite's sensors (Groom and Schumaker 1993).

Despite the methodological difficulties, it is important to continue our progress toward greater accuracy in deforestation estimates. Some of our progress will depend on the availability of satellite images and our ability to interpret the large amounts of data they make available. The rest will come from seeking uniformity in methodology, clarity in the definitions and assumptions used, and better fine-scale categorization of deforestation by habitat and by current land use. The resulting statistics will ultimately be the most powerful for use in planning conservation and development strategies.

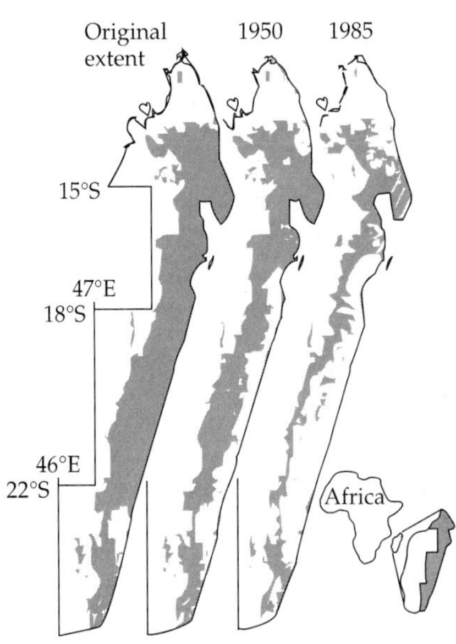

Figure B Distribution of rainforest in eastern Madagascar from before human colonization to modern times. Note the progressive loss of both overall forest cover and large blocks of forest. (From Green and Sussman 1990.)

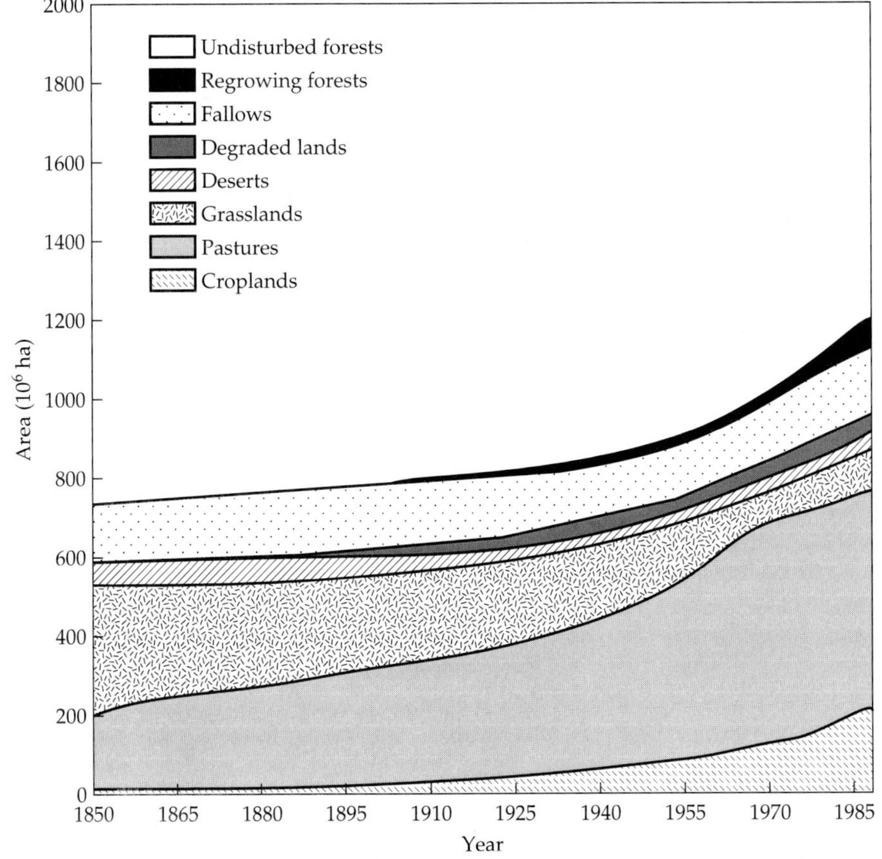

Figure 5.4 Changes in land use in Latin America from 1850 to 1985. Note the increase in pastures and croplands, and the losses of undisturbed forests and grasslands. (From Houghton et al. 1991.)

Table 5.3
Forest Land (km²) Deforested, Isolated, and Influenced by Edge Effects in the Brazilian Amazon in 1978 and 1988[a]

State	Deforested	Isolated	Edge effects	Total
1978				
Acre	2,612	18	4,511	7,141
Amapá	182	0	368	550
Amazonas	2,300	36	6,498	8,834
Maranhão	9,426	705	13,120	23,251
Mato Grosso	21,134	776	25,418	47,328
Pará	30,449	2,248	49,791	82,488
Rondônia	6,281	991	17,744	25,016
Roraima	196	4	812	1,012
Tocantins	5,688	337	6,584	12,609
Total	78,268	5,115	124,846	208,229
1988				
Acre	6,369	405	23,686	30,460
Amapá	210	1	689	900
Amazonas	11,813	474	36,392	48,679
Maranhão	31,952	2,123	28,147	62,222
Mato Grosso	47,568	2,542	71,128	121,238
Pará	95,075	6,837	116,669	218,581
Rondônia	23,998	2,408	52,345	78,751
Roraima	1,908	1	5,236	7,145
Tocantins	11,431	1,437	6,760	19,628
Total	230,324	16,228	341,052	587,604

From Skole and Tucker 1993.
[a]Note the tremendous increase in all categories in this 10-year span. Data were compiled using satellite imagery.

Such small, localized areas of endemism are unusually susceptible to unnoticed and large-scale extinctions. On a single forested ridge, Centinela, in the western Andes of Ecuador, there used to be as many as 90 endemic plant species. Although no comprehensive scientific analysis has been made, one can conjecture, on the basis of plant/animal relationships elsewhere, that the same habitat contained tens of times as many endemic animal species (mainly invertebrates). In the 1980s, the ridge's forest was cleared for agriculture, and the 90 plant species, plus their associated animal species, were eliminated (Dodson and Gentry 1991). In the words of E. O. Wilson (1992):

> Its name deserves to be synonymous with silent hemorrhaging of biological diversity. When the forest on the ridge was cut a decade ago, a large number of rare species were extinguished. They went just like that, from full healthy populations to nothing, in a few months. Around the world such anonymous extinctions—call them "centinelan extinctions"—are occurring, not open wounds for all to see and rush to stanch but unfelt internal events, leakages from vital tissue out of sight.

A detailed analysis of the processes leading to local extinctions is presented by James Karr in Essay 5A.

How shall we translate a 2% annual rate of forest destruction into an annual species extinction rate? One analytic path is revealed by the species–area relationship and the theory of island biogeography (introduced in Chap-

ESSAY 5A
Extinction of Birds on Barro Colorado Island, Panama

James R. Karr, University of Washington

To slow rates of biodiversity loss (or declines in biological integrity—see Essay 14A), we must take steps to minimize losses of components of the biota. But what steps? First we must understand the ecological and demographic processes that define how extinctions actually occur on a local scale. The birds on Barro Colorado Island, Panama, offer important clues to local extinction processes.

The avifauna of Barro Colorado, a small hilltop in central Panama, existed for thousands of years with only limited human influence. Change came first during the 19th century, when the eastern half of Barro Colorado was cleared for small subsistence farms, and then between 1903 and 1914, when construction of the Panama Canal dammed the Chagras River to form Gatun Lake, which flooded the lowlands around the hilltop. As a result, Barro Colorado became a 15 km^2 land-bridge island isolated from nearby lowland forests. In 1923 Barro Colorado Island was designated a biological reserve; with growing interest in tropical biology, the island became an ideal natural laboratory for the interplay of scientific theory, experiment, and observation.

One result of studies on Barro Colorado is that we know it now supports fewer species of birds than do nearby mainland forests. Three hundred seventy-five bird species are known from Barro Colorado in the 20th century; 209 species have been known to breed on the island. Since the island's isolation, many bird species have disappeared, apparently because of two factors: successional loss of second-growth habitats (32 species) and island effects (50–60 species), including ecological truncation (disproportionate losses of certain species, in this case large or specialized species). During 24 years of fieldwork in central Panamanian forests, my students and I have asked several questions about the processes involved in these extinctions.

Are species lost at random? I classified all resident land birds at a mainland site called Pipeline Road according to their food habits, habitat affinity (dry, wet, or foothill forest), and the vegetation layer in which they foraged (Karr 1982a). The Pipeline Road forest was contiguous with the Barro Colorado forest before construction of the canal. By comparing the distribution of species in the mainland fauna with the species missing from Barro Colorado, I could determine whether the missing species were a random subset of the mainland fauna. The distributions of mainland and Barro Colorado–extinct species did not differ as a function of food habits, but striking differences were found for both habitat type and foraging stratum. Among the strata, extinction losses were high for ground (2.4×) and undergrowth (1.4×) species, but low for canopy species (0.4×). Dry forest species had low extinction rates (0.1×), while foothill species had high extinction rates (3.7×). Clearly, the forest species missing from Barro Colorado are not a random set of species from the fauna on the nearby mainland.

Are certain demographic attributes associated with extinction? Extinction of species on a land-bridge island occurs when a population is no longer able to maintain itself and recolonization from the nearby mainland is not possible. In 1979, I initiated a long-term study of central Panama birds to evaluate the role of demographic attributes in the extinction process. Birds from the Pipeline Road site were captured, banded with aluminum bands, and released. Using statistical models for open populations, we estimated demographic parameters such as population size and mean annual survival rate for 25 species of mainland forest birds of the undergrowth (Karr 1990). Mean annual survival rates for the eight species absent from Barro Colorado Island were significantly lower than those for the 17 species still present there. When the species are arrayed in the sequence of their disappearance from Barro Colorado, the lowest survival rates identify not only the likelihood of extinction but also the sequence of loss from Barro Colorado.

Why are undergrowth species especially prone to disappearance? A common explanation for the high loss of terrestrial and undergrowth species on Barro Colorado is predation; high densities of small to medium-sized predators subject nests and adults to high predation rates. When one extinct species, the song wren, was reintroduced to the island, a period of successful reproduction was soon followed by a population decline, probably caused by heavy predation. Two experimental studies of nest predation on the island and mainland also showed higher nest predation rates on Barro Colorado than at the Pipeline Road site.

Does risk of nest predation vary among undergrowth species? Sieving (1992), who noted that 8 of 12 bird species in the terrestrial insectivore guild are now extinct on Barro Colorado, tested the hypothesis that interspecific variation in nest design and placement underlies differential avian extinction on the island. She selected five terrestrial insectivores for intensive study—two that are extinct and three that persist on Barro Colorado. She placed handmade mimics of the species' nests containing quail eggs in the forest undergrowth in microhabitats appropriate for each species and recorded predation on these mimics.

Losses of eggs to predators were higher on the island than on the mainland, and predation rates varied between Barro Colorado–extinct and Barro Colorado–persistent species. Paradoxically, loss rates for Barro Colorado–extinct species were lower than loss rates for Barro Colorado–persistent species. Sieving then discovered that absolute rates of nest loss were less important than the relative change in predation rate from mainland to island; that is, for species now extinct on Barro Colorado, predation on the island increased by 100% relative to the mainland rate for those species. For species that persisted on the island, predation rates increased by only 30%.

Apparently, species whose nests are less exposed to predation on the mainland are less able to renest after a loss to predation and therefore are unable to compensate for the higher predation occurring on Barro Colorado. Over evolutionary time, species-specific rates of nest loss associated with nest design and placement may determine a species' ability to replace clutches, thereby determining patterns of extinction on Barro Colorado Island. For each species, the interaction between intrinsic (autecological) and extrinsic (environmental) factors determined the fate of its population on the island (Sieving and Karr 1997).

Does inbreeding in small populations account for extinctions on Barro Colorado Island? Blood samples of birds from Pipeline Road, Barro Colorado, and other Gatun Lake islands were evaluated for genetic similarity using DNA fingerprinting. Inbreeding was detected in bird populations on Barro Colorado and nearby Gatun Lake islands (Sieving and Karr 1996). But this inbreeding does not seem to be a contributor to Barro Colorado extinctions, at least over ecological (<100 years) time scales.

Studies of avian extinctions on Barro Colorado provide insight into the number, identity, and attributes of species susceptible to local extinction. Extinction of birds on the island is not random at the species or guild level; it can be attributed to numerous factors, including disproportionate losses of large and specialized species and of species from undergrowth and foothill forest. In addition to these factors, demographic attributes (fecundity, rates of adult survival and recruitment, and population variability) interact in complex ways to vary the risk of extinction among species. Life histories that balance susceptibility to nest predation with the ability to replace clutches are essential for persistence on Barro Colorado. Differential extinction rates on the mainland and island demonstrate the importance of the local and regional habitat mosaic as a determinant of extinction probability. Genetic factors do not seem to be important, at least over ecological time scales. Environmental factors increasing the mortality rate at any life stage should be the focus for management of insular reserves.

---

ter 4), a well-established theory with supporting empirical evidence drawn from on-the-ground analyses around the world (MacArthur and Wilson 1967; Case and Cody 1987; Ricklefs 1990; Shafer 1991). The theory states that the number of species in a given area increases as the zth power of area, where z generally ranges between 0.2 and 0.35. (Recall from Chapter 4 that $S = cA^z$; the model is also discussed in greater detail in Chapter 9 and presented in Figure 9.5). This species–area relationship also means that the number of species declines as area is lost. So when a habitat loses 90% of its original extent, it can no longer support, as a very rough average, about 50% of its original species (Figure 5.5).

How likely is this estimate to be correct? It depends upon the status of the remaining 10% of habitat. If this relict expanse is split into many small pieces (as is often the case with remnant tracts of tropical forests), a further "islandizing effect" comes into play, reducing the stock of surviving species still more. Similarly, if most of the species concerned occur in small, local endemic communities, the percentage loss of species can be so high as to approach the percentage loss of area. On the other hand, if the species are largely widespread and not endemic to narrow regions, less than a 50% loss could occur with a 90% habitat reduction. So the 90%/50% species–area calculation for extinctions could be a minimum estimate, a reasonable estimate,

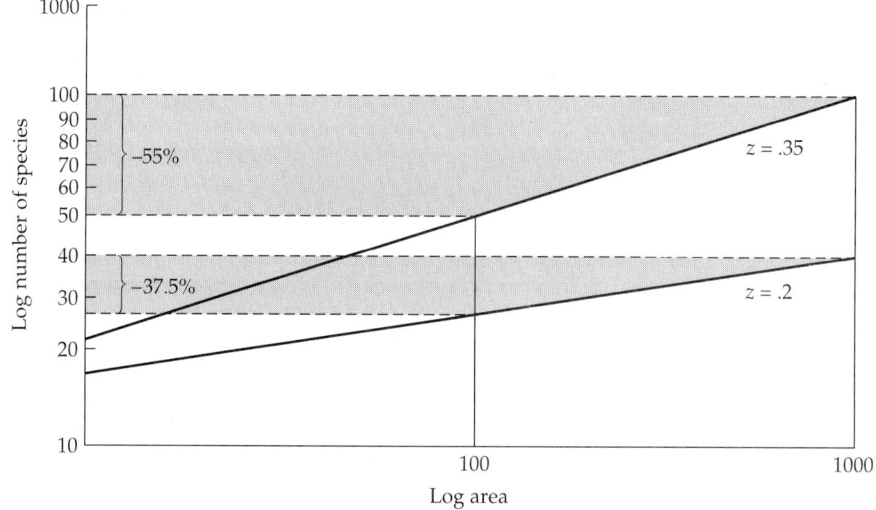

Figure 5.5 Species–area relationships based on the equation $S = cA^z$, with $c = 10$ and $z = 0.2$ or 0.35. Note that a 90% decrease in area, from 1000 to 100 ha, would result in a predicted loss of from 37.5% to 55% of the species, depending on the particular value of z. Greater z values (steeper species–area relationships) imply greater species losses per unit area.

or could overestimate losses, depending on the specific circumstances. These estimates are also a function of the quality of the remaining habitat, as well as the taxa involved. Certain taxa are more able than others to overcome habitat loss; for example, some birds and butterflies can disperse more readily than can other species.

The broadest application of island biogeography to tropical deforestation and species extinctions has been presented by one of the authors of the original theory, E. O. Wilson (1989, 1992). He has calculated that, on the basis of a 1% annual deforestation rate (as was assumed to be the case at the time of his analysis in the late 1980s), tropical forests have been losing between 0.2% and 0.3% of their species per year. Wilson further assumed that tropical forests contain only 2 million species, so he calculated that the annual tropical forest loss has amounted to somewhere between 4000 and 6000 species per year. But the annual forest destruction rate is now 2%, and the species stock is more realistically taken to be at least 5 million species (possibly 6 million, and conceivably many more). Using Wilson's analytic model, this means that the annual species loss in tropical forests could be between 20,000 and 30,000 per year, or 50 to 80 per day. Wilson has refined his earlier estimate upward in light of more recent and substantive data, postulating an annual loss of 27,000 species, or about 75 per day, in tropical forests alone (Wilson 1992).

Note, however (as Wilson has repeatedly emphasized), that these are optimistic calculations. If we employ a more realistic assessment, and qualitatively incorporate a number of factors other than habitat destruction, such as diseases, alien introductions, and overhunting, the annual total could be larger. The annual extinction rate in tropical forests alone means that we are witnessing a rate far above the "natural" rate of extinctions before the advent of the human era, considered to be perhaps one species every few years (Raup 1991a,b). So the present global extinction rate is roughly 100,000 times higher than the background rate.

A skeptic may ask, if extinctions are occurring in such large numbers right now, why are they not individually documented? How much solid evidence is there? To this, the pragmatic scientist responds that it is far easier to demonstrate that a species exists than that it does not. To achieve the first, all one has to do is to find a few specimens. To achieve the second with absolute certainty, one must search every last locality of the species' range before being sure. This is fine for the purist, but we live in a world with insufficient scientists, funding, and above all, time to undertake a conclusive check. Given that we are witnessing a mass extinction of exceptional scope, it seems sufficient to make a best-judgment assessment of what is going on, and in cases of uncertainty, assume that a species that has not been seen for decades is in fact extinct until it is proven to be extant.

This is the situation for large numbers of species. Recall the 90 endemic plant species of the Centinela ridge, where outright deforestation has eliminated all natural vegetation. Yet the plants have not officially been declared extinct; conservation organizations generally require that a species fail to be recorded for 50 years before it can be designated extinct. In peninsular Malaysia, a 4-year search for 266 known species of freshwater fishes turned up only 122 of them (46%), yet they are all "officially" regarded as still in existence (Mohsin and Ambok 1983). In Lake Victoria, two-thirds of the former stock of 300 cichlid fish species, all but one of them endemic, have not been seen for years; even though they are not yet "officially" extinct, this species extinction spasm must rank as the greatest single extinction episode of vertebrate species in modern times (Ogutu-Ohwayo 1990; Baskin 1992; Lowe-

Table 5.4
Numbers of Plant and Animal Species Known to Have Gone Extinct Since 1600, and Officially Threatened with Extinction

Taxon	No. extinct since 1600	No. presently threatened[a]
Animals		
Corals	1	—
Mollusks	191	354
Crustaceans	4	126
Insects	61	873
Fishes	29	452
Amphibians	2	59
Reptiles	23	167
Birds	116	1029
Mammals	59	505
Total	486	3565
Plants		
Ferns and fern allies	16	—
Gymnosperms	2	242
Monocotyledons	120	4421
Monocotyledons: palms	4	925
Dicotyledons	462	17,474
Total	604	23,062

From Smith et al. 1993a.
[a]Includes IUCN categories of "vulnerable," "endangered," and "probably extinct."

McConnell 1993). Dozens more such instances can be cited, even though we have scarcely started to document the situation overall (Wilson 1992).

There have been, of course, well-documented extinctions in recent times, and even these modest numbers should give us pause for thought (Table 5.4). Well over 1000 species of plants and animals have been officially recorded as extinct since 1600, but given the extremely conservative criteria for extinction and our vast lack of knowledge of tropical invertebrate faunas, this is certainly a minuscule proportion of actual extinctions.

Through all of this, it should be borne in mind that we are dealing with the irreversible loss of unique life forms. It is not always possible to detail the precise survival status of tens of thousands of threatened plant species and millions of animal species. In light of the irreversibility and uniqueness involved, perhaps the burden of proof (recall Figure 2.3) should be shifted onto the shoulders of the skeptics, who should be asked to prove that a species still exists, rather than the reverse.

This raises a key question concerning species extinctions that also applies to many other environmental issues: what is "legitimate scientific caution" in the face of uncertainty? Uncertainty can cut both ways. Some observers may object that, in the absence of conclusive evidence and analysis, it is appropriate to stick with low estimates of species extinctions on the grounds that they are more "responsible" (though one could ask "responsible to whom?"). But what about asymmetry of evaluation? A low estimate, ostensibly "safe" (again, for whom?) because it takes a conservative view of limited evidence, may fail to reflect the real situation just as much as does an "unduly" high estimate. In a situation of uncertainty in which not all parameters can be quantified to conventional satisfaction, perhaps we should not become obsessed with what can be counted if that is to the detriment of what counts. Undue caution can readily become recklessness, and it will be better for us to find we have been roughly right than precisely wrong. An example of scientific caution and great uncertainty in extinction is illustrated by the possible global decline of amphibian species, which has made a great deal of news in both the scientific and popular press. The patterns and controversies are summarized in Essay 5B by Joseph Pechmann and David Wake.

ESSAY 5B
Declines and Disappearances of Amphibian Populations

Joseph H. K. Pechmann, Savannah River Ecology Laboratory, and David B. Wake, University of California, Berkeley

The 1990s were rung in with alarm bells concerning declines and disappearances of amphibian populations (Wake and Morowitz 1991). To be sure, much of this news was not new; it has long been obvious that habitat destruction and alteration, introduction of exotic species, pollution, and other human activities have been exacting an increasingly heavy toll upon amphibians as well as other fauna and flora. The problems of frogs, toads, and salamanders, however, had hitherto been relatively neglected. A 1990 National Research Council workshop (Wake and Morowitz 1991) served as a wake-up call concerning the accelerating losses of amphibian biodiversity.

Some of the declines and disappearances of amphibian populations that had occurred since the 1970s were, however, new and unusual in one respect: their causes were unknown. These unexplained losses had taken place in isolated areas relatively protected from most human impacts. For example, the harlequin frog and the only known populations of the golden toad, as well as a number of other species of amphibians, disappeared from the Monteverde Cloud Forest Reserve in Costa Rica during the late 1980s (Crump et al. 1992; Pounds and Crump 1994). Twenty of the 49 species of anurans known to occur in the reserve were still missing in 1996, eight years following the crash (Pounds and Fogden 1996). A number of frogs endemic to the tropical and subtropical montane rainforest streams of eastern Australia disappeared (seven species) or declined (at least four) since the late 1970s, including the gastric-brooding frogs *Rheobatrachus silus* and *R. vitellinus* (Czechura and Ingram 1990; McDonald 1990; Tyler 1991; Ingram and McDonald 1993; Richards et al. 1993). Ranid frogs and bufonid toads suffered a similar fate in many parts of the western United States, including the areas in and around Sequoia, Kings Canyon, and Yosemite National Parks (Fellers and Drost 1993; Sherman and Morton 1993; Bradford et al. 1994a; Stebbins and Cohen 1995; Drost and Fellers 1996). Diurnal hylodine frogs and other species were reduced or lost in areas of the Atlantic forest of Brazil sampled by Heyer et al. (1988) and Weygoldt (1989). At the El Yunque forest reserve in Puerto Rico, two species of *Eleutherodactylus* became extinct, and five populations of three others apparently disappeared (Joglar and Burrowes 1996). In some of these locations the plot was complicated by the fact that not all sympatric amphibian species appeared to be affected.

Numerous hypotheses have been suggested to explain these puzzling changes in population sizes and distributions, including increased ultraviolet radiation resulting from ozone depletion or other aspects of global change, acid precipitation, pathogens (some perhaps introduced or spread by humans), long-distance transport of chemical pollutants, subtle habitat changes, introduction of nonindigenous species, and natural fluctuations. There is no support for the view that there is a single, global cause; rather, populations probably have declined or disappeared for different reasons. Also, several different factors may have affected any particular population, and the combined effect of several stressors can be worse than the sum of their individual effects.

While discussion of the competing hypotheses has at times been spirited (e.g., Blaustein 1994; Pechmann and Wilbur 1994; Blaustein et al. 1996; Licht 1996), scientific debate is not a sign of disarray. Rather, the questioning and testing of hypotheses is the lifeblood of the scientific method. There is a tension between this process and the need for conservationists and natural resource managers to reach a consensus and take action before it is too late to save populations and species (Blaustein 1994; McCoy 1994). It is difficult to mount a defense in those cases in which the enemy is unknown, however. If a population decline represents a natural fluctuation, no defense by humans may be necessary. Achieving the proper balance between scientific certainty and conservation action is a continual challenge.

In this essay, we discuss some of the hypotheses that have been proposed to account for the unexplained declines in amphibian populations. The reader should bear in mind that most of the threats to amphibians are well known, and that they threaten other biota as well. The decline and loss of many amphibian populations is beyond doubt, and the main cause—human activities—also seems clear. Knowing this, however, does not tell us in every case what particular dimensions of our activities have caused problems, nor why particular populations are in trouble.

Ultraviolet-B radiation has received much attention as a possible explanation for declines and losses of amphibian populations in comparatively undisturbed areas. The primary evidence for this hypothesis comes from a series of field experiments conducted in Oregon, USA, by Andrew Blaustein and colleagues (Blaustein et al. 1994a; Blaustein et al. 1995; Kiesecker and Blaustein 1995). These experiments demonstrated that egg mortality in the western toad, Cascades frog, and northwestern salamander was higher when the eggs were exposed to ambient levels of sunlight than when 100% of UV-B was blocked. UV-B had no effect on the survival of Pacific treefrog eggs in the same ponds. The Pacific treefrog was found to have higher levels of an enzyme, photolyase, that facilitates the repair of DNA damaged by UV-B.

The effects of UV-B throughout the life cycle of amphibians, including sublethal effects, should be examined in order to determine whether historical changes in UV-B and factors that influence its impacts are sufficient to have had effects on the population or landscape level. Ozone depletion is one factor that may have increased exposure of amphibians to UV-B, especially at mid- and high latitudes (Stolarski et al. 1992; Herman et al. 1996). Also, climate warming and anthropogenic acidification may have increased the depth to which UV-B penetrates aquatic habitats (Schindler et al. 1996; Yan et al. 1996). Perhaps in some cases UV-B acts primarily to increase the effects of other stressors. Kiesecker and Blaustein (1995) found that the effect of UV-B on western toad and Cascades frog eggs was virtually eliminated when a fungicide was used to remove *Saprolegnia*, a fungus known to kill eggs.

Pathogen infection is another appealing hypothesis that could explain losses of amphibians from many geographic regions. The experiment by Kiesecker and Blaustein (1995) found that *Saprolegnia* increased egg mortality even when the eggs were shielded from UV-B. *Saprolegnia* has been widespread in the environment in Oregon and worldwide for many years, however, so an interaction with some additional stress, such as drought or increased UV-B, must be invoked to explain recent losses (Blaustein et al. 1994b). Another possibility is that the stocking of fish, which carry *Saprolegnia*, has increased the incidence of the disease (Blaustein et al. 1994b).

Redleg (*Aeromonas hydrophila*) is a bacterial disease implicated in the disappearance of the boreal toad (*Bufo boreas*) from the mountains of Colorado (Carey 1993). As is the case for *Saprolegnia*, *Aeromonas* is a ubiquitous, long-established disease that affects fish as well as amphibians. *Aeromonas* is often a secondary infection that strikes animals weakened by natural or anthropogenic stressors. Carey (1993) has hypothesized that some unidentified anthropogenic stress has exacerbated the effects of *Aeromonas* on *B. boreas* in Colorado in recent years. Laurance et al. (1996) have hypothesized that an exotic epidemic disease, perhaps an iridovirus, is responsible for the catastrophic declines of Australian rainforest frogs. They have hypothesized further that human activities, such as the international trade in aquarium fishes, introduced the disease to Australia and elsewhere. Although some characteristics of the Australian declines are consistent with the disease hypothesis, they are also consistent with other hypotheses.

Acid precipitation has probably had negative effects on some amphibian populations, such as natterjack toads at heathland sites in Britain (Beebee et al. 1990). Experiments conducted by Harte and Hoffman (1989) on a Rocky Mountain population of tiger salamanders suggested that episodic acidification associated with the release of contaminants into breeding ponds during snowmelt resulted in deformities and mortality of embryos, and consequently a decline in population size during the mid-1980s. Wissinger and Whiteman (1992) documented a rebound in numbers in this population beginning in the late 1980s. They found that during their study, the salamanders either bred after the spring acidity pulse or the pulse was benign, and suggested that the 1980s decline may have been related to pond drying. Chemical analyses of water samples suggested that anthropogenic acid precipitation is an unlikely explanation for declines and disappearances of amphibians in other parts of the Rocky Mountains (Corn and Vertucci 1992; Vertucci and Corn 1996), the Sierra Nevada (Bradford et al. 1994b), the tropical rainforest of Australia (Richards et al. 1993), and the Monteverde Cloud Forest Reserve in Costa Rica (Crump et al. 1992). Additional data on within-year variation and long-term trends in acidity at breeding sites in these regions, and on the sublethal effects of acidity on species of concern, are necessary for definitive evaluation of the acid precipitation hypothesis.

Predation and competition from introduced species may have been responsible for the declines of some amphibians. The American bullfrog was introduced in California before the turn of the 20th century and has long been implicated in the disappearance of the red-legged frog from much of its range in the Central Valley and the Sierra Nevada foothills (Moyle 1973; Hayes and Jennings 1986). Its effect on populations of the lowland yellow-legged frog in northwestern California has been documented recently (Kupferberg 1996). The introduction of trout for sport-fishing is thought to have been an important factor in the disappearance of Sierra Nevada frogs (Hayes and Jennings 1986; Bradford 1989). All but 20 of the 4131 mountain lakes of the state were fishless in the 1830s (Knapp 1996). Stocking of lakes in Yosemite National Park reached a million fish each year in the 1930s and 1940s, and may have gradually reduced the number of permanent source lakes that harbored base populations of frogs. Thus as frogs gradually disappeared from small, semi-isolated lakes as a result of predation or drought, chances of recolonization became steadily reduced. Declines of amphibians were most dramatic many years after the most intense stocking activity, so it is unlikely that introduced fish are the main culprit (Drost and Fellers 1996).

Chemical pollutants that were previously undetected or whose effects have been underestimated represent another possible explanation for declines and disappearances of amphibians in areas that appear to be relatively undisturbed (Berrill et al. 1993; Stebbins and Cohen 1995). For example, atmospheric transport of pesticides from California's Central Valley to the Sierra Nevada has recently been documented (Zabik and Seiber 1993). Researchers have now begun to realize that extremely low doses of pesticides and other synthetic chemicals, especially mixtures of them, may mimic, block, or disrupt natural hormones (Stebbins and Cohen 1995; Arnold et al. 1996); these substances may affect embryonic development as well as adult reproduction (Guillette et al. 1995). Thus, levels of synthetic compounds that were previously considered "safe" for wildlife may have significant effects on populations.

Population sizes of amphibians, like those of other groups, may fluctuate widely due to natural causes. Drought, predation, and other natural factors may cause local populations to go extinct, necessitating recolonization from other sites. Some declines and disappearances of amphibian populations in areas little affected by humans may be natural occurrences from which the populations may eventually recover on their own, provided that source populations exist elsewhere in the general area (Blaustein et al. 1994c; Pechmann and Wilbur 1994). Natural processes have been hypothesized to account for the losses of the golden toad and harlequin frog (drought, Crump et al. 1992; Pounds and Crump 1994), declines and extinctions in the Atlantic forest of Brazil (severe frost and drought, Heyer et al. 1988; Weygoldt 1989), and the loss of some montane populations of the northern leopard frog in Colorado (drought and demographic stochasticity, Corn and Fogleman 1984). Natural fluctuations may also interact with human influences, resulting in losses from which recovery may be unlikely. For example, Bradford (1991) and Bradford et al. (1993) hypothesized that natural processes had eliminated some populations of the mountain yellow-legged frog, but that stocking of predatory fish in streams used by the frogs as dispersal corridors prevents recolonization of these sites.

Pechmann et al. (1991) used 12 years of census data for amphibians breeding at a pond in South Carolina to illustrate how extreme natural fluctuations may be, and how difficult it can be to distinguish them from declines due to human activities (see Figure 12.5; see also Semlitsch et al. 1996 for an update and data for additional species). Even "long-term" ecological studies rarely capture the full range of variability in population sizes (Pechmann and Wilbur 1994; Blaustein et al. 1994c), because the observed variation may continue to increase over time (even after 100 years for some insects, Hanski 1990). Several authors have argued that the unexplained declines and disappearances they have observed in amphibian populations over the last 20 years are too extreme, too widespread, or too long-lasting to be natural fluctuations (e.g., Drost and Fellers 1996; Laurance et al. 1996). However, inadequate data exist at present to formulate a "null model" of the expected distribution of trends in amphibian populations around the world, against which recent losses could be compared (Blaustein et al. 1994c; Pechmann and Wilbur 1994; Travis 1994).

Numerous documented declines and disappearances of amphibian populations remain unexplained, although many hypotheses have been proposed. The current thinking of the majority of researchers is that there are probably many interacting causes for these losses. Perhaps the only certainty is that *Homo sapiens* is a major culprit in the biodiversity crisis affecting amphibians and other taxa.

So much for the current extinction rate. What about the future? Through detailed analyses backed by abundant documentation, Wilson (1992) concludes that we face the prospect of losing 20% of all species within 30 years and 50% or more thereafter. Another long-standing expert in this area, Peter Raven (1990), calculates that one-sixth of all plant species, and, by implication, of all animal species, occur in the tropical forests of just three countries, Colombia, Ecuador, and Peru, and that these three countries appear likely to lose virtually all their forest cover within another three decades; hence, their species communities will be largely eliminated. Based on a further and more extensive calculation, Raven believes that half of all species exist in tropical forests that will be reduced to less than one-tenth of their present expanse within the same three decades. So in accord with island biogeography, Raven concludes that one-fourth of all plant species are likely to be eliminated during the next 30 years, and that "fully half of total species may disappear before the close of the 21st century." These estimates are in line with those of several other analysts (Myers 1986, 1990a,b; Diamond 1989; Club of Earth 1990; May 1992b).

Of course, the calculations leading to such extinction rate estimates are only as good as the assumptions and data that go into them. Actual estimates of species losses, like estimates of habitat losses, vary greatly. Box 5B discusses this issue and compares some of the extinction estimates that have been proposed, showing the variation involved. Regardless of the precision of these various estimates, the message is clear: large numbers of species are already

BOX 5B
Quantifying Extinction Rates
Approaches and Limitations

Martha J. Groom, North Carolina State University

Conservation biologists concur that human activities are accelerating the pace of extinction among most taxa across the globe. The expansion of human populations has caused extinctions of countless species, and threatens the persistence of still more, via overharvesting, exotic species introductions, environmental contamination, and widespread alteration of landscapes and climatic patterns. Yet, we know little about the details of the taxonomic and geographic patterns of extinction. We also have only an imprecise understanding of the mechanisms that drive increases in extinction probabilities.

Extinction rates have been measured in a variety of ways. Most commonly, and as presented to this point, estimates of the rate of habitat loss (particularly deforestation) are combined with estimates of species numbers (derived from species–area curves or from more direct data, such as field surveys) to produce an overall prediction of the numbers of species expected to go extinct over some time period. Table A provides a number of examples of predictions for global species loss due to tropical deforestation. These estimates vary enormously, primarily because authors have chosen different baseline estimates of (1) the number of species extant in the world (range 3–10 million), (2) the proportion of species found in tropical rainforests (range 25%–75%), (3) the shape of the relationship between habitat loss and extinction, and (4) the rate and extent of habitat loss (range 0.5%–2.0% annual global deforestation).

Extinction estimates such as these suffer from a number of limitations. Foremost among these is the enormous uncertainty in our estimates of the numbers of species worldwide, as has already been discussed. Here, I will stress that the extreme inequities in the degree to which particular taxa are known (e.g., contrast birds with insects or nematodes) will impinge on our ability to estimate extinction rates wherever undescribed or unstudied taxa dominate the total biodiversity (e.g., in tropical rainforests, the majority of the diversity may be insect taxa, the majority of which may be undescribed; Erwin 1982). However, we may be able to improve our estimates for such speciose, unstudied, and difficult-to-measure groups (such as insects, nematodes, fungi, microorganisms) by extrapolation of species numbers from carefully designed sampling protocols (Colwell and Coddington 1994; Hammond 1994).

The problems of estimating habitat loss were discussed in detail in Box 5A. Besides questioning the accuracy of habitat loss estimates themselves, we should ask which types of habitat alterations are included, and how they are predicted to affect extinction risk. For example, habitat loss usually is accompanied by several forms of habitat degradation, including fragmentation effects, and increased hunting pressures. Turner (1996) found that the majority of studies showed an increase in local extinctions with fragmentation of tropical forests. Thus, degraded forests may lose species, though perhaps not as rapidly as forests destroyed outright. Usually, losses due to habitat degradation are not included in extinction estimates (e.g., Wilson 1992), which therefore may tend to underestimate this component of extinction. Similarly, as cleared areas of forest recover, they will be able to support more species again. Extinction estimates usually ignore recovery processes, and thus may overestimate extinction rates.

We probably know the least about the shape of the relationship between habitat loss and extinctions. Authors must choose a relationship fairly arbitrarily, either set directly as a level of extinction per area of habitat lost or set indirectly using a species–area curve. For example, several authors have assumed that 50% of species will be so localized in their distribution that they will go extinct following local deforestation, whereas the remaining 50% will be broadly enough distributed, or sufficiently mobile, to persist in undisturbed areas. Existing data on species losses for even severely degraded areas suggest that this estimate may be too pessimistic. Avian extinctions in Puerto Rico and Singapore were 12% and 28% of the original species respectively, despite the loss of more than 99% of the primary forest cover (Brash 1987; Corlett 1992). However, the loss of 44% of the freshwater fish species in Singapore (Corlett 1992) may be more indicative of the probable losses of less mobile species. The use of species–area curves also lacks

Table A
Some Estimates of Global Species Loss Due to Tropical Deforestation, and Their Assumptions

	Assumptions			
Extinction estimate	**Total no. species (millions)/% tropical**	**Tropical forest loss**	**Extinction/area lost**	**Source**
1 species/hr by 2000	5–10/40%–70%	245,000 km^2/yr	50% of species extinct when 10% area left	Myers 1979
1 million species by 2000	5/40%	33% of remaining forests destroyed by 2000	50% of species in area will go extinct	Myers 1985
10% of all species by 2000; 25% of all species by 2015	4–5/50%	2% deforestation/yr	50% of species in area will go extinct	Raven 1988
17,500 species/yr	10/50%	0.7% deforestation/yr	50% of species in area will go extinct	Wilson 1988a
8.8% of all species by 2000	3–10/25%	12.3% deforestation between 1980 and 2000	Concave curve[a]	Lugo 1988
5%–38% of all species between 1990 and 2020	10/>50%	0.8%–1.6% deforestation/yr	Species–area curve; $z = 0.15, 0.35$	Reid and Miller 1989
27,000 species/yr	10 in tropical rainforests	1.8% deforestation/yr	Species–area curve; $z = 0.15$	Wilson 1992
20% of all Neotropical plant species between 1950 and 1992	60,000 in Neotropical forests	18.7% lost between 1950 and 1992	Simulation model	Koopowitz et al. 1994

[a]Corresponds to curve D in Figure 1, p. 329 of Lovejoy 1980.

Table B
Predicted Extinction Rates within Selected Vertebrate Groups Calculated from the Revised IUCN Threatened Species List[a]

Taxon	"Critical" %	"Endangered" %	"Vulnerable" %	Est.% extinct in 100 yrs	Est. no. yrs to 50% extinct
Boidae	6	12	35	17	365
Iguanidae	4	8	56	15	428
Anseriformes	5	8	20	16	404
Psittaciformes	7	8	24	15	421
Bucerotidae	10	30	40	34	166
Marsupiala	3	11	34	14	453
Canidae	6	12	21	16	403

Modified from Mace 1994.
[a]Categories proposed by Mace et al. 1992.

an empirical basis in many applications. Compounded, all these sources of uncertainty in extinction estimates can lead to extremely large errors (Simberloff 1986). Yet, despite the disparity in methods used, these extinction estimates all point to the same pessimistic conclusions (May et al. 1995).

Mace and her colleagues (Mace et al. 1992; Mace 1994) recently proposed an alternative approach to categorizing extinction risk, as well as estimating extinction rates in well-known taxa. Extinction risk is assigned according to a combination of several quantitative criteria, including rates of decline in population size, the size of the population (or average size of subpopulations in fragmented species), and the size of the species' geographic range (Mace 1994). Extinction rates can then be estimated from the distribution of taxa within four categories of predicted extinction risk: "critical" (50% risk of extinction in 5 years or 2 generations), "endangered" (20% risk of extinction over 20 years or 10 generations), "vulnerable" (10% risk of extinction in 100 years), or "safe" (0% chance of extinction in 100 years). This approach yields predictions for specific taxa (Table B) that are in rough agreement with those found in Table A, despite the great difference in the methodology used in their calculation. The approach advocated by Mace and her colleagues, as well as other approaches emphasizing the use of data bases of species numbers, such as the IUCN Red Data lists (e.g., Smith et al. 1993a,b), has the advantage that it emphasizes the use of information about species in calculating extinction risk, and thus may be more likely to produce accurate predictions. However, only for a few taxonomic groups is there sufficient information to make quantitative assessments of extinction risk; thus, these methods are not suitable for use in obtaining regional estimates of total extinction rate.

The most helpful aspect of the approach advocated by Mace may be its focus on strong predictors of extinction risk, or in other words, on the mechanisms of extinction, rather than on the crude trends in extinction statistics. By focusing on the mechanisms of extinction, we may be better able to design reserve systems and management strategies that will protect biodiversity. In this vein, researchers have surveyed mass extinction events in the fossil record to identify attributes that correlate with high extinction rates within and among taxa (e.g., Jablonski 1994), and have analyzed contemporary species loss data to identify extinction-prone guilds (e.g., for birds, Kattan et al. 1992; for insects, Thomas and Morris 1995; for plants, Leach and Givnish 1996).

Koopowitz et al. (1994) take yet another approach. Assuming that rarity in terms of the number of occurrences across a landscape confers a high extinction risk, Koopowitz and his colleagues took distribution profiles for Neotropical plant species and assessed total loss in plant biodiversity as a function of the rate of habitat loss and the number of sites occupied by each species. In general, their model suggests that approximately 3000 species have been lost over the past 40 years, and that a total of 37.4% of all Neotropical plant species would go extinct if 90% of the Amazon Basin were to be converted from primary forest to other uses. The use of such simulation studies, coupled with statistical analyses of detailed data sets, may hold promise for providing more detailed and accurate predictions of extinction risk.

Despite the many limitations to our methods of estimating extinction rates, it seems clear that a large extinction event is now occurring. Indeed, despite the variety of ways in which these estimates are calculated, all are chilling: 10–20% of most taxa are expected to go extinct over a period ranging from a few decades to a century. While it may be critical to obtain more precise estimates of losses in particular circumstances, imprecise estimates and the "need for further study" are no excuse for inaction. The crucial point is that these figures constitute a strong signal that we cannot ignore.

going extinct, and still larger numbers will go extinct unless prevailing patterns of habitat destruction stop, and are eventually reversed.

Critical Regional Losses: Hot Spots of Extinction

The above calculations based on species–area relationships represent a generalized mode of estimating the present extinction rate in tropical forests. This

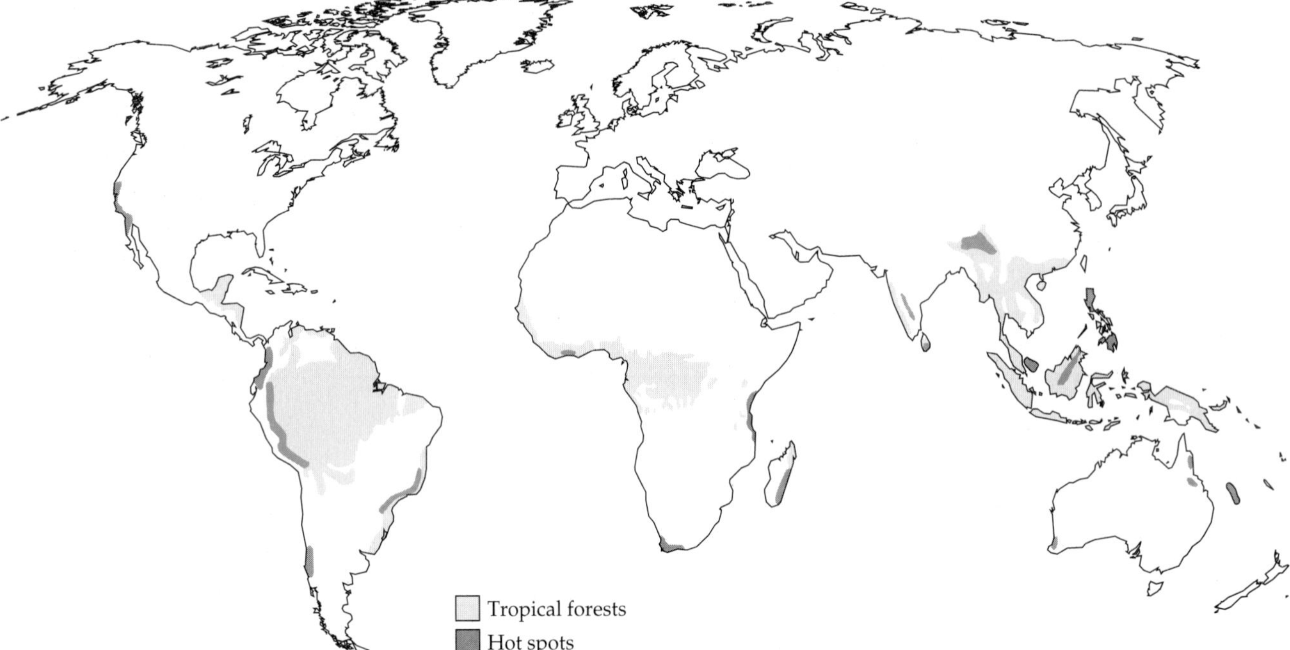

Figure 5.6 The extent of tropical forests ca. 1950, and the 18 global "hot spots" of biodiversity so far identified. These hot spots, mostly in tropical systems, contain a disproportionately high level of species diversity in very small areas.

method is applied at the biome level, making little allowance for local circumstances. Fortunately, we have a parallel set of calculations at the local level, in the form of a "hot spots" analysis relating to areas that feature exceptional concentrations of species with extraordinary levels of endemism, and face an exceptional threat of imminent habitat destruction (Myers 1988, 1990a, 1996).

The analysis reveals that 14 hot spots occur in tropical forests: Madagascar, the Atlantic coast of Brazil, western Ecuador, the Colombian Chocó, the uplands of western Amazonia, the eastern Himalayas, Peninsular Malaysia, northern Borneo, the Philippines, New Caledonia, southwestern Côte d'Ivoire, Tanzania, the western Ghats in India, and southwestern Sri Lanka (Figure 5.6; see also Table 4.3). Their collective expanse is less than the size of California, and constitutes less than 5% of remaining undisturbed forests. They contain more than 37,000 endemic plant species, or 15% of all plant species, in less than 311,000 km^2, or just 0.2% of the earth's land surface.

Four other hot spots occur in Mediterranean biomes: California, central Chile, the southern tip of South Africa, and southwestern Australia (Figure 5.6). They contain 12,720 endemic plant species in a collective expanse of 435,700 km^2, or 0.3% of the earth's land surface. Adding the two sets of hot spots together, 50,000 endemic plant species, or a full 20% of all plant species, face severe threat of habitat destruction in 746,700 km^2, or 0.5% of the earth's land surface (Myers 1990a).

The hot spots also contain a still higher, though unquantified, proportion of the earth's animal species (Myers 1988, 1990a). Species–area inventories in diverse sectors of tropical forests, among other biomes, suggest there are at least 40 animal species for every plant species, assuming a minimum planetary total of all species of 10 million. If the planetary total is in fact 30 million, and accepting that virtually all the additional species are animal species, then the 18 hot spots described contain a minimum of 2 million endemic animal species—threatened just as much as are the plant species.

Six of the hot spots (the Atlantic coast of Brazil, western Ecuador, the Philippines, New Caledonia, southwestern Côte d'Ivoire, and southwestern

Sri Lanka) have already lost 90% or more of their original habitat expanse, and if recent land use trends continue without acceleration, the rest are expected to lose 90% within the opening decade or two of the 21st century. If we apply the 90%/50% species–area relationship, these regions will lose at least half of their species within the foreseeable future.

Hot spots occur elsewhere, though as yet they have not been documented and analyzed in much detail. The most prominent of such localities are in certain wetlands (including swamps, rivers, and lakes), coral reefs, and montane environments. According to a preliminary and exploratory appraisal by Myers (1996), these additional hot spots may constitute the sole habitats of at least 5% of all plant species and a higher proportion of animal species. In turn, this means that at least one-fourth of all species are confined to hot spots. If we accept that, in the absence of conservation efforts of sufficient scope and scale, we can anticipate the loss of one-half of all species within the foreseeable future, the hot spots analysis suggests that we can make substantial progress simply by safeguarding a handful of top-ranked biodiversity areas.

The analytic strategy based on hot spots is supported by recent research on birds (Bibby et al. 1992). As many as 2609 species, or over one-fourth of the earth's 9000-plus bird species, are confined to just 2% of the earth's land surface. They are located in 221 endemic bird areas (EBAs) with a maximum expanse of 50,000 km^2; more than three-fourths of these areas are in the tropics, notably in tropical forests. These areas accommodate 70% of all bird species recognized to be threatened or endangered, and also are vitally important for the conservation of large numbers of species of plants, mammals and other vertebrates, and insects and other invertebrates. If these EBAs lost 90% of their habitats, and the remaining 10% were completely protected, we could still witness the eventual demise of half their bird species, well over 1000 species and more than 10% of the world's avifauna. Fortunately, half of the species are found in just 46 EBAs, lending themselves to hot spots treatment for strategic planning on the part of conservationists.

The protection of hot spots obviously should be a high global priority. But how are biodiversity protection priorities set in more general terms? How do we face the awesome task of protecting so much diversity that is being lost so quickly? Such issues are addressed in Essay 5C, by Russell Mittermeier and Adrian Forsyth.

ESSAY 5C

Setting Priorities for Biodiversity Conservation

One Organization's Approach

Russell A. Mittermeier and Adrian B. Forsyth, Conservation International

Maintenance of biological diversity is now recognized in many circles as the single highest conservation priority of our time. Biological diversity is our living natural resource base, our biological capital in the global bank. Unfortunately, although interest in the global environment is growing, and more resources are being made available, we still have only a tiny fraction of the resources, both human and financial, to get the job done. Consequently, we have to put available resources to use in the best possible ways, applying them to areas containing the highest concentrations of diversity and areas at immediate risk of disappearing. To do this effectively, we need priority-setting methodologies based on the best scientific information available.

In several ways, Conservation International has placed a great deal of emphasis on priority setting. We have done it at a global level, refining Norman Myers' concept of "threatened hot spots," 18 areas around the tropics that together occupy only 0.5% of the land surface of the planet, and yet may hold a third or more of all terrestrial species diversity and a much higher percentage of the diversity at greatest risk. We have done it with the "major tropical wilderness areas" concept, which recognizes the value of the last few major blocks of undisturbed tropical forest. We have done it with the "megadiversity country" concept, highlighting the importance of the political entities that harbor the largest chunks of global biodiversity. And we are now looking at a series of global priority-setting exercises for other major categories of ecosystems, such as deserts, dry forests, savannas, wetlands, Mediterranean biomes, and marine systems.

As the next step down in the "hierarchy of priority setting," we have focused on the regional workshop concept, in which a group of experts on a threatened hot spot, a major wilderness area, or a key country get together for several weeks and pool their information using the most up-to-date mapping data and computerized Geographic Information Systems. The maps and other materials emerging from such an exercise are powerful planning tools and can often serve to catalyze action in a way that goes beyond the actual data that they provide.

All of the above priority-setting exercises make use of the best available information (both published, and in the minds of the world's biodiversity experts) to provide the soundest scientific underpinning for the hard conservation choices that need to be made in the next few years. Inevitably, many information gaps exist simply because the field of biodiversity conservation is a new one and the amount of actual fieldwork that has been conducted is still minimal relative to the size of the priority areas identified. Although the 18 hot spots thus far identified occupy only 0.5% of the land surface of the planet, they still cover several hundred thousand square kilometers, only a tiny fraction of which has been properly inventoried. To fill some of the gaps in our knowledge and to refine our data base, Conservation International (CI) created the Rapid Assessment Program (RAP) in 1989.

RAP is a biological inventory program designed to provide the information necessary to catalyze conservation action and improve biodiversity protection. The purpose of RAP is to quickly collect, analyze, and disseminate information on poorly known areas that are potentially important biodiversity conservation sites. RAP works by assembling teams of top-notch tropical biologists and host country scientists to generate first-cut, on-the-ground assessments of the biological value of different sites.

The core members of the RAP team are four of the world's most experienced field biologists, representing more than 100 years of accumulated field time. They are combined with a number of other scientists who together examine an area's species diversity, its degree of endemism, the uniqueness of the ecosystem, and the degree of risk of extinction on a national and global scale. As a conservation tool, RAP provides a primarily qualitative assessment and precedes long-term scientific inventory and research by establishing the relative importance of the site in question in regional and global terms. This unique tool helps us further refine our conservation strategies.

We recognize the fundamental importance of long-term field studies at key sites and are actively involved in promoting such work. However, we believe that the tremendous time pressure under which we are operating makes it essential that we have this capacity for top-quality rapid assessment of as many unknown or poorly known ecosystems as possible in order to efficiently direct conservation activities. This is the principle role of the CI RAP team.

It is important to point out that, while the program is conducted under the auspices of Conservation International, its results are for the international conservation community at large. We readily make available all reports in draft form both to the host governments of the countries being surveyed and to any other interested scientists and organizations. The ultimate purpose of the RAP team is to generate the best possible conservation action on behalf of our planet's biological diversity, that legacy of life that is so critical to us all.

The priority-setting exercises discussed here are not a form of triage. The biological resources of all nations are valuable to them, and worthy of being conserved and used sustainably. By setting priorities, we are merely facing reality by suggesting that levels of investment be at least roughly proportional to the richness and uniqueness of different ecosystems and the degree of threat under which they exist.

Patterns of Species Vulnerability

So far we have looked at entire communities of species at risk. Let us now consider three categories of species that appear to be unduly vulnerable to extinction.

Rare Species. In *On the Origin of Species* (1859), Charles Darwin observed that "rarity is the attribute of a vast number of species in all classes, in all countries." Indeed, in most biotas studied, many, and sometimes the majority of, species are to some degree rare. That is, a few species tend to be very common and dominate the biota, some species are at an intermediate range of abundance, and many species are quite rare. This pattern is illustrated in Figure 5.7 for fish species in several streams of the central Savannah River drainage in South Carolina, where about one-third to three-fourths of the fauna may be said to be rare, depending on criteria chosen. In general, rarity should make a species more vulnerable to both natural and human-induced extinction.

But rarity is not a simple concept. A species may be rare in at least seven different ways, based on different distributional patterns (Rabinowitz et al. 1986). A species may be rare because of a highly restricted geographic range, because of high habitat specificity, because of small local population size, or because of various combinations of these characteristics (Table 5.5). Thus, for example, a species may be distributed across an entire continent (broad geographic range), be a habitat generalist (low habitat specificity), and yet be rare because it occurs at extremely low densities (small local population size) wherever it is found. Alternatively, a species may be locally superabundant, but be rare because it occurs in very specialized habitats that are geographically restricted.

Different types of rarity make species vulnerable to different extinction processes. For example, a locally abundant species that occurs at only one location (such as the Devils Hole pupfish, discussed earlier, or many other highly endemic species) is extremely vulnerable to local stochastic events or intentional habitat destruction. A broadly distributed species that exists at low population sizes may weather such events quite well, but be more vulnerable to loss of genetic diversity and inbreeding (discussed in Chapter 6). A broadly distributed habitat specialist, such as a wetland annual, is vulnerable to any broad influences that affect its particular habitat, such as pollution, reduced rainfall, or climate change. Narrowly distributed specialists may be even more vulnerable to extinction; Angermeier (1995) found that extinct species of Virginia fishes tended to be restricted to a single physiographic province, as well as being ecological specialists.

Recent, human-caused rarity may be more devastating than natural rarity if the species is not adapted to low numbers. Bighorn sheep of North America (Figure 5.8), which probably numbered as many as 2 million before European settlers arrived, now total only 5000 or so, living in small, widely scattered populations. Due to a lifestyle that induces each herd to form a strong attachment to its traditional range, the species is not inclined to colonize new territory, not even former habitat. Because the bighorn sheep is an exceptionally conservative creature, it now seems predestined to remain rare (Geist 1971).

Humans have also been known to drive very abundant species to or near extinction: witness the Passenger Pigeon, Carolina Parakeet, and bison of North America. Their former patterns of abundance did not prevent declines

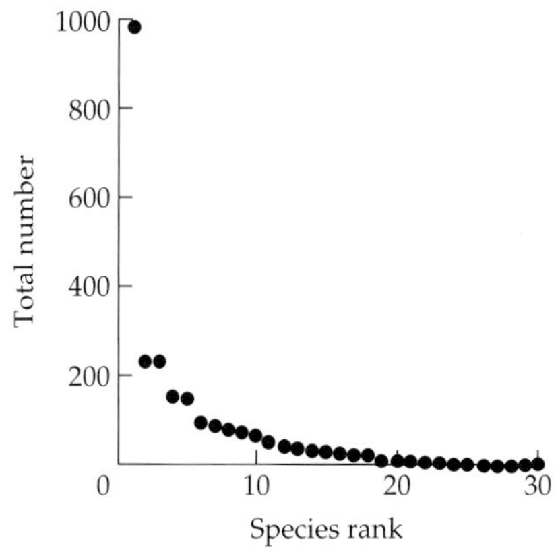

Figure 5.7 Rarity is a typical situation in most natural communities. In this assemblage of fishes from South Carolina streams, one species dominates, several are at intermediate levels of abundance, and many are naturally rare. (Data from Meffe and Sheldon 1988.)

Table 5.5
Seven Forms of Species Rarity, Based on Three Distributional Traits

Population size	Geographic range: Large		Geographic range: Small	
	Habitat specificity: Broad	**Habitat specificity: Restricted**	**Habitat specificity: Broad**	**Habitat specificity: Restricted**
Somewhere large	Common	Locally abundant over a large range in a specific habitat	Locally abundant in several habitats but restricted geographically	Locally abundant in a specific habitat but restricted geographically
Everywhere small	Constantly sparse over a large range and in several habitats	Constantly sparse in a specific habitat but over a large range	Constantly sparse and geographically restricted in several habitats	Constantly sparse and geographically restricted in a specific habitat

Figure 5.8 The bighorn sheep (*Ovis canadensis*), one of the examples of rarity that makes a species more vulnerable to extinction. Populations of the bighorn have been made very small by human activities, making the species more vulnerable to extinction due to small population size. (Photograph by David Scott.)

to extinction for the first two and near-extinction for the latter. Once driven to rarity, even once-abundant species are vulnerable. The Passenger Pigeon, hunted heavily by professionals in the late 19th century who were aided by railroad mobility and telegraph communication, was essentially prevented from successful colonial reproduction for two decades, driving it from superabundance to rarity to extinction (Blockstein and Tordoff 1985).

There are still other ways of becoming rare. The giant sequoia (*Sequoia gigantea*) of California was rare long before humans arrived on the scene. The tree has a restricted geographic range because it is a "relict" species, left over after geoecological change eliminated related species. The California Condor (*Gymnogyps californianus*) formerly had a broad geographic range, but its range contracted several centuries ago coincident with climate changes, and it became rare; its specialized lifestyle leaves it particularly vulnerable to further human disruption of its habitat.

There is a lengthy list of taxa that are even more restricted to small areas. An Arizona cactus survives in a valley less than 10 km long. The El Segundo blue butterfly (*Euphilotes battoides allyni*) lives on only a few hectares at the end of a runway at the Los Angeles airport. In Northern California, a critically imperiled butterfly, Lange's metalmark (*Apodemia mormo langei*), is confined to an 8 ha patch of sand dunes. The Laysan Teal (*Anas laysanensis*) inhabits the marshy shores of a 5 km^2 lagoon on a Hawaiian island. Numerous species of fishes, amphibians, and invertebrates occur in one or a few springs in desert regions. Rarity in all these cases lends itself to extinction vulnerability.

Rarity is especially a key characteristic of large numbers of tropical forest species (Elton 1973; Janzen 1975; Gilbert 1980). As previously noted, many species are confined to small areas, sometimes no more than a few tens or hundreds of square kilometers on an isolated ridge or in a single valley, and many have specialized lifestyles. Such species are particularly vulnerable to extinction through habitat disruption or destruction.

Thus, rarity of all types, be it natural or human-induced, is cause for special concern. This concern is even reflected in legal protection; almost by definition, most species listed under the U.S. Endangered Species Act or CITES are rare in some way. One of the keys to successfully stemming the tide of broad-scale extinctions is to act *before* species become rare, while they, and their habitats, are still common. This is one of the motivations behind setting aside lands and waters for conservation purposes; it not only protects the rare species in those localities, but should prevent the common species from becoming rare.

Long-Lived Species. Long-lived species typically have a suite of life history characteristics well suited to long-term predictability, but not conducive to rapid response to a human-disturbed world, let alone to population recovery in such a world. These characteristics include delayed sexual maturity (often one or more decades), low fecundity, reliance on high juvenile survivorship, and cessation of reproduction and protection of adults when times are bad. Together, they mean that long-lived species have great difficulty responding to environmental changes that reduce their populations; that is, they cannot easily "bounce back" from major population declines because their reproductive rates are so low and they take so long to mature. In short, they are closely adjusted to the long-term capacity of their habitats to support them—a fine strategy for their particular evolutionary histories, but one that is unsuited to a contemporary world experiencing abundant disruptions at the hands of humans.

These unfortunates in our modern world include species that are overexploited (e.g., whales, rhinoceroses, elephants) and species that are losing criti-

(A)

(B)

cal habitat (e.g., great apes, sea turtles, some freshwater turtles, and many cranes and other large birds). They also include many others that are restricted to small, stable habitats and suffer local extinction (Figure 5.9).

If, through whatever cause, a long-lived species loses a large proportion of its numbers, it may prove unable to build up its population again, no matter what protective measures are provided (see Essay 7A). Because these species are particularly vulnerable to extinction due to their life history characteristics, their populations should be closely monitored and their habitats accorded special protection. One of the unique conservation problems with this group is that population declines may take many years to be noticeable simply because individuals live so long. Consequently, particular attention should be paid to population age structure and recruitment of juveniles into the population. Thus, special conservation action is needed to safeguard long-lived species while their numbers are still well above what would be acceptable levels for other types of species.

Species Dependent Upon Keystone Species. In its most general sense, a **keystone species** (or group of species) is one that makes an unusually strong contribution to community structure or processes, out of proportion to its abundance. A keystone species may be a major predator, whose presence limits the abundance of prey and thereby reduces their competitive interactions; a unique food source, such as figs and palms that fruit during seasons of fruit scarcity for tropical frugivores; or a species that maintains critical ecosystem processes, such as nitrogen-fixing bacteria or phosphorus-mobilizing fungi. The concept of keystone species will be discussed in greater detail in Chapter 8; their critical feature for our purposes now is that the removal of these species can make many other members of the community vulnerable to extinction.

(C)

Figure 5.9 Long-lived species are vulnerable to extinction for a number of reasons, including (A) overexploitation, which affects African elephants (*Loxodonta africana*), or (B) habitat destruction, which affects many sea turtles, including this Pacific ridley (*Lepidochelys olivacea*). Other species restricted to small, stable but isolated habitats (C), such as these plants on a granite outcrop, are also especially vulnerable. (A, photograph © Joe McDonald/Visuals Unlimited; B, by C. R. Carroll; C, by Robert Wyatt.)

The goal of analyzing keystone species for any community is to determine membership in the sets of species that have disproportionate effects on the rest of the community and to focus our conservation efforts on those sets. It would be vastly impractical, if not impossible, to create a conservation plan that would apply to all seed dispersers in a tropical forest, for example. However, it is reasonable and productive to think of specific conservation plans for the small set of critically important keystone species that disperse large seeds, and then to embrace the many species of animals that disperse small seeds in a more general plan of habitat conservation.

Unfortunately, there are major gaps in our understanding of keystone species. We have only a rudimentary knowledge of which sets of species are keystones in particular communities, and even less knowledge about the ecology of these critically important species. Therefore, an important research priority

Figure 5.10 A Brazil nut tree, an example of a keystone species; in addition to its ecological role, the tree is widely used as a cash crop by humans. (Photograph by Chris Miller.)

in conservation is to identify keystone species and to understand how to conserve them and the species that depend on them. A corresponding policy priority is the creation of appropriate legislation to accord keystone species special protection.

An example of a keystone species "set" is tropical trees that produce large, oil-rich seeds, such as the family Lecithydaceae. A familiar example of this tree family is the Brazil nut tree (Figure 5.10), whose nuts are widely harvested in Amazonia as a source of cash. The huge tree is pollinated solely by an iridescent bee, a member of the euglossine subfamily. Likewise, the tree's nut depends for its germination on a sharp-toothed rodent, the agouti, which chews and softens the large woody pod before eating and dispersing the seeds (or simply leaving them free to germinate). So this towering tree requires, for its reproductive system, the services of a high-flying bee that pollinates flowers in its crown and a forest-floor rodent that disperses its seeds. Of the two creatures, the euglossine bee appears to be more important in that it also pollinates, among many other plants, orchids—and in turn, these plants often supply prime sources of food to sundry other insects, which pollinate other plants, and so on. The Brazil nut tree may be regarded as a keystone species in the sense that it provides a critical or pivotal food source in its large oil-rich seeds.

In another sense, we can view the euglossines as a different kind of keystone species, one known as a **mobile link species**. Because these euglossine bees are specialist pollinators of many species of orchids, aroids, and bromeliads, as well as pollinators of Brazil nuts and other trees, the reproductive success of these plants depends on the services provided by the bees. Thus, the success of all these plants is "linked" by the mobility of their specialist pollinators. Furthermore, plant hosts, by virtue of supplying food to extensive associations of mobile links, have been termed **keystone mutualist species** (Gilbert 1980; Terborgh 1986, 1988).

Many other cash crops, after the pattern of the Brazil nut tree, are pollinated by specialist insects, bats, or birds that depend in turn on the plants. Tiny midges and thrips pollinate rubber and cocoa; certain bees and other hymenopterans pollinate passion fruit and cucurbits; flies pollinate cashew, mango, and cola nuts; nocturnal moths and bats pollinate calabash, kapok, and balsa trees; and hummingbirds pollinate wild pineapple. All of these specialized pollinator relationships form part of larger food webs, often with their own mobile links and keystone mutualists.

This concept of pivotal linkages within tropical forest ecosystems can be extended to thousands of plants that, through their nectar, pollen, and fruits, supply critical support for multitudes of insects, mammals, and birds; an outstanding example is figs, with their 800 species worldwide, mostly in tropical forests. If, as a result of human disturbance of forest ecosystems, a keystone mutualist is eliminated, the loss may lead to that of several other species, which may, in certain circumstances, trigger a cascade of linked extinctions. Eventually, a series of forest food webs could become unraveled. Developed as they are through the coevolution of plants and animals that have sustained each other through ever more complex relationships, these food webs can become destabilized, with effects reverberating throughout their ecosystems. When human incursion causes the severing of a few threads, the damage can ultimately lead to a rending of the fabric from top to bottom.

Genetic Losses

There is more to the biodiversity crisis than the extinction of species in large numbers: there is also loss of diversity within species. While poorly reflected in many conservation strategies, this loss adds a further dimension to the loss of life on earth. Clearly, a species might not supply a full array of environmental services such as nutrient cycling, soil formation, disease resistance, or climate regulation (Ehrlich and Ehrlich 1981) if it has lost much of its genetic variability and the ecological adaptability that encompasses. The loss of genetic diversity is dealt with in great detail in Chapter 6; here we provide only a brief discussion.

Every species represents the outcome of evolutionary processes that have generated a unique amalgam of genetic variability. The individuals that make up a species are genetically differentiated, due to high levels of genetic polymorphism across many gene loci. So biodiversity ultimately comprises the sum of all variants constituting the genomes of all organisms on earth. In turn, this means that the total number of species is not the only standard by which we should evaluate the abundance and diversity of life; genetic variation within species represents another major level of biological diversity.

While intraspecific genetic differences may appear slight, they can actually be quite pronounced: consider, for example, the variation manifested in the many races of dogs or the specialized types of wheat developed by breeders. Yet even this gives only a crude picture. A typical bacterium may contain about 1000 genes, certain fungi may have 10,000, and many flowering plants and a few animals may have 400,000 or even more (Hinegardner 1976). Although many of these genes may not be expressed, their numbers provide some sense of the potential for genetic variation.

Within this context of the planet's genetic variability, we can recognize that biological depletion applies not only to species themselves, but to subspecies, races, and populations. A given species may consist of hundreds of genetically distinct populations. Many species are far from threatened—indeed, they flourish in unprecedented numbers—but their gene pools have been greatly reduced through the elimination of most of their populations. An example is wheat, a species that totals trillions of individuals every growing season; yet the wild and primitive cultivar relatives of modern commercial wheat have disappeared to the extent that the great bulk of the species' genetic variability has already been lost, and most of the rest is severely threatened (Yeatman et al. 1984; see also Myers 1995).

Much the same applies to virtually all our leading crops and to our breeds of domestic livestock (Brisbin 1995). Yet we know little about how far this biological depletion has proceeded, or how soon it may reach a threshold of critical genetic impoverishment beyond which a domesticated species loses its capacity to adapt to new diseases and other environmental threats (Soulé 1987). Most of our agricultural crops have very little remaining genetic diversity and are susceptible to disease and pest infestations.

The key to resisting such threats is the genetic diversity residing in wild stocks. Like biodiversity hot spots, certain areas of the world are especially critical as centers of crop genetic diversity because they either contain the wild ancestors of our domesticated crops or hold concentrations of modern agricultural germ plasm. Twelve of these regions have been identified: Mexico–Guatemala; Peru–Ecuador–Bolivia; southern Chile; Brazil–Paraguay; the United States; Ethiopia; Central Asia; the Mediterranean region; India–Burma; Asia Minor; Thailand–Malaya–Java; and China (Witt 1985). Particular regions, often very small areas, within these countries hold the key to crop genetic diversity because the wild ancestors of agricultural crops originated there and may still occur there. Such areas are critical to continued, let alone expanded, crop production (Witt 1985), yet they are being lost at a rapid rate.

Threats to Biodiversity

We have discussed the tremendous losses of biodiversity that are occurring and the major extinction episode we have entered. But what are the specific causes of this event? What are the threats to biodiversity? As discussed in Chapter 1, the ultimate threat is a burgeoning human population, and there is little indication of serious attention to our own, out-of-control growth rate. With 5.7 billion people in 1997, a population doubling time of 43 years, and a growth rate of some 11,000 people per hour, there is little secret as to the root cause of the biodiversity crisis. In addition to these large numbers is a high per capita resource consumption rate in developed countries (led by the United States), with many of those resources coming from undeveloped countries in tropical regions (Ehrlich et al. 1995; Myers 1997). There is also the problem of low efficiency of resource use, and a "throwaway" mentality that encourages one-time use of "cheap, inexhaustible" resources in the name of convenience. These factors together constitute the "root causes" of biodiversity loss, and should always be borne in mind when attempting to deal with any conservation issue. However, the more direct causes of biodiversity loss are varied, and more amenable to treatment and minimization. They constitute five broad classes of threats, which we address here.

Habitat Destruction, Fragmentation, and Alteration

By far the largest single threat to biodiversity worldwide is the outright destruction of habitat, along with habitat alteration and fragmentation of large habitats into small patches. The effects of habitat destruction are clear: habitat is lost, species dependent upon that habitat can no longer "make a living," and they fail to reproduce, die, or, if mobile enough, move elsewhere. The differences between an intact forest and a parking lot, or between a coral reef and a dredged sandbar, are self-evident, and we need not belabor the point that habitat destruction reduces biodiversity. More subtle processes occur when habitats are fragmented or modified (degraded), and we will spend more time on those issues.

Not all natural habitats will be destroyed outright within the immediate future, nor do they need to be to produce destructive effects on biodiversity. Fragmentation—the breakup of extensive habitats into small, isolated patches that are too limited to maintain their species stocks into the indefinite future—also will eliminate species. This phenomenon, treated extensively in Chapter 9, has been widely analyzed via the theory of island biogeography, and concerns about its effects have been strongly supported by empirical evidence, albeit with variations on the general theme (MacArthur and Wilson 1967; Williamson 1981; Case and Cody 1987; Wilcove 1987; Daily and Ehrlich 1996).

Habitat degradation is also likely to cause long-term losses of species. Habitat degradation is a more difficult concept than fragmentation because what constitutes degradation for one species may go unnoticed by another, or may even be a habitat enhancement. Thus, clear-cutting and exposure of soils is an obvious degradation for any species dependent upon a closed forest, but is a habitat enhancement for weedy annual species that require such conditions.

A complicating factor is the inertia of environmental degradation—especially degradation that has already occurred. Through inertia, degradation continues to exert an increasingly adverse effect into the future, no matter how vigorously we work to resist the process, because the potential damage is already "in the pipeline." An obvious example is acid rain, which will inflict injury on biotas in the future by means of pollutants already deposited, though not yet causing apparent harm. Similarly, many tropical forests will suffer desiccation through climatic changes induced by deforestation that has already taken place. Desertification will keep expanding through built-in momentum, and ozone-destroying CFCs now in the atmosphere will continue their work for a century or more, even if we were to stop releasing them immediately. There is potentially enough global warming in store due to past greenhouse gas emissions to cause significant climate change, no matter how much we seek to slow it, let alone halt it.

Introduced Species

The second leading cause of biodiversity loss is the effects of species introduced beyond their native ranges; this rampant phenomenon is causing widespread destruction. Familiar examples include kudzu vines in the southeastern United States, zebra mussels making their way through streams and lakes down the middle of North America, exotic birds in Hawaii, rats and goats on many islands throughout the Pacific, Africanized honeybees throughout the Americas, and hundreds of crop pests throughout the world. Such introduced species typically replace native floras and faunas through competition, predation, or parasitism, and may change the dynamics of system function. These phenomena will be discussed in detail in Chapter 8.

Exploitation and Overharvesting

A third category of threats comes from humanity's use and misuse of natural resources. These threats include

- direct commercial exploitation of wild living resources such as marine fishes or whales (discussed in Essay 5D by Carl Safina).
- the environmental side effects of collection of nonliving resources such as oil or other minerals (e.g., oil spills, habitat destruction from open-pit mines, toxins associated with mining activities).
- unintentional mortality of nontarget organisms, such as sea turtles caught in shrimp nets, dolphins and seabirds caught in drift nets, or the tremendous diversity of "by-catch"— fishes and invertebrates unintentionally caught in marine trawls.
- overhunting, as was evident in the extinction of the Passenger Pigeon (Blockstein and Tordoff 1985) and the near-extinction of the American bison, as well as the losses of flightless birds, tortoises, and other species on islands visited by sailors in the 17th through 19th centuries (Ehrlich and Ehrlich 1981).
- global trade in wildlife, which threatens wild populations. For example, Hunter (1996) listed estimates of numbers of individuals exploited annually for such trade, including 25,000–30,000 primates, 2–5 million birds, 500–600 million ornamental fishes, 9–10 million orchids, and 7–8 million cacti.

ESSAY 5D

Global Marine Fisheries

Depletion and Renewal

Carl Safina, National Audubon Society

When Henry David Thoreau wrote, "Give a man a fish and he eats for one day; teach him to fish and he eats for a lifetime," he committed two common errors: he was thinking of fish only as food, and he was assuming that the supply would last forever. We can forgive Thoreau these two errata in an otherwise very insightful metaphor, but lots of people whose careers are focused entirely on fisheries have committed the same errors. Their mistakes have stretched the oceans to their limits, resulting in depletion, ecological upheaval, human impoverishment, and threats to the food supply for many poor people around the world.

We have treated fish as mere commodities, forgetting that they are wildlife dependent on natural production in a wild environment. Instead of sensibly living off the biological interest of wild populations, we have been mining the capital, because the emphasis—in thinking, politics, and fisheries law—has been on economics over biology. And ironically, overemphasis on short-term economics has resulted in losses of billions of dollars to businesses and taxpayers.

In the 20th century, ocean fish catches increased 25-fold, from 3 million to a peak of about 82 million metric tons in 1989; then something quietly happened. In 1990 the catch declined by 3.5 million tons, and has been generally static ever since. All major regions in the Atlantic, Mediterranean, and Pacific now have declining catches; in some regions, catches peaked in the early 1970s and have since declined by more than 50%. Only in the Indian Ocean has the catch been increasing—through the same industrialized fishing methods that exceeded the limits in other oceans (Weber 1993, 1994; FAO 1995).

For decades, both public apathy and denial by fisheries experts allowed depletion of the oceans to proceed. However, in the last few years apathy and denial have been dashed by facefuls of cold water, as spectacular fishery collapses and massive unemployment and human dislocation removed all doubt that life in the oceans has been changed and that people have been affected. Meanwhile, some of the world's greatest "inexhaustible" fishing grounds and marine ecosystems—most notably the Grand Banks and Georges Bank of Canada and New England, which once spurred European settlement of the region—are now largely closed following their collapses. Canada is paying $2 billion in unemployment assistance, and overall in the United States, fishery depletions are costing $8 billion and 300,000 jobs annually (Sissenwine and Rosenberg 1993). Conservation issues are often pitched as "jobs versus the environment," but in the oceans, conservation makes jobs.

And lack of conservation can make enemies. Fishery conflicts—some of them violent—are erupting around the world as boats compete over dwindling resources. In one recent year, Norway, Iceland, the United States, Canada, Indonesia, Taiwan, Nicaragua, Russia, China, the Philippines, Japan, France, Britain, Spain, the Galápagos Islands, and others were involved in nearly thirty international conflicts over fishing. Guns have been fired, boats have been seized, and fishermen have been jailed and even killed (Maddox 1994; Camhi 1995a).

Converging Recognition of a Global Problem. Fishing accounts for about 1% of the global economy, but on a regional basis, marine fishing contributes enormously to human survival. In Asia, more than a billion people rely on fish as their main source of animal protein. Worldwide, about 200 million people—often quite poor—depend on fish for their livelihoods. The United Nations says fisheries have become "globally non-sustainable" (FAO 1995), and notes, "It is important to continue to single out overfishing (and its economic counterpart, overinvestment) as the main culprit" (FAO 1994). A workshop convened by the U.S. National Academy of Sciences identified "fishing activities" as the major threat to life in the oceans (NRC 1995). Pauly and Christensen (1995) remarked that, "Contrary to some terrestrial systems such as rainforests, of which large undisturbed tracts still exist . . . the overwhelming bulk of the world's [continental] shelves are impacted by fishing, leaving few sanctuaries where biomasses and biodiversity remain high."

A War on Fishes. In the 1950s and 1960s, fisheries began adapting military technolgies such as radar, sonar, and loran to peaceful efforts of food gathering, but from the fishes' perspective it might have seemed like a declaration of war. Radar allowed boats to fish in dense fog; sonar detected fish deep under the oceans' formerly opaque blanket, and loran turned the trackless sea into a grid so that fishers could return to within 50 feet of that secret ridge on the bottom where so many fish gathered. Later came satellite-originated maps of water temperature fronts, faxed directly onboard ships, indicating where fish are likely to congregate.

Many industrialized fishing ships are floating factories deploying giant fishing gear: 80 miles of longlines with thousands of baited hooks; drift nets up to 40 miles long (still in use in some European countries in defiance of a mostly successful global ban); and bag-shaped trawl nets large enough to engulf 12 Boeing 747 jetliners. From some exceptionally heavily hit populations—often rapidly diminishing ones—80–90% of the fish are taken each year (Sadovy 1993; Safina 1993a, 1994; NOAA 1994; FAO 1995; ICCAT 1995; Camhi 1996; NMFS 1996).

The world's industrialized fleet now has twice the fishing power needed to catch what the oceans can produce (Weber 1994). Consequently, fishing has turned into an extremely inefficient venture, so overcapitalized with excess killing capacity that $124 billion is spent each year to catch $70 billion worth of fish (FAO 1992), a $54 billion losing proposition that is depleting a significant portion of the oceans' ecosystems. Massive subsidies—including fuel tax exemptions, price controls, low-interest loans, and outright grants for gear or infrastructure—are a main reason that fishing power outgrew the ability of the fish to support the boats. Open access is itself a type of subsidy, as fishers pay no fee to profit from public common-property wildlife resources.

Problems Inherent in Fishing: By-catch, Ecological Effects, and Habitat Destruction. Virtually every kind of fishery catches unintended, unwanted creatures that, collectively, are known as by-catch or by-kill. Each year an estimated 27 million metric tons of dying or dead marine life are thrown overboard, one-fourth to one-third of the total catch. By-catch includes nontarget fishes, undersized target fishes, seabirds, marine mammals, and any other nontarget species. By-catch exceeds target catch in some fisheries; shrimp trawlers have the highest ratio of by-kill to targeted catch, ranging from 128% to 830%, accounting for over one-third of the global by-catch (Alverson et. al. 1994).

In addition to overfishing and by-catch, fisheries suffer from habitat destruction and pollution, some caused by the fisheries themselves. In many regions of the world's continental shelves, bottom-dwelling animals and plants (many of which feed and shelter fish) have been seriously damaged by commercial trawling (e.g., Dayton et al. 1995). Throughout the tropical Indo-Pacific region, many divers are now catching reef fish for export to China by stunning them with cyanide, a potent poison that kills corals (Rubec 1986; Veitayaki et al. 1995; Johannes and Riepen 1995).

Coastal fish habitats have also been subject to changes unrelated to the act of fishing (Stroud 1992; National Research Council 1995). Because roughly two-thirds of all commercially valuable fish spend the first and most vulnerable stages of their lives in shallow coastal waters, the loss of half the world's estuarine habitats has cost uncountable dollars and has had major social effects (e.g., Houde and Rutherford 1993). Agriculture, road building, and deforestation result in extensive land erosion and sedimentation of coral reefs and rivers, ultimately ruining fish habitat in much of the tropics and—along with dams—destroying some of the world's greatest salmon runs (e.g., Waldman 1995; National Research Council 1996).

Aquaculture: Not a Panacea. While the catch of wild marine fish is declining, each year the number of people in the world increases by an amount equal to the population of Mexico. Even if the fish that now become fertilizers and animal feeds—a third of the catch—were used for direct human consumption, this would maintain current consumption rates for only 20 years. Even improved conservation of wild fish would not keep pace with the growing human population. We will therefore witness in the next few years the heretofore unthinkable exhaustion of the oceans' ability to naturally satisfy humanity's demand for seafood.

Aquaculture—seafood farming—will have to double in the next 15 years to fill the gap between the demand and what nature can supply (FAO 1995). Indeed, aquaculture has been growing rapidly enough to compensate for the decline of wild fish in commerce. However, because aquaculture entails property ownership and focuses on high-value species for export to developed countries, it is unclear whether increasing aquaculture will translate into more food for hungry people; it might actually mean less (Weber 1994). And aquaculture faces challenges of its own, such as the coastal pollution that has already caused the stagnation of worldwide mollusk production. Many "cultured" fish (such as groupers and eels) cannot currently be bred and are raised in captivity from wild fry, but fry are getting scarce because the wild fish are declining. It is unlikely that aquaculture will take much pressure off wild populations or allow the oceans to recover. Increased shrimp farming—now the source of half the world's shrimp in commerce—has not led to decreased intensity of shrimp trawling. In fact, some shrimp farmers are now going fishing with fine-mesh nets to catch food for their shrimp (called "biomass fishing"). Aquaculture is likely to increase habitat losses as more of the world's mangroves and marshes are destroyed to make artificial ponds. Intensive aquaculture is itself a source of pollution, releasing excess feed, feces, toxic antibiotics, alien species, and alien pathogens, and creating overnutrification and oxygen deficiencies in waterways (Pillay 1992).

Management Problems. Few countries have achieved much success in fisheries management, and most are scarcely trying. In many regions, there are no data with which to manage; where data exist, they have largely been disregarded (Safina 1994; FAO 1995). The International Commission for the Conservation of Atlantic Tunas, for instance, has never since its inception in the 1960s been in compliance with its charter obligation to manage for sustainable yields, and has allowed overfishing and regional depletion of tunas and billfishes despite having the world's best data on regional population trends for these species (Safina 1993a). Many areas of the high seas are not covered by any fisheries agreements, and fishing proceeds unbridled and largely unmonitored. Where management exists, it often (1) fails to anticipate new markets that result in sudden high value and demand, as has happened with shark fins and juvenile eels (Musick et al. 1993; Bonfil 1994; Camhi 1995b; Cole 1996; Lee 1996; Waterman 1996); (2) fails to anticipate new, highly efficient fishing gear (e.g., Safina 1993b); or (3) has little enforcement power, and fishers break the rules. From 1986 to 1992, for example, fleets fishing the Grand Banks took sixteen times the allowed catch. Further, if a country does not like the restrictions in an agreement, it can ignore them (e.g., Italy and France ignored the United Nations' global ban on large-scale drift nets)—or it can simply quit, as Iceland has done with the International Whaling Commission (Weber 1993).

The United Nations says that 70% of the populations of fish, crustaceans, and mollusks in the world's oceans "are in need of urgent corrective conservation and management" (FAO 1995). Their main concern, at the global level, "is to control fishing effort and to reduce it where necessary." But between 1989 and 1992, the world added 136,000 fishing vessels. Correcting the situation will mean reductions in total world landings in the short and medium term, which will require controversial policy decisions backed by political will and enforcement. But governments have difficulty implementing such decisions (FAO 1995) because fishers have overt and subtle ways of influencing decision makers, such as routine financial contributions to politicians made by the fishing industry (e.g., Safina and Iudicello 1995).

Toward Saner Seas. Too many fisheries still show a "buffalo hunter" mentality, and I have painted an alarming picture because the many problems are indeed serious. But solutions, though difficult, are available. Improvements, though few, have occurred, enough to point the way. One of the most important things that can be done is to remove the subsidies that support fisheries incapable of existing on the resources. Indeed, fisheries would be configured more rationally with regard to the living resources if they were *taxed* for using common property resources, rather than subsidized.

We know enough about the human-induced problems to understand how to fix them. Recent advances in by-catch reduction, such as turtle excluders, successful techniques for releasing dolphins from tuna nets, and sonic devices for warning mammals of the presence of nets are all worthy of increased research and support for implementation. Recoveries of severely depleted fishes such as Atlantic herring, mackerel, and striped bass show that fish populations can rebuild and resume their ecological role and economic value if fisheries are managed seriously.

Even the political influence of exploitive users has begun to wane as the larger political consequences of resource depletion and consequent job losses make themselves felt, and as conservation organizations begin to understand that fish are wildlife too. With the hard work of some of these groups, several long-term goals have been achieved nationally and internationally, including the United Nations' new treaty on high seas fishing and its largely successful global ban on large-scale drift nets. Interest in and commitment to the oceans is much greater in the last few years than it has ever been before. The problems are largely a matter of political will, but politics reflects public opinion, and that means politics can be changed.

The end of a long era of mythical limitlessness and ideological freedom of the seas is upon us. This may seem a tragedy of sorts, but coming to grips with reality is always liberating in the end. Real management of human activities in the seas is in its infancy; this is a new field with many challenges and abundant room for positive involvement and influence. Perhaps we need to ask, as did Thoreau, "Who knows what admirable virtue of fishes may be below low-water-mark, bearing up against a hard destiny, not admired by that fellow creature who alone can appreciate it! Who hears the fishes when they cry?"

Pollution and Toxification

Another class of threats includes the familiar litany of problems associated with the release of synthetic substances, often by-products of beneficial processes, that are toxic to living organisms or otherwise modify their habitats. Such threats come from industrial releases into air, water, and soils, mining, transportation (exhausts, oil spills), and even light and noise pollution, such as lights that disrupt sea turtle nesting activities. We have now injected over 100,000 synthetic industrial chemicals into our environments worldwide, with little or no testing to determine their effects. In the United States the volume of these potentially hazardous materials released each year has topped three million tons, or 11 kilograms per American, and each year we add another 1000 or more such chemicals to our environment. Given what we have learned already through bitter experience about their toxic effects and other harmful impacts, whether on wildlife or humans or both, we can assume that many of these "chemical time bombs" will eventually cause profound and pervasive injury to creatures in contaminated environments (Colborn et al. 1996; Myers 1996).

Secondary Effects and Synergistic Interactions

Because the main mechanisms of extinction tend to be studied in isolation from one another, we know very little about the dynamic relationships between discrete mechanisms. Yet, **secondary effects** and **synergistic interactions** can be quite significant. A secondary effect occurs when the loss of one species leads to losses of others, and is especially prevalent in specialized mutualistic or predator–prey relationships. For example, if a predator relies entirely on one prey species, and that species goes extinct, obviously the predator's days are numbered. Likewise, if a specialized pollinator is responsible for all the pollination of a tree species (as is the case for many fig species and their euglossine pollinators, Janzen 1979), that tree's reproduction will cease if the pollinator disappears.

A synergism occurs when two stresses together have an effect greater than the sum of their independent effects. For example, in an experimental study, Long et al. (1995) demonstrated that survival of leopard frog (*Rana pipiens*) embryos was unaffected by either low pH or high levels of ultraviolet light, but in combination these two stresses significantly reduced survival, and may play a role in the current amphibian declines.

The likely outcome of several extinction mechanisms operating simultaneously is that their various effects will amplify one another. This means that synergisms, working collectively and with compounding effects on one another, will lead to greater extinction probabilities. In the more immediate term, they may cause the expected extinction episode to be compressed in time, especially in the early phases. This means that large-scale losses of species may occur even sooner than many observers anticipate. Indeed, the synergistic connection could prove to be a major phenomenon at work during the impending extinction spasm (Myers 1986, 1992c). To the extent that we can discern some of its possible workings, we can begin to understand some potential patterns and processes as the spasm works itself out, and be better able to anticipate and prevent some of them.

A good example of a synergistic influence is the potential effects of global climate change. For many species, a few degrees of temperature change, or

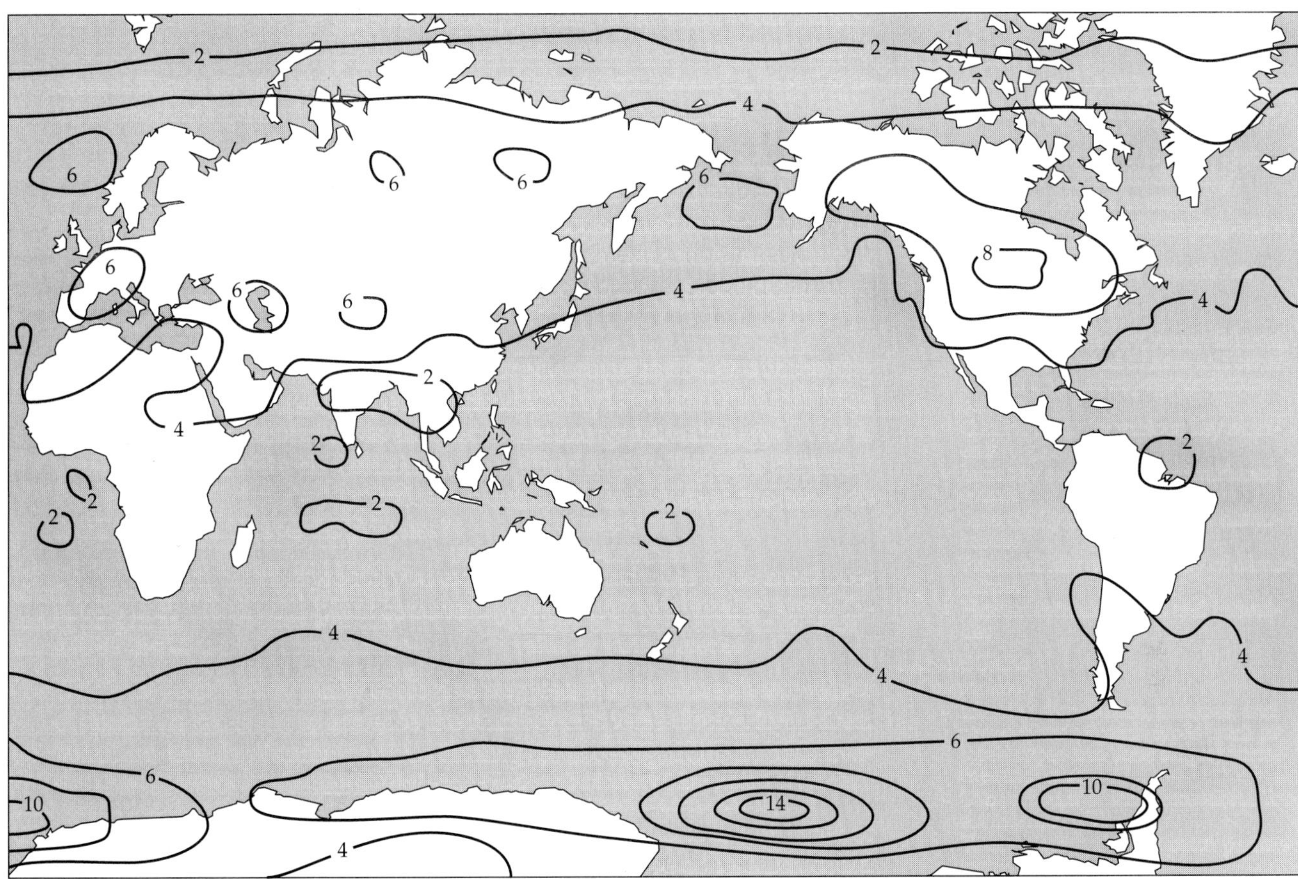

Figure 5.11 An example of a predicted global warming scenario. Each contour line represents a 2°C increase above current conditions. Higher temperature increases are expected at higher latitudes. These increases could interact in synergistic ways with a multitude of other human activities and result in great ecological upheaval. (Modified from Manabe and Wetherald 1987.)

slight changes in rainfall pattern, are the difference between survival and extinction; such changes will be unusually harmful for the many species that will already be stressed through other human activities. As the planet warms, higher temperature profiles are likely to move from the equator toward the poles (Figure 5.11), and rainfall patterns will change. Vegetation, trying to adapt by following temperature and moisture changes, will meet with limited success, for the changes will not only be large, but will emerge suddenly compared with previous climate changes (Intergovernmental Panel on Climate Change 1990, 1992). At the end of the last Ice Age, when the glaciers covering much of North America retreated, vegetation followed the ebbing ice northward at a rate of 50 km or so per century; the sudden arrival of greenhouse warming could require communities of plants and animals to migrate much faster. Many species will find it impossible to achieve this, and they will die out, or their ranges will be severely restricted.

Those species that can make a quick transition will encounter a further problem. In the past, they have enjoyed a "free run," with only geographic obstacles—mountains, rivers, and the like—blocking their paths. This time they will find their way blocked by farmlands, cities, and other effects of human communities, which are "development deserts" for many wild species. To a migrating forest, an urban sprawl may present a bigger barrier than a mountain range.

Given the severity of these problems, we should direct attention to synergistic interactions. Yet we are far from recognizing, let alone documenting and analyzing, the most prevalent manifestations of synergisms in the natural world today (Ehrlich 1986; Odum 1993). Still less have we attempted a methodical assessment of the ways in which multiple synergisms will affect the outlook for biodiversity.

The Future of Evolution: A Process at Risk

Mass extinction of species is far from the whole story concerning the current biotic crisis; also at risk are certain processes of evolution itself. The most serious repercussion of the species extinction spasm may lie with the eventual disruption of the course of evolution, insofar as speciation processes will have to work with a greatly reduced pool of species, populations, and genetic variability. This dimension of the biotic crisis has received little attention from biologists.

The forces of natural selection can work only with the "resource base" available. If that base is drastically reduced, the result could be disruption of the creative capabilities of evolution, persisting far into the future. Given what we can discern from the geologic record, the "bounce-back" time is likely to be protracted. After the late Cretaceous crash that occurred 65 million years ago, some 50,000–100,000 years elapsed before a new set of diversified and specialized biotas started to emerge; it took another 5–10 million years before there were bats in the skies and whales in the seas. In the case of coral reefs, which suffered more severely than most other biomes, there was a 10-million-year hiatus before a fresh community of reef-building species became established. Following the crash of the late Permian, when marine invertebrates lost roughly half their families, it took as much as 20 million years before the survivors could establish even half as many families as they had lost (Jablonski 1986, 1991; Raup 1988, 1991b).

But the evolutionary outcome this time could prove yet more devastating (Myers 1990b). The critical factor lies with the likely loss of key environments. Not only do we appear poised, in the absence of greatly expanded conservation efforts, to lose most tropical forests, but there is also progressive depletion of tropical coral reefs, wetlands, estuaries, and other ecosystems with an exceptional abundance and diversity of species and unusual ecological complexities. These environments have served in the past as "powerhouses" of evolution, meaning that they have produced more species than other environments. It has long been believed (Darlington 1957; Mayr 1982) that virtually every major group of vertebrates and many other large categories of animals originated in spacious zones with warm, equitable climates. It has likewise been supposed that the rate of evolutionary diversification—whether through proliferation of species or through emergence of major new adaptations—has been greatest in the tropics, especially in tropical forests (Stanley 1981; Stenseth 1984). In addition, tropical species, especially tropical forest species, appear to persist for relatively brief periods of geologic time, which implies a high rate of evolution.

Furthermore, the current mass extinction will apply across most, if not all, major categories of species. This is almost axiomatic if certain environments are eliminated wholesale. The result will contrast sharply with the end of the Cretaceous, when not only placental mammals survived, but also birds, amphibians, crocodiles, turtles, lizards, snakes, and many other non-dinosaurian reptiles. In addition, the present extinction spasm is likely to eliminate a large share of terrestrial plant species; by contrast, during most mass extinction episodes of the prehistoric past, terrestrial plants survived with relatively few losses (Hickey 1984; Knoll 1984; Traverse 1988), and supplied a resource base for new animal species. If this biotic substrate is depleted, the restorative capacities of evolution will correspondingly be diminished.

A mass extinction episode also could trigger an outburst of speciation in a few categories of species. As discussed in Chapter 3, a certain amount of "creative disruption" in the form of habitat fragmentation can readily lead to splitting off of populations, followed by differentiation and termination of interbreeding, so that a population becomes distinctive enough to rank as a new race, then a subspecies, and finally a species. An example is the case of Lake Nabugabo, a recent "offshoot" of Lake Victoria in East Africa, which has led to the development of six species of *Haplochromis* cichlids. The introduction of new food resources and other materials into existing species' habitats can also foster speciation, as has occurred in the case of bananas in Hawaii, which led to the emergence of several moth species of the genus *Hydylepta*, all of which are obligate feeders on banana plants. The marked acceleration of speciation through these processes will not remotely match the rate and extent of extinctions, however. Whereas extinction can occur in just a few decades, and sometimes in a year or less, the time required to produce a new species is much longer. It takes decades for the fastest speciators, such as certain insects, centuries to millennia for many other invertebrates, and hundreds of thousands to millions of years for most mammals.

Among the reduced stock of species that survives the present extinction episode will be a disproportionate number of opportunists. These are species that can rapidly exploit newly vacant niches (by making widespread use of food resources), are generally short-lived with short generation times, feature high rates of population increase, and are adaptable to a wide range of environments. All of these traits enable them to exploit new environments and to make use of disturbances and "boom periods"—precisely the attributes that enable a species to prosper in a human-disrupted world. Examples include the House Sparrow, the European Starling, the housefly, rabbits, rats, and other "pest" species, together with many "weedy" plants.

While generalist species will profit from the coming crash, specialist species, notably predators and parasites, will suffer disproportionately higher losses. Not only are their lifestyles specialized, but their numbers are also typically much smaller. Because specialist predators and parasites are often the creatures that keep down the populations of generalists, there may be little to hold pests in check. Today, probably less than 5% of all insect species deserve to be called pests (Pimentel 1991), but if extinction patterns tend to favor such species, the outcome could be a situation in which pests increase until their natural enemies can no longer control them. In short, our descendants could find themselves living in a world with a "pest and weed" ecology.

Overall, the prospect is that in the wake of the present extinction spasm, there will not be a mere hiatus in evolutionary processes. Rather, our distant descendants may find that many evolutionary developments that have persisted throughout the Phanerozoic have been suspended, if not terminated. To cite the vivid phrasing of Soulé and Wilcox (1980b), "Death is one thing, an end to birth is something else."

Concluding Thoughts

It is obvious that we are in the opening phase of a mass extinction of species, centered in tropical forests, but broadly occurring elsewhere as well. If, through lack of conservation responses of sufficient scope and scale, this mass extinction is allowed to proceed unchecked, it has the potential to eliminate one-fourth to one-half of all species within the next century or so. The same biodepletive processes will leave many surviving species with reduced population and genetic variability, and thus diminished environmental adaptability.

This extinction spasm will have an impoverishing effect on evolution's capacity to generate stocks of replacement species, causing a hiatus that could extend for million of years.

All this presupposes that we will fail to do a better job of preserving biodiversity. However dismal the prognosis presented here, it is *not inevitable* that we face a mass extinction of the scope delineated, for prediction is not destiny. Although our best efforts will fail to save many species, there is still the opportunity to save species by the millions—provided we immediately come to grips with the challenge.

Humankind is the sole species in the history of life with the capacity to eliminate other species in large numbers. We are also unique in that we possess the knowledge and capabilities to save species in large numbers. Fortunately, we still have time to turn an unprecedented problem into an unrivaled opportunity. But that time will run out in the early decades of the 21st century, after which the processes of habitat destruction will have gained so much momentum that they will be difficult to stem without much greater expense and with far less chance of success.

Summary

As a result of human activities and overpopulation, we are now witnessing a global mass extinction spasm. Species-rich biotas are being destroyed at high rates, especially in tropical lowland forests, but also in other tropical environments, coral reefs and other marine environments, freshwater lakes, and Mediterranean biomes, and other areas. In the process, biological diversity, including genetic, species, and ecosystem diversity, is in sharp decline. Estimates of habitat and species losses vary greatly due to the difficulties of gathering accurate data over broad expanses and the use of a variety of models and assumptions. Predictions of future losses also vary, but all unquestionably point to extinctions of significant percentages of existing life-forms, most of which are unknown at this time. One of the easiest and most efficient ways of stemming this loss would be protection of 18 identified "hot spots" of diversity, small areas of the earth that contain exceptionally high concentrations of species found nowhere else.

Not all species are equally vulnerable to extinction. Rare species and long-lived species are especially vulnerable. Additionally, keystone species or sets of species support many other species that are reliant on them. If these keystones are lost, the vulnerability of their many dependent species is high, and cascading extinctions are likely.

Species losses are only one component of biodiversity losses. Genetic diversity—the basis for evolutionary change and adaptation—and population diversity—the result of local adaptations—are also being lost at high rates. This problem may be especially critical with respect to losses of crop genetic diversity, which forms the basis for agricultural production. Most of the world's major crops and domestic animals have narrow levels of genetic variation, and the wild ancestors of many of these species are extinct or nearly so. As a result of this biotic impoverishment, the human sustenance base is increasingly vulnerable to pests, diseases, and changing environments.

In addition to outright habitat destruction, fragmentation and degradation of habitats are major threats to biodiversity. Creating ever smaller chunks of forest exposes the remaining habitats to edge effects, invasive species, and other ills that accelerate extinctions. Species introductions, overharvesting, pollution and toxification, and secondary effects and synergistic processes are the other major classes of threats to biodiversity. In particular, synergisms (interactions among multiple stresses) are poorly understood, but are likely to accelerate extinctions. Global climate change is certain to add to and complicate all the other problems leading to extinctions.

All of this change will result in risk to the processes of evolution itself. The actual course of evolution may be disrupted, as speciation processes will be working with a reduced pool of species, populations, and genetic variation. The events of the next few decades could have an impoverishing effect on evolution's course that will be felt for several million years, and could radically change the history of life on earth.

Questions for Discussion

1. Should our aim be solely to preserve a maximum number of species, or should we give differential emphasis to higher taxa such as families and orders, even if this goal conflicts with the first? Remember that we cannot do everything, if only because conservation resources—especially time—are in short supply in relation to the challenge.

2. Regardless of your answer to Question 1, should our sole aim be to preserve a maximum amount of biodiversity? Or—in light of what we know about food webs and ecosystem stability—should we seek to safeguard ecological processes?

3. Following from Question 2, recall that the most depauperizing effect of the present mass extinction could be its disruption of the future course of evolution. Consequently, should our predominant conservation strategies be geared to safeguarding evolutionary processes? If so, would this mean that we should give less attention to species that are "evolutionary dead ends" because they will not produce new species for millions of years? Notable examples of such "dead ends" include the whales, the rhinos, the elephants, the great apes, and certain other long-lived species. Should we not direct greater emphasis to those species, notably the insects and other invertebrates, that, by reason of their far more rapid turnover of population stocks, supply more of a "resource base" for natural selection to work on?

4. If conservation biologists accept that the biotic crisis demands a strong, action-oriented response, what does this imply in practical terms? Should they not only engage in on-the-ground efforts to save strategic habitats, but also strive to bring the matter to the attention of political leaders and policymakers? Or should they stick to what they are best at, their scientific disciplines, and leave politicking to others? Or should they expand their expertise from, for example, the flow of energy through ecosystems, to include the flow of influence through the corridors of power?

5. What does all of this say about the boundaries of conservation biology as a discrete discipline? Is it a subset of biology, strictly a life science? Or should it give equal prominence to social sciences such as economics, political science, law, and ethics?

6. In two or three decades' time, your children or other youngsters may ask you a question along the lines of, "When the biodiversity crisis became apparent in its full scope during the 1990s, what did you do about it?" What will your answer be?

Suggestions for Further Reading

Daily, G. C. (ed.). 1997. *Ecosystem Services: Their Nature and Value*. Island Press, Washington, D.C. The best statement to date of what biodiversity contributes to both the biosphere's workings and humanity's welfare, with lots of economic and other quantification.

Ehrlich, P. R. and A. H. Ehrlich. 1981. *Extinction: The Causes and Consequences of the Disappearance of Species*. Random House, New York. A first-rate and eminently accessible account of how and why we are triggering a mass extinction of species—and how and why we need to stem it quickly. Containing an abundance of hard science, the text is illuminated with a host of anecdotal insights, making the book a fine introduction to the mass extinction field for the neophyte and expert alike.

Elliott, D. K. (ed.). 1986. *Dynamics of Extinction*. John Wiley and Sons, New York. Curiously enough, we know little about the actual mechanisms of extinction in its final phases. What happens to a species when its numbers are brought below a critical level, what processes of ecological equilibration start to operate, how does demographic stochasticity work on the ground? A book you will return to time and again.

Myers, N. 1979. *The Sinking Ark*. Pergamon Press, Oxford. The first detailed account of the species extinction spasm that is overtaking the biosphere. Looks especially at social science factors that unwittingly promote extinction of species and populations and erosion of their genetic base.

Myers, N. 1992. *The Primary Source: Tropical Forests and Our Future*. (Expanded ed.). W. W. Norton, New York. A synoptic review and analysis of the biome that is the richest biotically and the most threatened through habitat depletion. A detailed account of what is at stake for us all in tropical forests, with a comparative assessment of deforestation rates, the main agents of deforestation, and what we can do to safeguard this, the principal locus of mass extinction.

Raven, P. H. 1990. The politics of preserving biodiversity. *BioScience* 40:769–774. A fine account of the "social science" aspects of biodiversity. Raven should know: he is a past president of the American Institute of Biological Sciences and the current home secretary of the National Academy of Sciences.

Reaka-Kudla, M. L., D. W. Wilson, and E. O. Wilson (eds.). 1996. *Biodiversity II: Understanding and Protecting Our Natural Resources*. National Academy Press, Washington, D.C. A marvelous compendium of papers by several dozen first-rank authors in the biodiversity arena. If you are looking for the best expertise on the basic biology, evolution, genetics, economics, ethics, and philosophy of biodiversity, you will find it here. If you plan to have just one biodiversity book by your bedside, make it this one.

Soulé, M. E. (ed.). 1987. *Viable Populations for Conservation*. Cambridge University Press, New York. Biodiversity exists within species as well as among species. This is the book that will bring readers up to speed on the crucial factors of genetic variability, especially as concerns key issues such as the critical minimum gene pool size of populations.

Wilson, E. O. 1992. *The Diversity of Life*. Belknap Press of Harvard University Press, Cambridge, MA. Far and away the finest general book on biodiversity: what biodiversity consists of, where it is primarily located, how fast it is disappearing, what we are losing, and what we can do to better safeguard it. Informative, illuminating, and highly readable—a wonderful combination by the guru of biodiversity.

II

Population-Level Considerations

6

Genetics

Conservation of Diversity within Species

Wild species must have available a pool of genetic diversity if they are to survive environmental pressures exceeding the limits of developmental plasticity. If this is not the case, extinction would appear inevitable.

O. H. Frankel, 1983

As indicated in Chapter 5, contemporary extinction rates are, or will soon be, as high as any that have ever occurred on earth. This unrestrained loss of species is accompanied by a more subtle but no less important process, the loss of genetic diversity. When a population or species disappears, all of the genetic information carried by that population or species is lost. When a contiguous population is fragmented through habitat destruction and many small, isolated populations result, genetic diversity within each may decay over time. In the words of Thomas Foose (1983), "Gene pools are becoming diminished and fragmented into gene puddles."

But why be concerned with something as detailed as genetic diversity when bigger problems such as large-scale habitat destruction, global warming, toxic wastes, and the spread of exotic species threaten wholesale destruction of ecological systems? Certainly, massive destruction of tropical rainforests, for example, does not lend itself to genetic solutions. Species in those systems will go extinct through loss of habitat, and all the genetic diversity in the world will not save them (other than, perhaps, genetically based human intelligence). Such situations of mass destruction require different approaches, at different scales (see chapters in Parts III and IV). However, there are many conservation challenges that require the guidance and direction that genetic data, collected and interpreted within the constructs of sound genetic theory, can provide. Rhinoceroses, grizzly bears, Pacific salmon, desert fishes, Siberian tigers, African elephants, and many other species are all benefiting from the input of geneticists (Figure 6.1).

(A)

(B)

(C)

(D)

Figure 6.1 Many species around the world are beginning to benefit from inclusion of genetic information in their management plans. These include (A) various species of rhinoceros, including the white rhinoceros (*Ceratotherium simum*); (B) Przewalski's horse (*Equus przewalskii*) from the Dzungarian Basin of Mongolia, Kazakhstan, and China; (C) numerous fish species, such as the Sonoran topminnow (*Poeciliopsis occidentalis*) from Arizona; and (D) the Red-cockaded Woodpecker (*Picoides borealis*) of the southeastern United States. (A, photograph © San Diego Zoo; B, by Ron Garrison © San Diego Zoo; C, by John N. Rinne; D, by Walker Montgomery.)

Why Genetics?

There are at least three biological reasons to believe that genetics can make important and critical contributions to conservation biology. First, the **Fundamental Theorem of Natural Selection** (Fisher 1930) tells us that the rate of evolutionary change in a population is proportional to the amount of genetic diversity available. When genetic diversity in a population decreases, the rate and scope of potential evolutionary change in that population in response to environmental challenges is reduced. Essentially, loss of genetic diversity reduces future evolutionary options.

Second, there is a consensus among population geneticists that **heterozygosity**, or high genetic variation within individuals or populations, is positively related to fitness. Heterozygosity at single or multiple **gene loci** (single-locus and multi-locus heterozygosity, respectively) may confer fitness advantages upon individuals. Heterozygosity will be discussed in greater detail below; for now we will say that reduced individual heterozygosity may lead to lower fitness.

Finally, the global pool of genetic diversity represents all of the information for all biological processes on the planet. Every biochemical product, every growth pattern, every instinctive behavior, every color morph is encoded in a genetic "library" of unimaginable global extent. Wilson (1985b) has calculated that the billion bits of genetic information carried in the DNA of a single house mouse, if translated into equivalent English text, would fill nearly all 15 editions of the *Encyclopedia Britannica* printed since 1768. Loss of such diversity will probably decrease the ability of organisms to respond to environmental change, and will also discard biological information potentially useful to humans, such as crop genetic diversity and valuable biochemicals. In essence, we are losing the "blueprints" of life.

Throughout this text we promote the evolutionary paradigm for conservation, which means that genetics should be prominent in its practice. Evolution is the single most unifying organizational concept in all of biology, and it should play a prominent role in conservation as well. Vrijenhoek (1989b) even called for an "evolutionary conservation ethic," which would place a long-term, evolutionary perspective at the heart of conservation. The role of evolution may be most evident with respect to genetic conservation, but it permeates all aspects of the field. Consequently, we encourage all students of conservation biology to develop a solid foundation of evolutionary knowledge, including genetics, and apply that mindset to conservation. As Ehrenfeld (1991) aptly put it, "The biosphere is a system, or a set of systems, with many millions of elements that are changing in time and are affected by myriad local irregularities and discontinuities and by countless historical singularities. As yet, there is no single comprehensive theory besides evolution that takes it all in. Quite possibly there never will be."

The basic problem linking genetics to conservation is that small populations, whether in the wild or in captivity, tend to lose genetic variation over time. This loss of variation may well increase the probability of population extinction or reduce opportunities for future adaptation through evolutionary change. Because habitat fragmentation and destruction will continue to produce small, isolated populations of plants and animals, and because by the time many species are recognized as threatened or endangered they are typically in small and isolated populations, understanding the genetic consequences of small population size is vital to good management and recovery efforts. The basic thrust of conservation genetics, the message to take from this chapter, is that we must maintain natural patterns of genetic diversity at many levels and thus preserve options for future evolution.

Before proceeding further, we state two important caveats. First, we assume that the student has a working knowledge of basic (Mendelian) genetics and at least a rudimentary knowledge of population genetics, including, but not limited to, patterns of inheritance, basic molecular genetic structure and function (DNA and chromosome structure), the meaning of **Hardy-Weinberg equilibrium**, and the concept of **natural selection**. If the student lacks this background, we recommend consulting a good introductory genetics text before proceeding, or other writings such as Chapter 2 in Wilson and Bossert (1971), or Chambers (1983).

The second caveat is that entire books have been written on conservation genetics, and the field has a large and growing literature. The application of genetics to conservation is also a young endeavor, with advances made quickly and arguments generated (though often not resolved) easily. We can provide only an introduction to the topic, and encourage the serious student to pursue more advanced topics in other texts or the original literature (such as Frankel and Soulé 1981a; Schonewald-Cox et al. 1983; relevant chapters in Soulé 1986a; and especially more recent works such as Ryman and Utter 1987; Falk and Holsinger 1991; Avise 1994; and Loeschcke et al. 1994).

Genetic Variation: What Is It and Why Is It Important?

A species' pool of genetic diversity exists at three fundamental levels: genetic variation within individuals (heterozygosity), genetic differences among individuals within a population, and genetic differences among populations. Each level is a genetic resource of potential importance to conservation, so each must be understood relative to the others.

Variation within Individuals

Heritable genetic variation is the basis for evolutionary change and is essential if natural selection is to operate. With the exception of identical twins and clones, every individual of a species is genetically unique. This is easily seen by looking around a college classroom: some resemblances may occur, but every individual is distinguishable from every other. Some of this **phenotypic**, or physically expressed, variation is due to variation in the **genotype**, or the genetic constitution, and some is due to **environmental modification**, such as differences in nutritional history or hair stylists.

Quantitative genetics describes this relationship between an organism's phenotype, its genotype, and environmental influences as

$$V_p = V_g + V_e + V_{ge}$$

where V_p is overall phenotypic variation among individuals, V_g is variation due to genotype (usually multi-locus), V_e is variation due to environmental influences, and V_{ge} is variation due to genetic–environmental interactions. A particular physical or behavioral character may be due entirely to genotype (such as eye color), to environment (such as loss of a limb in an accident), or, more likely, to a combination of both (such as skin color as an interaction between racial background [genetics] and recent exposure to sunlight [environment]). This relationship is the essence of the age-old "nature versus nurture," or genetics versus environment, debate, an argument about whether genetics or environment is more important as the basis for an individual's phenotype. The answer, of course, is usually "both." Suffice it to say here that genetic variation is important at the level of the individual because it forms part of the basis for its phenotype.

At any particular gene locus an individual has two **alleles**, or copies of the gene inherited from its two parents. At the *population* level, each locus may be said to be either **monomorphic** (both copies of the allele are always the same; there is no variation at that locus) or **polymorphic** (there are multiple types of alleles at that locus). For any particular *individual*, any polymorphic locus may be either **homozygous** (two copies of the same allele) or **heterozygous** (two different alleles); monomorphic loci, of course, are always homozygous. The overall level of heterozygosity, or the proportion of gene loci in an individual that contains alternative forms of alleles, is one measure of individual genetic diversity.

Rarely can we directly document alleles, however. We can more easily determine allele products, such as enzymes encoded by gene loci. The technique of protein **electrophoresis** is typically used to estimate the genetic constitution of individuals at selected gene loci. In electrophoresis, a tissue sample such as blood, muscle, or plant leaves is homogenized and placed in a gel medium, through which is passed an electric current. All of the enzymes and other proteins in the sample migrate various distances through the gel based on their relative sizes and electric charges, which are unique to each. When a protein-specific stain is applied to the gel, the locations of the particular forms of that enzyme (called **allozymes**) are revealed (Figure 6.2). In this way, one can determine the presumptive alleles carried by the individual that are responsible for the allozymes present, and infer the genotype of that individual.

The significance of within-individual variation as measured by techniques such as electrophoresis is that greater heterozygosity may correlate with higher individual fitness, a topic to be addressed below. The ultimate origin of

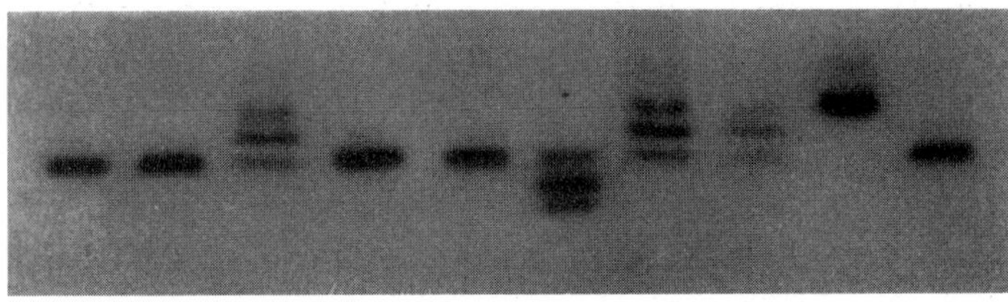

Figure 6.2 A protein electrophoresis gel showing the genetic diversity that can be detected with this technique. Each column represents a single individual of a greenhead horsefly (*Tabanus nigrovittatus*). Single lines in a column indicate homozygotes and multiple lines show heterozygotes for, in this case, the locus "isocitrate dehydrogenase." (Photograph courtesy of Robert C. Vrijenhoek).

such genetic variation is **mutations**, but within-individual variation is produced each generation by recombination during sexual reproduction.

What is the value of a focus on individual genetic variation? First, the individual is the level upon which natural selection acts. Genetic variation at the individual level can reflect the action of selection, or can indicate low levels of diversity relevant to conservation. Second, the individual is the level at which genetic problems such as inbreeding occur; this will be discussed below. Third, knowledge of individual genotypes may be important in captive breeding programs, in which mating schemes may be developed that attempt to maximize genetic diversity of offspring. Finally, genetic variation is always measured in individuals, but is then summed over populations and compared at that higher level. Rarely do we direct our conservation efforts solely toward individuals; more typically, populations or species are the units of concern. Consequently, we must understand genetic variation of groups, variation both within and among populations.

Variation within Populations

Population-level genetic variation consists of the types of alleles present and their frequencies across all members of a population considered together (the **gene pool**). Both the conservationist and the population geneticist are interested in the structure of that variation—how much there is and how it is distributed over space and time. The causes of change in this structure are of particular interest to the conservation biologist, who generally wishes to minimize major losses of genetic variation or changes in its natural distribution.

Genetic variation at the population level is described by the types and frequencies of alleles present, and by the particular combination of alleles (genotypes). Consider, for example, the gene locus that encodes an enzyme called phosphoglucomutase (PGM) in the club moss *Lycopodium lucidulum*, a primitive plant (Table 6.1). This locus has three possible alleles in this species, designated *a*, *b*, and *c*. Among four populations in New York and Connecticut, there are major differences in the presence and frequencies of these alleles. One Connecticut population has alleles *b* and *c*, another has only *b*; one New York population has only *a* and *b*, and the other has only *b*. Each population may thus be described by the types (*a*, *b*, *c*) and frequencies of occurrence of these alleles. With measurements across a broad spectrum of gene loci (Table 6.1), patterns often emerge that distinguish populations genetically.

Gene frequencies within a population generally change over time, due to selection, random processes such as **genetic drift**, or immigration from or emigration to other populations, called **gene flow** (Figure 6.3). It is these changes in gene frequencies, and especially losses of alleles, that are often of concern to the conservation biologist, and they will be discussed in detail below.

Variation among Populations

Species rarely exist as single, randomly interbreeding, or **panmictic**, populations. Instead, genetic differences typically exist among populations; these

Table 6.1
Gene Frequencies at Five Polymorphic Loci in the Club Moss *Lycopodium lucidulum*

Locus	Allele	Woodridge, CT	Litchfield, CT	Binghamton, NY	New Lebanon, NY
PGM					
	a	0.00	0.00	0.50	0.00
	b	0.86	1.00	0.50	1.00
	c	0.14	0.00	0.00	0.00
PGI-2					
	a	0.68	1.00	1.00	0.75
	b	0.32	0.00	0.00	0.25
G6PD-1					
	a	0.93	1.00	0.82	0.91
	b	0.07	0.00	0.18	0.09
G6PD-2					
	a	1.00	1.00	0.50	1.00
	b	0.00	0.00	0.50	0.00
LGGP-1					
	a	0.50	0.50	1.00	1.00
	b	0.50	0.50	0.00	0.00

From Levin and Crepet 1973.

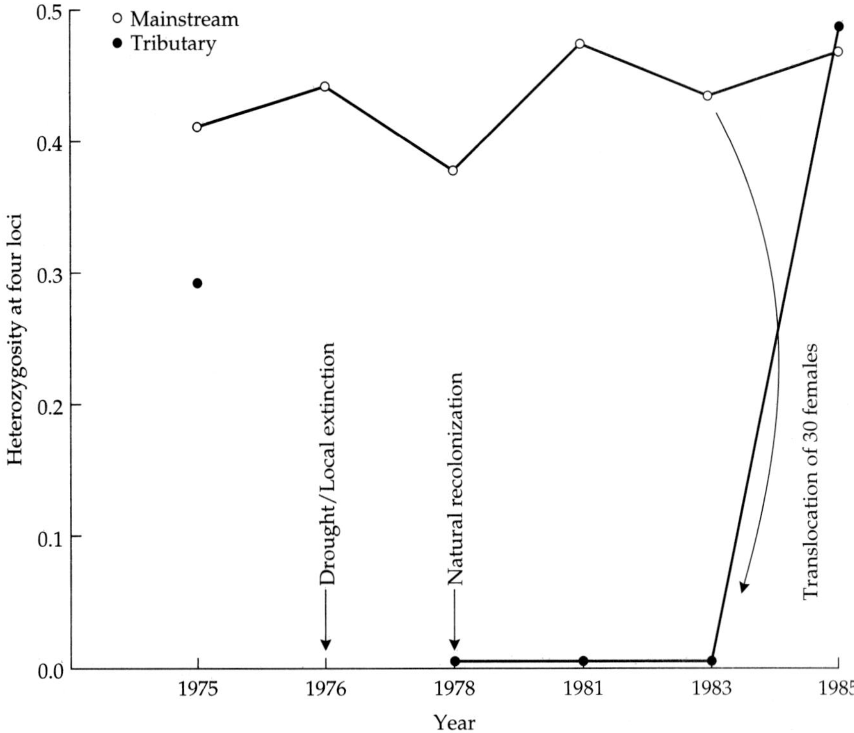

Figure 6.3 Example of gene frequency change due to local extinction and a founder event in a natural population of *Poeciliopsis monacha*, a small desert fish of Sonora, Mexico. Heterozygosity at four loci from fish in a small tributary dropped from near 0.3 in 1975 to zero after a drought and local extinction. Natural recolonization by presumably few individuals resulted in zero heterozygosity from 1978 through 1983, while heterozygosity in an adjacent mainstream population remained high. Translocation (gene flow) of 30 fish to the tributary population from the mainstream population restored heterozygosity in 1985. (Modified from Vrijenhoek 1989a.)

geographic genetic differences are a crucial component of overall genetic diversity.

To understand among-population variation, consider a hypothetical species consisting of three populations (Figure 6.4). Genetic diversity in this "species" consists of within-population diversity (mean individual heterozygosity level within a population) and among-population divergence (mean genetic difference among geographic locations). A simple genetic model of this diversity is

$$H_t = H_p + D_{pt}$$

where H_t = total genetic variation (heterozygosity) in the species, H_p = average diversity within populations (average local heterozygosity), and D_{pt} = average divergence among populations across the total species range (Nei 1973, 1975). Divergence may arise among populations both from random processes (founder effects, genetic drift, demographic bottlenecks, and mutations, discussed below) and from local selection.

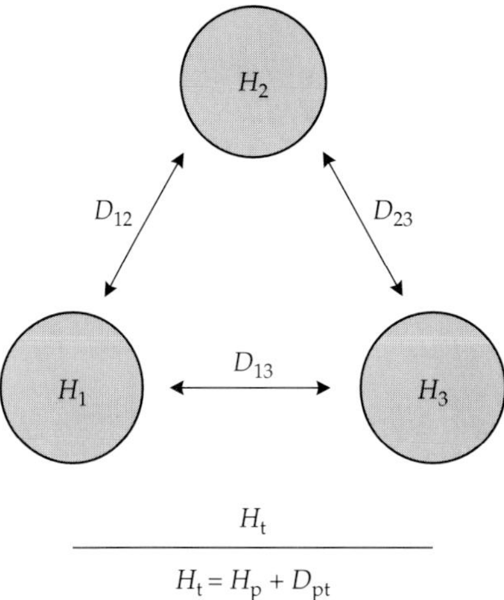

Figure 6.4 Partitioning of total genetic diversity, H_t, into within- and among-population variation. This schematic represents a species with three populations, each with some level of within-population heterozygosity (H_1, H_2, and H_3); mean heterozygosity is H_p. Among-population divergence (D_{12}, D_{23}, and D_{13}) is represented by the arrows between populations; mean divergence is D_{pt}.

The critical point is that a species' total genetic variation can be partitioned into component parts: within- versus among-population diversity. With that approach, one can determine how variation is spatially distributed and can thus define areas of particular conservation interest. For example, Stangel et al. (1992) found that the endangered Red-cockaded Woodpecker (*Picoides borealis*) in the southeastern United States had an overall mean allozyme heterozygosity level of 0.078 (or 7.8%), which is within the typical range of values for most bird species that have been sampled. Of the total genetic variation measured, 14% consisted of among-population differentiation (D_{pt}), and 86% was mean genetic diversity (H_p) within populations. The among-population component for these woodpeckers is higher than for most other bird species examined, whose vagility typically results in high genetic exchange and thus little local genetic differentiation. These woodpeckers are more site-specific than many birds, and consequently local populations tend to diverge genetically. Conservation programs for this species should therefore protect both components of genetic diversity in order to retain the maximum amount of total variation and maintain a natural population genetic structure. We will return to this topic in detail when we discuss management of genetic diversity in nature. An overview of levels of total heterozygosity (H_t) and the proportion of that heterozygosity attributable to among-population divergence (D_{pt}) in natural populations is offered in Table 6.2.

The Fitness Consequences of Variation

We stated earlier that genetic diversity is the basis for a species' evolutionary flexibility and responsiveness to environmental change. Let us now elaborate on that statement by looking at, first, the association between the genetic diversity of individuals (heterozygosity) and their fitness, and second, the importance of among-population genetic divergence.

An individual's **fitness** is defined by its lifetime reproductive success *relative to other individuals in the population*. In genetic terms, fitness is measured as the proportion of the next generation's gene pool represented by the individual's genotype. Fitness is thus a *relative* term, measured against the performance of all other individuals in the gene pool. Fitness is extremely difficult to measure in nature (Endler 1986), but characters that probably contribute to fitness (*fitness correlates*), such as size, fecundity, growth rate, or metabolic efficiency, often can be quantified. An important question, then, is whether these fitness correlates are related to heterozygosity. If so, then preservation of as much genetic diversity as possible is a matter of high conservation priority.

Table 6.2
Mean Total Heterozygosity (H_t) and Proportion Due to Among-Population Differentiation (D_{pt}) in Several Major Taxonomic Groups

Taxon	H_t	No. of species	D_{pt}	No. of species
Vertebrates				
Fishes	5.1%	195	0.135	79
Amphibians	10.9%	116	0.315	33
Reptiles	7.8%	85	0.258	22
Mammals	6.7%	172	0.242	57
Birds	6.8%	80	0.076	16
Invertebrates				
Insects	13.7%	170	0.097	46
Crustaceans	5.2%	80	0.169	19
Mollusks	14.5%	105	0.263	44
Others	16.0%	15	0.060	5

From Ward et al. 1992.
Note: Notice that the more vagile groups (birds, insects) have the lowest levels of among-population differentiation.

Many population geneticists agree that heterozygosity enhances fitness-related characteristics. The evidence for this is good (e.g., Figure 6.5, and summarized in Mitton and Grant 1984, and in Allendorf and Leary 1986), although there are counterexamples (Zouros and Foltz 1987) and cautionary guides (Hedrick and Miller 1992).

Although high heterozygosity levels may appear to be good, not all species or populations have high levels of heterozygosity, and there is no standard, "acceptable" level. Typical heterozygosity levels vary greatly among taxonomic groups (see Table 6.2), and heterozygosity may simply reflect the recent demographic history of a population. Measured values from natural populations range from 0 to over 0.3 (0% to >30%). Mean measured values are about 0.07 for plants, 0.11 for invertebrates, and 0.05 for vertebrates, with a great deal of variance around each mean (Nevo 1978). Thus, expectations of

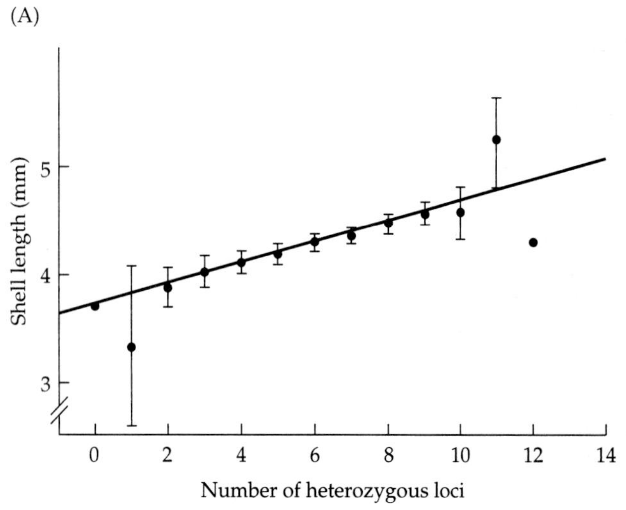

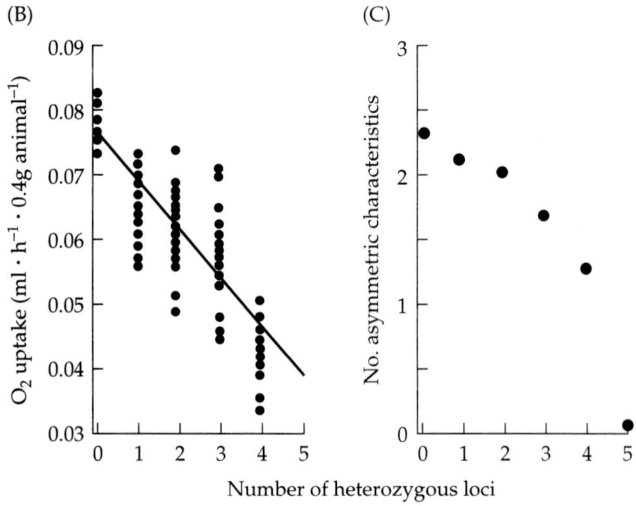

Figure 6.5 Three examples of correlations between heterozygosity level and a fitness-related character. (A) Growth rate in the coot clam *Mulinia lateralis* over a two-week period after collection as larvae. (B) Oxygen consumption in the American oyster (*Crassostrea virginica*); low consumption indicates greater metabolic efficiency. (C) Morphological asymmetry in rainbow trout (*Oncorhynchus mykiss*); greater asymmetry indicates less developmental stability. (A, from Koehn et al. 1988; B, from Koehn and Shumway 1982; C, from Leary et al. 1983.)

heterozygosity levels vary greatly, and a low level, or even no heterozygosity, does not necessarily indicate an anomaly. However, *loss* of heterozygosity in a population, especially over just a few generations, may indicate real problems.

The mechanisms that may translate higher heterozygosity into higher fitness are not clearly understood. In some cases, higher fitness may be due to **overdominance** at a single locus or multiple loci, wherein the heterozygous genotype is superior to either homozygote. This is clearly the case for the locus encoding the β chain of human hemoglobin in Africa. Two doses of the normal allele make the individual susceptible to malaria, a common parasitic disease in some areas. An alternative allele, in homozygous form, leads to severe anemia through sickling of red blood cells (sickle-cell anemia). A heterozygous individual, however, is protected from malaria and is only mildly anemic; the heterozygote clearly has higher fitness than either homozygote in a malarial environment, expressing the characteristic of overdominance. In other cases, higher fitness may derive not from individual heterozygous loci (overdominance), but by lethal or sublethal recessive alleles being masked by alternative alleles (called **dominance**). That is, homozygosity at these loci would be lethal, or would at least reduce fitness. This is particularly a problem in inbreeding populations, as discussed below.

An oft-cited example of a correlation between low heterozygosity and low fitness (at least in captivity) is the South African cheetah (*Acinonyx j. jubatus*). Fifty-five cheetahs from several populations examined had no detectable genetic diversity at 47 allozyme loci ($H = 0.0\%$), low heterozygosity ($H = 1.3\%$) of 155 soluble proteins, and no diversity in the major histocompatibility complex (O'Brien et al. 1983, 1985). These animals were so genetically uniform that skin tissue transplants were routinely accepted among all individuals; their immune systems could not distinguish between themselves and other individuals because they were virtually identical genetically. It was claimed that these animals had difficulty breeding in captivity, there were high rates of infant mortality in both wild and captive populations, males had sperm counts ten times lower than related cat species and 70% morphologically abnormal sperm, and the species was especially susceptible to an epizootic coronavirus under zoo conditions. Both genetic diversity and fitness in captivity in these populations are thus low.

However, the cheetah story is not without controversy, as is often the case in conservation. O'Brien and his colleagues attributed the low heterozygosity in cheetahs to multiple demographic bottlenecks, but this conclusion has been criticized by Pimm (1991) and others as unsupported and unrealistic. Also, there is evidence that male cheetahs in zoos, despite abnormal sperm, can fertilize females with high efficiency and produce normal offspring (Lindburg et al. 1993). Additionally, there is a problem of cause and effect, as there is no "control" group with which to compare these cheetahs. Do cheetahs have poor reproductive performance because of low genetic diversity, or low diversity because of a history of poor reproductive performance? Some have suggested that poor performance in captivity is merely due to poor husbandry (Caro 1993). Caro and Laurenson (1994) presented convincing evidence that low population densities and poor recruitment in the wild are due to heavy predation on juveniles (73% known mortality from predation), rather than lack of genetic diversity. Merola (1994) has argued that the low genetic diversity found in cheetahs is not unusual for terrestrial carnivores, and that habitat destruction is a major cause of the cheetah's decline in the wild, although O'Brien (1994) challenges this position. Whatever the cause, the fact remains that the cheetah has little measurable genetic variation and, at least in some cases, low fitness correlates in captivity.

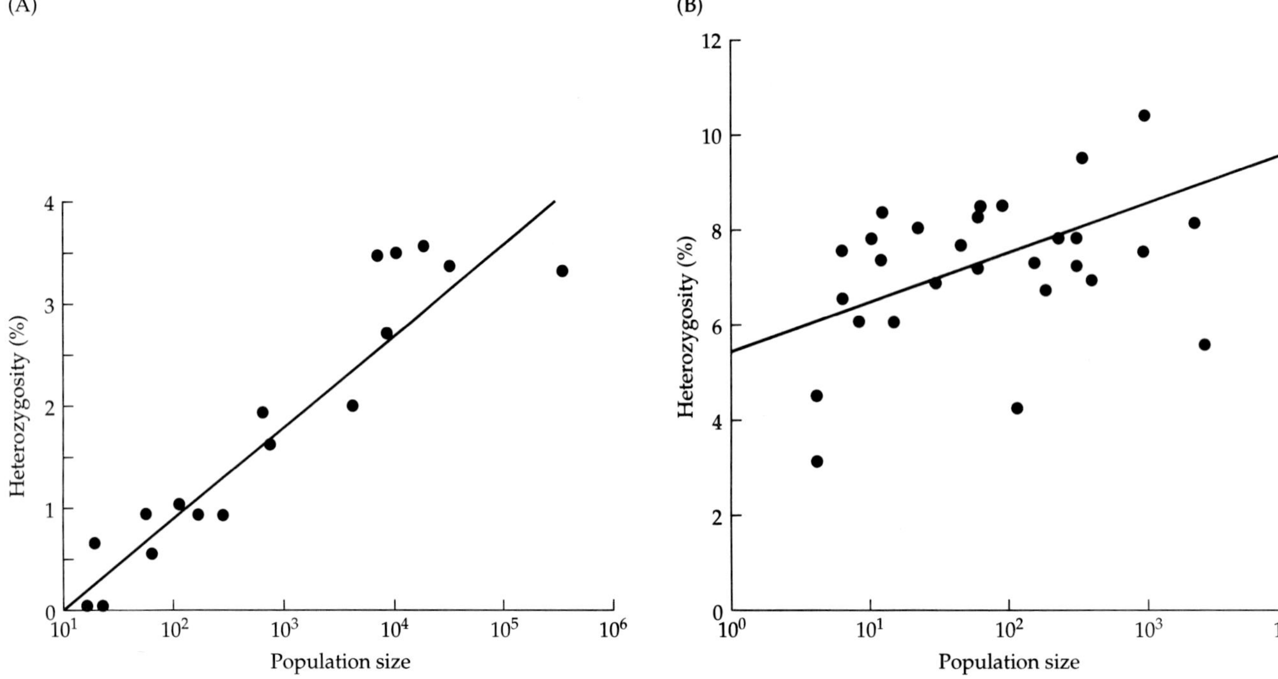

Figure 6.6 Relationships between heterozygosity level and population size in two species. (A) *Halocarpus bidwillii*, a coniferous tree from New Zealand ($r = 0.94$). (B) The Red-cockaded Woodpecker (*Picoides borealis*) from the southeastern United States ($r = 0.48$). (A, from Billington 1991; B, data from Stangel et al. 1992.)

Regardless of its actual fitness effects, heterozygosity is often higher at larger population sizes (Figure 6.6). This implies that small populations tend to lose heterozygosity over time, which is an argument for maintaining large populations, and thus large reserves, wherever possible. This topic will be revisited repeatedly in this and other chapters.

A cautionary note is in order relative to heterozygosity estimates for small populations of wild organisms. Low heterozygosity per se does not necessarily mean that a demographic bottleneck has occurred or that the population is in genetic danger. Sherwin et al. (1991) studied a small, endangered, and isolated population of the eastern barred bandicoot (*Perameles gunnii*), a marsupial, in southeastern Australia. No genetic variation was detected at 27 loci, suggesting an effect of small population size. However, two large "control" populations in Tasmania also had no variation at those loci, indicating that recent population size alone cannot account for the paucity of genetic diversity in this species. Too often, control populations for comparison are lacking. Many species in nature have little detectable genetic variation (Nevo 1978; Ward et al. 1992; Merola 1994), yet seem to do well; some of these clearly have had small populations in historical time, whereas others have not.

Among-population divergence also may play a critical role in local fitness and population survival, for two reasons. First, populations may be locally adapted, due to the long-term interaction of their genome with the biotic and abiotic environments of the region and selection for that region. Local adaptation is common, and is readily seen in many plant and animal populations; it may even lead to speciation (Chapter 3). Second, so-called **coadapted gene complexes** may arise in local populations (discussed in Essay 6A by Alan Templeton). These are gene combinations with a long history together in a population, and are thought to work particularly well in combination. For

ESSAY 6A
Coadaptation, Local Adaptation, and Outbreeding Depression

Alan R. Templeton, Washington University, St. Louis

When individuals of an animal or plant species from different geographic areas are brought together, as in captive breeding or translocation programs, they often hybridize with one another. Outbreeding depression occurs if these hybrids, or the offspring of the hybrids, have reduced fertility and/or survival abilities. There are two main causes of outbreeding depression: coadaptation and local adaptation. Coadaptation results when a local population evolves a gene pool that is internally balanced with respect to reproductive fitness. For example, the process of gamete formation normally requires a matched set of chromosomes (with the exception of the sex chromosomes). However, if the two sets of chromosomes differ in number or structure, fertility problems are possible. This type of coadaptation is illustrated by a reduction in fertility that occurred during captive breeding of the owl monkey, *Aotus trivirgatus* (de Boer 1982). It turned out that animals from different geographic populations had been mixed and that these local populations had different chromosome types. By pairing animals with similar chromosome types, successful reproduction was restored.

The second major cause of outbreeding depression is local adaptation. The geographic range of many species encompasses a variety of environmental conditions. Under such conditions, local populations often adapt to their regional environment, particularly if dispersal among populations is limited. Hybridization between individuals from different local populations often results in individuals that are not adapted to any or to the wrong local environment. For example, ibex (*Capra ibex*) became extinct locally in the Tatra Mountains of Czechoslovakia through overhunting. Ibex were then successfully transplanted from nearby Austria, which had a similar environment. However, some years later, a decision was made to augment the Tatra ibex population by importing animals from Turkey and the Sinai, areas with a much warmer and drier climate. The introduced animals readily interbred with the Tatra herd, but the resulting hybrids rutted in the early fall instead of the winter (as the native Tatra and Austrian ibex did), and the resulting kids of the hybrids were born in February, the coldest month of the year. As a consequence, the entire population went extinct (Greig 1979).

The problem of local adaptation is inherent in all translocation programs, which by definition involve the movement of organisms from one location to another. If the translocation program also involves moving organisms from more than one location to a common place, the problem of coadaptation is also present. Both local adaptation and coadaptation were factors in the reintroduction of collared lizards (*Crotaphytus collaris*) in the Missouri Ozarks.

Most collared lizards live in the deserts of the American Southwest. The Ozark populations therefore represent both a geographic and ecological extreme for the species as a whole. Although there are no true deserts in the Ozarks, the collared lizards can live in glades—open, rocky habitats characterized by a hot, dry microclimate. One of the few trees that can invade these hot, dry glades is the juniper, *Juniperus virginiana.* Prior to European settlement, the Ozarks were subjected to frequent fires that prevented junipers from becoming established in the glades. After European settlement, the suppression of fires has caused many former glades to become completely shaded over by junipers, leading to the extirpation of many glade inhabitants. As the role of fire in the Ozarks has become appreciated, fire regimes have been deliberately reestablished to restore glade habitat. The glade flora has returned remarkably well with little or no need for reintroductions. However, collared lizards will not disperse through even a few hundred yards of forest, so once extirpated from a glade, they are incapable of natural recolonization. Consequently, there was a need for reintroduction of collared lizards as part of a general glade community restoration program.

An examination of past reintroduction programs indicates that the probability of a self-sustaining reintroduced population increases with increasing geographic proximity of the site of origin of the propagules to the site of release (Griffith et al. 1989). Such a strategy minimizes the dangers of local adaptation. Local adaptation was a real danger for the Ozark collared lizards, which inhabit an ecological extreme for the species as a whole and which display many unique adaptive traits not found in their southwestern relatives (Templeton 1994). Therefore, all lizards obtained for the reintroduction program were captured from other Ozark glades whose habitats had not yet degenerated to the point of causing local extinction. Although this strategy minimized the problems associated with local adaptation, it accentuated the danger of coadaptation. The remaining glade populations are small in size, so only a handful of lizards could be collected from any single glade without endangering the natural glade population. This meant that releases into restored glades would have to involve lizards caught from several different natural glade populations. Moreover, molecular genetic surveys revealed that the different natural glade populations are genetically distinct from one another with little or no genetic contact, making the possibility of coadaptation even more likely. Despite the risk of coadaptation, it was decided to go ahead with a mixed release program.

The decision to accept the risk of coadaptation was based on an evolutionary consideration. Natural populations are the products of evolutionary change, and as long as they retain genetic variation, they will continue to evolve. Reintroduced populations are no exception. Hence, evolutionary change, and the factors that promote it or retard it, must be incorporated into strategic decision making. In general, when compromises must be made, genetic diversity and the potential for evolutionary change should always have priority over other considerations. We are simply not wise enough to anticipate all the challenges a reintroduced population will face. If natural or released populations have the potential for evolutionary change, they can evolve solutions to problems such as outbreeding depression or environmental change; without it, their adaptive flexibility is lost. We should never forget that the earth's biodiversity is the product of past evolution and is not, nor has it ever been, static. Hence, conservation programs should try to conserve processes (such as evolution) that affect living organisms and ecosystems rather than conserving the current status quo of the living world.

Mixing lizards from different glades would maximize their genetic variation, and hence they should be capable of overcoming outbreeding depression through evolutionary change, just as captive populations have been able to overcome inbreeding depression through evolutionary change (Templeton and Read 1984). To see if this was the case, and to monitor the success of the release program, a blood sample was taken from each lizard prior to release and scored with molecular genetic surveying techniques. After release, each population has usually been resampled once a year to monitor its success, to gather individual size and growth rate data, and to obtain blood samples from lizards born into the reintroduced population for genetic monitoring.

In terms of the primary goal (to establish self-sustaining genetically variable populations), the program has been completely successful: all six populations released between 1984 and 1989 still existed as of 1993, and are highly genetically variable. The genetic markers also allow individuals to be ranked in their degree of hybridity (the extent to which their ancestry represents mixtures of founders from different glades). By coupling hybrid rankings with data on adult size, growth rates, and reproductive success, the hypothesis of an outbreeding depression can be tested. The data are still being gathered, but preliminary analyses indicate no outbreeding depression. However, regardless of the ultimate outcome, valuable lessons will be learned.

Given the rate at which biodiversity is being lost, management decisions often have to be made with incomplete scientific knowledge. Conservation programs should be implemented in a manner that aids in the management of biodiversity as well as in finding answers to questions about biodiversity that can be generalized to other conservation needs. In this respect, reintroduction programs should be regarded and designed as both management programs and scientific experiments simultaneously.

---

both of these reasons, among-population divergence is an important component of overall genetic diversity, contributing to local uniqueness and evolutionary adaptability.

Loss of Genetic Variation

If genetic variation is important to fitness and adaptive change, then its loss should be of serious concern to conservationists. The central problems in conservation genetics are losses of genetic diversity in small populations and changes in the distribution of this diversity among populations. Losses of diversity can result in reduced evolutionary flexibility and declines in fitness, either from expression of deleterious recessive alleles or loss of overdominance. Changes in the distribution of diversity can destroy local adaptations or break up coadapted gene complexes (outbreeding depression). Both problems can lead to a poorer "match" of the organism to its environment, reducing individual fitness and increasing the probability of population or species extinction. A major concern of conservation biologists at the population level should be to maintain as much natural genetic variation as possible, in as nearly natural a geographic distribution as possible, so that evolutionary and ecological processes can continue. To do this, we need to understand how genetic variation is lost, both within and among populations.

Reduced genetic diversity within populations can arise from four factors that are a function of population size: founder effects, demographic bottlenecks, genetic drift, and the effects of inbreeding. However, it is not the absolute number of individuals, or census size (N_c), that is relevant to the distribution and abundance of genetic variation, but the so-called **genetically effective population size** (N_e), and we must describe that concept first.

Population geneticists have defined an "idealized population" as one in which every individual has an equal probability of contributing genes to the next generation. It is typically conceived of as a large, randomly mating population with nonoverlapping generations, a 1:1 breeding sex ratio, even distribution of progeny numbers among females, and no selection occurring. Because real populations never meet these criteria, but population genetic models are based on such idealized situations, corrections must be made in the sizes of real populations to accurately reflect the parameters affecting levels of genetic diversity. Such a correction is the genetically effective population size (N_e), which is typically smaller, and often much smaller, than the census size (N_c).

An analogy with the "wind chill factor" is helpful in understanding N_e. A winter day of 2°C will feel colder if there is a 20 km/hr wind than if the wind is calm. The effective temperature is reduced by wind; it is *as though* the actual temperature were lower than it really is, due to the chilling effect of wind. Similarly, the effective size of a population, in a genetic sense, may be substantially lower if breeding sex ratios are uneven, or reproductive success among females is uneven, or the population has undergone a major decline in size. The effective size of the population is reduced by these features; it is *as though* the actual population size were lower than it really is, due to the effects mentioned. N_e takes into account who is actually breeding and how many offspring they are contributing to the next generation.

Mathematically, N_e is affected by the sex ratio of the breeding individuals in the following way:

$$N_e = (4N_m \cdot N_f) / (N_m + N_f)$$

where N_m and N_f are the numbers of successfully breeding males and females, respectively. For example, a census population of 500 would have an N_e of 500 (at least with respect to sex ratio) if all individuals bred and there was a 50:50 sex ratio: $N_e = (4 \cdot 250 \cdot 250)/(250 + 250) = 500$. However, if 450 females bred with 50 males, $N_e = (4 \cdot 50 \cdot 450)/(50 + 450) = 180$; the genetically effective population size in this case would be only 36% of the census size because few males participate in breeding. Or, if there were only 114 breeding females and 63 breeding males, and the remaining 323 individuals were immature, N_e would be about 162. This relationship can produce some surprising results. For example, one male breeding with four females results in an N_e (3.2) not much less than that of one male breeding with nine females (3.6) (Seal 1985). Obviously, breeding systems and population structure are important concerns in effective population size and conservation of genetic diversity (Chesser et al. 1993, 1996).

N_e is also strongly affected by the distribution of progeny among females (family size), and is estimated as

$$N_e = 4N_c / (\sigma^2 + 2)$$

where σ^2 = variance in family size among females. Higher variance results in a smaller N_e, which makes intuitive sense: if one female produced the majority of offspring in a population (resulting in higher variance in progeny distribution), her genes would be disproportionately represented in the next generation. The effects of progeny distribution on N_e are clearly demonstrated in Table 6.3. Interestingly, N_e can actually be *twice* N_c if the variation in progeny distribution is zero because all alleles are equally represented in the next generation, and N_e is actually a measure of allelic representation.

Large population fluctuations also reduce N_e because every time a population crashes to a small size, it experiences a demographic bottleneck (discussed below). The harmonic mean of population sizes in each generation provides an estimate of N_e:

$$1/N_e = 1/t\,(1/N_1 + 1/N_2 + \cdots + 1/N_t)$$

where t = time in generations. Table 6.4 shows how a single population crash can produce a large reduction in N_e; in this hypothetical population, a single crash to 25 individuals drastically reduces N_e well below the mean census size.

Table 6.3
Effects of Variance in Number of Progeny among Females (σ^2) on Genetically Effective Population Size (N_e)

σ^2	N_c	N_e	N_e/N_c
0	100	200	2.0
1	100	133	1.3
2	100	100	1.0
5	100	57	0.57
10	100	33	0.33

Note: In all cases, the census population size (N_c) = 100.

Table 6.4
Effects of Population Fluctuations on Genetically Effective Population Size (N_e)

Year	N_c
1	800
2	1000
3	25
4	500
5	1000
5-year mean N_c^a	665
5-year mean N_e^b	110.5

[a]Calculation of 5-year mean N_c: (800 + 1000 + 25 + 500 + 1000)/ 5 = 665
[b]Calculation of 5-year mean N_e: $1/N_e = 1/5(1/800 + 1/1000 + 1/25 + 1/500 + 1/1000) = 1/5\ (0.04525) = 0.00905$; thus, $N_e = 1/0.00905 = 110.5$

To further complicate matters, there are actually two types of genetically effective population sizes. The *inbreeding effective size* (N_{ei}) measures the rate of loss of heterozygous individuals from a local population (a loss of variation within individuals), or simply the increase in inbreeding, while the *variance effective size* (N_{ev}) measures the rate of loss of total genetic variation from a population, whether the loss is experienced within or among individuals (Gliddon and Goudet 1994). Typically, the two numbers differ substantially only when population size is significantly increasing or decreasing (Crow and Kimura 1970), and for our purposes, the subsequent discussion applies to either type of effective population size. The real value of N_{ev} emerges when dealing with multiple or subdivided populations, in which case genetic models can become quite complex when social structure, mating tactics, and patterns of gene flow are considered (Chesser et al. 1993).

Unfortunately, there are no theories or equations that simultaneously handle multiple deviations from the ideal situation. Influences of bottlenecks, skewed sex ratios, and family sizes cannot at present be simultaneously estimated by these models. The important point is that, due to properties associated with sex ratio, family size, and population fluctuations, N_e is nearly always significantly smaller than the census population size. The use of N_e in a management scenario is discussed in Essay 6B by Fred Allendorf.

ESSAY 6B
Genetically Effective Sizes of Grizzly Bear Populations

Fred W. Allendorf, University of Montana

The fragmentation and isolation of populations is of increasing concern in management of endangered species. Loss of genetic variation in isolated populations of large mammals is especially serious because of their low population densities and large spatial requirements. Thus, even the largest protected reserves may be too small to maintain genetically viable populations of large mammals.

The most useful concept for estimating the expected rate of loss of genetic variation in isolated populations is effective population size (N_e). Knowledge of N_e allows prediction of the expected time when reduced genetic variation is likely to threaten continued existence of an isolated population. In spite of agreement about the importance of effective population size for making management decisions, considerable confusion persists about its estimation in natural populations. This is especially true for large mammals because of their complex demographics and numerous departures from the genetically "ideal" population.

Well-known studies with domestic animals have shown that loss of genetic variation has a variety of harmful effects on development, reproduction, survival, and growth rate. Studies with a variety of species in zoos indicate that similar effects probably occur in wild populations of animals (Ralls and Ballou 1986). For example, natural populations of lions (*Panthera leo*) that have lost genetic variation through recent population bottlenecks have more developmentally abnormal sperm and lower testosterone concentrations than adjacent populations that have not lost genetic variation through a bottleneck (Wildt et al. 1987).

The rate of loss of genetic variation generally has been measured by change in average heterozygosity per individual per locus (H). Heterozygosity is expected to be lost at a rate of $1/2N$ per generation in the theoretical "idealized" population of equal numbers of males and females that are all equally likely to contribute a sperm or egg to the next generation (Wright 1969). However, as described in the main text, a wild population of N individuals will lose heterozygosity much faster than $1/2N$ due to unequal sex ratios, fluctuations in population size, and nonrandom reproductive success, resulting in a smaller genetically effective population size (N_e).

A variety of methods provide estimates of N_e under different violations of the assumptions of the ideal population (Wright 1969), but several problems restrict the application of these estimations to wild populations. First, these formulas cannot be combined to estimate rate of loss of genetic variation in a wild population in which all of the assumptions are simultaneously violated. Second, many of the parameters needed to estimate N_e with these formulas are virtually impossible to estimate in wild populations. Finally, most populations do not consist of a single, randomly mating group. Existing formulas for estimating N_e have not been designed to incorporate the effects of gene flow between geographically separated local populations.

In 1975, the U.S. Endangered Species Act declared the grizzly bear (*Ursus arctos horribilis*) to be a threatened species. The number of grizzly bears in the contiguous 48 states has declined from an estimated 100,000 in 1800 to less than 1000 at present. Similarly, the range of the species within this area is now less than 1% of its historical range. The current verified range of the grizzly bear is approximately 5 million ha in six separate subpopulations in four states (Servheen 1985). The range reduction isolated subpopulations because continuous habitat was divided and movement corridors disappeared. Population decline accelerated because these isolated subpopulations were small and subject to stochastic demographic influences.

An estimation of the rate of loss of genetic variation in grizzly bear subpopulations is needed to determine population sizes necessary to maintain genetically viable subpopulations. Moreover, it is also important to determine what management actions can be taken to reduce loss of genetic variation in the remaining subpopulations. Current estimates of **minimum viable population size** (MVP) for the grizzly bear are based upon a comprehensive series of computer simulations of demographic structure (Shaffer and Sampson 1985); recovery targets for some of the six subpopulations are less than 100 individuals, a size that will lose genetic variation at a rate likely to decrease fitness if the subpopulations are isolated.

We have developed a simulation model to estimate effective population size (Harris and Allendorf 1989). The model is a discrete-time, stochastic computer program that follows the history and kinship of each individual. Values of life history parameters used in the simulations were taken from studies of grizzly bear populations in Montana, Wyoming, and British Columbia.

Our results indicate that the effective population size of grizzly bears is approximately 25% of census size (Allendorf et al. 1991). Thus, even fairly large isolated subpopulations, such as the 200 or so bears in Yellowstone National Park, are vulnerable to the harmful effects of loss of genetic variation. A moderate decrease in genetic variation in this population may decrease reproductive rates, further reducing population size, which would further accelerate the rate of loss of genetic variation. The population could thus enter an "extinction vortex" (Gilpin and Soulé 1986).

Exchange of bears among currently isolated subpopulations is likely to be required to decrease the rate of loss of genetic variation. We therefore extended our simulations to determine the amount of gene flow needed to reduce this loss to a more acceptable level. The introduction of only two unrelated bears each generation greatly reduced the rate of loss of genetic variation (Figure A). This agrees with analytic results that have shown that even one migrant per generation is expected to limit genetic divergence among subpopulations (Wright 1969).

Our results support the notion that even large and protected reserves are too small to maintain viable populations of large mammals if they are isolated. Genetically viable populations can only be maintained in such reserves by artificial gene flow among reserves. However, even if all available isolated reserves are genetically connected, there is insufficient habitat available for many species (Ralls and Ballou 1986). A combination of protected natural habitat preserves and ex situ preservation in zoos will become necessary for many species. Zoos will allow an increase in the total number of animals to be maintained and can also serve as sources of individuals to be used in gene exchange programs.

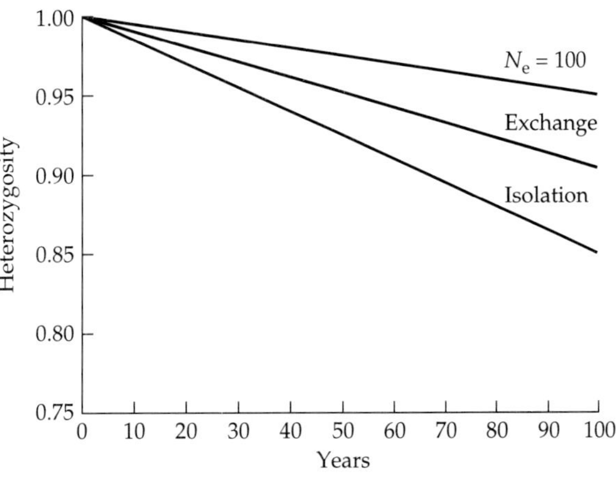

Figure A Expected rate of loss of heterozygosity in a population of 100 grizzly bears. The top line shows the expected rate of loss if the population behaved as an ideal population of 100 individuals. The bottom line shows the rate of loss estimated by computer simulations in an isolated population of 100 bears. The middle line shows the effect of introducing 2 unrelated bears every generation (10 years) into the population of 100 bears.

We can now return to the question of loss of genetic diversity within populations. There are several closely related mechanisms by which small populations lose genetic diversity.

First, a **founder effect** occurs when a few individuals establish a new population, the genetic constitution of which depends upon the genes of the founders. If the founders are not representative of the parent population, or if only a few founders are involved, then the newly established population is a biased sample of the larger gene pool from which it came, and may have lower overall genetic diversity (Table 6.5).

Second, a **demographic bottleneck** occurs when a population experiences a severe, temporary reduction in size. As a result, the genetic variability of all subsequent generations is contained in the few individuals that survive the bottleneck and reproduce, the same phenomenon that occurs in the founder effect. Some genetic variability will be lost in the process; the magnitude of the

Table 6.5
Examples of Genetic Diversity in Founder Populations Compared with the Larger Source Populations

Species	Mean observed heterozygosity: Source/founder	Mean number of alleles per locus: Source/founder	Proportion of loci polymorphic: Source/founder
Anolis grahami[a] (lizard)	0.078/0.064	1.75/1.50	0.50/0.29
Musca autumnalis[b] (fly)	0.053/0.038	1.55/1.46	0.36/0.29
Lymantra dispar[c] (gypsy moth)	0.053/0.002	2.10/1.05	0.50/0.05
Acridotheres tristis[d] (mynah)	0.05/0.03	1.43/1.15	0.31/0.13
Rhagoletis pomonella[e] (apple maggot)	0.189/0.095	2.8/1.5	0.59/0.24
Passer montanus[f] (Eurasian tree sparrow)	0.093/0.079	1.5/1.3	0.36/0.28
Theba pisana[g] (land snail)	0.083/0.056	1.24/1.16	0.22/0.16

From Howard 1993.
[a]Taylor and Gorman 1975.
[b]Bryant et al. 1981.
[c]Harrison et al. 1983.
[d]Baker and Moeed 1987.
[e]McPheron et al. 1988.
[f]St. Louis and Barlow 1988.
[g]Johnson 1988.

loss depends on the size of the bottleneck and the growth rate of the population afterward. The proportion of genetic diversity remaining from one generation to the next is $1 - (1/2N_e)$; this proportion can range from 0.5 (50% variation) with an N_e of 1 (the gametes of one individual carry, on average, 50% of the genetic diversity of the population), to near 1.0 (100%) with a large N_e, say, of 1000. The predicted relationship between population size and remaining genetic variation is shown in Figure 6.7. Generally, a bottleneck rarely has severe genetic or fitness consequences if population size quickly recovers in a generation or two.

Third, **genetic drift** is a random change in gene frequencies in small populations attributable to sampling error. That is, in small populations, by chance alone, some alleles will not be "sampled" or represented in the next generation. Mathematically, genetic drift simply represents a chronic bottleneck that results in repeated losses of variability and eventual fixation of loci (loss of alleles resulting in monomorphic loci). The proportion of variation retained is estimated by $[1 - (1/2N_e)]^t$, where t is the number of generations at that population size. Whereas a single-generation bottleneck of moderate size, say 10–50, may not severely reduce genetic diversity (Figure 6.7), a prolonged bottleneck of the same size, resulting in genetic drift, can have greater effects (Figure 6.8).

Population genetics theory tells us that perhaps more important than depletion of quantitative genetic variation by founder events, demographic bottlenecks, or genetic drift is loss of rare alleles from the population. However, empirical support for this idea is not abundant. We do know that rare alleles contribute little to overall genetic variation, but they may be important to a population during infrequent or periodic events such as unusual temperatures or exposure to new parasites or pathogens, and may offer unique responses to future evolutionary challenges. The expected number of alleles, $E_{(n)}$, remaining at a locus in each generation is estimated as

$$m - \sum_{1}^{j} \left(1 - p_j\right)^{2N_e}$$

where m = the original number of alleles, and p_j is the frequency of the jth allele (from Denniston 1978). The loss of alleles due to genetic drift is demonstrated in Table 6.6, in which rare alleles are seen to be lost rapidly from small populations, even though much of the overall genetic diversity is retained.

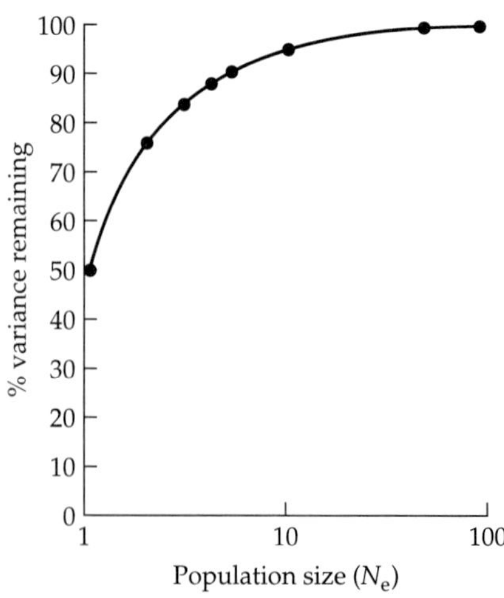

Figure 6.7 Average percentage of genetic variance remaining after bottlenecks of various sizes in a theoretical, idealized population.

Fourth, **inbreeding**, or mating of individuals related by common ancestry, is a potentially serious problem whose probability of occurrence increases in smaller populations if mating occurs at random (i.e., if mating with relatives is not actively avoided). Empirically, there is no absolute measure of inbreeding; the level of inbreeding is measured relative to that of a base population. The

Table 6.6
The Loss of Rare Alleles as a Function of Population Size

N_e	No. alleles remaining	% original alleles remaining	% quantitative variation remaining
1000	≈8.00	≈100.0%	99.95%
100	7.81	97.6%	99.5%
10	3.86	48.3%	95.0%
5	2.69	33.6%	90.0%
1	1.35	16.9%	50.0%

Note: In this hypothetical example, a large population starts with 8 alleles, 7 of which are rare. Original allele frequencies are 0.80, 0.07, 0.03, 0.03, 0.02, 0.02, 0.02, and 0.01. The average number of remaining alleles after one generation at various effective population sizes is shown. Notice that the percentage of allelic variation declines at a much faster rate than overall quantitative variation.

expected increase in inbreeding per generation, ΔF, is expressed, once again, as $1/2N_e$ if panmixia prevails. Inbreeding results in a predictable increase in homozygosity, and may be manifested as **inbreeding depression**, such as reductions in fecundity, offspring size, growth, or survivorship (Figure 6.9), changes in age at maturity, and physical deformities (Falconer 1981). Two competing hypotheses have been proposed for the mechanism leading to inbreeding depression. The *dominance hypothesis* states that inbreeding results in more instances of deleterious recessive alleles appearing in homozygous form, where they are clearly expressed, rather than being masked by dominance in the heterozygous condition. The *overdominance hypothesis* focuses instead on the loss of genome-wide heterozygosity and its presumed fitness advantages. In this model, inbreeding results in loss of heterozygosity with its attendant lowered fitness. These two hypotheses result in different predictions about relative tolerance to inbreeding. The dominance hypothesis suggests that inbred populations have already experienced exposure of deleterious recessive alleles, and most have probably been purged from the population; further inbreeding should not then have large effects on fitness. The overdominance hypothesis, however, predicts that further inbreeding should result in continued loss of fitness through further heterozygosity losses. Much evidence to date supports the dominance hypothesis (Charlesworth and Charlesworth 1987), indicating that homozygosity for deleterious recessive alleles is a major factor in inbreeding depression, although the matter is by no means settled.

Data from domesticated animals indicate that a ΔF of 10% will result in a 5–10% decline in individual reproductive traits such as clutch size or survival rates; in aggregate, total reproductive attributes may decline by 25% (Frankel and Soulé 1981). Data on inbreeding depression in the wild are difficult to compile, as the level of inbreeding is not easily determined. A few studies, however, have demonstrated severe inbreeding depression. In experimental studies, inbred and outbred land snails (Chen 1993) and white-footed mice (Jimenez et al. 1994) were released into the field and their survivorship followed. In both cases, inbred individuals had significantly lower survival rates. Heschel and Paige (1995) documented reduced seed size and germination success, and higher mortality during stress, in smaller compared with larger populations of the scarlet gilia plant; these results were attributable to inbreeding (and possibly genetic drift) in small populations. Keller et al. (1994) studied a natural population of song sparrows in which inbreeding coefficients were known through pedigree analysis. The population crashed during severe winter weather, and outbred individuals survived at a significantly higher rate than inbred individuals.

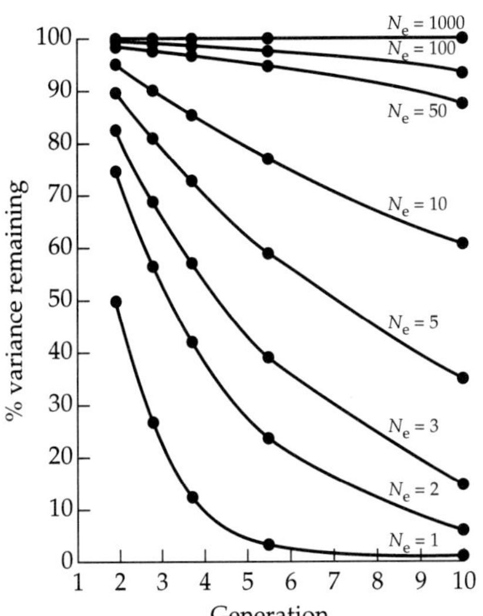

Figure 6.8 Average percentage of genetic variance remaining over 10 generations in a theoretical, idealized population at various genetically effective population sizes (N_e). Variation is lost randomly through genetic drift.

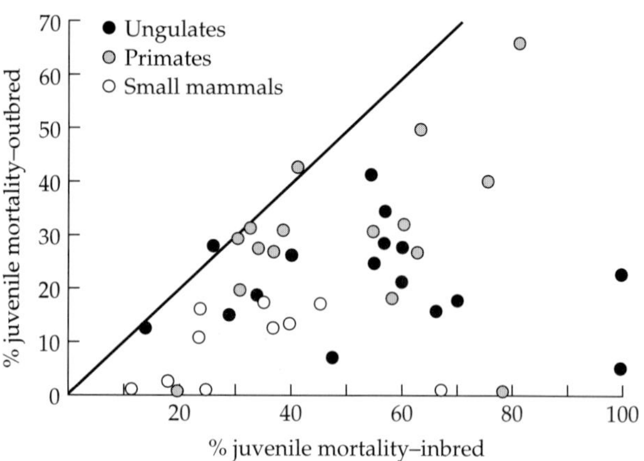

Figure 6.9 The effects of inbreeding on juvenile mortality in captive populations of mammals. Each point compares the percentage of juvenile mortality for offspring of inbred and noninbred matings. The line indicates equal levels of mortality under the two breeding schemes. Points above the line represent higher mortality from noninbred matings; points below the line, higher mortality from inbred matings. The distance of a point from the line indicates the strength of the effect of level of inbreeding. (From Ralls and Ballou 1983.)

Many species are known to avoid inbreeding in the wild (Pusey and Wolf 1996), further evidence that inbreeding depression is real and important. Inbreeding also may have a threshold relationship with extinction, wherein a population persists quite well until a particular level of inbreeding is reached, then suddenly declines to extinction (Frankham 1995).

Not all inbreeding is cause for alarm. Some natural populations apparently have experienced low levels of inbreeding for many generations with no ill effects (Thornhill 1993). In these cases, it is thought that slow inbreeding has given natural selection an opportunity to purge the population of deleterious recessive alleles (the dominance hypothesis). Sudden increases in inbreeding, however, can be damaging to a population, especially if it has little history of prior inbreeding. Inbreeding depression may therefore be more prevalent in a species or population with historically large population sizes that now occurs in small populations.

The fundamental point of this section is that small, isolated populations—which describes many threatened and endangered species—will lose some percentage of their original genetic diversity over time, approximately at the rate of $1/2N_e$ per generation. A population of 1000 will retain 99.95% of its genetic diversity (assuming a lack of selection) in a generation, while a population of 50 will retain only 99.0%. Such losses of diversity may seem small, but are magnified over many generations. After 20 generations, the population of 1000 will still retain over 99% of its original variation, but the population of 50 will retain less than 82%. Small population numbers over a prolonged period are thus to be avoided in conservation programs whenever possible. This principle is particularly apropos to captive breeding programs.

The theory and causes of loss of genetic variation are clear, but what about empirical evidence? Are populations of endangered species, for example, actually depauperate in genetic variation? Avise (1994) lists and discusses some 14 cases of endangered plant and animal populations with low to undetectable levels of genetic diversity, including northern elephant seals (Hoelzel et al. 1993), gray wolves (Wayne et al. 1991), the Asiatic lion (Wildt et al. 1987), and a narrowly endemic clover (Hickey et al. 1991). On the other hand, he also lists five endangered species with quite normal levels of genetic variation, including a flightless parrot from New Zealand (Triggs et al. 1989) and the manatee (McClenaghan and O'Shea 1988). Clearly, there should be concern about low genetic variation in small populations of endangered species, but it by no means is a universal pattern.

Loss of among-population genetic diversity occurs when historically divergent and isolated populations experience an artificially high rate of genetic exchange with other populations through human actions. This can occur when plants or animals are moved (intentionally or inadvertently) by people, or when new movement corridors are created. The uniqueness of formerly isolated populations may then be diminished or lost, as may their local adaptations and coadapted gene complexes.

It is important to remember that the total amount of genetic variation in a species (H_t) is a function of within-population diversity (H_p) and among-population divergence (D_{pt}), as described above. Simply looking at H_t does not provide a clear picture of genetic diversity, as overall diversity can be a complicated balance between the two individual components. For example, decreasing D_{pt} by homogenizing populations through gene flow will probably increase H_p, keeping H_t constant. However, an important component of genetic diversity, population uniqueness, may be lost in the process. Generally, an increase in one component of diversity results in a decline in the other, and this can be a complicating problem in management.

Management of Genetic Variation in Natural Populations

If evolution is the unifying feature and driving force of natural systems, then the primary goal of genetic management in nature should be to allow continued evolutionary change in the populations and species of concern. By definition, evolution is dynamic, and change is expected. Ecological systems are dynamic, and generally are not at equilibrium (see Chapter 1). The best way to "manage" such dynamic, changing systems is to permit and allow for change—a *conservationist* rather than a *preservationist* approach. Simply maintaining the status quo is inappropriate to long-term conservation at any level, including genetics. Rather, a fluid, evolutionary perspective will allow populations to continually adapt to inevitably changing conditions.

Time Scales of Concern

Genetic conservation actions should be compatible with three conservation goals, on three time scales of concern: maintenance of viable populations in the short term (extinction avoidance), maintenance of the ability to continue adaptive evolutionary change, and maintenance of the capacity for continued speciation.

The first level of concern, avoidance of population extinction, has a time scale of days to decades and is the first and most obvious goal of conservation. If this goal is not met, then further goals are automatically denied. Of course, some populations repeatedly undergo extirpation and recolonization cycles, such as "weedy" or "fugitive" species, and local extinction is a natural part of their dynamics. Such is the case of early successional plant species in forests, which appear only when light gaps are opened by tree-falls (Collins et al. 1985). The type of population extinction to be avoided is that which is not part of the natural system dynamics, probably does not have a recolonization source, and is usually caused, directly or indirectly, by human action.

Because all environments change, and change is being accelerated by humans, genetic management must also maintain the ability of populations and species to genetically adapt, or evolve. "Locking" a population or species into a genetic configuration from which it cannot easily escape, as through inbreeding or genetic drift in small populations, is poor long-term management. This concern has a time scale of decades to millennia.

Finally, speciation is the creative part of biodiversity, as extinction is the destructive part. The potential for continued speciation must be maintained, especially now that extinction rates are so exceedingly high. To consider only short-term preservationist goals is to adopt a narrow perspective and ignore the larger picture of the human role in earth's history. Retention of the ability to speciate is the ultimate goal of conservation, although its time scale, tens of thousands or more years, makes it difficult to appreciate.

Units of Conservation

Given the importance of genetic variation to short-term fitness, continued adaptation, and the speciation process, a difficult and practical question confronts the resource manager (Nielsen 1995): What are the units of concern in genetic conservation? What, in fact, should we conserve? Even casual reflection reveals that we cannot save every population, every morphological variant, every unique allele. How do we determine and define the biologically significant units within a species that are worthy of attention?

To answer these questions, we must return to our underlying premise that our main goal in conservation is to conserve evolutionary potential, which of course requires genetic diversity; this should be done irrespective of taxonomic status. Consequently, the population seems the most reasonable level at which genetic conservation should take place. The population, rather than the species, is the ecologically and evolutionarily functional unit. The population is where genetic changes take place over generations, and is where local adaptive change occurs. Natural geographically and genetically isolated populations are of particular interest, as they have the greatest potential for speciation. To conserve only at higher levels, such as species, overlooks important dynamics and attributes of individual populations and risks the loss of critical genetic diversity and local ecological function. On the other hand, to work below the level of populations in the wild, say, with alleles, is impractical at best, a micromanagement approach that is probably counterproductive in a larger, dynamic system.

If we accept the population as the unit of conservation, the problem then becomes how to define a population. The population geneticist has a ready answer—the **deme**, or local, randomly interbreeding group of individuals, is a good and worthy unit of protection. Unfortunately, the deme is often of greater theoretical than practical utility, as it is difficult or impossible to clearly delineate in the wild. How does one define the borders of reproductive isolation for a Michigan beech forest or a fan coral in the Caribbean? Also, a continuum of population types exists, from those that are clearly isolated (such as aquatic plants or animals in desert springs, or birds on small oceanic islands) to those that clearly have genetic exchanges with similar groups in other geographic regions.

Many populations, in fact, may really be members of **metapopulations** (Gilpin and Hanski 1991)—networks of populations that have some degree of intermittent or regular gene flow among geographically separate units (Figure 6.10). For example, the Bay checkerspot butterfly (*Euphydryas editha bayensis*) in California exists in many distinct habitat patches; individuals may move among patches, creating gene flow and recolonizing patches where populations have gone extinct (Ehrlich and Murphy 1987; Harrison et al. 1988). Such metapopulation structures are likely to become even more common as habitat fragmentation splits large populations into smaller units that manage to retain some gene flow. When we speak of populations, then, we may mean anything from a single, clearly isolated unit to a complex network of units with some degree of gene flow. Metapopulations will be discussed in greater detail in a landscape context in Chapter 7.

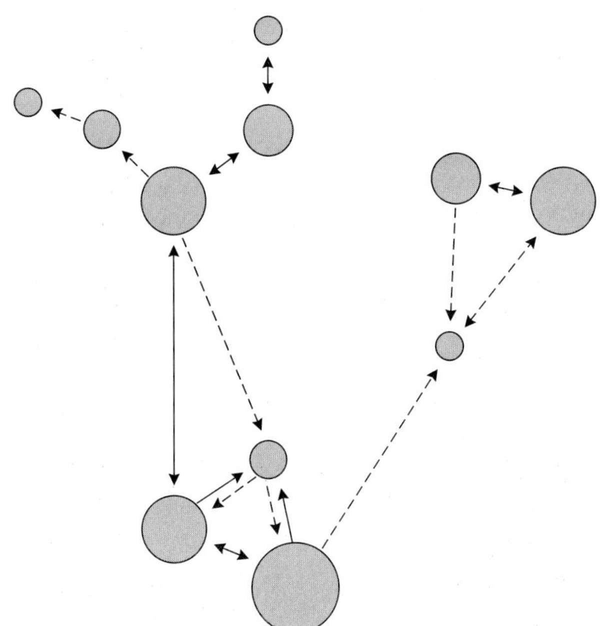

Figure 6.10 An illustration of a metapopulation. Each circle is a local population, with the circle size indicative of relative population size. Solid arrows indicate regular and free gene flow; dashed arrows indicate occasional or irregular gene flow.

Perhaps you can see that we are facing a problem inherent in many aspects of biology: that of trying to define breakpoints in a continuum in which breakpoints may not exist. This problem was discussed in Chapter 3 in the context of defining species: it cannot objectively and absolutely be done, and we must accept some "fuzziness" as a result. Populations exist along a continuum from completely isolated units to those that experience regular genetic exchange with similar units. In trying to define a population we must realize that most populations probably experience some level of genetic exchange with other populations, and that we will usually not find clear breaks. The best we can do is try to identify units that seem to have some ecological and evolutionary significance.

If we define our goal as protecting biological diversity within species, there are many potential ways to identify conservation units. For example, distinct phenotypes, such as different butterfly color morphs or distinct banding patterns in land snails, could qualify as conservation units. Long-term geographic isolation, such as that found in Galápagos tortoises or in fishes or snails in isolated springs, would certainly qualify populations as reasonable conservation units. Even geographic distance, in the absence of clear isolation, could be used to assign conservation unit status, protecting extremes of a species' geographic range. If populations occur under very different selective regimes that produce distinct life histories or behaviors, they could be considered conservation units. Basically, any biologically relevant characteristics could help to distinguish conservation units within the species level.

The U.S. Endangered Species Act addresses the question of conservation units in a more rigorous, legalistic sense, and provides further guidance. The definition of a "species" in the Act includes "any *distinct population segment* of any species of vertebrate fish or wildlife which interbreeds when mature" (italics added). The phrase "distinct population segment" is rather indistinct, of course, and federal agencies have struggled to find a consistent approach to interpreting "distinct."

A suggested solution (Waples 1991) says that a population is distinct if it represents an **Evolutionarily Significant Unit** (ESU) of the biological species. An ESU is in turn defined as a population that (1) is reproductively isolated from other conspecific population units and (2) represents an important component in the evolutionary legacy of the species. The use of the term "significant" is unfortunate, because it could be interpreted to imply that other units are "insignificant" and can be dispensed with. That is not the case. Virtually any biological unit, down to the single individual, has *potential* evolutionary significance. However, the ESU approach tries to identify levels of biological organization that presently appear to be of greatest importance because of their distinctness.[1]

Adoption of the ESU definition may be satisfying conceptually because it recognizes the evolutionary role, importance, and fate of populations, rather than just species. However, it is difficult operationally for two reasons. The first part of the definition essentially defines a deme, which, as we have already noted, is difficult or impossible to delineate in nature. The second part requires a subjective assessment of the population of concern relative to other populations of the species, which are equally undefined under the first part of the definition. However, as discussed next, an expansion of the simple genetic model presented in Figure 6.4 may offer a reasonable solution to these problems and allow adoption of the ESU approach in a functional, as well as conceptual, sense. Alternatively, Vogler and DeSalle (1994) propose an objective and testable method based on the phylogenetic species concept discussed in Chapter 3.

Hierarchical Gene Diversity Analysis

One approach to more rigorously defining ESUs in a genetic sense is called **hierarchical gene diversity analysis**, and it is based on the fact that species consist of a spatially hierarchical genetic structure. Our task is to partition overall genetic diversity into within-population and among-population components (the latter of which can be further subdivided, as will be explained shortly) and determine where biologically significant breaks in genetic diversity occur. At the lowest level of the hierarchy, interbreeding individuals within a population are genetically most similar. As we move through the hierarchy, we find greater genetic differences among more geographically separated or otherwise distinct populations (e.g., poor dispersers), until we reach the very large genetic differences between populations strongly isolated by physiography or geographic distance. This genetic hierarchy in fact extends beyond populations; under the biological species concept, different, closely related species simply represent very large genetic gaps, which are sometimes crossed in hybridization.

A genetic hierarchy exists because the divergence component of diversity (D_{pt}) can be subdivided based on any biologically meaningful *geographic* hierarchy in the distribution of the species. That is, populations of a species exhibit various levels of genetic divergence from other populations, based on the amount of gene flow among them. Populations that are geographically proximate, and that experience regular gene flow, will be more similar genetically than populations that are geographically farther apart and experience little or no gene flow. A species can thus be visualized as having a spatial genetic architecture. The species consists of a collection of populations with a hierarchical genetic structure based on the degree of genetic similarity among them. In turn, this structure is a function of geography and levels of gene flow.

---

[1] Note that the ESU is similar, but not identical, to the Evolutionary Unit (EU) discussed in Chapter 3. The EU (Clegg et al. 1995) does not stress reproductive isolation as a criterion, as does the ESU, for the practical reason that reproductive isolation is typically difficult to assess. Clegg et al. (1995) argue that the EU and ESU are likely to lead to similar results, especially for vertebrates.

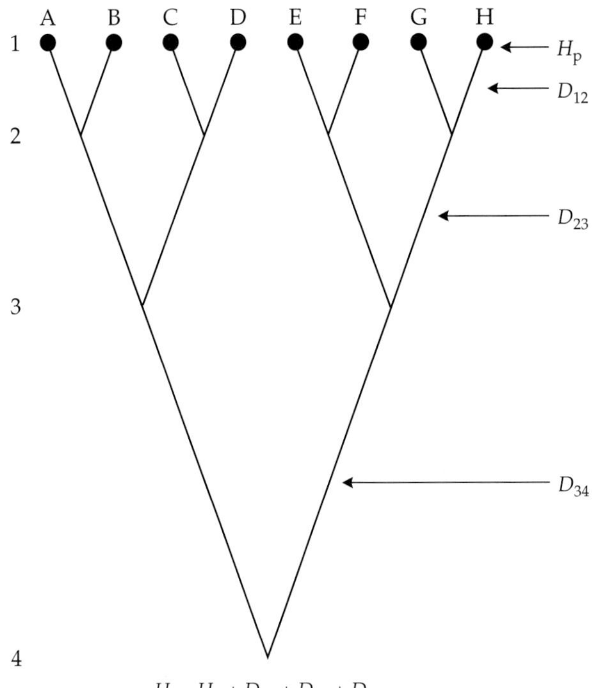

Figure 6.11 A schematic diagram demonstrating a hierarchical genetic structure of a species. The eight populations (A–H) may be grouped at different levels according to some objective geographic criterion. Level 1 in this hierarchy is mean heterozygosity within each population (H_p). The first level of divergence (D_{12}) is the mean genetic divergence between pairs of geographically adjacent populations. Divergence may also occur among the four pairs of two populations (D_{23}) and the two pairs of four populations (D_{34}).

Consider a hypothetical species with eight sampled populations with geographic relationships as shown schematically in Figure 6.11. The number of lines necessary to travel from one population to another is an indication of their geographic proximities. There are four levels of geographic structure in this example that are potentially reflected in genetic structure. Total genetic diversity (H_t) is composed of average heterozygosity of the eight populations (H_p), plus genetic divergence between pairs of adjacent populations (D_{12}), plus genetic divergence among the four groups of two populations (D_{23}), plus genetic divergence between the two groups of four populations (D_{34}).

Perhaps the clearest physical example of a geographic (and thus genetic) hierarchy involves riverine species, because rivers form a geographic structure with a natural hierarchy. River headwaters are called first-order streams, which combine to form second-order streams. Third-order streams consist of two or more second-order streams, and so forth. Consider, then, a species of fish (or plant or benthic invertebrate) that is found in a river drainage, for which 14 sites are sampled, as in Figure 6.12. The relevant questions for genetic conservation are: (1) What is a reasonable breeding unit of concern? and (2) How distinct (evolutionarily significant) are the different breeding units? The task is first to distinguish reasonable breeding units and then to determine what level of genetic divergence represents evolutionary significance.

Total genetic diversity in this case consists of average heterozygosity across all populations (H_p), plus average divergence among populations in first-order within second-order streams (D_{12}), plus average divergence among populations in second-order within third-order streams (D_{23}), plus average divergence among populations in third-order within fourth-order streams (D_{34}). Divergence could also occur among populations in different watersheds across the total range of the species (D_{wt}), or at any other reasonable level in a hierarchy.

Three hypothetical examples illustrate how genetic diversity might be partitioned in a species such as this, and how that information could be used to

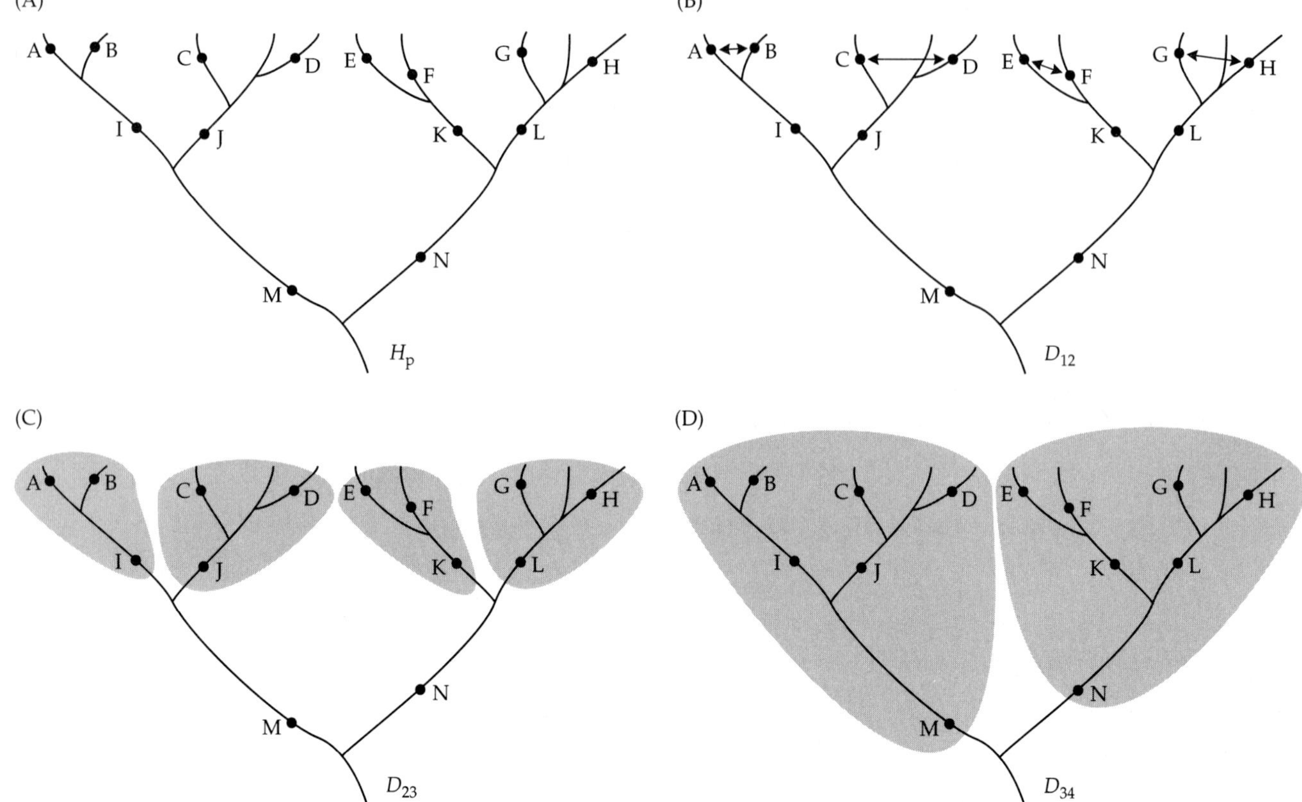

Figure 6.12 A genetic hierarchy in stream organisms based on an objective stream order classification, using 14 sampling sites distributed across the drainage. Total genetic diversity (H_t) may be partitioned into (A) heterozygosity within populations (H_p), (B) mean divergence among populations taken in different first-order streams (D_{12}), (C) mean divergence among populations taken in different second-order streams (D_{23}), and (D) mean divergence of populations taken in different third-order streams (D_{34}).

Table 6.7
Hypothetical Examples of Possible Genetic Hierarchies in Stream Fishes

Level of diversity	% diversity Example 1	Example 2	Example 3
H_p	70.0	70.0	70.0
D_{12}	17.7	0.2	0.6
D_{23}	11.1	22.3	1.3
D_{34}	1.2	7.5	28.1

define an evolutionarily significant unit (Table 6.7). For simplicity, we will assume that the heterozygosity (H_p) or within-population component of diversity is constant (70%) in all three cases. In the first example, 17.7% of genetic diversity occurs as the average divergence among populations in different first-order streams (D_{12}). This large number indicates that fish in different first-order streams experience some reproductive isolation and are good candidates for ESUs. That is, individual local breeding units in each headwater stream have high genetic divergence from similar breeding units in other headwater streams, and need to be managed as evolutionarily significant units. Divergence (11.1%) also occurs among second-order streams, but management at the lower level of first-order streams would automatically maintain divergence at the level of second-order streams.

In the second example, essentially no genetic divergence occurs at the level of first-order streams (there is so much movement and gene flow among fish in connected first-order streams that there is no detectable genetic divergence at that level), but over 22% of genetic diversity occurs as average divergence among fish in different second-order streams. In this case, fish in different second-order streams would be reasonable ESUs for management.

In the third example, significant divergence does not occur until we reach the level of third-order streams; different populations *within* third-order systems are not genetically structured. Because there is little divergence among first- or second-order streams, probably due to high mobility and gene flow throughout the system, any group of fish from any point within the third-order level of the hierarchy fairly represents the entire system. However, fish from different third-order streams are very different and should be treated as ESUs.

The question arises as to what constitutes "significant" genetic differentiation worthy of recognition and protection. There is no easy answer, and each conservation program must determine what is "significant" genetic differentiation in its particular circumstances. This determination should be guided by biological understanding of the system and good genetic data. For example, the cheetah may have extremely low, nearly undetectable levels of genetic diversity; however, what little among-population diversity remains, even if it represents a tiny percentage of overall variation, may be critical to protect. In a highly variable species, that same small percentage of among-population divergence may be unimportant by comparison. There are no cutoffs or rules of thumb here; understanding the biology of the organism and the ecology of the system is the best way to decide upon reasonable levels of genetic differentiation for identifying conservation units.

To date, real-world data are rarely as clear and comprehensive as the hypothetical example presented. Echelle (1991) compiled hierarchical genetic data for numerous fish species of western North America. The data (Table 6.8) allowed genetic diversity to be partitioned into only three levels: within-population diversity (H_p), divergence among samples within drainages (D_{sd}) and divergence between drainages (D_{dt}). (Note that the subscripts can be freely changed to reflect the particular situation; there is nothing set about the subscripts used, or the levels of diversity addressed). Echelle found a great deal of variation among these species in their hierarchical patterns of genetic diversity. Some, such as *Xyrauchen texanus* (razorback sucker) and *Cyprinodon bovinus* (Leon Springs pupfish), had nearly all of their genetic variation represented as within-population heterozygosity. Others, such as *Oncorhynchus clarki henshawi* (cutthroat trout) and *Gambusia nobilis* (Pecos gambusia), had a large proportion of their diversity represented as divergence among samples within drainages. Finally, some had appreciable variation between drainages, such as *O. clarki lewisi* (another cutthroat trout subspecies) and *C. macularius* (desert pupfish).

These data are of limited value because of incomplete geographic sampling; they are therefore only rough approximations of a hierarchical distribution of diversity. Also, they were collected by entire drainages rather than by stream order, and thus may not be fine-grained enough to determine ESUs. Nevertheless, we can see that for some species, local populations contain virtually all of the genetic diversity of the species. From a solely genetic perspective (ignoring for the moment ecological, demographic, and other factors of relevance to conservation decisions), conserving one population will conserve most of the genetic variation in the species. In other cases, strong geographic divergence (either within or between drainages) occurs, indicating the need to conserve multiple units in order to capture a representation of the species' genetic diversity. More comprehensive data sets than these would allow more detailed genetic analyses and better estimation of units of conservation.

Distance as a Genetic Hierarchy. Both the hypothetical example and the Western fish data involve clear geographic hierarchies (stream structure) upon which the genetic hierarchy can be based. If no obvious geographic hierarchy exists, however, this approach can still be used, with distance as the hierarchical unit. In this case, individuals are sampled across part or all of their range of occurrence, and different distances between samples are used as the structuring units (Figure 6.13). For example, oak trees in an oak woodland might have no obvious geographic structure other than distance, but this would not prevent a hierarchical analysis, because trees in closer proximity presumably

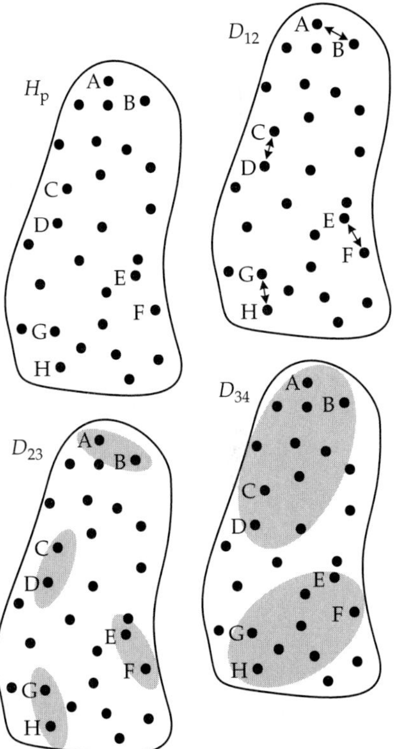

Figure 6.13 A genetic hierarchy based on geographic distance. In this example, eight populations (A–H) of oak trees are sampled across a landscape containing no obvious geographic structure. Total genetic diversity may be partitioned as in previous examples: mean heterozygosity (H_p) within all eight populations; mean divergence of adjacent populations taken at distances of, say, 100 m (D_{12}); divergence among groups of populations at a greater distance, say, 1 km (D_{23}); and divergence across groups over larger distances, say, 10 km (D_{34}).

Table 6.8
Distribution of Genetic Diversity in Endangered and Threatened Fishes of Western North America

Taxon	P/L	H_p	D_{sd}	D_{dt}
Salmonidae (trout and salmon)				
Oncorhynchus nerka	18/26	94.4	3.1	2.5
O. apache	5/35	90.5	9.5	—
O. clarki bouvieri	8/46	96.3	3.7	—
O. clarki henshawi	15/35	55.5	44.5	—
O. clarki lewisi	103/29	67.6	15.7	16.7
O. mykiss	38/16	85.0	7.7	7.3
O. gilae	4/35	86.4	13.6	—
Catostomidae (suckers)				
Catostomus discobolus yarrowi	3/45	54.8	—	45.2
C. plebeius	5/45	92.9	—	7.1
C. plebeius (second study)	4/27	11.3	—	88.8
Xyrauchen texanus	2/21	98.9	1.1	—
Cyprinodontidae (killifishes)				
Cyprinodon bovinus	5/28	98.6	1.4	—
C. elegans	7/28	89.2	10.8	—
C. macularius	3/38	70.1	—	29.9
C. pecosensis	6/28	92.3	7.7	—
C. tularosa	3/28	81.0	19.0	—
Poeciliidae (livebearers)				
Gambusia nobilis	16/24	48.4	51.6	—
Poeciliopsis o. occidentalis	10/25	59.3	40.7	—
Cichlidae (cichlids)				
Cichlosoma minckleyi	3/13	97.7	2.3	—
C. minckleyi (second study)	3/27	94.6	5.4	—
Cottidae (sculpins)				
Cottus confusus	16/33	53.9	46.1	—

Modified from Echelle 1991.
Note: P/L = numbers of populations/gene loci surveyed; percentage of total genetic diversity measured is separated into heterozygosity within populations (H_p), divergence among samples within drainages (D_{sd}), and divergence among drainages (D_{dt}). Dash indicates data not measured at that level in the hierarchy.

form more cohesive genetic units than trees farther apart, inasmuch as gene flow (pollen dispersal) is probably higher among closer trees. Divergence is more likely to occur at greater distances, and the hierarchical approach can detect this pattern. In this case, the hierarchical approach might consider distances of, say, 0.1 km, 1 km, and 10 km as the hierarchical units, and then determine at which level significant genetic divergence occurs.

The actual hierarchical partitioning of the genetic data is accomplished through an analysis called "*F*-statistics," introduced in Box 6A. More detailed consideration of *F*-statistics is beyond the scope of this book, and should be pursued elsewhere (Hartl and Clark 1990 provides a good, general overview; more detailed presentations may be found in some of the original literature, such as Crow and Kimura 1970; Nei 1975; Wright 1978).

The Data Needed for a Hierarchy. The data used in defining conservation units can be anything reliably quantifiable that has variation. Morphological or behavioral data can be used, but these are subject to environmental modi-

BOX 6A

Calculation of *F*-Statistics

Derrick W. Sugg, State University of New York, Geneseo

Fixation indices, or *F*-statistics, were developed by Sewall Wright (1922, 1965, 1969, 1978) as a means of describing how genetic diversity is partitioned in a population. By partitioning genetic diversity into different components, one can determine the relative amounts of diversity residing within individuals, subpopulations, and the overall population. Because adaptive evolution requires genetic variation, it is important to understand how much of the total variation is available for selection acting on individuals. More recently, conservation biologists have shown renewed interest in fixation indices because these indices provide a means to discover how natural populations maintain genetic variation (which is beneficial for developing management strategies) and a means to determine levels of genetic variation in threatened or captive populations (which is beneficial for assessing the success of management strategies).

Typically, when one calculates fixation indices, this is done for a structured population. The classic approach is to sample individuals from different subpopulations at fairly distinct geographic locations. Such a population is said to consist of three levels of structure: individuals (*I*), subpopulations (*S*), and the total population (*T*). One calculates the average individual heterozygosity by counting the number of heterozygous individuals in a subpopulation and dividing that sum by the total number of individuals in the subpopulation. This calculation is made for every subpopulation, and the average for all subpopulations is called the average individual heterozygosity,

$$\left(H_I = \frac{1}{k} \sum_{i=1}^{k} \frac{\text{No. of heterozygotes}_i}{N_i} \right)$$

where k is the number of subpopulations and N_i is the number of individuals in the ith subpopulation. At the same time one can use those individuals to determine the frequencies of alleles. These allele frequencies are used to calculate the expectations for heterozygosity in the average subpopulation ($\overline{H}_S$) and the total population (H_T). The expectation for the average subpopulation is

$$\overline{H}_S = \frac{2}{k} \sum_{i=1}^{k} p_i - p_i^2$$

where p_i is the frequency of the gene in the ith subpopulation. The expected number of heterozygous individuals for the entire population is given by

$$H_T = 2\left(\overline{p} - \overline{p}^2\right)$$

where p is the frequency of the gene averaged over all individuals in the population without respect to the subpopulation they came from. ($\overline{H}_S$) predicts the frequency of heterozygous individuals in subpopulations if they mate at random, and (H_T) predicts the same frequency if individuals are mating at random without respect to subpopulations.

These estimates of the observed and expected frequency of heterozygous individuals can be used to calculate the fixation indices, F_{IS}, F_{IT}, and F_{ST}. Values for F_{IS} determine whether or not subpopulations have fewer or more heterozygous individuals than expected.

This index is calculated from

$$F_{IS} = \frac{\overline{H}_S - H_I}{\overline{H}_S}$$

When there are fewer heterozygous individuals than expected,

$$\left(\overline{H}_S > H_I\right)$$

F_{IS} will be positive. When

$$\overline{H}_S < H_I$$

then F_{IS} will be negative. Therefore, negative values for F_{IS} indicate an excess of heterozygous individuals in subpopulations, and positive values indicate the

$$F_{IT} = \frac{H_T - H_I}{H_T}$$

opposite condition. F_{IT} is calculated in a similar manner:

and the interpretation of positive and negative values is the same, except that they apply to the total population instead of the subpopulations. Finally, the degree of genetic differentiation

$$F_{ST} = \frac{H_T - \overline{H}_S}{H_T}$$

among subpopulations (how unique they are) is given by

which is always greater than or equal to zero. High values for F_{ST} indicate that subpopulations have very different gene frequencies, and when $F_{ST} = 1$, then subpopulations are said to be "fixed" for different alleles; each subpopulation has a unique allele for each locus.

---

fication of the underlying genetic base. More typically, allozyme electrophoresis had proved to be a reliable, fairly inexpensive, and relatively easy procedure. The data generated, allozyme frequencies, are a direct function of genetic constitution and are not modified by the environment. Other genetic data may also be useful in defining conservation units, including the results of karyotype analysis (inspection of chromosome structure), mitochondrial DNA (mtDNA) analysis, and DNA sequencing.

A technique known as the polymerase chain reaction (PCR) can be quite useful in conservation studies because it can produce large quantities of DNA (a process called amplification) from tiny and even degraded samples, such as skin particles, hair, bone, epithelial cells in urine, or remains in gut contents of predators. Once amplified, the DNA can be analyzed by other means to acquire genetic data. John Avise provides an overview of the utility of these various molecular genetic techniques for conservation biology in Essay 6C.

ESSAY 6C
What Can Molecular Biology Contribute to Conservation?

John C. Avise, University of Georgia

Prior to the early 1960s, most genetic analyses of eukaryotes were confined to a small handful of species—such as fungi, Mendel's pea plants, maize, fruit flies, guinea pigs, and house mice—that could be maintained and bred under controlled laboratory conditions. From observed transmission patterns across generations, the genetic bases of various morphological or physiological attributes in these species were deduced, and indeed, the findings laid the empirical foundation for major principles of particulate or Mendelian inheritance. However, such breeding experiments could hardly be expected to capture the full flavor of genetic diversity across the earth's broader biota, nor the richness of variation in that vast majority of genes that do not contribute in any simple or obvious way to observable phenotypic differences at the organismal level. In the latter half of the 20th century, the invention and deployment of molecular techniques for revealing variation in proteins and DNA has changed this situation dramatically. No longer need genetic attention be confined to short-generation species that can be crossed in captivity, nor to the phenotypically overt mutations they carry. *The fundamental contribution of molecular biology to conservation has been to open the whole world of nature, from microbes to whales, to direct and extensive genetic scrutiny.*

Furthermore, because various genes or portions thereof evolve at widely different rates, the genetic data provided by molecular biology are relevant to a full spectrum of ecological and evolutionary time scales. Through the choice of appropriate loci, molecular assay methods, and procedures of data analysis, researchers now can examine genetic issues ranging from micro- to macroevolutionary. With suitable molecular markers, it is possible to empirically estimate such diverse genetic parameters as those relating to parentage assessment, kinship, population structure, dispersal and gene flow (contemporary and historical), reproductive compatibility, mating system, hybridization, introgression, phylogeny, and forensic identification at any level. Examples of the types of questions that can be addressed are presented in Table A. In perusing this list, a practicing conservation biologist should ask herself, "For the taxonomic group in which I am interested, would answers to any of these or related questions improve understanding of organismal biology in ways serviceable to conservation efforts?" I suspect that the answer often will be "yes." In support of this contention are case studies from a wide variety of plant and animal taxa in which molecular genetic markers already have been employed fruitfully in a conservation context (Avise and Hamrick 1996; Smith and Wayne 1996).

What follows are thumbnail sketches of a few of the molecular assays commonly employed in conservation biology. For detailed descriptions of these techniques, and their histories and applications, see Avise (1994) and Hillis et al. (1996).

Protein electrophoresis was the first method to be developed and widely adopted in the field. This method distinguishes allelic forms of particular genes on the basis of electrophoretic mobility differences in the proteins they

Table A
Examples of Questions That Can Be Addressed Using Molecular Genetic Data

1. Parentage and kinship
   - Who has successfully bred with whom?
   - Do field observations on social or mating behavior reliably predict true biological parentage?
   - What are the magnitudes of various influences on effective population size (N_e), such as interdemic gene flow, or male and female variances in reproductive success?
   - Is demic or social structure present?
   - What is the mating system?
2. Within-population genetic variability
   - What is the magnitude of genetic variation?
   - What is the level of inbreeding?
   - Is genetic variability or inbreeding related to fitness?
   - Are certain classes of genes of special fitness relevance?
3. Population structure and intraspecific phylogeny
   - What are the levels of interpopulation gene flow?
   - Are dispersal and gene flow gender-biased?
   - How does gene flow relate to demographic connectedness?
   - Do significant phylogeographic partitions exist?
   - What are the evolutionarily significant units? What are the potential management units?
   - Can regional phylogeographic provinces be identified?
4. Species boundaries, hybridization phenomena, and forensics
   - How distinct genetically are "endangered species"?
   - Does hybridization occur, and if so, how often, and between what taxa?
   - What are the magnitude, pattern, and direction of introgression?
   - What is the organismal source of an unknown biological sample?
5. Species' phylogenies and macroevolution
   - What are the phylogenetic relationships among particular species and higher taxa?

Modified from Avise 1996.

encode. The data consist of diploid genotypes of individuals, from which population statistics such as allele frequencies, heterozygosities, and genetic distances may be estimated. Typically, genotypic information from 20 or more loci is accumulated in a protein electrophoretic study, and the primary applications include categories 1–4 in Table A. Major strengths of this approach are its technical simplicity and comparatively low cost, and the multilocus nature of the data provided. A limitation is the technique's failure to detect the many nucleotide substitutions that do not alter protein charge in the genes examined, so that numbers of distinguished alleles per locus are typically low.

With respect to providing qualitative genotypic data accruable across multiple genes, two DNA-level analogues of protein electrophoresis involve assays of *minisatellite* and *microsatellite* loci. These loci contain variable numbers of tandemly repeated DNA units, each unit typically a few tens of nucleotides in length in the case of minisatellites, and two, three, or four nucleotides long in the case of microsatellites. Laboratory assays involve distinguishing alleles by size, i.e., by the numbers of tandem repeats. Many alleles (often a dozen or more) may exist at each such "DNA fingerprinting" locus, and these provide considerable resolution for microevolutionary questions such as those in categories 1–3 of Table A.

Unlike the procedures mentioned above, *mitochondrial DNA (mtDNA)* assays in effect provide information from only a single "gene." This disadvantage is balanced, however, by the fact that the non-recombining mtDNA molecule evolves rapidly and often exhibits a plethora of alleles (haplotypes) whose phylogenetic relationships can be estimated from the observed mutational differences (at the level of DNA restriction sites or nucleotide sequences). Because mtDNA is maternally inherited in most higher animals, different haplotypes can be thought of as "female family names," and the phylogenies interpreted as appraisals of matrilineal history. The prime areas of utility for conservation biology are in categories 3 and 4 of Table A.

In recent years, an important development for empirical conservation genetics has been the introduction of minimally invasive sampling methods for molecular assay. These involve the in vitro amplification of DNA via the PCR (polymerase chain reaction), using as a template small amounts of native DNA such as can be obtained from blood, hair, fin clips, single feathers, or even feces. When appropriately coupled with the available DNA assay procedures (e.g., of microsatellites, restriction sites, or nucleotide sequences), PCR-based methods can be adapted to address any of the categories of questions listed in Table A.

Typically, molecular genetic data are most rewarding in a conservation context when integrated with information from other relevant disciplines such as ethology, field ecology, natural history, demography, systematics, or paleontology. In the final analysis, biodiversity—the subject matter of conservation biology—*is* genetic diversity, at all levels. Molecular biology has provided the empirical means for direct appraisals of these historical treasures.

Biogeographic Models of Gene Flow

As we have said, undisturbed populations in the wild have some degree of genetic population structure based on biogeographic patterns. A single population or metapopulation exists somewhere along a spectrum of isolation and gene flow, from an extreme of complete isolation and no genetic exchange with other populations, to the opposite extreme of free genetic exchange among populations. These natural biogeographic structures have important implications for genetic management because they are often altered by human actions, which may seriously affect fitness and local adaptation.

As we have seen, populations diverge from one another as a function of genetic drift, mutation, and local selection. Drift can have a particularly strong effect on small populations, and is an inverse function of N_e. Countering the effects of these various divergent forces is gene flow via dispersal and reproduction (often expressed as migration rate, m, the proportion of individuals exchanged among populations per generation), which tends to homogenize populations and increase within-population variation.

The level of genetic divergence between two populations is the product of N_e and m. If N_e is small, populations will tend to diverge as a result of random genetic drift, and high rates of migration (m) are needed to prevent divergence. If $N_e \cdot m$ is greater than 1, local populations will tend not to diverge significantly in terms of the alleles present (Allendorf 1983). For example, a pair of populations with a mean N_e of 1000 and an m of 0.01 (an average of one individual exchanged per hundred generations) would not significantly diverge by chance alone, since $N_e \cdot m = 10$. However, a pair of smaller populations, with a mean N_e of 100 and the same rate of gene flow, would diverge more, since $N_e \cdot m = 1$; random genetic drift would be greater in the smaller populations, and a higher rate of gene exchange (such as $m = 0.02$) would be

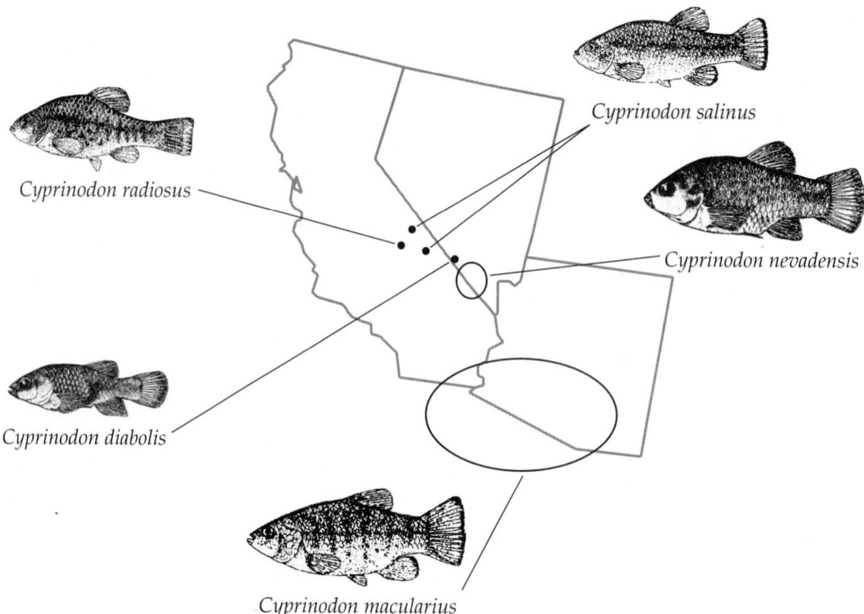

Figure 6.14 Pupfishes of southwestern American deserts, an example of local population differentiation and speciation through genetic isolation. These five closely related species have apparently been isolated for at least 10,000–12,000 years, since the end of the Pleistocene. They have differentiated in their respective drainages or single habitats into different forms, recognizable as species. The habitat of two pupfishes, *Cyprinodon diabolis* and *C. radiosus,* are shown in Figure 5.2 and Figure 11.9, respectively.

needed to prevent divergence. Of course, strong local selection can influence divergence as well (Endler 1973).

Some populations and species in nature have existed for long periods in complete isolation from other gene pools, and have diverged through genetic drift or selection (Figure 6.14). Notable examples include numerous species in the Galápagos Islands (Lack 1947; Levinton and Bowman 1981), and fishes and snails in isolated desert springs (Minckley and Deacon 1991). In these cases, natural movement among islands or springs was historically rare or nonexistent ($m \approx 0$), and strong divergence occurred. H_p is expected to be low and D_{st} high in such cases; virtually all of the total genetic diversity (H_t) in such a species could be due to the divergence component. The management implication of this scenario is that the separation of these naturally isolated populations should be maintained. This makes intuitive, as well as genetic, sense; no credible biologist would casually move finches or tortoises among the islands of the Galápagos, for example, without extraordinary justification.

Contrasted with this isolated, "island" model is the typical hierarchical model discussed earlier, in which genetic exchange occurs among populations in a hierarchical fashion. In this case, local populations may be only partially isolated from other gene pools, with some probability of gene flow among them. Geographically proximate populations would, on average, experience gene flow more frequently (m would be higher) than would more geographically distant populations. Genetic "connectedness" is then a function of geographic structure and spatial scale.

Most endangered species do not experience the equilibrium conditions implicit in a hierarchical model, however. By their very nature of being endangered or of special concern, their genetic structure has probably been altered, populations have been lost, and remaining populations are dangerously small and fragmented. Habitat destruction, blockage of migratory routes, drying or diversion of waterways, clear-cutting, urbanization, and other human activities isolate populations that normally would experience gene exchange with other populations. Such induced fragmentation and isolation will lead to loss of heterozygosity and divergence from other populations where gene exchange previously occurred. Leberg (1991), for example, found that Eastern Wild Turkey (*Meleagris gallopavo silvestris*) populations in Arkansas, Kentucky, Tennessee, and Connecticut were fragmented and had gone through bottlenecks because of human activity. Genetic divergence among these populations (10.2%) was among the highest recorded for birds, and much higher than for turkey populations that had not experienced known bottlenecks. Leberg attributed this divergence to human activity, including management manipulations.

Scenarios such as the Wild Turkey situation may call for the manager to simulate natural gene flow by artificial means: by moving individuals among now-isolated populations among which gene flow once occurred. The management challenge in the hierarchical model is to determine former rates and directions of gene flow among populations and try to mimic those rates in the face of human disturbance. The age and sex ratios of translocated individuals should match the natural history of the species, and care should be taken to not introduce parasites or pathogens in the process. This management prescription is in direct contrast to that for the island model, in which case the manager should not induce gene flow, but rather should protect the normal isolation of populations. But where natural gene flow has historically occurred and has been interrupted by humans, management should emphasize continuance of gene flow near historical levels. Such is now being done for the Florida panther (*Felis concolor coryi*), and genetic models have been used to design the program and evaluate its possible consequences (Hedrick 1995). This isolated population has experienced a decline in genetic diversity, but will now experience gene flow from Texas cougars (*Felis concolor stanleyana*) to bolster its heterozygosity levels.

The natural genetic structure of a species, and its normal rates of gene flow, may be inferred from geography, historical records, knowledge of the biology of the species, and genetic information derived from a hierarchical analysis (Slatkin 1987; Meffe and Vrijenhoek 1988). Assuming that the value obtained for the divergence component (D_{pt}) of total genetic variation (H_t) reflects a balance between the divergent influences of genetic drift and the convergent influences of gene flow, the effective migration rate historically experienced can be roughly estimated as

$$D_{pt}/H_t = 1/(4N_e m + 1)$$

(modified from Crow and Kimura 1970).

Thus, in a species in which the divergence component of genetic variation is 3%, $0.03 = 1/(4N_e m + 1)$; rearranging, $4N_e m + 1 = 33.3$, and $N_e m \approx 8.1$. In other words, an average of eight reproductive individuals per generation must move among the populations to maintain a divergence level of 3%. Compare that with the situation in a species with a high D_{pt}, such as 35%. In that case, $0.35 = 1/4N_e m + 1$; $4N_e m + 1 = 2.86$, and $N_e m = 0.46$; on average, less than one reproductive individual should be moved among the populations every other generation to maintain that level of divergence.

Echelle et al. (1987) studied four species of pupfishes in the Chihuahuan Desert region of New Mexico and Texas, and their data are amenable to calculating historical migration rates. These four species span a range of geographic distribution and isolation, and their estimated migration rates reflect this (Table 6.9). The geographically most isolated species (*Cyprinodon tularosa*) has the lowest estimated migration rate based on genetic data, while the highest estimated migration rate occurs in *Cyprinodon bovinus*, which occurs along a single drainage system that is at least occasionally connected when flooded.

In this section we have presented some simplified analyses of very complicated genetic situations. Such analyses are for illustrative purposes, to dem-

Table 6.9
Estimated Historical Rates of Gene Flow among Populations of Four Species of Western North American Pupfishes

Species	Distribution	D_{pt}	$N_e m$
Cyprinodon bovinus	A single, ≈8 km long section of spring-fed stream	1.4%	17.6
C. pecosensis	600–700 km of mainstream Pecos River	7.7%	3.0
C. elegans	Spring-fed complex of canals and creek, with partial isolation	10.8%	2.1
C. tularosa	Two isolated springs and associated creek in extremely arid area	19.0%	1.1

Modified from Echelle et al. 1987.
Note: D_{pt} is the proportion of total genetic diversity attributable to divergence among populations. The more isolated populations have a higher D_{pt} and consequently a lower estimated rate of gene flow.

onstrate basic principles, and should not be taken as the final word in genetic management. We caution that genetic management programs for species in the wild should not be approached lightly; effective programs require a good understanding of the biology and distribution of the species in question, comprehensive genetic data collected and analyzed properly, and proper models for predicting rates of change of genetic diversity and heterozygosity. However, complex genetic models are no substitute for sound biological knowledge, including basic natural history.

In some cases, genetic data for a hierarchical analysis are difficult to obtain, or there is no detectable genetic variation in the data. Large mammals, such as cheetahs, polar bears, and white rhinoceroses, may be especially prone to these problems. In such cases, the manager must do the best job possible with what is available and rely on historical records of distribution, inferences from the species' biology, or genetic knowledge from similar species. Genetics is only one aspect of a broader management picture, and provides only one type of data.

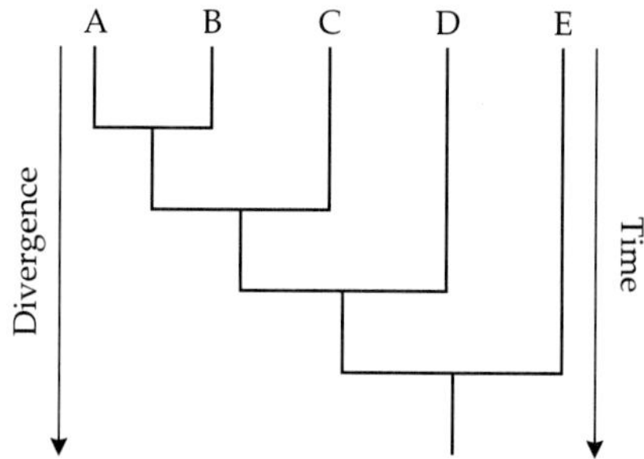

Figure 6.15 A schematic demonstration of deep versus shallow evolutionary separations. Level of genetic divergence and time both increase toward the bottom. Population E is the most divergent; all else being equal, that level of divergence should receive priority protection before other levels of (more recent) divergence.

Depths of Evolutionary Separation

The hierarchical gene diversity approach discussed throughout this chapter can not only outline the overall genetic structure of a species and estimate historical rates of gene flow, but can also help to discriminate "deeper" or older evolutionary separations from "shallower" or more recent divergences that have lesser evolutionary significance (Figure 6.15). This is possible because the degree of genetic separation between two populations is thought to correlate with the time since physical separation, and can be used as a sort of molecular genetic "clock." Because genetically based changes in protein structure are known to occur on a somewhat regular basis in evolutionary time, evolution of protein structure has been used as a calibrated standard for the time since separation between populations (Maxson and Wilson 1974; Sarich 1977); more genetic changes mean a longer ("deeper") evolutionary separation. This approach has been criticized due to difficulties in accurately standardizing the "clock," but its basic premise is that greater genetic change between two entities indicates a longer evolutionary separation.

The "molecular clock" method is a phenetic approach, which measures the degree of genetic divergence among various species, populations, or any taxonomic level of interest. A phylogenetic (cladistic) approach (see Chapter 3), in which unique character states identify groups of interest, would also work. In that case, those groups with the fewest evolutionary novelties (in this case, genetic changes) would be assumed to be the oldest, most primitive groups. More detailed discussions of selection of taxa for conservation based on uniqueness and evolutionary separation may be found in Vane-Wright et al. (1991), Crozier (1992), Faith (1992), and Moritz (1994).

The theme of evolutionary depth has been especially well elucidated by John Avise and his colleagues (Avise et al. 1987; Avise 1989; Avise and Ball 1990; Avise 1994), who are strong proponents of using molecular genetic data to determine **phylogeographic** relationships within species and to identify the deepest evolutionary separations. They argue that, because we cannot save every variant, the older lineages, all else being equal, should receive conservation priority, as they represent major branches. The newer, "minor" separations probably do not have such deeply rooted adaptations or such long histories in their present habitats, and should receive attention only after the deeper lineages are secure.

Greater evolutionary depth often corresponds to a major geographic separation in genetic structure, tying this concept back to the hierarchical gene diversity analysis. For example, a small, livebearing desert fish, the Sonoran topminnow (*Poeciliopsis occidentalis*), was found to exist in three major geographic groupings, based on allozyme studies and a hierarchical gene diversity study (Vrijenhoek et al. 1985). These three groups, two of which had already been recognized as subspecies, were estimated roughly to have been separated for periods ranging from 1.7 to 4.3 million years. These three major genetic groups should be the primary foci for genetic conservation and should receive priority attention, because within-group differentiation is much smaller by comparison. More genetic information would be lost if one of these three major groups went extinct than if an equivalent number of populations distributed across the species range went extinct.

Such major genetic groups can often be identified in species of conservation interest and should be the primary concern for genetic management. For example, Bischof (1992) used mtDNA to show that African elephants have a highly subdivided population structure. Unique genetic types exist in eastern and southern African regions, but there is also evidence of gene flow among regions, indicating the importance of migration corridors among reserves (see Chapter 10).

"Cookbook Prescriptions" in Genetic Conservation

Before we leave the topic of management of genetic variation in nature, we must raise the issue of standardized prescriptions and "cookbook" methodologies for management of diversity at genetic or other levels. It is tempting for a manager of any system to rely on developed, reliable procedures that produce a predictable outcome. The need for detailed knowledge of each system in order to make management decisions is an unwelcome message for many managers, because it demands more of their limited resources and involves less certainty. Unfortunately, biological systems are so complex and individualistic that at least some detailed knowledge of the specific system of concern is necessary for reasonable management; generalities are dangerous and destabilizing to a management scheme (Ehrenfeld 1991). Consequently, we caution against management approaches that rely on quantitative rules of thumb and cookbook procedures.

Early discussions of conservation of genetic diversity in small populations included the so-called "50/500 rule," which stated that a genetically effective population size (N_e) of at least 50 individuals is necessary for conservation of genetic diversity in the short term (several generations) and to avoid inbreeding depression, and that an N_e of 500 is needed to avoid serious genetic drift in the long term (Franklin 1980; Soulé 1980). These may in fact be reasonable order-of-magnitude estimates of the minimum numbers needed, based on simple genetic models, but they may also mislead in many cases (Lande 1988). For example, when considering the effects of mutations on inbreeding, Lande (1995) suggested that effective population sizes of 5000, rather than 500, may be needed to effectively conserve genetic diversity.

A prescription such as the 50/500 rule ignores demographic, ecological, and behavioral considerations. For example, many more than 50 or 500 individuals may be necessary in colonially breeding species that require large numbers to reproduce successfully, or in species that depend on large groups to feed successfully. The Passenger Pigeon became extinct not because populations slowly dwindled to very low numbers and then disappeared because of genetic decline, but because the species needed hundreds or thousands of individuals for its breeding colonies. When population sizes fell below these large, threshold numbers, the last populations of the species rapidly disappeared, even though genetically viable numbers remained (Brisbin 1968).

On the other hand, the 50/500 rule may discourage conservation attempts in situations in which fewer individuals than the prescribed number are available. Smaller populations may be "written off" as a likely loss because of their small numbers, yet they may be doing well and be worthy of attention. Some populations of desert fishes, for example, may have existed at population sizes of several hundred or less for many generations and have thrived (Deacon and Deacon 1979). Yet, a genetic rule of 50/500 would dictate that they are not worthy of conservation efforts because they are doomed to extinction through genetic deterioration. Likewise, Pére David's deer (*Elaphurus davidianus*) and Przewalski's horse (*Equus przewalski*; see Figure 6.1) both recovered from population sizes of less than 20 (Woodruff 1989). A suggestion was made, and rejected, that conservation efforts for the Orange-bellied Parrot (*Neophema chrysogaster*) of Australia be abandoned because fewer than 200 individuals remained (Brown et al. 1985). These examples raise interesting questions (Pimm 1991). Can a large population lose genetic variation? Perhaps that happened with the African cheetah, and it did not go through a demographic bottleneck. Why do some small populations not lose genetic variation? Why do some populations with low genetic variation seem to thrive anyway?

Our point is that strict *quantitative* rules should generally be avoided, or at least applied with a great deal of caution, because the historical and ecological circumstances of each species may make it more or less prone to losses of genetic diversity and the problems those losses cause. Every ecological scenario has the potential to be unique, and additional data, such as natural history, biogeography, or demography, should be acquired whenever possible to assess the case before management decisions are made. There are no easy fixes to most conservation problems.

Qualitative rules are another matter, and a number of good genetic guidelines have emerged based on our current knowledge (Table 6.10). These are

Table 6.10
Qualitative Guidelines for Genetically Based Conservation Practices

1. Large genetically effective population sizes are better than small ones because they will lose genetic variation more slowly.
2. The negative effects of genetic drift and inbreeding are inversely proportional to population size. Thus, avoid managing for unnaturally small populations.
3. Management of wild populations should be consistent with the history of their genetic patterns and processes. For example, historically isolated populations should remain isolated unless other concerns dictate that gene flow must occur. Gene flow among historically connected populations should continue at historical rates, even if that calls for assisted movement of individuals.
4. Low genetic diversity per se is not cause for alarm, because some species historically have low diversity. However, sudden and large losses of diversity in natural or captive populations are always cause for concern.
5. Avoid artificial selection in captivity. This is best done by keeping breeding populations in captivity for as few generations as possible, and also by simulating wild conditions as nearly as possible.
6. After a population crash, encourage rapid population growth to avoid a prolonged bottleneck.
7. Avoid possible outbreeding depression caused by breeding distantly related populations if other choices are available.
8. Avoid inadvertent introductions of exotic alleles into wild or captive populations.
9. Harvesting of wild stocks (hunting, fishing) can select for genetic changes that can affect the future evolution of the population or species. For example, culling the largest individuals can select for earlier maturity at smaller body sizes. Thus, avoid selection in harvesting wild stocks.
10. Maintenance of genetic diversity in captive stocks is no substitute for genetic diversity in the wild. Technological mastery over the genome should not be used as an excuse to overexploit or destroy species or populations in the wild.

not based on strict quantitative rules, but are consensuses on reasonable approaches to genetic conservation.

Other Uses of Genetic Information in Conservation

Much of this chapter has discussed two major uses of genetic data in the conservation of populations and species in the wild. The primary discussion emphasized ways of describing the quantity and geographic distribution of genetic variation in species, employing a hierarchical gene diversity analysis. That same approach was shown to be useful in estimating historical levels of gene flow among populations, information that could determine whether artificial gene flow is necessary to retain natural geographic patterns of genetic diversity. There are several other conservation uses to which genetic data can be put (treated in detail in Avise 1994), and we discuss these now.

Electrophoretic or other genetic data can be used to identify unique gene pools worthy of special protection. This is particularly true with reference to identification of unique alleles present in one population but absent in others. Such a scenario could dictate that special efforts be made to protect a population with unique genetic attributes. Echelle et al. (1989) studied 16 populations of a small endangered fish, the Pecos gambusia (*Gambusia nobilis*), from its four remaining, widely separated locations in the Pecos River system in New

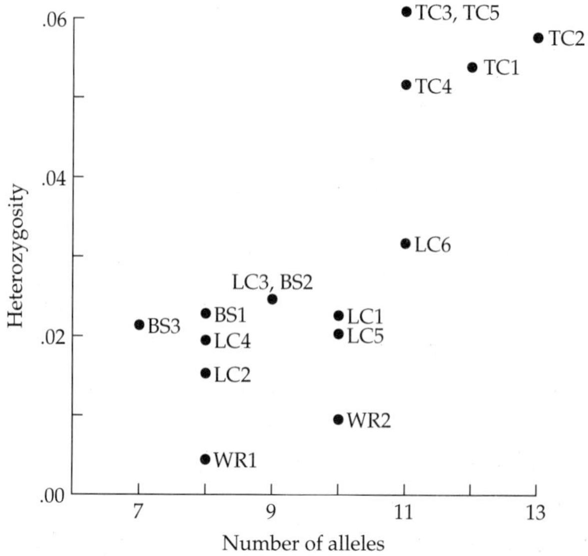

Figure 6.16 Heterozygosity plotted against number of alleles in the population for 16 populations of the Pecos gambusia (*Gambusia nobilis*) from Texas and New Mexico. The five Toyah Creek (TC) populations have the highest diversity and are the most divergent from other populations (BS, LC, and WR). (From Echelle et al. 1987.)

Mexico and Texas. They found that populations from a drainage called Toyah Creek had the highest heterozygosity and allelic diversity, and were the most divergent of all the populations (Figure 6.16). This group of fish should receive particular conservation attention, as it contains more genetic diversity than groups from other regions, and also has unique alleles that would be lost if these populations went extinct.

Genetic data can also make important contributions to taxonomic studies. Traditional taxonomies are usually based on morphological data, which may accurately reflect evolutionary relationships, or may be misleading due to local adaptations and phenotypic plasticity. Genetics can help to clarify relationships and guide conservation efforts toward truly divergent or unique taxa. Such analyses were discussed in Essay 3C.

Genetic data are also crucial throughout all aspects of captive breeding programs (see Essay 6D by Oliver Ryder). Captive breeding occurs at one end

ESSAY 6D

Conservation and Ex Situ Population Management

Oliver A. Ryder, Zoological Society of San Diego

Management of small populations for conservation looms as an increasingly important intervention for the preservation of biological diversity as the number of threatened and endangered species increases. Ex situ conservation programs (involving maintenance of gene pool resources off site) represent an important supportive strategy within the context of the larger goal of preserving habitats and ecosystems. The very fact that the number of endangered species is increasing dramatically suggests that additional conservation strategies, such as captive breeding and other ex situ conservation practices, may be necessary to provide sufficient assurance that important components of biological diversity are available to human society in the future.

Botanical gardens, aquariums, and zoological parks are established institutions with expertise in reproduction of living collections for conservation purposes. Furthermore, these institutions, because of their access to exotic and diverse biological resources, are in a unique position to contribute to conservation of genetic resources for the future through gene banking and cryopreservation of germ plasm. As the importance of ex situ conservation has become increasingly apparent, institutions such as zoos have contributed to conservation biology theory and practice through the establishment of long-term programs for the preservation of genetic diversity in individual taxa and for a broader representation of plants,

Suggestions for Further Reading

Avise, J. C. 1994. *Molecular Markers, Natural History and Evolution*. Chapman & Hall, New York. A very readable treatment of the various uses of molecular genetic data in biological studies, including conservation. Topics include descriptions of the tools and approaches, as well as applications.

Falk, D. A. and K. E. Holsinger (eds.). 1991. *Genetics and Conservation of Rare Plants*. Oxford University Press, New York. As the title implies, this multiauthored volume focuses on the genetic diversity of plants. The 14 chapters cover topics related to the population biology and genetics of rare plants, problems in sampling their genetic variation, management of rare plant collections, and strategies for protecting their genetic diversity.

Hartl, D. L. and A. G. Clark. 1990. *Principles of Population Genetics*, 2nd ed. Sinauer Associates, Sunderland, MA. A very good textbook on the basics of population genetics, offering more advanced topics than is possible here. A great "next step" for the serious student who wants to better understand population genetics and then apply it to species conservation.

Ryman, N. and F. Utter (eds.). 1987. *Population Genetics and Fishery Management*. University of Washington Press, Seattle. One of the oldest forms of resource management is fisheries biology. This book explains for fisheries managers (although it is applicable to many management scenarios) both basic and advanced topics related to genetics in a fisheries resource.

Schonewald-Cox, C. M., S. M. Chambers, B. MacBryde, and L. Thomas (eds.). 1983. *Genetics and Conservation: A Reference for Managing Wild Animal and Plant Populations*. Benjamin/Cummings, Menlo Park, CA. This classic book was among several that initiated broad concern for conservation of genetic diversity. Twenty-five chapters by experts in various aspects of genetic diversity lay out the principles and problems of the field.

Thornhill, N. W. (ed.). 1993. *The Natural History of Inbreeding and Outbreeding: Theoretical and Empirical Perspectives*. A thorough compilation of the state of our knowledge of inbreeding and outbreeding. Both theoretical and empirical perspectives are presented, as well as many taxon-specific reviews.

7

Demographic Processes

Population Dynamics on Heterogeneous Landscapes

In looking at Nature it is most necessary to . . . never forget that every single organic being around us may be said to be striving to the utmost to increase its numbers.

Charles Darwin, 1859

Few topics have attracted the attention of ecologists more than fluctuations in the numbers of plants and animals through time and their variation in abundance through space. Understanding population fluctuations, and thus population conservation, requires understanding the links between demographic processes—birth, death, immigration, and emigration—and the environments in which populations exist.

Some ecologists have been particularly impressed by the relative constancy of populations, while others have been impressed with their extreme variation. The former usually postulate an "equilibrium" population size and explain the observed equilibrium by reference to density-dependent factors, which prevent populations from getting either too small or too large. On the other hand, those impressed by the magnitude of population fluctuations usually see the world as consisting of many local subpopulations, each of which has a high probability of extinction due to the unpredictable nature of factors that operate independently of population density. Given the great diversity of organisms and environments and the fact that most ecologists study only a few species in a few places, there should be little surprise in such diversity of opinions.

Organisms clearly vary with regard to both their susceptibility to the vicissitudes of nature and the duration of their life spans in relation to the frequency of natural disturbances. Organisms also vary in the extent to which they live their lives in one location or experience a wide variety of environmental conditions in different locations. These facts alone account for much of the difference among species regarding the extent to which populations fluctuate in time and space. An entire generation of rotifers or thrips may experience an unusual cold spell that reduces reproduction and increases mortality, while in the next generation conditions may be optimal for the species. Individual whales and sequoias, on the other hand, experience thousands of separate cold and warm fronts, and the whales of one generation are quite likely to experience an average environment something like that experienced by the whales of other generations. Accordingly, whales and sequoias are much less likely to fluctuate wildly in population size than are thrips, and even if they did fluctuate as much, an ecologist observing them over the course of his or her career would be less likely to record the fluctuations.

Unfortunately, much of the theory of population ecology, particularly as it is presented at the undergraduate level, has been based on the fallacious notion that all organisms in a population experience more or less the same environmental conditions. A more modern point of view is that every organism exists as part of an open population in a heterogeneous landscape, and that different individuals in the same population experience different conditions for a variety of reasons, the most obvious of which is that they live in different places. Even if they live in similar habitats, they may experience vastly different conditions because similar patches of the same habitat are often out of phase with one another with regard to availability of essential resources or other environmental conditions. Furthermore, organisms may move from one habitat patch to another, resulting in an interdependence of the dynamics of the populations in various patches. Accordingly, conservationists must concern themselves with the spatial and temporal scales over which animals move and their environments change.

This chapter covers a variety of concepts that allow us to study and understand the demography and dynamics of natural populations on various temporal and spatial scales. It is only by viewing populations from these several perspectives at once that one can both appreciate the enormous complexities of population abundance and distribution and begin to organize and understand that complexity. This understanding is an essential prerequisite to developing a practical theory of population ecology that can aid in conserving biological diversity.

What Is Population Demography?

Demography embodies the intrinsic factors that contribute to a population's growth or decline, including natality (especially the birth rate associated with different age classes of individuals within the population) and mortality (especially juvenile and adult survivorship). Rates of dispersal between populations (immigration into and emigration out of habitat patches) are also components of demography. These four factors, *B*irth, *I*mmigration, *D*eath, and *E*migration, are often referred to as the "BIDE factors." The sex ratio of the breeding population and the age structure (the proportion of the population found in each age class) are also considered demographic factors because they contribute to birth and death rates.

These demographic factors are studied together because they are the means by which populations respond to short-term changes in their environments. Other population attributes, such as age at first breeding, are more difficult to alter in response to short-term stimuli, and are more likely to change in response to long-term changes in an organism's environment. These long-term attributes are often referred to as life history characteristics, and their value to conservation biology is discussed in Essay 7A by Justin Congdon and Arthur Dunham.

ESSAY 7A

Contributions of Long-Term Life History Studies to Conservation Biology

Justin D. Congdon, Savannah River Ecology Laboratory,
and Arthur E. Dunham, University of Pennsylvania

Life history studies can contribute to the conceptual basis of conservation biology by identifying the range of feasible suites of life history trait values that can exist within a given life history. Suites of feasible life history trait values are combinations of values that are physically and genetically possible; they are known to presently exist in some organisms. In the many cases in which trait values of a target species are not known, they can be estimated from well-studied organisms with similar suites of life history traits.

Making informed estimates of life history trait values requires an understanding of life history traits in general and how they coevolve, as well as reasonably complete life history data on a range of organisms. The ability to place realistic boundaries on trait values is extremely important in cases in which decisions may be based on projections from population modeling (Crouse et al. 1987), or when a conflict exists between harvesting and conserving a target species.

A case in point is sea turtle conservation and management programs aimed at stabilizing and restoring sea turtle populations (Frazer 1992). At present, it is technologically impossible to obtain complete sea turtle life history data, almost all of which are obtained from hatchlings and adult females at nesting beaches. Age of females at sexual maturity is estimated from minimum ages of females at nesting beaches; clutch frequency and survivorship of adult females is estimated from the return rates of females to nesting beaches (Frazer 1983). All of the above estimates are based on the assumption that the vast majority of females show strict nesting beach fidelity. Data on males are virtually nonexistent.

Without the empirical foundation that can only be provided by long-term life history studies, the permutations of assumed life history trait values for species like sea turtles are infinite. Although values of 3 to 30 years have been suggested for age at maturity in sea turtles as a group, it is unlikely that all values in this range are equally probable. If we are constrained only to data from sea turtles, opinions about probable ages at maturity remain without empirical boundaries. Presently, only existing studies of other long-lived organisms can provide life history data that are empirically sufficient to resolve some conflicting opinions about life history trait values of sea turtles and approaches to sea turtle conservation (Frazer 1992).

To illustrate the importance of associations of life history trait values in long-lived organisms, we created a set of graphs from life history data on common snapping turtles (*Chelydra serpentina*) on the University of Michigan's E. S. George Reserve. The relationship between juvenile and adult survivorship was determined for low (0.2, Figures A1 and A3) and high (0.8, Figures A2 and A4) nest survivorships, which might represent a worst- and best-case scenario for a sea turtle nesting beach. In one set of simulations, age at maturity was allowed to vary from 15 to 30 years of age (Figures A1 and A2), with fecun-

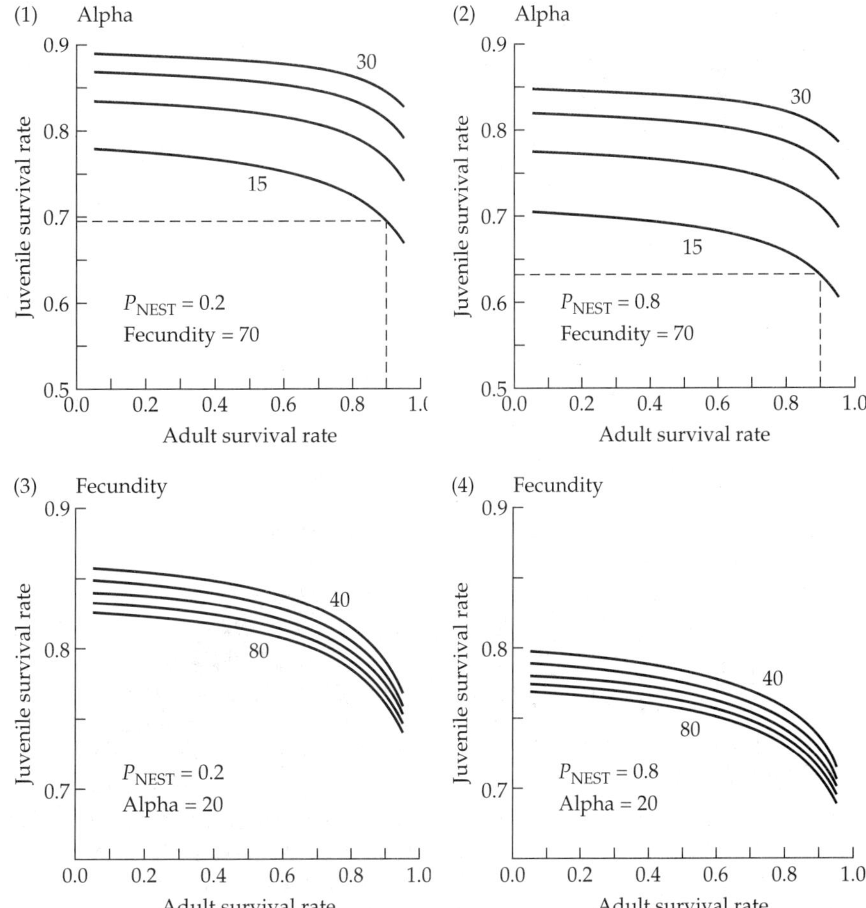

Figure A The relationship between adult and juvenile survival rates with P_{NEST} (probability of nest survival) set at 0.20 (1, 3) or 0.80 (2, 4). In (1) and (2) alpha (age at sexual maturity) varies between 15 and 30 years, and in (3) and (4) fecundity (annual production of female producing eggs) varies between 40 and 80. In all simulations, isoclines are produced where the population is stable ($r = 0$) for each combination of life history trait values. Values above or below isoclines represent increasing or decreasing populations, respectively.

dity fixed at 70 eggs annually, a value close to that reported for loggerhead sea turtles (Frazer 1984). In another set of simulations, fecundity was allowed to vary from 40 to 80 eggs, with age at maturity fixed at 20 years (Figures A3 and A4). These simulations result in a set of isoclines at which the intrinsic rate of increase (*r*) of the population is 0 (the population is stable); values above or below an isocline represent increasing or decreasing populations, respectively.

From Figures A1 and A2, it is obvious that, regardless of whether or not nest survivorship is high due to conservation efforts, age at maturity has a substantial effect on the levels of juvenile survivorship required to maintain a stable population. From Figures A3 and A4 it is also apparent that annual fecundity can double at either nest survival level, but juvenile survival rates still must exceed 70% to maintain a stable population. Under all conditions, lowering of adult survival levels (such as through harvest or accidental killing in shrimping nets) exacerbates the problem by increasing the already high required juvenile survival levels with even higher ones. Therefore, conservation efforts aimed at increasing nest survival and head-starting young juveniles are probably doomed to failure without a concomitant reduction in mortality of adults and juveniles.

Because all five species of sea turtles found in waters off the United States are listed as endangered or threatened by the Endangered Species Act of 1973, their populations are already substantially reduced from historical levels. Efforts should be and are being made to reduce existing sources of mortality and to prevent new sources of mortality being imposed on any age classes of sea turtles. A potential new source of mortality to young juvenile sea turtles is a proposal to harvest *Sargassum* (a floating brown alga), where juveniles live (Coston-Clements et al. 1991). The potential effects of *Sargassum* harvest on survival rates of juveniles are unknown, but it seems unlikely that harvesting can be undertaken without some level of increase in juvenile mortality. If age at maturity of sea turtles is set at 15 years, and survivorship of adults is 0.9, average juvenile survivorship cannot fall below 0.68 (Figure A1) or 0.63 (Figure A2) annually, with low and high nest survival, respectively. Thus, examination of Figure A can only lead to the conclusion that any increase in juvenile mortality will almost certainly have serious consequences for stable populations of sea turtles and potentially catastrophic consequences for populations that are already declining.

The combination of life history modeling and a long-term life history study of freshwater turtles at the University of Michigan's E. S. George Reserve has documented that in long-lived organisms, both juvenile and adult survival must be high to maintain a stable population. Since life history traits of age at first reproduction and longevity positively covary across many taxa (Charlesworth 1980; Charnov 1990), it is almost certain that all long-lived organisms, such as sea turtles, sharks, some bony fishes, tortoises, and freshwater turtles, delay sexual maturity. In addition, the whole range of trait values that make up a long-lived organism's life history combine to limit their ability to respond to increased mortality. They exist in populations that, when compared with shorter-lived organisms, require both high adult and juvenile survivorship. Thus, populations of long-lived organisms have limited abilities to respond to chronic increases in juvenile mortality and even lesser abilities to respond to increased mortality through commercial harvest of juveniles or adults (Congdon et al. 1993). Data obtained from long-term life history studies of species that are not of direct conservation concern are a resource that can contribute to developing concepts and solving problems related to management and conservation practices.

In this section we start with an example of the importance of demographic factors in a conservation strategy; other examples will follow when specific demographic topics are discussed. The Hawaiian monk seal (*Monorchus schauinslandi*), which is found in the northwestern Hawaiian Islands, has been in a population decline for several decades. The seals rest and give birth on the beaches of the mostly uninhabited islands. When the U.S. Coast Guard established stations on some of the islands, the seals shifted their activities to islands away from the Guard personnel, and the population began to decline precipitously (Figure 7.1). The Hawaiian monk seal was declared endangered in 1976 because of this population decline, and steps were taken to reverse the trend (Gerrodette and Gilmartin 1990).

The seals' decline was puzzling because the beaches they used were unchanged by the military presence, and the adults were not being killed or harassed by the Coast Guard personnel. The only effect on the species was that some of the Guard's recreational activities on the beaches caused the seals to move to previously unused beaches on other islands. Demographic studies revealed that juvenile survivorship on these alternative islands was drastically lower than on the original beaches. The shape of the new islands allowed waves to pass completely over the sandy beaches at high tide, sweeping young seal pups into the sea, where large numbers of sharks were waiting. The original beaches did not have a problem with large waves, and so the

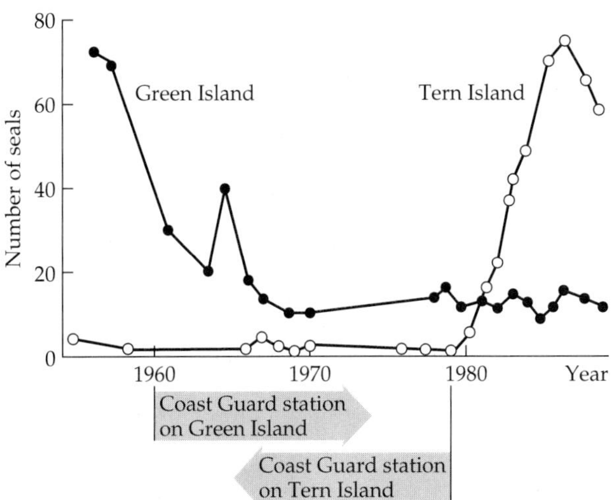

Figure 7.1 Total number of Hawaiian monk seals recorded during monitoring efforts at two islands in the northwestern Hawaiian Islands. Seals stayed away from Green Island and Tern Island while U.S. Coast Guard stations were present. During this time, seals used other islands where juvenile survivorship was very low, causing a population crash. (From Gerrodette and Gilmartin 1990.)

young seals, which are poor swimmers, did not suffer high mortality there. Few offspring survived during the years that the seals were restricted to the alternative islands, and therefore adults lost through normal mortality were not replaced, causing the population to become both smaller and older. When the Coast Guard personnel modified their behavior, the Hawaiian monk seals returned to their original "hauling out" beaches, juvenile survivorship increased, and the population began to recover.

Gerrodette and Gilmartin (1990) point out that simple population counts through monitoring programs failed to identify the seals' problem. It took a demographic analysis to uncover the low survivorship of juveniles and the resulting lack of recruits into the population. Correcting this demographic problem proved to be the key to the recovery process for this endangered species

Mechanisms of Population Regulation

Conservation biologists are interested in why some species are rare, and what keeps them so. Thus, conservationists are concerned with factors that might regulate population size. A population can be said to be regulated if it has the tendency to increase when rare and to decline when common. The concept of population regulation is closely tied to that of density dependence. Howard and Fiske (1911) introduced the distinction between "catastrophic mortality factors" that kill a constant proportion of a population independent of its density, and "facultative mortality factors" that kill an increasing proportion of the population as density increases. The same idea is now embodied in the distinction between density-independent and density-dependent factors affecting population growth, though density dependence can refer to birth rates as well as to death rates. **Density-independent** factors influence birth and/or death rates in a manner independent of population density, while the intensity of **density-dependent factors**, by definition, changes with population density (Figure 7.2).

For density-dependent factors to regulate population growth, either per capita mortality must increase or per capita natality must decline as population density increases. Although there are a myriad of factors that can, in theory, contribute to density-dependent changes in mortality and natality, most of

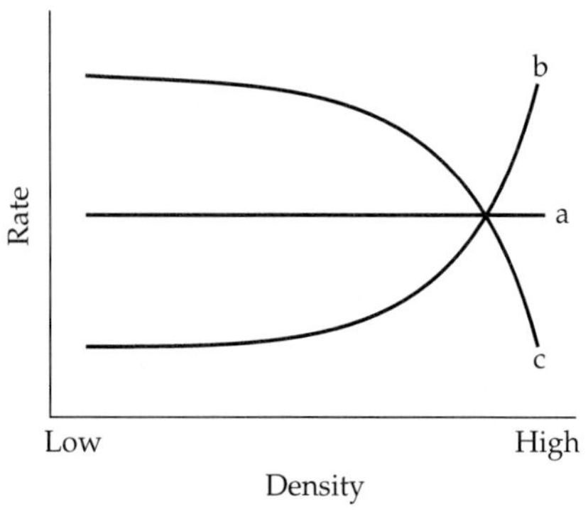

Figure 7.2 This figure demonstrates density-independent (a) and density-dependent (b and c) population responses. In the case of a density-independent response (a), density has no influence on a given parameter, such as mortality or birth rate. In the case of density dependence, a parameter such as mortality may increase at higher densities (b), while other parameters, such as clutch size or individual growth rate, may decrease at higher densities (c). The particular shapes of the response curves, of course, would vary greatly among taxa and environments.

these can be grouped into several categories or mechanisms of population regulation. Among the most prominent are the following:

- Increased mortality or decreased natality due to a shortage of resources
- Increased mortality due to increased predation, parasitism, or disease
- Increased mortality or decreased natality due to increased intensity of intraspecific social interactions

Of all of the density-dependent mechanisms that could lead to population regulation, the increased shortage of resources at high population densities is probably the best investigated. Many examples exist, ranging from the limitation of population growth in aquatic algae due to reduction of available nutrients at high algal densities, to the control of elk populations due to reduction of food resources when elk abundances are high (Coughenour and Singer 1996). The essential point is that, in each case, reduction in the resource (such as food, shelter, or space) is due to the presence and activity of large numbers of the resource consumer.

Mortality due to disease, parasitism, or predation may increase as the density of potential victims increases. Probably the best-known case of disease-related population regulation is the control of introduced rabbits by the *Myxoma* virus in Australia. In 1859, about 25 European rabbits were released from captivity in southeastern Australia. By the turn of the next century hundreds of millions of rabbits occupied an area in excess of 3 million km^2, and rabbits had become a major pest in Australian agricultural lands. In 1950 the *Myxoma* virus was introduced in an effort to control the rabbits. The virus spread rapidly and devastated the rabbit population over large areas by 1954. Thereafter, the incidence of the disease also declined. In the following decades there were cycles of recovery of the rabbits followed by subsequent outbreaks of the virus; however, during this time the virulence of the virus also declined, resulting in less dramatic oscillations in both rabbit and virus populations.

The effect of the infectious disease brucellosis is also strongly density dependent in the wild bison (*Bison bison*) population of Yellowstone National Park. The presence of this disease presents a conservation problem for managers of the park, because ranchers near Yellowstone insist that all bison wandering outside the park be killed so that the disease is not passed to local cattle populations. Dobson and Meagher (1996) examined the population ecology of the disease and its bison host, and concluded that eradication of the disease in wild bison is probably impossible because of the low population threshold at which the bison become infected.

There is no doubt that social behavior can play a direct role in regulating some animal populations, although in most, and perhaps all, cases social behavior interacts with resource shortage, disease, and predation to determine population size. In general, social behavior regulates access to resources such as food, cover, and breeding sites, and thereby affects survival and reproduction. For example, House Wrens (*Troglodytes aedon*) interfere with the breeding of many other species by puncturing the eggs in nests built within the wrens' territories. This interference may have played a major role in the near disappearance of Bewick's Wrens (*Thryomanes bewickii*) from the eastern United States, because Bewick's Wrens appear to be particularly susceptible to this kind of reproductive interference (Kennedy and White 1996). Populations also can be regulated by intraspecific social dominance behavior or aggression.

Occasionally, density and social behavior have the opposite effect in that birth rates may increase or death rates decrease at high densities. In some organisms, high population densities are required to stimulate courtship and breeding activity, or to otherwise allow reproduction. This phenomenon, called the "Allee effect," may affect breeding if the population drops below the required density (Allee et al. 1949). For example, pollen transfer may become difficult, if not impossible, among individuals of a rare, widely dispersed plant, resulting in failed reproduction (Bawa 1990). Colonially nesting birds may suffer poor recruitment if their densities become too low (Halliday 1980; see also Veit and Lewis 1996 for a theoretical model of Allee effects in models of avian population growth), and some fishes must nest in dense colonies to reduce predation rates on eggs and larvae (Hamilton 1971; Dominey 1981).

The above examples emphasize the facultative nature of the regulating factors whereby per capita mortality increases or per capita natality declines with increasing population density. Other mortality factors act independently of population density; that is, the magnitude of mortality or natality does not depend on population density per se. For example, in the northern United States, the winter ranges of many bird species are defined by severe winter weather (Root 1988). A series of unusually cold years will greatly decrease population densities in a region, regardless of the birds' densities during the previous summer. These population declines are therefore density independent.

Davidson and Andrewartha (1948a,b) investigated the causes of outbreaks of *Thrips imaginis*, a major pest on apples in Australia. In moist areas, such as irrigated suburban residential areas, these thrips persist even during dry years, but in drier habitats, their food supplies decline in midsummer, causing a catastrophic crash in the numbers of thrips. Although the crashes in thrip numbers occur following the peak of thrip populations in midsummer, there is no evidence for a density-dependent regulating mechanism, because the decline in food availability is due to an extrinsic factor, dry weather, rather than to the activity of the thrips per se. In other words, the food does not disappear because of overexploitation by thrips, but rather because of the weather, which is unaffected by the density of thrips.

It must be kept in mind that populations can be regulated by more than one factor, and that the simultaneous effects of several factors working in concert may be responsible for population changes. The extinction of *Trilepidea adamsii*, a New Zealand mistletoe, may have involved both density-independent and density-dependent factors (Norton 1991). The mistletoe was never widespread, so the extensive habitat destruction (a density-independent factor) that took place in New Zealand probably limited the plant to a few locations. Overcollecting by botanists and grazing by an introduced opossum were density-dependent forces that further reduced the species until it disappeared. (Scientific collecting is density dependent because as a species becomes more rare, specimens become more valuable, and field collectors may make a special effort to find and gather the last few individuals; of course, this practice also hearkens back to the discussion of ethics in Chapter 2.) This added pressure may have eliminated the few remaining *Trilepidea* populations.

A Hierarchical Approach to Population Regulation

Most models of population dynamics project future population sizes based on current population size and per capita birth and death rates. Some population models and studies go further by attempting to incorporate the causal factors that determine birth and death rates. Although the latter approach is sometimes described as incorporating the mechanisms of population regulation, there are mechanisms of population regulation that operate at more than one level in a hierarchy of causation. Thus, population regulation must be viewed as a hierarchical process.

An example of this view comes from studies of population fluctuations in granivorous birds such as sparrows. Typically, these studies have looked for regulatory factors by relating sparrow birth and death rates to spatial and temporal variations in food supply. All other things being equal, the survival of sparrows during winter is highest when and where seed production has been greatest (Pulliam and Parker 1979; Pulliam and Millikan 1982). Unfortunately, all other things are rarely equal, and, in the case of sparrows, not only food supply, but also habitat availability, varies dramatically from year to year. Sparrows live primarily in early successional habitats, and the availability of such habitats depends on a complex of factors ranging from the decisions of farmers to abandon land to the rate of old-field succession. Year-to-year variation in the abundance of wintering sparrows in the southeastern United States may depend less on how much food is available in each patch of habitat than on how habitat availability is affected by factors such as the influence of the global economy on the price of soybeans and the decisions made by farmers (Odum 1987).

As stated above, the population dynamics of animals needs to be viewed as a hierarchical process. In the case of the overwintering sparrows, local factors such as food supply affect sparrow populations at one level, while regional patterns of agriculture affect habitat availability for the sparrows at a very different level. To make population projections, one needs to know how many individuals there are, what habitats they occupy, and the characteristic birth and death rates for individuals in those habitats. A purely empirical model can be constructed based on population size and distribution and on habitat-specific demography. Such a model can be used to project future population sizes as long as (1) the habitat-specific birth and death rates do not change and (2) the fraction of the population in each habitat type does not change.

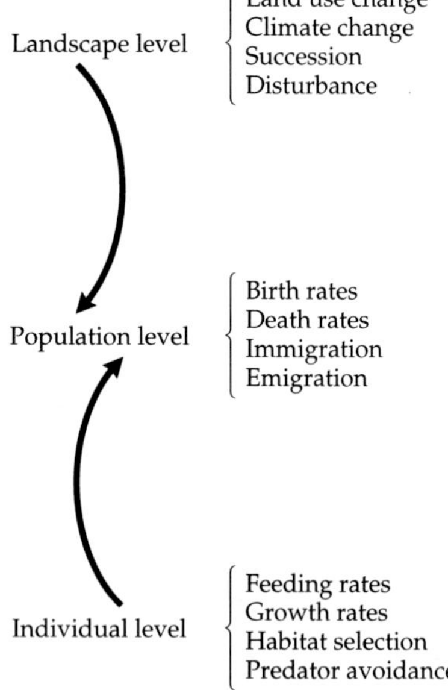

Figure 7.3 Population dynamics must be understood as resulting from a hierarchy of processes affecting populations at different levels. Landscape-level changes in the availability of habitat determine how much suitable habitat exists for a given species. The availability of suitable habitat and the behavior and physiology of individual organisms combine to influence the dynamics of populations.

This type of model can be used to examine the hierarchical levels of population regulation. The model can incorporate factors such as food supply, competition, disease, and predation that influence population growth by affecting birth and death rates within the habitats where individuals occur. Such a model is called a "mechanistic" model, and provides a "lower" or "individual-level" explanation of the phenomenon of population growth because it emphasizes factors operating within small-scale patches. These are the factors that ecologists have emphasized in population studies (Hassell 1978; Pulliam 1983; Werner et al. 1983).

There is, however, a "higher level" of explanation consisting of all those factors that operate at larger spatial and temporal scales, such as the factors that determine the availability of suitable habitat (Pearson 1993). In the case of the overwintering sparrows just discussed, the factors influencing availability of suitable habitat are at least as important in determining population dynamics as are the individual-level factors. Broad-scale geographic factors, such as land use and climate change, operate at a "landscape level," beyond the habitats where the population currently resides and often over relatively long periods of time. Factors at this landscape level determine the amount and location of suitable habitat for each particular species. Figure 7.3 illustrates this hierarchical approach. A complete explanation of past trends or a projection of future trends requires an understanding of both the "lower-level" factors determining birth and death rates within habitats and the "higher-level" factors determining regional trends in habitat availability. To understand the population dynamics of species of interest, conservationists therefore need to be concerned with environmental factors that operate at a variety of spatial scales. The next few sections discuss several key concepts that link populations to these higher-level factors.

Habitat-Specific Demography

Sources and Sinks

In many populations, individuals occupy habitat patches of differing quality. Individuals in highly productive habitats may be successful in producing offspring, while individuals in poor habitats may suffer poor reproductive success or survival. The fate of a population as a whole may depend on whether the reproductive success of individuals in the good habitats outweighs the lack of success by individuals in the poor areas. The idea that population dynamics may depend on the relative quality of good and poor habitats is called **source and sink dynamics**, and recently has been recognized as an important concept in conservation biology (Pulliam 1988; Doak 1995).

Good habitats are called **sources**, and are defined as areas where local reproductive success is greater than local mortality (see Box 7A for a more complete definition and treatment of sources and sinks). Populations in source habitats produce an excess of individuals, who must disperse outside their natal patch to find a place to settle and breed. Poor habitats, on the other hand, are areas where local productivity is less than local mortality. These areas are called **sinks** because, without immigration from other areas, popu-

---

BOX 7A
The Theory of Sources and Sinks

The population dynamics of an organism can be strongly influenced by the abundance and location of suitable habitat. The approach taken here is to attempt to understand how demography relates to habitat suitability and to relate population dynamics to the characteristics of real landscapes, including the location of suitable habitat. Consider a population of organisms living in a seasonal environment, consisting of a nonreproductive season or "winter" and a reproductive or breeding season. If the population has n_T individuals at the end of the winter, just prior to the onset of the reproductive season, and if none of the adults die during the breeding season, and each adult produces an average of b offspring, then at the end of the breeding season there will be $n_T + bn_T$ individuals alive (Pulliam 1988). Furthermore, if adults survive the nonbreeding season with probability P_A and juveniles survive with probability P_J, then at the beginning of the next breeding season the population size will be

$$n_{T+1} = P_A n_T + P_J b n_T = n_T (P_A + bP_J)$$

Let $\lambda = P_A + bP_J$. Lambda (λ) is the finite rate of increase for the population and gives the number of individuals at the beginning of year $T + 1$, per individual at the beginning of year T. The annual finite rate of increase (λ_t) can vary from year to year as the survival rates and/or reproductive rates vary. The geometric mean, $\bar{\lambda} = (\lambda_1\lambda_2 \cdots \lambda_t)^{1/t}$ of the rates over a sequence of t years characterizes the growth rate of the population in the sense that $n_t = n_0\bar{\lambda}^t$. Accordingly, if the long-term mean $\bar{\lambda}$ is less than 1.0, the population will decline, and if it exceeds 1.0, the population will grow. Obviously, the population cannot grow forever, so for a population that does not go extinct or become infinitely abundant, the long-term mean $\bar{\lambda}$ must be close to 1.0.

The mean finite rate of increase ($\bar{\lambda}$) can also be used to describe spatial variation in population growth rates. In this case, we refer to the habitat-specific rate of increase and calculate $\bar{\lambda}$ based on the birth and death rates that apply in a specific habitat or patch of habitat (Pulliam 1988). This concept of habitat-specific growth rate is complicated by dispersal. If each patch of habitat were isolated from all others, then the value of $\bar{\lambda}$ calculated for any one habitat would be the growth rate experienced by the population in that habitat. However, if habitats are connected, the growth rate experienced by the entire interconnected population is given by the weighted average across all habitats; that is, different parts of the population are growing at different rates.

Some habitats are clearly more suitable than others. Consider the simple case in which there are two habitats of different quality, and migration between them. Habitat 1 is the better habitat, called the source, and here reproduction exceeds mortality, so that the habitat-specific growth rate, $\bar{\lambda}_1$, is greater than 1.0. In habitat 2, the sink, mortality exceeds reproduction, so $\bar{\lambda}_2$ is less than 1.0. Assume that the subpopulation in the source grows at the rate $\bar{\lambda}_1$ until it reaches a maximum size (n_1^*), which represents the maximum number of breeding individuals that can be accommodated in the source. Once the source has reached its maximum size, there are $\bar{\lambda}_1 n_1^*$ individuals at the end of each nonbreeding season; of this total only n_1^* can remain to breed, and the remaining $n_1^*(\bar{\lambda}_1 - 1)$ must emigrate from the source habitat into sink habitat (Pulliam 1988).

In the absence of immigration, the sink subpopulation would soon disappear, because each year there would be fewer individuals than the year before. However, with the steady immigration of $n_1^*(\lambda_1 - 1)$ individuals from the source habitat, the sink population will grow to an equilibrium population of $n_2^* = n_1^*(\lambda_1 - 1)/(1 - \lambda_2)$. Note that $\lambda_1 - 1$ is the per capita reproductive surplus in the source habitat and $1 - \lambda_2$ is the per capita reproductive deficit in the sink habitat. Clearly, if the reproductive surplus in the source is much larger than the reproductive deficit in the sink, the sink habitat will contain far more individuals than the source habitat, despite the fact that the sink subpopulation is dependent on emigration from the source for its very existence. In other words, most of the individuals in a local population may exist in habitat that cannot maintain the population (Pulliam 1988).

---

lations in sink habitats inevitably spiral "down the drain" to extinction. The terms *source* and *sink* are also used to describe the populations found in these habitats: **source populations** are those found in source habitats, and **sink populations** are those found in sink habitats.

Population ecologists are discovering that many species have both source and sink populations (see Pulliam 1996 for a recent review). The excess individuals produced by source populations can disperse to sink habitat patches and maintain the populations found in these poorer habitats. A population that consists of several subpopulations linked together by immigration and emigration is called a **metapopulation** (Figure 7.4); this concept was introduced in Chapter 6 and is discussed more fully later in this chapter. *Metapopulation* is a broader term than *source* or *sink* because in metapopulations the demographic rates may or may not be the same in different patches of habitat. Sources and sinks form a special type of metapopulation in which some patches (sources) are substantially better than others (sinks). Metapopulations have been described in species as diverse as Scandinavian crickets and frogs, desert grasses in Israel, and Spotted Owls (*Strix occidentalis*) in the western United States.

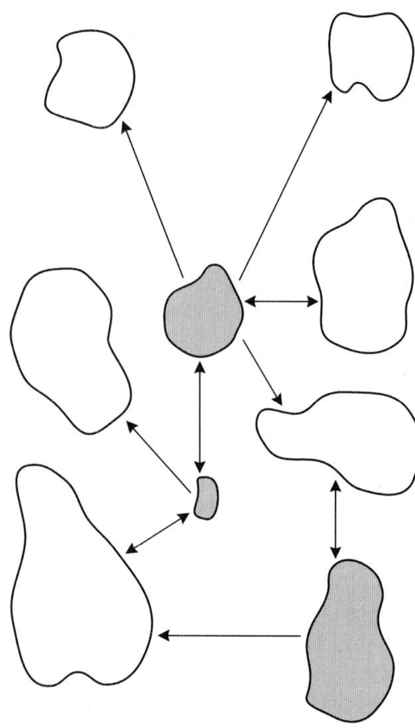

Figure 7.4 A schematic example of a metapopulation structure affected by source and sink patches. In this case, a few source habitats (shaded) provide excess individuals, which emigrate to and colonize sink habitats (open). The sink habitats may be spatially larger than the sources, and may even have higher population densities, but their populations would go extinct were it not for the presence of the source habitats. Arrows indicate directions of movement of individuals.

Several results from studies of source and sink dynamics have broad implications for conservation biology. First, theoretical models of sources and sinks have shown that a small proportion of the total population may be located in the source habitats. For instance, using demographic parameters that are reasonable for many natural populations, Pulliam (1988) showed that as little as 10% of a metapopulation may be found in source habitats and still be responsible for maintaining the 90% of the population found in the sinks. Such relationships may greatly affect the ability of conservationists to identify critical habitats for endangered species. Until recently, critical habitats were defined as the places where a species was most common. Source habitats, however, are defined by demographic characteristics—habitat-specific reproductive success and survivorship—not population density. Source habitats could easily (and mistakenly) be ignored if conservationists concentrated on preserving habitat only where a species is most common, not where it is most productive. If source habitats are not protected in a conservation plan, obviously the whole metapopulation could be threatened.

An example of the utility of considering source–sink dynamics in conservation is Wootton and Bell's (1992) analysis of the population dynamics of the Peregrine Falcon (*Falco peregrinus*) in California. Wootton and Bell modeled this population as two subpopulations (northern and southern California) linked by dispersal. Their analysis suggests that the northern population acts as a source for the smaller southern population. The regional management strategy for this species includes the release of captive-reared young, and is aimed primarily at the southern population, which Wootton and Bell show to be a sink. Management efforts would be more productive if they were directed at stabilizing and increasing the northern source population rather than the southern sink population.

Another major implication of the source–sink concept concerns reserve design. Pulliam and Danielson (1991) showed with a source–sink model that adding habitat to a reserve can actually result in a smaller metapopulation if most of the additional land is sink habitat. Individuals dispersing within the reserve may settle in the unproductive sink patches if the available source patches are too hard to find—in essence, the available source patches become lost in a sea of sink. Recent studies using a metapopulation model developed for Spotted Owls predict just such a problem with some reserve designs proposed for this species in the Pacific Northwest. These researchers have suggested that Spotted Owl reserves should have "hard boundaries"; that is, the reserves should be separated from similar-looking sink habitat, so that dispersing birds will not settle in unproductive territories (McKelvey et al. 1993).

Determining which habitats are sources and which are sinks requires a great deal of knowledge about the natural history of organisms. One needs to know the birth and death rates of individuals in each habitat type, details of dispersal behavior, and other aspects of the organism's life history. Without such knowledge, it is impossible to design a conservation plan that considers realistic population dynamics. Critics of this approach argue that this information is often difficult to gather and thus rarely available (Wennergren et al. 1995). Studies to obtain such basic information will be critical in the planning of management and conservation strategies that incorporate the natural variability found in most populations.

Metapopulation Concepts

Levins (1969) introduced the concept of the metapopulation to describe a collection of subpopulations of a species, each occupying a suitable patch of habitat in a landscape of otherwise unsuitable habitat. Because these subpopulations are linked together by the emigration and immigration of individuals between patches, a subpopulation can go temporarily extinct in a patch, which can then be recolonized. Fragmented populations that are not linked by dispersal of individuals do not fit the metapopulation model (Harrison 1991). In his classic model of metapopulations, Levins (1969) demonstrated that the fraction of suitable habitat patches occupied at any given time represents a balance of the rate at which subpopulations go extinct in occupied patches and the rate of colonization of empty patches (see Hanski 1989). The rate of local extinction depends largely on conditions within a patch and the stochastic (or random) nature of the dynamics of small populations. The rate of colonization of empty patches, on the other hand, depends on the dispersal ability of the species and the location of suitable patches in the landscape.

The subpopulation in each patch can fluctuate in size, and when a subpopulation is very small, local extinction can be prevented by occasional immigrants that arrive from neighboring patches. This has been termed the **rescue effect** by Brown and Kodric-Brown (1977), who argue that it is often a major factor in maintaining small populations. The rescue effect may also be important in maintaining high levels of species diversity, because poor competitors will not be excluded from patches by locally well adapted species if the populations of the poorer competitors are maintained through immigration (Stevens 1989). The rescue effect is in part responsible for one major characteristic of metapopulations: the proportion of habitat patches that are occupied is relatively constant through time, even though populations in the individual patches may go extinct relatively frequently.

Conservation biologists are using metapopulation models to describe the structure of populations that are found scattered across isolated patches and that are threatened or otherwise of management interest. In many of these metapopulation analyses, the goal is to identify particular subpopulations, habitat patches, or links between patches that are critical to maintenance of the overall metapopulation. Beier (1993) provides an excellent example of this type of analysis in his study of the cougar (*Felis concolor*) population of the Santa Ana Mountains of southern California. Beier used radiotelemetry data to show that the cougars form a series of semi-isolated populations found mostly in small mountain ranges linked by riparian corridors (Figure 7.5). A metapopulation simulation model showed that the overall population in the region is heavily dependent on movement by individual cats through the corridors to colonize empty areas. Beier's analysis showed that any loss of habitat (and corresponding decrease in population size) in this region would greatly increase the chance of extinction for the entire metapopulation.

Beier looked at the importance of specific habitat patches and corridors in maintaining the metapopulation. One corridor in the northern part of the study area linked a 150 km^2 patch (8% of the total area) with the rest of the region. When the study was published, this corridor was slated for development by the city of Anaheim. Beier's analysis demonstrated that loss of this corridor would mean that the northern habitat patch would eventually be unoccupied due to lack of immigrants, and that the cougar population as a whole would suffer greatly. Because the metapopulation model identified the importance of this corridor, Beier proposed that the development plan be modified to leave the corridor intact.

There has been much debate about how the number, size, and arrangement of suitable sites influences population persistence. This controversy can be illustrated by what has come to be known as the SLOSS debate. SLOSS is an acronym for "Single Large Or Several Small" and refers to whether conservation reserves are best designed as one big block of protected land or as several smaller reserves. The SLOSS debate mainly has been concerned with the effect of reserve design on the diversity of species protected, but the SLOSS logic can also be applied to the viability of a metapopulation by focusing on the two contradictory ways in which distance between suitable sites influences population persistence. If several populations are close to one another, migration between them may be common, and thus metapopulation persis-

(A) (B)

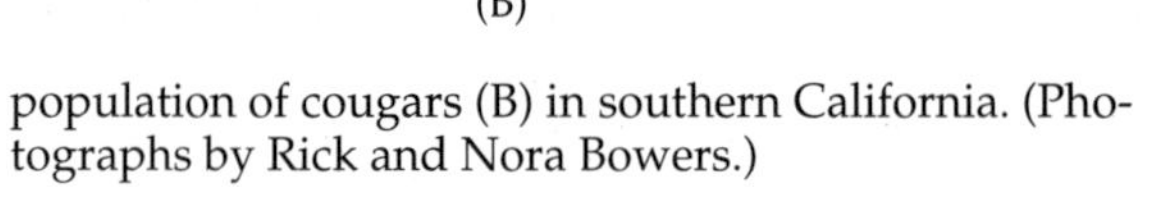

Figure 7.5 The use of riparian habitat (A) as corridors was shown to be a crucial element in the maintenance of a viable population of cougars (B) in southern California. (Photographs by Rick and Nora Bowers.)

tence may be promoted. On the other hand, sites close to one another are more likely to experience the same environmental conditions, including the same floods, fires, disease outbreaks, or other disturbances. This negative aspect of proximity leads to shortened metapopulation persistence by increasing the correlation between the dynamics of local populations, and thereby increases the likelihood that all local populations will go extinct at once.

There is no single answer to the SLOSS debate because the number, size, and location of habitat patches affect different species differently. Likewise, there is "no single 'magic' population size that guarantees the persistence of populations" (Thomas 1990). Extinction is best described as a probabilistic phenomenon: the larger the number of populations and the larger the size of each population, the lower the probability of extinction. For good dispersers, broadly separated sites that are close enough to permit adequate dispersal between them, yet far enough apart to experience different environmental conditions, might maximize population persistence. On the other hand, this arrangement might lead to the rapid extinction of a species with poor dispersal ability because no exchange of individuals among sites would be possible.

Compared with the SLOSS debate, much less attention has been paid to the overall size of complex landscapes that make effective conservation or management units. How large does a landscape need to be before the population dynamics within it are independent of events external to the landscape? Pulliam et al. (1995) define "spatial autonomy" as the level of population independence reached by a landscape of a particular size. Ideally, conservation and land management units such as refuges and forest districts should be large enough to confer a high degree of spatial autonomy on the populations being managed within the unit. Pulliam et al. present results of simulation models that suggest that spatial autonomy is a complex function of the size, quality, and quantity of habitat patches both within the landscape of interest and in surrounding regions.

Population Viability Analysis

Models of factors contributing to population viability are proving to be valuable additions to the conservationist's toolbox. The study of the ways in which habitat loss, environmental uncertainty, demographic stochasticity, and genetic factors interact to determine extinction probabilities for individual species has been termed **population viability analysis**, or PVA (Soulé 1987; Shaffer 1990). Although PVA is a relatively new approach, a number of excellent studies have demonstrated its utility (e.g., Murphy et al. 1990; Stacey and Taper 1992; Doak et al. 1994; Nantel et al. 1996). Our discussion of PVA is enhanced by Mark Shaffer, one of its developers, in Essay 7B.

ESSAY 7B
Population Viability Analysis
Determining Nature's Share

Mark L. Shaffer, The Wilderness Society

Until the human population stabilizes, a major challenge for conservation biology is to determine nature's share of the landscape. We must know how much land, and in what patterns, will allow natural dynamics to maintain the diversity of life in a global ecosystem that is already dominated by humankind. Population viability analysis is the branch of conservation biology that seeks to determine nature's share by understanding the relationship of habitat and species survival.

Since humankind began hunting, we have understood the importance of habitat *type* in determining the distribution and abundance of a species: you do not hunt for pronghorns in alpine meadows. Game management, both archaic and modern, extended this recognition to the equal importance of habitat *quality*. It reflects an understanding that there are degrees of habitat suitability for any species, and these are reflected in overall population features, such as abundance, fecundity, or average size. In fact, the very basis for modern game management is maintenance of habitat type and manipulation of habitat quality to achieve desired levels of distribution and abundance.

Over the past 30 years, studies of biogeography, particularly of island biotas, have shown us that habitat *quantity* is as fundamental to the survival of a species as is habitat type or quality. In other words, having the proper type of habitat, even of high quality, may not assure species survival unless there is enough of it.

In just the last 10 years, the controversy over the Spotted Owl and old-growth forests in the Pacific Northwest has taught us that habitat *pattern* is also crucial in determining a species' fate. Not only must we maintain the proper habitat of good quality in sufficient amounts, but that habitat must be arranged in an appropriate pattern across the landscape.

Like physicists searching for a grand unified theory explaining how the four fundamental forces (strong nuclear force, weak nuclear force, electromagnetism, and gravity) interact to control the structure and fate of the universe, conservation biologists now seek their own grand unified theory explaining how habitat type, quality, quantity, and pattern interact to control the structures and fates of species. Population viability analysis (PVA) is the first expression of this quest.

PVA seeks to determine how the likelihood of extinction changes in response to changes in habitat type, quality, quantity, and pattern. In a world with a fixed land area and a growing human population, competition for land use can only intensify. If land must be set aside from development to maintain habitat for certain species, how much land is enough?

The roots of PVA trace back to MacArthur and Wilson's (1967) island biogeography theory. In seeking to explain the relatively low species diversity of island biotas, they proposed that the number of species on an island at any time represented a balance between immigration of species to the island and extinction of species already present. Smaller islands had fewer species, in part, because they could support only smaller populations, and smaller populations should have higher extinction rates.

Given the pace at which modern civilization is fragmenting natural landscapes, it was not long before conservationists saw the similarity between an island and a stand of old-growth timber in a sea of clear-cuts, or a patch of coastal sage scrub in a sea of subdivisions. And it was not long before they began to examine the reasons why smaller populations have higher extinction rates (Soulé and Wilcox 1980; Shaffer 1981; Gilpin and Soulé 1986). Population viability analysis was born.

The reason small populations are fragile, it turns out, is because of chance events. Chance operates at several levels that affect the likelihood of extinction. Chance plays a role in determining when individuals die, how many offspring they have, or whether they can find suitable mates (called demographic stochasticity). Chance affects the weather, which affects the food supply and helps determine the rates of survival and fecundity (environmental stochasticity). Periodic major catastrophes such as floods, fires, and hurricanes can also be viewed as chance events; at least they are unpredictable (natural catastrophes). Chance even affects the genetic makeup of populations through genetic drift (genetic stochasticity).

All of these four chance factors become more important as population size gets smaller. Moreover, they can interact to reinforce one another's negative effects and draw small populations into what have been termed "extinction vortices" (Gilpin and Soulé 1986).

Among the earliest attempts to determine what all this means in real numbers for a real species was my work (Shaffer 1983) on the grizzly bear (*Ursus arctos horribilis*). Using very detailed data collected over a 12-year period in Yellowstone National Park and environs by John and Frank Craighead and their colleagues, I constructed a quantitative model of grizzly bear population dynamics that kept track of individual bears and incorporated the effects of chance events. The results demonstrated that if you want a grizzly bear population to have a 95% chance of persisting for a century, you have to have enough habitat to support 70–90 bears. If you want a higher probability of survival (say 99%), or the same probability but over a longer period of time (say 200 years), you must save even more habitat to support a larger, more durable population.

Although the above analysis was incomplete in that it did not include an assessment of the genetic effects of small population size or the impacts of natural catastrophes, it nonetheless captured the essence of what a PVA should be, namely, a data-based, quantitative assessment of the relationship between the likelihood of extinction and the amount of habitat available to a species.

Twenty years, and at least 28 PVAs, (Boyce 1992) later, we have made significant progress in understanding extinction dynamics. We better understand the threats to small populations and how these threats can interact to pull such populations toward extinction. And we are beginning to understand the geometry of extinction, how the loss and fragmentation of natural habitats can so dilute them across the landscape that they no longer support many of the species dependent on them. Efforts to devise a credible strategy for conserving the Spotted Owl have led to the first PVA for a true metapopulation (Thomas et al. 1990). This is a data-based, (partially) quantitative assessment of the relationship between the likelihood of owl extinction and both the amount *and* pattern of old-growth forest maintained across the landscape of the Pacific Northwest.

Still, we cannot say how much natural habitat is enough to perpetuate nature's diversity of species, for several reasons. First, the theoretical basis for assessing population viability is still developing. There is no single model of population dynamics sophisticated enough to simultaneously incorporate all classes of chance events. But even if our theory were perfect, we know virtually nothing of the details of the life histories of the vast majority of species. Conservation biology operates in a model-rich but data-poor world, and the tub of species we need to know something about is filling rapidly: The Nature Conservancy has identified 9000 species native to the United States that may be at some risk of extinction.

How then to proceed? One of the major lessons of more than 20 years of the Endangered Species Act is that we should focus our efforts on conserving natural habitats and ecosystems, and not on attempting to rescue one endangered species at a time. Similarly, we should not attempt a quantitative PVA for every threatened or endangered species. Instead, we need to concentrate our efforts on those species indicative of natural systems, species whose own area requirements for viability provide some index of the area requirements of the systems that support them. These will likely be top carnivores: large-bodied, long-lived, slowly reproducing species at the top of their ecosystem's food chain. If we can come to understand their requirements for viability, we will have gone a long way toward understanding the appropriate spatial requirements of the ecosystems that support them. In this way, PVA can assist in the quantification of landscape ecology, and in designing land use patterns that allow for perpetuation of overall biodiversity.

As far as we know, all populations eventually go extinct. Very large populations may last for hundreds, thousands, or even millions of generations, while small populations are much more vulnerable to extinction. Shaffer (1981, 1987) lists the following four categories of factors that influence the likelihood of population extinction:

1. Demographic uncertainty (also called demographic stochasticity)
2. Environmental uncertainty
3. Natural catastrophes
4. Genetic uncertainty (including the founder effect, genetic drift, and inbreeding)

We discuss the first three categories below; the fourth category, genetic uncertainty, was treated at length in Chapter 6.

Demographic uncertainty is usually taken to mean uncertainty resulting from the effects of random events on the survival and reproduction of individuals. An extremely skewed sex ratio is an example of an unusual demographic event that could occur in a small population. For example, the Dusky Seaside Sparrow (*Ammodramus maritimus nigrescens*) was doomed to extinction in 1980 when the last six known individuals all happened to be males (Kale 1983). **Environmental uncertainty** usually refers to unpredictable events, such as "changes in weather, food supply, and the populations of competitors, predators and parasites" (Shaffer 1987). One way of appreciating the distinction between these two categories is to think of demographic stochasticity as the variation experienced at the individual level, given a mean population mortality rate and/or rate of reproduction. Environmental uncertainty, on the other hand, refers to temporal and spatial variation in these mean rates. Even where different subpopulations are subject to the same mean rates, some subpopulations will, by chance, experience more mortality or reproduction than others during a particular interval of time. The final category of extinction factors to be considered in this chapter is **natural catastrophes**. These can be defined as extreme cases of environmental uncertainty, such as hurricanes or large fires, that are usually infrequent and short in duration, but widespread in their impact.

Demographic uncertainty, environmental uncertainty, and natural catastrophes are convenient labels for various forms of variation that influence the demographic process and thereby contribute to extinction probability. The lines between these categories are, however, somewhat arbitrary. For example, natural catastrophes such as floods, droughts, and fires are distinguished by their brief durations, severe effects, and infrequent occurrence. What constitutes a flood or a drought, however, is not always clear; accordingly, arbitrary definitions based on expected frequency are often used (i.e., "a 50-year flood"). A "catastrophe" that is repeated frequently may become part of the normal level of environmental uncertainty to which organisms must adapt.

As a general rule, genetic and demographic uncertainty are important factors in the viability of only very small populations (e.g., <50 individuals). Environmental uncertainty and catastrophes can affect the viability of much larger populations. Conservationists working with endangered species often must deal with the combined effects of all four factors, because many endangered species, especially large vertebrates, exist in small populations. The recovery plans for many endangered species set two goals for establishing viable populations: (1) create multiple populations, so that a single catastrophic event cannot eliminate the whole species, and (2) increase the size of each population to a level at which genetic, demographic, and normal environmental uncertainties are less threatening. This can be very difficult to do, especially with species that currently exist in a single small population, or are found in a single unique habitat patch.

A number of authors have suggested general guidelines for establishing viable population sizes (e.g., Gilpin and Soulé 1986). Populations of 10–50 individuals are often said to be too small because they result in rapid loss of genetic variability or because they are too prone to extinction due to a single natural catastrophe. Populations of 1000–10,000 individuals, on the other hand, are often said to be adequate to ensure long-term persistence. Such numbers can, however, at best be viewed as very general guidelines. The evolutionary record tells us that populations of 10,000 or more will almost certainly go extinct eventually, even though the expected persistence time is very long. Also, populations that appear to be safe for many years may suddenly decline if they are subject to threshold responses (discussed in Box 7B). Any attempt to estimate a population's viability must be done in the context of social goals and political realities, and with an understanding that any predictions are made in a context of uncertainty.

BOX 7B
Thresholds of Population Responses

Researchers and policymakers concerned about species extinction normally worry about very rare organisms. It is generally agreed that species whose total population has declined to just a few individuals are the most likely to go extinct in the immediate future. The history of human exploitation of plants and animals tells us, however, that common species, even abundant ones, can suffer huge population declines that threaten the species with extinction. The Passenger Pigeon (*Ectopistes migratorius*) was one of the most abundant birds in North America in the early 1800s. A century of overhunting and habitat destruction caused the bird to decline until the huge populations suddenly crashed over the span of a few decades. The Passenger Pigeon became extinct in the early 1900s, when the last few individuals died in zoos (Blockstein and Tordoff 1985). Similarly, overexploitation by humans has caused the collapse of a number of fisheries of formerly abundant species such as the Pacific anchovy and the Atlantic striped bass. Why have these common species declined so precipitously?

Part of the explanation of sudden population crashes lies in the nonlinear nature of population change. Populations do not always follow smooth trajectories such as those mapped in Figure 7.2. Under some circumstances, populations will exhibit threshold responses, dramatic changes in population size over short periods of time. Because threshold responses make it particularly difficult to design strategies for managing populations over time, it is important for conservation biologists to consider such population responses in their investigations. Lande (1987) developed a general metapopulation model for territorial species that is useful in the study of thresholds of population change. In the discussion below, we use this to model one kind of population threshold response. We consider how far habitat loss and land use change might proceed before there is any significant effect on the fraction of suitable sites that are occupied by a territorial species.

Lande (1987) considered metapopulation dynamics on a large landscape divided into many sites, each the size of one territory. In his model, the landscape consists of two habitat types (suitable and unsuitable) with a fraction h of the sites being suitable and a fraction $u = 1 - h$ being unsuitable. In the Lande model, the suitable and unsuitable sites are considered to be randomly interspersed. The model considers females only, assuming that females can always find a mate.

In the Lande metapopulation model, juveniles are assumed to inherit their mother's site with probability e; if they fail to inherit their natal site, they must disperse, in which case they can search up to m tracts (potential territories) before perishing. A juvenile survives only if she finds an unoccupied, suitable site, and the probability of doing this is

$$1 - (1 - e)\left(u + \hat{p}h\right)^{m}$$

where $\hat{p}$ is the proportion of the territories already occupied. Juvenile mortality during dispersal is thus density dependent, because as population size increases, more of the suitable sites are already occupied and juveniles have a lessened chance of finding a suitable unoccupied site before perishing.

Lande calculates the "conditional" lifetime reproductive success of those females that live to find a suitable territory. The product of this conditional reproductive success and the probability of a dispersing juvenile female finding an unoccupied, suitable territory gives the expected lifetime reproductive success, R_0, which according to the Lotka-Euler equation equals unity for a stationary population. Accordingly, Lande solves the equation $R_0 = 1.0$ for the value of $\hat{p}$ in order to get the equilibrium proportion of suitable territories occupied.

The utility of metapopulation models can be easily demonstrated by simplifying the Lande expression for the probability of a dispersing juvenile finding an unoccupied, suitable site before perishing. Lande assumes that dispersing juveniles search both suitable and unsuitable sites. This is probably a realistic assumption if suitable and unsuitable sites look the same superficially and must be explored in detail in order to differentiate them. In some cases, however, such as might be the case for suitable forest intermixed with unsuitable fields, potentially unsuitable sites may be so obvious that the dispersing female need not waste her limited number of searches on finding them. The female still must search for an unoccupied site, so the probability of finding an unoccupied site before perishing becomes $1 - (1 - e)\hat{p}^m$.

The probability $(1 - e)$ of not inheriting the natal territory depends on when the juveniles disperse. If, for example, juveniles disperse in the fall when their parents are sure to still be alive, this probability reduces to unity. These simplifying assumptions make it easy to solve for the equilibrium proportion of suitable sites occupied by setting the finite rate of increase equal to unity as follows:

$$\lambda = P_A + bP_j\left[1 - (1 - e)\hat{p}^m\right] = 1.0$$

and solving for $\hat{p}$, the equilibrium proportion of suitable sites occupied.

The above equation can be solved for the equilibrium proportion of suitable sites occupied. According to the model, all other things being equal, the equilibrium population size declines linearly as the proportion of the entire landscape that is suitable declines (Figure A1). The decline of population size with decreasing reproductive success or decreasing survivorship is, however, nonlinear and may indeed be very abrupt (Figure A2). This is because for high values of m, virtually all suitable sites are found, so equilibrium population size remains about the same so long as the same amount of suitable habitat is available and λ does not fall below 1.0.

Pulliam (1992) gives a hypothetical example based on this model in which the equilibrium population stays steady and then abruptly declines as the proportion of agricultural land in the landscape increases (Figure B). The example assumes that birds in territories next to agricultural plots are exposed to high levels of pesticide residues in the food they feed their young and, as a result, have lower reproductive success. Thus, as a greater proportion of the landscape becomes agricultural, the average reproductive success decreases. At some point the reproductive success drops so low that $\bar{\lambda}$ is less than 1.0, and the population abruptly goes extinct. If the ability of dispersing juveniles to find suitable sites is high (large m), the proportion of suitable sites occupied is essentially a step function, abruptly declining from near 100% to 0%.

Such abrupt declines in populations may be difficult to predict because the problem may well go undetected until a critical threshold is reached. Such threshold responses could apply to a variety of situations, including habitat loss, exposure to toxins, and habitat fragmentation. Since catastrophic population collapse has been documented in a number of real-world situations, such as the Passenger Pigeon and the commercial fisheries mentioned above, threshold responses are a major unsolved problem facing conservationists. Models such as Lande's are useful tools for studying population threshold responses.

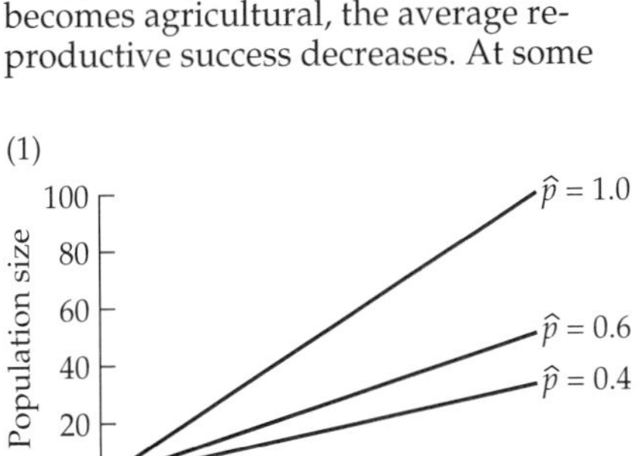

Figure A Population size depends on both the fraction of the landscape that is suitable and the demography of the species within suitable patches of habitat. In most cases, population size will increase linearly as the proportion of the landscape that is suitable increases. In Figure A1, $\hat{p}$ refers to the fraction of suitable sites occupied at demographic equilibrium. Population size can change abruptly with changes in demographic factors such as survival probability and reproductive success. In Figure A2, m refers to the dispersal ability of the species; higher values of m imply that the species is a better disperser and can therefore find a larger fraction of suitable sites.

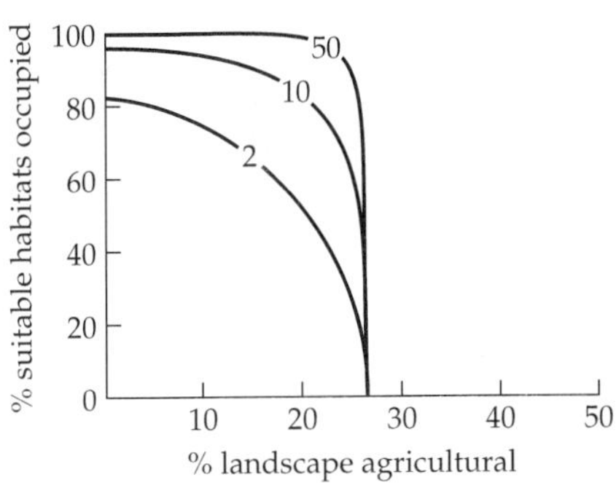

Figure B If reproductive success or survival depends on landscape structure, population size can change abruptly as landscape features change. In this example, suitable habitat patches that are adjacent to agricultural land where pesticides are used are characterized by low reproductive success. Consequently, as the fraction of the landscape in agriculture increases and a greater fraction of other habitat patches abuts agricultural land, reproductive success declines. When reproductive success reaches the threshold necessary to balance mortality, the fraction of suitable habitat patches occupied (and therefore the population size) declines abruptly. The numbers on the three lines refer to relative dispersal ability (m), as discussed above.

(A)

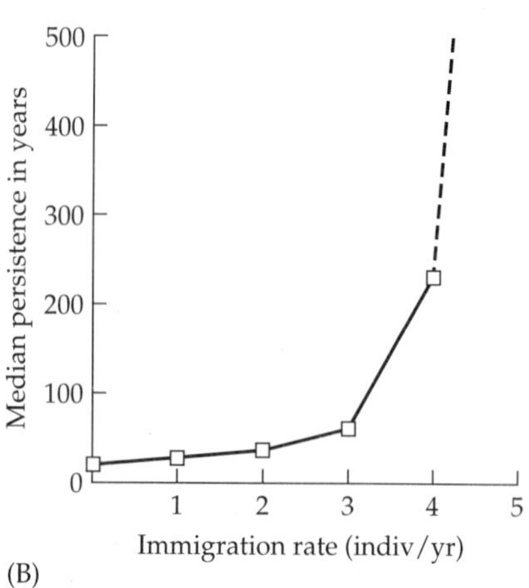

(B)

Figure 7.6 Small populations of Acorn Woodpeckers are found in isolated oak canyons (A) in New Mexico. (B) A population viability model showed that these populations could persist only if some immigration between populations occurred. Persistence times of populations increased quickly as the average number of immigrants per population increased. (A, photograph by Rick and Nora Bowers; B, from Stacey and Taper 1992.)

Most PVAs published to date have combined field studies of important demographic parameters with simulation modeling of the possible effects of various extinction factors. Generally, the object of these analyses is to generate a prediction of the probability that a population will go extinct in a given number of years (e.g., "a 95% probability of extinction within 1000 years"). Murphy et al. (1990) have proposed that two different styles of PVA will be needed for different types of organisms. Species with low population densities that are restricted to small geographic ranges (most endangered large vertebrates, for example) will require PVAs that include analysis of the genetic and demographic factors that affect small populations. This is the style of PVA that has been done most frequently to date. Smaller organisms, such as most threatened invertebrates, have a different set of problems. They frequently are restricted to a few habitat patches, but within those patches can reach high population densities. Murphy et al. propose that PVAs for these species will need to emphasize environmental uncertainty and catastrophic factors.

Stacey and Taper (1992) provide an example of a PVA for a nonendangered bird, the Acorn Woodpecker (*Melanerpes formicivorus*), which is found in the oak woodlands of the western United States and Mexico (Figure 7.6). This species is normally found in small, isolated populations scattered across large regions. Stacey and Taper developed a simulation model to predict the effect of environmental uncertainty on the viability of individual woodpecker populations. In the simulations, when total isolation was imposed, most of the populations went extinct within 20 years. With a small amount of migration between populations, however, most of the simulated populations lasted more than 1000 years. For their New Mexico study sites, Stacey and Taper have records showing that small woodpecker populations have survived for over 70 years, suggesting that migration must be important in maintaining these natural populations.

In general, population viability cannot be assessed by focusing on a single patch of suitable habitat and the organisms living in it. Most organisms live in islands of suitable habitat embedded in a larger landscape. As the Acorn Woodpecker study demonstrated, there is often an exchange of individuals among suitable habitat patches in the landscape. Because populations in the various patches are linked by the movement of dispersing individuals, the fates of the populations are interconnected. Population viability analyses of most organisms will therefore need to consider the importance of factors that link subpopulations within a metapopulation (see the section titled "The Landscape Approach," below).

Empirical Studies of Population Persistence

Thomas (1990) points out that, whereas estimates of population viability based on theoretical models are quite uncertain, a number of studies of real populations give us guidelines for predicting population persistence. For example, Thomas refers to the extinctions of birds in the California Channel Islands over an 80-year period (Jones and Diamond 1976; Figure 7.7). Of populations on islands with fewer than 10 breeding pairs, 39% went extinct during the 80-year period, but only about 10% of the populations numbering between 10 and 100 pairs went extinct in the same time. Only one population numbering between 100 and 1000 pairs went extinct, and no populations exceeding 1000 pairs went extinct. Thomas also refers to a study of birds on islands around the British coastline by Pimm et al. (1988), which found that populations of 1 or 2 pairs had a mean time to extinction of 1.6 years, populations of 3 to 5 pairs had a mean time to extinction of 3.5 years, and populations of 6 to 12 pairs had a mean time to extinction of 7.5 years. Thus, even among very small populations (1–12 pairs), the time to extinction increased with population size.

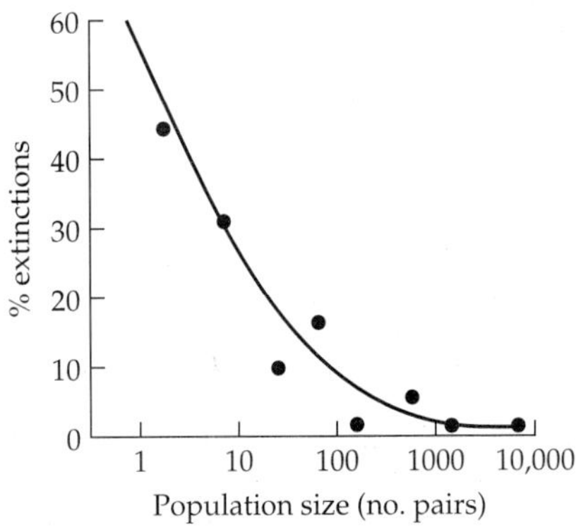

Figure 7.7 Extinction rates of bird species as a function of population size on the California Channel Islands. Plotted is the percentage of populations in various size classes that became extinct during the study. (From Jones and Diamond 1976.)

The above examples refer to persistence times of isolated populations receiving few or no immigrants. A number of studies have shown that the local populations of a metapopulation often go extinct, but studies directly relevant to the persistence times of metapopulations per se are extremely rare. One of the first theoretical analyses to consider the persistence of metapopulations is that of Hanski et al. (1996) who estimated "minimal viable metapopulation size" (the number of subpopulations required to support metapopulation persistence). Hanski et al.'s theoretical analyses suggest that many endangered species may be on a trajectory toward extinction due to inviable metapopulation size, in spite of protection of current subpopulations.

One of the best field studies of the persistence of a metapopulation is the long-term study of checkerspot butterflies (*Euphydryas editha*, Figure 7.8) near Jasper Ridge in northern California, briefly mentioned in Chapter 6 (Ehrlich et al. 1980; Ehrlich and Murphy 1987; Murphy et al. 1990). Checkerspot butterflies are found in scattered serpentine grasslands around the San Francisco Bay area. These grasslands have declined rapidly due to development. The butterflies at Jasper Ridge live in distinct demographic units or subpopulations despite the fact that the serpentine grassland habitat in which they occur is "essentially continuous" at Jasper Ridge and "uninterrupted by barriers to the butterfly's flight" (Ehrlich and Murphy 1987). The local demographic units are sufficiently connected by individual movement that they are probably part of the same genetic population. Ehrlich and Murphy describe the situation as a metapopulation that is "subdivided into groups that occupy clusters of habitat patches and interact extensively." More to the point, the demographic units fluctuate in size more or less independently of one another and are subject to local extinction and recolonization.

Figure 7.8 The checkerspot butterfly (*Euphydryas editha*) is the focus of one of the best long-term studies of metapopulation dynamics. See also Figures 9.15 and 10.12. (Photograph by P. R. Ehrlich.)

Although the checkerspot butterfly exists at a variety of locations in the San Francisco Bay area, not all populations are equal in their ability to resist environmental perturbations. The total population at Jasper Ridge is small, fluctuating from fewer than ten to a few hundred individuals. Such small populations are too small to maintain themselves indefinitely, particularly during periods of prolonged drought. Other populations are much larger and may persist through even the worst environmental conditions. Murphy et al. (1990)

Figure 7.9 Furbish's lousewort is found in small isolated populations that colonize riverbanks often affected by natural disturbances. (Photograph by Sue Gawler.)

review evidence that local populations in marginal areas frequently go extinct and are repopulated by emigration from nearby source habitats. While the small population at Jasper Ridge may go extinct occasionally, Murphy et al. (1990) conclude that the metapopulation should be resilient to extinction because of the presence of the large source subpopulation.

Although animals are generally thought to be better dispersers than plants, many plant species may also exist in metapopulations characterized by frequent local extinction and recolonization. One of the best studies of plant metapopulation dynamics is the work of Menges (1990; Menges et al. 1986) on Furbish's lousewort (*Pedicularis furbishiae*; Figure 7.9). This herbaceous perennial species is endemic to the Saint John River Valley in northern Maine, and lives in very unstable habitat patches along the riverbanks. Menges describes this lousewort as inhabiting "a disturbance/successional niche" defined by hydrology and vegetation response. The species is a poor competitor and seems to do best in low sites characterized by nonwoody vegetation, frequent flooding, and springtime ice scour.

Menges and his colleagues measured habitat-specific demographic variables and concluded that in the absence of catastrophic disturbance, these wet, early-successional sites cannot maintain viable populations. However, this system is characterized by catastrophic events that lead to local extinction due to ice scour and bank slumping. Menges developed a model incorporating much of the known biology of the species and its response to such catastrophic events, and concluded that local population extinction probability is high even at the best of sites. Thus, "individual *P. furbishiae* populations are temporary features of the riverine ecosystem," and metapopulation viability "depends on a positive balance between new populations and extinction" (Menges 1990).

The Landscape Approach

Individuals of the same species living in relatively close proximity to one another may experience quite different physical and biotic environments, even to the extent that some may not be able to survive and reproduce while others do very well. At spatial scales substantially larger than what one individual encounters, the landscape experienced by a population represents a mosaic of good and bad places for the species. The growth, or lack thereof, of the population is determined not only by the quality of the individual microsites occupied, but also by the spatial and temporal distribution of suitable and unsuitable microsites or patches of habitat.

Increasingly, conservationists are adopting the landscape perspective when designing management plans and analyzing the environmental factors affecting species of interest (Noss 1983). Conservation strategies must recognize that organisms move over heterogeneous landscapes, and therefore that saving a single patch of "critical habitat" will rarely be enough to maintain a population. Researchers working with aquatic systems were among the first to realize this principle, because a river or lake cannot be considered protected if the watershed that feeds the system is not included in the management plan. Similarly, recognition of concepts such as source–sink dynamics requires conservationists and land managers to adopt a landscape perspective. In many areas, this broader perspective requires planners to consider landscape patterns and land use strategies outside of the land unit (park, forest district, county) that they are working with directly (Noss 1983). Even in a region as large as Yellowstone National Park, wildlife managers are realizing that their management strategies must cut across artificial political and agency boundaries to establish a regionwide conservation plan (Goldstein 1992; Turner et al. 1995; see also Case Study 5 in Chapter 18).

How is this landscape perspective developed and applied in the field? First, we must define what is meant by a landscape. A landscape is *a mosaic of habitat patches across which organisms move, settle, reproduce, and eventually die* (Forman and Godron 1986). The size of a landscape depends on the organism. A field or woodlot that is a single patch of relatively uniform quality for a bird or mammal may, at the same time, be a mosaic of patches of quite different quality for individual nematodes or shrubs. For any species, the landscape containing a population can, in principle, be mapped as a mosaic of suitable and unsuitable patches. Such maps are the basic tool of the landscape ecologist. Each map is specific to the habitat requirements of one species and must be drawn at a scale appropriate to that organism. In general, the scale must be fine enough to resolve the areas occupied by individuals over significant portions of their lifetimes (Turner 1989; Turner et al. 1989).

In order to map the patches of suitable habitat for a particular species, one must have a set of criteria for drawing the habitat boundaries. Following Elton (1949) and Andrewartha and Birch (1984), a habitat boundary is chosen so as to circumscribe a "certain homogeneity with respect to the sort of environments it might provide for animals" (Andrewartha and Birch 1984). In managed landscapes, the drawing of habitat boundaries is usually simplified by the strong contrasts between habitats subjected to different management histories. For example, a pine plantation is clearly discernible from a neighboring old field or deciduous woodlot. In landscapes less dominated by human activities, habitat boundaries are often "softer" and more arbitrary. Boundaries are typically very ambiguous or absent altogether in marine systems, where application of landscape concepts is difficult and sometimes inappropriate; Essay 7C by Brian Bowen and Deborah Crouse addresses the unique aspects of demography in marine "landscapes."

ESSAY 7C
Landscape-Level Conservation in the Marine Realm

Brian W. Bowen, University of Florida, and Deborah Crouse, Center for Marine Conservation

Marine conservation entails many of the same principles as terrestrial and freshwater conservation: species require appropriate habitats to survive and reproduce, and ecosystems must remain above some minimal size in order to persist. However, conservation priorities can be quite different in marine ecosystems. For example, habitat fragmentation is recognized as a primary concern in terrestrial (including freshwater) conservation, but what does habitat fragmentation mean for a jellyfish? These species are typically distributed across entire ocean basins, and individuals may drift thousands of kilometers in a single generation. Hence, an anthropogenic gap in the distribution of a jellyfish species (caused by coastal pollution, for example) may be readily bridged by drifting individuals, and demographic processes within these species may be little changed by localized extirpations around human populations. In contrast, the same liquid medium that confers resilience on drifting jellyfish may carry additional insults (foreign diseases or parasites, for example) far beyond the original point of introduction. For this reason, marine refugia may be more vulnerable to invasion than their terrestrial or freshwater counterparts. These contrasts between marine and terrestrial/freshwater conservation cast doubt on the universality of conservation principles such as landscape management. Indeed, the very name "landscape management" seems to exclude over 70% of the earth's surface.

The differences between marine and terrestrial/freshwater conservation can be readily illustrated by the species that move between these realms. For example, salmon are subject to heavy fishing pressure in both oceanic and riverine habitats, but mortality in the riverine fisheries is much more likely to cause population extinctions. In the past, whole spawning populations have been destroyed by placing nets across a river channel. Oceanic fisheries, spread across thousands of kilometers, may greatly reduce stocks, but cannot yet approach the catastrophic efficiency of inland fisheries. A parallel observation may be made for aquatic pollution, which has extinguished riverine salmon stocks in many areas, but has not yet decimated oceanic stocks.

Thus, the size and nature of the oceans, a fluid medium defined in three dimensions, requires a different set of conservation priorities (Butman and Carlton 1995). Where *habitat fragmentation* is a primary concern in terrestrial/ freshwater ecosystems, *habitat degradation* and *overexploitation* hold a parallel level of concern for marine conservationists. Cases abound of heavily fished or heavily polluted coastal habitats that retain much the same species composition as before, but at vastly different densities (Norse 1993). Formerly common species (especially commercially harvested ones) become rare, but few disappear entirely. These species are not subdivided by habitat fragmentation, but may be reduced to levels that preclude a significant role in the ecosystem (see Butman et al. 1995). When species cease to function in ecological processes, the corresponding ecosystem is impaired, and cascading trophic effects can have far-reaching consequences.

One corollary of this emphasis on habitat degradation (rather than habitat fragmentation) is that broad distributions and long dispersal distances may buffer many marine species against range-wide extirpation. When commercially valuable species become economically extinct (too scarce to support commercial fisheries, Crouse et al. 1992), the fishery will often shift to other species, allowing the original target species to persist or recover over time. As a result, human-induced extinctions in the marine realm have been relatively rare (Carlton et al. 1991). This is due in part to the nature of the marine medium, and in part to the nature of the human presence. Marine species are usually harvested by nonspecific methods such as nets and dredges, approaches that may devastate the seabed (Riemann and Hoffmann 1991), but do not approach the efficiency of terrestrial and freshwater harvests. Obvious exceptions to this pattern are the air-breathing marine mammals and reptiles, which must return to the surface to breathe (and to the shoreline to reproduce, in many cases) and therefore can be hunted with methods similar to those applied to terrestrial animals. Indeed, any species that aggregates at some life stage, as for spawning or migration, will be vulnerable to human harvest.

Sea turtles, like salmon, cross the boundary between marine and terrestrial/freshwater habitats. At intervals averaging one to four years, mature turtles migrate hundreds or thousands of kilometers from feeding habitats to nesting areas. Females ascend surf-built beaches to lay eggs, and hatchlings depart the beach 45–65 days later. This brief terrestrial interlude is clearly critical to sea turtle survival. The marine segments of sea turtle life history are more complex and typically include multiple habitats. For example, juvenile loggerhead turtles feed along the edges of oceanic currents, while the subadults and adults occupy shallow coastal areas.

One remarkable feature of marine turtle biology is that females return to nest in the same region, often on the same beach, in successive nesting seasons. This female nesting-site fidelity prompted researchers to suggest that female turtles return to deposit eggs on their natal beach (Carr 1967). Population genetic studies, employing maternally inherited mitochondrial DNA (mtDNA), have confirmed that each nesting colony is an isolated group of female lineages, which is consistent with the natal homing hypothesis (Bowen and Avise 1995; Bass et al. 1996). A primary ramification of this natal homing behavior is that each nesting population is a distinct demographic entity. Processes such as hatchling production and mortality proceed independently in each nesting population, and colonies depleted by human or natural phenomena are not replenished readily by immigration from other (source) nesting colonies.

During the terrestrial segment of marine turtle life history, both eggs and females are extremely vulnerable to overexploitation. For example, the green turtle rookeries of the lesser Antilles hosted over a million nesting females prior to European colonization, but these nesting populations were largely hunted out by the end of the 17th century, and three hundred years later they have not been recolonized (Parsons 1962). Sea turtles can be harvested with high efficiency during their terrestrial stage, and a typically terrestrial outcome is observed: nesting colonies become extinct.

In contrast to the demographic isolation of nesting populations, tagging and genetic studies demonstrate that feeding grounds are usually occupied by turtles from several nesting colonies (Carr 1967; Bowen 1995). Hence, an increase in mortality on one feeding ground can reduce nesting colonies throughout an entire ocean basin. For example, Pacific oceanic fisheries incidentally capture and drown juvenile loggerhead turtles, and this mortality reduces recruitment into nesting populations in both Japan and Australia, the two primary nesting areas in the western Pacific (Bowen 1995). In this situation, human incursions into sea turtle feeding grounds have an effect typical in marine conservation: populations are greatly reduced across broad geographic scales, but may persist in reduced numbers. This does not diminish the conservation concern for such marine species, but may shift the weight of concern from *organismal extinction* to *ecological extinction* (Crouse et al. 1992). Long before marine turtles approach organismal extinction, they may be (and indeed already are in many cases) reduced to the point at which they no longer serve a viable function in marine ecosystems. The depletion of hawksbill sea turtles (one of very few consumers of sponges) may impair coral reef ecosystems, and the depletion of green sea turtles (one of the few large marine herbivores) will alter the sea-grass beds that function as nurseries for many fishes and invertebrates.

Marine ecosystems may be resilient in many respects, but conservationists do not yet understand the magnitude of this resilience. Like buffered solutions in a chemistry experiment, marine ecosystems may absorb considerable perturbations without apparent effect, then succumb to a seemingly minor insult once a threshold is passed. Until recently, marine turtles at sea were believed to be relatively immune to human perturbations. The advent of drift net and longline fisheries offshore, and intensive bottom-trawl fisheries near shore, has changed that perception. An estimated 5,000–10,000 juvenile loggerhead turtles perish annually in Mediterranean longline and drift net fisheries (Bowen 1995 and references therein), and prior to the recent introduction of turtle excluder devices, an estimated 5,000–50,000 benthic juvenile and adult loggerheads drowned annually in the shrimp trawl fisheries of the western Atlantic (National Research Council 1990). Crouse et al. (1987) demonstrated that populations of Atlantic loggerheads, which may require more than 20 years to reach maturity, are highly vulnerable to mortality in these juvenile stages (see Essay 7A by Congdon and Dunham). In general, late-maturing species cannot tolerate high juvenile or adult mortality, so the incidental capture of loggerhead turtles has the potential to induce both ecological and organismal extinction. This fact illustrates another high-priority issue for marine conservation: incidental bycatch of species that are not (or no longer) targeted by commercial fisheries is a serious cause of depletion and endangerment.

The marine turtles illustrate how demographic processes differ between marine and terrestrial organisms, and how caution must be practiced in extending terrestrial conservation principles to marine species. Landscape management principles may not readily apply to the marine realm, and an appropriate scale for ecosystem management may extend across thousands of kilometers. In these circumstances, marine conservationists are faced with a different set of challenges than those that beset terrestrial wildlife managers. Perhaps foremost among these challenges is the recognition that few marine ecosystems are confined to a single jurisdiction. Clearly, a new class of solutions must emerge in order to protect marine biodiversity.

Suitable sites for a particular species are often distributed as isolated patches embedded in a matrix of unsuitable habitat. Figure 7.10 provides an example of this type of landscape, showing suitable habitat for Bachman's Sparrow (*Aimophila aestivalis*), a species of management interest to the U.S. Forest Service. This bird is found on pinelands where timber is harvested. The maps in Figure 7.10 show distributions of suitable habitat on a 5000 ha tract of timberland at the Savannah River Site, a U.S. Department of Energy facility in South Carolina. At the Savannah River Site the sparrow is found in two habitats: frequently burned old-growth pine stands, and very young pine clear-cuts. Both of these habitat types have the appropriate vegetative structure (an open understory) and are therefore suitable breeding sites for this species (Dunning and Watts 1990). Hardwood stands and pine stands between 5 and about 80 years of age are unsuitable for Bachman's Sparrows. Figure 7.10B shows the distribution of suitable sites on the study area in 1990. Figure 7.10A shows the probable distribution of suitable sites 20 years earlier (1970) based on the known land use history of the area, while Figure 7.10C shows the projected distribution of suitable sites 20 years in the future (2010) based on a proposed management plan for the site (Liu et al. 1995). The maps indicate that the locations of suitable habitat patches change for this species on a relatively short time scale (20 years = 4–6 sparrow generations). The fact that the locations of suitable patches change from year to year could pose a problem for the sparrow, as field studies show that isolated, short-lived suitable patches often are not colonized. The sparrow's regional population may be reduced if a sizable portion of the suitable habitat is not occupied (Dunning et al. 1995).

A number of the factors that influence the location of suitable habitat for Bachman's Sparrow are quite general in that they influence the location of

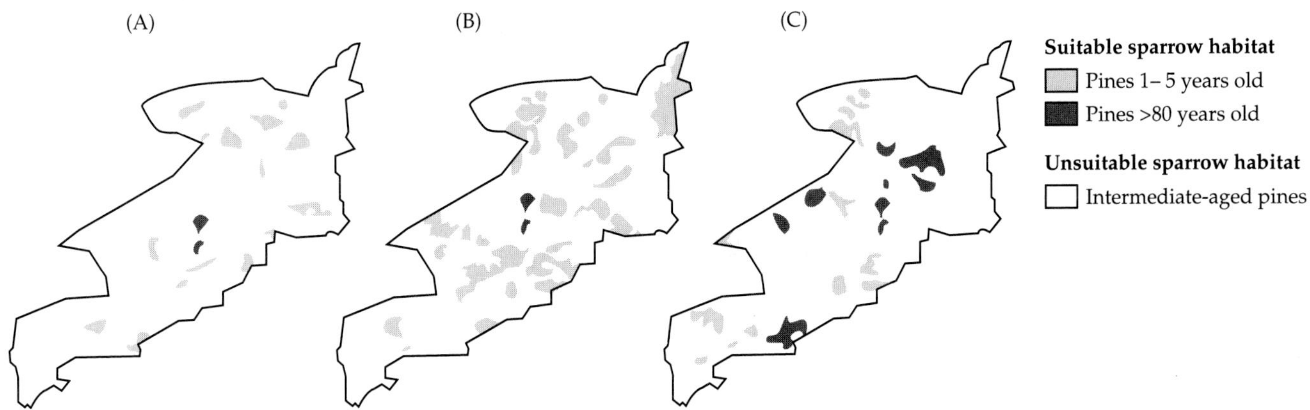

Figure 7.10 Distribution of suitable breeding habitat for Bachman's Sparrow in (A) 1970, (B) 1990, and (C) 2010 on a 5000 ha tract at the Savannah River Site, South Carolina. Bachman's Sparrow breeds both in older-growth pine forests and in young clear-cuts, but not in middle-aged pine stands. The distribution of habitats in 1970 is based on the land use history for the area; the distribution in 2010 is based on a proposed management plan. Notice the islandlike nature of suitable habitat patches.

habitat for many terrestrial species. Factors such as soil type, topography, and vegetative cover all provide information on the suitability of a site for a particular species, and all of these factors can be readily mapped. For Bachman's Sparrow, soil type and topography influence the rate at which seedling trees grow and, therefore, the ages of pine stands that have vegetation profiles suitable for the sparrow. In addition, time since disturbance, successional status, and management history may provide additional information on the suitability of a site. Knowledge of such factors improves our ability to map out suitable habitat patches for a species.

The combination of factors determining site suitability is different for every species. Such information alone is not enough to determine unambiguously the presence or absence of a species, but it can often be used to categorize habitats as suitable versus unsuitable, and in some cases to assign a probability of occupation. As discussed in the next section, a landscape map based on the number and location of suitable sites under existing or proposed land use patterns can be an invaluable tool for species management.

Spatially Explicit Models

Metapopulation models of the sort discussed earlier are very general conceptual models that do not attempt to incorporate the complexities of real landscapes. As Levins (1966) points out, general models typically offer general insights, but they are neither very precise nor very realistic. One of the primary themes of both conservation biology and landscape ecology is that details, such as the geometry of habitat patches in a landscape, can influence population trends and extinction probabilities. Metapopulation models make very unrealistic assumptions about the dispersal behavior of individuals and do not reflect the complexity of real landscapes. Whereas such models are useful for gaining general insights into population dynamics, they are not as well suited for managing particular species on particular landscapes. In contrast, spatially explicit models of the sort discussed below are well suited for incorporating realistic details of particular species and landscapes, but, because they are so specific, the conclusions reached from them cannot easily be generalized to other species and landscapes.

Spatially explicit population models incorporate the actual locations of organisms and suitable patches of habitat, and explicitly consider the movement of organisms among such patches. The *M*obile *A*nimal *P*opulation, or MAP, is a class of spatially explicit population models (Pulliam et al. 1992; Liu 1993; Liu et al. 1995) that simulate habitat-specific demography and the dispersal behavior of organisms on computer representations of real landscapes. In MAP models, the landscape is represented as a grid of cells, each of which is the size of an individual territory of the species being simulated (e.g., 2.5 ha for Bachman's Sparrow or 1000 ha for the Spotted Owl; see map inserts in Figure 7.12). Clusters of adjacent cells represent the size and location of forest tracts in the landscape; these tracts are assumed to be relatively uniform in terms of suitability for the species of interest. MAP models contain subroutines that specify forest management practices, succession, and, in some cases, the growth rates of tree species. Thus, such a model can depict the current landscape structure and project that structure in the future based on a management plan specifying a harvest and replanting schedule. Other management activities, such as thinning or burning stands, that might influence stand suitability can be incorporated easily into MAP models. The most realistic MAP models are run on landscape maps generated by **geographic information systems** (GIS, discussed further in Chapter 12), which incorporate the actual distribution of habitat patches in a region. Whereas most MAP models are run on landscapes of less than 10,000 ha, they are capable of simulating landscape change and population dynamics over 100,000 ha or more (Pulliam et al. 1995).

Analyses using MAP models have proved valuable in a variety of conservation situations. For example, BACHMAP, a MAP model developed specifically for Bachman's Sparrow, is being used to determine how forest management practices may influence the population viability of the sparrow in pine forests in the southeastern United States. One analysis using BACHMAP demonstrated that aspects of a management plan designed to improve habitat for one endangered species (the Red-cockaded Woodpecker) may cause a short-term decline in the sparrow's numbers, thus potentially creating a second species requiring management intervention (Liu et al. 1995). MAP models can help managers to avoid this type of unintended effect during the design of management plans (see Box 7C).

A spatially explicit model developed for Yellowstone National Park has been used to show that wintering herds of bison and elk respond to the local

BOX 7C
Conservation of Nontarget Species in Managed Landscapes
The Role of Population Models

Traditionally, wildlife management has focused on the preservation of single species. For many decades, public land management emphasized game animals or other species with economic importance. In more recent years, additional attention has shifted to threatened and endangered species. Single-species management, however, also affects dozens of nontarget species found in the same habitats. Such nontarget effects are rarely assessed prior to implementation of the management actions. As conservationists call for greater emphasis on management for biodiversity, it has become increasingly important to develop tools that allow one to assess the effects of a specific management strategy on a wide variety of organisms.

One potential tool for this purpose is population simulation models linked to maps that capture the complexity of real-world landscapes. With such models, the responses of many different organisms, including both target and nontarget species, to a specific landscape change can be modeled and assessed. Such an approach requires (1) a population model that is flexible enough to reflect the life history and behavior of species of interest, (2) realistic landscape maps, usually created through a geographic information system (GIS), and (3) habitat-specific information on the species' distribution and demography to parameterize the model.

One group of models that fits this description is the MAP models, designed to model *M*obile *A*nimal *P*opulations in complex landscapes (Pulliam et al. 1992). One MAP model has been developed to model the population dynamics of Bachman's Sparrow, a declining species of management interest in the southeastern United States. Conservationists have used this model to determine how this species may be affected by management strategies designed to preserve populations of the endangered Red-cockaded Woodpecker, which is found in some of the same habitats as Bachman's Sparrow.

Bachman's Sparrow is found in pine woodlands that contain a dense ground cover of grasses and forbs as well as relatively open understories with few shrubs (Dunning and Watts 1990). These conditions are found in the oldest of mature pine forests (>80 years old) or in early successional habitats such as 1–5-year-old clear-cuts. Mature pine forest managed for the Red-cockaded Woodpecker usually provides adequate habitat for Bachman's Sparrow. In many areas, patches of habitat suitable for the sparrow (either mature forest or clear-cuts) are found only as isolated islands embedded in a landscape of unsuitable habitat (see Figure 7.10).

Populations of the sparrow have declined since the 1930s to the point where the species is absent over much of its former range. Even where it is still reasonably common, the sparrow is locally distributed and absent from many patches of seemingly suitable habitat. This population decline, and the absence of the bird from many areas, may be related to the scattered distribution of suitable habitat patches, if the sparrows find it difficult to find and colonize unoccupied territories in isolated clear-cuts or mature stands. We analyzed landscape change and the population dynamics of Bachman's Sparrow using BACHMAP, a MAP model parameterized for the sparrow. In this analysis, we used landscape maps that reflect the complex habitat mosaics of the Savannah River Site (SRS), a large region of pine forest in South Carolina managed by the U.S. Forest Service for timber production and wildlife conservation.

We have used our MAP model to study the current management strategies at the SRS and their effect on nontarget organisms. The U.S. Forest Service has developed a 50-year Operation Plan that sets management strategies for meeting wildlife goals for the SRS. The Operation Plan is a model for multiple species management, because it lists target goals for over 42 species at the SRS. A majority of the specific management practices described in the Operation Plan, however, deal specifically with the endangered Red-cockaded Woodpecker, because the Endangered Species Act dictates that the needs of the woodpecker be given priority. We modeled the Operation Plan to determine how Bachman's Sparrow, a nontarget species of most of the specified management strategies, would fare under the Operation Plan.

Our studies have suggested that many aspects of management have a strong effect on the sparrow. For example, mature pine forest is now a rare habitat type in most areas of southern pine timberlands. Our simulations suggest, however, that it can be a very important habitat for the sparrows. Simulations that included a small amount of mature forest in the landscape almost always supported at least a small sparrow population. Without the mature forest patches, the sparrow populations often suffered extinction, even if a relatively large amount of clear-cut habitat was available (Pulliam et al. 1992). The mature forest acted as a source habitat that produced dispersers that would colonize the surrounding clear-cut habitat. As has been suggested in analytical models of source and sink habitats, a small population in a source habitat patch may be critical for supporting a much larger sink population (Pulliam 1988).

Our simulations suggest that in general the sparrow would benefit from the changes specified in the Operation Plan. To benefit the woodpecker, which is restricted to mature pine forest stands, the Operation Plan proposed increasing the overall age of the SRS forest. Since Bachman's Sparrows also use mature forest, over the long term these changes should result in a large increase in the sparrow population. Over the first 1–2 decades of the Operation Plan, however, our simulations suggest that the sparrow population will decline to a dangerously low level. This decline reflects the decrease in suitable habitat caused by the low numbers of clear-cuts created while the forests are allowed to age.

Thus, the Operation Plan as modeled may have some unintended negative effects on the sparrow, despite the fact that the sparrow shares a major habitat type—mature pine forest—with the main target species of the Plan. Several additional measures that the Forest Service has initiated may increase the amount of suitable habitat during these first few decades, which may help counter the negative effect on the sparrow population that we saw in our simulations. In particular, our simulations show that one management program, if expanded, would greatly increase the sparrow population. This program manages middle-aged pine stands (50–70 years old) in a manner that generates the ground vegetation found in mature pine habitat, and therefore provides suitable habitat for the sparrow in a wider variety of pine age classes. A series of MAP models, each parameterized for other nontarget species, would give the managers of the SRS a research tool that could be used to test the effects of the Operation Plan on a wide variety of species. Population simulation models linked to GIS landscape maps should prove to be increasingly valuable tools for land managers and conservation biologists in the future.

---

patterns of habitat diversity caused by large-scale fires (Turner et al. 1994; Pearson et al. 1995; Figure 7.11). The 1988 fires at Yellowstone, although dramatically large and well publicized, proved to be well within the range of disturbance to which the herds could respond. Spatially explicit population

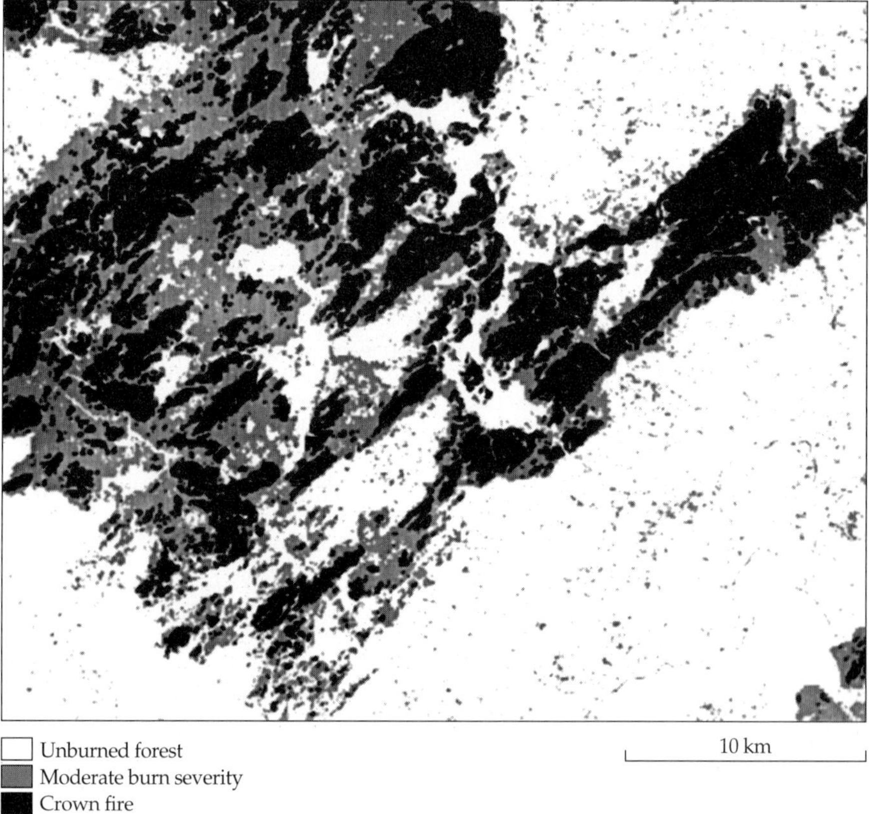

Figure 7.11 GIS map of part of Yellowstone National Park, showing the distribution of burned and unburned forest after the fires in 1988. Burned patches are oriented NE–SW due to prevailing winds during the fires. A spatially explicit model of this region showed that bison and elk herds were able to respond effectively to the new distributions of habitats caused by the fires. (From Turner et al. 1994.)

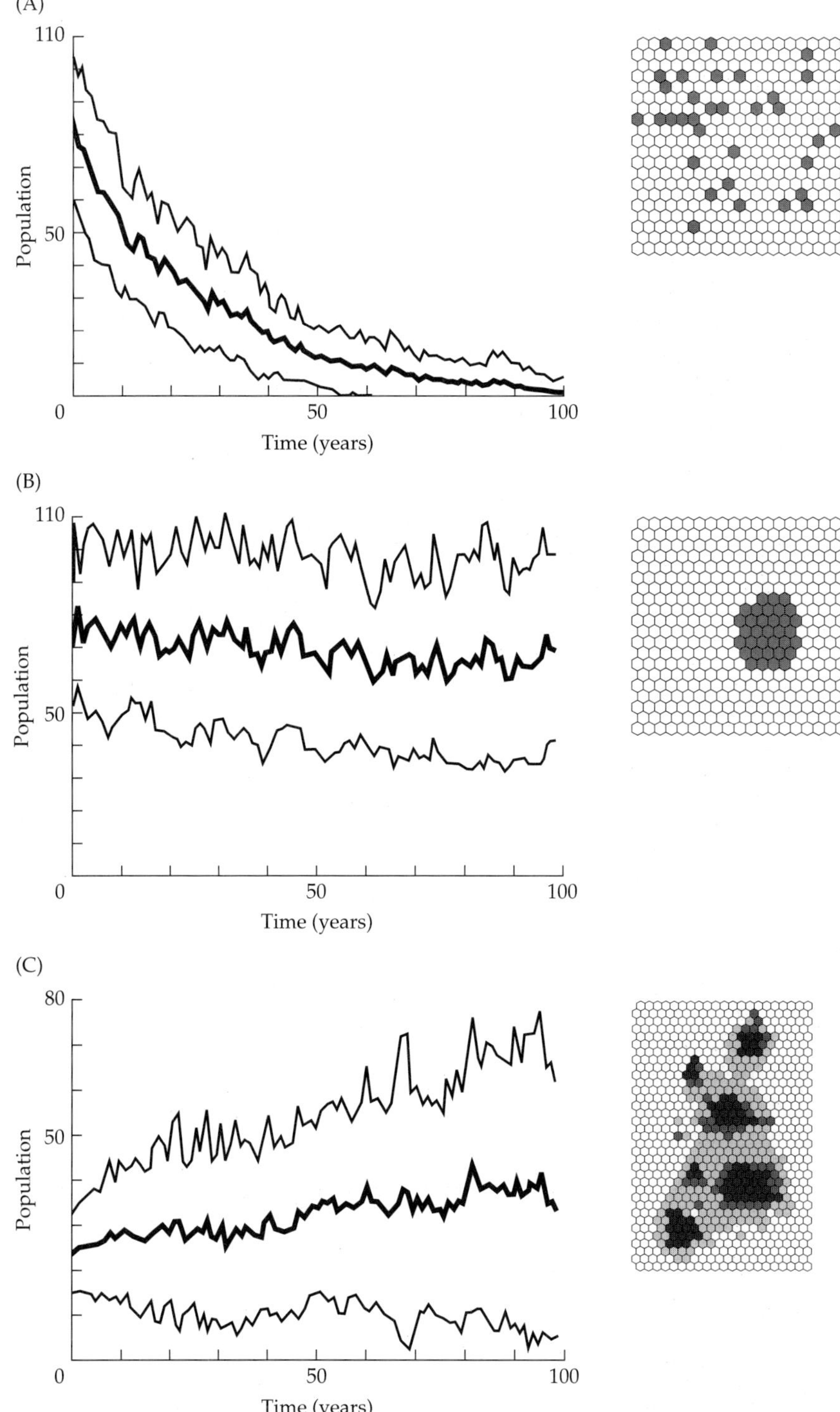

Figure 7.12 Results of a simulation model for Spotted Owls that varied only the configuration of suitable and unsuitable habitat; all other population parameters were held constant. All results are based on 30 simulations; the heavy line in each graph is the mean population response, and the thin lines are one standard deviation from the mean. (A) Suitable habitat is randomly scattered. (B) Suitable habitat is arrayed in one large block. (C) Clusters of suitable habitat are surrounded by marginal habitat (buffers). (From McKelvey et al. 1993.)

models developed for the Spotted Owl (McKelvey et al. 1993) have also proved to be valuable conservation tools (Figure 7.12). Much of the current conservation plan for the owl in the Pacific Northwest has been tested using the Spotted Owl model (Verner et al. 1992; McKelvey et al. 1993). An analysis of Spotted Owl populations in southern California using the spatially explicit Spotted Owl model has identified the owl populations in the San Gabriel and San Bernardino Mountains as being critical to the viability of the entire southern California metapopulation (Verner et al. 1992).

Spatially explicit models provide land managers with a new tool for predicting how management plans and land use changes may affect species of management concern. While some spatially explicit models are sufficiently well developed and parameterized to be used in conservation and management, for most species the relevant population parameters are not known, and several years of concentrated fieldwork will be required to collect the large amount of data needed to parameterize the models.

Summary

An understanding of the fluctuations in numbers of natural populations and the application of this understanding to the conservation of species must be based firmly on an understanding of the factors influencing spatial and temporal variability in population demography. All populations exist in heterogeneous landscapes, and different individuals experience different conditions depending on when and where they are located. Some locations (termed "sources") are highly productive and produce an excess of individuals, which often populate less productive locations ("sinks") where local mortality exceeds reproduction. In some cases, sink populations may be larger than the source populations that support them. Accordingly, great care must be exercised in the design of nature reserves to identify and protect source habitats.

Population viability depends not only on the quality of local habitat patches, but also on the number and location of patches and the amount of movement between them. The dispersal mode of a population is a key factor in determining its viability. In many cases population dynamics must be studied at the level of many local patches of habitat, and population models must incorporate immigration and emigration explicitly. Metapopulation models that consider the dynamics of many interacting subpopulations in a habitat mosaic demonstrate that the fraction of a landscape suitable for a given species and the magnitude of dispersal between suitable patches are critical components of population viability. Unlike metapopulation models, spatially explicit population models consider the exact locations of habitat patches and can incorporate detailed behavioral information about how dispersing individuals locate suitable habitat. Spatially explicit models can be useful tools for testing specific conservation strategies in a given region, while metapopulation models are more useful for investigating general landscape influences using hypothetical populations.

A number of theoretical models are now available for quantitative analyses of population viability and extinction probability. These models should be viewed as useful additions to the collection of tools available for understanding the dynamics of natural populations. The more realistic models are, however, very data hungry and are only as good as the natural history insights and field studies that support them.

Questions for Discussion

1. Traditionally, population studies have been done at a local scale on homogeneous populations. Recently there has been a shift toward landscape studies. What are some of the advantages of working at the landscape scale? Are there any disadvantages?

2. In a paper discussed in this chapter, Davidson and Andrewartha showed that thrip populations decline precipitously in dry summers when food is in short supply. Does this necessarily mean that thrips are food-limited, or

that they are regulated in a density-dependent manner? What further evidence would be required to demonstrate density dependence?

3. In the late 1960s, Furbish's lousewort came to national attention when a dam was proposed for the Saint John River in Maine. This dam would have eliminated floods and ice scour in the river valley, thus eliminating the creation of new habitat patches for this plant. How would this have affected the lousewort's population dynamics? Can you think of any management actions that could have been taken to mitigate the dam's impact?
4. How could management designed to improve conditions for an endangered species actually have negative effects on other species? Do you know of any cases in which this has actually occurred, or might occur in the future? What could a land manager do to prevent this situation from occurring?
5. Why is it necessary to consider population regulation from a hierarchical perspective? Can you think of a real population in which different factors at the local and the regional scales limit population growth? How could policies in effect at a regional scale make it difficult to manage populations by manipulating local factors?
6. This chapter emphasizes that conservationists must consider habitat quality as well as habitat quantity when managing for threatened organisms. What is meant by habitat quality, and how would land managers measure and/or improve it?
7. Many recent studies on local populations of migratory birds have found that birth rates are lower than expected, and, in some cases, that local birth rates are not as high as local death rates. Does this necessarily mean that the local populations are about to go extinct? How would this finding influence your attitude toward the need to preserve other habitats in the local area and the region?
8. Consider Figure 7.12. As a conservation biologist, how would you interpret the three outcomes for a forest manager? Discuss this both in terms of population trends and variance.

Suggestions for Further Reading

Andrewartha, H. G. and L. C. Birch. 1984. *The Ecological Web.* University of Chicago Press, Chicago. This book presents an excellent overview of how resources, mates, predators, and other factors influence population dynamics. Andrewartha and Birch view the environment of an organism as "everything that might influence its chance to survive and reproduce." The book is a good beginning source for readers who want more information on the topic of population regulation.

Dunning, J. B., D. J. Stewart, B. J. Danielson, B. R. Noon, T. L. Root, R. H. Lamberson, and E. E. Stevens. 1995. Spatially explicit population models: Current forms and future uses. *Ecol. Appl.* 5:3–11. Most population models do not consider space explicitly and, therefore, do not incorporate the ways in which the dynamics of populations might change as the relative shapes and positions of habitat patches change. This paper presents a summary of how spatially explicit models are being used to further our understanding of the role of spatial location in determining population processes. It emphasizes how such models are being used in conservation and management applications.

Gilpin, M. E. and M. E. Soulé. 1986. Minimum viable populations: Processes of species extinction. In M. E. Soulé (ed.). *Conservation Biology: The Science of Scarcity and Diversity*, pp. 19–34. Sinauer Associates, Sunderland, MA. A conceptual model for understanding and studying population viability. With this chapter,

Gilpin and Soulé started many people thinking about the causes of extinction and how they might be studied. They argue that many species are threatened because they experience a specific combination of life history traits and environmental conditions (called an "extinction vortex") that makes the species susceptible to extinction. One has to recognize the kinds of threats that a given species is likely to experience before one can design a plan to protect that species.

Hanski, I. and M. E. Gilpin. 1991. Metapopulation dynamics: Brief history and conceptual domain. *Biol. J. Linn. Soc.* 42:3–16. This paper provides a brief history of the metapopulation concept and presents a survey of metapopulation terminology. It also reviews a number of studies that have been conducted on single-species and multispecies metapopulations and relates those studies to conservation issues.

Pulliam, H. R. 1988. Sources, sinks, and population regulation. *Am. Nat.* 132:757–785. Although the idea of source and sink habitats had been described previously, this paper was the first to analyze the consequences of sources and sinks for population dynamics. Pulliam proposed that many organisms live in sink habitats where local reproduction is insufficient to balance local mortality. Large sink populations may be common in nature, being maintained by immigration from very productive source habitats. The paper also discusses the implications of sources and sinks for the study of population conservation.

Rhodes, O. E., R. K. Chesser, and M. H. Smith (eds.). 1996. *Population Dynamics in Ecological Space and Time.* University of Chicago Press, Chicago. This volume summarizes a wide variety of approaches to studying how populations change over large temporal and spatial scales. Chapters on large-scale population change in everything from birds to microbes relate our understanding of population dynamics at these scales to efforts to mitigate the effects of global climate change on ecosystems worldwide.

Shaffer, M. L. 1981. Minimum population sizes for species conservation. *BioScience* 31:131–134. This paper was one of the first to discuss the concept of a minimum population size necessary to maintain viability. Schaffer proposed that the probability of population extinction could be analyzed by focusing on the interaction of four factors: demographic uncertainty, environmental stochasticity, natural catastrophes, and genetic uncertainty.

We also suggest the following papers by the researchers who have developed the analytic and spatially explicit models for Spotted Owls. These papers describe the theory and data underlying these models and their results, and discuss how the models can be used in today's political environment.

Bart, J. 1995. Amount of suitable habitat and viability of Northern Spotted Owls. *Conserv. Biol.* 9:943–946. Response to published criticisms of owl studies.

Murphy, D. and B. Noon. 1992. Integrating scientific methods with habitat conservation planning for the Northern Spotted Owl. *Ecol. Appl.* 2:3–17. Description of the use of models in the Pacific Northwest political and management arena.

Noon, B. R. and C. M. Biles. 1990. Mathematical demography of Spotted Owls in the Pacific Northwest. *J. Wildl. Mgmt.* 54:18–27. Analytic modeling attempt to see whether owl populations are declining.

Verner, J., et al. 1992. *The California Spotted Owl: A Technical Assessment of Its Current Status.* U.S. Forest Service General Technical Report PSW-GTR-133. Complete description of data bases and modeling efforts for the California subspecies.

III

System-Level Considerations

8

Community- and Ecosystem-Level Conservation

Species Interactions, Disturbance Regimes, and Invading Species

A thing is right when it tends to preserve the integrity, stability, and beauty of the biotic community. It is wrong when it tends otherwise.

Aldo Leopold, 1949

Much of conservation, and much of our previous discussion, deals with single species and their welfare. The Endangered Species Act, CITES, genetic conservation, and ex situ preservation in zoos, aquariums, and arboretums all focus on the species as a unit. However, species must ultimately exist in natural settings, within functioning communities and ecosystems, interacting with other species and the abiotic environment. Therefore, conservation must also focus on species interactions and the ecosystem context within which these interactions occur.

The very nature of the problem with which we are dealing—the loss and protection of biodiversity—dictates that we consider collections of interacting species and not just properties and declines of single species. By definition, bio*diversity* ultimately means working at the community and ecosystem levels and dealing with the effects of species declines and losses on other species, on interactive processes, and on the functional ecosystem that provides their support. Unfortunately, the principles of community and ecosystem ecology are less certain than some other areas of ecology and evolution, and their application to conservation problems is less well developed. Consequently, we will focus less specifically on community and ecosystem ecology in this chapter than on particular and critical species interactions.

For the purposes of this chapter we use the term "*community*" to refer to a set of two or more interacting species, such as those in a trophic web, that live in a particular habitat. The term *"ecosystem"* adds another dimension by including those interactions of the community with the abiotic environment by which nutrient cycling and other important processes are influenced or even regulated. The ecosystem may be regarded as the "life support system" for the community. Here, our interest in ecosystems is focused on how they relate to biodiversity—to community support—rather than on the many biotic–abiotic interactions that characterize them.

Although some mention has been made in previous chapters of species interactions and system-wide conservation, in this chapter we will explore those topics in greater depth. In particular, we will examine the roles of keystone species, mutualisms, disturbance regimes, and the effects of invading species. We also will explore patterns of community-level and ecosystem-level changes over ecological and evolutionary time to search for lessons useful in understanding the effects of contemporary changes affecting conservation efforts.

Critical Species Interactions

Not all species in a community are equal in their contributions to community structure and processes, and not all interactions are vital. Some community members or species interactions are especially critical because they affect many other species, process materials out of proportion to their numbers or biomass, or have particularly strong links to other species or even other systems. Walker (1992) called these species, which tend to be responsible for system structure and function, "drivers." In contrast, some species may be quite removable from, or substitutable in, a community with little to no effect on its structure or function; these species are called "passengers." Conservation biologists should identify and focus research on those species or interactions that are especially critical to community and ecosystem dynamics—the "drivers" of the system—whenever possible (Holling 1992). We will discuss three classes of such critical interactions here.

The Role of Keystone Species

Figure 8.1 The sea otter is a keystone species that controls abundance of sea urchins, which in turn prevents overgrazing of kelp beds. (Photograph © Stephen J. Krasemann/DRK Photo.)

Some species, because of their trophic position, their production of food resources, or other interactions, play a disproportionately large role in community structure, and are called **keystone species**. We began to develop the idea of keystone species in Chapter 5, and will explore it further here. A classic example of a keystone species, the one for which the term was developed, is the sea star *Pisaster ochraceus*, which preys on invertebrate communities in the rocky intertidal zone along the North American Pacific coast. By conducting exclusion experiments in which sea stars were removed, Paine (1966, 1969) found that species richness of mussels, barnacles, snails, and other rocky shore inhabitants decreased from 15 with sea stars present to 8 without them. Sea star predation apparently kept densities of all species low, but especially those of the competitive dominant, a mussel (*Mytilus californianus*), which, in the absence of predation, usurped a large proportion of limiting space and thus excluded several other species. Consequently, *Pisaster* is known as a keystone predator.

The sea otter (*Enhydra lutris*, Figure 8.1), which preys on sea urchins (*Strongylocentrotus droebachiensis*) in large numbers, appears to be another keystone predator. When sea otter populations declined in the 20th century due to fur trapping and removal by fishermen, sea urchin populations expanded greatly and grazed heavily on algae and kelp. In some places, they effectively destroyed entire kelp forests, which in turn lowered the diversity of the other plants and animals in that habitat (Estes and Palmisano 1974).

Figure 8.2 Beavers fundamentally change the characteristics of aquatic systems, thus acting as keystone species through habitat modification. This particular beaver dam and lodge in northwestern New Jersey flooded a large tract of land, killing streamside trees and creating a lake environment. (Photograph by G. K. Meffe.)

Reintroduction of sea otters reversed this situation, and kelp beds recovered (Krebs 1988).

Terborgh (1986) described another type of keystone species, a keystone food resource. The tropical forests of Central and South America are not bountiful and constant Gardens of Eden, as they are often portrayed. The diverse animal assemblages of such regions, including many species of primates, bats, birds, and marsupials, depend on a diverse collection of fruits and seeds for much of their caloric intake. There is usually about a 3-month period in the year when production drops to or below the level of consumptive demands, and most animals must migrate or expand their diets. Figs, nectar, and certain fruits, representing less than 1% of plant species diversity, appear to be keystone resources because they sustain nearly the entire frugivore community through this period of scarcity. Without these few plant resources, the frugivore community would have a much more difficult time surviving this period.

Another type of keystone species is a habitat modifier, sometimes called an "ecosystem engineer" (Jones et al. 1994). Examples include the beaver *(Castor canadensis)* and the African elephant (*Loxodonta africana*). Beavers turn free-flowing, barrier-free streams into sluggish ponds and lakes, and create impediments to movement by fishes (Figure 8.2). Beaver dams change not only flow rate, but a myriad of other habitat characteristics, including nutrient dynamics, sedimentation rates, channel geomorphology, and biogeochemical cycles (Naiman et al. 1986); they also change habitat availability for terrestrial and amphibious species, and can kill large expanses of terrestrial forests, at the same time creating opportunities for aquatic or semiaquatic species (Feldmann 1995; Clements 1996; Snodgrass 1996).

The African elephant is an herbivore that browses on a variety of woody plants, supplemented by grasses. When feeding on shrubs, or small to large trees, the elephants strip bark and branches, and sometimes uproot entire trees. Dense woodlands can be transformed by elephant feeding into woodland–grasslands or even open grasslands (Figure 8.3). These areas may support more grazing ungulates, but are then more susceptible to fire, which further favors grasses over woody plants. This keystone browser thus can change the major plant features of entire landscapes.

Figure 8.3 Elephants greatly alter their environments and can change a forested area into a grassland. In Tsavo National Park, Kenya, elephants have stripped bare all large vegetation within the park, which is separated by a road, a railroad, and two fire breaks from a non-park area. By creating a more barren landscape, elephants are acting as a keystone species. (Photograph by D. B. Botkin.)

Yet another type of keystone species includes inconspicuous and even microscopic members of ecosystems whose biological processes are critical to the functioning of larger, more evident species. For example, mycorrhizal fungi are associated with the roots of many species of trees and enhance the plant's ability to extract soil minerals (Harley and Smith 1983). The fungi are critical to the growth and productivity of the trees, and may also protect the roots from infections by producing antibiotics. In the tropics, many trees are obligately dependent on mycorrhizal fungi, and the absence of appropriate fungi in the soil after large agricultural or natural disturbances may greatly retard reforestation (Janos 1980). Such fungi are no less important in temperate zones, especially for gymnosperm trees (Marks and Kozlowski 1973). Bacteria, tiny invertebrates, and algae and fungi all exist in soils and break down and decompose dead matter that would otherwise build up and remain unavailable to living species. The great cycles of nature would literally shut down were it not for these inconspicuous but keystone species (Wilson 1987).

So what exactly is a keystone species? Several examples have been given, but what do they have in common? And is there a good definition of keystone species? There is presently great debate within the scientific community about this concept, with concern that it will be overused and abused, and that most species will be designated keystones. This is especially a danger when "favorite" focal organisms become so obviously important to a researcher that they of course *must* be keystones; if this approach were taken to its extreme, the world would consist of little else but keystone species! Of course, this approach would be counterproductive and would make the concept meaningless.

Several scientists who have extensive experience with the keystone species concept met in 1994 to discuss and flesh out the issues (Power and Mills 1995). A consensus definition (though subject to change) was derived from that meeting: "*A keystone species is a species whose impact on its community or ecosystem is large, and disproportionately large relative to its abundance*" (Power et al. 1996; italics added). Thus, an abundant species is not a keystone species simply due to its abundance (unless its effects are out of proportion to that abundance), but rather is a community dominant (Figure 8.4). A true keystone species would be likely to be less abundant in a community, but have quite a large influence on other species and on community structure.

Removal, addition, or local changes in population size of keystone species have wide-ranging effects on other species, on processes and interactions, and even on landforms. As we have seen, in many cases keystone species are conspicuous, predaceous, or otherwise of direct interest to humans. In other cases they may be small and inconspicuous; they can even be rare and only a minor part of the biomass. Regardless, the nature of keystone species' effects is such that they typically play a part in trophic interactions—as predators on competitive dominants, mutualists such as pollinators and mycorrhizal fungi, major dispersers of seeds, herbivores that change vegetative conditions for

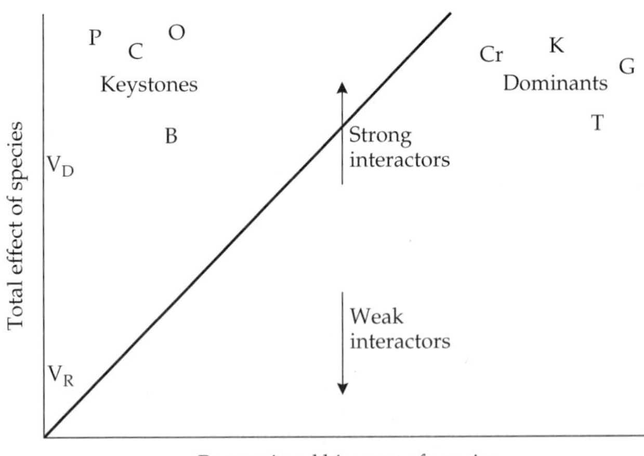

Figure 8.4. A visual representation of the concept of keystone species, which have large influences on communities beyond their relative abundances. The diagonal line represents species whose total impacts are proportional to their abundances. V_D is a distemper virus that might kill wild canids or felids, changing predator–prey interactions; V_R is a rhinovirus that might cause individuals to sneeze, a minor effect, and thus is not a keystone species. Other keystones include freshwater bass (B), the sea star *Pisaster* (P), the predatory whelk *Concholepas* (C), and sea otters (O), all of which have disproportionately large effects on their communities. Species such as reef-building corals (Cr), giant kelp (K), prairie grasses (G), and trees (T) dominate community biomass, but not disproportionately so, and are considered community dominants rather than keystones. (From Power et al. 1996.)

other grazers, or decomposers of dead matter. It is these trophic relationships that are largely responsible for the structure of natural communities and ecosystems; disrupting this structure can have repercussions far beyond the immediate and obvious interactions involved.

Despite the apparently clear relationships of some putative keystone species to their communities, the keystone species concept presents some problems in its application to conservation (Mills et al. 1993). First, as we have seen, it is only now rigorously being defined and the keystone concept still means different things to different people (Paine 1995). Second, there is a range in the strength of keystone species' effects, and manipulation of combinations of a few non-keystone species could have the same or greater effects than manipulation of the apparent keystone species. Third, a focus simply on protection of keystone species could fail to protect other species of interest or the system at large. Clearly, protection of a few keystones, even if we knew what they were, would not guarantee successful system conservation.

Mills et al. (1993) argue that "the complexity of ecological interactions and ignorance of them militates against the application of the keystone species concept for practical management recommendations . . . Instead, we advocate the study of interaction strengths and subsequent application of the results into management plans and policy decisions." We largely agree with this assessment; as we said earlier in this chapter, conservation biologists should focus their research on identifying and understanding the strongest interactions in communities, regardless of what we call them. Throughout this book we will continue to refer to "keystone" species and resources, but with the caveat that the term will simply refer to species and resources that have an effect on the rest of the community disproportionate to their abundance. Thus, related terms, such as "mobile links" in Chapter 5, may be used for particular circumstances, but the point remains that conservation biologists need to identify and focus on the most significant interactions.

Mutualisms

Mutualisms, relationships in which two or more species benefit from a specific and often highly coevolved interaction, can be especially important in conservation. For example, many angiosperms must be pollinated by a particular species of insect (a mobile link; see Chapter 5), and have evolved elaborate mechanisms to attract specific insects and thereby ensure that pollen is transferred to other individuals of their species (Figure 8.5). Likewise, seed dispersal is a critical function for many plants, and some have evolved elaborate mechanisms to disperse their seeds by animals (Figure 8.6). The very existence of fruit is attributable to the plant's need for seed dispersal. Legumes and their nitrogen-fixing bacteria in root nodules are another example of a plant mutualism.

(A)

(B)

Figure 8.5 Euglossine bees are important, specialized tropical pollinators of orchids, aroids, and other plants. (A) Euglossine bees visiting an aroid plant. Because individual plants are visited repeatedly by the same bee, these bees act as "mobile link mutualists." (B) Orchid pollen sacs (pollenia) adhere to the backs of bees. (Photographs by C. R. Carroll.)

(A)

(B)

Figure 8.6 Numerous mechanisms have evolved for efficient dispersal of seeds. Some seeds, such as those of this acacia (A), are attractive to birds, which ingest the seeds and later pass them. Other seed types are attractive to mammals, such as this agouti (B). (Photographs by D. H. Janzen and Winifred Hallwachs.)

Animals can form mutualistic relationships with other animals as well. A classic example is parasite pickers, which remove parasites from other species. Some birds are known to clean parasites from the bodies of rhinoceroses or other large mammals, and wrasses (small marine fishes) set up "cleaning stations" where large, often predaceous fishes come to be relieved of their parasites (Feder 1966; Snelson et al. 1990). A different type of animal mutualism is a nesting association. Some stream fish species spawn in the nests built by other species, and may help to fan the eggs and reduce predation rates on both species (Wallin 1989).

Because they affect more than one species, and often incorporate a critical function with far-reaching community effects, mutualisms should be identified and maintained whenever possible. It is easy to see that the loss of a seemingly insignificant species such as an insect could have much larger ramifications for the community as a whole if the insect is involved in a critical mutualism. For example, loss of a specialist pollinator could lead to local extinction of its host flowering annual (which could then lead to loss of other insects that might be associated with that annual); loss of a seed food resource for small mammals could reduce prey availability for snakes and birds, and so forth. As we mentioned earlier, tropical fig trees may be thought of as keystone species, but should their specialized wasp pollinators decline, this important resource would be in jeopardy. The importance of tightly coevolved species interactions is further elaborated by Douglas Futuyma in Essay 8A.

ESSAY 8A
The Evolution and Importance of Species Interactions

Douglas J. Futuyma, State University of New York, Stony Brook

Charles Darwin, a great thinker and an outstanding naturalist, remarked in *On the Origin of Species* that in England, red clover is pollinated exclusively by bumblebees (or humblebees, as they are called in England), that "the number of humblebees in any district depends in a great measure upon the number of field-mice, which destroy their combs and nests,"and that since "the number of mice is largely dependent, as every one knows, on the number of cats . . . It is quite credible that the presence of a feline animal in large numbers in a district might determine, through the intervention first of mice and then of bees, the frequency of certain flowers in that district!"

Darwin's perception of the complex interactions among the species in a community has been thoroughly substantiated. The abundance of every species is influenced by that of other species, which serve as its food, as mutualists, predators, parasites, or competitors, or which create its habitat or influence it indirectly though such interventions as

Darwin described. Consequently, substantial changes in the abundance of one species will often threaten the extinction of others.

Although some effects are obvious, such as those of exotic predators, other species interactions are more subtle, yet still fragile. Many of these have their origin in two evolutionary phenomena—the evolution of specialization and the coevolution of species—which often go hand in hand.

All species are ecologically specialized in one way or another, sometimes to an extraordinary degree. The koala eats only *Eucalyptus* leaves, for example, and some snakes eat only crayfish or termites or other snakes. Specialization reaches its apogee in many parasites that attack only one or a few related species of hosts, and in herbivorous insects. The majority of the more than half million species of herbivorous insects have diet restrictions like that of the Colorado potato beetle, which will feed only on potato and a few closely related plants, and will starve to death if confined to any other plant. Related species of insects often feed on related plants; for example, larvae of each of the 60 or more species of Neotropical butterflies in the tribe Heliconiini feed only on particular species of passionflowers (Passifloraceae). Thus, much the same feeding habit has been retained throughout the time it has taken for the ancestral heliconiine to give rise to all these species.

This long-term restriction in diet has persisted in some groups of insects for at least 40 million years, which suggests that the insects may have little potential for adapting to different kinds of plants. In my laboratory, we are studying genetic variation in several species of specialized leaf beetles, to determine whether they have the genetic potential for evolving changes in their willingness to feed on, or in their capacity to grow and survive on, plants other than their natural hosts. In some instances, they do have such a capacity, but in most cases we find no evidence that they could adapt even to plants that are the normal hosts of closely related species of beetles. A species that feeds only on ragweed, for example, shows no hint of a genetic potential to feed on goldenrod, a member of the same family that is the host of several species in the same beetle genus. An obvious conservation implication of this work is that loss of plant species could easily result in simultaneous losses of specialized insect species.

Coevolution is the process of reciprocal adaptation among interacting species. All kinds of ecological interactions may coevolve, but I shall cite examples only of mimicry and mutualism.

The heliconiine butterflies, mentioned above, are famous for their mimetic color patterns. They are distasteful to birds, and advertise their unpalatability by bright coloration that is recognized by birds that learn, after one unpleasant experience, not to attack them. Individuals of each of two or more unpalatable species gain advantage from possessing the same color pattern, since they then profit from the birds' experience with any of the other species. In tropical America, several species of heliconiines have an almost identical orange and black tiger-striped pattern, evolved independently in several evolutionary lineages; moreover, the same pattern has evolved in some distasteful ithomiine butterflies—a quite unrelated group—as well as in some other butterflies that are palatable, but gain protection from resemblance to the distasteful "models."

Mutualism is an ecological interaction in which each of two (or more) species profits by using the other as a resource. (It would be better called "reciprocal exploitation," because neither species is doing the other an altruistic favor.) Often the interactions are highly specialized. A spectacular example is provided by the more than 900 species of figs (*Ficus*) throughout the tropics and the tiny wasps (Agaonidae) that pollinate them. The astonishing fact is that almost every fig species is pollinated by only one species of wasp, which uses only one species of fig. It appears likely that the specificity of this interaction is responsible for the origin of new pairs of associated species, for if a genetic variant of one fig species were to be visited exclusively by a wasp variant that responds exclusively to that fig, it would form the basis of a new reproductively isolated species.

The biology of the fig/wasp interaction is extraordinary. The tiny fig flowers are enclosed within a hollow structure (syconium) with an opening that is occluded by scales that differ in form among fig species. The scales apparently prevent the wrong species of wasp from entering. In most fig species, the syconium contains male flowers and both short and long female flowers. The female wasp enters, bringing with her pollen, held in special structures, which she then actively places on the female flowers' stigmas. She inserts an egg into each of many female flowers, but her ovipositor can reach the ovaries of only the short flowers, and it is in these that the larvae develop. Seeds develop only from long flowers, in which a wasp egg does not hatch. The female wasp dies, and her offspring emerge and mate within the syconium. The males die within, but the females gather pollen from the male flowers and then emerge to repeat the cycle.

Space does not permit exploration of the many fascinating questions about evolution that the fig/wasp system raises. But we should note that this exquisite coadaptation of species to each other has far-reaching ecological and conservation effects. It has caused the evolution of an extremely diverse group of plants. In many tropical forests, figs of various species are abundant, and are extremely important resources for birds, bats, monkeys, various other mammals, and even fish, which all feed on the fruit. Wasps about 1 mm long, which no one but an entomologist would notice unless he or she already knew about them, are fundamentally important components—perhaps keystone species—of many tropical communities. The long history of evolution, often of small, obscure species, has given rise to intricate interactions on which the structure of many communities depends. Conservation of these communities is dependent on the retention of these myriad species interactions.

Indirect Effects and Diffuse Interactions

One salient feature of keystone predators is that their indirect interactions with non-prey species can be very strong; their presence in a community can have far-reaching effects, even on species they do not consume. These indirect effects, though less obvious than predation, may be critical to community structure and thus may be of great conservation relevance. Examples of such interactions are legion; two, one involving birds and one involving fishes, should suffice to illustrate this type of interaction.

Throughout its range in North America, the Peregrine Falcon (*Falco peregrinus*), a predator on other birds, declined in abundance over several decades of the 20th century due to pesticide effects on its reproduction. Recovery beginning in the 1970s restored the species to some of its former range. On Tatoosh Island, Washington, Peregrine Falcon abundance increased from the late 1970s through the 1980s. Paine et al. (1990) studied the falcon and other native birds on the island during this period. They found that some species of birds, especially two species of auklets, declined after falcons increased; these declines were a result of predation, a direct interaction. However, other species increased in abundance. In particular, Pelagic Cormorants (*Phalacrocorax pelagicus*) and Common Murres (*Uria aalge*) increased significantly in the few years after falcons became abundant, even though murres are subject to low levels of falcon predation. Paine et al. (1990) attributed these increases, as well as slight increases in Black Oystercatcher (*Haematopus bachmani*) abundance, to the effects of falcons on Northwestern Crows (*Corvus caurinus*). Crows formerly were major egg and nest predators on various bird species, but falcons both preyed directly on crows and suppressed their nest-raiding activities. Thus, a direct predatory effect of falcons on crows resulted in an indirect effect on other species, and an increase in their abundance.

In prairie streams of Oklahoma, an herbivorous minnow called the stoneroller (*Campostoma anomalum*) heavily grazes algae wherever it occurs and keeps algal growth on rock substrates to a minimum. The stoneroller in turn is preyed upon by largemouth (*Micropterus salmoides*) or spotted (*M. punctulatus*) bass, very effective fish predators. The natural distribution of these fishes is often complementary in different pools of a given stream; stonerollers are found only in pools without bass, either because they leave when bass appear or because they are eaten by the bass. In stoneroller pools, algae is typically cropped very closely, but algal growth is luxuriant in bass pools (Power and Matthews 1983; Power et al. 1985). Experimental manipulations of predator and prey fishes confirm this scenario: if a bass is tethered in a pool with stonerollers, algae grows luxuriantly within the range of the bass, because stonerollers avoid that area, but is cropped heavily just outside the range of the bass. Adding bass to pools containing stonerollers soon results in heavy growth of algae (Figure 8.7). Thus, the direct predator–prey interaction be-

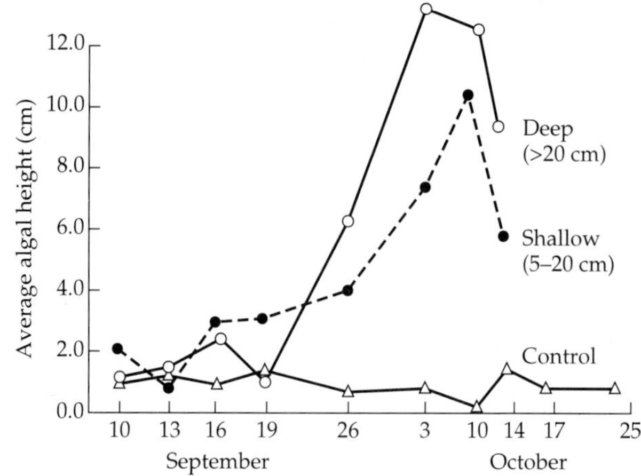

Figure 8.7 Algal standing crops in an experimental pool (to which bass were added) and a control pool (with no bass and only the algivore *Campostoma anomalum*) in a small stream in Oklahoma. The addition of bass inhibits or stops algal grazing by the herbivore, allowing algae to recover from heavy herbivory. This phenomenon is an indirect interaction between bass and algae. (From Power et al. 1985.)

Table 8.1
Classes of Possible Keystone Species/Mutualistic Interactions and the Potential Results of Their Losses

Class	Effects of losses
Top carnivores	Increases in abundances of prey species and smaller predators; overgrazing and overbrowsing
Large herbivores and termites	Habitat succession and decrease in habitat diversity
Habitat modifiers	Disappearance of habitat features
Pollinators and other mutualists	Reproductive failure of certain plants
Seed dispersers	Recruitment failure of certain plants
Plants providing essential resources during scarcity	Local extinction of dependent animals
Parasites and pathogenic microorganisms	Population explosions of host species
Mutualists with nutritional and defensive roles for their hosts	Increased predation, disease, and dieback of plants

Modified from Soulé and Kohm 1989.

tween bass and stonerollers indirectly controls algal distribution and abundance. Again, an indirect interaction influences community structure.

We conclude this section on critical species interactions by reiterating our warning that not every species interaction is crucial, its loss dooming the community. We know from numerous population or species extinctions that many species can be removed from a system without overriding harm to the remainder of the community. However, some species are especially important because of the central role they play in community processes (Holling 1992), and their loss could have a cascading effect. It is one of the challenges of conservation biology to identify these critical interactions and ensure that they are maintained.

A summary of critical keystone and mutualistic interactions, and the potential effects of their losses, is presented in Table 8.1. We will take a closer look at the results of the removal of certain types of species in the discussion of species introductions below.

(A)

(B)

(C)

Figure 8.8 A typical successional sequence from Hutchison Memorial Forest in central New Jersey. (A) The field in this photograph is 2 years old and dominated by herbaceous species. (B) A 10-year-old field, with some woody species and a higher overall diversity. (C) An older forest stand eventually results from the successional process. (Photographs by S. T. A. Pickett.)

Changes in Ecological Time: Disturbance Regimes and Invasive Species

The Importance of Disturbance Regimes

Much of the early historical development of theoretical ecology was premised on the comfortable notion that population dynamics and species interactions were at, or at least very near, an equilibrium state. In this view, nature could ultimately be understood if we only knew the appropriate deterministic rules that controlled ecology. More recently, theoretical and empirical interest has shifted away from purely deterministic viewpoints to place much more emphasis on the roles of various kinds of disturbances, patch dynamics (see Essay 9B), and other stochastic processes.

When one speaks of disturbance, of course, ecological succession immediately comes to mind. **Succession** is the familiar process by which an abandoned agricultural field eventually returns to mature forest (Figure 8.8), or a

(A)

(B)

(C)

Figure 8.9 Every type of disturbance patch, no matter how small, has relevance to the local ecology. Shown here are three types of soil disturbance patches. (A) A large *Atta* ant colony in Costa Rica; (B) a gopher tortoise burrow, with newly hatched tortoises moving from their nest into their mother's burrow; and (C) a tip-up mound from a tree blow-down. (Photographs by C. R. Carroll.)

coral reef rebuilds after destruction by a hurricane. The older literature described succession as an innate characteristic of a community; that is, the "natural state" of a community was defined by what was perceived to be the last, or "climax," stage of succession. A deciduous forest would therefore be called an "oak–hickory forest" (representing the apparent climax condition) rather than being named for an association more characteristic of a recent disturbance, such as "black locust–black cherry forest" or "sumac–elderberry forest," even though the latter may be common. Indeed, forests and many other communities tend to be labeled by the association that persists for the longest time.

In contrast, current thought emphasizes the dynamics of disturbance patches in both space and time, rather than the duration of a patch in a successional sequence. From this perspective, the characteristic biodiversity of a forest, a coral reef, or a prairie is a product of patch dynamics generated by particular disturbance regimes. Thus, as we emphasize throughout this book, nature does not keep a tidy house. A perception of nature in disequilibrium is much closer to reality than a "balance of nature" perspective. A celebrated question in ecology is, "What determines the number of species?" The research agenda associated with this enduring question now includes attempts to understand the interplay between deterministic and stochastic processes, and the effects of the scale, intensity, and frequency of those processes.

In ecology, there is always a creative tension between, on the one hand, the theorists and analytic modelers who wish to simplify nature and explore general processes, and on the other hand, the field ecologists and simulation modelers who focus on complexity in nature. This is particularly apparent in the body of research that addresses disturbance regimes. At one extreme, disturbance regimes can be generalized simply by allowing some parameter of mortality to vary. At the other extreme, every disturbance patch and event, from pocket gopher mounds and ant hills to landslides, is seen as having its unique natural history (Figure 8.9).

In conservation biology, the focus should be clear. Disturbance regimes are important to the extent that they influence probabilities of extinction and colonization and, thereby, the patterns of biodiversity in the landscape. It is clear that at least some kinds of disturbances greatly influence biodiversity, and often the effects are strongly influenced by scale, intensity, and frequency (see discussion of the "intermediate disturbance hypothesis" in Chapter 10). For example, we noted that in tropical forests, many trees are obligately associated with mycorrhizal fungi. If soil does not contain the fungi, the germinating seeds of these species cannot survive or compete with other species. A small soil disturbance patch, such as from a fallen tree, may retain, or quickly regain, its fungal inoculum. However, a large soil disturbance, such as from a landslide, may lose the fungal inoculum and regain it only very slowly. Thus, biodiversity will be maintained in a landscape characterized by small soil disturbances, but will decline if disturbances become large.

Fire frequency and intensity provides another example. As will be discussed in Chapter 12, a forest responds very differently to low-intensity than to high-intensity fires, and the effects of frequent fires are different than those of infrequent ones. The role of the conservation biologist, then, is to understand how systems respond to different types of disturbances and how those responses are influenced by changes in scale, intensity, and frequency. Because disturbance regimes are often important to the maintenance of biodiversity, conservation managers, especially of small areas where the disturbance regime may not occur naturally, may need to mimic natural disturbance regimes as part of their management plan. We will discuss the difficulties of implementing disturbance regimes in Chapters 11 and 12, but here we introduce the point that the role of disturbance regimes in conservation biology should be a priority for research.

Many of our conservation problems are associated with loss of the most mature stages of succession, such as old-growth forests in the northwestern United States and mature tropical lowland forests in many regions of the world, which may take many hundreds of years to reach a mature state. "Resetting" of these communities to earlier successional stages over large areas reduces the temporal and spatial diversity of habitat available, and many species associated with more mature successional stages cannot survive in the extensive earlier stages that are created. A major challenge of conservation is to retain both late successional stages and a mix of all successional types within a landscape, not to retain ecosystems as static and unchanging.

Species Invasions

A particular concern for native communities and species of conservation interest is the introduction of species beyond their native ranges. Known variously as "exotics," "aliens," "invaders," "non-natives," or "nonindigenous species," there are many examples of disastrous invasions by such species that have resulted in losses of native species, changes in community structure and function, and even alterations of the physical structure of the system (Mooney and Drake 1986; Drake et al. 1989; Simberloff et al. 1997). However, not all species invasions result in disaster, and fortunately so, because there are few areas that remain free of non-native species. In some cases, the use of exotics can actually have positive conservation value; this perspective is elaborated in Essay 8B by Ariel Lugo.

ESSAY 8B

Maintaining an Open Mind on Exotic Species

Ariel E. Lugo, Institute of Tropical Forestry, Puerto Rico

To consider only the invading species themselves in developing management programs or in recommending regulatory actions is tantamount to curing symptoms and not disease.

J. J. Ewel, 1986

Several reasons are given for the success of exotic species. They may do well because they are freed from natural enemies, competitors, and parasites. Consequently, a common strategy of control programs is to introduce organisms from the native habitats of target exotic plants to harm them; that is, eliminate exotics by introducing more exotics! Exotic species may also find little competition in the ecosystems they invade; empty niches may be available to exotics, which thus have little effect on the invaded ecosystem. The success of exotics has also been attributed to their being aggressive colonizers, fast growing, and highly fecund. However, Ewel (1986) noted that "species invasions often reflect the conditions of the community being invaded rather than the uniquely aggressive traits of the invader."

I subscribe to Ewel's point of view. When a good match is made between the genome of any species and the environmental conditions that support its growth, the result can be explosive population increases. This is why organisms that are rare in their natural habitats may suddenly become weedy in a new situation. The water hyacinth (*Eichhornia crassipes*) is fairly inconspicuous in its natural Amazonian habitats, but exhibits explosive growth in the slow-moving, highly eutrophic waters of artificial canals and reservoirs in Florida. Experiments show that it cannot grow as well when subjected to oligotrophic waters or fast flow. Close observation of successful exotic organisms usually yields similar results.

Ecological Functions and Services of Exotic Species

I have studied monoculture plantations of exotic trees in Puerto Rico and compared them with native forests of similar age. My studies include 73 comparisons of structure, composition, and function of these ecosystems. I cannot find a single comparison that suggests an ecological anomaly in the forests dominated by exotic species. These ecosystems function like native forests, with differences mostly in the magnitude of rates and state variables (i.e., biomass and other structural features).

No negative effects have been detected in the water cycle, accumulation of carbon and nutrients, or in any other site condition. Claims to the contrary, such as those leveled against *Eucalyptus* trees, cannot be substantiated when evaluated critically.

I have also found that native plant species grow and develop under canopies of exotic species established in degraded sites, including some where succession was arrested prior to planting exotics. Native birds are attracted to and use the native species understory of these exotic tree plantations. For these reasons, I and others have suggested that exotic species can be important tools for land rehabilitation and restoration of biological diversity in damaged sites where natural succession is arrested. For example, Vitousek and Walker (1989) documented nitrogen enrichment in nitrogen-poor lava flows in Hawaii by the exotic tree *Myrica faya*. The greater availability of soil nitrogen where the exotic occurs favors the entire ecosystem and results in higher productivity. One would expect that higher productivity would eventually result in a greater capacity to fix carbon, circulate nutrients, and support more species.

Will Exotic Species Dominate the World?

The dominance of exotic species on the landscape will be a function of the degree of human modification of the environment. In general, human activity fragments the landscape, favors establishment of exotic species, increases environmental heterogeneity, may cause species extinctions, and may augment the total number of species on the landscape. The Pacific Islands are instructive because they represent a worst-case scenario of the effects of intensive human activity on small land areas isolated from sources of biotic replenishment. In these islands, particularly the Hawaiian chain, isolation allowed the evolution of a highly diverse and endemic suite of organisms, originally exposed to merely a slow rate of invasion by exotic species.

Humans greatly accelerated that rate and in the process transformed the flora and fauna of the Pacific Islands. The process has been ongoing for some 2000 to 4000 years, and the results have been staggering in terms of species extinctions and transformation of biotic composition. The number of species across all taxonomic groups has increased from about 9000 to 12,000, but many see this trend as an erosion in global biodiversity because endemic forms are lost while pantropical weeds replace them. There is certainly truth to this argument, but it is not entirely accurate because many exotic species are neither weedy nor pantropical. Some may be rare and endangered species that find refuge in another, more favorable location and then become weedy. In Puerto Rico, for example, *Delonix regia* is a common naturalized species in danger of extinction in its native Madagascar habitat.

Species–area curves help to illustrate the size/isolation issue. I compared the density of species on two Caribbean islands with that of the Hawaiian Islands (Table A). If the area and plant species density values of the Hawaiian Islands are used to estimate the numbers of plant species expected in Cuba and Puerto Rico (same latitude as Hawaii), the results underestimate the actual number of species on the two Caribbean islands. This means that when area is corrected for, the density of species in the Caribbean is much higher than in the Hawaiian Islands. Part of this higher species density in the Caribbean is caused by the islands being closer to sources of propagules, but part is also explained by the Caribbean islands being six times older than the Hawaiian Islands. Could this mean that the Hawaiian Islands have a greater capacity to absorb additional plant species than do the Caribbean islands? The age of islands, as well as their degree of isolation, influences the density of species and invadability of their communities. In Hawaii, exotic species are the likely invaders of plant communities because they are actively transported from a large reservoir of genetic material (the whole world), while the native species evolve slowly and are constrained by founder effects.

I would expect that in the absence of significant climate change, environments that today support high species richness will do so in the future, but the species composition may be different. And we should not forget that the forces of evolution are not suspended for exotic species. One could argue that the enrichment of islands with exotic genomes provides fuel for the evolutionary process and greatly increases adaptive possibilities. This is particularly important in light of human-induced changes in the atmosphere, climate, geomorphology, and other environmental conditions.

The change in species composition taking place in the world today is not a chaotic process; it is a process that is responding to fundamental changes in the conditions of the planet. Age-old ecological constraints such as time, energetics, biotic factors, growth conditions, and opportunity are at play, regulating which species are successful and which are not in a specific location. Human activity generates the environmental change that powers the response of organisms through adaptation, evolution, or formation of new groupings of species and communities.

Management Strategies for a Changing World

I have highlighted contradictions in the way we deal with biodiversity issues in general and exotic species in particular. Even in Hawaii, where there is great concern about the degree of exotic species invasions and their potentially negative effects, the government actively and successfully introduces hundreds of insect species for agricultural pest control. We correctly worry about the negative effects of human activity, but forget that this activity started thousands of years ago at a time when people depended directly on the environment for survival. Even then, exotics were introduced and perhaps countless numbers of species were driven to ex-

Table A
Predicted and Actual Numbers of Plant Species in Cuba and Puerto Rico Using the Species–Area Relationship for the Hawaiian Islands ($S = cA^z$)

Island	Area (km^2)	z	Predicted number of plant species	Actual number of flowering plant species
Cuba	70,750	0.30	3100	6000
Hawaii	16,640	—	—	1750–2350
Puerto Rico	8960	0.30	1600	2200

Note: The z value is that for Hawaiian plants. Consideration of only fern species results in 143 species in Hawaii and 408 species in Puerto Rico.

tinction. I do not point these things out to excuse introductions of species nor to condone driving species to extinction. But we must maintain an open mind and analyze the issue of exotic species introductions and management as an intrinsic and continuous process in a world where our own species is a main agent of change.

It is in our power to take actions to mitigate the negatives of our activities and to enhance the positives. Actions that may help are learning to manage and control environmental change, recognizing when conditions are obviously beyond our control, avoiding condemning species because of successional stage or ecological function, improving our capacity to manage biotic resources, concentrating human activity to allow more space for native ecosystems, and encouraging environmental heterogeneity as a mechanism to maximize biodiversity. One thing is clear: the world will continue to change and become less familiar to those that walked on it or wrote about it centuries ago.

We face several critical questions in understanding invading species in a conservation context. What are the particular characteristics of invading species and invaded communities that determine the outcomes of such floral and faunal changes? Are there general rules by which the effects of such invasions can be predicted? Should some species cause more concern than others? Should there be special planning to eradicate some species if they establish a population? Or, if the invader cannot be eliminated, can it be managed to minimize its effects? Similar arguments arise when we consider the species that may be lost from communities due to invasions. We lack the resources to save everything, so which species are most important?

This section argues that the effects of invasions depend a great deal on which species and which communities are involved. Some species are more likely to invade than others, and some are more likely to be lost from a community than others (general patterns are summarized in Table 8.2). This means that conservation biologists need to identify the important invaders or important native species that will be vulnerable. The major questions we will ask are:

1. Which species are most likely to invade communities?
2. Which native species are communities most likely to lose?
3. Which species, once they do invade, will cause extensive extinctions of native species?
4. Which native species extinctions will lead to many further losses of species and change in community structure?

We will address each of these four questions in turn, and will argue that each has two sides. The answers depend both on the natural history of the species that may invade or be lost—their physiology, behavior, genetics, and ecology—and on community characteristics, especially the role of potential competitors with, and predators on, the invading species.

Which Species Introductions Succeed? Not all introduced species succeed. We often are not aware of the many accidental introductions that fail (the successes are obvious), but there have been enough deliberate introductions to provide some records of failures. Fishes, birds, and mammals have been introduced for sport, plants and birds for aesthetics, and insects for biological control of pests. Typically, the majority of introductions fail. Across various invertebrate and vertebrate taxa, success rates of over 50% are rare, 10%–40% are common, and, in some groups, any success is unusual (Lawton and Brown 1986).

Chance clearly plays a role, for repeated attempts with the same species in the same place are often necessary for success. Game bird biologists have successfully introduced seven species of pheasants, quail, and their relatives into the United States, but even under optimal circumstances, most of these introductions fail (Pimm 1991). Similarly, the European Starling (*Sturnus vulgaris*),

Table 8.2
Some Generalized Characteristics of Invasive Species and Invadable Communities

Characteristics of successful invaders
High reproductive rate, pioneer species, short generation time
Long-lived
High dispersal rates
Single-parent reproduction (i.e., gravid or pregnant female can colonize)
Vegetative or clonal reproduction
High genetic variability
Phenotypically plastic
Broad native range
Habitat generalist
Broad diet (polyphagous)
Human commensal
Characteristics of invadable communities
Climatically matched with original habitat of invader
Early successional
Low diversity of native species
Absence of predators on invading species
Absence of native species morphologically or ecologically similar to invader
Absence of predators or grazers in evolutionary history ("naive" prey)
Absence of fire in evolutionary history
Low-connectance food web
Anthropogenically disturbed
Characteristics of communities likely to exhibit large invasion effects
Simple communities
Anthropogenically disturbed communities

Modified from Lodge 1993.
Note: The list is not exhaustive, nor is every characteristic critical in a given situation. These are merely generalized trends, with many exceptions.

introduced in New York's Central Park in 1891, has spread to most of North America, but several introductions before 1891 failed (Long 1981).

Deciding which introductions are likely to succeed or fail requires a wealth of autecological information. We should know, for example, whether the species can tolerate the physical conditions of the new habitat. Indeed, we should ask how important is a match between, say, the climate of the potential new home and the existing one; for plants, a similar photoperiod can also be important. (Many introduced species do *not* show a good match in the climate of their old and new homes.) We should know how well the species can fare when it is at low density. Can it find mates? Can it reproduce quickly to overcome low numbers? Is it vulnerable to the genetic problems of inbreeding that haunt small populations? Will biological interactions with competitors, diseases, or predators prevent the species from invading? In any given case it may not be critical to have detailed answers to all these questions, but any one of these factors may be critical to an invasion's success or failure.

The role of competition in determining which species can invade has been of interest for a long time. Elton (1946) suggested that communities might be structured by competition. If so, there should be fewer representatives of each genus in any given community than would be expected at random because

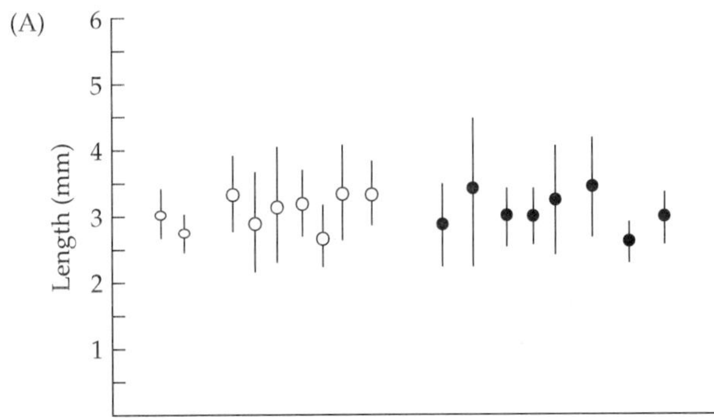

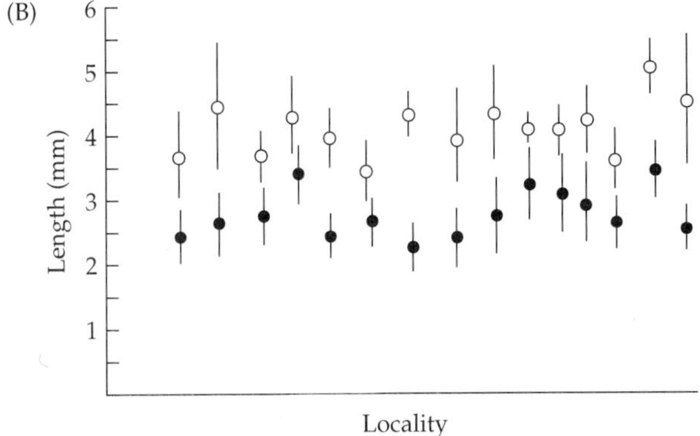

Figure 8.10 Two species of mud snails (*Hydrobia ulvae* [open circles] and *H. ventrosa* [filled circles]) tend to be the same size where allopatric (A), but diverge in size where sympatric (B). Shown are means plus and minus one standard deviation for several different localities. The phenomenon of size separation is thought to be due to competition for limited resources, and is called character displacement. (From Fenchel 1975.)

species in the same genus, by being ecologically similar, would tend to exclude each other through competition. Elton's competitive exclusion idea was extended to morphological similarity by Lack (1947). He proposed that competition is likely to be more intense between species that are similar because they are more likely than dissimilar species to share essential resources. This principle often is reflected in morphology: body size or the shape of a critical character may be divergent where two species co-occur, but more similar where they do not (Figure 8.10). Taxonomic or morphological similarity between an invader and a resident is more likely where there are more resident species, and sufficiently intense competition can prevent species introductions. Some of the most direct evidence of invasions being more difficult in species-rich communities comes from studies of introduced birds on islands (Moulton and Pimm 1983, 1985, 1986, 1987; Moulton 1985, 1993).

What is the role of predation in species invasions? Obviously, a native predator, if it preys on the invader, will make it harder for the invader to succeed, but nature can be more complex than this. Predators may also make it easier for a species to invade if they feed heavily on resident species and so reduce their competitive effects on the invader. There is no universal answer to this question.

Which Species Are Most Likely to Go Extinct? This may be the easiest question to answer. Species already at risk of extinction for other reasons may be further jeopardized by invading species. Rarity is by far the best predictor of the chance of extinction (Diamond 1984a,b; Pimm 1991), in large part because species numbers vary so much. Among Hawaiian birds, for example, there are some species with fewer than ten individuals, and others

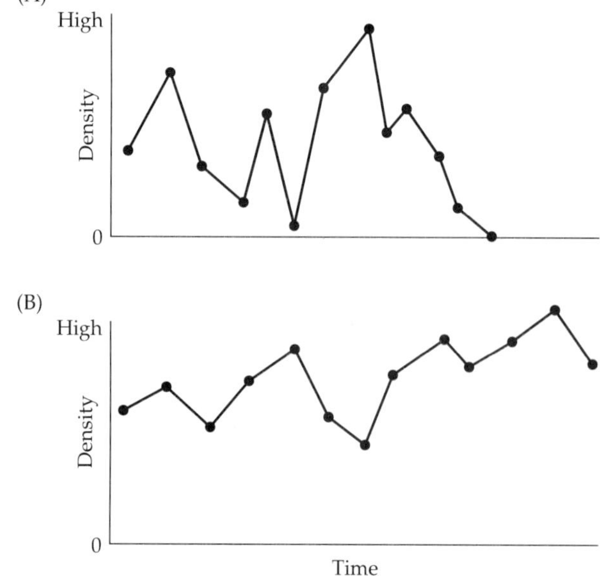

Figure 8.11 A highly variable population (A) has a higher likelihood of extinction than a population with lower variation (B), simply because it approaches low numbers more frequently. At that low point, it is more vulnerable to extinction due to demographic or genetic stochasticity, or to environmental variation (see Chapter 7).

with millions (Scott et al. 1986). Whatever other factors are important, a species six orders of magnitude more abundant than another is going to be less threatened.

Abundance is not the only factor, of course. Species differ in their risks of extinction at a given small population size (Pimm et al. 1988). Species also differ greatly in how much their numbers vary from year to year. Some species vary by only a factor of two over 20 years, others by four orders of magnitude over the same interval (Pimm 1991). Other things being equal, greater variability in population size may lead to greater risk of extinction (Figure 8.11).

What makes some species vary more than others? Environmental variability, the diversity of predators that exploit the species, the species' degree of trophic specialization, and its life history characteristics all contribute. An extended discussion of these effects is provided by Pimm (1991).

Which Invaders Will Cause Extensive Extinctions of Native Species? Not all alien species cause damage, and Simberloff (1981) has suggested that only a few do. However, the evidence for severe damage in particular instances is compelling, and there are many cases of communities devastated by alien plants and animals (Pimm 1991; Simberloff et al. 1997). Some of the best examples are native fishes of North American deserts that have gone extinct as a result of introductions of predatory exotic fishes (Minckley and Deacon 1991).

Are there repeat offenders or just vulnerable communities? Are some species the ecological equivalent of Genghis Khan, wreaking havoc wherever they invade? Are there species whose introductions should always be avoided and others that are never a problem? Or does the outcome depend on the community into which the species is introduced?

Two mosquitofish species (*Gambusia affinis* and *G. holbrooki*) of eastern and central North America are notorious for their devastating effects as exotic species in a variety of different community types (Courtenay and Meffe 1989). These small (<5 cm), harmless-looking, guppylike fishes have caused species reductions or extinctions (through their predatory habits) in a variety of community types (springs, ponds, lakes, slow rivers) when introduced in Australia, Europe, Asia, Africa, western North America, and especially on oceanic islands (reviewed in Courtenay and Meffe 1989; Arthington and Lloyd 1989). Several dozen species of fish (including large predators and game species) and numerous species of invertebrates have been negatively affected or extirpated after mosquitofish introductions. Similarly, in southern California streams, the introduction of *Gambusia affinis* and the crayfish *Procambarus clarkii* has been shown through field experiments to devastate populations of the once common California newt (*Taricha torosa*). These new predators apparently are not deterred by the potent chemical defenses of the newt that work well against native predators (as reported in Diamond 1996). The outcome of *Gambusia* introduction seems little affected by the community type or native species involved—yet, curiously, mosquitofish continue to be intentionally introduced for mosquito control (Swanson et al. 1996).

In a major review of introduced mammals and birds, Ebenhard (1988) recorded 59 introductions of domestic cats (*Felis domesticus*). A majority of these (38, or 64%) had detrimental effects, including extinctions of native prey populations. This percentage should be contrasted with that for all predator introductions: 32%. Cats thus seem twice as likely to cause damage as other introduced predators. The story is more complicated than this, however. Thirty-five of 49 (71%) introductions of cats to islands had detrimental effects, while only 3 of 10 (30%) introductions to mainlands, or islands once connected to mainlands, had such effects. Island communities are particularly vulnerable to introduced predators. The figure of 30% of introductions is still about three times the average for all mammalian predators introduced to mainlands (9%). Quite clearly, cats have an unusual potential to create problems, and they, along with the mosquitofishes just discussed, are a good example of a species whose introduction should always be avoided. Other examples of invasive species with a track record of severe effects include rats, goats, zebra mussels, fire ants, and plants such as kudzu (Figure 8.12). So yes, there are repeat offenders whose introductions should always be avoided.

Which Native Species Extinctions Will Result in Further Losses of Species and Change in Community Structure? Which species can we not afford to lose? Are there some species whose presence in a community is crucial? That is, if we do not make special efforts on their behalf, might we lose species that play keystone roles in maintaining the composition of the ecological community?

In practice, some species get much more protection than others, but not always for well-justified ecological reasons. Their protection may arise because they are large, feathered, or furred and they capture the public's imagination more than the small and the scaled. Although they may not always be critical species to their communities, large species typically require more space than small species, and thus their protection may protect other species or the community at large. Protect the Spotted Owl of old-growth forests of the Pacific Northwest, and nearly 200 other species are protected under its umbrella. But there are species that are important for reasons other than their size or public appeal; these are classes of species whose loss will cause extensive **secondary extinctions**.

The community consequences of particular species introductions and extinctions depend critically on which species are removed and the patterns of trophic interactions. Computer models of the process of removing species demonstrate several possibilities. Removing a plant species from the base of a simple food chain destroys the entire community (Figure 8.13A). However, the loss of one of several plant species used by a polyphagous herbivore in a more complex community (Figure 8.13C) causes few or no extinctions because

(A)

(B)

(C)

Figure 8.12 A number of invasive species repeatedly have been shown to be successful colonists and a major challenge to native communities. These include species such as (A) zebra mussels (shown growing on a native mussel, *Leptodea fragilis*), (B) kudzu overgrowing a native forest in the southeastern United States, and (C) Africanized honeybees that have taken over a Wood Duck nest box in Costa Rica. (A, photograph by D. W. Schloesser; B and C, by C. R. Carroll.)

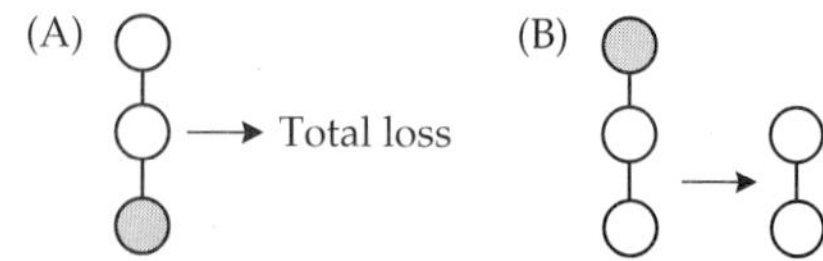

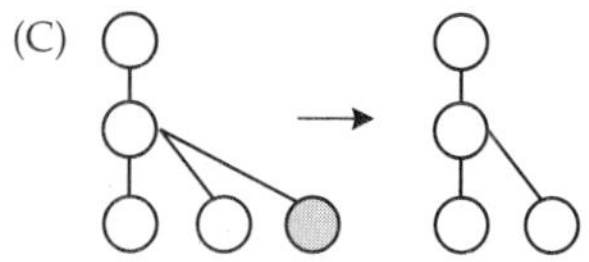

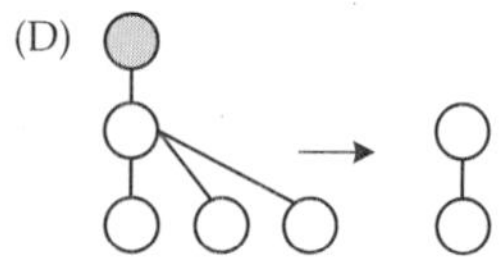

Figure 8.13 The effects of species removals depend on the complexity of the food web and the species' position in the web. (A) A plant removed from the bottom of a simple food chain causes the entire food chain to be lost. (B) A predator removed from the same food chain may have no effect. In contrast, a plant lost from a more complex web may have little effect (C), but a predator lost from the same web may release its herbivore prey and so lead to the loss of several species of plants (D). (From Pimm 1991.)

the herbivore is not so dependent on one species. Similar rules apply one trophic level up when contrasting polyphagous and monophagous predators. These effects are obvious and well known. Less obvious are the effects of removing species from the tops of food chains.

Removing a predator species that preys on a monophagous herbivore (Figure 8.13B) probably leaves the plant the herbivore eats at a lower density, but the plant is likely to survive. In a more complex community (Figure 8.13D), the predator's absence may lead to the herbivore exterminating all but one resistant plant species, which then regulates the herbivore's numbers.

In short, secondary extinctions are most likely when plants are removed from trophically simple communities. In more complex communities, the remaining species have alternative food supplies. Yet, secondary extinctions are more likely in complex communities than in simple ones following the loss of top predators because cascading extinctions from upper trophic levels can propagate more widely in complex communities (see Pimm 1991 for a detailed explanation).

These principles have simple extensions to discussions involving competitors. Removing the predator of a species that competes with many other species may cause many changes (see the discussion of keystone predators above). Removing a predator of a species that competes more locally may have fewer effects.

What kinds of introduced species are likely to cause the greatest community changes? We can predict the effects of introduced species from these conclusions about species removals. Adding a generalist herbivore to an island lacking predators may be equivalent to removing the herbivore's predator in the herbivore's native community. Highly polyphagous introduced species are likely to cause more damage than monophagous species, just as predator removals have more severe effects when their prey are polyphagous. A parallel argument suggests that polyphagous predators will cause more damage if they are introduced into areas containing no competitors or diseases.

Finally, the combination expected to produce the most profound changes is the introduction of polyphagous herbivores without their predators into relatively simple communities. Without predators, these herbivores may attain high densities, their generalized feeding habits may exterminate many species of plants, and the removal of a few plant species may cause the collapse of entire food chains. Oceanic islands invaded by goats often fall under this worst-case scenario.

To see how these various ideas about invaders and invaded communities apply, let us consider several examples of additions and subtractions of species, which will together present several sides of the invasion story.

Figure 8.14 The brown tree snake, *Boiga irregularis,* the cause of the loss of ten bird species on Guam, and a potential threat to Hawaii. (Photograph by Gordon H. Rodda.)

The Brown Tree Snake on Guam. We start with the case of the brown tree snake, *Boiga irregularis* (Figure 8.14), which is accused of exterminating all the forest birds on Guam, one of the Mariana Islands of the western Pacific. Our conservation interest here is whether special efforts are needed to prevent *Boiga* from spreading from Guam to the Hawaiian Islands of the central Pacific, the most remote archipelago on the planet. To answer this question, we must first establish what *Boiga* has done on Guam, and then try to understand the unique species and community characteristics of Hawaii that might have bearing on the question.

The brown tree snake's native range is from Australia north through New Guinea to the Solomon Islands. It arrived in Guam after World War II, probably in a military transport, and eventually spread across the entire island, remaining at low densities for two decades. Birds started disappearing from

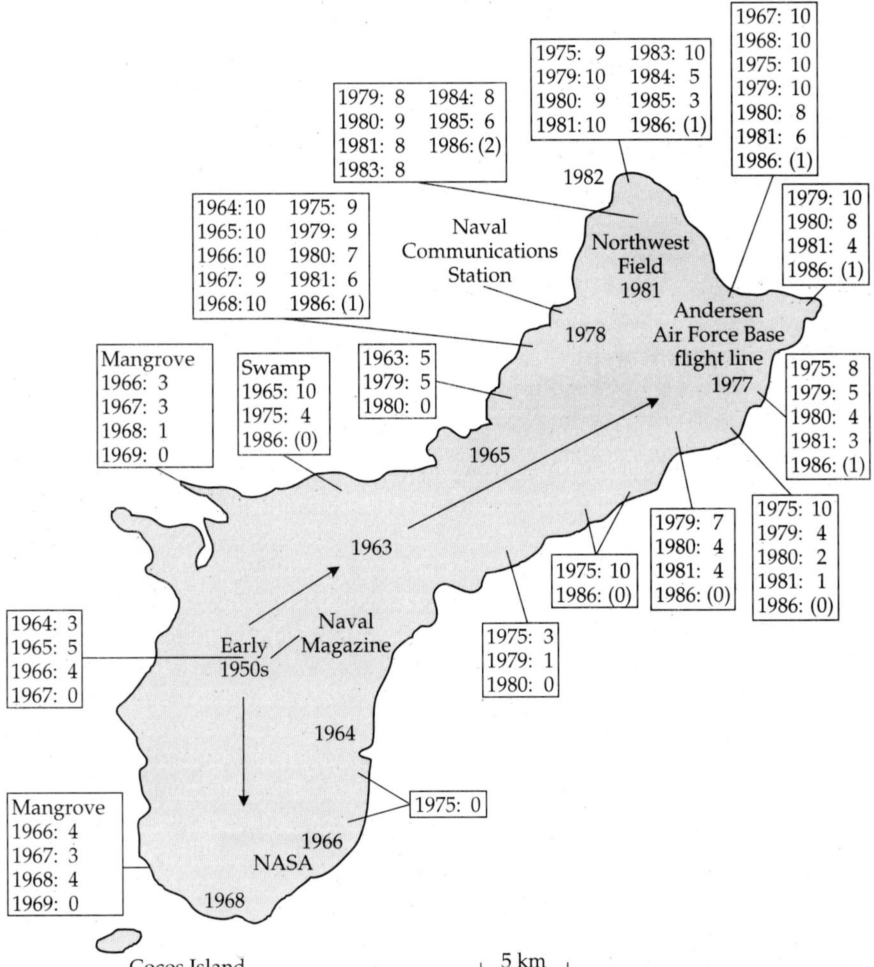

Figure 8.15 Map of Guam showing the spread of *Boiga* and the loss of forest bird species. *Boiga* colonized the southern part of the island after World War II, and progressively spread from there, as indicated by the arrows. Each box lists the number (out of a possible 10) of forest bird species found at that location in the year indicated. For 1986, the surveys were incomplete, and those numbers are in parentheses. (Modified from Savidge 1987.)

the middle of Guam in the early 1960s. At about the same time, the snakes appeared in large numbers—some well-fed in chicken coops, others reduced to carbon on power poles (surrogate trees!) after short-circuiting insulators and causing blackouts. Savidge (1987) noticed that ten species of forest birds followed a similar pattern of decline: the birds were gone from the forests of southern Guam by the late 1960s, and one by one, species were lost progressively farther north (Figure 8.15). In early 1983, ecologists found all ten species in one small patch of tall forest beneath a cliff line on the northern tip of the island. By 1986, they had disappeared from this area as well.

There was considerable debate about the causes of the decline in Guam's birds. Some scientists argued that pesticides were to blame, and others believed that avian diseases might be at fault. The native species might be susceptible to diseases carried by introduced birds or domesticated chickens and pigeons. Introduced birds might be directly responsible by competing with or harassing native species. There was also the familiar list of introduced rats, cats, and other mammals.

Not only did the forest birds decline, but the Fairy Tern stopped nesting on the island. However, on the small island of Cocos, a few hundred meters off the south coast of Guam (Figure 8.15) where there are no *Boiga*, it remains abundant. The tern's decline on Guam ruled out pesticides, because it nests in trees but feeds on oceanic fish, which would not be affected by pesticides. It is also a highly mobile species; were it declining on Guam due to disease, the population on Cocos would also have been infected. The cumulative evidence indicates that *Boiga* has driven ten bird species to extinction on Guam by predation; two of these species and one distinctive subspecies lived nowhere else. Four more bird species are so rare that their survival is unlikely.

Will *Boiga* colonize Hawaii in the coming decades and cause similar destruction? *Boiga* made it from the Solomons to Guam; the snake can survive far longer than the eight-hour plane ride from Guam to Hawaii, and dead *Boiga* have already appeared on airfields in Hawaii. *Boiga* can certainly reach Hawaii, but can it increase in numbers from a few founding stowaways, and can it devastate? Small populations run high risks of extinction from chance events (discussed in Chapters 6 and 7): individuals may not find mates; for species producing few young, there is a chance that those individuals will be of the same sex; inbreeding in small founder populations may quickly take its toll; all individuals may die early in the invasion for completely independent reasons. These factors are unavoidable at very low numbers, but they quickly become unimportant as the population increases in size. Every invading population not arriving in force must run this gauntlet of demographic and genetic accidents, but many succeed quite well. With *Boiga*, a female could arrive already gravid and lay a clutch of a dozen eggs (Cogger 1979). Thus, a single female could initiate a successful invasion.

Of course, invading species must also be able to survive the physical environment of their new home. Interestingly, a bad match between the climates of old and new homes may not prevent success; some species readily adapt to different conditions and climate in their new homes. The lush tropical forests of lowland Hawaii house a community of introduced birds, many of which are from temperate climates. In the case of *Boiga*, the physical environment of Hawaii is similar to that of Guam and appears quite suitable for the snake.

Whether an alien species succeeds or not also depends on the welcome afforded it by the community's established species. Do they provide it with prey, or do they prey on the alien? Do they compete with it by feeding on species that the alien also may feed upon? Do they harbor reservoirs of diseases fatal to the alien, or does it carry diseases fatal to them?

The nearest continent to Hawaii, North America, is more than 4000 km away, and consequently few species have arrived on the islands naturally; there is only one native terrestrial mammal (a bat) and no native reptiles or amphibians. There were once about 100 species of passerine birds, but they descended from just four colonizations (a crow, a finch, a flycatcher, and a honeyeater). Of the plants, only about 10% are found elsewhere; the remainder are endemic. Thus, the Hawaiian Islands are too remote to have native snakes that could be competitors, predators, or hosts of fatal diseases. Yet they are home to many native and introduced birds and introduced lizards on which the snake could feed; the large numbers of introduced birds in disturbed habitats around airfields and ports could provide *Boiga* with abundant prey. The community setting thus seems favorable to *Boiga*.

Oddly enough, the only enemy for *Boiga* may be another introduced species. Over a century ago, the small Indian mongoose was introduced to Hawaii to control rats. That effort was a conspicuous failure, perhaps because rats are nocturnal while the mongoose is diurnal. (Ecological insight has rarely been a close partner of deliberate species introductions.) The mongoose is an aggressive and generalized predator that might prey on *Boiga*, and this could prevent the snake's establishment. However, this is a slim hope at best, and we cannot bet the ecological future of Hawaii on such good fortune. Prevention of the establishment of *Boiga* offers the best chance of not repeating the Guam tragedy in Hawaii.

The evidence all points to *Boiga* being able to colonize Hawaii and damage its ecological communities. It has managed to exterminate one avifauna already, and its natural history and the features of Hawaiian ecological communities make a successful invasion and subsequent damage quite likely. Thus, we conclude that *Boiga* is more likely to succeed than many other invading species and more likely to cause harm if it establishes itself. Any conservationist would strongly recommend that special measures be taken to first prevent and then seek out and eliminate potential immigrants like *Boiga*.

The Loss of the American Chestnut Tree. The American chestnut (*Castanea dentata*) was once an important component of the deciduous forests of eastern North America. It ranged from Georgia in the south and Illinois in the west to as far north as Maine. In some forests it made up more than 40% of the overstory trees (Krebs 1985). Yet in the early part of the 20th century, chestnuts were driven almost to extinction by a fungal disease, chestnut blight, first noticed in an area near New York City (Figure 8.16). The species now survives only as rare, small individuals, which become infected and die as they mature. The fungus is thought to have been introduced on nursery stock from Asia, where it is endemic. It is found on other species of trees, but appears to kill only chestnuts. Our interest here is in the fate of the animal communities that depended on chestnuts. Many species might be expected to have used chestnuts, and therefore we might expect many animal extinctions.

Despite the numerical importance of the chestnut, there have been no extinctions of terrestrial vertebrates in eastern North America due to its decline. Seven species of Lepidoptera (moths and butterflies) apparently fed exclusively on chestnuts (Opler 1978), and all of them are now possibly extinct. Forty-nine other species of Lepidoptera also fed on chestnuts, but the tree made up only part of their diets. Hence, only 12% of Lepidoptera reported to have fed on chestnuts were so specialized that they may have become rare or extinct. None of these seven species supported very specialized species of insect predators, so the chestnut food web is probably like the one shown in Figure 8.13C: most of the herbivores are polyphagous, and the web is fairly

(A)

(B)

Figure 8.16 The American chestnut tree, *Castanea dentata*, formerly dominant in the eastern deciduous forest of North America, was nearly removed from the forests by chestnut blight. (A) A second-growth stand of chestnuts near Voluntown, Connecticut, in 1910 shows the former dominance of this species. (B) By 1922, near Oxford, Pennsylvania, large stands of the tree were dying from blight. (Photographs courtesy of the Connecticut Agricultural Experiment Station, S. L. Anagnostakis.)

resistant to the removal of one of its plant species. Thus, the American chestnut tree was lost with very few known effects on animal species. The significance of infective disease in biodiversity conservation is discussed in broader terms by Andrew Dobson in Essay 8C.

ESSAY 8C
Infectious Disease and the Conservation of Biodiversity

Andy Dobson, Princeton University

Dissect any population of vertebrates, invertebrates, plants, or fungi, and you will find a whole community of organisms living within their tissues. Furthermore, the richness of this community of parasites will increase as you examine the host's tissues at finer scales of resolution. Unfortunately, ecologists and conservation biologists often overlook the huge variety of biodiversity that lives in, upon, and often at the expense of free-living species. Parasites and microorganisms are a major component of biodiversity, perhaps as many as 50% of all living species (Price 1980; Toft 1991). Ironically, whereas few people worry about their long-term conservation (Sprent 1992), it is important not to ignore them, as many pathogens have profound effects at the physiological and individual levels that fundamentally affect the evolution of populations and the functioning of ecosystems.

To illustrate the dramatic effect that parasites can have at the population to ecosystem levels, consider the role of one pathogen species in the savanna ecosystem of East Africa. Rinderpest virus (RPV), a morbillivirus that causes widespread mortality in ungulates, was first introduced into East Africa at the end of the 19th century (Plowright 1982). Cattle were probably responsible for its introduction into the Horn of Africa, where they transmitted it to wild artiodactyls; over the next ten years it spread throughout sub-Saharan Africa, producing mortality as high as 90% in some species. Travelers through the region reported that in some places the ground was littered with carcasses, and the vultures were so satiated they could not take off (Simon 1962). Even today, the observed geographic ranges of some species are thought to reflect the impact of the great rinderpest pandemic.

The best way to examine the full impact of a pathogen on a host population is to remove it and monitor subsequent changes in host demography and behavior. This is possible for rinderpest, as an effective vaccine was developed in the late 1950s, at about the same time that long-term monitoring of wild game species began in Serengeti National Park in Tanzania and other East African game parks. At this time most cattle farmers perceived wild artiodactyls to be the reservoir of the rinderpest virus that caused regular epidemic outbreaks in their cattle. Vaccinating the large number of wild animals in the region was an impossible task, so the program focused only on vaccinating cattle to protect them from infection.

Vaccination produced a remarkable and unforeseen effect on the local ecosystem, particularly in the Serengeti, where long-term wildlife monitoring allowed rinderpest removal to be studied in some detail (Sinclair 1979; Dobson 1995). As vaccination coverage in cattle increased, the incidence of "yearling disease" (RPV in wildebeest and buffalo) declined rapidly, and calf survival in these and other wild artiodactyls increased significantly (Talbot and Talbot 1963; Plowright 1982). This led to a rapid increase in the density of those species; in the Serengeti, wildebeest numbers increased from 250,000 to over a million between 1962 and 1976, and buffalo nearly doubled over the same period and expanded their range. This increase in herbivore density produced a significant increase in some carnivore species, particularly lions and hyenas, thus refuting the hypothesis that ungulate numbers were regulated by their predators. Other species, such as hunting dogs and Thompson's gazelles, declined. The latter may have been due to increased predation by hyenas, while the reason for the decline of hunting dogs remains controversial.

In many ways rinderpest virus acts as a keystone species in the East African savannas. If the importance of keystone species varies inversely with their biomass (Power et al. 1996), then rinderpest is a keystone par excellence, as there was probably never more than a kilogram of RPV in the entire Serengeti, yet it caused changes in the densities of all the major vertebrates. Furthermore, there is increasing evidence that the first epidemic led to a pulse of plant recruitment when the density of herbivores was massively reduced (Prins and van der Jeugd 1993). Similar direct and indirect effects of pathogens on plants and herbivores have been crucial in shaping the structure of a number of well-studied communities (Dobson and Crawley 1994).

The mathematical conditions determining whether a pathogen can establish and maintain itself in a host population, or whether it dies out, have been examined by a range of authors (Kermack and McKendrick 1927; Anderson and May 1991; Heesterbeek and Roberts 1995). Such models typically contain an expression for the basic reproduction ratio of the parasite, R_0 (also known as the basic reproductive rate), and a threshold number of hosts that is required for R_0 to exceed unity. Expressions for R_0 are usually the product of the birth and transmission rates of the pathogen divided by the product of its mortality rates at each life cycle stage. The threshold number of hosts required to sustain the pathogen is obtained by rearranging the expression for the special case in which $R_0 = 1$.

At present, theoretical studies of R_0 far exceed experimental and empirical attempts to examine how transmission rates respond to changes in host biology (Grenfell and Dobson 1995). Obviously, endangered species of birds and mammals are not the best organisms with which to pursue such studies. Nevertheless, it should be readily apparent that rare species should be less prone to harboring specific pathogens than are more common species, as it is unlikely that their populations will be dense enough to continuously sustain infections. The more significant threat to endangered species may be pathogens acquired from species with large populations that do sustain continuous infections. In this case, the pathogen is present in one host species and invades another. At this stage two things can happen: the combined population densities of the potential host species are insufficient to sustain the pathogen, and it dies out, or the parasite sustains itself in the new community of hosts.

An important example of this pattern occurs in the Greater Yellowstone ecosystem, where bison and elk harbor *Brucella abortus*, the etiological agent of brucellosis. Although brucellosis is primarily a disease of the reproductive tract and nervous system, it exhibits different characteristics in different hosts (McCorquodale and DiGiacomo 1985). In elk, infection of females leads to abortion of the next calf; transmission occurs when uninfected individuals inspect the aborted fetus. In contrast, brucellosis in bison seems to operate as a sexually transmitted disease, and there are only two examples in this century of bison losing calves to brucellosis (Meagher and Meyer 1994; Meyer and Meagher 1995). As the Yellowstone bison population is growing at close to its theoretical maximum, it is unlikely that females are losing calves that are simply not found by researchers. Nevertheless, ranchers and federal officials regard bison and brucellosis as a threat to livestock, particularly cattle. Although there are no examples of transmission between bison or elk and domestic livestock, there are frequent proposals to eradicate brucellosis from Yellowstone.

Unfortunately, eradication of a disease requires reduction of the susceptible population below the threshold density at which the pathogen can sustain itself. For *Brucella,* this threshold may be very low, perhaps as few as 200 susceptible bison and similar numbers of elk (Dobson and Meagher 1996). As no effective vaccine is available for bison, and the vaccine is only partially effective in elk, eradication of *Brucella* from Yellowstone would require a massive reduction in the size of the bison and elk populations. This is unlikely to be acceptable on either ethical or political grounds. Instead, it may be sensible to establish a sanitary zone around the area in which cattle ranching is restricted to vaccinated, or castrated, animals.

Attempts to breed endangered species in captivity are frequently confounded by disease outbreaks, and translocation of individuals to bolster declining populations carries with it the risk of disease introductions. In Hawaii and other island ecosystems, the introduction of avian malaria and other pathogens has led to the decline of native species.

Such epidemiological problems are illustrated by the endangered Bali Mynah, the only endemic bird species on the Indonesian island of Bali. Its population has been reduced from between 1000 and 2000 birds to an all-time low of 18 birds in 1990 (van Balen and Gepak 1994). This precipitous decline is mainly due to illegal trapping and habitat degradation. Today the population stands at 55–60 birds; the increase is mainly due to translocation of captive birds bred in zoos. The current Species Survival Plan recommends increasing the wild population to at least 200 birds as soon as possible, with the hope that it might eventually reach 1000 birds; however, the remaining habitats are unlikely to support more than 200 birds (van Balen and Gepak 1994). Although many Bali Mynah chicks are produced in captivity, their survival rate has been low. Postmortem examinations reveal the consistent presence of a coccidian parasite, atoxoplasmosis (*Isospora* spp). Concern that this pathogen may be introduced into the wild population following translocation has led to construction of a quarantine facility at Surabaya Zoo in east Java.

The major unknown in the Bali Mynah recovery plan is whether or not atoxoplasmosis is present in wild birds. If it is, then captive birds should be exposed to the pathogen while in captivity to stimulate antibody production; otherwise, the shock of infection may reduce survival in translocated birds. In contrast, if atoxoplasmosis is absent in the wild population, then its introduction by captive-bred birds may increase mortality in the few surviving wild birds. Thus, it is crucial that birds scheduled for reintroduction and the few remaining wild birds be monitored for infection.

To summarize, parasites and pathogens remain an important consideration in the management of captive and free-living populations of threatened and endangered species. Epidemiological theory suggests that pathogens shared among several species present a greater threat to the viability of endangered species than do specific pathogens. However, there is a more optimistic side to parasites and pathogens that could be used to conservation advantage: pathogens could be effectively employed as biological control agents to reduce the densities of rats, cats, and goats that present the major threat to many endangered and threatened island species. Obviously, caution has to be exercised when considering the introduction of any pathogen into the wild, so this method of pest control should be restricted to isolated oceanic islands (Dobson 1988). However, the majority of extinctions recorded to date in wild populations have occurred on oceanic islands (Diamond 1989).

Clearly, parasites and diseases are emerging as important considerations in the management of endangered species. The enormous expansion of our ecological understanding of parasites and their hosts in the last 15 years means that ecologists now see a predictable structure in conditions that foster disease outbreaks. Epidemics can no longer be considered purely stochastic events that occur as random catastrophes. We now have a significant mathematical framework that delineates the general conditions under which a disease outbreak will occur (Anderson and May 1986, 1991; Grenfell and Dobson 1995). A major challenge for conservation biologists is to apply and extend this framework so that it can minimize the disease risk to endangered species of plants and animals.

The Loss of Plants and Birds in Hawaii. The contrast between the American chestnut experience and that of the loss of Hawaiian plants is striking. About half of the bird species of Hawaii went extinct after the islands' discovery by Polynesians over a millennium ago. Approximately half of the remaining bird species went extinct after Europeans colonized Hawaii in the early

(A)

(B)

(C)

Figure 8.17 A meliphagid and two drepanidids of Hawaii are all specialized as nectar feeders. The Hawaii O'o (A) and Molokai Black Mamo (B) are extinct. The I'iwi (C) is extinct on Lanai and Molokai and endangered on Oahu, but survives elsewhere. These birds' declines and extinctions may be a result of losses of the nectar-producing plants that constituted their food sources. (A and B, photographs by Bishop Museum; C, by Jaan Lepson.)

1800s, and about half of those remaining are now endangered (Freed et al. 1988). These patterns of extinction and survival are closely tied to plant species extinctions.

Two families of nectivorous birds are of particular interest. Three of the five endemic meliphagid species are extinct, and the other two are probably extinct. One meliphagid, the Hawaii O'o, and two related species of drepanidids, the Black Mamo and I'iwi, have peculiar nectar-feeding bills (Figure 8.17); the first two are extinct, and the third is extinct on two islands, very rare on a third, and has declined on others. All these extinctions may have followed the destruction of important nectar-producing plants by introduced goats and pigs. A native hibiscus, *Hibiscadelphus*, a rich source of nectar, is now exceedingly rare. Many of the native lobelliods (such as the genera *Trematolobelia* and *Clermontia*; Figure 8.18) have clearly evolved to be pollinated by the three drepanidids; they have corollas that fit the birds' unusual beaks (Figure 8.18). Some parts of this remarkable plant radiation are extinct, and other parts are very rare; at least one species has only one individual remaining in the wild.

Figure 8.18 *Trematolobelia kauaensis* is an example of the Lobeliacae, a family that experienced adaptive radiation on Hawaii. Many of these species, which were pollinated by nectar-feeding birds and provided major foods for those birds, are now extinct. The plant extinctions were likely caused by depredations of introduced pigs and goats, and in turn may have caused various bird extinctions. (Photograph by Stuart L. Pimm.)

Some surviving Hawaiian birds also seem to be unusually specialized species and are threatened as a consequence. Another rare drepanidid is the Akiapola'au, an insectivore, which feeds in forests of large koa trees. The koa forest is being lost because the trees are felled for their attractive wood. A granivore, the Palila, is endangered because it depends almost exclusively on the seeds of one tree, the mamane, which is declining because of introduced goats and sheep. The ranges of frugivorous thrushes in Hawaii are declining because the loss of a small number of fruiting species may prevent the thrushes from having a year-round food supply (van Riper and Scott 1979). Thus, in contrast to the loss of the American chestnut tree, most of whose herbivores were polyphagous, the loss of various Hawaiian trees is having a much more devastating effect on their specialized feeders. The problems of alien species in Hawaii, as well as efforts to deal with them, are further elaborated in Essay 8D by Lloyd Loope.

Species Invasions: A Summary. We wish to summarize the arguments we have presented by emphasizing four features of species invasions. First, all species introductions and losses are not equal in their effects on the community. Second, which species will invade depends on the particular characteristics of individual species and the potential host community. Which species will have major effects once they have invaded also depends on these characteristics.

ESSAY 8D

The Hawaiian Islands as a Laboratory for Addressing Alien Species Problems

Lloyd Loope, Biological Resources Division, U.S. Geological Survey

Alien species are increasingly recognized as a threat to biological diversity and human welfare worldwide, not just on islands. A gathering of representatives from 80 countries at a United Nations conference in mid-1996 produced the following conclusion:

> Invasive species were identified as a serious global threat to biological diversity, and in some countries the most important threat. Such species threaten the natural and productive systems which they invade and have in many cases caused disruption of ecological systems, homogenization of biota, and extinctions. This has often resulted in significant environmental, economic, health, and social problems, imposing costs in the billions of dollars and seriously affecting a large number of people. (Norway/UN Conference on Alien Species, 1996)

Although the Hawaiian Islands are by no means typical of the world, they provide a microcosm of alien species problems and attempts at solutions. Located near the middle of the Pacific Ocean, Hawaii is increasingly important as an international transportation hub. Honolulu International Airport is the 17th busiest in the world in terms of total passenger traffic; military air traffic is also substantial. The state is a social melting pot, with much movement of cultural trappings such as ethnic fruits and vegetables into and out of the islands. Tourism is the primary industry, and visitors come from all over the world. Some like Hawaii so much they decide to move there, and many bring attractive plants from home or from tropical areas throughout the world. Agriculture also is an important industry, resulting in much movement of living materials into and out of Hawaii. All this activity results in the frequent arrival of new alien species. An average of 20 new immigrant species of invertebrate animals per year established themselves in Hawaii between 1961 and 1990; about half of these are considered pests, and about 1 in 20 are serious economic threats.

What Is Biologically Special about Hawaii?

Over evolutionary time, the few animals and plants that reached Hawaii over thousands of kilometers of open ocean found remarkably diverse habitats. The approximately 10,000 species of land-dwelling animals and plants of Hawaii—most of them endemic—are believed to have evolved on the islands in near-complete isolation, arising from roughly 2,000 ancestors that arrived by chance over 70 million years. A few successful colonizing species are the sources of spectacular evolutionary adaptive radiations—the Hawaiian honeycreepers, the vinegar flies, and the silverswords, for example. The Galápagos Islands have gained considerable fame from Charles Darwin's observations of classic species radiations among the island group's animals during his 1835 visit-observations that subsequently contributed to Darwin's theory of evolution. The Hawaiian Islands, however, have become an even more important site for modern evolutionary studies because their native animals and plants have had a much longer period of evolution in isolation and a much greater variety of habitats to occupy.

Hawaii's Biodiversity Crisis and Efforts to Cope with It

Oceanic island ecosystems in general, and the Hawaiian Islands in particular, are highly susceptible to damage that is caused by humans and the alien plants and animals they bring with them. Because of their evolution in relative isolation and in the absence of many of the forces that affect continental organisms, ecosystems of the Hawaiian Islands are particularly vulnerable to invasion by alien species from continents. More native species have been eliminated in Hawaii than anywhere else in the United States and in most places in the world. Although habitat destruction has been a major cause of extinction and endangerment, the introduction of alien species has contributed in a major way in the past, and is now the predominant cause of biodiversity loss in Hawaii.

Until the 1970s, an open-minded approach to alien species—and acceptance of "inevitable" deterioration—prevailed in Hawaii. Events at Hawaii Volcanoes National Park in the 1970s began to change the mindset of managers of Hawaiian natural areas from acceptance of deterioration to proactive management, which attempts to reverse deterioration and safeguard the large and remarkably intact areas of persisting native biological diversity. Until 1970, 15,000–20,000 feral goats had the undisputed run of the park, and were well on their way toward eliminating the native vegetation. Although thousands of goats had been removed over the years, no lasting population reduction had been achieved. The demonstrated value of small, fenced feral ungulate exclosures proved a powerful impetus toward overcoming bureaucratic inertia. A small group of dedicated park managers initiated a program to fence the park boundary and to eliminate goats within the fence. Significant shifts in funding were made within the park, and new funding strategies were pursued aggressively. As of the 1990s, Hawaii Volcanoes and Haleakala National Parks are goat-free. Pig removal programs are also well advanced, and native vegetation is recovering in both of these prime natural areas. This has been achieved in spite of budget limitations, irate hunters (many of whom believed that hunting in the parks was not only their right but also an important part of their heritage), and animal rights activists.

Inspired by their successes in managing feral ungulates, managers have undertaken the equally challenging problem of alien plant proliferation. An integrated approach to this problem has been adopted within natural areas, including elimination of incipient populations to nip aggressive invasions in the bud, elimination of peripheral populations to slow their spread, control within Special Ecological Areas (largely intact stands of diverse native vegetation with associated fauna), biological controls, and concurrent basic and applied research. As of the 1990s, these approaches, which require extensive interagency cooperation, are being adopted island-wide and statewide.

Federal and state managers of protected areas in Hawaii (primarily National Parks, State Natural Area Reserves, and private reserves) are struggling, with some success, to mitigate the effects of alien species on the native biota. In recent years, there has been an increasing realization that the future of these protected areas may depend more than anything else on success in keeping new alien plant and animal species from becoming established. It is apparent that many aggressive plant and animal species not yet established in Hawaii (such as the brown tree snake, discussed earlier) could, if introduced, exploit and modify habitats not yet threatened by any established alien species. There is an understanding that unless this insidious threat is combated with ingenuity and commitment, alien species can be expected to proliferate and inundate all but the most resistant native ecosystems in protected areas of Hawaii. And in view of the difficulty and expense of controlling invasive species after they are established, preventing the establishment of new introductions appears not only cost-effective, but essential.

A Developing Alliance for Improved Alien Species Management in Hawaii

Much conceptual progress has been made in the 1990s in addressing the alien species problem in Hawaii. With leadership by The Nature Conservancy of Hawaii and the Hawaii Department of Agriculture, an alliance of biodiversity, agriculture, health, and business interests is emerging to address the pest crisis. This alliance has focused, for example, on the early formation of partnerships among parties regarded as key to any successful pest management program and on assessing the full costs of the impact of alien pests on Hawaii's economy. Emphasis is being placed on raising public awareness in order to build political support for the new tools needed to stem the flow of new alien species and to more effectively control those species that enter the islands. The most serious need is for tools that help to target problem species, especially in the form of risk assessment to identify potential pests, sampling systems to identify and monitor "leaks" in port-of-entry inspections, and surveillance to detect newly established pests while eradication or containment is still possible. The Hawaii program can serve as a useful model of these or other elements of national or global strategies for alien species management.

Third, decisions about which species invasions are likely to be important and which communities are likely to be vulnerable require a very broad range of ecological expertise, and may be quite complicated. Problems in conservation biology frequently do not fit easily into the small pigeonholes (physiological ecology, avian community ecology, and so forth) our academic training creates. Interdisciplinary thinking is necessary to understand these problems.

Finally, conservation biologists have to make decisions based on what we know now. Experiments may be impossible for many reasons, including lack of time or money. We must often choose priorities using incomplete knowledge of surrogate systems. Our recommendation that special attention be paid to the potential introduction of *Boiga* to Hawaii has only a little to do with what we know about the snake in its native range. It is based more on what we know about introductions of species in general, on the effects of this species elsewhere, and particularly, about the vulnerability of islands to exotics. Often, the evidence we must marshal is less than satisfactory, yet its conservation implications may be huge. For example, few, if any, stories of secondary extinctions are better than anecdotes. But we cannot afford to ignore the possibility of secondary extinctions just because it is hard to collect rigorous data and impossible to perform experiments. The problems are immediate, and the science will be driven by them, not by taxonomic or methodological preferences.

Overabundance of Native Species

An emerging problem in conservation biology that is separate from, but related to, the problem of species introductions is overabundance of native species (Garrott et al. 1993). In many places, anthropogenically altered environments have proved favorable to a subset of native species, resulting in expansions of their populations to the detriment of other native species. These expansions are not much different in their effects from invasions of exotics. Garrott et al. (1993) stated: "Similar to exotic species, overabundant or expanding native species can reduce natural diversity by monopolizing resources, introducing or spreading infectious diseases and parasites, changing the spe-

Table 8.3
North American Species That Have Proven a Problem in Their Native Habitats Due to Overabundance

Cattail	*Typha* spp.
Common sunflower	*Helianthus annuus*
Prickly pear	*Opuntia* spp.
Beaver	*Castor canadensis*
Brown-headed Cowbird	*Molothrus ater*
Canada Goose	*Branta canadensis*
Cottontail rabbit	*Sylvilagus* spp.
Coyote	*Canis latrans*
Gray fox	*Urocyon cinereoargenteus*
Gray squirrel	*Scirus carolinensis*
Gulls	*Larus* spp.
Muskrat	*Ondontra zibethicus*
Opossum	*Didelphus virginiana*
Pocket gopher	*Thomomys* spp.
Raccoon	*Procyon lotor*
Raven	*Corvus corax*
Red fox	*Vulpes vulpes*
Red squirrel	*Tamiasciurus hudsonicus*
Red-winged Blackbird	*Agelaius phoeniceus*
Striped skunk	*Mephitus mephitus*
White-tailed deer	*Odocoileus virginianus*

From Garrott et al. 1993

cies composition or relative abundance of sympatric species, and even causing local extinctions." They listed many examples of such species that have had negative effects on their native ecosystems due to their superabundance (Table 8.3); many of these are mid-sized omnivores that do especially well in domesticated landscapes. Such population expansions can be every bit as damaging as successful invasions of exotic species.

Changes in Evolutionary Time

We have seen that losses of keystone species or mutualists, or additions of exotic species, can have drastic, negative effects on communities and ecosystems, and that disturbance regimes are an important factor in determining levels of biodiversity. But how unexpected are changes in species composition in the long-term picture of ecological communities? Is it that unusual for species to drop out of or be added to a community? What are the long-term patterns, and what can they tell us about conservation of ecological communities? To answer such questions, we must examine communities over longer periods of time.

In addition to the normal, short-term changes that occur in ecological time and can be observed even within the lifetime of a single conservationist, long-term changes, over thousands to tens or hundreds of thousands of years, are also occurring. Studying these changes can shed further light on community patterns and processes relevant to conservation. For example, are communities stable and predictable over the longer haul? Do species associations and interactions remain constant over centuries? Do communities respond as a unit to global changes such as glacial advances and retreats? Or does community composition change over these longer time periods, with some species being lost as other species spread, and with fluid associations and interactions over time?

Evidence over both longer-term (millions of years) and shorter-term (tens of thousands of years) evolutionary time scales indicates that many plant and animal communities are in fact quite fluid and have changed appreciably throughout their histories. Addressing first the longer term, we know that diversity of marine invertebrates (Bambach 1986) and terrestrial plants (Knoll 1986) has increased over many millions of years (see also Chapter 4). In the case of marine organisms, this took the form of an increase in the number of guilds, as new methods of predation or new ways of exploiting a particular environment developed, rather than a packing of existing guilds more tightly. Also, as species of coral reef organisms disappeared over about 10 million years, reef structure did not collapse, but community structure changed. Thus, community structure, and therefore species interactions, do not remain stagnant, but change over evolutionary time.

The shorter-term geologic record contains even better evidence for the impermanence of community structure. Davis (1986) and Delcourt and Delcourt (1987) analyzed records of pollen deposition in Quaternary (from 2 million years ago) and Holocene (from 10,000 years ago) plant communities in North America. There were time lags of decades to centuries in the responses of some plant species to climatic changes such as glaciation, meaning that some species in a community shifted their distribution before others. Consequently, forest communities that are similar today may have quite different temporal histories, and a given species may have been in place for very different lengths of time in different locations (Figure 8.19). In New Hampshire, for example, maple (*Acer* spp.) arrived 9000 years ago, hemlock (*Tsuga canadensis*) 7500 years ago, and beech (*Fagus grandifolia*) 6500 years ago. In Wisconsin, maple

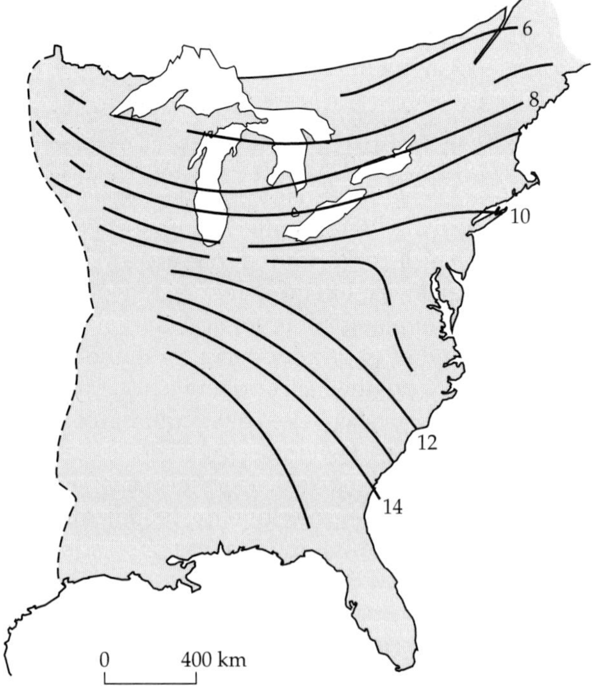

Figure 8.19 The northward range expansion of maple (*Acer*) in eastern North America from glacial refuges in the southern Mississippi Valley during the Holocene period. Lines represent thousands of years before present when maples first appeared at that point along the advancing front. The shaded area is the present range of *Acer*. (From Davis 1981.)

arrived 7000 years ago and hemlock and beech only 2000 years ago. Beech arrived before hemlock in central Michigan, but hemlock preceded beech in northern Michigan. Oak–hickory communities in southern Michigan have existed 5000 years longer than those in Connecticut (Davis 1981).

The point is, contemporary plant communities may have very different histories of association depending on their locations, and thus different histories of species interactions. These communities are not necessarily set in any particular configuration of species; if certain species are added or removed, the communities probably will continue to function normally. As stressed earlier, however, the question important to conservationists is: which species can be added or lost without major repercussions to the rest of the community? Although the overall mix of species commonly changes over long time periods, there is no evidence that strong mutualistic interactions are easily decoupled. An interesting question remains: "Are the species that are most likely to leave communities those that either have redundant ecological roles or are only weakly coupled to other species (e.g., the "passenger species" mentioned earlier in the chapter)?"

Delcourt and Delcourt (1987) indicated that contemporary North American temperate forests must be better understood in the context of long-term changes. In particular, because 90% of the Quaternary period has been glaciated, temperate zone plant communities have been shaped by conditions very different from those we see today. Vegetational dynamics in eastern North America range from a long-term equilibrium, to alternating periods of equilibrium and disequilibrium, to continual disequilibrium. For example, low-latitude forests have maintained the greatest integrity and stability in a dynamic equilibrium throughout the last 20,000 years. Mid-latitude forests were in one dynamic equilibrium state during glaciation, but shifted to a new equilibrium after glacial retreat. Postglacial forests at high latitudes were initially in disequilibrium, but tended toward an equilibrium in more recent times. In the Pacific Northwest, Douglas firs began domination of that area only about 10,000 years ago, and their old-growth forests have existed for only 5000 to 7000 years (Brubaker 1988). The species of a particular contemporary forest thus may have a relatively long period of association under relatively constant conditions, or its species composition may be a more recent phenomenon affected by disturbance and environmental change.

Animals show similar patterns of community change over the long term. Graham (1986) indicated that there were some 22 glaciations of the Northern Hemisphere during the last million years, during which northern and montane mammal species moved southward and downslope, respectively. Many arctic mammals occurred in presently temperate regions of the United States and Europe (Figure 8.20), and temperate species moved toward the tropics. In reference to these movements, Graham addressed the question of how old ecological communities are today. He concluded that distributional shifts during the Quaternary period were not wholesale, community-level movements, but individual species responses to environmental changes. Species migrated in different directions at different times and for different distances, thereby changing community structure at any location. There was great intermingling of mammalian faunas at different times, with no modern analogues for some of the resulting communities (Graham et al. 1996). In some cases, arctic and boreal faunas mixed with temperate faunas rather than displacing them. Modern mammalian communities in regions affected by glaciation are geologically young, less than 10,000 years old.

Van Devender's (1986) studies of packrat middens in the Chihuahuan Desert of North America confirm these patterns. Vegetation in that region

Figure 8.20 An example of change in geographic distribution of a small mammal after glacial periods. The Greenland collared lemming (*Dicrostonyx groenlandicus*) was found as far south as West Virginia during the late Pleistocene (dots), but occurs today only in boreal regions. (From Graham 1986.)

changed in the late Pleistocene (starting about 11,000 years ago) from pinyon–juniper–oak woodland to oak–juniper woodland to desert grassland, and finally to Chihuahuan Desert scrub about 4000 years ago. The ancient stashes of seeds and animal parts left by packrats indicate that many present desert animals lived in the same general places in the late Pleistocene, but in different habitats; they were not tightly associated with particular plant communities, but switched to new ones as plant communities changed. These changes, however, occurred slowly compared with patterns of contemporary habitat destruction and alteration.

Of course, not all communities have changed so drastically over evolutionary time. Some, such as the deeper parts of the oceans, are presumably more stable, having been little affected by sea level changes during glacial advances and retreats. Similarly, communities in tropical regions may have had longer periods of association, again having been disrupted less by global climatic change (although there is evidence of significant changes in community composition in the tropics, Colinvaux et al. 1989). Because of these possibly longer-term associations, such communities may have developed stronger coevolutionary relationships, and may be more cohesive units than more recently formed communities.

What does the age of a community association tell us about conservation efforts and policy? What does knowledge of an association's age tell us about the importance of retaining the system and species interactions intact? Older communities, those that have existed in something like their present states for longer periods, may be more vulnerable to outside disturbance and change than are younger systems. These older communities may have had time to develop more and tighter interspecific interactions such as mutualisms, and individual species may be more dependent upon such interactions. For example, there are many intricate and highly specific pollination and seed dispersal systems in tropical forests, more so than in temperate or boreal regions. If such systems are disturbed by humans, the disruption may have greater consequences than similar changes in temperate regions.

This is not to say that communities at higher latitudes, or those that regularly undergo natural disturbances, can be freely disturbed by humans and not be affected. Rather, such communities may be more resistant or resilient to anthropogenic disturbance than are the more complex communities of the tropics or the more stable communities of the deep oceans. But the picture is more complicated than that. Regions with low rates of productivity, such as tundra and deserts, are famous for the effects of even minor disturbances—such as wheel tracks from early pioneers—remaining visible for many decades or even centuries afterward. Productivity therefore must also be considered when estimating possible damage to a community from an artificial disturbance.

Understanding the short- and long-term historical changes evident in many communities makes their conservation today even more challenging. Contemporary biotic changes such as species additions and deletions are superimposed upon a dynamic and somewhat uncertain evolutionary history. We know that species composition changes over time, but we usually do not understand the local causes and effects of such changes. It would be easier to conserve contemporary systems if they were historically stable and unchanging; we could simply (at least in theory) strive to maintain native species compositions as we found them, or as we suspect them to have been before the influence of humans. However, ecological and evolutionary history tells us that there is no set endpoint for the biotic composition of communities. What constitutes a "natural" northern temperate forest or dry savanna? Because their species compositions have changed over time, there is no clear target for contemporary conservation.

What we can do is realize that these historical changes typically occurred over much longer time periods than the changes now being imposed on natural systems by humankind. Slow climatic changes over centuries, set in a completely wild matrix, afford ecological systems opportunities to gradually adjust to change, while eliminating a pollinator with pesticide application over one month, or introducing a novel predator over one season, does not. The anthropogenic influences throughout the world that are changing species interactions and community compositions are merely one more in a long series of ecological insults, but one for which the evolutionary history and genetic variation of species has not prepared them. Minimizing such influences is clearly a reasonable conservation goal.

Summary

By definition, conservation of bio*diversity* must ultimately reach beyond the species level and consider communities and ecosystems. Knowledge of a community's critical components and strong interactions, such as keystone species and mutualisms, can focus and guide conservation efforts. A species may be a keystone component because of some aspect of its trophic ecology, such as being an important predator, changing habitat structure through its foraging efforts, or providing a critical food resource. Mutualisms create critical links among species that perform a function, such as pollination or seed dispersal, that may be critical to continued community composition.

Changes occur in communities over ecological time for a variety of reasons, but especially relevant to conservation are natural disturbance regimes and introductions of exotic species. Virtually all natural communities experience a normal disturbance regime, such as fire, flooding, drought, herbivory, or storm damage. Understanding the scale, frequency, and intensity of natural disturbances is critical to conservation at the community level. Continuance of normal disturbance regimes at appropriate scales should be encouraged, and new, artificial disturbances should be avoided. An especially devastating type of new disturbance is invasion by exotic species. Many examples exist of the destructive effects of both plant and animal invasions. Their success depends on the characteristics of both the particular invader and the particular communities invaded, and is difficult to predict a priori. All species introductions to and losses from communities are not equal with respect to their community effects; some may be quite benign, while others can be devastating.

Long-term studies of ecological communities and ecosystems over evolutionary and geologic time shed more light on community and ecosystem conservation. Many communities, especially in temperate zones, have been dynamic over spans of thousands of years, and some may be relatively new in evolutionary time. Species additions to or deletions from communities over evolutionary time are often independent; that is, many communities do not seem to be cohesive, tightly woven units that remain together over time, but rather assemblages of species that continually enter and leave the picture. Such communities may be less susceptible to human disturbance than are communities with long-term associations that have evolved complicated species interactions. Thus, the changes wrought by humans on natural communities are superimposed upon a historical dynamism in many cases. This knowledge makes conservation more difficult, but provides another perspective on ecological change that should be incorporated into management efforts.

Questions for Discussion

1. How might you determine whether a particular species is a keystone species in a given area? What sorts of approaches might you use?
2. If species X is determined to be a keystone species in reserve Y, is that good evidence that it is also a keystone species in reserve Z, or outside of any reserves?
3. How could you determine what factors are important in predisposing a particular invasion to success or failure? What types of data for the species and the system would help you out?
4. If climatic change over evolutionary time repeatedly has caused shifts in species ranges and community structures, why should we be concerned with conservation of these communities today? Aren't human-induced

changes simply another form of the disturbance that natural communities have had to deal with for eons?

5. We stated that not all species interactions in a community are equal. How might you evaluate which interactions in a given community have disproportionately large effects?
6. Following up on Question 5, should we work harder to prevent a species' extinction if it is shown to be a strong interactor? That is, should a species' role in a community have bearing on conservation efforts to prevent its untimely extinction?

Suggestions for Further Reading

Brown, J. H. 1995. *Macroecology.* University of Chicago Press, Chicago. Brown proposes and advocates ecological studies on a broader, less detailed scale than the typical reductionist studies that are the norm of the field. He advocates a macroscopic view of ecology and conservation, emphasizing geographic and historical patterns, as a supplement to small-scale experimental studies to address the questions that concern us.

Diamond, J. and T. J. Case (eds.). 1986. *Community Ecology.* Harper & Row, New York. An excellent overview of issues in community ecology by a large group of authors. This book covers experimental methods in ecology, species introductions and extinctions, the relevance of spatial and temporal scales, equilibrium and nonequilibrium communities, the various forces structuring communities, and various types of communities.

Drake, J. A., H. A. Mooney, F. di Castri, R. H. Groves, F. J. Kruger, M. Rejmanek, and M. Williamson (eds.). 1989. *Biological Invasions: A Global Perspective.* John Wiley & Sons, New York. A very comprehensive review of biological invasions around the world. The topics cover a variety of ecosystems and numerous species and concepts. This book provides an excellent overview of biological invasions.

Pickett, S. T. A. and P. S. White (eds.). 1985. *The Ecology of Natural Disturbance and Patch Dynamics.* Academic Press, Orlando, FL. This seminal work stimulated the current interest in and awareness of disturbances and patches in ecological systems. Twenty-one chapters cover a broad array of disturbance topics relative to plants and animals.

Pimm, S. L. 1991. *The Balance of Nature? Ecological Issues in the Conservation of Species and Communities.* University of Chicago Press, Chicago. A good compilation of a large amount of information regarding community ecology and conservation. Pimm reviews such topics as community resilience, temporal variation of species and the environment, extinctions, food web structure, species introductions, and the vast and complex experimental and observational literature on communities.

Schultze, E.-D. and H. A. Mooney (eds.). 1994. *Biodiversity and Ecosystem Function.* Springer-Verlag, Berlin. The two broad themes addressed by the various authors of this book are the role of individuals in ecosystem function and the functional role of biodiversity in the ecosystem. Includes a general treatment of ecosystem function, functional groups (mostly fungi and higher plants), species interactions, and good treatments of important concepts such as keystone species, redundancy, diversity and succession, and stability.

Simberloff, D., D. C. Schmitz, and T. C. Brown (eds.). 1997. *Strangers in Paradise: Impact and Management of Nonindigenous Species in Florida.* Island Press, Washington, D.C. Despite its narrow focus on Florida, this very comprehensive overview of nonindigenous species problems has widespread relevance. Topics include the history and patterns of introductions, taxonomic reviews of introductions, methods for managing nonindigenous species, and the regulatory framework surrounding introductions.

Strong, D. R., Jr., D. Simberloff, L. G. Abele, and A. B. Thistle. 1984. *Ecological Communities: Conceptual Issues and the Evidence.* Princeton University Press, Princeton, NJ. This collection of papers covers many of the highly contentious issues in community ecology, and challenges some of the earlier concepts of community patterns and stability. It also emphasizes the more rigorous, experimental approaches to understanding community structure and function.

9

Habitat Fragmentation

frag•ment (frăg'mənt) n. 1. A part broken off or detached from a whole. 2. Something incomplete; an odd bit or piece . . .

The American Heritage Dictionary

Alteration of habitats by human activity is the greatest threat to the richness of life on earth. The most visible form of habitat alteration is direct habitat removal, as when a forest is clear-cut, a wetland is drained, a stream is dammed to create a reservoir, or a remnant prairie is converted to a shopping mall. However, if we step back and view the broader landscape, as from a mountain peak or an airplane, often the most striking pattern we see is the **fragmentation** of a once continuous natural landscape into odd bits and pieces.

Habitat fragmentation is generally considered to have two components: (1) reduction of the total amount of a habitat type, or perhaps of all natural habitat, in a landscape; and (2) apportionment of the remaining habitat into smaller, more isolated patches (Harris 1984; Wilcove et al. 1986; Saunders et al. 1991). Although the latter component is fragmentation in the literal sense, it usually occurs in tandem with widespread deforestation or other habitat reduction. Conservation biologists should perhaps try harder to separate literal fragmentation from the larger problem of habitat loss (Fahrig 1996); the two processes are not always coupled. For example, in managed forest landscapes, there are ways vegetation can be removed without fragmenting the remaining forest (Franklin and Forman 1987; Harris and Silva-Lopez 1992). In some cases, a landscape may be more "shredded" than fragmented (discussed in Essay 9A by Peter Feinsinger). In other cases, "variegation," or creation of a shifting, fuzzy-edged mosaic of varying suitability, more accurately describes the result from the standpoint of species' habitat requirements (McIntyre and Barrett 1992; Ingham and Samways 1996). Nevertheless, the end result of human settlement and resource extraction in a landscape is often a patchwork of small, isolated natural areas in a sea of developed land (Figure 9.1). The forces behind such landscape conversion, and their effects, are graphically illustrated in Essay 9B by Richard Knight and John Mitchell.

Studies in many regions have documented local extinctions, shifts in species composition and abundance patterns to favor weedy species, and other forms of biotic impoverishment in fragmented landscapes (Burgess and Sharpe 1981; Noss 1983; Harris 1984; Wilcox and Murphy 1985; Saunders et al.

ESSAY 9A

Habitat "Shredding"

Peter Feinsinger, University of Northern Arizona

When modern-day humans convert a landscape and reduce the original habitat to a small fraction of its former area, the term "habitat fragmentation" is most commonly employed. This label conjures up an image of circumscribed islands of natural habitat jutting from an advancing sea of agriculture or other form of land development, isolated by quite inhospitable terrain from one another and from the nearest unconverted "continent." The insularization analogy is compelling and powerful, with the result that most work on habitat remnants and nature reserves assumes, implicitly or explicitly, that these are configured as islands. For example, MacArthur and Wilson used a fragmentation example (1967; see Figure 9.1) to lead off their classic treatise on island biogeography.

Even the debate surrounding very different physical layouts—corridors and networks—now treats these as means of connecting remnant habitats of greatest concern, assumed to be islandlike, rather than as entities themselves of conservation interest. The island analogy also underlies models of the genetic and demographic consequences of small population size (Chapters 6 and 7). The observation that "nature is patchy" generates many potent ecological concepts, such as metapopulations, source–sink topographies, dispersal–diffusion processes, and landscape mosaics. When these concepts are used to model events on landscapes of conservation concern, again we often assume that natural habitat in such landscapes is insularized. And for many landscapes the assumption is valid (Figure A).

Other configurations are possible, however. In Latin America, and I suspect in other regions, it is often difficult to find landscapes that fit the image of insularization well enough for the island analogy and its corollaries to be applied with a clear conscience. Graphic examples abound, though, of "habitat shredding." Along many advancing agricultural frontiers, and even in some stabilized agricultural landscapes, land use practices *shred* the original habitat into long, narrow strips (Figure B) rather than fragmenting it into two-dimensional isolates. Shreds of native vegetation snake along watercourses or ridges, survive on disputed boundaries between different landholders, persist as buffers between different crops, or serve as cheap (if rather ineffective) fences for cattle pasture. Shreds may be several meters wide or several hundred, encompassing hectares or thousands of hectares. Typically, shreds are not isolates; they connect directly with the as-yet-unconverted habitat (which may itself be a protected reserve) that persists beyond the invasion front. Some shreds protrude as simple peninsulas, others link with one another in complex networks, and a few, corridorlike, run into a second large tract at the far end, although this last is rare.

Does it really make a difference to the biota, or to its investigators, whether habitats are fragmented or shredded? *Yes!* In shredded landscapes, populations of native plants and animals do not necessarily languish in isolated, two-dimensional patches; rather, they are tentacles extending from a corpus that still resides in unconverted habitat, probing the converted countryside. The key questions are not about who persists despite low population size for how long in which sizes of fragments; they are about which populations extend outward for what distance along which sorts of shreds. Long and narrow, shreds may be "all edge." Thus, edge effects and the interaction of a shred's contents with its landscape context are of paramount importance (Forman and Godron 1986). The investigator's focus must of necessity broaden beyond the focus on contents alone that often characterizes studies of fragments.

Metapopulation models, landscape mosaic metaphors, and other "nature is patchy" concepts do not fit the shred configuration well. Instead, shredded landscapes may demand that ecologists develop new or modified models of population dynamics, demography, dispersal, and genetics, or that they apply the principles of landscape ecology (Forman and Godron 1986). Most importantly, the conservation consequences of shredded habitats may differ significantly from those of fragmented habitats.

So, what questions might conservation ecologists ask of shredded landscapes? Here are a few; I trust that readers will be able to generate many additional ones.

At the population level:

- For a given plant or animal species, what demographic changes occur along a shred?
- What genetic structure characterizes the tentacular demes occupying shreds, as compared with demes in the intact habitat? Genetically speaking, are shred populations robust or decaying?

At the community level:

- What changes in species composition occur along a peninsular shred from base to tip? Who drops out, who appears, where do these changes occur, and why?
- What is the nature of species replacement (if any) along the shred? Is there a one-for-one replacement of natives by robust opportunists and exotics, or is there a monotonic shift in species richness?
- What happens to community function, structure, and dynamics? For example, do guild structure, life-form spectrum, community-level plant phenology, and internal disturbance regimes remain fairly constant, or do these attributes change with distance along the shred?
- Does the nature of species interactions change along a shred, and if so, what are the consequences to the interactors? For example, might pollination of native flora depend on animal populations centered in habitat beyond the invasion front, and thus decline along the shred's length? In contrast, might seed predation levels respond most directly to exposure to edge, and thus remain quite constant throughout the shred's length?

At the landscape level (see also discussions in Forman and Godron 1986):

- Are edge effects constant along the length of a shred?
- How do edge effects vary with the

shred's context? For example, what differences exist among the edge effects exerted by neighboring habitat consisting of (1) unimproved cattle pasture, (2) improved cattle pasture, (3) crops of various kinds with various levels of treatment with fertilizers and pesticides, (4) variously treated shrub or tree plantations, (5) second growth of various ages and consistencies?

What sorts of interchange occur between the shred's contents and its context, and how do these vary with different contexts? Do animals native to the shredded habitat exploit, on a daily or seasonal basis, resources in the context? Do animals resident in the context exploit resources in the shred?

Do shreds merely absorb exotics from nearby converted landscapes, or do shreds spray the converted landscapes with propagules of native species?

Are shreds doomed to decay, to fade into the species composition of the converted landscape, or might they serve as reservoirs of native species for eventual restoration of that landscape?

How do shreds themselves affect the ecology of their context? Aside from effects on physical attributes such as hydrology and nutrient flow, how do shreds affect their agricultural context regarding weed control, arthropod herbivores, natural enemies of herbivores, or pollinators of animal-pollinated crop plants?

What might shredded habitats tell us about corridor design?

Thus, what role might shreds, and various shred configurations, play in the management of converted landscapes?

Figure A A fragmented landscape: Islands of "chaco serrano," a dry subtropical thorn forest, surrounded by cattle pastures and forage crops, in Tucumán Province, Argentina. (Photograph by Peter Feinsinger.)

Figure B A shredded landscape: "Selva basal," a wet subtropical forest invaded by citrus groves and sugarcane fields, in Tucumán Province, Argentina. (Photograph by Peter Feinsinger.)

In short, shredded habitats invite empirical study and modeling in their own right as ecologically interesting and significant landscape features along agricultural frontiers, in the Neotropics at least. They should arouse conservation concern as possible refuges for native species, as corridors for or barriers to exotics, and as potential reservoirs of native species for future restoration of their surroundings. Shreds' manifest potential for interchange with the developed lands surrounding them suggests a potentially critical role for them in landscape management. But how much do we really know about the ecology of shreds and their role in conservation? Aside from extensive work in European landscapes, summarized by Forman and Godron (1986), very little (which has enabled me to speculate shamelessly here). Need a research topic? Think "shreds."

This essay is not intended to disparage the "nature is patchy" perspective, an approach that has tremendous explanatory and predictive power for most landscapes and a metaphor that has guided most of this author's own research career. Many converted landscapes may fit the island analogy well, and others that now display shreds may be doing so only temporarily, as a transitional phase on the way to true insularization. Nevertheless, rather than accepting without question the island analogy, conservation ecologists working at population or community levels should allow landscapes themselves to instruct them as to which metaphor—islands, shreds, or yet another—best fits the current layout of remnant habitats, and then ask the questions most appropriate to that layout.

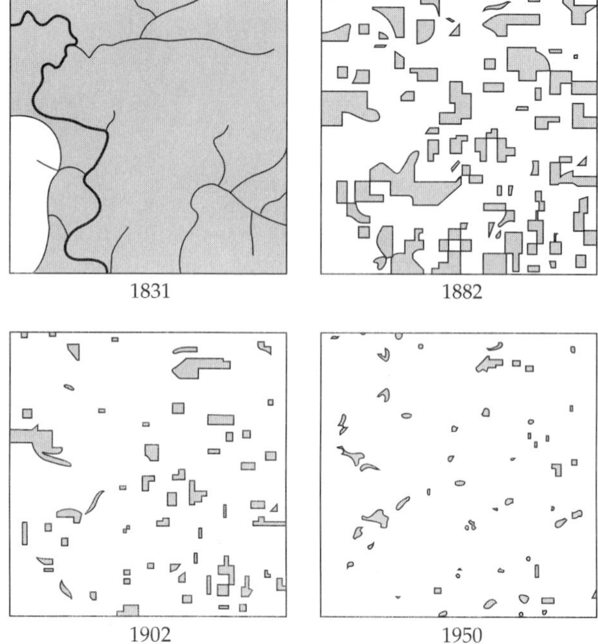

Figure 9.1 Changes in wooded area of Cadiz Township, Green County, Wisconsin, during the period of European settlement. Shaded area represents the amount of land in forest in each year. (From Curtis 1956.)

1991). Thus, fragmentation has become a major subject of research and debate in conservation biology. In this chapter, we review some differences between fragmented landscapes and naturally heterogeneous landscapes, discuss island biogeography and species–area relationships, and summarize the biological consequences of fragmentation. We conclude with recommendations for countering fragmentation, leading into the following chapter on conservation reserves.

ESSAY 9B
Subdividing the West

Richard L. Knight, Colorado State University, and John Mitchell, USDA Forest Service

It's boom time in the Rockies. Since the early 1990s, the Intermountain West of the United States has experienced population growth unlike any it has seen before. This region, consisting of eight states (Arizona, Colorado, Idaho, Montana, Nevada, New Mexico, Utah, and Wyoming) is not only the fastest-growing area in America, its growth rate rivals that of Africa and exceeds that of Mexico. For example, from 1992 to 1993, the net movement of people into this region from California alone was 72,500 (Larmar and Ring 1994). Fueled by the "floating baseline"—a concept that captures the imbalances between the high (though declining) quality of life in the West and that in other regions in America where crime, traffic congestion, air pollution, and the cost of living remain worse—it is projected that people will continue to move to this area for decades to come. Unlike past "booms" in the West, which were fueled by energy and mineral development, this growth is driven by expansion of the service, recreation, and information industries and is marked by the conversion of private agricultural lands to rural subdivisions. This "boom" may forever alter the native biodiversity of this vast region, on both private and public lands.

Until recently the West was principally urban, with most of its citizens living in cities while rural areas sustained low population densities on ranches and farms. Today, these once rural Western landscapes are experiencing rapid population growth, principally through people moving to small-acreage subdivisions. In most of America during the 1980s, metropolitan areas began growing at rates faster than nonmetropolitan areas, but not in the Intermountain West. It was the only region in America where rural counties grew faster than the metropolitan centers, such as Denver, Salt Lake City, and Albuquerque (Cromartie 1994; Theobald 1995).

In the American West, land that is not public is private, and what is not cities and towns is likely to be farmland and ranchland. Therefore, most of this rural growth is occurring on what were once farms and ranches. For example,

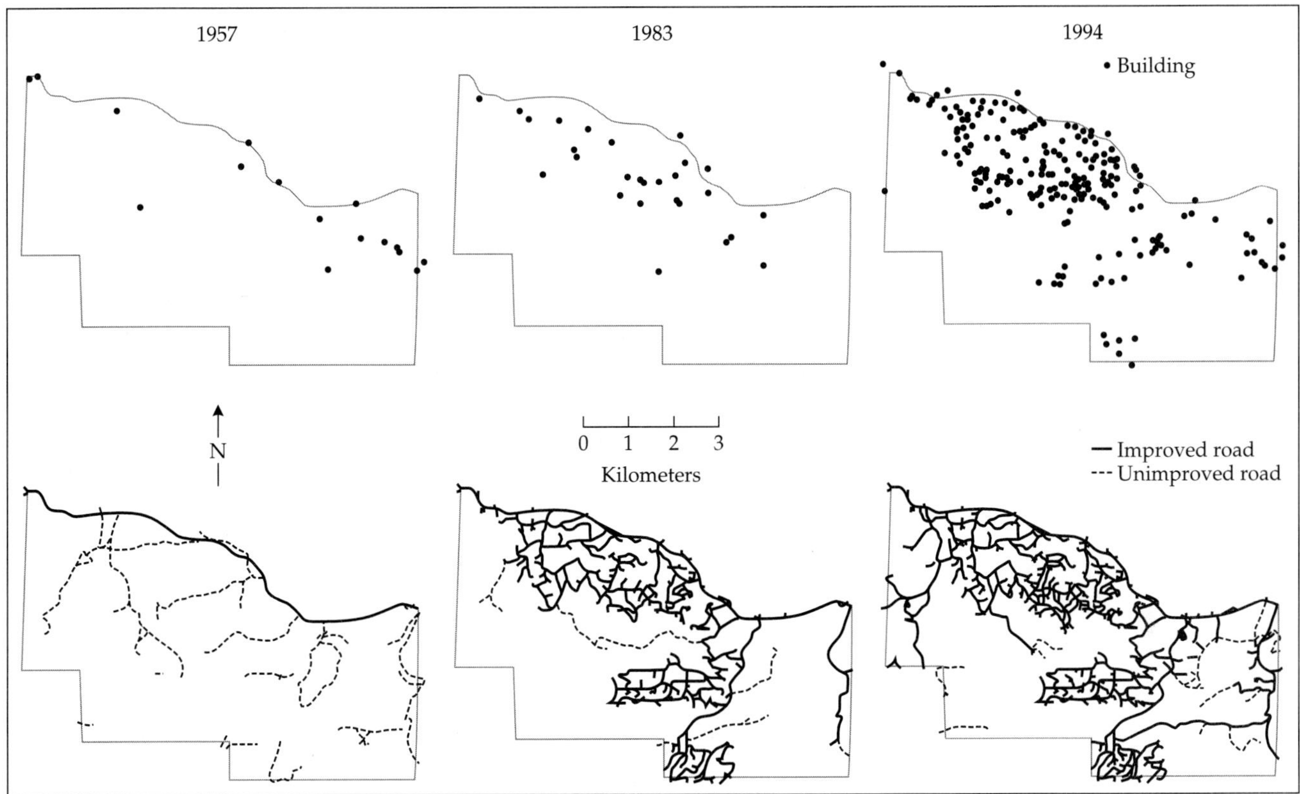

Figure A A ranch in Colorado that has been subdivided into ranchettes. The upper maps show the increase in the number of houses over time; the lower maps show the increase in access roads built to serve the ranchettes.

since 1978, Colorado ranchland and farmland has declined by 90,000 acres per year, most of it converted to subdivisions and commercial development (Colorado Department of Agriculture 1996). Between 1969 and 1987, 19% of the ranchland in Park County, Wyoming, was platted for subdivision, while in Teton County, Idaho, the rate was 16%; in Gallatin County, Montana, the rate was 23% (Greater Yellowstone Coalition 1994).

The New West is one of ranchette developments, rural subdivisions as vast as the former ranches they now occupy. This style of development is creating a new landscape, evenly sliced and diced into 20- to 40-acre parcels (Figure A). Because over half of the West is in public lands, private lands are in a minority. Because private lands are often at lower elevations and contain some of the West's most important wetlands, these areas are among some of the region's most productive sites. Based largely on the patterns of early settlement history, riparian areas became and have remained the cornerstones of much of the farmland and ranchland in the West. Today, prime development property includes wetlands, streams, and rivers. Whereas historically, human densities were low in riparian areas, today's homesites in those areas are measured in square feet rather than sections.

What are the conservation implications of this new settlement pattern in the West (Knight et al. 1995)? Two conspicuous changes associated with rural subdivisions are an increase in human density and an accompanying increase in buildings, roads, and fences (Figure A). These changes translate to more dogs and cats, more automobiles and road-killed wildlife, an increase in wildlife nuisance problems, more landscaping with nonnative plants, more security lights at night, more noise, and more people walking across the land (Figure B). Preliminary studies indicate that these changes will result in an overabundance of generalist and human-adapted species and a decline of species sensitive to humans and their activities (Vogel 1989; Tyser and Worley 1992; Schonewald-Cox and Buechner 1993; Engels and Sexton 1994; Jurek 1994; Beier 1995; Friesen et al. 1995; Knight et al. 1995; Blair 1996).

Ranches adjacent to public lands are also eagerly bought and subdivided. Suddenly, national parks, for-

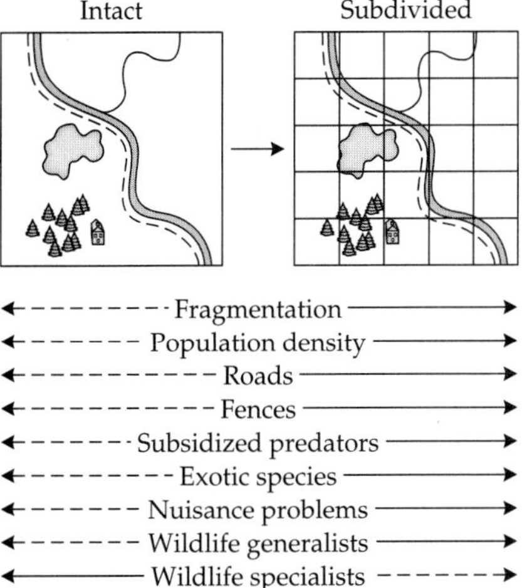

Figure B Ecological effects that result when land is subdivided into ranchettes. Solid lines indicate an increase in an effect; dashed lines indicate a decrease.

ests, and other public lands are ringed by homesites, with every home accessed by individual roads. This means a whole new suite of challenges for public land managers. Ecosystem management principles stress the management of landscapes based on ecological rather than administrative boundaries (see Essay 10A). When neighbors who view fire as a legitimate threat to their homes, rather than an ecological process that needs to be restored to the land, suddenly rim public land boundaries, does fire remain a management tool? When entry onto public lands is suddenly across the fence rather than through the entrance, what are the effects of the ranchette owner's chain saws, dogs, cats, weapons, garbage, and exotic plants? When these same lands are viewed as sources for black bears, mountain lions, and ungulates, all of which now become suspect as threats or nuisances, does wildlife win?

Given the continuing reruralization of the American West, what does the future offer for humans and the maintenance of the regional biological diversity? Will newcomers to this region come to understand how their dogs and cats, their exotic plants, their yard lights beaming through the once black night are altering the wilderness and silence they thought they were heading for? Will they come to learn how to manage their horses to minimize overgrazing, how to place their access roads to minimize soil erosion, how to live with rattlesnakes, black bears, and mountain lions? Will they learn to appreciate the sublime beauty of their own landscape so as not to build on its ridges and cliffines, or up against the streambanks? Do these ranchettes promise anything more than a crowded and congested Intermountain West (Brown and McDonald 1995)?

Because of these human settlement patterns and their associated influences, there will be a new West, one quite different from the old, and one that may very well last longer than the old. It is being created today, in the region and on the land, by the region's new inhabitants. How these once rural lands will appear, and what native biological diversity they will support, will depend on whether the new occupants listen to the land and hear what it says, and whether or not they understand and accept what the land can and cannot do (Orr 1994). Aldo Leopold gave us perhaps the best advice we can hope for when he penned these words (cited in Flader and Callicott 1991):

> But of course we must continue to live with it according to our lights. Two things hold promise of improving these lights. One is to apply science to land-use. The other is to cultivate a love of country a little less spangled with stars, and a little more imbued with that respect for mother-earth—the lack of which is, to me, the outstanding attribute of the machine-age.

Fragmentation and Heterogeneity

A superficial view of fragmentation portrays a large area of homogeneous habitat being broken up into small, isolated pieces. Thus, the unfragmented forest in Figure 9.1 is shown as uniformly gray. But the apparent homogeneity of this forest is an artifact of graphic art. If we zoom in and map forests at higher resolution (see Figures 9.2 and 9.3), we see that they are far from uniform. In fact, virtually all landscapes are mosaics at one scale or another (discussed in Essay 9C by Steward Pickett). At a landscape scale of analysis (a few kilometers across), the distribution of vegetation types typically corresponds to changes in elevation (which reflect temperature and precipitation gradients), slope, and aspect (which reflect gradients in soil moisture and other properties), as well as differences in soil parent material. This heterogeneity is vividly displayed in mountainous regions, such as the Smoky Mountains (Fig-

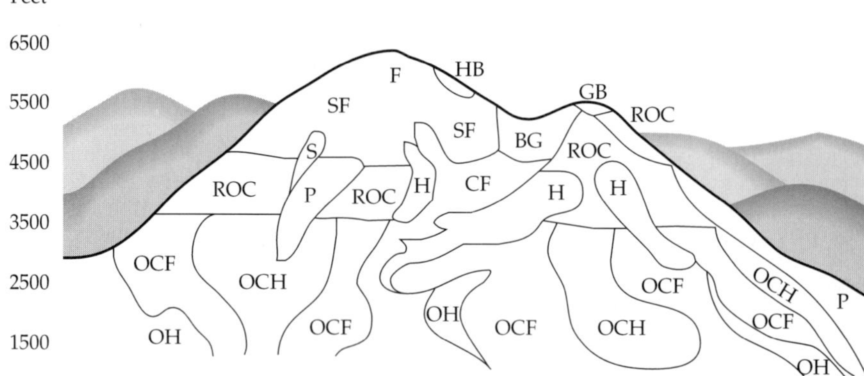

Figure 9.2 Topographic distribution of vegetation types on an idealized west-facing slope in the Great Smoky Mountains National Park. Vegetation types: BG, beech gap; CF, cove forest; F, Fraser fir; GB, grassy bald; H, hemlock; HB, heath bald; OCF, chestnut oak–chestnut; OCH, chestnut oak–chestnut heath; OH, oak-hickory; P, pine forest and heath; ROC, red oak–chestnut oak; S, spruce; SF, spruce–fir. (From Whittaker 1956.)

ESSAY 9C
Mosaics and Patch Dynamics

Steward T. A. Pickett, Institute of Ecosystem Studies, New York Botanical Garden

Mosaics are patterns composed of smaller elements, like the tile or glass works that reached an artistic zenith during the Byzantine era. One of the marvels of such mosaics is that in spite of being made of individual bits fixed in place by mortar, the best works seem animated and lively. It is ironic that a static entity can suggest such motion and liveliness.

Like mosaic art, most of the landscapes in which we must practice conservation are composed of smaller elements—individual forest stands, lakes, hedgerows, shrubland patches, highways, farms, or towns. Because the time scale of human observation is short relative to many landscape changes, people have often assumed mosaic landscapes to be static, with unchanging bits of nature and culture cemented into place.

Most often, landscape mosaics have been looked at only from the perspective of specific elements in them, rather than as an entire array that might interact. The focus may be on a stand of a rare plant, or the breeding ground of an unusual animal. The local spatial scale of observation is linked to a tacit assumption that the status of a particular population, community, or ecosystem can be understood by studying a particular patch in a mosaic. The conditions in adjoining or distant elements of the mosaic have been ignored.

Ecologists have learned, however, that these two assumptions often do not hold in the real world. First, virtually all landscapes are in fact dynamic. Although the mosaics of art only *seem* to vibrate and shimmer, mosaic landscapes *do* in fact change. Bormann and Likens (1979) coined the phrase "shifting mosaic" to label the insight that landscapes are dynamic. Landscapes may change in two ways. First, the individual elements, or patches, may arise, change size or shape, or disappear. For example, new patches may arise through logging, lightning fires, turning of prairie sod for farming, conversion of a farm to a suburb, or reforestation. Examples of changes in patch shape include encroachment of a forest into a field, or the spread of a bog into a pond. Second, the structure, function, or composition of individual patches may change. For instance, the species composition, and hence the rate of nutrient cycling, in an ecosystem may change as a result of succession. Patch dynamics is the term that incorporates all these fluid possibilities.

The second incorrect assumption about mosaics is that the elements act separately from one another. As ecologists began to look longer and more mechanistically at the dynamics of the specific sites they studied, it became increasingly clear that organisms, materials, and other influences can flow between systems, even when there are distinct boundaries between them. Thus, mammal populations in a forest may rely on food from outside the forest, certain insect populations may be maintained by migration, and some forest successions can be driven primarily by seed input rather than species interactions at the site. It is safer to assume that ecological systems in a mosaic landscape are open, rather than closed and isolated.

These changes within landscapes and fluxes among patches are crucial to conservation. Conservation strategies and tactics that ignore these two dynamic aspects of landscapes are doomed to failure. This conclusion is all the more germane in landscapes where humans, with their great mobility, energy subsidies, and insertions of novel organisms and materials into systems, are dominant influences. It is also important to realize that the dynamics of a landscape may reflect specific human behaviors and land uses, either now or in the past. So the dynamics of landscapes are in reality a complex mixture of human effects and natural effects such as land use, disturbance, and succession.

Successful conservation requires knowing what the patches are, how they change, and how they are affected by fluxes from outside the target area (or even the region). There may be important fluxes that have been halted or reversed by human activities in the landscape. Or there may be important population, community, or ecosystem processes within the site that no longer occur naturally. Conservation requires not only choosing areas in which the processes that are responsible for the existence of a conservation target are intact, but also compensating for natural or anthropogenic processes that no longer occur. Conservation is, in a sense, active maintenance of patch dynamics.

Some of the most important insights for conservation to arise from modern ecology concern the need to treat ecological systems, be they populations, communities, or ecosystems, as open to outside influences, and to manage systems to maintain the dynamics that created them. All landscapes in which we practice conservation should be treated as shifting and interconnected mosaics. The smaller or more delicate the target for conservation, the more critical the patch dynamic view becomes.

ure 9.2), but also exists in relatively flat landscapes such as the southeastern coastal plain of the United States. An elevation gradient of only a few meters in Florida may lead through a progression of longleaf pine (*Pinus palustris*) and turkey oak (*Quercus laevis*) on dry sandhills, down through flatwoods with longleaf pine, then slash pine (*P. elliottii*) on wetter sites, and sometimes pond pine (*P. serotina*) on the wettest sites. Slopes may have seepage bogs grading down into shrub swamps. This gradient-aligned vegetation pattern is a product of fire interacting with the slope moisture gradient (Wolfe et al. 1988; Noss and Harris 1990).

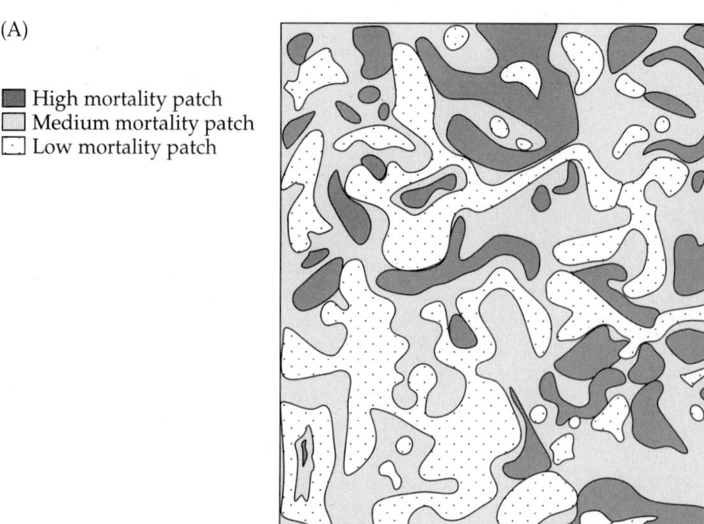

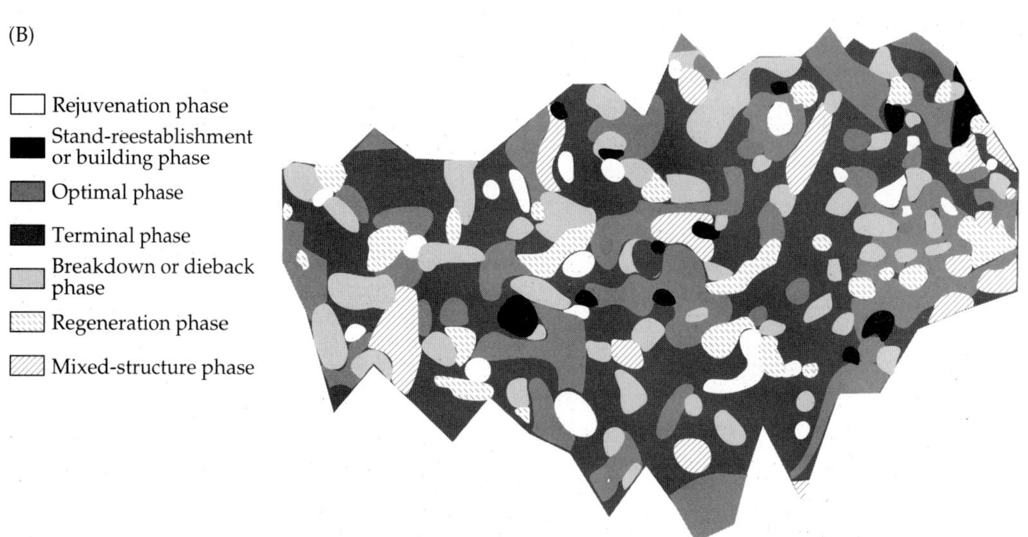

Figure 9.3 (A) Fire mortality patches for 1800 to 1900 in the Cook-Quentin study area, Willamette National Forest, Oregon. Scale is about 10 km from left to right. (B) Stand development phases in a 1 km wide section of virgin forest in Yugoslavia. Patches average about 0.5 ha in size. Phases represent stages in a continuous cycle of forest dieback and recovery. (A, from Morrison and Swanson 1990; B, from Mueller-Dombois 1987.)

Natural disturbances create considerable heterogeneity in forests and other vegetation, beyond that generated by the physical environment. The "grain" of a landscape is determined largely by the spatial scale of disturbance, that is, by the size and distribution of disturbance-generated patches. Relatively large disturbances, such as extensive fires, create a coarse-grained pattern (Figure 9.3A), whereas canopy gaps caused by death and fall of individual trees or small groups of trees create fine-grained patterns (Figure 9.3B). Because a given area often is affected by many different kinds and scales of disturbance, several grains of pattern may be overlaid on one another, increasing the diversity of the horizontal pattern. Furthermore, disturbances are typically patchy in time as well as space, so that new disturbances occur in some areas while previously disturbed sites are recovering. This continuously changing pattern has been called a space–time mosaic (Watt 1947) or shifting mosaic (Bormann and Likens 1979). Natural disturbances, especially when of moderate intensity or intermediate frequency of occurrence, generally increase the diversity of habitats, microhabitats, and species in an area.

The patterns portrayed in Figures 9.2 and 9.3 are examples of natural patchiness or horizontal complexity. Every landscape is patchy at one scale or another, and often at many scales, though some landscapes obviously are more patchy than others (Forman and Godron 1986). As a consequence of patchiness, habitat quality for species varies spatially, and many species may be distributed as metapopulations—systems of local populations linked by dispersal (discussed in Chapters 6 and 7). Because patches of habitat suitable to a species are often spatially separated, the persistence of a metapopulation is tied to the efficiency of dispersal by individuals or propagules from one patch to another (see Figures 6.10 and 7.4). If dispersal between patches becomes impossible due to distance or a lack of corridors, stepping-stone patches, or other habitats that the species of concern can travel through, then metapopulations may be destabilized.

Dispersal is more likely to maintain metapopulations in naturally patchy landscapes than in formerly continuous landscapes fragmented by human activity (den Boer 1970; Hansson 1991), probably because the organisms living in patchy landscapes are accustomed to traveling across a diverse mosaic. The metapopulation model also suggests that habitat patches currently unoccupied may be critical to species survival because they represent sites for possible recolonization. Establishing small populations on vacant patches may help prevent downward spirals in metapopulations (Smith and Peacock 1990). Although the classic model of metapopulations as sets of populations persisting in a balance between local extinction and colonization is too simplistic to depict the many types of population spatial structure found in nature (Harrison 1991, 1994), the basic model of spatially distinct population units connected by occasional dispersal seems to have considerable generality.

Recognizing that conservation biology is a value-laden science and that conservation biologists place high value on diversity, it is easy to conclude that patchiness is "good." Old-growth forests, for example, have been of interest to ecologists and conservationists in part because they are so heterogeneous. With trees of many ages, and canopies that are tall and uneven, old-growth forests have higher rates of gap formation than do younger stands (Clebsch and Busing 1989; Lorimer 1989). High levels of habitat heterogeneity, expressed horizontally and vertically, contribute to high species diversity.

But if patchiness is good, then why is fragmentation caused by humans perceived as bad? Surely fragmentation creates a patchy landscape; superficially, at least, the patterns in Figures 9.1, 9.2, and 9.3 are similar. Are conservation biologists just being misanthropic? Or are there fundamental differences between naturally patchy landscapes and fragmented landscapes? If so, what precisely are these differences? These are not trivial questions. Answering them may allow the design of land use plans and management practices that mimic natural processes and patterns and thereby maintain biodiversity; failing to answer them will probably lead to further biotic impoverishment.

The differences between naturally patchy and fragmented landscapes are only beginning to be explored scientifically. We can hypothesize that the following three distinctions are of major ecological significance:

1. A naturally patchy landscape has a rich internal patch structure (lots of tree-fall gaps, logs, and different layers of vegetation), whereas a fragmented landscape has simplified patches, such as parking lots, cornfields, clear-cuts, and tree farms with trees all of the same species and size.
2. Largely because of (1), a natural landscape has less contrast (less pronounced structural differences) between adjacent patches than does a fragmented landscape, and therefore potentially less intense edge effects.
3. Certain features of fragmented landscapes, such as roads and various human activities, pose specific threats to population viability.

In short, fragmentation creates a landscape different from that shaped by the natural disturbances to which species have adapted over evolutionary time (Noss and Cooperrider 1994). We will attempt to shed light on these differences in explaining how fragmentation threatens biodiversity. But we must admit at the outset that the mechanisms underlying the differences in the viability of populations in natural and fragmented landscapes are still largely inferred, not proven. Fragmentation is not simply the creation of habitat islands. There are many degrees and scales of fragmentation. It is a process with unpredictable thresholds, not simply an either/or condition. Furthermore, spatial heterogeneity and patchy distributions of species in intact landscapes lead to complex distributions when those landscapes are fragmented, often confounding predictions of biotic responses to fragmentation (Norton et al. 1995).

The Fragmentation Process

In terrestrial ecosystems, fragmentation typically begins with gap formation or perforation of the vegetative matrix as humans colonize a landscape or begin extracting resources there. For a while, the matrix (that is, the most common habitat type) remains as natural vegetation, and species composition and abundance patterns may be little affected (Figure 9.4). But as the gaps get bigger or more numerous, they eventually become the matrix, and the connectivity of the original vegetation is broken. By analogy, if the holes in Swiss cheese become much bigger than the cheese, the block of cheese collapses.

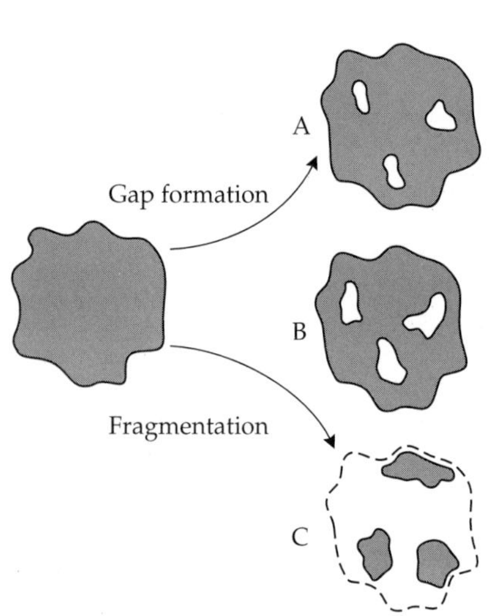

Figure 9.4 A fragmentation sequence begins with gap formation or perforation of the landscape (A). Gaps become bigger or more numerous (B) until the landscape matrix shifts from forest to anthropogenic habitat (C). (From Wiens 1989.)

Because fragmentation is a complex process involving many variables, no two landscapes are likely to show identical trajectories of change. Each landscape at any point in time will have its own unique structure, though landscapes in a given region subjected to the same kind of development or resource exploitation may have very similar patterns. Ecologists have suggested a number of measures of landscape pattern, including fractal dimension (a measure of patch size and shape complexity), contagion (the positive or negative association between patch types), and other spatial statistics (O'Neill et al. 1988; Turner 1989; Mladenoff et al. 1993; see Box 9A). Although the relevance of these statistics to conservation questions has not been firmly established, time series analysis of change in landscape pattern, as measured by various spatial statistics, can be related to changes in species composition and other expressions of biodiversity, and provides a powerful monitoring approach (Noss 1990).

The point in the fragmentation process at which biological integrity declines dramatically usually is not known, as few fragmentation studies have been conducted over a long enough period. Researchers may see the final outcome of fragmentation without observing the process; alternatively, they may observe the process, but not the long-term consequences. Fragmentation and

BOX 9A
Quantifying Landscape Pattern and Fragmentation

David J. Mladenoff, University of Wisconsin, Madison

Habitat fragmentation is an important aspect of landscape pattern, but how does one quantify fragmentation? A variety of analytic techniques exists to describe spatial patterns of landscapes (Turner and Gardner 1991), often based on the use of computerized geographic information systems (GIS) software that allows complex manipulations such as changing and combining maps and analyzing their content (Burrough 1986). These methods can produce simple summaries of mapped habitat types, including patch area, number, size class distribution, and relative abundance. Patch size class distributions can be analyzed, much the way tree size class distributions might be compared among forest stands.

Because maps often contain too much information to grasp visually, more complex indices can be calculated from basic map information, and many have been described and proposed (Turner 1989; Riitters 1995). But one must be cautious in selecting formulas that reduce great complexity to simple numerical values, as information can be lost. To select among various indices we might ask: (1) Is the scale of the map data, including the spatial extent of the mapped area, the detail of the map classes, and the resolution, appropriate to our question and analysis? (2) Does the index provide information that is biologically interpretable in relation to our question? (3) How is the index scaled numerically, and how can we interpret the range of values it generates from one landscape to another? All of these factors will affect the results of any index, so the map data must not only be appropriate to the question at hand, but must also be consistent among areas or landscapes if comparisons are made.

A number of indices begin by using the proportion *(p)* occupied by the various map classes or habitat types (O'Neill et al. 1988). The Shannon–Wiener diversity index can be used to measure landscape diversity based on the relative abundance of map classes. This is similar to how diversity might be calculated for plant or animal communities. Thus,

$$H = \frac{-\sum(p_k)\ln(p_k)}{\ln(s)}$$

Here, p_k is the proportion of the landscape occupied by map class or habitat k, s is the total number of classes in the map, ln s is the maximum diversity possible for s classes in the map, and dividing by this value scales the index from 0 to 1. Values approaching 1 indicate higher diversity or greater evenness of habitat classes in a landscape.

Other indices measure the complexity of habitat patch shapes in a landscape. For a given habitat patch area, a more complex shape will have a higher edge:interior ratio than a simpler shape, such as a circle. The amount of edge and interior can be measured directly on a map using GIS and the ratios compared, or the information can be used to calculate another type of index called the *fractal dimension.* This index is based on the relation

$$\log(A) \sim d \log(P)$$

where A is the area of a patch, P is the perimeter of the patch, and d is the fractal dimension (Krummel et al. 1987; Turner 1989). For all patches in a map or class, log (P) is regressed against log (A), yielding d, the slope of the regression line (Krummel et al. 1987). In this index, values are scaled from 1 to 2, with 1 indicating a simple, circular patch, and values approaching 2 indicating complex, convoluted patch shapes.

Another useful approach examines not only the relative abundance and shape, but also the distribution of habitat patches in order to assess their isolation. One metric of this type is called the *proximity index* (Gustafson and Parker 1992):

$$\text{PX} = \sum(S_k/n_k)$$

where S_k is the area of patch k, and n_k is the nearest-neighbor distance of patch k. The summation is calculated for a focal patch and each neighboring patch within a buffer distance that is determined by the user's needs.

Another useful group of metrics measures the contagion, or "clumpiness," of a habitat, indicating how aggregated a particular patch type is on the landscape. A related group measures the significance of association or adjacency relationships among different habitat types. Both of these metrics can reflect characteristics that may be important in assessing the quality of a landscape for particular species.

Another quite different group of techniques, known as spatial statistics or geostatistics, are not indices, but involve more complex statistical analysis of spatial patterns. For example, semivariograms are used to measure the spatial autocorrelation shown by the distribution of elements or points within a map (Burrough 1986).

The application of these tools to landscape patterns was demonstrated in a study that quantitatively compared forest patch size, shape, distribution, number, and spatial associations between an old-growth landscape and a young, managed forest (Mladenoff et al. 1993). The old-growth landscape contained a greater range of forest patch sizes. Although most patches in both landscapes were small (<5 ha), patches in the managed landscape ranged to only 200 ha, while those in the natural landscape ranged to over 1000 ha. Similarly, fractal dimension analysis showed that patches in the managed landscape were much simpler in shape than in the old-growth landscape. The natural landscape had a dominant matrix type with both larger patches and greater patch complexity, thus maximizing both forest patch interior (habitat) and interspersion (connectivity) at the same time.

Fractal dimension analysis also showed, somewhat surprisingly, that patch complexity did not increase linearly with patch size. Instead, there were three distinct peaks in patch complexity across the range of sizes for a given forest type in the natural landscape. This finding suggests that different processes may operate at various scales in patch creation of a particular forest type. Such a relationship did not occur in the managed landscape.

Adjacency analysis also showed that the natural landscape had certain significant associations of various forest types—for example, a positive association between upland hemlock *(Tsuga canadensis)* and lowland conifers—that did not occur in the more fragmented managed landscape. These relationships may be critical when a given species requires different habitat types in proximity to one another to fill different needs. They also may be important in tree species recolonization following disturbance.

The patterns we found illustrate the fragmentation of a forest into smaller, more dispersed patches that occurs within a managed landscape. This effect is increased by the greater proportion of successional types occurring in managed areas, which means that less common old forest patches are further isolated. At high forest cutting rates, these smaller, more isolated forest patches are likely to have high edge:interior ratios. The loss of a dominant matrix forest type with large, integrated forest patches and characteristic shape and adjacency relationships is the major change in managed forest landscapes.

As a result, natural, primary forest landscapes have different spatial patterns than human-disturbed or managed landscapes. Some of these patterns and their effects can be explained in relation to tree species dispersal and colonization and habitat use by animals. Analyzing landscape patterns can be useful in predicting the relative effects of management scenarios, in monitoring change through time (White and Mladenoff 1994), and in setting objectives for restoring spatial patterns hypothesized to be important for conservation and sustainable functioning of ecosystems (Mladenoff et al. 1994). Many of these hypotheses remain to be tested, and the patterns found would benefit from testing in other regions. The challenges in using these new and powerful techniques is in using them consistently, with appropriate data, and in ways that are interpretable and biologically meaningful.

---

edge effect studies in landscapes that are still largely forested typically fail to find deleterious impacts (e.g., Rudnicky and Hunter 1993) and sometimes find positive effects of fragmentation on such measures as bird diversity and abundances (McGarigal and McComb 1995). Site tenacity in birds is one of many factors that may create time lags in response to fragmentation and other disturbances. Individuals may return to a site where they have bred successfully in the past, sometimes several years after the habitat has been altered (Wiens 1985). Many models of habitat fragmentation or population subdivision ignore details of spatial structure, assuming that all habitat patches are equivalent in size or quality and that all local populations are equally accessible to dispersing individuals (Fahrig and Merriam 1994). For all these reasons, the study of fragmentation remains a topic of active research interest.

As we discuss the consequences of fragmentation in the remainder of this chapter, bear in mind that the process can occur at many different spatial and temporal scales and in any kind of habitat. Essentially, fragmentation is the "disruption of continuity" in pattern or processes (Lord and Norton 1990). At a broad biogeographic scale, regions that were once connected by wide (many kilometers) expanses of natural habitat may now be isolated by agriculture; the severance of such biogeographic corridors may take place over hundreds of years. The occasional interchanges that once took place between the faunas and floras of these regions are now precluded, with unknown evolutionary consequences. What if there had been no Bering Land Bridge or Isthmus of Panama? Migration of species in response to climate change, which in the past occurred over hundreds of kilometers (Davis 1981), may not be possible when regions are heavily fragmented (Peters and Darling 1985).

At an intermediate scale, the kind of landscape fragmentation portrayed in Figure 9.1 typically takes place over decades; this is the scale at which effects of fragmentation have usually been studied. Although sometimes we arrive too late to observe the mechanisms leading to species loss, intensive field studies of populations and communities in regions currently being fragmented may teach us a great deal.

At a finer scale, the internal fragmentation of once pristine natural areas by roads, trails, power lines, fences, canals, grazing livestock, and other human-related activities has not been well studied, but it has potentially dramatic effects on native biodiversity and ecological processes. Lord and Norton (1990) described structural fragmentation of short-tussock grasslands in New Zealand by grazing and other disturbances, which was followed by invasion of naturalized plants. They concluded that ecosystem functioning is more likely to be disrupted at finer scales of fragmentation, although the organisms affected are smaller and the overall process is less noticeable to human observers.

Insularization and Area Effects

Rapid settlement of regions such as the midwestern United States (see Figure 9.1) left behind scraps of the original vegetation as habitat fragments. The analogy with islands, though imperfect, was easy to make. Biogeographers have long known that as the area of any insular habitat declines, so does the number of species it contains. In 1855 the Swiss phytogeographer Alphonse de Candolle predicted that "the breakup of a large landmass into smaller units would necessarily lead to the extinction or local extermination of one or more species and the differential preservation of others" (cited and translated in Browne 1983). This statement may be the first written recognition of the potential negative effects of habitat fragmentation on biodiversity (Harris and Silva-Lopez 1992).

Recognition of a relationship between species number and land area goes back further, and is one of the great empirical generalizations of biogeography (see Chapter 4). Apparently the first recorded mention of a species–area effect was by Johann Reinhold Forster, a naturalist on Captain Cook's second tour of the Southern Hemisphere in 1772–1775. Forster noted that "islands only produce a greater or lesser number of species, as their circumference is more or less extensive" (Forster 1778, in Browne 1983). Subsequent studies have confirmed the species–area effect for many groups of islands and have extended it to "habitat islands" in terrestrial landscapes. More generally, a species–area relationship exists for sample plots of vegetation within continuous habitats, but the slope is less steep than for islands (Figure 9.5). On islands or in insular habitats, a tenfold decrease in habitat area typically cuts the number of species by about half (Darlington 1957).

What are the causes of the species–area relationship? This question has been long debated. As with most natural phenomena, many scientists have sought single causes for the relationship between species richness and area, although the phenomenon is almost certainly multicausal. The most straightforward explanation in many cases is habitat diversity. As area increases, so does the diversity of physical habitats and resources, which in turn support a larger number of species (Williams 1943; Lack 1976). Several studies have concluded that habitat diversity is better than area as a predictor of species diversity (Power 1972; Johnson 1975), though other studies have concluded that area itself, or some unrecognized factor correlated with area, is more important (Johnson and Raven 1973; Johnson and Simberloff 1974; Harner and Harper 1976). Disentangling the effects of area, habitat diversity, and other factors that contribute to species richness has proved difficult. Simberloff (1991) concluded that "probably, on all but very small sets of sites, the majority of the species–area relationship is accounted for by the fact that larger sites, on average, have more habitats than small ones." Studies showing that area and habitat diversity are both important for increasing species richness suggest that nature reserves should be both large and naturally heterogeneous (Freemark and Merriam 1986).

Although habitat diversity frequently provides the best explanation for species–area relationships, other factors often are at work. Possibly we could ignore biology and consider sampling theory. In a statistical population of many individuals of both rare and common species, larger samples would be expected to yield more species. Thus, passive sampling may be an appropriate null hypothesis for biological factors (Connor and McCoy 1979). Among biological explanations, species richness might increase with area because the

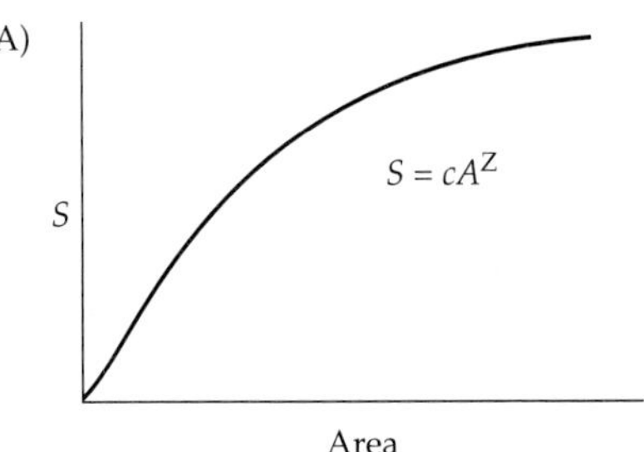

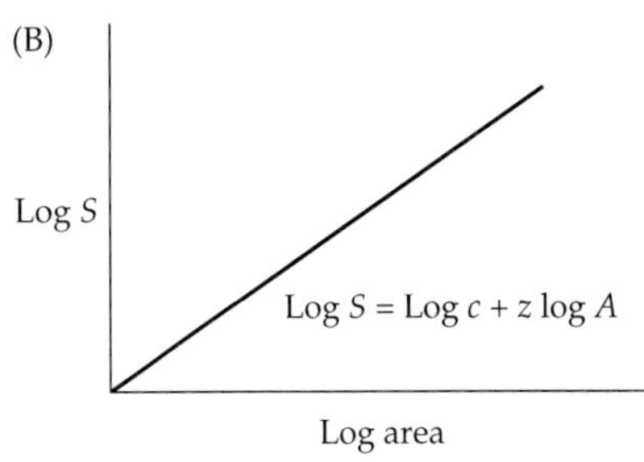

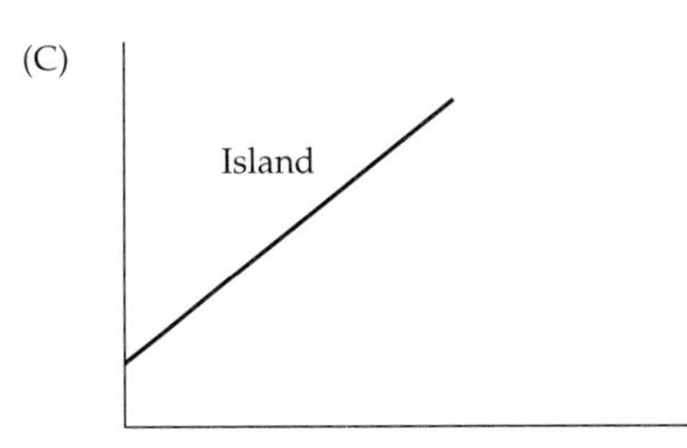

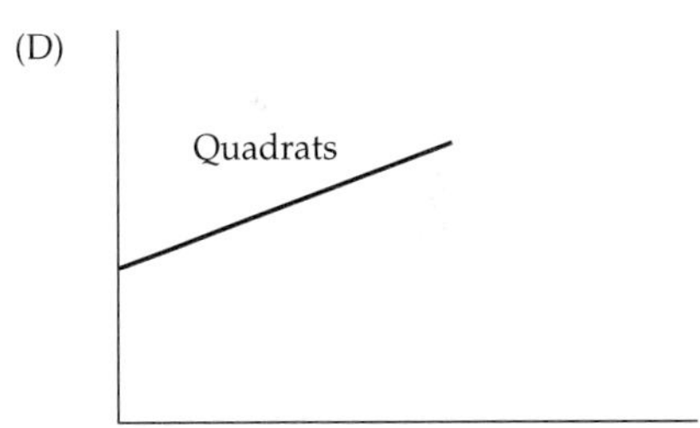

Figure 9.5 A schematic diagram of the species–area relationship. Shown on an arithmetic plot (A), species richness (S) increases rapidly with increasing area, then levels off. A log–log plot (B) linearizes the relationship. The slope of the relationship is steeper for islands or other isolated habitats (C) than for sample quadrats within extensive habitats (D). (From Harris 1984.)

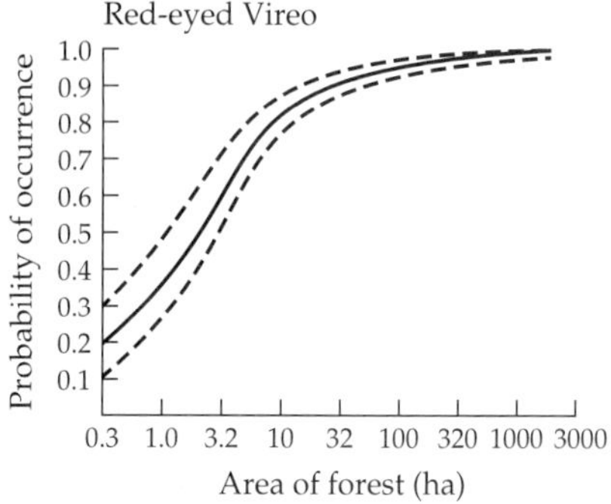

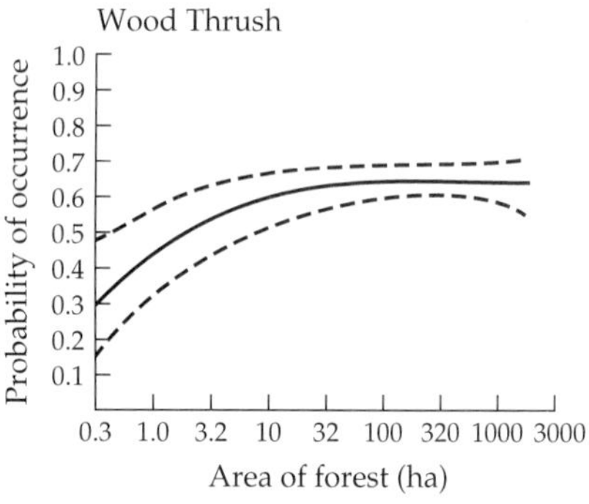

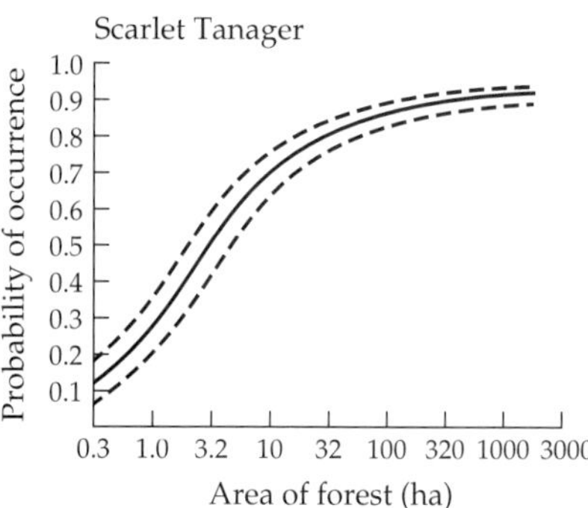

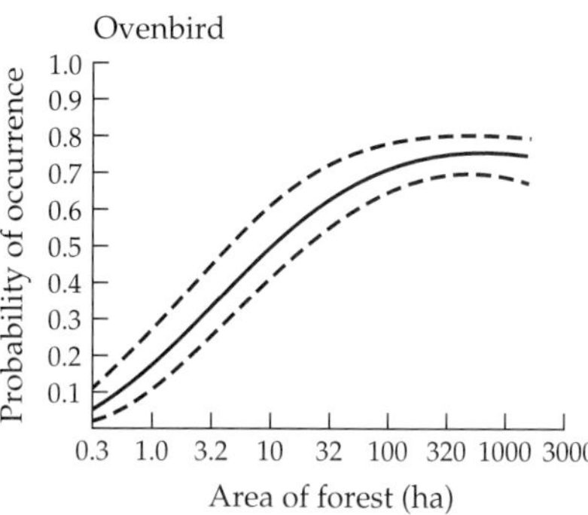

Figure 9.6 Probability of four species of common forest interior Neotropical migrant birds nesting in United States mid-Atlantic forests of various sizes, based on point counts. Dotted lines indicate 95% confidence intervals. (From Robbins et al. 1989.)

size of populations increases, thus reducing the probability of extinction (Preston 1960, 1962). We know from studies and models of population viability that large populations are less likely than small ones to go extinct due to various stochastic processes (see Chapters 6 and 7). All populations fluctuate through time; a small population is more likely to fluctuate down to zero.

A small island or nature reserve may be smaller than the territory or home range of a single individual of some species. For example, a cougar (*Felis concolor*) is unlikely to remain long within a 1000 ha park. In the Rocky Mountains of the United States and Canada, annual home ranges of cougars average over 400 km^2, and those of grizzly bears (*Ursus arctos horribilis*) average nearly 900 km^2 (Noss et al. 1996). Large carnivores and other wide-ranging animals are typically among the species most threatened by habitat fragmentation, in part because small areas fail to provide enough prey, but also because these animals are more likely to be killed by humans or their vehicles when they attempt to travel through fragmented landscapes (Harris and Gallagher 1989). Other species, for reasons not entirely understood, avoid settling in small tracts of seemingly suitable habitat. Studies in the eastern United States have confirmed that many songbird species are "area-sensitive" and usually breed only in tracts of forest many times larger than the size of their territories (Figure 9.6). Similarly, studies of birds on grassland remnants in several regions of the United States showed that several species occur only on fragments larger than 10 or even 50 ha, even though their territories are much smaller (Samson 1983; Herkert 1994; Vickery et al. 1994). In all these cases, the probability of finding breeding pairs of area-sensitive species increases with the size of the fragment.

The most famous and controversial explanation for the species–area relationship is the equilibrium theory of island biogeography (MacArthur and Wilson 1963, 1967). MacArthur and Wilson, though recognizing the role of habitat diversity in controlling species occurrence, suggested an ultimate explanation: the number of species on an island represents a balance between colonization and extinction (Figure 9.7). Over a period of time, species continually go extinct on an island, but other species immigrate to the island from the mainland or other islands. Islands near the mainland experience higher rates of colonization than remote islands because the dispersal distance is shorter. Large islands contain larger populations and consequently suffer lower rates of extinction. Size may affect immigration rates as well, as larger islands stand a higher chance of intercepting dispersing individuals. Islands closer to an immigration source can also be expected to have lower extinction rates, as declining populations can be bolstered by immigrants of the same species—a rescue effect (Brown and Kodric-Brown 1977). Therefore, equilibrium theory predicts that large, "near" islands will contain the most species, all else being equal.

The effect of isolation on diversity was noticed by Forster (1778, in Browne 1983), who observed that the number of species common to islands and continents decreased as islands became more distant from the mainland. However, Forster and other biogeographers of the time failed to recognize that inadequate dispersal was responsible for the absence of many species on islands, particularly distant ones. Forster attributed the depauperate condition of islands to peculiarities of their physical environments. Charles Darwin was among the first to recognize that species on islands had arrived from the continents, many of them subsequently differentiating into new species (Browne 1983).

A common distinction in island biogeographic studies is between oceanic and **land-bridge islands** (MacArthur 1972). Land-bridge islands were con-

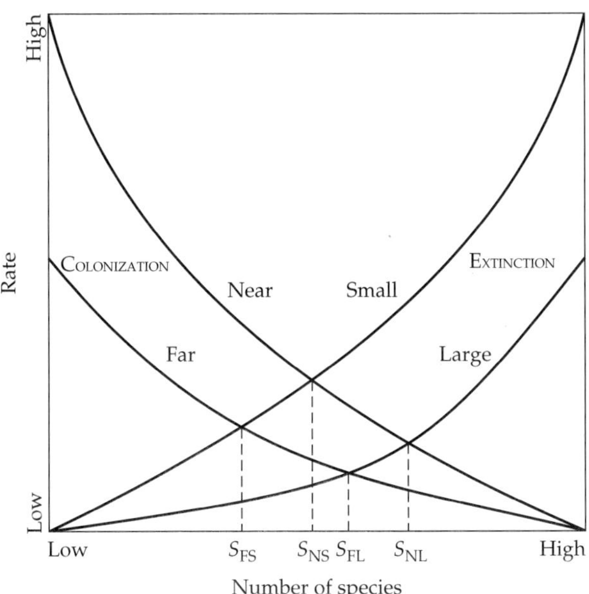

Figure 9.7 Predicted species richness on an island, represented as a balance between rate of colonization (immigration to the island) and rate of extinction, according to the equilibrium theory of island biogeography (MacArthur and Wilson 1967). In this model, colonization is affected mainly by island distance from the mainland (near or far); extinction is affected by island size. Species richness corresponds to the intersection of the colonization and extinction curves. The greatest number of species is predicted to occur on islands that are near and large (S_{NL}). (From Wilcox 1980.)

nected to each other or to continents during the Pleistocene, when sea level was as much as 100 m lower than today. Presumably, at that time, land-bridge islands contained numbers of bird species similar to those in areas of equal size on the mainland. Since becoming isolated, these islands apparently have lost species over time, a phenomenon called **relaxation**, with some species being more extinction-prone than others (Diamond 1972; Terborgh 1974; Faaborg 1979). However, equilibrium species richness on land-bridge islands is typically higher than on similar-sized oceanic islands that were never connected to larger landmasses (Figure 9.8; Harris 1984).

The analogy between land-bridge islands and terrestrial habitat patches isolated by development of the surrounding landscape was persuasive and spawned a series of papers proposing rules for the design of nature reserves (Terborgh 1974; Willis 1974; Diamond 1975; Wilson and Willis 1975; Diamond and May 1976). The usefulness of the land-bridge island analogy for conservation was marred by, among other problems, the weak evidence for relaxation being strongly related to island size (Abele and Connor 1979; Faeth and Connor 1979). Nevertheless, the many similarities between habitat fragments and land-bridge islands keep the analogy alive. For example, in national parks in western North America, the number of extinctions has exceeded the number of colonizations since the parks were established, and extinction rates are inversely related to park area—both as predicted by the land-bridge island hypothesis (Newmark 1995). Relaxation of species richness has also been documented in isolated reserves that were formerly connected to extensive wild areas. For example, in a cloud forest fragment in Columbia isolated for several decades, 40 species of birds (31% of the avifauna present in 1911) have gone extinct (Kattan et al. 1994). Similarly, 50.9% of the plant species in the Singapore Botanic Gardens, an isolated fragment of lowland tropical rainforest, have gone extinct over the last century (Turner et al. 1996). Furthermore, density-dependent models of population persistence show that fragmentation can greatly increase extinction risk (Burkey 1989), and empirical data on extinction rates on islands and in islandlike habitats show that sets of smaller islands lose more species than single large islands of the same total area (Burkey 1995).

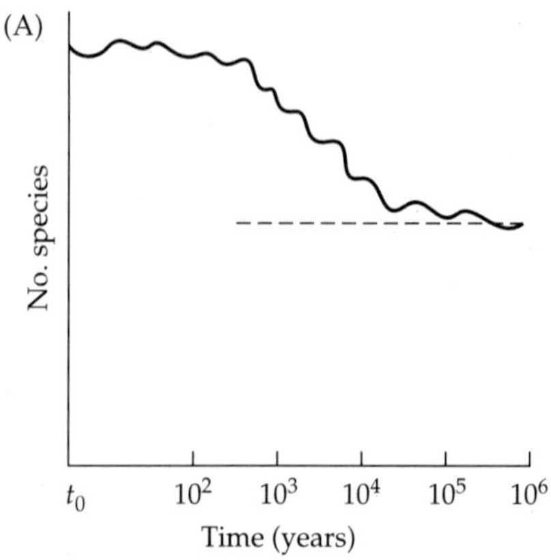

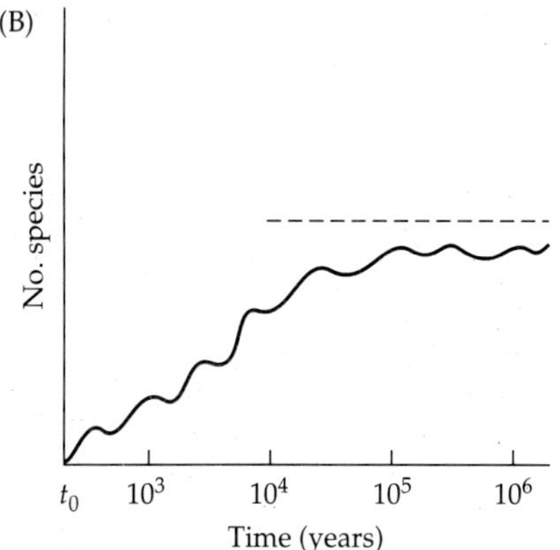

Figure 9.8 Predicted species richness over time for land-bridge islands (A) and oceanic islands (B). Land-bridge islands were once part of a large land area and contained more species than they could retain after their isolation by rising sea level; the decline in species richness after isolation is known as "relaxation." Oceanic islands, often of volcanic origin, are slowly colonized by long-distance dispersal, so species richness builds gradually to an equilibrium level (dashed line). (From Harris 1984.)

The response variable in the classic equilibrium model of species richness is a community-level property and not necessarily the most appropriate variable for conservation planning in fragmented landscapes. Subdivision or fragmentation of habitats may increase species richness, but often favors "weedy" species—those that thrive in areas disturbed by humans—over more sensitive ones. Many small, isolated nature reserves are quite rich in species, but exotic and other opportunistic species have replaced native species that have gone locally extinct (Noss 1983). In a 400 ha woodland park in metropolitan Boston, the number of native species has declined by 0.36% per year over the last century, while the number of exotic species has increased at a rate of 0.18% per year. The proportion of native species in the flora went from 83% in 1894 to 74% in 1993 (Drayton and Primack 1996). Thus, ratios of exotic to native species and population-level considerations of extinction and colonization are often more useful than species numbers in conservation planning and management (Haila 1990; Noss and Cooperrider 1994).

Island biogeographic theory has sometimes been supported by empirical studies and sometimes not. Often, researchers claiming support for the theory have failed to consider alternative or null hypotheses. The reserve design rules offered by Diamond, Terborgh, Willis, and others have been challenged as idiosyncratic and having many exceptions. Half of them do not even follow directly from island biogeographic theory (Simberloff and Abele 1976, 1982; Margules et al. 1982; Simberloff 1991). But despite problems with the theory and its sometimes uncritical application to reserve design, island biogeography has led to major advances in conservation. Above all, the theory has expanded the focus of scientists and conservationists to landscapes—to collections of sites, not just single sites—and got them thinking about the potential effects of habitat area and isolation on biodiversity. Considering the problem of habitat fragmentation, it would be difficult to think of a more meaningful contribution.

Biological Consequences of Fragmentation

Some effects of fragmentation on biodiversity have been conspicuous; others have been subtle and indirect. Some have occurred almost immediately after the initial disturbance, whereas others have developed over decades or are still unfolding. Fragmentation of some regions, such as the Georgia Piedmont (Turner and Ruscher 1988; Odum 1989), partially has been reversed through abandonment of agricultural fields and maturation of second-growth forests. However, fragmentation of other regions, such as the Pacific Northwest, Florida, and much of the tropics, continues. Most deforestation in Central America has occurred since 1950, and rates of deforestation are still increasing (Hartshorn 1992).

As suggested earlier, the effects of fragmentation can be seen at several levels of biological organization, from changes in gene frequencies within populations to continent-wide changes in the distributions of species and ecosystems. At the species level, there are essentially three options for persistence in a highly fragmented landscape. First, a species might survive or even thrive in the matrix of human land uses; a number of weedy species worldwide fit this description. Second, a species might survive by maintaining viable populations within individual habitat fragments; this is an option only for species with small home ranges or otherwise modest area requirements, such as many plants and invertebrates. Many of these species can meet all of their life history requirements and maintain viable populations within the boundaries of a single fragment; if so, they will persist there indefinitely, barring major environmental changes such as global warming.

A third way to survive in a fragmented landscape is to be highly mobile. Some mobile species can integrate a number of habitat patches, either into individual home ranges or into an interbreeding population. The Pileated Woodpecker (*Dryocopus pileatus*) has demonstrated adaptation to fragmented landscapes, particularly in eastern North America. Foraging individuals now travel among a number of small woodlots in landscapes that were formerly continuous forest, often using wooded fencerows as travel corridors (Whitcomb et al. 1981; Merriam 1991). White-footed mice (*Peromyscus leucopus*) and eastern chipmunks (*Tamias striatus*) maintain populations in fragmented landscapes only when dispersal between woodlots, aided by fencerow corridors (Figure 9.9), is great enough to balance local extinctions (Fahrig and Merriam 1985; Henderson et al. 1985). A species incapable of pursuing one or more of these three options is bound for eventual extinction in a fragmented landscape.

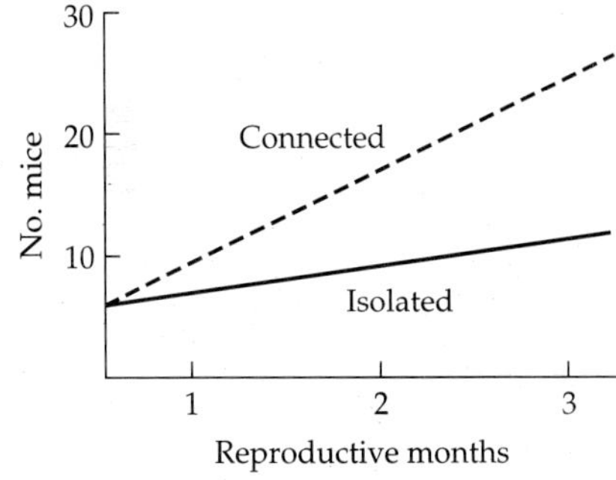

Figure 9.9 Isolated woodlots in a fragmented landscape are predicted by simulation models to have lower rates of population growth than woodlots connected by fencerow corridors. These predictions were verified by studies of white-footed mice in southern Ontario. (From Merriam 1991, based on Fahrig and Merriam 1985.)

Initial Exclusion

One of the most rapid and obvious effects of fragmentation is elimination of the species that occurred only in the portions of the landscape destroyed by development. Many rare species are endemics with very narrow distributions, occurring in only one or a few patches of suitable habitat. Recall the loss of up to 90 species of plants on the Centinela Ridge in Ecuador (Chapter 5) when that small patch of forest was destroyed by loggers (Gentry 1986). Similarly, Cerro Tacarcuna is a mountain on the Panama–Colombia border that supports at least 71 species of angiosperms (24% of the mountain's flora) that are "extremely endemic"; that is, these species have ranges of only 5–10 km^2, and could easily be lost through fragmentation (Gentry 1986). In Colombia and Ecuador, existing national parks do not include the ranges of most of the bird species unique to those countries (Terborgh and Winter 1983). If habitat outside the parks is eliminated, those species will be lost by exclusion unless they are capable of moving rapidly to suitable habitat elsewhere. Eventually, as habitat destruction continues, suitable habitat may not be available anywhere.

Barriers and Isolation

Isolation of habitats by barriers to movement is an effect of fragmentation as important as reduction in habitat size. Species that are restricted to certain kinds of habitat may depend on a constellation of habitat patches in relatively close proximity, if no single patch is large enough to meet the needs of individuals or groups (Figure 9.10). As noted earlier, the viability of metapopulations may depend on enough movement of individuals among patches to balance extirpation from local patches. Also, many animal species require a mix of different habitats with distinct resources—for example, food patches, roost sites, and breeding sites—in order to meet their life history requirements

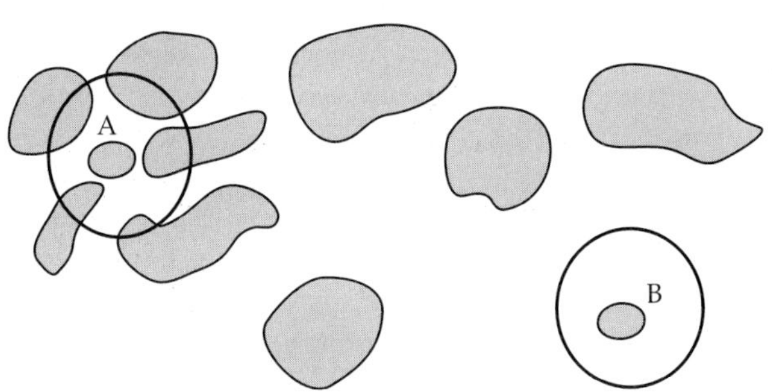

Figure 9.10 A constellation of separate habitat patches may be critical to the survival of individuals or populations. If a species requires resources in the shaded habitat patches, site A will be preferable to site B. Although no single patch is large enough by itself to support a population, the close grouping of patches in site A provides sufficient resources within the accessible part of the landscape (circle). In contrast, site B consists of one small, isolated patch and will not support a population. If human activities create impenetrable barriers to movement between the patches in site A, that site will no longer be superior to site B. (From Dunning et al. 1992.)

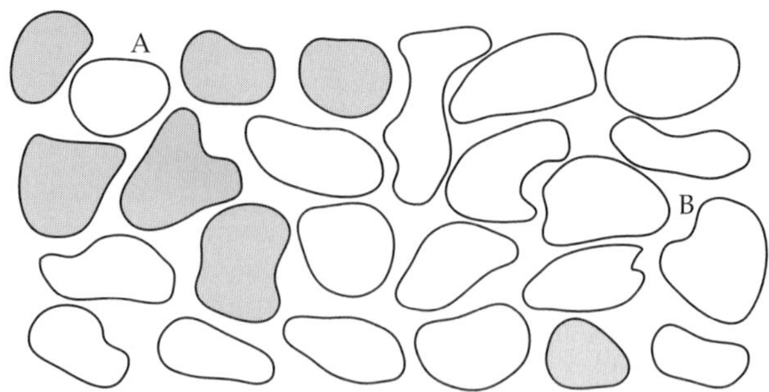

Figure 9.11 Many animals require a suite of different habitats or resources to meet life history needs. If a species requires nonsubstitutable resources found in two habitat types (shaded and open), regions of the landscape where the two habitats are in close proximity (site A) will support larger populations than regions where one habitat type is rare (site B). However, as in the example in Figure 9.10, barriers between habitat patches will destroy any advantage of site A. (From Dunning et al. 1992.)

(Figure 9.11). If these critical areas become separated by barriers, populations may decline rapidly to extinction.

What constitutes a barrier to movement is highly species-specific; a hedgerow that is a barrier to the movement of some species (e.g., livestock) may serve as a corridor to others. Unfortunately, very little information exists on the qualities of suitable dispersal habitat or on barriers for various species. Species- and habitat-specific dispersal studies are essential for gaining a better understanding of fragmentation effects. What we do know, however, suggests that human-created structures and habitats—roads, urban areas, agricultural fields, clear-cuts—can greatly inhibit the movements of many kinds of animals and, potentially, plants (especially those dispersed by animals).

One significant type of barrier in many landscapes is roads. Habitat fragmentation is usually accompanied, and augmented, by road building. To the extent that individual animals hesitate to cross roads, roads fragment populations into smaller demographic units that are more vulnerable to extinction. A study in southeastern Ontario and Quebec found that several species of small mammals rarely ventured onto road surfaces when the road clearance (distance between road margins) exceeded 20 m (Oxley et al. 1974). In Oregon, dusky-footed woodrats (*Neotoma fuscipes*) and red-backed voles (*Clethrionomys occidentalis*) were trapped at all distances from an interstate highway right-of-way, but never in the right-of-way itself, suggesting that these rodents did not cross the highway (Adams and Geis 1983). In Germany, several species of carabid beetles and two species of forest rodents rarely or never crossed two-lane roads (Figure 9.12); even a narrow, unpaved forest road, closed to public traffic, served as a barrier to these species (Mader 1984). Another study found that roads and railroads inhibited normal movements of lycosid spiders and carabid beetles; although crossings were rare, longitudinal movements along these barriers were stimulated (Mader et al. 1990).

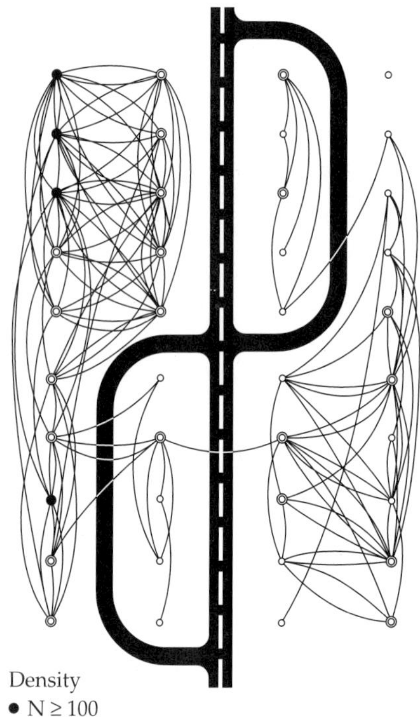

Figure 9.12 Roads can be significant barriers to the movement of small vertebrates and invertebrates. In this example, populations of the forest-dwelling carabid beetle *Abax ater* were almost completely divided by a road and even by parking loops. Lines represent movements of marked beetles between capture and recapture points. (Modified from Mader 1984.)

Road clearances can be barriers in a wide variety of habitat types. In a study of the effects of a highway on rodents in the Mojave Desert (Garland and Bradley 1984), only one white-tailed antelope squirrel (*Ammospermophilus leucurus*), out of 612 individuals of eight rodent species captured and 387 individuals recaptured, was ever recorded as having crossed the road. A 9-year study in a Kansas grassland found that very few prairie voles (*Microtus ochrogaster*) and cotton rats (*Sigmodon hispidus*) ever crossed a dirt road 3 m wide that bisected a trapping grid (Swihart and Slade 1984). Many other studies have documented the barrier effects of roads, even for animals as large as black bears (*Ursus americanus*) (Brody and Pelton 1989). In the latter study, the frequency at which bears crossed roads of any type varied with traffic volume. An interstate highway was the most significant barrier, and bears that attempted to cross it were often killed. Roads are the largest source of mortality for endangered Florida panthers (Figure 9.13) and many other large mam-

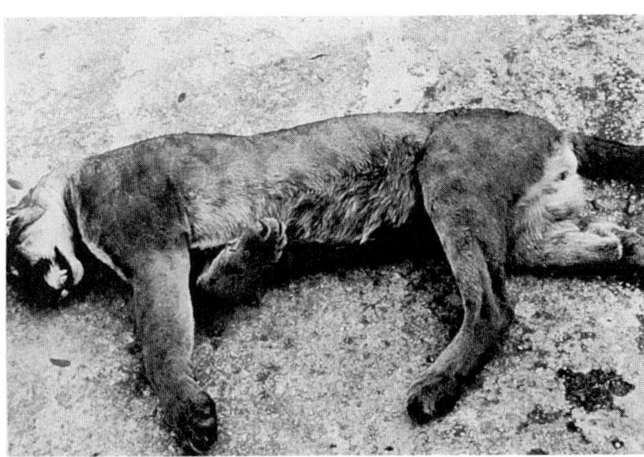

Figure 9.13 A road-killed Florida panther. Automobile collisions are the largest single source of mortality for Florida panthers. (Photograph by R. C. Belden.)

mals, and have been implicated in widespread amphibian declines as traffic volume has increased in many regions (Fahrig et al. 1995).

The long-term effects of roads and other dispersal barriers on population dynamics and genetic structure are generally unknown. Effects of isolation are usually only inferred. Low rates of genetic interchange among populations (on the order of one successful migrant per generation) may be sufficient to prevent inbreeding depression and other genetic problems in many cases (see Chapter 6). However, a German study found that separation of populations of common frogs (*Rana temporaria*) by highways reduced the average heterozygosity and genetic polymorphism of those populations (Reh and Seitz 1990). A Canadian study of white-footed mice failed to find any significant effects of road barriers on genetic structure, but hypothesized that such effects could be important in cases in which roads are absolute barriers (Merriam et al. 1989).

The genetic structure and persistence of plants, as well as animals, may be affected by isolation. For a tropical tree, *Pithecellobium elegans*, three measures of genetic variation were lowest in populations that were smaller and more isolated from other populations (Hall et al. 1996). Isolation also increases extinction probabilities in herbaceous plants of the Florida scrub (Quintana-Ascencio and Menges 1996).

Although inbreeding depression and genetic drift may increase extinction risk in small, isolated populations, in other cases fragmentation may increase the among-population component of genetic diversity (Simberloff and Cox 1987; Simberloff 1988). As discussed in Chapter 6, the creation of fragmented distributions and population bottlenecks by human activities has apparently increased genetic differentiation among populations of Wild Turkeys (*Meleagris gallopavo*) in three regions of the eastern United States (Leberg 1991). However, these increases could be offset in the long run by the erosion of genetic diversity within the family of populations that were once connected.

Barrier effects are both relative and cumulative. A city block can be expected to be more of a barrier to most forest species than a cornfield, which will be more of a barrier than a pine plantation. The cumulative effects of many barriers are probably what finally extinguishes populations in many cases. In a multiple-species context, the landscape matrix in which habitat islands are embedded is better seen as a "filter" than as a barrier because it allows individuals of some species, but not others, to pass through. Individual features, such as a river or a highway, are also filters because individuals of some species, but not others, cross them (Figure 9.14).

The amount of structural contrast between habitat fragments and the matrix in which they exist is one measure of fragmentation (Harris 1984); that is, as the landscape around fragments is progressively altered, the functional iso-

Figure 9.14 Natural or artificial barriers to movement are perhaps better understood as filters, because individuals of some species will cross them but others will not. The Columbia River defines range limits for some species and subspecies of terrestrial animals because it is an essentially permanent barrier to movement. For other species, such as most birds, the river is only a partial barrier at most. However, logging and urban development in lowland areas of western Oregon and Washington have created a "bottleneck," or area of restricted interchange, for forest species such as the Northern Spotted Owl (*Strix occidentalis caurina*) that once crossed the river. It is unknown whether interchange presently occurs between Spotted Owl populations in the two states. (Photograph by B. Csuti.)

lation of those fragments increases. A structurally rich matrix may serve as marginal habitat for some species and buffer population fluctuations; it may also encourage dispersal among patches. However, a low-contrast matrix may be dangerous in situations in which habitat selection is imperfect and individuals are drawn to low-quality (sink) habitats (see Chapter 7). Dispersing individuals may settle in the matrix, but then fail to survive or reproduce. For example, Northern Spotted Owls (*Strix occidentalis caurina*) usually nest in old-growth forests, but occasionally nest in younger forests, including second growth. Available data suggest that reproduction is poor in the latter habitats; that is, they are potentially population sinks (McKelvey et al. 1993). In such cases, it may be better to surround habitat fragments with highly dissimilar habitat than with marginally suitable forest. The presence of old-growth species in a managed forest matrix may give the impression that these species are not dependent on old growth, but once old-growth source populations are eliminated, populations in the matrix may disappear rapidly.

Nevertheless, for many species, as the landscape matrix departs more and more from natural habitat, isolation increases as individuals are less willing or able to travel from one patch of natural habitat to another. This process is a very common one, and occurs when the intensity of development or resource extraction increases in a landscape. Landscape-scale studies are needed that measure birth and death rates in different habitats, as well as dispersal among those habitats. Only then can we say with assurance which kinds of matrix are optimal for a network of natural areas.

Although the examples above come from terrestrial ecosystems, as these have been better studied with regard to fragmentation, human-created barriers also fragment aquatic habitats. Dams, for example, not only block access of migratory fishes to upstream areas, but also prevent recolonization of stream segments by any species whose local populations have vanished due to natural or anthropogenic causes (Moyle and Leidy 1992). The flattened musk turtle (*Sternotherus depressus*) has been lost from over half its range in the Warrior River Basin of Alabama because modification of stream and river channels has fragmented suitable habitat. The remaining populations are small and isolated, and therefore at high risk of extinction (Dodd 1990). Catherine Pringle takes up the topic of fragmentation of aquatic systems in Essay 9D.

ESSAY 9D
Fragmentation in Stream Ecosystems

Catherine M. Pringle, University of Georgia

Although much attention has been focused on habitat fragmentation in terrestrial ecosystems, fragmentation can also occur in aquatic systems, where it can have deleterious effects on ecosystem integrity. Streams and rivers have been likened to "blueprints" of the ecosystem, integrating processes occurring in both the atmosphere and the terrestrial environments that they drain. Riverine systems reflect the interaction of many factors, including hydrologic modifications, erosion, and nutrient runoff resulting from land use changes, and acid rain.

Fragmentation of stream ecosystems can occur when (1) the longitudinal continuum is disrupted (e.g., by dams or severe pollution) or (2) when lateral connections are severed between the stream channel and adjacent wetlands or riparian zones (e.g., through channelization, wetland drainage, or groundwater exploitation).

Stream habitat destruction and fragmentation is occurring at a rate unprecedented in geologic history, contributing to dramatic losses in global aquatic biodiversity and associated ecosystem integrity. The United States has lost over half the wetlands that existed at the time of the American Revolution. Of the 3.2 million miles of streams in the lower 48 states, only 2% remain free-flowing and relatively undeveloped. Currently, only 42 free-flowing rivers of over 125 miles in length exist; the other 98% of U.S. streams have been fragmented by dams and water diversion projects (Benke 1990). Here I discuss the effects of this fragmentation of stream corridors at levels from genes to populations to ecosystems.

Genetic and Species-Level Changes

As streams become increasingly fragmented by dams, water abstraction, or pollution, populations of aquatic organisms are subject to reduced gene flow and loss of genetic variation. The Cherokee darter (*Etheostoma scotti*) provides one example. This small fish is endemic to portions of the Etowah River system in the Piedmont region of Georgia in the southern United States (Bauer et al. 1994). Because of its current isolated range, which is fragmented by degraded habitat (urbanization and other human land use), there is no potential for genetic exchange among populations. For obligate riverine species with large home ranges, impoundments may similarly fragment the range, causing losses in genetic diversity and local extinctions.

The genetic and species-level effects of dams on economically important migratory fishes such as salmonids have received much attention (Pacific Rivers Council 1993). Over 100 major salmon and steelhead populations or stocks have been extirpated on the West Coast of the United States and Canada, while at least 214 more are at risk of extinction (Nehlsen et al. 1991). Less is known about the genetic and species-level effects of stream fragmentation on North American biota of less economic importance (nongame fishes, freshwater shrimps, other invertebrates). In tropical areas such as the Amazon, fish migratory patterns are so complex—covering huge drainage areas—that the direct effects of dams and other forms of stream fragmentation are unknown for even economically important fish species (e.g., Goulding et al. 1996).

Population- and Community-Level Changes

Some North American mussel species have been extirpated or are declining because their migratory host fish species have been removed by dams and other hydrologic modifications. One example is the dwarf wedge mussel (*Alasmidonta heterodon*). In the past 20 years, known populations of this mussel have dropped from 70 to 19 (Middleton and Liittschwager 1994). A leading theory for the cause of its demise is that the fish species that serves as its host during the critical early stage of development may also be in decline. It is suspected that the host fish is anadromous, and that dam construction has blocked its access to upstream mussel populations. Consequently, the recovery of the host fish may be pivotal to successful recovery of the mussel. The problem is compounded by the fact that the mussel is also extremely sensitive to the siltation that results from dams and riverbank erosion and to toxic chemicals in agricultural runoff and industrial effluent.

Degraded downstream areas can act as population sinks (Chapter 7) for native riverine species and, alternatively, as sources of exotic species or facultative riverine species. For example, in his studies of streams draining urban areas in the Apalachicola–Chattahoochee–Flint River Basin of the southeastern United States, DeVivo (1996) found highly variable fish faunas and atypical age structures that may be related to high heavy metal and pesticide levels. Only those fishes most tolerant of degraded conditions (often exotic species) had established populations. Consequently, stream reaches upstream of degraded downstream reaches are vulnerable to invasion by exotic species common to degraded areas, which then serve as source populations of exotics.

Ecosystem- and Landscape-Level Changes

When dominant faunal components of an ecosystem are excluded from upper portions of the watershed as a result of downstream human activities, a cascade of ecosystem-level effects may occur, particularly when the extirpated component was an important food source, predator, host species, or habitat modifier. For instance, populations of Bald Eagles and other animals that depend on migrating salmon as a food source may decrease dramatically if this food source is eliminated (Spencer et al. 1991).

Faunal components that are vulnerable to stream fragmentation can play key roles in ecosystem-level properties and processes such as water quality and nutrient cycling. For example, salmon remove fine particulate organic matter in bed sediments during spawning (R. Naiman, University of Washington, personal communication), and also release nutrients when they die after spawning, affecting algal biomass and primary production (Kline et al. 1990) as well as secondary insect consumers (Schuldt and Hershey 1995). This nutrient release is considered essential for maintaining the productivity of nursery areas for future salmon stocks (Mathisen 1972). Consequently, when dams block salmonid migration routes, patterns of nutrient cycling in entire riverine ecosystems can be altered.

The loss of mussel species from streams where they were once diverse and abundant is yet another legacy of anthropogenic disturbance that often goes unacknowledged. Ninety percent of the world's freshwater mussel species are found in North America, and 73% of all mussel species in the United States are at risk of extinction or are already extinct. The prognosis is not good: in 1990, 90% of the listed mussels were still declining, and only 3% were increasing (Master 1990). Given that mussels filter an enormous amount of water, and that they were once plentiful throughout North America, we must wonder about their role in maintaining ecosystem and landscape integrity before they were reduced in diversity and number.

Groundwater exploitation in stream watersheds can sever lateral connections between stream channels and adjacent springs and wetlands, resulting in landscape-level changes in the drainage network and the distribution of biota. The increasing exploitation of groundwater reserves for municipal, industrial, and agricultural use is having profound effects on riverine ecosystems as groundwater tables are lowered. For example, populations of the anadromous striped bass (*Morone saxatilis*) are dependent on coldwater refuges within riverine systems during hot summer periods because of their high oxygen requirement. In the southeastern United States, spring-fed stream systems are home to healthy and productive populations of striped bass. These streams have a high thermal diversity, and the fish can actively search out and use spring-fed areas as refuges (Van Den Avyle and Evans 1990). Extensive groundwater withdrawals threaten the springs, and thus the survival of biota dependent on coldwater refuges.

A Case Study

The complex problems caused by stream fragmentation in the largest natural forest left in the Caribbean Islands, the Caribbean National Forest (CNF) of Puerto Rico, illustrate the challenges facing resource managers in their attempts to balance water use and biological integrity.

The CNF (11,269 ha) is located in the northeastern corner of Puerto Rico and is drained by nine major rivers, which are characterized by a simple food chain dominated by shrimps and fishes, typical of oceanic islands. Almost all of the shrimps and fishes living in these rivers must spend some part of their lives in the estuary to complete their life cycle. In the case of shrimps, newly hatched larvae migrate downstream and complete their larval stage in the estuary (March et al. 1996). Upon metamorphosis, the juveniles migrate upstream, where they live as adults. This life cycle is known as *amphidromy*. In contrast, two species of fish spend most of their lives in fresh water, but migrate to the sea to breed (*catadromy*).

Migratory fishes and shrimps are food sources for both aquatic and terrestrial organisms (including humans), and their migrations form a dynamic link between stream headwaters and estuaries. When water is removed for human use (drinking water, irrigation, etc.), this results in direct mortality of shrimp larvae migrating to the ocean. At present, all except one of the nine stream drainages within the CNF have dams and associated water intakes on their main channels. The extent of water abstraction is so severe that on an average day, over 50% of riverine water draining the forest is withdrawn into municipal water supplies before it reaches the ocean (Naumann 1994). Moreover, several rivers have no water below their water intakes for much of the year, resulting in highly fragmented systems. Water abstraction in the lower reaches of one of the main rivers within the CNF resulted in 59% mortality of shrimp larvae, as measured over a two-month non-drought period during 1995 (Benstead et al. 1996). During periods of drought, larval mortality can be much greater, reaching up to 100% when all of the water is abstracted. Although the small dams at water intakes do not appear to be physical barriers to the upstream migration of returning juvenile shrimps, they function as a predation gauntlet for the juveniles due to the concentration of both freshwater and marine predaceous fishes below the dam (March et al. 1996; Benstead et al. 1996).

In all of these ways, the fragmentation and alteration of streams by humans has a dramatic effect on ecosystem integrity and biological diversity.

Crowding Effects

When an area is isolated by destruction of the surrounding natural habitat, population densities of mobile animal species may initially increase in the fragment as animals are displaced from their former homes. This packing phenomenon has been called a "crowding on the ark" and has been described for tropical (Leck 1979) and temperate (Noss 1981) forest reserves. The initial increase in population densities in isolated fragments is followed by collapse in most cases. The crowding effect has been convincingly demonstrated in tropical forest patches in the Minimum Critical Size of Ecosystems Project in the Amazonian forest of Brazil (Lovejoy et al. 1986; Bierregaard et al. 1992). In this study, the capture rate of understory birds in an isolated 10 ha fragment more than doubled in the first few days following its isolation, but rapidly fell in subsequent days. Longer-term crowding effects are likely in many cases, but have not been proven. The biological consequences of the crowding effect have been poorly studied. In Maine, densities of Ovenbirds (*Seiurus aurocapillus*) increased in forest fragments newly formed by logging; however, density was inversely related to offspring production, as pairing success was lower in fragments than in nonfragments (Hagan et al. 1996). For these and other reasons (see below), many fragments may be population sinks, despite an abundance of birds and other organisms.

Local and Regional Extinctions

Metapopulation dynamics suggest that even once-common species are not immune to the effects of widespread habitat alteration and fragmentation. When local populations become isolated, they face a higher probability of extinction. For example, the Middle Spotted Woodpecker (*Dendrocopos medius*) is a sedentary forest species with poor powers of dispersal. A population in Sweden, isolated since about 1950, remained relatively stable at 15–20 pairs from 1967 to 1974, then declined rapidly to extinction in the period from 1975 to 1983. The proximate causes of extinction were mortality from cold weather and, more importantly, reproductive failures due to reduced fecundity, probably related to inbreeding depression (Pettersson 1985). The White-backed Woodpecker (*Dendrocopos leucotos*) has disappeared from parts of Sweden where habitat fragmentation has resulted in a low density of suitable habitat patches; recolonization of vacated patches in such areas is too low to maintain the metapopulation (Carlson and Aulen 1992).

Species Vulnerable to Fragmentation

What kinds of species are most vulnerable to local and regional extinction following habitat fragmentation? Consideration of life histories suggests some answers to this question. Among the categories of species predicted to be most vulnerable are the following:

Naturally Rare Species. Terborgh and Winter (1980) concluded that rarity is the best predictor of population vulnerability. But there are many potential reasons why a particular species is rare (Rabinowitz et al. 1986; Chapter 5). Some plants and animals are rare because humans have driven them to that condition; other species are rare naturally. Two major categories of naturally rare species are (1) species with limited or patchy geographic distributions and (2) species with low population densities. Some species, of course, fall into both categories. The first category includes narrowly endemic species, which fragmentation may eliminate by initial exclusion. The second category includes animals with large territories or home ranges (see below), although plants with small populations are also likely to go extinct in fragmented habitats (Fischer and Stocklin 1997). As we have seen, small populations are generally more vulnerable to extinction due to demographic, genetic, or environmental stochasticity (Shaffer 1981).

Wide-Ranging Species. Some animals, such as large carnivores and migratory ungulates, roam over a large area in the course of their daily or seasonal movements. Even large fragments may not provide enough area for viable populations of these species; thus, they must travel widely and often attempt to move through heavily fragmented landscapes. In so doing, they encounter roads, people with guns, and other sources of mortality (Mladenoff et al. 1994; Noss et al. 1996). As discussed above (see Figure 9.11), animals of heterogeneous landscapes, such as amphibians and other species that depend on distinct habitats for different phases of their life cycles, also are vulnerable to roads and other barriers. Resplendent Quetzals (*Pharomachrus mocinno*), which require fruits from spatially separated habitats at different times of the year, cannot maintain year-round populations in small reserves; if reserves are isolated by fragmentation, these birds will not be able to migrate to track fruiting schedules and will probably go extinct (Wheelwright 1983; Powell and Bjork 1995).

Nonvagile Species. Species with poor dispersal abilities may not travel far from where they were born, or may be stopped by barriers as seemingly insignificant as a two-lane road or clear-cut. Many insects of old-growth forests are flightless and are poor dispersers (Moldenke and Lattin 1990). Clear-cuts are substantial barriers to carrion and dung beetles in Amazonian forests being fragmented by pasture development (Klein 1989). Perhaps surprisingly, some species of birds have very low colonizing abilities and will not cross areas of unsuitable habitat (Diamond 1975; Opdam et al. 1984; van Dorp and Opdam 1987). Without the occasional arrival of immigrants to provide a rescue effect and bolster genetic diversity, populations of nonvagile species may not persist long in habitat fragments. Variation in dispersal ability has been shown to be a critical determinant of survival for mammals in fragmented tropical forests in Queensland, Australia (Laurance 1990).

Species with Low Fecundity. A species with low reproductive capacity cannot quickly rebuild its population after a severe reduction caused by any number of factors. Neotropical migrant birds, for example, often have low reproductive rates in comparison with permanent resident species, which may be one factor responsible for their decline in fragmented eastern forests of the United States (Whitcomb et al. 1981).

Species with Short Life Cycles. Populations of animals with long life spans (which usually also have large bodies) tend to persist longer than short-lived species (Pimm 1991). Several studies also have shown that plants with short life cycles are more extinction-prone than longer-lived plant species in habitat fragments. For example, in the Singapore Botanic Gardens, mentioned earlier, individual longevity was strongly correlated with persistence of species; fewer species of trees were lost after isolation than shrubs, climbers, or epiphytes (Turner et al. 1996). In the Florida scrub, herbaceous plants are more extinction-prone than longer-lived shrubs (Quintana-Ascencio and Menges 1996). And in remnants of calcareous grassland in Central Europe, local extinctions have been more common among plant species with short life cycles, as well as those with small local populations and high habitat specificity (Fischer and Stocklin 1997).

Species Dependent on Patchy or Unpredictable Resources or Otherwise Highly Variable in Population Size. Species with specialized habitat or resource requirements often are vulnerable to extinction, especially when those resources are unpredictable in time or space. When resources fluctuate seasonally or annually, species dependent on those resources also fluctuate. Populations may also fluctuate in response to weather extremes or other variation in the physical environment. Whatever its cause, population variability predisposes species to extinction. The higher the level of fluctuation, the greater the chance of extinction (Karr 1982b; Pimm et al. 1988; for some interesting exceptions, see Pimm 1993). Drought years, for instance, often cause population crashes of wading birds, amphibians, and other species dependent on ephemeral wetlands. Reductions in fruit or mast abundance due to drought affect frugivorous and mast-dependent animals. Habitat fragmentation makes such species vulnerable in two ways: by reducing the number of sites that contain critical resources, and by isolating suitable sites and making them harder to find.

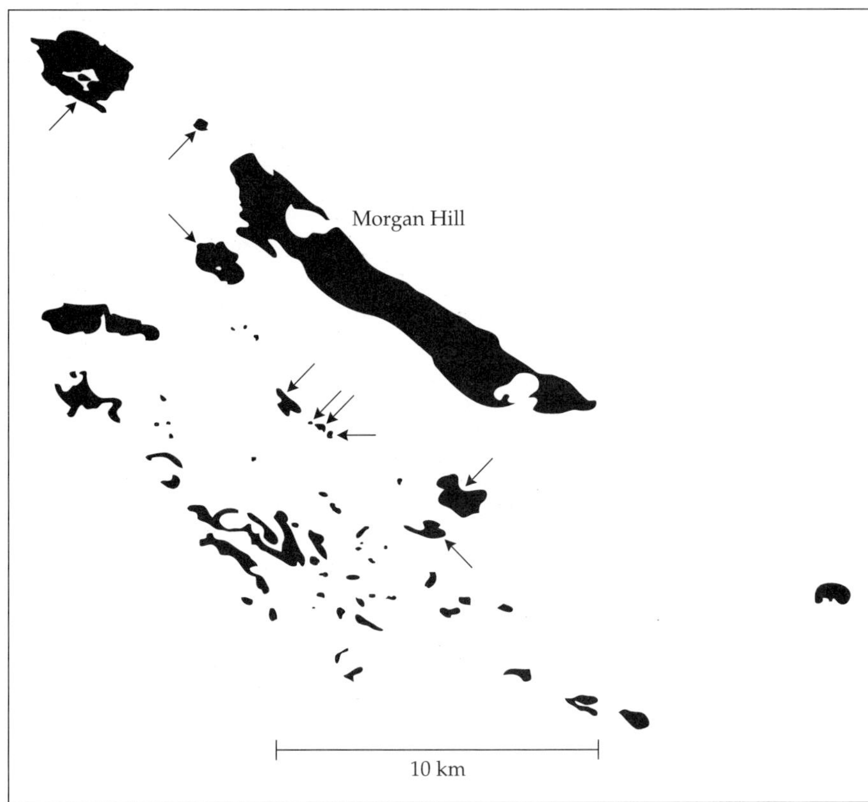

Figure 9.15 Habitat for the Bay checkerspot butterfly (*Euphydryas editha bayensis*) metapopulation is fragmented due to natural and anthropogenic factors. The black areas represent the butterfly's serpentine grassland habitat. Of the small patches of grassland, only those closest to the large Morgan Hill population (denoted by arrows) are usually occupied, suggesting that this butterfly is a poor disperser. Extinctions in small patches are apparently common and can be reversed only when isolation is minimal. (From Harrison et al. 1988.)

Studies of metapopulation dynamics in the Bay checkerspot butterfly (*Euphydryas editha bayensis*) suggest that local extinction is frequent on the small patches of serpentine grassland to which the species is now restricted due to fragmentation of the original, more extensive native grassland (Figure 9.15; see also Chapter 7). Persistence of the metapopulation is heavily dependent on dispersal from a source population to recolonize vacated patches. Because the species is a relatively poor disperser, stepping-stone habitat patches that reduce isolation may be important (Murphy and Weiss 1988). However, only those patches of suitable habitat closest to the large source population were found to be occupied by Bay checkerspots (Harrison et al. 1988).

Ground Nesters. Nesting on or near the ground is another life history trait ill suited to ecological conditions in fragmented landscapes. Ground-nesting birds are highly vulnerable to various "opportunistic mesopredators" that abound in landscapes with high ratios of edge to interior habitat (Wilcove 1985; see below). On the other hand, ground nesters seem less susceptible than shrub nesters to brood parasitism by Brown-headed Cowbirds (Robinson 1992b).

Large-Patch or Interior Species. Some species occur only in large patches of forest, prairie, shrubland, or other habitats, and are absent from small patches with little or no true interior habitat. In the shrub–steppe of southwestern Idaho—a community type that until recently was not known to contain fragmentation-sensitive species—three shrub-obligate bird species were found to be restricted to large, unfragmented patches of shrubs (Knick and Rotenberry 1995). California red-backed voles (*Clethrionomys californicus*) in southwestern Oregon are restricted to remnants of old-growth forest, preferring the interiors of forest remnants to the edges and making little use of regenerating clear-cuts (Mills 1995). In a hardwood forest in northern Florida, four breeding bird species showed significantly reduced densities within 50 m of the forest edge (Noss 1991a). Harris and Wallace (1984) found that isolated northern Florida hardwood forests smaller than 30 ha lack many of the birds characteristic of this community. Forest interior birds in the eastern Usambara Mountains of Tanzania are more vulnerable to extinction in fragmented landscapes than are edge species, perhaps because they avoid crossing large clearings; populations are therefore easily isolated (Newmark 1991). In Amazonian Brazil, understory hummingbirds, which readily use gaps, edges, and second growth, are far less vulnerable to fragmentation than insectivorous birds, which are unwilling to cross open areas (Stouffer and Bierregaard 1995).

In some cases, populations of forest interior birds in habitat fragments are lower than might be estimated from counts of singing males. In Missouri, about 75% of territorial male Ovenbirds in forest fragments were unmated, compared with 25% in larger sites (Gibbs and Faaborg 1990). For this species, fragmentation probably reduces pairing success by altering dispersal dynamics and habitat selection by females (Villard et al. 1993).

Species Vulnerable to Human Exploitation or Persecution. Some species are actively sought by people for food, furs, medicine, pets, or other uses, whereas others, such as snakes and large predators, may be killed on sight. Most habitat fragments are readily accessible to humans due to high edge: interior ratios and the ubiquitous presence of roads. In traveling between habitat fragments, animals may easily be seen and killed or collected by people. The Iberian lynx (*Felis pardina*), the most endangered carnivore in Europe, is declining because fragmentation of its habitat has increased human access and has led to high levels of illegal trapping, road mortality, and hunting with dogs (Ferreras et al. 1992; see also Case Study 6 in Chapter 13).

For purposes of comparison, studies of fragmentation should concentrate on species predicted to be vulnerable due to the kinds of traits reviewed above, as well as on related species with similar and dissimilar life histories. Land managers might also concentrate monitoring and conservation efforts on vulnerable species. Knowing more about the autecology of such species will be fundamental to conservation success (Simberloff 1988).

Edge Effects

The structural contrast between habitat islands and the landscape matrix is an indicator not only of isolation, but also of the strength of **edge effects**. The outer boundary of any habitat island is not a line, but rather a zone of influence that varies in width depending on what is measured (Murcia 1995). Sunlight and wind impinge on a forest island from the edge and alter the microclimate. Edge zones are usually drier and less shady than forest interiors, favoring shade-intolerant, xeric plants over typical mesic forest plants. In southern Wisconsin forests, edge zones of shade-intolerant vegetation may extend 10–15 m into a forest on the east, north, and south sides, and up to 30 m on the west side (Ranney et al. 1981). In Douglas fir (*Pseudotsuga menziesii*) forests of the Pacific Northwest, increased rates of blow-down, reduced humidities, and other physical edge effects may extend two to three tree-heights, or over 200 m, into a forest (Harris 1984; Franklin and Forman 1987; Chen and Franklin 1990). These physical edge effects have been shown to increase growth rates, elevate rates of mortality, reduce stocking density, and differentially affect regeneration of conifer species in old-growth forests up to 137 m from clear-cuts in Washington and Oregon (Chen et al. 1992). Elevated rates of canopy and subcanopy damage, as well as proliferation of disturbance-adapted plants, occurred up to 500 m from edges of tropical forest fragments in Queensland, Australia (Laurance 1991).

In some cases, animals are attracted to edge habitat, which functions as an "ecological trap" (Gates and Gysel 1978). Many passerine birds were attracted to a field–forest edge in Michigan and nested at greater densities near the edge than in the forest interior. However, birds nesting near the edge suffered higher rates of nest predation and brood parasitism by Brown-headed Cowbirds, and as a result had greatly reduced fledging success (Gates and Gysel 1978). Roads and powerline corridors as narrow as 8 m may produce significant edge effects by attracting cowbirds and nest predators to the corridor and the adjacent forest (Rich et al. 1994). Cowbird parasitism can be significant for hundreds of meters into a forest from an edge and is a major reason for the decline of forest birds in heavily fragmented landscapes (Brittingham and Temple 1983; Robinson et al. 1995). Increased rates of nest predation by animals such as jays (e.g., *Cyanocitta cristata*), crows (*Corvus brachyrhynchos*), raccoons (*Procyon lotor*), opossums (*Didelphis marsupialis*), foxes (e.g., *Vulpes fulva*), squirrels (*Sciurus carolinensis*), skunks (*Mephitis mephitis*), and other opportunistic predators may extend hundreds of meters from edges in eastern North America (Figure 9.16). Similar problems have been observed in Swedish forest fragments (Andren and Angelstam 1988). Nest predation in agricultural landscapes in central Spain was found to be lower in farmland than in forest patches, perhaps because small specialist predators "packed" into small remnant forest patches (Santos and Tellaria 1992). Furthermore, predation and parasitism edge effects are not limited to forests. A study of birds in tallgrass prairie fragments in Minnesota found higher rates of nest predation in smaller fragments, in areas close to wooded edges, and in vegetation that had not recently burned. Rates of brood parasitism by cowbirds were also higher near wooded edges (Johnson and Temple 1990).

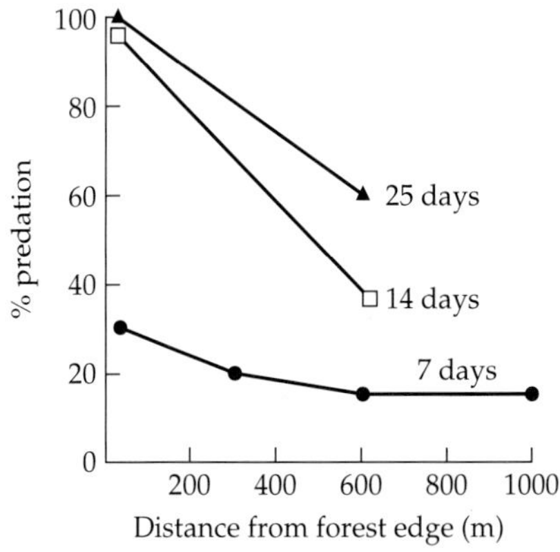

Figure 9.16 Percentage of experimental nests (quail eggs) preyed upon as a function of distance from forest edge. Graph shows losses after 7, 14, and 25 days. Results indicate that edge-related predation extends 300–600 m into the forest. (From Wilcove et al. 1986.)

Some studies have failed to confirm the ecological trap hypothesis with regard to nest predation (Ratti and Reese 1988) or have found inconsistent or conflicting evidence (Paton 1994; Murcia 1995). Part of the problem relates to inconsistencies in study design and to biases associated with the use of artificial nests (Murcia 1995; Haskell 1995). The strongest evidence for an ecological trap is for distances only up to 50 m from an edge (Paton 1994). In heavily fragmented landscapes dominated by disturbed lands, such as southern Illinois, edge effects may not be observed because all remaining patches of natural habitat are saturated with nest predators and brood parasites. Cowbirds saturate even the largest available tracts (ca. 2000 ha) and areas more than 800 m from edges (Robinson 1992a). In such situations, nesting success of forest birds may be so low that the entire region is a population sink. Persistence of forest interior birds in such landscapes is tenuous and may depend on immigration from landscapes with greater forest cover and better reproductive success (Temple and Cary 1988; Robinson 1992b; Donovan et al. 1995; Robinson et al. 1995).

The matrix surrounding habitat patches in terrestrial landscapes clearly distinguishes these patches from real islands; much of the variation in the results of edge effect studies undoubtedly relates to differences in matrix type, management regime, and other uncontrolled factors (Murcia 1995). Generally, the greater the structural contrast between adjacent terrestrial habitats, the more intense the edge effects. However, Janzen (1983a) found that problems with weedy species invading natural disturbance sites in pristine forests in Costa Rica were greater when the forests were surrounded by successional habitats rich in weeds than when they were surrounded by croplands and heavily grazed pastures. Janzen (1986) found invasions of weedy plant species and various human disturbances at least 5 km into a forest. In Maryland, nest predation rates are higher in woodlots surrounded by suburbs than in woodlots surrounded by agriculture, probably because garbage and other food subsidies in suburban landscapes encourage proliferation of opportunistic predators (Wilcove 1985). Similarly, in Ontario, the diversity and abundance of songbirds in forest blocks surrounded by suburbs was much lower than in forests with few or no nearby houses, probably because populations of house cats, squirrels, and other nest predators are higher in suburbs (Friesen et al. 1995).

The pervasiveness of edge effects implies that habitat patches below a certain size will lack the true interior or "core" habitat that some species require. If 600 m is determined to be the penetration distance of significant nest predation, then a circular reserve smaller than 100 ha (250 acres) will be all edge (Wilcove et al. 1986). Using a conservative, two-tree-height edge width of 160 m, patches of old-growth Douglas fir forest in the Pacific Northwest smaller than 10 ha (25 acres) are all edge; a landscape that is 50% cut over in a typical checkerboard harvest system contains no true interior forest habitat (Franklin and Forman 1987). Temple (1986) assumed a 100 m edge width for forest fragments in south-central Wisconsin. Sixteen bird species were found to be sensitive to fragmentation in this landscape, breeding less frequently or not at all in smaller fragments. In a comparison of two forest fragments, one without any core habitat (due to its shape) lacked successful breeding by interior birds. The other fragment, with a similar total area but with a core area of 20 ha (50 acres), contained successful breeding pairs of 6 of the 16 fragmentation-sensitive bird species (Figure 9.17).

Deleterious edge effects contradict the message, often promoted by wildlife managers, that edge habitat benefits wildlife. One popular wildlife textbook urged managers to "develop as much edge as possible" because "wildlife is a product of the places where two habitats meet" (Yoakum and Dasmann 1971). It is true that most terrestrial *game* animals in the United States are edge-adapted, as are many animals characteristic of urban and intensive agricultural landscapes (Noss 1983). Forest fragmentation, some of it intentional for the production of game, has increased deer densities so much in the upper

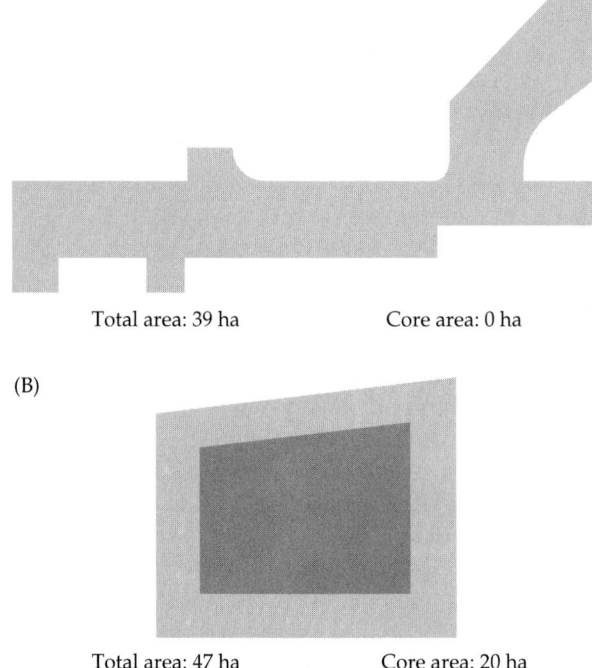

Figure 9.17 A comparison of breeding success of fragmentation-sensitive birds in two forest fragments with similar total areas but vastly different core areas (forest interior). Fragment A is entirely edge habitat (light); fragment B contains 20 ha of core habitat (dark). Of 16 species known to be sensitive to fragmentation, none bred in fragment A, and 6 bred in fragment B. (From Temple 1986.)

Midwest that regeneration of several tree species may be at risk because of heavy browsing (Alverson et al. 1988). The game-management bias of many wildlife biologists may have blinded them to the negative effects of edge in fragmented landscapes. Increased interest in nongame wildlife, which constitutes a far greater proportion of the biota than game species, has coincided with concern about deleterious edge effects and other problems related to habitat fragmentation.

Changes in Species Composition

The edge effect studies reported above suggest that species composition and abundance patterns will change in fragmented landscapes. For example, birds characteristic of forest interior habitats may be unable to maintain their populations in landscapes where edge is abundant; instead, the landscape may gradually become dominated by edge-adapted species not in great need of conservation. Species composition is altered in fragmented landscapes because some species are more vulnerable than others to reduced area, increased isolation, edge effects, and other factors that accompany the fragmentation process.

Species loss from fragmented habitats, then, may follow a predictable and deterministic sequence (Patterson 1987; Blake 1991). In studying habitat patches of various sizes, a pattern of **nested subsets** (not to be confused with "nesting" for reproduction) in the distribution of species is often observed (Figure 9.18). A nested subset is a biogeographic pattern in which larger habitats contain the same subset of species found in smaller habitats, but add new species to that subset. Thus, a set of the most common species is found in all habitat sizes, from smallest to largest, but progressively larger habitats add subsets of species found only in larger areas. The species found only in larger areas are generally those most vulnerable to fragmentation.

Boreal mammals and birds on mountain ranges in North America's Great Basin, which are natural habitat islands, show a nested distribution pattern that may be a consequence of selective extinction of area-dependent species on smaller habitat islands. In this case, extinctions have occurred in the same basic sequence throughout the region, despite considerable variation in extinction rates (Cutler 1991).

Distribution of bird species among woodlots in agricultural landscapes is typically nonrandom; the species found in small woodlots are also found in the larger patches. In east-central Illinois, the most highly nested pattern was found for species requiring forest interior habitat for nesting and for species that migrate to the Neotropics (Blake and Karr 1984; Blake 1991). A similar nonrandom pattern, with all species occupying large patches but many species absent from small patches, has been documented for birds on islands in Swedish lakes, in forest patches in central Spain, and in many other temperate communities (Nilsson 1986; Tellaria and Santos 1994). Studies of birds in the Wheatbelt of Western Australia have documented the loss of many species in small habitat remnants since isolation (Saunders 1989), a relaxation effect predictable from island biogeographic theory. Such results support previous suggestions that although a collection of small sites may harbor more species, large sites are needed to maintain populations of species sensitive to human disturbance. Recognizing that "conservation strategy should not treat all species as equal but must focus on species and habitats threatened by human activities" (Diamond 1976), an optimal conservation strategy in most cases would avoid fragmentation of large natural areas.

Nested species distribution patterns do not always have straightforward explanations. There can be other reasons for nested subsets besides a pre-

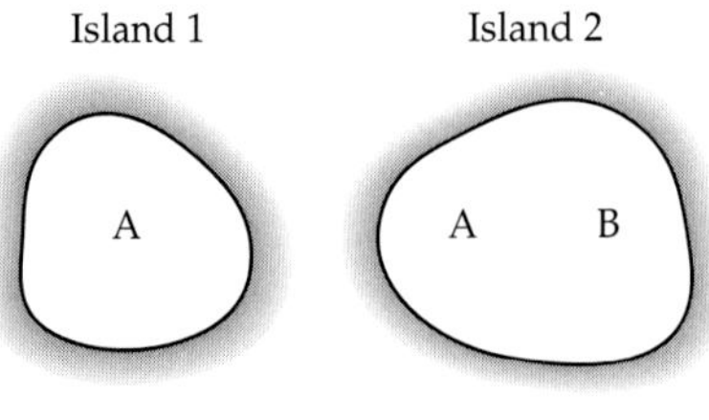

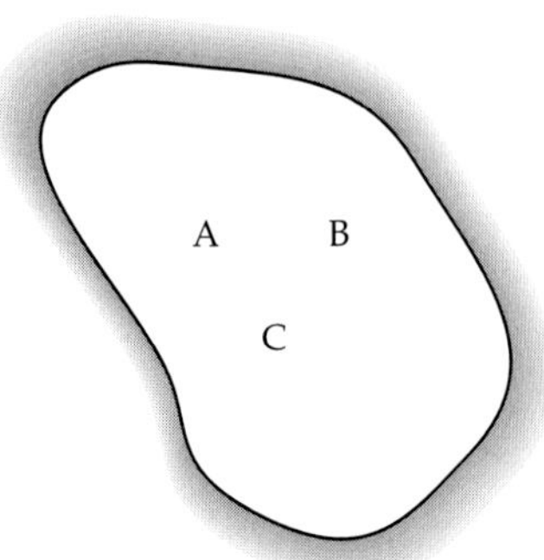

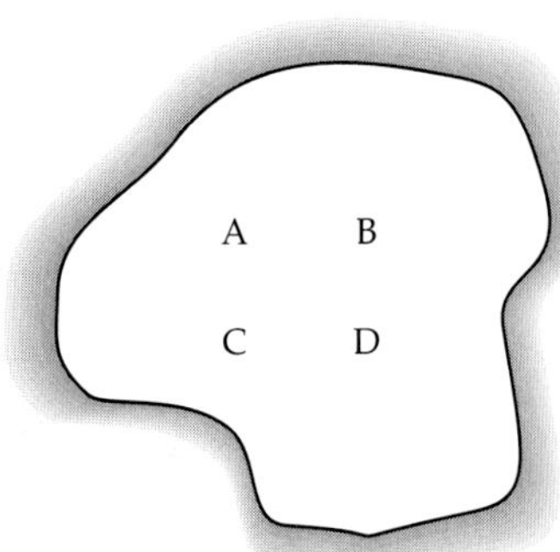

Figure 9.18 Hypothetical nested subset distribution of species on islands of different sizes. The letters A through D represent different species. Species are added in a predictable sequence with increasing island size and number of habitats. The largest island contains all four species. (From Cutler 1991.)

dictable sequence of extinctions as habitats are progressively fragmented. An examination of nestedness from the perspective of individual species showed that different kinds of factors, most related to habitat requirements, determined the distribution patterns of different species (Simberloff and Martin 1991). Moreover, most studies suggesting loss of bird species from small forest fragments have failed to test the null hypothesis that bird assemblages in small patches are simply "samples" from the larger regional pool of bird species.

A study of breeding birds in forest fragments in the southern taiga of Finland confirmed predictions from the null model that the location of breeding pairs varies randomly among fragments from year to year, and that the pattern of species additions with increasing sample size is similar to that expected for random sampling (Haila et al. 1993). Thus, local turnover of species in small fragments may represent simple changes in territory locations from year to year, rather than true "extinctions" and "recolonizations." These studies do not, in our view, negate the evidence that fragmentation is harmful—there is simply too much evidence to the contrary. However, such studies suggest a need for greater experimental rigor, so that the true effects of the fragmentation can be separated from statistical artifacts.

The addition of species to fragmented landscapes is as important to consider in conservation as is species loss. Many of the species that invade fragmented landscapes are exotics or are otherwise considered weedy. Increases in the number of species at a local scale due to invasions by weedy or exotic species are often accompanied by declines in diversity at a regional or global scale as sensitive native species are progressively lost, even though overall species richness may remain the same or even increase. As cosmopolitan species invade more and more regions, regional biotas are homogenized and lose their distinctness—a "mongrelization" of the global landscape. This process of homogenization is one of the most prominent forms of biotic impoverishment worldwide.

Fragmentation generally increases the rate of exotic species invasion, often through the creation of disturbed habitats through which exotics travel rapidly. For example, many exotic plants, exotic insect pests, and fungal diseases of trees are known to disperse and invade natural habitats in the western United States via roads and vehicles (Schowalter 1988). Sometimes habitat fragments can be relatively resistant to invasion. Alien plants were found along the edges of old-growth forest patches in Indiana, but forest interiors were virtually free of aliens (Brothers and Springarn 1992). The dense wall of vegetation that developed along the edges of the fragments in this study was thought to discourage invasion by reducing interior light levels and wind speeds. In a North Carolina study, however, exotic species such as Japanese honeysuckle (*Lonicera japonica*) penetrated forests up to 60 m or more from south-facing edges (Fraver 1994). With time, some exotic species become well established in forest interiors and outcompete natives.

Effects on Ecological Processes

Ecological processes may change substantially as a result of edge effects and other accompaniments of habitat fragmentation. Unfortunately, ecological processes in fragmented landscapes have received little research attention. The best-studied processes, as reviewed earlier, have been nest predation and brood parasitism of birds. Increased nest predation rates may be, in part, a consequence of higher densities of opportunistic mesopredators made possible by the elimination of large predators (Wilcove et al. 1986; Soulé et al. 1988). Predator removal, in turn, is facilitated by habitat fragmentation. Other studies of species interactions in fragmented landscapes are scarce, but include work on seed dispersal and herbivory as they vary near forest edges (Murcia 1995).

Probably some of the strongest effects of fragmentation on ecological processes will turn out to involve the invertebrate community. Invertebrates are critically important in decomposition, nutrient cycling, disturbance regimes, and other natural processes in ecosystems, and they appear to be quite sensitive to disruption of microclimate and other effects of fragmentation (Didham et al. 1996). Climatic edge effects may explain why dung and carrion beetle communities in 1 ha and 10 ha forest fragments in Brazil contain fewer species, sparser populations, and smaller beetles than do comparable areas within intact forest (Klein 1989). The drier conditions in small fragments, which are largely edge habitat, may lead to increased fatal desiccation of beetle larvae in the soil. Loss of beetles results in reduced decomposition rates of dung and probably other "ripple effects" throughout the ecosystem (Klein 1989). Other processes that depend on invertebrates and are known to be disrupted by fragmentation include pollination, seed predation, and parasitism (e.g., control of phytophagous insects by parasitic Hymenoptera), all of which require serious study (Didham et al. 1996).

The disruption of natural disturbance regimes by habitat fragmentation has been little studied, but may have striking effects on biological communities. When a landscape is fragmented, for example, natural fires that once spread for dozens or even hundreds of kilometers from their ignition points are stopped by artificial firebreaks such as roads, farm fields, and urban areas. Lightning is unlikely to strike small habitat fragments often enough to support fire-dependent communities such as grasslands and savannas. For example, censuses of small prairie remnants in Wisconsin showed that 8 to 60% of the plant species were lost over a 32- to 52-year period in the absence of fire (Leach and Givnish 1996). Losses were highest among short, small-seeded, and nitrogen-fixing plants, in addition to those growing in the wettest and most productive sites; rare plant species experienced the heaviest losses. These findings support the hypothesis that passive fire suppression caused by landscape fragmentation leads to loss of native species and that plants with the poorest competitive abilities in fire-suppressed habitats will be most heavily affected (Leach and Givnish 1996). Prescribed burning and other active management is urgently needed in such cases.

The Problem of Climate Change

Fragmentation is a threat to biodiversity even in a relatively stable world. If we add the phenomenon of rapid climate change, then we have perhaps the most ominous of all potential threats to biodiversity (Peters and Lovejoy 1994). Species migrating in response to climate change have always had to cope with dispersal barriers such as rivers, lakes, mountain ranges, and desert basins. The additional set of barriers created by human activities will make migration all the more difficult (Peters and Darling 1985). New climates will render reserves set aside to protect certain species or communities unsuitable for them. Weeds may dominate many fragments.

Even natural rates of climate change threaten species restricted to fragments surrounded by inhospitable habitat. The increased rates of change predicted with greenhouse warming may eliminate all but the most vagile species as they fail to track shifting climatic conditions. High-elevation and high- latitude habitats may be lost entirely. Although wide habitat corridors and artificial translocations of populations northward and upslope may help some species in some areas, these solutions will not suffice for whole communities, especially if climate change is as rapid as predicted.

Conclusions and Recommendations

This chapter has reviewed evidence that fragmentation occurs at many spatial scales and may have a variety of short-term and long-term effects. Some species benefit from fragmentation, whereas many others are placed at increased risk of extinction. Global biodiversity can be maintained in large part by devoting conservation resources to those species and ecosystems most at risk, and by controlling or reversing the processes that place them at risk. However, species not currently at great risk from fragmentation must also be addressed in conservation planning, lest continued habitat alteration worsen their status and make their conservation more difficult. There is also a need to develop effective management strategies for landscapes that are already fragmented, including management of the internal dynamics of remnant natural areas and the external influences on those areas.

Strategies for countering fragmentation follow logically from consideration of the fragmentation process and its effects. Because fragmentation causes reduction in the size of natural areas and isolation of remaining areas in a sea of unsuitable habitat, corrective action should include maintenance or restoration of large, intact core areas that span large portions of regional landscapes (Noss and Cooperrider 1994). These core areas will contain the source populations of many fragmentation-sensitive species (Robinson et al. 1995). Where circumstances prohibit establishment of truly large reserves, biodiversity can be well served by land use practices—for example, clustered developments and reduced road building—that minimize fragmentation and optimize connectivity of similar natural habitats. Connectivity must be defined functionally as the potential for movement or genetic interchange of target species or, on a broader spatiotemporal scale, migration of floras and faunas.

Large, interconnected nature reserves are only part of the solution to the fragmentation problem. Entire landscapes, including private and multiple-use public lands, should be managed in ways that minimize destruction and isolation of natural habitats. Opportunities to reduce and reverse fragmentation abound on public lands in the United States. Unfortunately, fragmentation continues on these lands (Noss and Cooperrider 1994). Between 1972 and 1987, average forest patch size in two ranger districts of the Willamette National Forest, Oregon, decreased by 17%, the amount of forest clear-cut edge doubled, and the amount of forest interior at least 100 m from an edge declined by 18% (Ripple et al. 1991a). In the Olympic National Forest, Washington, more than 87% of the old growth in 1940 was in patches larger than 4000 ha; in 1988, only one patch larger than 4000 ha remained, and 60% of the old growth was in patches smaller than 40 ha. Of the remaining old growth in 1988, 41% was within 170 m of an edge (Morrison 1990). Stopping destructive management practices on public lands is essential to conserving biodiversity in the United States. Nevertheless, at this writing, the U.S. Congress is pushing for increased, unsustainable, and destructive logging and other resource production on public lands. The situation is seldom better in other countries.

Some recommendations for maintaining biodiversity in fragmented landscapes (or those in danger of being fragmented) follow from the information presented in this chapter:

1. Conduct a landscape analysis. Determine the pattern of habitats and connections, and relate these to the needs of native species in the landscape. Where are the major, unfragmented blocks of habitat? Can natural connections among habitats be maintained or restored?

2. Evaluate the landscape of interest in a larger context. Does it form part of a critical linkage of ecosystems at a regional scale? What is the significance of this landscape to conservation goals at regional, national, and global scales?
3. Avoid any further fragmentation or isolation of natural areas. Developments, resource extraction activities, and other land uses should be clustered (and minimized) so that large blocks of natural habitat remain intact. In planning reserves, emphasize large areas whenever possible.
4. Minimize edge effects around remnant natural areas. This can be done by establishing buffer zones with low-intensity land uses. Be careful, however, not to produce population sinks that lure sensitive species out of reserves and into areas where mortality is high or reproduction is reduced.
5. While conserving large, unfragmented patches of habitat, do not "write off" the small fragments. Such areas may be the last refuges for many species in highly fragmented regions and can maintain populations of many species for decades. Moreover, these small fragments contain the sources for recolonization of the surrounding landscape, should destructive activities cease (Turner and Corlett 1996).
6. Identify traditional wildlife migration routes and protect them. Steer human activities away from critical wildlife movement areas.
7. Maintain native vegetation along streams, fencerows, roadsides, powerline rights-of-way, and other remnant corridors in strips as wide as possible in order to minimize edge effects and human disturbances.
8. Minimize the area and continuity of artificially disturbed habitats dominated by weedy or exotic species, such as roadsides, in order to reduce the potential for biological invasions of natural areas.
9. Small fragments often suffer from disruption of natural processes, such as fire regimes. Active management will be needed to maintain the native flora and fauna of these fragments.

Summary

Fragmentation, the loss and isolation of natural habitats, is one of the greatest threats to regional and global biodiversity. Whereas natural disturbances and other processes create heterogeneous landscapes rich in native species, human land uses often create islands of natural habitat embedded in a hostile matrix. Such fragmentation reduces or prevents normal dispersal, which is critical to long-term population viability for many species, and increases edge effects and other threats.

Fragmentation acts to reduce biodiversity through five major mechanisms. First, because remaining fragments represent only a sample of the original habitat, many species will be eliminated by chance (initial exclusion). Second, the modified landscape in which fragments exist may be inhospitable to many native species, thus preventing normal movements and dispersal (isolation). Third, small fragments contain fewer habitats, support smaller populations of native species, which are therefore more susceptible to extinction, and are less likely to intercept the paths of dispersing individuals (species–area effects). Fourth, climatic influences and opportunistic predators and competitors from the disturbed landscape can penetrate the fragments, reducing the core area of suitable habitat (edge effects). Many terrestrial game animals in North America are adapted to habitat edges and thrive in fragmented landscapes, which has encouraged wildlife managers to promote edge habitat at the expense of sensitive species adapted to habitat interiors. Finally, disruption of natural disturbance regimes and other processes in fragmented landscapes will lead to changes in biological communities.

Nine kinds of species have been identified that are likely to be especially vulnerable to the effects of fragmentation: rare species, species with large home ranges, species with limited powers of dispersal, species with low reproductive potential, species with short life cycles, species dependent on resources that are unpredictable in time or space, ground-nesting birds, species of habitat interiors, and species exploited or persecuted by people. Some of the most ominous effects of habitat fragmentation may not become apparent for decades or centuries, such as the effects of fragmentation on ecological processes, and the inability of species in isolated fragments to track changes in habitat conditions related to changing climate.

Some strategies for countering fragmentation are available: (1) do not destroy or fragment intact wildlands and other natural areas, few of which remain in most regions; (2) minimize road construction, clearing of vegetation, and creation of other barriers to dispersal; (3) maintain or restore wide habitat corridors or other forms of functional connectivity among natural areas; (4) minimize creation of artificial dispersal corridors (such as weedy roadsides) that encourage proliferation of exotic species; and (5) actively manage habitat fragments to compensate for disrupted natural processes.

Questions for Discussion

1. Lake Gatun was formed when the Panama Canal was built in 1914, creating the 17 km^2 Barro Colorado Island (see Essay 5A). Since then, careful observations have documented a 25% decline in the island's avifauna. Speculate on the reasons for this decline.

2. The Northern Spotted Owl, an obligate resident of old-growth coniferous forests in the Pacific Northwest, is thought to be sensitive to high temperatures, feeds on small mammals (many of them arboreal), and is subject to predation by the Great Horned Owl, a habitat generalist. Old-growth forests within the range of the Northern Spotted Owl once covered 60%–70% of the region, but have been reduced by 90%. How might different approaches to forest management affect the long-term viability of Spotted Owl populations?

3. Much of southern California was once covered by coastal sage scrub, a vegetation type dominated by California sagebrush, buckwheat, and herbaceous sages of the genus *Salvia*. A number of species endemic to this vegetation type, including the California Gnatcatcher (federally listed as threatened) and many plant species, have been proposed for listing under the Endangered Species Act. Development, mostly residential, has destroyed nearly 90% of this habitat. How might future developments or other land uses be controlled to protect biodiversity in coastal sage scrub?

4. Many species of small vertebrates and invertebrates are sensitive to the barrier effects of roads, refusing to cross even two-lane roads in some cases. Larger animals, including endangered species such as the Florida panther, are vulnerable to roadkill. How might these kinds of problems be corrected?

5. Recent population models suggest that the grizzly bear in the northern Rocky Mountains may require about 30 million acres of wilderness habi-

tat for long-term viability. Yellowstone National Park, by comparison, has only 2.2 million acres (see Essay 6B). Thus, habitat fragmentation at a regional scale is a threat to grizzly bear survival. The grizzly bear is vulnerable to fatal encounters with humans, many related to livestock production or road access by poachers. Housing subdivisions are also being constructed in grizzly bear habitat. How might conservation strategy address these regional fragmentation problems? What kinds of information—biological and otherwise—might be used to determine necessary reserve sizes, linkage widths, and management guidelines?

6. The longleaf pine–wiregrass ecosystem was once the dominant vegetation of the southeastern coastal plain of the United States, but has declined by 98% since European settlement. The dominant plants of this ecosystem depend on frequent (2–5-year intervals) low-intensity ground fires that control invading hardwoods and other competitors and maintain the characteristic open structure of the ecosystem. Fire suppression, in addition to logging, has been a major reason for the decline of this ecosystem. How might habitat isolation by roads, agriculture, and urbanization contribute to this decline?
7. Suppose you are the manager of a small (20 ha) forested nature reserve in the midwestern United States. What kind of management would you consider to reduce edge effects and maintain ecological integrity in this reserve? What variables (biotic and abiotic) would you monitor to determine whether or not your management plan is effective?

Suggestions for Further Reading

Burgess, R. L. and D. M. Sharpe (eds.). 1981. *Forest Island Dynamics in Man-Dominated Landscapes*. Springer-Verlag, New York. This text was the first book-length treatment of fragmentation problems. The chapters, by a number of prominent authors, focus on species–area effects, edge effects, and other problems in small fragments of eastern North American deciduous forest. Most of the studies reported were carried out in southeastern Wisconsin or Maryland.

Harris, L. D. 1984. *The Fragmented Forest: Island Biogeography Theory and the Preservation of Biotic Diversity*. University of Chicago Press, Chicago. Larry Harris won considerable acclaim with this book on fragmentation problems and potential solutions in the western Cascades of Oregon. More than any book before and virtually any since, this book spells out the advantages of taking a "big picture" approach to conservation by looking at landscapes and regions instead of only at individual sites.

MacArthur, R. H. and E. O. Wilson. 1967. *The Theory of Island Biogeography*. Princeton University Press, Princeton, NJ. This book, now a classic, formally presented and explored the idea that the number of species on an island is dependent on its size, distance from the mainland, and biogeographic history. Although the equilibrium theory proposed here remains controversial, this book stimulated more research in conservation than did any other work in history.

Noss, R. F. 1987. Protecting natural areas in fragmented landscapes. *Natural Areas J.* 7:2–13. This article reviews threats to biodiversity in fragmented landscapes and offers an approach for designing regional reserve networks composed of core areas, buffer zones, and corridors. Case studies are presented for southern Ohio and Florida. The basic model developed here has since been proposed for many regions.

Noss, R. F. and A. Y. Cooperrider. 1994. *Saving Nature's Legacy: Protecting and Restoring Biodiversity*. Defenders of Wildlife and Island Press, Washington, D.C. This award-winning book reviews the processes that create and destroy biodiversity and offers a detailed and comprehensive strategy for designating reserves and modifying land use practices to better conserve biodiversity, with emphasis on the United States. Specific options for reducing fragmentation are provided throughout.

Robinson, S. K., F. R. Thompson III, T. M. Donovan, D. R. Whitehead, and J. Faaborg. 1995. Regional forest fragmentation and the nesting success of migratory birds. *Science* 267:1987–1990. This landmark paper is the culmination of many years of research on the effects of fragmentation on forest birds in the midwestern United States. Major proximate threats (nest predation and cowbird parasitism) are discussed, and regional source and sink populations are identified. The authors urge the protection of large, unfragmented core areas in each region.

Saunders, D. A., R. J. Hobbs, and C. R. Margules. 1991. Biological consequences of ecosystem fragmentation: A review. *Conserv. Biol.* 5:18–32. This review of the literature on fragmentation problems starts with the observation that most fragmentation research to date has provided little of practical value to managers. After reviewing the literature on the physical and biotic effects of fragmentation, the authors conclude that research and management efforts should focus on controlling external influences on fragments and that an integrated approach to management of whole landscapes is needed.

Soulé, M. E. and D. Simberloff. 1986. What do genetics and ecology tell us about the design of nature reserves? *Biol. Conserv.* 35:19–40. In addition to being an excellent review of the general literature in conservation biology, this paper reconciles the two opposing viewpoints of the SLOSS (single large or several small reserves) controversy: multiple reserves in different habitats and regions will sample more species, but each reserve ideally should be large enough to maintain viable populations and normal ecosystem processes.

Wilcove, D. S., C. H. McLellan, and A. P. Dobson. 1986. Habitat fragmentation in the temperate zone. In M. E. Soulé (ed.), *Conservation Biology: The Science of Scarcity and Diversity*, pp. 237–256. Sinauer Associates, Sunderland, MA. Wilcove and co-authors present one of the most concise and comprehensive treatments of the problems arising from habitat fragmentation, with emphasis on temperate forests. The model presented suggests that further fragmentation of even already heavily fragmented regions may lead to rapid species loss, and that insularization can cause extinctions independent of habitat reduction. The advantages of large reserves, close reserves, and circular reserves are underscored.

10

Conservation Reserves in Heterogeneous Landscapes

It is from the earth that we must find our sustenance; it is on the earth that we must find solutions to the problems that promise to destroy all life here.

Justice William O. Douglas

The last several millennia have seen the earth transformed from an expanse of contiguous habitats, interrupted only by natural barriers or localized natural disturbances, to a patchwork of natural, human-modified, and thoroughly destroyed habitats. As explained in Chapter 9, habitat modification and degradation on many scales has fragmented natural areas into habitat patches separated by highways, cities, agricultural fields, plantation forests, mines, railroads, deforested wastelands, and countless other barriers. Because this trend will continue in the foreseeable future, conservation efforts must proceed with the understanding that only a small, critical fraction of the world's habitats may survive as natural or seminatural areas. This makes it all the more crucial that stewardship of these remaining areas be undertaken in a responsible and biologically sound manner through reserve development and protection. But reserves are and will remain only a small proportion of the overall landscape. A focus strictly on reserves will miss many opportunities for good conservation, and we must include the landscape matrix in our thinking for conservation planning.

Protection of habitat in reserves is a recent phenomenon, dating back only about a century, although habitat has been protected indirectly for millennia as hunting reserves and for other amusements of royalty. Many of the original reserves in the United States, including Yosemite, Glacier, Yellowstone, and Grand Canyon National Parks, were created not to protect biological resources, but as geologic attractions and for their aesthetic appeal (Figure 10.1). Sequoia and Kings Canyon National Parks were established not to protect the giant sequoia trees, but rather to protect the watershed serving the large agricultural interests in California's Central Valley. The largest protected area in the eastern United States, Adirondack Park, was protected as New York City's water source. Many existing reserves, therefore, do not effectively capture crit-

(A)

(B)

(C)

(D)

Figure 10.1 Many of the large, attractive natural reserves in the United States, such as (A) Grand Canyon, (B) Death Valley National Monument, (C) Yosemite, (D) Kings Canyon, and other national parks, were created as geological attractions and for their aesthetic appeal. Consequently, they may not be especially effective in biological conservation. (A and B, photographs by G. K. Meffe; C, © J. Hughes/Visuals Unlimited; D, by C. R. Carroll.)

ical biotic regions, nor are they designed in a manner conducive to biological conservation. Conspicuously missing, for example, at least in the United States, are protected natural areas of highly productive flatlands, including native prairies. Generally, reserves are remnants of low-productivity lands that have marginal agricultural value.

Today, about 4.25 million km^2 (about half the size of the United States), or about 2.8% of the world's land surface, is protected in reserves worldwide (Western 1989). For many of these reserves, though, protection is nominal at best: they exist on planning maps but do not function in their intended sense because of continued destructive land uses such as poaching, mining, agriculture, and logging. The goal recommended by the International Union for Conservation of Nature and Natural Resources (IUCN) is preservation of a cross-section of all major ecosystems. Its plan calls for the preservation of 13 million km^2, or 8% to 10% of the earth's surface (Western 1989b). How these areas are selected and protected is of utmost importance.

This chapter will not specifically address the theory behind conservation reserves, because much of that has been covered, directly or indirectly, in the previous chapters on biodiversity, genetics, demography, communities, and habitat fragmentation. We will instead build on information from those chapters to explore real-world issues in conservation reserve design. We will also stress the need to include the landscape matrix in reserve planning, not only because the matrix is the major landscape component, but also because it harbors many species of conservation interest, as well as threats to reserves. The importance of looking beyond the artificial boundaries of reserves and other natural areas is discussed by Richard L. Knight in Essay 10A.

ESSAY 10A

Lines across the Land

Richard L. Knight, Colorado State University

It is a fact, patent both to my dog and myself, that at daybreak I am the sole owner of all the acres I can walk over. It is not only boundaries that disappear, but also the thought of being bounded. Expanses unknown to deed or map are known to every dawn, and solitude, supposed no longer to exist in my county, extends on every hand as far as the dew can reach.

Aldo Leopold (1949)

In the course of settling and building nations that spread across continents, humans inevitably draw lines across the land. Whether these brushstrokes reflect different political jurisdictions, partition private from public lands, or are simply survey boundaries by which land is measured (e.g., sections, townships, ranges), our world has been, and continues to be, artificially fractured, fragmented, and fissured. It seems that the very endeavor of being human involves partitioning, dividing, and allocating resources along a variety of human-defined borders.

Due to our pervasive inclination to draw lines upon the land, it seems inevitable that public lands, nature reserves, multiple-use areas, and parks would have boundaries defined by human constructs. Had our public land units been designed by ecologists, rather than surveyors acting on administrative orders, their shapes, sizes, and locations might have been quite different from their actual appearance today. For example, rather than a gunbarrel-straight line defining one border of a national park, the boundary might reflect the inherent winding line of a watershed or ridgeline. Instead of a forest reserve boundary being demarcated by a state border, the management unit might instead end at the edge of a broad climate pattern or a major vegetation type. Up until a short time ago, these would have been no more than ecological musings, but a change in how we perceive land management offers hope that the future will see administrative lines more closely mirroring ecological boundaries.

For a variety of reasons, natural resource managers have behaved as though their borders were inviolable by forces from without (Pickett and Ostfeld 1995). This belief certainly simplified their lives, for if one assumed that boundaries were like steel walls that would prevent biotic and abiotic fluxes from passing across them, there was little need to consider what took place on the other side. Accordingly, a National Park employee would not have to communicate with the staff of an adjacent National Forest, nor would a BLM office have to interact with the private land owners contiguous to their boundary.

Thus, it became customary to view parks and other public lands as islands of protection in seas of development. Within their closed borders, resource managers could retain a seemingly ideal world that captured the balance of nature (Wagner and Kay 1993). Systems were viewed as self-regulating, disturbances were exceptional, and a single endpoint defined where the area would remain in equilibrium (Pickett and Ostfeld 1995).

The past decade has seen a substantial shift from this idealized world of closed systems. Indeed, the belief that humans can command nature has come to be viewed as a "pathology" that permeates natural resource management (Holling and Meffe 1996). Today, agencies responsible for managing ecosystems are encouraged to replace a view of nature as ordered and under their control with one that recognizes and embraces the dynamic nature of ecosystems captured in the phrase "the flux of nature" (Pickett and Ostfeld 1995). This new perspective accepts the natural variation in ecological systems and believes that this flux is essential if ecosystems are to retain their resilience.

As we approach the 21st century, federal and state land management agencies in the United States are addressing the challenge of managing ecosystems (Interagency Ecosystem Management Task Force 1995). This has necessitated a shift in focus, from concern for specific administrative units to concern for the health and land use practices of the more broadly defined ecosystem. Because the new and emerging issues of biodiversity and ecological integrity cut across lands under a variety of ownerships (public and private alike), the need for collaboration among agencies, owners, and stakeholders becomes paramount. Ecosystem management at the landscape level can be achieved only by creating an interactive network of ideas, information, and skills. This perspective recognizes the diversity of legitimate interests and capabilities in a pluralistic society, and the fact that information, values, resources, and power are distributed across geographic boundaries, social groups, organizations, agencies, and disciplines (Wondolleck and Yaffee 1994). The new focus on the management of landscape-scale ecosystems suggests the need for a far greater level of coordination, cooperation, and collaboration across jurisdictional and property boundaries in order to achieve the goal of healthy, diverse ecosystems and meet the diversity of needs typically found among a variety of public and private stakeholders.

There is evidence that a shift to cross-boundary management through cooperation and collaboration is occurring (Wondolleck and Yaffee 1994). The U.S. Fish and Wildlife Service is participating in biological diversity initiatives using watershed boundaries, rather than traditional artificial borders. Furthermore, watersheds have been clustered into ecosystem units, and ecosystem teams have been formed to develop ecosystem plans for the watersheds in these units. Recently, a National Forest and Bureau of Land Management office in Colorado "dimmed" their artificial boundaries by merging their two units into a single, much larger area that more closely reflects ecological boundaries.

Administrative boundaries are artifacts of human occupancy and management of the land. Surprisingly, many believe that these boundaries are permanent, stamped indelibly upon the landscape. Because even ecological boundaries are in a constant dynamic, it is certainly erroneous to assume that administrative boundaries are immutable. For a moment, can we imagine a future with fewer boundaries and a more integrated landscape that would facilitate movement of both humans and wildlife? One whose administrative borders are more aligned with natural demarcations upon the land, such as rivers, ridgelines, and changes in major vegetation types? One where administrative boundaries are modified, softened, or even abandoned? Given the breadth of different types of boundaries, and the complexity of social and biological issues associated with transboundary topics, how can we better manage lands created by administrative boundaries?

These are unanswered questions that land stewards will grapple with for as long as people cultivate a land ethic. The important thing is that, by accepting the dynamic boundaries of ecosystems and the impositions people place on the land, we are moving in the right direction.

The phrase "reserve design" is actually something of a misnomer. There are increasingly small chances that conservationists will have the luxury of actually "designing" reserves. Perhaps it remains a possibility in the Amazon Basin and when deciding how to clear-cut much of the small remaining area of old-growth forest in the United States. However, in most cases, the reality is that conservation interests will take what they can get, and will work within the constraints of what is available, regardless of any optimal theoretical designs that may or may not be accepted at the time.

For example, several years and great intellectual energies were spent on the "**SLOSS**" debate—the acronym stands for "Single Large Or Several Small." Conservationists asked whether, given limited money, time, and personnel, it would in general be a better practice to develop one large reserve or several small reserves *of the same total size*. The debate raged for years with no clear resolution. Rather than probing the details of this debate, which is now largely relegated to historical interest (Soulé and Simberloff 1986), we will let it serve as a reminder that developing sound conservation reserves is more complicated than simply adopting a general principle that, even if agreed upon, would rarely present itself as a real-world decision to be made.

Given that conservationists will seek and accept whatever reserves they can acquire, the key questions focus more on how to convince the human populace that large reserves are needed, and how to manage the internal dynamics of and external threats to reserves once acquired. No longer at issue is whether bigger reserves are better; we knew all along that, *all else being equal*, large reserves hold more species, better support wide-ranging species, and have lower extinction rates than small reserves. The problems are more complicated than that. We must instead determine what other physical and biological features are important in supporting viable populations, communities, and functioning ecosystems at given localities.

Considerations and Goals for Conservation Reserves

As we have already seen, the prevailing paradigm of ecology well into the 1970s was the equilibrium, "balance of nature" perspective. Ecological systems were thought to have a stable-point equilibrium, such as a predictable climax state, and to be structurally and functionally complete and self-regulating. Most species populations within an ecosystem were relatively stable from year to year, and kept each other's numbers in check. If disturbed from a given physical configuration, a climax ecosystem would return to it (Figure 10.2A). The conservation implications of this paradigm included the notions that (1) a particular unit of nature is conservable by itself in a reserve; (2) such units will maintain themselves in a stable and balanced configuration; and (3) if disturbed, the system will return to its former, balanced state (Pickett et al. 1992). Under this paradigm, reserves would probably succeed as long as they were locked up and protected from human influences. If only it were that easy!

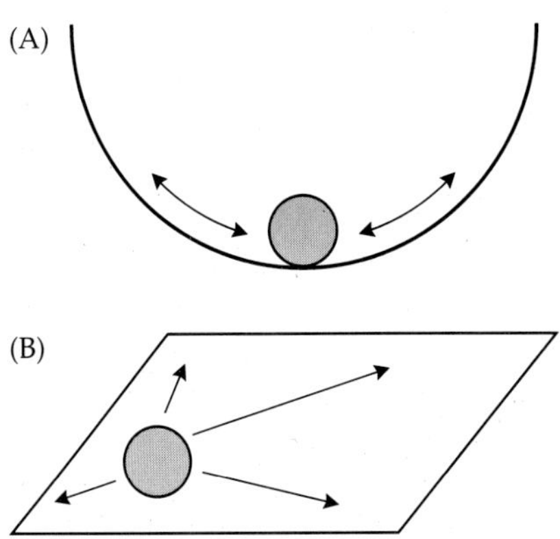

Figure 10.2 Conceptual models of (A) equilibrium and (B) nonequilibrium ecological systems. If disturbed, the equilibrium system eventually returns to its original state, but the nonequilibrium system can assume a new state. The latter perspective also more explicitly recognizes the importance of external disturbances.

As we have repeatedly emphasized, the last two decades have witnessed a shift in the prevailing paradigm toward a new worldview, stimulated by empirical contradictions with the equilibrium perspective (e.g., Botkin and Sobel 1975), by recognition of the prevalence and effects of natural disturbances in ecological systems (Sousa 1984), and by a change in scale of focus, from very coarse-scaled to finer-scaled views (Pickett et al. 1992). This "nonequilibrium" paradigm (Figure 10.2B) recognizes that ecological systems are rarely at a stable point, are open to exchange of materials and energy with their surroundings, are not internally self-regulating, and are very much influenced by periodic disturbances that affect their internal structure and function. It is a perspective that emphasizes processes, dynamics, and context, rather than endpoint stability.

The definition of "disturbance," and what actually constitutes a disturbance in a given community, has been much debated. Useful definitions include those of White and Pickett (1985), who defined a disturbance as "any relatively discrete event in time that disrupts ecosystem, community, or population structure and changes resources, substrate availability, or the physical environment," and Petraitis et al. (1989), who included as a disturbance any "process that alters the birth and death rates of individuals present in the patch."

One of the most important concepts in the study of disturbance, and one relevant to conservation reserves, is the **intermediate disturbance hypothesis** (Connell 1978), which states that maximum species richness in many systems occurs at an intermediate intensity and frequency of natural disturbance (Figure 10.3). High disturbance levels allow the persistence of only those species that are disturbance-adapted, while low disturbance levels allow competitive dominance by some species, causing local extinction of others. However, many species can coexist and persist at intermediate levels of disturbance, especially if patches of different disturbance types and intensities exist.

The conservation implications of the nonequilibrium paradigm include the following: (1) a particular unit of nature is not easily conservable in isolation from its surroundings, and therefore the matrix must be incorporated into conservation planning; (2) reserves will not maintain themselves in a stable and balanced configuration over long periods of time; and (3) reserves will incur natural disturbances (as well as human disturbances) and are likely to change state as a result (Pickett et al. 1992). The nonequilibrium paradigm tells us that reserves will not succeed simply by being locked up and protected from humans; disturbances and influences from the matrix, including human societies, will affect reserves, resulting in changing species compositions and changing rates and directions of natural processes. This dynamism needs to be accommodated when managing conservation reserves.

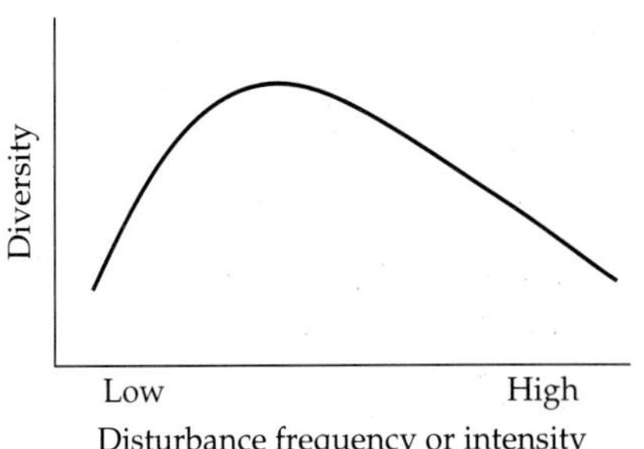

Figure 10.3 Model of the intermediate disturbance hypothesis. Species diversity is lowest at high and low levels (frequencies or intensities) of disturbance, and highest at an intermediate level. (Modified from Connell 1978.)

Application of the nonequilibrium paradigm makes conservation in reserves more difficult because reserves must be able to incorporate often unpredictable magnitudes and directions of change and still maintain species diversity and ecological processes. Regardless of the difficulties associated with the nonequilibrium perspective, to the best of our current knowledge this appears to be how natural systems function, and conservation reserves must operate under this paradigm. *The nonequilibrium paradigm should be the underlying model and motivation for all decisions affecting selection and management of conservation reserves.*

In very large reserves these nonequilibrium processes largely develop from naturally occurring disturbance regimes, and may add to habitat and species diversity. However, as the sizes of reserves decrease, disturbances may become destructive to diversity, and intervention through management may become necessary. For example, a tree blow-down in a small reserve of, say, 100 ha may allow colonization by exotic species from adjacent areas off the reserve. Mechanical removal of those colonists and planting of native species may be necessary. There are great conceptual and practical difficulties in finding relevant types and levels of management that mimic natural processes; these are discussed in detail in Chapters 11 and 12.

Goals of Conservation Reserves

The purpose of conservation reserves should be to retain the diversity of biological elements and ecological processes inherent in nature that would otherwise be lost through continuing habitat degradation. This being the case, it is important to realize that reserves are often relatively small, remnant parts of larger ecosystems, strongly influenced by a matrix of variously modified and perturbed systems surrounding them. Even rather large reserves are influenced by external events at local to global scales, and reserves by themselves will never suffice to protect all of biological diversity.

Nature reserves are typically developed with one or more of three primary biological motivations (Soulé and Simberloff 1986). First is the preservation of large and functioning ecosystems. Large expanses may be protected for their local and global "ecosystem services" (Ehrlich and Mooney 1983), for example, watersheds for flood control and water recharge, as occurred in Sequoia and Kings Canyon National Parks. Complete, functional units such as intact watersheds are most desirable as primary, critical resources to be set aside for their free ecosystem services to both humans and nature (Figure 10.4).

Figure 10.4 The Coweeta watershed of North Carolina, a Long-Term Ecological Research (LTER) site, is an example of the type of complete, functional unit that should be protected in reserves. (Photograph courtesy of USDA Forest Service.)

(A)

(B)

(C)

Figure 10.5 Conservation reserves are often motivated by single-species protection. The protected species are often large, high-profile vertebrates, such as (A) the African elephant (*Loxodonta africana*), (B) the giant panda (*Ailuropoda melanoleuca*), or (C) the Bengal tiger (*Panthera tigris*). (A, photograph by Gary J. James/Biological Photo Service; B, by Ron Garrison © San Diego Zoo; C, by Vivek Sinha/Biological Photo Service.)

A second motivation for nature reserves is to preserve biodiversity. This reserve strategy focuses on areas of high species richness, such as tropical rainforests or coral reefs, or unique areas with high rates of endemism, such as Madagascar or some desert regions (one such reserve, Ash Meadows, is the topic of Essay 10C, later in this chapter).

Finally, reserves are also developed to protect particular species or groups of species of special interest. These are typically either severely endangered species or otherwise highly visible taxa, and include the California Condor, African elephants, rhinoceroses, pandas, and large carnivores such as tigers and jaguars (Figure 10.5). Many other species and entire ecosystems are preserved as a secondary benefit under the "umbrella" of these high-visibility, so-called "charismatic" vertebrates, which invariably require large expanses. As discussed in Chapter 3, for example, current laws in the United States recognize endangered species, but not endangered ecosystems. However, because the protected plants or animals are an integral part of their ecosystems, their habitats are also protected by law, as are other species inhabiting those areas. A case in point is the protection of old-growth forests in the Pacific Northwest through legal protection of Northern Spotted Owls (*Strix occidentalis caurina*) and Marbled Murrelets (*Brachyramphus marmoratum*).

These three reserve types are not mutually exclusive, of course. A reserve intended to protect a single, high-profile species may also protect an intact ecosystem (although not necessarily); likewise, an ecosystem reserve will probably protect a large amount of diversity. Ideally, the more a reserve can protect at all three levels, the more desirable and successful it will be.

An additional motivation for reserves, which we will not directly address here, but which nevertheless can have important effects on habitat use and preservation, is perpetuation of plants or animals for harvest. In particular, great quantities of wetlands have been protected by waterfowl hunting groups as duck habitat, some estuaries are protected as fish and invertebrate nurseries, and forest tracts are often managed for improvement of deer, quail, or turkey habitat, or for eventual logging. Although these efforts are motivated by concerns for single- or multiple-species harvest rather than biodiversity or ecosystem function, they still have positive influences on broader aspects of conservation, if for no other reason than precluding development in these areas.

If a reserve is managed too intensively for one species, however, then biodiversity in general may decline, or particular aspects of diversity may be lost. For example, large predators that are thought (usually erroneously) to compete with hunters for game species may be purposely eliminated, and game densities may become so high that they damage their habitat. Forests managed for low plant species diversity or low structural diversity, which may favor a particular game species or may benefit logging, also tend to support lower diversities of vertebrates than do high-diversity, multispecies stands (Pianka 1967; Cody 1975).

Concerns in Conservation Reserve Development

There are three major classes of concerns in the development of conservation reserves, which require disciplinary integration. First and perhaps foremost are the biological considerations we have just discussed—the siting of reserves for protection of ecological processes, an intact biota, or a special, identified subset of a biota. These goals require consideration of the location, size, and shape of the reserve, its connections and spatial relationships with other natural areas, population sizes needed to maintain critical species, local colonization and extinction dynamics of the biota at large, ecological dynamics within the reserve, and threats posed by land uses surrounding the reserve.

The second concern is for the reserve's anthropological or cultural effects. Wherever possible, a biological reserve should not disrupt the traditional, sustainable cultures of indigenous peoples, and should be compatible with the cultural norms of local societies (Figure 10.6). This is recommended both because ethics demand that all human societies deserve such consideration, and because it is less likely to cause strife and resentment, and thus failure of the reserve. Social support for a reserve by local people, paying visitors, and the general public will greatly enhance its chances for success.

Figure 10.6 The traditional, sustainable cultures of indigenous peoples should be considered in the design of any nature reserve. The reserve should be compatible with traditional and sustainable cultural norms of local societies. Shown here are the Chief and Chieftess of the Ecuadorian Siona people. As elders, they are the principal repositories of indigenous knowledge, and can have great bearing on the success or failure of a reserve. (Photograph by Eduardo Asanza.)

Finally, conservation reserves need to work within the political and economic constraints and realities present at local to global levels; if those constraints seem unreasonable, they must be modified through public education or, at times, court action. There are usually trade-offs to be made with, and battles to be fought against, competing interests for land. Land and its products are and will continue to be limiting resources for an expanding global human population, and conflicts will arise among groups with diametrically opposed viewpoints concerning land use. The more these conflicts can be defined, understood, and minimized at the outset, the easier it will be to maintain successful reserves.

Six Critical Issues in Reserve Success

Wilcox and Murphy (1985) summarized the problems and challenges facing conservation reserves when they said, "Habitat fragmentation is the most serious threat to biological diversity and is the primary cause of the present extinction crisis." Fragmentation of natural habitat in a matrix of degraded or inhospitable urban, industrial, and agricultural lands is the common pattern of human land use. This fragmentation results in habitat loss, isolation of remaining habitat, strong influences from the new matrix, and creation of edges exposed to that matrix.

There are at least six critical issues to be considered in developing and maintaining successful conservation reserves that have a chance of functioning ecologically within the larger landscape matrix despite habitat fragmentation. All of these hearken back to the basic premise that ecological systems are dynamic and nonequilibrium, and they tell us that successful reserves will be managed on that basis. Species will go extinct in reserves despite our best efforts, and plant and animal community structure will change over time within reserves—that is the essence of natural systems. Reserves must be designed to accommodate these changes rather than to resist natural change. Ideally, this is done by creating reserves of the largest size possible, by including spatial and temporal heterogeneity, by considering the geographic context of the reserve, by connecting reserves on a regional basis, by considering natural landscape elements, and by creating zones of different uses within reserves.

Reserve Size

Larger reserves are better for maintenance of individual species, biodiversity, and ecological functions than are smaller reserves, for at least two reasons. First, the basic species–area relationship (Chapters 4, 5, and 9) tells us that larger reserves capture a greater number of the species within a region than do smaller reserves. More species are thus supported in larger reserves. Second, the persistence of individual species in a reserve may depend on the size of the reserve; some species, especially large vertebrates, tend to be lost from smaller reserves. However, persistence varies greatly by taxon and life history characteristics. Many species can persist with no problem in small reserves—witness the success of gray squirrels (*Sciurus carolinensis*) in eastern North American city parks—whereas other species will disappear in decades from our largest protected wilderness areas (discussed below). It is the latter type of species that is usually of concern when reserve size is considered.

The reserve size needed may also vary as a function of the habitat quality of the area. That is, reserve size may be partly a surrogate for a critical amount or type of resources. A reserve with low-quality resources for a target species may need to be larger than another reserve with higher-quality resources simply to accommodate the number of individuals needed to maintain a viable population.

Much of the concern about extinctions of large vertebrates in reserves comes from analyses of minimum viable populations (MVP), a concept discussed in Chapter 7. This approach to conservation addresses individual species and their long-term probability of population persistence in reserves of various sizes. Its goal is to maintain viable populations of selected species, usually large vertebrates, over long periods of time in the face of likely biotic and abiotic challenges, and to identify the population sizes, and thus reserve sizes, necessary to do this. (Note that the goal is not to maintain a *minimum* number, but to identify a population size below which extinction is quite likely, and then maintain populations well above that size). This is done through a population viability analysis (PVA), "a structured, systematic, and comprehensive examination of the interacting factors that place a population or species at risk" (Shaffer 1990). The serious practical difficulties involved in actually applying PVA in reserve management are discussed in Chapter 7 and reviewed by Boyce (1992).

In general, large-bodied, low-density, upper-trophic-level species with large individual ranges need a greater area to maintain viable populations in the long term than do smaller-bodied, higher-density, lower-trophic-level species with smaller ranges. Among plants, larger areas are required for species that are obligate outcrossers than for facultative selfers; larger areas are also needed for species that are disturbance specialists or that require forest "gaps" than for habitat generalist species. Among animals, large mammals and birds generally require larger reserves than other animal or plant taxa, and carnivores require larger reserves than herbivores (Figure 10.7). Thus, much of the concern regarding reserve size has centered on mammals.

The potential for loss of large animals from even a large area is illustrated by changes that have occurred in Florida's large mammalian fauna in the last few centuries (Harris and Atkins 1991). Florida supported 11 species of large mammals (>5 kg) until 200 years ago: bison, manatee, black bear, monk seal, white-tailed deer, key deer, Florida panther, red wolf, bobcat, otter, and rac-

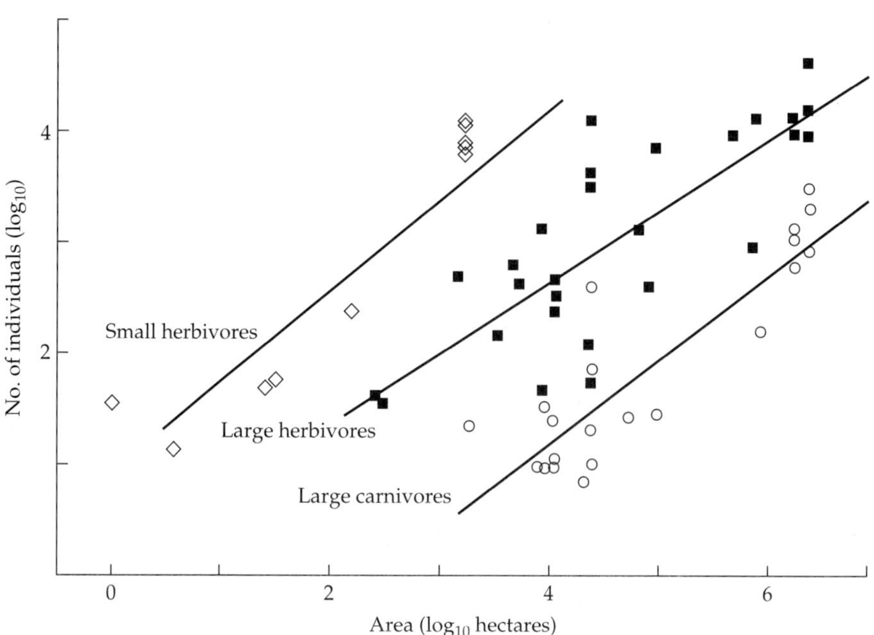

Figure 10.7 Population sizes supported by reserves of various sizes around the world for small and large herbivores and large carnivores. (From Schoenwald-Cox 1983.)

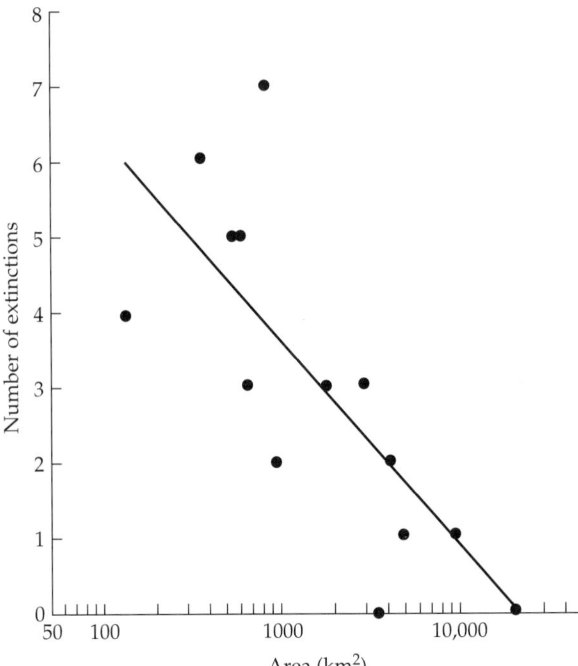

Figure 10.8 Naturally caused extinctions that occurred after reserve establishment as a function of park area in 14 western North American national parks. (From Newmark 1987.)

coon. Three of these species, the monk seal, the bison, and the red wolf, are locally or globally extinct (largely due to hunting and predator control); three others, the manatee, the Florida panther, and the key deer, have been so reduced that they are federally listed as endangered; and three more, the black bear, the bobcat, and the otter, are listed as threatened species by the state of Florida or are listed by the Convention on International Trade in Endangered Species (CITES). Only the white-tailed deer and the raccoon (two habitat generalists, an herbivore and an omnivore, respectively) are doing well in Florida.

Newmark (1987) reported on cases of natural extinctions of mammals in 14 western North American national parks over a period from 43 to 94 years after park establishment. He found a strong negative relationship between park size and extinction (Figure 10.8): the largest parks had few or no extinctions, whereas the smallest parks had up to seven mammalian species disappear since legal protection of the parks. In a subsequent study (Newmark 1995), he found that the total number of extinctions (29) of mammal species in these same 14 parks exceeded colonizations (7). Survival time within a park was a function of initial population size, taxonomic affiliation (lagomorphs—pikas, hares, and rabbits—were most susceptible to extinction), and generation time. Species with large initial populations (and therefore occurring in large parks) and long generation times were less likely to go extinct. Picton (1979) found that loss of large mammal species from isolated mountain ranges in the northern Rocky Mountains was a function of habitat size (Figure 10.9). It is clear from these data that many of our reserves simply are not large enough to maintain viable populations of large vertebrates indefinitely without management intervention.

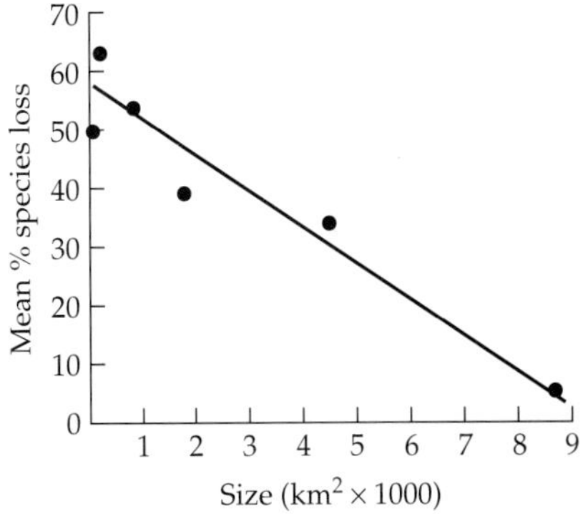

Figure 10.9 Percentage loss of large mammal species since European settlement as a function of area of isolated ranges in the northern Rocky Mountains. (From Harris 1984; data from Picton 1979.)

The danger of small reserve size was given further credence by the modeling exercises of Belovsky (1987). His mathematical extinction models indicate that from 0% to 22% of current parks worldwide can be expected to support the largest mammalian carnivore species (10–100 kg) for 100 years; none of these species are expected to persist for 1000 years. Large herbivores have slightly better prospects; from 4% to 100% of reserves should allow persistence for 100 years, and 0% to 22% for 1000 years. For persistence in evolutionary time (10^5–10^6 years), Belovsky estimates that reserves of 10^6 to 10^9 km^2 are needed for large mammals (>50 kg). However, the majority of all reserves worldwide are under 10^5 km^2 (Frankel and Soulé 1981).

Grumbine (1990) summed up thoughts on reserve size with the following: "The assumption that our current parks and preserves are in any meaningful sense protecting large, wide-ranging native mammals has little factual basis. For most areas (100,000 ha or less) this lack of protection seems to include the short term (decades). For the long term (centuries), it is likely that all current reserves are incapable of supporting minimum viable populations of large carnivores and herbivores." Likely, at least, without active management.

Another concern related to reserve size is the maintenance of genetic diversity, discussed more fully in Chapter 6. The smaller populations maintained in smaller reserves will in general contain less genetic diversity and be more subject to genetic stochasticities with negative effects on population viability. These smaller populations are more likely to suffer loss of heterozygosity due to genetic drift or founder effects, are more likely to experience inbreeding, and are more likely to go extinct due to random demographic influences (Lande 1988).

Reserve size also has implications for the expected degree of edge effects, addressed in Chapter 9. Smaller reserves have a greater edge:interior ratio, thereby increasing edge effects and decreasing the amount of true interior habitat. This shift can make the reserve more vulnerable to invasion by exotic and edge species, and subject it to edge environmental influences such as temperature extremes and increased winds (Saunders et al. 1991).

Finally, larger reserves are more likely to be able to accommodate disturbances, either natural or anthropogenic. All of a small reserve of several hundred hectares, for example, could be affected by a fire or hurricane, and its residents left with no suitable habitat patches. This happened in 1938 in Harvard Forest, when all of the mature timber was blown down in a single hurricane (White and Bratton 1980). A reserve of hundreds of thousands of hectares, by comparison, is more likely to have some patches unaffected by the same disturbance, leaving appropriate habitat available. The topic of heterogeneity is pursued more fully in the next section.

Heterogeneity and Dynamics

Spatially and temporally heterogeneous areas are generally superior to homogeneous areas as conservation reserves if the goal is to maintain high biological diversity. This principle stems from the observation that nature is dynamic and changes over time and space through biotic and abiotic disturbance. Spatial heterogeneity of habitat "patches" within a reserve accommodates disturbance better than does a homogeneous reserve by offering species a diversity of habitat types at any given time. If a particular habitat patch is altered or destroyed by disturbance, or if it undergoes succession and becomes unsuitable for a given species, then other appropriate patches may be available for colonization within the reserve.

Patches are perhaps best discussed in terms of α and β diversity (Chapter 4). A single habitat patch supports a particular group of species at any point in time, and has an α-, or within-patch, diversity. Species differences among different patch types constitute β-diversity. High overall diversity in a reserve may arise from α-diversity, β-diversity, or both.

The presence or absence of a species in a given habitat patch is a function of local colonization and extinction rates in that patch for that species. Overall patch diversity is therefore a function of colonization and extinction dy-

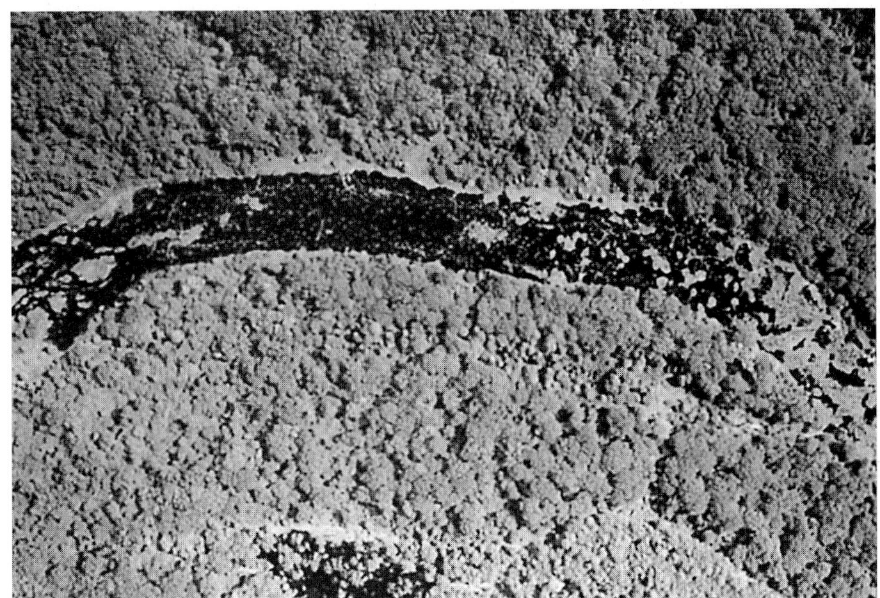

Figure 10.10 Most landscapes consist of habitat patches created by various natural processes, including disturbances, resulting in a patchwork of habitat types, such as this area along the Savannah River in South Carolina. (Photograph courtesy of Savannah River Ecology Lab.)

namics across the pool of species. Because conservation reserves are typically the last bastion for many species, the probability of colonization from external sources may be reduced or eliminated. In that case, extinction dynamics become the dominant force in species diversity for the reserve, and species diversity will ultimately decline. In order to retain species, then, rather than depending on recolonization from external sources, the reserves themselves need to provide the source areas—thus the need for internal heterogeneity of patches in a reserve.

This emphasis on heterogeneity within reserves (or **patch dynamics**) was developed by Pickett and Thompson (1978), who stressed the importance of the internal dynamics of habitat patches in maintaining overall diversity. Habitat patches in a landscape are created by disturbance regimes, which result in a patchwork of habitat types of different sizes, shapes, successional stages, and persistence times (Figure 10.10). Types of natural disturbances that create habitat patches include fires, storm tree-falls, and insect damage in forests; wave action on marine shorelines; floods and droughts in streams; and herbivory and soil disruption by mammals in grasslands. Each of these disturbances modifies or destroys some component of the existing biota, creating a habitat patch of an earlier successional stage. Anthropogenic disturbances, often of greater size or intensity than natural disturbances, also create patches (Figure 10.11).

The internal structure of the reserve, including species composition, population densities and dispersions, and organic geometry, is defined by the disturbance pattern and longevities of the patches. A reserve is thus a mosaic of patches of various sizes and ages, and its diversity depends partly on the dynamics of these patches. Patches change through time, new patches are created by disturbance, and spatial relationships among patches change.

The patch dynamics perspective does not mean that reserves should be chopped up into many small patches. Rather, the natural disturbance regime and the resultant size and frequency of disturbance patches must be ascertained, as well as successional patterns for the landscape. Ideally, then, the size of reserve necessary to include the various natural patch types can be determined. The types of disturbance, their usual magnitude and frequency, and the typical responses of the biota are requisite information. It is also important

Figure 10.11 Anthropogenic disturbances, such as this clear-cut in an old-growth forest in Washington State, create new types of patches on the landscape. (Photograph by G. K. Meffe.)

to understand and incorporate rare but extensive disturbances, such as hurricanes or monsoon floods, into reserve design—those severe disturbances that may occur at frequencies of once in hundreds to thousands of years, but which can have drastic consequences for a reserve based on "normal" magnitudes of disturbance.

Pickett and Thompson (1978) recommended that reserve size be based on a **minimum dynamic area**, which is the smallest area with a complete, natural disturbance regime. This would maintain internal recolonization sources and minimize extinction by maintaining a complete diversity of patches at any given time. Such a minimum dynamic area can be determined only by empirical knowledge of each system; it could vary, for example, from perhaps tens of hectares in a rocky shoreline community to hundreds of thousands of hectares in a lowland rainforest, but in any case should be considerably larger than the largest disturbance patch, including rare and extreme disturbances.

Another empirical fact argues for habitat heterogeneity in reserves. A review of the conservation literature suggests that many, perhaps most, species in nature may exist not as single or isolated populations, but as groups of populations, or metapopulations, in different habitat patches (see Chapters 6, 7, and 9 for detailed discussions). Metapopulation structure may indeed be widespread, but too few studies have been conducted to provide much insight into just how common it is. As you will see in the discussion that follows, an assumption of metapopulation structure has important implications for the management of conservation areas. Determining the existence of metapopulation structures (through studies of population structure and movements) and their distribution among taxonomic groups and different environmental conditions should be a high research priority in conservation biology. When metapopulation structure exists, then interactions occur among the populations through movement among habitat patches, which affects genetic structure of individual populations, habitat patch occupancy, and recolonization of patches after local extinction.

Metapopulations have important implications for patch dynamics and heterogeneity of reserves. When similar habitat patches are spatially separated across a reserve, individual species may have a metapopulation structure, with populations occurring in different suitable patches. The patch dynamics perspective assumes that dispersal among similar successional patches is possible, countering local extinction processes. In order for patch dynamics to work, of course, multiple habitat patches need to exist and to be accessible to metapopulations of species appropriate to each patch type. That is, reserves need to be internally heterogeneous.

Murphy et al. (1990) point out that the metapopulation perspective may be more critical for "small" biota, such as annual plants, invertebrates, and small vertebrates, than for the megavertebrates championed as the "umbrella" species under which many other species are protected. These smaller species, with short generation times, small body sizes, high rates of population increase, and, sometimes, high habitat specificity, are more vulnerable to localized density-independent environmental factors than are the megavertebrates. Thus, a large, local population of a threatened butterfly, such as the Bay checkerspot (*Euphydryas editha bayensis*) in California (discussed in previous chapters), could be lost because of annual variations in temperature or rainfall that would not affect even sparse populations of vertebrates (Figure 10.12). A metapopulation structure, with repeated patches inhabited by this species, may have kept the Bay checkerspot from going globally extinct in the face of numerous local extinctions (Ehrlich and Murphy 1987). It is important to note also that, although small-bodied species may be more directly influenced by environmental disturbances than are large-bodied species, the higher rate of population growth found in small-bodied species also means that they recover from perturbations more quickly (Minckley et al. 1991).

The emphasis on habitat heterogeneity in conservation reserves is an outgrowth of the realization of the importance of processes, rather than just patterns, in ecological systems. A patch dynamics approach fosters continuation of natural processes and change in a reserve, which means that disturbance events should generally not be controlled or eliminated. In fact, lack of disturbance may become a problem.

One of the important questions in reserve management is how to ensure that disturbance regimes are maintained (see Chapters 11 and 12). For terrestrial communities, the role of fire provides an instructive case in point. In large, intact forests before human settlement, fires were usually the result of lightning strikes, and occurred rather frequently, but at low intensity (Heinselman

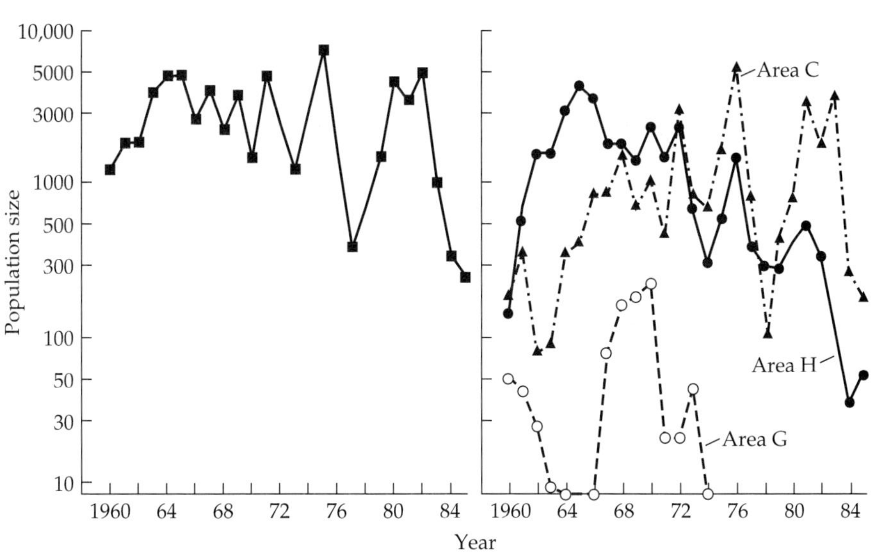

Figure 10.12 Size changes in three populations of the Bay checkerspot butterfly (*Euphydryas editha bayensis*) southeast of San Francisco, California. Numbers of the combined metapopulation are shown at left; the separate population dynamics are shown at right. Note the extinctions and recolonization in area G. (From Ehrlich and Murphy 1987.)

1973). In preindustrial societies fires were sometimes used to manage habitat for game production or to clear small areas for agriculture. Under these conditions, fires tended to be small and patchy, thereby creating an important disturbance regime or patch dynamic. Today, unless prescribed fires are explicitly used to manage habitats, fires tend to be suppressed and are thus rare, but extensive and intensive when they do occur, as in the 1989 Yellowstone National Park fires, which covered thousands of hectares and destroyed large forest stands. Under such conditions, fire is less an agent of disturbance and patch dynamics than an agent of large-scale habitat conversion.

When patch heterogeneity must be generated through management, the goal should be kept clearly in mind. If the goal is to maintain the characteristic biodiversity of the region, then management should be used to mimic the magnitude, frequency, and spatial scale of natural processes that generate patch heterogeneity. However, management of heterogeneity simply to maximize numbers of species per se would result in the transformation of a landscape into a mosaic of edges and patches, and might make it more vulnerable to invasion by exotic species (Hobbs and Huenneke 1992).

Landscape Context

Biodiversity in reserves is influenced both by the patch dynamics within the reserve and by the context of the larger landscape, which must be considered at multiple scales. At the within-reserve scale, each patch type is spatially located in the context of other patch types. Patch inhabitants must be able to move among similar patches and recolonize new patches if metapopulation structure is to continue. Some species also use different patch types seasonally or at different life history stages, and must be able to find those patches within the larger context of the reserve. For example, elk must have access to low-elevation winter grazing and to high mountain meadows during summer. Some salamanders develop as larvae in ponds, but spend their adult lives in a terrestrial "patch."

Figure 10.13 Satellite image of the U.S. Department of Energy's Savannah River Site in South Carolina, adjacent to the Savannah River. Note how this 780 km^2 area of largely forested lands (dark circle) stands out from the surrounding region of heavy agricultural use and suburban development. (Satellite image courtesy of Savannah River Ecology Lab.)

At a larger scale, the entire reserve functions in the context of a surrounding, nonreserve matrix (Figure 10.13), which can have critical consequences, both positive and negative, for the reserve. Conservation reserves are dynamic, with extensive movements by plants and animals, as well as material transport and energy flux, occurring within and among habitats. Consequently, the boundaries or edges of reserves have received a great deal of attention, and may be critical factors in the protection of interior habitat, because edges determine the dynamics of immigration and emigration. The landscape surrounding the reserve also requires attention. It may be a combination of urban, suburban, industrial, or agricultural or forestry lands, offering a mixture of threats ranging from domestic plants and animals to crop monocultures to pathogens to severe pollution. It may also offer positive features, such as source populations for some species. It is important to remember that most of the world is, and will continue to be, matrix, not reserves.

The importance of edges in reserve success was emphasized in a boundary model developed by Schonewald-Cox and Bayless (1986). This model recognizes that the administrative boundary of a reserve is often designated by political or legal, rather than ecological, considerations, within the constraints of previous land ownership and conflicting public demands. This legal boundary acts as a filter, controlling human activities within and outside of the reserve, and often differs from natural, ecological boundaries or edges, which control biological and physicochemical events.

The administrative boundary typically results in the creation of a generated edge, a false edge that is the result of the effects of greater protection within a reserve and lesser protection outside (Figure 10.14). The generated

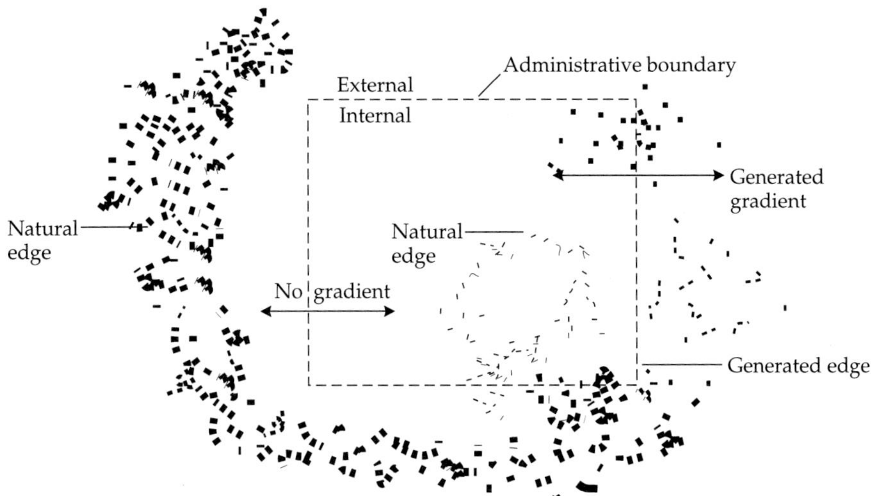

Figure 10.14 Boundary model of a reserve, illustrating natural ecological edges and generated edges created by an ecologically artificial administrative boundary. (Modified from Schonewald-Cox and Bayless 1986.)

edge may be close to or far from the legal boundary; if deep within the reserve, it reduces the effective reserve size. These various boundaries and edges create gradients that affect movements into and out of the "legal" reserve, and thus affect population dynamics, community structure, and ecosystem function.

The incongruity of the legal and biotic boundaries of reserves was explored by Newmark (1985) for the eight largest reserves or reserve assemblages in western North America. He compared the identified legal boundaries with the biotic boundaries, which he determined by watershed locations and the estimated areas needed to maintain viable populations of the nonflying mammals with the largest home ranges. Newmark found that seven of the eight reserves have biotic boundaries larger than their legal boundaries by factors of 1.2 to 9.6 for MVPs of 50, and 6 to 96 for MVPs of 500. Seven of the eight reserves also have legal boundaries smaller than the simple minimum area requirements of one or more mammalian species. This approach reinforces the earlier message that even our largest North American reserves are too small to maintain some species in perpetuity, and emphasizes the conservation significance of the semi-wild public and private lands that may surround reserves as a buffer. The message? Watch the matrix!

The **area/perimeter ratio** of a reserve is important when considering reserve boundaries (Buechner 1987); if the ratio is low (as in small or elongated reserves with proportionately more perimeter length per unit of interior area), then the average distance from interior points to the boundary is small, and interior species, those requiring undisturbed habitat away from edges, presumably will do poorly. If the ratio is large, then the interior is farther removed from edge influences (see Chapter 9). A lower area/perimeter ratio also means that more management, and thus more energy, money, and time, is necessary to maintain the interior characteristics of a reserve. From an edge perspective, a more circular reserve, with a higher area/perimeter ratio, would be preferable to an elongated reserve (Figure 10.15).

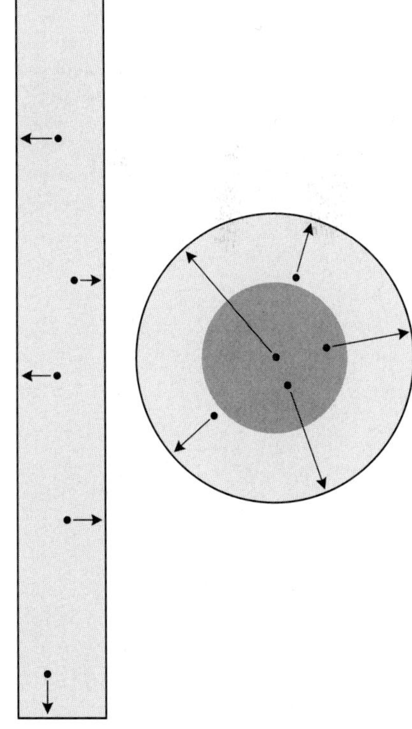

Figure 10.15 A schematic diagram showing the relationship between area and edge in two hypothetical reserves of the same area. In the rectangular reserve, there is no true interior habitat; all points are close to an edge (light shading). In the circular reserve, there is some true interior habitat (dark shading).

There is another critical point to be made here. A narrow reserve with no core habitat is less sensitive to further habitat loss because the area is already essentially all edge habitat. In contrast, a circular reserve with core habitat can be strongly affected by even small habitat losses because they bring edge effects farther into the core (Figure 10.16). For example, inholdings in large natural areas can have effects much larger than their area might suggest simply because they extend edge effects into core areas.

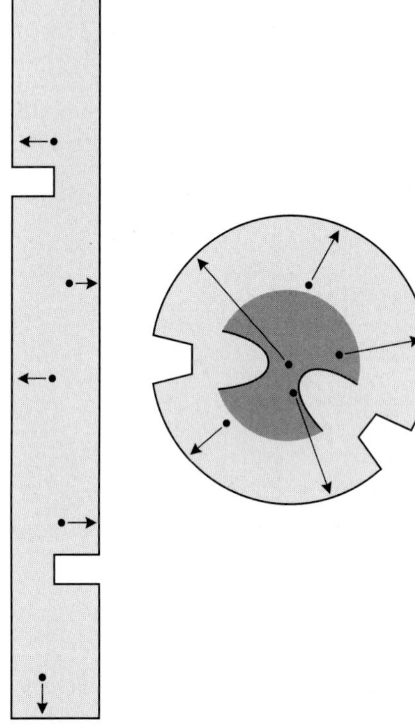

Figure 10.16 The same hypothetical reserves from Figure 10.15, with small pieces of edge habitat destroyed. In the rectangular reserve, little real effect is realized, because the reserve was previously all edge. In the circular reserve, the new habitat loss extends edge habitat far into the core, effectively reducing the size of the core reserve.

The boundary model encourages the creation of buffers around reserves to increase available habitat (even if suboptimal) and to decrease exposure to adverse conditions from the developed world. The buffers can have some limited exploitative function, such as selective timber harvest, hunting, or low-density development, and still function in a protective role. If the generated edge forms within the buffer rather than within the reserve, that is an added positive feature.

Even on a small, localized scale, buffers may be critical to ecological function and species survival. Burke and Gibbons (1995) studied freshwater turtles in wetland habitats in South Carolina that are legally protected by federal wetlands statutes. However, because turtles inhabiting the wetland nest and hibernate in the surrounding uplands, the legal buffer around this particular wetland protected none of the turtle nest and hibernation sites (Figure 10.17). A buffer 30.5 m wider protects 44% of sites, a buffer of 73 m would protect 90% of sites, and protection of all turtles would require a buffer of some 275 m.

Context must also consider human intervention, both direct and indirect, legal and illegal. Direct intervention includes activities such as legal harvest (hunting, logging), poaching, industrial and agricultural activities, mining, and urban and suburban development, and raises a number of questions in each instance. For example, will a proposed or existing reserve be encroached upon by new development? If so, how will drainage patterns change? What are the likely effects of domestic animals on the reserve? What types of cultivated plants are likely to escape into the reserve? Will adjacent agricultural activities affect the reserve through use of fertilizers and pesticides? Will industrial expansion affect the reserve through increased air and water pollution or legal or illegal dumping of wastes? Mitigation of these adverse effects is the concern of reserve management (Chapters 11 and 12); however, as we discuss below, reserves can be created so as to minimize some of these risks using buffers and zoning.

Indirect human influences can affect reserves as well, and include regional and global changes such as acid rain, global climate change, and regional land use activities. These effects are less subject to control or mitigation, but nevertheless should be considered in reserve selection and management. For example, are regional land use activities so heavily urban that it is unlikely that a reserve can effectively function as other than a green space for human use? If so, then monies should not be devoted to unrealistic goals of species preservation. Is acid rain so intense that continuous neutralization of lakes will be necessary to maintain fish populations? If so, then perhaps resources should be directed toward other species more likely to persist under such conditions.

Janzen (1983a, 1986) has been especially adamant about the context of reserves. He argues that mainland "insular" reserves are in fact not at all insular, but are under constant threat from the surrounding landscape and all of its evils, both natural and anthropogenic, a problem he calls the "eternal external threat." Such evils include pesticides, fire (or lack of it), local or global climate modification, migration of reserve animals into surrounding areas, movement of animals and plants (especially alien species) into the reserve from adjacent areas, and food subsidies from lands adjacent to the reserve. Unfortunately, most of the biotic movement and subsidy will come from successional species of disturbed habitats or species from croplands, which will invade reserves from edges inward. The smaller the reserve, the greater the effect of the surrounding habitat as a source of problems, and the greater the need for habitat buffers that minimize habitat differences between the core reserve and adjacent areas.

The invasion of a reserve by species from surrounding, "unbuffered" lands is clearly illustrated by a study of a natural tree-fall gap in a 10 ha patch of original forest surrounded by old pastures and secondary successional forest in Santa Rosa National Park, in northwestern Costa Rica (Janzen 1983). Nearly all the plant species that grew after creation of this 124 m^2 gap came from second-growth vegetation of anthropogenic origin outside of the park, from a minimum of 60 m away. This patch presumably will not regenerate as primary forest, but will form a long-lasting patch of disturbance vegetation uncharacteristic of the mature forest of this region. More important, perhaps, than the loss of species in the gap is that species interactions and processes inherent in the original vegetation will be altered. Insolation levels will change, soil moisture and drainage may be altered, nutrient cycling will be different from that in the surrounding forest, and coevolved relationships among the biota will be disrupted. Attention to context, including incorporation of a buffer zone, could have significantly reduced these unnatural effects of a natural disturbance.

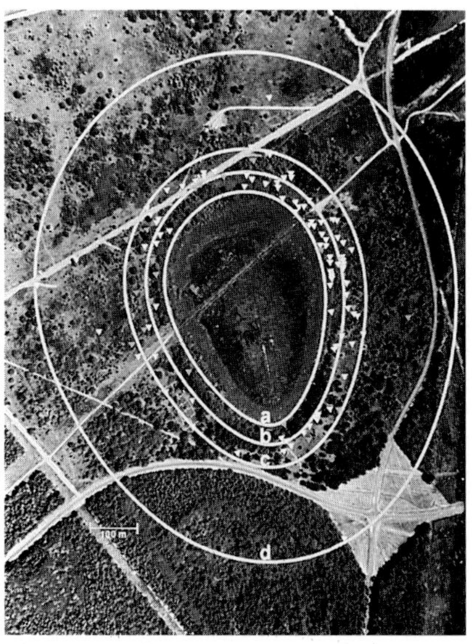

Figure 10.17 The federal wetlands delineation line (ring a) surrounding this wetland habitat in South Carolina protects none of the known nesting or hibernation sites for freshwater turtles. More stringent state laws that encompass an extra 30.5 m (ring b) protect more habitat and include 44% of turtles sites, but larger buffers are needed to protect 90% (ring c) or 100% (ring d) of the turtles. (From Burke and Gibbons 1995.)

Connecting Fragmented Habitats

As we saw in Chapter 9, human activities around the planet have created widespread habitat fragmentation and isolation in virtually every ecosystem type. Because these activities are a major contributor to the loss of biodiversity, it makes intuitive sense that reconnection of habitats would be a major step toward solving that problem. This is the basis for the idea of connecting reserves through corridors, or strips of habitat connecting otherwise isolated habitat patches. Corridors have been promoted as important features of reserves that allow movement, and thus recolonization, among high-quality habitats.

Corridors may be necessary even across small disturbance areas, as species differ greatly in dispersal capabilities. A nocturnal mammal, for example, may have no problem traversing a 100 m wide clear-cut, whereas a forest interior bird or a diurnal snake may find it an insurmountable barrier. A given corridor may actually serve as a selective filter, allowing movement by some species and blocking movement of others (Noss 1991b).

Wildlife corridors have two major purposes. The first is to allow periodic movements among different habitat types used for different purposes, such as breeding, birthing, feeding, or roosting (Soulé 1991b). Such movements range from annual migrations of large herbivores between summer and winter grazing areas to daily movements of birds between feeding and roosting sites. The second is to allow permanent immigration and emigration of individuals among habitat patches in a metapopulation context, allowing gene flow and recolonization after local extinction.

Noss (1991b) described three types of wildlife corridors needed at different spatiotemporal scales, because specific problems exist at different scales of both time and space and at different levels of biological organization. The scale of concern for a given situation depends on the biota involved and the conservation goals. The **fencerow scale** connects small, close habitat patches, such as woodlots, using narrow rows of appropriate habitat, such as trees or shrubs, for the movement of small vertebrates, such as mice, chipmunks, or passerine birds (Figure 10.18). These corridors are entirely "edge" habitat and thus are not useful for habitat interior species.

Figure 10.18 A fencerow corridor in northeastern Georgia. Such fencerow corridors connect small habitat patches such as woodlots, and may be effective for movement of small vertebrates. These corridors are entirely "edge" habitat and are not at all effective for habitat interior species. (Photograph by G. K. Meffe.)

The second type of corridor functions at the **landscape mosaic scale**. These are usually broader and longer corridors that connect major landscape features rather than small patches (Figure 10.19). They may function for daily, seasonal, or more permanent movement of interior as well as edge species,

Figure 10.19 A strip corridor, in this case a riparian forest along the Río Tempisque in Costa Rica (center of photo). Strip corridors are broader and longer than fencerow corridors and connect major landscape features. Strip corridors can promote daily or seasonal movements of interior and edge species, and create a landscape-level mosaic of reserves. (Photograph by C. R. Carroll.)

and result in a landscape-level mosaic of reserves. This type of corridor would include large strips of forest that connect otherwise separate reserves, riparian forests along streams, or habitats that follow natural gradients or topographic features such as mountainous ridges.

The **regional scale** is the largest corridor scale, and connects nature reserves in regional networks (Figure 10.20). This last type of corridor is further discussed below.

The benefits of corridors can be high (Noss 1987), even though corridor inclusion has potential costs, and corridors may not be desirable in all situations (as discussed below). Because fragmentation is one of the greatest threats to biodiversity, countering its effects through reconnection of prime habitats through the landscape matrix should be considered whenever possible. One of the best arguments for corridors is that the original landscape was largely interconnected, but then fragmented by human actions; reconnection will move the situation slightly back toward the original state (Noss 1987). Corridors should be considered on an individual basis for each reserve, and included or rejected on the basis of data pertinent to each system.

If corridors are desirable for a given situation, what form should they take? Again, there is no set answer, and only an empirical approach tailored to each situation, combined with generalized knowledge about the biology of the species involved, will suffice. The solution will depend partly on what types of biota are to be preserved and their mobilities, the distance between reserves to be connected, how likely it is that human interference will occur in the corridors, the availability of corridor habitat, and other factors unique to each situation. Corridors may be as simple and mundane as a hedgerow, a powerline cut, or a highway median of pine trees that allows movements of birds and small mammals. Such simple corridors, consisting entirely of edge habitat, are called **line corridors**. In contrast, **strip corridors** are broader, and contain some interior habitat with intact and functioning communities, such as a swath of tropical forest several hundred meters wide. Ideally, such corridors would be large enough to experience their own patch dynamics.

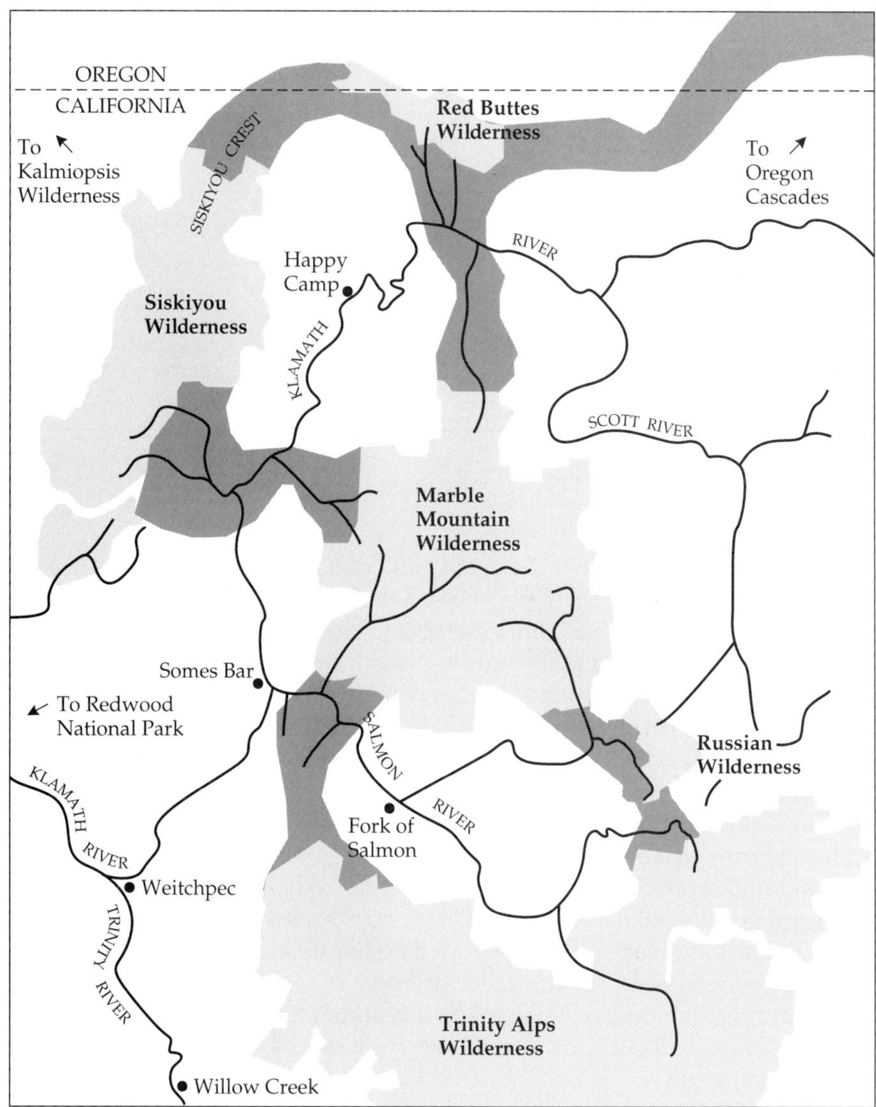

Figure 10.20 Proposed corridors (dark shading) that would connect various wilderness areas (light shading) into a regional mosaic in the Klamath area of northern California/southern Oregon. Arrows show directions of other nearby wilderness areas. (From Pace 1991.)

Riparian zones can serve as excellent strip corridors and protect important habitat at the same time. Especially in arid areas, many species are drawn to riparian areas from upland zones, and are at least periodically dependent on the resources there. Riparian strips can also connect highland and mountain habitat with the lowlands and thereby provide for elevational migrations. However, riparian corridors are not the answer to all problems in connectivity. They will not serve as corridors, for example, for upland species that avoid mesic conditions.

Corridors connecting reserves that are farther apart may need to be wider in order to be effective (Harrison 1992), because large, wide-ranging animals such as some mammalian predators require interior habitat in order to travel very far. One cannot expect a grizzly bear to travel many kilometers among reserves in a corridor 50 m wide. Knowledge of average home range sizes for individuals or groups can help in estimating necessary minimum widths for corridors (Table 10.1).

Table 10.1
Estimates of Minimum Corridor Widths Based on Average Home-Range Sizes in Several Mammals

Species	Location	Minimum width (km)	Source
Wolves	Minnesota	12.0	Nowak and Paradiso 1983
Wolves	Alaska	22.0	Ballard and Spraker 1979
Black bears	Minnesota	2.0	Rogers 1987
Mountain lions	California	5.0	Hopkins et al. 1982
Bobcats	South Carolina	2.5	Griffith and Fendley 1982
White-tailed deer	Minnesota	0.6	Nelson and Mech 1987
Dwarf mongoose	Tanzania	0.6	Rood 1987

From Harrison 1992.

Soulé (1991) warned that the quality and effectiveness of corridors need to be considered, not just their size, shape, and position. This means that the objective of the corridor, usually in terms of viability of specific target species, needs to be clearly stated at the outset. A corridor that does not function in its intended way can actually be detrimental by serving as a "death trap" or "sink corridor" that pulls individuals away from source areas and exposes them to increased mortality, but does not effectively deliver them to the intended reserve.

Lindenmayer and Nix (1993) studied corridor use by marsupials in Australia and provided evidence for Soulé's warning; they found that home range size and minimum corridor width were not the only important factors in corridor use. Additional factors influencing corridor use included the larger landscape context of the site, habitat structure (such as number of trees with hollows or size of stream in the corridor), and the social structure (solitary/colonial; monogamous/polygamous), diet, and foraging patterns of the target species. Thus, each corridor configuration should be the result of a detailed ecological analysis.

Noss and Harris (1986) point out that conservation strategies that focus on individual reserves while ignoring the larger landscape are unrealistic for several reasons: (1) isolated reserves are static, and do not effectively deal with continuous and expected biotic change within reserves; (2) they are focused on the *content* of individual reserves rather than the *context* of the entire landscape matrix; (3) they emphasize populations and species rather than the systems in which they occur and interact; and (4) these strategies are oriented toward high species diversity rather than toward maintaining the natural and characteristic diversity of the area.

Noss and Harris (1986) proposed an approach to regional reserve design called "Nodes, Networks, and MUMs." A **node** is an area with unusually high conservation value; for example, a region with high species diversity, high endemism, or that contains critical resources, such as breeding or feeding grounds for a species of particular interest. The criteria for selection of nodes can span the entire range of the biological hierarchy, from genetics to ecosystems. Nodes also may be dynamic, moving in space in response to environmental change, and must be permitted to track shifting environments through time.

Individual nodes, however, will rarely, if ever, be large enough to maintain and protect all the biodiversity within their borders indefinitely. That was demonstrated earlier with North American large mammals, and East (1981) has also argued that the large herbivores and carnivores in African savanna reserves will not persist for long in their current configuration. Consequently, **networks** of reserves need to be developed by connecting the various nodes through corridors of suitable habitat. These corridors connect the nodes into a landscape scheme that allows flow of species, genes, energy, and materials among them.

Multiple-use modules, or **MUMs**, as proposed by Harris (1984), consist of a central, well-protected core area surrounded by a series of buffer zones of increasingly heavy use by humans farther from the central core. The core would be inviolable, allowing no development or avoidable human impacts, whereas the buffer zones would be used for human endeavors ranging from bird-watching and backpacking near the core, to hunting, logging, and low-density residential development farther from the core. Management of all areas, however, would be consistent with preservation of the core or node. This approach resolves conflicts between "hands-on" conservation/management and "hands-off" preservation through zoning of individual components, further discussed below. An example of a MUM network for northern Florida and southern Georgia was proposed by Noss and Harris (1986; Figure 10.21). Interestingly, they note that the major impediment to development of MUMs is not lack of money, but lack of cooperation among federal, state, and local land management and regulatory agencies and private landowners.

Corridors: A Caveat. We have just discussed the conservation role of corridors in largely favorable terms, while at the same time calling for more

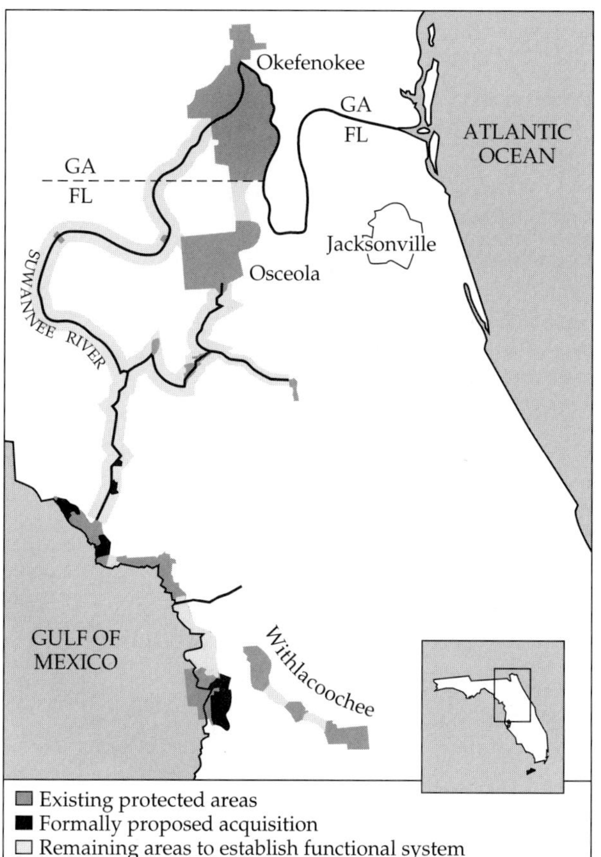

Figure 10.21 An example of a proposed multiple-use module (MUM) network in southern Georgia and northern Florida. The various nodes (existing protected areas) could be connected by proposed riparian and coastal corridors. (From Noss and Harris 1986.)

empirical studies. There are good reasons to expect that corridors, if designed properly, can enhance population viability in fragmented and otherwise isolated habitats. However, there are important "real-world" considerations that urge caution. First, the empirical basis for our confidence in corridors is poorly developed. Most of the studies on corridors have simply demonstrated whether or not the target organisms can be found there. We do not know how often existing putative corridors are really used for movement between major habitat patches, or the probability of mortality should an individual attempt to disperse. Experimental studies testing efficacies of corridors are virtually nonexistent. Second, the establishment of new corridors, especially of extensive systems intended to facilitate the movement of many species, requires the commitment of resources that might otherwise be used to enlarge existing reserves or buy new ones. If a fixed number of acres is to be set aside, then inclusion of corridors could reduce the size of core areas for the reserves.

The real utility of corridors remains to be demonstrated, both as a general principle and in specific cases. Even if corridors seem to work generally, every case of planned corridor use should involve some assessment of the likelihood of real contributions to reserve success. These themes are discussed further in Simberloff and Cox (1987) and Simberloff et al. (1992).

Natural and Modified Landscape Elements

Landscape elements are the "basic, relatively homogeneous, ecological elements or units" (Forman and Godron 1986) that make up the overall landscape (Figure 10.22). *Natural* landscape elements include features such as drainage basins, ridges, ecotones, salt marshes, slopes, canyons, habitat penin-

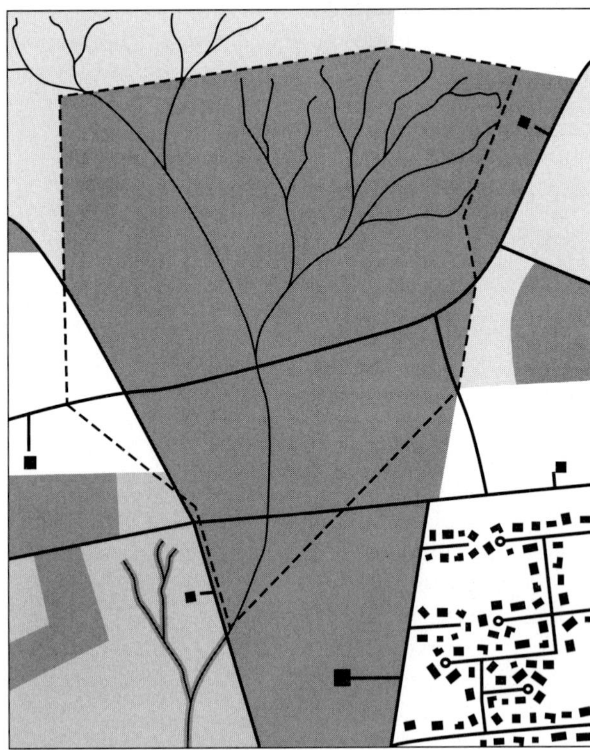

Figure 10.22 A schematic diagram showing various natural and modified landscape elements in and around a newly created reserve. The reserve is denoted by the dashed line. The dark shading is primary forest, light shading is second-growth forest, and white areas represent present or former agricultural fields. Dwellings are indicated by black squares, roads by solid black lines. Note that both natural and modified landscape elements are contained within and outside of the reserve.

sulas, or any other identifiable piece of natural landscapes. *Modified* landscape elements include roads and highways, agricultural fields, timberlands, industrial zones, and cities. Natural and modified landscape elements should be identified at the outset in reserve design and incorporated, accounted for, or excluded as appropriate. As a general rule, a diversity of natural landscape elements (i.e., habitat patches) will enhance the conservation value of reserves, and modified elements will detract from it.

Inclusion of the entire extent of a particular natural element, rather than a portion, permits control and protection of the entire unit. For example, a reserve or system of reserves that includes an entire drainage basin is preferable to one in which part of the basin is out of the reserve, especially upstream from it. In the former case, reserve management has control over activities within the whole basin; in the latter case, the reserve is subject to upstream events, such as pollution or stream modification, outside of the control of reserve managers.

Exclusion of modified landscape elements cannot always be accomplished, and conservation reserves must incorporate such elements at the outset and determine how to minimize their detrimental effects. For example, a major highway may run through a proposed reserve, effectively cutting it in two, or creating a population sink via highway mortality. An upstream sewage treatment facility may be dumping secondary effluents into a river that runs through a downstream reserve, reducing the quality of the water through eutrophication. In cases such as these, the problematic element must first be identified, then its effects must be reduced as much as possible. This effort could include measures to minimize the effects (such as highway underpasses for wildlife [Figure 10.23] or installation of tertiary treatment facilities), or mitigation measures elsewhere to create replacement for habitat reduced or lost through the activity.

The above are examples of point-source problems, discrete problems at identifiable locations. Analysis of landscape elements must also consider non-point-source avenues of impact, which may be more difficult to control. For example, chemical pesticides, nutrients, and invasive species are not confined by reserve boundaries; typically, as agricultural and timber production intensifies, chemical leakage and invasion of natural areas by weedy plants, animals, and pathogens also increase (Carroll 1991). Furthermore, agricultural crops near reserves may become important food resources for a subset of reserve animals and thereby distort their effect on other populations. Such species include food generalists such as raccoons and corvids (crows and jays) in the temperate zone, whose enhanced populations seriously threaten nesting bird species (Wilcove et al. 1986), and granivorous birds (e.g., quelea and parakeets), rodents, bandicoots, and other generalists in the tropics. Insects on crops may also cause expansion of populations of generalist predators and parasitoids, which may then invade natural habitats and attack the much smaller and potentially more vulnerable populations of insects in natural systems, as Howarth (1985) has shown in Hawaii.

The use of landscape elements around natural areas is rarely constant, and hence the influence of surrounding land use on natural areas also changes. Land use patterns change in response to technology, external markets, population growth and decline, war, government policies, land degradation, and other socioeconomic factors. The complexity of these land use possibilities and historical changes makes it difficult to determine the extent to which contemporary biological patterns are the product of purely biological processes or are strongly influenced by a particular history of resource exploitation. To use

(A)

(B)

Figure 10.23 Highway mortality of endangered Florida panthers and other species is being minimized by extensive fencing (A) along highways through the Florida Everglades, complete with underpasses (B) that permit movement under the highway by wildlife species. (Photographs by G. K. Meffe.)

African elephants as an example, Caughley (1976) argued that Zambian elephants have natural long-term population cycles. Abel and Blaikie (1986) countered with the argument that apparent long-term elephant population cycles were really the consequences of hunting pressure and agricultural land use changes that were, in turn, greatly influenced by the 18th and 19th century slave and ivory trades. Thus, modified landscape elements and changing land uses near reserves may affect elephant populations within reserves. Further perspectives on landscapes in conservation reserves are provided by Richard Forman in Essay 10B.

Buffer Zones

Conservation reserves may use **zoning** to influence land use activities around reserves and make them more compatible with the conservation goals of the

ESSAY 10B

Designing Landscapes and Regions to Conserve Nature

Richard T. T. Forman, Harvard University

Future biodiversity depends largely on our success in designing landscapes in places such as New Jersey and China. Today, nine-tenths of the land shows a significant human imprint, and the global human population still doubles about every generation. Tropical mega-reserves are desirable, but with their extraordinary disappearance rate, it is unwise to count entirely on their survival. Rather, I believe we must design whole landscapes and regions that mesh humans and nature, including biodiversity. Several key issues are outlined here, but all focus on the central attribute of landscapes, namely, the spatial arrangement of elements in a mosaic.

If you are a physician who keeps people's livers working, you would like to know how liver cells function. But if given a choice, you would prefer to know how livers are connected to the heart, lungs, intestine, and brain, because a live liver depends on a living body. So it is in protecting species. You would like to know the fine-scale details of genetics and demography, but success depends more on understanding the broad-scale configuration of ecosystems and land uses within a landscape or region.

Spatial Elements of Landscapes

A patch–corridor–matrix paradigm, in which every point is within a patch, a corridor, or the background matrix, provides generality for use in a forested, arid, agricultural, suburban, or any other landscape (Forman and Godron 1986; Forman 1995).

Patch Size and Number. Large patches of natural vegetation are essential to protect aquifers, habitat interior species, species with large home ranges, natural disturbance regimes, and sources of species dispersing through corridors and the matrix. Small patches act as stepping stones for dispersal across the landscape, decrease wind and water flows and erosion in the matrix, and occasionally provide habitats for small-patch-restricted species. In short, large patches provide several major benefits, and small patches provide minor, supplementary benefits (Forman 1995).

How many large patches are needed to protect the species of a particular landscape? We do not know, but apparently more than three large patches of a habitat type are generally required (Forman et al. 1976; Game and Peterken 1984; Margules and Austin 1992).

Boundaries and Patch Shape. Nature provides a rich assortment of landscape boundaries that have major effects on both species use and movement. The most common natural boundary types are (1) curvilinear (with lobes and coves) and (2) a strip of mosaic; less common are (3) straight and (4) self-similar fractal boundaries. Yet civilization geometricizes the land; hard straight lines replace the soft curves of nature. The ecological effects of this process may be large. For example, plant colonization patterns, herbivore browsing, and wildlife movement and usage are strongly affected by the curvilinearity and cove sizes of a boundary (Hardt and Forman 1989; Forman and Moore 1991).

The literature agrees that round patches are the ecologically optimum shape for reserves based on edge:interior ratios, yet this may not always be true. Based only on considerations of species conservation, a patch should provide (1) a large core and interior area, (2) dispersal of species from the patch to the matrix and other patches, (3) a "drift-fence effect" to aid in recolonization of the patch, and probably other functions. Many useful shapes are possible, and the optimum shape will reflect a balance among the functions provided (Forman 1995).

Corridors and Networks. Wooded strips, where forest habitat was formerly continuous in a landscape, play key roles as species habitats, conduits, and barriers, in controlling wind erosion, and in creating a landscape grain or mesh size. Stream and river corridors normally are the most important strips because of their numerous ecological roles, and their ecologically based minimum width varies markedly along the corridor system. Species also move along stepping-stone patches, which are equivalent to corridors with major gaps. Movement requires continuous suitable habitats not squeezed too tightly by unsuitable habitats. The key step in implementing corridor and stepping-stone systems for species conservation is to determine the optimum locations, types, and designs. Corridors often form dendritic or rectilinear networks that provide optional routes for species movement (Forman 1992, 1995).

Context. Adjacency or juxtaposition effects are familiar; examples include seeds blowing into an oasis and herbivores moving from woods to clearings. But how are the species in a patch affected by the number of adjacent habitats? Or the number of adjacent habitat types? Or the sizes of adjacent habitats? To answer such questions we could compare a forest surrounded by, for example, cropland, versus cropland and marsh, versus four types, versus *n* types.

The landscape mosaic surrounding a patch or corridor normally contains a variety of ecosystem types, each with its own species pool. Each local ecosystem in the mosaic is a source, as well as a sink, for species. In addition, resistances to movement across a landscape vary from low to high. Thus, the equilibrium island biogeographic theory is of only tangential use on land, since the central mosaic attribute of landscapes swamps the model assumption of islands in a homogeneous, inhospitable matrix. Only portions of an ecomosaic theory have solidified as yet (Turner and Gardner 1991; Forman 1995), but they are highly useful in understanding and planning the landscapes and regions around us.

Landscape Change and Planning

In the mosaic dynamics of landscape changes such as deforestation, suburbanization, or desertification, an ecologically optimum pattern or mosaic sequence of landscape changes may exist, and is worth a search. If successful, one could pinpoint the worst element, or the best element, to change at any point along the sequence.

For example, logging of dispersed forest patches has been studied to understand its effects on biodiversity, windthrow, fire ignition, game populations, and other parameters in a whole landscape (Franklin and Forman 1987; Hansen et al. 1992). In examining the mosaic sequence progressing from 100% forest through a 50% checkerboard pattern to 0% forest, ecologically important thresholds were detected. The dispersed-patch cutting sequence is highly detrimental ecologically compared with several other cutting patterns considered. Indeed, a limited number of mosaic sequences can describe almost all types of landscape change (Forman 1995).

To attain the support required for sustained species protection, two or three major ecological objectives should be concurrently addressed. Thus, a large reserve protects both biodiversity and an aquifer. A stream corridor enhances fish populations, mineral nutrient absorption, and biodiversity. If a community or a farmer has a soil erosion problem, planting a row of exotic shrubs may help. But an ecologist would combine erosion control and biodiversity, planting rows of several native species with roots and canopies at different levels, which provide food and cover for diverse animals over the year.

A sustainable environment is an area in which ecological integrity (including biodiversity) and basic human needs are concurrently maintained over generations (Forman 1990). Saving species depends on designing sustainable landscapes and regions. Aggregating land uses in large patches, maintaining small outliers in fine-grained areas, and providing connectivity for species movement are ready handles for wise planning, management, and policy.

Finally, a "spatial solution"—that is, a pattern of ecosystems or land uses that can conserve the bulk of, and the most important attributes of, biodiversity and natural processes in any region, landscape, or major portion thereof—has emerged (Forman 1995; Forman and Collinge 1996). Not every species, every soil particle, every nutrient, and every portion of key water bodies can be protected, but most can. The ecological spatial solution incorporates: (1) indispensable patterns for which no known or feasible alternative exists; (2) an aggregate-with-outliers pattern for optimally fitting different land uses together; and (3) strategic points in a landscape. Ample research frontiers for the spatial solution and its use exist.

But society does not have to wait for detailed ecological surveys before taking effective action. The spatial solution, with its few simple patterns and principles, combined with only a general survey of landscape area, is highly effective in conserving nature. Its use is especially critical during the first 40% of removal of natural vegetation in a landscape (Forman 1995; Forman and Collinge 1996). The spatial solution should become our top priority in conservation and land use planning.

---

reserves. This practice helps to avoid conflicts among various user groups and may be the only way to secure a reserve in the first place, due to fears of exclusionary wilderness use. Through a carefully planned zoning approach, a conservation reserve system can allow for habitat and species protection, experimental scientific research (including manipulations), human habitation and development, and limited use of natural resources.

A zoning approach might proceed as follows (Figure 10.24): A reserve system should have a central core consisting of a protected natural area that is subject only to nondestructive activities such as ecological monitoring, photography, hiking, and bird-watching. Often, these cores may already exist within established national parks or monuments, wilderness areas, or state

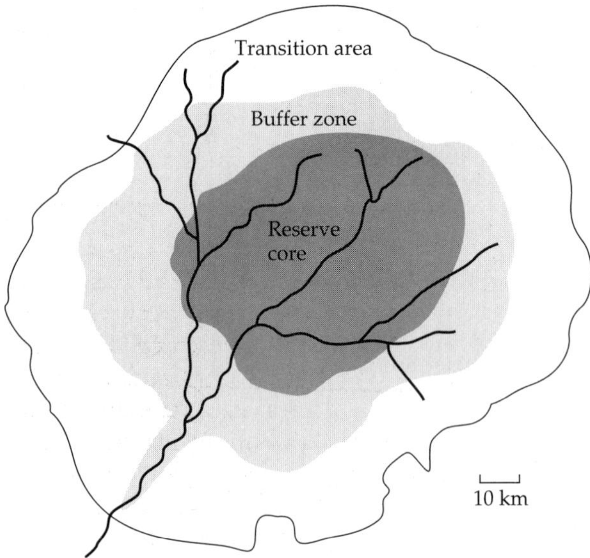

Figure 10.24 A schematic diagram of a zoned reserve system, showing the possible spatial relationship between a core area, a buffer zone, and a transition area. Human activities in each zone should be appropriate to the goal of that zone and especially to the protection of the reserve core.

wildlife areas. Surrounding or adjoining the core is a buffer zone, which may be a mix of public and private lands in which activities compatible with protection of the central core are allowed; these could include manipulative research, education, habitat rehabilitation, ecotourism, and traditional, low-impact land use, including sustained harvest of natural crops such as nuts or mushrooms. Outside of the buffer zone, and lacking distinct boundaries, is a transition area, which typically would include human settlements and associated activities such as fishing, forestry, agriculture, and other sustainable economic pursuits consistent with protection of the core area. Transition areas may extend indefinitely and link several reserve systems in the region.

It may seem intuitively obvious that the vegetation and other community characteristics of buffer zones should resemble those of the protected natural areas they surround. However, there are situations in which the transition from core reserve to buffer zone should be abrupt, and the buffer zone habitat very different from that of the core reserve. Whether to have an abrupt or a gradual transition in the buffer zone needs to be considered on a case-by-case basis. If vulnerability to fire is severe, then eliminating highly combustible weedy and second-growth vegetation around forested reserves may be important. Where the protection of ground-nesting birds in the reserve is an important management goal, it may be useful to surround the reserve with habitat unsuitable for generalist predators. Where the reserve is fragmented and vulnerable to invasion by exotic species, it may be important to create buffer habitat that excludes those weedy species that are likely to be successful colonists of the fragmented reserve.

The Problem of Certain Change and Uncertain Direction

Despite our most careful planning and prediction efforts, biological, cultural, economic, and political changes will affect conservation reserves over the long term. These changes will occur over and above the dynamic changes expected in biological systems, as discussed repeatedly to this point. Flexibility therefore becomes a key to reserve success. Although many changes cannot be predicted with respect to extent or direction, some classes of changes are more likely than others, and can be included in planning for conservation reserves. A good example is global climate change.

All indications point toward an average global warming trend of several degrees over the next century through accumulation of so-called "greenhouse gases" produced by human activities (Grover 1990; Kareiva et al. 1992). These gases, including CO_2, methane, and chlorofluorocarbons, trap infrared energy as it reradiates into space from earth, increasing the temperature of the lower atmosphere. This thermal increase will probably be accompanied by changes in precipitation patterns, soil conditions, and sea levels. In some regions, the frequency of extreme events such as droughts may rise, increasing the ecological effects of environmental stochasticity. Such changes portend major effects on species and communities in reserves (Peters and Darling 1985; Gates 1993).

Past global climate changes, such as those that have occurred repeatedly in the coming and going of ice ages, offer clues to the expected effects of human-induced global warming. Latitudinal shifts in community types and species ranges of hundreds of kilometers were typical of global warming and cooling of only a few degrees, the same magnitude that is predicted for our present warming scenario. During Pleistocene interglacials, when average global temperatures were only 2–3°C higher than at present, manatees occurred in New Jersey, tapirs and peccaries foraged in Pennsylvania, and Osage oranges grew in southern Canada (Dorf 1976). This indicates that major changes can be expected in the imminent greenhouse warming.

A great deal of habitat would probably be altered and made unsuitable for existing species in a global warming scenario. For example, a model based on biogeographic species–area relationships in montane small mammals (McDonald and Brown 1992) predicts loss of 9–62% of the species currently inhabiting 19 isolated mountain peaks in the Great Basin of the western United States. This estimate was based on areal habitat loss expected in a 3°C temperature rise. Such boreal species would have no place higher and colder to go during a warming event.

The impact of global changes on conservation reserves may be great, and should be considered at the outset and planned for wherever possible. Species whose entire ranges are confined to reserves with little altitudinal variation are likely to experience climatic changes beyond their tolerance levels and could be in danger of global extinction if other populations are not available for recolonization. Additionally, species in reserves are often remnant populations with reduced genetic diversity, living in isolated areas with little chance for movement to new regions outside the reserve. Climate change would only place further pressures on such species, including physiological stress and changes in competitive, predatory, mutualistic, or parasitic interactions (Peters and Darling 1985). The lowered genetic diversity of small reserve populations would reduce their likelihood of responding to added challenges through selective change (see Chapter 6). Certain types of species and habitats are more likely to be affected by global climate change than others (Peters and Darling 1985); these are summarized in Table 10.2.

(A)
Future reserve
RL
(B)
Reserve
RL
(C)
New RL
Former reserve
Old RL

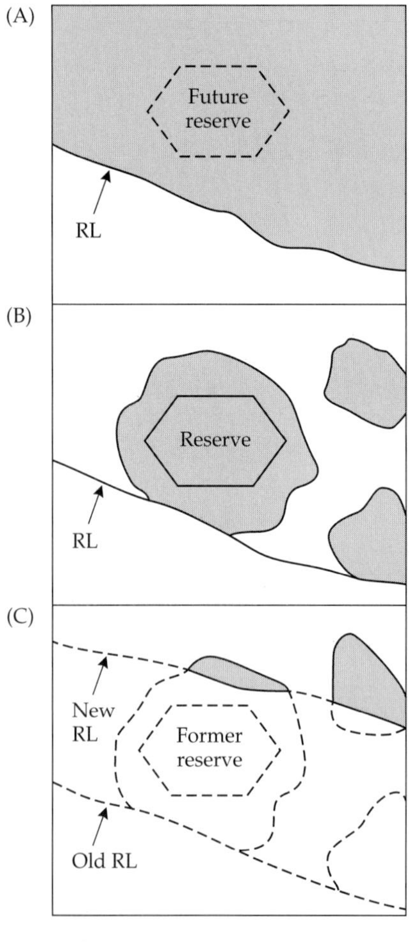

Figure 10.25 Schematic diagram of a reserve relative to latitudinal changes in temperatures. Shaded regions show suitable remaining habitat for a given species. The range limit of the species (RL) moves north as a result of global climate change (A–C), making the reserve ineffective. (From Peters and Darling 1985.)

The implications of global climate change for reserve function are profound, and increased management of reserves will be necessary because of it. For example, individual animals or plants may need to be transported among reserves in response to altered climate or rainfall patterns, or natural disturbances in reserves (such as fire) may need to be simulated. Consequently, management of conservation reserves should anticipate climate change. One approach might be to locate reserves near the present northern limits of the ranges of critical species, rather than at the southern ends, which will only become warmer and less likely to support the desired species (Figure 10.25). Reserves located in an area of maximum heterogeneity of topography and soil types will increase the "choices" of the biota; especially important will be access to a range of elevations and permanent water sources.

Maximization of the number and size of reserves will also increase the likelihood of species survival. Connection of reserves through corridors, especially north–south oriented or high–low elevation corridors, would allow movement of species in response to changing conditions. Long north–south corridors would, of course, be costly and politically difficult to establish, but not insurmountably so. In the United States, national forests are already largely arrayed in north–south strips along the Appalachian, Rocky, and Cascade Mountain ranges; better connections among them would help to address the global warming scenario. Riparian forests frequently offer north–south habitat, and we should look more closely into the role of riparian corridors in the siting of new reserves. Finally, buffers around reserves with flexible zoning retain options to shift reserve boundaries in the future in response to climate changes.

Anthropological and Cultural Implications of Conservation Reserves

A conservation reserve may be doomed to eventual failure, regardless of its biological soundness, if its planning does not consider and include the needs

Table 10.2
Types of Species and Communities Most Likely to Be Affected by Global Climate Change

Type	Predicted effect
1. Peripheral populations	Populations near the edge of the species' range would be more likely affected by range shifts due to warming.
2. Geographically localized species	Local endemics would be unlikely to have populations in areas of suitable habitat after a range shift due to climate change.
3. Genetically impoverished species	Species or populations with low genetic diversity may lack the variability necessary to adapt to changing climatic or habitat conditions.
4. Specialized species	Specialized species generally are less tolerant of environmental change and often require a narrow range of conditions.
5. Poor dispersers	Sedentary or less mobile species would have difficulty spreading their distributions into newly created suitable habitat during climate change.
6. Annual species	Complete reproductive failure in one year by an annual species spells local extinction. Such failure is more possible during climate change in annual than in perennial species.
7. Montane and alpine communities	Species distributions would shift to higher elevations during global warming, occupying smaller areas with smaller populations, making them more vulnerable to extinction. Species originally at the highest elevations would have nowhere higher to go.
8. Arctic communities	Temperature increases in arctic regions are expected to be greater than in equatorial areas, and those communities may undergo greater stress.
9. Coastal communities	It is expected that upwelling patterns in coastal areas will be altered, and that sea levels will rise, flooding coastal habitat. Both events will stress coastal communities, which will likely not be able to follow rising waters inland due to human development.

Modified from Peters and Darling 1985.

and desires of people. An exclusively preservationist approach, which locks nature away for safekeeping, only causes increased conflict between people and nature, and can backfire to the detriment of the protected area. Planned and controlled inclusion of people in the reserve will ensure greater cooperation with, and more positive attitudes toward, the reserve.

For example, since 1986, Costa Rican and American scientists have been cooperating in an effort to rehabilitate and restore a 75,000 ha dry tropical forest in Guanacaste National Park in northwestern Costa Rica (Figure 10.26). Degraded over the last three centuries by agriculture, ranching, and alteration of natural fire patterns, the natural communities that existed in the precolo-

Figure 10.26 The Guanacaste project is a major effort to rehabilitate and restore a 75,000 ha dry tropical forest in northwestern Costa Rica. This area was degraded over the last three centuries, but natural systems are being reconstituted through a cooperative effort with local residents. Shown here is a degraded dry forest. (Photograph by C. R. Carroll.)

nization state are now being re-created (Allen 1988). Doing this, however, requires more than knowledge of the regional biology.

The project is based on a philosophical approach called "biocultural restoration," which incorporates local people into all aspects of the reserve's development and protection. The idea is to embed biological understanding and appreciation in the local culture through education about, and interaction with, the park. Early on, these scientists realized that an important reward for local people is an intellectual understanding of their environment and the complexities of the world around them, recreating an understanding of the land that their grandparents had, but which they may have lost in the modern world.

The goal of the project is to create a "user-friendly" park that contributes to the quality of the people's daily lives. This is accomplished by making Guanacaste a "living classroom" through formal educational programs, encouraging independent exploration of the area, and creating apprenticeships in the areas of ecological research or law enforcement. Some local farms are being purchased, but the former owners are allowed to remain there and work toward restoration or protection. A family that formerly raised cattle may now be involved in raising and managing a dry tropical forest. Once the forest is restored, residents may be trained as park guards and own land nearby. The formula for such a project is strictly "home-grown" and not a generic textbook model (there is no such thing). Such formulas need to be developed independently in each case according to the local situation and the needs of the people and wildlife (Western and Wright 1994). Nevertheless, the general approach used in the Guanacaste National Park restoration project is a good model to adopt elsewhere, and we will return to it in Chapter 14 when we discuss restoration.

At least three "user" groups need to be considered in the development of conservation reserves. First and foremost are local residents who are already established in the region, perhaps having been there for centuries. Every effort should be made to allow continuation of their normal mode of life, including *sustainable* use of natural resources. If lifestyle modifications are necessary to meet the biological goals of the reserve (such as stopping poaching or illegal timber cutting), these need to be introduced in a cooperative, rather than confrontational, manner; voluntary adoption is much more likely to succeed than enforced changes. Implementation of such modifications will typically require education, economic programs, and any other assistance necessary to smooth the transition with minimal interruption of traditional lifestyles.

If local land use patterns are not sustainable, then conflict may be a necessary requisite to good reserve management. This is evident in the current conflicts between loggers and conservationists over remaining old-growth forests in the western United States. The (recent) traditional use of the land, clear-cutting of forests whose trees are 200 to over 1000 years old, is clearly not sustainable and must be altered if any forests are to remain as reserves. Likewise, corporate-style agriculture, in which large expanses of land are cleared, tilled, and sprayed with chemical fertilizers and pesticides, may be incompatible with conservation reserves. In cases such as these, there may be no alternative to direct conflict over land use. The reasonable approach is to help residents make the necessary changes in their lifestyles and livelihoods.

The second "user" group is the population at large, whether local (tribal, city, county), regional (state), national, or international. This population must be supportive of reserves to ensure the necessary long-term funding and to provide the political base to resist development contrary to the biological interests of the reserve. If citizen support is lacking, it is unlikely that a reserve or reserve system will be able to resist developmental incursion for any extended period.

Finally, the needs of visitors must be included as part of conservation reserves, as they will often be a major source of revenue and public support for the reserve. Even if the local constituency does not initially support a particular reserve, those opinions may change if economic benefits of tourism are realized in the local area. Ecotourism is a developing industry worldwide; its use should be considered whenever its presence would not interfere with the ecological aspects of the park (see Case Study 3 in Chapter 18).

Most people seem to have an inherent positive attitude toward natural areas and nature in general (termed **biophilia** by Wilson [1984]), and will work toward their protection if they understand the value of the system, and if conflicts between conservation and their economic needs are minimized. The key is to identify and alleviate these conflicts during the planning stages of a reserve through active inclusion of the various user groups. They know the area, and they will be affected by the reserve; communication and cooperation with such people is not only pragmatic, but ethically proper.

Many examples exist of reserves that failed to either preserve native biodiversity or protect indigenous cultures because the needs of people were not adequately considered in the original planning. If it is seen as inhibiting the welfare of local inhabitants, or if their needs are not met elsewhere, a reserve will usually be exploited for its resources in an unsustainable manner (see Case Study 4 in Chapter 18). For example, when banana plantations closed in southwestern Costa Rica, one of the few opportunities left for the displaced workers was to become part of illegal gold mining efforts in nearby Corcovado National Park. The mining caused serious damage to the terrestrial, and especially the aquatic, ecosystems, contaminating rivers with silt and mercury (Tangley 1988). Unemployment and hunger are strong motives to exploit whatever resources are available, regardless of their designated level of protection. A reserve will be protected from exploitation only when local economies are sound and people's basic needs are satisfied.

Long-established cultures have been destroyed by the development of well-intended biological reserves that ignored or did not meet the needs of the people. It may be argued that this anthropological loss is every bit as devastating as losses of biodiversity. One African tribe was displaced from its ancestral homeland in the creation of the Kidepo National Park in Uganda; its culture soon disintegrated (Turnbull 1972). The Waliangulu people of Kenya, traditional elephant hunters, likewise suffered cultural disintegration when the Tsavo National Park was established (Murrey 1967). The Vedda society of Sri Lanka broke down due to a development project to expand rice production, together with the creation of the Madura Oya National Park, established to mitigate the effects of the rice project on wildlife. This 2000-year-old culture of hunter–gatherers has shown no tendency to take up rice cultivation, and their knowledge of sustainable existence in tropical forests is being lost with their societal collapse (Burgess 1986, in Dasmann 1988).

Fortunately, negative examples such as these are countered by positive examples of reserve development in which the welfare of indigenous peoples was included in the planning. For example, the economic value of wildlife is being used in Zimbabwe to the benefit of local people. Some 200 local conservation councils control wildlife use on private lands and are overseen by the national government to ensure protection of rare and endangered species (Dasmann 1988). The local communities benefit from the sale of wildlife products such as meat and hides, and are therefore motivated to protect the resource as their own. Communal lands are controlled by the national government, with economic benefits still going to local communities. This program, called CAMPFIRE, is discussed in Case Study 4 of Chapter 18.

A different problem was addressed in a World Wildlife Fund project on the western slopes of the Andes in Colombia, an area of high biological diversity. A 1600 ha ranch was purchased for protection of a forested plateau. However, the ranch was threatened with degradation by probable development in the surrounding area. Adjacent to the ranch lived the Awa/Cuayquer people, who traditionally employed sustainable land use practices consistent with biodiversity protection. To protect the ranch forest, a reserve system was created that included zoning outside the central core, with protected, manipulative, and administrative zones. These zones were established in consultation with the Awa/Cuayquer, and provided for the satisfaction of their basic needs, including programs in education, nutrition and health, and agroecology. Strong community support developed for the reserve system, which included Awa/Cuayquer land (Dasmann 1988).

Through programs such as these, natural biodiversity is more likely to be protected, and traditional cultures, which often enjoy sustainable and low-impact lifestyles, are served as well. Bullying of any culture, from Peruvian Indians to American ranchers, will never serve the best interests of conservation. Conflict is often unavoidable, but should be approached with an understanding and appreciation of the local culture, with every attempt made to accommodate their concerns and fears.

Political and Economic Constraints on Conservation Reserves

Up to this point in our discussion of conservation reserves, we have focused on biological or anthropological considerations. Now we will introduce some political realities into the discussion. The issues raised in this brief section are explored in more detail in the following chapters, and are illustrated in a real-world scenario in Essay 10C, by Jack Williams.

Conservation biology can inform us regarding the ecological, genetic, and other biological aspects of reserves, but conservation biologists often have little or no input into a reserve's selection, configuration, or relationship to the larger landscape matrix. For publicly owned reserves, such as state and fed-

ESSAY 10C
Pupfish, Politics, and Reserve Management in the Arid Southwest

Jack E. Williams, Bureau of Land Management

The desert oasis named Ash Meadows has been the scene of many battles over land and water use. Endangered fishes—mostly species of pupfish—have been the focal point of concern. One pivotal battle between the diminutive Devils Hole pupfish (*Cyprinodon diabolis*) and agricultural interests intent on withdrawing water from the aquifer that supplies the only spring habitat of the species was ultimately decided in the United States Supreme Court. On June 7, 1976, the Court upheld a lower court ruling for a permanent injunction on groundwater pumping until a safe water level for the pupfish could be established. During the court proceedings, the fate of the pupfish became the rallying cry for both conservationist and development interests (Figure A). Now, more than two decades later, and despite numerous endangered species listings and the creation of a National Wildlife Refuge at Ash Meadows, questions still remain concerning the survival of the Devils Hole pupfish and the area's many other endemic species.

Ash Meadows, located along the Nevada–California border approximately 145 km (90 miles) northwest of Las Vegas, consists of dozens of crystal-blue springs, wetlands, and alkaline uplands surrounded by the Mojave Desert. With 26 endemic taxa of fishes, springsnails, aquatic insects, and plants within the 94.7-km^2 oasis, it is the smallest area with such a rich and specialized flora and fauna in the United States (Deacon and Williams 1991)

As in most preserves, protection of Ash Meadows has come in fits and starts. On January 17, 1952, President Harry S. Truman declared 16 ha (40 acres) around Devil's Hole a disjunct portion of Death Valley National Monument. The natural values of Devil's Hole received further protection through court rulings during the 1970s. The major breakthrough for protection of the entire Ash Meadows area, however, came in June of 1984, when 5154 hectares (12,736 acres) was acquired with the help of The Nature Conservancy and designated by Congress as the Ash Meadows National Wildlife Refuge. This halted plans for a large commercial and residential development, but not before some spring systems were drained and ditched and their flows diverted to create reservoirs. Some areas within the refuge boundary remain privately owned, while others are managed by the Bureau of Land Management.

During the 1940s, early investigations of Ash Meadow's unique fauna found numerous populations of introduced bullfrogs and crayfish already established. Introduction of non-native species has continued to be a problem at Ash Meadows. During the 1960s, an illegal tropical fish farm provided the source for a wide variety of exotic species that flourished in the warm spring waters. Large populations of introduced mosquitofish (*Gambusia affinis*) and sailfin mollies (*Poecilia latipinna*) persist in many areas. Largemouth bass (*Micropterus salmoides*) have been introduced into reservoirs and have invaded springpools, where they prey on the native pupfish and speckled dace.

How are the problems of introduced species and groundwater management to be handled? Introduced species such as mosquitofish are notoriously hard to control in areas like Ash Meadows, with its many interconnected waterways. Chemical treatment has been tried, but the effects of such control efforts on nontarget species, such as the tiny native springsnails, can be severe. Removal of groundwater from areas outside Ash Meadows also may have long-term negative consequences by reducing springflows within Ash Meadows. With deep groundwater throughout much of the state slowly flowing from northeast to southwest, proposals by the city of Las Vegas to buy ranches and pump their groundwaters for municipal uses are cause for concern.

These issues cannot be easily resolved by the National Wildlife Refuge system, which traditionally has focused on waterfowl production and hunting. Even fishing activities on the refuge's reservoirs may conflict with protection of the endemic spring-dwelling species because of the likelihood of introducing and managing for predatory fishes, such as largemouth bass. Restoration of natural springs, their outflows, and desert wetlands may conflict with desires for improved vehicle access, recreational facilities, and our tendency to intensively manage landscapes. And, as with the groundwater concerns, we are finding that ecosystem boundaries seldom conform to the administrative boundaries of the preserve.

To date, many urban and agricultural centers of the arid West have flourished with little regard for water consumption rates or effects on native biota. There are better alternatives for meeting the growing urban needs for Western water than tapping our already depleted surface and groundwaters. Professor James Deacon of the University of Nevada, Las Vegas, has questioned why society should spend billions of dollars on new water projects when it would be cheaper and environmentally more sound to "get serious about retrofitting Las Vegas for water efficiency [and] then get serious about converting agriculture in the Colorado River basin to water efficiency and use the savings for urban needs—in both Nevada and California."

Water use, whether surface waters on the refuge or groundwater from outside, will continue to garner political attention. How society responds to these issues may be the ultimate court case for the Devils Hole pupfish and the other members of the Ash Meadows community.

Figure A Preserves protecting species such as the Devils Hole pupfish typically provoke visible responses on both sides of the development/conservation debate. (Photographs by Edwin P. Pister.)

(A)

(B)

(C)

(D)

Figure 10.27 The results of multiple uses of public lands in the United States. Activities such as off-road vehicles (A), clear-cutting (B), geothermal energy extraction (C), and cattle grazing (D) all degrade public lands. In reserves that serve multiple functions, biodiversity protection may be a minor aspect of a larger and more environmentally destructive agenda. (A and D, photographs courtesy of Bureau of Land Management; B, by Barry R. Noon; C, by Edwin P. Pister.)

eral parklands, decisions about the reserves and about conservation in general are part of the larger political/economic/sociological landscape, and are made within a much broader context than biological expediency. Even privately owned reserves are subject to political and economic pressures. Reserves may serve multiple functions, as do National Forest lands and the range and desert lands of the Bureau of Land Management in the United States. In these reserves, mining, timber harvest, grazing, hunting and fishing, and off-road vehicle recreation are just some of the more prominent uses (Figure 10.27); conservation of biodiversity is only part of a crowded agenda for these multiple-use reserves. In some countries, even national parks may be exploited for minerals, timber, and game. The Organic Act of 1917, which established the National Park Service in the United States, permits restricted grazing in U.S. national parks.

With the exception of the National Park Service, the management authority for publicly controlled reserves in the United States seldom comes from a single agency; usually multiple agencies are involved. Protection of wetlands on the east coast may jointly involve the Army Corps of Engineers, the Environmental Protection Agency, the Fish and Wildlife Service, the National Park Service, and numerous state and local agencies. The agency authorized to take action within a reserve is usually not the same agency that principally controls activities on lands adjacent to the reserve. This can create special difficulties for reserve management. In the western United States, for example, the national parks, which are managed by the Department of the Interior, are usually surrounded by National Forest lands controlled by the Department of Agriculture, or by lands controlled by the Bureau of Land Management, or by state-owned lands. Logging, mineral mining, petroleum extraction, and power plant operations on these adjacent lands can cause serious pollution in the air and waters of reserves.

Air pollution and energy extraction on public lands are considered to be the two most important external threats to United States national parks. Oil-fired power plants, smelters, and even distant metropolitan areas create severe air pollution and impaired visibility in Grand Canyon National Park (Figure 10.28); oil and gas extraction on public lands adjacent to Glacier National Park is considered to be the park's most serious external threat (Freemuth 1991). As of this writing, a proposed gold mine 2.5 miles from the border of Yellowstone National Park, which threatened the rivers of the Greater Yellowstone Ecosystem with severe pollution, has been stopped.

The many forms that reserves can take, in terms of ownership, management authority, and use, can create serious obstacles to achieving conservation goals. Usually, these problems are tackled in an ad hoc fashion through various management programs. It would be far better if these problems could be ameliorated during the process of designing the reserve. For example, land exchanges between public agencies are common and can be used during the establishment of a reserve to reduce the number of agencies involved in reserve operations and authority. Earlier in this chapter we discussed a major problem in conservation: many reserves may be too small to support viable populations of the species they are supposed to protect. In the United States, it is possible to greatly increase the effective sizes of reserves, especially in Western states, by aggregating or connecting (through habitat corridors) adjacent or nearby lands controlled by different public agencies. For example, many Western national parks are surrounded by national or state forests or Bureau of Land Management lands. If the agencies involved would develop compatible conservation goals and management programs, the total conservation areas would be greatly expanded. As Grumbine (1990) remarks, "To

(A)

(B)

(C)

Figure 10.28 Air pollution in Grand Canyon National Park, Arizona, as shown in a fixed camera at the Desert View Watchtower on three different days; visibility is (A) 303 km, (B) 156 km, and (C) zero. Visibility can change daily as a result of air pollution from copper smelters and power plants in the region, and smog from metropolitan areas such as Los Angeles. (Photographs courtesy of U.S. National Park Service.)

preserve biodiversity in national parks, national forests, or anywhere else, we can no longer afford fragmentation in our management efforts any more than we can afford habitat fragmentation in natural ecosystems."

We usually think of politics and economics as forces acting to limit the size of reserves. Sometimes, though, reserves may be expanded in order to meet political and economic objectives. Transnational reserves, so-called "peace parks," may be established as part of a larger foreign policy agenda. Glacier International Peace Park connects Glacier National Park in the United States with Banff and Waterton Lakes National Parks in Canada. In Central America, two peace parks are under development, one on the Atlantic watershed between Nicaragua and Costa Rica, and the other connecting Costa Rica's La Amistad National Park with Panama's proposed Boca del Toro National Park.

The most obvious situation in which economic considerations can lead to expanded reserves is where the reserves protect critical economic resources. In Venezuela, it was discovered that Oilbirds are important seed dispersers of trees in forested watersheds that border important shipping channels for petroleum tankers. To provide long-term protection of the watershed forest, and thereby reduce erosion and landslides that would damage the shipping lanes, a small reserve containing cave nest sites for Oilbirds was expanded to include large watersheds. There is still considerable opportunity for the development of additional reserves in watersheds and catchment basins that provide irrigation and drinking water. In such cases, reserve configuration will not only be based on conservation science, but will also be part of the larger planning effort for economic development.

Summary

The selection and development of conservation reserves should be conducted under a nonequilibrium paradigm that recognizes the dynamism of natural systems and the importance of natural and anthropogenic disturbance to their ecology. Biological motivations for reserves include ecosystem protection, conservation of biodiversity, and protection of selected target species. However, biological motivations are not the only concerns for conservation reserves; their anthropological and cultural effects, as well as political and economic influences, must also be considered.

Within the biological arena, at least six critical issues should be considered relative to conservation reserves: reserve size; heterogeneity and ecological dynamics within the reserve; the landscape context of the reserve; connections of the reserve to other reserves or natural areas; the landscape elements, both natural and modified, that will influence the success of the reserve; and accommodation of human activities. All of this planning must be conducted with some degree of flexibility due to the uncertainty of change. For example, global climate change over the next century is quite likely, but the specific directions of changes and their effects on particular reserves are less certain.

Reserves are unlikely to meet their conservation goals if the human presence is not included in their planning. Anthropological and cultural considerations include concern for traditional peoples in and around reserves. Sustainable practices should be continued and included in conservation reserves; nonsustainable practices that conflict with reserve goals will need to be changed through education and other supportive measures. Reserve success will be enhanced by political and economic practices congruent with conservation objectives. In particular, multiple-agency mandates that do not work at cross purposes with each other and with conservation objectives are more likely to achieve reserve goals than are fragmented agencies working in opposition.

Questions for Discussion

1. The metapopulation concept is central to conservation reserves, particularly with respect to connected networks of reserves. Yet, data relevant to metapopulations are rare. Discuss the possible characteristics of plant and animal populations that might predispose them to having a metapopulation structure.
2. Discuss how the presence or absence of a metapopulation structure would affect the desirable levels of patchiness and spatial connections within a reserve.
3. Many reserves are developed at least partly to protect a visible and popular segment of the biota, such as tigers, elephants, or coral reefs. Develop arguments that might be used to convince legislators and the local populace that developing reserves to protect the following is in the public interest: (a) endemic snails in springs on western United States grazing lands; (b) a diverse but mostly unknown assemblage of beetles in a Bornean forest; (c) wading birds in a Japanese wetland that is about to be drained for a corporate headquarters; and (d) six endemic mussel species in a Virginia river under heavy recreational and industrial use.
4. Information on the utility of corridors is too limited for us to confidently prescribe many expensive corridors connecting habitats or reserves; yet the concept seems reasonable. Discuss how you might collect data or design experiments to test the efficacy of corridors for conservation reserves.
5. How might you go about determining the minimum dynamic area for a particular reserve and disturbance regime? How might you use active management to augment limited reserve area?
6. Discuss some problems and approaches that might be used in establishing a reserve for a large carnivore in an area with mixed cultural values and multiple land ownership.

Suggestions for Further Reading

Forman, R. T. T. and M. Godron. 1986. *Landscape Ecology*. John Wiley & Sons, New York. Forman and Godron produced this first textbook on landscape ecology several years ago, but it remains a definitive work. It defines landscape ecology, outlines its principles, emphasizes dynamics, and discusses management at the landscape scale.

Hudson, W. E. (ed.). 1991. *Landscape Linkages and Biodiversity*. Island Press, Washington, D.C. Hudson has put together a strong grouping of papers touting the benefits of linked landscapes in conservation. The collection presents a broad perspective on biological and political aspects of linkages in landscapes.

Kareiva, P. M., J. G. Kingsolver, and R. B. Huey (eds.). 1992. *Biotic Interactions and Global Change*. Sinauer Associates, Sunderland, MA. A rich compilation of 29 chapters on global climate change, including patterns and determinants of change, physiological, population, evolutionary, and community responses, habitat fragmentation and landscape change, and community research on global change.

Pickett, S. T. A. and J. N. Thompson. 1978. Patch dynamics and the design of nature reserves. *Biol. Conserv.* 13:27–37. This classic paper is central to the idea that heterogeneity and patches are important in the development of conservation reserves. A "must read" for a heterogeneity perspective.

Shafer, C. L. 1990. *Nature Reserves: Island Theory and Conservation Practice*. Smithsonian Institution Press, Washington, D.C. A thorough overview of the design of nature reserves from the perspective of island biogeography theory. Because of its focus on island theory, the book is limited in its scope, but is thorough with respect to that area.

Szaro, R. C. and D. W. Johnston (eds.). 1996. *Biodiversity in Managed Landscapes: Theory and Practice*. Oxford University Press, New York. A large volume by the best theoreticians and practitioners in the business, focused on managed landscapes. Topics include principles, inventory and monitoring, various strategies for biodiversity maintenance, the practice of landscape-level management, and policy and social considerations.

IV

Practical Applications and Human Considerations

11

Management to Meet Conservation Goals

General Principles

Applied ecology is difficult, but not impossible. Action has to be taken, but the problems cannot be solved by off-the-shelf answers. Solutions will require intellectual and empirical depth well beyond what is now available, as well as commitment, money, organization, and work. Most significantly, applied ecology requires rethinking the basis of how ecological problems and their solutions are approached. It is almost too late to start, but tomorrow is even later.

L. B. Slobodkin and D. E. Dykhuizen 1991

Why Is Management Necessary?

In Chapter 1 we said that conservation biology was a crisis discipline. A species is threatened with extinction, and something must be done quickly. An aggressive invader establishes itself in a sensitive natural environment, and a program for eradication must be developed and implemented. Cattle are carrying disease into a population of desert bighorn sheep, and some intervention is necessary. Heavy metals from urban runoff are contaminating a stream that is the only water source for a large wetland reserve, and funds must be found for diverting the stream and drilling wells to supply the wetland with groundwater. These are examples of the immediate crises that occupy much of the professional lives of conservation managers. They are, however, symptoms of more systemic and larger problems. As we argue throughout this book, conservation biology will remain a crisis discipline until we stop parasitizing the natural environment in order to maintain ever-expanding economies and human populations.

Not only are there many different kinds of crises, but the contexts in which the crises occur are also important. For example, wildfires can be essential natural processes when they occur at the right frequency and intensity, and a disaster otherwise. Wildfires are more acceptable in remote wilderness areas than they are in more heavily visited natural areas. This is true even when park visitors accept the idea that fire is an essential natural process for maintaining the ecosystem that supports the animals and plants they find so appealing.

Crises in conservation take many forms, and good management, in equally varied forms, is the appropriate response. Because there are so many different challenges, all of which are strongly influenced by the environmental and social context in which they occur, management requires an eclectic set of approaches. There is no theoretical base specific to conservation management, though good management approaches have a strong dependence on the wealth of theoretical and empirical studies in biology. There is no particular field of training that prepares one to be a good conservation manager. Management approaches have changed over several decades, and continue to evolve. The history of wildlife conservation management, elaborated by Curt Meine in Essay 11A, elegantly demonstrates that we have come a long way in our understanding of and appreciation for diverse natural systems, and have developed a more sophisticated and sound philosophy toward biological diversity.

ESSAY 11A

Conservation Biology and Wildlife Management in America

A Historical Perspective

Curt Meine, International Crane Foundation

"All through college I was trained to create edge, edge, and more edge. Now all I'm hearing is that edge is bad!" The words were those of a district-level wildlife manager in the U.S. Forest Service. He and two dozen colleagues were attending an agency-sponsored continuing education program designed to keep them up to date on innovations in habitat management. But after several days of patient participation, this agency veteran could no longer contain his confusion. What he was hearing (this was the late 1980s) and what he had been told in college (perhaps 20 years before) simply did not jibe.

His exasperation revealed much, not only about recent changes in our view of edge effects, but about longer-term changes within (and surrounding) the field of wildlife management generally. The immediate source of his confusion could be surmised. Probably none of his college instructors had explained—perhaps they did not realize themselves—the origins and development of the edge effect concept and its application in wildlife management. None cautioned that the creation of edge habitat was a management tool, the appropriate and effective use of which (like that of all tools) is a function of timing, location, and ecological context. None recounted how, in the 1930s, maximization of edge habitat was seen as a progressive technique in the then-new field of game management, and was used to restore game populations in a Midwestern landscape that, after decades of intensive agricultural development, retained little edge, little cover of any kind, and only incidental remnants of its originally extensive biotic communities. None foresaw how the too-eager use of this tool, especially in forest settings, could have detrimental effects on interior-dwelling species.

But the manager's complaint revealed a still deeper frustration. Beyond concerns about the proper application of this or that technique, he was confronting the rapidly changing role and context of wildlife management as it entered the 1990s. The reconsideration of edge effects has been only one outward sign of a more basic reappraisal of means and ends in the effort to conserve, in the face of intensified human impacts, wild places and the flora and fauna they contain. The emergence of conservation biology itself, with its special emphasis on protection and maintenance of biological diversity, has been another important indicator of this reappraisal.

Seen from one angle, conservation biology directly challenges many of the assumptions and priorities that have guided wildlife management for five decades. These include the profession's heavy emphasis on a narrow range of species, especially game animals and those select few (usually higher vertebrates) with obvious economic, aesthetic, or symbolic value; a tendency to adopt single-species approaches in research and management, and to underestimate the importance of broader, system-wide approaches; education and training programs that stress the development of technical skills while downplaying conceptual clarity and intellectual flexibility; and a relatively rigid disciplinary framework that carries over from the classroom to the agency department—and ultimately to the landscape. These tendencies, though, are not unique to wildlife management, but find analogous expression within agriculture, forestry, range management, fisheries management, and other resource-related professions (Meine 1995).

The roots of conservation biology lie in many fields, within and beyond the sciences proper. Wildlife management is only one, but its contributions have been disproportionate. It was the arena in which biological knowledge and ecological principles were first applied in a systematic manner to the conservation of organisms and their natural habitats. As such, it played a leading role in advancing conservation beyond the point where success was measured solely in human economic terms (whether that measure was board feet produced, deer "harvested," fingerlings released, acre-feet retained, or tourists admitted). In this, it helped initiate the process—still far from complete—that would redefine conservation as the effort to protect, manage, and restore healthy and diverse ecosystems. Seen from this perspective, conservation biology represents not so much a radical departure from the past, but a further stage in conservation's continual evolutionary process. Along the way, it has given "traditional" wildlife management the opportunity to return to its roots, and to revise and reaffirm many of its founding (if sometimes neglected) principles.

At the time of its own emergence as a distinct profession in the 1930s, wildlife management itself represented a significant departure from conservation's status quo. As Aldo Leopold noted in his seminal text *Game Management* (1933), "the thought was that restriction of hunting could 'string out' the remnants of the virgin supply [of game animal populations] and make them last a longer time. . . . Our game laws . . . were essentially a device for dividing up a dwindling treasure." Leopold introduced the idea, profound in its implications, that populations of wild animals and plants could best be perpetuated through the active study, protection, and, where necessary, restoration of their habitats. He called upon science "to furnish biological facts" and "to build on them a new technique by which the altruistic idea of conservation can be made a practical reality."

Some sense of how this new approach transformed wildlife conservation in America can be gained by summarizing several key developments in the crucial decade of the 1930s.

- In 1930, virtually all of those involved in the management (as distinguished from the *study* or *protection*) of wild animal populations focused on game species. In 1936, the one-word term "wildlife" came into common usage, signaling the broadened purview of the field. By 1940, "wildlife" was standard terminology, and included for many not just "nongame" vertebrates, but invertebrates and plants as well.
- Prior to 1930, "management," such as it was, entailed mainly captive breeding programs, persecution of predatory species, tighter legal restrictions on hunting, and essentially ad hoc creation of refuges and sanctuaries. By 1940, the basic shift in approach was complete, and primary emphasis was placed on the provision of suitable habitat.
- In 1930, understanding of the science of ecology was confined to a select few, mainly within academia. By 1940, ecology was the cornerstone of wildlife management.
- In 1930, there existed no textbooks, journals, or professional organization devoted exclusively to the emerging field. By 1940, it had its text (Leopold's *Game Management*), its journal (the *Journal of Wildlife Management*), and its professional society (The Wildlife Society).
- In 1930, one could count on one hand the number of research projects set up specifically "to furnish biological facts" relevant to the conservation of wildlife. By 1940, a national system of financial and institutional support for wildlife research (the Cooperative Wildlife Research Unit program) had been established.
- In 1930, opportunities to study wildlife management were virtually nonexistent, confined (at best) to an occasional lecture in a forestry or agriculture class. By 1940, courses and whole departments devoted to wildlife management were in place in dozens of universities (particularly the nation's land-grant universities).
- And perhaps most significantly, in 1930, few appreciated the connections between wildlife ecology and management, other basic and applied sciences, and economics, philosophy, and other fields. By 1940, at least the first inklings of the broad implications of conservation were being heard, spurred on in no small part by the new generation of "wildlifers."

Even as wildlife management was securing these professional footholds, its conceptual foundation continued to broaden. During these years of ferment, the focus had expanded well beyond Leopold's (1933) original aim of "making land produce sustained annual crops of game for recreational use." The shift toward the more inclusive term "wildlife" reflected not just an interest in a wider spectrum of species, but a deeper realization of the pervasive importance of the science of ecology. Leopold himself saw this clearly. In a 1939 address to a joint meeting of the Society of American Foresters and the Ecological Society of America, he described ecology as "a new fusion point for all the natural sciences." He noted that ecology challenged traditional notions of utility, even as it highlighted the basic importance of biological diversity. "No species," he proposed, "can be 'rated' without the tongue in the cheek. The old categories of 'useful' and 'harmful' have validity only as conditioned by time, place, and circumstance. The only sure conclusion is that the biota as a whole is useful, and biota includes not only plants and animals, but soils and waters as well" (Leopold 1939).

Leopold was by no means alone in this realization. In every field of natural resource management there were "dissenters" (to use Leopold's term) who came to the same conclusions: that an understanding of natural phenomena and human environmental impacts could be gained not simply through dividing reality up into smaller and smaller bits—the method of reductionist science—but by attending to the connections and relationships in nature at various scales of time and space. For the conservation professions this had important practical implications. One could not simply manage soils, or trees, or game animals, or any other "resource" as discrete entities; one had to treat as well the ecological processes that kept the system as a whole healthy. And this meant that, departmental and disciplinary labels notwithstanding, integration was essential to all conservation work.

This line of thinking would endure even the tumult of World War II. As an inherently integrative endeavor, wildlife management was partially immune to the postwar trend toward hyperspecialization. Through the 1950s, there was close, active, and regular interaction among academic ecologists, other biologists, and the applied wildlife management programs in the universities and the state and federal governments (Wagner 1989).

By the end of the 1950s, however, even wildlife management began to suffer from "hardening of the categories." As Wagner (1989) notes, new directions in the underlying sciences "would send academic ecology and applied wildlife management down somewhat different paths and dissolve the close association of previous decades." And in the ensuing decades, these widening gaps—between theoretical and applied scientists, between scientists and managers, between departments in the agencies and universities—would make consensus ever more difficult, even as threats to the biota, at all geographic scales, intensified. In short, the "glue" that first allowed wildlife management to come together and stick together—an expanding appreciation of biological diversity and ecosystem processes, broad training in the natural sciences, collaborative research projects, and integrated approaches to resource management—was allowed to break down. For a generation, fragmentation would become increasingly evident, not only in the modern landscape, but in the modern mindscape (Cooperrider 1991).

The quickening pace of environmental degradation and biological impoverishment in the 1960s and 1970s would outstrip the ability of the various conservation-related sciences, acting in isolation, to respond. In a world beset by complex, large-scale, interrelated environmental concerns, including deforestation, air and water pollution, global climate change, human population growth, and misguided international development projects, wildlife management as generally practiced seemed less and less relevant or responsive.

The newly energized environmental movement sought to confront these trends through ambitious conferences, management programs, and legislative initiatives at the national and international level. Yet, these measures alone could not reverse the trends. Ultimately, conservation goals could only be attained through understanding and changing the entrenched patterns of resource use that threatened plant and animal populations, degraded their habitats, and disrupted the functioning of ecosystems. This was, in many ways, the proper domain of wildlife management, but in order to respond, the profession has had to rethink its priorities, broaden its mission, and reintegrate itself with the other resource management professions (Meine 1992). For many within wildlife management, that process has in fact gone on under the name of conservation biology.

The rise of conservation biology has all but inevitably provoked defensiveness on the part of some in the "traditional" conservation fields. But it has also allowed many—from the agency head to the district-level wildlife manager—to step beyond, and return to, their respective areas of expertise with a deeper sense of their professional roots, their shared goals, and the special contribution they can make to the common cause. Conservation biology treats the world not as a disaggregated collection of specialties, but as an interconnected whole to which each of the specialties can bring emphasis, insight, and perspective. In this, it is not so much a challenge to wildlife management as a fulfillment of the conservation vision to which wildlife management has always given so much. As wildlife management redefines its own future role accordingly, it can take justifiable pride in its historic efforts to promote what Leopold (1933) called "that new social concept toward which conservation is groping."

The basic message of this chapter is that conservation management, while critically important, is only a set of tools and approaches whose usefulness and appropriateness are measured by the extent to which they contribute to long-term conservation of natural patterns and processes. Because management is very often an intervention to reverse or mitigate the negative consequences of human activities, managers must be more than good biologists. Indeed, good management requires a blending of many skills beyond those learned in biology classes (Figure 11.1). There is a real need for managers to have training and experience in other fields, such as resource and ecological economics, sociology, anthropology, and philosophy, and to meld those skills to develop a more complete vision of the management world. As conservation managers, we may not be able to reorder national or international priorities for environmental stewardship and protection, though we should all work toward that goal. However, we can take more proactive approaches to management and thereby anticipate problems before they become crises. Much of this chapter and the next provides guidance for developing these proactive approaches for conservation management.

In our view, management is bad, or at least woefully inadequate, when it is seen as an end in itself, as a technological "fix." However, management that is logically linked to long-term solutions, to stewardship of the environment, can provide the critical intervention needed to conserve biodiversity. Thus, for example, elaborate breeding programs to maintain genetic diversity in captive populations of endangered species have limited usefulness if they are conceived as ends in themselves. But breeding of captive populations can become

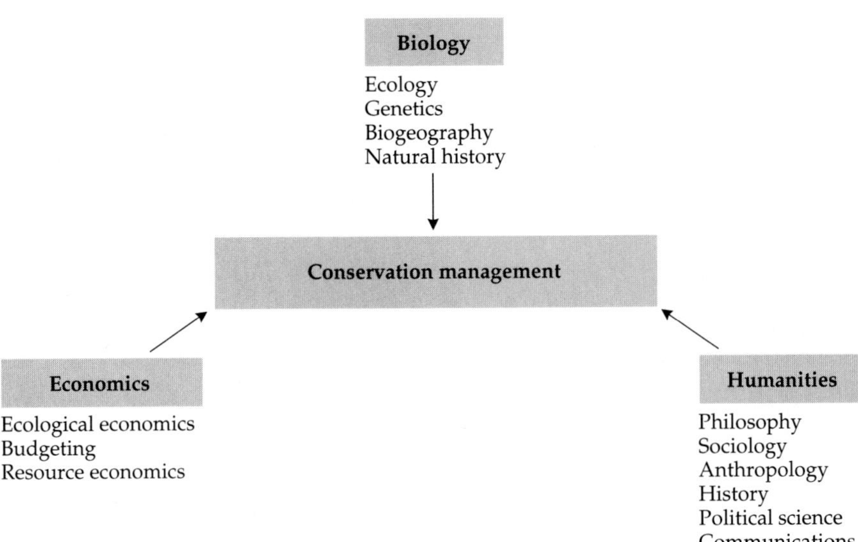

Figure 11.1 Conservation management is a complicated mix of biological, economic, and humanistic concerns. Some expertise in each of the three major axes of concern is desirable in a manager, although detailed expertise in all areas is unusual. Some aspects of management, such as risk assessment or restoration ecology, involve mixes of skills from all three axes.

a critical management option when it is part of a larger effort to restore and protect natural habitats so that the endangered species can be released into the wild with a greater chance for survival and a capacity to adapt to environmental change.

By the time you have reached this chapter, you should be thoroughly disabused of the romantic notion that nature seeks a balance and that everything would be just fine if we would only stop interfering with natural processes. For those still unconvinced, we pose the following questions: do we really need to manage natural areas and their populations? Why can't nature take care of its own? To begin to address these questions, we must understand that across the globe, human actions have directly and indirectly undercut the self-sustaining and natural regenerative capacity of many ecological systems. This has led to a number of serious problems that require direct management, such as the following:

- Because protected areas are frequently too small to support all of the species they might once have held, intervention management is necessary to maintain populations at viable levels.
- Similarly, protected areas are often too small to contain the normal patterns of disturbance that generate important processes of resource diversity. Management frequently must simulate those disturbances.
- Protected areas are often so fragmented and isolated that natural migration is unable to balance local extinctions. Under these conditions, managers may have to translocate individuals between management areas.
- Protected areas are typically surrounded by hostile anthropogenic environments that harbor invasive species (weeds, diseases, and generalist predators) and degrading processes (siltation and pollution). Management must minimize or remove such influences.
- Some protected areas are under direct pressure for development, for release of their natural resources for human use, or for use as agricultural lands for rapidly increasing and desperately poor human populations.

It is important to remember that natural systems, even those remote from humanity, change: they are dynamic rather than constant. For example, relative species abundances and even absolute species composition in a particular

(A)

(B)

Figure 11.2 Habitats can change greatly from year to year, even without catastrophic events, as demonstrated by these two photographs of a central Texas prairie in spring in two different years. (A) The prairie habitat in one year is rich in spring wildflowers. (B) In the same habitat a year later, few wildflowers appear. Slight variation in spring rainfall apparently resulted in a nearly complete failure of the spring wildflowers, with subsequent declines in solitary bee populations. (Photographs by C. R. Carroll.)

habitat can change over periods as short as a few years (Figure 11.2). This temporal change in biodiversity may be purely a reflection of natural processes of local extinction and colonization, which makes it difficult to determine whether management is working. On top of this natural variation are the pervasive intrusions of human economic activities into natural systems. The preagricultural natural landscape of 10,000 years ago has been replaced by a highly fragmented and human-dominated landscape where natural areas are few, often degraded, and isolated. Consequently, local extinction rates of native species can be high, colonization rates low, and rates of invasion by exotics greatly increased.

In such a context, a laissez-faire or passive approach to protection without active management would lead, in many cases, to rapid rates of local extinction, to increased probability that some species would become extinct, and to further habitat degradation. To return to the general question (Is management necessary?), nature can "take care of its own," but only if the ecosystem is sufficiently large and intact, and external forces not too intrusive. Because some level of management seems generally necessary, perhaps our earlier questions should be recast: "In order to achieve specific conservation goals, what is the minimum level of management required?"

Four Basic Principles of Good Conservation Management

To find our way through the maze of possible management options, it is critical that we operate from basic, scientifically grounded, principles of management. Any good ecological manager could, and should as a matter of practice, articulate a list of the management principles and corollaries that guide them in making management decisions. We give priority to the following four principles of conservation management, although others could certainly be added:

1. Critical ecological processes and biodiversity composition must be maintained.
2. External threats must be minimized and external benefits maximized.
3. Evolutionary processes must be conserved.
4. Management must be adaptive and minimally intrusive.

Principle 1: Critical Ecological Processes and Biodiversity Composition Must Be Maintained

We need to move beyond a fragmented, species-by-species approach to management and instead think in terms of maintaining critical ecological processes and biodiversity composition. We can appreciate the limitations of a species-based management approach by remembering that even small management areas contain hundreds to thousands of species interacting in a near infinity of ways. Consequently, structure can be quite complex in even a simple community.

It should be apparent that management plans cannot be created, much less put into effect, for every species in a management area. So what is to be done? There are two common, and not necessarily mutually exclusive, tactics: one is to focus on species of special interest, and the other is to focus on ecosystems. In species management, plans are developed for a few species that, for various reasons, are thought to be important. Typically, these are species that are highly visible, are relatively large ("charismatic megafauna"), are aggressive exotics, or are particularly characteristic of the environment represented by the management area. The conservation management of these species, when they are chosen judiciously, can serve as an "umbrella" of protection for many other species. For example, in the Greater Yellowstone Ecosystem, the grizzly bear (*Ursus horribilis*) is central to much management planning; maintaining habitat of sufficient quality and size to support a viable grizzly bear population will also support most of the species characteristic of the northern Rocky Mountains.

The other, increasingly important, management approach is to emphasize important ecological processes and their interactions with human activities. We refer to this approach as **ecosystem management**, and will expand on its meaning later in this chapter and, in Chapter 12, show how it is implemented.

Principle 2: External Threats Must Be Minimized and External Benefits Maximized

Because the management area is likely to permit human activities, or at the very least, to be embedded in a region dominated by human activities, we must pay particular attention to three questions: (1) How can we shelter the management area from negative outside influences such as pollutants? (2) How can the management area benefit from potentially positive outside influences, such as semi-wildlands that form a buffer zone around it? (3) How can management decisions become participatory, so that the various stakeholders in the area are included in the process?

Land-based natural areas may be metaphorically described as "islands of natural habitat," but they differ ecologically from real oceanic islands in several ways. The most important difference is that, unlike oceanic islands, land-based reserves are surrounded by landscapes that produce invasive species, degradative pollutants, and intrusive processes (Figure 11.3). Thus, as Janzen (1986) cautions, reserves are faced with the "eternal external threat." On the positive side, it may be possible to use land outside the conservation area to ameliorate three serious problems: boundary effects, small reserve size, and fragmentation.

Figure 11.3 A habitat "island" surrounded by external influences. The San Joaquin Freshwater Marsh of the Natural Reserve System of the University of California (right of center near top) is one of few remaining naturally occurring freshwater marshes in southern California and is completely surrounded by the city of Irvine. (Photograph courtesy of the California Natural Reserve System.)

Boundary Effects. Boundary effects occur in the transition zone between the management area and the outside world (Figure 11.4). By definition, this is the zone where influences from outside have a significant effect on management goals. In the ideal situation, boundary effects may be limited to a narrow edge. For example, populations of birds that nest on or near the ground

Figure 11.4 The boundary of a small (45 ha) reserve near North Augusta, South Carolina, showing the severe edge effect that can influence species and processes in the reserve. In this case, a powerline cut has created the sharp boundary. (Photograph by G. K. Meffe.)

may be depressed by scavengers and generalist predators, such as raccoons and opossums, that commonly occur near edges with agricultural lands, but will not venture far into interior habitat. Other boundary effects may penetrate deeply into the conservation area, as, for example, when agrochemicals are carried into a stream that enters the reserve. In small reserves, of course, the entire area may be affected.

In many cases, the conservation manager will need to work with the owners and managers of land surrounding the reserve to reduce negative influences that may come from their land use practices. The following three examples illustrate this need.

Figure 11.5 Public lands in the United States, from deserts to mountains, are used for cattle grazing under an allotment scheme that sets the number of head of cattle that can graze. Overgrazing can damage and despoil desert springs, streams, and range habitat. (Photograph by E. P. Pister.)

1. In U.S. deserts, ranchers hold federal grazing allotments that permit them to stock public lands with cattle (Figure 11.5). The cattle range widely and may use springs near protected reserves, springs that may be important for animals of the reserve as well. Reserve managers might work with local ranchers or, more commonly, with federal agencies such as the Bureau of Land Management to provide drinking troughs for cattle while fencing off sensitive natural springs to protect them from contamination and trampling by cattle.
2. In biological reserves located near urban centers, problems with trespassing and petty vandalism can be severe, and simply erecting higher fences and posting more "No Trespassing" signs may be inadequate. In these circumstances, good community relations assume great importance, and encouraging schools and private conservation organizations to use the reserve for environmental education is a major means of improving community relations. Managers should always look for appropriate ways to use their reserves for public environmental education. Also, problems with vandalism are more likely to get attention from local law enforcement if the reserve provides important services to the community.
3. In the southeastern United States, much of the forested land is privately held and used for timber. Thus, privately held upland pine

> forest constitutes most of the southeastern pine ecosystem. In this region, conservation of pine forests must involve cooperative agreements with the families and corporations that own most of the pinelands. Recently, for example, Georgia-Pacific, one of the largest timber companies and landowners in the Southeast, agreed to a conservation plan to protect the endangered Red-cockaded Woodpecker (see Figure 6.1D), which nests in cavities in large pines on Georgia-Pacific lands. If these woodpeckers are not protected on private timberlands, it is doubtful that sufficient protected habitat will be available to ensure their survival.

Traditional or "indigenous" rights create special management problems, but sometimes opportunities as well. In some places, local people have long traditions of using reserve lands for hunting, fur trapping, fishing, and gathering medicinal plants. Sometimes these traditions long predate establishment of the protected reserve, as do, for example, harvesting of saguaro cactus fruits in Arizona desert reserves by Pima Indians, harvesting of medicinal plants in eastern Ecuadorian national parks by Siona Indians, or harvesting of ginseng plants (used in oriental medicine) and mushrooms by longtime residents of the southern Appalachian Mountains. There are some ambiguous cases and gray areas, but generally it is easy to distinguish between long-term traditions of land use that should be continued, as long as they do not jeopardize the conservation objectives of a reserve, and irresponsible poaching that should be stopped.

Long-term residents often have considerable indigenous knowledge about natural resources that could be useful to managers. In particular, families that have lived in a region for several generations may have important information about how the natural landscape and land uses have changed over long periods. You may learn, for example, that 40 years ago extraction of hemlock trees for the tanbark industry was intense in one part of an eastern forest but absent in other hemlock forests; such information may help to explain the current spatial pattern of hemlock and rhododendron thickets. In some reserves, such as Guanacaste, Corcovado, Braulio Carillo, and other national parks in Costa Rica, local residents have been hired by the park service, at least in part for their natural history knowledge of the area. One should not overly romanticize the value of long-term residents, though. Sometimes they, as individuals or organized groups, are simply hostile to the reserve, and legal restraints may be required to prevent damage to the reserve through arson, poaching, vandalism and the like. The value of indigenous knowledge systems is the topic of Essay 11B by Mark Plotkin and Adrian Forsyth.

ESSAY 11B
Retaining Indigenous Knowledge Systems as a Management Tool

Mark J. Plotkin and Adrian Forsyth
Conservation International

The philosopher-naturalist Laurens Van der Post recently remarked that the most damning legacy of colonialism has been its relentless tendency to separate tropical peoples from their land and culture. "The great mistake people make is in thinking about the aboriginal races in South Africa—the Bushmen and Hottentots and the like—as primitive peoples. They were actually very sophisticated societies and cultures with immense awareness and very important values."

The sophistication of many indigenous cultures is most evident in their agricultural systems. Over 200 years ago, a Jesuit priest in lowland Bolivia, Francisco Eder, noted that an extraordinary irrigation system in the local savannas, which had been devised in pre-Columbian times, still supported an enormous population of Mojeno Indians. Thanks to the influence of the Padre and his cohorts, as well as introduced diseases, this Amerindian agricultural system was abandoned, and the savannas that once fed the teeming local populace today are covered with a scrub vegetation supporting a few mangy cows.

The chinampa system, developed in pre-Columbian Mexico, remains in use, albeit in a much more restricted range than it once covered. Usually constructed in swampy or lacustrine environments, chinampas consist of garden plots created by building small islands using layers of vegetation and mud. The surrounding waters seep in and provide the necessary moisture, while mud scooped up from canals around the plot is periodically added as fertilizer to the garden on top of the island. According to Jim Nations of Conservation International, chinampas not only produce food and other useful crops year-round, they do not deplete the soil or require artificial fertilizers or pesticides.

A similar system is now being studied in the altiplano of northwestern Bolivia. Alan Kolata of the University of Chicago had long been intrigued by a series of ridges and depressions in this remote region that seemed to indicate some form of agricultural system that involved raised planting beds surrounded by canals. The local Aymara Indians, however, employed no such system. Kolata and his colleagues worked with the Aymaras to dig a series of raised beds surrounded by ditches; the results were a crop yield seven times greater than the local average.

Here we see three different fates for three independently evolved agricultural systems: the Mojeno system has been lost, the chinampa system still exists, and the altiplano system would have remained lost if it had not been for an intrepid anthropologist and his indigenous colleagues. How many other equally valid and possibly even more productive systems have completely disappeared without a trace? The superiority complex that drives outsiders from Western societies to want to replace "primitive" systems with ill-suited ones developed on foreign soils continues to this day: the Indonesian government is currently trying to get tribal peoples in highland New Guinea to forgo their traditional and highly productive agricultural system based on sweet potatoes and sago palms, and replace it with rice, an inappropriate crop. This colonial attitude comes from cultural biases and a lack of understanding.

Yet, the problem we face is not just the loss of agricultural systems themselves, but extinction of cultivar diversity as well. Indigenous agricultural systems typically contain many different varieties of a single crop, much as a farmer in the industrialized world may grow several different types of corn: one to feed his family, another to feed his animals, still another to make popcorn, and another to sell as a cash crop. The Amerindian farmer in the Amazon usually cultivates distinct varieties of cassava for the production of bread, beer, meal, porridge, and whatever other end products he desires. The Tirio Indians of northeastern Amazonia have at least 15 varieties of cassava in their gardens, while other tribes like the Machiguenga of Peru may cultivate several dozen. Time and again, these often obscure varieties from indigenous gardens are crossed with commercial varieties to increase yield and increase resistance to pests and diseases. A barley plant from Ethiopia was crossbred with barley in California, providing resistance to the lethal yellow dwarf virus, which threatened an industry worth $160 million per year. The yield of cassava in Africa has been increased tenfold because of disease resistance provided by cassava from the Amazon. And scientists have recently found that a variety of sunflower being cultivated by the Havasupai Indians in the American Southwest offers resistance to a blight attacking sunflower crops in the Old World.

The late economic botanist Edgar Anderson once stumbled across an Indian garden in Guatemala that initially seemed more of a rat's nest than a productive agricultural plot. It was only after careful study that he realized how much more sophisticated than the botanist was the farmer:

> In terms of our American & European equivalents the garden was a vegetable garden, an orchard, a medicinal plant garden, a rubbish heap, a compost heap, and a beeyard. There was no problem of erosion though it was at the top of a steep slope; the soil surface was practically all covered and apparently would be during most of the year. Humidity would be kept up during the dry season and plants of the same sort were so isolated from one another by intervening vegetation that pests and diseases could not readily spread from plant to plant . . . It is frequently said by Europeans and European Americans that time means nothing to an American Indian. This garden seemed to me a good example of how an Indian, when we look more than superficially into his activities, is budgeting his time more efficiently than we do. The garden was in continuous production but was taking only a little effort at any one time . . . I suspect that if one were to make a careful study of such an American Indian garden, one would find it more productive than ours in terms of pounds of vegetables and fruit per man-hour per square foot of ground. Far from saying time means nothing to an Indian, I would suggest that it means so much more to him that he does not wish to waste it in profitless effort as we do.

At a time when there are ever more mouths to feed on this planet, we suggest that Anderson's admonition to look more closely at the form and function of indigenous systems is advice worth following. Modern management techniques often overlook and disparage these indigenous systems, which are based on centuries of in situ sustainable existence, in favor of high-tech but often inappropriate and expensive systems that fail. We can learn a great deal about environmental management (and humility) from such cultures. This was succinctly summarized by anthropologist David Maybury Lewis, who said,

> It's an irony that while tribal peoples with few resources strive mightily to keep their ties to the earth, we, with huge resources, strive mightily to leave it behind. We need no more power for the children to live another thousand years. We need the old wisdoms of the last one hundred thousand, those wisdoms that lie at the common fundament of all humanity. Wisdom of the different, yet common family. Wisdom of the different, yet common myths. Wisdom of the different, yet common home.

Reserve Size. Management areas are often small with respect to the resource needs of the species they contain. This is especially true for large-bodied species, species with long generation times, large predatory vertebrates, and highly migratory species. For these species, the area required to maintain a minimally viable population may greatly exceed the actual size of the reserve (see Chapters 7 and 10 for extended discussions of this problem). Semi-wild lands around a protected area could increase its effective size. The game reserve system of East Africa provides a good illustration of this strategy. The core reserves act as refuges for large game animals, but the mixed agricultural fallow and brush lands that surround the reserves are important grazing and hunting grounds for game and other wild animals. In the United States, protected natural reserves are commonly surrounded by public and private semi-wild lands, including multiple-use national and state forests, Army Corps of Engineers lands around lakes and reservoirs, Bureau of Land Management lands in the Western states, and large portions of state and national parks and monuments.

Habitat Corridors. The expansion of human-dominated landscapes has increasingly fragmented and isolated natural habitats. One of the most active debates in the conservation community concerns the advantages and disadvantages of reconnecting fragmented habitats. Because the conservation of fragmented habitats was extensively treated in Chapters 9 and 10, we simply remind you here of two of the most salient points.

First, the habitat corridors that may have to be established to connect habitat patches should facilitate movement among patches and minimize mortality within the corridors. The corollary is that the corridors should be designed so that they are not misinterpreted by the species as resident habitat. This is important because the high edge:interior ratio of corridors may enhance the density of generalist predators and scavengers, and therefore the longer an individual takes to move through a corridor, the greater the risk of mortality. Therefore, managers need to understand, for each species, what is perceived as an acceptable environment for migration versus what is seen as acceptable environment for longer-term residency.

Second, reconnecting existing habitat patches may be cheaper than establishing new large habitat blocks, but there are still real costs to be paid. Corridors may have to extend long distances and cross significant barriers such as highways. The engineering required to assist migrants in crossing these barriers may be expensive, and the right solutions are not always obvious. Indeed, it is easy to find crossings that are used by habitat generalists such as white-tailed deer; that is, the solution is easy for species that probably do not need connected habitat in order to maintain viable population densities. But how would you engineer a highway crossing for pine martins, arboreal predators that seldom leave the tree canopy to cross open ground? If barrier crossings are not adequately designed, a corridor can become a death trap.

Principle 3: Evolutionary Processes Must Be Conserved

Species should not be protected as though they were static museum pieces, but rather as participants in evolutionary processes. We asserted in previous chapters that two fundamental objectives of conservation biology at the species level are keeping populations large enough to ensure against stochastic causes of extinction, and ensuring that species retain sufficient genetic diversity to permit adaptation to changing environments. These two objectives are related in that small populations are more likely to lose genetic diversity through chance processes, and are also more vulnerable to stochastic environmental events. Obviously, a reserve manager cannot maintain the optimal mix of genes (who could predict what it should be?), but ecological conditions can be maintained that will favor maintenance of genetic diversity at reasonable levels. And in general, the processes that increase population size will also favor increased genetic diversity. Chapters 6 and 7 discuss the significance of genetics and demography to conservation issues and explain the influences that environmental and demographic factors have on the likelihood that a species will go extinct.

Typically, genetic management of a species is not explicitly included in a management plan until its populations have declined to some precariously low level. Thus, by the time genetics becomes a management issue, much diversity will already have been lost, and managers may have to deal with additional genetic problems such as inbreeding depression. For these reasons, Templeton (1990) reminds us that "rather than establish captive populations as acts of desperation, it is better to establish them as "insurance policies" when the natural populations are still sufficiently large to contain much genetic diversity."

Principle 4: Management Must Be Adaptive and Minimally Intrusive

Insofar as possible, management should be gentle and minimally intrusive. Because environmental conditions may change and new problems arise, management should also be adaptive; that is, it should remain flexible in order to meet new contingencies, rather than stubbornly adhering to a written plan simply because it has survived a bureaucratic maze and is supported by "headquarters." As a corollary to the general attributes of good management discussed above, contingency plans should be included in the event that the original strategy fails to work. The following question should be asked of every management plan: If the plan fails, will the biotic community be worse off than if the plan had not been executed? If the answer seems to be "yes," then special attention should be given to contingency plans to minimize negative effects on the biotic community.

Of the many institutional changes that the implementation of good management requires, two seem particularly fundamental. First, institutions should facilitate innovative approaches to management. Institutions develop their own culture, their way of "doing business," or what many would refer to as "an agency bureaucracy." Institutional cultures are adaptive strategies for survival in the political world, but may be maladaptive when substantive changes are needed. Institutions must become more flexible, accommodating change rather than reflexively resisting it, in order to support innovative resource management. Good management, whether at the level of species or ecosystems, requires institutional flexibility and provides some mechanisms by which it may be achieved. For example, the U.S. Forest Service has for years worked under the mandate to "get the cut out," meaning that timber yields were of paramount importance in forest management planning. Because Forest Service budgets were, until recently, closely linked to timber receipts, this narrow emphasis on logging was not surprising. Now the Forest Service, along with other federal natural resource management agencies, has a new mandate to balance extraction and production of natural resources with protection of biodiversity. Because federal agencies are now less focused on maximizing receipts for the sale of natural resources, they are freer to explore and incorporate other management goals.

Second, management should incorporate people and their socioeconomic concerns into the landscape. Good management, especially at the level of ecosystems, is far more than having an ecological perspective on our natural resources; it involves the integration of people and their interests into the landscape in a way that does not harm the ecosystem processes upon which we depend. The inclusion of people as part of the ecosystem is really an extension of the writings and thinking of Aldo Leopold (1938), who spoke of "the oldest task in human history: to live on a piece of land without spoiling it." Leopold never tried to exclude humans from the landscape, but wanted to better integrate people as part of the landscape in a way that the land could support without being degraded. Modern ecosystem management is essentially that: attempting to devise a healthier relationship between a growing human population and a shrinking resource base. To accomplish this, we must mesh ecological, sociopolitical, and institutional perspectives in ways that protect the interests of all, while not diminishing the interests of others or the ability of the land to support our activities.

Our four principles of good management will not tell you what to do in any particular situation, but they will provide guidance, a mindset, to help you make the right decision. As much as we need new scientific knowledge to help us become better stewards, we need to change our priorities and perspectives. These principles form the core of a promising management approach—ecosystem management—that has emerged in recent years, and to which we devote the remainder of this chapter.

Ecosystem Management

Conservation management can focus on many different levels, ranging from protecting genetic diversity and population viability, to habitat manipulations for single species, to protection of natural areas for native communities, to landscape-level protection or restoration (Table 11.1). All of these are legitimate management approaches, and all have a place in conservation management. However, a recent emphasis on what has variously been called "the "ecosystem approach," "adaptive ecosystem management," or, most commonly, "ecosystem management" has dominated conservation management and will provide the focus for the remainder of this chapter and the next. This approach does not eliminate or replace any other management approaches but in fact takes them into account to build a larger, overarching perspective.

The Defining Characteristics of Ecosystem Management

The ecosystem approach to conservation is the result of an evolutionary (not revolutionary) process in natural resource management over many decades. It was most recently motivated in the United States by policy driven by the Vice

Table 11.1
Examples of Management at Different Environmental Scales

Scale	Management example
Population	Population vulnerability analysis leading to estimates of minimum viable population densities
Habitat	Using prescribed burning to maintain natural patterns of vegetation heterogeneity
Landscape	Protecting riparian wetlands against pollution from agrochemicals by developing vegetation buffers between agricultural fields and wetlands

President's National Performance Review (Gore 1993), developed at the highest levels of the federal government (Interagency Ecosystem Management Task Force 1995), and endorsed by all federal agencies. Ecosystem management as a new and more holistic approach to conservation is being embraced by natural heritage organizations, including public agencies such as the U.S. Forest Service, Bureau of Land Management, Environmental Protection Agency, U.S. Fish and Wildlife Service, and the Biological Resources Division of the U.S. Geological Survey, as well as by private organizations such as The Nature Conservancy. Indeed, ecosystem management has become the centerpiece of environmental policy in the late 20th century.

Our elaboration of ecosystem management is a synthesis arising from many different sources of information, from academic to highly practical, social to ecological, institutional to individual. It is also grounded in many different kinds of experience, including our involvement in management issues both national and international, training of resource managers, interactions with academic, agency-based, and nongovernmental scientists, and countless illuminating discussions with resource managers and other stakeholders in the outcome of management decisions.

What exactly is "ecosystem management"? Is it an important new direction for stewardship, a devious cover for the "tyranny of ecology," as one book's dust jacket asserts (Chase 1995), an assault on private property rights, or just a mantra to cover business as usual by those who would unduly exploit nature? Because it is identified with such widely disparate labels, there must be considerable confusion about the true nature of ecosystem management. Part of the confusion arises because people who pursue personal agendas tend to embrace popular slogans in order to advance their cause. Thus, a logging company might wish to assert that clear-cutting is ecosystem management, just as an environmental protectionist might wish to place all Western rangelands off-limits to cattle as a precondition to "good" ecosystem management. We strongly maintain that ecosystem management is a critically important new direction for stewardship, and for that reason, it is essential that its true meaning not be debased by those who would use it as a marketing label to advance their own narrow purposes.

Box 11A presents some of the definitions of ecosystem management that have appeared in the recent literature. Each of these definitions has some merit. A skeptic might look at them and conclude that, because ecosystem

BOX 11A
Some Definitions of Ecosystem Management

"Management of natural resources using system-wide concepts to ensure that all plants and animals in ecosystems are maintained at viable levels in native habitats and that basic ecosystem processes are perpetuated indefinitely."

Clark and Zaunbrecher 1987

"The careful and skillful use of ecological, economic, social, and managerial principles in managing ecosystems to produce, restore, or sustain ecosystem integrity and desired conditions, uses, products, values, and services over the long term."

Overbay 1992

"The strategy by which, in aggregate, the full array of forest values and functions is maintained at the landscape level. Coordinated management at the landscape level, including across ownerships, is an essential component."

Society of American Foresters 1993

"A strategy or plan to manage ecosystems to provide for all associated organisms, as opposed to a strategy or plan for managing individual species."

Forest Ecosystem Management Assessment Team 1993

"To restore and maintain the health, sustainability, and biological diversity of ecosystems while supporting sustainable economies and communities."

Environmental Protection Agency 1994

"Protecting or restoring the function, structure, and species composition

of an ecosystem, recognizing that all components are interrelated."
U.S. Fish and Wildlife Service 1994

"Integrating scientific knowledge of ecological relationships within a complex sociopolitical and values framework toward the general goal of protecting native ecosystem integrity over the long term."
Grumbine 1994

"Any land-management system that seeks to protect viable populations of all native species, perpetuates natural disturbance regimes on the regional scale, adopts a planning timeline of centuries, and allows human use at levels that do not result in long-term ecological degradation."
Noss and Cooperrider 1994

"Ecosystem management is the integration of ecological, economic, and social principles to manage biological systems in a manner that safeguards long-term ecological sustainability. The primary goal of ecosystem management is to develop management strategies that maintain and restore the ecological integrity, productivity, and biological diversity of public lands."
U.S. Bureau of Land Management 1994

"The ecosystem approach is a method for sustaining or restoring natural systems and their functions and values. It is goal driven, and it is based on a collaboratively developed vision of desired future conditions that integrates ecological, economic, and social factors. It is applied within a geographic framework defined primarily by ecological boundaries."
Interagency Ecosystem Management Task Force 1995

"The application of ecological and social information, options, and constraints to achieve desired social benefits within a defined geographic area and over a specified period."
Lackey 1996

"Ecosystem management is management driven by explicit goals, executed by policies, protocols, and practices, and made adaptable by monitoring and research based on our best understanding of the ecological interactions and processes necessary to sustain ecosystem composition, structure, and function."
Christensen et al. 1996

"A collaborative process that strives to reconcile the promotion of economic opportunities and livable communities with the conservation of ecological integrity and biodiversity."
The Keystone National Policy Dialogue on Ecosystem Management 1996.

---

management cannot be unambiguously defined, it is not developed enough to be put into practice. This would be an unfortunate assumption, for there is a great deal of commonality among these definitions: they emphasize large-scale, system-wide perspectives, they focus on the composition and processes of ecological systems and their complexities, they recognize the need for integration across multiple scales of concern—ecological, economic, and cultural—and long-term sustainability of the ecosystem is their implicit, and often explicit, management goal.

A good way to envision ecosystem management is as three interacting circles (Figure 11.6). These circles represent ecological, sociopolitical, and institutional perspectives, all of which influence how we use and interact with natural systems. A successful ecosystem approach occurs at the intersection of all three circles; dwelling in any single circle indicates too narrow a perspective. For example, concern *only* with immediate institutional capabilities, funding, or performance ignores how institutions will affect ecological systems, or how they will be received by society. Likewise, concern *only* for preservation of ecosystems (an ecological focus) is unrealistic because it ignores society's interests in those systems as well as institutional momentum that could have a strong bearing on how those systems are used.

Even working at the intersection of two of the three circles is insufficient for a good ecosystems approach. For example, there may be strong popular support for restoring a particular ecosystem, along with the ecological knowledge of the system needed to do it well, but if the institutions that need to do the work are not engaged, or not capable of performing the tasks, then the effort will fail. Thus, a successful ecosystem approach must incorporate ecological, sociopolitical, and institutional perspectives.

With this conceptual model and the several definitions from the literature as our background, we will adopt the following as our working definition of ecosystem management: *Ecosystem management is an approach to maintaining or restoring the composition, structure, and function of natural and modified ecosystems for the goal of long-term sustainability. It is based on a collaboratively developed vision*

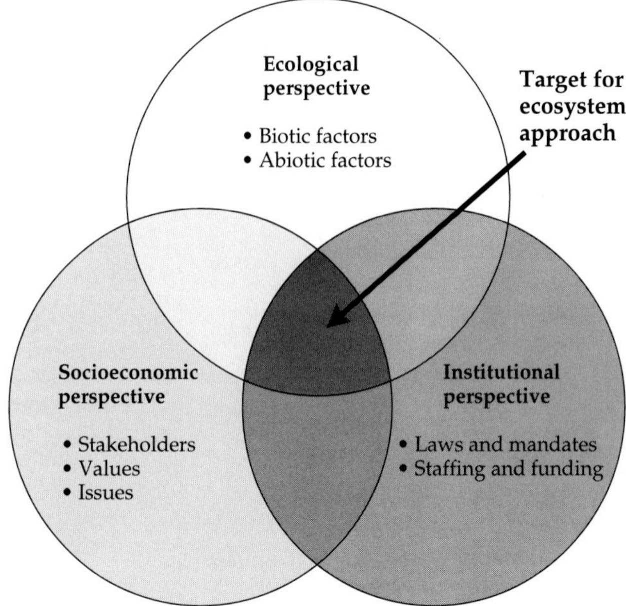

Figure 11.6 A conceptual basis for ecosystem management. Good ecosystem management lies at the intersection of ecological, socioeconomic, and institutional perspectives. (Modified from Dennis A. Schenborn, personal communication.)

of desired future conditions that integrates ecological, socioeconomic, and institutional perspectives, applied within a geographic framework defined primarily by natural ecological boundaries.

Ecosystem management will not succeed if ecological perspectives dominate to the exclusion of human welfare, if narrow economic considerations prevent good ecological stewardship, or if institutions remain rigid and cannot change to incorporate alternative perspectives and ideas. All three of the circles in Figure 11.6 must be addressed and integrated in a balanced manner for true ecosystem management to prevail.

This integration of numerous perspectives is not necessarily easy, and it takes time and effort. An excellent example of a successful approach is the Applegate Partnership in Oregon, discussed in Case Study 2 in Chapter 18. Here, disparate groups with varied and sometimes conflicting interests in the land came together, identified common interests, and developed plans for long-term sustainability of their ecosystem.

Our conception of ecosystem management encompasses the many existing kinds of ecological systems, ranging from natural systems such as wilderness areas—where social and economic demands are mainly nonconsumptive—to moderately modified systems such as national forests or rangelands—where social and economic needs are greater and often consumptive—to highly modified areas such as suburban parks and the urban landscape. Ecosystem management encompasses the entire range of landscapes that together determine the health and integrity of ecological and human systems.

The successful realization of ecosystem management is predicated on the inclusion of several scientific and social components. In order to work effectively toward the long-term sustainability of ecological systems, we must use the best available science, recognizing that ecological systems are dynamic, and hence, that management results will be uncertain and surprises common. Management therefore must be adaptive, and monitoring of appropriate indicators continuous, in order to respond to the dynamic and uncertain nature of ecological systems.

Table 11.2
Comparison of Traditional and Ecosystem Approaches to Management of Natural Resources

Traditional Management	Ecosystem Management
Emphasis on commodities and natural resource extraction	Emphasis on balance between commodities, amenities, and ecological integrity
Equilibrium perspective	Nonequilibrium perspective
Ecological stability	Dynamics, resilience
Climax communities	Shifting mosaics
Reductionism	Holism
Prescription; command and control management	Uncertainty and flexibility; adaptive management
Site specificity	Attention to context
Solutions imposed by resource management agencies	Solutions developed through discussions among all stakeholders
Optimization; problem simplification; search for single best answer	Multiple solutions to complex problems
Confrontation; single-issue polarization; public seen as adversary	Consensus building; multiple issues; public invited as partners

The spatial and temporal scales of ecosystem management must be appropriate to the particular ecological system. These scales will usually require that a landscape mosaic of habitats contains sufficient resources to meet the life cycle requirements of populations under the expected conditions of significant interannual environmental variation. Because research into long-term climate change suggests that the amplitude of climatic variation, at least for precipitation, is increasing (Tsonis 1996), managers should err on the liberal side in defining the appropriate landscape mosaic.

From the outset, we want to be clear that we recognize that many practitioners of natural resource management are dissatisfied with the current state of affairs; indeed, we have yet to meet a manager who was completely satisfied with the status quo. Furthermore, many managers know what kinds of institutional changes need to be made, but are frustrated by the many disincentives and barriers to change that block the development of more rational approaches to natural resource management. Table 11.2 illustrates some of the contrasts between traditional management and ecosystem management, that is, management as it has been for several decades contrasted with what we think management should become.

Key Elements of an Ecosystem Approach

Ecosystem management is essentially an expansion of natural resource management and human–land relationships in three dimensions: time, space, and degree of inclusion (Figure 11.7). First, the temporal dimension is expanded because we are concerned with the health and vitality of ecosystems into the indefinite future, rather than simply what they can do for us here and now. Our time frame must go beyond the next year or the present budget cycle to include decades and even centuries. This does not mean that ecosystems should be "frozen in time"—that is, managed such that natural change is not permitted. Rather, management goals must include ensuring that ecosystem dynamics occur within ranges that do not exceed the resilience of the system. In the long run, ecosystem management would not attempt to constrain the ecosystem in the face of major climate change. It makes no sense from an ecosystem perspective to hold only a short-term view when the effects of human activities on ecosystems can last for decades and even centuries.

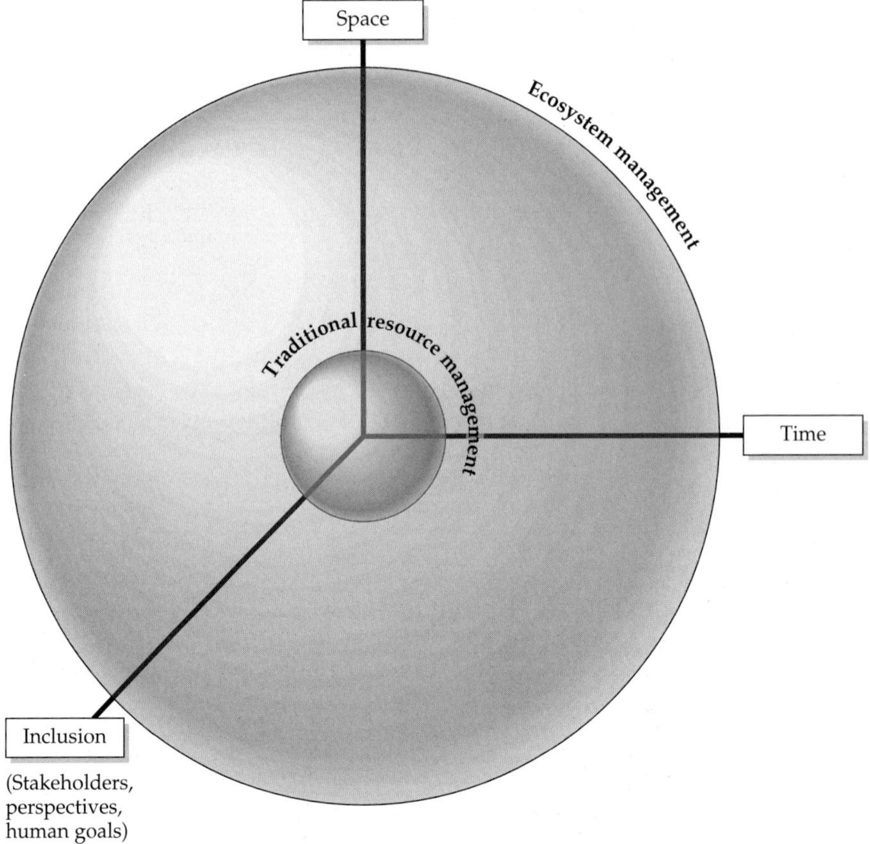

Figure 11.7 Ecosystem management is an expansion of traditional natural resource management in three dimensions. Temporal and spatial scales of concern, as well as degree of inclusion in decision making, are all expanded by ecosystem management.

Second, the spatial dimension is expanded beyond a particular small plot of ground to include the larger landscape and connections to other landscapes. No longer is it satisfactory to work solely within a national park or local preserve when we know that our decisions have effects across its boundaries and are in turn affected by external events. We must begin to recognize and understand the spatial connections present in nature to more effectively manage these systems. Ideally, the spatial scale should include sufficient heterogeneity to provide resources for species during years of scarcity. Beyond food, these resources could include such things as habitat cover that facilitates movement throughout the landscape, and, for plants, an adequate supply of pollinators, seed dispersers, and good germination sites.

Finally, the human dimension is expanded to include a broader diversity of interests, talents, and perspectives in natural resource decision making. Single-institution, top-down, command-and-control decision making will not suffice in true ecosystem management, for it can exclude the majority of persons and interests affected by the decision and can ignore relevant information and talents that could contribute to problem solving.

A number of elements of an ecosystem approach have been proposed, with a great deal of overlap among them. These elements together create a different mindset in natural resource management, a new mentality in dealing with land stewardship.

Grumbine (1994), in an already classic paper called "What is Ecosystem Management?" summarized ten dominant themes of ecosystem management that have emerged in the scientific literature. These themes have appeared repeatedly in writings on the topic and seem to represent areas of agreement about ecosystem management:

1. *Hierarchical context.* There are many levels in the biological hierarchy (genes through landscapes). Connections among levels should be sought and understood by managers. No single level can be managed or manipulated without affecting other levels.
2. *Ecological boundaries.* We must work across administrative and political boundaries, with a focus on ecological boundaries.
3. *Ecological integrity.* We must protect complete native diversity (genes, populations, species, communities, ecosystems) along with the ecological patterns and processes that create and support that diversity. Note that "integrity" will have somewhat different meanings depending on the land use context. Ecological integrity in a national park wilderness will have a different form than ecological integrity in multiple-use lands such as national forests and rangelands. Ecological integrity is an important concept that is difficult to express in operational terms; for one approach using reference ecosystems, see Essay 14A .
4. *Information base.* An ecosystem approach requires more ecological, social, and economic knowledge and better use of existing data to make informed decisions. Scientific data are the basis for good decision making.
5. *Monitoring.* Monitoring is a critical aspect of the feedback loop that is necessary for adaptive management, as it allows evaluation of the results of management actions and modification of those actions. Monitoring must be linked to carefully chosen indicators that reflect management goals.
6. *Adaptive management.* Because our knowledge is limited and ecosystem dynamics are complex, we must continually learn how to manage better; consequently, management should be approached as an experiment. Flexibility and adaptation in the face of uncertainty are critical.
7. *Interagency cooperation.* Working within ecological boundaries demands cooperation among multiple federal, state, and local agencies as well as private parties. No single entity can or should be doing all the work and decision making.
8. *Organizational change.* Resource management agencies must change their structure and methods of operation to accommodate the flexibility necessary for an ecosystem approach. Entrenched, inflexible agencies that follow a prescriptive rather than an experimental approach *cannot* do good ecosystem management.
9. *Humans are embedded in nature.* People are a fundamental part of nature; they influence ecological patterns and processes, and are influenced by them. People—their needs and desires—must be considered from the outset and throughout the management processes if ecosystems are to be protected.
10. *Values.* Human values will always drive management goals.

The Interagency Ecosystem Management Task Force (1995), a presidentially appointed group of representatives from most federal departments, characterized the ecosystem approach in the following ways: more partnerships and greater collaboration; broader program perspective; broader resource perspective; broader geographic and temporal perspective; more dynamic planning processes; less reactive and more proactive. Their key elements of ecosystem management include the following:

1. Develop a shared vision of the desired ecosystem condition that takes into account existing social and economic conditions in the

ecosystem, and identify ways in which all parties can contribute to, and benefit from, achieving ecosystem goals.

2. Develop coordinated approaches among federal agencies to accomplish ecosystem objectives, collaborating on a continuous basis with state, local, and tribal governments and other stakeholders to address mutual concerns.
3. Use ecological approaches that restore or maintain the biological diversity and sustainability of the ecosystem.
4. Support actions that incorporate sustained economic, sociocultural, and community goals.
5. Respect and ensure private property rights and work cooperatively with private landowners to accomplish shared goals.
6. Recognize that ecosystems and institutions are complex, dynamic, characteristically heterogeneous over space and time, and constantly changing.
7. Use an adaptive approach to management to achieve both desired goals and a new understanding of ecosystems.
8. Integrate the best science available into the decision-making process, while continuing scientific research to improve the knowledge base.
9. Establish baseline conditions for ecosystem functioning and sustainability against which change can be measured; monitor and evaluate actions to determine if goals and objectives are being achieved.

Note that these elements are a mixture of ecological, socioeconomic, and institutional considerations (see Figure 11.6), not dominated by any one concern. They recognize, for example, certain underlying ecological realities such as dynamics, complexity, and heterogeneity, while also recognizing private property rights, the need for interinstitutional cooperation, and the desire for continued economic benefits from the environment.

A group of largely academic scientists produced a report on the scientific basis for ecosystem management for the Ecological Society of America (Christensen et al. 1996). This report emphasized details of the ecological basis for ecosystem management, and offered the following components:

- *Sustainability.* Intergenerational sustainability should be a precondition for management rather than an afterthought. Ecosystems cannot be degraded and yet expected to provide goods and services to future generations.
- *Goals.* Goals should be stated in terms of specific "desired future trajectories" and "desired future behaviors." Obviously we cannot reach ecosystem goals if they are not stated.
- *Sound ecological models and understanding.* Research is needed that emphasizes the role of processes and interconnections in ecosystems.
- *Complexity and interconnectedness.* Complexity and interconnectedness are inherent components of all ecosystems. They provide resistance to and resilience from human disturbances, and should be retained to the fullest extent possible.
- *Recognition of the dynamic character of ecosystems.* Striving to attain or retain a status quo is not ecosystem management, because we know that ecosystems are dynamic and changing. We must allow for and expect change over time in ecosystems.
- *Context and scale.* Because ecosystem processes operate over a broad range of spatial and temporal scales, there is no single appropriate spatial scale or time frame for management. Also, all ecosystems are embedded in larger landscapes, whose structure and dynamics affect and are affected by them.

- *Humans as ecosystem components.* Humans are integral components of the ecosystem who must be engaged as stakeholders to achieve sustainability.
- *Adaptability and accountability.* Ecosystem management is evolutionary, and will change as our knowledge bases in ecology, economics, sociology, and other relevant disciplines develop. Management goals and strategies are merely hypotheses to be tested by research and management actions, updated with new information, and modified. There is no single, prescriptive way to properly manage at the ecosystem level.

These various aspects and features of ecosystem management are now being implemented at many organizational levels, including the U.S. federal government. Examples of this approach by practitioners are provided in Essay 11C by Michael Dombeck (former Acting Director of the Bureau of Land Management and current Chief of the U.S. Forest Service) and Chris Wood.

ESSAY 11C
Ecosystem Management on Publicly Owned Lands

Michael Dombeck and Christopher A. Wood, U.S. Forest Service

Nearly 30% of the land in the United States is collectively owned by its citizens. Four federal agencies—the Bureau of Land Management (BLM), the Forest Service, the National Park Service, and the Fish and Wildlife Service—are responsible for managing over 90% (627 million acres) of these lands. Public lands contain some of the most remarkable cultural, archaeological, and historical sites in the world. They often provide the best, and sometimes last, habitats for rare plant and animal species. For example, of the 214 stocks of Pacific salmon that Nehlsen et al. (1991) identified as being at some risk of extinction, Forest Service and BLM managed lands contain habitat for 134 and 109 stocks, respectively (Williams and Williams 1996).

Each year, tens of millions of Americans use public lands for recreational activities such as hunting, fishing, hiking, backpacking, camping, and cycling. Extractive industries such as mining, ranching, logging, and oil and gas development provide jobs to rural communities that depend on the production of natural resources from these lands.

Public expectations of public lands have changed over the past 20 years, making resource management more complex. Changes in demand, taken together with growing public concern over the health of waterways, grasslands, and forests, an increasingly complex set of legal mandates, and greater knowledge of how to manage natural resources on a sustainable basis, pose significant challenges for federal agencies.

It is increasingly clear that federal agencies cannot protect individual species or habitats without managing them in the context of larger ecosystems. Instead of traditional species- by-species or commodity production-based approaches, BLM, the Forest Service, and other federal land management agencies now focus on working with all interested parties to manage ecological systems in their entirety—an ecosystem management approach.

Principles of Ecosystem Management

Regardless of whether one works for a federal land management agency, a state wildlife agency, or manages private land, there are essentially nine "operating principles" of the ecosystem approach (USDI BLM 1994a):

1. Sustain the productivity and diversity of ecological systems.
2. Gather and use the best available scientific information as the cornerstone for resource allocation and other land management decisions.
3. Involve the public in the planning process and coordinate with other federal, state, and private landowners.
4. Determine desired future conditions based on historical, ecological, economic, and social considerations.
5. Minimize and repair damage to the land.
6. Adopt an interdisciplinary approach to land management.
7. Base planning and management on long-term horizons and goals.
8. Reconnect isolated and fragmented parts of the landscape.
9. Practice adaptive management. Be flexible and willing to change as new information becomes available.

The first principle is the cornerstone of the subsequent eight. Our overriding priority must be to maintain the health, diversity, and productivity of the land. We simply cannot meet the needs of people if we do not first secure the ecological integrity of the land. At its root, ecosystem management involves providing values, products, and services from the land in a manner that safeguards long-term ecological sustainability (Wood 1994). The simplest distillation of the concept is that ecosystem management entails working within the limits of the land in order to maintain ecological sustainability.

Effective conservation and restoration strategies must recognize that ecological processes occur on varied temporal and geographic scales (FEMAT 1993). Similarly, ecosystem approaches should operate across a succession of scales.

It is also increasingly clear that resource managers cannot protect individual species or habitats without managing them in the context of larger ecosystems. In the words of John Muir (1869), "when we try to pick anything out by itself, we find it hitched to everything else in the universe." For example, land ownership patterns rarely coincide with distinct topographic boundaries. Long-term conservation and restoration strategies cannot overlook the relationship between the health of federal lands and the condition of adjoining state and private lands. The ecosystem approach embraces the active participation of all who use, value, and influence the land's health.

Resource Advisory Councils

Communities whose economies depend on public lands are often the most seriously affected by ecological degradation; they are also often the most knowledgeable about the land. As a result, federal land management agencies are forming partnerships with federal, state, and local governments, interested private landowners, and other public land users to ensure local involvement in managing public lands.

The western United States has the nation's fastest-growing population with the largest proportion living in urban areas, and also contains most of the nation's public lands. Generally city-dwelling or suburbanite and highly mobile, this new generation of users appreciates public lands most for their aesthetic, spiritual, and recreational values.

In order to integrate the full array of interests and to involve more people in the management of public resources, BLM created 24 citizen Resource Advisory Councils that provide advice and recommendations on management of public lands. These councils help to ensure that citizens can share their knowledge with local resource managers. They are composed of people who:

- hold grazing permits or leases; represent interests associated with transportation or rights-of-way; represent developed outdoor recreation, off-highway vehicle users, or commercial recreational activities; represent the commercial timber industry; or represent energy and minerals development.
- work for nationally or regionally recognized environmental organizations; dispersed recreational activities; archaeological and historical interests; or nationally or regionally recognized wild horse and burro interest groups.
- hold state, county, or local elected office; are employed by a state agency responsible for management of natural resources, land, or water; represent Indian tribes within or adjacent to the area; are employed as academicians in the natural sciences; or represent the public at large.

As the nation continues to change, and more demands are placed on public lands, the diversity and balance of these councils will help to provide a shared and common vision for managing publicly owned resources.

Examples of Collaborative Stewardship

Collaborative approaches to land stewardship count on broad-based support from local communities and often require specialized local expertise. Fortunately, we have many examples to draw upon.

The Pacific Northwest Forest Plan. The Pacific Northwest forest plan is an ecosystem-based strategy for sustainable management of 25 million acres of federal land in the Pacific Northwest within the range of the Northern Spotted Owl, and is a blueprint for improving interagency coordination. The forest plan will enable federal agencies and other cooperators to restore degraded watersheds while allowing local communities to produce a sustainable level of wood products.

PACFISH (Pacific Salmon and Steelhead Recovery Strategy). In February 1995, the BLM and the Forest Service developed a joint strategy to conserve and restore anadromous salmon habitat. The strategy, known as PACFISH, establishes conservation and restoration measures for watersheds used by Pacific salmon and steelhead on public lands in the West. PACFISH stresses the integration of sound scientific and research information with on-the-ground management. The PACFISH strategy forms the aquatic and riparian components of the Pacific Northwest Forest Plan.

The Owl Mountain Partnership. In northwestern Colorado, representatives of multiple federal, state, and county agencies, as well as private ranchers, jointly manage 240,000 acres of mixed-ownership land. The partnership was formed to develop an integrated decision-making process. The intent of the partnership is to serve the economic, cultural, and social needs of the community while developing adaptive, long-term landscape management programs, policies, and practices that ensure ecosystem sustainability. Initially a project to solve livestock/wildlife conflicts, the Owl Mountain Partnership has protected and improved resources across the watershed, including habitat for waterfowl and upland wildlife, big game hunting, and fishing.

The Canyon Country Partnership. The Canyon Country Partnership was created to coordinate planning and management actions in the canyon country of southeastern Utah and adjacent Colorado. The partnership consists of five federal agencies, Indian tribes, state agencies, county governments, and private landowners, and was initiated by BLM to coordinate the planning and management actions of all land and resource managing agencies and organizations in the area. The goal of the partnership is to maintain the basic health and sustainability of ecosystems while meeting the social and economic needs of local people. The partnership extends beyond land use planning to allow resource managers, interest groups, and the public to develop common solutions to common resource problems in the Colorado Plateau.

Coos Watershed Association. The Coos Watershed Association encompasses 587 square miles of western Oregon. The watershed is composed of private lands owned by Weyerhauser and Menasha, state and federal lands, private agricultural lands, and tribal and county government lands. Working together, this coalition raised nearly half a million dollars to improve dwindling salmon runs, riparian and aquatic habitats, and fish passage. This partnership between the public and private sectors emphasizes the importance of education, community involvement, and maintaining open lines of communication. For example, local fishermen whose jobs were lost as a result of the declining fishery were hired by the Association to visit with private landowners to discuss the importance of healthy watersheds. The Watershed Association offered these landowners free labor and materials if they agreed to fence off critically important riparian areas.

Trout Creek Mountains. In the high desert country of southeastern Oregon, local ranchers are working with BLM, Oregon Trout, the Izaak Walton League, the Fish and Wildlife Service, the Oregon Department of Fish and Wildlife, and others to improve watershed health through better land stewardship. In 1991, grazing on 523,000 acres of public lands faced potential shutdown when the Lahontan cutthroat trout, a federally listed threatened species, was discovered in Willow and Whitehorse Creeks. A local working group composed of ranchers, environmental activists, and state and federal agencies began a dialogue and, using a consensus-based process, identified common goals and avoided costly litigation and shutdown. A deferred rest/rotation grazing program helped woody vegetation to return, native trout populations to rebound, and riparian areas and water quality to improve. No ranchers were forced out of business, and the process brought different people together to restore and maintain the health of the land.

Ecosystem approaches are either unlikely to be initiated, or once accomplished, to endure, if those people who affect ecosystem health do not support both the work itself and the maintenance required thereafter (Cairns, in press). All the technical expertise in the world cannot overcome public disinterest in, or worse, distrust of conservation and restoration activities. Education and communication are perhaps the most critical tools available to resource managers.

Ecosystem management is a collaborative process. Thus, federal agencies' first priority should be to work with user and interest groups, academia, local communities, and others to develop shared goals for healthy ecosystems. Developing "ecological sideboards" or thresholds that measure ecosystem health provides managers and citizens with performance measures. As Leopold (1947) said, "the only progress that counts is that on the actual landscape of the back forty."

BLM has worked through Resource Advisory Councils, academia, conservation groups, commodity users, and others to develop ecological standards for public lands throughout the West. These state or regional standards will measure progress toward, or movement away from, ecosystem goals. Before such measures can be implemented or enforced, however, people must understand the consequences of poor stewardship and the benefits of healthy ecosystems. Too often, federal agencies allow operating procedures to complicate relatively straightforward missions and, consequently, public acceptance and effectiveness.

Resource management agencies cannot become complacent. Ecosystem management can, and does, work when resource professionals spend more time on the land with representatives of local interests, community leaders, user and conservation groups, state officials, and others, communicating ideas, educating people, and building community support for healthy, diverse, and productive ecosystems.

Acknowledgments. The authors wish to thank the many resource managers from state and federal agencies such as BLM and the Forest Service whose knowledge, experience, and hard work are helping to maintain and restore the health of public lands.

We recognize the potential for conflict between meeting the desires of stakeholders and meeting requirements for ecosystem sustainability. Indeed, a major task for social research is to understand the conditions under which stakeholders might replace narrow and short-term self-interest decisions with ones that are long-term, contribute to ecosystem sustainability, and are socially cooperative.

Perhaps just as important as discussing what ecosystem management is, is pointing out what it is *not*. Because the ecosystem approach is relatively new and still developing, there are numerous misunderstandings about what it is supposed to do and how it will affect citizens. The Interagency Ecosystem Management Task Force (1995) outlined common misunderstandings about the ecosystem approach, presented here in Box 11B.

BOX 11B
Common Misunderstandings about Ecosystem Management

- *The "private lands" issue.* The ecosystem approach is seen by some as a thinly veiled attempt by government to take over management of private lands. In fact, ecosystem management expressly recognizes the rights of private landowners, who may increase their influence on public agency decisions through stakeholder involvement.
- *Difficulty in defining ecosystems.* Because ecosystems are not precisely defined, and can be addressed at many spatial scales, some argue that an ecosystem approach is meaningless. However, prior definition of precise boundaries is not necessary for ecosystem management; boundaries should merely reflect some natural bounds of interest (such as a watershed or mountain range) as well as the interests of relevant

stakeholders. Ecosystem management is an approach to problem solving, not a map exercise.

- *Expansion of authority.* Some have expressed concern that an ecosystem approach is a way for federal agencies to expand their authority over state and local land use planners. In fact, ecosystem management gives no additional authority to federal agencies, and demands that existing authority be used in a more cooperative, rather than confrontational, manner.
- *Top-down imposition.* Again, some feel that ecosystem management is an avenue for federal agencies to impose solutions on local communities in a top-down manner. This would be antithetical to good ecosystem management, in which cooperation, grass-roots initiatives, and stakeholder involvement are encouraged in developing a shared vision for the future. A top-down imposition is not ecosystem management and should be rejected.
- *Reduced environmental protection.* Some have charged that the ecosystem approach is a way for resource managers to compromise away environmental protection. Once again, the ecosystem approach neither adds to nor detracts from federal agency authority on environmental issues. Rather, it allows communities of stakeholders to develop solutions to environmental problems in a cooperative manner.
- *Ecological myopia.* Some feel that ecosystem management considers only ecological systems and not human needs or land uses. This is blatantly false according to the definitions of ecosystem management laid out here and elsewhere, which explicitly include people in the landscape, living in a sustainable manner.
- *Cure-all.* Some people believe that the ecosystem approach is a magic solution to the problems of natural resource management and will resolve all conflicts. However, natural resource management is a complex, difficult, and sometimes nasty job with many conflicting demands. Ecosystem management is merely a tool to help resolve the conflicts and accommodate multiple perspectives in a way that is not destructive to the environment or human needs and desires. It is evolving and should improve over time. Right now, it seems to be the best tool available for the task at hand.

Modified from IEMTF 1995.

Ecosystem Scale, Adaptive Management, and Stakeholders

We view ecosystem management as a process that consists of three essential components. First, it recognizes the *ecosystem* as the appropriate management unit. Second, a flexible and ongoing *adaptive management* model is used. Third, *stakeholders* in the management area are brought into the process of decision making, from establishing research priorities and identifying problems through the implementation of management decisions. Here we discuss the meaning and significance of each of these components.

The Ecosystem as the Appropriate Management Unit. Biology textbooks commonly define an "*ecosystem*" as a community of organisms interacting among themselves and with their physical environment. In this sense the ecosystem represents a higher level of organization beyond the population or the community because it also includes abiotic components. In Chapter 12 we will go beyond the biophysical definition of *ecosystem* to show how it is used in the context of ecosystem management.

Ecosystems are dynamic, not static, and the limits to ranges of variation in ecosystem structure and function must be identified. All ecosystems have a natural range of variation in structure and processes, and this range is ecosystem-dependent. For example, over a month, the composition and structure of woody species in an old-growth deciduous forest typically will not change in a significant way; unless a major disturbance occurs, the forest will consist of the same trees in the same positions. However, over a decade, and certainly over a century, the forest may experience great variation in composition and structure: trees will die, others will replace them, diseases or herbivores will attack the forest, fire may break out, and so forth. There is an expected range of variation over the long term for this system.

All natural systems have expected ranges of variation, both short-term and long-term. Many, though not all, kinds of short-term variation are relatively easy to incorporate into management plans; rarer, more extreme events are more difficult to incorporate. Yet the uncommon, extreme events—the so-called episodic events—unduly shape ecosystems because their impacts are not softened by evolutionary adaptations. A major, and unanswered, question in ecosystem management is, "How are extreme but rare events incorporated into management plans?"

Because ecosystems experience so much natural variation from so many sources, yet are not fundamentally altered by any but the most severe natural (and human) disturbances, they are said to possess *resilience*. Resilience is the magnitude of disturbance that can be absorbed or accommodated by an ecosystem before its structure is fundamentally changed to a different state (Holling 1973, 1986)—for example, before a shrubland becomes a grassland, or a grassland becomes a desert. Of course ecosystems do not have a single resilience property; rather, any ecosystem may be resilient to some disturbances and vulnerable to others. For example, a system with dense vegetation may be resilient to damage caused by ice storms, but, because of fuel loading, have poor resilience to fires.

Any ecosystem is expected to be resilient to disturbances and variations that are within the normal "repertoire" of what it has experienced over ecological time (millennia). Consequently, rivers are expected to be resilient to flooding, chaparral and longleaf pine wiregrass systems to frequent fires, and high-latitude aquatic systems to winter freezing. In fact, ecosystem composition and structure may change significantly when those disturbances do *not* occur, as when riverine flows are stabilized by dams, or fires are suppressed where they normally occur. Then, the normal range of variation is not experienced, and ecosystems change.

The importance of variation and disturbance is nicely illustrated in a model developed by Holling (1995), who discussed the *constructive* role that variation and disturbance play in maintaining the integrity of ecosystem function (Figure 11.8). Holling's model is, of course, a generalized abstraction of the real world, but it provides a useful construct for comparing the behavior of particular ecosystems. In his model, terrestrial ecosystems go through four functional stages as they develop. The first stage is *exploitation*, or early succession after a disturbance. In this stage, rapidly growing pioneer and opportunist species dominate and exploit the open space. The system then moves toward the *conservation* stage, in which more mature communities (i.e., com-

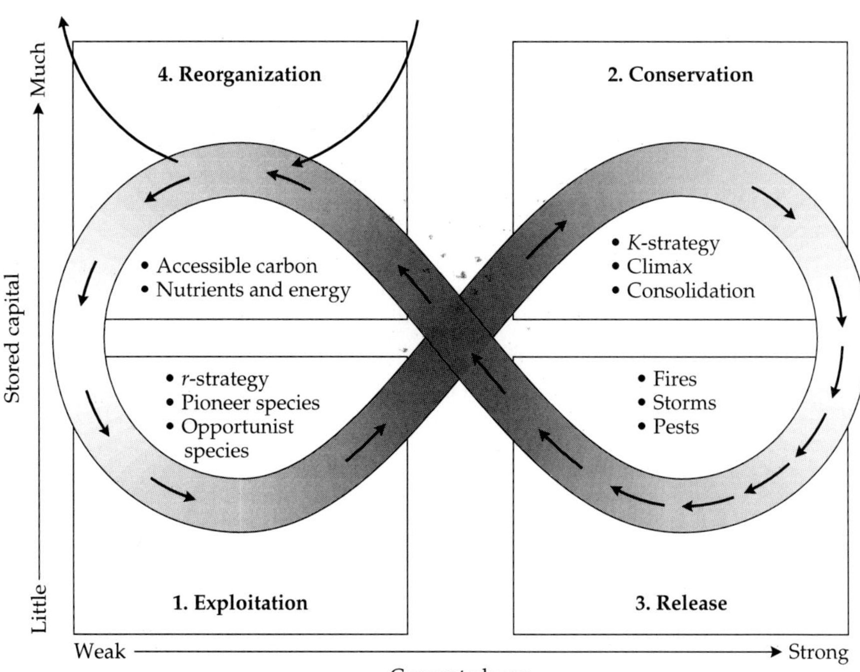

Figure 11.8 Holling's model: The functional stages of ecosystem development and the flow of events between them. (Modified from Holling 1992.)

posed of longer-lived species) develop. In this stage, which can last a long time, a complex community structure develops and strong interspecific relationships, especially mutualistic ones, prevail.

As system organization and "connectance" increase, the system becomes more "brittle," meaning that it is more susceptible to biotic and abiotic disturbances such as insect infestations, storms, fires, or pathogens. At some point, a major disturbance occurs, quickly shifting the system into the *release* phase, whereupon its complexities, structure, and stored energies are quickly released and disorganized. Although the release destroys structure, it also creates opportunity, in the sense that the system can begin to reassemble; this concept is called *creative destruction* and is an important aspect of disturbance. This rapid and chaotic release phase is followed by *reorganization,* in which the system begins to rebuild. The time spent in the stages of this model is uneven: the exploitative stage is moderate in length, the conservation phase can be very long, the release phase is very rapid, and reorganization is also rapid. Holling's model is critical in appreciating the dynamism of ecosystems and landscapes. Perhaps the most critical aspect of the model is the view of the release or disturbance phase as "creative destruction." By ending opportunities for a continued, complex community structure, major disturbances can create new opportunities for reorganization. Indeed, quite different opportunities may arise, as indicated by the arrow sweeping through the reorganization phase in Figure 11.8.

Holling's model seems to reflect reality in fire-prone forest ecosystems, but its generality remains to be demonstrated. Some ecosystems, particularly riparian and coastal zones, may be better characterized by shorter, pulsing patterns produced by the daily and lunar cycle hydroperiods. In these cases, tidal flow and seasonal changes in water level periodically provide energy and material subsidies to the ecosystem (Odum et al. 1995). When appropriate, indicators of sustainability should reflect regular or periodic pulsing events and respond to conditions of too much or too little energy and material subsidy. For example, one set of indicators that might be used in evaluating the experimental pulse release of water from Lake Powell into the Grand Canyon is the extent to which amounts of material accumulation in the form of sandbars and other sediment deposits approach desired levels. The main point is that ecosystems undergo characteristic cycles of change. While the length of the cycles and the type of change is specific to the particular ecosystem, maintenance of change is essential to ecosystem management.

Ecosystems with keystone species and those with few compensatory responses and low redundancy present particular problems. In these systems, small changes to the key players can produce very large responses. This phenomenon has been most rigorously studied in northern temperate oligotrophic lakes. In these lakes, variation in predator–prey interactions can cause a "trophic cascade" of effects through the plankton and thereby influence ecosystem processes (Carpenter and Kitchell 1993).

A major difficulty in pursuing ecosystem sustainability is the risk of management decisions either pushing an ecosystem well beyond its normal range of variation experienced over ecological time, or suppressing natural variation to the point that the system cannot function in a normal way and loses resilience as a result (Holling and Meffe 1996). When a system is constrained to behave within artificially narrow limits, the resilience of the system is compromised. When events then occur that the system formerly could have absorbed, they may cause unusually harsh disruptions. The artificial constraint of ecological systems, and the resultant management problems that ensue, have been termed "the pathology of natural resource management" by Holling (1986, 1995) and

Holling and Meffe (1996). This simple but potentially far-reaching concept can be stated as follows: "*When the range of natural variation in a system is reduced, the system loses resilience.*" That is, a system in which natural levels of variation have been reduced or constrained by management activities will be less resilient than an unaltered system when subsequently faced with external perturbations, either of natural or anthropogenic origin.

Holling and Meffe (1996) offered several examples of this pathology, of which fire suppression in fire-prone ecosystems is the most relevant to ecosystem management. Fire suppression tends to be successful in reducing the short-term probability of fires on public lands and in suburban, fire-prone regions. But the result of constraining natural system behavior is an accumulation of fuel that eventually produces fires of much greater intensity, extent, and human cost than if fires had never been suppressed (Kilgore 1976; Christensen et al. 1989). Through fire suppression, the system becomes less resilient to major fires, and may fundamentally change state after a fire finally erupts; this was strikingly demonstrated in the Yellowstone National Park fires of 1988. This example does not argue that we should never suppress fire. Rather, it is presented as an instance of what happens when natural variation is suppressed: systems lose resilience and are more vulnerable to unpredictable external events.

Whether management goes beyond the natural ranges of variation or suppresses them, the system may change to a fundamentally different state as a result, and may not continue to function as it normally would. Consequently, identifying the driving disturbances and typical ranges of variation in a given ecosystem is critical to understanding the system and managing it in a sustainable way that does not alter its resilience.

Development and Use of Adaptive Management Models. Traditional resource management has followed a strongly hierarchical chain-of-command model, with decisions made at the top and carried out at the bottom. This rigid, command-and-control approach to decision making is the antithesis of ecosystem management. Such rigidly hierarchical approaches to natural resource management have significant liabilities. Ecological systems are complex and are characterized by many nonlinear processes and indirect effects. Such systems inevitably have threshold responses and produce surprises. Furthermore, to varying degrees, colonization and extinction processes constantly shuffle the biological players in most local communities, thereby changing biological interactions. Economic development in the management area can also greatly affect ecological processes through habitat fragmentation, release of toxins, spread of exotic species, withdrawal of water, and increased frequency of wildfires, among other insults. Consequently, taking a rigid hierarchical and prescriptive approach to the management of ecological systems that are inherently dynamic and difficult to predict is a serious mismatch.

Natural resource agencies have begun to recognize the need to build more flexibility into local management. For example, forest plans developed periodically by the U.S. Forest Service set broad goals, but now allow for considerable local modification of the plan by district rangers. However, much more change is needed. Ecosystem management requires an adaptive management model characterized by a program of continual monitoring of indicators that measure progress toward goals, ongoing analyses of policy alternatives, and an institutional capacity to change management practices when better alternatives are available and current practices are not achieving their objectives.

Adaptive management also approaches all management actions as scientific experiments. In its "purest" form, an experimental approach would involve the use of treatment and control units whose behavior can be statistically compared. Though this is an excellent idea, in practice it is rare that actual, tightly controlled management experiments can be conducted on a large scale with true replicates. Short of that, however, management can still be *treated* like an experiment in the sense that smaller, prototype management trials can be instituted, sufficient time given to judge their results (with statistical analyses where feasible), and assessments made as to the effectiveness of the approach, after which the approach can be accepted, modified, or rejected. Regardless of its similarity to a true experiment or the level of satisfaction with the outcome, the management approach should be revisited periodically to both judge its continued relevance and to search for further improvements. *An adaptive ecosystem approach has a beginning, but no end; it requires continual reassessment and innovation.*

Finally, adaptive management recognizes that mistakes or errors are not cause for punishment, but opportunities for learning and improvement. Management errors should not be "swept under the carpet," hidden from public view in fear of reprisals, for that is the best way to ensure that the same errors will occur again. To be adaptive and useful, mistakes should be openly aired so that all may learn from them and avoid repeating them. This requires a different institutional mindset, one that is less defensive and more forgiving, one that realizes that management is a continual experiment and that mistakes will be made, and one that is assured enough in its vision and mission to learn, adapt, and modify, even if it means recognition of human flaws and limitations.

Participation by Stakeholders. Natural resource agencies have traditionally kept management planning within the agency. When people outside the agency were consulted, they usually fell into one of two classes: scientists were contracted to answer narrowly defined technical questions, or the ranchers, miners, and loggers who held public land leases were consulted about the possible economic consequences of proposed changes in policy.

Through their requirements for more frequent and timely public hearings, the National Environmental Protection Act, the Endangered Species Act, and other environmental legislation have begun to open up the process of decision making in public resource agencies to greater public participation. However, one of the tenets of ecosystem management is that long-term public support for environmental protection requires that all stakeholders participate in decision making (see Box 11C for a definition of stakeholders). Traditionally, public participation has been limited to the opportunity to comment during public hearings. If stakeholders are not brought more fully into the management

BOX 11C
What Is a Stakeholder?

Stakeholders are people who want to or should be involved in a decision or action because they have some interest or stake in the outcome. Their level of interest can vary from mild or passing to intense. People can be stakeholders for a variety of reasons:

1. They have a real or perceived interest in the resource, its use, its protection, or its users.
2. They believe that management decisions will directly or indirectly affect them.
3. They are located in or near areas about which decisions are being made.
4. They have an interest in the decision-making process.
5. They pay for the decisions.
6. They are in a position of authority to review the decisions.

Inclusion of stakeholders in decision making helps to ensure that their concerns are met early on, and that they "buy into" the decision through partial ownership, thus being more likely to support it later.

Modified from Dennis A. Schenborn, personal communication.

process, the sentiment that environmental protection unfairly restricts private property rights will continue to grow and will erode public support for environmental protection.

Effective ecosystem management involves a willingness to give up some degree of control. Much of the history of natural resource management is a history of control and domination: of people, of land, of resources, of other organizations. This is antithetical to good ecosystem management, wherein cooperation, consensus, and inclusion are surer roads to success. Political boundaries on a map are meaningless in an ecosystem context, but are often treated by institutions as territories to be jealously protected. Thus, in the traditional view, national forests are seen as different and isolated from national parks, which have no relation to military lands, which are separate from private lands. In reality, all of these lands are interconnected, and activities on one will have consequences for the others. Institutional territoriality, which acts to "control" a designated piece of a map, does nothing to integrate the landscape in an ecosystem fashion, but merely perpetuates a closed, command-and-control mentality that is ultimately detrimental to both the health of the land and human prosperity.

In addition to giving up some control, institutions must be willing to accept responsibilities and break down internal barriers to the flow of information. Another way of stating this is that institutions must be willing and able to learn and adapt (Lee 1993a). An example of the types of changes that must be incorporated into institutional "psyches" was graphically presented by Westrum (1994; Table 11.3).

Ecosystem management requires a greater degree of partnership among stakeholders, including interagency cooperation at all levels of government and government cooperation with private citizen advocacy groups, research scientists, business interests, and nongovernmental organizations. Managers have been severely constrained by budgets that are barely adequate to support basic programmatic needs, much less allow them to respond to new innovative proposals. It is through these broad partnerships that consensus on complex issues can be reached while significant new sources of financial support for management can be developed. It is worth noting that broad-based financial support has two important consequences for the manager that go beyond just increasing the size of the budget. First, the risk of losing financial support is spread among the various sources of funds, thereby reducing dependency on government appropriations. Second, managers may be freer to develop innovative programs when they are less dependent on restricted funds from state and federal sources.

Table 11.3
Stereotypes of Three Types of Organizations and How they Handle Information and Responsibilties

Pathological Organization	Bureaucratic Organization	Generative, Adaptive, or Progressive Organization
It doesn't want to know	It may not find out	It actively seeks information
Messengers are shot	Messengers are listened to—if they arrive	Messengers are trained
Responsibility is shirked	Responsibility is compartmentalized	Responsibility is shared
Bridging is discouraged	Bridging is allowed but neglected	Bridging is rewarded
Failure is punished or covered up	Organization is just and merciful	Failure results in learning and redirection
New ideas are crushed	New ideas present problems	New ideas are sought and welcomed

Modified from Westrum 1994.

Living with Uncertainty and Risk

Managers often have to take quick action to reduce the ecological risk arising from some hazard. Frequently, decisions must be made before all information is available, or when the quality of some of the information is suspect. California Fish and Game biologist Phil Pister once saved an entire species, the endangered Owens pupfish (*Cyprinodon radiosus*), by collecting the fish in buckets and coolers when he discovered their single habitat (Figure 11.9) rapidly drying up (Pister 1993). He was forced to take action although there was considerable uncertainty and risk, both biological and political. He literally held the evolutionary fate of the entire species in his hands as he carried the fish in buckets across the desert, with no contingency plan, and where tripping over a rock could mean extinction of the species. A large part of a manager's responsibility is identifying ecological risks before they reach such a crisis stage and, keeping the four principles of good conservation management in mind, developing risk management plans to minimize the negative consequences.

In the most general sense, ecological risk assessment involves estimating the likelihood that an identified hazard will have a negative effect, and estimating the ecological consequences of that negative effect. A typical example might involve the risk of damage to a lake ecosystem if a particular pesticide were applied to agricultural lands in the lake watershed. Generally, risk assessment has two phases. The first involves identifying what is at risk, the environment in which it occurs, and the size and distribution of the sources of the hazard. The second phase is assessment of how the recipient environment will be exposed to the causal agents and what the environmental effects will be for various exposure regimes. The information from risk assessment is then integrated into a decision analysis process that typically includes cost-benefit and other economic analyses and policy studies. Essay 11D by Lynne Maguire provides a fuller exploration of the important area of decision and risk analysis.

Figure 11.9 The single native habitat of the Owens pupfish, *Cyprinodon radiosus*. The fish nearly went extinct in August 1969 when the habitat dried up because of unexplained reduction in spring flow combined with unusually high evapotranspiration rates on hot afternoons. The species was rescued only through unplanned, unapproved action by a California Fish and Game biologist. (Photograph by E. P. Pister.)

ESSAY 11D
Decision Analysis in Conservation Biology

Lynn A. Maguire, Duke University

Suppose that the manager of a tiger reserve in India has been successful at controlling poaching within the reserve, and the tiger population has increased to the point where tigers sometimes leave the reserve, causing trouble in adjacent villages, where they are often killed. The manager suspects that the reserve may be too small to maintain a stable, self-contained tiger population and worries that continuing the present management strategy may lead to high levels of human/tiger conflicts and a declining tiger population.

One solution to this problem might be intensive management of the reserve's tigers, adding and removing tigers of certain ages and sexes to maintain a stable population within the reserve and to minimize human/tiger conflicts. Because tigers have a complex social system, such intervention might backfire, causing increased mortality from territorial disputes and infanticide. In addition, moving tigers will be very expensive. How can the manager satisfy demands from conservationists for protection of tigers, demands from politicians for protection of people, and demands from everyone for financial efficiency?

This problem embodies dilemmas typical of conservation decisions: there are multiple interest groups with many, sometimes conflicting, objectives; the outcomes of alternative management actions are far from certain; and any decision may have serious consequences. Are there any ways to improve on unguided intuition when facing such dilemmas?

Decision analysis, a structured way of analyzing decisions under uncertainty, can help. The first step is to identify the decision maker and her objectives: in this case, the reserve manager, who must improve tiger population status, minimize conflicts between tigers and humans, and minimize financial costs. The next step is to propose alternatives: continuing to protect the reserve under the present strategy, or actively adding and removing tigers. The next is to identify uncertain events that could affect how each management alternative might turn out. Whether or not the reserve *is* too small to maintain a viable tiger population will determine whether the tiger population is stable or declining and whether the level of conflict is high or low. Whether or not mortality increases will determine tiger population status under the "add and remove" alternative. The alternatives, uncertain events, and verbal descriptions of possible outcomes for all three decision objectives can be shown graphically on a decision tree (Figure A).

Sometimes just this structured description of the problem can help clarify the dilemma and suggest a solution; for many problems, a more quantitative analysis is helpful. Which alternative is better depends on *how likely* it is that the reserve is too small or that intervention will increase mortality, *how much* better it is to have a declining population with low levels of conflict than a declining population with high levels of conflict, and *how much* more money you are willing to spend to improve tiger status and minimize conflict. Resolving the dilemma requires a quantitative representation of the decision maker's beliefs about the facts of the matter and the preferences she has for different outcomes.

Beliefs about facts include estimates of the probabilities of the uncertain events that can affect outcomes, and predictions of the consequences of all the possible combinations of management actions and uncertain events. Sometimes there are historical observations (such as weather records) that can be used to estimate the probabilities of uncertain events directly. More often, lack of historical data and unique features of the current situation necessitate using **Bayesian statistics** to combine evidence from empirical data, theoretical models, and expert judgment. Structured questioning techniques have been developed to quantify a decision maker's intuition about uncertain events, or "subjective probabilities"; in this particular case, we will suppose that the decision maker assigns a probability of 0.4 to the likelihood that the reserve is too small to maintain a viable tiger population.

Quantifying the verbal descriptions of outcomes requires the decision maker to specify observable criteria for measuring how well each decision objective is met, e.g., population growth rate as a measure of population status, number of human/tiger conflicts per year as a measure of conflict, and dollars as a measure of financial cost. Models of tiger population/habitat relationships and of tiger/human interactions might be used to predict population growth rates and rates of conflict under the two

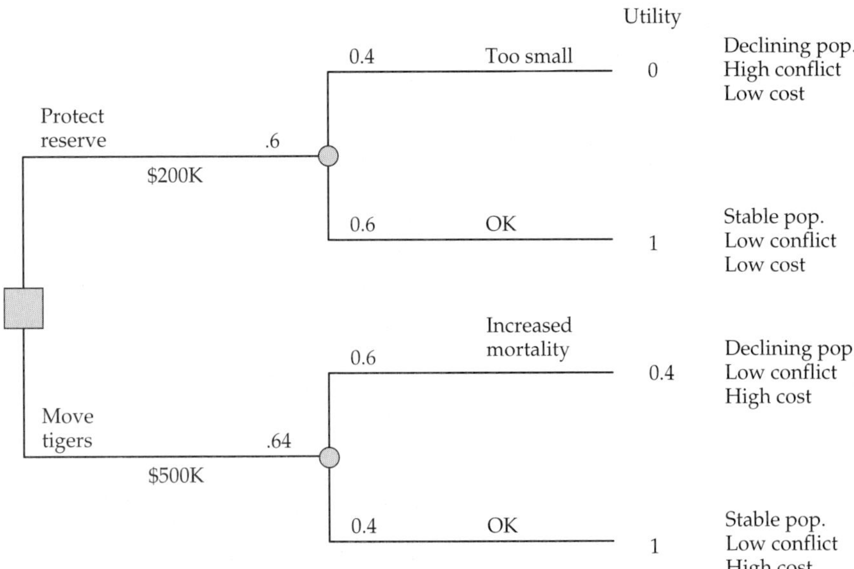

Figure A An example of a decision tree.

scenarios, "reserve too small" and "reserve OK," and similarly, for the intervention alternative, under the two scenarios, "increased mortality" and "OK."

These predictions may not accurately reflect the decision maker's preferences among outcomes; she may not think that 200 tigers are twice as good as 100 and half as good as 400. "Utility" measures relative preferences among outcomes, often on a scale of 0 to 1. Using a structured questioning technique, the decision maker can be guided from the verbal descriptions of tiger population status and human/tiger conflicts to a numerical value that combines these two criteria (leaving financial cost separate for now). Suppose the decision maker considers a stable population with low conflict the best outcome (utility = 1); a declining population with high conflict the worst (utility = 0); and, with the help of structured questions, finds that a declining population with low conflict has an intermediate utility value of 0.4.

To analyze the decision quantitatively, the decision maker applies a decision rule; maximizing expected utility is a common one, but others are possible. First, she calculates expected utility for each alternative by multiplying the utility of each outcome by its probability. For "protect reserve," the expected utility is (0.4)(0) + (0.6)(1) = 0.6; for "move tigers," the expected utility is 0.64. The action with higher utility, "move tigers," is preferred, but not by much.

The next step is to take account of any other criteria, in this case, financial cost: is it worth an extra $300,000 to improve expected utility (representing tiger population status and human/tiger conflict) from 0.6 to 0.64? Sometimes the answer to such trade-off questions is obvious. If not, there are again structured sets of questions that can help the decision maker articulate her willingness to trade additional dollars for improved population status and/or reduced conflict.

One advantage of imposing a quantitative structure on a decision problem is the ability to see how sensitive the choice of action is to changes in probability or utility values. If the probability of increased mortality under the "move tigers" option were 0.7, instead of 0.6, the expected utility of this option would be 0.58, instead of 0.64, and the "protect reserve" option would be superior for all objectives. Sensitivity analysis identifies which components of a problem have the greatest effect on choice of action, guiding further analysis and research. Sensitivity analysis can also be used to represent the views of different decision makers, or different interest groups, who may not share the beliefs or values of the reserve manager, pointing out where disagreements about facts or values do or do not lead to disagreements about actions.

Decision analysis addresses some of the major difficulties of conservation decisions in the following ways: (1) the structured framework helps the decision maker describe the problem accurately and make full use of available information; (2) making uncertainties explicit helps the decision maker use subjective, as well as objective, information about probabilities rationally, a task that is difficult in intuitive decision making; (3) identifying specific decision objectives, measurement criteria, and utility scores makes the value structure used by the decision maker explicit and open to scrutiny; (4) an explicit decision rule guides the choice of action; and, (5) the explicit and graphical format of decision analysis aids communication and negotiation when conservation decisions are in dispute.

To illustrate this process, consider a comprehensive evaluation of an agricultural project in the Pacific coastal zone of Honduras (Figure 11.10). Multinational lending institutions such as the World Bank and the Inter-American Development Bank require impact assessments as part of their lending

Figure 11.10 An agricultural landscape in southwestern Honduras. Erosion from these fragile slopes contributes large silt loads to downstream estuaries and shrimp ponds. (Photograph by C. R. Carroll.)

requirements. In the river bottoms of this region, melons for the U.S. and European markets are an important commercial crop. Because U.S. and European consumers demand cosmetically perfect melons, large amounts of pesticides are used in their production. Imagine that the government of Honduras requests international credit to build irrigation systems for export melon production. Part of the environmental risk assessment would involve the possible transport of agricultural chemicals into rivers that drain into estuaries of the economically and ecologically important Bay of Fonseca. This bay borders three countries, contains one of the largest intact mangrove ecosystems along the Pacific coast, and is the location of an important export shrimp mariculture industry (Figure 11.11). Further analysis would determine the fate and transport of the chemicals and their likely ecological effects on aquatic populations.

Figure 11.11 A commercial shrimp pond in Honduras. Silt from eroding farmland and pesticides from commercial export farming threaten the shrimp production industry. (Photograph by C. R. Carroll.)

A cost-benefit analysis might be conducted that would weigh the benefits of increased agricultural productivity and sales against potential losses to estuarine-based fisheries and shrimping, or the cost of cleanup should chemical pollution occur. It is unlikely, however, that biodiversity losses would be included in a cost-benefit analysis, except possibly as a comment in the text. If a decision to proceed with the irrigation project were made, it might incorporate a risk management approach to minimize the environmental effects. For example, policies might be developed so that economic incentives or government regulation would favor minimal use of toxic chemicals or prohibit those known to affect aquatic ecosystems. In its classic form, cost-benefit analysis does not include nonmarket "goods." In other words, if the costs and benefits cannot be expressed in monetary units, they are not included in the analysis. Obviously, the classic form of cost-benefit analysis does not count losses in natural biodiversity as part of the "cost."

The process of risk assessment and risk management has become much more inclusive in recent years. We must now develop risk assessment and management approaches that explicitly incorporate the protection of biodiversity and the cultural integrity of native peoples (Figure 11.12). This will not be an easy transformation, because cost-benefit analysis grew out of a need to make market-based investment decisions. Attempts to find ecologically meaningful surrogate units for market value in cost-benefit analyses have so far been unsatisfactory. Most of these surrogate measures, such as "willingness to pay" or "maximum travel to visit," treat natural areas and biodiversity protection as if they were amusement parks; that is, their "value" is determined by how much people are willing to pay for their existence or by what they are willing to give up in order to ensure their continuance.

Figure 11.12 A Brazilian rubber tapper in the Amazon Basin. Rubber tappers who extract raw latex from wild rubber trees are conducting sustainable use of tropical forests. Protection of the cultural integrity and needs of such indigenous peoples should be incorporated into any management plans. (Photograph courtesy of National Archives.)

The illogic of assigning some measurement of market value to biodiversity loss is perhaps made more apparent by considering an analogy. Just as extinction is forever, so is the loss of a classic painting. We can assign a transaction value to the painting, that is, how much money one museum would demand from another in order to be willing to sell the painting. We could even assign a kind of societal value to the painting by asking art lovers how far they would be willing to travel to view the painting or what maximum admission price they would be willing to pay. In these ways, we would have a quantitative assessment of value. However, suppose some wealthy madman wanted to buy the painting so that he could burn it? One would hope that, under those circumstances, a museum would be unable or unwilling to assign a market value to the painting. So it is with attempts to assign a monetary value to the loss of biodiversity.

Conservation management decisions are premised on an analysis of the costs of planning and implementation, and on ecological trade-offs; the former are measured in money or time and effort, and the latter in biological units that are not easily specified, and are almost always nonmarket values. However, the limitations of the analysis are set more by various sources of uncertainty in the system's ecology than by the inability to define homogeneous units for costs and benefits. The causes of uncertainty must be explicitly understood in order to minimize risk. Our focus will include the following four principal sources of uncertainty (other than investigator error and poor data collection): environmental stochasticity, indirect effects, nonindependent effects of stresses, and extrapolation from incomplete knowledge.

Environmental Stochasticity. Environmental stochasticity introduces uncertainty that is characteristic of the kind of environmental change being measured, the taxa involved, the ecosystem, and the scale at which measurements are made. For example, a large storm can uproot individual trees in a forest. At the scale of meters, near an affected tree, the influence of this stochastic event would be large and exist for a long time. On a larger scale—the entire forest—the event may have minimal spatial and temporal influence. In streams flowing through the forest there may be no influence beyond a temporary increase in runoff. Stochasticity in this type of storm event would generate moderate to high uncertainty in studies of tree species, but little uncertainty in studies of aquatic species. Very often, computer models can be used to explore the significance of stochastic effects for management plans. For example, the introduction of environmental stochasticity did not influence the threshold for extinction in computer-modeled population dynamics of the Northern Spotted Owl (McKelvey et al. 1993).

Indirect Effects. Indirect effects may involve species that are not directly affected by a particular stress. For example, when a pesticide eliminates a predator, its loss may influence the population densities of the predator's normal prey, as well as competitors of the prey species. The resurgence of secondary pests in agricultural fields following pesticide treatments is a very common example of this phenomenon. Indirect effects are likely when particularly important species, such as strong interactors and keystone species, are removed.

Nonindependent Effects. Nonindependent effects of stresses, such as synergisms between toxic chemicals, may introduce errors when the effects of stress are estimated separately. For example, heavy metals are toxic to fish, but the joint toxicity of two metals, such as copper and zinc, can be greater than their independent additive toxicities (Lewis 1978; Finlayson and Verrue 1982). Another illustration of nonindependence is the effects of stress events that occur so frequently that the system cannot recover in the short intervals between stresses; these are sometimes referred to as "cumulative time effects." For example, the frequency of anthropogenic fires can be so high that even classic fire climax communities such as chaparral can be degraded.

Cumulative Space Effects. Cumulative space effects can occur when management units cannot be treated independently of other management units or private lands. The obvious example, and one that has been discussed frequently throughout this book, is that of fragmented forests. As fragmentation increases, the survival of species in each patch is increasingly dependent on immigration among patches. The importance of cumulative space effects is an argument for pursuing management of fragmented habitats at the scale of landscapes. Cumulative effects are often ignored in management planning, but the cost of ignoring them can be high.

Extrapolation is often made from limited measurements at a lower level of biological organization in order to estimate an effect occurring at a higher level. For example, life history studies of individual populations are sometimes used to estimate effects at the level of communities. Uncertainty is introduced when reductionist studies are used to understand the behavior of larger systems. The most common form that this extrapolation takes is the use of so-called **indicator species** as surrogates for the community or even the ecosystem. For example, the Northern Spotted Owl requires large tracts of old-growth forest in the Pacific Northwest, and has sometimes been called an indicator species for high-quality old-growth forest habitat. But this would be true only for very large forest patches. The owl would be a poor surrogate for the many species, such as voles, that also flourish in small patches of old-growth forest. Using the occurrence of the owl as an indicator of habitat quality would underestimate the conservation value of small, high-quality forest patches, just as the use of voles as indicators of high-quality habitat for large mobile vertebrates would result in error. Good management planning explicitly recognizes these sources of uncertainty and develops policy priorities to minimize their magnitude and effects.

Uncertainty and risk will always be a central part of conservation management. It cannot be avoided, largely because ecological systems are so inherently complex and dynamic, and because the forms of human influences on systems are so diverse. There is always the danger in management of "paralysis by overanalysis"—doing nothing because of continued uncertainty. Such a non-decision is in fact a decision to do nothing. This may be the correct decision in many cases, but that decision should be made overtly, after careful analysis of all the information at hand, not covertly by default and inaction. Conservation management will always have some risk and uncertainty, and indeed, some mistakes will be made. However, reliance on general ecological and evolutionary principles, combined with knowledge of the system at hand, and divorced from biologically unsound bureaucratic pressures, should result in good management policy decisions in most cases.

Summary

It is important for conservation managers to move beyond an ad hoc approach to management, in which each day brings new and unexpected problems, to a more systematic approach that helps managers to identify and anticipate management needs. Although it is not an exhaustive list, we have identified and discussed four general principles of good conservation management that will help managers develop a more systematic approach to decision making and planning:

1. Critical ecological processes and biodiversity composition must be maintained.
2. External threats must be minimized and external benefits maximized.
3. Evolutionary processes must be conserved.
4. Management must be adaptive and minimally intrusive.

By building these principles into management plans, as discussed in the next chapter, managers can anticipate and prevent many crises.

Ecosystem management has become the centerpiece for conservation management in recent years, and is an approach we promote here. Although definitions of ecosystem management abound, and serve many different interests, we believe that it consists of simultaneous attention to ecological, socioeconomic, and institutional concerns, and satisfaction of each in management. If approached at appropriately large spatial and temporal scales, in an adaptive manner, and with inclusion of all relevant stakeholders, ecosystem management offers the best opportunities for progress in today's difficult management environment.

Uncertainty and risk are inherent in conservation management. Understanding and dealing with the contributions of sources of uncertainty and risk, such as environmental stochasticity, nonindependent effects, and cumulative effects, is essential to good management planning.

Questions for Discussion

1. Imagine you are the director of a 500 ha private reserve owned by a local conservation organization. The reserve is on an isolated mountain located in the Mojave Desert of California at an elevation of about 1000 meters. The reserve was established to protect a small herd of desert bighorn sheep. Additionally, you have a use agreement to manage 15,000 hectares of public multiple-use land that surrounds your private reserve. The public land includes several springs that contain water in years of average or greater rainfall, but only one has continual flow in drought years. Ranchers have been given grazing allotments on the public land to stock cattle at densities of one head per five ha. Identify the critical management issues from your perspective and from a cattle rancher's perspective. Discuss possible means for resolving conflicts. How might you make use of the "cultural knowledge" of the ranchers? Are there, perhaps, more environmentally benign ways to raise cattle? What information would you need in order to develop a management plan for the protection of the bighorn sheep?

2. Do you think that economic cost-benefit analysis has any place in conservation management? What can you offer in its place to assist the decision-making process?

3. Suppose you are the lead manager for the Spotted Owl in Oregon. You understand that the owl needs large expanses of old-growth forest to survive, and also understand that the larger issue is protection of those few remaining forests, and that the owl is the most powerful legal means to do so. The owl is not popular among loggers, whose livelihoods depend on those forests; in fact, many loggers would like to kill owls to open up more logging opportunities. Discuss the relevant management issues from the perspective of ecosystem protection, endangered species protection, and the economic viability of the region.

4. Suppose that a panel of experts is asked to define the management objectives of the National Park Service and that they come up with the following statement: "The purpose of the national parks is to maintain the biotic assemblages that existed prior to the discovery of America by Europeans." Is this a reasonable objective? Take any national park and develop the outline of a management plan to meet this objective. How might you change the objective?

5. We generally promote ecosystem management in this book. Are there any "downsides" to this approach? Some might argue that there is too much compromise involved in consensus decision making, and that ecosystem management gives away too much biodiversity. What do you think? Are there better alternatives?

Suggestions for Further Reading

Chase, A. 1995. *In a Dark Wood.* Houghton Mifflin Company, New York. The author of this book, which was written for a general audience, is an influential critic of ecosystem management. It is worth reading to gain an understanding of a cogently argued position taken by someone who cares deeply about conservation, but opposes what he sees as excessive domination of policy by eco-technocrats.

Edwards, P. J., R. M. May, and N. R. Webb (eds.). 1994. *Large-Scale Ecology and Conservation Biology.* Blackwell Scientific Publications, London. This publication came from the 35th Symposium of the British Ecological Society and Society for Conservation Biology. Within its 16 chapters are many good examples from the British and European literature, but the geographic coverage is generally broad. The book is particularly useful for its discussions of scale-dependent processes, a critical view of the metapopulation concept, and community changes during the Holocene.

Grumbine, R. E. 1992. *Ghost Bears: Exploring the Biodiversity Crisis.* Island Press, Washington, D.C. This book's general thesis is that the protection of biodiversity depends on large interconnected wildlands. The public's acceptance of such massive changes in land use will require fundamental changes in our value system. This is an important critique of the "species-by-species" approach to conserving biodiversity.

Knight, R. L. and S. F. Bates (eds.). 1995. *A New Century for Natural Resources Management.* Island Press, Washington, D.C. A very important series of chapters that maps an ongoing transition from traditional to innovative conservation management, with an eye toward the new century. The contents cover biological, economic, sociological, ethical, and educational issues.

Samson, F. B. and F. L. Knopf (eds.). 1996. *Ecosystem Management: Selected Readings.* Springer, New York. A compilation of papers from the literature that are pertinent to the new movement toward ecosystem management. They cover the general topics of understanding diversity, restoring ecological processes, emphasizing biotic integrity, and promoting ecological sustainability.

Schelhaus, J. and R. Greenberg (eds.). 1996. *Forest Patches and Tropical Landscapes.* Island Press, Washington, D.C. The 19 chapters of this book cover a wide range of conservation issues that relate to landscape heterogeneity. Just a sampling of some of the topics should give you the eclectic flavor of this book: pollination, gallery forests, managed forest patches and bird diversity, and arthropod diversity in forest and agricultural patches. The geographic coverage emphasizes the New World, but some chapters include the "sacred groves" of Africa, remnant forests in Indonesia, and restoration in India.

The Keystone National Policy Dialogue on Ecosystem Management. *Final Report.* 1996. The Keystone Center, Keystone, CO. The result of a year and a half long dialogue among 50 individuals representing diverse interests including federal, state, and local resource and regulatory agencies; tribal organizations; forest management, housing, agriculture, and ranching industries; environmental organizations; congressional staff; academia; and others. They developed a concise and enlightened vision of a sustainable ecosystem management approach.

12

Management to Meet Conservation Goals

Applications

Regardless of whether we wish to protect nature as it is, reconstitute it, correct imbalances, or merely keep options open, will we have the ability to plan such complex exercises, and the techniques to implement them?

David Western, 1989

How Are Management Decisions Made?

In ideal circumstances, conservation managers would focus their time and efforts on the protection and restoration of biodiversity and would head off crises by good advance planning. The unfortunate reality is that many of the decisions made by conservation managers are made in a rather ad hoc fashion simply because there are often so many different kinds of small crises and contingencies to deal with. In a single day, a manager might have to decide the best way to prevent trail erosion, respond to requests from school groups to take nature walks through sensitive natural areas, resolve a conflict between scientists over the location of research plots, file permits to work with a federally listed endangered species, and attend a public hearing concerning the possible effects of a nearby development.

On a day-to-day basis, few managers of large conservation areas or projects have the luxury to contemplate the "big issues" in conservation, such as the ones addressed throughout this book; instead, their days are ruled by a "tyranny of many small decisions." Yet, it is these same conservation managers who, in many cases, must create the management programs for conserving critical resources, protecting sensitive species, and identifying areas where research is needed.

How can a conservation manager function in such a confusing and demanding environment? We cannot offer a recipe or a generic solution for this problem because the constraints vary considerably, depending on whether the manager works for a public or a private agency, on the kinds of land use or other agreements in place, or on whether the manager is responsible for multiple resources over a large area or for the conservation of particular species. We can, however, offer some general advice on planning management activities, based on our experience in both tropical and temperate zone management, in humid and semiarid regions, and on many conversations with managers. The general characteristics of the planning process, applicable to all scales of conservation management, are presented in Box 12A.

BOX 12A
The Development of Management Plans

The planning process should have several general characteristics. It should be focused on achieving the principal management goals and not try to encompass too much. It should lead to an adaptive and flexible management plan; that is, there should be periodic evaluations of how well the plan is achieving the goals, whether or not the goals have changed, and what modifications to the plan need to be made. The plan should also develop around and implement the principles of good management discussed throughout Chapter 11. A sound plan for making and implementing management decisions can be developed from this ten-point agenda:

1. Review/revise the mission statement. Conservation management always needs to proceed from clear goals and objectives. The absence of a clearly stated mission can easily lead to management inefficiency and to conflicting programs.
2. Learn the history of the site or program. Learning as much as possible about the history of a site or program is important for two reasons: it is useful to know what changes have taken place in the landscape (Figure A), and a historical review can reveal important information about how neighboring private landowners perceive the reserve or the program, and thus help in enlisting their support.
3. Identify specific problems that require management. In many cases the problems will be evident, while others will emerge from research and from dialogue with stakeholders. The role of the manager is to identify problems at an early stage, while they are still manageable, to determine the essence of the problem, and to develop and implement plans for solving the problem or mitigating the effects.
4. Establish a group of formal or informal advisors. The particular choice of advisors should, in part, be

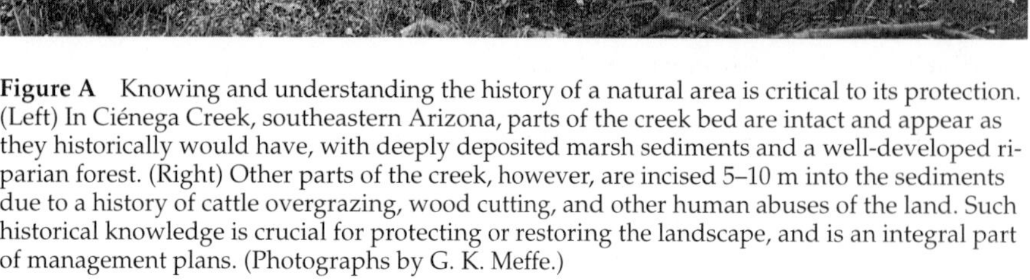

Figure A Knowing and understanding the history of a natural area is critical to its protection. (Left) In Ciénega Creek, southeastern Arizona, parts of the creek bed are intact and appear as they historically would have, with deeply deposited marsh sediments and a well-developed riparian forest. (Right) Other parts of the creek, however, are incised 5–10 m into the sediments due to a history of cattle overgrazing, wood cutting, and other human abuses of the land. Such historical knowledge is crucial for protecting or restoring the landscape, and is an integral part of management plans. (Photographs by G. K. Meffe.)

linked to the identification of major management problems, but should encompass more than mere technical advice. The advisory group should include all relevant points of view: scientists, managers of similar reserves or programs, representatives of appropriate resource management agencies, representatives of conservation advocacy groups, the local community, and various business interests. Because the solution to many conservation problems will involve sociological and economic considerations as well as biology, the wise manager will seek stakeholder advice from all quarters.

5. Develop an adaptive management plan. The previous four steps should all lead to the development of a comprehensive management plan, which defines the major goals and objectives to be accomplished, the actions to be undertaken, and the indicators of progress to be monitored, and projects the resources needed. Generally, a five-year time frame is reasonable; anything beyond five years for planning purposes is probably speculation. A management plan should also include the physical plant (such as buildings, roads, and waste disposal) and zoning for different uses (for example, public use areas, areas for manipulative research, areas for observational research only, wilderness areas, and areas for educational use). All management plans should include milestones (interim goals) to evaluate progress in meeting the long-term goals and objectives. Management plans should be reviewed annually, or even more frequently for rapidly changing projects. The review and evaluation process will be effective to the extent that institutional and budgetary mechanisms that support innovation and flexibility are in place.
6. Develop annual work plans. Management plans are general planning documents, but they do not specifically tell you what to do during the year to actually implement the plan (such as establish five 10 ha research grids with marked coordinates, or radio-collar 20 adult bobcats), nor do they tell you what the line items of your annual budget will include. For these purposes, you will need to develop detailed annual work plans. Often these work plans lock the manager into a rigid set of priorities for the year, so they should be developed with considerable thought.
7. Develop an inventory of resources and a site description. Various kinds of inventories will be useful. For a conservation area, lists of species occurrences and site locales, a reference museum, and photographs and other historical documents of land use and changes will be appropriate. For a species management or recovery program, it may suffice to simply collate reports and other "gray literature" that is not broadly available. The use of spatially explicit information, generally developed through the application of geographic information system (GIS) methods, is rapidly becoming an essential tool for managers. The significance of GIS methods is that various kinds of information, from ecological to social, can be linked to particular locations, and any changes can be depicted as temporal trends. Furthermore, when GIS and dynamic modeling are coupled, it is possible to explore the future consequences of land use decisions before actually modifying resource use.
8. Identify key areas where research is needed. Good management of conservation problems involves identifying priority areas where research is needed to support management decisions. The advisory committee, with its interdisciplinary mix and diverse makeup, can be put to good use in formulating research questions. It is also helpful and efficient to develop and maintain good relationships with universities and agencies where research talent can be found. If seed money is available to attract graduate students, this can be a particularly valuable means to leverage larger research efforts.
9. Maintain good relationships with the local community. Managers should understand that the community is a critical resource, and that long-term successful conservation will depend on having good community support. Inviting community participation on the advisory committee, making the management area available as an outdoor classroom for local schools, and providing nature tours are just a few of the many ways in which the reserve or conservation program can become an integral part of the community.
10. Develop cooperative agreements. Examples include developing a memorandum of understanding with a public agency such as the Bureau of Land Management that would allow researchers access to adjacent agency land, or formal or informal agreements with private landowners. These kinds of agreements are important for three reasons. First, management areas are frequently too small to provide all the resources needed to maintain biodiversity (see Chapters 9 and 10); agreements to use surrounding lands as a buffer zone may increase the viability of the management area. Second, agreements with neighboring landowners and managers can be an effective means to reduce "external threats", such as contamination of streams, pesticide drift, and wildfires. Third, entering into land use agreements may provide access to a larger pool of human and physical resources.

Underlying the ten-point agenda presented in Box 12A, however, must be a healthy and rigorous philosophy toward conservation management. "Good management" really is a function of how one defines the goals and directions of the endeavor, and the same management action may be judged positively under one value system and negatively under another. For example, clear-cutting old-growth forests is considered good resource management if the goal is short-term timber production, and the manager who produces more board feet is commended and rewarded under that value system. Under a value system based on conservation of ecosystem composition, structure, and function, the same action is considered objectionable and even unconscionable. Thus, like beauty, "good management" is in the eye of the beholder, and depends on the particular philosophical underpinnings and value system. An example of such disparate value systems in management is discussed with respect to conservation of desert fishes in Essay 12A by Edwin P. Pister.

ESSAY 12A

The Importance of Value Systems in Management

Considerations in Desert Fish Management

Edwin P. Pister, Bishop, California

To one who started his career in 1953, managing game fish populations for the California Department of Fish and Game in the state's vast and heavily tourist-impacted eastern Sierra and desert regions, it has been encouraging to note how, during the ensuing 45 years, the priorities of society have grown more sophisticated in matters relating to conservation. Unfortunately, programs of resource management agencies have been slow in recognizing and responding to the public will.

During the two decades following World War II, most government fisheries management effort in the United States was directed toward satisfying the desires of a nation freed from wartime constraints and eager to explore outdoor recreation. This was the era of huge production trout hatcheries and reservoir management programs. Agency leadership assumed a complacent attitude that such programs would satisfy society's needs forever. All one had to do to accomplish this was build more fish hatcheries, and introduce into the reservoirs any alien game fish (regardless of the source or ecological consequence) that showed promise of improving angling for a while. Into this management scenario entered a cadre of fisheries biologists/managers, emerging in vast numbers from burgeoning fish and wildlife schools and eager to apply their newly learned technologies to satisfying angler demand and, where this proved to be inadequate, to top off the harvest by calling for yet another hatchery truck. The term "biodiversity," yet unborn, lay dormant in the womb of a society unaware of adverse changes in fish communities that, even at this early date, were beginning to occur throughout the American West. In the context of this essay, the terms "manage" and "conserve" are essentially synonymous. What we are attempting to do now is manage for the conservation of biodiversity.

As one might expect, considering the basic need of fish for water, changes were first noted in the desert areas of North America, where negative biological impacts of water extraction and diversion by humans were soon recognized (Miller 1961). Government agencies in the Southwest (and nationwide) soon found themselves faced with responsibilities for which they were ill-prepared: management and preservation of a native fish fauna with which they were almost totally unfamiliar (or even unaware), known essentially only to academic researchers. Ironically, most agency knowledge of this component of the fauna derived from inventories conducted following chemical poisoning projects designed to eradicate native fishes. Up to that point, nongame fishes had been viewed primarily in the very negative context of being unwanted competitors with economically important, introduced game species (Pister 1991).

Agencies were caught off-guard from two major perspectives: (1) their knowledge of the biology of many of these species and related ecological interactions was totally inadequate to assure the continued existence of an intact fauna, and (2) few individuals within these agencies were of a philosophical bent that encouraged enthusiasm for nongame management. Those that were, were constantly plagued by a question posed by their peers and society: "What good are they?"—a question that, unfortunately, remains with us even today. The infancy of nongame species management is reflected in the fact that when Robert Rush Miller and I wrote a paper in 1971 on the management of the Owens pupfish, it was the first paper ever published in the *Transactions of the American Fisheries Society* relating to the management of a nongame, or commercially unimportant, species (Miller and Pister 1971).

It was the certain knowledge that government inertia in this respect would persist for at least a decade that caused a group of concerned scientists in 1969 to form the Desert Fishes Council, essentially to "hold the fort" until such time as fully funded management programs for native fishes could be implemented (Pister 1991). At this writing, over 25 years later, we still await full implementation, as both state and federal agencies struggle with perpetually underfunded programs in an often futile effort to fulfill their obligations under the provisions of the Endangered Species Act, and to conserve biodiversity within their jurisdictions. Federal suppression of environmental and endangered species programs during the environmental "Dark Ages" of the 1980s, a syndrome from which we are hopefully now emerging, was a major factor impeding development of a concerted national recovery effort.

Native fish faunas are in trouble primarily because of habitat destruction and change and because of introduced predacious and competitive species. Efforts to manage or conserve native fishes to date have taken several directions, chronicled in the *Proceedings of the Desert Fishes Council* and other publications. They include establishment of small refuges, free from alien species and designed to emulate as closely as possible the evolutionary habitat of the species or species complex, restoration of damaged habitat, artificial rearing facilities such as the Dexter National Fish Hatchery, operated by the U.S. Fish and Wildlife Service near Roswell, New Mexico, and acquisition and protection of major habitat areas, utilizing an ecosystem integrity approach. In this latter instance managers must often learn to live with the existence of alien fishes and inexorable change due to increasing societal demands for water. Recent research on habitat preferences of desert fishes allows this information to be incorporated into operational plans of water development projects, thus assisting in management and recovery efforts.

The long-term importance of the refuge management approach cannot be overemphasized. If a North American desert fish species is not currently listed as endangered, it will not be long before it reaches that point. From all indications, urban development in the desert will continue indefinitely into the future, and each time a new dwelling is connected to a domestic water supply, it either directly or indirectly impacts an aquatic habitat. Very few desert aquatic habitats today even approach pristine, and the situation continues to deteriorate. We must live with the possibility that much of our desert aquatic fauna may eventually exist only in artificial refuges, or in greatly altered native habitats. The ethics and evolutionary practicality of such a scenario provide much discussion for biologists and philosophers as we enter the next century.

Recovery efforts to date have primarily been holding actions, and very little "recovery" per se has been effected. This rather depressing situation will in all likelihood continue for as long as ever-increasing numbers of people demand an ever-increasing standard of living. We can only hope, before it is too late, that the values inherent in maintaining natural biodiversity will become sufficiently clear, and society will be willing to make the minor sacrifices necessary to retain it. Indiana University's Lynton Caldwell put it this way (Miller 1988):

> The environmental crisis is an outward manifestation of a crisis of mind and spirit. There could be no greater misconception of its meaning than to believe it to be concerned only with endangered wildlife, human-made ugliness, and pollution. These are part of it, but more importantly, *the crisis is concerned with the kind of creatures we are and what we must become in order to survive.* (emphasis added)

Successful conservation management must be applied at different levels of ecological organization, from the population to the landscape, depending on place and circumstance. With this background in developing a sound management decision agenda, we can now look at some specifics of managing for different levels of ecological organization, and the different and sometimes conflicting goals of conservation management.

Managing at the Population Level

Managing for Sustained Yields

Managers of timber, fish, and game are interested in maintaining populations that can be logged, fished, or hunted in perpetuity; that is, they are interested in maintaining sustained yields. A sustained yield, whether by people catching fish, lions hunting zebra, or rabbits eating plants, simply means that the harvested individuals are not removed at a rate faster than they can be replaced in the population through reproduction. In practice, this simple relationship becomes complicated and difficult to achieve. This is true for even the most sophisticated harvest schemes.

The difficulty arises because we are seldom interested in taking just a few individuals. In human terms, "yield" implies an economic harvest, whether of commercial fish, recreational game animals, or timber. We usually want to know how close we can come to the **maximum sustained yield** (MSY) without jeopardizing the population. If a population behaved according to the classic logistic equation $dN/dt = rN[1 - (N/K)]$ for growth with density-dependent mortality and birth rates, then its growth from a small to a large population would follow an S-shaped curve that is symmetrical around its inflection point (Figure 12.1). The MSY corresponds to the point on the curve that represents the maximum rate of recruitment into the population. In small populations, the individual reproductive rate is high, but numbers are few; in high-density populations, crowding lowers individual and population reproductive rates. In this symmetrical growth curve, the maximum rate of recruitment occurs at the inflection point; hence the point of MSY is $K/2$.

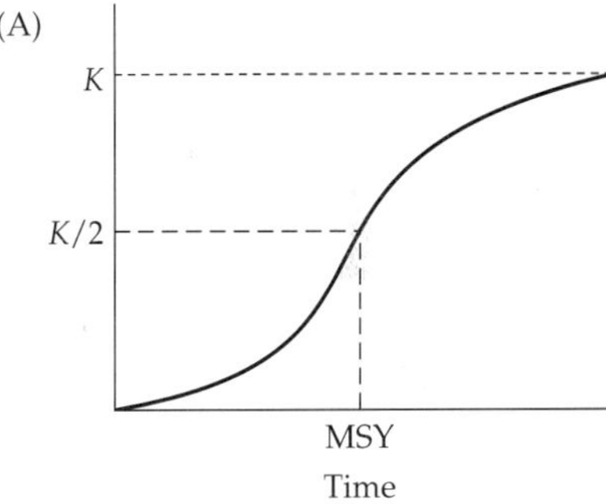

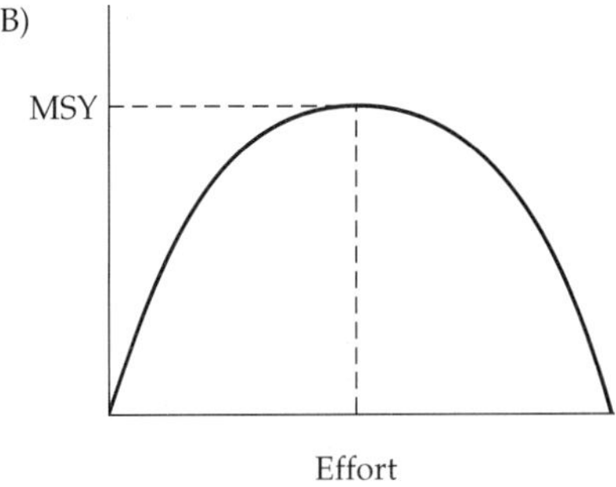

Figure 12.1 Logistic growth curve (A) with point of maximum sustained yield, $K/2$, indicated; (B) redrawn as a yield-per-effort curve.

So, all one has to do is harvest at a rate such that the population is kept at $K/2$, no higher and no lower, and MSY will be achieved. If it is that simple, why do we not have a very clear idea of the MSY for any species? The answer embraces all the complexities of population and ecosystem dynamics. First, populations are not controlled by the deterministic logistic equation. As Hall (1988) has pointed out, only a few artificial laboratory populations appear to follow the logistic growth curve. Second, K is essentially impossible to identify accurately, and because the environment is never constant, it is not a constant value. Third, because there are important sources of environmental stochasticity that influence birth and death rates, the intrinsic rate of increase (r) is not a simple function of population density (N) and reproductive physiology. Fourth, mortality pressure (harvest) is usually increased for larger and older individuals, and relative survivorship is increased among younger individuals. This is the reverse of the pattern of age-specific mortality normally found among natural populations, and could lead to evolutionary changes in life history parameters. Finally, population growth is often strongly influenced by the number of individuals moving into and out of the population; that is, by immigration and emigration. Net migration in any one population is, in turn, influenced by the spatial pattern, the quality of habitats, and population densities in the surrounding landscape.

Time lags in population processes cause particular difficulties for natural resource managers. All of the population processes described in life tables require time before their effects on population change are fully expressed. Commercial, recreational, and subsistence hunting and fishing are just special forms of mortality that may be specific to particular age or size classes or even to one sex. Because mortality can affect age structure, sex ratios, and social systems, the full population effects of hunting and fishing in any one year may take several years to be expressed, particularly in longer-lived species such as whales or sea turtles. Thus, an increased harvest effort may result in a short-term increase in yield, but a sustained decrease over a longer time. Management decisions based on short-term responses could be counterproductive in the longer term.

In forests managed for timber production, tree density, growth rates, and reproduction can all be managed through various silvicultural methods to produce high yields (Figure 12.2). On National Forest lands, trees are cut to meet a mandate for MSY for each harvested species. Thus, for managed temperate zone forests, one would think that the necessary population parameters for determining MSY would be known with considerable precision. Additionally, the long generation times of trees mean that tree populations are less susceptible to short-term environmental stochasticity. However, whether or not timber management in national forests is meeting the mandate for maintaining maximum sustained yields is debatable. First, few stands have been harvested for more than one or two cutting cycles, so the empirical basis for determining whether or not MSY has been reached is very incomplete. Second, the resource management principle that natural systems can be harvested on a sustainable basis loses much of its meaning if the natural system is transformed into a production system. Silvicultural practices that include intensive site preparation, removal of potentially competing species, replanting with single species, and extensive use of herbicides and fertilizers fundamentally change the natural forest ecosystem. Under these conditions, a forest managed for maximum sustained yield has a closer ecosystem analogy with a wheat field than with a natural forest.

(A)

(B)

(C)

Figure 12.2 (A) High-density loblolly pine monoculture grown for pulpwood; (B) lower density loblolly pine monoculture grown for timber; (C) mixed pine/hardwood system for both wildlife and timber. (Photographs by C. R. Carroll.)

In commercial fisheries, population estimates are far less precise, and significant immigration and recruitment from areas remote from the area of har-

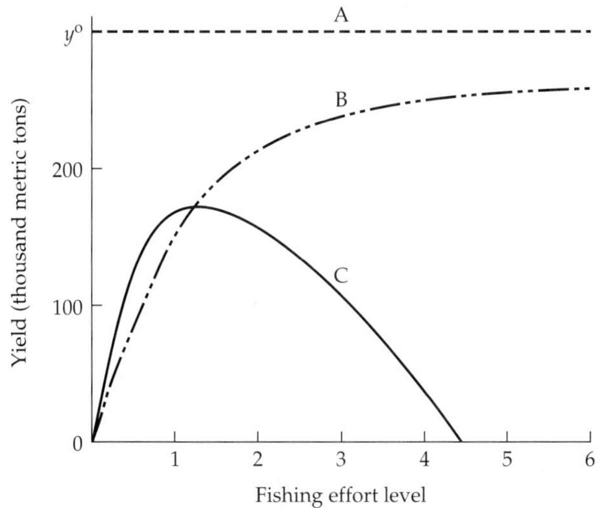

Figure 12.3 The effects of mesh size of fishing nets on the sustainability of a South African anchovy fishery. Curve A represents the theoretical ultimate maximum sustained yield (y^o) that could be attained if it were possible to select any age class for harvest. Curve B represents the effect of harvesting age class 3 and older. Curve C represents a harvest of age class 1 and older. (From Getz and Haight 1989.)

vest are common. Fisheries management has therefore relied heavily on the use of techniques for estimating population density from partial samples, combined with sophisticated computer modeling. Mistakes are to be expected in this approach, and a major objective is to make management as adaptive as possible so that corrective measures can be taken. For example, Figure 12.3 shows how different mesh sizes in fishing nets can be used to selectively harvest different size classes in an anchovy fishery. Because each size class makes a characteristic contribution to population growth through size-specific fecundity and mortality rates, it is possible to achieve sustainable yields by using the appropriate mesh size in nets. A mesh size that would release age classes younger than 3 would provide a sustainable fishery (curve B). A nonselective mesh size, which captures all size classes, would produce the highest initial yields with the lowest fishing effort (curve C), and thus would be economically most efficient in the short term, but would not be sustainable in the long term. The addition of more fishing boats would have little effect on curve B, but would rapidly degrade the nonselective fishery (curve C). Getz and Haight (1989) and Clark (1990) are good sources for an advanced treatment of the use of such models in population harvesting.

Even for our "best" examples of sustainable use, however, forests are frequently overcut, and fisheries are typically depleted and then abandoned. Why does that happen? Clark (1990) has convincingly argued that the deliberate overexploitation of biological resources possessing low rates of return—that is, low rates of biological growth—is widespread. As he notes, "If forests, marine mammals, or grazing lands are incapable of replenishing themselves at sufficiently high rates, economically rational owners will tend to overexploit these resources."

From this brief discussion of population management for sustained yields, we can take three important lessons for management of individual species populations: (1) our ability to maintain a population at a particular level through management is limited by the inherent difficulties in estimating critical population parameters and by the time lags characteristic of biological systems; (2) where the population is managed as a renewable natural resource for economic gain, there will typically be a conflict between managing for sustained yield and harvesting for the maximum economic return; and (3) strategies to enhance population densities of harvested species must take into account their effects on other species or ecosystem properties.

Conflicts in Single-Species Management: Lessons from Game Management

In Chapter 11, we emphasized the limitations of managing for single species, and stressed that management should be focused on how best to maintain the ecosystem that supports the composition and structure of biodiversity and functional processes. This does not mean that recovery plans for endangered species or other single-species management efforts are unimportant, but rather that, if we hope to develop proactive approaches to conservation, we will have to develop the more holistic goals of ecosystem management. Within these holistic goals, single-species management remains an important approach.

Management of single species can lead to maximizing production of a few species without regard to the community/ecosystem in which they occur. Achieving high densities for one species may cause serious habitat degradation and reduce biodiversity. For example, deer populations can be increased and held at high levels by providing special plantings of forage, but the resulting high deer densities may have negative effects on natural vegetation. In Georgia, white-tailed deer populations have grown exponentially over the past several decades (Figure 12.4); throughout much of their range, plants have been directly affected by high deer densities, and a few plants have been affected secondarily as deer modify the habitat (Table 12.1).

The effects of non-native game species on habitats and biodiversity can be particularly harmful. Until the latter part of the 20th century, there were few regulations in the United States controlling the transplant of native game species into new geographic ranges, or even the introduction of exotic game species. This reflected a common attitude that nature was simply scenery and a source of recreational enjoyment. The consequences of those early unregulated times continue to plague conservation biologists today. Western rainbow trout introduced into eastern hatcheries carried pathogens (furunculosis) that were devastating to eastern brook trout (Piper et al. 1982). European boar introduced into the United States by private hunting clubs are wreaking havoc by rooting up large tracts of Hawaiian forests (Stone and Scott 1985) and have virtually eliminated oak regeneration in some localities in the California coastal ranges. Asian Pheasants may displace native Prairie Chickens, and Axis deer may displace native deer when forage quality declines.

Many important conceptual contributions and, especially, field techniques have come from single-species studies. Some examples include mark–recapture and other techniques for estimating population sizes; radiotelemetry for determining movement patterns and habitat utilization; various methods for deter-

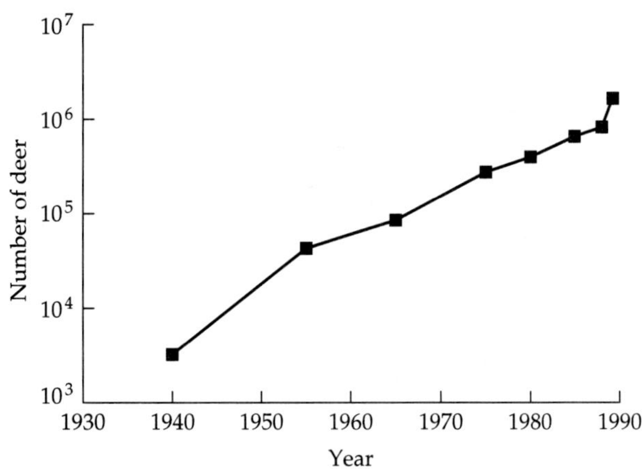

Figure 12.4 Populations of white-tailed deer in Georgia have grown exponentially for the past several decades. (From Odum 1988.)

Table 12.1
Plant Species Known to Be Affected by Large Deer Populations

Plants	Effects
Yew, white oak, live oak, pin cherry, sugar maple, white ash, yellow birch, eastern hemlock, blackberry, orchids, lilies	Decline when deer density is high
Leatherwood, wood sorrel	Indirectly affected by decline in eastern hemlock caused by deer browsing
Ferns, black cherry	Abundance increased by deer browsing
Tree seedlings	Seedling species diversity decreases
Deciduous trees	Affected more than coniferous vegetation by deer browsing

Note: See Carroll 1992 for sources.

mining diet from stomach contents and fecal analysis; methods for aging individuals and thereby permitting life table analyses; techniques for assessing the significance of parasites and pathogens; measures of "health" and reproductive status from body fat, hormone titers, and fecal analysis; and methods of determining the relationship between habitat quality and carrying capacity. We have also learned from game studies a very important lesson, the value of native predators, and many contemporary conservation programs now involve predator reintroductions, a topic taken up in Essay 12B by Robert Warren.

ESSAY 12B

An Emerging Management Tool

Large Mammal Predator Reintroductions

Robert J. Warren, University of Georgia

Early species transplantation and reintroduction efforts conducted by wildlife managers in North America were designed to restore game animals to areas from which they had been extirpated in the late 19th and early 20th centuries. These early wildlife restoration efforts were funded by hunting license sales and taxes on sporting arms and ammunition. Thus, state and federal agencies appropriately directed most of their efforts toward reintroducing game species.

Today, with the greater level of interest in nongame wildlife and in community- and ecosystem-level management, wildlife and conservation biologists are investigating the potential of predator reintroductions in efforts to restore wildlife communities in specific areas. However, the decision and process whereby one implements a program to reintroduce predators requires one to consider more than merely biological and ecological questions. Of equal importance are social and political questions. In this essay I present some general considerations for a predator reintroduction program by using examples of current mammalian predator reintroduction efforts—three for felid species and two for canid species.

Obviously, for predator reintroduction to be successful, suitable habitat must be available, which requires an abundant supply of prey. However, of equal importance is the area's degree of isolation. Almost all sites to which predators have been reintroduced are large, rather isolated areas of public land, such as national parks or wildlife refuges. An appropriately sized area is obviously important, given the relatively large home range sizes of most wild felids and canids.

One also must consider land ownership patterns and land uses surrounding the area proposed for the predator reintroduction. Except in the instance of islands, predators are likely to move off of the reintroduction site, and may represent a source of problems to surrounding landowners. Some of the red wolves (*Canis rufus*) reintroduced to Alligator River National Wildlife Refuge, North Carolina, had to be recaptured after wandering off the refuge. Indeed, such movements can be fatal to the reintroduced predator. On November 29, 1995, one of the red wolves reintroduced to the Great Smoky Mountains National Park was shot and killed by someone on the North Carolina side of the park. Even an island cannot ensure that predators will not leave a reintroduction area. One bobcat (*Felis rufus*) reintroduced to Cumberland Island National Seashore (CINS), Georgia, swam 1–2 miles of salt marsh and open water to return to the mainland.

The next consideration for predator reintroduction is the source of individuals. It is most desirable to translocate wild-trapped individuals from areas that are ecologically similar to the proposed reintroduction site. Such individuals are most likely to be genetically adapted to the reintroduction area, and are likely to have a greater chance of successfully establishing themselves than captive-reared individuals. My colleagues and I live-trapped bobcats from coastal Georgia for reintroduction to CINS. We also recruited local fur trappers to assist in the trapping effort by paying them more for an uninjured, live bobcat than the trappers could obtain by selling the animal's pelt. Diefenbach et al. (1993) describe the detailed procedures for housing, handling, and transporting wild-trapped bobcats prior to reintroduction to CINS. In general, wild-trapped individuals should be quarantined for a few weeks and tested serologically to ensure that they are free of disease. Davidson and Nettles (1992) describe some of the wildlife disease concerns associated with reintroduction of wild species in North America.

In the case of of endangered or threatened predator species, individuals for translocation may not be readily available in the wild. Therefore, some endangered predator reintroduction programs require captive breeding. The 1982 Endangered Species Act Amendments provided for the experimental reintroduction of populations of endangered species. Most red wolf reintroduction efforts to date have been conducted with captive-reared individuals. The recovery effort for Florida panthers (*Felis concolor coryi*) uses individuals injured on highways for captive breeding. This recovery effort also includes field research on panthers in southern Florida to obtain the ecological data necessary to reintroduce captive-reared or wild-trapped panthers to northern Florida. These researchers also have experimentally introduced sterilized, radio-collared mountain lions captured from western Texas into northern Florida (Belden and Hagedorn 1993). Such use of surrogate panthers can help to determine whether panthers can survive in northern Florida before risking reintroduction of an individual of the endangered subspecies.

Public and political concerns are the most important consideration for any predator reintroduction effort. Stipulations of the National Environmental Policy Act (NEPA) (Public Law 91-190) apply to any predator reintroduction on public land. NEPA requires federal agencies to consider the environmental effects (including the human environment) of any proposed action. This usually is accomplished by preparation of an Environmental Assessment (EA) or an Environmental Impact Statement (EIS), which describes the proposed action and its possible environmental effects. These documents must be sent out for public review and comment. Wildlife and conservation biologists should be careful in the preparation of these documents, because public perceptions or misconceptions regarding predators may interfere with the proposed reintroduction efforts. Warren et al. (1990) and Brocke et al. (1990) describe important biopolitical lessons they learned in dealing with public, political, and media concerns while attempting to reintroduce bobcats and lynx (*Lynx canadensis*), respectively.

The 1995 reintroduction of gray wolves (*Canis lupus*) to the Yellowstone Ecosystem in Idaho, Montana, and Wyoming (Fritts and Carbyn 1995) has been publicly and politically controversial. This controversy involves several federal and state agencies, as well as park visitors and surrounding ranchers. The potential environmental effects of this reintroduction were so great that Congress ordered the U.S. Fish and Wildlife Service (FWS), in consultation with the National Park Service and U.S. Forest Service, to prepare a detailed EIS. The EIS included evaluations of historical evidence for the gray wolf in the area, the sociological and economic effects of wolf reintroduction (this assessment included public and park visitor attitude surveys), and the management and ecological effects of wolves in the ecosystem (NPS and FWS 1990). The 1995 gray wolf reintroduction plan called for the capture of wolves in Canada and their release in the United States over a three-year period; 29 were released in 1995 and 37 were reintroduced in 1996. Because of the controversy, the reintroduction plan allowed biologists to kill any wolves that attacked livestock, and to compensate ranchers for livestock losses. One of the wolves released in 1995 had to be killed for attacking sheep, and the rancher was paid for the dead sheep. One of the other wolves was found dead near a highway, and one was shot illegally. In the case of the illegally killed wolf, the offending person was convicted and sentenced to six months in prison and fined $10,000.

Opposition from some segments of the public to the reintroduction of gray and red wolves has been so great that it has included legislatively and genetically based attacks. Western senators succeeded in shifting $200,000 from the FWS's budget for the 1996 gray wolf reintroduction project to a project on trout diseases. However, private funding contributions helped offset these federal funding cuts. State-level political opposition led to requests that the gray wolf be removed from the endangered species list in Montana, or that it be changed from "endangered" to "threatened" status, either of which would reduce federal protection for this species. Public forces opposing the red wolf reintroduction program have even resorted to genetically based arguments to have the red wolf removed from the endangered species list, citing recent mtDNA evidence that the red wolf may be a hybrid, and therefore not protected under the Endangered Species Act's definition of a species (Nemecek 1996).

Predator reintroduction programs should not be justified on the basis of restoring control over a particular prey population, because the ecological interactions between most predator and prey populations are very complex. Predators are only one of a myriad interacting factors that may affect the number of individuals in prey populations in a particular area. The reintroduction of bobcats to CINS was described as a "failure" in some media stories despite the fact that the reintroduced bobcats met the project's criteria of survival and reproduction on the island. Two news articles were published one year after reintroduction, stating that the original justification for bobcat reintroduction had been to control the white-tailed deer (*Odocoileus virginianus*) population on the island, and that the bobcats had "done little to control the deer population" (Warren et al. 1990).

Finally, it is important that wildlife and conservation biologists evaluate the success of their predator reintroduction efforts. A species reintroduction effort is successful only if it results in a self-sustaining population; hence, information on survival and reproduction of the reintroduced predators must be obtained. The endangered red and gray wolves that have been released in the United States, as well as the nonendangered bobcats reintroduced on CINS, have been released with radiotransmitter collars, which reveal the location of females in dens so that production of young can be documented. A special signal is emitted if the predator dies. These data on reproduction and survival provide the basis for computer models that evaluate population viability (Diefenbach 1992; Fritts and Carbyn 1995) and point to management actions that might be necessary in the future to maintain the reintroduced predator population. In essence, the work of a predator reintroduction project has only just begun once the releases have occurred.

Managing Species as Surrogates of the Larger Community

Because it is not possible to include all species in management plans, management for biodiversity sometimes focuses on management of indicator species that can act as surrogates for the larger community. This strategy requires providing suitable habitat for species that are known to be sensitive to habitat fragmentation, pollution, or other stresses that degrade biodiversity, and monitoring their populations. For example, with the growing evidence of a widespread decline in amphibian populations, Vitt et al. (1990) have suggested that amphibians may be useful indicators of environmental degradation because they may be more sensitive to environmental stresses than other vertebrates. However, they may be inappropriate indicator species on other grounds. Pechmann et al. (1991) analyzed long-term data sets on amphibian populations in South Carolina and showed that their population densities can fluctuate greatly from year to year, even with no human influences (Figure 12.5; also see Essay 5B). This implies that the population dy-

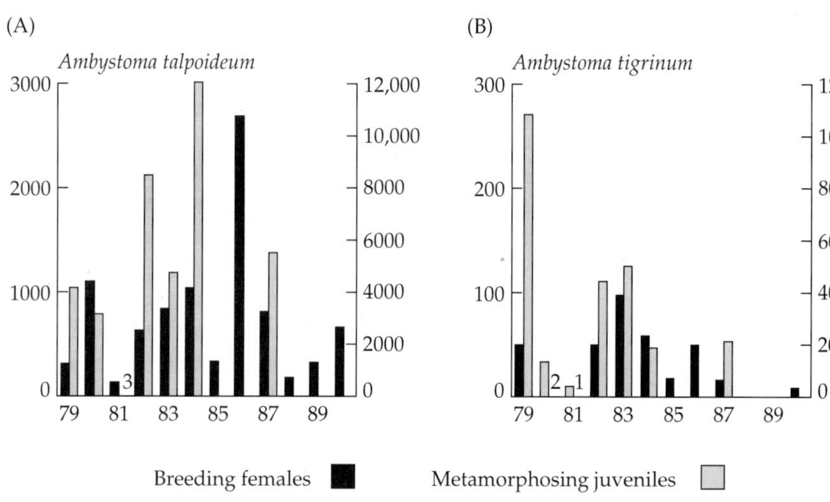

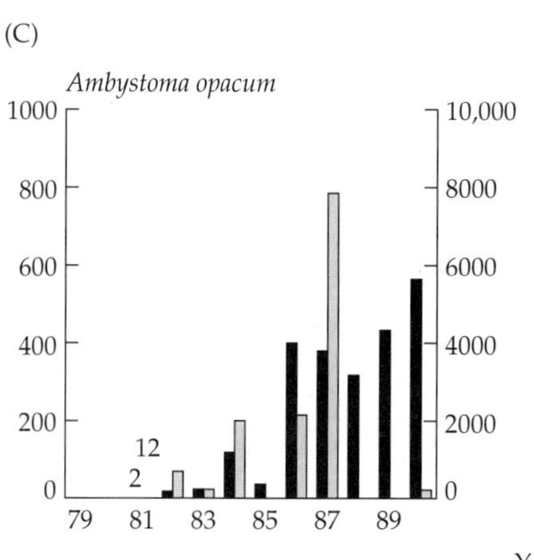

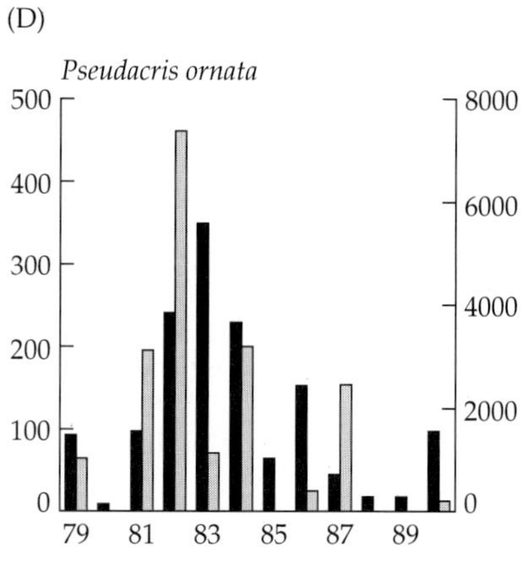

Figure 12.5 Natural fluctuations in population size of three species of salamanders (A–C) and one species of frog (D) in a temporary pond, Rainbow Bay, in South Carolina from 1979 to 1990. Both breeding females (left axis) and metamorphosing juveniles (right axis) vary greatly annually, and some species disappear from and reappear in the system. Such species may be poor choices as indicator species for the larger system, since their natural, or background, population fluctuations are so large. (From Pechmann et al. 1991.)

namics of at least some amphibians are too "noisy" for them to be good indicators of habitat change; that is, they may respond to environmental events that may be insignificant to the larger community. On the other hand, they may be good indicators of normal temporal dynamics of at least a subset of other species.

Another problem with potential indicator species involves longevity. Long-lived species may persist in an altered habitat for decades, but not reproduce. This occurred with razorback suckers (*Xyrauchen texanus*) in several reservoirs in the Colorado River drainage in Arizona. Adults persisted for 40 years or more in reservoirs after the dams were constructed, but there has been no evidence of recruitment (Minckley 1983), making the presence of adults poor indicators of environmental change. The choice of appropriate indicator species that can act as surrogates for the larger community is difficult, and this strategy probably will never be completely successful. Great caution must be applied, or the concept can be easily misused. This should not be surprising, given the complexities and diversities of taxa and life histories that are represented in any habitat.

Habitat Management

Management at the scale of habitats has been most intensively investigated for forests, deserts, and rangelands; that is, management has emphasized systems that are harvested for timber or grazed by livestock and native ungulates. The history of forest management provides the most comprehensive view of habitat management. Formerly, game management was often part of forest management plans, and multiple-use forest management in some regions was synonymous with production for trees, deer, and turkey. Now, U.S. federal forests are mandated to manage for nongame biodiversity as well.

The most common private forest management practice in the southeastern United States is conversion of mixed-age hardwoods and pine to a monoculture of even-aged, short-rotation pine, typically loblolly or slash pine (Figure 12.6). These plantations are seldom allowed to grow for more than about 30 years before harvesting. Forest conversion to simple monocultures must have major effects on the diversity of other forest organisms, though investigations of these likely effects have only recently begun.

Once conversion to monoculture has taken place, the rapid successional process that follows also forces changes in forest biodiversity. In a 14-year study of wildlife responses to loblolly pine conversion in Alabama, Johnson (1986) found major effects on selected plants and game animals. Forb and vine cover declined after about the fifth year following pine planting. Populations of quail, raccoon, and opossum all declined in the later years of succession. Interestingly, even though deer forage was poor in the later successional years, deer populations remained high. The highly mobile deer herds were probably helped by the mosaic of conversion plots in the region that were in various stages of succession: the older conversions provided shelter but poor food, while younger conversions offered poor shelter but high-quality food. Thus, the regional habitat mosaic maintained deer density.

Forest management, however, need not be analogous to monoculture crop production. Indeed, some management schemes attempt to use ecological principles to achieve sustained harvest while maintaining natural biodiversity. Polycyclic management is a method of harvesting mature trees from uneven-aged stands. Forest vertical structure has long been known to be an important

Figure 12.6 A short-rotational pine plantation. The loblolly pines in this photograph from the Georgia Piedmont are approximately 20 feet tall and 5 years old. (Photograph by C. R. Carroll.)

determinant of forest bird diversity (MacArthur and MacArthur 1961), and the uneven-aged stand structure maintains some of the heterogeneous physical structure found in natural forests.

Another example of forest management compatible with biodiversity maintenance is the use of small strip clear-cuts. This form of management is designed to mimic the natural "gap-phase dynamics" of temperate and tropical forests (Figure 12.7). In unmanaged mature forests, a gap is created when a large tree falls and creates an opening in the canopy. The increase in light penetration allows saplings in the gap to grow rapidly, and until the canopy again begins to close, the gap is filled with small trees, shrubs, and herbaceous plants. Birds and other animals forage in these resource-rich gaps and disperse seeds throughout the forest. Obviously, the frequency and size of gaps will be related to the age distribution and species composition of the forest trees, and gaps in even-aged monoculture plantations will be scarce. A strip clear-cut forestry method developed in the Palcazú Valley of Peru is based on ecological principles learned from studies of gap-phase dynamics in natural forests, and is discussed in detail in Chapter 18, Case Study 1.

Figure 12.7 This approximately 70 m tall tree in Costa Rica was toppled during a windstorm. Natural tree-falls in tropical forests create light gaps, which are required by many species of tropical trees for their regeneration. Forest management that mimics light gap dynamics is much preferable to clear-cutting and may be sustainable in the long term. (Photograph by C. R. Carroll.)

In the United States, various forest management schemes have been developed for enhancing game species while still permitting economic return from timber harvests. Typically, these programs are based on pine harvests; they require lower pine planting densities than maximum yield harvest schemes and include some admixture of hardwoods and understory forbs and shrubs. For the most part, these methods are designed to improve habitat quality for a few game species, such as deer and turkey, and larger issues of biodiversity are incidental.

The National Forest Management Act of 1976 requires that protection of biodiversity be included in U.S. National Forest management plans. It is likely that management for biodiversity will become mandated for all federal lands. At present, we do not know what the optimal management plan to maintain biodiversity in any particular forest would look like. In general, the twofold objective will be (1) to produce sustainable management practices that provide for multiple sources of revenue, such as timber, recreation, hunting leases, and other extractive uses; and (2), at the same time, to maintain the biological integrity of the forest ecosystem. This is no small task, and it is not at all evident that both objectives can be satisfactorily achieved, but some innovative attempts have begun.

One approach gaining acceptance in the southeastern United States is the development of selective harvesting techniques that ultimately generate uneven stands of pine–hardwood mixtures and thereby mimic natural forest structure and, to some extent, tree and understory diversity (Hunter 1990). It is also important that such management schemes be based on scales larger than individual stands. It will be necessary to develop comprehensive management schemes that contain subprograms applicable to the scale of individual stands, and to integrate these subprograms at the higher level of regional landscapes. An example of this approach, as developed by Pulliam and his students for Bachman's Sparrow in pine stands, was discussed in Chapter 7.

Ecosystem Management

In Chapter 11, we discussed the underlying basis for ecosystem management and the general principles that it follows. Here, we begin to connect those principles to actual management practices as they are occurring, or should occur, and illustrate some of the problems and opportunities associated with ecosystem management.

The Biophysical Ecosystem

Generally, the management areas that are appropriate for the considerable time, effort, and costs associated with the ecosystem management approaches we described in Chapter 11 are large and encompass more than a single type of biophysical ecosystem. For example, if an ecosystem scientist were describing a large watershed comprising coniferous forest, lakes, and rivers, the description would be given in terms of three ecosystems with distinct properties, but which were ecologically linked in many ways. Although an aquatic-minded ecologist might focus studies on the ecosystem properties of the lakes or rivers, the ecosystem scientist would also be cognizant of transport of organic matter from the watershed, water from surface runoff, and other inputs.

Therefore, we need to make an important distinction between ecosystems as biophysical units and the meaning of "ecosystem" as part of the phrase "ecosystem management." To this point, we have been discussing ecosystems as biophysical units. Our emphasis has been on a level of biological organization above that of populations and communities that includes interactions between the biota and the physical environment. In this usage, people are included to the extent that their activities modify the structure and processes of the biophysical ecosystem. Ecosystem takes on an expanded meaning when it is used in ecosystem management; in this sense, the entire management area may be called an ecosystem, even though that area may be so large that several biophysical ecosystem types are included.

An example of a major ecosystem management project that includes several biophysical ecosystem types is the "Greater Yellowstone Ecosystem (GYE)," discussed in detail in Case Study 5 of Chapter 18. The GYE includes, at a minimum, the following biophysical ecosystems: coniferous forests, grasslands, hot springs, rivers, lakes, grazing rangelands, and agricultural fields. What is the management logic and scientific rationale that justifies calling such a heterogeneous landscape an "ecosystem" and enclosing it in a single, huge management unit? The answer is that such a strategy makes sense, both managerially and scientifically, if the management area is a network of biophysical ecosystems that are linked through ecological interactions or through social institutions.

For example, herds of large grazing animals—mainly bison, elk, and pronghorn—have adapted to the Yellowstone landscape by migrating seasonally to the most favorable regions. One of the most significant of these migrations was the winter movement of herds down from the high plateaus to the valleys and river bottoms, regions that are now developed for agriculture and second homes. Other important migratory routes led to national and state forest lands that surround the park. Through their need to migrate, the bison, elk, and pronghorn are dependent on access to, and utilization of, these surrounding non-parklands. They utilize several biophysical ecosystems, all of which must be considered in an ecosystem management approach.

In choosing the boundaries of the management area, there are three biophysical considerations, which we list in descending order of importance. First, an ecosystem, as a biophysical unit, should be completely enclosed within the management area. Attempting to manage only a stretch of a river or half of a lake is unlikely to be successful. Second, if the area includes multiple biophysical ecosystem types, the decision to include or exclude them should be based on the degree to which they have functional linkages, as with lakes and watersheds or estuaries and rivers. The inclusion of different ecosystems that are functionally linked is logical because management decisions that directly affect one ecosystem might indirectly affect another. A third, less commonly used biophysical consideration brings together ecosystems that are independent—that is, have no or only weak linkages—but are affected by the same stresses. Common examples include management programs to mitigate pollutants such as acid precipitation and other industrial fallout that can be transported long distances and across heterogeneous landscapes.

Generally, areas under ecosystem management must be large in order to encompass the resources needed by the various populations that constitute the biotic components of the ecosystem. The significance of spatially explicit landscape information to ecosystem management derives from three well-established principles: (1) the spatial configuration of food sources will influence which food sources are utilized; (2) resources may not always be available at a particular place, but their absence may be compensated by their availability at some other site; and (3) some parts of the landscape may not be used because cover is poor and/or risk from predators is too great. Thus, the management plan should encompass sufficient area and landscape heterogeneity so that populations can maintain themselves in spite of temporal variation in resource abundance. This spatial scale, what Fleming et al. (1994) refer to as the "functional landscape mosaic," largely defines the boundaries of the "ecosystem" in the context of ecosystem management.

Adaptive Management as a Flexible Decision-Making Model for Ecosystem Management

A major consequence of the dynamic nature of ecosystems is that their management must also be dynamic—that is, flexible and responsive. Management that responds in creative and innovative ways to changes in complex systems is "adaptive management" (Holling 1978; Walters 1986), and as discussed in Chapter 11, is a salient feature of ecosystem management. The change and dynamics in ecosystems does not mean that they are chaotic. Ecosystems are predictable at some spatial and temporal scales. A forest today is likely to remain a forest tomorrow, unless a hurricane arrives tonight. It is exactly that sort of unpredictability, at many scales, that needs to be incorporated into management programs and appreciated by managers.

The inherent dynamics of change in ecosystems makes *prescriptive* management difficult and ineffective. Consequently, management must follow a different strategy: it must be flexible, adaptive, and predictive. This means accepting a range of possible outcomes of any management action, with some probability of each outcome occurring; approaching management as an experiment, learning from results, and modifying future actions; and personal and institutional willingness to admit to mistakes and learn from them rather than minimizing them or defending status quo practices.

Adaptive management approaches have found utility in a wide array of complex systems, from policy analysis to industrial organization. Consequently, many analytic tools and models have been developed. The majority of these analytic approaches represent some form of simulation modeling, which is commonly used to explore potential consequences of different management decisions. When simulation modeling was first applied to adaptive management more than twenty years ago, it was considered a major conceptual and practical breakthrough. Simulation of management decisions allowed managers to substitute computer programming for actual decisions, some of which might have been prohibitively expensive or their consequences difficult to reverse were they to be proven wrong.

Uncritical use of simulation modeling, however, can unduly shape the goals of environmental management. For example, one of the first applications of simulation modeling was for the management of an important forest pest in Canada, the spruce budworm. In the model, the forest was valued for pulpwood production rather than for biodiversity or other ecosystem values. Therefore, no major restrictions were placed on the use of pesticides to control the spruce budworm; consequently, simulations of various pest control strategies suggested that low-level spraying was the best management option. Had the forest been valued for ecosystem protection, the use of pesticides might not have been a management option (McLain and Lee 1996).

If simulation modeling is used to explore the consequences of complex ecosystem management decisions, a mix of models, each having different structures and underlying valuation assumptions, is more appropriate than a single model. For example, Liu et al. (1994) coupled a population viability model for Bachman's Sparrow with a standard model for projecting forest timber revenue. The use of two models made it possible to evaluate the tradeoffs between probabilities of extinction for the sparrow and changes in timber revenue under different timber harvest practices. Recent advances in linking ecological and economic processes have included the coupling of models to relate economic yields and bird community responses under various silviculture regimes (Hansen et al. 1995).

Large-scale environmental management programs may include different biophysical ecosystems, more than one public or private institution with management responsibilities, commercial interests, advocacy groups, private citizens, and the constraints of layers of local through national law. In this case, adaptive management must go far beyond simple simulation models in order to explore complex management options. For example, an innovative approach to understanding how the greater Everglades ecosystem can be maintained is being developed by the U.S. State Department's Man and the Biosphere Program, Human-Dominated Systems Directorate (Harwell et al. 1996). In this holistic approach, geographic information systems and simulation models are being used to develop land use and hydrology scenarios that, if implemented, would provide various degrees of protection of water flow and quality for the Everglades while permitting some economic development in South Florida. These scenarios range from land uses and patterns of water flow to the Everglades that mimic those of early, pre-European settlement of Florida and greatly constrain economic development, to a pattern of land use and water flow that supports rapid economic development with only minimal protection of the Everglades. Each scenario is then evaluated by teams that represent social and ecological perspectives in a process known as "Scenario–Consequence Analysis." What has emerged from this study is a perspective that modest changes to water use in the agricultural areas around the Everglades would serve two purposes: they would maintain appropriate water recharge to the Everglades, and they would contribute to the sustainability of South Florida agriculture.

Should Ecosystem Management Mimic Natural Processes?

We have stated all along that ecological systems are dynamic and disturbance-driven on many different temporal and spatial scales. Consequently, it seems reasonable that an ecosystem approach should incorporate natural disturbances into management regimes in an adaptive fashion. However, this is easier said than done. In practical terms, it can be difficult to adequately define the historical frequency, magnitude, and extent of natural disturbances, and even more difficult to mimic them. The point of this section is not to discourage such an approach (in fact, we strongly encourage the use of natural disturbance regimes in management), but to point out the limitations involved and to suggest that, in the absence of precise knowledge, approximations of natural disturbance regimes may be the best we can do. This is quite acceptable if we pursue such regimes in an adaptive manner with a willingness to learn from our management experiments and improve our methods.

When, and in what manner, should ecosystem managers intervene to restore natural processes? This question assumes that the manager understands and can recognize for each of these processes the acceptable range of variation in the ecosystem and knows when these ranges have been exceeded. This level of understanding goes beyond just knowing something about historical patterns. It requires a deeper understanding of when the extremes become so great that they will cause long-term, inappropriate changes to the ecosystem—that is, when the resilience of the system is exceeded. For example, a forest manager may learn something about the historical frequency of fires by examining fire scars and tree rings. But it is probably more important for the manager to understand how frequently fires can occur before the ecosystem makes a fundamental shift to a different kind of ecosystem, as depicted in Holling's model (see Figure 11.8).

Historical information about the patterns of occurrence of natural disturbances such as fires, killing frosts, damaging storms, or floods helps to guide management decisions. We should keep in mind, however, that mimicking historical patterns of disturbance may not produce the intended management results because contemporary ecosystems are usually embedded in landscapes that are very different from ancestral conditions. Fragmentation, isolation, and reduced areal size all influence how the ecosystem responds to disturbance regimes, translocation of populations, invasion by exotic species, or any other potentially disruptive process. Managers need to know the resilience of their ecosystem to various kinds, intensities, and frequencies of perturbations.

To get this kind of information, managers may need to conduct experiments on rather large scales in an adaptive fashion. Examples include burning

Figure 12.8 The National Science Foundation maintains a network of field sites (indicated by dots) for long-term ecological research in the United States, Puerto Rico, and Antarctica.

experimental forest blocks at different frequencies to find the threshold at which regeneration fails, increasing the amplitude of water released from reservoirs to find the point at which downstream riffle habitats for fish spawning begin to degrade, or increasing stocking densities of native ungulates or cattle in desert grasslands to find the threshold at which cactus and other unpalatable plants begin to replace desert grasses.

In the United States, these kinds of medium- to large-scale experiments are being conducted in a system of Long-Term Ecological Research sites (LTER) with support from the National Science Foundation and often in partnership with federal and state agencies. The distribution of these LTER sites (Figure 12.8) indicates extensive, but still incomplete, coverage of ecosystem types in the United States. Medium- to large-scale experiments designed to probe the limits of ecosystem resilience need to be conducted more widely. The primary role of public lands is to protect our natural resources, but these lands (and waters) should also be seen as *natural laboratories* to help us understand the limits to management.

To return to the question, "Should management imitate natural processes?" it would be extremely difficult for managers to mimic natural processes exactly. Moreover, there are compelling reasons why managers should not be preoccupied with attempts to precisely imitate natural processes. Selecting a particular regime of management processes that exactly imitates nature implies that an appropriate historical period of reference has been selected and that the natural processes operating during that time are known and can be duplicated by the manager. The selection of such a period of reference would be something of an arbitrary process. For North America, should that period be pre-industrial development, pre-European contact, pre-human disturbance, or some other period? And, of course, the further back in time we place our period of Eden, the less we know about the natural processes that were then in place. Even if we knew those processes, the vast differences in spatial scales and connectivity of habitat patches between landscapes that existed hundreds of years ago and today's fragmented landscapes make it unlikely that a manager could duplicate the original processes in any meaningful way.

Consider the dilemma for managers posed by the following historical analysis. The semiarid highlands where the states of New Mexico, Arizona, Colorado, and Utah meet is known as the "trans-Pecos" region. Truett (1996) asked the fundamental question, "Are current population densities of bison and elk representative of population densities in the region when indigenous cultures were dominant?" Using information such as the composition of the animal remains in ancient Indian midden piles and early accounts of European explorers, he came to the conclusion that current densities are much higher than pre-settlement densities. Two factors seemed most likely to contribute to the higher densities found today. First, stock tanks and other impoundments for cattle have greatly increased the amount of available water in this semiarid region. Second, hunting pressure from Indians during the pre-settlement period imposed much greater mortality than current sport hunting practices.

Here, then, is the dilemma for managers in this region: If they adopted a management goal of recreating ecological systems as they existed before the landscape was modified by ranches, mining, and other development, they would have to remove artificial sources of water, reestablish migratory routes, and perhaps cull bison and elk. What they would achieve by this effort, of course, would not be re-creation of an ancient ecological system, but rather a pale image of certain elements of ancient times. What, then, should the ecological manager do?

We do not believe that the proper role of ecosystem management is to "freeze" a system in some arbitrary time period. In the real world, resource managers must balance many competing concerns. The human imprint on nature, in its myriad forms and intensities, will always be present; it is not new. For thousands of years, humans have been major contributors to the form and function of most terrestrial and freshwater ecosystems and have been stakeholders in the benefits and costs of natural services that are supplied by those ecosystems. The oak savannas of California, the oak woodlands of Europe, the open glades ("balds") on southern Appalachian mountaintops, inter-Andean valleys, African savannas, and salt marshes all have long histories of strong influence by people.

The ecological manager cannot precisely imitate natural processes or recreate historically remote environments. But, at the other extreme, in this era of rampant population growth and development, neither can ecological managers responsibly take a laissez-faire approach and become mere spectators to the continuing erosion of biodiversity and the loss of our natural heritage. In Box 12B we use fire, a nearly ubiquitous tool for terrestrial ecosystem management, to explore how managers might seek a rational balance between mimicking natural processes and meeting immediate management concerns.

BOX 12B
The Use of Fire in Ecosystem Management

Fire is both a naturally occurring agent of disturbance and a management tool that can be used to reduce risk of property damage and to manipulate habitat patterns. Fires that are intentionally set and controlled by managers (prescribed burns) represent the most common terrestrial ecosystem management practice. Prescribed burns reduce the likelihood of catastrophic wildfires by reducing the amount of accumulated "fuel"in the form of woody debris, dry brushy undergrowth, and other highly flammable vegetation. Prescribed burning is also used to create habitat, to generate spatial heterogeneity, and to remove undesirable vegetation. Prescribed burns are often touted as a "natural" management tool because fires occur naturally in most terrestrial ecosystems.

Let's first explore what information would be required to use prescribed burning as a natural process. We would want to know, for some historical time period, the answers to several questions. How frequently did fires occur, and during which parts of the annual cycle? Were the lengths of intervals between fires normally distributed, or did years with fires tend to be clustered or overdispersed? Were the fires "hot," that is, did they leave cleared, mineralized land and volatilize large amounts of soil nitrogen, or were they "cool," leaving patches of vegetation untouched? Were the fires localized or widespread? Did the fires cover a simple topography, or a complex one, such that post-fire vegetation and animal population responses varied? Finally, we would need an answer to this critically important question: "If we imposed a historically accurate fire regime, would the ecosystem respond now in the same manner as it did in the past?" This is another way of asking whether the imposition of historically accurate disturbance regimes would exceed the resilience of contemporary ecosystems. First, we will explore what is needed to understand historical fire regimes. Then we will explore how fire can be used to assist ecosystem management.

Scars of old fires, preserved in the annual growth rings of trees, allow the occurrence of fires to be dated through dendrochronology, that is, by counting annual tree rings from the present back to the location of the fire scar. Although the dating of a particular scar in a tree is straightforward, determining the temporal distribution of fire intervals, the areal extent of fires, and differences in these patterns between sites requires a rigorous analytic approach. Suppose, for example, a manager wanted to know the distribution of fire intervals in two different management areas in order to implement a prescribed burning regime that followed the "natural" historical pattern. Assuming that the choice of the historical period of reference could be logically defended, the ecologically minded manager might reasonably ask several questions: How often did fires occur? Is the mean interval between fires an adequate estimator of fire frequency for management purposes, or should the variance and temporal trends of the interval lengths also be considered? The manager might also want to know whether the historical patterns differed between the two management areas.

In pursuing answers to these questions, the manager would need to establish an appropriate sampling regime for analyzing tree ring data. To do this properly, so that statistical models could be used for evaluation, every tree in the study area old enough to span the time period of interest must have an equal probability of being included in the sample. If different areas or different time periods are going to be compared to see whether their fire histories differ, a particular statistical model has to be chosen. A negative binomial distribution would be appropriate if fires have an equal probability of occurring every year. However, if the probability of a fire (or of a particular tree suffering scarring) is thought to be an increasing or a decreasing function of length of time since the last burn, then a different statistical model has to be used, such as a Weibul distribution. These fire frequency models and methods are considered at length by Johnson and Gutsell (1994).

Knowing the historical patterns, no matter how accurately, is still insufficient for implementing a regime of prescribed burning if it is to closely mimic natural processes. The behavior of naturally occurring fires is not only a function of the interval length since the previous fire, but is also influenced by atmospheric conditions such as wind and humidity. Yet, the atmospheric conditions of high wind and low humidity that enhance large, hot fires are not the conditions a cautious manager would choose to conduct a prescribed burn. Consequently, prescribed fires generally result in patchy burns that may imitate some kinds of natural burns, but would not, for example, imitate the effects of a hot fire that volatilizes large amounts of nitrogen, sterilizes seedbeds, and removes all of the accumulated coarse woody debris. Considering the onerous burden, in terms of time and funds, that an investigation of this sort would impose, the ecological manager might well ask, "Is it worth it?"

We are left with some important questions that trouble all ecological managers who are attempting to recreate historical patterns of disturbance, whether by fire, flood, or any other agent. If we are trying to mimic natural patterns of disturbance through management intervention, how close does the approximation need to be? What indicators should be used to monitor success or failure of the disturbance regime? Related to this concern, what if closely mimicking historical natural disturbance patterns and processes would cause an erosion of the contemporary native biodiversity of the ecosystem, enhance the establishment and spread of exotic species, or reduce the inherent fertility of the soil? Given these undesirable outcomes, the manager is likely to implement a different, albeit more artificial, disturbance regime in order to maintain the ecosystem. This is an ecologically rational response because it recognizes that historically accurate disturbance patterns and processes might exceed the resilience of contemporary ecosystems.

These concerns become especially important in the intensive management that is often required in small protected areas. For example, if historical patterns of fire intervals and average areal extent of burns were used to establish prescribed burning regimes in a small reserve, much of the reserve might be represented by a single stage in post-fire recovery, thus reducing habitat heterogeneity.

Where do all these considerations leave us with regard to the development of fire management regimes? First, historical records of fire frequency are a useful "first cut" for developing prescribed burn plans (see Lesica 1996 for a successful example of the use of fire history to establish prescribed burns). The next step involves evaluation of any other concerns that might mitigate against the use of historical fire patterns. This evaluation phase, of course, requires significant involvement by stakeholders in the management area. Discussions should be framed in such a way that they can lead to tentative fire management plans that can be implemented, tested, and modified in the context of adaptive management. This is not an easy process. Because fire can affect large areas, and because there is always some risk that fires will escape containment, the public is wary of the deliberate use of fire for management. Furthermore, the increasing density of homes and other development adjacent to public lands makes public acceptance of the use of fire more problematic. Indeed, an organization that has unexpectedly become involved with fire management issues is the American Lung Association, because of its concern over the release of smoke particulates as a health hazard.

Many conservation managers now face major opposition to the use of fire, and countering this opposition will only become more difficult as private homes and development increasingly surround national parks and wilderness areas and inholdings continue to proliferate on public lands. Here, then, is a classic example of the need for public education to help people expand their perspective from pure self-interest to one that understands the social value of ecosystem sustainability.

Including Stakeholders in Decision Making

By now it should be clear from our discussion that decision making in ecosystem management must be highly participatory. Furthermore, the ecosystem management approach explicity includes people as integral parts of the ecosystem. This does not mean that natural ecosystems should be managed to maximize their economic value, as the misnamed "Wise Use" movement would have it, nor does it mean that all other species have a standing equivalent to that of humans, as some in the animal rights movement would maintain. Rather, people are included for a suite of reasons. First, through the sheer size of the human population, coupled with our material desires and needs, we have a pervasive influence on virtually all ecosystems; no culture, lifestyle, or political system is completely exempt from this influence. Second, for reasons that are ethical or religious, we have a responsibility to act as stewards to counter the potential degradative consequences that our economic lives have for natural ecosystems. Third, we cannot understand the dynamics of ecosystem function, nor the variation in ecosystem structure, without explicitly including people, in a sense as a "keystone species." Fourth, long-term successful management of ecosystems requires the cooperation of stakeholders, as broadly defined in Box 11C.

Principal stakeholders are those people whose livelihoods or residences are connected to the management area, and those institutions—public and private—with activities in the management area. Principal stakeholders should play major roles in the development, implementation, monitoring, and evaluation of the ecosystem management plan. Participation by minor stakeholders is best served through forums for public commentary.

A contradiction frequently exists when stakeholders are brought into decision making. Individuals often make decisions about resource use that are based on short-term and self-interest perspectives. Yet the same stakeholders, under other circumstances, may make decisions that are long-term, community-based, and which favor sustainability of the resource. In order for participatory decision making to contribute to ecosystem sustainability, mechanisms must be found to balance self-interest with the overriding need for resource sustainability. For example, community education and local project involvement can reduce mistrust, minimize narrow self-interest decisions, and contribute to what Crance and Draper (1996) call "socially cooperative choices." An example of an applied stakeholder-inclusion approach is offered in Box 12C.

BOX 12C
Natural Community Conservation Planning

Land planning and zoning are commonly employed to regulate land uses ranging from single-unit family dwellings on large lots to apartment houses and commercial uses such as shopping malls and industrial complexes. Although land planning as a means of influencing development has a long history, it has only recently been applied to resolve conflicts among advocates for conservation of natural areas, public agencies charged with protecting species or critical habitat, private landowners, and commercial land developers. Some individual private landowners, of course, have willingly foregone a portion of the potential market value of their property through conservation easements or by joining land trusts to provide long-term conservation protection for their land. But community-level conservation planning is a new approach, albeit one with some significant problems to be resolved.

This process, known as Natural Community Conservation Planning, or NCCP, is an application of conservation biology principles to local land use planning within the social, political, and legal contexts of land use (Reid and Murphy 1995). It emphasizes habitat conservation rather than single species-oriented conservation, and allows planned, controlled development while protecting natural areas. An example from Orange County and surrounding areas in Southern California that has been featured in the news media is a plan to protect the coastal scrub habitat of a federally protected bird, the California Gnatcatcher. Among the major players in this NCCP are the federal and state agencies that are charged with enforcement of the Endangered Species Act, county and municipal land planning and fire control agencies, The Irvine Company as the major land owner and developer in the region, The Nature Conservancy, and various citizen groups. The Nature Conservancy, under the guidance of Steve Johnson, the TNC Land Steward, has played the lead role in negotiations.

The uncertainty that potential enforcement of the Endangered Species Act introduced into the development market provided a major incentive for pro-development players to enter the negotiating process. Although the process has not been easy, it has been facilitated by the presence of the single major land developer, The Irvine Company, which has a history of accommodating conservation goals, such as through wetland mitigation processes. When completed, the conservation plan will set aside critical coastal scrub habitat and allow development to occur outside the set-aside area without fear of future intervention in the form of enforcement of the Endangered Species Act.

NCCP is an innovative approach to meeting conservation objectives in areas that are under threat of development. It has, however, three aspects that remain problematic. First, it is uncertain whether the negotiation process and successful land planning will occur when many different land developers are involved. Second, this approach may be limited to habitats that contain federal- or state-protected species, and may be ineffective without the associated litigation threat. Third, the conservation plan "freezes" the habitat of the species to what is circumscribed in the plan, thus violating an essential principle of adaptive management, that is, the need to revise and modify protection plans. However, in regions where development pressures are intense, such community-based conservation land use plans may be the only realistic option for protecting biodiversity.

We believe that the principles of ecosystem management articulated in Chapter 11 offer managers reasonable mechanisms for establishing rational goals. The principle of long-term sustainability calls for managers to establish functional landscape mosaics that contain the necessary resources to support biodiversity and ecosystem functions. The principle of adaptive management allows the manager to make decisions in a climate of uncertainty and, through continuous monitoring and the use of indicators, to make necessary corrections. The principle of stakeholder involvement in decision making allows managers to find an acceptable balance between exclusionary preservation at one extreme and total economic exploitation at the other extreme.

Contributions from the Landscape Scale

The large spatial scales typically involved in ecosystem management require some special techniques for data gathering and analysis. Such techniques include **remote sensing** and geographic information systems (GIS). Remote sensing may be based on low-altitude aerial photography or high-altitude satellite imagery (Figure 12.9). The former provides high resolution of relatively small areas, thereby sacrificing general information over large landscapes; the latter provides low resolution of relatively large areas, thereby sac-

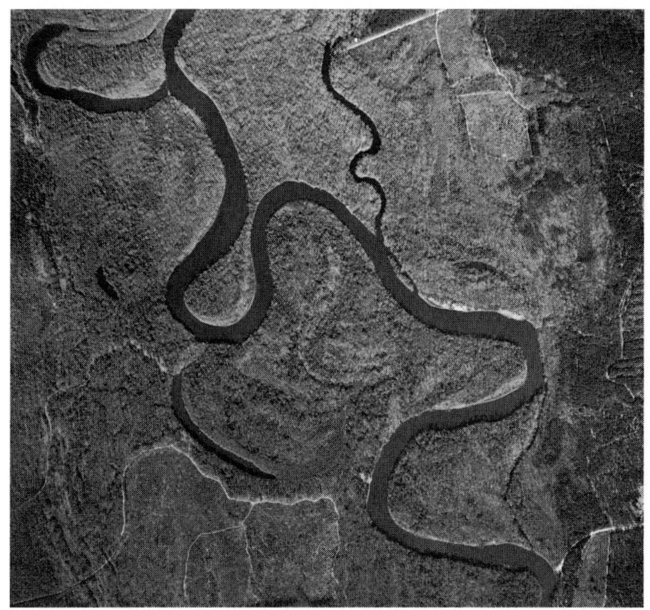
(A)

(B)

Figure 12.9 Both (A) low-altitude aerial photography and (B) high-altitude satellite imagery provide valuable data sets for conservation practices dealing with landscape-scale issues. Both images are of the Savannah River, separating South Carolina (on right) from Georgia. The site in (A) is 3.75 km on a side, and is shown as an inset of the larger image in (B), which is 15.6 km on a side. Note the greater detail in (A), but the better overall landscape perspective in (B). Choosing the correct scale of landscape analysis is a matter of the particular interests and questions in each case. (Photograph and satellite image courtesy of the Savannah River Ecology Laboratory.)

rificing detail for broad geographic information. The use of special films and filters allows different portions of the electromagnetic spectrum to be emphasized, and thus permits a focus on particular kinds of information. For example, photographs of landscapes taken with infrared film can show spatial variation in surface temperatures. Vegetation cover can easily be seen in these photographs and can be distinguished from rock, bare soil, or water. An international symposium on technology in natural resource management (ASPRS/ACSM/RT 1992) provides a good treatment of the application of GIS and remote sensing to resource conservation.

It is important, however, to understand the limits of these techniques. Infrared film will easily detect vegetation, but only if it covers most of a pixel (a dot that forms the smallest unit of photographic resolution). Therefore, these photographs will present a biased picture of vegetation cover by lumping areas of sparse vegetation with areas that lack vegetation. In desert regions, where plant cover is sometimes highly dispersed, infrared photography would fail to detect a substantial fraction of the total vegetation.

Remote sensing is especially useful for detecting major changes in land use, such as deforestation and conversion of forestlands to agriculture (Figure 12.10). Because the reflectance properties of plants vary somewhat by species and the physiological condition of the plant, it is possible to correlate conditions on the ground with remote imagery. This technique can be used in detecting signs of habitat degradation, such as large changes in plant species composition or loss of cover due to overgrazing. Geostationary satellite imagery can be used to record environmental changes in a particular region over time through sequential photographs.

Computer-based geographic information systems are used to analyze spatially related data sets. GIS can be used, for example, to highlight topographic relief, vegetation patterns, or any physical feature that can be displayed from remote sensing data. GIS can be a useful tool for selecting the best locations for reserves by facilitating the mapping of centers of species richness, and for improving reserve design by emphasizing physical features, vegetation pat-

Figure 12.10 A satellite image of the northern California coast between Klamath and Trinidad. The remaining old-growth stands of redwoods (*Sequoia sempervirens*) and Douglas fir (*Pseudotsuga menziesii*) in parks appear dark in contrast to brighter areas of secondary forests and pastures. The image was developed using the near-infrared reflectance from a Landsat Multi-Spectral Scanner scene obtained on April 8, 1988, and demonstrates the utility of remote sensing for detecting land use changes over time and space. (Satellite image courtesy of the Savannah River Ecology Laboratory.)

terns, habitat delineation, and drainage basins (Figure 12.11). An important application of GIS is so-called **gap analysis**, developed by Michael Scott and his colleagues at the University of Idaho (Scott et al. 1987), and discussed here by Mike Scott and Blair Csuti in Essay 12C.

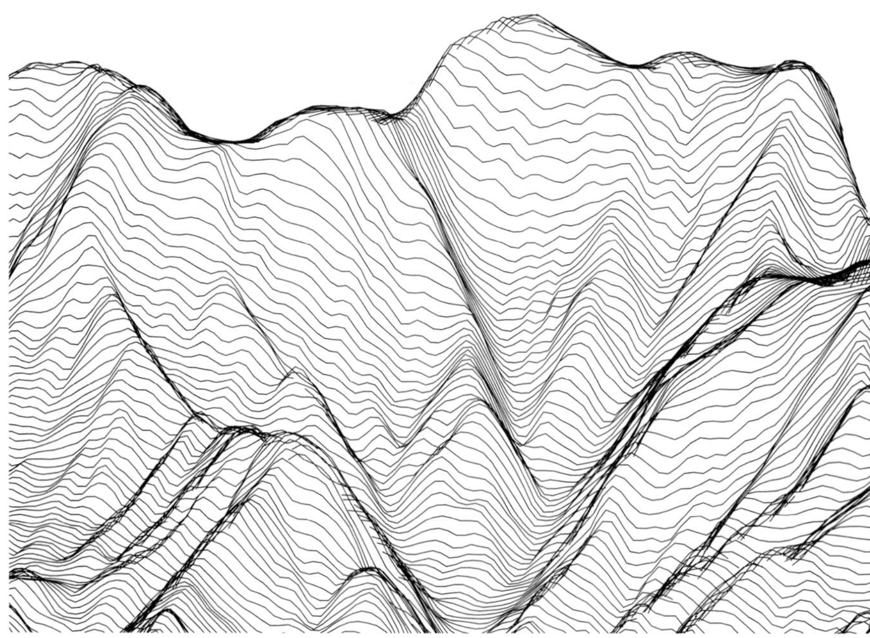

Figure 12.11 Geographic information system techniques can be used to emphasize topographic features. This figure represents an exaggerated relief of a basin in the Coweeta Hydrologic Laboratory in North Carolina. (Courtesy of Kurt Saari.)

ESSAY 12C

Gap Analysis

Assessing Landscape Trends in Diversity

J. Michael Scott, Biological Resources Division, U.S. Geological Survey, and Blair Csuti, University of Idaho

The claim that a squirrel could travel from the Atlantic Ocean to the Mississippi River without touching the ground may be an exaggeration, but it captures the essence of the pre-Columbian landscape of eastern North America. The original Eastern deciduous forest is essentially gone, lost one farmstead at a time to the pioneer's axe. The exploitation of primeval forests and other natural resources has largely taken place at a local scale, without knowledge of, or regard for, the larger context or consequences of human activities on the continent's biodiversity.

Because biodiversity has spatial properties at every level in its hierarchy, from genes to the biosphere, studies of its distribution, status, and conservation encompass a variety of disciplines, including systematic biology, ecology, and geography. The need for an ecological data base that can be used to address research and management questions relevant to the conservation of an area's species, ecosystems, ecological processes, and biological phenomena is pressing. Only with this landscape-scale information can we make intelligent decisions about identification, selection, and design of natural areas, or prescribe appropriate management practices on multiple-use wildlands. In the United States, such an effort is being pursued by the U.S.G.S. Biological Resources Division's Gap Analysis Program, which attempts to provide the elements of an ecological data base at a landscape scale needed to answer research and management questions about our nation's natural resources (Scott et al. 1996).

The Gap Analysis Program, a cooperative effort among regional, state, and federal agencies and private groups, draws on several branches of science to assess the status and trends of some elements of biodiversity over large areas. The program has a four-point mission: (1) map the land cover of the United States; (2) map predicted distributions of vertebrates for the United States; (3) document land cover types and vertebrate species in areas managed for long-term maintenance of biodiversity; and (4) provide this information to scientists, educators, the public, natural resource managers, planners, and policy-makers.

Gap analysis makes use of two technologies that have emerged over the past two decades—satellite remote sensing and geographic information systems—to examine the distribution of natural resources and human impacts at landscape, regional, and national scales. Because of practical constraints, we focus on three accessible levels of the biodiversity hierarchy: (1) ecosystems, delineated and typed by dominant vegetation; (2) sets of species; and (3) individual species. There are three steps in any conservation planning effort: identification, selection, and design. Gap analysis deals primarily with the first, but the second and third require site-specific investigation of the structure and function of all elements of biodiversity.

It would seem axiomatic that you cannot effectively manage something if you do not know its location, configuration, or extent. Perhaps the most ambitious and critical contribution of the Gap Analysis Program to natural resource management is the development of a seamless, national, mesoscale (1:100,000) map of current land cover. Although myriad local, state, and federal agencies have created maps for small project areas, there are no up-to-date, consistently classified maps for larger regions of the United States at a scale larger than 1:7,000,000. The lack of consensus on a national vegetation or ecosystem classification system (Orians 1993) is a major roadblock to regional land cover analysis. The Gap Analysis Program is part of a cooperative effort to fill this void and establish a national vegetation classification system.

Because information about the distribution of large terrestrial organisms is better known and documented, we are developing distributional data bases for several classes of these species (amphibians, reptiles, birds, mammals, and in some states, butterflies). Traditional sources (museum specimen records, breeding bird surveys, literature records) are supplemented by expert opinion to develop a geographic representation of the probability of a species occurring in an area. Species maps are linked to land cover, elevation, rivers, wetlands, temperatures, and other habitat features by factoring in the habitat associations of each species. While our inability to map microhabitat elements important to many species, such as springs, cliffs, or downed logs, prevents us from applying these maps at local scales, comparisons with known lists for well-studied natural areas have shown these maps to be sufficiently accurate (ca. 80% overall, Edwards et al. 1996) for regional planning purposes.

The final information layer needed for conservation evaluation is on land stewardship patterns, consisting of generalized land ownership and land management status. Although individual parcels of private land are not identified, lands in public ownership are mapped according to managing agency. These public lands are then classified according to their management prescriptions. While there are many possible insights to be gained by comparing the distribution of elements of biodiversity with land ownership and management status, the most obvious is a simple report of the current representation of each element of biodiversity on lands managed for natural values. The geographic data may also be displayed to highlight the location of land cover types or species not well represented in current natural areas.

Because only a small fraction of any nation's land area will be managed for conservation (Pressey 1994), gap analysis data may be sampled to find the most efficient subset of areas in which all, or nearly all, species or land cover types will be represented. While areas especially rich in overall species diversity ("hot spots") are appealing candidates for conservation, more systematic analyses can identify sets of areas that complement one another's species or cover type composition, thus capturing elements of diversity that may not be represented in hot spots (Pressey et al. 1993). A number of heuristic and linear programming algorithms are available for these spatial analyses (e.g., Kirkpatrick 1983; Margules et al. 1988; Bedward et al. 1992; Nicholls and Margules 1993; Csuti et al., in press). We must emphasize that gap analysis data sets provide useful information on the location of areas with high potential for natural resource value, but do not address issues of habitat quality, population viability, or community and ecosystem dynamics. These topics must be addressed by biological field studies as well as the sociological and economic studies used to design a natural area.

Early gap analysis results on the status and trends of land cover types are available for a few Western states (Caicco et al. 1995; Davis et al. 1995; Edwards et al. 1995; Kiester et al. 1996). In general, relatively few land cover types are well represented (i.e., >20% of their total area) in existing natural areas. However, statistics comparing the current areal extent of land cover types with the locations of natural areas can be misleading, because they do not account for historical losses of natural land cover. Using relatively subjective data, Noss et al. (1995) identified 126 ecosystem types in the United States that have lost over 70% of their original area; thirty of these have lost over 98%. Conversely, and not surprisingly, many ecosystem types that have experienced little or no decline and are well represented in natural areas tend to be isolated, high-elevation, sparsely vegetated alpine systems with little or no economic potential. On the optimistic side, there are many natural communities that retain much of their compositional, structural, and functional biodiversity when subjected to sustainable levels of multiple-use resource extraction (Scott et al. 1990).

The promise of gap analysis is to provide land managers with comprehensive and contextual information on important elements of the biodiversity under their stewardship. Gap analysis can provide 1:100,000 scale maps from which the success of land management practices may be judged through comparison with future mapping efforts. Gap analysis is already providing spatial information about biological resources to both public and private resource managers, information that has been used for purposes as diverse as locating research projects, siting sawmills, and open space planning for a seven-county area in Southern California (Scott et al. 1996).

All this exciting technology must come with a warning: the products from GIS applications can be quite eye-catching, and it is easy to become seduced by the technology and to forget that GIS is simply a useful tool for answering questions about large spatial scales. To be properly used, it must be combined with good ecological knowledge and good decision-making capabilities. Computers hold only data, not the answers to vexing conservation problems. These answers will always need to come from competent and creative conservationists.

An Example of Ecosystem Management: The Chesapeake Bay Program

Throughout the inhabited world, coastal zones are experiencing the greatest degree of economic development. In the United States, coastal counties constitute 11% of the land area, but in recent years have accounted for more than half of all new home construction (World Resources Institute 1994). Nearly half of the U.S. population is expected to live within 85 km of the coast by the year 2010 (Culliton et al. 1990). Consequently, the nearshore marine environment is highly vulnerable to degradation, especially from the polluting effects of sewage discharges and stormwater runoff from urbanized landscapes.

But each coastal region also has its unique set of problems. In the wet tropics, the major problem is rivers carrying high sediment loads due to soil erosion; in parts of the Mediterranean region, it is excessive discharge of poorly treated sewage; in the Gulf of Mexico, petrochemicals pollute estuaries and contaminate beaches; in Florida bays, the prop wash from overpowered pleasure boats tears up beds of sea-grass. In most cases, threats to the coastal zone stem from one systemic problem: our propensity to mask unsustainable economic growth by dumping its waste into the ocean.

The Chesapeake Bay, on the mid-Atlantic coast of the United States (Figure 12.12), is famous for its rich harvests of blue crabs, oysters, and fish; from 1983 to 1992, nearly 90 million pounds of blue crabs were harvested annually from the bay (Reshetiloff 1995). The bay and its surrounding wetlands are also home to Bald Eagles, Osprey, many species of waterfowl, and other birds. The Chesapeake Bay is one of the largest, most economically important, and, from a biodiversity perspective, richest coastal ecosystems in North America.

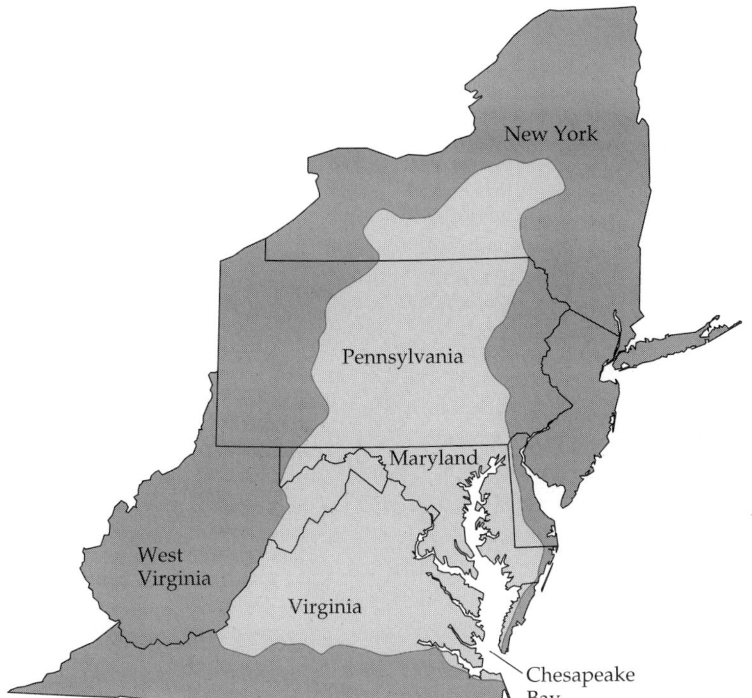

Figure 12.12 The Chesapeake Bay and its drainage watershed (light shading).

But for many decades the bay also has been the recipient of a soup of pesticides, fertilizers, heavy metals, and other toxins as runoff from the hundreds of thousands of hectares of lawns, golf courses, farm fields, and asphalt surfaces that have developed through much of its watershed, as well as a huge volume of waste from homes and factories that flows directly from treatment plants into the bay. These decades of stress took their toll on the bay and its estuary ecosystems. Blue crab harvests were threatened, finfish catches declined, sea-grass beds—important as nursery habitat for crabs and many fishes—were fragmented and greatly reduced in extent. Because the rivers that empty into the estuary carried heavy loads of sediments, nutrients, and toxins, parts of the main estuary were depleted of oxygen and became lethal to fishes and crabs for several months each year.

In response to these deteriorating conditions, the Chesapeake Bay Program (CBP) was initiated in 1983. This multilevel partnership includes federal and state agencies and many cooperating county, municipal, and nongovernmental stewardship organizations, as well as commercial interests and citizen advocacy groups. From the outset, the primary purpose of the CBP has been to restore the living resources of the bay and estuaries and to reach this goal through ecosystem management. Currently, the partners in CBP include:

- Nine federal agencies, including the Environmental Protection Agency (EPA) and the National Oceanic and Atmospheric Administration (NOAA)
- A regional Chesapeake Bay Commission representing Maryland, Pennsylvania, and Virginia that facilitates interstate collaboration on policy development
- State governments of Maryland, Pennsylvania, Virginia, and the District of Columbia
- County agencies within the watershed
- Local organizations, including municipalities and private voluntary organizations.

Research sponsored by the nine participating federal agencies has generated an enormous amount of information, maintained on 129 data bases and GIS projections for the basin (Federal Agencies Committee 1995). Just a few examples include aerial surveys of phytoplankton blooms, spatial/temporal patterns of dissolved oxygen, blue crab population distributions, bird distributions, and waste discharge patterns. In a recent interagency workshop, 104 new data sets, not currently in existence, were identified as priority needs to support the CBP. A major effort is being made to make these data sets compatible among the agencies and to make them more accessible to the public. For example, several data sets, and their graphical representations, can be downloaded from the Internet, and the goal is to make all nonrestricted data sets easily accessible.

This brief discussion of data bases and their accessibility relates to ecosystem management in two important ways. First, because information is shared among all stakeholders, no single group holds dominion over information that would allow them to control decision making. Thus, access to data may facilitate participatory decision making or, at least, improve discussions in public forums. Second, long-term data sets are important for adaptive management, one of the fundamental principles of which is that the project be modified if it is not achieving its objectives. In order to assess progress, a substantial monitoring effort is necessary. Long-term data sets can support these monitoring needs, if they are designed for that purpose. Unfortunately, in many cases there is little relationship between the data sets generated by researchers and the needs of managers. The Chesapeake Bay Program seems to be a refreshing exception, with the selection of data sets closely tied to indicators of progress and requirements for monitoring. For example, stabilizing blue crab populations is one goal for restoration. To measure progress toward this goal, data sets that allow monitoring of crab populations are maintained along with data sets on commercial harvests, on declining sea-grass beds, on various pollutants, and on anoxic conditions, all representing major threats to the blue crab.

Is the Chesapeake Bay Program a successful example of ecosystem management? The program can certainly point to a number of significant improvements to the ecosystem of the bay and to a reduction in some of the major threats to the bay. An overview of the vital signs of the Chesapeake Bay ecosystem shows the following (Chesapeake Bay Program 1995):

- Current land use is approximately 60% forested, 30% agricultural, and 10% urban/suburban. By 2000, urban/suburban land use is expected to increase by 35%. Recognizing that the location of forest losses is important, state programs have emphasized protection and restoration of riparian forests.
- Between 1982 and 1989, the watershed had a net loss of 19,500 acres of wetland, mostly forested wetlands.
- Population growth is rapid: the human population increased from 8.4 million in 1950 to 14.7 million in 1990 and is expected to reach 17.4 million by 2000. Wastewater discharge is increasing at a rate greater than the population growth rate.
- Despite increased wastewater discharges, phosphorus loads from municipal sources have decreased by about 70% since 1970, largely through improvements to municipal treatment plants funded by a Federal Construction Grants program.
- Rates of nitrogen discharge from treatment plants have decreased since 1985, but still remain positive.
- Rivers integrate both point-source and nonpoint-source pollutants. All rivers emptying into the bay show recent declines in phosphorus loads

and a leveling off of nitrogen loads since about the mid-1980s. A goal of 40% reduction in pollution loads has been set for 2000. The 40% reduction goal, especially for phosphorus and nitrogen, is projected to significantly improve levels of dissolved oxygen in the bay and estuaries. Through the use of mathematical models, the tributaries and river stretches that contribute the majority of the pollutant loads have been identified for intensive strategies of pollution reduction.

- There is no trend in improvement of low levels of dissolved oxygen, nor in reductions in algal blooms. The legacy of many years of nutrient accumulation in bay and estuary sediments means that a long lag time will occur before pollution reduction efforts affect dissolved oxygen levels and algal blooms.
- Of the toxic contaminants that reach the bay, trace metals (e.g., arsenic and mercury) and polycyclic aromatic hydrocarbons represent the greatest environmental concern. Data on spatial patterns in the concentration of these contaminants have allowed managers to designate "Regions of Concern" and to develop action plans to reduce contaminants in these regions. As a result of two federal acts, the Clean Water Act and the Clean Air Act, contaminant loads to the bay have been reduced. New state and local programs are designed to encourage industrial efficiency and to discourage new industries that discharge contaminants.
- The total abundance of intact, submerged aquatic vegetation has increased 75% since the 1970s, though the exotic *Hydrilla* has contributed to some of this increase. A restoration goal of 114,000 acres has been set bay-wide and is expected to be reached by 2005. Sharp boundaries exist between vegetated and nonvegetated areas, consistent with small changes in water quality. It is worth noting that these sharp transitions in abundance are examples of the many nonlinearities that characterize ecosystems.
- The abundance and composition of zooplankton are used as indicators of water quality and to measure the productive base for secondary consumers such as fishes. High concentrations of zooplankton, such as those found in the Choptank River, have been associated with high spawning success of striped bass.
- Benthic communities, including oysters, remain degraded in regions with low dissolved oxygen levels and in regions where sediments are contaminated with toxins.
- Striped bass (*Morone saxatilis*) populations have greatly increased due to the restoration of beds of submerged vegetation that serve as nursery habitat and changes in harvest regulations to reduce catch limits. Sexually mature females represented only 10% of the female fish stock in 1988 and 1989, but increased to 50% by 1992.
- American shad (*Alosa sapidissima*) populations remain low, due in large part to dams, culverts, and other stream barriers that prevent successful spawning runs by this andromonous fish. A priority of the CBP is to reopen spawning streams. Currently, 160 miles of streams have been cleared of barriers and, over the next ten years, 1,357 stream miles are scheduled to be freed of barriers to shad runs. Shad populations had been increasing, albeit slowly, until a major decline occurred in 1993. In subsequent years shad populations again began to increase. The 1993 decline was coast-wide, reminding us that as large as an ecosystem management area might be, conditions external to the management area remain important.
- Blue crab (*Callinectes sapidus*) populations remain stable, even though approximately 75% of the adult stock is harvested each year. Crab popu-

lations independent of harvest levels are sampled with summer trawls and winter dredges. Harvest samples from commercial and sport fisheries provide information on stock removal rates. The two principal management approaches are restoration of sea-grass beds to protect juveniles and harvest regulations to control stock removal.

- The Chesapeake Bay satisfies only part of the habitat needs of migratory waterfowl, hence factors that affect population growth or decline may be largely outside the Chesapeake Bay management area. For example, winter populations of Canvas-back Ducks on the bay may be more strongly influenced by droughts in the pothole regions of the upper Midwest, where they breed, than by habitat quality in the bay. Some species of waterfowl are highly dependent on bay habitat and food resources. Redhead Duck populations have declined to very small numbers, largely because their food base, submerged aquatic vegetation, has declined. Black Ducks require that nesting habitat and brood-rearing habitat be in close proximity. Populations have declined because habitat fragmentation due to development has decoupled the duck's nesting habitat (remote marshes) from its brood-rearing habitat (alder-fringed streams). Canada Geese are declining due to poor reproduction in recent years and from overharvesting. Scoters, Old-squaw, and Golden-eye are also declining. Other species of waterfowl, such as Mallards, Canvas-backs, Buffleheads, and Mergansers are increasing.

Encouraging some level of participation by all stakeholders is an important principle of ecosystem management. Citizen monitoring groups play an important role in assessing the quality of the bay environment. For example, the Chesapeake Bay Citizen Monitoring Program (CBCMP) is run by trained volunteers who collect samples for water quality analysis, watch for the appearance of exotic zebra mussels, and monitor changes in living resources. CBCMP volunteers collect data at 110 stations and follow a tested protocol so that baseline data are assured to be of high quality. CBCMP is not the only volunteer organization that monitors the bay; more than 21 citizen monitoring groups are active in the watersheds of the Chesapeake Bay.

The Chesapeake Bay Program is an example of ecosystem management on a grand scale. Given the complexity of the bay and watershed ecosystems, the many sources of stress to the bay, the rapidly growing population in the region, and the years of accumulated nutrient and toxin loads, the Chesapeake Bay Program can point to many successes. Because the problems of the bay ecosystem are clearly recalcitrant to easy solutions, the CBP must be recognized and embraced by citizens as a long-term contributor to the quality of life in the Chesapeake Bay region. The nearly 1000 community organizations, volunteer groups, and schools in Maryland alone that are active in bay restoration projects are testimony to the high level of citizen commitment. Furthermore, Maryland's private Chesapeake Bay Trust, funded through gifts, state tax check-offs, and purchase of commemorative Chesapeake Bay license plates, has given over $6 million in grants to citizen groups between 1985 and 1994 (Chesapeake Bay Trust 1995).

Summary

The world of the conservation manager is challenging and complex. Many decisions on many fronts need to be made on a daily basis, with few opportunities for "cookbook" guidance and easy answers. However, we offer ten key planning activities that are common to most management scenarios, which should provide a basis for strong and informed management of conservation landscapes.

Conservation management proceeds at several spatial scales of interest. At the single-species or population level, there is a long history of management for sustainable yields, especially of game and commercial species. The results of such management are mixed at best, and no good examples of maximum sustained yield of a commercial animal species without eventual collapse exist. Single-species management is also the focus when using species as surrogates, or indicator species, for larger systems. Again, there are few examples of successful management on this basis.

The next level of scale, habitat management, shows promise for conservation if habitat manipulation for biodiversity, and not just for single species of interest, is pursued. Modification of existing habitat-scale practices, especially forest management and harvest techniques, to make them compatible with biodiversity conservation, would make important contributions toward conservation at the habitat level.

Management at the ecosystem and landscape levels offers the most promise for successful biodiversity conservation. Identification and management of critical species or processes, such as keystone species or nutrient cycling, hold the promise of great advances in conservation practice. Technological advances such as remote sensing, satellite imagery, and geographic information systems are helping to advance the utility of landscape-level management.

Conservation at these higher levels of organization and, usually, larger spatial scales requires that natural ecological boundaries be used to delineate the management area. The identification of strong functional linkages among biophysical ecosystems within the landscape provides an objective and scientifically defensible means for identifying natural boundaries.

These two chapters on management offer only an initial look at the complex, challenging, and sometimes frustrating world of the conservation manager. It should be clear that there are no set prescriptions, no clear and consistent rules by which conservation management actually proceeds. Every situation is unique, and each has its own complications and constraints. The best advice is to obtain as much relevant biological, sociological, economic, and political information as is available regarding a management situation, and act according to your best intuition on behalf of long-term perpetuation of biodiversity. Seven real-world examples of conservation management follow in the case studies in Chapter 13. There, you will recognize many of the problems and opportunities that were discussed in more abstract terms in these last two chapters. There, you will see conservation management in action.

Questions for Discussion

1. What are the various ways in which the multiple-use mandate for public lands creates conflicts with the protection of biodiversity? What can be done to resolve these conflicts?

2. Some people have criticized the use of geographic information systems and remote sensing as just a fancy way to impress the people who control funding. Can you think of important issues in conservation that can best be addressed using these techniques?

3. For a natural habitat in your area, discuss which species are likely to be keystone species and what is needed to protect their populations.

4. Do you think that legislation is needed to protect landscapes that provide important environmental services, such as flood control, recreational amenities, or protection of urban drinking water? What are some important environmental services in your area that are provided by natural environments?

5. For any habitat you wish to consider, describe how its biodiversity is influenced by natural and anthropogenic disturbances. How can these be approximated by some management method? Discuss this question in terms of type, scale, frequency, and intensity of disturbance.

6. Actions that are taken to protect vulnerable species and habitats may affect some people's livelihoods. Because the decision to protect biodiversity is an expression of the public's will, do you think that the government also has a social obligation to assist families and businesses that may be dislocated by a conservation plan?

7. Houses are scattered throughout the fire-prone foothills of southern California, making prescribed burns a problematic option either for maintaining the "fire climax" vegetation patterns or for preventing catastrophic wildfires. What alternatives to prescribed burns might be possible?

8. Herds of African goats are being used experimentally at some fire-prone sites to reduce vegetation and, hence, fuel loading. Do you see benefits and risks associated with this novel approach?

Suggestions for Further Reading

Agee, J. K. and D. R. Johnson (eds.). 1988. *Ecosystem Management for Parks and Wilderness*. University of Washington Press, Seattle. This collection of articles treats conservation management at the "system level" rather than at the level of individual populations. It is a good introduction to both the limitations of and the potential for managing ecosystems rather than individual species.

Clark, T. W., R. P. Reading, and A. L. Clarke (eds.). 1994. *Endangered Species Recovery: Finding the Lessons, Improving the Process*. Island Press, Washington, D.C. A critical assessment of endangered species programs with the intention of drawing lessons from past experience and improving future efforts. The chapters include case studies and various theoretical perspectives. An excellent introduction to the critical thinking and assessment that is much needed in conservation management.

Gunderson, L. H., C. S. Holling, and S. S. Light (eds.). 1995. *Barriers and Bridges to the Renewal of Ecosystems and Institutions*. Columbia University Press, New York. A deeply considered, problem-oriented approach to real management in a real world. This book offers a solid basis for new, system-level thinking, and provides excellent case studies that demonstrate the difficulties and opportunities for ecosystem management throughout the world.

Hansson, L., L. Fahrig, and G. Merriam (eds.). 1995. *Mosaic Landscapes and Ecological Processes*. Chapman and Hall, New York. The 12 chapters in this book provide an excellent overview of landscape ecology and will give you good insight into how patterns and processes at the landscape scale relate to ecosystem management.

Hunter, M. L. 1990. *Wildlife, Forests, and Forestry: Principles of Managing Forests for Biodiversity*. Prentice Hall, Englewood Cliffs, NJ. A good general treatment of modern forest management in the context of conservation of biodiversity.

Interagency Ecosystem Management Task Force. 1995. *The Ecosystem Approach: Healthy Ecosystems and Sustainable Economies*. Volume I: Overview. Volume II: Implementation Issues. Volume III: Case Studies. National Technical Information Service, Springfield, VA. An outstanding and clear presentation of the ecosystem approach by a task force of U.S. government agencies. The principles of ecosystem management are clearly laid out, as well as how the approach can be implemented through various institutions.

Turner, M. G. 1989. Landscape ecology: The effect of pattern on process. *Annu. Rev. Ecol. Syst.* 20:171–197. One of the best reviews of landscape ecology as it relates to functional linkages among ecosystems and the ecological significance of spatial patterns in the landscape. For anyone interested in how heterogeneity in the landscape might influence ecological processes, this remains the best review.

Western, D., R. M. Wright, and S. C. Strum (eds.). 1994. *Natural Connections: Perspectives in Community-Based Conservation.* Island Press, Washington, D.C. A good global view of many community-based conservation projects. Among the twelve detailed case studies, one of the best is on the CAMPFIRE program on Zimbabwe communal lands. The geographic coverage includes Nepal, India, Indonesia, Africa, Australia, Latin America, the United States, and the United Kingdom. General issues such as land tenure, cultural traditions, and economic dimensions are well covered. The final five chapters that make up the "Overview" section alone make the book worth reading.

13

Conservation Management Case Studies

The land is too various in its kinds, climates, conditions, declivities, aspects, and histories to conform to any generalized understanding or to prosper under generalized treatment.

Wendell Berry, 1977

In Chapters 11 and 12 we developed the important principles of conservation management and discussed how these principles and methodologies have been applied at scales ranging from individual populations to ecosystem management. In this chapter, we present seven case studies that provide in-depth descriptions of important management issues, and which weave in many of the themes and problems discussed in previous chapters.

Although we place a heavy emphasis on ecosystem management in this book, there is still a place for single-species management within the ecosystem perspective. Indeed, much of management has a species-level focus. Ecosystem management certainly does not preclude that focus and in fact can nicely incorporate single-species issues within its purview. Thus, the first three case studies focus on the management of endangered species, or groups of species, and their systems. Black-footed ferrets, sea turtles, and Spotted Owls are all high-profile organisms that have received a great deal of attention in scientific circles and various news media. You will see the various problems and challenges facing managers in these three very different scenarios, ranging from the need to understand the biology of secretive species, to the motivation of indigenous peoples to protect a traditional resource, to the tangled political and legal webs that managers are often caught in.

The next four studies all deal with management of larger conservation areas. One focuses on management of multiple systems, or conservation units, using the Costa Rican National System of Conservation Areas as a model; it illustrates the multitude of management challenges facing anyone wanting to go from the theoretical world of concerns for reserve size, heterogeneity, and context to the real world of reserves, with its issues of bureaucracy, fund-raising, and public acceptance and use. Next, one of the major examples of ecosystem management, the Florida Everglades, is addressed. Its history of hydrologic change and human use is now being melded with attempts to restore natural processes while maintaining a human presence in the system.

The human presence is even more evident in the next study, of Doñana National Park in Spain. This critically important region has been occupied and altered by humans for many centuries, and is under assault from all sides as agriculture and society expand and demand ever more resources from the region. Finally, we take a global management perspective with a look at conservation of the world's 15 crane species. These efforts encompass every imaginable aspect of conservation, from genetic and captive breeding concerns, to landscape conversion, to Cold War politics, to the social and biological ravages of war.

You will probably find that these studies are not very tidy. Management in the real world is usually a far cry from the neat, clear, and logical layout of topics in textbooks. Messy issues such as lack of funding, conflicts among individuals or groups with different value systems, impacts on people's livelihoods, historical contingencies, and lack of cooperation or understanding by political leaders inflict themselves on the best-laid plans of conservation managers. The answer is to be flexible and adaptive, and to try to understand each management scenario as completely as possible, while keeping the overall goals of the program in mind.

CASE STUDY 1

Management of an Endangered Species: The Black-Footed Ferret

Dean E. Biggins, Biological Resources Division, U.S. Geological Survey, Brian J. Miller, Universidad Nacional Autónoma de México, Tim W. Clark, Yale School of Forestry, and Richard P. Reading, Northern Rockies Conservation Cooperative

The black-footed ferret program is the oldest recovery program for an endangered species in the United States, an example of the single-species management strategy that remains a major approach to declining biodiversity. Among the management lessons illustrated are the need to conserve natural habitat to receive captive-bred individuals, the importance of landowner cooperation, the need for flexibility and innovation in dealing with contingencies such as unexpected disease outbreaks, and especially the many negative social influences on endangered species recovery, including agency momentum and political fear, which prevent rapid institutional learning and adaptive management.

Figure 13.1 The black-footed ferret (*Mustela nigripes*) is highly endangered, due largely to habitat loss and intentional extermination of its primary prey, various prairie dog species. (Photograph by D. E. Biggins, U.S. Fish and Wildlife Service).

Brief Description of the Problem

North America's black-footed ferret (*Mustela nigripes*, Figure 13.1) is a 600–1400 g mustelid (weasel family) whose closest relatives are the European (*M. putorius*) and Siberian (*M. eversmanni*) polecats. The recent historical range of the black-footed ferret coincided with the ranges of the black-tailed (*Cynomys ludovicianus*), Gunnison's (*C. gunnisoni*) and white-tailed (*C. leucurus*) prairie dogs, which collectively occupied about 100 million acres of intermountain and prairie grasslands. Despite this large range, ferrets declined precipitously over the 20th century; they were rare by the 1960s (Henderson et al. 1969), listed as endangered under the Endangered Species Act of 1973, and unlocatable by the time the U.S. Fish and Wildlife Service (FWS) approved the first recovery plan in 1978.

Black-footed ferrets were rediscovered near Meeteetse, Wyoming, in 1981 (Schroeder and Martin 1982). During the next several years, field research enhanced understanding of the behaviors and ecology of the ferrets (Biggins et al. 1986; Clark 1989), building on a base of studies conducted in South Dakota in 1964–1974. By May 1985, a plan was formulated to begin captive propagation of the ferrets, starting with six animals to be taken from Meeteetse in late summer 1985. However, in July of 1985, a severe decline in prairie dogs was noticed, accompanied by a decline in ferrets; plague (*Yersinia pestis*) was discovered in the prairie dogs, stimulating a massive campaign to halt its spread. The operation concentrated on killing fleas, the plague vector, by dusting 80,000 burrows with the insecticide carbaryl.

In October 1985 six ferrets were captured to begin the breeding program, but all died from canine distemper when two of them carried the disease from the field into the holding facility, exposing the other four. Six additional ferrets subsequently were captured to start the captive population. The low point for the ferrets was reached in the winter of 1985–1986, with four known survivors at Meeteetse, plus the six captives. There were no kits born in the captive population in 1986, but two litters were produced at Meeteetse. A decision was made to take the few remaining ferrets from Meeteetse, bringing the captive population to 18 by early 1987, and placing the future of the species in the hands of the captive breeding program.

After a tenuous start, the captive population expanded and has been maintained at 200–300 adults. Coordination of captive propagation is the responsibility of the Species Survival Plan working committee (under the auspices of the American Zoo and Aquarium Association), which includes participants from each ferret propagation facility. The primary objective of the SSP is to produce kits for reintroduction as efficiently as possible, and to serve as the ultimate hedge against extinction. Allocation of surplus ferrets for reintroduction is the responsibility of the FWS.

By 1991, sufficient ferret kits were being produced to start reintroduction. The Meeteetse prairie dogs continued to decline, eliminating reintroduction possibilities there. An alternative site near Medicine Bow, Wyoming, received 228 ferrets in 1991–1994, and in 1994–1995, an additional 90 ferrets were released in South Dakota and 78 in Montana. Each summer following a release, a few litters of wild-born ferrets have been found.

Pages of supporting detail could have been inserted between each of the sentences of the brief chronicle above (see Clark 1988; Miller et al. 1996, for additional discussion), but we have chosen to devote the remainder of this treatise to the biological and social challenges faced by the ferret program and the lessons learned that could be applied to future conservation programs. The primary value of recounting the history of the ferret program is not in presenting an orderly series of events, but in analyzing the challenges and how well the recovery process worked when trying to meet them.

Biological Challenges

Causes of Decline. A critical component of any recovery program is identifying the cause of decline. A major problem for black-footed ferrets was the destruction of prairie dogs, which constitute about 90% of the ferrets' diet and dig the burrows that serve as shelter for the ferrets. From 1900 to 1960, prairie dogs were reduced to about 2% of their former geographic range (Marsh 1984), largely due to agricultural development and extensive poisoning campaigns in the Great Plains, where prairie dogs are considered pests (Figure 13.2). Sylvatic plague, probably introduced to North America in about 1900 (Eskey and Haas 1940), also caused massive die-offs of prairie dogs (Barnes 1982).

(A)

(B)

Figure 13.2 (A) The black-tailed prairie dog (*Cynomys ludovicianus*) is one of the species critical to ferret survival, but has been actively exterminated by ranching and farming interests. (B) Note the symbolic use of prairie dogs as "pests" on the sign. (Photographs by D. E. Biggins, U.S. Fish and Wildlife Service).

The prairie dog ecosystem supports many species, and one of the most tightly linked is the black-footed ferret. Fragmentation of ferret habitat (prairie dog colonies) eliminated or reduced ferret populations, making remaining populations more susceptible to extinction by disease, genetic problems (Chapter 6), demographic events (Chapter 7), or natural catastrophes. Sources of immigration were undoubtedly destroyed, and recolonization and genetic exchange were hampered (Chapter 9). Under these circumstances, risk of extinction may rise more rapidly than habitat destruction, and reduction of one species may produce secondary extinctions (Wilcox and Murphy 1985).

In addition to habitat loss (e.g., prairie dog decline), the black-footed ferret is very sensitive to canine distemper. In the 1970s, some black-footed ferrets died after vaccination with a modified live virus safely used to immunize other ferret species (Carpenter et al. 1976). Erickson's (1973) prediction that "the hazards of exposure of the highly sensitive black-footed ferret to canine distemper virus may be substantial" was fulfilled by the apparent involvement of that disease in the loss of ferrets at Meeteetse (Forrest et al. 1988). More recently, black-footed ferrets living in outdoor pens have died from plague infections, showing unexpectedly high sensitivity to the disease that decimates their prairie dog prey (many other carnivores are relatively resistant to plague). Because plague was widespread at Meeteetse in 1985, canine distemper should no longer be held solely responsible for the demise of the Meeteetse ferrets.

In summary, the ferrets were set up by a deterministic event (habitat destruction) and were probably knocked out by one or more stochastic factors (Biggins and Schroeder 1988; see "Secondary Effects and Synergistic Interactions" in Chapter 5). The twin challenges of protecting habitat and avoiding diseases are daunting. A habitat program has been proposed that involves protected areas, public education, legal recognition of the prairie dogs' delicate status, and conversion of the federal subsidy for poisoning prairie dogs into a positive incentive for ranchers who manage their land in the interest of wildlife and livestock (Miller et al. 1994a). At present, researchers at the Wyoming State Veterinary Laboratory are working on a distemper vaccine to protect both captive and released animals, and plague research has begun to address several questions.

Captive Breeding. Biological challenges in the captive breeding program include increasing propagation efficiency, rearing kits so as to maximize survival behaviors after release, protection from disease, genetic management, and proper husbandry (e.g., diet, photoperiod, stress).

An unresolved dilemma has arisen concerning maximizing production and genetic management. The males that breed best are most likely to become overrepresented genetically. Balancing the genetic influence requires reducing their use as breeders, but that is likely to reduce kit production. Also, the black-footed ferret program has not completed a genetic analysis of founders, resulting in a studbook with a weak foundation (Miller et al. 1996).

In captivity, about two-thirds of the prime females produce kits. Although this rate is not radically different from that in other captive mustelids (e.g., mink, *M. vison*), it seems lower than the rate for the free-ranging population at Meeteetse, suggesting an opportunity for improvement. High neonatal mortality is one factor decreasing production. Its causes could include crowding of ferrets, excessive human disturbance, or inbreeding. A rigorous research agenda should address these and other captive propagation questions. This research may involve risk to individual animals and was discouraged when ferret numbers were low, but a different philosophy should prevail now that imminent extinction is not a threat.

Captive breeding was necessary for the ferrets, was successful in preventing their extinction, and is now producing animals for reintroduction.

However, it is not a panacea for every species, and should be employed with caution. It is expensive, risky, and must be closely tied to reintroduction needs.

Reintroduction. To increase chances of the ferrets' survival after release, we tested reintroduction techniques with the closely related Siberian ferret (*M. eversmanni*; Figure 13.3) in 1989 and 1990 (Biggins et al. 1990, 1991; Miller et al. 1990a,b, 1993), and recommended a field test on black-footed ferrets that were to be released in 1991 (USFWS, 1990). Pre-release conditioning was not used in 1991, but it was attempted with 18 animals released in Wyoming in 1992. In that year, ferrets reared in outdoor pens survived significantly better than cage-raised counterparts and demonstrated different behaviors (Biggins et al. 1993; Vargas 1994). A replicate test, postponed until 1994, produced similar results in Montana. Predation, primarily by coyotes (*Canis latrans*), caused 88% of the known deaths of radio-tagged ferrets in Wyoming, and 100% of the deaths in Montana. In 1995, ferret deaths were substantially reduced in Montana when coyotes were aerially hunted and electric fencing was used to exclude them from the reintroduction sites. Coyotes have also been killed in Wyoming, but not in South Dakota. In addition, several release strategies (holding animals in various types of cages for acclimation, varying degrees of provisioning) have been used over different years and sites. Each of the coyote management and ferret release methods has its proponents, but lack of testing with sound experimental designs has left us with ambiguous data that fuel continued debate. Debates and delays notwithstanding, improved reintroduction efficiency is within reach.

Additional evidence of diseases, however, is disconcerting. Canine distemper is ubiquitous in other carnivores sampled at all reintroduction sites; plague is present at reintroduction sites in all states except South Dakota; and reintroduced ferrets in Shirley Basin, Wyoming, declined abruptly in 1994 as plague increased dramatically (Dold 1995). Also, the ultimate effect of inbreeding remains to be seen. Our failure to understand fully the potentially interactive causes of the ferrets' decline, ineffectiveness at reestablishing habitat (or even halting losses), and the looming question regarding diseases serve to emphasize the uncertain future of operational reintroductions. This is one of several reasons reintroductions of ferrets should be considered experimental for some time to come, and be designed to maximize the chance of detecting factors that may limit future recovery.

There are several interrelated questions for which there will be no easy answers, even if we obtain biologically relevant data to provide guidance. For example, is it reasonable to extend the Noah's Ark model (Hutchins and Conway 1995) for zoo production and release of animals to a scenario of "repeated floods"—that is, if viable, self-sustaining black-footed ferret populations seem unachievable due to recurring diseases or lack of habitat, should we artificially maintain nonviable populations through periodic restocking? What is the smallest population worth sustaining, and what level of perpetual restocking is justifiable?

(A)

(B)

(C)

Figure 13.3 Black-footed ferrets are so rare that technologies and techniques are often worked out on "surrogate" species, such as these Siberian polecats (*Mustela eversmanni*). Young polecats reared and conditioned under varying procedures were tested using predator models such as (A) stuffed owls and (B) a "robo-badger," a remote-controlled, stuffed and motorized badger, and their behaviors and survival were finally compared during trial releases (C). (Photographs by D. E. Biggins, U.S. Fish and Wildlife Service).

Social Challenges

The social challenges of black-footed ferret recovery are equally daunting. Indeed, the attitudes and values people hold toward wildlife are at the root of the ferret decline. A Montana attitudinal study suggested that the recovery program must address the antagonism of ranchers, develop support among undecided or uninformed individuals, and simultaneously maintain the support of conservationists (Reading and Kellert, 1993). Cutlip and Center (1964) suggested pressure, purchase, and persuasion to change attitudes. Persuasion, attempted mostly by overburdened wildlife officials rather than by trained public relations experts, was the only technique used in Montana. The preliminary effort at education was unsuccessful at garnering local support and alienated some conservationists (Reading 1993), but attitudes may have improved somewhat after local residents were able to personally view ferret reintroduction efforts. The difficult task of education becomes monumental with some federal, state, and local government programs continuing to sponsor prairie dog poisoning, reinforcing the misconception that these species have little value (Miller et al. 1996). Ironically, programs to control coyote populations are generally well-received by ranchers. In this case, coyote control would also enhance the ferret recovery program.

The perceptions of recovery program participants also vary. Most programs involve multiple groups, and each has different definitions of the problem, goals, methods of operation, values, perspectives, and ideologies. Although diverse views can strengthen a program by providing multiple approaches, they also can instigate conflict and power struggles that deflect attention from recovery. Clark and Harvey (1988) and Miller et al. (1996) discuss power struggles in the ferret program and their negative effects. Each participating agency strives to appease its primary constituents, but constituencies differ. Should local groups, or states, or the country's population as a whole control the ferrets' destiny (in part, a recurring question of interpreting the U.S. Constitution)? The majority of ranchers at reintroduction sites do not favor prairie dogs or ferrets. State fish and wildlife agencies are in the difficult position of being primarily funded by sportsmen who often use private ranches, at times the same ranches and leased lands that contain potential ferret habitat. Access to the lands may depend on a smooth relationship between the wildlife agency and the landowners. The federal agencies involved, mostly funded through general tax funds, try to represent everyone, an impossible task.

In making crucial decisions, the pace has seemed sluggish at times, perhaps in part due to fear of failure and a mistaken notion that failure due to "natural causes" (no action) is better than failure due to a bad choice. Within public agencies, risk aversion is understandable because agencies are castigated from every conceivable angle. The ferret program is replete with examples, including criticism from: (1) the Sierra Club Legal Defense Fund, which challenged the nonessential experimental designation of the release sites for providing too little protection for the ferrets; (2) the Wyoming Farm Bureau, which complained that the ferret had too much protection and the ranchers too little; and (3) the American Humane Society, which was upset over the release of adult ferrets rather than kits.

Use of Science and Program Goals. In the early management of the Meeteetse program, everyone agreed with the following goals: (1) learn as much as possible about the biology of this little-understood animal; (2) do everything possible to conserve the only known population at Meeteetse; and (3) plan for species recovery. Each of these goals, nevertheless, conflicted in some way with the others. Goal 2 was adopted as the first priority objective at Meeteetse during the early 1980s. To some degree, the research implied by goal 1 and the removal of animals for translocation and/or captive breeding implied by goal 3 are inconsistent with the complete protection implied by goal 2. The situation was further confused by the realization that the direct manipulations required for some research could place some part of the population at risk, but results from that research could advance recovery of the species.

During early reintroductions, the primary objective was to achieve some predetermined survival rate for a specified period (often 20% for 30 days); as a result, the intensity of monitoring designed to maximize learning from early reintroductions was limited. Again, anything that *might* have increased the impact on the released animals was not tolerated, including some research designs and monitoring methods.

The general tendency in these examples is for short-term, geographically localized goals to take precedence over longer-term species recovery goals. Intensive study and monitoring can have localized benefits (e.g., radiotelemetry sometimes enabled rescue efforts on animals that otherwise would have perished), but its focus is to provide information that will help future efforts, often at another site or in another state. The conflict has been misstated as research versus operational ferret recovery. Everyone in the program is working toward the goal of recovery, but perceptions differ on which process will achieve recovery quickest. Demographic goals are appropriate for ferret recovery, especially in long-term considerations (e.g., the recovery plan), but learning-focused goals should not always be subordinate to them (Clark 1996).

An issue related to goal setting is interpreting success and failure. With the present emphasis on numbers of ferrets conserved or established, "success" can occur with little learning, which increases the chance for a long-term, large-scale failure. Conversely, a "failure" could teach us something so dramatic that it becomes far more valuable than localized "successes" such as meeting short-term survival goals. The definition of success should be refined (aided by carefully prioritized goals) so that it does not stifle risk taking, innovative thinking, and experimentation. A high-risk experiment may be warranted if the potential reward is great enough. The utility of success/failure characterizations is related mostly to public relations (your supporters may turn into detractors with too many "failures" and too few "successes") and legal issues (a demographic "success" is prescribed for down-listing the ferret from endangered to threatened).

The original recovery plan implied the highest priority for learning during early reintroductions of ferrets; we argue that learning was given a low priority from the beginning. The best solution at this point in the program may be to designate a reintroduction site as truly experimental (all sites thus far have a legal "experimental" designation related to the Endangered Species Act). At this site, novel approaches, experimental design, and intensive monitoring would be emphasized, but the goal of population establishment would not be ignored. Likewise, other sites should not abandon experimentation and monitoring. Population establishment and experimental goals are not mutually exclusive.

Funding. Funding inconsistencies continue to be a major impediment to the captive breeding program. Six zoos are producing approximately half the surplus ferrets under their own funding. The other half are produced at a facility in Wyoming, supported over the years by federal funds (mostly from Endangered Species allocations) and money from the Wyoming Game and Fish Department. The program was in jeopardy in 1995 with greatly diminished state and federal funding. Private funding (PIC Technologies) rescued the effort temporarily, but uncertainty still exists. Numbers of captive ferrets cannot fluctuate with available money, so greater stability is needed.

Planning and Implementation. This critical part of organization determines how well skills, funds, resources, organizations, and people are coordinated to meet the challenges of recovery. Common problems of weak program organization include slow decision making, decision making without the benefit of outside expertise, decision making that consolidates control at the expense of scientific and management priorities, rewarding of organizational loyalty instead of creativity, faulty information flow (or even blockage), failure to develop objectives that can be used to accurately evaluate program success, deviation from plans during implementation, and a rigid bureaucratic hierarchy that impedes effective action. Plans can be altered substantially during implementation by incompetent execution, by deliberate delay by people who oppose the plan, or by yielding to local political pressure. The ferret program has been criticized for all of these (Miller et al. 1996; Clark, in press).

One way of avoiding such problems (or at least decreasing their intensity) is the formation of high-performance recovery teams to make recommendations (Clark et al. 1989; Clark and Cragun 1994). A recovery plan is essential, but should not replace a team (Miller et al. 1994b). Plans can outline goals, but only teams, communicating freely and efficiently, can respond to rapidly changing events. Information flow within and between teams and working groups improved substantially when the FWS began coordinating monthly conference calls. Representatives of teams should be selected for their expertise and not simply to represent an agency. It makes no more sense for a team of upper-level agency managers to issue judgment on highly technical research plans than it does for a group of specialized scientists to try to generate and coordinate funding for the program. In addition, when advisors come from a high level of any organization, their recommendations may reflect politics more than biology (Miller et al. 1996). Because even good plans and devoted teams can outlive their usefulness in a dynamic venture, there should be a periodic outside review of the entire program to determine how well the process is working and to avoid letting institutional momentum determine its direction. The American Zoo Association recently began such a review of the black-footed ferret program at the request of FWS.

How far should we go to save the black-footed ferret? It is the only North American ferret; there is nothing else much like it on this continent, and it occupies a unique niche in a declining biotic assemblage, the prairie dog ecosystem. Saving this "flagship" species will ensure a place for many of its associates. Eliminating it will, in the words of Rolston (Essay 2A), "shut down a story of many millennia, and leave no future possibilities." The challenges we have described in saving the ferret are not trivial, but we fervently hope that the task can be accomplished.

CASE STUDY 2

Nhaltjan Nguli Miwatj Yolngu Djaka Miyapunuwu: Sea Turtle Conservation and the Yolngu People of North East Arnhem Land, Australia

Rod Kennett, The Australian National University, and Djalalingba Yunupingu, Djawa Yunupingu, Botha Wunungmurra, Nanikiya Munungurritj, and Raymattja Marika, Dhimurru Land Management Aboriginal Corporation

This study, although it also focuses on single-species conservation (six species are involved), contrasts strongly with the ferret study because the project it examines is community-based and incorporates indigenous knowledge. The Aboriginal people of north east Arnhem Land, Australia, have harvested sea turtles and their eggs for millennia. Recent population declines as a result of influences from Western societies necessitate new approaches to turtle management that combine modern scientific knowledge with ancient, indigenous insights.

Sea turtles have occupied the world's oceans for some 100 million years. During their long evolutionary history they have witnessed dramatic upheavals and rearrangements of the continents and oceans, and major shifts in the earth's climate. These global events undoubtedly had profound effects on sea turtles—on their nesting and feeding grounds and their migration routes—and we know from the fossil record that not all sea turtle species survived. Despite their long tenure on earth, however, the last few hundred years has seen a dramatic decline in sea turtle numbers, and the last seven extant species of sea turtles are in imminent danger of extinction. The destruction of foraging and nesting habitats, the intentional and unintentional slaughter of turtles in fisheries, and the slow poisoning of the world's oceans with pollutants have taken their toll. Most populations are declining, and many are extinct.

People have exploited sea turtles for thousands of years, and it is likely that most of the subsistence turtle fisheries around the world have been managed sustainably for much of that time. But human populations have exploded, and in many cases, especially in the Indo-Pacific region, the exploitation of sea turtles far exceeds that of even a few hundred years ago. It is within this new context of declining sea turtle populations that indigenous turtle fishers and managers, including the Yolngu people of northern Australia, have begun to reevaluate the ways in which they "look after" their turtles.

The Yolngu live in north east Arnhem Land in the Northern Territory of Australia (Figure 13.4). Arnhem Land is a vast area of tropical wet-dry Australia—some 97,000 km^2 of mainland and 6,000 km^2 of offshore islands—that is owned and managed by Aboriginal people. Unlike much of the rest of Australia, it remains largely unmodified by European settlement and is sparsely populated. It is home to a suite of unique flora and fauna and has enormous conservation significance.

Non-Aboriginal scientists believe that Aboriginal people have occupied northern Australia for somewhere between 40,000 and 100,000 years. According to the Yolngu, they have occupied the land since the creation beings first formed the landscape and bestowed law and knowledge on the ancestors of today's traditional owners. Regardless of whose interpretation of the past is correct, Aboriginal people have been the caretakers of Australia for a long time, and possess a rich culture of law, ceremony, oral history, and detailed traditional ecological knowledge.

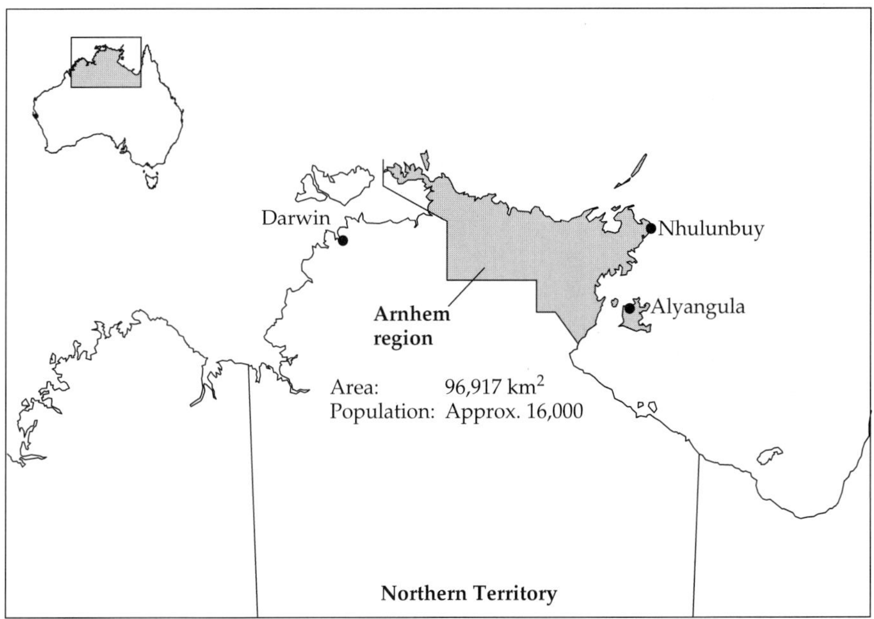

Figure 13.4 The north east Arnhem Land region of Australia, where Aboriginal peoples are working to ensure the continued persistence of sea turtles. (Courtesy of the Dhimurru Land Management Aboriginal Corporation.)

This close bond between people and country remains especially strong for the Yolngu. Throughout much of Australia, Aboriginal people were dispossessed of their land and marine estates as British colonization spread. Geographic isolation, the harsh tropical climate of northern Australia, and the difficulties encountered in trying to apply European agricultural systems combined to spare the Yolngu from the degree of colonial impact that was felt in southern areas of the continent. Today, the Yolngu maintain a lifestyle that accepts and even embraces much of non-Aboriginal (or balanda) culture, but in which Yolngu cultural practice remains paramount. Many live in remote coastal settlements where hunting and gathering native foods, including sea turtles and their eggs, remains an important part of life.

The Yolngu's strong sense of identity and culture, and determination to manage their own affairs, is reflected in the formation of the Dhimurru Land Management Aboriginal Corporation. Dhimurru was originally established to manage recreation areas created around the township of Nhulunbuy for the predominantly balanda workforce of a large, open-cut bauxite mine. More recently it has expanded its role to include the facilitation of land and resource management by traditional owners of the region.

Dhimurru employs five Yolngu rangers and two non-Aboriginal administrative staff. The Corporation works closely with rangers from the government conservation agency called the Parks and Wildlife Commission of the Northern Territory (PWCNT). Dhimurru embraces a two-way approach to conservation activities, emphasizing the value of traditional ecological knowledge and practice while recognizing that non-Aboriginal science can inform traditional owners in developing contemporary resource management strategies. The sea turtle, or *miyapunu*, project is regarded as a flagship project, combining traditional knowledge and practice with modern biological knowledge and techniques.

Aims

The miyapunu project commenced in early 1995 in response to concerns by senior Yolngu about apparent declines in sea turtle numbers. One of the possible causes of the decline is overharvesting (Figure 13.5). As Djalalingba Yunupingu, Senior Cultural Ranger, explains, "In the Northern Territory, where we live, I think we catch too many turtles. We dig up too many turtle nests and we don't let them hatch and let the baby turtles go back to the sea and grow and become adult turtles." However, other factors, such as mortality as bycatch in Australian fisheries, increasing subsistence and commercial harvests in the Indo-Pacific region, and habitat loss in other parts of the turtles' range, are also affecting turtle populations in north east Arnhem Land.

Figure 13.5 A nesting loggerhead turtle (*Caretta caretta*). A female can lay more than 100 eggs in a single nest, which she then covers and leaves alone. Such nests are highly susceptible to human and animal predation. (Photograph by John Domant; courtesy of the Center for Marine Conservation.)

The major aims of the project are to quantify the harvest of eggs and turtles by Yolngu; to identify and quantify other regional factors, such as mortality resulting from commercial fishing and recreational activities, that affect local populations; and to improve our basic knowledge of the distribution and abundance of sea turtles in the region. Gaining the active participation and support of Yolngu is vital to the project, and it is hoped that the project will foster an awareness and appreciation of traditional ecological knowledge among "mainstream" resource scientists and managers. The ultimate goal is to enable Yolngu to make informed decisions on contemporary management guidelines and thereby ensure a sustainable subsistence harvest of sea turtles.

Significance

Data from the project on sea turtle distribution and abundance will substantially contribute to sea turtle conservation within the Indo-Pacific region. Australian sea turtle populations are believed to be among the healthiest in the world, but there are worrisome signs. For example, loggerhead turtles, a species known to migrate between the Arnhem Land coast and southern Queensland, have declined by 85% over the last 15 years (Limpus and Reimer 1994). Data from tagging programs and genetic studies in Queensland and Western Australia show that many of our Australian turtles spend at least part of their lives in Papua New Guinea or Southeast Asia, where they are killed in commercial and subsistence harvests (Limpus and Miller 1993). The levels of harvest in Indonesia—30,000 green turtles per year in Bali alone—are unlikely to be sustainable and so may be causing declines in northern Australian populations (Limpus 1993). At present, we lack the data needed to make robust estimates of sea turtle numbers in the Northern Territory and hence to determine the extent of any declines.

From a global perspective, the miyapunu project has enormous significance. Six of the seven sea turtle species in the world occur in north east Arnhem Land, and five of these are known to nest in the region. All are regarded as endangered or vulnerable by national and international conservation agencies (although the flatback is not officially listed). All are of enormous cultural significance to Yolngu, who know them as Dhalwaptu (green turtle), Garriwa (flatback turtle), Garun (loggerhead turtle), Guwarrtji (hawksbill turtle), Muduthu (olive ridley turtle), and Wurrumbili (leatherback turtle).

Both the Yolngu and the turtles live in a region that is currently free of many of the development pressures threatening sea turtle habitats elsewhere in the world, and where major habitat modification has not occurred. However, the recent stranding on the Arnhem Land coast of more than 55 turtles in fishing nets discarded in international waters shows that other threatening processes are occurring. Inevitably, coastal developments and the potential threats they present to sea turtles will eventually arrive on the Arnhem Land coast. The skills and knowledge that Yolngu learn through the miyapunu project will assist them in protecting their sea turtle resources while allowing them to benefit from these developments.

Community Involvement

The miyapunu project represents a remarkable cooperative effort involving federal and state governments and nongovernmental agencies (Dhimurru, the PWCNT, The Australian National University, and the Australian Nature Conservation Agency). However, it is the response of the Yolngu who live on the 400 km of coastline and offshore islands within the Dhimurru management area that will determine its success. Botha Wunungmurra, Dhimurru ranger, confirms the significance of the project to the Yolngu. "Yes, it is an important job for us all. Not only for Dhimurru or the Dhimurru staff, or the Dhimurru workers. It involves all the outstations, or all the interested persons who want to do this miyapunu research with us. But we already know our culture, our tradition, how we catch a turtle. We know where its feeding grounds are or where it's coming from or how the tide is taking the turtles. All Yolngu know these things about the turtle, and what the turtles' names are. So we can save all this information and our culture for the next generation."

Activities

Regular beach surveys are providing data on nesting activity and egg harvest (Figure 13.6). In a 15 km section of beach that is regularly visited by Yolngu, egg collection is as high as 90% of all nests. Concern over this level of harvesting has prompted Dhimurru to close off vehicle access to a 5 km section of beach. Dhimurru rangers are already reporting larger numbers of emerging

Figure 13.6 Dhimurru ranger Botha Wunungmurra and biologist Rod Kennett work together to measure eggs from a Guwarrtji, or hawksbill turtle (*Eretmochelys imbricata*), nest. Such data are part of the regular surveys now being conducted by the miyapunu project. (Photograph courtesy of R. Kennett.)

hatchlings. Other management strategies are being developed to minimize the effects of recreational vehicle activity on the beaches that remain open to access.

A monitoring program is being tested in schools to collect data on the harvest of turtles and eggs. Schoolchildren ask elders to help them to fill in a data sheet when a turtle is caught or eggs are collected (Figure 13.7). Hunters are also asked to return turtle heads to Dhimurru so that a tissue sample can be taken for population genetics studies. Dhimurru ranger Djawa Yunupingu outlines the program: "Whenever we dig up a turtle nest we count up the eggs and record them on an information sheet that we always carry with us and put an "X" on the location where we collected the eggs. It could be Nanydjaka or Djulpanyurra or at Yelangbara, and we write down the names of the Yolngu who collected the eggs, what sort of turtles laid the eggs, whether it was an olive ridley, flatback, or green turtle, or whatever. We have already sent some miyapunu kits and information sheets to all the homeland centres that are along the coast about collecting turtle eggs or catching a turtle, who caught the turtle, what sex it was, male or female, was the turtle harpooned or was it caught on the beach while nesting."

Yolngu hunters also participate by returning tags from hunted turtles, and tagged turtles from Western Australia and Queensland are regularly caught. Recently Yolngu hunters captured a turtle that was tagged in North Western Australia by a research team that included local Aboriginal people, the Bardi. As a result, Yolngu and Bardi are exchanging information about turtles, and Dhimurru rangers plan to visit the Bardi to explain the miyapunu project.

Now that Yolngu are tagging turtles themselves, it is felt that the rate of tag return will increase. Djawa Yunupingu describes the excitement of tagging the first turtle: "We saw a Garriwa (flatback turtle) come up the beach . . . when it had finished laying its eggs, covered the eggs, and was making its way back to the sea, it was then that we flipped it over on its back and tagged both its front flippers. It was the first turtle to be tagged by Dhimurru and all of us are very proud of it too."

I.D NUMBER ______________

DHIMURRU - CCNT MARINE TURTLE RESEARCH PROJECT

INFORMATION SHEET - MIYAPUNU

COMMUNITY [ ]

WHO CAUGHT THE TURTLE? [ ]

WHEN WAS THE TURTLE CAUGHT?

CIRCLE THE MONTH

JANUARY FEBRUARY MARCH APRIL MAY JUNE JULY
AUGUST SEPTEMBER OCTOBER NOVEMBER DECEMBER

HOW WAS THE TURTLE CAUGHT? [ ]

IS THE TURTLE MALE OR FEMALE?

CIRCLE ONE

DARRAMU MIYALK YUTA YAKA MARNGI

HOW BIG IS THE TURTLE?

MEASURE THE SHELL

COLLECT THE TURTLE HEAD

TAKE THE PLASTIC TAPE OFF THIS SHEET AND TIE IT TO THE TURTLE HEAD. PUT IT IN THE PLASTIC BAG.

GIVE THE TURTLE HEAD AND INFORMATION SHEET TO LAYNHA AIR

Figure 13.7 A data sheet used in the miyapunu project. This easily completed sheet provides critical information on sea turtle harvest practices and population characteristics. (Courtesy of the Dhimurru Land Management Aboriginal Corporation.)

An ongoing program of community visits and oral interviews with hunters to record traditional knowledge of sea turtles is under way. As part of this program, a community workshop was held at Dhanaya on Port Bradshaw in November 1995. Yolngu elders and hunters from the nearby communities spent two days "talking miyapunu" with Dhimurru rangers and balanda scientists. The workshop yielded significant data on sea turtle distribution and generated a great deal of community interest and pride in the project.

After learning that tagged loggerhead turtles had traveled from Queensland to the Northern Territory, Dhimurru rangers visited the Mon Repos Sea Turtle Research Centre in Queensland. At the centre, they participated in the research on loggerheads and green turtles and solved the ancient mystery of "where does Garun nest?" Djalalingba Yunupingu explains, "Garun [loggerhead] do not come up on our beaches to nest. . . . They come up to nest and lay eggs in Bundaberg, Queensland, or in Western Australia. . . .The reason why I came here was to see a Garun, because back home we wondered where did Garun lay its eggs and you people thought that Garun lays its eggs in the water. Nothing, it just travels around the feeding grounds and travels up here to lay its eggs and the eggs hatch here." Garun also told the Yolngu another important story—that to care for turtles in their waters, Yolngu must work with people in the other places where their turtles travel.

Dhimurru has produced an informational video on the miyapunu project (Figure 13.8), and plans to distribute it to other Aboriginal communities and

Figure 13.8 Filming of an information video for the miyapunu project. Yolngu hunters demonstrate how to find Guwarrtji mapu (hawksbill eggs). (Photograph courtesy of R. Kennett.)

perhaps to indigenous turtle managers elsewhere in the world. The Yolngu hope that the video will help them to establish links with other indigenous managers of turtles. Such links will be welcomed by the IUCN marine turtle specialist group, who identify the participation of indigenous people as one of the key issues in sea turtle conservation and management (IUCN 1995). This is especially true in the Northern Territory, where, without the active involvement and support of Aboriginal people, sea turtle conservation efforts will fail.

Yolngu see the miyapunu project as a continuation of their long custodianship of Australia and its animals, and know that its importance extends beyond their lifetimes and beyond their region. Nanikiya Munungurritj (senior ranger) and Raymattja Marika (educator) explain,

> What we would like to do now is create an awareness and understanding of the turtle and how we can help maintain and preserve and respect it through our knowledge and beliefs, through our clan stories and songs, so that in the future Yolngu and Balanda generations throughout the world can be educated about the life of a turtle in its environment. The turtle takes a long time to become a full-grown creature and lay its eggs. All these things we have to take into consideration so that we don't wipe out the family of turtles through careless fishing by fishing trawlers or constantly hunting them. So that there is some left for our children and our great grandchildren.

CASE STUDY 3

Management of the Spotted Owl: The Interaction of Science, Policy, Politics, and Litigation

Barry R. Noon, U.S. Forest Service,
and Dennis D. Murphy, Stanford University

Knowledge of scientific methods is not always enough in conservation management. Political pressures, legal proceedings, and policy decisions often

dictate success or failure in a management scheme. The Spotted Owl epitomizes the high-visibility struggle that sometimes ensues when protective legislation restricts use of a resource. Success or failure in management often is determined by skills other than ecological knowledge.

The requisite skills for effective conservation planning, reserve design, or species management entail more than knowledge of the theoretical and applied principles of population, community, or ecosystem ecology. These principles, plus an understanding of relevant species' ecologies, life histories, and habitat relationships, are essential components of any effective conservation strategy, but by themselves are insufficient to conserve most of the species about which we are concerned.

The process of developing a scientifically sound conservation strategy defensible to political attacks, likely to be adopted by society, and subsequently implemented, is often the most difficult and least discussed aspect of conservation biology. Many strategies, even those built on a firm foundation of defensible science, will fail if the biologists involved are inept at defending their plan against inevitable criticisms, or are unable to convince decision makers of the true costs to society of failing to implement the conservation actions.

Drawing on our experiences in conservation planning for both the Northern (*Strix occidentalis caurina*) and the California (*S. o. occidentalis*) Spotted Owls, our goals in this case study are to (1) briefly review the logic and methods used to produce scientifically credible plans; (2) focus on the tactics necessary to make a conservation plan resilient to attack; (3) contrast the Northern and California Spotted Owl plans; (4) discuss ways to explicitly address scientific uncertainty and incomplete information; and (5) provide suggestions to decrease the adversarial nature of conservation planning, and increase the influence of scientists and managers in the formulation of natural resource policy.

The Northern Spotted Owl

Perhaps more than any threatened or endangered species, the Northern Spotted Owl (Figure 13.9) epitomizes the struggle between groups representing disparate value systems in a land of limited resources and unlimited demands. The debate has been oversimplified as a choice between employment and economic vitality on one hand, versus species survival and rich, functioning ecosystems on the other. This dichotomy has provoked lawsuits and intense public and scientific disagreement; with rapidly diminishing options, it led the U.S. Congress and President Clinton to judge the Spotted Owl/timber harvest situation a conflict to be resolved at the highest political levels.

Figure 13.9 The Northern Spotted Owl (*Strix occidentalis caurina*), a focal point of conflicts between endangered species preservation and short-term economic interests. (Photograph by David Johnson.)

One effort at resolution arose from a 1989 amendment to an appropriations bill in which Congress directed the U.S. Fish and Wildlife Service, U.S. Forest Service, National Park Service, and Bureau of Land Management to convene an Interagency Spotted Owl Scientific Committee (ISC) to "develop a scientifically credible conservation strategy for the Northern Spotted Owl." As members of the ISC, we struggled to develop a scientific protocol, using the rigor of strong inference (i.e., hypothesis testing, discussed below), that would allow consideration of both biological and nonbiological factors in development of a habitat conservation plan. The strategy developed by the ISC and presented to Congress (Thomas et al. 1990) is not the most recent proposal for resolution of the Northern Spotted Owl conservation crisis (Thomas and Verner 1992). However, the process, logic, and rationale employed has formed the foundation for all subsequent reserve design proposals for the subspecies.

Conservation planning for the Northern Spotted Owl has a long and complex history that reads like the plot of a political novel. Protagonists, antagonists, confrontations, disputes, secret memos, political pressure, litigation, media distortion, and personal attacks have been everyday players and events. Set against this background of political and legal turmoil, our challenge was to bring to the forefront all information pertinent to the preservation of the species and to provide a defensible conservation plan that appropriately considered scientific uncertainty and competing value systems.

The California Spotted Owl

Concern with, and studies of, the California Spotted Owl are more recent than for the northern subspecies. Consequently, its ecological associations are less well known, and it has not yet accumulated the contentious history of legal, political, and scientific debate that characterizes its northern counterpart.

Scientific and management interest in the California Spotted Owl was largely stimulated by release of the ISC report (Thomas et al. 1990), and by concern that some environmental groups were about to petition the Fish and Wildlife Service to list the California subspecies as threatened. In response, the Forest Service, California Department of Forestry, and other state and federal agencies established a scientific team to evaluate the status of the California subspecies and, if needed, to recommend changes in land management practices. The expectation was that a proactive management response would preclude the need to list this subspecies at a later date.

Contrasting Conservation Strategies

The ultimate measure of the success of a conservation strategy is long-term persistence of populations in the natural habitats that support them. Nonetheless, the immediate targets of conservation planning are not normally populations of specific sizes, but explicit management guidelines, habitat reserves, or other set-aside lands that are designed to assure species persistence. Conservation plans can differ widely in their design and subsequent implementation. Two extremes are represented by (1) plans that designate fixed, or static, reserve boundaries—spatially referenced distributions of habitat blocks designed to support locally stable populations given the condition of facilitated dispersal among habitat blocks—similar to the strategy for the Northern Spotted Owl; and (2) plans that restrict management activities within certain habitats in order to retain suitability for target species or to render them suitable at some future time—such as the plan for the California Spotted Owl, which did not specify the boundaries of a fixed reserve system.

The reserve strategy is most appropriate for species that occur in largely stable (or climax) communities that are in decline due to habitat loss and fragmentation. For such species, population declines must be arrested by stabilizing both the amount and distribution of suitable habitat (see discussion in Lande 1987; Lamberson et al. 1992; Lamberson et al. 1994). In contrast, dynamic management plans may be appropriate for species that do not demonstrate immediate and significant local population declines, but are exposed to ongoing, landscape-wide degradation of their habitat.

In these two distinct planning exercises, two important features prove central to producing conservation science that is credible, defensible, and repeatable. The first is the rigorous application of the scientific method, both in the process of gathering and analyzing data and in communicating the results to land use planners. The second is the development of clear operational definitions for the crucial terminology that recurs in legislation, management standards, and guidelines. Good science is rendered worthless when delivered to meet vague goals that are phrased as abstract biological concepts.

Creating a Scientifically Rigorous Conservation Plan

The conservation planning process is dependent on spatially explicit ecological information—particularly the distributions of populations, habitats, and resources. That information is best portrayed as independent map layers, including such information as political boundaries and ownership, topographic features, vegetation types, distribution of roads, and elevation demarcations. When overlaid to form a composite map, these layers collectively provide an initial outline of habitat "polygons" that are candidates for inclusion in a reserve network. This preliminary reserve design map has many spatial properties that can be expressed as falsifiable hypotheses and subjected to testing.

Scientific rigor is often difficult to achieve because most ecosystems are not amenable to experimental manipulations. The targets of study by conservation biologists are usually large, mobile species that exhibit complex behaviors and can be widely distributed across highly diverse landscapes that typically have been logged, grazed, cultivated, drained, roaded, and beset by introduced species. This study arena appears terribly opaque to systematic, rigorous experimental design. As a result, most management decisions are made on the basis of incomplete information drawn from disparate sources. Nevertheless, all management plans have properties that can be stated as falsifiable hypotheses and subjected to testing with data.

In the conservation planning process, a hypothesis can be defined as an assertion of a map property that is subject to tests with empirical information and theoretical predictions. When test conclusions fail to confirm one or more properties of a preliminary reserve design, such as the location, size, shape, or spacing of habitat patches, the configuration of the proposed reserve system is adjusted. Successive map iterations are sequentially tested with available information. The final product, a conservation strategy, is then portrayed as a map of reserve boundaries or special management zones.

For the Northern Spotted Owl, the ISC used data from all pertinent biological studies and inferences drawn from those data to test the properties of the map—including the number of reserve or habitat conservation areas, their current habitat condition, distribution, configuration, and spacing, and the nature of the landscape between the reserves. When one or more properties of the map were falsified, test results were used to refine the map to be consistent with existing information. The new map then generated a new set of falsifiable hypotheses. This process continued iteratively until all relevant data had been examined and all map properties had been tested.

The basic tests of hypotheses and emerging guidelines that dictate the number, size, shape, and spacing of reserve areas for the static reserve design are also applicable to dynamic management designs. Implementation of a management-based conservation plan, however, can be considerably more complex. To be successful, managers must be able to project the shifting configuration of the de facto reserve system that will result from expected management actions. For the California Spotted Owl, this ongoing process will require the use of dynamic maps integrated with vegetation succession models (best handled with a geographic information system) to forecast where, and at what future time, degraded habitat will become suitable. The ultimate task in dynamic planning is to schedule contemporary management actions to ensure that essential habitat components will be present at all future times within the planning horizon. This challenging process should also be carried out within a hypothetico-deductive framework.

Hypotheses Tested and Reserve Design Principles Invoked

To determine whether the Northern and California Spotted Owls were threatened subspecies and in jeopardy due to logging practices, we tested the following null hypotheses:

1. The finite rate of population change (λ) of owls is ≥ 1.0 (i.e., the population is growing).
2. Spotted Owls do not differentiate among habitats on the basis of forest age or structure.
3. No decline has occurred in the areal extent of habitat types selected by Spotted Owls for foraging, roosting, or nesting.

The Northern Spotted Owl. For the Northern Spotted Owl, the first null hypothesis was rejected based on the observation that λ was significantly less than 1.0 at two long-term study sites (Thomas et al. 1990). Subsequent tests of this hypothesis, based on additional study sites and additional years of data (USDI 1992), indicate that populations of resident, territorial females declined significantly, at an estimated rate of 7.5% per year, during the 1985–1991 period. No studies have found areas of stable or increasing populations.

The majority of Northern Spotted Owl habitat studies supported rejection of the second null hypothesis and provided evidence in favor of selection of old-growth forests, or forests that retained the characteristics of old forests (Thomas et al. 1990). The exception to this pattern was in coastal redwood forests of northern California (<7% of the owl's range), where owls are also found in younger forests that retain some residual old-growth components. Since the ISC report, numerous studies have confirmed that Northern and California Spotted Owls prefer old-growth habitat, providing additional falsification of hypothesis 2 (Solis and Gutierrez 1990; Buchanan 1991; Ripple et al. 1991b; Bart and Forsman 1992; Blakesley et al. 1992; Carey et al. 1992; Lehmkuhl and Raphael 1993).

The rejection of hypothesis 2 led to the test of hypothesis 3. Based on data from National Forest lands in Oregon and Washington, the ISC found significant declines in the extent of owl habitat, a trend that was projected to continue into the future (Figure 13.10). Additional analyses since the ISC report have provided evidence of significant habitat declines in California (McKelvey

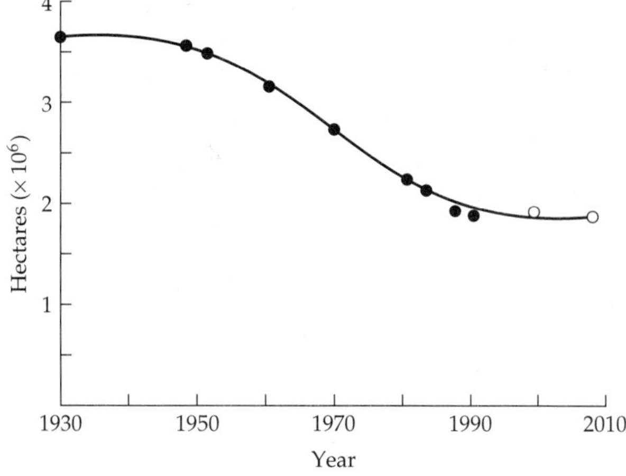

Figure 13.10 Estimated trend in the areal extent of suitable Northern Spotted Owl habitat in National Forest lands in Oregon and Washington from 1930 to 2010. Estimates beyond 1990 are projections based on National Forest plans.

and Johnston 1992); regionally specific estimates of habitat loss are provided in the Draft Recovery Plan (USDI 1992).

Subsequent development of the conservation strategy was based, in large part, on the results of map-based tests of five basic principles of reserve design (Wilcove and Murphy 1991), stated as falsifiable hypotheses:

1. Species that are well distributed across their ranges are less prone to extinction than species confined to small portions of their ranges.
2. Large blocks of habitat containing many individuals of a given species are more likely to sustain that species than are small blocks of habitat with only a few individuals.
3. Blocks of habitat in close proximity are preferable to widely dispersed blocks of habitat.
4. Contiguous, unfragmented blocks of habitat are superior to highly fragmented blocks of habitat.
5. Habitat between protected areas is more easily traversed by dispersing individuals the more closely it resembles suitable habitat for the species in question.

Particularly relevant to a territorial species with obligate juvenile dispersal, such as the Spotted Owl, was the prediction from theoretical models of sharp thresholds for species extinction (Lande 1987; Thomas et al. 1990; Lamberson et al. 1992; Lamberson et al. 1994; see also Chapter 7). One threat arises when the amount of suitable habitat is reduced to such a small fraction of the landscape that the difficulty of finding a territory becomes an insurmountable barrier to the population's persistence. Another occurs if population density is so low that the probability of finding a mate drops below that required to maintain a stable population.

One area of scientific uncertainty relevant to Spotted Owl reserve design was the size and spacing of reserve areas. Existing biogeographic principles were helpful, but too broad for specific application to the Spotted Owl problem. To address this uncertainty, we used computer simulation models, premised on Lande (1987), structured and parameterized in terms of the life history of the Northern Spotted Owl. The ISC determined the goal for conservation to be a 95% certainty of range-wide persistence for 100 years. Given estimates of the current amount of habitat, and its ability to regrow within 100 years, model results suggested that a minimum habitat size for locally stable populations would be a network of blocks, each capable of supporting at least 20 pairs of birds (Figure 13.11; Thomas et al. 1990; Lamberson et al. 1992, 1994).

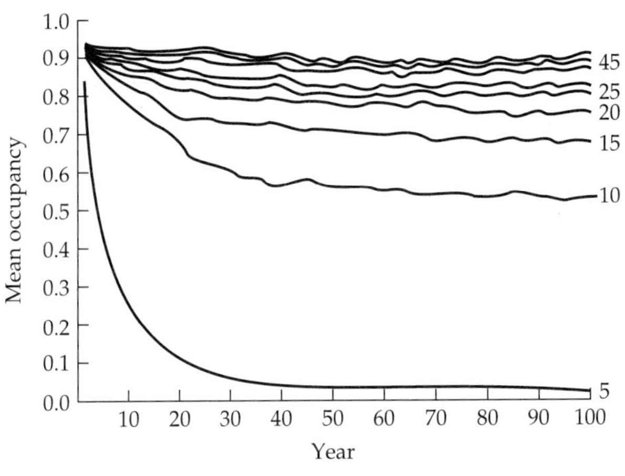

Figure 13.11 Some of the predictions for Spotted Owl persistence upon which management is based come from computer modeling. Shown here are predictions of mean occupancy rates of suitable sites by pairs of Spotted Owls over time for various sizes of clusters (blocks of suitable habitat sites), assuming that 60% of the sites within a cluster are suitable. Numbers on the right are total sites per cluster. These results predict that clusters with more individual sites will support more owls.

The California Spotted Owl. Demographic studies have been conducted for long enough to compute estimates of λ for two study populations of the California Spotted Owl in the northern Sierra Nevada of California. Estimates of λ for the Sierra Nevada populations were not significantly less than 1.0 (Noon et al. 1992). Even though hypothesis 1 was not rejected for these study populations, Verner et al. (1992) proceeded to test hypothesis 2, because the tests for hypothesis 1 had low power, and the point estimates of l were less than 1.0 (Noon et al. 1992). Hypothesis 2 was rejected at both the landscape and home-range scale for both Sierra Nevada populations (Gutierrez et al. 1992). At both spatial scales, owls selected stands of large, old trees with closed canopies. This pattern was particularly pronounced in nest and roost stands.

Consistent rejection of hypothesis 2 led to tests of hypothesis 3. Forests in the Sierra Nevada have been markedly affected by human activities within the last 150 years (McKelvey and Johnston 1992). A combination of logging and natural attrition of old-growth forest has led to a decline in the number of large, old trees (particularly pines), has broken up the patchy mosaic of the natural forest, and has encouraged development of dense understory conifer regeneration. The result has been rather uniform, landscape-wide loss of old-growth forest elements (e.g., large, standing live and dead trees and large downed logs) strongly associated with the habitat use patterns of Spotted Owls.

Based on current Forest Service land management plans, loss of old-growth forest elements was projected to continue, resulting in forests susceptible to fire disturbance and nearly devoid of large, old trees. Given these projections, Verner et al. (1992) proposed interim (5–10 year) guidelines that both reduced allowable harvest levels and restricted silvicultural activities in habitats selected by Spotted Owls. These restrictions, invoked at a landscape scale, would serve to retain the large tree components in harvested stands in order to greatly accelerate the rate at which these degraded stands would become suitable habitat in the future. The locations of suitable blocks of habitat would shift dynamically across the landscape, but with reduced harvest levels, an adequate amount and distribution of suitable habitat would always be available.

Why Two Different Conservation Strategies?

At both landscape and home-range scales, the Northern and California Spotted Owls select habitats that retain old-growth forest characteristics. Consequently, timber harvest of old-growth forests, or their components, threatens both subspecies' long-term persistence. Given the wide acceptance by the scientific community of the ISC reserve design for the northern subspecies, why was a similar strategy not adopted for the California Spotted Owl? There are several reasons (Verner et al. 1992).

First, during the past 50 years, the number and distribution of Northern Spotted Owls may have been reduced by as much as 50% from pre-20th century levels (Thomas et al. 1990). No evidence of similar declines in number or distribution exists for California Spotted Owls, despite the fact that forests in the Sierra Nevada have been logged for the past 100 years. Currently, Spotted Owls in the Sierra Nevada are widely distributed throughout the conifer zone.

Second, the primary silvicultural method in the Pacific Northwest, west of the Cascade crest, has been clear-cutting. Because clear-cutting practices have dominated in the Pacific Northwest, particularly over the last 50 years, habitat within the range of the Northern Spotted Owl is either undisturbed and suitable, or cut within the last 50 years and unsuitable. The result has been an island-like distribution of suitable habitat. The ISC opted for a Northern Spot-

(A)

(B)

Figure 13.12 Two forest management types: (A) clear-cutting and (B) selective harvesting. In the latter, an 80-year-old stand of Douglas fir was thinned (selectively harvested) to 50 trees/acre at age 40 and planted with hemlock in the understory. (A, photograph by Barry R. Noon; B, by John Tappeiner.)

ted Owl strategy that clearly differentiated habitat reserves from areas where logging could occur. In contrast, selective tree harvest has been the predominant harvest method over most of the range of the California Spotted Owl (Figure 13.12). Current data indicate that some level of selective harvest does not render habitat unsuitable for owls, at least over the long term. As a result, the current distribution of Spotted Owls in the Sierra Nevada is comparatively uniform in both the conifer zone and adjacent foothill riparian/hardwood forest. Imposing a static reserve design here would leave many owls outside of reserves and vulnerable to habitat loss.

Third, fire is not a major threat to forests west of the Cascade crest in Washington or Oregon (Agee and Edmonds 1992). Despite the fact that fire spreads contagiously, even large contiguous blocks of old-growth forest within this region would face little risk of catastrophic loss. On the other hand, the Sierran mixed conifer forests, where most California Spotted Owls occur, are drier, and given a history of fire exclusion, very prone to catastrophic fires. A habitat reserve strategy there could deal with the uncertainties of logging, but not fire.

Collectively, the above considerations led Verner et al. (1992) to propose an interim landscape-level conservation strategy that would retain the old-growth forest components apparently needed by owls for roosting and nesting. Based on continuing research and adaptive modifications to the interim plan, such a strategy would preserve future options for Spotted Owl management.

Issues that Arise after the Conservation Plan Is Put Forward

Confronting Scientific Uncertainty. Contentious debate surrounding the value of threatened and endangered species like the Spotted Owl inevitably arises if their conservation is accompanied by significant economic costs. As a result, conservation biologists and their colleagues in forestry, range sciences, and wildlife biology have been swept into public debates that take them from the status of sequestered experts to that of key players in the development of public policy. Scientists have been drawn into the land use decision-making process, have been required to defend the merits of their field studies in public forums, and are finding themselves defending their science against often savage criticism.

Scientists are trained to treat facts with doubt and to question their validity, a circumstance that lawyers use to advantage. Uncertainty is inherent in the scientific process because the goal of science is to incrementally reduce levels of uncertainty by subjecting alternative hypotheses to rigorous tests. Thus, scientists do not construct conclusions from data; rather, they construct hypotheses that are tested with further data. They cannot prove the truth of an assertion; rather, they fail to disprove that assertion, and thus support it.

Special interest groups employ lawyers and consultants to seek flaws and weaknesses in scientific analyses and data. And in those cases in which no obvious flaws exist, critics will note how little scientists actually know. They exaggerate and misconstrue the inherent, inevitable uncertainty that accompanies the best scientific efforts.

In the courtroom, the tactic used most frequently is to exploit the areas of uncertainty inherent in the scientific process—or worse, to use disinformation and distortion in an attempt to discredit the scientist. Also, critical data that could significantly contribute to problem definition and resolution may be purposely excluded as lawyers manipulate the litigation process so that the critical issues are never put on the table.

A disproportionate amount of criticism of the ISC strategy, both in industry press releases and during litigation, was directed toward the computer simulation models and the inferences drawn from them. Models are ready candidates for criticism because any model simple enough to be operational is necessarily too simple to be completely realistic. Like all simulation models, those used in the conservation assessments of both owl subspecies were characterized by abstractions and simplifying assumptions. And, like all models, they were open to criticism if one demands (unrealistically) that a model be a complete representation of the real world. Because of these perceived weaknesses, the scientists responsible for the models were frequent targets during litigation.

The motivation to discredit both conservation strategies rested on the simple fact that owl protection meant reducing allowable tree harvest. From the timber industry's perspective, access to large-diameter, economically valuable trees on public lands would simply be too restricted. This stipulation, however, was not a consequence of the model results, but was dictated by the habitat associations of the Spotted Owl.

Burden of Proof in Conservation Debates. The allocation of burden of proof can often determine the results of decision making. Some entity must assume the responsibility for providing sufficient information to compel a decision maker to adopt a solution. In the Northern Spotted Owl litigation, the strategy of the timber industry, and to some extent the federal agency lawyers, was to put the burden on the scientists to prove an adverse effect of timber harvest on Spotted Owl persistence. In the absence of compelling information and arguments, the lawyers argued, the status quo (high levels of harvest in late seral stage forests) should continue. Failure to make a decision to change management practices for Spotted Owls was a de facto decision to continue current practices.

Federal environmental laws do not require judges to be scientific experts. Rather, the law requires public agencies to fully disclose all pertinent information, and to openly consider competing interpretations of this information. Despite attacks on the credibility and objectivity of the Spotted Owl scientists, these courtroom tactics failed because the judges ruled that existing environmental laws require a full disclosure and analysis of existing data. The analyses provided by the ISC and other scientists provided convincing evidence of risk to the species, thus mandating conservation action. Defensible science and open debate prevailed in the courtroom, and eventually led to more responsible decision making.

Ethics and Science. Most people involved in conservation science are motivated by a strong sense of responsibility to the biota and to future generations. Lawyers attempt to label such scientists as "advocates" who are therefore biased, and refuse to recognize that one can support a position in the absence of bias; bias does not necessarily follow from advocacy. Science is not value-free, nor should it be. Environmental science and environmental law have a clear ethical foundation, which is appropriate. "Resource stewardship" is not a buzz phrase, but a meaningful expression of responsibility to future generations. Conservation scientists recognize that meeting this responsibility will often come at the expense of maximizing short-term economic gain.

Some scientists involved in the Spotted Owl debates chose not to participate in the normative process to render data scientifically credible (e.g., peer review and publication). Instead, they exploited the uncertainty inherent in the scientific process to justify maintaining the status quo or to obscure reasonable hypotheses. They were often able to stir up doubt, not because a hypothesis was unreasonable, but simply because irrefutable proof was a standard that could not be met.

Improving the Role of Science in Conservation Policy

The courts have assumed an increasing role in rendering land management decisions based on procedural aspects of law, as well as deciding substantive issues that should be discussed and resolved in other arenas. Because of society's continuing failure to acknowledge that hard choices must be made, and then to move forward and make them, we have lacked an adequate forum and process for environmental problem resolution.

We need to develop alternative strategies for problem resolution, and scientists should be key contributors to this process. The forum for decision making must be expanded to include all affected parties, representing a diversity of perspectives. Given such a forum, behavior must be governed by a set of rigidly enforced ground rules, including: (1) participating parties must treat one another with professional respect; (2) the strength of any argument put on the table should be a function of the information content of the argument; (3) no pertinent data may be withheld or suppressed; and (4) the reliability of the data should be judged by the degree to which they have been exposed to the scientific process of peer criticism and repeated attempts at falsification.

Such a forum for problem resolution would be a significant step toward solving emerging crises in land use and natural resource management. Once solutions were offered, the final responsibility would be to conduct risk assessments to accompany each of the alternative management plans. Thus, the decision makers would be the final arbiters of which conservation plans were implemented and would be obligated to make known the risks, to both present and future generations, associated with the decisions they made.

Ultimately, the decisions we make as a society regarding management of declining resources come back to a fundamental question: "Does the value gained from the continued existence of a species equal the cost incurred to assure its persistence?" How we respond to this question will determine the fate of many species, including the Spotted Owl.

CASE STUDY 4

Managing Beyond Borders: The Costa Rican National System of Conservation Areas (SINAC)

Christopher Vaughan, Universidad Nacional, Costa Rica, and Carlos Manuel Rodreguez, National System of Conservation Areas, Costa Rica

National planning can contribute to successful management of conservation areas by facilitating the coordination of resource and development agencies,

by involving the civil society and encouraging participation by private landowners in conservation decision making, and by supporting decentralized and flexible regional planning. Stable, long-term funding is essential so that national planning can be implemented.

Protected natural areas have traditionally been viewed as islands, independent of and protected from their surroundings. However, natural areas affect neighboring lands, and are affected by external ecological, physical, cultural, and social influences. If protected areas are to survive in the long term, they must be complementary to, and not isolated from, the general landscape, and must take into account human influences and needs. Integration of protected areas into regional development plans as multiple-use areas is necessary to obtain maximum sustainable natural resource conservation and production without losing future use options. The case of Costa Rica's attempt to integrate protected areas into regional land use programs is explored here, and the management challenges of such an approach are emphasized.

Few countries worldwide can boast of Costa Rica's recent degree of success in wildland conservation and management. Two decades ago, the country was faced with one of the world's highest population growth rates, a huge international debt, land-hungry rich and poor, the world's highest deforestation rate, and a legal system that promoted deforestation (Leonard 1987). However, visionaries changed political and public opinion, received international financial and political support, and established a world-famous wildlands conservation and management system, which by the late 1980s included 29% of the national territory (14,500 km^2) in 78 protected national and private areas (Figure 13.13A).

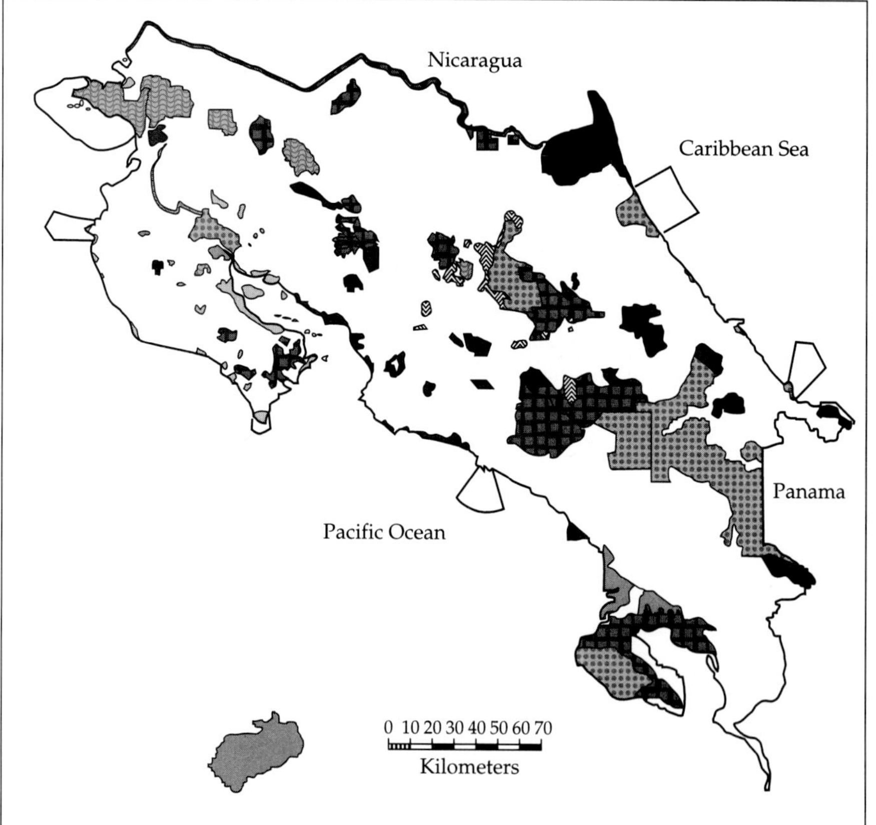

Figure 13.13 The evolution of Costa Rica's Conservation Areas: (A) up to 1990; (B) 1990–1994; (C) 1996. Note the progressive integration of the Conservation Areas into the larger landscape and society.

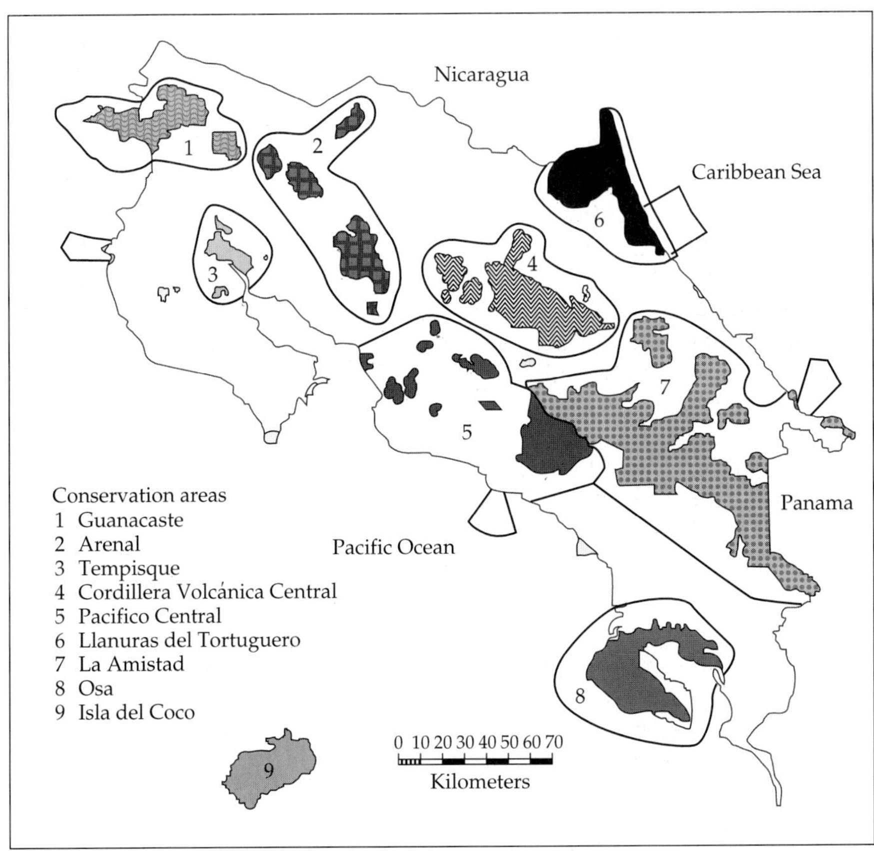

Nicaragua
Caribbean Sea
Panama
Pacific Ocean
1
2
3
4
5
6
7
8
9
Conservation areas
1 Guanacaste
2 Arenal
3 Tempisque
4 Cordillera Volcánica Central
5 Pacifico Central
6 Llanuras del Tortuguero
7 La Amistad
8 Osa
9 Isla del Coco
0 10 20 30 40 50 60 70
Kilometers

(B)

Nicaragua
Caribbean Sea
Panama
Pacific Ocean
1
2
3
4
5
6
7
8
9
10
Conservation areas
1 Guanacaste
2 Arenal
3 Tempisque
4 Cordillera Volcánica Central
5 Pacifico Central
6 Llanuras del Tortuguero
7 Amistad Caribe
8 Amistad Pacifico
9 Osa
10 Isla del Coco
0 10 20 30 40 50 60 70
Kilometers

(C)

Before 1995, the majority of these protected areas was managed by four separate government institutions: the National Parks Service, the General Forestry Directorate, the Wildlife Service, and the National Indian Affairs Commission. Several private organizations, including the Tropical Science Center and the Organization for Tropical Studies, also owned private reserves. Although wildland areas often shared borders, each institution managed their areas independently, with little effective coordination.

By the beginning of the 1990s, it was apparent that the existing wildland system was not accomplishing its principal objectives of maintaining ecological processes and essential natural systems in undisturbed communities and ecosystems, restoring natural processes in disturbed communities, preserving biological diversity, and providing for sustainable use of species and ecosystems. Twelve major problems made it difficult to achieve these objectives:

1. The overabundance of legislation and institutions involved in wildland management posed problems in defining institutional jurisdiction and priorities.
2. The size and shape of protected areas could not guarantee perpetuation of biological processes and biodiversity conservation.
3. Increasing pressures from human activities inside and around protected areas (banana cultivation, cattle ranching, fires, uncontrolled ecotourism, poaching, firewood collection, and deforestation) were causing both biogeographic insularization and conflicts with local residents.
4. Limited existing scientific information promoted species and ecosystem protection through isolation, rather than active management through restoration and development of biosphere reserves.
5. Budgetary and human resources were unstable and even decreased in some years, while wildland surface area and institutional responsibilities increased.
6. Local communities were increasingly hostile to wildland policies, partly because residents had never participated in wildlands decision making.
7. Centralized decision making from the capital city of San José had inhibited local area management.
8. Forest reserves, protected zones, and wildlife refuges were not managed as such.
9. Monitoring of natural and socioeconomic processes was insufficient in the protected wildland areas.
10. Private property within the national parks amounted to about 7% of the total area.
11. The existence of development policies that created competitive use of the soils and the forest cover favored agriculture, livestock and urban uses.
12. There was a lack of national environmental policy as well as a tendency for conflicting sectorial policies within the executive branch.

Thus, the disjunct wildlands system and its biological riches were increasingly threatened by people wanting to exploit resources to improve their standard of living. Management of the wildlands system was uncoordinated among institutions, which had neither sufficient human and economic resources nor innovative programs to guarantee the system's long-term survival. Biological conservation principles, such as minimum reserve size or active management through restoration ecology, were not being applied.

An Innovative Approach

A new approach to Costa Rican wildland management was devised by the Costa Rican National Parks Service, working with several NGOs and professionals. By 1989, a concept of conservation areas began to develop, without legal backing, within the Ministry of the Environment (MAE). Called the National System of Conservation Areas (SINAC), it seemed the best option to achieve wildland objectives, evolve within modern Costa Rican society, and overcome the many limitations of the existing wildlands system. SINAC would consolidate protected areas conservation and management, while orienting wildlands toward satisfying the socioeconomic needs of the local communities as well as other national and international interests. Biological conservation concepts would be incorporated into this new system, with special attention to minimum population sizes, restoration ecology, and long-term monitoring.

But in 1995, two events occurred that radically changed the orientation of SINAC. First, there was strong political support from the incoming government to consolidate SINAC along "sustainable development" lines. Second, two dynamic Costa Rican professionals with strong environmental and public and private administrative backgrounds were hired to administer it. In several months' time, SINAC's original wildlands management approach became a mandate involving natural resource management at a national landscape level.

One of the first steps in this direction was the merger of the forestry, wildlife, and wildlands agencies into SINAC to facilitate national planning and executive processes directed toward sustainable natural resource management. This was a landmark decision, because these three agencies within MAE had carried out similar functions in wildland and wildlife management. These agencies were administratively and operationally disjointed due to bureaucracies with inefficient and duplicative management; for example, vertical administrative structures had involved up to 17 decision-making levels. Worse, this situation was occurring in triplicate among the three agencies, with three general directors, separate legal departments with 17 lawyers in San José, three personnel management offices, three separate accounting systems, and all in a totally centralized system. In contrast, SINAC now has one director in charge of biodiversity, one lawyer in San José, and one lawyer in each Conservation Area who lives with, experiences, and resolves legal problems in situ, not by telephone.

A second major step was to promote public participation in SINAC. In general, local communities had never been consulted about changes affecting their lives, including prohibitions on their use of resources such as hunting or firewood extraction. This resulted in misunderstandings of and hostility toward conservation efforts (Vaughan and Flormoe 1995). SINAC promotes participation by all groups who share the common objective of preservation, restoration, and protection of ecological equilibrium and biodiversity. Eventually, SINAC aspires to place the civil society in charge of most aspects of management, concessions, and research, with the state involved in facilitation and financing (Figure 13.14). SINAC now functions as a technical organization decentralized from MAE with a legal mandate that permits great flexibility in carrying out its mission.

SINAC Structure

In its original form, SINAC consisted of three managerial components: central office headquarters, Satellite Areas, and Conservation Areas. The headquarters was the administrative body responsible for managing, regulating, guiding, auditing, and consolidating the conservation and satellite areas. It also set

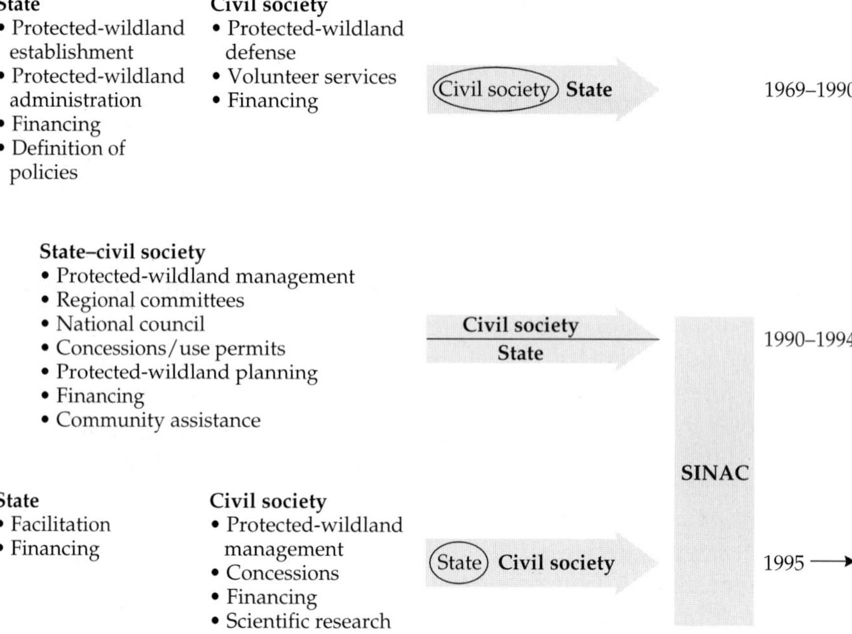

Figure 13.14 A diagram of state and civil society participation in the evolution of SINAC.

guidelines, long-term objectives, and policies for SINAC with the Minister and Vice Minister of MAE. The Satellite Areas were dispersed protected areas, not belonging to any particular Conservation Area due to their geographic isolation. They also were not technically or administratively integrated into any Conservation Area.

The nine Conservation Areas were a group of contiguous or clustered wildlands placed in one of several management categories depending on their characteristics, regional influences, and participation by local inhabitants (see Figure 13.13B). Each Conservation Area included one or more core or nucleus areas—consisting of one or more existing wildlands such as national parks—for biodiversity conservation, plus surrounding buffer zones for sustainable development activities. Government wildlands (forest reserves, wildlife refuges, and protected areas) or private lands adjacent to the core areas served as buffer zones, where, depending on the management criteria, rational, sustainable uses of natural resources were promoted, including controlled timber or firewood extraction, wildlife management, and ecotourism.

As of mid-1996, SINAC administers all biodiversity in Costa Rica. The ten Conservation Areas have evolved into territorial units (state protected areas, private property, and urban zones) governed under one development and administrative strategy in which private, local, and federal management and conservation activities are interrelated, and solutions based on sustainable development are sought jointly with the civil society (see Figure 13.13C). The reforms selected were based on surveys, over 50 workshops of SINAC's 700 employees using participatory methodologies, and short courses during a six-month period. Among the conceptual reforms that have been implemented are:

1. *Decentralization.* During the transformation process, economic resources, staffing, and decision making are being transferred to the Conservation Areas to improve efficiency and regional services.
2. *Democratization.* The civil society is taking an active, direct, and decisive role in the decision-making process in SINAC. When the evolution of SINAC is complete, the civil society will manage the system, and the state will act as a provider and financier (Figure 13.14).

3. *Processing.* The new institutional framework will better execute processes aimed at fulfilling the vision and mission of SINAC. This includes activities that consume resources and provide a product or service to a customer.

From the above, we derived a vision, mission, and proposition, defined by SINAC's employees:

Vision: To constitute a well-organized and consolidated system that offers an efficient service to the client (society), aiming at responsible management and conservation of the natural resources, and contributing to improve the quality of life of Costa Rica's inhabitants.

Mission: To consolidate SINAC, integrating and planning it with other MAE dependencies so that the authority and competence is delegated toward the regions, and ample participation is given to the civil society in decision making, thus offering quality and efficient service to its clientele.

Proposition: To administer and promote sustained natural resource use in accordance with the economic and social development of Costa Rica while including an elevated degree of civil society participation.

Funding Strategies: A Key to Success

A new funding strategy is a fundamental part of the decentralizing process that guarantees independence and autonomy for Conservation Area operation. Over a decade ago, the norm was that some small but popular national parks and biological reserves (Carara, Manuel Antonio, Poas) took in large sums of money from tourist entrance fees, which subsidized the operational costs of other parks. The rest of the money needed to finance the Conservation Areas came from endowments, trust funds, and donations (40%) and government funds (30%). Consequently, there was great financial dependence of one Conservation Area on another, with a dangerous proportion of the economic resources depending on international sources and the central government.

Under the new funding principles, the Conservation Areas should be financially self-sufficient, and all income generated in each area should be retained for that area. The specific parameters of the financing strategy consist of the following (Figure 13.15):

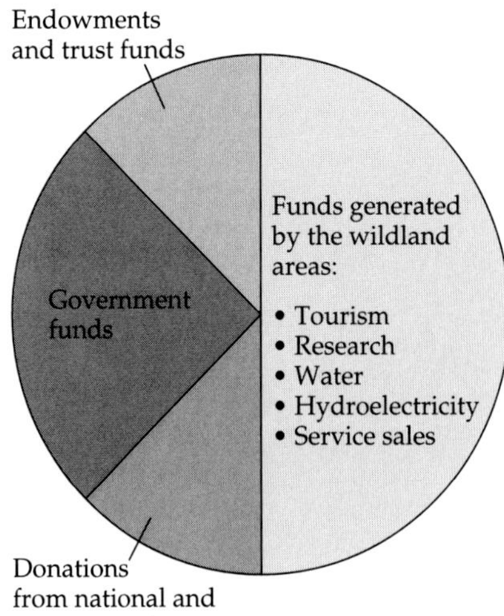

Figure 13.15 Funding strategy for the national system of Conservation Areas, showing the broad funding base.

50% of the funding will be produced by

- general entrance fees to wildland areas
- research permits and royalties from commercial products (medicines, agricultural products, industrial products) as a result of research in biodiversity prospecting
- charges for environmental services (water for human consumption and energy production; projects in carbon fixing)
- income from concessions, licenses, and use permits, administration or services

15% of the funds will be produced by

- international aid (GEF, BID, ASDI, NORAD, USAID, NGOs)

15% of the funds will be produced by

- investment interest from endowments, trust funds, and debt swaps (all of the Conservation Areas have constituted endowments to provide funds and produce financial resources that guarantee their long-term stability)

20% of the funds will be produced by

- the General Budget of the Costa Rican government, financed by congressional decision

This strategy for financing the Conservation Areas seeks autonomy, independence, and operational security in the long term, healthy competition among the Conservation Areas, and, most important, the sustainable use of biodiversity for the well-being of the Costa Rican society.

An Example of Conservation Area Organization

SINAC has united 71 of the 78 wildlands, agroscapes, and urban areas within ten Conservation Areas: La Amistad, Arenal, Cordillera Volcánica, Tempisque, Guanacaste, Llanuras de Tortuguero, Amistad Pacífico, Amistad Caribe, Osa, and Isla del Coco (Figure 13.13C). Each Conservation Area has its own administrative body, and its own unique characteristics and problems to resolve. A detailed summary of one area, the Osa Conservation Area (ACOSA), is presented as an example of how these organizations function.

The Osa Conservation Area is located in south-southeastern Costa Rica and includes an area of 4,104 km^2 (8.6% of the national territory), which includes the cantons of Osa, Golfito, and Corredores (Figure 13.16). ACOSA had a human population of 100,763 inhabitants as of late 1995, or a density of 26.2 inhabitants per km^2. Much of the area of ACOSA is dedicated to agriculture, and large areas were in banana production by the United Fruit Company until the early 1980s. Today, African oil palm plantations, cattle raising, and rice planting dominate the agroscape.

To provide greater coverage of ACOSA and offer better service to residents, four offices have been established in the largest towns of the region. The new focus by MAE in ACOSA and each of the other Conservation Areas is grounded in three major sectors: Promotion, Control, and Protected Areas. The goal of the Promotion sector is to establish and execute a process that facilitates and promotes responsible management and active conservation of natural resources by private enterprises, and to integrate them sustainably into the economic and social development of the area.

The Control sector focuses on promotion and execution of programs of natural resource control. Its greatest work ahead is to coordinate protection activities with the persons in charge of the operational centers, similar institutions, and NGOs in the region. The functions of this sector will be carried out both inside and outside of protected areas in ACOSA. Also, ACOSA will train employees and civilian groups so that they will be able to protect natural resources in the region.

The Protected Areas sector focuses on management actions within protected areas. It is responsible for all aspects of development of controls and actions relative to biodiversity and other landscape elements in ACOSA. There is a program of training sessions for technical, administrative, and field personal to achieve this end.

ACOSA includes approximately 160,000 ha in ten national wildland areas on the Osa Peninsula, which contains the last remaining large tract of lowland, humid tropical forest on Mesoamerica's Pacific coast (Figure 13.17) and protects an immense amount of biological diversity, including many endemic species. Rainfall varies from 3–4 meters per year on the coasts to 5–6 m per year at the highest points (600 m). On the Osa Peninsula alone, there is one national park, one forest reserve, one mangrove reserve, one wildlife refuge, and two Indian reserves, all created in the last 20 years (see Figure 13.16).

The great biological richness of the Osa Peninsula has interested scientists for many years. Over 500 species of trees have been identified in Corcovado

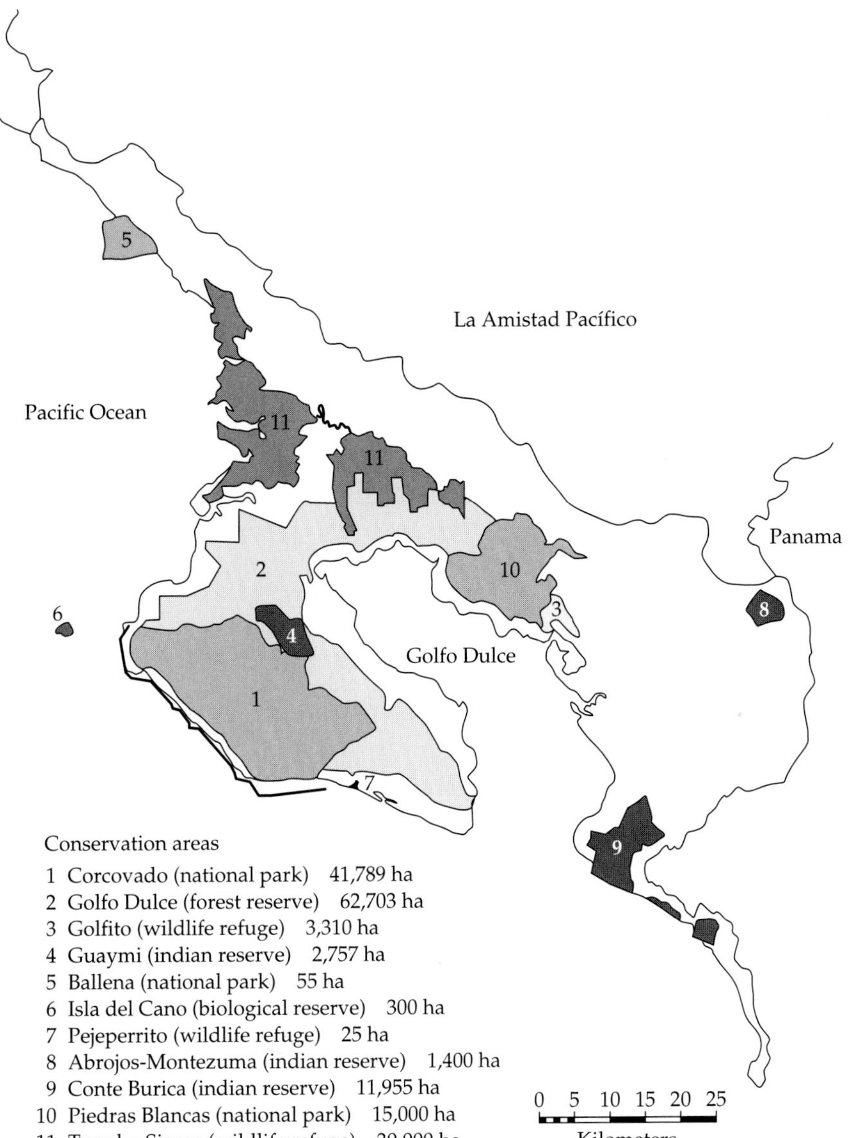

Figure 13.16 Detailed map of the various units making up the Osa Conservation Area (ACOSA). Note the contribution of national forests, Indian lands, parks, and other types of lands with different historical uses.

National Park, with more than 100 species/ha found in some areas. The Conservation Area is home to 140 mammal, 367 bird, 117 reptile and amphibian, 40 freshwater fish, and at least 6000 insect species. These include endangered large mammals such as the jaguar, cougar, ocelot, and tapir, and one of the largest populations of Scarlet Macaws in Mesoamerica (Vaughan 1981).

Corcovado National Park, the first wildland area created on the Osa Peninsula in 1974 and the cornerstone of ACOSA, resulted from a land trade with a multinational company, publicity created by the international scientific community, and relocation of several hundred inhabitants from the park area (Vaughan 1981). However, this park was not large enough to protect natural ecosystems on the Osa Peninsula. Exploitation of untouched wilderness increased in the middle 1980s for three reasons: (1) the opening of a year-round highway into the peninsula permitted access for the first time by loggers and squatters; (2) gold deposits found in Corcovado National Park and its expanded areas created a conflict between the government and gold panners;

Figure 13.17 The Osa Peninsula is the largest remaining tract of lowland rainforest in the area, containing huge specimens of trees such as this *Ceiba pentandra*. Holding up the tree is Mario Boza, first director of the Costa Rican National Parks Service. (Photograph by Christopher Vaughan.)

and (3) abandonment of lands controlled by banana companies elsewhere in southwestern Costa Rica caused high levels of unemployment and an exodus to the Osa Peninsula, considered the last frontier in southern Costa Rica.

These colonists had little understanding of the limitations of land use on the peninsula. Poor soils, steep slopes, and high precipitation imposed severe limitations on yields for farmers who practiced slash-and-burn agriculture. Farming destroyed forests and watersheds. Uncontrolled hunting, small to moderate gold mining efforts, and small-scale timber operations also had detrimental effects on biological communities on the peninsula.

ACOSA was established in 1990 to avert an ecological disaster while allowing for a sustainable human presence on the peninsula and elsewhere in southwestern Costa Rica. Regional planning is ongoing. ACOSA works with local community organizations and NGOs, focusing on finding ways to encourage environmentally sound economic alternatives for the lands surrounding the core areas. At present, the Conservation Area, in cooperation with the Forestry Directorate, National Parks Service, and Mining Directorate, serves as the coordinating agency for formally organized programs in agroforestry, research, ecotourism, protection, land organization, environmental education, and mining.

Success or Failure?

Although human and economic resources are scarce, SINAC seems to be working. The basic administrative infrastructure is in place, and environmental education, agricultural and scientific research, and environmental monitoring have begun in all conservation areas. Costa Rican wildland areas are increasingly popular for foreign and Costa Rican ecotourism and scientific use. These visitors are attracted to Costa Rica because its natural beauty and tropical biota are accessible, and because the country is safe for travel due to its stable political system and well-developed infrastructure.

Nationally, there is a strong commitment from government agencies, NGOs, local development agencies, and national development organizations and conservation groups to continue and fortify SINAC. Many projects have been implemented with support from local communities near or within the Conservation Areas. International support for Costa Rica's conservation efforts has been strong, and the SINAC initiative comes at a time when the world is looking for new approaches to managing wildlands and surrounding human communities. One of the most important concepts put into place is charging the resource user for the natural resources contained in each Conservation Area. The pace at which progress has been made is remarkable; this nationwide coordination project, complete with infrastructure and funding, has come together in three years.

Can the Costa Rican Model Be Generalized?

The key ingredients of the SINAC model that make for successful conservation area management are coordination of agencies, involvement of private landowners, regionalized plans, flexible policy, and long-term support. Can these ingredients be transposed to other tropical countries? In principle, yes, but in practice it will be difficult. Few countries give conservation the priority it receives in Costa Rica, and few tropical countries have the political stability and level of education enjoyed by Costa Rica.

There is perhaps an important lesson here for conservation management in the United States and elsewhere. Coordination by public agencies in the United States does occur, but usually it is due either to efforts of progressive individuals or to a legal requirement such as the Endangered Species Act. Citizens are usually not brought into the decision-making process, and their input is typically limited to commentary on proposed agency plans or, more forcefully, initiation of legal injunctions that block a state or federal action. Regional planning does occur, but is often constrained by federal guidelines. For example, National Forest management plans are regionalized, but they have to meet federal guidelines for timber harvest. Conservation of biodiversity is not given priority, but is simply one of many competing management objectives. Finally, funding and policy often shift with election year cycles. The United States and other developed countries could learn a great deal from Costa Rica about how to develop effective national and regional resource management policy.

CASE STUDY 5

The Everglades: Trials in Ecosystem Management

Lance H. Gunderson, University of Florida

One of the most visible attempts at ecosystem management is occurring in the Florida Everglades. With huge and unabated population growth in the region, as well as an important and entrenched agricultural base, the challenges for good management are as difficult here as anywhere. Management of the Everglades must be based on an understanding of the key driving forces that structure the system, the many complexities and surprises associated with human manipulations, and the cross-scale processes that influence the natural system.

The Everglades is one of the most widely recognized ecosystems in the world. During the 20th century, dramatic changes in population numbers and human development have transformed this large, once contiguous wetland into a partitioned, highly managed system for water control. Because water is central to both the ecological and human systems, ecosystem-level management in the Everglades has been and continues to be centered on hydrologic processes. Floods, droughts, fires, storms, and other landscape-scale processes are key self-organizing elements in the remnant wetland ecosystem. Human management institutions have been forced to adapt to these cycles, and have undergone periodic shifts and reforms in response to unanticipated variation or surprises resulting from these ecosystem processes (heavy rainfall, hurricanes, droughts, eutrophication), or brought about by the maturation of latent management deficiencies.

In the coupled human and natural systems, the recurring sequence appears to be that unforeseen ecological changes are perceived as crises, and are followed by periods of dramatic institutional reform. These crises provide opportunities for innovation, creativity, and renaissance. Indeed, the relatively rapid dynamics of the ecosystem have produced many crises and surprises during the 20th century. The trials of the Everglades provide a useful case study for lessons in management at the ecosystem level, which is only beginning to embrace the concepts of ecosystem management as discussed in earlier chapters.

Although Everglades management has long focused on ecosystem-level processes (primarily the hydrologic system), until recently that focus took the form of controlling unwanted variation in the hydrology by compartmentalization, drainage, impoundment, and the use of technology for moving and cleaning water. Other pieces of an ecosystem management approach—sustainability, system resilience, cross-scale issues, and adaptive management—are only beginning to be addressed in an effort to revive and sustain ecological values around the notion of ecosystem restoration.

This case study is structured in three parts. The first is a brief review of the cross-scale relationships of the Everglades ecosystem, presented as a way of compressing the complexity of ecological relationships into a framework that provides understanding. The second recounts the history of water management during the 20th century, revealing the coupling between ecological and institutional dynamics. The lesson here is that human institutions must adapt to unpredictable changes in the ecosystem. The final section describes incipient ecosystem management activities focused on ecosystem restoration.

Understanding the Ecosystem

One of the precepts of ecosystem management is that it should be based on ecological understanding at multiple scales. That is, ecosystem management does not just refocus the scale of management concerns, like changing ocular power on a microscope, but attempts to deal with issues by understanding how ecosystems are structured and function across spatial and temporal scales (Figure 13.18). Consequently, this section portrays elements of the Everglades ecosystem in snapshots at three spatial scales, and addresses how structures and functions interact across scales. These three snapshots, at the local habitat scale, the landscape scale, and the regional scale, will be used to illustrate the structures and processes that are objects of management at each of these scales and how they interact.

The Alligator Hole. A characteristic habitat of the Everglades is the alligator hole (Figure 13.19), which is surrounded by a variety of emergent marsh plants, including sawgrass—the most common plant in the Everglades. The area of open water is kept free of plants by the activity of alligators. At this scale, patterns are created by biotic processes such as competition for light and nutrients as well as animal activity. Many processes, including photosynthesis, respiration, decomposition, nutrient mobilization, soil accretion, and bedrock dissolution, occur at smaller scales than seen here, but may be partly apparent at this scale. Many small aquatic organ-

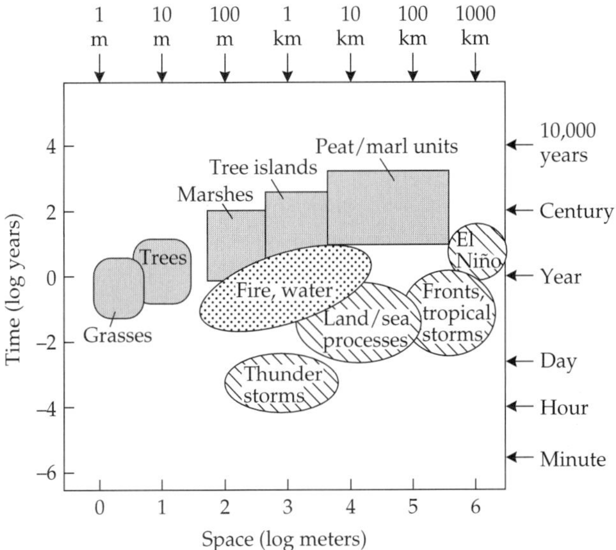

Figure 13.18 Spatial and temporal domains of critical ecosystem components in the Everglades. The squares represent the domains within a vegetation hierarchy of individual plants, associations, and landscape units. The cross-hatched ellipses represent the atmospheric hierarchy, the primary sources of water input. The mesoscale processes of fires and surface water conditions are in an intermediate position, and integrate the vegetation and atmospheric hierarchies. (From Light et al. 1995.)

isms (grass shrimp, water fleas, mosquitofish) spend their lives within a single alligator hole, while other organisms, including alligators, require larger spatial scales for survival. During droughts, the holes are refugia for many aquatic organisms (Craighead 1971), offering resilience for populations over broader spatial scales. The habitat window is the scale at which populations of plants, small aquatic animals, and alligators are monitored, but most management in the Everglades occurs at broader spatial scales, especially at the landscape level.

The Everglades Landscape. In the Everglades ecosystem, the biota are adapted to and interact with a few key landscape-scale processes—surface water hydrology, fires, storms—that fluctuate on time scales of decades and cover areas up to hundreds of square kilometers. The interaction of these variables across space and time generates much of the landscape structure seen in Figure 13.20. The large tree islands are characteristically teardrop-

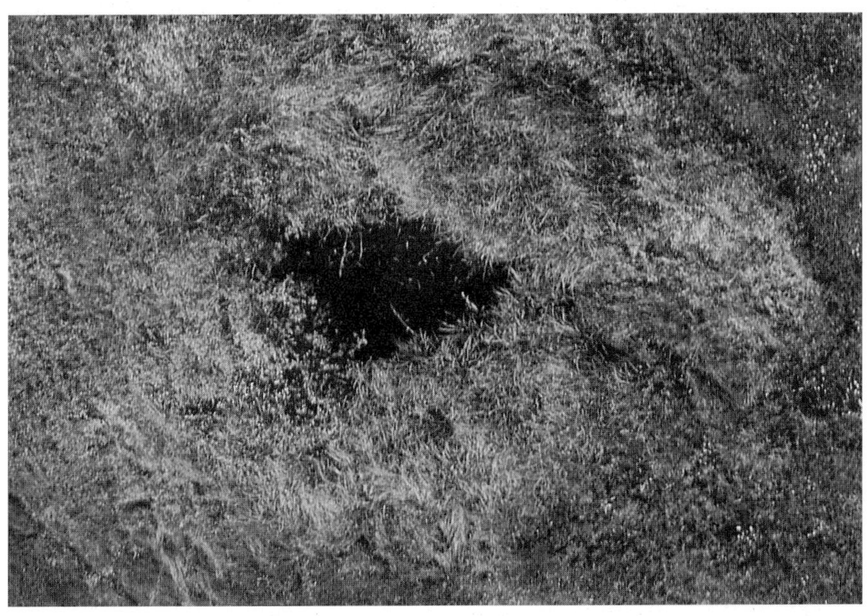

Figure 13.19 Aerial photograph (10 m window) showing the landscape mosaic in a conserved area (Everglades National Park) at the scale of a single alligator hole. Visible are tree islands, sawgrass marshes, and wet prairies. (Photograph courtesy of the South Florida Water Management District.)

Figure 13.20 Aerial photograph (1 mile window) of the landscape mosaic in conserved areas in the southern Everglades, showing tree islands, sawgrass marshes, and wet prairies. (Photograph courtesy of the South Florida Water Management District.)

shaped and oriented to overland water flow patterns. The underlying topography of both the bedrock and the soil surface is very flat, with elevation differences between the highest, driest hardwood forests and the lowest alligator holes of less than one meter.

Fires have been part of the ecosystem for as long as the wetland complex has existed, and occur at multiple frequencies, with annual and decadal intervals. Severe, peat-consuming fires lower soil elevation, leave little organic matter or local vegetation propagules, and generally result in dramatic shifts in vegetation assemblages (Craighead 1971). Less severe fires generally consume aboveground biomass, leaving viable roots and allowing rapid regeneration of vegetation similar in composition and structure to that before the fire. The visible patterns of gray sawgrass stands and darker wet marshes (Figure 13.20) are created by this interplay of severe fires, which create the wet prairies, and less severe fires and hydrology, which moderate the slow spatial spread of remnant sawgrass stands.

The landscape scale contains the home ranges of a suite of small animals (fish, small mammals), but is only a part of the foraging area of wading birds. The wading birds are a critical cross-scale link, as they feed over larger spatial scales up to a regional level. Fire management (control and prescribed fires) is applied at the landscape scale, whereas water management is applied at the regional scale.

The Region. The Everglades wetland is part of a larger watershed that covers most of the southern peninsula of Florida (Figure 13.21). The watershed comprises three sub-basins: the Kissimmee River basin, Lake Okeechobee, and the Everglades. Rainfall is the primary input, with an annual mean of about 130 cm (range 95–270 cm, MacVicar and Lin 1984). Most rainfall occurs during the summer months and is associated with convective thunderstorms, but other oscillation periods (3 months and 12 years) indicate cycles at longer and shorter time frames (Gunderson 1992); the longer-term cycles of flood and drought have been linked to El Niño activity (Rasmussen 1985; Ropelewski and Halpert 1987).

The annual pattern of wet and dry seasons is one of the dominant cycles organizing energy flow through the system. Water levels rise during June and remain high into early fall due to summer rains; water levels then slowly decline through the fall and winter months. In spring, high temperatures, high evaporation, and little or no rain result in the lowest water levels of the year. This rainfall variation translates into large spatial variation in water depths. In the wet season, most of the system is inundated, resulting in high primary and secondary aquatic productivity. As the system dries, the spatial extent of wetted area decreases, and aquatic organisms move with the drying front, concentrating their numbers and providing forage for predators such as alligators and wading birds. If the drought is severe, most of the organisms die or are consumed, leaving little stock for recovery; if it is less severe, the remnant stocks allow for rapid recovery when water returns.

Development within the Everglades is scarcely 100 years old. Human population growth in the region has been dramatic, exploding from fewer than 30,000 people at the turn of the century to just over 5 million in 1990. Development was predicated on several factors that enabled humans to control undesirable aspects of summers in southern Florida, including air conditioning, mosquito control through pesticide application, and control of natural flooding in many areas, including the eastern marshlands of the Everglades.

Human land uses and geologic and hydrologic features are key structures apparent at the regional scale (Figure 13.21). Land in the historical Everglades (excluding the Kissimmee River Basin and Lake Okeechobee) is divided among four types of use: urban, agriculture, water control, and protected park. Urban systems cover 12% of the area, and can be seen as the lighter, mottled patterns along the eastern rim of the Everglades. Various forms of agricultural uses cover 27% (Everglades Agricultural Area, EAA), most of it found in the northern Everglades and south of Lake Okeechobee. The central third of the historical marshland has been designated Water Conservation Areas (the large, dark polygons in the middle of Figure 13.21). About 21% of the historical system is preserved in Everglades National Park or Preserve, at the southern terminus of the freshwater wetland. Of the original Everglades ecosystem, less than half remains in areas where conservation is the primary management objective (Gunderson and Loftus 1993; Davis et al. 1994).

The geologic features underlying the Everglades have structured much of the region's development and management history. The deepest soils—categorized as peats and mucks—are Holocene sediments, which occur in the northern Everglades and have attracted agriculture. The higher coastal ridge is where urban development has occurred. These geologic features have also contributed to the low-nutrient, or oligotrophic, status of the historical Everglades system.

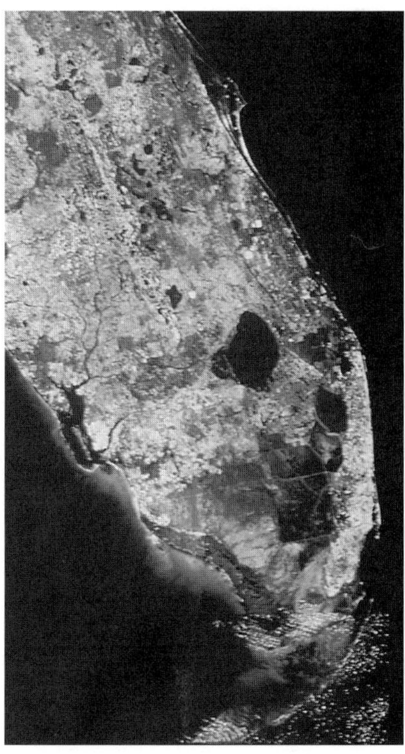

Figure 13.21 A recent satellite image of South Florida, showing the hydrologic system of the Everglades and current land uses. The Everglades was once the southern third of a hydrologic system that included the Kissimmee River Basin and Lake Okeechobee (the large lake near the center of the photograph). Land uses of the Everglades ecosystem are indicated by the Everglades Agriculture Area in the north, Water Conservation Areas (dark areas), urban development along the east coast, and the national park and preserve in the south. (Photograph courtesy of the South Florida Water Management District.)

Development of Water Management

In the 20th century, the Everglades ecosystem has been transformed from a vast subtropical wetland into a highly managed multiple-use system as a result of one of the largest public works projects in the world. This transformation was not a linear process, but rather was characterized by turbulence and punctuated change. For the most part, management was driven by a series of events perceived as crises that threatened exploitation of the resource. Each crisis precipitated actions resulting in a reconfiguration and emergence of a new system.

These crises appear to have arisen from two kinds of causes: those created by external environmental events and those that result from human activities. The former are mostly exogenous to the region, and arise from larger-scale processes, such as hurricanes or too much or too little rainfall over the system. The latter occur over a longer period of time, tend to be endogenous to the system, and reflect chronic problems defined by slower variables, such as water quality degradation that leads to dramatic shifts in dominant taxa. These crises originate as a result of human development of natural resources, and are associated with agricultural activities, primarily in the form of soil loss and water pollution.

These crises have resulted in at least four major eras of water management (Light et al. 1995), based on a recurring theme of flooding effects. The first two eras were a result of flooding due to high rainfall events, the third was related to drought, and the fourth resulted from attempts to rectify latent or previously unaddressed problems.

The earliest settlers were intent on reclaiming land "lost" to natural flooding in order to farm the rich muck soils. Early attempts at drainage were able to control water levels during average water conditions; the approach was to dig canals and drain the land as fast as possible. Periods of dry years allowed for agricultural expansion, at least until the next wet year. However, these attempts at drainage were unable to cope with the full variation in climatic regimes. Flooding crises occurred in 1903 as a result of high rains and in 1926 and 1928 due to severe hurricanes.

In 1947, the same year Everglades National Park was established, over twice the normal amount of rain fell on South Florida, severely affecting the coastal communities and inundating some areas for several months. This acute flooding resulted in the implementation of a widespread plan to avoid this type flooding in the future. The massive control plan, developed by the U.S. Army Corps of Engineers, called for the creation of specific land use areas (agriculture, water conservation, and national park) and a water management infrastructure (2240 km of canals and levees, pumping stations with 3.8 billion liters/day capacity, and requisite water regulation schedules) to regulate floodwaters. This era of water management lasted from 1947 through the early 1970s.

The crisis that precipitated the next era of water management was a drought in 1971. Less than 82 cm of rain fell over the system, creating the worst drought in 40 years (Blake 1980). By the early 1970s, the human population of South Florida had topped the 2 million mark, and sugarcane production in the EAA had more than tripled following the Communist takeover in Cuba and the subsequent U.S. ban on Cuban sugar imports. The low rainfall, coupled with increased urban and agricultural water demands, prompted concern over the adequacy of the water supply. Serious problems arose in trying to retool a system designed for flood control to meet water supply concerns. The situation was exacerbated by the difficulty inherent in decisions involving trade-offs among water use categories. The major reform that resulted was the creation of state water management districts, which would manage the system for water supply on a watershed-wide basis.

The history of water management in the Everglades provides a few lessons for ecosystem management. First, there will always be uncertainty inherent in the dynamics of the system being managed; consequently, management institutions must be capable of adapting, renewal, and learning. Second, the focus of management must be on multiple scales, in both space and time. Management focused on one scale (e.g., local drainage of farmland) is likely to result in surprises and crises at larger scales. Third, a key lesson is that the success of ecosystem management is not just in clear articulation of its goals, but in what kind of management framework is established to meet those goals and to encourage learning while managing. Conservation, preservation of ecological structures and processes, and minimizing external threats while maximizing external benefits are noble objectives, and in one shape or form have always been part of the history of conservation in the Everglades. Yet clearly management has failed in at least half a century of trying. The final section looks at some of the reasons and possible solutions for this failure, and discusses the most recent attempts at adaptive ecosystem management around the goal of ecosystem restoration.

Restoring the Everglades for Conservation

Since the early 1980s, the focus of management in the Everglades has been on ecosystem restoration. Water management via water control has benefited both urban and agricultural interests. However, conservation and preservation of the remnant wetland has been less successful, and is now being pursued through ecosystem restoration. That restoration is predicated on resolving current resource issues and conflicts, and on re-creating as many of the historical attributes of the ecological system as possible. The historical ecosystem was characterized by three attributes: it supported a suite of animals with large spatial requirements, it was oligotrophic, and it supported a spatially diverse vegetation mosaic.

Vegetation Issues. The key vegetation issues include changes in spatial distribution due to water management, losses in native cover types due to land use conversions, changes in species composition due to nutrient inputs, and invasions of exotic flora (Gunderson 1994). Vegetation changes have been related to modifications of the hydrologic regime. Sawgrass and tree island communities have been replaced by open-water marshes in areas of water impoundment. Where water levels have been reduced, broad-leaved hardwoods and exotic trees have replaced the grassy marsh vegetation.

Nutrient enhancements or additions change the species composition of both macrophytic and periphytic assemblages (Davis 1991). The addition of phosphorus-laden water (linked to runoff from agriculture) to portions of the Water Conservation Areas has resulted in a shift in dominance from sawgrass to cattail communities. In these same areas, the periphyton (algal community) has shifted to dominance by pollution-tolerant taxa.

Although about 17% of the flora is alien (from areas outside of Florida or the southeastern coastal plain), only a handful of species have become aggressive invaders. The main invasive trees are the melaleuca (*Melaleuca quinquenervia*), Australian pine (*Casuarina* spp.), and Brazilian pepper (*Schinus terebinthifolius*). Melaleuca invades the drained marshes of the eastern glades, where water levels have been lowered and fires burn frequently (Myers 1983). Australian pine invades the southern and eastern glades, but on slightly higher sites. Brazilian pepper is found on unburned upland sites and on abandoned farm fields. All are adapted to short periods of flooding.

Animal Issues. Many changes have been noted in the fauna during the 20th century. Most notable are an increase in non-native species, the endangerment and extirpation of some native species, and dramatic changes in populations of key taxa. Several hundred species of exotic animals have become naturalized along the southeastern coast of Florida; of these, a few dozen (primarily fishes) exploit altered niches within the Everglades system (Gunderson and Loftus 1993). Exotic fishes live primarily in canals, drainage ditches, and borrow pits throughout the region, although a few species survive in the mangrove/freshwater ecotone. Exotic birds have become naturalized in the coastal ridge area. As a rule of thumb, the abundance of exotic animals declines with distance from the coastal area.

At least 17 taxa from South Florida have been recognized as federally endangered or threatened; most notable are the Florida panther, Cape Sable Seaside Sparrow, and Wood Stork. Although many of these taxa have small populations and are vulnerable to extinction, none has disappeared from the wetlands of the Everglades. Extirpations have occurred in the fauna of the upland communities due to conversion to human uses, with habitat loss cited as the primary cause.

The most dramatic changes in the fauna have been observed in nesting populations of wading birds (Frederick and Collopy 1989; Bancroft 1989; Ogden 1994). From the 1920s through the 1960s, the Everglades provided the primary nesting area for populations in the southeastern United States. Since then, only 5–10% of the populations that once nested there continue to use the area (Ogden 1978, 1994), possibly due to a spatial decrease in early wet season habitat caused by development, less water flow through the system, alteration of the hydrologic regimes necessary for successful feeding and breeding, or higher quality of other sites in the Southeast. In spite of the loss of nesting habitat, the Everglades still continues to provide an important feeding area for wintering and transient populations.

Other Issues. A number of other issues haunt the Everglades, including the presence of toxins such as mercury, which settles from the atmosphere, is trapped by organic sediments, and is then mobilized in food webs. There is also a growing recognition of linkages between the Everglades and other areas, such as the freshwater flow into the estuaries of Florida Bay, and the importance of the area as an feeding stop for migrating and overwintering birds.

Attempts at Recovery. By the late 1980s, a group of scientists from the South Florida Water Management District and Everglades Park began a process to synthesize existing ecological understanding and to translate that understanding into restoration strategies. A symposium was held, followed by three years of workshops, in which a computer model to improve communication among scientists, engineers, and resource managers was developed and tested. The synthesis emerged in a book (Davis and Ogden 1994) in which, for the first time, changes to the system are described, restoration goals are defined, and restoration polices are prescribed.

The major conclusion of this informal collaborative effort was that enough is known about the Everglades ecosystem to begin rehabilitation efforts (Holling et al. 1994; Walters and Gunderson 1994), the focus of which should be hydrology. Tinkering—defined as dealing with a subset of the system—has not worked, nor have single, quick-fix structural solutions. The group discovered that restoration will require composite policies; that is, integrated sets of structural and operational changes will have to be devised to satisfy restoration goals and provide for existing water needs of the region. Moreover, there must be more than one set of "composite" policies, so that the region will not be dependent on one set of unforgiving rules.

The process of hydrologic restoration can be distilled to a few key points. First, more water should flow through what is left of the system, into the estuaries of Florida Bay (Walters et al. 1992). Second, that water should be clean. Third, there is enough water in Lake Okeechobee, the EAA, and the urban sectors to supply restoration needs. There are specific costs associated with improving water quality in each of these water sources. Finally, restoration should move forward as an adaptive process, with management actions viewed as experiments derived from working hypotheses that deal with the many uncertainties of the system.

An adaptive management framework provides hope for restoring and conserving key properties of this world-famous ecosystem.

CASE STUDY 6

Conservation Management of a European Natural Area: Doñana National Park, Spain

Carlos Fernández-Delgado, University of Córdoba, Spain

In contrast to the Americas, Europe has been settled by technological Western cultures for thousands of years, and these people have had a long time to leave their mark upon the land. Consequently, fewer natural areas remain in Europe than in many other regions, and fewer opportunities are available to manage them in a semi-pristine state. The challenges of managing the remaining natural areas are great, as the relatively small remnants exist in a matrix dominated by humanity. Here is one example of the special challenges involved in managing a European natural area.

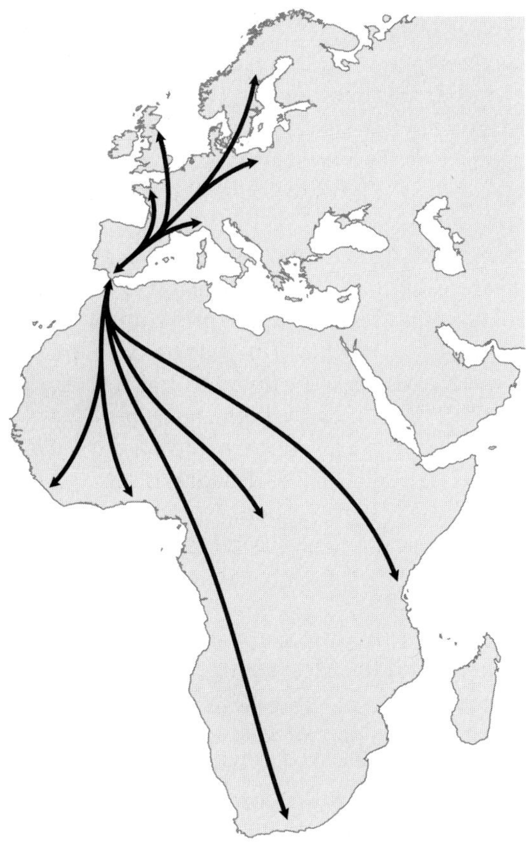

Figure 13.22 Doñana National Park is located in a critically important area of southern Europe on the Iberian Peninsula. Major bird migration pathways for the entire European and African continents pass through Doñana.

The 50,720 ha Doñana National Park, located in Andalucía on the southwestern coast of Spain (Figure 13.22), is part of the Guadalquivir River Basin. The Guadalquivir is one of the largest rivers in the country, and the only navigable one. The area has a subhumid Mediterranean climate, influenced by the Atlantic Ocean, with alternating dry and rainy seasons (Emberger et al. 1976; Font 1983). Some three thousands years ago, during the pre-Roman period, a lake (*Lacus Ligustinus*) covered much of the area. The lake remained during Roman colonization until approximately the 4th or 5th century A.D., after which alluvial deposits due to severe deforestation in the uplands transformed the lake into a marsh with a tidal influence, and ultimately into a marsh with a pluvial influence (Bernúes 1990). It is on this marsh that most of present-day Doñana National Park is located (Figure 13.23).

Doñana has three dominant ecosystem types: fixed dunes, or "cotos," mobile dunes, and marshes. The fixed dunes are affected by the depth of the water table, the mobile dunes are driven by substratum mobility, and the marshes are created by seasonal rains (García-Novo et al. 1977). The mobile dunes of Doñana, which run parallel to the coastline for 30 km, are the most important dunes on the Iberian Peninsula and some of the most extensive in Europe. They move an average of 4–6 m/year, with some sections moving up to 20 m/year (García-Novo et al. 1976).

The marshes of Doñana National Park occupy some 27,000 ha, and are highly productive and seasonally variable, with winter water depths up to 1 m and little to no water during the summer (Figure 13.24). The broad ecotone between the marshes and uplands has a complex vegetational structure and a high faunal diversity, including many herbivores and predators (Figure 13.25).

(A)

(B)

Figure 13.23 (A) This alluvial plain was once a lake; it has silted in over a period of centuries as a result of deforestation in the upper parts of the drainage. (B) Seasonal marshes form after heavy rains, and are critical feeding habitats for resident and migratory birds. (A, photograph by G. K. Meffe; B, by Carlos Fernández-Delgado.)

The Biogeographic Importance of Doñana

Doñana's geographic position, between the European and African continents and between the Atlantic Ocean and the Mediterranean Sea, results in a rich flora and fauna, with some 800 species of vascular plants, 30 species of fishes, 11 amphibian species, 19 reptiles, 348 birds, and 29 mammals recorded (Valverde 1960, 1967; Rivas-Martínez et al. 1980; Fernández 1982; García et al. 1989; Llandres and Urdiales 1990; Fernández-Delgado et al. 1994). The park is especially critical to bird diversity, as some three-fourths of all European species are found in Doñana due to its position on the migratory routes of many species (see Figure 13.22) and its abundant food resources (García-Novo et al. 1977; Amat 1980). During spring and autumn migration, it is easy to observe more than 200 species of birds.

Many Doñana species are endemic, threatened, or endangered, or otherwise of ecological interest. These include an endemic cyprinodontid, the Iberian Toothcarp *(Lebias ibera)*, the White-headed Duck *(Oxyura leucocephala)*, European Bittern *(Botaurus stellaris)*, Squacco Heron *(Ardeola ralloides)*,

Figure 13.24 In the area of contact between the mobile dune system and the marshlands, a permanent lagoon has been formed by water draining from the dunes. During severe droughts (such as when this photo was taken in 1995) this is one of the few remaining water bodies in the entire park and supports large bird populations. (Photograph by G. K. Meffe.)

(A)

(B)

Figure 13.25 Overabundance of herbivores and introduced species are two major environmental problems in Doñana. (A) A large herd of red deer running through the marshland during the dry season. In the background is the introduced eucalyptus forest. (B) Wild pigs in the ecotone formed where the dune systems and the marshlands meet. In the background is the introduced pine forest. (Photographs by Carlos Fernández-Delgado.)

Marbled Teal *(Marmaronetta angustirostris)*, Ferruginous Duck *(Aythya nyroca)*, Crested Coot *(Fulica cristata)*, Andalusian Hemipode *(Turnix sylvatica)*, Curlew *(Numenius arquata)*, Black Tern *(Chlidonias niger)*, Ruddy Shelduck *(Tadorna ferruginea)*, Slender-billed Gull *(Larus genei)*, Spanish Imperial Eagle *(Aquila adalberti)*, Purple Gallinule *(Porphyrio porphyrio)*, the only European species of mongoose *(Herpestes ichneumon)*, and the Iberian Lynx *(Felis pardina)*, one of the most threatened felids of Europe.

This rich biota means that Doñana is one of the most important wetlands in Europe. This was recognized when it was declared a National Park by the Spanish government in 1969, an International Biosphere Reserve in 1981, and a Natural Heritage Preserve by UNESCO in 1995.

Human History in Doñana

Human habitation and use of the Doñana area goes back thousands of years. All the great European civilizations have passed through and utilized this area, including Phoenicians, Greeks, Romans, Visigoths, and Arabs (Equipo 28 1985). Prior to 1262, the area was controlled by Arabs, and the marshlands were used for grazing by Arabian horses, while the surrounding hills were used for timber extraction and wax and honey harvesting from beehives. In 1262, after conquering the area, the Christian King Alfonso X established a hunting area in Doñana, beginning a hunting phase that lasted 400 years (Granados 1987). Hunting centered on wild pigs and red and fallow deer in the forest, and on waterfowl in the marshes. This activity largely protected the forest, which served as a shelter for game species. However, hunting encouraged the eradication of predator species such as foxes, wolves, birds of prey, lynx, and mountain cats. There were large rewards for each animal killed, which greatly reduced the predator populations, while the herbivore populations, freed of their enemies, increased considerably.

In 1628 the introduction of cattle began a new phase in Doñana (Granados 1987). In addition to cattle grazing, people were able to cut firewood for their personal needs. Excessive cattle populations resulted in overgrazing, reduced the Doñana cork-oaks, and increased dune formation. Growing interest in forest development led to a forestry phase. In the beginning, forestry was centered on cork-oaks, white and black poplars, willows, ashes, and junipers (Granados 1987). Many animal species that were unable to adapt to the changes were locally extirpated, including the Black Stork *(Cico-*

nia nigra) and the Swan *(Cygnus* sp.). Forestry activity increased with the introduction of pines in 1737, which was so successful that they are the principal component of the forest today, with a resulting loss of oak mast.

Toward the end of the 19th century, river red gum *(Eucalyptus camaldulensis)* was introduced, of which a large population still exists in the northern part of the park, eliminating a thicket habitat. This represented the largest human intervention in Doñana in recent years. Besides river red gum, an additional 50 plant species were introduced; most of these, however, became scarce because of inappropriate conditions and low soil fertility.

This forest phase lasted until modern scientific interest began in the 1950s with expeditions led by the Spanish naturalist José A. Valverde (Mountfort 1958). The area was eventually visited by renowned naturalists such as Guy Mountfort, Roger Tory Peterson, and the Nobel laureate Sir Julian Huxley, which raised its public visibility. In 1964, with help from the World Wildlife Fund (WWF), a Spanish scientific group (Consejo Superior de Investigaciones Científicas) bought 6794 ha in the Doñana area and established the first protected area as the Doñana Biological Station. In 1969 Doñana National Park was officially created with an initial extension of 35,000 ha; this was enlarged in 1978 when the present boundaries were established, ushering in the present conservation phase.

Conservation and Management Problems in Doñana National Park

In the present conservation phase, human activities in Doñana have drastically diminished, and its traditional uses have begun to be managed. But the new prohibitions and regulations in the name of conservation have not been welcomed by many inhabitants of the region, and have led to deterioration of the relationship between the park administration and the surrounding villages. Of course, this makes the management job more difficult.

One of the conflicts centers on agriculture. The beginning of the conservation phase coincided with recent agricultural development of lands surrounding Doñana. Until that time, most of the marshlands of the Guadalquivir estuary were, from an agricultural perspective, unproductive; however, with advances in agricultural technology, these impoverished soils became usable. Large hydraulic works built to improve agriculture in areas around Doñana directly influenced water flow within the park. Natural canals have been cut, blocked, or transformed depending on the particular interest surrounding each. Illegal irrigation wells proliferated throughout the area, drastically lowering water table levels during the summer dry period and threatening the park's vegetation (Castells et al. 1992). These wells also represented a threat to many vertebrate species, including lynx, which fell into them and drowned (EBD 1991); most wells are now covered. Heavy pesticide use on agricultural fields kills birds in large numbers; in 1973 and 1986, 50,000 and 20,000 birds died, respectively (Castroviejo 1993).

Hunting has increased considerably in areas around the park because of the large numbers of birds that are attracted to Doñana. Predators are also attracted to the park, and adjacent landowners set illegal traps or poison them; this is the leading cause of death for many carnivores, including the Imperial Eagle and the lynx, both endangered species (EBD 1991). Proliferation of electrical cables also contributed to bird loss; mortality was so high that all of these structures are now subterranean.

Another negative impact on the national park has its origin in the cultural aspects of the area, especially in a religious tradition centered in the nearby village of El Rocío, where pilgrims have gathered annually since the 12th century to celebrate the Virgin of Rocío. Initially this was a local celebration, but today it is a national event, with the number of visitors (called "romeros") increasing every year. The pilgrimage, or "romería," is a festival lasting one week, during which up to a million visitors arrive with a variety of vehicles, including nearly 250,000 horses. A diversity of groups, or "brotherhoods," use traditional roads to get to the village, one of which crosses the national park from south to north (Figure 13.26). In 1995, 10,000 people and 3000 vehicles left 20 tons of waste inside the park. One of the biggest problems is that this activity takes place over one of the most delicate parts of the national park during spring, when many birds are reproducing. Elimination of this traditional activity is not possible, however, due to the strong public outcry and revolt that it would engender.

Matalascañas, an old fishing village on the beaches of Doñana, has become a major urbanized tourist area that threatens the water table, increases coastal organic pollution, and is the main source of domestic animals in the park (Figure 13.26). It is also a primary source of road mortality in summer and on weekends for Doñana vertebrates (amphibians, reptiles, nocturnal birds, and mammals, including lynx).

Another negative effect is contamination by mining industries through the dumping of heavy metals in the bodies of water closest to the park (Cabrera et al. 1984, 1987). The organic contamination coming from the neighboring villages (the majority of their wastewater has not been purified) is also important, and large amounts of urban and agricultural debris surround Doñana (Arambarri et al. 1984; Castells et al. 1992)

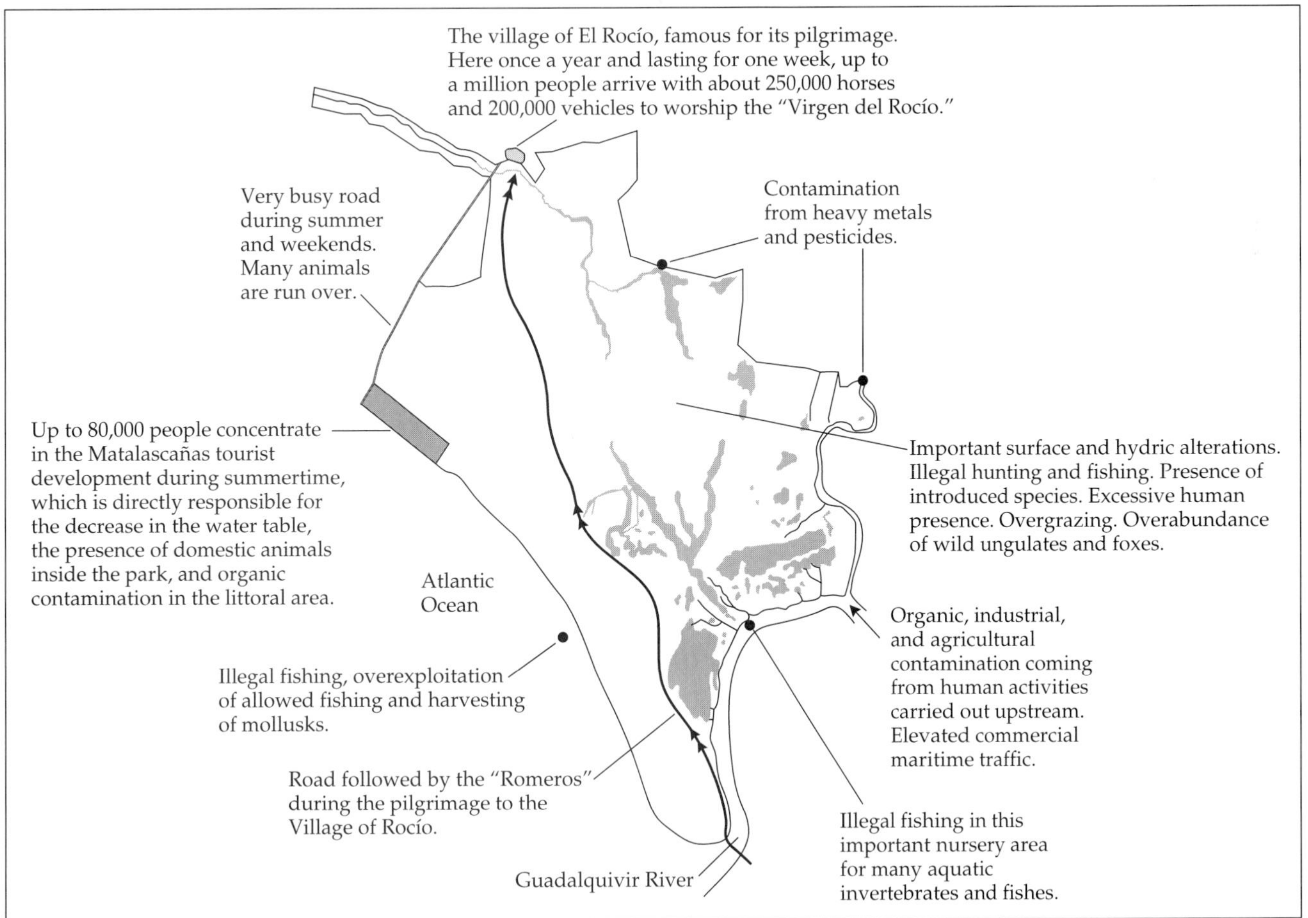

Figure 13.26 A schematic overview of the many conservation problems facing Doñana National Park.

Many companies, attracted by the natural and cultural importance of the area, want to set up businesses near Doñana. In 1991, the "Costa Doñana" project attempted to construct a large tourist area, with more than 30,000 hotel beds, on the park boundary, but national and international pressures stopped the project. Presently, there is a plan to construct a large dam in the Guadalquivir near Doñana in order to retain water for surrounding agricultural fields. This project could destroy the entire estuarine ecosystem (Fernández-Delgado 1996).

Inside the national park there are also problems. The red and fallow deer populations are so large that they must be controlled artificially. Vegetation damage by cattle, still present in the park due to pressures from the neighboring villages, is high (Figure 13.27). Foxes and wild pigs are also superabundant and difficult to control because of their high reproductive rates; the density of foxes in Doñana is one of the highest in Europe (Rau 1987). Rabbit populations, the basic prey for most of the carnivorous species, have decreased because of introduced viral infections (myxomatosis and hemorrhagic viral disease). Botulism, an endemic illness in Doñana affecting waterfowl, may become a major problem if water quality declines (INITAA 1992). The accumulation of heavy metals and pesticides, especially in birds of prey, threatens to reduce their reproductive success in the near future (González et al. 1984; Hernández et al. 1986, 1988). Illegal hunting and fishing inside the national park are also major problems. Doñana's 70 guards (a large number by some standards) are not enough to control poachers.

Most of the water management in Doñana has been oriented toward waterfowl; thus, many sluices were built to prevent fresh water from flowing from the park into the Guadalquivir River. This management has isolated the various water bodies of the park from the river, preventing fishes and invertebrates from colonizing after a dry period. Additionally, the few remaining hectares with some tidal influence have been eliminated.

Exotic species have markedly changed the ecology of Doñana. The most spectacular effect has been due to the intentional introduction of the red swamp crayfish *(Procambarus clarkii)* in 1974. This species is so well adapted to the region that it has not only altered trophic relationships, but has also influenced the economy of the region (Montes et al. 1993). Presently, the crayfish occupies nearly all of the Iberian Peninsula, and annual harvest in

Figure 13.27 Hundreds of cattle still live within Doñana National Park. These cattle are drinking water from one of the few remaining water bodies in the marsh during a drought. (Photograph by Carlos Fernández-Delgado.)

the Doñana area is 3000–5000 tons. Other introduced American species, including the eastern mosquitofish *(Gambusia holbrooki)* and the mummichog *(Fundulus heteroclitus),* threaten the endemic pupfish (*Lebias ibera*) with near extinction in Doñana (Fernández-Delgado et al. 1994). These exotics, along with introduced largemouth bass *(Micropterus salmoides),* also have contributed to the disappearance of the stickleback *(Gasterosteus aculeatus)* in Doñana (Fernández-Delgado 1987).

Measures to Protect Doñana

At the present time, two programs are being developed to protect Doñana National Park, one focused on the interior and the other on the surrounding areas. Conservation measures within the park fall under "The Doñana National Park Management Plan," locally known as PRUG (BOE 1991). This plan is run by a committee of 25 people who represent local, regional, and national governments, universities, communities, and conservation associations. The group is in charge of fulfilling the objectives included in PRUG, whose guiding philosophy is that conservation takes priority over any other activities within the park, and that the park's natural richness depends on conservation in the surrounding areas.

The park has been divided into four zones: the Zones of Special Use (173 ha), which include installations for park management and visitor information centers, the Zones of Moderate Use (382 ha), intended for the traditional roads that cross the park, the Zones of Restricted Use (100 ha) near the information centers, where people are allowed to walk about freely, and the Reserve Zones (50,065 ha), the bulk of the park, with entry restricted to managers, researchers, landowners, and other authorized people.

The program is designed for management of natural resources, research, public use, compatible extractive uses, and improving the relationship between the park administration and its neighbors. Included in the natural resource management plan is an attempt to restore the park's water system to its state before the transformations adjacent to Doñana. Managers are also trying to maintain and/or recover the vegetation formations characteristic of Doñana by eliminating exotic species, controlling plagues and illnesses, and preventing fires.

Both the flora and fauna are managed toward preservation of native species, protection of threatened or endangered populations, control of overabundant species, and elimination of exotic species where possible. Two management programs are being conducted on the most visible and charismatic species of Doñana: the lynx and the Imperial Eagle. Both programs are oriented toward habitat improvement, which will benefit many other species as well. Additionally, densities of ungulates (red deer, fallow deer, wild pig) and foxes are being controlled, and the most abundant introduced plants are being eradicated.

The management plan allows the park's use by local residents for traditional resource extraction, such as coal mining, beekeeping, harvest of mollusks on the beach and pinecones in the forest, hunting and fishing in designated areas, and extensive cattle grazing. Because of high unemployment in the surrounding villages, this program has created problems for park managers due to the high number of requests. The number of licenses for some activities has been increased through political pressure, resulting in overexploited stocks, especially of mollusks.

A public use program provides visitors with information about the national park and argues for the need for its conservation. Seven reception centers have been built at various points to inform visitors of Doñana's history and natural richness. But these reception centers and the high number of visitors they draw have been criticized by conservation associations for their effects on the park. Obviously there is a trade-off between public educationl/involvement and resulting damage to the park. A series of outreach activities is attempting to improve the relationship between the national park and the residents of surrounding areas. These activities include environmental education programs in the neighboring villages; information points about the park have been established in several of them.

Finally, a buffer zone of 56,930 ha surrounding Doñana has recently been designated. The buffer is managed by the regional administration in Seville, with a lower level of protection and a limited budget, while the national park is managed by the national administration in Madrid. Human activities in the buffer zone are little controlled, and it remains to be seen whether it will have much of a positive influence on the park.

A second plan to protect Doñana, approved in 1995, is "The Sustainable Development Plan for Doñana's Neighboring Areas," which foresees an investment of some $525 million (U.S.) through the year 2000 to improve the economy of the surrounding villages. The majority of this investment is for water management (31%), equipment and road infrastructure (25%), and agriculture (21%). The rest will pay for a variety of programs such as environmental education, developing cattle ranching outside of the park, and promoting ecotourism.

There are also attempts to change agricultural practices in the region by replacing crops that need large amounts of water and pesticides with more xeric crops and organic approaches. Water management also is changing, with a new emphasis on water conservation and water quality. The water delivery systems of the area are being modernized, stream and riverine habitats will be restored, and water treatment plants are being installed. In short, the idea behind the plan is to improve the economy of the villages affected by Doñana's proximity and make their activities compatible with conservation of the area and its exceptional natural values.

The Future of Doñana

Two questions remain: Will Doñana ultimately be saved from the human pressures that surround it? And what will be its conservation status when it passes to the next generation?

The greatest long-term threats to Doñana come from the surrounding lands. Human pressures are so high that the area is being degraded unintentionally in a slow but continuous fashion. The fundamental problem is that the survival of the people of the Doñana area is at stake. Andalucía, with an unemployment rate of nearly 34%, is one of the poorest areas in Europe. It is politically difficult to control or limit the negative environmental activities of the few companies that generate jobs in this area, and the few measures followed often are interpreted as restriction of economic development by the national park. To change this opinion, it is necessary to invest large amounts of money in the region, but unfortunately there are many other depressed areas in Spain also in need of economic development. The Sustainable Development Plan for Doñana's Neighboring Areas is a good start, but these investments end in 2000, and it is uncertain what will happen next.

International cooperation seems essential to the long-term protection of Doñana. Because it plays a vital role in the migratory routes of many bird species from throughout Europe, it is critical that these other countries become involved in protection of the park at every level, including economic development. The natural resources of Doñana National Park are essential to the biota of the European and African continents. Because effective conservation here will benefit so many, it is appropriate that the costs be shared as well.

CASE STUDY 7

Putting the Pieces Together: International Management of Cranes and Their Habitats

Curt D. Meine and James T. Harris, International Crane Foundation

The world's 15 species of cranes offer some of the most complex challenges imaginable to conservation managers, who potentially must come to grips with all possible aspects of conservation biology simultaneously. Crane conservation efforts must deal with biological, sociological, economic, and political issues, language and cultural barriers, funding challenges, international cooperation, and myriad other issues to succeed. Their successes offer a model from which others may learn.

The cranes (Family Gruidae) belong to one of the world's most ancient families of birds, with fossil records dating back more than 50 million years. The 15 extant species in the family (Figure 13.28) are widely distributed, occurring in more than 110 countries on five continents; only South America and Antarctica lack cranes (Johnsgard 1983). Primarily birds of open wetlands, grasslands, and savannas, cranes have in some cases been able to adapt to and even thrive within humanized landscapes; however, over the last 150 years cranes have had to cope with accelerated loss of habitat and other threats. As a result, cranes now constitute one of the world's most threatened bird families, with seven species currently included on the IUCN Red List of Threatened Animals, and four more likely to be added (Groombridge 1993; Meine and Archibald 1996).

Cranes have long commanded the respect and admiration of their human neighbors, a cultural value that now plays a critical role in drawing

Figure 13.28 The world's 15 species of cranes are here depicted in a wall poster, that can be used as an attractive educational tool. (Original artwork by David Rankin; photograph courtesy of the International Crane Foundation .)

attention to their biological plight. Even as cranes have declined in numbers, their beauty, dramatic migrations, and striking calls and behavior have inspired widespread conservation efforts. Since the early 1970s, a global campaign has been undertaken to develop conservation programs focused on cranes and the ecosystems that serve (in part) as crane habitat. This unusual effort, centered on a single family of birds, yet international in scope and integrated in its approach, offers lessons of broad relevance to conservation biologists. In contrast to management efforts involving particular species in a particular place, crane conservation offers an example of what might be called "meta-management"—coordinated efforts to conserve an entire group of species throughout the world.

Conservation Status of Cranes

The loss, degradation, and overexploitation of wetlands represent the most important threats to cranes, affecting their distribution, movement, and breeding success, and involving habitats used by migratory and nonmigratory species alike throughout the year (Archibald et al. 1981; Harris 1994). Species that use upland grasslands and savannas have also been heavily affected by conversion and degradation of these ecosystems. Because of the cranes' low reproductive potential—in most species, pairs do not breed until 3–5 years of age, and raise on average about one chick per year—increases in mortality caused by hunting, poisons, and powerline collisions can easily depress crane populations. Other important threats to cranes include dam construction, water diversions, urban expansion, invasive plant species, artificial concentration of populations, genetic and demographic problems associated with small populations, disturbance, lack of effective environmental law enforcement, and political instability. As a result of these multiple threats, 11 of the 15 species of cranes may be listed as threatened under the recently revised IUCN Red List criteria (Table 13.1).

The challenge in crane conservation has been to identify the combinations of actions that are available, and required, to respond to the highly varied circumstances on the ground. Conservation programs for cranes entail a wide range of actions, including: stronger legal protections; development of international agreements and cooperative international programs (including the United States–Canada Migratory Bird Treaty, the Ramsar Convention for wetlands protection, and the Convention on the Conservation of Migratory Species of Wild Animals); development of community conservation projects; establishment and management of protected areas; habitat protection, restoration, and management; monitoring and research; support for nongovernmental organizations; public education and professional training; and captive propagation and reintroduction. In some cases, as with the Whooping Crane, necessity has often been the mother of invention, dictating important short-term steps. In other cases, as with the endangered cranes of East Asia, conservationists have taken steps incrementally and opportunistically, amid complicated sociopolitical circumstances.

Three cases from around the world illustrate how crane conservationists have responded to need and opportunity.

Cranes of the Amur River Basin

The Amur River along the Russia–China border is the world's eighth longest river, and the longest without a dam on its main stem. Its basin is rich in species diversity, a reflection of its unique mix of elements from the northern coniferous forests, southern deciduous forests, and Eurasian steppes. For migratory birds, the Amur Basin is an important link between

Table 13.1
Proposed Conservation Status of Cranes under the Revised IUCN Criteria

Taxon	Conservation status (proposed)
Black Crowned Crane (*Belearica pavonina*)	Vulnerable
West African Crowned Crane (*B. p. pavonina*)	Endangered
Sudan Crowned Crane (*B. p. ceciliae*)	Vulnerable
Grey Crowned Crane (*Belearica regulorum*)	Vulnerable
South African Crowned Crane (*B. r. regulorum*)	Endangered
East African Crowned Crane (*B. r. gibbericeps*)	Vulnerable
Blue Crane (*Anthropoides paradiseus*)	Critically Endangered
Demoiselle Crane (*Anthropoides virgo*)	Lower Risk (least concern)
Wattled Crane (*Bugeranus carunculatus*)	Endangered
Siberian Crane (*Grus leucogeranus*)	Endangered
Sandhill Crane (*Grus canadensis*)	Lower Risk (least concern)
Lesser Sandhill Crane (*G. c. canadensis*)	Lower Risk (least concern)
Canadian Sandhill Crane (*G. c. rowanii*)	Lower Risk (least concern)
Greater Sandhill Crane (*G. c. tabida*)	Lower Risk (least concern)
Florida Sandhill Crane (*G. c. pratensis*)	Lower Risk (near threatened)
Mississippi Sandhill Crane (*G. c. pulla*)	Critically Endangered
Cuban Sandhill Crane (*G. c. nesiotes*)	Critically Endangered
Sarus Crane (*Grus antigone*)	Endangered
Indian Sarus Crane (*G. a. antigone*)	Endangered
Eastern Sarus Crane (*G. a. sharpii*)	Endangered
Australian Sarus Crane (*G. a. gilii*)	Data Deficient
Philippine Sarus Crane (*G. a. luzonica*)	Extinct
Brolga (*Grus rubicundus*)	Lower Risk (least concern)
White-naped Crane (*Grus vipio*)	Vulnerable
Hooded Crane (*Grus monachus*)	Vulnerable
Eurasian Crane (*Grus grus*)	Lower Risk (least concern)
Whooping Crane (*Grus americana*)	Endangered
Black-necked Crane (*Grus nigricollis*)	Vulnerable
Red-crowned Crane (*Grus japonensis*)	Endangered

Note: See IUCN 1994 for a summary of the revised categories and criteria. Under the revised criteria, "Threatened" includes the categories "Critically Endangered," "Endangered," and "Vulnerable." (At the time of publication these listings for the cranes had only been proposed, and remain subject to further review by crane specialists.)

arctic breeding grounds and temperate wintering areas. It is also a center of diversity for cranes, with six species (four of which are threatened) occurring in the region (Halvorson et al. 1995).

International tensions have for decades prevented intensive development of the Amur Basin; however, in recent years, development pressures have been growing. A series of dams has been proposed for the Amur River, threatening the river itself and adjacent wetlands. Rapid agricultural conversion of wetlands in the associated Sanjiang Plain in China is depriving Red-crowned and White-naped Cranes and other wetland species of critical breeding habitat. In Russia, economic uncertainty has contributed to inefficient agriculture and exploitive forestry.

Since 1980, cranes have played a key role in stimulating regional conservation initiatives. Important wetlands in Russia and China have been protected, including international reserves at Lake Khanka on the Russia–China border and in the China–Mongolia–Russia border region. A Russian NGO, the Socio-Ecological Union (SEU), has established Muraviovka Park

Figure 13.29 Entrance to a crane refuge in the Amur Basin. (Photograph courtesy of the International Crane Foundation.)

(Figure 13.29), the first private nature reserve in Russia since 1917, by leasing prime crane habitat. Muraviovka is located amid farmlands; crucial community support has been fostered through an exchange program involving schoolteachers and student conservationists from the area and from the United States. In 1992, a landmark workshop brought together conservationists from six countries to share information and consider how to integrate conservation with development in the basin (Halvorson et al. 1995). Khinganski Nature Reserve, along the Amur River, has received vital financial support from a consortium of American zoos for an experimental reintroduction program for Red-crowned and White-naped Cranes. The American zoos have sent eggs to Khinganski for releases, while the Russians have sent captive cranes to bolster the genetic diversity of North America's captive population.

Eastern Sarus Cranes in Southeast Asia

The Eastern Sarus Crane (Figure 13.30), the rarest subspecies of Sarus Crane, formerly occurred throughout Indochina. Over the last 50 years it has been decimated throughout its historical range. Decades of war in Vietnam resulted in massive disruption of one of its last strongholds in the wetlands of the Mekong River delta. Extensive ditching, drainage, and conversion of the wetlands, along with the disturbance and hunting that often accompany warfare, were thought to have resulted in the loss of the subspecies. In 1984, however, local Vietnamese officials reported that the birds had reappeared at a 7500 ha impoundment, the Tram Chim wetland (Brehm Fund 1987). The exact location of this population's breeding grounds has yet to be determined, but Eastern Sarus Crane nests have recently been confirmed at three sites in northeastern Cambodia (Barzen 1994).

Following rediscovery of the flock, several international initiatives were immediately undertaken to protect the population and its habitats. The main wintering area in Vietnam was protected, and is now designated as the Tram Chim National Reserve. Research and management has since focused on restoration of the natural hydrologic processes of these wetlands. In the meantime, safeguarding wild resources has become more difficult as popu-

Figure 13.30 The Eastern Sarus Crane in the Tram Chim wetlands, Vietnam. (Photograph courtesy of the International Crane Foundation.)

lation pressures in Vietnam have resulted in many people being relocated to lands surrounding the reserve.

Broader conservation measures have also been undertaken. International cooperation on behalf of the Eastern Sarus Crane has been enhanced through a workshop convened at Tram Chim in 1990, and through the signing of a Memorandum of Agreement by Cambodia, Thailand, and the International Crane Foundation (ICF) in 1992. The agreement outlined plans to study the breeding grounds in Cambodia, to conduct collaborative field studies in the Mekong Delta, and to participate in international training programs. ICF has also sponsored the preparation of a population and habitat viability analysis for the subspecies. In 1994, a team of wetland managers from Vietnam visited natural floodplain wetlands in northern Australia to study and compare wetland management techniques. And in 1996, ICF, in partnership with several other NGOs, organized an international workshop on sustainable development alternatives in the Mekong River watershed. Such watershed-scale approaches will be increasingly important as the region's human population and its economies continue to expand.

Blue Cranes in Southern Africa

The Blue Crane is endemic to southern Africa, with the vast majority of the population occurring in eastern and southern South Africa. It remains abundant in parts of its range, but has declined significantly since the mid-1970s, and its distribution is now the most restricted of the 15 crane species.

As recently as 1980, there was little conservation concern about the Blue Crane. The species, however, has occasionally caused considerable crop damage, and intentional and unintentional poisoning by farmers, as well as extensive loss of its grassland habitat to afforestation, have significantly affected both its distribution and numbers (Allan 1994). Although the total population is still estimated at 21,000, its rapid decline has caused great concern and a spate of conservation activity among South African conservationists. Recent measures include stricter legal protection for the species; local and national surveys of the population; expanded field research; increased attention to habitat management (through, for example, appropriate fallowing and planting of lure crops), particularly on private lands; the emergence of several NGOs with Blue Crane conservation programs; and development of educational programs focusing on the species.

Especially important have been the efforts of the Overberg Crane Group, which in 1993 developed *A Conservation Programme for the Blue Crane in the Overberg* (Scott and Scott 1996). This comprehensive program emerged from a 1992 Blue Crane workshop, involving broad representation from the local community. The program's goals are to assess the status of the Blue Crane in the Overberg region, address problems that cranes have caused for farmers, and expand conservation measures. Nine specific conservation projects were outlined, and coordinators have been assigned to monitor progress and provide feedback to the group. Conservation agency officials contribute to the program as part of their assigned duties, while volunteers from the farming community, universities, and other institutions also participate. The Overberg Program has met with considerable success. Farmer participation, for example, was key to developing a simple solution to the problem of Blue Crane depredations in sheep feedlots. A single low strand of wire, strung entirely around the feeding trough, does not impede access of sheep to their food, but does impede cranes, which are unwilling to enter such a confined space. The work of the Overberg Crane Group provides a useful model for conservationists elsewhere.

Coordinating Crane Conservation Response

As these examples illustrate, cranes provide important opportunities to build conservation programs that combine various goals, activities, and techniques. Limits of time, money, and personnel have forced crane conservationists to develop ways of coordinating their efforts at the regional and international levels. A number of mechanisms and organizations have emerged to help integrate the various components of a balanced and comprehensive conservation program.

Recovery Teams and Recovery Plans. The U.S. Endangered Species Act of 1973 provides for the development and implementation of recovery plans for endangered species. These plans are prepared and periodically updated by recovery teams appointed by the U.S. Secretary of the Interior. The U.S. Whooping Crane Recovery Team was appointed in 1976, and the USFWS published its first Whooping Crane Recovery Plan in 1980. The plan has been revised twice, in 1986 and in 1994 (USFWS 1994). The Canadian Whooping Crane Recovery Team was established in 1987 to coordinate recovery activities within Canada. Its first plan was published in 1988 and revised in 1994 (Edwards et al. 1994).

Recovery activities have been closely coordinated between the two nations. In 1995, a Memorandum of Understanding on Conservation of the Whooping Crane was signed, calling for the preparation of a combined plan and the formation of a single recovery team comprising five U.S. and five Canadian members. These steps are especially important as precedents for other nations that share endangered migratory crane populations. For example, in 1995, representatives of the range nations of the rare Central and Western populations of the Siberian Crane met for the first time in Moscow, laying the foundation for the establishment of a Siberian Crane Recovery Team.

International Crane Foundation (ICF). Since 1973, the International Crane Foundation (located in Baraboo, Wisconsin, U.S.A.) has carried out conservation programs around the world. ICF's programs in field ecology, aviculture, research, education, and training have helped to strengthen the

(A)

(B)

Figure 13.31 (A) The International Crane Foundation, near Baraboo, Wisconsin, has facilities for holding and rearing the world's 15 species of cranes, including (B) these endangered Whooping Cranes. (A, photograph courtesy of David Thompson, International Crane Foundation; B, by G. K. Meffe.)

global network of crane conservationists. Its publications, including workshop proceedings as well as *The ICF Bugle*, a quarterly newsletter, provide communication links for that network. The Ron Sauey Memorial Library for Bird Conservation serves as a central repository for the world's scientific literature on cranes, their habitats, and their conservation.

ICF maintains a "species bank" of threatened cranes on-site, and is one of the three primary breeding facilities for the Whooping Crane (Figure 13.31). ICF has successfully bred all 15 species in captivity, developing new techniques that have been used in the propagation of other endangered birds. ICF's ex situ efforts now focus on the rarest species (primarily the Siberian and Whooping Cranes), and on the integration of captive crane management with field conservation measures (including crane reintroduction, ecosystem restoration, and habitat management programs). ICF also provides training opportunities for biologists, managers, and educators, and supports a wide range of public education projects at its headquarters and around the world.

IUCN/SSC Crane Specialist Group. In 1970 the International Council for Bird Protection (now BirdLife International) asked George Archibald (then conducting doctoral studies on crane biology at Cornell University) to organize a World Working Group on Cranes. Some 40 crane researchers joined the working group. In 1973, Archibald and Dr. Ron Sauey cofounded the International Crane Foundation to carry out the Working Group's activities. Core members of the group in turn formed the IUCN Crane Specialist Group. Reports of the group's activities appear regularly in *Species*, the newsletter of the IUCN Species Survival Commission. In 1996, the group published its first conservation action plan (Meine and Archibald 1996).

Crane Working Groups. Crane working groups have played a key role in supporting research, information exchange, and development of conservation programs. Crane working groups have been organized at the regional, national, and local levels. At the regional level, working groups are active in North America and Europe. A Soviet Working Group on Cranes was active until 1989. An East Asian working group is now forming to coordinate activities in this most species-rich region. National-level working groups are best developed in Europe. China's crane researchers formerly met on a regular basis, but economic constraints have impeded meetings in recent years. Local groups include the Friends of the Brolga in southeastern Australia and the Highlands and Overberg Crane Groups in South Africa. Several local

Figure 13.32 Training workshops, such as this one in Maun, Botswana, are critical for gaining the support and sharing the information needed to accomplish the many and complicated objectives in crane conservation. (Photograph courtesy of the International Crane Foundation.)

working groups in South Africa have recently joined together under the umbrella of the South African Crane Working Group.

Global Captive Crane Working Group. The appropriate integration of captive propagation techniques with field management techniques is a critical need that challenges the ingenuity of conservationists. For example, avicultural research has yielded methods for testing the viability of eggs in wild Whooping Crane nests. One egg can be removed from nests that have two viable eggs, and either brought into captivity or placed in a nest where both eggs are bad. With few exceptions—the West African Crowned Crane, Wattled Crane, and Hooded Crane—all the species can now reliably be bred in captivity. Based on this success, the emphasis in captive programs has shifted from management of individual birds to management of healthy populations to meet conservation needs. In 1993, a Global Captive Crane Working Group was organized to set regional target populations, define genetic and demographic objectives, allocate limited space among species, and coordinate work with field conservation projects. In addition, captive management techniques have now been summarized in a crane propagation and husbandry manual (Ellis et al. 1996).

Crane Workshops and Meetings. Since 1975, some 35 national, regional, international, and species-specific crane workshops and meetings have been held (Figure 13.32). These gatherings provide important forums for information exchange, allowing scientists and conservationists from throughout the world to meet and learn from one another. Proceedings from most of the workshops have been published, making this information available to an even broader audience.

Lessons for Conservation Biologists

Each of the 15 crane species requires a different suite of conservation actions to ensure a secure future, and crane conservationists have had to integrate conservation programs under diverse circumstances. A number of basic guiding principles can be derived from this collective experience.

- *Conservation measures must be solidly grounded in the natural sciences, but should also involve the social sciences, humanities, law, education, economics, and other fields.* Fortunately, cranes are among the best-studied groups of organisms on earth. Effective conservation, however, requires that scientific knowledge be linked with an understanding of the human dimensions of the challenge—the social forces and trends that affect crane populations and habitats. Consequently, in situ conservation programs must be broadly conceived, and must combine research with legal protection, habitat protection and management, education, community participation, and other components. All of these features can and must contribute to balanced programs that sustain crane populations, crane habitats, and local human communities.
- *Conservation measures should be envisioned at multiple scales of time and space.* Conservation programs for cranes have spanned broad temporal and spatial scales, from highly localized and immediate efforts to save threatened habitats and populations, to longer-term programs in, for example, ecosystem restoration, watershed-scale planning, and maintenance of viable populations in captivity.
- *Conservation measures should seek to harmonize species-oriented and ecosystem-oriented approaches.* As well-known birds that serve as "umbrella" and "flagship" species, cranes have drawn attention to, and provided protection for, a broad array of other species as well as the processes that maintain ecosystem health. In the long run, cranes must be viewed within a larger landscape, watershed, or ecosystem context, and conservation activities must be coordinated at these scales. In particular, managers must appreciate the roles of flooding, fire, vegetation change, and other processes in these dynamic systems.
- *Conservation measures should take into account biological attributes and processes at all levels of the biological hierarchy.* Crane conservation has required attention to problems at the genetic, individual, population, subspecies, species, and family levels. Especially in the case of the Whooping Crane and the other highly endangered species, these problems need to be considered simultaneously to minimize risk.
- *Conservation measures should work across national, cultural, and ecological boundaries.* Because most cranes are migratory, and all occur in more than one country, successful conservation requires a clear consensus on goals and responsibilities among parties from different parts of the species' range, constant communication of reliable scientific information, and support from various governments, international institutions, and non-governmental organizations.
- *Conservation measures should seek to address local community development and conservation needs in an integrated fashion.* Efforts to conserve cranes—especially the 12 species occurring in Asia and Africa—are interwoven with the challenges of local sustainable development. Wild resources of wetlands and their watersheds cannot be conserved without active involvement, and leadership, from the resource users. In many cases, local people have vital clues to the best solutions for the threats confronting cranes.
- *The relationship between in situ and ex situ conservation measures should be well defined.* Captive propagation and reintroduction programs should be undertaken only as a last resort, and not as a substitute for in situ programs. Should ex situ programs become necessary, they should be developed based on clear goals and management guidelines. Priority should be placed on the maintenance and enhancement of genetic diversity

within crane populations, on safe and effective methods for reintroduction, and on assurance of high-quality care for captive cranes.
- *Education should be integrated into all conservation programs.* Ultimately, the conservation of cranes requires an informed public that understands and supports activities that sustain cranes and their habitats. Throughout the world, crane conservation programs have taken advantage of the opportunity that cranes provide for communicating basic information about wetlands and endangered species management.

Cranes, along with much of the world's biodiversity, will face difficult circumstances in the coming decades. History provides somber lessons about the speed with which even abundant species can become threatened. Although the survival (or, in some cases, recovery) of the cranes cannot be assured, many steps can be taken to enhance their chances. Compared with the prospects 50 years ago—when most crane species and populations were dwindling, scientific knowledge was scarce, and conservation efforts were essentially nonexistent—there is reason for cautious optimism. And in safeguarding cranes, we may ensure a more secure future for other members of the ecosystems in which cranes occur, including people.

Questions for Discussion

1. Black-footed ferrets were reintroduced into the wild in several small, isolated populations. Discuss the possible genetic consequences of this aspect of the recovery plan and the possible implications for the ferrets' long-term susceptibility to canine distemper. What alternative approaches might be possible?
2. There is currently considerable debate about the best way to manage endangered species. At the extremes, one school of thought holds that a species-based approach is essential, while the other school argues that we cannot protect all species, so we should shift to an ecosystem-based approach. In the context of the studies presented here, discuss the pros and cons of each approach. Are they mutually exclusive approaches to biodiversity protection?
3. Computer models of sea turtle conservation options (Crouse et al. 1987) show that protecting the larger juveniles and adults will result in faster recovery of populations than protecting eggs and hatchlings. Because of this, some conservationists argue that protection of nests and eggs is misguided, and that we should concentrate our efforts on protecting the larger, older turtles. Others argue that new turtles can only come from eggs, and that if we abandon protection of early life stages, the species will still go extinct as the older individuals die off from natural causes and are not replaced due to excessive egg and hatchling mortality. What do you think?
4. The Australian Aboriginal peoples are becoming important players in sea turtle conservation and management, partly because of their long-term use and knowledge of the various species. Are there indigenous peoples near you that have lived on the land long enough to have gained insight that would be relevant and useful to conservation managers? How might you incorporate them into local management scenarios?
5. Compare the Conservation Area approach to multiple use of public lands in Costa Rica with the multiple-use approach taken by the U.S. Bureau of

Land Management and the Forest Service. How would each deal with conflict between the need to protect biodiversity and the need to extract economic value from the lands?

6. Recall the Spotted Owl case study. Imagine that you are a biologist who has been invited to present testimony to a Congressional committee concerned about resolving the conflicts between biodiversity protection and local economic growth. How would you respond to the following statement from a Congressional committee member: "My aide tells me that the Spotted Owl also occurs in southern California and the a genetic study showed that the populations were the same [an electrophoretic study that indicated the populations were identical for 29 loci], and the owl doesn't need old-growth forest in southern California. Why can't we just harvest the old-growth forest and let the owl live in southern California?"
7. In Doñana National Park, a generally poor population seeking jobs and natural resources is pressing in upon this reserve with its critical wetlands, fragile dunes, and many endangered species. How would you convince such a populace that this area needs to be protected, and that it may be in their own best interest to do so?
8. The Everglades ecosystem is besieged with problems ranging from invasive exotic plants, to a deeply entrenched and politically powerful agricultural lobby, to an encroaching human population encouraged by real estate speculation. Why might an ecosystem approach be the best, and perhaps the only, way to address these multiple problems?
9. Cranes exemplify the need for conservation managers to think simultaneously across various spatial and temporal scales, across boundaries, and at different levels of biological organization in planning and implementing conservation measures. Choose another family of organisms and consider how these needs do or do not apply in planning conservation measures.
10. Every taxonomic group provides us with unique educational opportunities. Cranes, for example, because they are large, conspicuous, charismatic birds with broad cultural appeal, have provided rich opportunities for education about not only the cranes themselves, but also endangered species management, wetlands and grasslands, and sustainable development. Select three other species or families and identify their special attributes that might be used to convey conservation lessons to the general public.

Suggestions for Further Reading

The following suggested readings are meant to supplement the case studies by focusing on management in ecosystems that are not covered in this chapter.

Clausen, B. 1993. A survey of protected areas management by state and provincial Fish and Wildlife Agencies in Western states and provinces. *Nat. Areas J.* 13: 204–213. This survey of habitat management programs included agency staff in 13 Western states and two Canadian provinces. The upside of the survey shows a high level of management activity, while the downside suggests that resources are inadequate and declining, and that integration among agencies is weak.

Gibson, D. J., T. R. Seastedt, and J. M. Briggs. 1992. Management practices in tallgrass prairie: Large- and small-scale experimental effects on species composition. *J. Appl. Ecol.* 30:247–255. The authors examine the effects of burning and mowing on community composition in Kansas tallgrass prairie. In addition to their description of grassland management practices, they provide a good discussion of the significance of scale of management.

Hamilton, L. S. 1993. Status and current developments in mountain protected areas. *Mountain Res. Dev.* 13:311–314. Because of their relatively low productivity and fragile slopes, mountains are particularly vulnerable to mismanagement. At the same time, mountainous regions represent some of the most significant remaining natural habitat, and, in a future of climate change, their broad environmental range may provide important refugia.

MacKenzie, S. H. 1996. *Integrated Resource Planning and Management: The Ecosystem Approach to the Great Lakes Basin.* Island Press, Washington, D.C. One of the major ecosystem efforts is taking place in the Great Lakes region of the United States. This book addresses that effort in detail, including a historical analysis of water resource planning, assessment of ecosystem management successes in the region, planning and implementation processes, and the institutional structural changes necessary.

Marine Protected Areas. *Oceanus* 36(3), Fall 1993. This issue focuses on marine protected areas, from coastal to oceanic, polar to tropical. The marine environment produces more animal protein than poultry or beef, is the recipient of pollution carried by rivers and sewage systems, and along its coastal fringes is subject to intense development pressures. The need for marine protected areas is evident, but is largely overlooked by the conservation community.

Polis, G. A. (ed.). 1991. *The Ecology of Desert Communities.* University of Arizona Press, Tucson. Most publications that deal with management of desert lands emphasize their use for dryland agriculture or cattle and sheep range; thus, these works have limited usefulness for conservation managers. While this book does not dwell on management issues explicitly, it provides a good discussion of the factors (equilibrial and nonequilibrial) that influence desert communities.

Yaffee, S. L., A. F. Phillips, I. C. Frentz, P. W. Hardy, S. M. Maleki, and B. E. Thorpe. 1996. *Ecosystem Management in the United* States*: An Assessment of Current Experience.* Island Press, Washington, D.C. This book is just what the title implies: an assessment of 105 efforts toward ecosystem management throughout the United States, aimed at both practitioners and decision makers. It includes the status of each effort, factors that constrain or facilitate progress, and contact information for follow-up.

Zedler, J. B. and A. N. Powell. 1993. Managing coastal wetlands. *Oceanus* 36(2): 19–27. A good account of the complexities and uncertainties involved in wetland management. The unexpected outcomes in managing even reasonably intact wetlands should give pause to those who believe that we can re-create them. This is a useful extension of Essay 14B by Zedler.

The following papers, read in combination, provide a good overview of new approaches—and their attendant problems—for management at the scale of large landscapes.

Noss, R. F. 1993. A conservation plan for the Oregon Coast Range: Some preliminary suggestions. *Nat. Areas J.* 13(4):276–290.

Povilitis, T. 1993. Applying the Biosphere Reserve concept to a greater ecosystem: The San Juan Mountain Area of Colorado and New Mexico. *Nat. Areas J.* 13(1):18–28.

14

Ecological Restoration

The acid test of our understanding is not whether we can take ecosystems to bits on pieces of paper, however scientifically, but whether we can put them together in practice and make them work.

A. D. Bradshaw, 1983

One goal of conservation biology is to preserve biological diversity. Traditionally, this work has been carried out in wilderness or "natural" areas where human influence has been minimal or, as may be the case with some indigenous peoples, in areas where human use has maintained high biological diversity. In recent years, however, a growing number of conservationists have turned their attention to more or less severely altered areas, such as abandoned farm fields, utility corridors, highway rights-of-way, degraded wetlands, eutrophic lakes, ditched and leveed rivers, and even mined lands. Such areas present opportunities to contribute to the conservation of biodiversity not merely by protecting and maintaining populations and communities that persist on such sites, but by enhancing the sites through an active program of ecological restoration. We pursue that approach here.

What Is Ecological Restoration?

Though it was barely recognized as a conservation strategy as recently as a decade ago, and has gained recognition as a discipline only in the past few years, **restoration ecology** is now playing a significant role in the planning and programs of government agencies such as the National Park Service and the Army Corps of Engineers as well as nongovernmental organizations (NGOs) such as The Nature Conservancy, the Audubon Society, and the Sierra Club. Ecological restoration is a burgeoning field, as witnessed by the growth of two scientific societies, The Society for Ecological Restoration (created in 1987) and the Ecological Society of America, and their production of new journals, *Restoration Ecology* and *Ecological Applications*, respectively. Today, restorationists are in the process of opening up a second conservation frontier: the conservation of biodiversity and other features of the natural landscape in areas written off as a "lost cause" by earlier generations of conservationists.

The term *ecological restoration* is actually one of a family of related terms referring to various approaches to the task of ecological healing or rehabilitation. These terms include *restoration* itself, as well as *rehabilitation, reclamation, re-creation*, and *ecological recovery*, which are defined and discussed in Box 14A.

BOX 14A
Definitions of Common Terms Used in Restoration Ecology

Restoration: The word *restore* means "to bring back . . . into a former or original state" (Webster's New Collegiate Dictionary 1977). Ecological restoration simply means doing that to an ecological system. Restoration is often regarded as a distinctive form of conservation management, differing from "preservation," "conservation," "stewardship," or even "management" itself. There is no sharp distinction among these various forms of manipulation. All of them involve a series of attempts to compensate in a specific, ecologically effective way for alterations typically caused by human activities.

Rehabilitation: This is a broad term that may be used to refer to any attempt to restore elements of structure or function to an ecological system, without necessarily attempting complete restoration to any specified prior condition; for example, replanting of sites to prevent erosion.

Reclamation: This term typically refers to rehabilitative work carried out on the most severely degraded sites, such as lands disturbed by open-cast mining or large-scale construction. Though reclamation work often falls short of restoration in the fullest sense (a copy of a native ecosystem is not achieved), it is clearly a necessary step in the process of restoration under such conditions. In a sense it is the first step to restoring a more natural ecosystem. Unfortunately, the disciplines of reclamation and restoration have developed more or less independently, and only recently has significant communication between them occurred.

Re-creation: Re-creation attempts to reconstruct an ecosystem, wholesale, on a site so severely disturbed that there is virtually nothing left to restore. The new system may be modeled on a system located outside the range of the historical system, or may be established under conditions different from those under which it occurred naturally. Such efforts are not restoration in the strictest sense, but they can lead to important insights into the systems involved and the conditions that support them that can be invaluable in restoration efforts (Aber 1987; Jordan et al. 1987).

Ecological recovery: Recovery involves letting the system alone, generally in the expectation that it will regain desirable attributes through natural succession. This zero-order approach to restoration may or may not work. It is best regarded as a key *component* of restoration—the contribution of the system itself, as it were. In such cases the restorationist seeks to complement and reinforce natural processes.

Of these terms, *restoration* is both the most clearly defined and points toward the most ambitious objectives. This being the case, most of the principles, techniques, and issues relevant to the other forms of ecological rehabilitation at work pertain to restoration and can be discussed under this heading. For this reason, we confine ourselves here to a discussion of restoration.

To begin our exploration of restoration ecology, some discussion of the characteristics of people who call themselves restorationists is in order.

1. The restorationist acknowledges that the system has been altered in some way as a result of direct or indirect human influences, and makes explicit value judgments about the desirability of reversing this change. This viewpoint is important because it recognizes from the outset something that conservationists have sometimes been tempted to downplay: that human beings, like all other species, are continually interacting with ecosystems, that this interaction is ultimately unavoidable, and that it inevitably alters the ecosystems. This recognition is a critical first step toward managing any system in such a way as to conserve its historical qualities.
2. The restorationist makes an explicit commitment to the conservation of a specified system or landscape with specific, historically defined properties. In contrast, rubrics such as "management," "stewardship," and even "conservation" leave room for considerable vagueness in the definition of goals. This is one reason why restoration has proven especially liable to criticism: it promises a particular result that can be objectively judged.
3. The restorationist acknowledges that the return of the system to its historical condition—or its maintenance in the presence of novel influences—generally involves deliberate manipulations to compensate for those influences. In other words, it is an active as well as a passive process. This viewpoint represents a clear recognition of both

the beneficial role humans can play in the recovery of a degraded system, and their responsibility for playing that role.

4. Insofar as possible, the restorationist is also committed to re-creation of the entire system in all its aspects; these include dynamic and functional ecosystem properties as well as concrete elements such as the system's biotic and abiotic components.

The Role of Ecological Restoration in Conservation

Until recently, protection and management of natural areas have been the major components of conservation practice, while the role of explicit restoration has been minor or nonexistent. There are a number of reasons for this. First, at least in the Western Hemisphere, natural or unaltered areas have been relatively plentiful, and conservationists have been preoccupied with attempts to identify them and protect them from undue human influence before they disappear. Second, there is a widely shared feeling that, in some sense, "restored" systems are intrinsically inferior to their natural counterparts. Third, some feel that true restoration of ecosystems is not possible. Finally, there is a concern that the promise of restoration might be used to undermine arguments for the conservation of existing natural and wild lands. That is, if we have the ability to restore any ecosystem, is there a need to preserve some in situ?

During the past few years several developments have resulted in a growing interest in the practice of restoration, even among those who remain properly skeptical about our ability to produce authentic replicas of historical ecosystems. These developments include (1) legislation requiring rehabilitation of areas disturbed by certain kinds of mining, as well as restoration or creation of wetlands to compensate for—or "mitigate"—damage to wetlands by activities such as mining or construction (Brenner 1990); (2) increased use of restorative procedures, including use of native vegetation in engineering applications such as utility corridors, rights-of-way, and watercourses (Crabtree 1984); (3) growing interest in native vegetation as an element in ornamental landscapes (Diekelman and Schuster 1982; Smyser 1986); and (4) the sheer level of ecological destruction that has made restoration necessary and attractive.

The decline in opportunities for conservation, as existing natural areas have either been lost or brought under conservation status, has led conservationists to reconsider disturbed areas as objects for conservation action. Similarly, events such as the irruption of animal populations in some protected areas, the catastrophic fires in Yellowstone National Park in the summer of 1988, and a heavy fire year throughout the West in 1996 have drawn the attention of the general public and the professional conservation community alike to the need for more active management, even in protected areas. In addition to the factors listed above that influence the desire to implement restoration efforts, there is a general increase in the consciousness of the public about the deterioration of landscapes, whether natural or managed (Anderson 1995).

In the political arena, restoration may be perceived as an alternative to conservation, a very dangerous perspective. In fact, they are not alternatives, but complementary parts of a comprehensive conservation strategy. In a sense, conservation is the objective, while restoration is one means of reaching that goal. Seen in this way, restoration is not an alternative to conservation; rather, it is a subset of conservation and a means of achieving it—not only under extreme conditions, but in any landscape subject to unwanted influences. The first principle of restoration, borrowed from the medical tradition, is "first, do no harm."

Some Central Concerns of Restoration Ecology

The value of ecological restoration is the prospect it offers for actually reversing losses, allowing the conservationist to go on the offensive in the struggle to conserve natural landscapes. While initial gains may be modest, the potential of restoration efforts adds a new dimension to the work of protecting reserves, and to management and conservation generally. The development and acceptance of restoration leads to conservation that involves ecologically upgrading existing reserves, their expansion and diversification by restoration on adjacent, degraded lands, and even creation of new reserves in heavily developed or other ecologically degraded areas (see, for example, Hughes and Bonnicksen 1990).

Several basic concerns are common to all types of restoration projects. These concerns include the product or goal being strived for, the feasibility of producing an authentic product, the scale of the project, and its costs. Recently, such concerns have been placed in a more conceptual framework by Hobbs and Norton (1996), who list the steps they consider important in a restoration effort:

1. Identify and deal with processes leading to degradation in the first place.
2. Determine realistic goals and measures of success.
3. Develop methods for implementing the goals.
4. Incorporate these methods into land management and planning strategies.
5. Monitor the restoration and assess success.

The Product

The fundamental goal of restoration ecology is to return a particular habitat or ecosystem to a condition as similar as possible to its pre-degraded state (Figure 14.1). Restoration may also involve upgrading habitat for native species—

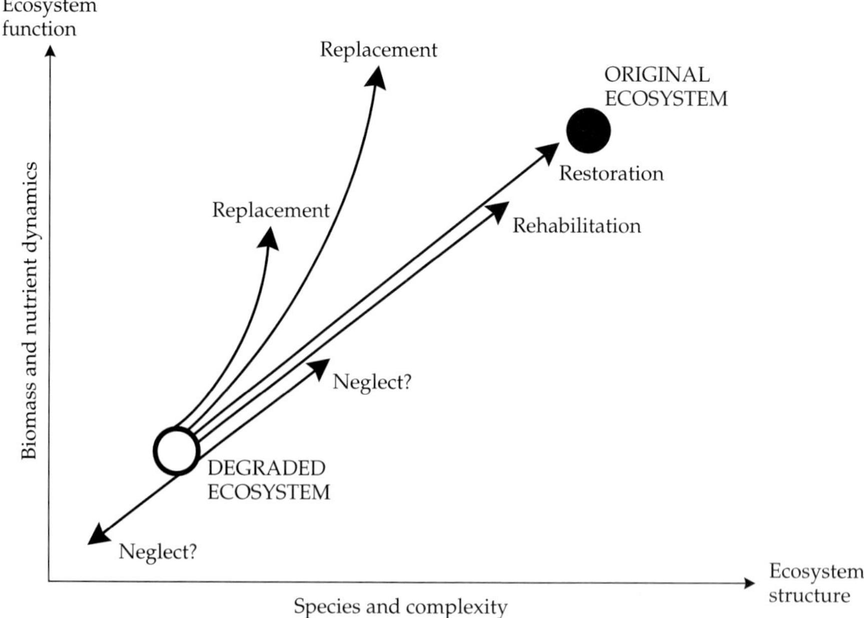

Figure 14.1 The trajectory of a restoration project may be viewed in terms of ecosystem structure and function. A change in both dimensions occurs upon degradation; the restoration process is an attempt to direct the system back toward the original state. Complete restoration would involve return to that state; partial return, or other trajectories, would result in rehabilitation or replacement by a different system. (Modified from Bradshaw 1984.)

in some cases for a specifically targeted rare species. To achieve any of these goals, some knowledge of the previous, undegraded state of the system is necessary, including knowledge of its structure (the species present and their relative abundances) and its function (the dynamics of biotic and abiotic interactions, including hydrology and nutrient cycling). Of course, for most ecological systems, we have only incomplete knowledge of structure and function, but at least some idea of the dominant species present is necessary to develop a "target" for the restored system. The level of knowledge of the former system at least partly determines how closely we can approximate it in restoration, and how well we can judge success. One approach to defining the target, an "Index of Biotic Integrity," was developed by James Karr, and is discussed by him in Essay 14A.

ESSAY 14A
Measuring Biological Integrity

James R. Karr, University of Washington

Environmental change has always been a reality, and it is continuous. Change on our planet is driven by wind and water, geologic activity, astronomical events, and the work of microorganisms, plants, and animals. These forces are active everywhere and at all scales in space and time. Usually the forces with the greatest potential for cataclysmic change are rare (like volcanic eruptions), local (like tornadoes or lightning fires), or slow to play out (like the advance and retreat of ice sheets).

Over the past two centuries, however, this pattern has changed. The activity of one species, *Homo sapiens*, has become the principal driver of change on the earth's surface. Human influences are massive, incessant, and global. For the first time in the earth's history, a biological agent—a single species at that—rivals geophysical forces in shaping the earth.

Human-caused change may be positive, neutral, or negative. The challenge faced by conservation biologists and other environmental scientists is to detect and interpret change, to distinguish among its causes, and to understand and explain its consequences, especially those that alter living systems. Resource and environmental managers want to detect and treat changes that have negative consequences, but at the same time they wish to avoid wasting resources to treat changes with neutral or positive consequences.

Negative consequences—that is, risks—were identified and assessed historically in terms of their effects on human health; a toxic chemical spill, for example, clearly presents a direct risk to human well-being. But direct risks to human health are not the only environmental risks that society faces; other, ecological risks also pose a threat to our well-being.

Human actions that increase ecological risks range from toxic chemical spills and excessive nutrient release from agricultural runoff to the destruction and fragmentation of natural habitats and the introduction of exotic species. For decades, modern society has behaved as if it were immune to ecological risks; conventional wisdom held that these risks could be easily detected and then remedied before serious damage occurred. This behavior has left a legacy of degraded environments.

To effectively restore degraded areas, or to protect existing high-quality areas, we must be able to define the attributes of "normal," undegraded, or "healthy" habitats as a model. Otherwise, how can we objectively assess whether mitigation or restoration techniques are succeeding, or are even necessary? One way of setting a baseline and measuring restoration success is to define the normal "biological integrity" of a system, and then measure deviations from it.

The phrase *biological integrity* was first used in 1972 to establish the goal of the U.S. Clean Water Act: "to restore and maintain the chemical, physical, and biological integrity of the Nation's waters." This mandate clearly established a legal foundation for protecting aquatic biota. Unfortunately, this vision of biological integrity was not reflected in the act's implementing regulations.

Integrity implies an unimpaired condition, or the quality or state of being complete or undivided. Biological integrity is defined as "the ability to support and maintain a balanced, integrated, adaptive biological system having the full range of elements (genes, species, and assemblages) and processes (mutation, demography, biotic interactions, nutrient and energy dynamics, and metapopulation processes) expected in the natural habitat of a region" (Karr 1996). Inherent in this definition are the assumptions that (1) living systems act over a variety of scales from individuals to landscapes; (2) a fully functioning living system includes items one can count (the elements of biodiversity) plus the processes that generate and maintain them; and (3) living systems are embedded in dynamic evolutionary and biogeographic contexts that influence and are influenced by their physical and chemical environments.

Unfortunately, regulations implementing the Clean Water Act were aimed at controlling or reducing releases of chemical contaminants (pollution) and thereby protecting human health; the integrity of biological communities was ignored (Karr 1991). As a result, aquatic organisms and aquatic environments have declined precipitously in recent decades. The present water resource crisis extends far beyond pollutant-caused degradation of water quality; in addition, we face losses of species, homogenized biological assemblages, and lost fisheries. Water resource programs have not protected, and are not protecting, biological integrity in the nation's waters because society continually fails to see rivers, and the landscapes they drain, in their entirety. Until an integrative perspective dominates our collective conscience, the condition of rivers will continue to decline.

Under Section 305(b) of the Clean Water Act, states are required to report the status of water resources within their boundaries, yet the dominance of numerical chemical criteria in water quality standards results in chronic underreporting of actual degradation. In one state, conventional chemical evaluations failed to detect 50% of the damage to surface waters when compared with the more comprehensive, sensitive, and objective assessment provided by biological evaluations. Today more resource managers are recognizing the weaknesses of the chemical contaminant approach, and state and federal agencies are moving to incorporate sophisticated biological criteria—numerical values or narrative expressions that describe the characteristics of a living aquatic assemblage.

To implement biological criteria, managers need formal methods for sampling the biota of streams, evaluating the resulting data, and clearly describing the condition of sampled stream reaches. I developed a measurement system, called the *index of biological integrity* (IBI), to fill this need. The complexity of biological systems, and the varied effects humans have on them, require a broadly based, multimetric index that integrates information from individual, population, and assemblage levels.

The IBI, like conventional economic indexes such as the index of leading economic indicators, provides a convenient measure of the status of a complex system. Both require an index time or baseline state against which future conditions are assessed. For IBI, that baseline—biological integrity—is the condition at a site with a biota that is the product of evolutionary and biogeographic processes in the relative absence of the effects of modern human activity.

The IBI metrics were chosen because they reflect specific and predictable responses of the stream biota to human activities across the landscapes those

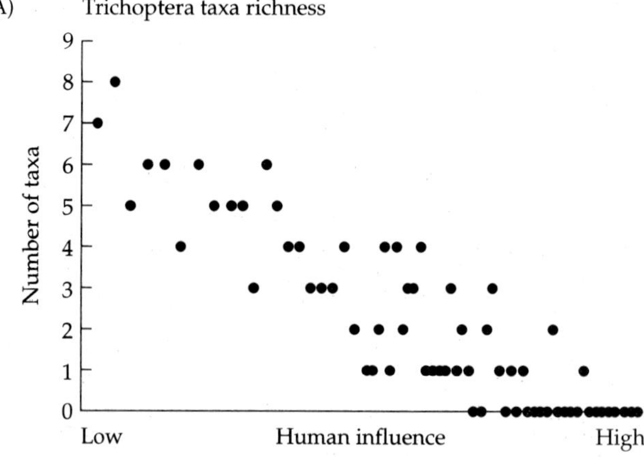

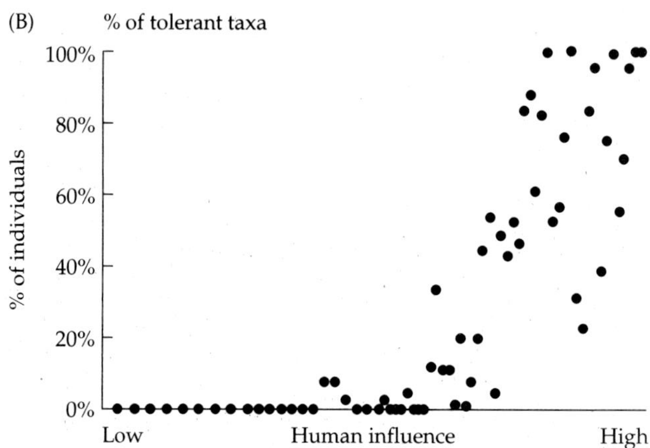

Figure A Biological responses across a gradient of human influence in watersheds can serve as "ecological dose–response curves." Human influence is measured as chemical pollutants or dams and weirs in a watershed, and amount of riparian corridors removed. As human influence increases, the number of Trichoptera (caddisfly) taxa in Japanese streams declines (A), and the number of invertebrates tolerant of organic effluent, sedimentation, and reduced oxygen levels in streams increases (B).

streams drain (Figure A). These responses are similar to the dose–response curves measured by toxicologists, in which an organism's response varies with the dose of a toxic compound. Because they provide an integrative measure of the cumulative effects of all human activities in a study watershed, IBI metrics can be viewed as ecological dose–response curves. The IBI is based in empirically defined metrics because (1) such metrics are biologically and ecologically meaningful; (2) they increase or decrease as human influence increases; (3) they are sensitive to a range of stresses; (4) they distinguish stress-induced variation from natural and sampling variation; (5) they are relevant to societal concerns; and (6) they are easy to measure and interpret.

The IBI metrics evaluate species richness, indicator taxa (stress intolerant and tolerant), relative abundances of trophic guilds and other species groups, the presence of exotic species, and the incidence of hybridization, disease, and stress-related anomalies such as lesions, tumors, or fin erosion (for fish) and head capsule abnormality (for stream insects). To determine an IBI for a stream, metric values from the stream are compared with the values expected for a relatively undisturbed stream of similar size in the same geographic region. Each metric is assigned a value of 5, 3, or 1 depending on whether its condition is comparable to, deviates somewhat from, or deviates strongly from the "undisturbed" reference condition. Metric scores are then summed to yield an index (in the case of midwestern United States rivers, based on 12 metrics) that ranges from a low of 12 in areas with no remaining fish to 60 in

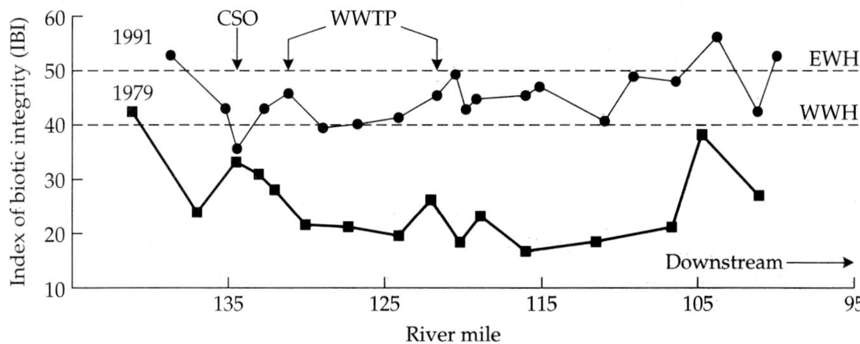

Figure B Longitudinal trend in fish IBI for the Scioto River, in an area downstream from Columbus, Ohio, 1979 and 1991. Locations of wastewater treatment plants (WWTP) and combined sewer overflow (CSO) are indicated by arrowheads. Dashed lines indicate standards for designated uses: WWH = warmwater habitat; EWH = excellent warmwater habitat. An IBI below 40 indicates that a reach does not attain water quality standards under biological criteria according to the Ohio Environmental Protection Agency. Improvements in IBI between 1979 and 1991 are largely due to improvements in the effluent from wastewater treatment plants. Some river reaches do not attain EWH largely because of physical habitat degradation and unresolved chemical contamination.

areas with fish faunas equivalent to those in pristine or relatively undisturbed areas.

IBI or its conceptual clones are now used on six continents and in freshwater and marine systems. As of 1996, 47 U.S. states were adopting biological criteria to assess the condition of water resources. The Ohio Environmental Protection Agency, for example, uses IBI to establish and maintain use designations for water bodies (Figure B) and to support their so-called Section 319 Clean Water Act nonpoint-source program, Section 305(b) CWA water quality inventory reports, and National Pollution Discharge Elimination System (NPDES) discharge permits. The conceptual underpinnings of IBI have now been applied to a variety of aquatic environments (Davis and Simon 1995), including large rivers, lakes, estuaries, wetlands, riparian corridors, and reservoirs. Taxa studied in developing IBIs have included algae, benthic invertebrates, and fishes (Ohio EPA 1988; Lyons et al. 1995; Fore et al. 1996).

A key to successful restoration, mitigation, and conservation efforts is having an objective way to assess and compare the biological integrity of damaged sites. IBI provides a tool for doing so and, at the same time, allows managers to set specific biological integrity targets for restoration programs.

The process of restoration actually involves setting the system on a new developmental trajectory toward its particular "target," its former state. How far along that trajectory the system goes depends on a number of things, including the level of knowledge of the previous state; how perturbed the system is; the availability of biota for restoration; the genetic variation of the biota; the level of alteration of hydrology, soil, and geomorphology; cost and available funding; and political will. Many times the product will not be an exact replica of the former system, but rather will represent a major change in trajectory toward the target.

The design and planning of restoration projects to achieve the product goal can be complex and may cover a large variety of problems and issues. The National Research Council (1992) has developed a checklist of questions appropriate for restoration projects, including questions to be addressed during project planning and design, during the project itself, and in the post-restoration phase (Table 14.1). Asking such questions helps restorationists to define the product, guide the project toward that product, and evaluate the product and make relevant adjustments.

Feasibility and Authenticity

Because the process of restoration is guided by its objectives, restorationists have devoted a considerable amount of attention to questions related to how objectives for restoration projects should be defined, how the results can be evaluated, the extent to which restoration can actually be carried out, the quality of restored ecosystems, and the feasibility of carrying out high-quality restoration work on an environmentally significant scale (see for example, Jordan 1990).

Table 14.1
A Checklist of Appropriate Questions for Planning, Conducting, and Evaluating Restoration Projects

Project Planning and Design

1. Has the problem requiring treatment been clearly understood and defined?
2. Is there a consensus on the restoration program's mission?
3. Have the goals and objectives been identified?
4. Has the restoration been planned with adequate scope and expertise?
5. Does the restoration management design have an annual or midcourse correction point in line with adaptive management procedures?
6. Are the performance indicators—the measurable biological, physical, and chemical attributes—directly and appropriately linked to the objectives?
7. Have adequate monitoring, surveillance, management, and maintenance programs been developed along with the project, so that monitoring costs and operational details are anticipated and monitoring results will be available to serve as input in improving restoration techniques used as the project matures?
8. Has an appropriate reference system (or systems) been selected from which to extract target values of performance indicators for comparison in conducting the project evaluation?
9. Have sufficient baseline data been collected over a suitable period of time on the project ecosystem to facilitate before-and-after treatment comparisons?
10. Have critical project procedures been tested on a small experimental scale in part of the project area to minimize the risks of failure?
11. Has the project been designed to make the restored ecosystem as self-sustaining as possible to minimize maintenance requirements?
12. Has thought been given to how long monitoring will have to be continued before the project can be declared effective?
13. Have risk and uncertainty been adequately considered in project planning?

During Restoration

1. Based on the monitoring results, are the anticipated intermediate objectives being achieved? If not, are appropriate steps being taken to correct the problem?
2. Do the objectives or performance indicators need to be modified? If so, what changes may be required in the monitoring program?
3. Is the monitoring program adequate?

Post-Restoration

1. To what extent were project goals and objectives achieved?
2. How similar in structure and function is the restored ecosystem to the target ecosystem?
3. To what extent is the restored ecosystem self-sustaining, and what are the maintenance requirements?
4. If all natural components of the ecosystem were not restored, have critical ecosystem functions been restored?
5. If all natural components of the ecosystem were not restored, have critical components been restored?
6. How long did the project take?
7. What lessons have been learned from this effort?
8. Have those lessons been shared with interested parties to maximize the potential for technology transfer?
9. What was the final cost, in net present value terms, of the restoration project?
10. What were the ecological, economic, and social benefits realized by the project?
11. How cost-effective was the project?
12. Would another approach to restoration have produced desirable results at lower cost?

From NRC 1992.

Of these questions, the most fundamental relates to the definition of the goals and objectives for restoration projects. It would seem that such definition would be simple, but it is often complex and involves difficult decisions and compromises. Ideally, restoration reproduces the entire system in question, complete in all its aspects—genetics, populations, ecosystems, and landscapes. This means not merely replicating the system's composition, structure, and function, but also its dynamics—even allowing for evolutionary as well as ecological change. Thus, one practitioner argued that objectives for restoration projects should be defined as "motion pictures" rather than "snapshots" (Dunwiddie 1992). A limitation here is that objects such as species are generally easier to specify in planning restoration projects—and to monitor when evaluating their success—than are processes such as ecosystem function and community dynamics, to say nothing of evolutionary changes. As a result, there is still a tendency to portray restoration projects in more or less static terms.

This having been said, just how good a job are restorationists able to do, given the current state of the art? How feasible is it to restore authentic ecosystems? Answers differ for each ecosystem type, and depend, of course, on the nature and extent of the influences or degradation involved. A satisfactory answer takes into account not only the *accuracy* of the resulting system—that is, how closely it resembles the model or reference system with respect to ecological parameters such as composition, structure, function, and dynamics—but also its *authenticity* in a larger sense, including consideration of its historical and aesthetic value. Most of these issues have not been investigated in detail, and studies of even the most straightforward ecological parameters defining a successful restoration effort are still in their infancy (Society for Ecological Restoration 1990). Indeed, restoration poses a fundamental challenge to the ecologist: the challenge of identifying those aspects of an ecosystem that are most important.

The most extensive work in this area has been conducted on wetlands. Mandated by law in some situations, wetland restoration has become a booming business, but there is concern among conservationists about the quality of the resulting systems. In the few cases in which attempts have been made to compare restored systems with their natural counterparts, interpretation of the results has varied widely. In one broadly cited study of a tidal marsh that appears to be restored in San Diego Bay, California, the investigators found that, although the restored wetland resembled the reference system with respect to the rate of nitrogen fixation in the root zone, it differed significantly with respect to ten other measures of structure, composition, and function (Zedler and Langis 1991). Essay 14B by Joy Zedler expands on these experiences.

ESSAY 14B

Restoring the Nation's Wetlands

Why, Where, and How?

Joy B. Zedler, San Diego State University

Over the past two centuries, over 53% of the wetland area of the contiguous United States has been destroyed, mostly through drainage for agriculture (Dahl 1990). That's an average rate of about 1 acre per minute, for a total loss of over 116 million acres in 200 years. The lower 48 states have only about 100 million acres of wetlands left. No wonder conservation leaders have developed a policy of "no net loss of wetland acreage and function" (The Conservation Foundation 1988), and the National Research Council (1992) has called for restoration of 10 million acres by 2010. This essay considers why, where, and how we should go about meeting that goal.

Why wetlands should be restored relates to their many landscape-level functions. Wetlands act as "sponges," providing flood protection by reducing flood peaks and shoreline erosion. To downstream water users, they are the "kidneys" of the landscape because they filter sediments, nutrients, and contaminants from inflowing waters, thereby improving water quality. To local and migratory animals, they are "supermarkets" that provide a wide variety of foods. Wetlands produce timber, waterfowl, and other products of economic value. In addition, they are aesthetically pleasing, which is part of the reason that over 160 million Americans spend $14.3 billion each year observing, photographing, and enjoying nature (Duda 1991). Resource agencies and managers agree that wetlands perform critical functions that benefit humankind.

Where wetlands should be restored is a more controversial issue, and one that can be argued from various perspectives. Because California has lost the greatest proportion of its historical wetlands (91%), perhaps it should have highest priority. Because Florida has suffered the greatest acreage loss (over 9 million acres, Dahl 1990), the need may be greatest there. On the other hand, Louisiana is currently losing wetlands at the highest rate.

Perhaps the greatest future threat to wetlands looms over coastal wetlands. Only 7% of the nation's remaining wetlands occur along the coast, toward which the bulk of the population is moving, bringing increased pressure to develop wetlands. Coastal wetlands are also potentially threatened by rising sea level due to global warming. A 3°C increase in temperature by 2100 is predicted to raise sea level 1 m and to eliminate 65% of the coastal marshes of the contiguous United States (Park et al. 1989). Thus, coastal wetlands may have the greatest need for restoration.

Wetlands restoration is not always feasible, but it can take place where wetland topography and hydrology are restorable and where the economic trade-off is not unreasonable. For example, many wetlands have been ditched or tiled for agriculture, but have been only marginally productive; their drains can easily be plugged and their wetland character allowed to redevelop without great cost. Such marginal agricultural lands offer the greatest opportunities for wetland restoration at the landscape level (National Research Council 1992).

The most difficult question is *how* wetlands can be restored on a large scale. In some places it is a relatively simple matter of recreating the hydrology that allowed natural wetlands to develop. North of Florida's Everglades, managers plan to return the Kissimmee River to its historical winding channel by undoing the 90 km straight channel that was cut in the 1960s, which eliminated 45,000 acres of river floodplain wetlands and reduced waterfowl populations by 90% (Koebel 1995). Forcing the river back into its natural meandering channel will rejuvenate much of its floodplain (Toth et al. 1995). This project has a high potential for success because the river channel is still intact and native wetland species occur nearby (Harris et al. 1995; Trexler 1995; Weller 1995).

In other places, restoration is more difficult. Southern California's salt marsh restoration attempts may represent the greatest challenge. In the San Diego area, 85% of salt marsh is gone, watersheds have been greatly modified, streams have been dammed, and degraded waters flow into each coastal wetland. Wetland sites are surrounded by urban uses, with no buffer between the wetland and development. Many of southern California's coastal wetland species are considered "sensitive" or threatened with extinction; for example, the sensitive species list for Tijuana Estuary includes one plant, seven invertebrates, two reptiles, and fourteen birds.

Considerable attention has been given to restoring nesting habitat for one bird on the U.S. endangered species list, the Light-footed Clapper Rail (*Rallus longirostris levipes*). This bird is a year-round resident of southern California salt marshes. As mitigation for damages to natural wetlands caused by highway widening, a new freeway interchange, and a new flood control channel, two marshes have been created at San Diego Bay expressly for Clapper Rails. The first mitigation project was a 12 acre series of islands and channels constructed in 1984. In 1990, an additional 17 acre site was excavated from the dredge spoil. To date, rails have not nested at either site.

Some of the inadequacies of these constructed salt marshes, compared with natural reference marshes, include less abundant epibenthic invertebrates (Scatolini and Zedler 1996), shorter vegetation (Zedler 1993), and lower concentrations of soil organic matter and soil nitrogen (Langis et al. 1991). From the standpoint of the Clapper Rail, the short stature of the plants may be the biggest problem: when the tide rises, the plant canopy is fully submerged, leaving no cover for rails, their nests, or their chicks.

A chain of events explains the short plant canopies at these constructed marshes. The sandy sediments do not retain nutrients well, so nutrients do not accumulate. Nitrogen limits plant growth, especially height. Low organic matter concentrations further limit nitrogen fixation rates, and perhaps the invertebrates that help to recycle nutrients. Finally, the short vegetation appears to be inadequate for use by beetles (*Coleomegilla fuscilabris*) that consume scale insects (*Haliaspis spartina*), which are native herbivores on the cordgrass vegetation (Boyer and Zedler 1996). Scale insect outbreaks further impair cordgrass growth. Experiments to augment soils with both organic matter and nitrogen improved plant growth in the first two years, but scale insects reduced plant growth in year three. Current experiments aim to produce tall plants before scale insect populations can irrupt.

From the problems that have plagued restoration attempts in San Diego Bay, we conclude that we are not yet able to recreate self-sustaining salt marshes or to reestablish self-sustaining populations of our endangered salt marsh birds. It is not yet clear how to guarantee long-term success. Our endangered species may well be the most difficult components to restore to wetland ecosystems. Because of their high habitat specificity, they are the first to decline when sites are modified and perhaps the last to return when artificial habitats are created.

We know *why* wetlands need to be restored: to replace hydrologic, water quality, and habitat functions. We have some ideas *where* the greatest gains can be made in the shortest period of time: marginally productive agricultural lands. We know *how* to restore wetlands where sites are not too damaged and where regional biodiversity is not too depleted: restore the hydrology, transplant the native vegetation, and wait for the animal populations to expand into the new habitats. What we cannot yet guarantee is replacement of habitat for the most sensitive species in regions where sites are highly disturbed and populations of critical food web components are no longer abundant. This is where students and researchers can make a huge difference.

Summing up their impressions of the success of attempts to restore a variety of wetlands, Kusler and Kentula (1990) concluded:

> Total duplication of natural wetlands is impossible due to the complexity and variation in natural as well as created or restored systems and the subtle rela-

> tionships of hydrology, soils, vegetation, animal life, and nutrients which may have developed over thousands of years in natural systems. Nevertheless, experience to date suggests that some types of wetlands can be approximated and certain wetland functions can be restored, created, or enhanced in particular contexts. It is often possible to restore or create a wetland with vegetation resembling that of a naturally occurring wetland. This does not mean, however, that it will have habitat or other values equaling those of a natural wetland nor that such a wetland will be a persistent, i.e., long term, feature in the landscape, as are many natural wetlands.

In addition to the work on wetlands, considerable work has been done in evaluating efforts to restore lakes (Cooke et al. 1986) and rivers and streams (Gore 1985). In contrast, evaluations of attempts to restore terrestrial ecosystems are often unsystematic and of limited applicability (Jordan 1990). Most studies address only a few features of the system—typically composition and structural features—rather than the more elusive functional and dynamic attributes. Nevertheless, ecologists' comments on some of the highest-quality projects, such as Greene Prairie at the University of Wisconsin Arboretum (Cottam 1987; discussed below) and the estuary of the Salmon River in Oregon (Morlan and Frenkel 1992), suggest that restoration of at least some ecosystems is possible under favorable conditions.

One point that is clear from restoration studies to date is that the feasibility of restoration varies enormously from system to system. Some systems, such as certain tidal wetlands, that have few species of plants and a relatively simple structure have been restored quite readily under favorable conditions. Others, such as peat bogs where the peat has been removed or disturbed, seem refractory to restoration. Thus, it is impossible to provide a general discussion of the restorability of ecosystems. This admission itself represents an important advance in conservation and restoration thinking.

An additional caveat should be inserted here, and will be repeated later. As mentioned above, when goals are established for a restoration project, one must be mindful that most ecological systems are ever-changing and thus represent a moving target for the restorationist. The traditional view that natural ecosystems are always in balance or equilibrium has caused problems in conservation biology in general (Sprugel 1991) and has turned out to be incorrect so often that ecologists have shifted to the newer nonequilibrium paradigm, discussed throughout this book (Wu and Loucks 1995). This reality is ever more obvious in restoration studies (Wyant et al. 1995).

Scale

The size of a restoration project is a central question that has great bearing on its potential success or failure. Complementing questions about the quality or authenticity of restored ecosystems are questions about the temporal and spatial scales on which restoration can be carried out, and the extent to which restoration efforts can be scaled up without unduly sacrificing quality (Figure 14.2). The National Research Council (1992) gives four considerations to be taken into account in determining the size of a restoration project:

1. The project should be large enough to minimize deleterious effects of boundary conditions and events on internal dynamics.
2. The project should be of a size such that managers can readily add, control, or eliminate, as necessary, disturbances to the system.
3. The project should be large enough so that various effects can be measured to assess project success.
4. The project should be an affordable size.

One might suppose that the best restorations are those conducted on a modest scale, involving relatively labor-intensive procedures. One might also

Figure 14.2 Temporal and spatial scales of restoration. The ideal situation is to work with a high degree of detail at large spatial scales with a long time scale in mind. More typical cases involve working on smaller temporal and spatial scales, and sacrificing detail. (From NRC 1992.)

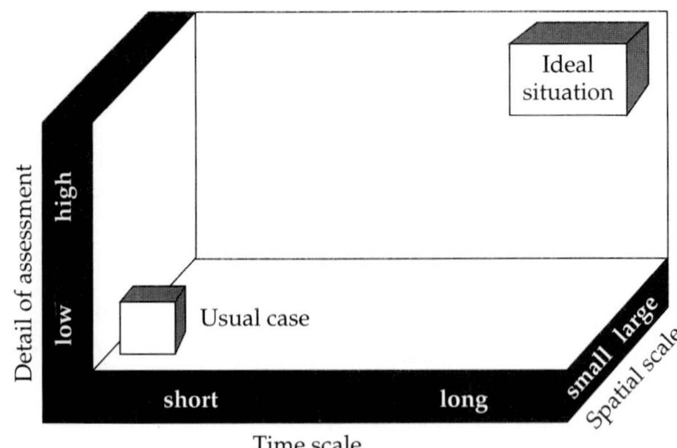

assume that attempts to "scale up" in space or time would necessarily entail compromises in quality. In some cases this is true. At present, the best restored prairies, for example, are those that were planted using labor-intensive ("horticultural") methods, and are relatively small (Figure 14.3). Greene Prairie at the University of Wisconsin Arboretum, for example, is only 16 ha. A portion of prairie planted at the Morton Arboretum in suburban Chicago is probably the most meticulously planted prairie anywhere and covers only a few hectares. This area is of higher quality, with respect to the presence and distribution of vascular plants, than portions of the prairie that were added later using less labor-intensive methods. Attempts to scale up to 250 ha in a restored prairie at Fermilab have resulted in further sacrifices in quality. Problems include lower diversity of native species, underrepresentation of rare species or species difficult to propagate or handle, and higher proportions of exotic species.

Observations such as these can lead to a certain pessimism regarding the value of restoration in conservation practice. Here the restorationist appears to be caught in a bind between ecological considerations on the one hand and technical and economic limitations on the other. Ecological quality depends, in part, on size: bigger is typically better, owing to various functional and island biogeographic considerations (see Chapter 10). In contrast, scaling projects up, though it may benefit the entire ecosystem, is likely to be carried out at the expense of some system components—at least in the short run.

There are several reasons to suppose that it may be possible to produce restored ecosystems of high ecological quality on a large scale. First is the

Figure 14.3 A prairie restoration experiment at the Curtis Prairie, ca. 1985. The highest-quality prairies have been planted using such labor-intensive horticultural methods, and consequently are small in scale. (Photograph courtesy of the University of Wisconsin Arboretum.)

principle, based on island biogeographic theory, that larger size actually helps. A larger site has a more complete functional infrastructure (a wider range of soils and exposures, more extensive and complete hydrologic systems, and so forth), and can support more species. Similarly, large sites have a greater capacity for self-repair than do smaller sites, and will, in effect, pull the restoration effort along more effectively toward the target. Given even a modest effort to ensure the timely introduction of species and the perpetuation of disturbance processes such as burning or grazing over the years, large-scale projects might be expected to improve gradually through what might be called "subsidized succession" until they achieve an even higher quality than more intensively restored, small-scale projects.

A second, related consideration is the realization that an abiotic system that remains either intact or fairly easily repairable, even despite drastic alteration in the biotic components, provides a solid foundation for reassembly of the ecosystem components. An excellent example is the recent discovery by prairie restorationists that simply throwing seed of prairie plants into an old-field sod often results in a prairie with more "conservative," or difficult to reintroduce, species than does the more laborious and costly traditional method that begins with plowing to set back competing species and open up space for prairie species. The old method disrupts the ecosystem; the newer approach both builds on the existing ecosystem and takes advantage of the rich assortment of establishment possibilities provided by the existing system, even if it is comprised entirely of exotic species. This work suggests that it may be possible to circumvent the quality–quantity trade-off, allowing restoration of high-quality systems on a large scale.

Restoration projects undertaken on a large scale (hundreds to thousands of hectares) typically emphasize the reintroduction, removal, or manipulation of ecosystem-scale processes such as burning, grazing, or hydrologic processes. Little if any direct manipulation of these communities, through reintroduction of native species or elimination or control of exotics, is possible, given the sheer size of the system. Thus, the restoration of thousands of hectares of tropical dry forest at Guanacaste National Park in Costa Rica (discussed below) has, so far, involved cessation of grazing and burning to reverse the effects of centuries of these practices (Jordan 1987). Likewise, large-scale wetland restoration projects frequently involve little more than restoration of appropriate hydrologic regimes—all that is necessary in some cases to ensure gradual recovery of the community. A project along these lines is the restoration of the Kissimmee River, Florida, which targets the floodplain of a 166 km river course and is expected to cost $372 million (Dahm 1995; Toth 1995).

Costs

Cost per hectare for restoration is, of course, an important consideration because it places a price on the ecosystem, linking its ecology with the human economy, as well as placing limits on the scope of projects. Cost is one of several considerations that will eventually determine the position of the equilibrium between restored natural systems and other forms of land use in human-dominated landscapes. A project must be realistically defined within proper financial bounds; an overambitious, overscaled project will soon run out of funding and possibly fail entirely, simply because it went beyond the financial constraints set upon it.

Because the costs of restoration projects vary widely, it is impossible to specify in any meaningful way the "going rate" for restoring a hectare of, say, tallgrass prairie or salt marsh. Moreover, costs and fees for projects are often the bases of business competition, discouraging publication of such information, so the figures available are likely to be incomplete, dated, or otherwise misleading (Guinon 1987). Despite these caveats, a few "ballpark" numbers may be helpful. Thompson (1992) reports that establishing a prairie in Iowa from seed may cost $625 per acre, while maintenance costs are $12–$18 per acre over a three-year period. Forests, depending on how trees are reestablished, may cost appreciably more. In arid areas, where land prices are low and restoration difficult, restoration costs, including site preparation, are often several times the per hectare market price of the land, and may total several thousand dollars per hectare.

The Restoration Process

In a simplistic sense, there are two general approaches to restoration, which differ considerably. The first, and most familiar, approach is to restore a disturbed area to its "natural state." However, we seldom know what the "natural" state was—we can see only what exists now. Many sites have undergone an unknown history of use by humans in ways such that we have little idea how they would appear without human influence. Even historical accounts are based on landscapes that may have been altered by prehistoric inhabitants. The second approach to restoration is to create a system that, while it does not mimic the natural situation, has a series of favorable traits that make the area better than it was before restoration. In both cases, either consciously or unconsciously, the restorationist is mimicking the natural process of succession.

Over the last 25 years, ecologists have been attempting to codify the theory underlying succession of natural communities. To an increasing extent the results of this activity have found their way into the literature of applied ecology and restoration, specifically recommending that successional theory be applied to problems of resource management and restoration (Hutnik and Davis 1973; Wali 1979; Bradshaw and Chadwick 1980; Dvorak 1984; Green and Salter 1987; Cairns 1988; Hossner 1988; Redente and DePuit 1988). A careful review of what natural resource managers do suggests that, in most cases, they are actually managing the process of succession to meet a certain goal—often without realizing that they are doing so.

Most management procedures are designed either to shorten the natural successional sequence—to speed up succession (Moore 1993)—or to hold a community in a particular stage of succession that is considered to have some desirable attributes. For example, the removal of juniper trees to increase cattle forage is, whether recognized or not, an attempt to set back succession and maintain a community dominated by highly productive grasses. Similarly, planting young trees in clear-cuts is an attempt to hasten succession to a forest rather than waiting for natural colonization of a site. The conscious use of restoration principles based on natural successional processes should be more economical than trying to plant vegetation and transport animals using methods based on traditional agricultural techniques.

A Succession Primer

Suppose an ecosystem is disturbed. The exact nature of the disturbance determines its potential path of recovery, mainly because the disturbance determines what remains to initiate the repair process. In a general sense, no disturbance completely destroys a site; there usually remain some propagules of plants or animals, some organic matter from the previous ecosystem, or other remnants, as well as the abiotic properties of the site. We can refer to these remnants of the previous system as **residuals,** or legacies (Figure 14.4). These

Figure 14.4 Residual components of the former ecosystem may be critical to restoration efforts. In this extreme case of a residual, a single conifer remains at this site after the eruption of Mount St. Helens in 1980. (Photograph by James A. MacMahon.)

residuals are, in essence, the raw materials available to rebuild the ecosystem. Clearly, the type, extent, timing, and intensity of a disturbance affects the assortment of residuals. Two forest fires in the same forest type can have dramatically different influences on the subsequent trajectory of succession depending on their areal extent, the heat of the fire, the time of year of the burn, and other variables. Similarly, a clear-cutting operation in that same forest type leaves different residuals than the fires.

Soon after disturbance a site is invaded by animals and plants, an invasion that goes on for the life of an ecosystem. In many cases the invaders are quite predictable because they live close to the disturbed area and are specifically adapted for colonizing disturbed sites. However, species that are neither geographically proximate to the site nor specially adapted to disturbance may also be early colonists if they have a high capacity for dispersal and if the site, even in its disturbed state, offers suitable habitat. After the eruption of Mount St. Helens, the early colonizing birds included juncos, ground-nesting birds that can use fallen trees as nest sites. They are not adapted to volcanic landscapes, but the ability to fly got them to the area, and the downed trees offered critical habitat for their breeding.

For both residual species and migrants, the site must offer appropriate conditions for establishing viable populations. Although species may survive a disturbance event, conditions at the site following disturbance may not be conducive to their subsequent breeding and persistence. Similarly, while a migrating species may reach a disturbed site, that does not ensure that conditions will allow it to become established and flourish.

Once established, species interact with one another in all the myriad of biotic interactions that characterize normal ecosystems. Such interactions include predator–prey relationships, parasitism, mutualisms, and competition. Under these conditions, some species will flourish, while others will simply be "edited" out of the species mix. If one of a pair of true mutualists survives, it cannot persist without its obligatory partner. Similarly, a voracious predator could extirpate a surviving prey population.

As groups of species become established, they often change the conditions of the site. Imagine, if you will, a forested site laid bare by a fire. Plants requiring shade cannot establish themselves or persist. Under such conditions residuals and migrants alike must be sun-tolerant. Species that become established change the light regime, providing opportunities for shade-tolerant species that were previously unsuccessful. Similarly, the digging activities of colonizing fossorial mammals, such as pocket gophers (*Thomomys*), may change the residual soil conditions in a way that permits establishment of a different suite of plants than could have occurred without the animals' activities.

Changes in the composition of the system's components will continue until a mixture of species persists and coexists for a long enough period that it is in some sort of equilibrium, often termed the climax. Of course, this "climax" is, in fact, an illusion, because the process of succession is always occurring. Species are added to and subtracted from an ecosystem for a variety of reasons all the time. There are constant disturbances of various magnitudes, and new colonists are always arriving. We might perceive little change because our vision of ecosystems is usually dominated by large, long-lived perennial plant species that appear not to change over time. Closer inspection would reveal that many species are highly volatile in their comings and goings. The fact that we may not perceive community composition continually changing can lead to problems in the restoration process. As mentioned earlier, we frequently choose a target ecosystem as a goal for restoration of an area, but that reference system changes over time. Thus, when we try to restore the disturbed site to the condition of the reference system, we are trying to hit a moving target. A further complication is that changes in an ecosystem are often discontinuous rather than continuous, and the presence of threshold phenomena may make comparisons to reference sites difficult and misleading (Friedel 1991).

It should be obvious that each subprocess of succession can dramatically affect the overall outcome and thus change the nature of the evolving ecosystem. It may not be as obvious that these processes are of differing importance in different environments (MacMahon 1981, 1987). It has been proposed, for example, that in arid areas establishment may be more important than some of the other processes, because arid areas have unpredictable abiotic environments (Reith and Potter 1986). Under such conditions the right sequence of temperature and rainfall may not occur each year as predictably as in more mesic sites (Figure 14.5). Thus, while there may be sufficient rain to permit

Figure 14.5 In arid regions, establishment of plants is highly dependent on the right sequence of temperature and rainfall. In the Sonoran Desert, wildflowers such as these poppies germinate and bloom only after winters of particularly heavy rainfall; seeds may otherwise lay dormant for years. (Photograph by John Hoffman.)

seeds to germinate, the seedlings may not experience subsequent conditions favorable to their establishment, growth, and reproduction. In contrast, very mesic areas such as rainforests may foster rapid growth and establishment of plants. Under these conditions, it is not the establishment phase that is critical, but the fact that plants become established so rapidly that they may preempt a particular site and slow down other aspects of the successional process. Therefore, when we attempt to apply our knowledge of succession to the restoration process, we have to be mindful of which processes are key in a particular environment.

Although hardly perfect, our knowledge of succession is good enough that ecological principles can serve as important bases for the restoration process. These principles have been used to restore communities varying from tundra (Cargill and Chapin 1987) to rainforests (Jordan and Farnworth 1982). In fact, three books are available that identify successional theory as the specific basis for restoration strategies (West et al. 1981; Majer 1989; Luken 1990), and many case studies support this perspective (e.g., Cairns 1995).

Examples of Restoration Projects

We will now explore several examples of restoration efforts that illustrate different problems, approaches, and scales of activities. The first example is presented in great detail to demonstrate the intricacies often involved in restoration; subsequent examples will be progressively less detailed, and will instead illustrate the breadth of principles, problems, and opportunities in restoration. These examples together begin to demonstrate the complexities, challenges, and rewards of restoration ecology and its role in larger conservation issues.

Restoration Following Mining Activities in Arid Lands

Because energy production and resource use in the United States often involves the mining of coal, uranium, or other minerals in arid areas, the ability to restore sites following such disturbances is of great practical importance. However, because plant establishment is slow and contingent upon a narrow window of climatic conditions, it is difficult and costly to restore lands in arid regions. While the goal of contemporary post-mining restoration includes substrate stabilization, it also includes development of a community characteristic of the area that will form a self-sustaining system that need not be managed in the future. This requirement for establishment of a persistent desirable ecosystem state implies more work and therefore higher costs.

For this example we will look at a restoration study in an area that underwent surface strip-mining for coal (Parmenter and MacMahon 1983; Parmenter et al. 1985, 1991). The study was conducted on the Pittsburgh and Midway Coal Mining Company's Elkol-Sorenson Mine, located 8 km southwest of Kemmerer, in western Wyoming (2103 m elevation). Precipitation averages 22.6 cm per year, mostly as snow, and is highly variable. May and June are the "wet" months, with approximately 2.5 cm precipitation each. Mean monthly temperatures range from –8°C in January to 17°C in July.

The terrain is characterized by rolling hills, and the presumed native vegetation is shrub steppe (West 1983). Dominant shrubs in the area include big sagebrush (*Artemisia tridentata*), rabbitbrush (*Chrysothamnus viscidiflorus*), and Gardner's saltbush (*Atriplex gardneri*), with occasional individuals of bitterbrush (*Purshia tridentata*), winterfat (*Ceratoides lanata*), serviceberry (*Amelanchier alnifolia*), and gray horsebrush (*Tetradymia canescens*) (Figure 14.6). A variety of common grasses are found on the site, and the soils are coarse, calcareous loams.

Figure 14.6 Typical vegetation near the Kemmerer mine site. Note the natural clumping of plants. (Photograph by James A. MacMahon.)

Following the mining process, the first step is to evaluate the state of a site, because not all surface-mined sites are equal. For example, during mining, turning over and mixing of soil horizons can dilute topsoil, expose toxic materials, or dramatically change soil structure. Knowledge of these effects is crucial because the overall potential for restoration often depends on the residual soil properties (Bentham et al. 1992). Along with soil changes comes the question of what plant propagules might be left. These problems were recognized early by reclamationists who recommended that, as the topsoil is scraped away, it be removed to storage piles adjacent to the mining sites. When the mined pit is closed and recontoured, the topsoil can then be respread on the surface to act as a fertile seedbed (Figure 14.7).

The initial arrival of plants on mined sites is usually a human-mediated process. The common scenario is for the mine operator to plant seeds or seedlings to initiate and speed up site recovery. Rapid recovery is important so as to minimize soil erosion and encourage residual seed banks to germinate while still viable. The planted vegetation is intended to stabilize the soil and to provide a source of organic matter that will begin soil regeneration. The intent is that desirable, seeded species will succeed, and that some of the residual species from the stored topsoil may also become reestablished.

(A)

(B)

Figure 14.7 (A) Stored topsoil pile at a coal mine site. (B) Respreading topsoil is the first step toward restoration. Saving and replacing such elements of the site may be critical to its ultimate restoration. (Photographs by James A. MacMahon.)

This particular study was designed to determine (1) whether managing the establishment phase by planting seedlings rather than seeds would permit more rapid restoration of mined lands in arid areas; (2) whether planting in dispersion patterns (clumps) and densities characteristic of arid areas would encourage establishment of plants and favorably alter soils; and (3) whether providing appropriate architecture of the plant component of the ecosystem would encourage animal reestablishment.

To deal with the problems of the establishment phase in an arid environment, seedlings (grown from seeds collected on an adjacent site), rather than seeds, were used (Figure 14.8). Although more expensive than seeding, the extra initial costs of planting would be recovered because the established plants would not have to be irrigated or fertilized, nor would the seedlings as readily fail because of a drought; thus, the site would not require a reseeding effort.

Figure 14.8 Planting of seedlings at the Kemmerer mining site, using a detailed experimental planting regime. (Photograph by James A. MacMahon.)

The species selected for planting were three woody perennials: big sagebrush, rabbitbrush, and Gardner's saltbush. One of each of these species formed a "planting unit" or triad, an equilateral triangle (40 cm on a side) with one plant at each apex. These triads were placed in plots representing three dispersion patterns: random, regular, and clumped. Because the goal of restoration was to create a functioning ecosystem that mimicked a reference area, attaining natural plant densities was also important. Native vegetation in the region contains about 16,000 woody plants per hectare. The study used a series of experimental plantings at four different plant densities, each applied to the three dispersion patterns. These densities included values above, equal to, and below the native density.

A large suite of measurements of many aspects of the reestablishing community was made, including both meso- and micrometeorology, plant establishment, growth, seed production, the movement, establishment, and effectiveness of mycorrhizal fungi, and recolonization of the site by animals.

Results indicated that, in terms of both survivorship and production of new plants through seeds, plants established in clumps were more successful than those in the regular or random patterns. This can be demonstrated by comparing two extreme planting scenarios. Figure 14.9A shows the planting pattern of triads in a low-density, regular dispersion plot, while Figure 14.9C shows the planting pattern of triads in a high-density, clumped dispersion plot. Figures 14.9B and 14.9D depict the actual persistence and size increment of the plants after three years. In the low-density plot, few triads had all three plants surviving, few of the plants had increased appreciably in size, and there was virtually no recruitment of new individuals. In contrast, the high-density plot had a marked increase in size of plants, a higher proportional survivorship, new recruits, and had even coalesced into larger clumps.

A prediction made in the study was that planting in clumps would be beneficial because clumps would trap organic matter and the spores of mycorrhizal fungi. This prediction was tested by measuring the establishment rate of the mycorrhizal association, the numbers of mycorrhizal spores in the soil, and the soil organic matter levels. As predicted, all of these measures were higher in clumps than in any other dispersion pattern, and were generally more favorable at the higher densities.

Reestablishment of animals was a more complicated process. Because of limited space on the mine site, plots were a maximum of 0.5 ha; this was too small to accurately measure changes in populations of highly vagile vertebrate species. However, censuses of insects indicated that they recolonized the site rapidly, and cursory observations of vertebrates suggested a better response to clumped sites.

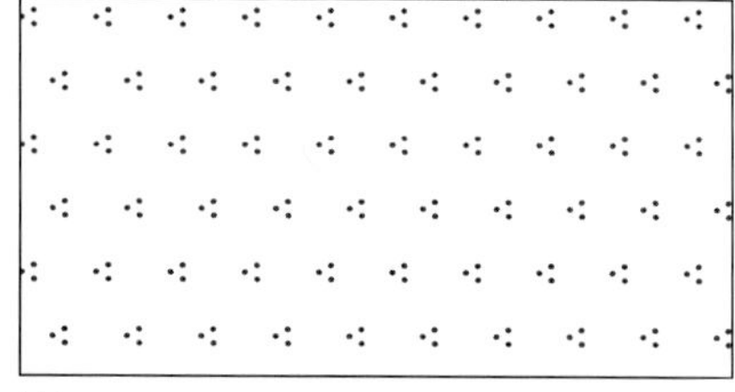

(A)

(B)

(C)

(D)

Figure 14.9 (A) Planting array of triads in a low-density, regular dispersion plot at the Kemmerer site. Each plot is 16 × 32 m. (B) Status of plants in A after three years. Positions and sizes of circles indicate actual positions and sizes of plants on the site. (C) Planting array of triads in a high-density, clumped dispersion plot. (D) Status of plants in C after three years. Note clumping, the larger sizes of some plants, and more recruitment of new plants from seeds compared with (B).

Two main themes emerged from this study. First, the use of seedlings rather than seeds in this arid region resulted in high success rates. A seeding study was conducted simultaneously, and those plots were less successful. Commonly, mine sites such as these need to be reseeded several times before plants become established, but the seedling approach was successful the first time. Second, the clumped pattern of planting fostered establishment of the mycorrhizal association, as well as increasing organic matter in the soil. Thus, this pattern of planting, in itself, enhanced the restoration process and was a major cause of successful plant establishment and subsequent growth. Overall, the use of ecological theory provided a sound and economical basis for restoration.

Restoration of a Tropical Dry Forest in Guanacaste National Park

Of all tropical forest types, deciduous dry forest has been the most severely affected by human activities (Figure 14.10). On a pantropical scale, these forests have been largely replaced by crops such as sorghum and cotton, and especially by cattle ranching. In Mesoamerica, dry forest formerly extended from the southwestern coast of Mexico south through northwestern Costa Rica and parts of Panama. Today, the forest consists mostly of isolated small remnants that persist in inaccessible sites such as deep ravines. In aerial photographs these forest patches look like tiny islands in a sea of grass and scrub.

Restoring these forests, even on a limited scale, is a formidable challenge. First, the conditions that caused the forest losses in the first place must be changed, and this requires a fundamental change in land use practices. Second, there must be enough forest nuclei left to act as a source of seeds for restoration. Third, though the animal component of these forest nuclei is very different from that of the original forest, it must at the very least contain those animals critical to the survival and expansion of the regenerating forest; that is, the appropriate numbers and kinds of pollinators and seed dispersers.

One of the few places where dry forest exists in nuclei large enough to support the ecological conditions prerequisite for restoration is in Guanacaste National Park in northwestern Costa Rica. The 10,700 ha park is located in the lowlands, and spans an altitudinal range from sea level to 317 m. The original forest of this region consisted of canopy trees 20–30 m in height, an understory layer of trees 10–20 m tall, and a shrub layer with many spiny species and woody vines. Two 4 ha forested plots in this region contained 44 and 68 tree species, as compared with two 4 ha plots in the Atlantic rainforest that contained 88 and 112 tree species. In all plots, the 10 most common species made up 45% or more of the total basal area (Hartshorn 1983). Thus, the species richness difference between tropical dry forest and tropical wet forest is the larger number of rare species in the wet forest. As a restoration goal, establishing the 10 most common tree species would represent, at minimum, nearly half of the woody biomass diversity of the dry forest.

Much of the landscape in Guanacaste has been completely converted to pastures, largely monocultures of African grasses. All but a small fraction of the remaining land has been degraded to a savanna-like landscape of a few tree species scattered through weedy fields, shrubby thickets, or species-poor second-growth forest. Fire is a key process in degradation, and fire suppression is a critical part of the restoration process. It is important to note that fire is not a significant part of the natural disturbance regime in this region, at least not at the frequency needed to maintain grasslands, because lightning strikes occur in the wet season. Ranchers set fires, typically on an annual basis in the dry season, to prevent encroachment of tree species on their pastures. In the absence of fire, grass is replaced by native woody species.

(A)

(B)

Figure 14.10 (A) Pacific lowland forest at Guanacaste National Park in northwestern Costa Rica, one of the few remaining tracts of intact tropical deciduous dry forest. (B) Most of the Pacific lowland forest has been degraded to poor-quality ranches or farmlands like this site near Guanacaste National Park. (Photographs by C. R. Carroll.)

For more than a decade, Costa Rican biologists with the National Park System, along with U.S. collaborators, have been restoring the dry forest on these lands using sound ecological principles and simple techniques. Their management strategy has two tactics: reducing wildfires and enhancing seed dispersal of forest trees. Wildfires had to be eliminated in order to stop the continuing process of forest degradation and exotic grassland enhancement. Seed dispersal had to be enhanced because the remaining forest is fragmented into small and isolated patches, and many of the normal dispersal agents are missing. Alternative, cost-effective ways to move seeds from forest patches into the grasslands had to be found.

The first problem the managers faced, and solved, was gaining management authority over the park land so that public use could be regulated. With this authority, unnecessary roads were closed, campfires and camping locations were restricted, and uncontrolled grazing by cattle was eliminated. In order to reduce wildfires, the managers needed to reduce the amount of highly flammable African grasses, which make up most of the pastures in the region. Because these grasses can grow more than 2 m high, they can support very hot and rapidly moving fires that penetrate fragmented forests. Along road edges, the grasses were mowed, grazed, or carefully burned to reduce accidental and intentional fires.

Once fire is kept out of the grasslands, the native woody vegetation quickly begins to invade. For example, at one site close to a large forest patch, the grassland was converted to early second-growth forest after only eight fire-free years (Figure 14.11). However, as the distance between forest patches

Figure 14.11 (A) If fires can be suppressed in grasslands such as this one, natural and enhanced seed dispersal processes can result in a rapid conversion back to forest. (B) Eight years of fire suppression allowed this young, second-growth forest to develop from a grassland. (Photographs by C. R. Carroll.)

(A)

(B)

Figure 14.12 Livestock can effectively disperse the seeds of many forest trees. Emerging from this pile of dung is a seedling of a large canopy tree, *Enterolobium cyclocarpum*. (Photograph by D. H. Janzen.)

increases, naturally occurring seed dispersal becomes a limiting factor in the rate of forest restoration. To enhance seed dispersal into grasslands, horses are fed meal containing the seeds of important large forest trees, especially seeds of the "Guanacaste tree" (*Enterolobium cyclocarpum*, Fabaceae). As the horses wander through the grasslands, they deposit the seeds in rich piles of manure, a highly cost-effective approach to revegetation (Figure 14.12). As these trees mature, they will become attractive "stopover" stations for other birds and mammals migrating among forest patches. Thus, isolated trees become the foci for additional seed dispersal. Trees that appear to lack effective long-distance seed dispersal, such as the large-seeded legume *Hymenaea courbaril*, are planted manually.

This approach to restoration seems to be working. Areas of the park that only a decade ago were pure expanses of African grasses are now healthy secondary forests of native species (Figure 14.13).

Two general lessons about restoration are illustrated by this example. First, degraded tropical forests can be recovered on reasonable time and spatial scales as long as some forest still exists to serve as a source of seeds and dispersal agents. Second, once the causes of degradation are understood, relatively simple techniques may be sufficient to initiate the restoration process. In this case, fire suppression and enhanced seed dispersal were two simple, but key, techniques for restoration. This observation demonstrates the value of devising and implementing a conceptual framework for restoration, as mentioned earlier.

Restoration of Native Prairies

Some of the earliest restoration efforts were conducted on the degraded tallgrass prairies of the midwestern United States, begun as Civilian Conservation Corps projects during the depression of the 1930s. By the end of the 19th century, tallgrass prairie had been all but eliminated over its formerly huge range, especially in the eastern, "corn-belt" portion of the range, largely through extensive agriculture. Only tiny remnants existed, often in very small patches where native vegetation was left undisturbed, such as railroad rights-of-way or cemeteries. Although outwardly appearing to be simple systems, prairies actually had quite high plant species diversities, and were spatially heterogeneous systems. Restoration efforts over the last half century have attempted to restore some of that diversity (Stevens 1995).

Figure 14.13 These satellite images show changes in forest cover at Guanacaste National Park between 1979 (A) and 1985 (B). Forest types are indicated by shading: the lightest shade is young, second-growth forest; the medium shade is older, more mature forest; the darkest shade is swamp forest. Note the replacement of light shading in several areas over time, especially at the upper right of the image. (Satellite images courtesy of Elizabeth Kramer.)

(A)

(B)

(A)

(B)

Figure 14.14 (A) Initial efforts by the Civilian Conservation Corps at restoring the Curtis Prairie at the University of Wisconsin Arboretum, ca. 1935; (B) Curtis Prairie as it looked in 1980. (Photographs courtesy of the University of Wisconsin Arboretum and Archives.)

Prairies have been a focal point of restoration attempts because they lend themselves to experiments on a small scale and in the short term. Prairie patches of less than a hectare can be restored, although restorations orders of magnitude larger have also been attempted or suggested. Few sweeping generalizations can be made about prairie restoration due to great regional and temporal variation in conditions, and each effort has its own set of unique circumstances, including climatic conditions, seed and plant sources, fire history and use in restoration, and planting methods employed (Kline and Howell 1987). Despite the variations involved, there are two basic groups of problems associated with prairie restoration: increasing the populations of native prairie species, and eliminating exotic herbaceous and woody species.

The oldest and probably most famous restoration project involves the Curtis and Greene prairies at the University of Wisconsin Arboretum (Figure 14.14). These sites had been used for crops or pasture for the previous century, and their original vegetation had been almost entirely eliminated. Restoration at the sites began in the 1930s (Cottam 1987). Site preparation for prairie restoration can involve a variety of techniques, depending on local conditions, and several were used at these sites. If the site is entirely taken up by exotic vegetation, then those plants may be eliminated through herbicide use, soil cultivation, or soil sterilization. However, more extreme treatments, such as sterilization, are more destructive to soil organisms, and often result in longer establishment periods for new vegetation and soil organisms. If some desirable vegetation is present, selective raking, soil disking, or burning may eliminate exotic species and open space for natives.

Planting techniques also vary. Transplanting of prairie sods, or plants grown individually, has a high success rate, but is costly. Alternatively, if existing prairie is available, it may be mowed late in the season, and the "hay" transferred to the restoration site. Seeds in the hay then seed the new site.

Observations of restored prairies at the Curtis and Greene sites over several decades indicate that these are very dynamic systems, with a great deal of unpredictability in species composition and community structure. Detailed surveys of the prairies every 5 years indicate that community composition at a location changes over time, and that entire communities change locations "in an amoeba-like movement that seems to be a response to the short-term climatic events of years immediately preceding the survey" (Cottam 1987). Such dynamism over a 24-year period is evident in Figure 14.15.

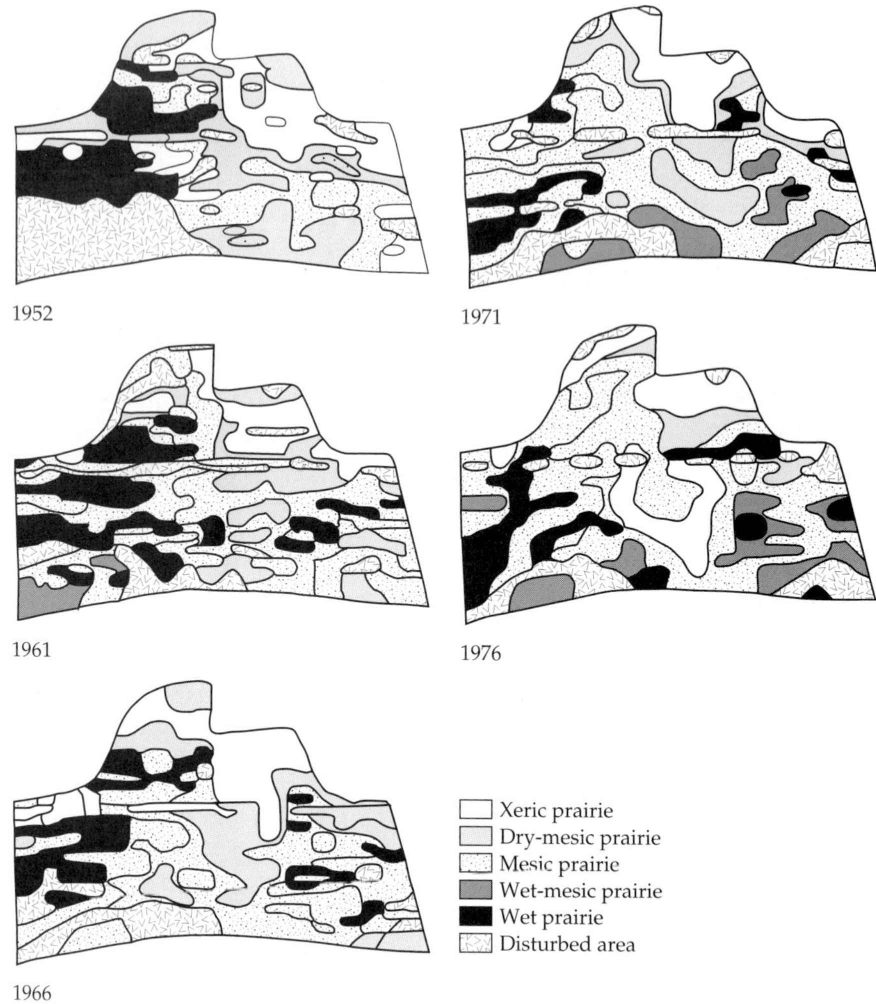

Figure 14.15 The temporal dynamics of prairies as illustrated by the Greene Prairie from 1952 to 1976. Changes were partly due to shifts of species toward more optimal sites, reflecting short-term variations in climate. (From Cottam 1987.)

Several classes of questions are relevant to the successful restoration of prairies (Kline and Howell 1987) and need further attention. The first involves disturbance. We know that prairies historically experienced disturbances in a dynamic mosaic pattern. How can we develop long-term, relevant disturbance regimes? Historical disturbances included fire, mound-building ants, and the actions of bison. Such disturbances are probably critical in maintaining native species and removing exotics, but what particular disturbance patterns are important?

Second, what is the relevance of population explosions of some plant species? For example, in the Wisconsin prairie projects, a plant called rattlesnake master (*Eryngium yuccifolium*) has completely covered Curtis Prairie, although it is usually abundant (and never dominant) only on mesic native prairies (Cottam 1987). What causes such explosions, will they last, and do they cause declines of other native species?

Third, it is generally recommended that locally adapted strains be used for plantings. But how important is that? Are there advantages to using more distant genetic varieties, perhaps to increase genetic diversity? Should strains from warmer climates be used to anticipate global climate changes? On the other hand, will nonlocal strains have reduced success rates, or conversely, will they outcompete other local species or strains? Obviously, many questions remain regarding the details of prairie restoration.

Since the earliest restoration efforts in the prairie region during the 1930s, many hundreds of projects have been initiated, often by amateurs (Packard and Mutel 1996). Many, developed for educational or ornamental purposes, are small, but projects on the scale of 10 to 20 ha are common. Further development of techniques, including successional restoration (involving seeding directly into existing sod) and the use of customized farm equipment for operations such as seed gathering and planting, have led to a general scaling up of projects in recent years.

A landmark project inside the proton accelerator ring at Fermi National Laboratory in suburban Chicago began in the mid-1970s, and now covers roughly 200 ha (Nelson 1987). The McHenry County Conservation District is now working on a project that will eventually include some 600 ha in northeastern Illinois, and The Nature Conservancy of Illinois is embarking on its "Chicago Wilderness" project, a program that will restore hundreds of hectares of prairie and other ecosystem types in the Chicago area. A project by the U.S. Fish and Wildlife Service at Walnut Creek, in central Iowa, will eventually include some 2800 ha of prairie, most of it on abandoned farmland (Drobney 1994). Still other projects, such as those on The Nature Conservancy's holdings in Kansas and Nebraska, which employ upgrading of existing prairies rather than restoration from nothing, involve tracts of many hundreds of hectares.

Of course, even tens of thousands of hectares is still only a small fraction of the millions of hectares of tallgrass prairie that existed in central North America before European settlement. Thus, even what appears to be minor progress is highly significant from the perspective of biodiversity conservation. These projects have resulted in reintroduction of prairie to regions from which it had been essentially eradicated, and they provide expanded habitat for hundreds of species of native plants and animals. Some of these species were extremely rare and had been reduced to a tiny fraction of their former range. Many prairie restoration projects now include a number of species on state or federal lists of rare or endangered species. Though no comprehensive figures are available, the work of restorationists during the past three decades has undoubtedly led to a slight increase in prairie acreage in the Midwest, reversing a two-century pattern of decline, and has provided a rich information base on how to restore prairie ecosystems.

Examples of Aquatic Restoration

Aquatic systems—lakes, streams, rivers, and wetlands—are critical resources in any region, but have a history of abuse throughout the world. Damming, channelization, groundwater pumping, diversion, and use as open sewers are just a few of the many ills experienced by aquatic systems. Fortunately, many of these problems are reversible, often just by removing the particular agent of destruction; others require greater restoration efforts. A few examples will illustrate some of these problems and potential restoration solutions.

Lake Washington is an 87 km^2 lake near Seattle, Washington. The lake was affected by raw and treated sewage from Seattle for much of this century, and by 1955, increased phosphorus loads had resulted in large blooms of blue-green algae (*Oscillatoria rubescens*), a species not previously found in the lake (NRC 1992). The presence of *Oscillatoria* is a classic indicator that water conditions in a lake are rapidly deteriorating (Lehman 1986). Because of sewage releases and resultant heavy algal blooms, water quality continued to deteriorate in Lake Washington, culminating in strong public concern over the destruction of this resource. A local government agency was formed, and provided funds to divert sewage releases into the Pacific Ocean at Puget Sound.

By 1967, four years after diversion began, 99% of the previous sewage input no longer flowed into Lake Washington. The resultant decrease in nutrient loading had rapid effects on the lake: water clarity greatly increased, phosphorus levels declined from 70 to 16 μg/l, and chlorophyll levels (a measure of algal growth) decreased from 35 to 4 μg/l (NRC 1992). Although diversion of sewage from the lake to Puget Sound only seems to redirect the problem elsewhere, in fact the comparatively huge size of that water body makes the additional input of nutrients relatively trivial. The conditions in Lake Washington were improved tremendously simply by removing sewage dumping. A compelling and readable account of the Lake Washington story is provided by Edmondson (1991).

Such eutrophication is a common problem in lakes in the United States and around the world. Increased levels of nutrients such as phosphorus and nitrogen from sewage outfalls or agricultural fertilizer runoff stimulate algal growth, fundamentally changing the biological, chemical, and physical conditions of the system. Such waters typically become warm, green, and overproductive. When algal blooms die, they sink to the bottom and decompose; this process depletes the water of oxygen, and the bottom can become anoxic, killing larger organisms such as invertebrates and fish. The restoration approach in such cases is standard and uncomplicated: eliminate the source of extra nutrients. The complications, of course, come in the form of the legal clout and political will necessary to make the changes.

A different type of problem affects many rivers throughout the world: fundamental changes in channel morphology, usually as a result of dredging, flood control projects, or agricultural activities in floodplains. Such actions result in unintended changes in river morphology and flow, usually causing greater problems for people than the original river behavior they were intended to change. An example is the San Juan River in southwestern Colorado. In the 1930s, willows along the banks of the San Juan were burned away, and bottomlands along the river were plowed for agriculture. This created an unstable and unnatural channel system broken into several "braids" that meandered across the river valley (NRC 1992). Riverbank soils were badly eroded because willow trees no longer held them in place, adjacent land was washed away, water quality declined, and roads and irrigation projects were damaged.

In an effort to restore the river to its former condition, a hydrologist was called upon to study the natural flows of undisturbed rivers in the area and to design a restoration program for the San Juan. He constructed a new river channel, floodplains, and river terraces based on the meander patterns, width-to-depth ratios, and flow patterns of stable streams in the region. He employed so-called "soft engineering" technology, which uses natural materials and heeds the natural tendencies of river flows. Rather than building a concrete and steel channel or relying on "riprap" (large rocks used to artificially stabilize the bed), he used natural materials such as tree trunks, boulders, roots, and vegetation to reinforce the new river channel. The new meander pattern has remained stable for five years, transports sediments as it should, and handles full flood capacity with no problem. The project demonstrated that understanding natural and predictable riverine flows is the key to restoring a system without the use of heavy technology and creation of an artificial state. The "soft" technology will eventually allow the river to return to a more natural state than would artificial materials, at a lower cost. This project was part of the rationale for a massive release of dammed water into the Colorado River in the spring of 1996 to reestablish its former geomorphology—a massive, high-intensity, short-duration restoration effort that early results indicate was quite successful.

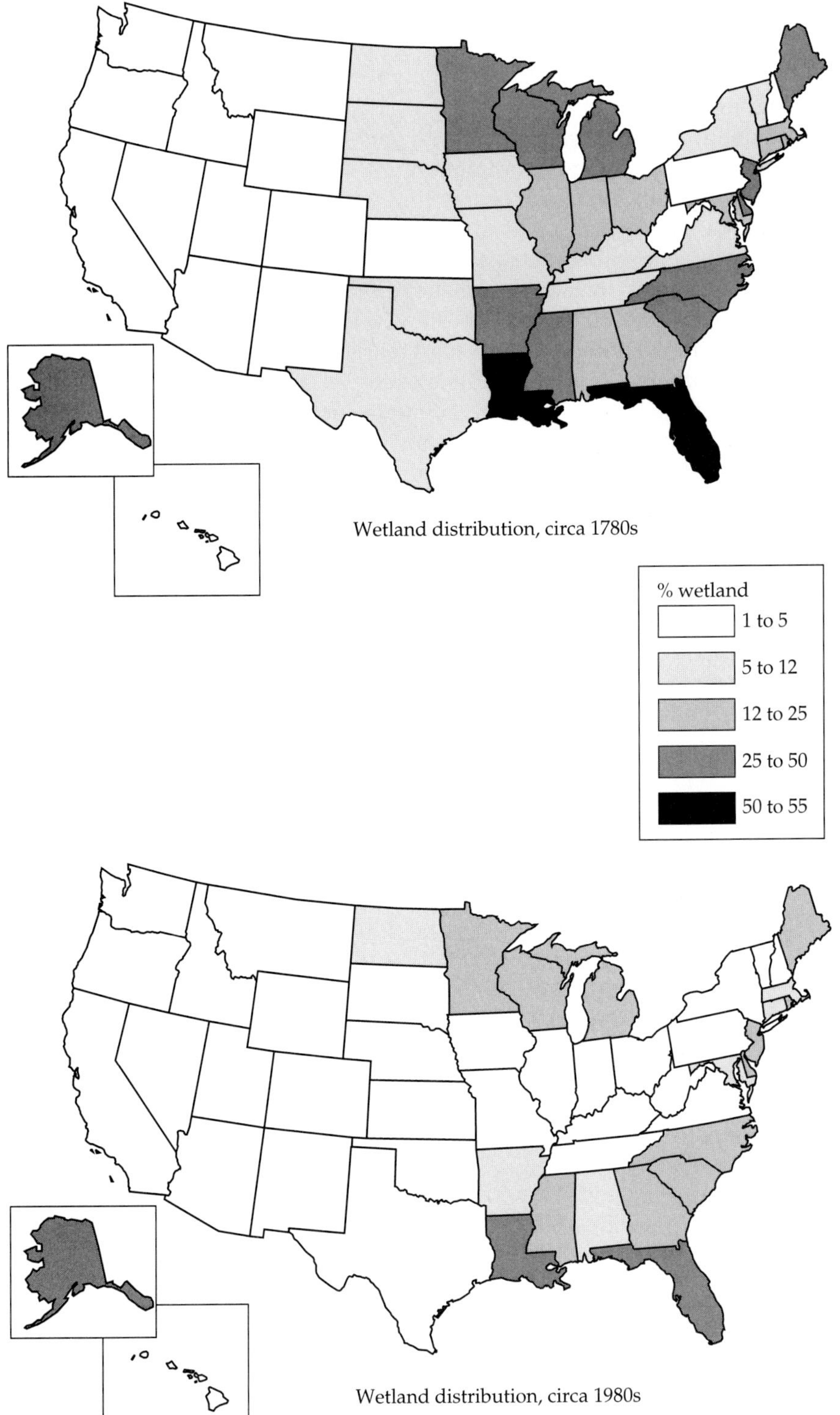

Figure 14.16 Wetland distribution in the United States in the 1780s and the 1980s. The percentage of wetland habitat has declined in every state over this 200-year period, and continues to do so. (From Dahl 1990.)

Finally, wetlands throughout the world have declined extensively over the last few centuries. In the contiguous United States, some 53% of the estimated original extent of wetlands has been lost in the last two centuries (Dahl 1990; Figure 14.16). Swamps, floodplains, bogs, sloughs, marshes, springs, and other wetlands that serve vital ecosystemic functions and are centers of biological diversity have been drained, ditched, pumped, and diked. The obvious restoration action in such cases is to reinstate the former hydrologic conditions by reestablishing historical water flows. Ditches may be closed, pumping stopped, dikes removed, and so forth.

A potentially limiting and complicating factor in this form of restoration is the availability of propagules or immigrants to the newly restored wetland. If only a few years have elapsed since drying, viable seed banks may still exist in the local soils, so that the native plant community can reestablish itself. If habitat corridors to other wetlands or associated uplands have not been destroyed, then natural migrations may bring wetland animals, such as amphibians and reptiles, back to the system. However, in the absence of natural recolonization, it may be necessary to reestablish the plant community, as was done in the prairie and arid mine site examples above. Likewise, it may be necessary to bring fish and other invertebrate populations to the site, and even to "inoculate" the system with water and substrate containing invertebrates and microbes from a comparable system.

General Observations on Restoration

Jackson et al. (1995) have argued that success in ecological restoration is determined by four overall factors: the specific ecological circumstances under which restoration proceeds, the various judgments made about the process, the values that are brought to the project or under which it must work, and the social commitment to the project and its goals (Figure 14.17). The best

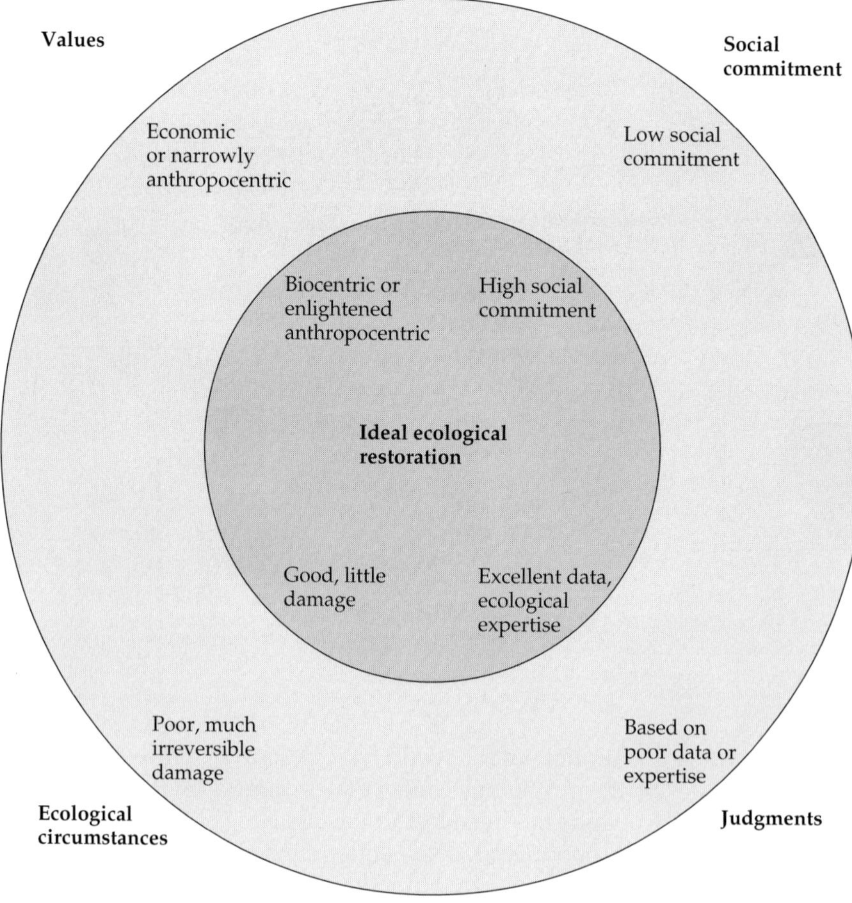

Figure 14.17 A model of four factors that determine the success of restoration projects. The closer one can come to the ideal state, (toward the center) the more successful the restoration will be. (From Jackson et al. 1995.)

restoration outcomes will occur when all four of these factors approach the ideal state; the further any particular factor is from the ideal state, the more difficult it will be to attain the stated goals. Obviously restoration is a complicated process that goes well beyond ecological considerations.

As evidenced by the several examples given, planning and conducting a restoration project requires consideration of a myriad of site conditions and selection of appropriate techniques from a huge array of alternatives. Of special importance is the recognition that the factors addressed in restoration—essentially those factors that limit, constrain, or influence the natural recovery process—vary enormously from system to system (MacMahon 1987). On the prairies, a key limiting factor is typically the genetic material available to the restorationist. The major restoration effort goes into finding and introducing native species in appropriate proportions while eliminating or excluding exotics, but relatively little attention is paid to patterns of distribution. On the shrublands of the arid West, pattern and structure are critical, and the distributions of species, even at the individual level, may be important attributes of the system crucial to successful restoration. In aquatic systems, restoration may be as simple as eliminating the major source of phosphorus or restoring a natural hydrologic pattern, or as complicated as restructuring a stream channel. In a megascale restoration such as the Guanacaste project, restoration focuses on eliminating human disturbance regimes and changing land use practices to allow recovery of native vegetation, assisted by intentional seed dispersal of native species.

Other factors, often of a very different nature, come into play when dealing with distinctly different kinds of systems, such as cliffsides, alpine regions, or vernal pools. For some systems, especially forests, the sequence of species introductions is a key, and often challenging, concern. In other systems, the particular soil type and structure may determine success or failure. There is literally no end to special considerations, and they are the subject of a growing body of literature. Successful restoration depends on identifying these key limiting factors and dealing with them effectively.

Similar considerations apply to restoration efforts undertaken in systems that have experienced different degrees or kinds of alteration—differences in the disturbance process. Restoration may involve rejuvenation of a system that, though altered or degraded in some way, offers basic structure to work with, provided it has not, in the jargon of the auto-body shop, been "totaled." There frequently *is* something to work with—residuals or legacies—even though this is not always obvious. The time and trouble spent in identifying and taking advantage of residuals is likely to be repaid later. In fact, recognition of what is available to work with may be the most important single step in successful restoration. Close observation of the system, often over a period of years, may be required. A classic example is the work being done to locate relict prairies in old cemeteries and along rights-of-way in northeastern Illinois, and then to restore them, principally by judicious hand weeding and reintroduction of fire (Betz and Lamp 1992). In many cases this has led to the recovery of respectable stands of prairie on sites so heavily infested with exotic species that prairie species were suppressed and difficult to find.

Despite such successes, there is a tendency to skip this first step in restoration, ignoring what is there and wiping the slate clean, as it were, with plow, ax, or herbicide. Unfortunately, this strategy frequently entails destruction of elements of the functioning ecosystem that can actually provide the best base for the restoration effort. If these elements are removed or destroyed, they may be nearly impossible to reconstruct. An intriguing example of this principle, mentioned previously, is the recent development of successional restoration of prairies in which, rather than clearing the ground with plow or pesticides, the restorationist merely throws seed of prairie species onto existing sod. The development of prairie is relatively slow under such conditions, but results suggest that this method favors species that may be difficult to establish on bare-soil sites. Not only is it an easier and cheaper process, but the resulting prairie may also be of higher quality than that achieved by more intensive methods. This method provides a way of avoiding the trade-off of quality for quantity that, in the past, has limited the value of prairie restoration as a conservation strategy.

This principle obviously has important implications for the practice and application of restoration. Recognizing that even low-key work with relatively intact systems is actually restoration will help the practitioner to think more clearly about the work at hand, including identification of disturbances, definition of goals, and so forth. This approach will also discourage the tendency to hide faulty or unclear thinking and planning behind softer, more ambiguous terms such as "management," "stewardship," or even "preservation."

One wishes that there could be a universal measure of ecosystem status or health (Rapport 1989) that could guide our planning and assessment of progress. Microbes may represent a group with some potential to help the restorationist. They are clearly important in ecosystems in general (e.g., Allen 1991) and in restoration projects in particular (Kieft 1991), as they were in the coal mine study described herein. Some researchers have recommended microbes as indicators of restoration progress, at least for terrestrial restoration projects (Bentham et al. 1992). Whatever organisms, processes, or system states turn out to be good indicators of restoration progress, we must always keep our restoration goal in mind, even if the vagaries of natural systems make that goal somewhat elusive. In the past, measuring progress was a simple matter of comparing the restoration project to a reference area. We now realize that this comparison is difficult, perhaps imperfect (Pickett and Parker 1994), but still has utility (Aronson et al. 1995).

Our relative neglect of animals in this discussion reflects the state of our knowledge, both in research and in the practice of restoration. Most studies tend to concentrate on vegetation, and usually on the most obvious species. Animals can play a vital role in restoration efforts (as was seen in the Guanacaste program), but systematic study of most of them, from a restoration perspective, is still in its infancy. (For an introduction to research on animals in restoration, the reader should refer to Panzer 1984 on insects in restored prairies; to Green and Salter 1987 and Majer 1989 on animals in general; and to Holl 1996 for an example of a failure to restore Lepidoptera on a reclaimed mine.)

Restoration has a valid and important role to play in conservation. The number of degraded ecological systems around the world grows as the number of relatively pristine systems declines. Concentrating only on the latter and ignoring the former throws away tremendous conservation opportunities. Most lands and waters around the globe are degraded to some degree, but many are usable as important conservation areas and buffers for wildlands. Growing attention to these degraded areas as the matrix within which centers of wilderness exist can only serve to enhance overall efforts to stem the loss of biodiversity. Restoration ecology is a key to our conservation future and is likely to be most efficient if conducted using sound ecological and conservation principles.

Summary

Restoration ecology is a tool in the arsenal against biodiversity loss, not an end unto itself. Protection of natural habitat before it is damaged by humans is the preferred course of action in conservation, but sometimes restoring damaged habitat is a viable and necessary option. Restorationists work in systems that have been damaged or degraded by human action, with the explicit intention of guiding those systems back toward their former, natural state through deliberate manipulation. Restoration ecology has been advanced by a number of factors, including legislation requiring habitat rehabilitation after human damage, increased use of restoration techniques in various engineering applications, a growing interest in cultivating native as opposed to exotic vegetation, and increased awareness of ecological destruction worldwide. But restoration runs the political risk of appearing to allow ecological destruction that can be fixed later, a false impression. Restoration is not an alternative to conservation, but a complement to and subset of conservation.

Basic concerns common to all restoration efforts include defining the desired product, determining the feasibility of the project, assessing the authenticity of the results, working at an appropriate and feasible scale, and working within realistic cost constraints. A "target" should be established for any restoration project, which can be based on good knowledge of the pre-disturbance system, knowledge of a similar, undisturbed system, or simply an ecologically more desirable condition than the present, degraded state (Bradshaw 1995). The system is then sent on a new developmental "trajectory" toward that state. The feasibility of restoration depends on a myriad of factors, including the present condition of the site (such as level of disturbance and condition of hydrology and soils), availability of biological materials for restoration (including their genetic diversity), and the cost of restoration and availability of funding. The scale of a project has great bearing on its potential success. In general, quantity sacrifices quality; that is, details cannot usually be tended to as readily in larger projects. The reality of cost also has great bearing on restoration success.

Much of restoration simply involves manipulation of succession, either to speed up the successional process or to halt it in an earlier state. Within this successional context, residuals or legacies of the undegraded system should be identified and used to advantage. Remnants of the former system provide not only raw materials for restoration efforts, but also information about the unperturbed state.

We have discussed several examples of restoration projects that demonstrated various concerns, challenges, and techniques used in restoration ecology. Collectively, they demonstrate that each restoration project is unique, and each must be designed and conducted for the particular site. As with most of conservation biology, there are no standardized, "cookbook" prescriptions that substitute for good local ecological knowledge.

Questions for Discussion

1. Imagine that you are given the job of restoring a prairie. What would you need to think about to begin the task? Prepare a list of questions to address regarding what you would need to know and what you would need to do in order to get the prairie restored.
2. Repeat Question 1 for another habitat, such as an estuary that has been degraded by dredging, a small swamp that has been drained for agriculture, or an alpine meadow that has been trampled by cattle and people. How does the list differ from that in Question 1?
3. If you successfully restored the prairie in Question 1, could those same techniques be transferred to another prairie restoration project 50 km

away? 500 km away? What are some factors that might have to be considered in modifying the techniques and approach used?

4. How worthwhile is it to attempt a restoration project when you are certainly not guaranteed success? What are some of the ecological and political pitfalls that might be encountered in a failed restoration attempt? How far along the restoration path should one travel, putting time and money into the project? Can you develop some guidelines (ecological, economic, political) that could suggest when to abandon (or not attempt) a restoration project?

Suggestions for Further Reading

Bradshaw, A. D. and M. J. Chadwick. 1980. *The Restoration of Land: The Ecology and Reclamation of Derelict and Degraded Land.* Blackwell Scientific Publications, Oxford. Two British authors show how a scientific approach to the management of derelict lands can pay substantial dividends in restoring land to a useful state. Many examples of work in Great Britain and Australia are given.

Buckley, G. P. (ed.). 1989. *Biological Habitat Reconstruction.* Belhaven Press, London. Topics related to habitat reconstruction, from the viewpoints of over 30 authors, are addressed, including the development of new habitats as well as the ecological principles of habitat reconstruction.

Cairns, J., Jr. (ed.). 1995. *Rehabilitating Damaged Ecosystems.* 2nd ed. CRC Press, Boca Raton, FL. This volume, edited by one of the pioneers of restoration ecology, contains a wealth of information concerning the reclamation of sites as disparate as coal slurry ponds and salt marshes. It contains a very readable first chapter by Cairns that lays out some of the problems of restoration ecology.

Dahm, C. N. (ed.). 1995. Special Issue: Kissimmee River Restoration. *Rest. Ecol.* 3(3):145 238. This entire issue is devoted to the Kissimmee River Project and includes detailed consideration of the ecosystem approach to this vast restoration project.

Jordan, W. R. III, M. E. Gilpin, and J. D. Aber (eds.). 1987. *Restoration Ecology: A Synthetic Approach to Ecological Research.* Cambridge University Press, Cambridge. This book was one of the first to invite a group of ecologists to address problems of restoration from theoretical as well as practical viewpoints. It has been used as a textbook in a number of university courses devoted to restoration ecology.

Luken, J. O. 1990. *Directing Ecological Succession.* Chapman and Hall, London. Luken specifically applies successional theory to the problems of management of disturbed lands in a detailed presentation.

Majer, J. D. (ed.). 1989. *Animals in Primary Succession: The Role of Fauna in Reclaimed Lands.* Cambridge University Press, Cambridge. This book deals with the role of animals on reclaimed lands as well as in primary succession in nature. A variety of case studies of reestablishment of fauna on reclaimed lands is presented.

National Research Council (U.S.), Committee on Restoration of Aquatic Ecosystems. 1992. *Restoration of Aquatic Ecosystems: Science, Technology, and Public Policy.* National Academy Press, Washington, D.C. This book has been hailed as an important statement of how restoration can be accomplished in aquatic systems. It includes restoration case studies of wetlands, lakes, and rivers, as well as a series of general principles that can be applied to any wetlands.

Nilsen, R. (ed.). 1991. *Helping Nature Heal: An Introduction to Environmental Restoration.* Ten Speed Press, Berkeley, CA. The publishers of *The Whole Earth Catalog* provide an extremely readable presentation of environmental restoration theory as well as practice in the United States. While not especially scientific in nature, this book is quite practical and makes restoration more accessible to anyone.

Stevens, W. K. 1995. *Miracle Under the Oaks: The Revival of Nature in America.* Pocket Books, New York. This treatment of the prairie restoration movement is presented in a fascinating style by a science writer for the *New York Times.*

Thompson, J. R. 1992. *Prairies, Forests, and Wetlands.* University of Iowa Press, Iowa City. Thompson addresses the restoration of forests, wetlands, and prairies in Iowa, offering a single perspective on a variety of types of restoration. This is quite a useful approach, given that most people are involved in the restoration of only one type of biotic community.

Wali, M. K. (ed.). 1992. *Ecosystem Rehabilitation*. Vol. 1: *Policy Issues;* Vol. 2: *Ecosystem Analysis and Synthesis*. SPB Academic Publishing, The Hague, The Netherlands. Wali is a pioneer in the area of restoration and reclamation ecology. This work is merely the most recent of a number of edited and original works that Wali has contributed to the field. In this case, the two volumes address policy issues as well as more esoteric scientific aspects of restoration.

Some journals that treat ecological restoration:

Ecological Applications
Environmental Management
Journal of Applied Ecology
Restoration and Management Notes
Restoration Ecology

15

Ecology, Politics, and Economics

Finding the Common Ground for Decision Making in Conservation

The ideas of economists and political philosophers, both when they are right and when they are wrong, are more powerful than is commonly understood. Indeed, the world is ruled by little else. . . . Madmen in authority, who hear voices in the air, are distilling their frenzy from some academic scribbler a few years back.

John Maynard Keynes

As we have seen throughout this book, planetary biodiversity is in serious jeopardy for a multitude of reasons: habitat destruction, pollutants and pesticides produced by industrial societies, human population explosions in desperately poor countries, introductions of exotic species, acidic deposition associated with the combustion of fossil fuels, direct exploitation of particular species, and a myriad of other processes. The reasons individuals interact detrimentally with the biosphere vary with culture, the structure of economies, and the social status of the actors. In this chapter, we will explore some of these reasons by focusing on economic and political aspects of decision making in conservation.

Conserving biodiversity requires that people both change how they interact with the biosphere in a great number of ways (see Chapters 16 and 19) and address a plurality of reasons why they should do so. Furthermore, the decision to change must be a collective one; people acting individually cannot conserve much biodiversity for their progeny. Given the myriad ways and reasons biodiversity is being lost, finding a common ground for framing and negotiating a collective agreement is proving to be a major challenge.

Discussing and negotiating less destructive modes of human interaction with the biosphere has proved difficult for two reasons. First, the problems involve many different actors in various positions doing different things for a variety of reasons. These differences make it inherently difficult to find common ground for agreeing on less destructive modes of interaction. Second, to facilitate analysis and communication, people simplify the complex problem of biodiversity loss in different ways. Some think of it as driven by human population growth, some by our social structure, others by our materialism, still others by our choice of technologies. Each explanation is partially correct, but agreement on the big, complex picture has been stymied by arguments among those who each insist that their limited perspective is better than that of others. Each small, simplified picture of the problem pins the blame differently and suggests a different, simple solution that appeals to different interest groups. In fact, the blame is largely indirect and widely dispersed, and the solutions will be multiple and complex. But, to date, the politics of reducing biodiversity loss largely has been carried out among groups who seek particular combinations of simple censure and new directions that meet self-serving ends.

As efforts to develop community consensus for management decisions become a central part of conservation planning, a fundamental contradiction in human behavior must be resolved. When livelihoods are involved, people tend to make decisions that maximize their self-interest in the short term. However, the same people may attach great importance to the opposing values of intergenerational equity and ecocentrism when they are presented in the abstract. How to help people and institutions move from decisions that are narrow in focus and limited in time to decisions that are more holistic, sustainable, and long-term is not the mandate of economics; however, the many varied perspectives of economics can significantly clarify these discussions.

Reaching a collective understanding of how to conserve biodiversity will require going beyond debate over simple explanations and solutions. For this to occur, those concerned with conserving biodiversity need to become familiar with the variety of simple perspectives being put forward and begin to see how they interrelate. That is the objective of this chapter. These separate perspectives are neither right nor wrong, merely too simple. Surprisingly, the perspectives of those favoring environmental conservation, as well as the views of those favoring greater material consumption, are both rooted in the history of economic thought. While conservation biologists are challenging the course of economic development, their perception of the processes of biodiversity loss is driven by historical economic reasoning. Even environmental ethicists argue in the context, or in opposition to the context, of thinking dominated by economic philosophers during the past two centuries.

Economic Philosophy and the Roots of the Biological Crisis

Background

Somewhat more than two centuries ago, economics emerged from moral philosophy at a time of great social change and scientific promise (Canterbury 1987; Nelson 1991). Long-standing moral principles with respect to the obligations of individuals to larger social goals were being challenged by the development of markets and by scientific advances that brought new opportunities for personal material improvement and fed great hopes for a plentiful future. In the second half of the 18th century, as today at the end of the 20th, people were concerned that following one's own economic interests might hurt society as a whole. Economists, then as now, argued that markets guided individual behavior, as if by an "invisible hand," toward the common good.

There is a critical difference between the times, however. Historically, material security had been the reward for good moral conduct, but increasingly after the Renaissance it was argued that material security was needed to establish the conditions for moral progress. Scarcity caused greed and even war; scarcity forced people to work so hard that they did not have time to contemplate the Scriptures and live morally. Material progress, in short, was necessary to establish the conditions for moral progress. Thus, two centuries ago, the individual pursuit of materialism was justified on the presumption that once their basic material needs of food, shelter, and clothing were met, people would have the time and conditions to pursue their individual moral and collective social improvement. Today, these earlier concerns with moral and social progress largely have been forgotten, while individual materialism for many people has become an end in itself.

Two centuries ago, as now, technological optimists were convinced that the essentials of life would eventually be assured through the advance of human knowledge leading to a mastery of underlying natural laws. The presumption has been that such laws are relatively few and that their mastery will make superfluous our dependence on the particular ways that nature, and people's place therein, evolved. To those concerned only with material well-being, the expectation of such mastery has meant that people do not have to be concerned with long-term scarcities or how their activities otherwise might affect the future (Simon 1981). Over the past two centuries, scientists have touted the goal of eventual mastery of nature and have justified their research on this basis. The belief that scientific progress will inevitably lead to dominion over nature and material plenty is still popularly held and frequently invoked, even by scientists, to support further population increases, technological change, and economic development along their historical, biologically destructive, paths (Simon 1981).

Economic thought evolved in the context of these dominant moral, material, and scientific beliefs, and will continue to do so. Reality, however, does not always unfold as expected; the social and environmental problems associated with economic development have dampened earlier ruling beliefs and empowered other interpretations. Thus, today most scientists are more humble, and many—conservation biologists most notably among them—argue that we need to direct the best of our scientific expertise and far more of our educational effort toward learning how to work *with* nature (Ehrenfeld 1981; Meffe 1992). Similarly, environmental ethicists are challenging the vacuity of individual material progress for its own sake, and economic thought is now evolving in this new context as well.

Adam Smith and the Invisible Hand

Adam Smith (1723–1790), widely recognized as the founder of modern economics, was a moral philosopher. While economics assumed a scientific gloss and a technical application late in the 19th century, ethical issues have always been embedded in its theory. And the key ethical issue has always been whether the pursuit of individual wealth can be in the interest of society as a whole. Smith reasoned, in the tradition of key liberal social philosophers such as Hobbes and Locke, that society is merely the sum of its individuals. If two people who are fully informed of the consequences of their decision choose to enter into an exchange, it is because the exchange makes each of them better off. Appealing to Judeo-Christian images of God, Smith invented the metaphor of the "invisible hand," arguing that markets induce people to behave in the common interest as if they were guided by a higher authority.

Thomas Malthus and Population Growth

The Reverend-turned-economist Thomas R. Malthus (1766–1834) explained the prevalence of war and disease as secular, material phenomena rather than acts of God. He argued that human populations were capable of increasing exponentially and would do so as long as sufficient food and other essentials of life were available (Malthus 1963). He further hypothesized that people could expand their food supply only arithmetically through new technologies and expansion into new habitats. Given the geometric potential of population growth, and the arithmetic food constraint, population would periodically surpass food supply. At these times, Malthus argued, people would ravage the land, go to war over food, and succumb to disease and starvation. Human numbers would consequently drop to sustainable levels, whence the process would repeat again (Figure 15.1). This simple model was widely used by biological scientists; both Darwin and Wallace acknowledged that Malthus's model was key to their formulation of the theory of natural selection.

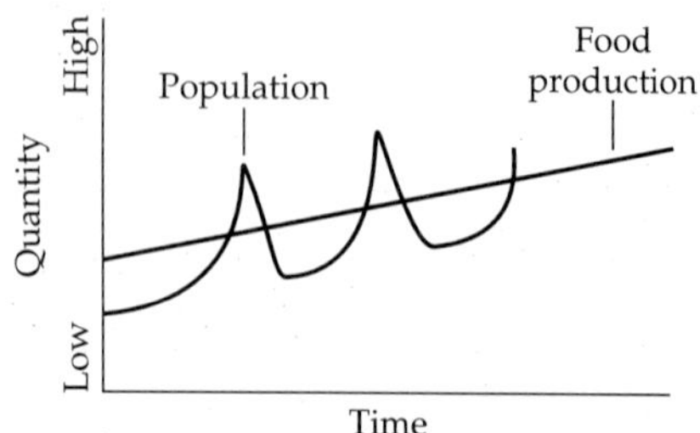

Figure 15.1 Thomas Malthus's model of population growth and collapse. Collapse occurs when population exceeds food production or carrying capacity.

Malthus's model is charmingly simple, but subsequent human demographic history generally has not supported it. Yet, periodically and in specific places, Malthus's model has been confirmed, and history may yet confirm it globally. Few question that the human population must ultimately be stabilized in order to sustain human well-being at a reasonable level (but see Simon 1981). The expansion of human populations into previously unpopulated or lightly populated regions, the intensity with which resources are collected, and the push to increase food production through the modern agrochemical, monocultural techniques that are so harmful to biodiversity are driven over the long run by population increase. The continued rapid rates of population increase in the poorest nations threaten to keep them poor.

Whether or not one finds our demographic history consistent with Malthus's model, it has become a part of human consciousness. This makes it difficult to contemplate, let alone discuss, the issues of population increase and its effects on biodiversity without Malthus's framing becoming central to the discussion. The success of his model stems from its simplicity. But the dynamics of population growth and the ways in which people depend on the environment are much more complex than Malthus's model. Thus, while Malthus has provided us with a powerful model, its simplicity restricts its usefulness for policymaking beyond the obvious prescription that fewer people would probably be better.

David Ricardo and the Geographic Pattern of Economic Activity

David Ricardo (1772–1823) introduced a second model of how economic activity relates to the environment (Figure 15.2), not because he was concerned

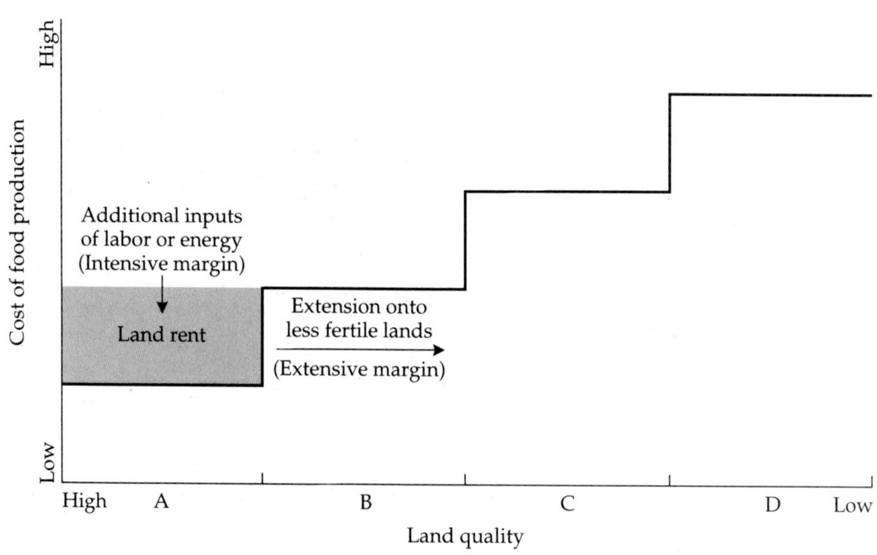

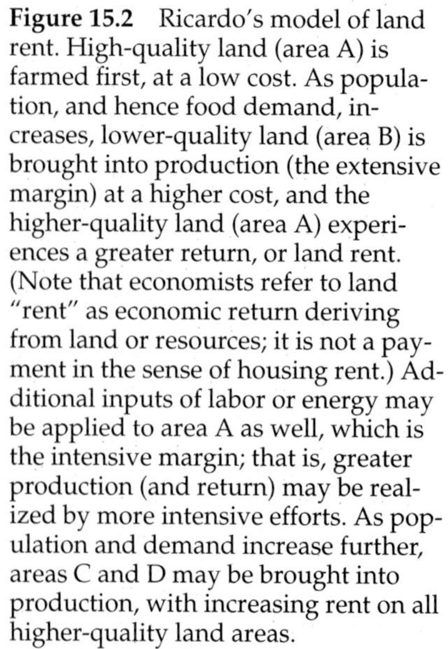

Figure 15.2 Ricardo's model of land rent. High-quality land (area A) is farmed first, at a low cost. As population, and hence food demand, increases, lower-quality land (area B) is brought into production (the extensive margin) at a higher cost, and the higher-quality land (area A) experiences a greater return, or land rent. (Note that economists refer to land "rent" as economic return deriving from land or resources; it is not a payment in the sense of housing rent.) Additional inputs of labor or energy may be applied to area A as well, which is the intensive margin; that is, greater production (and return) may be realized by more intensive efforts. As population and demand increase further, areas C and D may be brought into production, with increasing rent on all higher-quality land areas.

with environmental degradation or human survival, but rather because he wished to justify why landlords received a rent from their ownership of land (Ricardo 1926). Ricardo argued that people would initially farm the land that produced the most food for the least work. As population increased, farming would extend to less fertile soils requiring more labor; economists refer to this additional land as the **extensive margin**. Food prices would have to rise to cover the cost of the extra labor on the less fertile land. This means that the initial land would earn a rent, a return above production cost, because it would now be more valuable. Higher food prices, in turn, would also induce a more intensive use of labor on the better land; economists refer to these additional inputs as the **intensive margin**.

Ricardo's model shows how increasing population drives people to farm in previously undisturbed areas and how higher food prices lead to intensified efforts, and in modern agriculture, the greater use of fertilizers and pesticides, on prime agricultural lands. This model also provides insights into how fluctuations in food prices can result in the periodic entry and exit of farmers on the extensive margin and in shifts in farming practices on the intensive margin. Ricardo's model also helps us to understand why 20% of North American farmland has gone out of production as modern technologies have driven the price of food down. Ricardo's model of the way agricultural activities are patterned on the land in response to population growth and changes in food prices is critical to our understanding of the complex interrelations between human survival and biodiversity.

John Stuart Mill and the Steady State

John Stuart Mill (1806–1873) was the son of social philosopher James Mill (1773–1836), who also wrote on economics. J. S. Mill expanded on the linkages between individual behavior and the common good proposed by Adam Smith, arguing that competitive markets are critical to individual liberty. As a social philosopher seriously concerned with liberty, Mill also wrote on the immorality and waste of subjugating women to men. At the same time, he neither saw material prosperity as an end in itself nor foresaw that continuous growth in material well-being was possible. Mill envisioned economies becoming mature and reaching a steady state in which people would be able to enjoy the fruits of their earlier savings, or of their material abstinence, necessary for the accumulation of industrial capital. The idea that economies would reach a steady state was consistent both with the Newtonian worldview of the time and with natural phenomena. Change was common, unceasing growth was not, and relatively steady states, rather than random change, were perceived as natural. Contemporary ecological economist Herman Daly argues (from Mill) for a steady-state economy, in which flows of resources into production and of pollutants back to the environment are fixed at a steady level. Mill's and Daly's visions of a steady-state economy mesh with our understanding of how ecological systems operate (Daly 1991). The steady-state metaphor could become critical to finding common ground for slowing the loss of biological diversity. Essay 15A by Herman Daly extends this argument.

ESSAY 15A
Steady-State Economics

Herman E. Daly, University of Maryland

Any system in a steady state is characterized by balanced, opposing forces or fluxes. This does not imply stagnation; indeed, steady-state systems may be highly dynamic internally. For example, as long as the environment does not change in a major way, the species composition of an old-growth forest will remain in a steady state, neither losing nor gaining species overall, although considerable turnover of species may be occurring locally and seasonal changes will occur. Similarly, an economic steady-state system may be highly dynamic, but, on average, the many flows and exchanges are balanced.

The worldview underlying standard economics is that the economy is a system isolated from the natural world, a circular flow of exchange value just between businesses and households. In such an isolated system neither matter nor energy enters or exits, and the system has no relation with its environment; for all practical purposes there *is* no environment. Thus, standard economics ignores the origin of resources and the fate of wastes; they are "external" to the economic system. While this vision may be useful for analyzing exchange between producers and consumers, as well as related questions of price and income determination, it is useless for studying the relation of the economy to the environment. It is as if a biologist's vision of an animal contained a circulatory system, but no digestive tract. The animal would be an isolated system, completely independent of its environment. If it could move it would be a perpetual motion machine.

Whatever flows through a system, entering as input and exiting as output, is called "throughput." Just as an organism maintains its physical structure by a metabolic flow and is connected to the environment at both ends of its digestive tract, so too an economy requires a throughput, which must to some degree both deplete and pollute the environment. As long as the scale of the human economy was very small relative to ecosystems, one could ignore throughput, since no apparent sacrifice was involved in increasing it. The economy has now grown to a scale at which this is no longer reasonable.

Standard economics has also failed to make the elementary distinction between *growth* (physical increase in size resulting from accretion or assimilation of materials; a *quantitative* change), and *development* (realization of potentialities, evolution to a fuller, better, or different state; a *qualitative* change). Quantitative and qualitative changes follow different laws. It is clearly possible to have growth without development or to have development without growth.

The usual worldview, the one that supports most economic analysis today, is that the economy is not a subsystem of any larger environment, and is unconstrained in its growth by anything. Nature may be finite, but it is just one sector of the economy, for which other sectors can substitute without limiting overall growth in any important way. If the economy is seen as an isolated system, then there is no environment to constrain its continual growth. But if we see the economy as one subsystem of a larger, but finite and nongrowing, ecosystem, then obviously its growth is limited. The economy may continue to develop qualitatively without growing quantitatively, just as the planet Earth does, but it cannot continue to grow; beyond some point it must approximate a steady state in its physical dimensions.

The worldview from which steady-state economics (Daly 1991) emerges is that the economy, in its physical dimensions, is an open subsystem of a finite, nongrowing, and materially closed total system—the earth-ecosystem or biosphere. An "open" system is one with a "digestive tract," one that takes matter and energy from the environment in low-entropy form (raw materials) and returns it to the environment in high-entropy form (waste). A "closed" system is one in which only energy flows through, while matter circulates within the system. A steady-state economy is an open system whose throughput remains constant at a level that neither depletes the environment beyond its regenerative capacity nor pollutes it beyond its absorptive capacity. A result of steady-state economics is sustainable development, or development without growth—a physically steady-state economy that may continue to develop greater capacity to satisfy human wants by increasing the efficiency of resource use, but not by increasing the resource throughput.

Economic growth is further limited by the complementary relation between manufactured and natural capital. If the two forms of capital were good substitutes for one another, natural capital could be totally replaced by manufactured capital. But, in fact, manufactured capital loses its value without an appropriate complement of natural capital. What good are fishing boats without populations of fish, or sawmills without forests? And even if we could convert the whole ocean into a fishpond, we would still need the natural capital of solar energy, photosynthetic organisms, nutrient recyclers, and so forth. The standard economists' emphasis on substitution while ignoring complementarity in analyzing technical relations among factors of production seems a reflection of their preference for competition (substitution) over cooperation (complementarity) in social relations.

In an empty world, increasing throughput implies no sacrifice of ecosystem services, but in a full world it does. The ultimate cost of increasing throughput is loss of ecosystem services. Throughput begins with depletion of natural stock and ends with pollution, both of which are costs in a full world. Therefore, it makes sense to minimize throughput for any given level of stock. If we recognize that the economy grows by converting ever more of the ecosystem (natural capital) into economy (manufactured capital), then we see that the benefit of that expansion is the extra services from manufactured capital and its cost is the loss of service from reduced natural capital.

The efficiency with which we use the world to satisfy our wants depends on the amount of service we get per unit of manufactured capital, and the amount of service we sacrifice per unit of natural capital lost as a result of its conversion into manufactured capital. This overall *ecological–economic efficiency* is the ratio of manufactured capital services gained (MK) to natural capital services sacrificed (NK), or MK/NK. In an empty world there is no noticeable sacrifice of NK services required by increases in MK, so the denominator is irrelevant. In a full world any increase in MK comes at a noticeable reduction in NK and its services.

The steady-state economic view recognizes that economic systems are not isolated from the natural world, but are fully dependent on ecosystems for the goods and services they provide. Inasmuch as the overall size of the natural world cannot increase (and in fact decreases steadily at the hands of humankind), our economic systems cannot continually increase; they must operate as a steady-state system, one which does not quantitatively grow without bounds, but which can qualitatively develop. The internal workings of the economic machine must fully account for the raw natural materials consumed and the resultant wastes eliminated. The ultimate accounting rules for a realistic economy are the first and second laws of thermodynamics, which are inviolable.

Karl Marx and the Ownership of Resources

Karl Marx (1818–1883) addressed, in his multiple critiques of capitalism, how the concentration of land and capital within a small portion of society affected the way economies worked. There is an extensive literature written by scholars influenced by Marx, some of it now addressing the sustainability of development, and the way ownership of resources affects the path of development (Redclift 1984; Blaikie and Brookfield 1987). Neoclassical models also readily show how resource ownership affects resource use (Bator 1957). However, for a variety of political reasons, this facet of neoclassical economics was ignored in the West during the Cold War. Indeed, in the United States, economists who were concerned with the **distribution** of ownership of resources were politically disempowered because of their association with a central concern of Marx. Western neoclassical economists, including resource and environmental economists, addressed questions of the **efficient allocation** of resources, leaving their initial distribution among people as given. We now know that the initial distribution of rights to resources and to the services of the environment is critically important to resource and environmental conservation (Howarth and Norgaard 1992).

It has long been known that the way economies allocate resources to different material ends depends on how resources are distributed among people—owned by or otherwise under the control of different individuals—in the first place. Peasants or others who work land and interact with biological resources owned by someone else have little incentive to protect them. Landlords can counteract this lack of incentive only by diverting labor from other productive activities and employing it to monitor and enforce their interests in protection, a diversion that would not be necessary with a more equal distribution of control. Furthermore, especially wealthy landlords may have little interest in protecting any particular land or biological resource for their descendants when they hold land in abundance.

Imagine two countries with identical populations and identical resources allocated by perfect markets. In the first country, rights to resources are distributed among people approximately equally, people have similar incomes, and they consume similar products, perhaps corn, chicken, and cotton clothing. In the second country, rights are concentrated among a few people who can afford luxury goods such as beef, wine, caviar, fine clothes, and ecotourism, while those who have few rights to resources, living nearly on their labor alone, consume only the most basic of goods, such as rice and beans. In each country, markets efficiently allocate resources to the production of products, but the way land is used, the types of products produced, and who consumes them depend on how rights to resources are distributed. Under different distributions of rights, the efficient use of resources is different.

Within the 20th-century global discourse on development policy, many have argued that economic injustices within nations and in the international economic order have limited the development options of poor nations and thereby, in the long run, those of rich nations as well. Similarly, within the late 20th-century global environmental discourse, many are arguing that environmental injustices and the international ecological order limit the possibilities for conservation. The vast majority of the people on the globe still consume very little. The poor are poor for two reasons: First, they do not have sufficient long-term access to resources to meet their ongoing material needs. Second, they are well aware that others consume far more than they do—that their poverty is relative—and they rightfully strive to improve their own relative condition. Striving to meet their material needs and aspirations without the long-term security of adequate resources, the poor have little choice but to use the few resources at their disposal in an unsustainable manner. The poor, excluded from the productivity of the fertile valleys or fossil hydrocarbon resources controlled by the rich, are forced to work land previously left idle because of its fragility and low agricultural productivity: the tropical forests, steep hillsides, and arid regions.

Environmental justice also speaks to the excessive material and energy consumption of the wealthy 20–30% of the total population, made up of the middle classes and rich in the Northern industrialized nations as well as the elite in middle-income and poor nations. The global access to resources by the rich means that many of the environmental and resource effects of their consumption decisions occur at a great distance, beyond their view, beyond their perceived responsibility, and beyond their effective control.

The relationships between unequal access to resources, unsustainability of development generally, and the loss of biodiversity in particular were major themes of the United Nations Conference on Environment and Development held in Rio de Janeiro in June 1992. Because they have more to lose, rich peoples and political leaders of Northern industrialized countries generally have had some difficulty participating in this discourse, and even greater difficulty participating in the design of new global institutions to address the role of inequity in environmental degradation.

Our understanding of the environmental consequences of concentrated ownership and control is rooted in economic thinking, especially that of Karl Marx. Questions of equity are extremely important in the process of biodiversity loss and in the possibilities for conservation. For example, the occupation and ecological transformation of the Amazon has been driven partly by the concentration of land ownership in the more productive regions of Amazonian nations among a few people, and partly by the economic power (and political influence) of the rich that has enabled them to obtain subsidies to engage in large-scale cattle ranching. The ongoing efforts to establish international agreements on the management of biodiversity have been repeatedly forestalled by debate over the ownership and control of biological resources. But this is not simply a debate over fairness. The structure of the global economy and the ways specific economies interact with nature in the future will depend on which nations—the nations of resource origin or those of the Northern commercial interests, the likely discoverers of new uses for biodiversity—receive the "rent" from biological resources.

A. C. Pigou and Market Failure

Alfred C. Pigou (1877–1959) formally elaborated how costs that are not included in market prices affect the way people interact with their environment. Such a cost, or **externality**, is considered external to markets and hence does not affect how markets operate, when in fact it should. Consider, for example, pesticide use in agriculture and the associated loss of biodiversity (Figure 15.3). Normally, as the price of food increases, the **supply**—the quantity of food that farmers are willing to produce—increases. As prices rise, however, the **demand**—the quantity of food that consumers are willing to purchase—decreases. The market reaches equilibrium when the quantity supplied equals the quantity demanded—at price P_0 and quantity Q_0.

Now, imagine that we could measure the value of the biodiversity that is lost because of pesticide use—currently considered an externality—and add this to the cost of using pesticides to produce food. This would reduce the quantity of food that farmers could produce at a given price, shifting the supply curve, the price of food, and the quantity of food supplied. By including the cost of biodiversity lost due to farmers' decisions to use pesticides, we

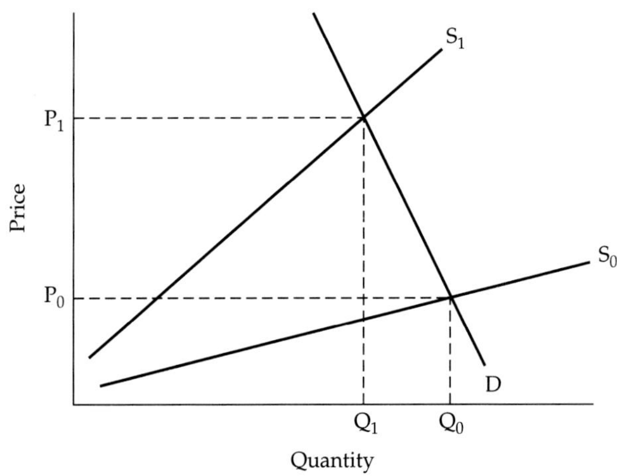

Figure 15.3 Model of a market and its distortion due to an external cost. S_0 (the supply curve) represents the willingness of farmers to supply food at different prices (P). As the price of food increases, the quantity of food (Q) that farmers are willing to supply increases. D is the demand curve, illustrating that people purchase lesser quantities of food at higher prices. The market reaches equilibrium when price $P_0 = Q_0$. If an externality, such as the cost of biodiversity loss resulting from pesticide use, is added to the cost of the food, the price of the food shifts to P_1, the quantity of food supplied to Q_1, and the supply curve to S_1.

internalize a cost that was previously external to the market, and thus affect how the market operates. Following the logic of Pigou and numerous environmental economists since, *biodiversity is not adequately protected because its value is not included in the market signals that guide the economic decisions of producers and consumers and thereby the overall operation of the economic system.*

This logic of market failure has led conservationists and some economists to argue that species need to be incorporated into the market system (Hanemann 1988; McNeely 1988; Randall 1988). When it is possible to give private individuals or local communities the rights to use a certain species, exploitation of that resource by others will be averted. This means that the community may benefit from conserving the species and thereby choose to do so; consumers will then pay a higher price, reflecting the costs of managing the species in a more sustainable manner. It is important to keep in mind, however, that incorporating species into the market system might *not* result in their conservation, and indeed, could even accelerate their extinction. Species within the market system, for example, will not be conserved if their value is expected to grow at less than the rate of interest, unless other controls are also placed on their harvest (see the discussion below on the rate of interest).

The processes of biodiversity loss also interact with one another in a larger, reinforcing process of positive **feedbacks**. The degradation of any particular area increases the economic pressure on other areas. For example, the loss of woody species through extensive clear-cutting reduces total carbon fixation and thus reduces opportunities to ameliorate climate change. To bring a system into equilibrium, negative feedbacks are needed. Economics helps us to understand why biodiversity is decreasing: few genetic traits, species, or ecosystems have market prices, the negative feedback signals that equilibrate market economies. In market systems, prices increase to reduce the quantity demanded when supplies are low, and drop to increase the quantity demanded when supplies are high, keeping demand and supply in equilibrium. By placing economic values on species, and by including them in market signals, biodiversity loss might be reduced.

The idea that we need to know the economic values of species is compatible with conservationists' understanding that, if the true value of species to society were understood, more species would be conserved. Clearly, if we knew the value of biological resources, we would be in a better position to manage them more effectively. And to the extent that these values could be included in the market system, markets themselves could assist in the conservation of biodiversity. In many cases the situation could be improved through amending market signals—for example, by heavily taxing pollution or use of rare species or ecosystems. At the same time, it is important to remember that market values exist only within a larger system of values, which for many people includes the preservation of nature as their ethical or religious underpinnings (Sagoff 1988). An alternative view, of the dangers of economically valuing species, is offered by Ehrenfeld (1986) and by Mark Sagoff in Essay 15B.

ESSAY 15B
A Noneconomic View of the Value of Biodiversity

Mark Sagoff, University of Maryland

What is the value of a plant or animal—such as the American burying beetle—that is threatened with extinction? Many people recognize that biodiversity represents the foundation of human existence; this tells us nothing, however, about the value of any *particular* species. To reason that every part is valuable if the whole is valuable—for example, that the seepage in your basement is valuable because water is essential to life—is the "fallacy of division." That some species, such as the bacterium *Thermus aquaticus*, possess great utility, moreover, tells us nothing about any other species—for example, the Ebola virus. We know that we cannot get along without biodiversity in general, and that species with known uses, such as wheat, are valuable in particular. But what are the reasons for preserving the "next" or "marginal" endangered species, such as the Karner blue butterfly, which occupies prime real estate and has no known economic use?

Many economists believe that the "reasons for caring about biodiversity are instrumental and utilitarian" (Randall 1991). Instrumental reasons for preserving species, as botanist David Given observes, are of two kinds. First, organisms possess direct economic value "as resources for humanity, both now and in the future." Second, species provide goods and services indirectly as "important parts of the web of life" (Given 1994). On the other hand, there are biologists, philosophers, and others who question economic arguments for protecting species and wonder whether metaphors like "the web of life" take full account of the vagaries of evolution. David Ehrenfeld, founding editor of the journal *Conservation Biology*, has written that the value of biodiversity does not depend on "the uses to which particular species may be put, or their alleged role in the balance of global ecosystems." Ehrenfeld (1988) argues that, owing to changes in our needs and in our technology, instrumental approaches to valuation "are shifting, fluid, and utterly opportunistic in their practical application. This is the opposite of the value system necessary to conserve biological diversity over the course of decades and centuries."

To see Ehrenfeld's point, consider whales. Two centuries ago, whale oil fetched a high price because it served as a principal fuel for household lighting. As that resource dwindled, the price of illumination rose to many times what we pay today (Yergin 1992). One might argue that whales, being a limited resource, represent the kind of "natural capital" that constrains economic growth. But with the development of modern innovations in the lighting industry—gas and kerosene lamps, then electric bulbs, then compact fluorescent bulbs—we have seen the amount of fuel required for, and the price of, a unit of household lighting halved again and again (Lovins 1990). By replacing one resource flow with another and by getting more economic output per unit of input, technology continues to make many commodities—not just household illumination—less expensive and more abundant relative to demand.

Why, then, do conservation biologists care about saving whales or, for that matter, any other threatened species? Is it for instrumental reasons? Are they concerned about maintaining a strategic reserve of blubber? Do they worry that the seas might fill up with krill? No; as whales have lost their instrumental value, their aesthetic and moral worth have become all the more evident. The extinction of whales represents an aesthetic and moral loss—something like the destruction of a great painting or the death of a friend. Whale *oil* has substitutes—petroleum-based fuel and lubricants—but whales do not.

More than 80% of Americans in a recent survey agreed with the statement that destroying species such as whales is wrong "because God put them on this earth." As the anthropologists who conducted the survey concluded, "It seems that divine creation is the closest concept American culture provides to express the sacredness of nature" (Kempton et al. 1995). By huge majorities, Americans, whether religious or not, believe that animals such as wolves and whales possess a dignity or intrinsic worth and thus make a legitimate claim on our respect and concern. As philosopher Ronald Dworkin points out, most of us attribute intrinsic value to other species: "We think we should admire and protect them because they are important in themselves, and not because we or others want or enjoy them" (Dworkin 1994).

While conservation biologists are plainly moved by the same spiritual, aesthetic, and cultural commitments to save species that motivate society as a whole, many lack the courage of their ethical convictions and instead offer economic or instrumental arguments for preserving biodiversity. In so doing, they support the economist's credo that it is irrational to value anything but our own well-being and, therefore, that we should protect whales and other species not because they are intrinsically valuable or deserve our respect, nor because of religious, moral, or cultural beliefs, but on economic grounds, insofar as whales or other species contribute to our well-being or welfare.

To shore up this economic rationale for protecting biodiversity at the margin, conservationists frequently argue that the "next" species to be lost could harbor a new crop or a lifesaving drug. To be sure, any of the more than 235,000 flowering plants and about 325,000 nonflowering plants (including mosses, lichens, and seaweeds) could have an application in agriculture, but there are good reasons why farmers cultivate rice, wheat, and corn rather than, say, Furbish's lousewort. It is hard enough to get people to eat their broccoli and lima beans; it is harder still to develop consumer demand for new foods. About 20 species, not one of which is in any way endangered, provide 90% of the food the world takes from plants, and only about 150 plants are extensively cultivated. Drug companies, moreover, generally find it far more efficient to design drugs on computers than to prospect for them in the wild.

Conservationists often argue that even if the in situ protection of the "marginal" or "next" endangered species cannot be justified by its potential as a source of pharmaceutical, agricultural, or other raw materials, each species nevertheless plays a role in supporting the ecosystem services and processes on which all life depends. As Paul and Anne Ehrlich (1981) have written, "A dozen rivets [on an airplane wing], or a dozen species, might never be missed. On the other hand, a thirteenth rivet popped from a wing flap, or the extinction of a key species involved in the cycling of nitrogen, could lead to a serious accident."

This instrumental argument for preserving biodiversity encounters three difficulties. First, many biologists believe that the functional redundancy of species is so immense that ecological processes would function perfectly well—other plants and animals would fill in—even if all the creatures now threatened, and a great many more besides, went extinct (e.g., Lawton and Brown 1993). Ecosystem function depends on interactions among relatively few species, not on the dwindling populations that are rare or endangered. The Global Biodiversity Assessment (Perrings 1995) makes this point, as does Holling (1992): "Although any ecosystem contains hundreds to thousands of species interacting among themselves and their physical environment, the emerging consensus is that the system is driven by a small number of biotic and abiotic variables on whose interactions the balance of species are, in a sense, carried along."

Second, it is hard to determine a species "baseline" for any ecosystem—that is, the mix of species that is appropriate for its health, resilience, or integrity. "Current ecological thinking argues that nature at the level of biological assemblages has never been homeostatic. Therefore, any serious attempt to define the original state of a community or ecosystem leads to a logical and scientific maze" (Soulé 1995). For example, the species composition of Cape Cod when the Pilgrims landed in 1620 had changed greatly by 1855, and has changed greatly again since then (Cronon 1983). Were these thoroughgoing changes bad or good? The land where the Pilgrims died—a howling and hostile wilderness, according to them—had to be tamed, domesticated, settled, and developed to be even remotely habitable. At which point in this history of ecological change do we say the "right" mix of species was present for "sustainability" of the human economy?

Third, ecologists have not agreed upon a way to classify the ecosystems or communities they study into natural categories and kinds. Therefore, they cannot say at what point a changing ecosystem collapses and is replaced by another ecosystem of a different kind. Indeed, because ecologists have no common view of which ecosystem qualities are constitutive or essential and which accidental, they cannot meaningfully predicate normative concepts such as "resilience," "health," or "stability" to ecosystems. The blight that caused the extinction of the mighty American chestnut, for example, caused changes in the species composition of the southeastern deciduous forest. Did the forest itself continue as the same ecosystem (and therefore exhibit resiliency), or did it give way to a different kind of forest? Suppose a large timber company replaced all the trees in a forest, one by one, with high-tech bioengineered silvicultural wonders, the improved photosynthetic efficiency of which made the forest more productive. Ecologists have no criteria for determining whether these trees would constitute the same forest—and thus whether the forest would or would not be "resilient."

The real reason for protecting species in their habitats is neither economic nor instrumental; it has to do with moral, cultural, and spiritual commitments to goals beyond our own welfare or well-being. Wilson (1992) elegantly takes up this theme in arguing that every kind of organism—the flower in the crannied wall—"is a miracle." Wilson adds, "Every kind of organism has reached this moment in time by threading one needle after another, throwing up brilliant artifices to survive and reproduce against nearly impossible odds."

To study these artifices—to appreciate the toil that each species endures to prevail in the vast labor of evolution—is to be moved by more than economic considerations. It is to feel reverence and awe in the presence of the creative force of nature, which is found as much in the smallest organism as in the most majestic landscape. Unfortunately, rather than affirming these moral, cultural, and spiritual reasons to protect nature, many environmentalists contrive economic arguments about benefits and costs. In this way they validate the view that only one kind of value is important—instrumental value for human well-being—and thus they protect not nature, but the very economic framework and perspective most likely to undermine it.

Even when species or ecosystems cannot be better conserved through the market, knowing their economic value can help to convince people and their political representatives that the species or ecosystems deserve protection. Environmental valuation can also improve our analyses of the benefits and costs of development projects that affect biodiversity. Techniques for such valuation include determining—through questionnaires and analyses of expenditures to observe interesting environments and particular species—people's willingness to pay to maintain biodiversity (Mitchell and Carson 1989). Essay 15C by Robert Costanza elaborates this perspective.

ESSAY 15C

Valuation of Ecological Systems with Sustainability, Fairness, and Efficiency as Goals

Robert Costanza, University of Maryland

The issue of valuation is inseparable from the choices and decisions we have to make about ecological systems. Some argue that valuation of ecosystems is either impossible or unwise, that we cannot place a value on such "intangibles" as human life, environmental aesthetics, or long-term ecological benefits. But, in fact, we do so every day. When we set construction standards for highways, bridges, and the like, we value human life—acknowledged or not—because spending more money on construction can save lives. Another frequent argument is that we should protect ecosystems for purely moral or aesthetic reasons (e.g., Essay 15B), and we do not need valuations of ecosystems for this purpose. But there are equally compelling moral arguments that may be in direct conflict with the moral argument to protect ecosystems—for example, the moral argument that no one should go hungry. All we have done is to translate the valuation and decision problem into a new set of dimensions and a new language of discourse, one that, in my view, makes the valuation and choice problem more difficult and less explicit.

So, although ecosystem valuation is certainly difficult, one choice we do not have is whether or not to do it. Rather, the decisions we make as a society about ecosystems imply valuations. We can choose to make these valuations explicit or not; we can undertake them using the best available ecological science and understanding or not; we can make them with an explicit acknowledgment of the huge uncertainties involved or not; but as long as we are forced to make choices, we are doing valuation.

Valuation and Social Goals

Valuation ultimately refers to the contribution of an item to meeting a specific goal. A baseball player is valuable to the extent that he contributes to the team's goal of winning games. In ecology, a gene is valuable to the extent that it contributes to the goal of survival of the individuals possessing it and their progeny. In conventional economics, a commodity is valuable to the extent that it contributes to the goal of individual welfare as assessed by willingness to pay. One cannot state a value without stating the goal being served.

Conventional economic value is based on the goal of individual utility maximization. But other goals, and thus other values, are possible. For example, if our goal is sustainability, we should assign value to something based on its contribution to achieving that goal. We can also assign value based on multiple goals—for example, to sustainability we can add individual utility maximization, social equity, or any other goals that we may deem important. This broadening is particularly important if our goals are potentially in conflict.

At least three broad goals have been identified as important to managing economic systems within the context of the planet's ecological life-support system (Daly 1992): (1) ensuring that the scale of human activities within the biosphere is ecologically sustainable; (2) distributing resources and property rights fairly within the current generation of humans, between this and future generations, and between humans and other species; and (3) efficiently allocating resources as constrained and defined by goals 1 and 2 above, and including both market and nonmarket resources, especially ecosystem services.

Several authors have discussed the valuation of ecosystem services with respect to goal 3—allocative efficiency based on individual utility maximization (e.g., Farber and Costanza 1987; Mitchell and Carson 1989; Costanza et. al. 1989; Dixon and Hufschmidt 1990; Pearce 1993; Goulder and Kennedy 1996). We need to explore more fully the implications of extending these concepts to include valuation with respect to goal 1—ecological sustainability—and goal 2—distributional fairness (Costanza and Folke 1996). A "Kantian" or intrinsic rights approach to valuation (cf. Goulder and Kennedy 1996) is one approach to goal 2, but it is important to recognize that the three goals are not "either-or" alternatives. While they are in some senses independent "multiple criteria" (Arrow and Raynaud 1986), they must all be satisfied in an integrated fashion to allow human life to continue in a desirable way. Similarly, the valuations that flow from these goals are not "either-or" alternatives. Rather than a "utilitarian versus intrinsic rights" dichotomy, we must integrate the three goals and their consequent valuations.

Society can make better choices about ecosystems if the valuation issue is made as explicit as possible. This means taking advantage of the best information we can assemble and making uncertainties about valuations explicit. It also means developing new and better ways to make good decisions in the face of these uncertainties. Ultimately, it means being explicit about our goals as a society, in both the short and the long term. Basing valuation on current individual preferences and utility maximization alone, as is done in conventional economic analysis, does not necessarily lead to ecological sustainability or social fairness (Bishop 1993). A "two-tiered" approach that combines public discussion and consensus building on sustainability and equity goals at the community level with methods for modifying both prices and preferences at the individual level to better reflect those community goals may be necessary (Rawls 1971; Norton 1995; Costanza et al. 1997). Estimation of ecosystem values based on sustainability and fairness goals requires treating preferences as endogenous and coevolving with other ecological, economic, and social variables.

Table A
Valuation of Ecosystem Services Based on the Three Primary Goals of Efficiency, Fairness, and Sustainability

Goal or value basis	Who votes	Preference basis required	Level of discussion required	Level of scientific input required	Examples of appropriate methods
Efficiency	*Homo economius*	Current individual preferences	Low	Low	"Willingness to pay"
Fairness	*Homo communicus*	Community preferences	High	Medium	"Veil of ignorance"
Sustainability	*Homo naturalis*	Whole-system preferences	Medium	High	"Modeling with precaution"

Valuation with Sustainability, Fairness, and Efficiency as Goals

We can distinguish at least three types of value that are relevant to the problem of valuing ecosystem services (Table A). Efficiency-based value (E-value) is based on a model of human behavior sometimes referred to as "*Homo economius*"—that humans act rationally and in their own self-interest. Value in this context is based on current individual preferences that are fixed or given. Little discussion or scientific input is required to form these preferences, and value is simply people's revealed willingness to pay for the good or service in question.

Fairness-based value (F-value) would require that individuals vote their preferences as members of the community, not as individuals. This different species (*Homo communicus*) would engage in discussion with other members of the community and come to consensus on the values that would be fair to all members of the current and future community (including nonhuman species), incorporating scientific information about possible future consequences as necessary. One method of implementing this might be Rawls's (1971) "veil of ignorance," in which everyone votes as if they were operating with no knowledge of their own individual status in the current or future society.

Sustainability-based value (S-value) would require an assessment of the contribution to ecological sustainability of the item in question. The S-value of ecosystem services is connected to their physical, chemical, and biological roles in the long-term functioning of the global system. Scientific information about the functioning of the global system is thus critical in assessing S-value, and some discussion and consensus building is also necessary. If it is accepted that all species, no matter how seemingly uninteresting or lacking in immediate utility, have a role to play in natural ecosystems (Naeem et al. 1994; Tilman and Downing 1994; Holling et al. 1995), estimates of the value of ecosystem services can be derived from scientific studies of the role of ecosystems and their biota in the overall system, without direct reference to current human preferences. Humans operate as *Homo naturalis* in this context, expressing preferences as if they were representatives of the whole system. Instead of being merely an expression of current individual preferences, S-value becomes a system characteristic related to the item's evolutionary contribution to the survival of the linked ecological–economic system. Using this perspective, we may be better able to estimate the values contributed by, say, the maintenance of water and atmospheric quality to long-term human well-being, including protecting the opportunities of choice for future generations (Golley 1994; Perrings 1994). One way to get at these values would be to employ systems simulation models that incorporate the major linkages in the system at the appropriate time and space scales (Bockstael et al. 1995). To account for the large uncertainties involved, these models would have to be used in a precautionary way, looking for the range of possible values and erring on the side of caution (Costanza and Perrings 1990).

In order to fully integrate the three goals of sustainability, fairness, and efficiency, we also need a further step, which Sen (1995) has described as "value formation through public discussion." This can be seen as the essence of real democracy. As Buchanan (1954) put it: "The definition of democracy as 'government by discussion' implies that individual values can and do change in the process of decision-making."

Limiting our valuations and social decision making to the goal of economic efficiency that is based on fixed preferences prevents the needed democratic discussion of values and options and leaves us with only the "illusion of choice" (Schmookler 1993). So, rather than trying to avoid the difficult questions raised by the valuation of ecological systems, we need to acknowledge the broad range of goals being served as well as the technical difficulties involved, and get on with the process of value formation in as participatory and democratic a way as possible, but in a way that also takes advantage of the full range and depth of the scientific information we have on ecosystem functioning.

While several techniques for estimating the value of biodiversity are producing interesting results, valuation is by no means an easy task, and estimates should be used cautiously. A major difficulty is related to the systemic nature of economics, ecosystems, and the process of loss. Market systems relate everything to everything else. When the price of oil changes, for example, the price of gasoline changes, the demand for and hence the price of products such as automobiles that use gasoline change, the demand for and hence the price of coal changes, and so on. Prices bring markets to equilibrium, and their flexibility is essential to this task. Similarly, the "right" price for a given species or ecosystem will depend on the availability of a host of other species or ecosystems with which it is interdependent, as well as on the availability of other species and ecosystems that may be substitutes or complements in its use. To assume that a species or ecosystem has a single value is to deny both ecosystem and economic system interconnections. Nevertheless, the valuation of genetic diversity, species, and ecosystems can assist us in understanding their importance and conveying this understanding to the public to improve the political process of finding common ground.

Common Property Management

Pigou also elaborated what came to be popularized as "the tragedy of the commons" (Hardin 1968). Resources used by multiple users without rules governing their use will be overexploited. Both traditional and modern societies typically develop rules for the use of resources held in common. Common ownership itself is not a tragedy; many resources have been successfully managed as commons. The absence or destruction of institutions regulating the use of resources used jointly by people, however, leads to a tragedy. Societies in transition between traditional and modern form frequently experience the tragedy of overuse when neither traditional nor modern forms of common control prevail. Similarly, resources for which access is difficult to restrict, such as the open sea and wildlife that crosses national boundaries, are frequently overexploited (Berkes 1989). The absence or destruction of institutions regulating commons has led to the extinction of diverse species and the genetic impoverishment of many more.

H. Scott Gordon (1954) formulated the problem of common property and open-access resources as shown in Figure 15.4. Imagine an open-access fishery (i.e., no restrictions) with total costs and total revenues from fishing effort as shown. Profits from the fishery are maximized at level of effort E_1, but with unrestricted access, people can put more effort into fishing, until the level E_2 is reached, at which no profit would be earned from fishing (costs would equal revenue). Additional fishing beyond E_2 would not be worth the effort because costs would now exceed revenues. Because more fish are caught at E_2, overfishing is more likely to occur in an open-access fishery than in a fishery managed as a commons with restricted access.

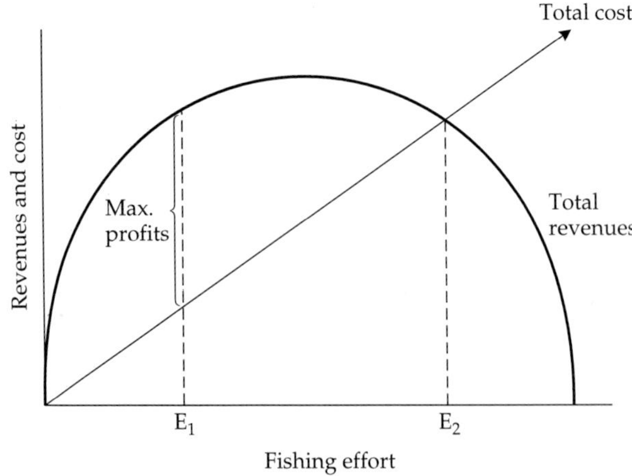

Figure 15.4 Excessive fishing effort occurs in an open-access fishery because existing fishermen expand their effort and new fishermen enter the fishery beyond level E_1, the point of maximum profit. Each fisherman makes a profit by increased fishing up to level E_2, where the industry as a whole breaks even (total revenues equal total costs). Further fishing beyond this point is economically counterproductive because costs exceed profits.

When genetic traits, species, and ecosystems cannot be owned by individuals and incorporated into market systems, common management institutions need to be established or strengthened. In some cases, traditional common property institutions can be maintained in the face of modernization. In other cases, new institutions will be needed. Common property institutions may be local, regional, national, or global. The health of institutions at all of these levels will be critical to conserving biological diversity. We will return to common properties and the tragedy of the commons in Chapter 19.

Harold Hotelling and the Efficient Use of Resources over Time

Harold Hotelling (1895–1973) developed a model of efficient resource use over time that helps to explain how species are driven to extinction (Hotelling 1931). According to Hotelling's model, even when market prices fully reflect the value of a biological resource, it will be efficient to exploit a species to extinction or totally degrade an ecosystem if the value of the species or the ecosystem over time is not increasing at least as fast as money deposited in an interest-bearing bank account. Hotelling's logic was distressingly simple. If the value of a biological resource is not increasing as fast as the rate of interest, both individual owners of the resource and society at large are *economically* better off exploiting the resource faster and putting the returns from the exploitation in the bank. Those returns can then be invested in the creation of human-produced capital that earns a return greater than the rate of interest. In this solely economic view, biological resources are merely a form of natural capital that can be converted into human-produced capital, and should be so converted if they do not earn as high a return as human-produced capital.

This argument both describes why economically rational owners of biological resources exploit them to extinction or destruction, and prescribes that they "should" do so. So long as we assume that markets reflect true values, historical and ongoing losses of genetic, species, and ecosystem diversity are efficient and "should" occur. Hotelling's reasoning currently dominates resource economic theory and policy advice from economists. However, in light of the principle of intergenerational equity (discussed below), Hotelling's model is inappropriate for most decisions regarding conservation.

The Rate of Interest

Hotelling's argument highlights the importance of interest rates in the management of biological resources. If a person can earn an 8% return per year by investing in industrial expansion through stock or bond markets, he or she has little economic incentive to invest in trees that increase in value at only 3% per year, or in the preservation of tropical forests, which may have no immediate economic return. By strictly economic logic, biological resources that are not increasing in value as fast as the rate of interest "should" be exploited, and the revenues put into industrial capital markets. This logic is a form of "discounting the future." The rate of interest affects how, by economic reasoning, people discount the future. If the rate of interest is 10%, one dollar one year from now is worth only $0.91 today, because one can put $0.91 in the bank today and, earning 10% interest, it will be worth $1.00 next year. The problem is that, at 10% interest, one dollar one decade from now is only worth $0.39 today, two decades from now a mere $0.15 today. Clearly, discounting at 10%, a species has to have a very high value in the distant future to be worth saving today. With a lower rate of interest, it would be discounted less, and hence worth more. Thus, lower interest rates appear to favor conservation.

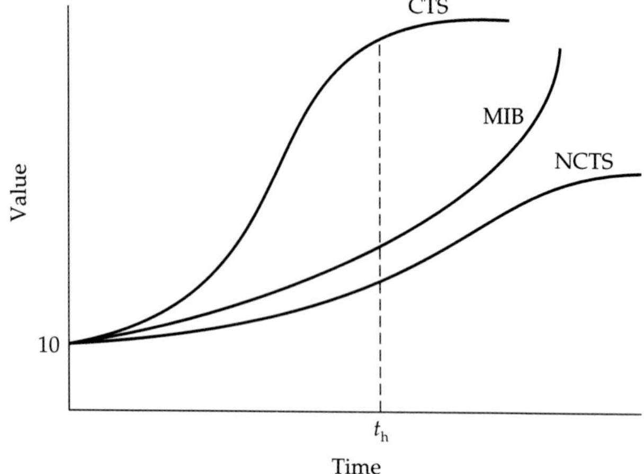

Figure 15.5 Commercial tree species (CTS) are those that grow faster in their early years than does money in the bank (MIB). When their rate of return equals or is less than return from MIB, it is, economically, time to harvest (t_h). Noncommercial tree species (NCTS) are those that always grow more slowly than money in the bank, and thus are not economically attractive.

It has long been argued, for example, that trees that grow more slowly than the rate of interest will never be commercial. Imagine that it costs $10.00 to plant a tree seedling, and that the rate of interest is 10%. An entrepreneur has the choice of putting $10.00 in the bank to earn 10% or planting the tree seedling and harvesting it at a later date. Each year, the money in the bank increases in value: to $11.00 at the end of the first year [$10.00 + ($10.00 × 0.1) = $10.00 × 1.1], to $10.00 × $(1.1)^2$ or $12.10 at the end of the second year, to $10.00 × $(1.1)^3$ or $13.31 at the end of the third year, and so on. As long as the value of the tree grows faster than the money in the bank, it is a commercial tree species, and it pays to invest in the tree (Figure 15.5). Eventually, of course, the tree begins to grow more slowly, and when it is growing in value only as fast as money in the bank, it pays to cut the tree. But if the tree never grows in value faster than money in the bank, it is a noncommercial tree species, and it never pays to plant the tree in the first place. Slow-growing trees such as teak and many other hardwoods will be cut down and not replanted when interest rates are even moderately high. This principle has had an enormous effect on development projects. For example, the World Bank considers returns of 15% to be acceptable, and hence has rarely financed timber projects except those with very fast growing species such as eucalyptus. Historically, development aid has financed the replacement of natural forests of mixed species with monocultural forests of fast-growing species based on this understanding of economic efficiency. High interest rates encourage transformation of natural ecosystems toward faster-growing species or other uses of land.

Clearly, interest rates affect the way biological resources are managed, and hence affect the rate and direction of ecosystem transformation and species extinction. Any species or ecosystem that cannot be managed such that it generates a flow of services at a rate greater than the rate of interest should—under economic perspectives—be depleted. Since even many economists find exploitation to extinction rather crass, there has been considerable interest in whether the interest rate produced by private capital markets accurately reflects social interest, and whether, when these interests are factored in, a social rate of interest would not be significantly lower than the private interest rate. Might private capital markets be working imperfectly, generating rates of interest that are too high and hence lead to excessive biodiversity loss (Marglin 1963)? There are good reasons to expect that lower interest rates would generally favor the conservation of biodiversity, though there are some situations in which this would not be the case. This has not been simply an academic argument. The World Bank now realizes how its own evaluation policies have hastened biodiversity loss and, in part for this reason, now has a policy of not financing the transformation of natural forest habitat.

Preserving Biodiversity as an Option

Many assumptions about the efficient use of resources over time underlie the logic of Hotelling's argument. Assumptions are made about the substitutability of human-produced and natural capital, people's ability to comprehend how the future will unfold, and the appropriateness of current peoples exposing future peoples to the risks of not having biological diversity that they might later find of value. These complications have led economists to argue, given the irreversibility of biodiversity loss (Fisher and Hanemann 1985), that it is appropriate to some extent to maintain biological diversity as an *option* even though narrow economic reasoning suggests otherwise. "Better-safe-than-sorry" reasoning has led to the introduction of the concept of **option value**, an upward adjustment of price to help assure conservation of the resource (Bishop 1978). The quantity analogue to option value is a *safe minimum standard* (see Chapter 2), the setting of a lower limit on the quantity of a resource that must be maintained (Wantrup 1952). In Essay 15D, David Newman and Robert Healy show how mainstream neoclassical economics can be used to evaluate alternative land use options. They show that timber extraction from a proposed nature reserve in Belize is marginally profitable at best. By including the option value of biodiversity protection and future revenue from ecotourism and fees for scientific research, they argue that protecting the land as a nature reserve represents its economic "best use."

ESSAY 15D
Evaluating the Opportunity Costs of Establishing a Nature Reserve

David H. Newman, University of Georgia, and Robert G. Healy, Duke University

For poor countries, any decision to restrict the use of natural resources, and thereby possibly forgo revenue, must be made carefully. If land with potential value for timber production is proposed as a nature reserve, a key question of government officials and local stakeholders will be, "What are the trade-offs?" When projects are evaluated by resource economists, these trade-offs are measured as the *opportunity cost*, the value forgone from the next best alternative use. If timber harvests are reduced or eliminated in a nature reserve, the forgone net revenue from timber sales represents the opportunity cost of the reserve. We provide an example from Belize to show how opportunity costs can be used to evaluate proposed nature reserves.

The proposed Bladen Reserve is located in a basin of the Bladen Branch, a major arm of the Monkey River, in southern Belize, Central America. Its steepness, inaccessibility, and distance from population centers have spared it from major deforestation and heavy hunting pressure, thereby preserving an unusually intact moist forest ecosystem (Brokaw and Lloyd-Evans 1987). Proposals were made throughout the 1980s to set aside approximately 35,000 ha of the Bladen as a nature reserve for wildlife conservation and tourism. The government of Belize, although sympathetic to the idea of creating more nature reserves, expressed concern over the economic trade-offs involved in designating a large reserve at Bladen Branch. What would be the impact on Belize's timber industry? How much timber revenue for the government would be forgone? Would the economic value of nontimber activities (research, tourism) be sufficient to offset the forgone timber income?

Our overall impression of the region of which Bladen is a part is that it is poised for dramatic changes in the near future. This relatively underdeveloped region is becoming inundated with colonists and refugees from other countries, who practice subsistence, slash-and-burn agriculture in competition with larger landholders controlling the better arable land. Similar scenarios have been played out throughout Central America, and the results are generally disastrous for environmental integrity. Farming moves to lower-quality, higher-elevation lands, which are quickly depleted. Hunting pressure kills much of the wildlife, and overall biological diversity becomes degraded.

Forestry Activities in the Region

The primary timber species harvested from the area are mahogany (*Swietenia macrophylla*), cedar (*Cedrela mexicana*), and pine (*Pinus caribaea*). In addition, some precious and luxury hardwoods are also harvested in the area: rosewood (*Dalbergia stevesonii*), bastard rosewood (*Swartzia* spp.), mayflower (*Tabebuia rosea*), and granadillo (*Platymiscium yucatanum*). Secondary hardwoods are also harvested, or have the potential for being harvested, including banak (*Vi-*

rola koschynia), yemeri (*Vochysia hondurensis*), Santa Maria (*Calophyllum braziliense*), cotton (*Ceiba pentandra*), nargusta (*Terminalia amazonia*), and sapodilla (*Manilkara zapota*).

No unprocessed logs are exported from Belize. Mahogany, cedar, and Santa Maria are used in both internal and export markets, while pine and the other secondary hardwoods have been used solely as lumber for internal markets.

Government royalties from timber harvests in 1988 for the individual species were: primary hardwoods, B\$0.60/ft^3; precious hardwoods, B\$20.00/ton; secondary hardwoods, B\$0.12/ft^3; and pine, B\$0.20/ft^3. Sale prices of finished lumber products were also controlled by the government, with retail prices set at B\$1.25/board foot (bf) for primary hardwood lumber; B\$3.00/bf for precious woods; B\$0.77/ bf for secondary rough hardwood lumber; and B\$0.70/bf for rough pine lumber. These prices are not actually followed in the market, as demand exceeds supply at these prices.

Forestry in the Bladen region presents significant opportunities, but also significant problems. As throughout the country, the sawmills are small, use antiquated equipment, and are undercapitalized. Product quality is generally low, and there is considerable production waste. However, given the extremely short harvesting season, low volumes per acre, short license duration, and poor infrastructure, it is unlikely that more heavily capitalized and efficient operations could be established.

The timber industries are an important component of the regional economy. The total annual salary income from the mills is near B\$650,000, and government royalties from timber harvests are about B\$90,000.[1] This compares with approximately B\$400,000 in royalty payments in 1985/1986 for the entire country (Arnold et al. 1989). The importance of the timber industry should not be ignored when determining the optimal mix of land uses for overall regional development.

Economic Analysis of the Bladen Branch Timber Resource

Our analysis is based on the information detailed in the few available studies of the Bladen watershed (Wright et al. 1959; Johnson and Chaffey 1974; Johnson and Woods 1976; King et al. 1986; Brokaw and Lloyd-Evans 1987). The paucity of accurate inventory data partly rests with the perceived inaccessibility of the area for commercial timber operations. Physical accessibility generally relates to the steepness of the slopes, the characteristics of the soil, and whether safe access for workers and equipment currently exists. Economic accessibility is more varied, as it has a value component and a temporal component. If sufficient timber quantities or values exist, most physical limitations can, to some extent, be overcome. Roads can be built and logging systems can be developed that physically allow access to the timber for harvesting.[2]

Due to the difficult physical access, the effective government policy has been that the steep granitic area on the slopes of the Maya Mountains be maintained in "protection forest." Only in the alluvial floodplains of the small tributaries and on the Bladen itself was small-scale agriculture or forestry even contemplated (Wright et al. 1959). The most recent land use study confirmed and expanded these recommendations (King et al. 1986). In line with this belief, only 4% of the granitic soil types in the Bladen area forest reserves were considered accessible, with an additional 16% considered partially accessible (Johnson and Woods 1976).

Stocking of the primary and precious hardwood species, based on the 1976 study, is very low. For trees greater than 50 cm (20 in), only 7.5 mahogany stems and 2.9 cedar stems per 100 ha were estimated for the limestone soils, and none for the granitic soils. With normal good stocking of merchantable trees considered 1 tree per ha, this must be considered very low stocking.

Accessible Timber Area and Volume

Four areas of relatively accessible timber within the upper Bladen Branch watershed are proposed for the reserve. Accessibility is relative, however—although these areas may be harvestable, it may be quite expensive to get to them. The accessible harvesting area is approximately 3000 ha, with virtually all of it on the limestone-derived soils. Using the average volumes taken from Johnson and Woods (1976) for the primary species and allowing for growth since the survey, the standing volume of primary species would be at most 45,000 ft^3. For the secondary species the total volume is larger, but more difficult to calculate; most are currently not harvested for processing. The total estimated harvestable volume of currently or potentially utilizable secondary species is 3,857,500 ft^3. Allowing for the potential of utilizing other species and for ingrowth, we estimate an expected harvestable volume of 4,500,000 ft^3.

Direct Costs and Benefits of Timber Production

The potential government royalty revenue from the likely-to-be-harvested standing timber is B\$567,000 (B\$0.60/ft^3 $\times$ 45,000 ft^3 + B\$0.12/ft^3 $\times$ 4,500,000 ft^3). Even if we assume higher stocking than the average described by Johnson and Woods, or more hectares available for harvesting, and increase the volumes by a further 25%, the total royalty revenue would be only B\$708,500. Naturally, this value could increase further if the government raised its royalty rates, but the ultimate effect of this would be uncertain, as it might reduce the total amount of timber harvested. Using current and proposed milling capacities, it would optimistically take at least ten years to harvest the timber from the area. Harvesting equal volumes over a period of ten years would give a present value (the value in current dollars) of B\$320,367 (B\$567,000/10 $\times$ 5.6502) at a 12% discount rate, or B\$417,318 (B\$567,000/10 $\times$ 7.3601) at 6%.

Only rough estimates of the other costs of production can be made. These costs include extraction and milling labor and equipment, road building, additional forest management costs, and capital costs. Arnold et al. (1989) present high and low estimates for logging and milling costs for primary and secondary hardwoods that range between a low of B\$0.55/bf and a high of B\$0.90/bf. Using these costs and the available timber results in a total production cost of B\$15,000,000 to B\$24,500,000 (B\$0.55/bf or B\$0.90/bf $\times$ 6 bf/ft^3 $\times$ 4,545,000 ft^3). Given that much of the timber lies in difficult terrain and is far from existing roads, it is likely that the production costs will be on the high side.

The value of the final timber product from this harvest comes from the sale of lumber and veneer on the wholesale market. Using government-controlled prices, the timber has a current lumber-equivalent value of B\$21,127,500 (B\$1.25/bf $\times$ 6 bf/ft^3 $\times$ 45,000 ft^3 + B\$0.77/bf $\times$ 6 bf/ft^3 $\times$ 4,500,000 ft^3). Because there is relatively little volume in primary or precious species in the area, the Bladen's timber is not of great importance to the export market.

Comparing the costs and revenues gives an idea of the relative value of the standing timber. Ignoring the royalty costs for the moment, the net total value of the timber ranges from –B$3,415,500 (B$0.75/ft^3) to B$6,129,000 (B$1.35/ft^3). It is difficult to calculate a present net value for the timber, as certain expenditures (primarily road building and equipment costs) must be in place prior to initiation of timber removals. However, we will optimistically assume that half of the total costs are spread out equally over the first four years and the remaining half over the remaining six years. Assuming that revenues occur equally over the ten-year harvesting period and that all prices and costs stay constant in real terms results in a PNV (present net value) that, at a 12% discount rate, ranges from B$3,000,000 to –B$2,700,000 (B$4,200,000 to –B$3,000,000 at 6%) or B$0.66/ft^3 to –B$0.59/ft^3 (B$0.92/ft^3 to –B$0.66/ft^3)

If we include the royalty costs, they will naturally lower the present net value derived from timber production by at least 10% and possibly much more, depending on the assumed costs. Likewise, given that the high-cost scenario gives negative returns, it is unlikely that a significant amount of harvesting would be performed in the currently inaccessible areas, as those would be considered high-cost (i.e. low-profit) areas. Thus, it is likely that the only steeper-sloped areas that would be logged would be those that contain high amounts of the primary species. Because the Bladen Branch has relatively low stocking levels of these species, under current price and cost conditions, the steep-sloped granitic and limestone areas will remain economically submarginal.

Indirect Costs and Benefits of Timber Production

A number of indirect costs and benefits, either intended or unintended, result when timber harvesting takes place. Often these results are difficult to quantify in economic terms and are ignored in economic analyses. However, it is important to consider both the positive and negative effects that timber harvesting may have on development of the upper Bladen Branch resource.

Clearly, the most immediate effect of harvesting is the physical removal of trees and the building of roads and trails to bring out the trees. Given the current Forest Department policy of strict diameter limit cutting rules, the harvesting itself would have relatively little effect on the ultimate composition of the remaining forest. Some feel that this policy will cause the forest to degrade over time, as favored species may have difficulties regenerating under forest cover (Arnold et al. 1989). However, more thorough cutting practices may in fact cause additional regeneration problems by favoring low-density, nonmarketable, fast-growing species (Johnson and Woods 1975). An additional benefit of the selective cutting method is that relatively little runoff occurs, as a smaller percentage of the ground is left bare. The high quality of Belize's streams, even though timber harvesting has been going on for over 150 years, is a direct result of these practices (Hartshorn et al. 1984).

The major long-term effect of timber harvesting, especially in an isolated area such as the Bladen, is due to road construction. Roads open up an area, allowing access for purposes other than logging. The most serious potential problem for this area is an influx of hunters and unplanned milpa farming activity. The resulting damage to the exceptional wildlife population in the Bladen from these activities could be dramatic. At the same time, improved access is needed if the Bladen is to develop as a tourist attraction.

Another concept that should be considered when the development of an irreplaceable asset such as the Bladen is contemplated is its *option value*. This is a term used in economics to emphasize the idea that, once irreversible development of an asset occurs, the owner (in this case the Belize government) loses the option of developing the area for other uses. Thus, there is a value in delaying any irreversible activity, such as logging, until better, more complete information on all options is available. Because the Bladen is considered one of the least disturbed large forest areas in Central America, its option value for research, tourism, biodiversity, and wilderness is high. Barring extensive hurricane damage, its timber values will not diminish over time, as worldwide supplies of high-quality tropical timbers continue to decline and prices rise. The cost of forgoing conservation options must be balanced against the benefits from any planned activities for the area that would foreclose these options.

Conclusions

From this analysis, timber harvesting in the Bladen Branch area seems a marginal operation at best. The government of Belize, in the end, agreed with these results, and declared a 393 km^2 portion of the Bladen Branch an official Nature Reserve in 1990. The area has been set aside strictly for research, and receives only minimal tourist use. Thus, the Belize government has in effect determined that the option value of the Bladen is sufficient to justify reserve status. Because this is not an irrevocable act, the government maintains the option of changing the use of the Bladen at some time in the future.

The power of an economic analysis in evaluating the opportunity costs of land use choices is that it can make explicit the costs of various decisions. The implication of this study is that it is not *always* the case that forests will be harvested for the immediate returns that timber can provide.

1. Royalty income is calculated using an average royalty payment of B$0.20/ft^3 and a conversion factor of 6 board feet to 1 cubic foot.
2. A former logger in the Bladen Branch area recounted how he actually drove a tractor over the Maya Mountain divide, winching his machine from tree to tree up the mountainside, at times hanging the tractor in midair. Clearly, even if this account is not strictly accurate, this area would not be considered "economically accessible."

The Economics of Biodiversity Conservation

The foregoing models of the ways in which people interact with the environment are generally understood among environmental economists and have become a part of the understanding of conservation biologists and environmental policy analysts as well. To the extent that common ground has been found for conservation decision making among people of diverse interests and situations, these models are proving critical to the framing of policies to ameliorate biodiversity loss. Several caveats must be kept in mind, however.

First, we have presented these simple economic models and arguments to highlight the special contribution of each to our understanding of the process of biodiversity loss. It is important to keep in mind that the different processes each model emphasizes are interactive. In reality, we are dealing with Malthus's concern with population growth, the patterns of land use suggested by Ricardo's model, the maldistribution of rights to biological resources highlighted by Marxian thinking, the problems of open access and other forms of market failure identified by Pigou, and the questions regarding the appropriateness of interest rates and the quality of information about the future used by economic actors highlighted by Hotelling's model, all at once. Reducing the rate of biodiversity loss will almost always entail multiple instruments for adjusting economic decision making. A single instrument, such as inclusion of the values of biological resources in the economic evaluation of development projects, will rarely be sufficient. Finding common ground has been difficult because people mistakenly think that one explanation and solution is correct, and the others are wrong, then argue over which is correct. Different mixes will be correct in different places, but understanding this requires increased sophistication. Furthermore, implementing different mixes of solutions across different areas is much more difficult than imposing one simple solution universally.

Second, environmental economists, conservation biologists, and environmental policy analysts share these understandings of how biodiversity is lost, but the consensus does not extend to economists in general, to policymakers less directly linked to environmental issues, and to most political representatives. Environmental economic understanding is not widespread because environmental economic models complicate or raise serious questions about the general model of neoclassical economics, the role of economics in the policy process, and the possibility of making general policy conclusions. In light of environmental economic models, for example, the general "rule" of economists that government interference in markets and trade should be minimized does not hold. Most economists still downplay the complexities of the interactions between economies and environmental systems, because if they conceded that such complexities were important, economic analysis would be much more difficult and would result in much more complex economic policies (Figure 15.6). The vast majority of books on economic theory, whether beginning or advanced, rarely even refer to environmental complexities as a special problem, let alone as a general problem.

Thus, whatever shared understanding of the process of biodiversity loss exists, it has not provided sufficient common ground for finding a broad political consensus for the conservation of biological diversity. Economics as a science of systems is relatively insignificant compared with economics as a collection of rhetorical arguments that support one political ideology or another. Biodiversity is being lost, in part, because most economists, policy analysts, and politicians refuse to admit complexities that confound or blatantly contradict their political economic ideologies. In short, the process of loss is intimately related to the human beliefs that the world is a relatively simple system that people can control through relatively simple knowledge, that it is resilient to human influences, and that it has infinite potential for human exploitation through new knowledge and technologies. These beliefs are deeply rooted in economic thinking, and they blind economists—and thereby politicians—to the more sophisticated economic models that complement biological understanding.

Figure 15.6 Many economic models ignore real-world complexities and limitations such as resource exploitation or waste disposal. Including such factors would make the models more realistic, but also more complicated.

Third, although economic explanations of the process of biodiversity loss are quite helpful, they have serious weaknesses. On the one hand, a concerted effort is needed to bring what is now conventional understanding among environmental economists into the mainstream of economics, policy analysis, and political discourse. On the other hand, our understanding of the process of biodiversity loss needs further improvement. Some new explorations under way are discussed below.

New Directions in Economic Thought

The Rights of Future Generations

Much of conservationists' concern with biodiversity is rooted in concern for our descendants (Partridge 1981; Norton 1986; Weiss 1989; Laslett and Fishkin 1992). Economists have also worried about how economic logic treats future generations, but the formal models economists have advocated for use in the policy process to date have implicitly assumed the existing between-generation distribution of resource rights, as defined by existing property law, government programs, and social mores. These economic models show how the current generation can efficiently exploit resources, rather than how resources might be shared more equitably with future generations. Environmental economists, though concerned with the future, have also followed this tradition in economic thinking, false to their own theory, of looking for *the single* most efficient allocation of resources, when in fact there are many efficient allocations defined by moral criteria beyond economic values. Moral criteria with respect to our obligation to future generations are especially important. Only recently have economists constructed models that allow them to understand how resources can be both efficiently used now and equitably shared with future generations. These recent models are based on the concept of utility.

Figure 15.7 The concept of utility and its interaction with intergenerational equity. Curve *U* represents the frontier of possible utility; the dashed line at 45° represents the points at which the needs of current and future generations are equally satisfied. A move from point *A* at some distance from the possibility frontier to point *B* on the frontier results in greater efficiency. Points *B* and *C* are both efficient. However, at point *B*, utility to current generations is high, but utility to future generations is low. Moving from point *B* below the 45° line to point *C* above the line represents a redistribution (a change in equity) between generations that promotes sustainability—the situation in which the utility to future generations is equal to or greater than the utility to the current generation.

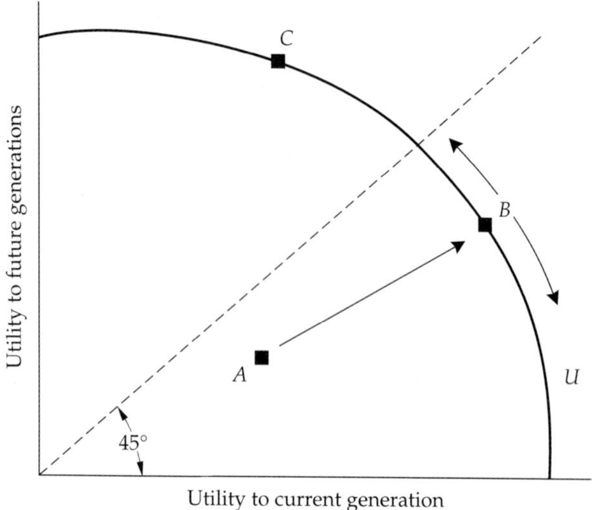

Utility is defined as personal satisfaction of some economic desire, or the want-satisfying power of goods. If one good (say, a wilderness experience) provides more satisfaction to an individual than another good (say, a day at the local mall), it is said to have higher utility. A major concern of environmental economists is the relationship between satisfying the needs and desires of the present generation, and satisfying those of future generations. Because utility has real limits, including resource limits, at the societal level, the limitations form a utility possibility frontier, represented as a curve in Figure 15.7. In this conceptual model, the frontier represents the highest utility possibly available to people in future generations, given the utility for people in the current generation.

If collectively we are not at the possibility frontier (say, we are at point *A*), then by improving economic efficiency we can reach a point on the frontier (point *B*) where more desires can be satisfied. But where we fall on the utility frontier curve is critical to future generations. If we do not care about leaving resources for future generations, we will satisfy our current desires close to the x-axis; that is, we will use many resources now so that utility to the current generation is very high, while that to future generations is low. To the extent that we are willing to make sacrifices by leaving part of current desires unsatisfied in order to leave resources for future generations, the utility function will move upward along the frontier curve toward the y-axis. The 45° line represents sustainability—the point on the frontier at which utility is equally satisfied between the current and future generations.

The models used by economists to date, even in the most recent economic literature on sustainability, are inappropriate for addressing intergenerational equity. The emphasis has been on internalizing externalities to increase overall efficiency—that is, on moving the economy from a position such as point *A* toward a position such as point *B*. Unfortunately, neither of these positions is sustainable for future generations—both points fall below the 45° line, and thus satisfy current utility at the expense of future utility. Note that simply transforming nonmarket goods—such as biodiversity—into a quantitative evaluation will not necessarily lead to their sustainable use. Biological resource valuation as currently conducted, for example, derives prices that would move an economy toward point *B*, increasing efficiency, helping future generations relative to point *A*, but not necessarily making the economy sustainable. Wholly new ways of thinking about environmental valuation will be needed; an example is offered in Essay 15E by Michael Balick and colleagues.

ESSAY 15E

Valuation of Extractive Medicines in Tropical Forests

Exploring the Linkage to Conservation

M. J. Balick, R. Mendelsohn, R. Arvigo, and G. Shropshire
New York Botanical Garden

The discovery of new pharmaceuticals from tropical forests to add to the war chest of modern medicine is an enticing reason to conserve tropical ecosystems. For example, the importance of the rosy periwinkle (*Catharanthus roseus*) in treating childhood leukemia and Hodgkin's disease is frequently cited in popular and scientific articles about the need for conserving rainforests. But another, perhaps more pressing, argument for conservation is the use of forests as pharmaceutical "factories" to produce local medicines used in primary health care.

New therapies for major diseases such as AIDS or cancer may be living in tropical forests. For various reasons, this potential is unlikely to result in significant conservation in the short term unless carefully constructed mechanisms are adopted. First, the development of a new pharmaceutical product from wild plants is a decade-long process, at best. Plants studied today, if found to be of value in medicine, will only yield royalties many years later, and cannot meet the immediate needs for money to support conservation activities.

Second, only a small fraction of plants studied actually reach the pharmacy shelves. Although there are undoubtedly numerous valuable chemicals to be derived from forests, these are hidden among tens of thousands of species and billions of hectares, and the net value of securing these areas may be small.

Third, when medicines are found, their extraction has historically led to destructive, not sustainable, use. *Pilocarpus* species, shrubby trees native to northeastern Brazil, are a case in point. The leaves of the trees are harvested by local people and processed by chemical companies to yield pilocarpine, a compound used in glaucoma treatment. The leaves have been wild-harvested from northeast Brazil for many decades without concern for continuity of the supply, and vast populations of *Pilocarpus jaborandi*, *P. microphylla*, and *P. pinnatifolius* are now extirpated.

Finally, local people traditionally have not benefited from discoveries of new medicines, and so have little incentive to manage forests to encourage discovery. Recent programs initiated by drug companies and developing countries address these last two points. However, it remains unclear to what extent these new efforts, while promising, will significantly contribute to global ecosystem conservation.

An additional, and more immediate, incentive for conservation may be the role of tropical forest ecosystems in providing traditional medicines and rural health care where local plants comprise 95% of the ethnopharmacopoeia. The World Health Organization estimates that 2.5–3.5 billion people worldwide use traditional medicines as part of their primary health care program. In Belize, Central America, where we are completing an inventory of ethnobotanical knowledge, up to 75% of the primary health care is provided by traditional healers using plant remedies. Both primary and secondary forests are sources of the plants processed into medicine. In many cases people known as "hierbateros" collect and sell these plants to the "curanderos," or traditional healers, actually providing the health care.

We conducted a series of forest inventories, combining ethnobotanical investigation with studies of the market value of the plants locally used in medicine (Balick and Mendelsohn 1992). We identified two 1 ha plots, one in a 30-year-old forest (plot 1) and another in a 50-year-old forest (plot 2). The two plots yielded 308.6 and 1433.6 kg dry weight, respectively, of medicines whose value could be judged by local market forces. Local herbal pharmacists and healers purchase unprocessed medicine from hierbateros and small farmers at an average price of U.S. $2.80/kg. Multiplying the quantity of medicines found per hectare by this price suggests that clearing a hectare of medicines would yield the collector between $864 and $4014 of gross revenue. Of course, the collector has costs he or she must bear to harvest this material. On a per-hectare basis, harvesting required 25 person-days on plot 1 and 80 person-days on plot 2. Given the local wage of $12/day, the total harvest costs for the plots were $300 and $960 respectively. When these costs are subtracted from gross revenue, the net revenue from clearing a hectare was $564 and $3054 on plots 1 and 2 respectively. However, the labor costs go back to the local economy, so they are not really lost from the system.

These value estimates of using tropical forests for medicinal plant harvest compare favorably with alternative land uses in the region; for example, milpa (corn, bean, and squash cultivation) in Guatemalan rainforest yields $288/ha. We also identified commercial products such as allspice, copal, chicle, and construction materials in the plots that could be harvested and added to the medicinal value. Thus, use of at least some areas of rainforest as extractive reserves for medicinal plants appears to be economically justified. A periodic harvest of medicinal plant materials seems a realistic and sustainable method of utilizing the forest. For example, with a 50 ha parcel of forest similar to the second plot analyzed, one could clear one hectare of medicines per year indefinitely.

As a postscript to our original study, the Belize Association of Traditional Healers is now negotiating with the government of Belize to allocate a 2430 ha parcel of land to be used as an extractive reserve for medicinal plants. Its management would be in the hands of the traditional healers and herb gatherers, with input from researchers. Larger-scale experiments aimed at developing sustainable extraction techniques for stems, roots, bark, and tubers would be carried out in this setting, in collaboration with local people who utilize these plants for health care.

On a global level, there are approximately 3 billion people using wild-harvested medicines. Assuming each person uses $2.50–$5.00 worth of medicine per year, the annual value of this resource could range between $7.5 billion and $15 billion. This is a significant aggregate value, and a large portion of it represents tropical forest species. The entire global pharmaceutical trade is estimated at $80–$90 billion annually. New drugs from tropical forests would have to compete for a substantial share of the modern drug market before they would be as valuable as the natural factory of local medicines. Thus, local rainforest medicines worth billions of dollars today could, if properly managed, have a more immediate effect on conservation than a new drug developed from a plant commercialized a decade from now.

Another issue is the replacement costs (substitution costs) of commercial pharmaceutical products when and if local plant resources become exhausted. The cost of replacing the type of primary health care delivery system now in place would be many times that of the present system; thus, a vast constituency ranging from individuals to governments has a vested interest in maintaining adequate supplies of forest medicines. One of the most effective and least expensive ways of accomplishing this is through in situ conservation of these resources in tropical forests.

We do not wish to underestimate the potential benefits of pharmaceutical drug discovery for tropical forest conservation. However, the importance of traditional medicines from tropical forests is another powerful argument for their conservation. Additional work is needed in order to properly understand and evaluate this issue and, if possible, harness it for maximum benefit to the conservation enterprise.

With respect to the rate of interest, the intergenerational models have an exciting theoretical result. When the current generation decides to assure assets for future generations, the rate of interest goes down. Economists have been reasoning backward in their search for reasons why interest rates perhaps should be lower in order to protect future generations. When we decide to protect future generations, interest rates *become* lower.

The intergenerational models elaborating the relationship between efficiency and intergenerational equity highlight the need for economic reasoning to work in conjunction with ethical criteria—a larger system of values—exercised through politics. While many economists will continue to argue in political arenas that protecting biological resources for future generations is inefficient, their arguments violate economic logic. There are more efficient and less efficient ways to protect biological resources, but caring about the future is not a matter of economic efficiency alone. Adopting the existing distribution of rights between generations is merely a convention of economic practice; it has no roots in economic theory. Changing this convention is critical to conserving biodiversity.

Distancing and Economic Globalization

The relationship between the environment and the modern global economy is clearly different than its historical interface with more local or regional economies. While considerable environmental concern has been expressed in hemispheric and global trade negotiations, economics is surprisingly ill-equipped to address the effects of globalization of the economy on environmental management. Whether they possess dominantly market or centrally directed economies, modern societies are undergoing a historical process that is most simply and effectively understood as **distancing**. Increasing specialization distances scientists from one another, impeding a collective scientific consciousness of how we are interacting with nature, let alone how we could. Increasing dependence on modern technologies shifts environmental and social problems from the local and immediate to the distant and future. Increasing specialization in the production process distances industrialists and workers from an overall consciousness of production technologies. Increasing urbanization distances people from the soil and water on which they depend. Increasing globalization distances people from the environmental and social effects of their consumption. Distancing makes it more difficult for people to be environmentally aware and to design, agree to implement, and enforce environmental management strategies.

At the same time, global communication is now nearly instantaneous and affordable for many. Some individuals are acquiring new perceptions of our global environmental predicament and are working to address it through nongovernmental organizations, which are less prone than government agencies to the communication barriers of disciplinary and professional specialization. There is now a discernible tension between bureaucratized but formal channels of power and less bureaucratized, informal channels of global communication and agreement.

The globalization of regional economies has been rationalized by the logic of trade, but falsely so. The logic of trade is simply that when two choosers decide to enter into an exchange, it is because the exchange makes each of them better off. To argue that free trade is good policy, one must also ensure that there are no costs and benefits external to those who choose; otherwise, new international institutions must be created to internalize those costs and benefits. Clearly, nations are having sufficient difficulty internalizing externalities nationally; international institutions are inherently more complicated and necessarily weaker. But the false application of the logic of trade to justify globalization is even more fundamental than this. Economists have always assumed that it is individuals and corporations who should be free to choose. Interestingly, the logic of trade is indifferent to whether the choosers are individuals, communities, bioregions, or nations. The logic does not say "individuals (and multinational corporations) should be free to choose, but communities or nations should not." But this is exactly the way the logic has been misinterpreted. The association of trade with individualism reflects the dominant premise in modern political thought. It reflects Western culture, not economic logic. The difference between individual and community interest, of course, is intimately tied to the systemic character of environmental systems. Nature cannot readily be divided up and assigned to individuals, hence the failure of markets to reflect its value.

The Coevolution of Modern Societies

Neither neoclassical nor Marxist economic models are adequate to preserve biodiversity. Each implicitly incorporates assumptions about the interrelationships of science, technology, and materialism that have driven the development and the accelerated biological transformation of the past century. A new, more comprehensive model is needed if we are to find common ground on these larger issues.

Consider development as a process of coevolution among knowledge, values, organization, technology, and the environment (Figure 15.8). Each of these subsystems is related to each of the others, yet each is also changing and affecting change in the others through selection. Deliberate innovations, chance discoveries, and random changes occur in each subsystem and affect, through selection, the distribution and qualities of components in each of the other subsystems. Whether new components prove fit depends on the characteristics of each of the subsystems at the time. With each subsystem putting selective pressure on each of the others, they coevolve in a manner whereby each reflects the others. Thus everything is coupled, yet everything is changing (Norgaard 1994).

In this coevolutionary perspective, environmental subsystems are treated symmetrically with the subsystems of values, knowledge, social organization, and technology. New technologies, for example, exert new selective pressures

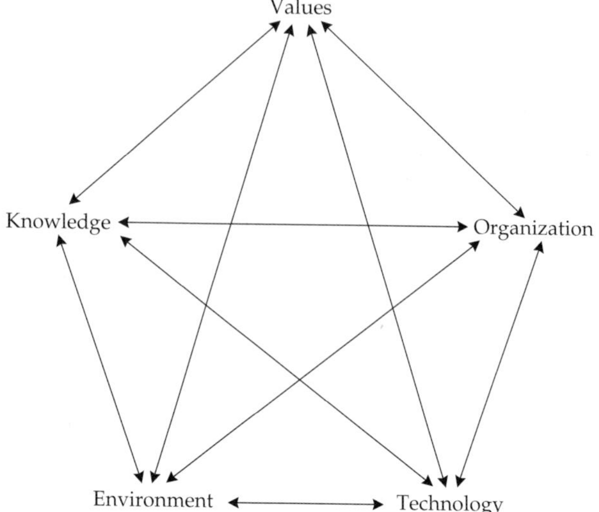

Figure 15.8 A coevolutionary model of development showing the interrelationships involved. Social and environmental change can be understood as a process of innovations (mutations) and introductions in the various subsystems and selection among them. Coevolutionary "development" occurs when this process favors the continued well-being of people.

on species, while newly evolved characteristics of species, in turn, select for different technologies. Similarly, transformations in the biosphere select for new ways of understanding the biosphere. For example, the use of pesticides selects for resistance and secondary pest resurgence, which in turn select both for new pesticides and for more systematic ways of thinking about pest control. Pests, pesticides, pesticide production, pesticide institutions and policy, our understanding of pest control, and the way we value chemicals in the environment demonstrate an incredibly tight and rapid coevolution in the second half of the 20th century.

In the short run, people can be thought of as interacting with the environment in response to market signals or their absence. The coevolutionary model, however, incorporates longer-term evolutionary feedbacks. To emphasize coevolutionary processes is not to deny that people directly intervene in and change the characteristics of environments. The coevolutionary perspective puts its emphasis on the chain of events thereafter—how different interventions alter the selective pressure on, and hence the relative dominance of, environmental traits, which in turn select for values, knowledge, organization, and technology and hence subsequent interventions in the environment.

While a coevolutionary perspective treats changes in the various subsystems symmetrically, we can use this model to address technology in particular. People have interacted with their environments over millennia in diverse ways, many of them sustainable over very long periods, many not. Some traditional agricultural technologies, at the intensities historically employed, probably increased biological diversity. There is general evidence that many traditional technologies, again at the level employed, included biodiversity-conserving strategies as a part of the process of farming. Technology today, however, is perceived as a leading culprit in the process of biodiversity loss. Modern agricultural technologies override nature, but do so only locally and temporarily. They do not "control" nature. Pesticides kill pests, solving the immediate threat to crops. But when a competitively dominant pest is eliminated, other species may quickly become pests. Pesticides also drift away from the farm to interfere with the agricultural practices of other farmers, and pesticides and their by-products accumulate in soil and groundwater aquifers to plague production and human health for years to come. Each farmer strives to control nature on his or her farm in each growing season, but creates new problems in other places and times. It is noteworthy that preharvest crop losses due to pests since World War II have remained at about 35%, while pesticide use has increased dramatically (Pimentel 1988).

Similarly, use of fertilizers can reduce the vagaries and limits of relying on nitrogen-fixing bacteria and other soil microorganisms that assist in nutrient uptake, microorganisms that are supported by traditional agricultural practices. But in the process of overriding them, these natural properties of ecosystems are lost, while the effects of nitrogen and phosphate pollution in groundwater aquifers and surface waters accumulate. While there is no doubt that modern crop breeding has produced far more productive varieties of rice, wheat, corn, and other grains, these varieties depend on irrigation, fertilization, pesticide technologies, and expansive monocultures, and thus have substantial environmental costs beyond agriculture and over time. The accelerated evolution of plant diseases associated with the monocropping of a limited number of varieties makes further improvements in crop disease resistance necessary. Whether or not modern agriculture can be thought of as less dependent on nature, it is surely more dependent on continual advances in agricultural research.

The contradictions of modern agriculture have stimulated a new interest in how traditional agricultural technologies conserve biodiversity and in the potential for combining modern scientific understanding with traditional techniques (National Research Council 1993). Clearly, people must still interact with the environment: the question is not whether, but how. While modern agriculture certainly causes environmental degradation, it is also clear that it feeds many people who would otherwise have to be supported through the use of more land devoted to agriculture, further threatening biodiversity. Traditional agricultural practices in areas of rapidly increasing population result in the expansion of farming into previously undisturbed regions. Furthermore, with the onset of modern development, the social relations and traditions that conserve resources break down, further hastening environmental degradation.

Beyond modern agriculture, fossil fuel-based technologies support industry, transportation, and thereby the concentration of people in urban areas. While packing people into cities reduces their direct impact on the land, and hence on biodiversity, fossil fuel-based transport, residential heating and cooling, and industry produce the vast majority of carbon dioxide and other greenhouse gases driving climate change. More immediate threats from ongoing air, soil, and water pollution, as well as from accidents such as oil spills, are also inextricably linked to fossil fuel-based technologies.

Improved technologies can increase energy and material efficiency, reducing energy and material flows and thereby the rate of environmental transformation. But technologies that merely reduce the consequences of existing approaches may offer little hope in the longer run. The multiplicative effects of increasing population and materialism on resource use and environmental transformation have outpaced efficiency increases to date.

New technologies that work *with* natural processes rather than overriding them are sorely needed (Wann 1996). During the past two centuries, technologies have largely descended from physics, chemistry, and, at best, microbiology; ecologists have never had the opportunity to systemically review such technologies. A few agricultural technologies, such as the control of agricultural pests through the use of other species, have arisen from ecological thinking. But research and technological development in biological pest control was nearly eliminated with the introduction of DDT after World War II. Research on and development of agricultural technologies requiring fewer energy and material inputs eventually received considerable support in industrialized countries after the rise in energy prices during the 1970s and the farm financial crises in the United States during the early 1980s. Support for agroecology, however—for technologies based on the management of complementarities among multiple species, including soil organisms—is still minimal. Learning how to use renewable energy sources will be a long and difficult process because most of our knowledge has developed to capture the potential of fossil energy. Our universities and other research institutions are still structured around disciplinary rather than systemic thinking (discussed in Chapter 16), and public understanding of the shortcomings of current technologies and the possibilities of ecologically based technologies is weak.

From the coevolutionary perspective, we can now see more clearly how economies have shifted from coevolving with their ecosystems to coevolving around the combustion of fossil hydrocarbons. In this transformation, people were freed from the environmental feedbacks of their economic activities that they once experienced relatively quickly as individuals and communities. The feedbacks that remain occur over longer periods and greater distances, and are experienced collectively by many peoples, even globally, making them more difficult to perceive and counteract (Norgaard 1994).

By tapping into fossil hydrocarbons, Western societies freed themselves, at least for the short term, from many of the complexities of interacting with environmental systems. With an independent energy source, tractors replaced animal power, fertilizers replaced the interplanting of crops that were good hosts of nitrogen-fixing bacteria, and pesticides replaced the biological controls provided by more complex agroecosystems. Furthermore, inexpensive energy meant that crops could be stored for longer periods and transported over greater distances.

Each of these accomplishments was based on the partial understanding of separate sciences and separate technologies. At least in the short run and "on the farm," separate adjustments of the parts seemed to fit into a coherent, stable whole. Agriculture was transformed from an agroecosystem culture of relatively self-sufficient communities to an agroindustrial culture of many separate, distant actors linked by global markets. The massive changes in technology and organization gave people the sense of having control over nature and being able to consciously design their future, while in fact they were merely shifting problems beyond the farm and onto future generations.

The unsustainability of modern societies arises from the fact that development based on fossil hydrocarbons has allowed individuals to control their immediate environments in the short run while shifting environmental impacts to broader publics and longer time frames. Working with these collective, longer-term, and more uncertain interrelationships is at least as challenging as trying to control nature had been historically. People's confidence in the sustainability of development is directly proportional to their confidence in our ability to address these new challenges.

The coevolutionary perspective helps us to see that the solution to biodiversity loss is not simply a matter of establishing market incentives to adjust the way we interact with nature. Nor is conservation simply a matter of intergenerational equity. Our values, knowledge, and social organization have coevolved with fossil hydrocarbons. Our fossil fuel-driven economy has not simply transformed the environment; it has selected for individualist, materialist values, favored the development of reductionist understanding at the expense of systemic understanding, and preferred a bureaucratic, centralized form of control that works better for steady-state industrial management than for the varied, surprising dynamics of ecosystem management. The coevolutionary model also points out that our abilities to perceive and resolve environmental problems are severely constrained by the dominant modes of valuing, thinking, and organizing.

Ecological Economics

Ecology and economics have been separate disciplines throughout their histories. While each certainly has borrowed theoretical concepts from the other, and the two have shared patterns of thinking from other sciences, they have addressed separate issues, utilized different assumptions to reach answers, and supported different interests in the policy process. Indeed, in their popular manifestations as environmentalism and economism, these disciplines have become juxtaposed secular religions, preventing the collective interpretation and resolution of the numerous problems at the intersection of human and natural systems. Many people understand the importance of bringing these domains of thought together. After numerous experiments with joint meetings between economists and ecologists, the International Society for Ecological Economics (ISEE) was formed in the late 1980s, its journal, *Ecological Economics,* was initiated, and major international conferences of ecologists and economists have been held since. Many ecological economic institutes have been formed around the world, and a significant number of books have appeared with the term *ecological economics* in their titles (e.g., Costanza 1991; Peet 1992; Jansson et al. 1994; Costanza et al. 1996).

Ecological economics is not a single new paradigm based in shared assumptions and theory. It represents a commitment among economists, ecologists, and other academics and practitioners to learn from each other, to explore together new patterns of thinking, and to facilitate the derivation and implementation of new economic and environmental policies. To date, ecological economics deliberately has been conceptually pluralistic, even while particular practitioners may prefer one paradigm over another (Norgaard 1989).

Robert Costanza, the founder and first president of ISEE, views ecological economics as encompassing economics and ecology; their existing links are shown in Figure 15.9 (Costanza et al. 1991). Ecological economists are rethinking both ecology and economics, extending the energetic paradigm of ecosystem ecology to economic questions (Hall et al. 1986), and participating in the

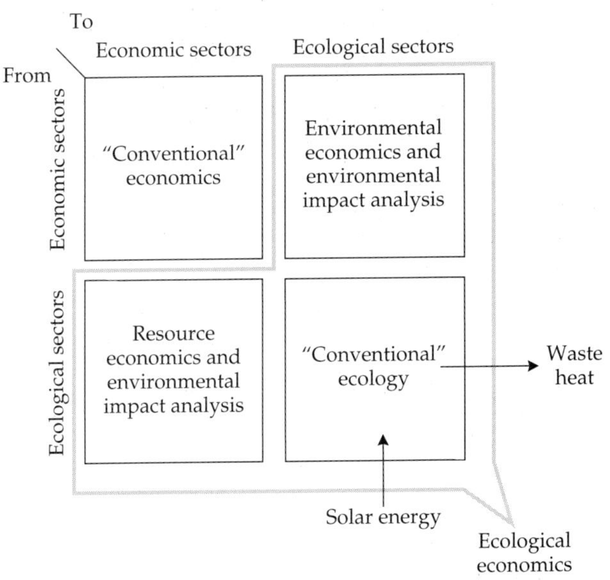

Figure 15.9 Ecological economics addresses the interactions between economies and ecological sectors. It encompasses conventional economics and ecology as well as environmental and resource economics and environmental impact analysis. The overall system is driven by the sun and dissipates waste heat. (Modified from Costanza et al. 1991.)

effort to include environmental values in national economic statistics such as measures of national income (Costanza and Daly 1992). This melding of economics and ecology must proceed if we are to have a realistic chance of developing an environmentally sustainable existence.

Summary

Those in search of common ground for deciding upon sustainable modes of interacting with the environment largely use patterns of reasoning developed within the history of economic thought. Conservation biologists invoke the population model of Malthus, rely on economic arguments to emphasize the value of diversity, use economics to design and argue for new social institutions to change individual behavior, and have become entangled in international debates over free trade and global inequity. At the same time, economics more generally remains the bastion of technological optimism and the overseer of the old development agenda. With economic arguments being used both by those who want to change the course of history and those who want to stay the course, considerable economic sophistication is required to make sense of and constructively participate in the effort to find common ground.

Like the multifaceted, hierarchical systems character of biodiversity itself, the loss of biodiversity has many, nested economic explanations. The politics of framing a more viable future is a cacophony of different voices, of diverse peoples using separate economic arguments to explain their understanding of the world's problems and to articulate their interests. The global political discord is unfamiliar, even frightening, to the untrained ear. We will find common ground when enough people understand how the diverse economic arguments evolved, how they all interrelate, how they all help to explain the human dilemma, and how they all need to be understood together in order to go beyond any one of them individually.

Questions for Discussion

1. Explore how some of the simple economic explanations interact. How, for example, might population growth and inequity interrelate with each other and with biodiversity loss, externalities, and globalization of the economy?
2. Which specific political interests (e.g., Northern developed vs. Southern undeveloped countries, capitalists vs. laborers) might find which particular economic models more attractive than others?
3. The advantage of market prices is that they adjust to give economic actors appropriate signals under different conditions. What is the significance of this to the valuation of species or ecosystems?
4. If we argue that we should forgo consumption of some resources now in order to save resources for future generations, how can we deal with the following argument that many people raise: technology will create substitutes for the resource, so there is no need to conserve it, and resource scarcity merely increases incentive to find alternative resources.
5. The early development of neoclassical economics was said to be "value-free." Do you think that any form of economics can really be "value-free?"
6. Traditional economists sometimes argue that conservationists should not be overly concerned about exploitation of renewable resources because

the rate of exploitation will decline as the resource becomes scarce. Discuss this perspective in light of information such as that provided by conservation genetics, the concept of minimum viable populations, and the behavior of nonlinear biological systems.

7. How does Ricardo's model of land use relate to capital-intensive agriculture and fisheries? That is, how does the purchase of expensive equipment such as harvesters or ocean-going fishing boats influence "rent," and thus resource exploitation?

Suggestions for Further Reading

Barbier, E. B., J. C. Burgess, and C. Folke. 1994. *Paradise Lost? The Ecological Economics of Biodiversity*. Earthscan Publications, London. The authors fully develop the importance of biodiversity to ecology and economics, explore the processes of loss by major ecosystem types, and fully develop lessons for management and policy.

Bellah, R. N., R. Madsen, W. M. Sullivan, A. Swidler, and S. M. Tipton. 1991. *The Good Society*. Alfred A. Knopf, New York. The authors present an excellent critique of the economic worldview and show how it has broken down many of the important social relationships of communities. The final chapter discusses the conceptual parallels with ecosystem transformation and the importance of reestablishing communities for the protection of natural systems.

Berkes, F. (ed.). 1989. *Common Property Resources: Ecology and Community-Based Sustainable Development*. Bellhaven Press, London. Berkes has assembled a lively set of essays on social organization and environmental management in traditional and modern societies. Institutions for the management of common property resources are critically important to the conservation of biodiversity.

Blaikie, P. and H. Brookfield (eds.). 1987. *Land Degradation and Society*. Methuen, London. Blaikie and Brookfield, along with numerous additional contributors, develop the paradigm they call "political ecology" and give excellent examples of how inequities prevent good environmental management in developing countries.

Costanza, R. (ed.). 1991. *Ecological Economics: The Science and Management of Sustainability*. Columbia University Press, New York. Costanza has compiled the best of the early papers on ecological economics. This volume documents the conceptual diversity and breadth of application of the work of this new group of activist-scholars.

Ehrenfeld, D. 1978. *The Arrogance of Humanism*. Oxford University Press, New York. Ehrenfeld's book on the errors wrought by Western science's hopes to control nature has become a classic among biologists. A philosophical treatise that is accessible and informative.

Hall, C. A. S., C. J. Cleveland, and R. Kaufman. 1986. *Energy and Resource Quality: The Ecology of the Economic Process*. John Wiley and Sons, New York. This book provides insightful analyses of the relationships between energy, environmental systems, and the economy. It critiques neoclassical economic thinking and use the best of it along with energetic analysis.

McNeely, J. A. 1988. *Economics and Biological Diversity: Developing and Using Economic Incentives to Conserve Biological Resources*. International Union for the Conservation of Nature and Natural Resources, Gland, Switzerland. McNeely combines sound analysis with numerous applications of economic principles. This book is readily accessible to readers with little or no economic training.

Norton, B. G. (ed.). 1986. *The Preservation of Species: The Value of Biological Diversity*. Princeton University Press, Princeton, NJ. An excellent compendium on biodiversity and values, with good coverage of economics as well as the way it fits into a larger scheme of environmental and other values.

Perrings, C. K.-G. Mäler, C. Folke, C. S. Holling, and B.-O. Jansson. (eds.). 1995. *Biodiversity Loss: Economic and Ecological Issues*. Cambridge University Press, Cambridge. Perrings et al. explore the dynamic interrelationships between economic and biological systems in the process of biodiversity loss. The explorations are stimulating theoretically while providing new insights into practical policy changes.

16

The Role of Institutions and Policymaking in Conservation

Politics is the art of taking good decisions on insufficient evidence.

Lord Kennet

The obscure takes a while to see, the obvious, longer.

Anonymous

When all is said and done, and the history of conservation advances and the role of conservation biology is written in coming decades, one thing will stand out clearly: the success of conservation efforts will be measured not in numbers of research grants garnered, nor numbers of students trained, nor papers published, nor amount of money spent by governments, industry, or nongovernmental organizations on environmental issues, although these will all contribute to success. Rather, success will be measured by how well we succeed in achieving a vision of a world that simultaneously serves the needs of humans and preserves nature. Success or failure will be determined by whether or not species extinction rates are stabilized and then lowered, by how many truly natural habitats remain, by how many intact ecosystems endure, and by the degree of social justice and equity we have achieved, since these are integral to the conservation of nature. And this, in turn, will be determined not by conservation or ecological theory alone, but by how well that theory, and knowledge, and experience in all forms, are put into practice. Transforming ecological knowledge into public practice is largely the domain of institutions and policymaking.

Regardless of how well we understand the natural world, how sophisticated our theories, how accurate our computer models, how complete our empirical knowledge, or how well we incorporate indigenous knowledge, none of this will be of value if it is not put into practice. All of the information in this book and other scientific volumes is worthless until it contributes to sound conservation policy and appropriate action. Consequently, policy and the institutions that drive it are the focus of this chapter. The following chapter will present the knowledge and tools needed for the scientist to become more effective in crafting and promoting sound conservation policy.

As we begin to address the topics of policy and the institutions that put policy into action, three principles should be kept clearly in mind that should drive our understanding of policy:

1. *The humility principle*: We must recognize and accept the limitations of human knowledge, and as a result, the limits of our capacity to manage the planet.
2. *The precautionary principle*: When in doubt (and uncertainty is more the norm than the exception), we must think deeply and act thoughtfully.
3. *The reversibility principle*: We must not make irreversible changes.

We need humility to recognize that our knowledge and understanding will always be limited; "completeness," like the Holy Grail, is an unachievable goal. This places an added burden on the scholar/scientist, the activist, the manager, and the policymaker. "Managing Planet Earth," the title of the September 1989 issue of *Scientific American*, is merely a fantasy. We must recognize from the start that our limited capacity to manage nature, even at the smallest scale, makes planetary management unlikely at best, and unwise and perhaps disastrous at worst (Ehrenfeld 1993a).

The precautionary principle tells us to be very cautious when making decisions about systems we do not fully understand, which describes our relationship to both the natural and the human world. If significant doubt exists regarding a choice to be made, or a technology to be used, the decision should be made with as much caution as possible, and with long-range consequences as fully thought out as we are capable of doing (Figure 16.1). This principle also tells us not to do something that cannot be reversed later if our decision is wrong. For example, many scientists feel that destruction of tropical forests, in addition to eliminating a great deal of biological diversity, is dangerous because it could change planetary climate patterns. Although this is not certain, the reversibility principle tells us it would be unwise to continue deforestation, as it is largely irreversible.

"Let's concentrate on technology for a couple thousand years and *then* we can develop a value system."

Figure 16.1 The precautionary principle would dictate that we be very careful about new technologies or policies affecting the natural world. This creates a need for a well-developed public value system that recognizes the potential hazards of policies that are not well considered. (Modified from an unidentified source.)

Before we move further into the policies and institutions that address environmental problems, we must stop and ask what exactly we mean by an environmental "problem," or, for that matter, any type of problem. Because policies and institutions are developed to deal with "problems" of some description, a definition is in order. Most philosophers would argue that a "problem" is not defined by the present and particular situation, but by the distance between the present situation and a vision of a desired state sometime in the future. This formulation emphasizes the importance of defining and envisioning the desired, rather than the present, state. It also emphasizes analysis of where we really are and forces us to distinguish between what is *symptom* and what is *underlying cause*.

Our goal is to try to create systemic change to achieve our larger vision, not simply to focus on individual events. Therefore, along with its role in defining environmental research (below), there is a value in environmental researchers working consciously and formally with policymakers and stakeholders to envision a desired state. "Problem," then, is redefined as *the path between the present and the desired state*. Solutions require analyzing how to get from here to there, and working backward from there to here, in order to free our thinking from the potential straightjacket of the present.

"Sustainability" is a much discussed goal, particularly since the U.N. Conference on Environment and Development held in Rio de Janeiro in 1992. Much of the discussion treats sustainability as a thing to be achieved, as if one day we would become "sustainable" after a long period of unsustainability.

This confuses the issue because sustainability is a social construct, a vision that will be ever-changing (further discussed later in this chapter).

You may find parts of this chapter upsetting to your long-held notions about science, conservation, the education process, the policy process, and/or various institutions with which you are often in contact. We will challenge the status quo, accepted policies, institutions, and ways of doing business. We have no choice here, for the status quo has not worked well to date. If institutions and environmental policies were succeeding, there would be no need for this book, or for the field of conservation biology. The mere existence of this field indicates that there is something very wrong with our policies, institutions, and humanity's way of conducting its affairs. To continue along the same institutional and policy paths would merely extrapolate the present trends of degradation well into the future. Insanity, it has been suggested, is doing the same thing over and over again while expecting a different result. We challenge students and professional scientists alike to question all present conservation practices and policies (including those presented throughout this book) and to ask whether these are the best means of achieving the long-term security of biological diversity and sustainability of the human species. Are our systems and institutions working? If not, what needs to be done to achieve appropriate system change? What new practices, policies, and institutions must be developed, replacing the tired solutions that have failed?

Types of Institutions and Their Roles in Conservation

There are a number of institutions in Western society that directly and indirectly bear on the development and outcome of conservation actions and policies, both locally and throughout the world. Each has the potential to contribute significantly to conservation efforts, or to serve as a barrier to such efforts. As with all human institutions, some are functioning better than others with respect to meeting the joint needs of nature and humankind. As human institutions, they must be challenged to meet the needs of present and future generations. Our observations relate directly to the United States and do not attempt to be comprehensive, for to do so would require volumes rather than a chapter. They are meant to provoke thought about institutions with which students and scientists in the United States are familiar.

Educational Institutions

There are a number of problems facing universities and other higher educational research institutions that prevent them from being as effective in conservation as they might be. Too often they have cut themselves off from society. There is clearly a place for narrowly defined and elegant disciplinary research driven by the curiosity of researchers, but if universities are truly to be citizens of the communities in which they are located, and of the world, they must respond appropriately to the broader social concerns at the intersection of the biotic system and the human system. New incentives are needed, from within and without, that will permit students and scholars to develop competencies that can contribute to this goal.

No one today seriously denies the breadth, depth, and importance of ecological concerns to present and future generations. Yet each year, colleges and universities graduate hundreds of thousands of young men and women who will be active citizens and leaders, but who are completely unaware of, and unschooled in, matters of basic ecology that relate to their daily lives. Just as these institutions over the years have defined certain requirements as to what it means to be an educated individual, it is now necessary for colleges and universities to ensure that their graduates are ecologically literate (Orr 1992). David Orr develops this theme in a special, extended essay (Essay 16A).

ESSAY 16A

Liberalizing the Liberal Arts

From Dominion to Design

David W. Orr, Oberlin College

After reflecting on the state of education in his time, H. L. Mencken concluded that significant improvement required only that the schools be burned down and the professorate be hanged. For better or worse, the suggestion was largely ignored. Made today, however, it might have found a more receptive public ready to purchase the gasoline and rope. Americans, united on little else, seem to be of one mind in believing that their educational system, K through Ph.D., is too expensive, cumbersome, and ineffective. But they are divided on how to go about the task of reform. On one side of the debate are those who argue that the failure is due mostly to the lack of funding for laboratories, libraries, equipment, salaries, and new buildings—a view, not surprisingly, held most avidly by professional educators. On the other side are those, such as Benno Schmidt, the former president of Yale University, who propose to make education over as a business.

Both sides of the debate, nonetheless, agree on the basic aims and purposes of educational institutions, which are, first, to equip our nation with a "world-class" labor force in order to compete more effectively in the global economy, and, second, to provide each individual with the means for maximum upward mobility. In these, the purposes of education both higher and lower, there is great assurance and repose.

Education from an Ecological Perspective

There are, however, better reasons to rethink education, having to do with the issues of human survival that will dominate the world of the 21st century. Those now being educated will have to do what we, the present generation, have been unable or unwilling to do: stabilize a world population now growing at the rate of over a quarter of a million each day, reduce the emission of greenhouse gases that threaten to change the climate (perhaps disastrously), protect biological diversity now declining at perhaps 100–200 species per day, reverse the destruction of rainforests (both tropical and temperate) now being lost at the rate of 300 km^2 or more each day, and conserve soils being eroded at the rate of 65 million tons per day. They must learn how to use energy and materials efficiently. They must learn how to use solar energy. They must rebuild the economy in order to eliminate waste and pollution. They must learn how to conserve resources for the long term. They must begin the great work of repairing, as much as possible, the damage done to the earth in the past 200 years of industrialization. And they must do all of this while reducing poverty and egregious social inequities. No generation has ever faced a more daunting agenda.

For the most part, however, we are still educating the young as if there were no planetary emergency. It is widely assumed that environmental problems will be solved by technology of one sort or another. Better technology can certainly help, but the crisis is not primarily one of technology. Rather, it is one of mind, and hence one within the minds that develop and use technology. It is first and foremost a crisis of thought, perception, imagination, intellectual priorities, and loyalties. It is ultimately a crisis of education that purports to shape and refine the capacity of minds to think clearly, to imagine what could be and is not, and to act faithfully. Resolution of the great challenges of the next century will require us to reconsider the substance, process, and purposes of education at all levels and to do so, in Yale historian Jaroslav Pelikan's (1992) words, with "an intensity and ingenuity matching that shown by previous generations in obeying the command to have dominion over the planet."

From Dominion to Design

Liberal arts institutions have a crucial role to play in reshaping education. We cannot know for certain what particular skills the young will need in coming decades, but we know with great certainty that they will need to be liberally educated in the fullest sense in order to do the work of designing households, farms, institutions, communities, corporations, and economies that (1) do not emit heat-trapping gases, (2) operate on renewable energy, (3) conserve biological diversity, (4) use materials and water efficiently, and (5) recycle materials and organic wastes.

The old curriculum was shaped around the goal of extending human dominion over the earth to its fullest extent. The new curriculum will be organized around development of the analytic abilities, ecological wisdom, and practical wherewithal needed for making things that fit in a world of microbes, plants, animals, and entropy: what can be called the "ecological design arts." Ecological design requires the ability to comprehend patterns that connect, which means getting beyond the boxes we call disciplines to see things in their larger context. Ecological design is the careful meshing of human purposes with the larger patterns and flows of the natural world, and the careful study of those patterns and flows to inform human purposes.

Competence in ecological design means incorporating intelligence about how nature works into the way we think, build, and live (Wann 1990, 1996). Design applies to the making of nearly everything that directly or indirectly requires energy and materials or that governs their use. When houses, farms, neighborhoods, communities, cities, transportation systems, technologies, energy policies, and entire economies are well designed, they are in harmony with the ecological patterns in which they are embedded. When poorly designed, they undermine those larger patterns, creating pollution, higher costs, social stress, and ecological havoc. Bad design is not simply an engineering problem, although better engineering would often help. Its roots go deeper.

Good designs everywhere have certain common characteristics, including right scale, simplicity, efficient use of resources, a close fit between means and ends, durability, redundance, and resilience. They are often place-specific, or in John Todd's words, "elegant solutions predicated on the uniqueness of place." Good design also solves more than one problem at a time and promotes (1) human competence instead of addiction and dependence, (2) efficient and frugal use of resources, (3) sound regional economies, and (4) social resilience. Where good design becomes part of the social fabric at all levels, unanticipated positive side effects multiply. When people fail to design with ecological competence, unwanted negative side effects and disasters multiply.

By the evidence of pollution, violence, social decay, and waste all around us, we have designed things badly. Why? There are, I think, three primary reasons. The first is that, while energy and land were cheap and the world relatively empty, we simply did not have to master the discipline of good design. We developed extensive rather than intensive economies. Accordingly, cities sprawled, wastes were dumped into rivers and landfills, houses and automobiles got bigger and less efficient, and whole forests were converted into junk mail. Meanwhile, the know-how necessary for a diverse, frugal, intensive economy declined, and words like "convenience" became synonymous with habits of waste.

Second, design intelligence fails when greed, narrow self-interest, and individualism take over. Good design is a community process requiring people who know and value the positive things that bring them together and hold them together. Old Order Amish, for example, refuse to buy combines, not because combines would not make farming easier or more profitable, but because they would undermine the community by depriving people of the opportunity to help their neighbors. This is pound-wise and penny-foolish, the way intelligent design should be. In contrast, American cities with their extremes of poverty and opulence are the products of people who believe that they have little in common with each other. Greed, suspicion, and fear undermine good community and good design alike.

Third, poor design results from poorly equipped minds. Good design can only be done by people who understand harmony, patterns, and systems. Industrial cleverness, on the contrary, is mostly evident in the minutiae of things, not in their totality or in their overall harmony. Good design requires a breadth of view that causes people to ask how human artifacts and purposes fit within a particular culture and place. It also requires ecological intelligence, by which I mean an intimate familiarity with how nature works in a particular place.

A contemporary example of ecological design is to be found in John Todd's "living machines," which are carefully orchestrated ensembles of plants, aquatic animals, technology, solar energy, and high-tech materials that purify wastewater, but without the expense, energy use, and chemical hazards of conventional sewage treatment technology. In Todd's words:

> People accustomed to seeing mechanical moving parts, to experiencing the noise or exhaust of internal combustion engines or the silent geometry of electronic devices, often have difficulty imagining living machines. Complex life forms, housed within strange light-receptive structures, are at once familiar and bizarre. They are both garden and machine. They are alive yet framed and contained in vessels built of novel materials. . . . Living machines bring people and nature together in a fundamentally radical and transformative way. (Todd 1991)

Todd's living machines resemble greenhouses filled with plants and aquatic animals. Wastewater enters at one end, purified water leaves at the other. In between, the work of sequestering heavy metals in plant tissues, breaking down toxics, and removing nutrients has been done by an ensemble of organisms driven by sunlight.

Ecological design also applies to the design of public policies. Governmental planning and regulation require large and often ineffective or counterproductive bureaucracies. Design, in contrast, means

> . . . the attempt to produce the outcome by establishing criteria to govern the operations of the process so that the desired result will occur more or less automatically without further human intervention. (Ophuls 1977)

In other words, well-designed policies and laws get the big things right, like prices, taxes, and standards for fairness, while preserving a high degree of freedom for people and institutions to respond in different ways. Design focuses on the structure of problems as opposed to their coefficients. For example, the Clean Air Act of 1970 required car manufacturers to install catalytic converters to remove air pollutants. Several decades later, emissions per vehicle are down substantially, but with more cars on the road, air quality is about the same. A design approach to transportation would cause us to think more about creating access to housing, schools, jobs, and recreation that eliminates the need to move lots of people and materials over long distances. A design approach would cause us to reduce dependence on automobiles by building better public transit systems, restoring railroads, and creating bike trails and walkways.

Implementing Ecological Design in the Institution

What does ecological design have to do with educational institutions? The starting point is to ask how those institutions work within the larger patterns and flows of nature on which they depend for energy, materials, water, food, and into which they discard their wastes. What impact do institutional purchases and operations have on the diversity of life on the earth? Do these institutions have a clear policy to implement state-of-the-art energy efficiency? Do they use nontoxic materials in new construction and renovations? Do they recycle organic wastes and paper? Do they purchase recycled paper and materials? Have they begun to phase out toxic substances in landscaping and maintenance? Do they use their institutional buying power to support local and regional economies? Have they begun to invest their endowments in things that preserve biological diversity and move the world in more sustainable directions? In short, do those same institutions that purport to induct the young into responsible adulthood act responsibly and imaginatively in making decisions that shape the world the young will inherit?

These are difficult and complex questions. But many colleges and universities are making significant progress in redesigning institutional operations to reduce environmental impacts while saving money at the same time. The State University of New York- Buffalo saved $3 million in 1991 by implementing a systematic energy efficiency program. They also significantly reduced the University's contribution to global warming and acid rain. For the same reasons, other institutions are implementing systematic energy policies. Hendrix College in Conway, Arkansas, is buying as much of its food as possible from local farms, thereby cutting transportation costs, improving the quality of its dining service, helping local farmers, and reducing the environmental impacts of its food service. Dozens of colleges and universities have implemented full-scale recycling programs. The University of Kansas has established an Environmental Ombudsman office to pursue cost-effective environmental reforms throughout the institution. Nationally, the Student Environmental Action Coalition in Chapel Hill and the National Wildlife Federation are helping to organize informed student involvement in issues of campus ecology (Eagan and Orr 1992).

The redesigning of institutional resource flows is a visible sign of an institution's commitment to the future. Done with intelligence and persistence, it can save money, but it also represents a significant educational opportunity. From a student's perspective, global problems appear to be abstract, remote, and mostly unsolvable. They invite apathy, or what's worse, posturing and hypocrisy. Problems in campus resource flows, in contrast, are visible, immediate, and at the right scale to be solved. Participation in projects that aim to improve the fit between the campus and the environment by increasing energy efficiency, closing waste loops, using recycled materials, supporting local economies, and designing low-impact buildings provides students with opportunities to learn the analytic and practical skills of ecological design. Such projects also provide opportunities to learn the realities of how institutions work and how, sometimes, they do not work.

This emphasis on ecological design requires an institution-wide commitment to environmental literacy that crosses discipline boundaries. Charles Knapp, President of the University of Georgia, decreed in 1991 that the university would no longer graduate environmentally illiterate students, and then set forth to develop coursework in a variety of departments to meet that goal. Tufts University has established an Ecological Literacy Institute, a summer program that attracts faculty from all departments. The Institute offers instruction and information about environmental issues and enables faculty to revise courses to include the environment and to develop new courses. There is good reason to extend the goal of environmental literacy to include administrative officials, staff, and trustees as well.

Competence in the ecological design arts finally requires extending the curriculum to include new fields of knowledge such as conservation biology, restoration ecology, ecological engineering, environmental ethics, solar design, landscape architecture, sustainable agriculture, sustainable forestry, energetics, industrial ecology, ecological economics, and least-cost, end-use analysis. A program in ecological design would weave these and similar elements together with the goal of making students smarter about systems and how specific things and processes fit in their ecological context.

Instruction in the ecological design arts aims to develop the habits of mind, analytic skills, and practical competence necessary to solve problems that are insuperable within the context that caused them in the first place. Its inclusion as an integral part of education at all levels is a recognition that the crisis of environment is solvable, but on nature's terms, not our own.

At the research level, universities have too often defined themselves along narrow disciplinary lines, with little communication among these disciplines. Thus, former biology departments have split into departments of zoology, botany, microbiology, physiology, genetics, molecular biology, and other narrow fields. The very action of dividing life sciences into separate disciplines means that communication among them is stifled, reductionism is encouraged, and, in some very important ways, knowledge is lost. David Ehrenfeld observes that " loss of knowledge and skills is now a big problem in our universities, and no subject is in greater danger of disappearing than our long-accumulated knowledge of the natural world. . . . We are on the verge of losing our ability to tell one plant or animal from another and of forgetting how the known species interact among themselves and with their environments" (Ehrenfeld 1989). When an environmental issue is confronted, it is done by groups of disparate specialists who see only a narrow slice of the overall problem, often in a way that advances their particular specialty, but does little toward addressing the real problem. This "discipline-defined approach," as opposed to an "issue-defined approach," will be discussed below.

The need for ecological literacy is critical, and the process should begin early in a student's education. At early ages it is possible to take full advantage of the natural curiosity of young people about the world around them. The environment is both gray and green—both urban and rural—and students should be introduced to ever-widening ecosystem concerns, beginning in their neighborhoods and expanding to the globe. If primary and secondary educational institutions, and all of the other institutions where young people learn (clubs, churches, television, movies, and so forth), do not do this, these students are less likely to cultivate an interest in and appreciation for environmental issues later in life. Public conservation education for all ages is discussed by Susan Jacobson in Essay 16B

ESSAY 16B
Nature Conservation through Education

Susan K. Jacobson, University of Florida

- *Declining populations of seabirds . . .*
- *Contaminated river systems . . .*
- *Ecosystems in need of prescribed fire . . .*

Solutions to conservation and resource management challenges such as these have been found through conservation education programs.

Education is an essential management tool that recognizes the central role of people in all nature conservation efforts. Indeed, although a conservation goal may be focused on a biological problem, effective conservation strategies must incorporate communication and education programs designed to affect people's awareness, attitudes, and behaviors toward natural resources and land management.

The goals of conservation education are many, and include

- Increasing public knowledge and consequent support for the development of appropriate environmental management and conservation policies
- Fostering a conservation ethic that will enable responsible natural resource stewardship
- Altering patterns of natural resource consumption
- Enhancing the technical capabilities of natural resource managers
- Incorporating resource management concerns into private sector and government policymaking processes

Most conservation education programs aim to influence long-term behavior, a goal of great complexity. Debate rages among educators regarding the relationship between people's conservation knowledge and attitudes and their subsequent behaviors, and how to best target these domains through education programs. Increased awareness of a conservation problem rarely guarantees meaningful behavioral changes in support of conservation. Conservation educators initially suggested that the learning process necessary for conservation action passes from ignorance to awareness, appreciation, understanding, concern, and finally action (e.g., Henderson 1984). Yet other researchers have found that many factors affect environmentally responsible behavior.

One popular model includes an individual's knowledge of environmental issues and action strategies, action skills, and several personality factors. Among these factors are the degree of responsibility and commitment felt toward the environment, one's attitudes toward the environment, and the perception of one's ability to effect change (Hines et al. 1986/1987). These variables influence people to act in accord with a stewardship ethic. Thus, conservation education programs must affect not only their audience's knowledge about the environment, but also other beliefs and behavior, in order to promote environmentally responsible actions in the future.

Systematic planning enables conservation educators to incorporate cognitive as well as affective and behavioral domains into a program. An assessment of needs involving all stakeholders in conservation problems can help to determine appropriate educational interventions and can identify and involve target audiences in the process (Jacobson 1995). Once specific goals and objectives for an education program are delineated, alternative methods and approaches for each audience can be considered. The examples that follow highlight the plethora of methods that have been successfully integrated with conservation programs to achieve specific results. These projects demonstrate the need for baseline information to compare with data collected after programs are implemented. This information provides concrete evidence of changes in participant knowledge, attitudes, or behaviors, and ultimately in the targeted wildlife or landscape. This form of program evaluation is helpful not only in providing accountability for program success, but also in revealing program areas that need modification.

The ingredients of a conservation education program that dramatically reversed the decline of seabird populations, such as Razorbills (*Alca torda*), Common Murres (*Uria aalge*), and Atlantic Puffins (*Fratercula arctica*), along the north shore of the Gulf of St. Lawrence in Canada included the following activities: residential youth programs on seabird ecology and wildlife law held at an island sanctuary; local student instructors with environmental training; conservation clubs; school seabird curriculum materials and theater productions; ornithological and pedagogical training for 50 local volunteers and staff; seabird posters, calendars, and other publications; radio, film, and television specials on seabirds; and study tours for leaders of national and regional conservation groups.

The Quebec-Labrador Foundation, in collaboration with the Canadian Wildlife Service, developed the conservation education program as part of their seabird management plan in 1978 (Blanchard 1995). The education program resulted in decreasing human predation on seabirds and eggs, as well as positively changing the conservation knowledge and behaviors of local residents. Initial interviews with residents of communities where bird population declines were most severe revealed a lack of public knowledge concerning wildlife regulations and a high occurrence of illegal hunting. Ten years after implementation of the education program, significant increases in seabird populations were recorded. A concomitant follow-up survey of community members revealed an improvement in residents' attitudes concerning seabirds and a decrease in perceived need to consume them.

This program demonstrates many aspects of successful conservation education. The audience participated in all aspects of program development. Experiential and interdisciplinary approaches were employed, from hands-on monitoring of seabirds to community theater productions starring puffin-costumed children. A comprehensive system was designed to monitor and evaluate program success—in this case through censuses of the biological resources and through before/after surveys of the knowledge, attitudes, and behaviors of the targeted audiences.

Understanding the knowledge levels and attitudes of the public is essential for effective resource management and the first step in designing an education program. An example from a Department of Defense land management initiative demonstrates the importance of assessing and involving key audiences in the process. The Natural Resources Division staff at Eglin Air Force Base in the Florida Panhandle realized the need for public support as they adopted an ecosystem management plan in the early 1990s. The new plan called for increased prescribed fires on the 463,000-acre forested base. Fires covering up to 50,000 acres/year were needed to restore the longleaf pine forest, which was once the most widespread ecosystem in the Southeast, but has dwindled to only 2% of its former range.

A survey of the public in surrounding counties, however, revealed that only 12% of the residents realized that fire was a natural and beneficial process in the longleaf pine ecosystem (Jacobson and Marynowski 1997). Imagine the public indignation if large fires and the accompanying smoke disturbed their communities unannounced. Fortunately, Eglin resource managers incorporated a comprehensive public education program into their management plan. Educational materials—mass media, publications, and public events—significantly increased audience awareness of the benefits of fire. Continuity and repetition of conservation information should continue to increase public knowledge and support for appropriate forest management at Eglin as the ecosystem plan is fully implemented.

Holistic approaches to conservation education such as these are less common within the formal school system. However, because most environmental attitudes are formed during childhood, schoolchildren are an important target for conservation educators. Conservation education in schools varies among countries in content, scope, and disciplinary base, and often is overlooked or ignored relative to traditional subjects. Extracurricular materials and innovative curricular supplements often provide the main exposure for students to environmental conservation knowledge and skill formation.

A challenge for conservation educators working in the schools is finding instructional strategies that can enable students not only to learn about local and global conservation issues, but also to learn how to act in response to environmental problems. To be effective, conservation education cannot be confined within the boundaries of a classroom, but rather must operate within the context of the environment it seeks to conserve. The Global Rivers Environmental Education Network (GREEN) exemplifies an ideal approach—hands-on, participatory, and interdisciplinary—to involving children in the complexities of environmental problem solving. The GREEN program, developed by the University of Michigan (Stapp et al. 1995), is a water quality monitoring program that has been adopted in more than 60 countries.

GREEN began in a Michigan biology class on the banks of the Huron River in 1984. Students became alarmed about water quality when several windsurfers, including a student at Huron High School, contracted Hepatitis A after falling off their boards into the river. The students' concern and subsequent testing of the polluted water by the teacher prompted a University of Michigan class to develop a water quality monitoring program appropriate for the secondary school students. The program included instructional materials, such as maps of the local watershed, a manual outlining standards for performing nine water quality tests, material on monitoring water for macroinvertebrates, a slide-tape presentation, and a set of water quality testing kits.

At the Huron River, students found high fecal coliform counts—over 2000 colonies per 100 milliliters of water (counts should not exceed 200 for activities such as windsurfing and swimming). Student actions resulted in the discovery of faulty underground storm drains as the pollution source, and led to correction of the problem by the city. Enthusiasm for the program from this initial school resulted in the expansion of GREEN nationally and globally. Now an international communication network allows students to share their experiences of watershed quality and diversity across geographic and cultural boundaries. International workshops held in 18 countries have allowed educators to exchange ideas on watershed programs appropriate for different geographic areas around the world. For countries with access to computers, a series of GREEN International Computer Conferences have been established, providing an interactive computer network with an international data base on water quality, as well as a source for the exchange of ideas on river conservation and restoration. The network now has more than 3000 participants from 80 countries.

Despite success stories such as these, conservation education around the world still lacks funding, resources, and support. Widespread methods for reaching adult and youth audiences are still lacking, and conservation education has not been institutionalized into the formal educational system in most countries. A survey of teenagers in England, Australia, the United States, and Israel revealed that mass media—radio, television, and the press—were students' most important source of information on environmental issues (Blum 1987). Yet conservation educators typically rely on publications and curriculum supplements (Archie et al. 1993), and biologists seldom embrace the media or the public.

Conservation education is needed at many levels and in many forms. New approaches by conservation educators that incorporate mass media tools and innovative advertising techniques would strengthen public awareness of the need for conservation. Concurrently, more widespread programs incorporating participatory, experiential techniques into project activities would further pro-conservation attitudes and behaviors. Toward this end, conservation education programming must become better integrated into conservation strategies. Only people's values and their consequent motivation and action will dictate whether we preserve our planet's wild species and the ecosystems that support us all.

Governments

Virtually all government institutions, whether their focus is local, state, regional, national, or international, suffer from the same problem: they are vertically oriented. Thus, there are agencies that deal separately with education, agriculture, finance and the economy, international affairs, commerce, health and safety, defense, the environment, and so forth (Figure 16.2). It is a fact, however, that most human and environmental problems are horizontal, and do not fit neatly into the boxes of a bureaucratic structure. This is especially true of such major concerns as biodiversity protection and human population growth. Each of these problems affects, and is deeply affected by, actions in any of the traditional areas. These effects are often exacerbated by the fact that, for example, ecosystem concerns are measured in decades and generations, whereas the political "needs" of traditional agencies are often measured in the months and years leading up to the next election.

Processes for adjudicating conflicts between these horizontal concerns and traditional, vertically structured agencies are largely missing. There is an urgent need to find out on whose desk the buck stops, and to ensure that that person can reflect the needs and desires of both present and future generations. Unless government institutions that seriously concern themselves with the long-term public good can be developed, ecosystem and human losses will continue. Political time frames (especially reelection) are much shorter than ecological (let alone evolutionary) time frames; this is a major reason why institutions focus on such short-sighted goals. There is unfortunately no perceived political constituency for the future, nor any politics of sustainability.

Many government agencies work at cross-purposes with other agencies (see Essay 1C). For example, the U.S. Forest Service has, as a major mandate, the production of harvestable timber in the billions of board feet per year. At the same time, it and the U.S. Fish and Wildlife Service have a legal obligation to maintain biodiversity that is directly dependent upon those trees. Thus, while the Forest Service cuts old-growth forests, Fish and Wildlife tries to maintain endangered species such as the Spotted Owl and Red-cockaded

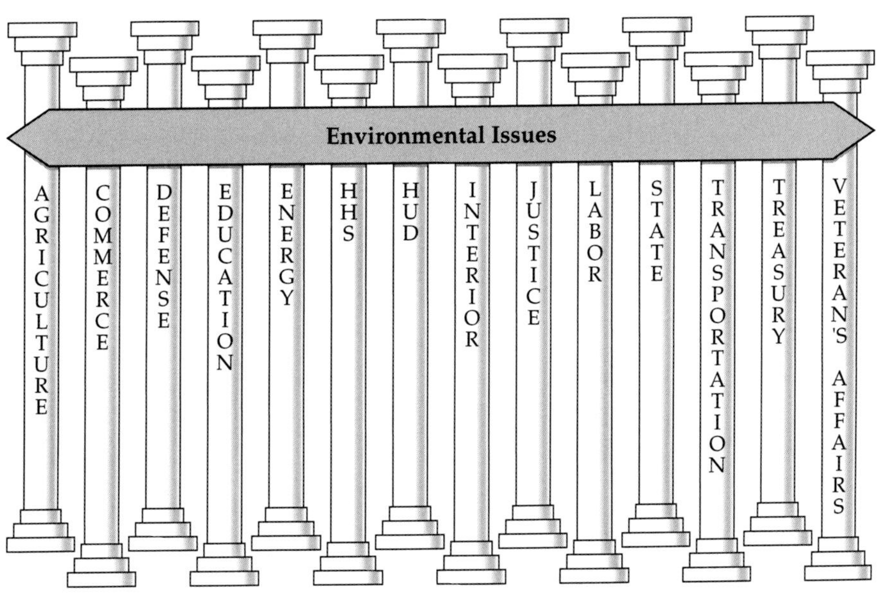

Figure 16.2 The federal government of the United States is organized in a vertical fashion around 14 departments that have representatives on the President's Cabinet. Each department is concerned with a particular aspect of human existence, but many issues, including environmental ones, cut across the boundaries of all the departments.

Woodpecker. Departments of public health in many states actively raise mosquitofishes (*Gambusia affinis* and *G. holbrooki*) and distribute them in natural water bodies in the mistaken belief that they will eliminate mosquitoes (Courtenay and Meffe 1989), while other agencies simultaneously work to remove mosquitofishes as exotic pests because they are so dangerous to native faunas. The U.S. Department of Agriculture spends large sums of money subsidizing tobacco farmers, while the Department of Health and Human Services spends large sums educating citizens to the deadly dangers of smoking. Thus, the government inadvertently subsidizes production of lung cancer while promoting higher health care costs. These examples could go on for pages.

It would seem logical that government agencies, which all fly the same national flag, should all be on the same side, whether in conservation, human health, or any other issue. Horizontal policy consistency seems a reasonable goal, but it is difficult to achieve within the vertical structure of government agencies. This problem parallels the lack of real interdisciplinarity in universities, which of course is where policymakers receive their training.

Part of the reason that government agencies frequently work at cross-purposes is that there are no fundamental, underlying visions and philosophies that guide all government action regardless of political party in power or short-term needs. For example, adopting ecological design principles as the underlying philosophy of our existence and our vision of the future (see Essay 16A; Wann 1996) would clearly dictate how all government agencies should operate. It would also ensure that money spent and directions taken by one administration would not be undermined by the different philosophies of the next administration, which are yet again dismantled by the following administration.

Instead, each agency seems to have its own, separate mission, fiercely defended and divorced from the missions of other agencies. Witness the decision in November 1993 of the Food and Drug Administration to allow the use of a genetically engineered drug, bovine somatotropin, to increase the amount of milk produced by dairy cows, without taking into account the social and economic effects of the drug's introduction, especially on agriculture: smaller dairy farmers are likely to be forced from their farms as the price of milk falls and as production on larger farms increases. The corporate scientists who developed the drug were not responsible for assessing the unanticipated consequences of its introduction; they were simply practicing traditional, linear scientific thought.

Rather than agencies continuing on a course of aggressively seeking expanded funding and protection of their own policy territories, what is needed is a vision of a desirable future, created in a truly participatory process involving scientists, policymakers, activists, and other stakeholders, that would serve to bring together disparate goals, perspectives, and mandates into a coherent whole.

Nongovernmental Organizations

It is hard to categorize nongovernmental organizations (NGOs) under one heading. Some are massive, with large budgets and global concerns, like the World Resources Institute, the Environmental and Energy Study Institute, the New York Botanical Garden, and The Nature Conservancy. Others are small and focus on a single community, region, or ecosystem, such as the Oregon Natural Resources Council, the Southwest Network on Environmental and Economic Justice, the Desert Fishes Council, and the SouthWest Organizing Project. Some carry out research with or without a policy focus, and in some respects are indistinguishable from universities. Some, both large and small, are potential consumers of knowledge as they organize and advocate for the environment at community, state, regional, national, or global levels.

Unfortunately, the media refers to "environmental groups" and "environmentalists" without making distinctions among them. The larger, traditional groups, often located in Washington and New York, are staffed by "experts"—lawyers, scientists, economists. They may have dues-paying members, but they are usually not accountable to them. They are often prepared to compromise to get the best deal possible, without taking into account or consulting with those who suffer most from environmental problems. Community and grassroots groups reflect "experience"—their members are often the objects of environmental assaults. These groups are accountable to members and are more holistic in their approach to solutions because they understand that jobs, environment, health, housing, civil rights, and other issues cannot be separated in the real world (see Shabecoff 1993; Gottlieb 1993; Bullard 1993; Bryant 1995; Dowie 1995).

The nongovernmental community plays an important role by providing a window on the real world for conservation scientists. NGOs can assist in the process of identifying knowledge needs because they are often in a position to listen to the needs of stakeholders and policymakers more directly than are scientists. As organizers and advocates at local, state, national, and even international levels, NGOs that are accountable to their constituencies can reflect the voices of people who are not usually heard in policy debates. As such, they can contribute to democratic decision making. NGOs can also serve as policy analysts and policy synthesizers, taking the results of more narrowly defined research and packaging them for various audiences. Finally, NGOs are potentially important employers of graduates in conservation biology, whether their interests are in further research or in the uses of research for social goals.

Coalition building among the traditional nongovernmental organizations and among the grassroots and community groups is increasing. Unfortunately, there is still too little cooperation between the traditional and the grassroots groups, in part because of their different experiences and different cultures. Alliances based upon trust and mutual understanding could contribute greatly to the democratization of the environmental movement. Linkages with other organizations concerned with health, jobs, justice, and other social concerns could also contribute greatly to efforts to deal with problems that do not come in tidy boxes labeled "environment" or "conservation." Anything that contributes to more holistic solutions will benefit people and nature.

Nongovernmental organizations often play an essential role in experimenting with new approaches to old problems. The Center for Rural Affairs in Walthill, Nebraska, for example, has developed an innovative approach to saving economically viable family farms, preserving communities, and promoting environmentally sound and sustainable agriculture. Funds raised through a unique bond issue will help younger family farmers to buy land from older farmers wishing to retire. The Center will help to develop the farm plans, and will also provide technical assistance for implementing environmentally sound and economically viable farming methods. Preservation of the farms will also contribute to community revitalization.

Business

Businesses, and the economic frameworks upon which many business decisions are made, present serious challenges to the conservation of biodiversity. So long as the concern of business seems to be the bottom line after the next quarter, rather than quality of life and community integrity after the next quarter century, ecosystem protection is not likely to be given high priority (see Chapter 15). So long as a standing redwood, or an Amazonian rainforest, has no "economic value" until it becomes lumber, nature will be consumed. So long as industrial tragedies (such as the oil spill from the *Exxon Valdez*) and natural tragedies exacerbated by human follies (such as the flooding of the Mississippi River in the summer of 1993) are contributors to the calculation of the nation's gross national product, nature will be shortchanged. So long as waste from production processes is seen as an "eternality" and not as a real cost of doing business, the biosphere will lose. Farmer, novelist, and essayist Wendell Berry has defined a community as "a neighborhood of humans in place plus the place itself: its soil, its water, its air, and all the families and tribes of the non-human creatures that belong to it" (Berry 1993). So long as production and place are separated, corporations are likely to have little commitment to place, and as a result, to the humans and ecosystems in place. So long as the market system gives little value either to equity or to ecology, ecosystems will be disadvantaged.

There is little doubt that businesses at all levels can be more environmentally sensitive (Hawken 1993; Figure 16.3). Whether business philosophy and practice can truly be congruent with conservation remains a great, unanswered question. For the sake of ecosystems and humankind, we must try to ensure that the answer is yes. Unfortunately, however, the evidence to date suggests that the need for institutional and system changes is only vaguely perceived by some, and accepted by fewer, although road maps for environmentally sensitive businesses and economies have been laid out (Daly 1991; Hawken 1993; Ashworth 1995). The often-used term "sustainable corporation" is an oxymoron. Corporations can and are achieving greater environmental sensitivity in their products and processes. They cannot, however, under present systemic constraints, address the issues of democracy, community, and justice that are essential elements of a vision of sustainability (Viederman 1996). These views are further pursued in Chapter 19 in the section on "the tragedy of the commons."

"Sir, would you take this latest warning of ecological disaster and pooh-pooh it for me?"

Figure 16.3 Business interests the world over generally have a poor reputation regarding their concern for, or understanding of, environmental issues. Many business interests are now "greening," that is, becoming more environmentally astute; this often makes economic as well as ecological sense. (Drawing by Dana Fradon; © 1992 The New Yorker Magazine, Inc.)

Consumers

Obviously, consumer preferences will have an important effect on the conservation of biodiversity. Consumers are limited in their choices to the goods and services that businesses are willing to provide—and those businesses often create wants that people had not had before. However, consumers can, have, and will continue to change the way business does business if they can be organized effectively; for example, witness the growing demand for "dolphin-free tuna" and many other environmentally friendly products in the United States (Figure 16.4). To continue and grow, this trend will require a much deeper understanding of the importance of the environment for oneself and one's children. The environment cannot be perceived as a special interest, but must be recognized for what it is: the playing field on which all human interests occur. Like businesses, consumers will have to understand the full social costs (as differentiated from prices) of their activities, and ultimately exhibit a willingness to pay those costs (Durning 1992). Until now, many businesses and consumers have been getting a free lunch, paid for by the environment.

Figure 16.4 Environmentally "friendly" or "green" product lines, such as these paper and cleaning products, are experiencing greater consumer demand and are becoming more available. (Photograph by John Goodman, courtesy of Seventh Generation.)

Legal Institutions

Much is made of the fact that the United States is a litigious society. However, it is important to understand the roots of the legislative emphasis that has given so much attention to the courts. Environmental regulation did not come about simply because Congress or other legislative bodies wanted to take control. It was a response to the failure on the part of various actors, including businesses, to perform voluntarily in ways that met the needs of the common good. For example, chemical companies were slow to react to the observation of the ozone hole and the need to stop production of CFCs. The Clean Air Act and international environmental legislation seemed to be the appropriate mechanisms at a given point in time to reduce pollution that was deleterious to the health and safety of society. Today there are still circumstances in which businesses are fighting regulations when, by meeting them, they would actually reduce their own costs. Understanding and change occur slowly. Change often involves a sense of repudiation of what one has done before, which is psychologically difficult for any of us to accept. Change is also difficult when time frames are perceived narrowly.

Underlying much of the concern about regulation is the assertion, usually from business, that we are a paranoid society that is too risk-averse. Part of the problem, however, is in the very definition of risk and how we assess it. In the first place, risk is rarely assessed by the people who are exposed to the risk. Second, our methods of assessment are at best primitive. We may be able to determine, for example, the relationship of one pollutant to the incidence of one kind of cancer. However, in the real world, we are all exposed to a "pollution soup," a variety of pollutants delivered in different concentrations, in different media—air, water, food. In addition, we are all different in our physical and genetic characteristics, and therefore react differently to the "pollution soups" we are served. There is new evidence that the "soup" may be more toxic by some orders of magnitude than one might assume from simply summing the parts (Arnold 1996; Colborn et al. 1996). Thus, how can one even approximate a serious assessment of risk from pollution? Here, the precautionary principle comes into play: better to be safe than sorry. Ginsburg (1993) addresses such questions in greater detail.

Consider the case of Rose Marie Augustine of South Tucson, Arizona. There are 30 tidy, simple houses on her block in a predominantly Hispanic area. Twenty-eight of the 30 families in those houses have experienced deaths from cancer, or have a cancer patient still living. Their drinking water is believed to have been polluted with the industrial solvent trichloroethylene, TCE, which was used in great quantities by the Hughes Aircraft plant nearby. Scientists who studied this neighborhood did not deny the correlations that were all too obvious, but they were unwilling to assign causation (Lavelle and Coyle 1992). Humility would suggest that we cannot know the cause of the cancers for sure, but the evidence argues that the problem is real. Perhaps the question to be asked is whether the scientists who performed the risk assessment would themselves be willing to live next door to Ms. Augustine and drink the water, given the situation they have observed. If not, then how much credence should be given to their findings? As biochemist Erwin Chargoff (1980) has observed, "where expertise prevails, wisdom vanishes."

It is often argued that the United States as a whole has become risk-averse, and that we are also afraid of the wrong risks. It is suggested, for example, that we pay too much attention to a chemical that might cause one extra cancer death in 10 million, while allowing cigarette smoking and car driving by millions of people, both of which kill people by the hundreds of thousands. There is, of course, legitimacy to this argument. What it fails to take into account, however, is the unequal distribution of the risks. Cigarette smoking and driving are volitional—we can choose to do them or not. Exposure to chemicals is, however, disproportionately felt by minorities and the poor. Chemical exposures are imposed upon people rather than subject to their free will and choice (Chavis and Lee 1987; Lavelle and Coyle 1992).

Alternative means of regulation have been proposed, and it is clear that we should explore all avenues to a better system. However, most that have been proposed to date are significantly flawed. For example, to assume that voluntary compliance for the common good will preserve systems is at best naive, given the fact, as already noted, that regulation became necessary in the absence of voluntary compliance. Similarly, while so-called market-based approaches may have some applicability, the market, by failing to deal adequately with both equity and ecology, starts as a flawed instrument.

Religious Institutions

There has been a long debate among scholars concerning the role that Judeo-Christian teachings have played in humankind's destruction of the environment (see Chapter 2). Do these teachings suggest that we are conquerors of the land—"be fruitful and multiply"—or stewards? Has the Judeo-Christian ethic done more harm or good for the environment?

Whatever the past debate, organized religion in the United States is now beginning to take the challenge of stewardship seriously (Baker 1996). Churches and synagogues are preaching on the environment, and there is pressure for church-owned lands to be managed in a sustainable and environmentally sound manner. Theological schools are training seminarians about the interface between religion and the environment. These efforts are all part of a major interfaith program instituted late in 1993 that will underline the injunction to revere God's creation and to protect it (Joint Appeal 1992). Because changes in the underlying value systems of human societies are critical to achieving conservation goals, religious values and teachings can play a vital role in creating a new human relationship with the earth. However, those teachings must move beyond self-salvation for an afterlife to incorporate planetary salvation now.

Examples of such a transformation can be found in rural parts of Latin America and the Philippines, where a religious movement known as "liberation theology" has begun to make connections between poverty and environmental degradation. Clergy in this movement have recognized a common pattern: poor farmers are displaced from relatively fertile lands by highly capitalized commercial agriculture. These displaced farmers often end up either in urban slums or on ecologically fragile and agriculturally marginal lands. Because sustainable agriculture is not possible on these marginal lands, the farmers continue to exploit new lands, usually by cutting forests, inadvertently destroying biodiversity. These experiences have led some clergy to argue that marginalized small farmers and degradation of biodiversity are endpoints of the same process—exploitative economic growth—and they are actively working to change this pattern.

The Media

Western industrial society at the end of the 20th century suffers from "infoglut," a satiation of information, made all the more apparent in cyberspace. Consequently, it is likely that all messages become weakened. In addition, the messages come in small boxes, and the interrelationships among the boxes are hardly ever drawn. For example, during the 1993 New York mayoral election, the front page of the *New York Times* showed side-by-side articles on crime and the economy; neither mentioned the other issue, and the linkages between the two were never made.

The range of opinions voiced through the media frequently reflects the needs and positions of the well-to-do, while the needs of the earth are heard only partially, if at all. For example, in 1993, the *New York Times* published three "advertorials" supporting NAFTA (the North American Free Trade Agreement), but the high cost of advertising in these special sections precluded the participation of NGOs opposing NAFTA.

The news media, almost by definition, focuses on immediate problems and not on long-term education and trends. Thus, it is difficult to build up the base of knowledge that makes it possible for the citizenry as a whole to understand events in their systemic context. Furthermore, it is not clear whether the plethora of "nature" programs on television, picturing animals and ecosystems near and far, contribute more to the true appreciation of nature and the desire to experience it and save it, or to the passivity of the "couch potato."

When one also considers the decline in literacy and reading in the United States, and the focus on television as our main source of news and information, the problem becomes exacerbated. If it is not visual and quick, the message is unlikely to get through. Many of the changes that concern conservation biologists are not of the dramatic sort that lend themselves to this form of public information. And then again, after a while, people may just tire of seeing what they perceive to be the same thing they have seen before. Do all the pretty places and exotic animals eventually begin to look alike?

Another problem with the media relates to scientists themselves. Journalists suggest that scientists do not know how to speak effectively to them and through them to laypeople. When asked a question, scientists may offer reprints of their published papers, rather than explaining their work in understandable terms. Or, perhaps worse, scientists go into a detailed and complicated explanation as if they were speaking to a colleague rather than a communicator. Scientists need to learn how to communicate in ways that maintain the integrity of their thinking without glazing over the eyes of the people they are trying to reach. They must understand and use the language and culture of the people with whom they are speaking, rather than assuming a superior air that destroys their capacity to communicate. This can be a great challenge, however. Ecological or economic concepts are generally too complicated for the short "sound bites" that have become the currency of the modern news media. Similarly, the media also need to change the way they present this type of information to the public. An example of how the media present an environmental issue is illustrated in Essay 16C by Erika Sherman and Ron Carroll.

ESSAY 16C

Newspaper Coverage of the Spotted Owl/Old-Growth Forest Controversy
Information or Polarization?

Erika Sherman and C. Ronald Carroll, University of Georgia

A highly polarized debate continues over saving the Northern Spotted Owl in the ancient Douglas fir forests of the Pacific Northwest. This debate has become one of the most divisive and bitter in U.S. environmental history. Timber workers say environmentalists are trying to take away their livelihoods. Environmental advocates say the timber industry has already destroyed most of the forest, and has itself put timber workers in jeopardy. Politicians toss arguments back and forth in a continuing stalemate, while government agencies question each other's policies, and the courts weigh various points. Although research scientists from the public agencies charged with protection of the owl and management of the forest, as well as university-based researchers, have much to contribute toward resolving the conflict, their views are seldom represented in news media coverage.

Before the debate began, jobs in the Northwest timber industry had already begun to decline. According to the U.S. Department of Labor's *Occupational Outlook Handbooks*, this decline began as early as the mid-1970s. At that time, the Department of Labor projected that employment in logging and lumber mills as a whole would decline through the 1980s, due to labor-saving machinery and modernization of logging and milling procedures. This decline was projected despite expected increases in the demand for lumber. However, due to recession, demand did not increase as much as predicted, so the job decline was worse than expected. In addition, other factors played a role in job declines in the Northwest timber industry, such as an increase in exports and the movement of some of the industry to the South. The news media's attention to the Spotted Owl's plight occurred in this milieu.

The issues surrounding protection of the owl reflect difficult societal choices that must be made to achieve stewardship of our natural heritage. Among these are how we balance economic and ecological considerations in the management of our few remaining ancient forests and other natural lands and waters, the future of timber and other industries that depend on natural resources, and how we handle our social responsibilities toward changing industries and displaced workers. The media have covered parts of the Spotted Owl debate, reporting on events as they occurred. Although the news media often deny that they are primarily a public information forum, it is likely that these news stories have been the main source from which the public has obtained most of its knowledge about the issues involved. The implication here is that the public's (and even politicians') knowledge, attitudes, and actions regarding such heated environmental issues could partly depend on the type of information available from the media.

In this context, it makes sense to analyze how the media have covered the Spotted Owl/old-growth forest issue. Have the media tended to portray the inflammatory, polarizing nature of the issues (i.e., owls vs. jobs), or have they attempted to chronicle the complex context of the problem? One way to analyze the media's approach is to examine the sources used in news stories and the different parts of the issue's context that have been covered. For example, if the most common sources were environmental advocates and industry representatives, the resulting picture might be more polarized than if the most common sources were the scientists and economists studying the issues and developing management plans. In terms of context, we would want to know whether only owls have been mentioned as a cause of timber industry problems, or whether other factors have been discussed as well.

The selection of sources directly affects what information is reported and emphasized. It seems obvious that the use of credible scientific sources can affect the way science stories are reported, and how they are received by the public. Yet studies show that authoritative scientific sources are little used by the news media, even in stories that deal primarily with scientific issues. Frequently, the few independent scientists who are consulted tend to be "celebrity scientists" (Nobel Prize winners, book authors, and the like) who have no direct involvement in the research (e.g., see Sheperd 1981).

A study of television coverage of environmental crises (Nimmo and Combs 1985) showed the following breakdown of sources used: government or corporate officials: 54%; citizen bystanders: 28%; scientific experts and interest group representatives combined: 18%. A study by Greenberg et al. (1985) of television environmental news sources found that 35% of the stories gave no sources at all. Scientists who had direct connections to the environmental issues generally were used only in longer "investigative" pieces. A most telling finding was that sources with contrasting viewpoints were used twice as often as would be expected by chance.

The emphasis that the news media place on providing contrasting viewpoints is a naive and illusory pursuit of "balance." Carried to its extreme, this approach gives the opinions of the lone dissident equivalent standing to the consensus viewpoint of a large scientific community. By this denigration of science, the news media mislead the public.

We located newspaper articles dealing with the Northern Spotted Owl or the old-growth forests of the Pacific Northwest using two data base indices. The Newsbank Electronic Index was used to obtain articles from small regional newspapers throughout the United States. This data base was crucial in providing articles from smaller newspapers in the Northwest, though articles about the Spotted Owl from any newspaper in any region were included in the study. Ninety-eight separate articles from 26 different newspapers were obtained, covering January 1990 to August 1992, the period of greatest interest by the news media in this issue. The Newspaper Abstracts data base, which indexes 29 major U.S. newspapers, was used to locate national news articles on the Spotted Owl, covering April 1989 to September 1992; 198 articles were obtained from 11 newspapers. In both data bases, the terms "Spotted Owl," "ancient forests," "Northwest forests" and "old-growth forests" were used to locate the articles. Editorial and other commentary articles were eliminated from consideration, as were articles repeated in identical form in morning and evening papers or in several newspapers through a wire service. Our sample gives a comprehensive picture of all newspaper articles dealing with the Spotted Owl/old-growth forests issue published during the years when these stories were most frequent in the media.

In the 98 articles from smaller, regional newspapers, the following breakdown of sources was found: industry representatives, 110; environmental advocates, 67; politicians, 67; government agency spokespersons (non-research), 66; research scientists, 14; miscellaneous, 11; academic economists, 4. (Each number represents one source cited in one article, no matter how many times it was used in that one article. Some sources were used in more than one article, and some were used more heavily than others within a single article. There were no instances in which a source fit in more than one category at the same time.)

In the 198 articles from major newspapers, the breakdown of total sources used was as follows: industry representatives, 180; environmental advocates, 150; politicians, 94; government agency spokespersons (non-research), 91; miscellaneous, 20; research scientists, 17; academic economists, 2.

In terms of the factors mentioned as contributing to the timber industry's problems, the following breakdown was found in the regional newspaper articles: owl only, 58 articles; log exports, 9 articles; mismanagement/overcutting, 8 articles; soft demand/recession, 8 articles; automation, 4 articles; environmental protection needs, 4 articles; aging industry cycle, 1 article; poor restocking of trees, 1 article.

The distribution of factors was similar in the articles from major newspapers: owl only, 129 articles; log exports, 29 articles; automation, 15 articles; mismanagement/overcutting, 14 articles; soft demand/recession, 9 articles; aging industry cycle, 9 articles; shift of industry to South, 4 articles; Canadian imports, 2 articles; industry takeovers, 1 article.

News articles on the Spotted Owl controversy used few scientists, economists, or experts as sources. Perhaps such sources, if well chosen, could have brought more information and a better sense of the larger context to the coverage of this issue and, by reducing polarization, could have contributed to a more reasoned resolution. The heaviest reliance in these articles was on industry representatives and environmental advocates, clearly polarized groups. In terms of the many factors contributing to the plight of the Northwest timber industry, overwhelming emphasis was placed on the owl, with minimal discussion of other factors in this complex context. It seems likely that the public did not have enough information to perceive the controversy as more than a power struggle between owl advocates and timber workers. Our findings closely parallel those of Glynn and Tims (1982), who conducted a content analysis of 511 news articles on the snail darter/Tellico Dam controversy of the 1970s, an Endangered Species Act case similar to that of the owl in debate intensity.

There are several reasons why reporters make poor use of scientific experts. Journalists rely on spokespersons who are likely to be administrators or "celebrity" authorities because these are the people who most frequently offer science news items (Sheperd 1981). Technical experts often are not adept at making highly complex information understandable (Salomone et al. 1990), and many scientists are unwilling to deal with journalists (Dunwoody 1986). Scientific issues do not lend themselves to being handled in the usual "who-what-when-where-why" format of standard news stories. Many journalists covering science are untrained in science (Friedman 1983). Daily deadlines do not allow journalists enough time to find and reach many experts (Friedman 1986). Editors and news producers consider technical/scientific information uninteresting and give it little space and time (Salomone et al. 1990). Finally, scientific sources tend not to fit into the journalistic paradigm of balancing the various "sides" of an issue (Greenberg et al. 1989).

How can coverage of environmental issues be improved? One such effort is the Media Resource Service of the Scientists' Institute for Public Information, which has a toll-free telephone system (and other resources) that journalists can use to quickly locate appropriate scientific experts willing to serve as sources for a news story. Another approach being developed is a series of environmental casebooks for journalists. These casebooks would explain the scientific bases of critical environmental issues at national/international and regional levels. They also would provide directories of credible and appropriate scientists who are willing to interact with journalists (scientists who are considered experts by other scientists). Such casebooks could be developed in part through workshops designed to improve communication between journalists and environmental scientists. The bottom line is that we must find better ways to develop consensus among all stakeholders so that environmental conflicts may be reduced. Even in the best of circumstances, such consensus is difficult to achieve; polarizing media approaches only make the situation more difficult. Conservation biologists must find effective ways to work with the press, to understand their unique circumstances, and thereby to carry science to the people.

Institutional and Policy Challenges for Conservation Biology

Students and professionals in conservation and other scientific fields often slip into a narrow, comfortable, and naive worldview: that conservation (or their particular discipline) is central to public thought, that everyone else cares about the discipline as much as they do, and that if only politicians, bureaucrats, and activists would adopt their perspective, then all would be well. The world is, however, much more complex than that. The public and policymakers usually do care about the issues, but often do not know how to respond to scientists and conservationists, whose frequently contradictory views add confusion rather than confirmation to their perceptions of the actions needed. Consequently, conservation scientists have to work especially hard to have their knowledge and messages incorporated into society (how to do this will be explicitly pursued in the next chapter).

Scientific perspectives are suspect to many, especially when the clash of different "experts" leaves the public and policymakers confused. In reality, these "experts" are typically specialists, often reflecting narrow perspectives rather than holistic approaches. Policy is, and will continue to be, made with or without the input of scientists, regardless of the relevance of their information. Consequently, a number of major challenges related to institutions and policy development face conservation biologists and others interested in contributing to policy through their theoretical and empirical insights. We discuss six of these challenges here.

Defining Appropriate Environmental Research

Much of ecological and conservation research is rooted in particular scientific disciplines. Geneticists have their domain, as do population biologists, ecophysiologists, landscape ecologists, and so forth. However, real-world environmental issues rarely lend themselves to strictly disciplinary solutions. An environmental issue is not bounded or defined by a particular scientific discipline, even conservation biology. Thus, the knowledge needed for the solution of problems needs to be defined by the issue, not by the discipline, if it is to contribute effectively to policy formation and implementation.

The difference between a discipline-driven approach and an issue-driven approach is that the former, almost by definition, begins and ends with its own set of tools for dealing with its own particular issues. Discipline-driven research usually begins with the curiosity of the investigator, who wants to understand some particular phenomenon. Any particular application or implication, other than a deeper understanding of nature, is usually absent. The desire is to "discover" something new, and the audience is usually the investigator's peers.

Presumably, one reason conservation biology began was to enlarge the tool kit and encompass broader perspectives. Issue-driven research is different than discipline-driven research because it starts with real-world issues and then tries to determine what methods, knowledge, and information might be available or needed to help resolve the problems. For example, rather than asking a discipline-driven question such as "What is the effect of trade on biodiversity?" an issue-driven question might be framed as "What would a trading system look like that valued cultural and biological diversity, equity, and democracy?"

We need to break through disciplinary and interdisciplinary boundaries if we are to make much progress in policy research for conservation. In most cases that research will need to be shifted from a discipline orientation to an issue orientation. A particular environmental issue is not simply the domain of genetics, while another answers to ecosystem ecology or economic theory. Environmental problems are complex and multidisciplinary; the answers should embrace the tools of the appropriate disciplines, but not be limited by them. These disciplines go well beyond environmental science and conservation biology, embracing psychology, philosophy, and the humanities, as well as other social sciences and ecological economics. As Wendell Berry (1989) reminds us: "The answers to human problems of ecology are to be found in the economy. And answers to the problems of the economy are to be found in human culture and character."

Incorporating Broader Sources of Information

The frame of reference for defining environmental issues and the research needed for the amelioration and prevention of environmental assaults should be broadened by listening to the people most affected. All stakeholders must have an opportunity to be heard, and all must also listen carefully to the views of others. The issue is not what scientists and researchers believe to be important in some idealized sense, but what is useful and can be used, as identified by several groups:

- people most affected by environmental assaults
- people who have historically maintained sustainable societies
- people who are charged by virtue of election or appointment to make and implement policy
- people who may produce the knowledge to assist and inform the policy process

In the area of conservation, there is the issue of who speaks for "the families and tribes of non-human creatures that live in the place," and who speaks for future generations. This is a moral and ethical issue of great importance, for which all stakeholders bear responsibility. This voice is the one most often lacking, however, because it is a reflection of values that may legitimately be in conflict with those of other stakeholders. Conservation biologists have a potentially important role to play here. In the absence of these voices, environmental research has a lesser chance of being substantively relevant to the policy process. Appropriate inclusion also increases the chances of solutions working politically.

In 1990, the U.S. Environmental Protection Agency's Scientific Advisory Board presented to its Administrator its assessment of the worst environmental problems. It revealed that hazardous and toxic wastes and underground storage tanks, the issues that topped the public agenda, were not on the scientists' list, and that climate change and radon, near the top of the scientists' list, were near the bottom in the public's view. Scientists reviewing this discrepancy usually suggest that it reflects a lack of understanding on the part of the public of "real risks," their fears having been irrationally fanned by activists who pay little attention to "acceptable risk levels." The public most affected by the environmental assaults see the scientists as insensitive and uncaring, and too abstract. They also see the scientists as not subject to the same exposures, so that their research "findings" blind them to the needs of people at risk.

There is an important lesson here: scientists, policymakers, representatives of the public, and the stakeholders most deeply affected and concerned all need to be consulted. The "scientific assessment" and the "public assessment" of key problems are both based upon an implicit or explicit analysis of who wins and who loses, of possible trade-offs, and of opportunity costs. These are important calculations. By definition, however, they are neither value-free nor ethically neutral, though often cloaked in the language of a "value-free" science. They must be reconciled in a democratic society.

If the public is "ill-informed," the scientific community concerned with contributing to the solution of environmental problems bears partial responsibility and has an obligation to work to overcome this alleged ignorance. At the same time, the scientific community has an obligation to listen to the public, and particularly to the people most affected by environmental assaults, often minorities and the poor. Cost-benefit analysis can work only if we are clear on how we measure costs and benefits, taking into account alternative values, especially those that cannot easily be quantified. For example, the value of a human life is usually imputed from projected lifetime earnings, making a poor person "less valuable" than a conservation biologist, who in turn is less valuable than a Donald Trump or a Michael Jordan. A socially and ethically adjusted cost-benefit analysis can become the basis for setting priorities for the funding of environmental research. What may appear to be the public's lack of scientific information may in fact be a reflection of different values given to that information, and/or a lack of trust in the purveyor of the information, whether the government, the academy, or business.

Understanding the Policy Process

There is a tendency among scientists to argue the centrality of scientific information in the policy process. Knowledge is clearly better than ignorance, but "good science" does not necessarily make "good policy." Science is necessary, but not sufficient, because policymaking is the process of reflecting what we value in a society, which is at heart a matter of ethics and values. Often, the scientist and policymaker have difficulty even communicating at the same level (Figure 16.5).

The question then becomes, what is good science for policy? What is the nature of the knowledge needed and attainable in the time frame available for action? And how can that knowledge best be utilized? Policy to "solve" environmental problems in a democratic society is a process of adjudicating the conflicting values of different legitimate interests in different time frames. Thus, science is not sufficient in and of itself; rather it is, and can only be, one input, albeit an important input, to policy.

To design a policy-relevant conservation agenda, it is essential to take into account the culture of the policy process, recognizing the differences between executive and legislative branches, and between different levels of government. Some aspects of that process are listed here, admittedly painted with a broad brush:

- There are usually no institutional structures for effectively integrating economic, environmental, and political concerns.

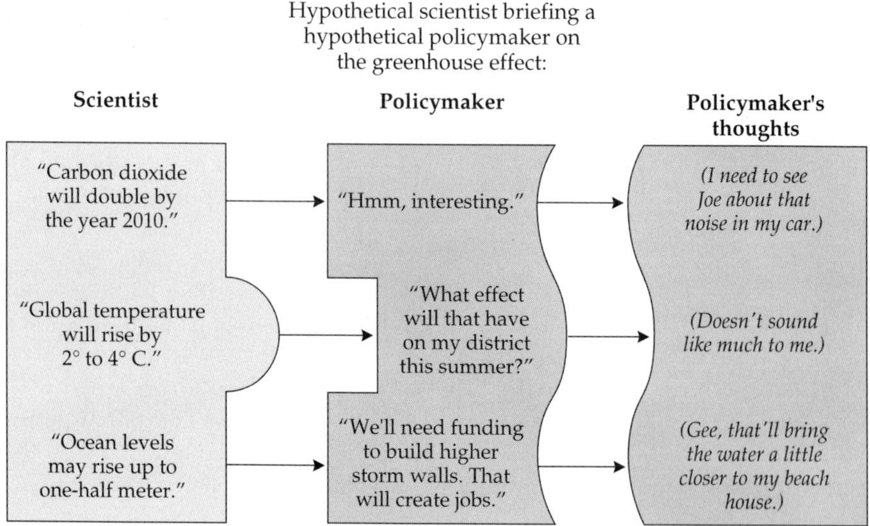

Figure 16.5 The scientist and policymaker often have problems communicating with each other. Their backgrounds, vital interests, and goals often differ enough so that they work toward very different ends, and may even have problems communicating simple ideas. (Modified from Byerly 1989.)

- No one is in charge, but there are lots of people involved in dealing with pieces of the problem.
- Policymakers, more often than not, have plenty of information (although perhaps not enough from the scientist's viewpoint), often conflicting, and plenty of demands for action, also conflicting.
- Policymakers do not want more problems; they want silver bullets, or quick answers, for those problems (an approach fraught with danger).
- Information for policymakers is usually imperfect, and there is often little or no organized demand for specific information by policymakers.
- Information, when requested, is often not available in the time frame needed, or in a form that is usable or useful.
- Scientists disseminate their work through publications, conferences, and the mailing of reprints, but rarely place great emphasis on increasing the utilization of their findings by policymakers.
- Scientists often want to provide information on what interests them, rather than what may be needed.
- Requests for information from policymakers are often quite sincere; frequently, however, such requests are excuses for postponing action.
- Requests for information from policymakers are often framed in ways that make it difficult for scientists to respond effectively; there are differences of culture and too few opportunities to overcome those differences.
- Policymakers generally perceive global change as small, barely perceptible, somewhere else, and/or far in the future, and they perceive the demands on them as a need for action in response to a specific event, here and now.
- Policymakers, as a corollary to the above, first deal with pressing problems with short-term solutions, putting off the long-term, recognizing that the first law of politics is to get reelected.
- Bureaucrats in academia, government, and nongovernmental organizations, especially in larger organizations, are extremely sensitive to the explicit and implicit incentive systems of the organizations in which they work, reacting more to those incentives than to the statements of outsiders or to larger value systems (see Byerly 1989).

It is clear that the policy process is not linear, and it is certainly not pretty. In that sense it is very human, and often differs from textbook models. "Muddling through" is the way one observer described it some years ago. Scientists and other relevant parties must be involved in the policy process throughout, both as listeners and as speakers, to ensure that the results of their research will be used and the best policy decisions will be made. Utilization of scientific results cannot be left to chance. Scientists have an obligation to make clear their findings and how they apply in specific circumstances. As economist Thomas Michael Power (1996) observed, "to the charge of advocacy, I plead guilty. To the claim that advocacy undermines the pursuit of useful knowledge, I take strong exception." The link between policy and science is examined in much greater depth in Chapter 17.

The Nature of Knowledge in Environmental Policymaking

There is a need for more and better interactions among scientists and the users—real and potential—of scientific knowledge: policymakers, activists and organizers, and affected citizens. These interactions can help to determine the nature of the knowledge that will be useful and used in the solution of environmental problems in an appropriate time frame. The primary foci in policy are political, economic, administrative, and organizational, and, under the best of circumstances, moral and ethical. This, in turn, greatly influences the nature of the scientific knowledge that will be usable and utilized in the policy process. As David Orr (1991) has observed, "As important as research is, the lack of it is not the limiting factor in the conservation of biological diversity."

Integrating Politics, Economics, and Administration. To achieve environmentally sensitive policy, we must have the political will to effect change: to stop, to conserve, to restore, to prevent. This process must take into account the claims of the various stakeholders who may lose, as well as those who may gain, from a particular policy position. For example, many Brazilian policymakers and politicians are fully aware of the social, ecological, and economic absurdity of destroying tropical Amazonian rainforests. It is not a need for new knowledge that keeps them from acting in line with their understanding; it is a lack of political will, based on their analysis of the political pressures upon them, and on their own desire to get reelected or reappointed.

Policy problems are economic in the sense that over the years we have conscientiously avoided paying attention to real costs. The food and fiber sector of the United States economy is a $700 billion per year enterprise. But we do not take into account an approximate additional $250 billion of environmental and social "externalities" involved in the production, distribution, and processing of food- and fiber-related products (Viederman, unpublished data), such as groundwater and air pollution and effects on worker health. This is but one example of the ways in which neoclassical economics fails to take account of nature as a source of capital and as a sink for the wastes of the productive system.

From a narrow disciplinary perspective, we find ourselves in the situation of identifying so-called side effects and by-products. In economics, for example, the well-known concept of "externalities," simply put, means those effects that economists choose not to address (Chapter 15). In the real world, however, there are no such things as side effects or by-products, which are only fictions created by too narrow a paradigm; there can only be effects and products. For example, when your doctor prescribes an antibiotic to treat an infection and informs you that a "side effect" might be nausea, to the doctor the nausea is a side effect because you are perceived only as the infection. To you, however, the nausea is very much an effect. A possible "side effect" of tamoxifen, an important treatment for breast cancer, is uterine cancer!

Solutions to environmental problems will require the adjudication of conflicts among values and political needs that are exacerbated by inadequate or cumbersome administrative structures and organizational arrangements. Thus, for example, the U.S. Secretary of the Interior, as head of both the Bureau of Land Management and the Fish and Wildlife Service, has conflicting mandates to use and to preserve nature's resources. Similarly, the number of committees in Congress responsible for preparing agricultural legislation makes coordination among them almost impossible. The Carnegie Commission on Science, Technology, and Government (n.d.) estimates that there are at least 16 federal agencies and departments involved in policies and activities related to the greenhouse effect (Table 16.1).

As David Ehrenfeld (1991) has observed,

> Rarely is expert knowledge sufficient for analysis, prediction and management of a given [environmental] situation. This is because in order to limit the number of variables they have to contend with, experts make the assumption that the systems they are working with are closed. Real-life systems are hardly ever closed. . . . The reductionist methods of science, which can work extremely well in closed systems, tend to break down under the open-endedness imposed by biological complexity and by the interacting complexities of political, economic and social systems.

Table 16.1
United States Federal Agencies Involved in Various Aspects of Policies and Activities Related to the Greenhouse Effect

Policy/activity	Agency[a]															
	EOP	DOE	EPA	NOAA	DOC	STATE	AG	DOI	NASA	USTR	TRE	NSF	DOT	FEMA	DOD	JUST
Conduct periodic assistance	x	x	x	x	x	x	x	x	x	x	x	x	x	x	x	
Increase stockpiles						x	x							x		
Identify adaptive business opportunities		x			x		x			x						
Develop insurance/emergency warning systems			x	x	x	x	x		x					x		
Manage ecosystems strategy			x					x								
Civil works/build infrastructure/ water and coastal zones					x		x	x								
Promote agricultural research						x	x									
Promote energy conservation/efficiency		x	x		x			x					x			
Promote solar energy		x			x											
Promote natural gas		x						x								
Promote nuclear energy		x				x										
Introduce carbon tax	x	x	x		x			x		x	x		x			x
Improve land use			x				x	x								
Expand hydropower		x	x				x									
Develop biomass energy		x	x				x									
Reduce coal use		x			x			x		x						
Adopt ambient greenhouse gas standards		x	x	x					x							
Promote reforestation			x			x	x	x								
Explore geoengineering		x	x	x		x						x				
Research weather modification			x	x		x	x	x	x						x	
Liability/compensation:																
Domestic		x	x		x		x	x		x	x					
International																x
Conduct international negotiation	x	x	x	x		x			x	x	x	x			x	

From Carnegie Commission on Science, Technology, and Government Task Force on Environment and Energy (no date).
[a]EOP, Executive Office of the President; DOE, Department of Energy; EPA, Environmental Protection Agency; NOAA, National Oceanic & Atmospheric Administration; DOC, Department of Commerce; STATE, Department of State; AG, Department of Agriculture; DOI, Department of the Interior; NASA, National Aeronautics & Space Administration; USTR, United States Trade Representative; TRE, Department of the Treasury; NSF, National Science Foundation; DOT, Department of Transportation; FEMA, Federal Emergency Management Agency; DOD, Department of Defense; JUST, Department of Justice.

Developing an Issue-Driven Science. A different scientific approach, an "issue-driven" science, will be needed to address the realities of conservation problems. It will not pretend to be either value-free or ethically neutral, although it will certainly need to remain objective and unbiased in its approaches, and must continue to be based on rigorous hypothesis testing. The scientific enterprise in this new paradigm will have to accept the world as it is, rather than trying to recreate it in ways that are more susceptible to its research needs. The circumstances that demand this new paradigm, as Funtowicz and Ravetz (1991) have observed, are that "facts are uncertain, values in dispute, stakes high and decisions urgent." As a result, the new paradigm will focus attention on the qualitative assessment of the quantitative data available, recognizing that uncertainty exists. It will also extend the peer community involved in assessment to all stakeholders, as the only way to arrive at decisions that are both scientifically sound and politically tenable.

An "issue-driven" science will therefore begin with a problem orientation that is nondisciplinary or transdisciplinary, recognizing at the outset that the situation is fraught with uncertainties. This orientation distinguishes it from curiosity-driven science, in which the effort is to minimize uncertainties. In this respect the new paradigm can be called "postnormal," to differentiate it from the scientific paradigm that is now considered "normal." The characteristics of this postnormal paradigm will include:

- Pragmatism and plurality: use of tools and conceptual frameworks appropriate to the solution of the problem, rather than being limited by the tools and conceptual frameworks of a particular discipline
- Acceptance of uncertainty as a given: asking questions about the real world that at present we do not know how to answer
- A focus on data quality rather than data completeness
- Use of a systems approach that is comprehensive, holistic, global, long-term, and contextual
- Incorporation of an explicit concern for future generations, sustainability, and equity
- A concern for dynamics, process, nonequilibrium, heterogeneity, and discontinuity
- Social as well as individualistic points of view
- Concern for the processes through which the behaviors of individuals and institutions change

The ongoing training and research efforts to develop a new ecological economics, for example, are reflective of the approaches of an "issue-driven, postnormal" science.

The Nature of the University and the Problems of Research

What are the criteria for assessing the capability of universities and other organizations to be effective providers of the training and research needed for environmental policymaking? Among others, the future requirements for good conservation research and policy are a transdisciplinary, issue-driven approach, a systems orientation, and flexibility.

By and large, universities are not presently organized to effectively carry out research and training along the lines of the paradigm described above. The guild system of the disciplines has a stranglehold on effective change, particularly at the more prestigious institutions. Investigator-initiated, peer-reviewed research is not likely to solve the world's problems by itself. Cross-disciplinary barriers in universities and elsewhere must be brought down so that effective, issue-driven research can be promoted. An example of this approach is the Organization for Tropical Studies (OTS), a university-based education program that crosses disciplinary barriers. OTS is discussed by its present and former executive directors, Gary Hartshorn and Donald Stone, in Essay 16D.

Derek Bok, who retired in 1992 from the presidency of Harvard University, observed:

> Our universities excel in pursuing the easier opportunities where established academic and social priorities coincide. On the other hand, when social needs are not clearly recognized and backed by adequate financial support, higher education has often failed to respond as effectively as it might, even to some of the most important challenges facing America. Armed with the security of

tenure and time to study the world with care, professors would appear to have a unique opportunity to act as society's scouts to signal impending problems long before they are visible to others. Yet rarely have members of the academy succeeded in discovering emerging issues and bringing them vividly to the public attention. What Rachel Carson did for risks to the environment, Ralph Nader for consumer protection, Michael Harrington for problems of poverty, Betty Friedan for women's rights, they did as independent critics, not as members of a faculty. Universities will usually continue to respond weakly unless outside support is available and the subjects involved command prestige in academic circles. (Bok 1990)

ESSAY 16D
OTS as an Institution for Conservation Biology

Donald E. Stone, Executive Director Emeritus, and
Gary S. Hartshorn, Executive Director, Organization for Tropical Studies

Slides, videos, and engaging professors can make conservation biology very exciting. However, there is no substitute for the real thing when it comes to studying the dynamics between humans and nature, and more particularly, to gaining insight into why these dynamics are occurring. It is these building blocks of conservation biology that the Organization for Tropical Studies (OTS) stresses in its hands-on courses in Costa Rica and Brazil, which promote an understanding of the complexities of tropical ecosystems and engage the participants in a dialogue as to how these ecosystems can be sustainably managed.

Understanding the role of OTS' courses in the broadly defined area of conservation biology requires an appreciation of the institution itself. OTS dates back to the early 1960s, when most of the world viewed tropical forests as an unlimited expanse of timber and biological diversity. OTS was formed by a small consortium of United States universities and the Universidad de Costa Rica to engage in "training, research and the wise use of natural resources in the tropics" (Stone 1988). Over the past 34 years the consortium has grown to 55 institutions. OTS has its operational base in Costa Rica, where it provides training for graduate students and policymakers, and operates three field stations (La Selva, Las Cruces, and Palo Verde) used by students and researchers from throughout the world. Quite simply, OTS is a world-class convenor of field-oriented courses in natural sciences and facilitator of tropical research.

Precisely what OTS does in conservation biology is best viewed in terms of its programs in Costa Rica: intensive field courses for graduate students and policymakers, and a new undergraduate semester abroad. The graduate student program, which is the prime justification for consortium membership, includes courses entitled *Tropical Biology: An Ecological Approach; Tropical Conservation Biology; Tropical Biodiversity;* and *Tropical Plant Systematics.* These English-language courses are complemented by the Spanish-language courses *Ecología Tropical* and *Agroecología.* In collaboration with Brazil's Instituto Nacional de Pesquisas da Amazônia (INPA), Universidad Estadual de Campinas (UNICAMP), and the Smithsonian Institution, OTS offers a Portuguese-language course, *Ecologia da Floresta Amazônica*, in Manaus. These courses run the gamut from traditional field biology to specific applications, but no matter what the subject, the impact of human interests cannot be ignored.

Other participant groups are also beneficiaries of an OTS education program soundly based in conservation biology. Policymakers in the United States are offered the short course *Interdependence: Economic Development and Environmental Concerns in Tropical Countries*, whereas the Latin American constituency, consisting mainly of mid-level government officials, is served by *Principios Ecológicos para Toma de Decisiones y el Manejo de los Recursos Naturales en América Latina.* These courses look at the direct effects of governmental policy on natural resources in the tropics. Undergraduates too have become a part of the OTS education program. OTS recently initiated an Undergraduate Semester Abroad program to introduce outstanding students to tropical biology; the curriculum includes Spanish language, Costa Rican culture, tropical conservation biology and natural history, and environmental issues. The Costa Rican people are also beneficiaries of OTS environmental education projects, which include collaboration with field station neighbors on projects of mutual interest.

What makes the OTS approach to conservation biology unique can best be appreciated by examining our course *Tropical Conservation Biology.* This course is designed for graduate students in their formative years of choosing a dissertation research topic. Some 20–22 competitively selected participants are brought to Costa Rica to experience a contrasting range of ecosystems (cf. Janzen 1983b), from sea level to 3000 m, from deciduous dry to evergreen wet forests, and from pristine to highly manipulated landscapes. This field course focuses on faculty-led field practica and discussions of actual conservation problems in Central America. Each student also researches and presents a paper on a topic of personal interest. The pace and focus over the four-week course are intense and unrelenting, seven days a week. The principal instructors, called course coordinators, and a graduate teaching assistant establish the intellectual framework and set the tone for the course, but the pace and rigor are maintained throughout by inviting a series of scientists to share their knowledge at one or more field sites. It is not uncommon for the students to be exposed to the expertise of a dozen or more world-class scientists.

To support its educational mission, OTS owns and operates three field facilities in Costa Rica: La Selva Biological Station (cf. McDade et al. 1994) in the wet lowlands of the northeast; Palo Verde Field Station in the monsoonally dry Pacific lowlands; and Las Cruces Biological Station in mid-elevation, Pacific slope cloud forest in the southwest. OTS's goal is to provide the basic infrastructure and security for scientists and students to conduct their research. La Selva adjoins the northern terminus of Braulio Carrillo National Park, and hence is able to offer attractive research opportunities on altitudinal patterns of biodiversity, corridor effects, forest recovery, and species dominance and migration. Researchers at La Selva pioneered the use of native tree species to rehabilitate degraded pastures in the region.

Las Cruces is famous for its beautiful Wilson Botanical Garden, which contains excellent collections of the major monocot groups such as orchids, bromeliads, gingers, and palms. Though Las Cruces' forests are modest in area, numerous patches of forest occur in the Coto Brus region, which have stimulated considerable interest among conservation biologists studying metapopulations and island biogeography effects on biodiversity. There are exploratory efforts to recreate a forest corridor that would connect Las Cruces with a 7000 ha Guaymí Indian reservation some 5 km away, and possibly with the more distant Golfo Dulce Forest Reserve.

The Palo Verde station is situated in the heart of Palo Verde National Park. It offers numerous applied problems in managing wildlife and wildfires while maintaining habitat diversity, particularly the 500 ha seasonal marsh between the station and the Río Tempisque.

These three field stations are the principal sites for most OTS field courses. The considerable amount of accumulated information on species and habitats at each of the stations provides a wealth of background material for students and researchers. To promote student research in particular, OTS offers an array of financial assistance that ranges from below-cost tuition for United States and Latin American students from member institutions, to post-course awards that enable students to immediately follow up on course-generated research questions, to larger fellowship awards that enable a few OTS alumni to return to our field stations to conduct graduate research. OTS fellowships are an important complement to our education program that significantly expands opportunities for graduate students to conduct research in all aspects of tropical biology.

So what does the OTS experience add up to when the exhilaration wears off? For most participants it becomes a reference point against which to measure future studies in the biological sciences, and for many it becomes the cornerstone for research careers in conservation biology. For those who become educators, the tropical experience permeates their future teaching, and for policymakers, the experience provides a framework for making decisions based on their first-hand experiences. For all alumni, the excellent networking opportunities, in addition to the enviable possibility of returning to the tropics, are benefits of the OTS experience that cannot be understated. In a sense, it is this aspect of OTS that nourishes the sustainability of the organization and permits progressive updating of the OTS courses in conservation biology. Through its remarkable partnership with Costa Rica, OTS has made significant contributions to our understanding of the tropics and the critical role humans must play to maintain these fragile resources in a sustainable manner.

Universities often reward reductionism, which is contrary to most needs of the environment. For example, in many disciplines, elegance is more honored than relevance. Traditional concerns, such as taxonomy and natural history, are put on the waste heap for more "exciting," and certainly more lucrative, ventures such as molecular biology (Wilson 1994). The university incentive system, especially within the traditional departmental structure, does not reward knowledge generation of the sort needed for policy. This is especially true for younger faculty members without tenure, who accept considerable risk in entering what is perceived to be the "softer" field of environmental policy research. Interdisciplinary efforts are usually the first to go in times of budget stringency. It is also true for graduate students who want to assist nongovernmental organizations in dealing with "real-world" problems, only to be thwarted by their academic advisers because the topic chosen allegedly does not lend itself to "good science," defined as a discipline-driven approach.

The Sufficiency of Knowledge and Some Roles for Environmental Research

Knowledge measured by the canons of a "normal" science is rarely adequate for environmental problem solving, but policy action cannot be postponed in the hope that "complete" information will become available. In all conservation endeavors, use should be made of all available knowledge, and when the time frame for decision making permits it, new research should be undertaken, guided by the needs of the policy process, not those of the researcher. An additional, and often overlooked, necessity is assessment of the possible political, social, environmental, cultural, and economic consequences of the policy action in order to avoid doing harm (Viederman 1991). As historian Edward Tenner (1996) observes, technology has made us healthier and wealthier, but what he calls "revenge effects," or unanticipated consequences, have created new problems or exacerbated old ones.

We often have enough information to make informed decisions with respect to conservation. However, much of this information is not used because it is in forms that are not always valued by the scientific community—for example, indigenous knowledge—or because it is the product of persons working outside the "normal" scientific system—for example, nonprofit or advocacy organizations. Even if there is no impending disaster, there are many problems, such as global warming and ozone depletion, where the windows of opportunity are narrowing and action would best be taken now, based on the best available information. Prudence may be more important than certitude. As has been observed, "it is better to be approximately right, than precisely wrong."

Nothing stated above should be taken to suggest that science—particularly a new, issue-driven science—does not have a critical role to play in policy, for it does. Such a science will not only ask the traditional questions—what do we need to know?—but will also recognize the limits of our capacity to know and to manage something as complex as the biosphere and human behavior. As such, it will also seek to minimize what harm we might do.

Here we list only a few of the important ways in which science can contribute to the solution of environmental problems; others easily may be added.

1. *Early warning systems* need to be developed to identify environmental problems before they become severe. The work of early researchers on global warming and the ozone hole are good examples, although the initial cool reception of their work underscores the problems of researchers who are ahead of their colleagues. Attention should also be directed to the development of "vital signs" that can signal issues on the horizon. A key issue is what constitutes appropriate measures of real change, as indicators frequently do not measure what they claim to measure. Thus, for example, library usage may no longer be a good measure of literacy because libraries are now good sources of videos and also provide shelter for the unemployed and the homeless.
2. *Technology assessment* needs to be developed in order to better understand the anticipated, and especially the unanticipated, political, social, economic, cultural, and ecological consequences of technological development over the short, medium, and long term. Technologies tend to develop more quickly than does our ability or motivation to question their appropriateness or desirability. Today's problems are all too often yesterday's solutions. It does not require sophisticated science to recognize, for example, that the introduction of bovine growth hormones, which increase a cow's production of milk, will (1) lower the price of milk paid to the farmer because of increased supply, (2) adversely affect small farmers, which in turn will (3) harm the economies of farming communities, encouraging (4) migration to cities over the long term, while at the same time (5) contributing to the vertical integration of agribusiness.
3. *Research for ameliorating the consequences of environmental assaults and developing benign technologies to restore natural systems* is a high priority, particularly research using nature as its model. Todd's (1988) work on solar aquatic treatment of wastewater, discussed in Essay

16A, is a good example. By imitating the way nature cleans dirty water—using various life-forms that ingest the organic material in sewage—Todd's system purifies municipal wastewater and sewage without using chemicals and without creating significant amounts of hazardous sludge products. The system also requires considerably less energy and money than conventional treatment facilities.

4. *Psychological and organizational research* is necessary to understand how to encourage needed environmental behavioral changes in individuals and institutions. More information and changes in values and attitudes are important, but are not sufficient, for behavioral changes. How can changes in consumption patterns be encouraged? Why does it take us so long to adjust to the inevitable global limitations that face us? We spend more time envisioning where we want to be than we do figuring out how to get there. Increasing our understanding of and capacity to change the behavior of individuals and institutions is an essential component of any effort to conserve biological and human resources.
5. *Agroecological and farming systems research* is needed to assist farmers in different climatic zones who wish to make the transition to a sustainable agriculture that is also economically viable and helps to revitalize rural communities.
6. *Conceptualization and implementation of an "ecological economics"* that will marry ecology and the economy, taking into account nature as resource and as sink. Among the issues of importance are the development of socio-economic-ecological accounting systems that combine qualitative and quantitative measures.

Conclusions

Moving from the elegance of science in its traditional and normal form to the messy world of politics, policy, program, and management is difficult for many. Not all conservation biologists need to be working in the trenches of policy. All, however, should be aware of policy needs and of the relationships of policy and science that we have tried to lay out here. Scientists have dual roles as scientists and citizens (Meine and Meffe 1996; Meffe 1996). Their goal should be not only to create knowledge, but to see that the knowledge is used to protect the very subjects of their study, the species and ecosystems of the world.

Some conservation biologists in university settings will take personal risks to their careers to make the leap. This is an unfortunate necessity, given the status of many of the institutions that we have discussed. We can hope that many institutions will begin processes of change: to train people differently (and better) for policy purposes, and to encourage, or at least recognize as equally valid, the needs of relevance and elegance.

The world of policy presents a real challenge to the conservation biologist. It requires incorporating in greater detail than would otherwise be the case the nature of other human systems as they are affected by and affect the ecosystems that are at the heart of conservation biology. Individually, the ecosystem and the human system are each extraordinarily complex; any effort to combine the two into one system is daunting. If we accept the limits of our knowledge, and as a result the limits of our capacity to "manage the planet," if we become more comfortable with uncertainty and are willing to assess our actions in order to avoid harm as best we can, then there is yet hope for us all.

Summary

If conservation biology is to be successful in its ultimate mission of biodiversity protection, its concepts and models must be transformed into rational policies that reflect our knowledge of human influences on the natural world. This transformation is the realm of institutions and policymaking. The principles of humility, precaution, and reversibility should guide policymaking with respect to the environment. This will require new ways of defining problems, as well as changes in the way many institutions conduct business. The fact that the status quo is not working toward improved environments for humans or most other species on earth is a strong argument for change.

A number of institutions have direct bearing on our ultimate success or failure at conservation of biodiversity. These include educational institutions, governments at all levels, NGOs, businesses, consumers, legal institutions, religious institutions, and the media. All can contribute in various ways to the promotion of reasonable conservation progress, or can impede that progress to the detriment of all. The policymaking process presents numerous challenges for conservation biology. These challenges include defining appropriate and useful environmental research programs, using broad information bases to define environmental issues and research agendas, understanding the policy process, and developing an issue-driven science to provide better input to policy. The world of policy and institutions can be messy, but it is critical that conservation biologists participate in it. If they do not, the decisions that most affect conservation will be made by those perhaps least qualified to do so. The creation of conservation knowledge will be of real utility only when it is transformed into policy action. That seems obvious, but as has been observed, the obscure takes a while to achieve, the obvious longer.

Questions for Discussion

1. In what ways do you feel that your training in conservation biology—including this text—could be better organized to increase your opportunities to contribute to public policy now and in the future?
2. Who defines the priorities, sets the agendas, and frames the problems for research? What, for example, are the sources of funding for research at your university, and how might they influence the nature of the research being done?
3. How does scientific research and scientific knowledge influence policy?
4. What alternative structures might provide a firmer base of science for public policy?
5. How can we balance the need for objective science and the need for subjective judgment in the policy process?
6. In determining the most important issues for scientific research for policy, who speaks for nature? Who are the surrogate stakeholders for nature? Who speaks for future generations? Who are their stakeholders?
7. How do stakeholders become a part of the process of identifying research needs and using research results? How can a better balance be achieved between the research needs perceived by researchers and by the public?
8. What changes in policies, practices, and institutions are needed to conserve biodiversity and sustain humanity? Can they change sufficiently

given present circumstances? Is reform possible? Is transformation possible? What new institutions and systems are needed?

9. What is your vision of a sustainable future that preserves ecological integrity while enhancing economic security and democracy?
10. What do you see as the most important challenges to the conservation of biological resources in the next five to ten years? What can, should, and will conservation biologists do about them?

Suggestions for Further Reading

Benedict, R. 1991. *Ozone Diplomacy: New Directions in Safeguarding the Planet.* Harvard University Press, Cambridge, MA. The author, chief United States negotiator of the Montreal Protocol on Substances that Deplete the Ozone Layer, combines science, politics, economics, and diplomacy in his portrayal of how the agreement came to be accepted.

Funtowicz, S. O. and J. R. Ravetz. 1990. *Uncertainty and Quality in Science for Policy.* Kluwer, Dordrecht, Netherlands. In response to the need for a method of expressing judgments of uncertainty and quality in science for policy, the authors present a notational system that is convenient, robust, and nuanced.

Funtowicz, S. O. and J. R. Ravetz. 1991. A new scientific methodology for global environment issues. In R. Costanza et al. (eds.), *Ecological Economics: The Science and Management of Sustainability,* pp. 137–152. Columbia University Press, New York. The uncertainty of traditional scientific methods used to address environmental problems demands new methodologies. The authors contrast applied science, professional consultancy, and a new, postnormal science.

Grumbine, R. E. (ed.). 1994. *Environmental Policy and Biodiversity.* Island Press, Washington, D.C. A collection of papers by and interviews with scientists on science and the policy process, emphasizing the strengths and limitations of science in policy. A realistic and honest assessment of science and policy today.

Ludwig, D., R. Hilborn, and C. Winters. 1993. Uncertainty, resource exploitation, and conservation: Lessons from history. *Science* 260:17, 36. The title tells it all in this critique of the status quo of resource exploitation; humanity has repeatedly overexploited natural resources despite our best efforts to the contrary.

National Research Council, Commission on Life Sciences, Committee on Environmental Research. 1993. *Research to Protect, Restore, and Manage the Environment.* National Academy Press, Washington, D.C. A review of federal support for research on the environment, and a proposal for reorganizing the research effort to make it more effective in supporting policy. It tends to focus more on what scientists have to offer than what the policy process needs, being insufficiently critical of what does not work.

Power, T. M. 1996. *Lost Landscapes and Failed Economies: The Search for a Value of Place.* Island Press, Washington, D.C. Argues that the quality of the natural landscape is an essential part of a community's permanent economic base and should not be sacrificed in short-term efforts to maintain employment levels in industries that are ultimately not sustainable, especially resource extraction industries.

Rubin, E. S., L. B. Lave, and M. G. Morgan. 1992. Keeping Climate Research Relevant. *Issues in Science and Technology* VIII, no. 2. A serious critique of federal support for research on acid rain and its failure to provide policy-relevant information in a timely fashion.

Tenner, E. 1996. *Why Things Bite Back: Technology and the Revenge of Unintended Consequences.* Alfred Knopf, New York. Things do go wrong with the technologies that are designed to make our lives better. Tenner addresses many instances of the downsides of technology.

17

Conservation Biologists in the Policy Process

Learning to be Practical and Effective

Other approaches may appear to offer simpler or easier solutions, but each usually turns up lacking in important ways—not the least of these being their relative inability to help one think and understand and hence to become a more humane, creative, and effective problem solver.

Garry D. Brewer and Peter deLeon, 1983

Conservation biologists want nature to be taken seriously in public policy, and they want issues such as endangered species, biodiversity, ecosystem management, and sustainability to be addressed as though they really mattered—which they do! If there is one overriding common interest shared by human beings everywhere, it is a healthy environment. But to date, conservation biologists have not been as effective as we need to be in influencing policy processes, achieving the outcomes we want, or significantly changing society's environmentally destructive practices. Why? Perhaps we have not been practical enough in our efforts, or perhaps we do not really understand what the policy process is and how to participate in it effectively. The previous chapter addressed the realities of the policy process and institutional roles in that process. Here, we discuss the "how to's" of effective policy practice.

Numerous problems must be overcome if a more practical and effective environmental policy is to be developed. First, much public policy regarding the environment seems to lack realism and rationality and reflects instead parochialism, politics, and often questionable justifications for decisions. Second, the practices and outcomes called for by many current policy decisions are clearly harmful to the environment and thus to the sustainability of humans and the planet's biodiversity. Third, policy thinking is very different from scientific thinking. Conservation biologists tend to be trained in science and technical issues and are not necessarily skilled participants in policy processes.

What can conservation biologists do to solve these problems? One alternative is simply to continue using our past approaches but with renewed commitment, energy, and resources. However, a more useful approach might be to learn more about the policy process, upgrade our policy analytic skills, develop influence, and truly affect policy practices and outcomes. This does not mean giving up our privileged positions as scientists in society, nor does it mean becoming narrow partisan advocates. It means instead that we conduct our science with an explicit policy orientation. If we do not become more successful, we can expect a continuing loss of biodiversity, reduced well-being for humans, and a further loss of public support for science.

This chapter places our conservation activities in their larger social context by looking at the perspectives and strategies of conservation biologists as well as the role of values, influence, and power. It offers analytic tools that allow biologists comprehensively and realistically to "map" the rationality, politics, and morality in any policy process. And it will help conservation biologists to develop new skills in policy analysis and policy participation. To introduce the perspectives and potential roles of scientists in the policy process, Ron Pulliam, former Director of the National Biological Service, offers his "insider" observations in Essay 17A.

ESSAY 17A

Who Speaks for Conservation Biologists?

H. Ronald Pulliam, University of Georgia

Endangered species preservation, the protection of wilderness and other natural areas, and the conservation of natural resources are among the most contentious issues currently faced by our society. Conservation biologists and ecologists are arguably the most reliable sources of scientific information about these issues. Why, then, do conservation biologists and ecologists play such a small role in framing and resolving the major conservation issues of our time? And if scientists are not leading the way in providing scientific advice to policymakers, who is?

Conservation biologists and ecologists are relatively new to their efforts to advise policymakers at the national level, and we do not yet know how to be fully effective in the public policy arena (as discussed throughout this chapter). Many practicing conservation biologists, particularly those in the university community, have no formal training and little or no experience in public policy issues. Rather than participating directly in the policy arena themselves, many expect their professional and scientific societies to speak and act on behalf of their profession. Some societies, such as the Wildlife Society and the American Fisheries Society, have long-established public outreach and congressional affairs offices and are, in fact, quite active on Capitol Hill. Whenever an issue comes before Congress that will affect fish or fisheries, Congress receives scientific input from the American Fisheries Society; whenever an issue affects wildlife, Congress hears from the Wildlife Society. Both societies are frequently called upon to testify before Congress because they are recognized for their scientific expertise and credibility. These societies are broadly interested in natural resources in general, but for better or worse, historically they have been most effective when they have focused narrowly on scientific issues dealing with fish and wildlife per se. Similarly, Congress hears from the Range Management Society on any of the scientific issues affecting rangelands, and from the Agronomy Society on any issues concerning soils.

Who speaks for conservation science on the broader issues of ecosystem protection, biological diversity, global change, and sustainable development? There are several scientific societies that represent the full spectrum of issues dealt with by ecologists and conservation biologists, but these societies have less of a track record in public policy and legislative outreach activities than do many of the more narrowly focused professional groups. For example, the Ecological Society of America has been in existence since 1915, but did not open its Public Affairs Office in Washington until 1983. The Society for Conservation Biology is a much younger organization, and it has yet to establish a formal presence in Washington.

Congress and other policymakers hear from a dazzling array of scientific specialists, but what they hear is often confusing and contradictory. When there is scientific confusion and uncertainty, Congress sometimes turns to the National Research Council of the National Academy of Sciences for a consensus scientific viewpoint. NRC reports, such as recent ones on "Science and the Endangered Species Act" and "Salmon and Society in the Pacific Northwest," can be influential in the long term, but the NRC can rarely respond in time to have an effect on fast-moving legislation.

Congress also had its own "in-house" research and assessment capability in the Office of Technology Assessment. The OTA was created in 1972 as the "analytical arm of Congress" to provide Congress with "independent and timely information" about the potential effects of technology. Recently, Congress eliminated the OTA. In certain areas in which the OTA had sufficient internal expertise, it produced excellent assessments; for example, its recent report on "Harmful Non-indigenous Species in the United States" is the best documentation available of the magnitude of the nonindigenous species problem. However, the OTA had a very small budget and staff, and focused its limited resources on a few high-priority issues. In fact, because of these limitations, requests for OTA studies could only have been made by chairmen and ranking minority members of standing committees of the House of Representatives or the Senate.

Congressional action on important environmental legislation often moves much faster than does the slow and tedious process of producing well-researched national assessments by the NRC or the OTA. When it comes to putting the big picture together quickly and evaluating the overall effects of new environmental laws or regulations, policymakers usually get their information from one of three sources: environmental groups, industry lobbyists, or federal agencies. Both environmental and industry groups have a "special interest" in the outcome of the legislative process and are therefore viewed as trying to present the available evidence in a way favorable to their own causes. This self-interest does not escape the attention of lawmakers, who often either collaborate with one faction or the other to further their own political ends or stand on the sidelines and denounce one or both sides as unreliable or biased.

Federal agencies such as the Fish and Wildlife Service, the Environmental Protection Agency, and the Forest Service play a central role in carrying out the environmental and natural resource laws passed by Congress. All of these agencies hire their own scientists and try to devise rules and regulations based on good scientific principles. In most cases these scientists work directly for the managers and regulators who apply the results of the scientific studies. Because the agencies are part of the executive branch of government and the agency heads are usually political appointees, these federal agencies are often directly involved in political battles between the administration and Congress. As a result, the agencies are too often viewed as using science to support their predetermined views, and the science is consequently open to criticism as being censored or biased.

In an attempt to avoid the conflict of interest that can emerge when scientists work directly for regulators who use science to justify their regulations, the Department of the Interior created an independent, nonregulatory, nonadvocacy science agency, the National Biological Service. The NBS was created to provide decision makers both inside and outside of government with unbiased, peer-reviewed scientific information. Unfortunately, legislation to create the NBS came before Congress just at the time when the "wise use movement" was beginning to gain influence in Washington, and the NBS became the focus of an intense debate about how biological information might be used to curtail private property rights. Fears that the Department of the Interior (DOI) would use the information collected by the NBS to increase federal regulations and control over private landowners led some in Congress to call for the abolishment of the NBS, thereby threatening a 50-year history of biological research in the DOI. In the end, the biological science capability of the DOI was rescued by merging NBS with the U.S. Geological Survey, previously the physical science research agency in DOI. This merger has provided the DOI with a unique opportunity to develop an integrated environmental science capability independent of the management and regulatory agencies in the department. Only time will tell whether this latest restructuring of science within the DOI will lead to better scientific information being incorporated into environmental policy.

This essay points out some of the difficulties encountered in trying to bring unbiased scientific information to bear on controversial conservation decisions. What can be done to improve the current situation? First, conservation biologists must become more aware and informed about the role of science in the public policy process and about how environmental laws and regulations are created and enforced. Accordingly, public policy courses should be available as a regular part of conservation biology curricula at both the undergraduate and graduate levels, and such courses should be taught by faculty both knowledgeable about the conceptual issues and experienced in the public policy arena.

Second, professional and scientific societies, particularly those with a broad interest in the full spectrum of environmental issues, should become more active in the public policy arena. Professional societies can be a primary source of unbiased scientific opinion concerning the major environmental and conservation issues of the day. But to be effective, such information must be readily available and must represent the prevailing majority view of members of the society. Thus, professional societies must put into place mechanisms to anticipate what issues will be forthcoming in public policy debates and must strive to synthesize the relevant scientific information in a timely manner. In some cases this may result in the publication of consensus documents that synthesize and interpret the technical literature in a manner comprehensible to decision makers. In other cases it may require rapid preparation of written and oral testimony that can be presented at congressional hearings and other public fora. Professional societies should also provide more opportunities for their members to learn about the public policy process and to become active in it. These opportunities could range from society-sponsored workshops and short courses to the sponsorship of congressional fellowships and legislative internships.

Additionally, all conservation biologists and ecologists must become aware of the obligations they have as individuals to share their information and knowledge with students, the public, and decision makers. In many cases, the greatest contribution that an individual scientist can make will be in the classroom, training not only the next generation of specialists, but also future lawyers, politicians, teachers, business men and women, real estate developers, journalists, and so forth, all of whom need to understand the basic concepts of conservation biology and ecology. Because industry and environmental groups play an integral role in both influencing public policy and managing natural resources, conservation biologists can play a key role by working with these groups and helping to ensure that sound science is considered in their management and policy decisions.

Finally, conservation biologists should come to view public service—at a local, state, or national level—as a routine part of their careers. University law faculty and economics professors routinely leave the ivory towers and take government posts for a few years, only to return to their home universities after their public service. Why should this not be a regular part of the career track of an ecologist or conservation biologist? In whatever way best fits our individual talents and dispositions, we should all seek ways to use our science to influence public policy and the kind of environment that we leave for future generations.

Understanding People in the Policy Process

Progress has been made in environmental policy and management in the last few decades, to be sure, but much remains to be done. Conservation biologists are keenly aware that too few policies give sufficient weight to biodiversity and other environmental considerations, such as clean air and water, and soil preservation. Yet influencing the *policy process*—the endless, dynamic, interactive flow of values, decisions, and practices from local to international scales—is key to conserving biodiversity and sustaining the human enterprise. Clearly, we have an important role to play in working toward the common interest of a healthy environment. But just how should we go about doing this?

Let's look at a real example that will be used throughout this chapter. Concerns surfaced in 1990 about the degradation of a salt marsh in a medium-sized city on the East Coast. The following year, conservation biology students, affiliated with an institute for watershed and coastal policy and management at a big university, set out to restore the marsh. Based on their scientific studies, they concluded that a 1919 tide gate, located at the mouth of the river running through the marsh, had significantly limited tidal flows and degraded the marsh. Their research on flora, water quality, and fauna revealed that significant changes had taken place. Water above the gate had become brackish, causing reeds (*Phragmites australis*) to take over. The gate itself, which prevented normal tidal fluxes, was dilapidated and needed replacement. They also discovered that the state Department of Environmental Protection (DEP) would pay for a new self-regulating tide gate, which would restore flows into upper reaches of the marsh at no cost to the city. The DEP had put new gates in other areas, which resulted in dramatic recovery of the marshes within a few years, so there was a good precedent for this solution. One of these projects, in fact, is considered a national model for salt marsh restoration.

This seemed to be an opportunity for the city, the DEP, local citizens, and the students to work together to restore the marsh. Encouraged, the students presented their scientific studies and a proposal for a new tide gate to the mayor, fully expecting that this information would result in his "buy-in" and swift action. The mayor, however, wrote back that he was not interested in tide gate replacement.

The students' assessment was that the mayor was concerned about the economic well-being of the city and his own personal power, and that from his standpoint there was nothing to be gained by marsh restoration. Furthermore, the mayor had previously constructed a sports facility on the floodplain of the river near the marsh, which had been acclaimed as a major improvement to the city. One student speculated that the mayor opposed tide gate replacement because it might change the water table and flood the sports facility, which would embarrass the mayor and city for building on a floodplain.

The students continued their baseline biological studies, supported by grants, but after four years of work, they seemed no closer to their goal than when they began. Clearly, something was going on in this policy process that the conservation biology students did not understand initially, nor address effectively over the years. Perhaps they brought inadequate concepts and tools to the task. Perhaps their scientific, technical outlook prevented them from understanding the process they were trying to influence and how to participate in it successfully.

Clarifying One's Standpoint

Even problems that appear to have simple solutions, as in the marsh restoration case, require participants to understand their own roles in the public policy process that they wish to influence. Clarifying one's own standpoint involves understanding the perspective one brings to the process, choosing strategies to influence outcomes, and moving from a conventional to a functional understanding of the process.

Perspective. The perspectives people bring to a policy issue reflect their individual identities, expectations, and demands. In fact, the policy process—whether it is about marsh restoration on the East Coast, large carnivore conservation in the Rocky Mountains, or global climate change—is really about reconciling the perspectives of multiple participants. It is, in other words, *a social process for finding individual and collective meaning* (Bruner 1990).

Everyone has an *identity* (personality or self-system), shaped by biology, family, culture, location, training, and experience. Part of the identity of conservation biologists is their training in science. Scientists share a fundamental outlook or frame of reference that differs from that of people who do not have the same training and socialization. There are multiple sides to everyone's identity—professional, national, family, social—and some parts of one's identity may be in direct conflict with other parts, as, for example, when a proponent of democracy uses his technical knowledge to limit the role of others in public decision making.

We all operate with culturally determined and individually tempered premises and methods of understanding our experience of reality. At a basic level, we screen and sort data about the world. The result of this process is the recognition—actually, the creation—of meaning and the development of our ability to discriminate (Miller 1985; Berger and Luckman 1987; Dryzek 1990). Anthropologists call these basic operational premises—which are held by every individual and every group—*myths*. A myth consists of a core of beliefs, rules for conduct, and a variety of symbols. As a technical, functional term, the word *myth* differs from its use in everyday conversation, in which it denotes a false belief. Myths, in the technical sense, are taken for granted by most people, who are seldom conscious of the underlying premises from which their deliberations or actions spring. This is true of conservation scientists as well. We have become socialized and intellectualized to the premises, vocabulary, and norms (or myths) of the discipline of conservation biology, and we must recognize and acknowledge these to understand ourselves and our relationships with others.

Our identities give rise to certain *expectations* about how the world works. One common expectation of scientists, for instance, concerns the role of science and scientists in policymaking. According to this view, scientists have a privileged position in society as experts who produce technical knowledge so that decision makers can then make rational choices based on that knowledge. This expectation is unrealistic and usually remains unsatisfied for several reasons, both scientific and political. Scientific research often does not focus on policy-relevant issues (Ascher 1993), and it may not be presented in terms that are useful or even understandable to decision makers. In addition, the generalizability of scientific findings from their original context to another context is almost always open to question. As a result, decision makers may ignore scientific implications, or they may be unaware of the limitations of applying complex scientific knowledge to particular cases. Being able to assess the realism of one's own expectations about the policy process (or those of others) can help participants gauge what they ought to do.

Finally, we all make *demands* or claims on society's time, attention, or resources based on our identity and expectations. Our demands are really our preferences for policy outcomes and practices; they reflect our values. As conservation biologists, we want effective biodiversity protection, ecosystem management, global sustainability, and more. Such demands are on the order of those made by many other groups in society. The experience of having one's expectations and demands unsatisfied can be disconcerting and sometimes traumatic. After a repeated lack of success in affecting policy, some biologists entrench themselves even more deeply in their scientific perspective and myths, attribute their failure to "politics," and eventually become cynical and give up. These people never look empirically, systematically, and objectively at their own perspectives as a variable.

Let's review briefly. Conservation biologists are scientists who have a certain outlook, have undergone years of training and socialization to a certain identity, have built up certain expectations, and tend to make certain kinds of demands on society. From the perspective of conservation biologists, one of their most important missions is to bring all their scientific knowledge together in a way that accurately, clearly, and objectively conveys to policymakers the extent to which biodiversity is at risk and what can be done about it (see Brown 1995). This seems obvious: people need reliable information about the current state of affairs, its causes, and what might happen in the future. But resolving policy problems involves much more than supplying needed knowledge. It requires attention to "ideology, ethics, politics, economics, and other considerations. . . . Policy is determined by the complex resolution of all the relevant factors, of which rational analysis is but one" (Brewer and deLeon 1983). Conservation biologists must be vigilantly conscious of the limitations and biases, as well as the strengths, of their own identities and expectations. Demands made without this awareness will probably fail, and, personally and scientifically, conservation biologists will be vulnerable to public discredit as irrelevant, idealistic, or arrogant.

When conservation biologists enter the policy process, they leave the "hard high ground" of positivistic and objectivistic science and enter the "swampy lowlands" of practical politics—or so the comparison is often construed. Some scientists view themselves as being corrupted or violating their basic standards when they enter the policy process; the pejorative terms "advocate" and "politician" are often used by their peers to describe such persons. Yet scientists cannot successfully promote their demand for biodiversity conservation by holding fast to perspectives that do not fit realistically with the well-founded demands of the rest of humanity. Scientists should not delude themselves that what they do is somehow superior to the workings of the world and that other people should defer to their expertise. Neither scientists nor any other group with a particular perspective can hope to transfer knowledge across "rationalities" to another group simply by bringing information to the attention of the other (Dery 1984). It takes more than that to have influence and change policy.

The way to proceed in such a situation is for scientists to clarify their own standpoint by accounting for their own biases in perspective and accepting that—like all other participants—they are partisan players. Too many participants in policy processes proceed unconsciously based on unexamined myths and assumptions about themselves, other people, social processes, and the role of science in society. There are no value-free positions in the policy arena (Bahm 1971; Primm and Clark 1996). Although scientists strive for neutrality and objectivity in their work, in the policy process—which deals first and foremost in values—they bring their own value-laden demands, which have important value consequences.

At this point, let us return to the student conservation biologists and their efforts to restore the salt marsh. The students seemed to be operating from a scientific identity and myth. They seemed to have expected, initially at least, that conducting biological research on the marsh, presenting the mayor with a report of their results, and recommending tidal gate replacement was all that was needed for the marsh to be restored, especially because it would be done by the DEP at no cost to the city. They expected that city officials would welcome their concern about the marsh, heed their scientific knowledge, and use it responsibly. They were puzzled by their lack of influence, and it became obvious to some of them that achieving their goals had little to do with scientific information about marsh ecology and tide gates and much to do with other issues.

The students did not understand that when they entered the policy process, they and their knowledge were only one of several participants, perspectives, and values at play, and that other participants, including the decision makers, might judge other values to be more important. By failing to appreciate that city officials did not share their perspective on the significance of their studies or on how decision making does or should take place, the students discredited themselves. Their myths and practices consigned these otherwise effective participants to "policy irrelevancy."

Strategy. Besides being attentive to perspectives, conservation biologists need to be knowledgeable about the strategies available to influence policy outcomes and practices. *Strategies* are ways of managing resources to affect policy outcomes and achieve one's goals (Lasswell 1971). Resources may include an existing power base such as money, but they also include such things as knowledge and skill, people's well-being, their sense of what is morally right, the respect of their peers, or the affection of family and friends. All human beings have resources of these kinds, although some people have more resources than others. It is easy to see that a well-paid and highly respected corporate executive has more resources to influence policy than an uneducated prisoner of the state. The goal of the global human rights movement is to ensure that all humans have a base of resources with which to influence and control the quality of their own lives—including a healthy environment—and their prospects for a sustainable future.

People's perspectives usually include some inherent notion of which strategies are appropriate, or even available, in given situations. Four major classes of strategies are recognized, and each one includes a range of methods from persuasive to coercive. *Ideological strategies* appeal to ideas. They can be effective means of changing public policy; education, for example, is a widely accepted ideological strategy. *Diplomatic strategies* involve specialized communication among elites in the policy arena. (Elites are the most influential people or groups in any social setting; they have considerable resources at their command, such as power, wealth, and knowledge.) *Military strategies* use resources as weapons and build up armed forces to threaten or overpower opponents. "Holy wars" and extreme environmental "monkeywrenching" (such as blowing up bulldozers or spiking trees) are examples of military strategies. *Economic strategies* bestow or withhold wealth (land, money, and products) as a means of influencing policy. Because wealth is so closely tied to power, knowledge, and all other values, the creation, destruction, and distribution of wealth are powerful ways of influencing public policy.

In practice, individuals, groups, and nations use a mix of strategies to achieve their demands. A group that opposed wolf reintroduction to Yellowstone National Park, for instance, might first try to influence policy by asking its members to write letters to local newspapers voicing their concerns and opposition. It might also send the group's elite (executive director, board of directors, or wealthy benefactors) to visit personally with the superintendent of Yellowstone or surrounding states' game and fish departments to try to block reintroduction. The group might instigate a nationwide tourist boycott of the park to put pressure on government administrators. Eventually, if frustrated by the failure of all these efforts, some members of the group might resort to violence—threatening or harming agency personnel or shooting reintroduced wolves.

In the marsh restoration case, the students' strategy was largely ideological. They communicated their research to the policy elites to persuade them to replace the tide gate. But this strategy did not get them what they wanted, so they need to rethink their strategy and try again.

Conventional and Functional Understanding. There are two different, but related, ways of understanding policy processes. A *conventional* understanding sees events, situations, values, and decisions largely in customary, even habitual, ways. It uses common images and accepts standard labels for the relationships and interactions among entities. For example, many people draw on everyday notions about personalities and politics in choosing a candidate in national elections. But conventional images, notions, and language are not useful for comparing interactions in the policy process. General catch-all labels, such as dismissing a co-worker's activities as "political" or as a "personality quirk," do little to elucidate policy dynamics.

A *functional* view, on the other hand, goes beyond conventional wisdom to explore and understand the similarities and differences in processes of interaction—that is, to understand the structure and functioning of systems. The distinction is like that between a layman who understands a landscape in terms of meadows, trees, hills, and animals that he likes or dislikes, and an ecologist who understands a landscape in terms of structure and process—dynamic vegetative communities, land use changes through time, stream flows, succession processes, predation, biogeochemical cycling, energy flows, and so forth. A functional understanding of process is a tremendous advantage when it comes time to manage a landscape for ecological health. Such a frame of reference is also useful for understanding the policy process in order to develop influence and participate in it; neither conventional perspectives on politics nor the concepts of conservation biology are adequate for functional policy understanding.

A functional understanding depends on a stable frame of reference of integrated concepts, categories, and language from which to compare situations of perhaps widely different content (Lasswell and McDougal 1992). Such a comprehensive, yet precise, approach can enable conservation biologists to perform indispensable intellectual tasks in their analysis of situations and decision making. Functional analysis should be used to confront conventional images, which are often short on insight, explanation, and guidance. At the same time, conservation biologists need to cultivate conventional language in order to explain and justify matters to rank-and-file citizens, colleagues, and other participants in conservation and environmental policy. The practical advantage of a functional outlook is that it maximizes the likelihood that its holders will have influence and power over policy outcomes and practices.

The Shaping and Sharing of Values

Policies create or bestow values as well as determine how they will be distributed; in other words, the policy process is about the "shaping and sharing" of values (Lasswell 1971). Policy scientists recognize eight fundamental human values—*power, wealth, enlightenment, skill, respect, rectitude* (moral outlook), *well-being,* and *affection* (Table 17.1). These functional categories describe what all people strive to achieve in life, no matter what their culture, age, or situation. In addition, as discussed above, these values are the resources that people use to achieve their demands.

Table 17.1
Values or Bases of Influence and Power Potentially Open to Conservation Biologists Wanting to Affect Policy Outcomes and Practices

Value	Doctrine	Example	Professionals	Institutions
Power	Political doctrine	Victory or defeat in fights or elections	Presidents, politicians, leaders	Government, law, political parties
Enlightenment	Standards of disclosure	Scientific discovery, news	Scientists, reporters, editors	Scientific establishment, universities, mass media
Wealth	Economic doctrine	Income, ownership, transfer	Financiers, bankers, business people	Stock market, banks, businesses
Well-being	Hygiene, health	Medical care, protectors	Doctors, nurses, health care providers	Hospitals, recreational facilities
Skill	Professional standards	Instruction, demonstration of proficiency	Teachers, craftspeople	Vocational schools, professional schools
Affection	Code of friendship	Expression of intimacy, friendship, loyalty	Friends, intimates, family, community	Familiar and friendship circles
Respect	Code of honor	Honor, discrimination, exclusion	Social elites, societies, leaders	Social classes and castes
Rectitude	Moral code	Acceptance in religious or ethical groups	Ethicists, religious leaders	Ethical and religious associations

Modified from Lasswell and Kaplan 1950; Lasswell and McDougal 1992.

Policy decisions have outcomes and effects that bestow certain values on certain people and may deprive others. Oligarchy, for instance, is a form of government that concentrates power in the hands of a few while depriving the majority. Numerous policies, including minimum wage laws and social security programs, aim to distribute wealth more widely. Other policies, such as civil rights laws, are established to distribute power and respect more widely. Many environmental regulations seek to protect the natural world, which directly and indirectly affects the health and well-being of people. The U.S. Constitution and the United Nations' Universal Declaration of Human Rights both articulate an overriding goal for human civilization—"a commonwealth of human dignity" or democracy, which calls for the widespread shaping and sharing of all values and the equality of rights (McDougal et al. 1988; Lasswell and McDougal 1992).

Values are exchanged through social interactions; all eight are involved to some degree in any interpersonal interaction. For instance, anti-discrimination policies that seek to improve respect for certain deprived groups and satisfy the rectitude standards of certain groups may also effect changes in the economic standing, enlightenment holdings, or power base of these same people or other groups. The sum of all the value interactions in a society constitutes the *social process*, while the pattern of distribution and enjoyment of all eight values is the *social structure* (Lasswell and Kaplan 1950). Perspectives and strategies can also be defined in terms of values: functionally, perspectives are value priorities, and strategies are ways of managing value resources to affect value outcomes (Lasswell 1971).

Influence is the capacity of people to produce effects on others by intangible or indirect means. Through interpersonal and intergroup relationships, people make claims to certain values. Influence can be seen as the value position of a person or group as well as the potential for change in that position. To have influence within a community is to have a high position with respect to all the values important to that community. Within the scientific community, for instance, knowledge and skill are the preeminent values. Conservation biologists must draw on whatever values they possess and use them effectively to influence decision making and develop power.

The values at play in any given policy arena must be determined empirically. Although scientists would never think of conducting experiments without explicitly understanding the relevant concepts and checking facts empirically, when it comes to policy, these same scientists too often abandon their empirical rigor and jump into the fray without adequate policy theory or empiricism.

Power is participation in decision making. Power differs from influence in that it is only those people who participate in decision making whose acts really matter. To have power means that one's perspective must be taken into account by decision makers. Power, which may derive from myth, faith, and loyalties as much as interests, controls the value outcomes of policies and practices.

The salt marsh restoration case is a conflict of values, as are many other environmental and public policy issues. What the students wanted was to have influence in an area that was of concern to them. The students drew on their enlightenment, skill, and other value holdings and used them to seek power and respect. Instead, they found their value position wanting relative to those of other policy players. Having started out with little appreciation of what they were getting themselves into, the challenge for them now is to be as smart as possible in assessing their own and others' perspectives, strategies, and values in order to be effective in influencing future policy. They must clarify their perspective and their societal role as professionals, and they must find the necessary tools to analyze the policy process and develop influence and power.

An Analytic Method for Mapping Policy Processes

The concepts and terms introduced above all come from the social sciences, specifically the policy sciences. This field, developed by Harold D. Lasswell and his colleagues at the Yale Law School in the middle of the 20th century, grew out of research in anthropology, law, political science, sociology, and many other fields. The policy sciences provide a method of analyzing and mapping the policy process. We now have over 50 years' experience with this method, which has proved invaluable in addressing many complex policy problems. It is a method for interdisciplinary problem solving—whatever the content of the issue—and it provides an inclusive model of the policy process in which all problems and participants are embedded (Lasswell and Kaplan 1950; Lasswell 1971; Lasswell and McDougal 1992).

Policy-oriented conservation biologists need a method of making maps so that they can navigate the dynamic policy terrain successfully, and the policy sciences constitute such a guide (Figure 17.1). The policy sciences include analytic tools that allow conservation biologists to "map" the rationality and political issues in any policy process, but more specifically, they can help all of us to clarify and secure our common interest democratically. This method focuses attention on the problem itself so that it can be analyzed in full and in relation to its context. It provides guidelines to comprehend the context. It also enlarges the scope of inquiry to encompass a wide range of methods from many disciplines. And finally, it asks us always to justify our decisions and actions by reminding us of our own role as well as the consequences of our policymaking activities. An essential point to remember is that in policy problem solving—as in ecological problem solving—every detail is affected by its interaction with the *entire context* of the problem. Therefore, the problem

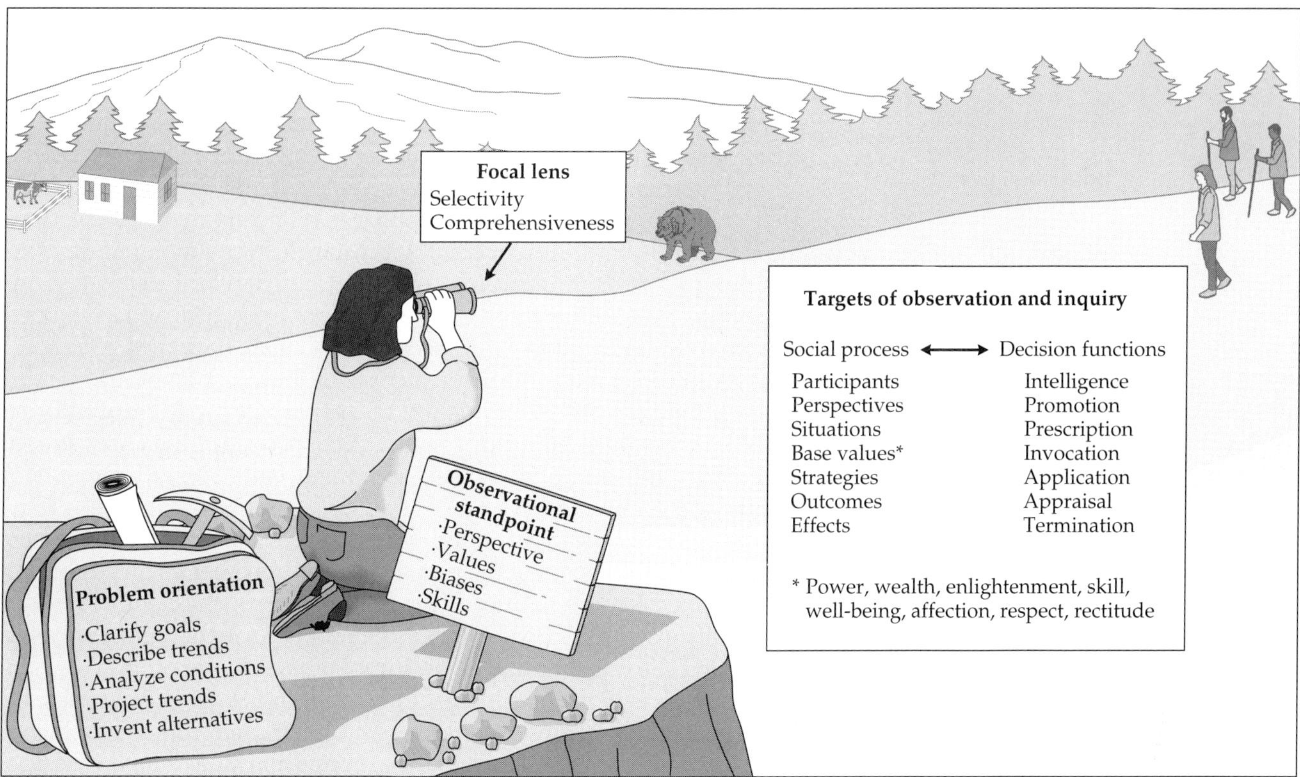

Figure 17.1 The integrated concepts and categories for interdisciplinary problem solving. (Modified from Lasswell 1971; Brewer and deLeon 1983; Reisman and Schreiber 1987.)

solver must use a method that places the problem within its context and continually makes reference to the societal and environmental setting.

There are three components to this mapmaking procedure: (1) problem orientation, (2) mapping of the social process or context, and (3) mapping of the decision-making process. Together these three components give the user a relatively complete picture of the policy arena and its processes for whatever issue is of concern. *Problem orientation* deals with issues of rationality both in the content of the problem and in the process itself. Mapping the context requires the use of the *social process model*—which looks at participants, how they interact, and the outcomes of their interactions (in terms of values)—and the *decision process model*—which focuses attention on a seven-function process by which participants formulate and implement policies. Based on sound concepts and categories, the method constitutes a stable frame of reference that allows participants (and observers, such as analysts) to examine a complex flow of events both systematically and comprehensively. Using conventional approaches, many people get lost and do not know how to order the myriad details systematically in a way that produces insight, improves judgment, and generates solutions.

Problem Orientation: Maximizing Rationality

Problem orientation is a strategy for constructing more rational policies (Brunner 1995). When people make policy decisions, according to the logic of rational choice, they will choose the alternative that they expect will be the best means of realizing their goals, based on everything they know about the problem and potential solutions. Practically speaking, rationality is the process of adapting alternatives (means) to goals (ends), and vice versa. An adequate strategy of problem solving involves what Lasswell (1971) called five intellectual tasks, which allow the user to "define" problems more clearly and to invent and evaluate possible solutions. Contrary to popular thought, problems are not out there waiting to be found; they are constructs in people's minds concerning the discrepancy between a desired state of affairs and an observed state, and they include basic notions about causes and solutions.

The first task is to *clarify the goals* of those involved in or affected by the problem and its solution. This is not as easy as it sounds: any community is composed of people with differing perspectives reflecting their values. Considerable differences have been evident, for instance, even among those committed to the goal of saving species, as evidenced by recent debates about reauthorization of the Endangered Species Act (see Noss 1996 and associated papers). Moreover, many people cannot clearly articulate their own goals, perspectives, or values, let alone reconcile them with those of others.

Second, *describe the trends* and history of the problem with respect to the goals. This task involves empirical data collection on, for instance, animal population sizes and numbers as well as human land uses, identities and expectations, and economic factors.

Third, *analyze the conditions* under which these trends have taken place. These may include the causes of the problem as well as other factors that have influenced or affected the situation. This is a task at which scientific inquiry has traditionally excelled; indeed, there are some who see this as the only significant task and the one that leads directly to solution of the problem.

The fourth task is to *project possible future trends* in the problem. It asks, for example, whether the decline of biodiversity in the United States will continue, or what the likelihood is that financial support for the Endangered Species Act will reverse or change ongoing trends and conditions.

Finally, based on the preceding information, the participants must *invent alternatives* to solve the problem and to realize their goals, evaluate how well each alternative might work, and choose one (or a combination) to implement. Practical problem solving is an exercise in successive approximation, not a one-time completion of these intellectual tasks or a final commitment to a policy (Table 17.2). Problem solving should be an iterative process; the five tasks should be revisited repeatedly.

The marsh restoration example shows that, despite a fairly conventional approach, the student conservation biologists did carry out some tasks of a useful problem orientation. They began by finding a discrepancy between a

Table 17.2
One Way to Apply the Five Tasks of Problem Orientation

1. Goals: What outcomes do we prefer? What are the problems with respect to these goals? (Problems are discrepancies between goals and actual or anticipated states of affairs.)
2. Alternatives: What alternatives are available to the participants and others to solve the problems?
3. Evaluation of alternatives: Would each alternative contribute toward solution of the problems or not?
   a. Trends: Did each alternative work or not work when tried in the past on relevant occasions?
   b. Conditions: Why, or under what conditions, did it work or not work?
   c. Projections: Would it work satisfactorily under these conditions?
4. Repeat the procedure to refine and supplement considerations of goals, alternatives, and evaluation so far.

Note: These tasks have been reconfigured here into a worksheet-like format after Brunner 1995. Ask these questions of your conservation problem.

desired state of affairs (an ecologically intact salt marsh) and what lay before them (the degraded marsh resulting from an outdated tide gate). Without defining this "problem" in terms of their own goals or the goals of any other community, they proceeded directly to documenting ecological aspects of the degradation, determining its proximate causes, and pursuing a "solution." The students did not identify who was affected by the problem and how they were affected (what groups were being indulged or deprived of what values). The students did document some biophysical trends and partially fulfilled the task of examining causes and conditioning factors. They might have broadened the scope of their trend research to document the effects of marsh degradation on local economies, human health, and other facets of the surrounding communities (that is, how the community was deprived of or indulged in certain values). A wider search for conditioning factors might also have revealed the significance of the new sports facility and other land uses. Such an exercise would have been helpful in framing this problem not simply as an ecological one with a technological solution (a new tide gate), but as a policy problem with a significant political dimension. It is not clear that the students considered future developments very thoroughly either. It would have been helpful for them to have projected the effects of continued marsh degradation in terms of water quality (salinity and flows), aesthetics, changes in vegetation, and possible effects on community well-being, as well as the effects of various alternatives.

Finally, the single solution proposed—restoring the marsh with a self-regulating tide gate—was not evaluated rigorously (although the success of other self-regulating tide gates in the state did bolster their case). Was the students' preferred alternative adequate to solve the problem? What aspects of the problem did it fail to address? What other alternatives might have compared favorably with it? What would happen if it did not work? These questions could not be answered, of course, without reference to some specified goals of some specified community, and without a thorough analysis of the history, conditions, and projected trends of the problem. A more complete problem orientation would have bolstered their appeal to the city by incorporating more realistic and reliable data. Instead of appealing to the city council to restore the marsh in order to improve wildlife habitat—which was probably seen by officials and other community members as a narrow scientific or environmental goal—they could have addressed wider community values and made a more convincing argument. Fundamentally, theirs was a problem-blind, rather than a problem-oriented, approach.

Mapping Social Process: Revealing the Context

In addition to bringing as much rationality as possible to problem-solving efforts, the policy-oriented conservation biologist must be consciously and explicitly aware of the social process in which problems are embedded. Indeed, the constant interaction between problem solving and social process indicates that mapping of social processes is as important as, and should be conducted simultaneously with, problem orientation.

The basic premise of social process mapping is the *optimization postulate*, which says that people are predisposed to act in ways that they perceive will leave them better off than if they had acted differently. In other terms, people pursue *values* (see Table 17.1) through *institutions* using *resources* that affect their *environment*. Social process can be viewed functionally as unceasing human interaction in an attempt to achieve preferred value outcomes (such as more power or wealth). Institutions are relatively fixed societal patterns for the shaping and sharing of values. For example, the institution of government shapes and shares power, the university shapes and shares enlightenment, and the hospital shapes and shares health or well-being. All people and institutions are part of many ever-changing social processes. Mapping these processes clarifies fundamental value–institutional interactions and their effects on the problem at hand as well as possible solutions.

There are seven steps to the conservation biologist's task of social process mapping:

1. Identify the *participants,* both individual and institutional. These should include not only those who are active in solving a problem, but also those who are affected by the problem and those who may be affected by the solution (see the discussion of stakeholders in Chapter 11).
2. Determine the *perspectives* of all the participants in terms of identities, expectations, and demands. As part of this step, try to understand the myths that motivate them as well as clashing counter-myths. This is the basis for all justifications or appeals to morality; all demands are justified relative to the myth's basic premises.
3. Describe the *situation* or arena and how it affects the participants. This refers to the zones of interaction—the geographic setting, the natural and human environment, the organizations involved—and the sequence of events, as well as the existence of any crises that might bear on the problem.
4. Describe the *base values* (or value resources) of the participants. Determine the value shapers and sharers, that is, who is indulged in what values and who is deprived. The perspectives and capabilities of the participants will give insight into their values.
5. Determine what *strategies* are being used by the participants and how they are deploying base values to affect outcomes.
6. Describe the *outcomes* of the interaction in terms of how individual and institutional participants are either indulged in certain values or deprived of others. We often speak of outcomes as choices or decisions—was a policy decision made one way or another?
7. Identify the post-outcome events or *effects* of the interaction, again in terms of values and institutions. The essential question about institutional effects is whether new practices have appeared or old practices have been diffused or restricted.

Although this exercise may seem to result merely in description, it is the basis for analyzing who wants what in the policy arena and why, how they might try to achieve it, how they might be thwarted, and how to achieve a better distribution of values for all involved or affected. A careful mapping of the social process can give tremendous insight into human interactions.

The students in the marsh restoration case may have seen themselves as the only players initially, but they should have realized that the issue affected many other people in many ways. If they had done nothing and the marsh had continued to degrade, it would have affected people; if they had achieved their goal of installing a new tide gate, that would also have affected people.

By 1995, a few of the students realized that the group's initial perspective and strategy were lacking, and they began to devise methods to investigate their own problem-solving approaches as well as the social and decisional processes they wanted to influence. Some enrolled in university courses that taught them how to apply a policy orientation to their scientific and conservation work. They started by carrying out an appraisal of their activities and the overall policy process to date, including a functional value analysis. This required them to examine their own perspectives and strategies and to produce a contextual map—all based on empirical data. They conducted a wide-ranging search, not only for people and groups involved in the decision-making process, but also for those who might have other interests in the salt marsh (e.g., health concerns, economic stakes, or political interests), including those who might oppose restoration. They began asking questions about people's perspectives: had anyone suffered health problems, for instance, or were people offended by the appearance of the area? Did the city or the developers make a lot of money from the sports facility, or did respect for the mayor grow because of it? What did people expect would happen? What did they want to happen?

The students concluded that the local community is deprived of well-being under current marsh management policy. There are health risks because of pollution and poor water quality. Changes in vegetation have increased fire danger as well as the threat of Lyme disease (because of increased numbers of deer ticks). Environmental aesthetics have been reduced. The community's stock of affection has also been reduced because there are few opportunities for outdoor community and family activities (such as picnics and sports) near the degraded marsh. Moreover, the residents have limited decision-making authority over their own neighborhood and the watershed, and are thus deprived of power.

The students characterized the neighborhoods surrounding the marsh in terms of income, existing institutional influences, governmental power structure, institutions beyond the immediate vicinity (such as the construction industry), and other ongoing issues of concern (looking for such potential conditioning factors as a housing crisis or new jobs at the sports center). They looked at the value distribution in the community. Who was wealthy? Who was poor? Who was powerful in the neighborhoods or in city government? Highly respected? Well-educated? Did anyone have strong principles about what was right for the marsh? The students determined that, given the context, the local community had little ability to increase its own well-being, affection, and power without help: they lacked skills, wealth, and knowledge.

Mapping the Decision Process: Making Policy

While the social process is the "who" and the "what" of any problem's context, the decision process is the "how." The *decision process* is the course of action by which participants formulate, implement, and enforce the rules or policies by which society lives. Because policy, even simple policy, involves diverse participants with equally diverse perspectives, values, and strategies, politics is inevitable. Yet, as Brunner (1995) points out, people must at some level reconcile their policy differences in order to secure their common interests. The decision process is a means of managing or reconciling conflicts among policies through politics. Scientists—with their strong scientific identity and their preferred strategy of communication or persuasion—may view decision processes as irrational and illogical. They often believe that their role is to supply all the facts, and that once the participants share a common fund of knowledge, they will all agree about its meaning and uses. *But shared knowledge cannot obviate the conflicts that arise from inherent differences in values and perspectives.*

A decision is commonly thought of as the point at which a commitment is made to a particular policy. But decision making is more accurately described as a process than as an event. It consists of several activities that lead up to the commitment and several that follow (Table 17.3). It may proceed sequentially or may skip, overlap, or repeat operations, or one function may be protracted. Knowledge of the functions of decision making and the particular difficulties

Table 17.3
The Seven Functions of Decision Making

Function term	Activity
Intelligence (planning)	Information gathering, planning, prediction (e.g., fieldwork, social surveys, models, pluralistic discussion)
Promotion (open debate)	Advocacy of alternatives (e.g., forums needed, pluralistic discussion, recommendations)
Prescription (setting rules or guidelines)	Enactment of general rules of operation (e.g., recovery plans and other agreements for species/habitat conservation)
Invocation (compliance or enforcement)	Carrying out of general rules in practice (e.g., work in field or lab and management)
Application (dispute resolution)	Based on peer review, authority, or other mechanisms (e.g., open, pluralistic forums, internal and external means)
Appraisal (review)	Continuous assessment of success and failure (e.g., formal and informal and internal and external evaluations)
Termination (termination)	Ending of rules and framework for their implementation (e.g., stopping what's not working, moving to a new beginning)

Modified from Lasswell 1971, in which these terms are described in detail.

that can occur in each is very useful. It permits participants to locate themselves in the process, anticipate and prepare for later operations, understand what functions have been skipped, and analyze how well each one has been carried out.

The first function is the *intelligence* or planning operation. At this point, information about a problematic situation is gathered, organized, and brought to the attention of decision makers. Intelligence should be collected from all relevant sources and people and communicated to key people. Part of this process involves the clarification of goals and other aspects of contextual problem orientation.

The second activity is *promotion*, or open debate about what to do. Participants begin to take sides and mobilize resources to advocate different alternatives. People need to think about what values are being promoted by what groups and about who will be indulged and who will be deprived by each alternative being promoted.

The third function is *prescription*, or the enactment of rules, policies, or guidelines for action. The implications and consequences of the rules must be considered: will they fit with existing rules already in use? Will they be binding?

Fourth is *invocation*, or enforcement of the general rules. The rules are put into practice and are applied to actual cases. Programs are set up, teams organized, and work begins. Enforcement, or compliance, is important to make sure that the program, teams, and operations are consistent with the rules prescribed. Invocation establishes accountability.

The fifth function is *application*, or dispute resolution. Participants must interpret the rules, and different interpretations often give rise to conflict. For conflict to be resolved, there must be enforcement as well as continuous review and approval or disapproval of behavior.

This operation is followed by *appraisal*, or review. All the other operations must be judged on their success or failure. Participants also need to question who the program really serves and who is responsible for its success or failure.

The last step is *termination*, or moving on to a new decision process. Termination cancels the past prescription as well as the program for its implementation.

The decision process in the marsh restoration case began when the students first got involved. Their principal activities were intelligence gathering, although this was limited to ecological information (which was one of their fundamental problems). Based on this information, the students defined the problem in a particular and narrow way—as marsh degradation—and promoted a solution—tide gate replacement. The new tide gate they sought would have constituted a new prescription, enacted by the city government through the authoritative decision process. But the policy promoted by the students conflicted with established policy or policy that other people wanted, and the policy elites effectively stopped their push for termination of existing marsh management and adoption of a new prescription. Their intelligence and promotion operations continued for some time. But because the students had only partly oriented to the problem, had carried out only limited social process or contextual mapping, and had failed to understand the decision process they wanted to influence, their intelligence and promotion activities were ineffective, and they were left frustrated by their experience.

As part of their new approach beginning in 1995, the students analyzed the "problem definitions" that seemed to be used by various key participants—the mayor, the city parks and recreation department, the state DEP, the university, citizens, and the scientific community. They discovered that these definitions were quite different and conflicting. The students have recommended a new problem definition that takes the common interest into greater consideration, and they hope to promote it successfully given their new insights. Several scientific questions remain unanswered, to which ongoing student projects will provide answers. The students have received additional grants to characterize the watershed in more biophysical detail and to conduct restoration ecology experiments. They are also seeking to build better maps of social processes within the community most directly affected. In addition, they are constructing better maps of the decision process, involving the community as well as city and state organizations. Specifically, they are analyzing effective power processes, identifying rigidities in the decision process, and determining how to overcome them through new strategies.

It is important to keep in mind that the decision process is the means by which the common interest—or at least a working specification of it—is found and implemented. The students and city officials (and other participants) advocated different policies, and it was not possible to satisfy all of these special interests at the same time. However, the decision process will not be over unless the students want it to be. They can develop new strategies to continue promoting their preferred alternative.

Learning to use these mapmaking tools—the problem-oriented and contextual approach of the policy sciences—requires experience and judgment. Some people, trapped in convention, will never appreciate their practical significance (Brunner 1996a), and some will never make the effort to learn them nor take the time to practice them. And some—some scientists among them—will never accept this functional way of understanding the complexity of the policy process and their own role within it (Brunner and Ascher 1992). But for those who see effective participation in the policy process as the key to achieving conservation goals, this method will pay off in practical results, in better understanding of policy, and in knowing when, where, and how to intervene to make improvements.

Effective Use of the Policy-Oriented Approach

There are many outstanding examples of basic knowledge being used by decision makers to produce good policies, and it is abundantly clear that science and technology have improved the lot of many humans and ameliorated some environmental problems. But relying only on the scientific perspective can be counterproductive. Science is essential, but it is also rare in environmental policymaking. Many policy decisions that affect biodiversity are less than rational, despite the availability of ever-increasing scientific knowledge (Colborn 1995; Healy and Ascher 1995). The expectation that science will influence policy outcomes often reinforces existing problems and controversies in the political arena rather than solving them. In fact, the beliefs of traditional science have been called into question by philosophers, cognitive psychologists, sociologists, political scientists, and the public (e.g., Dryzek 1990; Brunner and Ascher 1992; Colborn 1995; Healy and Ascher 1995; White 1995).

Conservation biologists largely share in the basic perspective or myth of science, which includes certain assumptions about science, rationality, and politics (Brunner 1996b). In this conventional view, the purpose of science is the prediction of consequences of possible changes in a system and the discovery and use of objective laws of nature for this purpose. Adopting a policy-oriented approach, however, provides new insights. A policy-oriented professional sees that the purpose of science in human affairs is "freedom through insight" by bringing more factors more reliably into conscious awareness for purposes of decision making. It is understood that prediction is not always possible because consideration of all factors compromises the ability to forecast accurately.

Similarly, the conventional view of rationality is that scientific predictions reduce uncertainty and that policy decisions must depend on them in order to be rational, cost-effective, and comprehensive. This view assumes that goals are fixed. The policy-oriented scientist, on the other hand, assumes that it is more rational, given the uncertainty and ambiguity in the world, to field-test multiple, discrete alternatives and to select, diffuse, and replicate the successes through the adaptation of both goals and alternatives. (Note that this is how natural selection operates: generation of variation followed by perpetuation of the most successful alternatives. Also, see the parallels with adaptive management in Chapters 11 and 12.)

Concerning politics, the conventional perspective holds that political consensus depends upon objective scientific knowledge and that scientists deserve a special position above and outside politics because their inputs to policy decisions are value-free and objective. The policy-oriented scientist realizes that the purpose of politics is to reach consensus, that doing so depends on trust and credibility derived from experience, and that the values and beliefs of scientists, like those of all other participants in politics, should be transparent to the public and their representatives.

The norms of professional behavior and the roles of professionals are currently undergoing dramatic reorganization in all sectors of society. Conservation biology is no exception. This changing situation leaves practitioners with some complicated professional choices (Schön 1983, 1987; Brunner and Ascher 1992; Clark 1993; Schön and Rein 1994; Sullivan 1995; Clark, in press). The issue of professionalism is being widely debated in many fields of science and policy, including the pages of the journal *Conservation Biology*. Some authors promote a more science-based, doctrinaire approach, while others advocate more policy-oriented thinking as the way to develop more creative, effective, and socially responsible professionals.

Developing a problem-oriented, contextual outlook does not mean abandoning good science or becoming a narrow partisan advocate. The policy-oriented approach *complements* science by enhancing rational consideration of social and decisional factors, providing methods for working effectively within the political arena, and offering a moral precept to clarify and secure, not special interests, but the common interest. A policy orientation permits practitioners to determine empirically and rigorously how their knowledge is used in policy and how well the policy process is working, and it permits them to upgrade the outcome of the process from their standpoint (see Lasswell 1970; Clark et al. 1992).

Over the course of the marsh restoration effort, the students have moved from a strictly scientific approach to a much more policy-oriented approach. Their initial perspective led them to treat the marsh issue as a technical problem; as they understood it, the only limitation on restoring the marsh was a lack of scientific information, and they continued to press forward on this front. But a reconceptualization of the problem and the communities affected by it, their roles in the policy process, and the range of potential solutions has created new options for the students.

There are two additional approaches that conservation biologists can use to achieve practical, effective participation in the policy process, which we address next.

A Coalition Approach

The policy-oriented practice of conservation biology should emphasize collaboration in its new mix of strategies. An opportunity almost always exists to form a *coalition* around a common interest, such as protecting biodiversity. In addition to environmental groups, participants might include community-based civic improvement groups, neighborhood block-watches and greening groups, block beautification and health care groups, and local civic and religious institutions. Each of these groups is organized around the convergent interests of its members. It may be difficult for conservation biologists to have much policy influence when working alone, and the best policy effect may come from joining forces with organizations with large memberships and community groups that already have good positions in the appropriate power process. Such organizations have standing, a history of success, and leaders who may have at least an implicit policy orientation developed from experience.

Thinking functionally about coalitions in policy illustrates how values are shaped and shared in the power process. An effective coalition often contains leaders who have a broad base of values available to them as resources and who are both problem-oriented and contextual. Many improvements have arisen from the vision and hard work of dedicated individuals who learned over time which approaches worked and which did not. As a result, successful individuals have developed a perspective rooted in rectitude, power, skill, and other values, although they may have little explicit, systematic knowledge about the policy process. The key to setting up or joining a coalition is to offer a larger and more powerful array of resources to the joint demand. Combined resources will bolster or augment whatever strategies are being used.

Since becoming more policy-oriented, the conservation biology students in the marsh restoration case have identified some natural allies and are reaching out to them. Likely allies include the local community most affected by current marsh management, government departments such as parks and recreation and the state DEP, and organized conservation groups in the region. The students are likely to benefit from membership in a larger, more powerful coalition, and they will also learn more about practical politics and policy processes.

To build a coalition to promote marsh restoration to the mayor and city aldermen (and as part of their general contextual mapping), the students carried out a survey of public values of people in the watershed, especially those living in the most polluted and degraded lower end. They found that local residents use existing parks along part of the marsh for recreation (walking, jogging, nature appreciation, and fishing), although these people generally perceive the area to be unsafe and polluted. When asked how they would like the marsh improved, residents said first that they wanted the pollution and garbage cleaned up (at that time, volunteer clean-up efforts extracted a daily average of 400–600 pounds of refuse from the river and marsh), and second, that they wanted the environment improved for plants and animals. However, the results indicated mixed attitudes toward the river and marsh: some citizens wanted to clean it up, whereas others viewed it as a dump. The students have learned that a better understanding of human values is essential for developing a successful policy for the watershed and for forming a workable coalition.

The students plan to follow up with local meetings about the marsh and watershed, more slide shows designed for public outreach, meetings with the city planner, the parks and recreation department, and DEP, and site visits with local, city, and state representatives (including fire and public health departments). They also plan to get substantial media coverage of the coalition they hope to develop around marsh restoration. Unfortunately, the mayor still sees marsh restoration as a non-issue and remains focused on the city's economy—the ability of the city to market itself successfully, as he puts it. Perhaps a powerful coalition can be built to influence the mayor, or perhaps tide gate replacement will have to wait for a new city administration.

An Innovation Approach

Another approach consistent with a policy-oriented outlook in terms of perspective and strategies is *innovation*, or the bringing of new practices into existence. Practice-based improvements are a proven, logical way to proceed in addressing difficult problems. As better science becomes available to innovators, it can be used to inform practice-based management and policy decisions. Innovation—or practice-based learning, as it is sometimes called—is an attractive and often overlooked approach to policy improvement. Brunner and Clark (in press), for instance, concluded that practice-based approaches in ecosystem management make the most of the limited human capacity to cope with ecological and policy complexities.

Innovations can be initiated through prototyping. A *prototype* is a trial change in a system, an attempt to try something new. Many industries, such as the auto industry, build and test prototypes. Policy systems can also develop prototypes that introduce new ways of interacting into social systems. Such changes are usually small in scale and intended to discover how to solve a problem; that is, they are created as learning situations, with further adaptations expected. They are like controlled experiments in that they have a clear goal, but unlike them in that they are flexible enough that programmatic details can be adapted as unexpected problems arise. If successful, a prototype can be "diffused" or transferred and adapted elsewhere to solve similar problems. Such innovative approaches offer much promise for improved conservation policy and management.

Thinking about the new tide gate as a innovation/prototyping exercise may be helpful to the students. The installation of self-regulating tide gates elsewhere in the region over the preceding years was nothing more than a series of individual prototypes or innovations to solve a particular problem. The students plan to study in some detail the processes of innovation, adaptation, and diffusion that led to the success of a new tide gate in a nearby city. In their study, the students will have to be explicitly and systematically policy-oriented, and they will have to seek lessons specifically useful for promoting their own successful prototyping exercise.

Conclusion: The Big Picture

These efforts all depend on keeping the big picture in mind—understanding how competing perspectives (grounded in differing myths) create vast gulfs between people that must be reconciled in order to secure our common interest of a sustainable future. Biodiversity will not be protected as long as the prevailing myth devalues it. But myths (or paradigms, as they are sometimes called by scientists, Kuhn 1965) may take decades or centuries to shift in response to changing contexts. Myths shift only when what people know no longer fits what they believe, so that the beliefs must change to conform to their experience of reality. Shifts in myths may be traumatic to the point of revolution and destruction of society's values and institutions.

The current predominant myth uses science, technology, and the epistemology of positivism instrumentally. These conspire to reinforce a worldview that sees humans apart from nature and nature free to be exploited. This current paradigm includes the notions that individuals are rational, profit-seeking entities, that our collective welfare is derived from individual welfare, that efficiency in the allocation of resources is the highest goal of society, and that this can be achieved only through private property and capitalism—thus elevating individual greed to the status of a positive social good, according to U.S. Congressman George Brown (1995).

There is much talk about finding a new myth for humankind (e.g., Berry 1988; Flannery 1994; Stanley 1995), and there are many ideas about the content of new paradigms. The concept of sustainability (with many variations) is one such idea (e.g., Goodland 1995; Doob 1995). Aldo Leopold's (1949) Land Ethic is another formulation that takes nature more into account in policymaking and in daily life than does the current predominant paradigm. Recently, some "ecological" myths have gained ground, such as Lovelock's (1988) Gaia hypothesis, which embodies a structure for understanding the earth's geophysical and biological systems, and "deep ecology," which grants humans no special claim, morally or otherwise, above other species (Devall and Sessions 1985; Naess 1989).

Conservation professionals must keep this big picture in mind as we carry out our professional work. We can play a key role in promoting a new myth that values biodiversity as the condition of human existence. We can promote flexibility in policies and practices to facilitate a revaluation of biological diversity. Our efforts can support a new myth that truly strives for a sustainable, democratic human enterprise in a healthy, biologically diverse world. This should be our overriding goal!

Summary

Conservation biologists need to be practical and effective in the policy process if they expect society to deal seriously with problems of endangered species, biodiversity, ecosystems, and sustainability. They can accomplish this, first, by learning about themselves and what they inherently (and even subconsciously) bring to policy processes, including their own perspectives, strategies, and values. Second, conservation biologists would benefit by taking more policy-oriented approaches—systematically orienting to problems and comprehensively mapping the social and decisional processes of which they are a part. Third, they can develop new professional strategies, such as building coalitions and introducing innovative prototypes into policy systems.

Questions for Discussion

1. Review the students' perspective (i.e., identity, expectations, and demands) and strategy in the marsh restoration case and compare these with your own perspective and preferred conservation strategy. (This can be done in an open discussion in class.)
2. Choose a local conservation issue and carry out a problem orientation exercise (five intellectual tasks), map the context of the issue (the social process), and analyze the decision process in play (seven decision functions). Judge how well the decision process is being carried out. Now integrate and synthesize all of this information. Assuming you wanted to intervene in this case, what would you do, why, and how? (This can be carried out in small working groups or as a class exercise.)
3. Design a conservation biology curriculum to develop policy-oriented professionals. Be problem-oriented yourself as you address this question. Remember that you will be a practitioner in a few short years and that you must be practical and effective!

Suggestions for Further Reading

Brewer, G. D., and T. W. Clark. 1994. A policy sciences perspective: Improving implementation. In T. W. Clark, R. P. Reading, and A. C. Clarke (eds.), *Endangered Species Recovery: Finding the Lessons, Improving the Process*, pp. 391–413. Island Press, Washington, D.C. This chapter describes the value of the policy science perspective in conservation biology and endangered species restoration. Other chapters in this volume also discuss a policy orientation in professionalism.

Brewer, G. D. and P. deLeon. 1983. *The Foundations of Policy Analysis*. Dorsey Press, Homewood, IL. The policy sciences are introduced to people interested in improving their analytic skills in problem solving.

Brunner, R. D. and W. Ascher. 1992. Science and social responsibility. *Policy Sci.* 25: 295–331. This outstanding paper examines the role and responsibility of science in society. It is recommended reading for all scientists.

Clark, T. W. and R. D. Brunner. 1996. Making partnerships work in endangered species conservation: An introduction to the decision process. *Endangered Species Update* 13(9):1–4. The seven functions of the decision process are described in the context of partnerships for endangered species recovery.

Clark, T. W., A. P. Curlee, and R. P. Reading. 1996. Crafting effective solutions to the large carnivore conservation problem. *Conserv. Biol.* 10:940–948. This paper carries out a problem orientation exercise for a practical problem—the conservation of large carnivores.

Lasswell, H. D. 1971. *Pre-view of the Policy Sciences*. Elsevier, New York. The basic primer on the policy sciences' approach to problem solving. Although it is somewhat difficult for readers who are not used to social science theory, it contains the single best synopsis of the integrated concepts and tools of this field.

Schön, D. A. 1983. *The Reflective Practitioner: How Professionals Think in Action*. Basic Books, New York. Professional practitioners can develop systematic "reflective" skills of thinking about their work and its relation to society that will enable them to tackle difficult policy- and management-related problems.

Weiss, J. A. 1989. The powers of problem-definition: The case of government paperwork. *Policy Sci.* 22:97–121. How people define problems has many consequences for how society formulates and implements solutions. Problem definition helps people to analyze problems, mobilize interest groups, and change institutions and practices.

18

Sustainable Development Case Studies

The first step toward a sustainable human future must be to break the grip that the growth myth retains on our thinking and institutions. Growth-centered development is itself inherently unsustainable. Sustainability does not depend on ending human progress, only on abandoning the myth that erroneously equates such progress with growth.

David C. Korten, 1991–1992

In the 1980s, the concept of **sustainable development** emerged as the means by which biodiversity and natural ecosystems would be saved while enabling humanity to continue to prosper. The concept was first promoted by the *World Conservation Strategy* (IUCN/UNEP/ WWF 1980), a global conservation blueprint that grew from the United Nations Conference on the Human Environment, held in Stockholm in 1972. This was followed by *Our Common Future*, the so-called Brundtland Commission Report (World Commission on Environment and Development 1987), a document adopted by many governments and global institutions as a guide to environmentally compatible development. A more recent successor is *Caring for the Earth: A Strategy for Sustainable Living* (IUCN/UNEP/WWF 1991). All of these documents promote sustainable development as a reasonable means of balancing the demands of nature and people.

But what exactly is sustainable development? Does it mean the same thing to everyone? Is it a legitimate alternative to continued outright destruction of nature? Does it hold the answer to the many conservation problems faced today and in the future? These and many other questions surround sustainable development, and many remain unanswered.

Sustainable development has been defined in various ways. The earlier reports—the *World Conservation Strategy* and the Brundtland Commission report—were largely anthropocentric: they focused on human aspirations and well-being, with the natural environment providing the means by which this was to be accomplished (Robinson 1993). For example, the concept of development used in the *World Conservation Strategy* emphasized that we should "satisfy human needs and improve the quality of human life." Conservation of biodiversity would ensure that we "yield the greatest sustainable development to present generations while maintaining its potential to meet the needs and aspirations of future generations." The Brundtland Commission report of 1987 modified this only slightly to define sustainable development as that which "seeks to meet the needs and aspirations of the present without compromising the ability to meet those of the future." Finally, the more recent global document, *Caring for the Earth*, defines sustainable development as "improving the quality of human life while living within the carrying capacity of supporting ecosystems." (Quotes taken from Robinson 1993.)

In all of these cases sustainable development is defined entirely around one species, *Homo sapiens*, and promotes continued and even expanded economic prosperity. All of these definitions are utilitarian—they perceive the environment as merely the means to an end (human happiness), rather than having inherent good apart from human gain. The definitions do not promote biological diversity other than as a means toward human happiness and well-being; if elements of biodiversity do not contribute to humanity, then presumably they can be discarded. This is perhaps not surprising, as economists and political leaders wrote these definitions.

These definitions may not go far enough in recognizing the extraordinary complexities of nature and the diversity of life-forms, in addition to the services they provide to humanity. They also tend not to recognize the fundamental, underlying problems that create a need for sustainability in the first place. For example, Korten (1991–1992) observed that "The [Brundtland] report's key recommendations—a call for the world's economic growth to rise to a level five to ten times the current output and for accelerated growth in the industrial countries to stimulate demand for the products of poor countries—fundamentally contradicted its own analysis that growth and overconsumption are root causes of the problem. Where ecological reality conflicted with perceived political feasibility, the latter prevailed." It is interesting that a subsequent addendum to the report (World Commission on Environment and Development 1992) stepped back from this recommendation for economic expansion and placed higher priority on population control (Goodland 1995).

The Ecological Society of America produced a "Sustainable Biosphere Initiative" in which a research agenda was proposed to help move the world toward sustainability (Lubchenco et al. 1991). In it, they defined sustainability as "management practices that will not degrade the exploited system or any adjacent system." They also recognized that a prerequisite to this vision is "consumption standards that are within the bounds of ecological possibility and to which all can aspire."

Obviously, human population growth and inequitable environmental demands must both be addressed in a realistic definition. Perhaps a more enlightened definition of sustainable development was offered by Viederman (1992):

> A sustainable society is one that ensures the health and vitality of human life and culture and of nature's capital, for present and future generations. Such a society acts to stop the activities that serve to destroy human life and culture and nature's capital, and to encourage those activities that serve to conserve what exists, restore what has been damaged, and prevent future harm.

In this case, although humanity still takes center stage, as perhaps it should in a definition of development, it more broadly recognizes the role and rights of the remainder of the world and places limits on human activities relative to that world. We offer a working definition of sustainable development that goes even further, and also acknowledges the inherent worth of biodiversity apart from its benefits to humanity. Thus, we define truly sustainable development as *human activities guided by acceptance of the intrinsic value of the natural world, the role of the natural world in human well-being, and the need for humans to live on the income from nature's capital rather than on the capital itself.*

There is a most critical distinction to be made between sustainable *growth* and sustainable *development*. Growth is a *quantitative* increase in the size of a system; development is a *qualitative* change in its complexity and configuration. An economic, social, political, or biophysical system can develop without growing, and thus can be sustainable. It can also grow in size without developing or maturing; this is *not* sustainable development. "Sustainable growth" is a self-contradictory term—an oxymoron. Continued, indefinite growth on this planet or any subset of the planet is a physical impossibility. Eventually, limits of some type (space, food, waste disposal, energy) must be reached; the point at which that will happen is the only aspect open to debate. (Some extreme "cornucopians," however, insist that there are no real limits because as one resource is depleted, others will be discovered or invented to take their place; consequently, the earth can sustain its present rate of human population growth for thousands of years, accommodating hundreds of billions of people [Simon and Kahn 1984; Simon 1990].) "Sustainable *development*" is the issue of concern. Can we make *qualitative* changes in complexity and configuration within existing human systems that do not place increasing *quantitative* demands on natural systems, and are in fact compatible with their continued existence?

If we are to attain such a goal, we must first understand the patterns of human behavior and desires that brought us to this crisis in the first place. These have been outlined by Viederman (1992) and modified as follows:

1. We have consistently failed to accept the fact that the economic system is an open system in a finite biosphere. The economic system is not a closed system, separate from the biosphere, as most traditional economists would have us believe (see Essay 15A); it requires inputs from and exports to living ecosystems, which impose real limits at both ends. Additionally, much of our attention has focused on resource constraints and substitutability, rather than sink constraints—the disposal of wastes.
2. We have consistently failed to recognize that the environment is the basis for all life, including our own, and all production. The natural world should not be merely another special interest competing for our attention, but the playing field upon which all interests compete (recall the "ecological theater" of Chapter 1).
3. We have continued to exhibit a disdain for nature, and a belief that we can master and control it (called by Ehrenfeld [1981] the "arrogance of humanism").
4. We do not question our uncritical acceptance of technology as the answer to all problems, despite a multitude of examples of today's problems being yesterday's solutions (Tenner 1996). This "techno-arrogance" (Meffe 1992) results in a disdain for the "natural" and a love of the "technical."
5. We have not distinguished between growth and development, perhaps due to our belief in technology as savior. Likewise, we fail to recognize that growth will not automatically lead to equity and jus-

tice within and among nations; that is, an "economic trickle down" effect is an unlikely and unfair assumption, and simply an excuse for a few to amass personal wealth at the expense of many.
6. We mistakenly have placed our faith in market systems as the principal mechanism for realizing social goods, such as economic sustainability and justice. Yet, in its failure to value nature's capital or human health, the market system has failed to deal adequately with that which we seek to protect: human life and culture, and nature's capital.
7. We have failed to consider the needs of, and our obligations to, future generations. This concern must be at the core of any conceptualization of sustainability.

These "sources of unsustainability" as Viederman calls them, help to explain how we have arrived at the precarious position we occupy today. They also imply that changes are needed in each of these areas to attain sustainability for the good of humanity and the natural world. Viederman (1992) guides us further by providing seven *principles of sustainability*:

1. Nature should be understood to be an irreplaceable source of knowledge, from which we can learn potential solutions to some of our problems.
2. We should understand that issues of environmental deterioration and human oppression and violence are linked in analysis and action. Gender and racial oppression and efforts to dominate nature have a common root.
3. Humility must guide our actions. Good stewardship begins with restraint.
4. We must appreciate the importance of "proper scale." Place and locality are the foundation for all durable economies, and must be the starting point of action to deal with our problems. Solutions are local and scale-dependent.
5. Sufficiency must replace economic efficiency. The earth is finite, and that fact must be accepted in order for humanity to adopt limits. Living within our needs on a planetary scale does not mean a life of sacrifice, but of greater fulfillment. We must distinguish between "needs" and "wants."
6. Community is essential for survival. The "global community" should reflect and encourage diversity while being interdependent.
7. Biological and cultural diversity must be preserved, defended, and encouraged.

Finally, Bartlett (1994) proposed nine hypotheses regarding sustainability (as discussed by Goodland 1995). We present them here in modified form (Table 18.1) as another window on the sustainability perspective. You might ask yourself how these hypotheses might actually be tested.

With these guidelines providing the basis of sustainable development, we will examine five case studies of potential sustainability. They will illustrate the principles and problems discussed thus far, and show the complexities inherent in managing interacting systems of humans and nature. We say "potential" sustainability because none of these have yet been proven in the long term, as none have existed for very long. All offer some promise of maintaining natural systems while satisfying human needs, if properly managed. Afterward, we will offer some cautionary comments and alternative perspectives on sustainable development.

Table 18.1
Some Hypotheses Regarding Sustainability

1. For the 1997 average global standard of living, the 1997 population of the earth exceeds carrying capacity.
2. Increasing population size is the single greatest and most insidious threat to representative democracy.
3. The costs of programs to stop population growth are small compared with the costs of population growth.
4. The time required for a society to make a planned transition to sustainability increases with increasing size of its population and the average per capita consumption of resources.
5. Social stability is a necessary, but not sufficient, condition for sustainability. Social stability tends to be inversely related to population density.
6. The burden of the lowered standard of living that results from population growth and from the decline of resources falls most heavily upon the poor.
7. Environmental problems cannot be solved or ameliorated by inceases in the rates of consumption of resources by society at large.
8. The environment cannot be enhanced or preserved through continual compromises.
9. By the time overpopulation and shortage of resources are obvious to most people, the carrying capacity has been exceeded. It is then too late to pursue sustainability in a reasoned, deliberate manner.

Modified from Bartlett 1994.

CASE STUDY 1

Sustainable Tropical Forestry

Gary S. Hartshorn and William Pariona A., Organization for Tropical Studies and Proyecto Especial Pichis-Palcazú

Limited sustainable use of tropical forests can be attainedif the natural dynamics of the particular forest under consideration are understood, and if local people are included in the planning and have a stake in successful management.

Despite growing national and global concerns about tropical deforestation, forests still dominate landscapes over much of the humid lowland tropics. For example, most of the forest-rich countries have more than one-third of their national territory still in forest cover (Table 18.2). Just ten countries account for 65% of our planet's remaining tropical forests, covering an area about the size of the United States. Yet, global loss of tropical forests continues at an ever-increasing rate; an area of tropical forest the size of the state of South Carolina was lost in 1992 (WRI 1995).

Many countries rich in tropical forests have made significant efforts to create a national system of protected areas. However, few forest-rich countries have exceeded the IUCN recommendation of a minimum of 10% of the country in protected areas (Dinerstein and Wikramanayake 1993; WRI 1995). Unprotected forests are usually available for development, but traditional development is virtually synonymous with deforestation. Without major progress in the sustainable use of tropical forests, it is unlikely that unprotected or unmanaged forests will survive well into the 21st century. Thus, the challenge of finding and testing techniques for using tropical forests economically and

Table 18.2
Status of Tropical Forests in Ten Forest-Rich Countries

Rank	Country	Remaining forests (km²)	% forest cover	Annual loss (km²)	% loss/yr
1	Brazil	5,611,070	66	36,709	0.65
2	Zaire	1,132,750	48	7,322	0.65
3	Indonesia	1,095,490	57	12,120	1.11
4	Peru	679,060	53	2,712	0.40
5	Colombia	540,640	47	3,670	0.68
6	India	517,290	16	3,390	0.65
7	Bolivia	493,170	45	6,247	1.27
8	Mexico	485,860	25	6,780	1.40
9	Venezuela	456,900	50	5,991	1.31
10	Sudan	429,760	17	4,817	1.12
	Subtotal	11,441,990	65	89,758	0.78
	World total (90 countries)	**17,562,990**		**154,000**	**0.88**

Data recalculated from WRI 1995.

sustainably, without destroying their ecological functions and the millions of species they harbor, is not only enormous, but extremely urgent. We do not have the luxury of conducting a decade or two of experimental research before recommending how to sustainably use tropical forests.

A Theoretical Basis for Tropical Forest Management

While conducting field research on the demography of a dominant tropical tree species in Costa Rica in the early 1970s, the senior author noticed a high incidence of large canopy trees falling and creating gaps in the old-growth canopy. Having read the classic literature on the antiquity and stability of tropical forests, the slow growth rates of most tropical trees, and the dearth of natural regeneration, he feared that his study forest was literally collapsing. However, monitoring of tree-fall frequency and the rebuilding of forest structure in gaps led him to the revisionist conclusion that this tropical forest is extremely dynamic (Hartshorn 1978). Other studies at several sites have caused a surprising change in our thinking about tropical forests, revealing that canopy gaps are important foci for natural regeneration and rebuilding of these very dynamic forests. Detailed observations of hundreds of tree species in the La Selva old-growth forest in Costa Rica indicated that about 50% of the native tree species are dependent on gaps for successful regeneration (Hartshorn 1980).

The frequent occurrence of gaps in the forest canopy due to tree-falls and the surprisingly high number of species dependent on gaps for successful regeneration support the intermediate disturbance theory of community diversity (see Figure 10.3). Just as has been shown for the marine intertidal zone, frequent disturbance in tropical forests prevents competitive exclusion of many species by the actual or putative dominant species. In pragmatic terms, tree species dependent on gaps in the forest canopy are able to grow rapidly and close the gaps from beneath (Pickett 1983; Brokaw 1985; Uhl et al. 1988). When these gap species attain the canopy (in as short a period as 10–20 years), they may become reproductive long before slower-growing, shade-tolerant tree species can reach the canopy.

Such gap-phase or patch dynamics are also important to other groups or guilds of species, as well as to overall community functions. For example, shade-intolerant understory plants commonly colonize forest gaps and provide a patchy nectar source for hummingbirds. Young gap-phase forest patches also attract mixed-species flocks of insectivorous birds characteristic of the primary forest understory. Even more intriguing is the strong fidelity of some flightless grasshoppers to young gaps in the primary forest (Braker 1991). It is clear that undisturbed old-growth tropical forest is extremely dynamic due to the high frequency of tree-falls and the rapid rebuilding of forest structure. These dynamic processes create a heterogeneous community that is patchy in time as well as space. The stochastic occurrence of intermediate levels of disturbance in tropical forests is a key reason for the persistence of the very high levels of biotic diversity there (Hartshorn 1980; Menges 1992).

As concerns about tropical deforestation gained momentum in the 1970s, there was growing frustration that forest management offered little hope for the survival of tropical forests. The primary ecological bases for this perception of insustainability were the almost universal failure to obtain acceptable natural regeneration of commercial species and the extremely slow growth rates of most tropical trees. A key element of these failures was the narrow focus on just a few of the most valuable and preferred timber species, such as the mahoganies, ebonies, and rosewoods.

The serendipitous presentation of four key papers at a 1976 symposium (Ashton 1978; Hartshorn 1978; Oldeman 1978; Whitmore 1978) opened the door to revisionist thinking about tropical forest dynamics. It became evident that a cause of poor natural regeneration could be that a single tree-fall gap might not be large enough to promote seedling establishment or juvenile growth of the preferred species. Furthermore, the high tree species richness of most tropical forests may drastically reduce the probabilities of successful seedling establishment under stochastic ecological processes. Hartshorn (1979, 1981, 1989) thus proposed simulating gap-phase dynamics by creating long, narrow strip clear-cuts as a forest management technique.

Yánesha Forestry Cooperative: The Palcazú Project

The strip-cut technique of tropical forest management has been pioneered by the Yánesha Forestry Cooperative (COFYAL) in the Central Selva region of Peruvian Amazonia. With major funding from the U.S. Agency for International Development (USAID), the Palcazú Project was initially designed as a typical rural development project based on agricultural colonization of the forest, facilitated by construction of a road into the Palcazú Valley. Because of U.S. Congress regulations in the Foreign Assistance Act, USAID was required to do an environmental assessment of the proposed development project before signing a loan agreement with the Peruvian government. That comprehensive, multidisciplinary assessment stated in very clear terms that agricultural development of the Palcazú Valley would fail due to excessively high rainfall (ca. 7000 mm/yr) and infertile soils.

Production forestry seemed the only viable development option for the valley, and we recommended that the strip-cut technique be tested as a forest management model. A companion social-soundness analysis of the proposed project noted that the project area's human population was about 60% Amuesha Indians, a small tribe of Arawakan Indians now largely confined to the Palcazú Valley. As a consequence of these environmental and social assessments, USAID required the Peruvian government to officially recognize and legally title all Amuesha native community lands in the Palcazú Valley as a precondition for disbursement of the funds; this was necessary because Indians in Peru typically do not hold title to their lands. Eleven native communities' land claims were accepted in the central and southern sectors of the lower Palcazú Valley (300–500 m elevation).

It took two years of technical assistance and political advocacy to create the Yánesha Forestry Cooperative, founded by five native communities and 70 individual Amuesha Indians (Stocks and Hartshorn 1993). COFYAL was the first Indian forestry cooperative in South America. Its objectives were (1) to provide a source of employment for members of the native communities; (2) to manage the communities' natural forests for sustained yield of forest products; and (3) to protect the cultural integrity of the Yánesha (Amuesha) people. Though political strife in Peru eventually disrupted and shut down COFYAL activities, the Amuesha native communities have used their experience with COFYAL to launch small forest industries focused more on medicinal plants.

Strip cuts were the cornerstone of the COFYAL management system for production forestry (Figure 18.1). Commercial strips were 30–40 m wide (about 10–15 m wider than the diameter of an average tree-fall gap) and of variable length depending on topography and logistics; in practice, strips were usually in the range of 100–300 m long. In contrast to traditional forest felling, in which only the largest trees are felled on top of standing smaller trees, strip cutting begins with a machete cleaning of the understory (all stems smaller than 5 cm). Harvesting begins with small pole-sized stems and proceeds through ever-larger trees. Each cut tree is immediately delimbed and hauled off the strip, so worker and oxen mobility on the strip is not seriously impeded by the crowns of felled trees.

COFYAL technicians classified forest that was suitable for timber management, identifying the size and boundary of each production stand, including the locations of all strips, hauling roads, and areas to be excluded from harvesting—such as steep slopes, streamside buffer areas, and swampy lands. Once all the strips to be harvested were determined and located on the ground, the harvesting cycles and sequence were assigned so as to maximize the persistence of mature or advanced regrowth forest bordering any recently harvested strip. For example, a four-cycle spatial harvesting sequence of strips is . . . |1|3|2|4|1| . . . , while a six-cycle harvest sequence is . . . |1|3|5|2|4|6|1| . . . . In either repetitive series, all parallel strips of the same

Figure 18.1 A demonstration strip in Peru six months after cutting. Note the intact adjacent forest and the lack of erosion at the strip site. (Photograph by Gary S. Hartshorn.)

Figure 18.2 A strip-cut site after 28 months of regeneration. Note the size of saplings and the presence of a thick herbaceous layer. (Photograph by Gary S. Hartshorn.)

number are harvested before cutting strips of the next higher number. Depending on the size of the production stand, it may take 6–10 years to complete one cycle of strip cuts. We projected a 30–40-year rotation between the harvesting of any given strip. Again, this surgical insertion of a narrow strip in the matrix of forest is fundamentally different from the classic advancement of the agricultural frontier that cuts entire patches of forest to create ever-larger treeless fields or pastures.

The principal ecological purpose of strip cutting in tropical forests is to promote natural regeneration of native tree species. Detailed inventories of natural regeneration of trees on two demonstration strips cut in 1985 (Figure 18.2) indicated superb regeneration and growth of hundreds of tree species (Hartshorn 1988, 1989; Hartshorn and Pariona 1993). Because harvested strips are not burned or used for agricultural crops, about 13% of the trees regenerating in a strip are exclusively from stump sprouts, and the rest are from natural seed germination, stump sprouts, or both. The high tree species richness on the regenerating strips includes many individuals of the valuable heavy hardwoods, which are purportedly slow-growing. Silvicultural interventions should occur every 3–5 years, however, to control aggressive, sun-loving lianas and to reduce competition among trees. Continued monitoring of tree regeneration on the strip cuts indicates that even with thinning, very few of the hundreds of native tree species have been eliminated or lost on the regenerating strips. If COFYAL members prefer to enrich a strip with a highly preferred tree species or to favor particular individuals in the regenerating strip, these silvicultural treatments are acceptable.

COFYAL had a timber processing complex on land ceded to the cooperative by the Shiringamazú native community. Timber processing facilities included a sawmill with a small bandsaw and a portable circular saw, a portable steel kiln for converting scrap wood to charcoal, and a network of 44 PresCaps, which fit over the butt end of logs (5–30 cm diameter) and use hydraulic pressure to replace the sap with chemicals for preserving posts and poles (Figure 18.3).

Local processing of wood enabled COFYAL to harvest most of the timber on a strip cut, averaging 250 m^3/ha. The pole preservation facility used trees normally too small for sawmilling. Local production of sawn wood enabled

Figure 18.3 The pole preservation facility of the Yánesha Forestry Cooperative (COYFAL). Here, wood from the areas that were strip cut was made into finished products, providing further employment to local citizens. (Photograph by Gary S. Hartshorn.)

COFYAL to market many more species of trees than would be acceptable as logs at national sawmills; some of the woods were of sufficiently high quality that COFYAL exported small quantities to specialty markets such as musical instrument makers and wood artisans in the United States and the United Kingdom. Sales of processed wood brought in U.S. $30,000 in 1991. Profits were distributed to community and individual members, who used the cash to build schools and health clinics, hire resident teachers, and improve housing.

Appropriate technologies were used by COFYAL wherever they were cost-effective and environmentally sound. For example, oxen were used to extract logs from the strip cuts. Though slower from a volume production perspective, oxen logging does far less damage to the fragile forest soil than does heavy machinery such as skidders, bulldozers, or tractors. Oxen dragged the logs to a patio at the end of a strip along a graveled road, from which a flatbed truck or tractor and wagon hauled the logs to the processing center. Where logistically feasible, a winch mounted on a truck was used to extract logs from the proximal part of a strip cut.

The strip-cut model for tropical forest management is being tested in other countries, including Bolivia, Costa Rica, and Papua New Guinea. Preliminary observations indicate that, as in the Palcazú Valley, narrow strip cuts promote outstanding natural regeneration of native tree species. Thus, the strip-cut model appears to be an increasingly robust technique for sound ecological management of complex tropical forests. In the race to find ways and techniques of using tropical forests without destroying them, many more projects like COFYAL must be tested and expanded to larger commercial scales.

As has been amply demonstrated by the COFYAL project, however, an environmentally sound management system alone is not sufficient. Sustainable development must also be integrated across disciplines. Unless these initiatives and projects are economically viable, socially responsible, politically acceptable, and ecologically sound, they have little chance of being sustainable, but more likely will be added to the long list of failed development projects. Tropical forests *can* be managed on a sustained-yield basis for timber or non-timber forest products while protecting biotic habitats and ecological services, generating adequate economic returns to local communities, promoting local well-being, and providing politically acceptable models for sustainable development.

CASE STUDY 2

Sustainable Temperate Forestry: Two Cases

Temperate forests can also be harvested sustainably, although the approaches will be different than in rapidly regenerating tropical forests. Here are two examples of sustainable use of forests in northern California and southern Oregon. In the first, a private forest, selective logging and attention to many aspects of diversity result in a harvested but healthy forest. In the second, the people of an entire watershed are deciding how best to balance the many human demands on natural resources with maintaining a sustainable system.

Forest products have always been, and will continue to be, a critical resource for all humanity. Whether used in construction, in paper products, or as fuel, forest products are a central feature of human existence. Although they are renewable in theory, practices for their harvest and use can be anything but sustainable if approached incorrectly. Tree harvest practices in the temperate zone have a long history of one-time, hit-and-run approaches that leave behind ecological and social devastation. However, a number of examples of good, planned, sustainable forestry practices are emerging that offer a model for economic, social, and ecological sustainability.

Certification and the Collins Pine Corporation

Fred Euphrat, Forest, Soil & Water, Inc., Healdsburg, California

As a consulting forester, I was not ready for my meeting with the forest managers of Collins Pine. "We want to take care of the bugs and the lichens," said forester Barry Ford, and his words were echoed by Bill Howe, the chief forester. Their goal was to develop a management plan that provides for wood, water, wildlife, soils, insects, fungi, and people's needs. Collins wanted its plan to demonstrate productive, sustainable forest management to the state of California, to guarantee good economic returns to the owners of Collins Pine, and to serve as a blueprint for succeeding generations of managers. The plan is a continuation of Collins' certification for sustainable forest management.

In its goals and situation Collins is unique, although the lessons it can teach us are generic. Owned jointly by the Methodist Church and the Collins family, Collins Pine manages over 94,000 acres of productive timberland in northeastern California. Its mill is the largest employer in the town of Chester, on the shores of Lake Almanor. Collins produces about 30 million board feet from its managed lands each year, all of which is certified as sustainably produced by Scientific Certification Systems (SCS), a member of the international Forest Stewardship Council. Collins' goals are to maintain the flow of logs through the mill, to maintain jobs in Chester, and to take care of the land and its ecosystems; that is, the corporation seeks ecological, economic, and social sustainability.

Collins Pine began selective cutting in the 1940s based on a European model of individual tree selection. Relatively gentle slopes, fast growth, and high-value wood on its lands helped to make this a feasible option. Collins cuts white fir, sugar pine, ponderosa pine, incense cedar, and Douglas fir. Permanent inventory plots allow its foresters to observe changes in stand composition and measure growth and tree regeneration. The corporation's sustained-yield planning provides a check on the system of selective forestry, requiring the development of cutting and forest management models to maintain a viable forest and wood production stream.

Figure 18.4 An example of the managed and harvested Collins Pine forest in northern California. Contrast this scene with clear-cut approaches to timber harvest, as shown in Figures 10.11 and 13.12A. (Photograph by Fred Euphrat.)

Figure 18.5 Lake Almanor and Mount Lassen as seen from the Collins Pine area. Such views demonstrate the potential for creating recreational activities in this area while still enjoying the economic benefits of timber harvest. (Photograph by Fred Euphrat.)

Certification was an important step on the road to public acknowledgment of Collins' sustainable practices. Among many other parameters, SCS evaluated growth versus harvest on Collins' entire landholdings to ensure that cutting did not exceed long-term forest production. The certifiers evaluated the harvesting and road systems to ensure that no resource damage was occurring at unreasonable levels—reasonability being based on the local and regional experience of the evaluators. They looked at management of soils, of downed wood, and of standing snags for nutrient cycling and wildlife habitat. And they looked at Collins' role in the Almanor area and the Chester community to see whether the company was a good employer and a good local steward of the landscape.

The feeling of working on Collins land is unique. First, the land is dispersed over half a million acres among the holdings of other timber owners, community and power reservoirs, and National Park, Forest Service, and other public lands. There are no gates and there are no "Keep Out" signs. The surrounding communities actively use the Collins land for fishing, hunting, and camping; there are several active grazing leases as well. There are moments when one feels flung back a century in time to see open meadows within forests of large trees, cattle wandering in open range, and trust and respect among neighbors. The country is wild, with salmon, black bears, cougars, goshawks, and bald eagles as the "charismatic megafauna," as well as a wide variety of "non-charismatic microfauna," such as Barry's lichens.

Can certification offer enough guidance and incentive to provide for the non-charismatics, the "boring" species that are, in fact, the building blocks of the forest ecosystem? The answer is probably yes, but maybe not in the most simple and literal of applications.

What is Collins doing differently from other companies? How does its land and forest look? Collins' land contains tall pine and fir forests (Figure 18.4). Where it occurs, the understory is manzanita, ceanothus, madrone, and tan oak. There are no clear-cuts, though in some areas the landscape opens up with rocky or young volcanic soils, and you can see vistas of Lake Almanor and Mount Lassen (Figure 18.5). The forests have a "parklike" feel: you can see underneath the tall overstory, due to shading and brush control, and, if you look carefully, find the stumps from the previous harvest. The whole area is selectively logged about once every 15 years, so each year foresters create logging plans for about 6% of the land.

The Collins land is interspersed with meadows, lakes, and creeks (Figure 18.6). Salmon, steelhead, and trout use the streams for spawning, rearing, and migration. The meadows, which are also grazed, are popular sites for fishing and camping. Collins is concerned about the quality of streams within the meadows, and has an active program of riparian fencing. Collins' riparian areas contain willows, cottonwoods, and alders. The land has been managed—logged, mined, grazed, and used for recreation—since before 1900, and has been under Collins' selective logging regime since 1946.

Under Collins' selective harvesting plan, individual, large trees or small groups of trees up to one-fifth acre are cut. "Biomassing"—whole-tree harvesting for wood chips—reduces dense regrowth by removing stems smaller than eight inches in diameter. Large trees are generally cut with spacing guidelines from 15 to 40 feet, leaving good growing room between trees following harvest. Collins foresters manage individual trees for future growth and adjust spacing to maximize that growth, rather than harvesting all the best trees at once.

Stream zones are carefully managed, too, with harvests removing less than 30% of trees in logically constructed zones larger than required by California law. Roads and erosion processes have been evaluated in selected watersheds

Figure 18.6 Streams within the Collins Pine forest run clear and are little affected by the timber operations, as evidenced by their populations of salmon and trout. (Photograph by Fred Euphrat.)

to determine ways to reduce the total sediment load in the streams. The feeling at Collins is that if sediment load is a problem in streams, it is up to the corporation to do its part in reducing that load, even if its share, compared with natural and other ownerships' erosion, is small.

Harvesting at Collins is conducted with standard logging practices for the region: road-based harvesting using bulldozers and skidders. The biomassing is done with a whole-tree harvester that snips tree trunks at the ground, working in tandem with a chipper. The roads in use were built in the 1950s and earlier. Where problem erosion exists on Collins land, it can generally be traced to old roads or skid trails, which would not be built today. Future harvesting may incorporate cable systems for the steepest slopes, and erosion reduction will require rehabilitation and/or closing of some roads.

At present, Collins is developing a Sustained Yield Plan (SYP). This document evaluates the effects of timber harvest in terms of tree growth and habitat outcomes over the next century. The intent of the plan is to evaluate the effects of harvest to date, to see whether the present system will generate the desired future conditions, and to quantify expected habitat changes over the foreseeable future.

One element that is difficult to work with in the Collins landholdings is fire. While it is known that fire is an important part of the ecosystem, the interspersed landholdings and the danger of an escaped control burn make fire, at this time, a difficult ecosystem management tool. An escaped fire could create such a burden through lawsuits or outright destruction of the forest that it would destroy the corporation. In this case, the managers must weigh the correct ecological path against the necessary economic path. Biomassing is being used in place of fire to reduce competition and undergrowth, and to create forests that are productive as well as aesthetically pleasing.

Certification and the SYP process provide guidance via feedback between the review team, which brings region-wide expertise to the evaluation, and the land managers. The team may require inventory information not presently available on trees and non-tree resources, such as soil, water, wildlife, brush species, burn history, or snag density and use. The need for this information for continued certification stimulates the corporation to work with the experts to develop effective data bases to describe the land, its productivity, and its uses.

When landowners implement monitoring, they can see for themselves and demonstrate to others the results of their improved management. With a monitoring program in place, forest managers can begin the process of adaptive management: inventory, implement management strategy, monitor, change strategy, monitor, and repeat.

Certification also increases the value of Collins products due to their differentiation in the marketplace. Collins supplies wood to Home Depot stores for its "Greenprint" series of products, which give consumers an environmental alternative within the store. A recent study by the Institute for Sustainable Forestry in Redway, California, found that most consumers were willing to pay an additional 5% for a sustainable product made from certified wood.

Certification also increases the value of the forest land itself. A well-managed landscape is worth more, in terms of the land's productive capacity and reduced restoration needs, than other, less well managed lands. Certification is stewardship, locally defined for incorporation into the broader marketplace— certification is a way of giving ecological goals a market value—certification is a way to gain value for both trees and lichens—no wonder Barry wants lichen-oriented forestry!

The Applegate Partnership

Su Rolle, USDA Forest Service and Bureau of Land Management

In 1992, a pair of unlikely collaborators, Jack Shipley (an avid environmentalist) and Jim Neal (a long-time logger), were fed up. They were tired of all the gridlock and fighting about "lizards and logs," and figured it was worth trying a different approach. Shipley and Neal began discussing the idea of managing the half-million-acre Applegate watershed in an entirely different way—one based on collaboration between private landowners and land management agencies.

The Applegate watershed is located in southwestern Oregon and northern California and includes USDA Forest Service, USDI Bureau of Land Management, state, county, and private lands (Figure 18.7). Approximately 70% of the watershed is under federal management, with most of the remainder in private ownership. There are about 12,000 people living in the Applegate watershed; about 4000 live in Grants Pass, Oregon, and the rest in rural areas with no incorporated towns.

Shipley and Neal talked informally with neighbors, loggers, environmentalists, and natural resource agency personnel for months. These grass-roots discussions reinforced their belief that these people had more common ground than differences. People wanted "healthy forests and healthy critters" as well as healthy humans. They soon found that folks shared interests in maintaining the long-term health of the watershed and the stability of local economies. With cautious but hopeful interest from diverse individuals, a coalition of people formed a "Board of Directors" and soon agreed on a vision, goals, and objectives. The Applegate Partnership now includes community residents, people affiliated with environmental groups, timber, farming, and ranching interests, schools, natural resource agencies, and anyone else interested in the Applegate watershed. The Partnership's first board meeting resulted in this vision:

> The Applegate Partnership is a community-based project involving industry, conservation groups, natural resource agencies, and residents cooperating to encour-

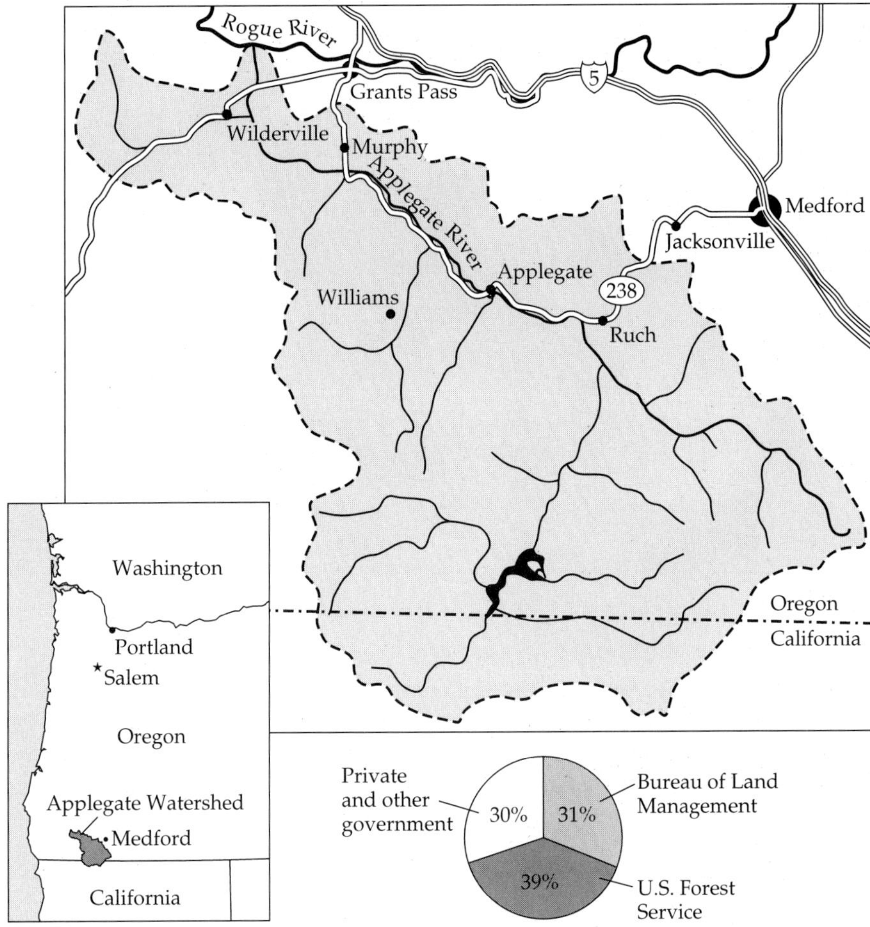

Figure 18.7 The Applegate watershed of southern Oregon and northern California (location in inset), showing the various rivers, towns, and roads of the region. The pie chart shows the land ownership pattern of the Applegate watershed. (Courtesy of the Applegate Partnership.)

> age and facilitate the use of natural resource principles that promote ecosystem health and diversity. Through community involvement and education, this partnership supports management of all land within the watershed in a manner that sustains natural resources and that will, in turn, contribute to economic and community stability within the Applegate Valley. (Applegate Partnership, 1992)

The group has been meeting nearly once a week for several years, with regularly scheduled meetings open to all (Figure 18.8). Initially, volunteer facilitators assisted in conflict resolution, which was particularly important given the long history of animosity among the various groups. Ground rules for communication were developed by the group, but attention to group process issues is still needed, and may always be. The group's motto is "Practice trust—them is us."

Though people are aligned with various constituencies, the meeting dynamics encourage them to come together as caring individuals, respectful of differing values, rather than as representatives of interest groups. Positions and agendas are "checked at the door." Still, the problem of balancing power and affiliation exists. George Stankey, a social science researcher, recently posed this question:

> Given the powerful role of special interests, how can collaborative decision-making structures, designed to achieve social learning and a consensus of views, avoid the perception of co-optation by the 'parent' groups whose individual members participate? (Stankey 1994)

Figure 18.8 The Applegate Partnership meets regularly to discuss the myriad issues that confront them. Meetings are open to all interested persons and are designed for the free exchange of information with no hidden agendas. (Photograph by Su Rolle.)

There is no easy answer. The Applegate Partnership, like most partnerships, strives toward win–win solutions, but compromise is inevitable. Because many individuals in the Partnership are connected to other constituencies, they maintain dialogue and information exchange with other local, regional, and occasionally national groups. Challenges arise when the "extended" constituencies get out of the information loop or disagree with directions in which the Partnership is headed. Other partnerships have similar challenges with regard to this balance of local and extended participation. It puts tremendous demands on the local people to maintain relationships with the local partnership and with their extended constituencies. A board member affiliated with several environmental groups, Chris Bratt, acknowledged, "It seems like a new thing every day. I have to continually deal with new challenges. Make new responses. There's so much paper and so much hand-holding. 'Oh, OK. How are you feeling now guys? Is everybody else OK?'" (Sturtevant and Lange 1995).

Though Jack Shipley is recognized as the charismatic leader of the Applegate Partnership, his style is such that leadership and responsibility are shared equally among participants. All people have equal access to power, information, and action. Decisions are made through consensus. When considering issues or projects, a common question asked is, "Who else needs to be at the table?"

Especially important to the Applegate Partnership is its community focus. Each person brings genuine and powerful feelings about this common place and the people who live in it. This strong attachment to place is a significant factor in the ability to unite and re-create community despite conflicting interests (Sturtevant and Lange 1995). And the very act of getting outside, on the ground, encourages people to see what they have in common more easily. The Partnership frequently takes field trips to federal and private projects (Figure 18.9).

The merging of maps across all ownerships through a Geographic Information System (GIS) has reinforced the perspective that the Applegate watershed is unique and merits a comprehensive, integrated approach to its management. Training of community members in the use of GIS and making computers accessible to students and residents is ongoing.

Figure 18.9 One of the keys to success in partnering is to get individuals out to see and participate in projects so that they will feel a sense of ownership. The Applegate Partnership does this regularly. (Photograph by Su Rolle.)

Most of the Applegate Partnership's focus for projects is on restoration while also creating opportunities for local employment. Examples include riparian planting on private lands, installation of fish screens, fencing off streams, obliterating roads, and reducing the risk of wildfires. For example, Billie Joe Hunter's feedlot has been around since the mid-1950s, serving the ranching community by boarding cattle in the winter when other feed is in short supply. The animals wandered back and forth across the creek to get from the feed bunks to the upslope bedding ground. The area was becoming an eyesore, with bare soils and subsequent erosion. Billie Joe would have liked to have done something else, but the marginal operation could not support investment in fences.

The Applegate River Watershed Council, a subcommittee of the Partnership, was able to secure a grant from the state of Oregon to begin restoring the site. Volunteers installed over 3000 feet of fencing, seeded native grasses, planted willows along the stream, and planted thousands of trees on the slopes (Figure 18.10). This project excludes the cows from most of the creek and improves water quality and fish and wildlife habitat.

Maintaining the rural community is important to the Applegate Partnership. A directory of businesses in the Applegate watershed is being developed for distribution. Members of community-supported agriculture groups pay farmers for weekly deliveries of fresh produce. The *Applegator*, a bimonthly newspaper focusing on natural resource and community issues, is distributed by the Partnership to every household in the watershed.

The Partnership works actively with the natural resource agencies to encourage landscape projects that will improve the overall health of the watershed. The Applegate Adaptive Management Area was created to include most of the federal lands in the Applegate River watershed in order to explore innovative opportunities for managers, scientists, and citizens to work together. Projects include timber sales to thin stands to increase the vigor of trees (and reduce their vulnerability to insects, disease, and wildfires), watershed restoration, and reintroduction of fire. The Partnership has encouraged people and various agencies to work together across jurisdictional, administrative, and political boundaries. Creative collaboration is expected among

Figure 18.10 Streamside restoration projects have been carried out by volunteers in the Applegate watershed. (Photograph by Su Rolle.)

diverse citizens, scientists, and managers. By opening up bureaucratic processes to interested community members and other government units, the agency personnel are gaining local knowledge, challenging traditional ways of doing business, generating more ideas and innovations, reaching better decisions, and shifting the "we/they" mentality toward an "us" perspective, with the agencies and communities working together.

Regardless of the success of its various projects, the Partnership can be called a success simply because it has moved beyond the deeply entrenched animosity and polarity around the issues that had been so pervasive. In place of the gridlock, "positive relationships developed between polarized groups, agencies and the community; a common vision was attained" (Wondolleck and Yaffe 1994). Connie Young, a board member of the Partnership, pointed out the importance of people learning to manage their own conflicts:

> We're going to have to come to some kind of agreement where we can all co-exist and where we can protect our natural resources and take care of God's world. The miracle is that these people will sit down and listen to each other. . . . they don't just shout at one another. . . . I have to give a little just like I see Chris Bratt [another board member and an environmentalist] giving a little. . . . his perspective on the watershed is totally different than mine. (Sturtevant and Lange 1995)

The Partnership is careful not to suggest that this model of collaboration be dropped on any other community. Each community is distinct in the variety of people and values present. But regardless of the setting, some lessons of the Applegate Partnership apply: respectful dialogue among all players, the sharing of dreams, and a willingness to work together seeking solutions is far better than fighting.

> What we're talking about here really isn't very sophisticated and it's not . . . high tech. In fact it's old stuff. It's old common sense stuff . . . probably the pioneers had to rely on community or not survive. (Jack Shipley, Applegate Partnership video, 1994)

CASE STUDY 3

The Role of Ecotourism in Sustainable Development

Robert Mendelsohn, Yale University

Ecotourism is emerging as a popular approach to protecting natural areas throughout the world. In general, ecotourism can be benign and consistent with sustainable development, although there are important exceptions that require careful management. Unfortunately, only a few ecotourism sites are sufficiently unique and desirable to be economically self-sufficient. Ecotourism will generally be most effective in generating income to supplement other nondestructive uses of wildlands. Ecotourism has a mixed record of sharing economic benefits with local people and thereby assuring their cooperation.

It is well known that wildlands in the United States and throughout the world are under heavy pressure for development. As the world human population rapidly expands beyond 5.7 billion on its way to 8 or 10 billion, "underutilized" wildlands are becoming the target for new settlements and economic activities. To balance this pressure, conservationists increasingly must demonstrate the benefits of maintaining lands in their natural state. With a growing world enthusiasm for ecotourism, this new form of leisure has become a popular rationale for conservation. Ecotourism tends to be benign compared with many economic uses, and the demand is growing. What, then, is the role of ecotourism in a sustainable development portfolio?

Ecotourism has a long history. Nineteenth-century travelers in the United States and Canada took trains from the crowded East to look upon the splendor of the Western wildlands. High on the visitation list were horseback trips into the wilderness and hunting for big game. With the rapid improvement of ground transportation, ever larger populations suddenly gained access to these same sites, leading to millions of visits to national forests and parks each year. Air transport made hitherto inaccessible regions suddenly available at the end of a single day of travel, spawning a vast international travel business. Even middle-class families could get on a plane and find themselves in a tropical Peruvian forest or African savanna the next morning. Ecotourism has consequently expanded from the adventures of a few wealthy men to the experience of a large population of families.

Ecotourism is a large and rapidly growing industry; it is currently estimated to be a $2 billion industry across the world (Herliczek 1996). In 1991, 30 million Americans participated in wildlife viewing, another 35 million adults went fishing, and 14 million adults went hunting (U.S. Fish and Wildlife Service 1992). In the process, the wildlife viewers spent $18 billion, the fishers spent $24 billion, and the hunters spent $12 billion. National park visitors alone numbered 260 million in 1991 (Norris 1992). At just one national park in Ontario, Canada, bird-watchers at the peak of the spring birding season, 24 days in May, spent $3.8 million; $2.1 million of this was spent locally (Figure 18.11).

The same explosion in travel is occurring internationally, especially in the tropics. In 1988, approximately 15 million tourists visited South and Central America, and many of these came to see the flora and fauna of natural areas (Figure 18.12). In Argentina, there is a huge tourist demand to see a single species, the Magellanic Penguin; thousands of tourists come to view a huge colony of 200,000 penguins (Figure 18.13). Visitor records of selected eco-

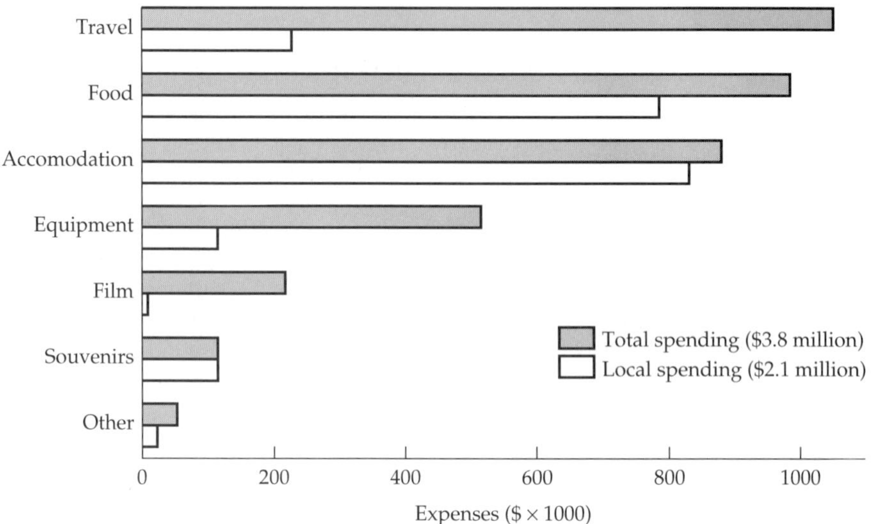

Figure 18.11 The money generated by ecotourism can be significant. In 1987, Bird-watchers at Point Pelee National Park, Ontario, spent $3.8 million from May 1 through May 24, the peak of the bird-watching season. With the exception of travel costs, the bulk of that money was spent locally. (From Hvengaard et al. 1989.)

tourism destinations show steadily growing attendance over the last decade (Harrison 1992). In Belize, visitation grew from 99,000 in 1987 to 215,442 in 1991 (Belize Tourist Board 1992). The Monteverde Cloud Forest Reserve in Costa Rica experienced increases from 471 visitors in 1974 to 40,000 by 1991 (Menkhaus and Lober 1996). Visitors to Nepal have increased from 10,000 in 1965 to 250,000 by 1990. Ecotourism is the fastest-growing component of tourism worldwide (Herliczek 1996).

Ecotourism can be a strong motivation to conserve natural sites. It provides a political base that demands highly valued experiences in nonconsumptive activities such as casual nature walks, bird-watching, whale watching, other wildlife viewing, photography, nature education, and canoeing and kayaking. Ecotourism has tremendous economic potential for local sustainable development. The revenues generated can support the well-being of local people and can be a funding source for further conservation work. Ecotourism also offers a compelling opportunity to engage in environmental education (Boo 1990). Surrounded by the beauty of a pristine site, it is relatively easy to sway visitors toward more sympathetic views of nature.

Figure 18.12 Ecotourism is a rapidly growing economic venture in many areas of the world. Here, an ecotourist photographs a sea lion (*Zalopus californianus*) on Seymour Island in the Galápagos. To minimize their effect on the environment, visitors are restricted to a trail marked by white stakes, and a park naturalist must accompany each group. (Photograph by Tim M. Berra.)

Ecotourism is not a perfect solution, however, and there are problems and limitations associated with its use. First, it is not always sustainable. The very process of bringing large numbers of people into remote areas for close contact with wildlife can be disruptive and in some cases destructive. Second, not all lands can be supported by ecotourism, which depends upon uniqueness, comfort, and accessibility. Third, the link between conservation and ecotourism needs to be strengthened. Although ecotourism has the potential to support conservation, it often has failed to realize this potential. We will explore these three issues in turn.

Is Ecotourism Sustainable?

The vision of a handful of people delicately walking down a graceful trail leaving no traces of their presence would suggest that ecotourism has no impact on visited lands. Although this view is accurate in many instances, one must be careful not to carry the argument to extremes. Ecotourism is less destructive than many other uses, but it definitely has effects, some of which are unavoidable costs of this activity, others of which can be managed to achieve a balance between preservation and development. There are several issues to be considered with respect to the sustainability of ecotourism.

(A)

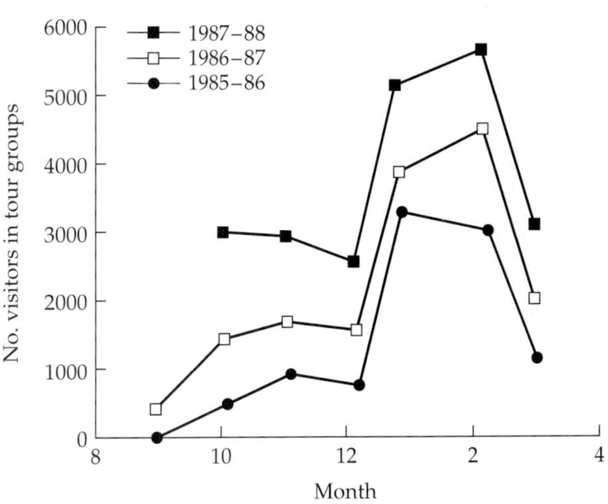

(B)

Figure 18.13 Magellanic Penguins are a major tourist attraction at Punta Tomba, Argentina. Huge numbers of the birds (A) have drawn increasing numbers of human visitors (B) who are willing to pay to see these spectacular aggregations. (A, photograph by Dee Boersma; B, modified from Boersma et al. 1990.)

First, even nonconsumptive visitation, if done by sufficient numbers of people, can subtly affect ecosystems. Animals that are used to minimal contact with humans may be affected by having thousands of gaping tourists trampling through their territories. Subtle behaviors may be altered, breeding grounds may be disturbed, and potential prey may be frightened away (Knight and Gutzwiller 1995). One cannot help but speculate that having two hundred people lining a road taking pictures must have some effect on a grizzly bear taking a meal in a meadow. These intrusions can lead to changes in animal behavior that may hamper, but not directly threaten, wildlife (Boyle and Samson 1985; Knight and Gutzwiller 1995). However, other intrusions may seriously affect populations by inhibiting reproduction. For example, visitors have antagonized nesting seabirds on remote islands (Boyle and Samson 1985) and sea turtles coming ashore at night to lay eggs in the sand (Jacobson and Lopez 1994).

Second, ecotourism can result in littering and other forms of local pollution (Herliczek 1996). Although tourists are encouraged to pack out what they bring in, objects tend to be left behind along most well-used trails. Over time, this can reduce the quality of the experience and degrade a site for future use. Similarly, lavatory facilities in remote locations may not be able to handle high volumes of users and may pollute water. Commercial operations that support ecotourism must develop adequate mechanisms to deal with these problems to prevent deterioration of site quality.

Third, ecotourism can lead to site degradation. When backcountry hiking and camping is conducted over a vast territory, the effects are dissipated and visible to only the most sensitive observer. However, certain key spots in the landscape, such as lake sites and alpine meadows, can attract excessive attention, leading to overuse and degradation. Some sites can be "too successful" (Figure 18.14), and need to be carefully managed so as to minimize the impact of high-density use. For example, boardwalks can be built to sustain short but heavily used nature trails. Networks of trails can be built in more remote areas to disperse visitors. Land managers can try to regulate and restrict use to already damaged areas. Unfortunately, the very remoteness and ruggedness of backcountry sites makes enforcement both expensive and unpleasant. Although damaged sites tend to be few in number, they are an acknowledged consequence of ecotourism.

Fourth, ecotourism reserves must be big enough to support the populations of animals and plants people want to see. As discussed in Chapter 10, if

Figure 18.14 Many popular areas for ecotourists and outdoor enthusiasts, such as Grand Canyon National Park, are under great pressure from human visitation, and require special efforts for protection because of their heavy use. (Photograph © Scott Berner/Visuals Unlimited.)

reserves are too small, they may not be effective for species or ecosystem protection. If reserves begin to resemble islands surrounded by a matrix of land used for conflicting purposes, the species being protected will have small population sizes, may not be able to migrate to other protected areas, and ecosystem processes may begin to break down. Issues such as minimal numbers of breeding pairs and insufficient territory sizes become critical in very small reserves, threatening the viability of the reserve as a whole.

Which Lands Are Suitable for Ecotourism?

It is largely unknown how much land, or which lands, should be set aside for ecotourism. Early studies and initial development have focused on unique natural sites supporting high-profile species such as lemurs (Maille and Mendelsohn 1993), elephants (Brown and Henry 1989), or grizzly bears (Creed and Mendelsohn 1993), or ecosystems with obvious public appeal such as tropical rainforests (Tobias and Mendelsohn 1991), marine coral reefs (Svendsen et al. 1993), and national parks such as Yellowstone. Places that are rare and have special characteristics that people value highly have been successfully developed for ecotourism. However, more common and abundant sites do not have the same appeal to visitors and cannot generate the same interest or income per hectare.

These insights into what ecotourists are looking for suggest that ecotourism is likely to result in isolated, specialized reserves scattered around the world, rather than vast protected tracts. Consequently, ecotourism will function as a large-scale, sustainable development strategy only in concert with other protective measures. Scattered, specialized ecotourism reserves would have the effect of protecting some (though not all) of the larger and more charismatic vertebrates from extinction. However, they would not be extensive enough to protect the broader diversity of plants and animals that is currently being jeopardized by land conversion. Also, ecotourism may not bring in enough revenue to support the large areas that megafauna require for persistence. Ecotourism thus has a role in conservation because it will contribute to protecting the species that the public values the most. That role is limited, however, and the positive effects of ecotourism fade quickly as one moves from key, high-profile reserves to surrounding areas.

A potentially overlooked requirement of sites is that they must offer viewing potential of the desired species. Species that prefer privacy may keep themselves hidden and offer few viewing opportunities. Ecotourists spend large amounts of money to actually see these animals. If the animals remain hidden, the quality of the experience will be reduced, and the reserve could fail economically. Denali National Park has relatively low populations of large mammals such as elk and moose; however, the open terrain of the park provides excellent viewing opportunities over large landscapes. Sites that have dense cover, in contrast, may have denser populations, but they may remain hidden. Reserve managers could establish viewing sites to overcome this problem; for example, reserves could establish hidden viewing shelters near waterholes or other places that large, charismatic vertebrates are likely to visit. Another approach is to focus on natural viewing sites. For example, many tourists are interested in seeing colorful birds, which are often most common or observable along forest edges. Unfortunately, if reserves include just the viewing sites, the critical forest interiors necessary to support these sites may not be protected.

Linking Ecotourism and Conservation

Ecotourism currently generates substantial rewards for tourists: seeing exotic animals and plants close up, and experiencing a sense of wildness. For ecotourism to be effective as a conservation strategy, however, the land use decision makers at the site must find it economically rewarding. Ecotourism must provide at least as high a standard of living as would alternative, and more destructive, uses of the land. This requires two steps that are typically not yet in place: the sites must generate revenue from the tourists, and this revenue must be distributed to the people who will either preserve or destroy the local landscape. That is, the funds must be used to encourage conservation, both by professional staff and by local citizens.

At most ecotourism sites, tourist access is either free or involves a minimal charge. Foreign tourists who have a high desire to visit these sites are being charged a very low price. Because many tourists are willing to pay more than they are being charged, the tourists, rather than local citizens, are currently the main beneficiaries of these sites. For example, at sites in Madagascar, foreign tourists are willing to pay between $275 and $360 per trip to see lemurs (Maille and Mendelsohn 1993). In Belize, it is estimated that foreign tourists are willing to pay about $350 per trip to dive on the coral reefs (Svendsen et al. 1993). In Costa Rica, foreign tourists are willing to pay hundreds of dollars for site access, but are currently charged only $5–$10 per site. With low or no fees being charged, little revenue is available to compensate local people as an incentive to protect the resources or to fund employment. In countries such as Costa Rica, Madagascar, and Belize, fees in the range of $100 to $200 per person could be charged to visit the country for ecotourism purposes. Multiplying by the number of visitors in each case yields potential annual revenues in the millions of dollars.

In order to tie ecotourism back to conservation, a second link must also be forged: the collected funds must be used for conservation purposes. There are two activities that need funding: the local people who are likely to convert the land to alternative uses must benefit directly from the tourist revenue being collected, and a professional staff must be paid. If central bureaucracies in the nations' capitals collect all the revenue, the local people will have no incentive to protect the reserves, and there will be no staff to practice conservation management. In contrast, if local people share in the benefits of a reserve, they are far more likely to protect the reserve and this source of income. Professional staff are important to natural areas because they can help plan sustainable use, protect the safety of visitors, and supervise local economic participation.

In addition to income, there are other mechanisms to win the cooperation of people who reside in the vicinity of reserves. Local people can be granted exclusive rights to harvest in the reserve in exchange for keeping others out. Citizens also can be given employment as guides and service workers supporting the tourist industry. Although these opportunities may appear to offer low wages from the perspective of international travelers, they often are extremely attractive to unskilled rural laborers. Reserves can also offer local services, such as health care and environmental education in local schools, as incentives for protection and cooperation.

The need to charge higher fees for ecotourism reinforces the earlier point that sites have to be relatively scarce for ecotourism to work. If people establish a reserve in an ordinary forest and then charge high fees, tourists will simply go to alternative sites in nearby forests; there is little potential ecotourism revenue in common sites. Sites that can be set aside solely for ecotourism are likely to be few in number and small in extent. However, ecotourism as one of several uses of a natural setting as a supplement to other sources of income could be widespread.

Although prime ecotourism locations involve rare and unique ecosystems, there is always a need for natural areas near large metropolitan areas. Such sites merely have to promise natural open space. For example, the million-acre Pinelands National Reserve in southern New Jersey is a major ecotourism region for the crowded cities of the Northeast such as New York and Philadelphia. Muir Woods outside of San Francisco protects only a small stand of redwoods, but their presence so close to a large metropolitan area is a valuable asset.

Conclusions

Ecotourism can make an important contribution to sustainable development throughout the world, particularly in developing tropical regions. Coupled with a mechanism to collect and distribute revenues from this activity, ecotourism can become an active force for conservation and sustainability. If practiced carefully and managed with the interests of the local site and local people in mind, ecotourism can be a sustainable source of income that will promote the conservation of many unique habitats throughout the world. However, it has only limited potential to protect natural areas, and must be conducted in ways that minimize threats of degradation from tourist activities.

CASE STUDY 4

Reconciling Conservation in African Game Parks with Human Needs

Richard F. W. Barnes, University of California, San Diego

Reserves designed to protect game or other species must include local citizens in their planning and must incorporate their traditional lifestyles into the reserve if they are to be sustainable. Reserves cannot be "locked away" from humans; they can provide sustainable means of sustenance and thus receive critical local support.

Africa is famous for its wealth of protected areas. The first African national park was created in 1925 in the Belgian Congo (now Zaire), and many more were declared during the colonial era. After independence in the 1960s, most of the new governments continued the same conservation policies and created many more protected areas; some countries have set aside very large areas for conservation (Table 18.3). However, national parks and game reserves are often unpopular within Africa, largely because protected areas are an alien concept—based on the Western ideal of national parks—that has been uncritically transplanted to the African context (Harmon 1987).

The concept of protected areas developed in the educated middle classes of Europe and North America in the late 19th century, rooted in a view that wilderness has its own intrinsic worth, and a belief that government has the right take control of certain lands on behalf of the general public and forbid their traditional use by the original residents (Marks 1984). This concept is difficult for rural Africans to comprehend, yet it has been widely applied across the continent. It usually means that people are not able to enter areas they have traditionally used, and sometimes it means that they have to be moved away; forced resettlement of indigenous groups has been a common feature of protected area establishment in Africa. The social consequences are devastating, as people lose not just their homes and farms, but also their identities. The most extreme example is that of the Ik, whose society disintegrated when they were moved out of the Kidepo Valley in northern Uganda (Turnbull 1972).

The benefits of protected areas include conservation of biological diversity; maintenance of genetic resources; protection of representative ecosystems, unique landscapes, or other features; protection of endangered species; recreation; opportunities for scientific research; stabilization of water catchments; ecotourism; education of the local citizenry; and preservation of the cultural

Table 18.3
Examples of the Investments, in Terms of Land Area, That African Countries Have Made in Protected Areas

	% of country covered by protected areas	
Country	**National parks**	**All protected areas**
West Africa		
Senegal	5.2	11.4
Cote d'Ivoire	5.5	6.2
Burkina Faso	1.8	9.6
Central Africa		
Gabon	0.0	6.3
Zaire	3.6	5.1
Chad	0.3	0.4
East Africa		
Uganda	3.5	20.5
Tanzania	4.1	14.6
Rwanda	12.4	13.6
Southern Africa		
Zambia	8.5	29.8
Botswana	15.1	17.2
Namibia	10.9	13.5

Data from IUCN 1993.

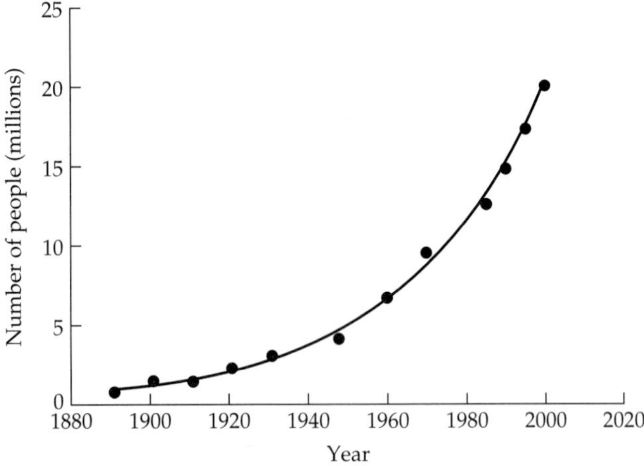

Figure 18.15 An example of human population growth in Africa: Ghana during the 20th century. Data for 1891, 1901, and 1911 are from Boateng (1970); data for 1921–1970 are from Twum-Barima (1981); figures for 1980 onward are predictions from Bos et al. (1993). An exponential curve has been fitted to the points, which describes a mean rate of increase of 2.9% per annum.

heritage for future generations. While these values may be appreciated by educated elites, they often have no meaning for rural inhabitants, many of whom wonder how one could justify placing so much land under government protection.

Some argue that tourism in protected areas provides tangible benefits by stimulating the economy and providing employment (as discussed in Case Study 3). Tourism can indeed be the most profitable land use in marginal areas. For example, the total revenue from Amboseli National Park was estimated by Western and Henry (1979) to be about 40 times the potential income from farming the same area. Each lion in the park was estimated to be worth $27,000 per year in tourist revenue. Similarly, Brown (1989) estimated that the game viewing value of elephants was worth between $22 and $30 million to Kenya's economy.

On the other hand, the balance sheet may show a net loss. Central and local governments must make heavy initial investments (roads, airports, hotels), which may not be balanced by later receipts from game viewing. A high percentage of profits goes to foreign companies such as airlines and hotel operators (Pullan 1984). Ordinary citizens living around a park often receive nothing, but still suffer crop damage caused by wild animals from the park. Thus, for many rural people, protected areas are a burden that imposes severe costs with no corresponding benefits. As human populations grow in Africa (Figure 18.15) and land becomes scarce, many people consider the land within park boundaries to be a wasted asset. This attitude can become self-fulfilling: when attention to maintenance of the infrastructure and protection of biodiversity languishes, the revenue from tourist visits will decline.

Changes in Conservation Philosophy

African protected areas have faced many social problems. First, even a huge, remote park can be dominated by outside human pressures on a local, national, and international scale. Second, some problems have arisen because people have been moved out; humans have long been part of the African landscape, and ecological changes occur when the human influence is removed. Third, if incentives to poach are great enough, then even a paramilitary guard force may not be able to defend a park from local people. Fourth, it is impossible to protect high-value species like elephants and rhinos over large areas with the resources typically available to conservation authorities (Albon and Leader-Williams 1988). It has become clear that the "defensive" approach to park management cannot succeed in the long term, and that the failure to involve local people in the creation and management of a park generates attitudes that eventually destroy it; indeed, a whole protected area system can be destroyed by such attitudes (Marks 1984).

There has also been a recognition of the injustices that were visited upon people unfortunate enough to live in or near conservation areas. Gradually, African conservationists began to rethink the management of protected areas. There was a growing realization that the narrow approach to natural resource management, in which a block of land had just one use—protection of biodiversity—was not working. A more broad-minded approach, with less emphasis on protection and more on multipurpose land use, was required. Conservationists realized that they must reconcile conservation with the need to enhance welfare in the surrounding communities.

Many community wildlife programs have now been established, usually based around a protected area. The emphasis is on understanding the needs of the local population and working through indigenous institutions such as the traditional chief or village committees. In many cases nongovernmental organizations (NGOs) work closely with the people. Government wildlife agencies are usually involved as well, to provide technical advice on such questions as hunting quotas. There is a spectrum of degrees of involvement of local communities. A national park might provide facilities such as clinics, schools, clean water, and roads to the community, with a goal of persuading the people that they benefit from the park and so dissuading them from hunting illegally within it. In other places people are allowed to use the protected area for traditional activities with little ecological impact, such as honey gathering or collecting wild herbs. There may be a system of land use zonation, with zones allowing different intensities of use by people, domestic animals, and wild animals, to minimize conflict. There may be programs allowing the local people to hunt in defined areas adjacent to the park, which acts as a reservoir of animals for the hunting area.

At the same time, there has been a movement toward management of wildlife on *unprotected* lands. A large proportion of Africa's wildlife is found outside parks and reserves. In marginal lands, exploitation of wildlife resources may bring a greater return to the people than traditional practices of agriculture and pastoralism, or may supplement those practices.

These various problems and opportunities are collectively illustrated in the six examples that follow. These examples demonstrate the various trials, tribulations, and successes in the protection of large landscapes in Africa.

The Togolese National Parks. The colonial powers established a large number of forest reserves in Togo in the early 1900s (Figure 18.16, site 1), but they ignored the traditional land use practices and rights of the residents. The reserves were very unpopular, and were invaded by the local people following independence. The newly independent government evicted the people and strictly protected the reserves, and in the 1970s it created three new national parks (Keran NP, Fosse-aux-Lions NP, and Fazao NP), forcibly relocating people living within their boundaries. Later, two of the parks were expanded and a large game reserve (Oti-Mandouri GR) was created. In each case residents were forcibly expelled, often with little warning, and their homes burned.

A two-year period of political unrest began in 1990. The opposition targeted the protected areas and the wildlife therein as symbols of the repressive government. It encouraged people to invade the national parks and game reserves and slaughter the animals. Many who had been expelled in the 1970s

Figure 18.16 Map of Africa showing the sites used as examples in the text: 1, national parks of northern Togo; 2, the M'Passa Biosphere Reserve, Gabon; 3, Ruaha National Park, Tanzania; 4, Parc National des Virungas (PNV), Rwanda; 5, Nazinga Game Ranch, Burkina Faso; 6, Nyaminyami, Zimbabwe.

returned to rebuild their former homes. Today you can see little wildlife in the former national parks, where natural vegetation is being cleared for settlement and agriculture. The government has realized that the former policies were counterproductive, has reversed its attitudes toward rural populations, and is now negotiating new boundaries for the protected areas. The new areas will be smaller, but if they are accepted by the rural communities, their survival is more likely. In return, the people will be secure in their homes because there will be guarantees that the protected areas will not be enlarged.

The M'Passa Biosphere Reserve, Gabon. The M'Passa Biosphere Reserve (Figure 18.16, site 2) was created in the early 1970s as an example of the rich rainforest of northeastern Gabon. Much valuable research in rainforest ecology has been conducted there (UNESCO 1987). Unfortunately, the local people were not consulted when the reserve was created. The boundaries of the reserve enclose a large area of forest close to several villages on the road west of Makokou (Figure 18.17). Consequently, the villagers woke up one day to find that their former hunting areas were now out of bounds. Strange foreign scientists, many from the former colonial power, roamed through the forests, from which the local citizens were now banned.

Hunting and fishing have great cultural significance and are also the main sources of protein for forest people. Because the reserve had no legitimacy in their eyes, the people simply ignored it and continued to hunt as before. Now the much-studied monkeys and antelopes have been shot and eaten, and cul-

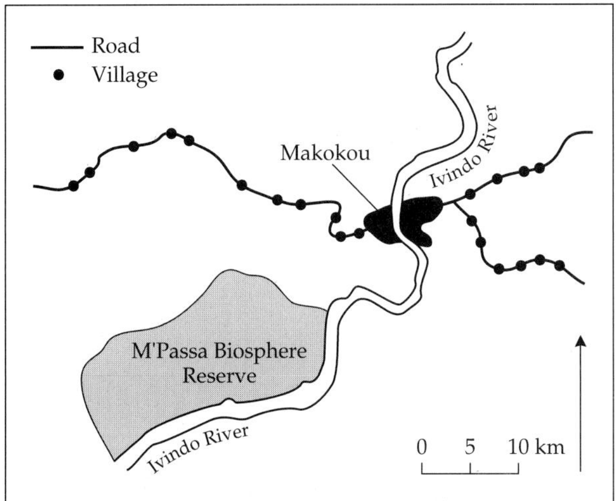

Figure 18.17 The M'Passa Biosphere Reserve, showing the surrounding villages and the nearby town of Makokou.

tivators are encroaching upon the reserve. Consequently, it has been lost as a site for conservation of forest biodiversity.

Ruaha National Park, Tanzania. Ruaha (Figure 18.16, site 3), Tanzania's second largest national park, covers 10,300 km^2 and is part of a vast wilderness with a wealth of plant, bird, and mammal life. Originally there were small settlements scattered through this vast area of woodland and bushland. The inhabitants lived by subsistence hunting and farming, but asked to be moved away following a long period of drought and crop failure in the 1940s, and the area became a national park.

In the mid-1950s the drought ended, and was followed by 15 years of good rains. An abundance of food increased elephant birth rates, calf mortality decreased because of human absence, and the surrounding and expanding human population drove elephants into the park. These factors caused a steady increase in the elephant population (Barnes 1983). The changes in the woodland caused by burgeoning elephant numbers posed a dilemma for Tanzania National Parks (TNP) authorities in the 1960s and 1970s. Should they cull thousands of elephants in a park established for their protection, or should they do nothing and risk losing the park's vegetative cover?

Ironically, the fate of the Ruaha elephants was decided not by the TNP authorities, but by the combined effects of the world ivory trade and Tanzania's economic recession. In the 1970s the economies of the western Pacific Rim, especially Japan, were developing rapidly, and the demand for luxuries such as ivory increased (Barbier et al. 1990). The demand for ivory drove up the price and triggered a surge of elephant poaching across the African continent.

Tanzania was in a deep recession at the time, and life was hard, encouraging the impoverished villagers around the park to turn to elephant poaching. The park staff could not cope with the poachers; the guards were ill-paid, ill-equipped, and demoralized. Consequently, between 1977 and 1984, about 60% of the Ruaha elephants were killed (Barnes and Kapela 1991), and the black rhino population was destroyed.

The intense harassment by poachers forced elephants to concentrate in the area around the park headquarters, resulting in accelerated habitat change there: conversion of woodland to bushland to open grassland, and loss of shady riverine groves of *Acacia* trees. In only a few years there was a massive ecological change, manifested by large-scale changes in vegetation cover and in large mammal biomass.

A survey of the local people in 1992 found that few understood why the park existed, and that three-fourths believed that it brought them no benefits. In the following year a project was begun to direct benefits from wildlife to the communities in the buffer zone adjacent to the park (Hartley 1995). This plan will allow local people to hunt game in the buffer zone, with an annual quota set by the government. They will also receive the meat and a proportion of the fees paid by tourist hunters who shoot big game in the buffer zone. These mechanisms will allow the people to benefit from the area adjacent to the park; the park itself will act as a wildlife reservoir. However, there are also plans to negotiate rights for the villagers to enter the park for honey gathering and fishing, activities that will have little ecological impact (Hartley 1995).

Parc National des Virungas. The Virunga Volcanoes straddle the frontiers of Rwanda, Uganda, and Zaire (Figure 18.16, site 4). Their montane forest and high-altitude plant communities form an island habitat surrounded by dense human cultivation. The Rwandan side is protected by the Parc National des Virungas (PNV), which covers about 200 km^2. Rwanda is one of the poorest countries in the world, and its human population density is the highest on the continent—about 270 people per km^2, growing at over 3% per annum; around the PNV the density is even higher.

The forests play a vital hydrologic role, absorbing moisture during rains and releasing it as streamflow during the dry season. Weber (1987) believes that this hydrologic function is the most important feature of the volcanoes for the local people. After part of the forest was felled for agriculture in 1968, some streams ceased flowing in the dry season.

The volcanoes have become famous as the realm of the mountain gorilla (*Gorilla gorilla berengei*). Gorilla numbers dropped from about 450 in 1960 to 270 in 1973 as the forests were felled or degraded by cattle grazing. The first efforts on the Rwandan side to protect the gorillas were based on the notion that the park had to be defended against the native hordes. Protection was confrontational, and some gorillas may have been shot in revenge for the brutal tactics used to dissuade poachers.

Nevertheless, these tactics bought time until a more enlightened approach was adopted. In 1979 a consortium of international conservation organizations launched the Mountain Gorilla Project (MGP) on the Rwandan side. The MGP worked on the principle that the park, the volcanoes, the natural communities, and the local people were all part of a larger system that required an integrated management approach.

The conservation program had three main components. First, park protection was improved by reorganizing the guard force. Second, ecotourism based on gorillas was initiated with the aim of improving the financial viability of the park (Figure 18.18). Several gorilla groups were habituated to allow one visit per day, for one hour, by six tourists. Third, a conservation education program was started. A mobile unit toured the villages and schools around the park, giving lectures and showing films.

The program was a spectacular success. Poaching declined, and gorillas on the Rwandan side reproduced better than those on the Zaire side, where there was no MGP. No gorillas were killed by poachers after 1984, and their numbers increased to about 300. Furthermore, despite fears that regular tourist visits would disturb the gorilla groups, those visited by tourists had the highest reproductive rates. The attitudes of the local people toward the park changed as they saw the prosperity brought by tourism. Revenues from tourism increased twentyfold in five years (Harcourt 1986); gorilla tourism became Rwanda's second largest foreign exchange earner.

Figure 18.18 Mountain gorillas are an important component of park protection in Rwanda. In addition to a high recognition factor and nearly universal desire for their protection, gorillas also generate income for the local economy through ecotourism. (Photograph © Peter Veit/DRK Photo.)

Everything changed when civil war broke out in 1990. The park was occupied at various times by the combatants and by refugees, and the park infrastructure was destroyed. The staff bravely continued to monitor the gorillas until the massacres of 1994 forced them to flee. Fortunately, only one gorilla is known to have been killed on the Rwandan side of the volcanoes during the fighting. The war ended in 1994, but the park remains insecure because of continuing political instability, ethnic tensions, very large numbers of refugees not far away in Zaire, and the mines laid in and around the park. The war and ethnic massacres have destroyed the economy and infrastructure of the region, yet revenues from the park could play a part in rehabilitating the country. A major effort is being made by the government and outside organizations to rehabilitate the park.

The Nazinga Game Ranch. Recognizing that standard methods of conservation were failing, Burkina Faso set out to try new forms of management based upon the rational use of biological resources. An experimental project was established in 1979 at the Nazinga Game Ranch (Figure 18.16, site 5), which is more of a game reserve than a ranch in the American sense. The project area covers about 2000 km^2 and includes ten villages adjacent to the reserve. Each village used to have its own private hunting territory in which game was abundant; however, during the preceding 30 years there had been a marked decline in wildlife (Belemsobgo 1995).

The project has two main objectives. The first is to rehabilitate and conserve the wildlife populations. Habitat protection and management strategies include controlling bush fires, building and maintaining dams, building a network of roads, and training village guards. There is also a program of applied research and ecological monitoring.

The second objective is to promote the rational and sustainable use of wildlife resources for the benefit of the local people (Belemsobgo 1995). To achieve this end, the local communities must be integrated into the project by encouraging their participation in reserve management. The project provides employment, and local people gather materials and foodstuffs (honey, firewood, thatch, wild plants for food and medicines) in the reserve. The project also encourages other development activities such as building wells and training craftspeople. Roads have been improved, and a dispensary and a school have been completed.

By 1993 there had been an encouraging increase in the biomass of large mammals (Belemsobgo 1995). The game resources in the reserve are being exploited through cropping for game meat, trophy hunting, game viewing, and fishing. In addition, each village has established its own formal hunting zone adjacent to the reserve. The fees paid by hunters in each hunting zone go into a savings account for improvements within the village. A regular flow of tourists each year, combined with the other revenue-generating activities, means that the project is on its way to becoming financially self-sufficient (Belemsobgo 1995).

The Zimbabwe CAMPFIRE Program. The Department of National Parks and Wildlife has established the CAMPFIRE program (*Communal Areas Management Programme for Indigenous Resources*) in Zimbabwe (Figure 18.16, site 6). This program is based on the principle that rural populations should take responsibility for wildlife on their lands and draw a direct benefit from management of those resources (Martin 1986). CAMPFIRE was made possible by the 1975 Parks and Wildlife Act, which gave landowners, including District Councils, responsibility for managing wildlife on their lands (Pitman 1991).

An example is the Nyaminyami district of northern Zimbabwe, where the local people have suffered for years from elephants that ravage their crops. The CAMPFIRE program in that area has twin goals. One is to reduce the elephant damage by shooting persistent crop raiders, dividing up the area into specified land use categories such as cultivation, pasture, and wildlife, and constructing electric fences where necessary. The second goal is to raise revenues from elephant management through a combination of game viewing, walking and photographic safaris, and trophy hunting (Russell 1993). Revenues are expected to be about Z$6 million per annum, with a quarter coming from hunting and the rest from the various forms of tourism. This money will not go to the central government, but will be used for community development projects and for cash payments to individual households. When individuals and families benefit directly in this manner, they will begin to see wildlife as an asset rather than a liability.

Challenges for the 21st Century

A range of approaches for involving local communities in protected area management are being tried. The details vary according to the ecological situation, human distribution and demography, cultural attitudes, and political and economic realities. There is reason for optimism (as in the Nazinga and CAMPFIRE examples), but these are long-term projects, and it is too soon to judge their success. There are many conflicts of interest that have yet to be settled, and changes are required in the visions of the various groups involved: wildlife authorities and other civil servants, local government, nongovernmental organizations, and the rural people themselves. Although in a given country the upper echelons of the government wildlife service may be enlightened, those in the lower ranks who were recruited and trained long ago may still be steeped in the old ideas, and they are the ones who have day-to-day contact with local residents. The legacy of mistrust and suspicion on the part of local people toward government wildlife agencies, born of years of conflict and repression, must be overcome.

There are many administrative hurdles yet to surmount. There is the question of who owns the resource or the right to exploit it. Usually it is the state, but the program will work best when rights are vested in local communities. Mechanisms must be worked out within communities for controlling harvests: who may hunt and how many animals they may kill per season. Even so, the system may not work as intended. For example, a local resident might have access to a clinic and clean water provided by a park development plan, but he might also continue hunting in the park, because by so doing, he would maximize the benefits he obtains (Gibson and Marks 1995).

Development requires that the environment be changed (by building roads, clearing land for clinics or schools, pumping water from a river to the village), and often these changes will affect ecologically sensitive species or communities. In other words, development and conservation are not always compatible (Robinson 1993). Careful planning can avoid some problems, but conservationists often will have to make compromises between the degree of human disturbance permitted in the project area and the needs of sensitive species.

Some plant and animal communities are very sensitive to disturbance (e.g., the Afro-alpine communities in the PNV) and must be protected by strict nature reserves where no human activity is allowed. These will survive only if they have the goodwill of the local people. If these sites are otherwise unproductive, then maintaining that goodwill poses a permanent challenge to conservationists.

Integrated conservation and development projects can provide only a temporary buffer against the greatest threat to protected areas: the exponential growth of human populations (see Figure 18.15). An increase of 3% per annum means that food production must double every 23 years *just to maintain the status quo.* Yet the best land is already being cultivated, and in many places soil fertility has been exhausted, which means that yet more land must be cleared. Thus, there is an ever-accelerating demand for new land to cultivate. Protected areas will soon become islands of fertile land in a sea of degradation; as human densities increase, hungry eyes will turn toward protected areas. Many such sites are small, or now harbor depleted wildlife populations or degraded woodlands. Inevitably, the people will decide they would be better off by cultivating the land instead.

We now understand that protected areas are not ecological islands, but must be considered elements of a landscape mosaic. The old patterns of thought, which had their roots in the colonial era, still linger, but for the most part they are disappearing. The movement toward community involvement is gradually changing the face of conservation; however, it will not guarantee the survival of national parks and game reserves. The challenges of Africa in the 21st century will require conservationists to be ever more flexible.

CASE STUDY 5

The Greater Yellowstone Ecosystem

Mark S. Boyce, University of Wisconsin-Stevens Point

To anyone concerned about the conservation of nature the very name Yellowstone is like a battle cry. This is where it all started; Yellowstone was the first wilderness set aside for a national park, and it remains an inspiration and the confirmation that dreams can be made to come true.

HRH Prince Philip (from Sutton and Sutton 1972)

Sustainability at the landscape level is a laudable goal and the ultimate form of protection, but it faces many obstacles. Local people and their lifestyles must be accounted for, previous resource exploitation must be made compatible with ecological goals, and tourism must be limited.

One approach to sustainable development is to set aside large tracts of land as reserves, but allow a combination of human economic activities within the reserves. Activities such as moderate grazing, extraction of minerals, timber removal, agriculture, hunting, fishing, and tourism can all be compatible with biodiversity protection, if done properly. If the set-aside area is large enough to encompass entire ecosystems, then more complete control over activities can be achieved. One example that begins to approach this ideal is the Greater Yellowstone Ecosystem (GYE) in the United States.

Since its establishment as the world's first national park in 1872, Yellowstone has been a paradigm of nature preservation. Today, Yellowstone National Park and the adjacent wild lands are frequently proving grounds for changing perspectives in resource management, exemplified by recent debates over fire management policy, ungulate population control, and wolf reintroduction. The pivotal issue in these debates usually is how human development can interact with our attempts to preserve a large ecosystem. We may not yet understand ecological processes well enough to accomplish sustainable development in the context of ecosystem preservation, but there are few places remaining in the world where we have a better opportunity to make it work than in the GYE.

Ecological Issues

The GYE encompasses an area of some 60,000 km^2 in the Rocky Mountains of Wyoming, Idaho, and Montana, with most lands managed by the U.S. Forest Service and the National Park Service (Figure 18.19). The area is high in elevation (1500–4200 m), with a short growing season, low to moderate productivity, and relatively low species diversity. The GYE is well known for its natural beauty, spectacular geothermal features, and a fauna rich in large mammals, including elk (*Cervus elaphus*), moose (*Alces alces*), mule deer (*Odocoileus hemionus*), pronghorn (*Antilocapra americana*), bison (*Bos bison*), bighorn sheep (*Ovis canadensis*), black bear (*Ursus americanus*), and of course, the threatened grizzly bear (*Ursus arctos*). Few endemic species of conservation significance occur in the area, exceptions being the Ross bentgrass (*Agrostis rossiae*), restricted to the Upper Geyser Basin of Yellowstone National Park, and the Jackson Lake sucker (*Chasmistes muriei*), which is presumed extinct.

Because of its low species diversity and relatively few threatened or endangered species, the GYE would not rank high as a site on which to focus attention for the preservation of biodiversity. Rather, the value of the GYE lies in its relatively intact status, affording a unique opportunity to protect a large, major landscape (recognizing that the common use of the term "ecosystem" in reference to the GYE is a misnomer, and that many ecosystems make up this landscape). In practice, however, the strongest motivation for conservation in the GYE is the protection of aesthetic wilderness values.

Ecological Process Management. National parks can serve a valuable function as ecological baseline preserves. Such areas can be managed with a minimum of human interference in order to document change through time relative to other areas where human influence is greater. Such management usually implies a "hands-off" policy, and ecological processes are allowed to take their course unimpeded. Sometimes this is insufficient, and because of prior human disturbances or influences occurring beyond the boundaries of

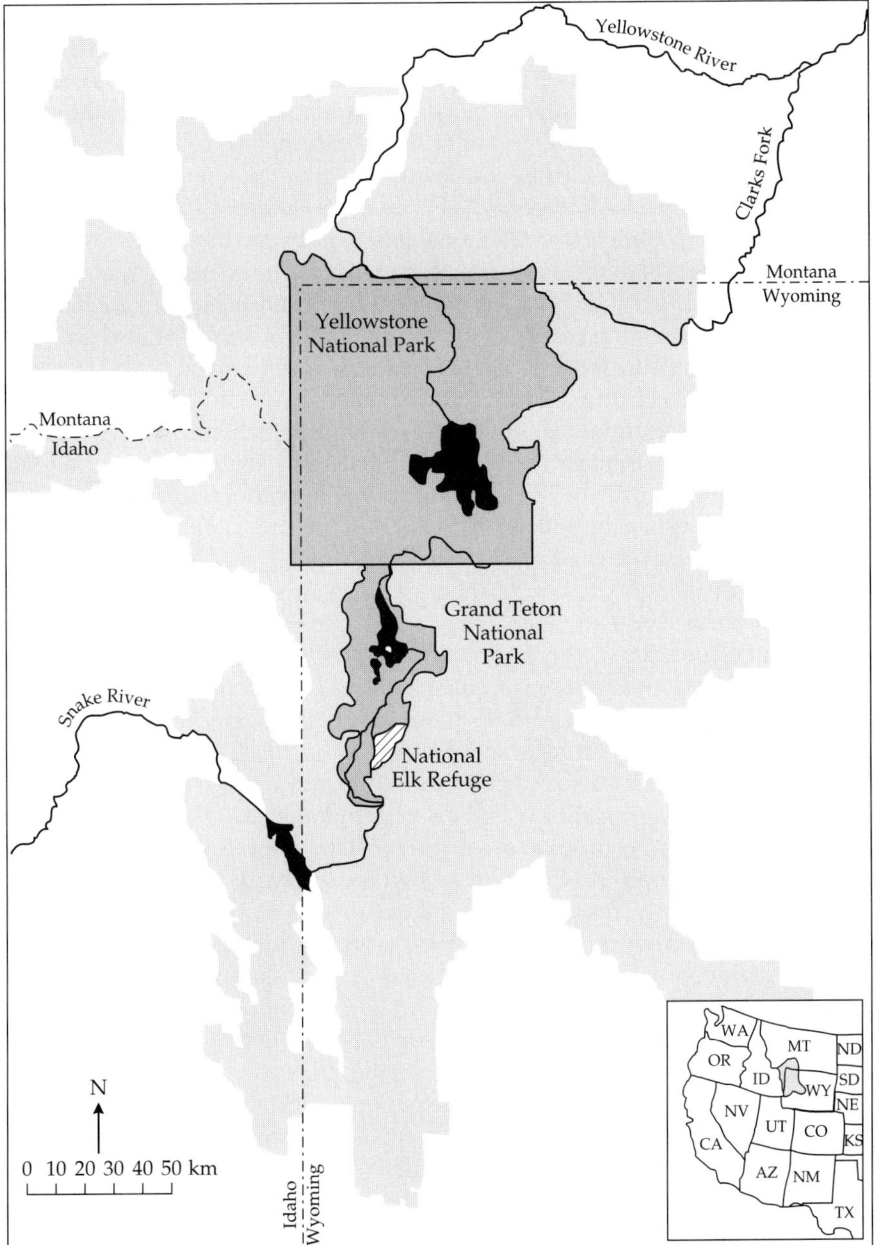

Figure 18.19 The Greater Yellowstone Ecosystem. Note the relationship of Yellowstone and Grand Teton National Parks (dark shading) to the various surrounding national forests, wildlife refuges, and other wild lands (light shading).

the park, intervention may be necessary to restore natural ecological processes to the landscape.

The legal boundaries of Yellowstone National Park established by Congress in 1872 (Figure 18.19) do not coincide with the ecological processes governing nature in Yellowstone. For example, large numbers of elk, mule deer, and bison regularly cross park boundaries to find winter ranges outside the park. Wildfires cross boundaries with complete disregard for agency jurisdictions. Even ecosystem boundaries may be arbitrary, and a number have been proposed for the GYE (Patten 1991). But to capture a geographic unit that makes any biological sense requires extending the boundaries of Yellowstone onto national forest lands on all sides. Transcending these agency boundaries to accomplish ecological process management has proved difficult in many instances.

At least in spirit, ecological process management prevails in the national parks of the GYE. Although lands adjacent to Yellowstone National Park are mostly Wilderness Areas, Congress has imposed constraints that preclude ecological process management as a priority in national forests. In particular, the Forest Service must provide multiple-use options for resources occurring in national forests, even if those uses conflict.

Fire Ecology and Management. During the summer of 1988, approximately one-half of Yellowstone National Park was burned by wildfires. Large-area fires are typical of the Yellowstone area, but occur at low frequency, with major large fires every 350 years (Romme and Despain 1989). Fire is clearly an integral part of the forest ecosystems throughout the Rocky Mountains, and one may envisage the Yellowstone landscape as comprising a dynamic, ever-changing mosaic of burned and unburned areas. Fire maintains aspen (*Populus tremuloides*) communities and enhances wildlife habitats. Recognition of the ecological importance of fire formed the basis for "let-burn" policies, established in the early 1970s, for natural fires in wilderness regions of Yellowstone and adjacent national forests.

But people fear fires and their destructive capabilities. Political objections to the fires of 1988 resulted in challenges to the fire management policies of the Forest Service and the Park Service. Despite extensive reviews, the fire management policies of the National Park Service and Forest Service have largely remained intact. Yet strict constraints have been imposed that reduce the chances that wildfires could burn out of control as they did in 1988. Nevertheless, given the low frequency of large fires in the GYE, we have several centuries to wait for a more enlightened administration.

Ungulate Management. Elk and bison populations have increased to near carrying capacity, and in some areas the consequences of herbivory on vegetation are pronounced. Both aspen and willow (*Salix* spp.) communities are browsed extensively, resulting in changes in vegetation communities, especially on winter ranges. However, such plant–herbivore dynamics are expected to change vegetation communities, and probably have done so for millennia.

Range managers argue that allowing native ungulates to heavily graze ranges in Yellowstone reflects a double standard because comparable grazing levels by domestic livestock outside the park would be unacceptable to federal land management agencies. However, managers in the National Park Service have quite a different charge—fostering native species—from those in the U.S. Bureau of Land Management and the Forest Service, who are required to manage for multiple use, including cattle grazing. Claims of "overpopulation" and "overgrazing" by native ungulates on Yellowstone's ranges appear to be without merit. The presence of cattle is not ecologically or ethically equivalent to the presence of native ungulates, and recreational users of public lands in the West are becoming increasingly intolerant of heavy livestock grazing.

A substantial fraction of bison and elk carry brucellosis, a bacterial disease, causing another ungulate management concern in the GYE (Figure 18.20). The disease is contagious and can cause livestock ranchers substantial economic losses because infected cattle must be destroyed. No practical methods have been devised for controlling the disease other than seasonally minimizing contact between wildlife and domestic livestock. Thus, wildlife dispersal out of the park is viewed as a threat by the livestock industry and the U.S. Department of Agriculture, and they have leveraged Yellowstone National Park into destroying bison as they migrate into Montana during the winter. Curiously, such draconian measures have not been implemented for the Jackson elk herd, despite the fact that 40% of the cow elk carry the disease.

Figure 18.20 Bison may damage fences and other agricultural development and may carry brucellosis, which can infect domestic livestock. (Photograph by M. S. Boyce.)

There are no easy solutions to ungulate population problems in the GYE. The public finds it unacceptable to kill wildlife inside park boundaries, and enjoys having abundant ungulate populations for viewing. Certain conservation groups have argued that eliminating livestock grazing on public lands in the GYE would resolve most conflicts, but this is an impolitic proposal in a region so traditionally dominated by ranching interests, and would violate the current multiple-use mandate of the Forest Service.

Wolf Recovery. Wolves were fairly common in the GYE until extirpated by U.S. Government hunters and trappers during the 1920s. The restoration of wolves to the GYE is deplored by local ranchers, who fear that wolves will prey on their livestock, and by hunters, who fear that wolves will compete with them for game. Furthermore, the mining industry opposes wolf recovery because the presence of yet another threatened/endangered species might further restrict the public lands available to them for mineral development. Thus, the release of wolves into Yellowstone National Park in January 1995 met with strong political resistance.

The release was done under the "experimental nonessential population" designation of the Endangered Species Act, which gives federal agencies authority to control the population when needed. After the initial release of 14 wolves in 1995, an additional 17 were released in 1996. One wolf was killed by federal agents because it attacked domestic sheep, but most wolves have thrived on elk and other native ungulates. Two family groups of wolves have been relocated back into Yellowstone National Park after they denned in areas outside the park where they were likely to come into conflict with humans.

Characterizing wolf recovery in Yellowstone as a success story may be premature. Recovery appears to be a boon to tourism, with increased visitation to portions of the park where wolves are frequently sighted. Ungulate numbers will be reduced by wolves (Boyce 1992b), so wolf recovery should reduce some of the perceived problems caused by elk and bison "overpopulation." Careful monitoring will be required to document the consequences of wolf predation for ungulate populations, and possibly for the vegetation that is influenced by the ungulates.

Development Issues

Traditionally, commodity extraction, including both mining and renewable resource development, has been an important component of the economy of

Figure 18.21 Ski lift at Teton Village, west of Jackson, Wyoming, an example of recreational development in the Greater Yellowstone Ecosystem. (Photograph by M. S. Boyce.)

the GYE. Gradually, demands for development in the GYE are shifting to include construction of vacation homes, ski resorts, tourism facilities, and new roads and trails to facilitate access (Figure 18.21). Whereas commodity development has always been an issue primarily involving the national forests in the GYE, recreational facilities are also being developed within the national parks.

Commodity Development in National Forests. Because of its multiple-use mandate, the Forest Service is obligated to provide opportunities for mining, timber harvest, and grazing in national forests. However, endangered species legislation gives the Forest Service license to place certain areas off limits for incompatible uses if they might jeopardize habitats for threatened or endangered species. For example, in the GYE, the Shoshone and Custer National Forests have banned oil and gas exploration and development on prime grizzly bear habitats. In Bridger-Teton National Forest, oil and gas leases may be granted in grizzly bear habitat or on steep slopes, but no surface occupancy by oil rigs is allowed. Still, throughout most of the GYE, oil and gas exploration is permitted, and is frequently at odds with wildlife and recreational uses of the area.

In the same year that Yellowstone was designated a national park, Congress also passed the mining law of 1872, encouraging hard-rock mining on public lands. In the GYE, mining primarily for gold and palladium occurs in the spectacular Beartooth Mountains north of Yellowstone National Park in Custer National Forest. A controversial gold mine has been proposed near Cooke City, Montana. Modern gold-mining techniques involve bathing ore in a cyanide bath, which carries the risk of chemical spills that could devastate stream biota.

In contrast to mineral extraction, logging and grazing are potentially sustainable uses of the national forests. Yet neither is particularly profitable in the GYE, and in many cases these uses conflict with wildlife habitat and recreational values. Every national forest in the GYE loses money on its timber program (O'Toole 1991), and cattle ranching is declining in the area despite the low fees charged for grazing on federal lands.

Conflicts between cattle and elk on winter range were responsible for the establishment of the National Elk Refuge near Jackson, Wyoming (Figure 18.22), where some 7500 elk are provisioned with alfalfa each year in lieu of

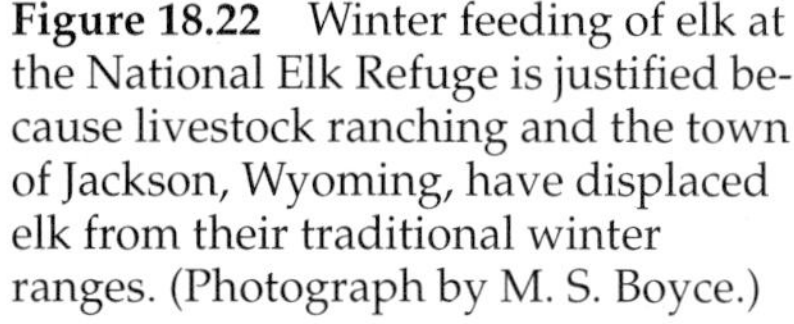

Figure 18.22 Winter feeding of elk at the National Elk Refuge is justified because livestock ranching and the town of Jackson, Wyoming, have displaced elk from their traditional winter ranges. (Photograph by M. S. Boyce.)

their natural winter range. More than 44% of the GYE's public lands are open to cattle and sheep grazing, resulting in competition with native wildlife, degradation of riparian habitats, and conflicts with predators. One-fifth of the grizzly bear deaths in the GYE have been linked to conflicts with domestic sheep grazing.

Despite these problems with livestock grazing in the GYE, there is much local support for ranching. The rugged lifestyle of the cowboy adds flavor to the tourism experience in the GYE, and ranching is viewed by the public as less in conflict with natural resources than are other forms of development. Many of the problems with livestock grazing in the GYE could be resolved by more conscientious grazing management on public lands—a responsibility of the Forest Service.

Resistance to ecosystem management on the part of the Forest Service may also relate to the fact that its financing comes partly from timber sales. O'Toole (1991) argues that greater attention to noncommodity interests could be secured if recreational users of the national forests were charged a user fee, which the Forest Service could then use to support its management programs.

Recreation-Based Development. The GYE is gradually changing to a recreation-based economy, which would appear more benign than a commodity-based economy (Figure 18.23). But recreational uses are not without consequences to the ecological integrity of the ecosystem (Knight and Gutzwiller 1995). For example, in recent years snowmobiling has become a popular recreational activity in Yellowstone during winter. Roads used by snowmobiles become snowpacked, creating corridors for movement of snowbound bison, resulting in shifts and expansion of their distribution. Conflicts with humans occur when these movements take bison beyond the boundaries of the park. We do not yet know the consequences of snowmobile corridors for the bison population, but it appears that they have substantially increased the available winter range.

One might argue that virtually any development will alter the system, and therefore that the best management for the GYE would be to minimize human visitation and use. Yet much of the support for conservation of Yellowstone comes from people who have enjoyed their experiences in the area.

Figure 18.23 A horse corral maintained for a trail ride concession within Grand Teton National Park. Development is often required to support recreational use within national parks. (Photograph by M. S. Boyce.)

Therefore, it is unrealistic to envision extreme protection; rather, a balance between preservation and development is needed.

Striking the Balance

Because ecosystem boundaries cross agency jurisdictions, any attempt to manage the GYE will require interagency coordination. Yet attempts at cooperative planning by federal and state agencies in the GYE have been blocked by political pressures driven by development interest groups.

Nevertheless, the transition to an ecosystem management philosophy appears to be happening throughout the GYE, despite lobbying pressures. Many people believe that the priority for management in the GYE should be recreational and tourism values, simply because of their overwhelming economic importance in the area. This transition has already led to the closing of sawmills, abandonment of grazing leases, and restrictions on mining and oil and gas exploration in certain areas. Yet incentives for development persist, and ensuring that it is done properly will require vigilance on the part of environmental organizations.

Ecologists have argued that there is value in maintaining ecosystem structure and function, but such values seem esoteric to many people. From a pragmatic perspective, perhaps Yellowstone's greatest value is as one of America's great playgrounds. In 1992 Yellowstone hosted more than 3 million visitors. Maintaining its wilderness character and avoiding tawdry development has secured the GYE's attraction for recreation and tourism. Consequently, ecosystem protection in the GYE can be justified economically.

But keeping the GYE pristine extracts a cost. Resources not exploited in the GYE in order to protect ecosystem structure and wilderness values there will be exploited somewhere else. It would be tragic if these resources were to come from tropical regions where biodiversity is greater, but environmental regulations are more lax. Perhaps nature conservation priorities need reevaluation in the context of a global human population now at 5.7 billion people and growing rapidly. Should the utilitarian justification for preservation of genetic resources take precedence? If so, preserving the GYE may be a poor choice.

How we manage Yellowstone will be a model of conservation and sustainability for the rest of the world. One alternative that we might foster is a model of preservation; that is, showing that we are willing to make sacrifices to protect large areas for their ecosystem and wilderness values. Another alternative is to demonstrate that sustainable development can be achieved by integrating commodity uses with amenities and recreation, while still preserving biological diversity. Yellowstone will have greater global relevance if we develop the latter conservation paradigm.

General Conclusions

These five studies demonstrate various aspects of and opportunities for sustainable development, and the many problems encountered in implementing it. These and similar approaches around the globe seem to offer some promise for the conservation of biodiversity and natural systems, but not everyone is impressed by their potential. Many skeptics feel that sustainable development is a camouflaged, "politically correct" approach to further and perpetual economic growth and continued, but less overt, environmental destruction under the guise of conservation. For example as one commentator wrote, "Sustainable development of the WCED [World Commission on Environment and Development] variety means business-as-usual. This satisfies business interests, government officialdom around the world, powerful international institutions such as the World Bank, the International Monetary Fund, UN Food and Agricultural Organization, and national elites whose international assets are relatively safe from the erratic fluctuations of their own economies . . . the World Bank (1994) contends that growth is the key to eradicating poverty and protecting the environment" (Clark 1995).

Ecological economist Herman Daly has said that sustainable development "should be rejected as a bad oxymoron" (quoted in Hardin 1993). Donald Mann, president of Negative Population Growth, Inc., said that "the concept of sustainable development is little more than a gigantic exercise in self-deception," because advocates really mean "sustainable economic growth," which, in a limited world, he termed "a thundering oxymoron if ever there was one" (quoted in Hardin 1993).

Herman Daly furthermore pointed out that Norwegian Prime Minister Brundtland, chair of the Brundtland Commission, "insisted that global economic growth must increase by a factor of 5 to 10 to make so-called 'sustainable development' possible. The amount of global pollution generated if the world turnover of nature's bounty were to become 5 to 10 times greater than it is now should give pause to even the most 'optimistic' of anticonservatives." Few economists have bothered to say a word against Brundtland's "optimistic" remedy for the world's ills. Natural scientists, however, delight in quoting the words of Kenneth Boulding, former president of the American Economic Association: "Only madmen and economists believe in perpetual exponential growth" (Hardin 1993). So, can sustainable development really work, or is it merely a ploy by economists to justify continued development? Let's take a look at the "downside" of these issues.

Some argue that there has never been a case of successful sustainability over the long term; the resource has inevitably been overexploited. This is particularly apparent in commercial fishing, in which the concept of maximum sustained yield (MSY) has driven policy for decades. Under this concept, harvest is done at a rate such that the exploited population is maintained at a level of maximum production (see Figure 12.2). Although this makes sense in theory, in reality it has typically resulted in losses of fisheries after a period of overexploitation (Larkin 1977). It is impossible to accurately estimate the point of maximum yield; that point changes over time and space, and no known population grows according to a logistic curve, as assumed by the model. If the sometimes considerable uncertainties involved in estimating MSY curves are not taken into account, these are dangerous models to use for predicting sustainability.

Beyond fishery failures, why have models of sustainability not worked thus far? Ludwig et al. (1993) offer these common features of our failures at sustainability:

1. Wealth or the prospect of wealth generates political and social power that is used to promote unlimited exploitation of resources.
2. Scientific understanding and consensus is hampered by the lack of controls and replicates, so that each new problem involves learning about a new system.
3. The complexity of the underlying biological and physical systems precludes a reductionist approach to management. Optimum levels of exploitation must be determined by trial and error.
4. Large levels of natural variability mask the effects of overexploitation. Initial overexploitation is not detectable until it is severe and often irreversible.

They go on to say:

> It is more appropriate to think of resources as managing humans than the converse: the larger and the more immediate the prospects for [economic] gain, the greater the political power that is used to facilitate unlimited exploitation. The classic illustrations are gold rushes [or old-growth forests]. Where large and immediate gains are in prospect, politicians and governments tend to ally themselves with special interest groups in order to facilitate the exploitation.

In a response to Ludwig et al. (1993), Rosenberg et al. (1993) indicated that multiple examples of sustained fisheries do exist, although many failures have indeed occurred. These failures, they argue, are less a function of inadequate scientific understanding than of frequent "failure of resource managers to follow scientific advice." Resource managers, they say, have frequently ignored scientific evidence and allowed higher harvest levels than are sustainable. Thus, attaining truly sustainable development seems as much a problem in changing human behavior and value systems as it is a biological or ecological problem. Unless human value systems change globally, and political and economic power no longer favors overexploitation, the prospects for sustainability appear dim. Ludwig et al. (1993) offer five principles of effective management that would help to promote truly sustainable development:

1. Include human motivation and responses as part of the system to be studied and managed.
2. Act before scientific consensus is achieved. Calls for additional research may be mere delaying tactics.
3. Rely on scientists to recognize problems, but not to remedy them. The judgment of scientists is often heavily influenced by their training in their respective disciplines, but the most important issues involving resources and the environment involve interactions whose understanding may involve many disciplines.
4. Distrust claims of sustainability. Because past resource exploitation has seldom been sustainable, any new plan that involves claims of sustainability should be suspect. One should inquire how the difficulties that have been encountered in past resource exploitation are to be overcome.
5. Confront uncertainty. Once we free ourselves from the illusion that science or technology (if lavishly funded) can provide a solution to resource or conservation problems, appropriate action becomes possible.

We do not offer these counter-perspectives to discourage a drive toward sustainable development or to denigrate the concept. Indeed, several of the case studies incorporated these points, and a truly sustainable global society, combined with a stable (zero growth) human population, seems the only real hope for avoiding the massive biological extinctions and ecosystem collapses discussed in earlier chapters, as well as massive human misery. Instead, we caution that blind acceptance of the sustainable development approach can be dangerous to conservation interests because there are so many potential problems and pitfalls, and because the concept can be abused to the benefit of further growth. Healthy skepticism, combined with honest attempts to balance the needs of natural systems against actual, long-term human needs, seems the most sensible approach.

There is another facet of sustainability that must be acknowledged: it is not a clear endpoint that will either be achieved one day or not. We may never achieve "true sustainability," whatever that is, but we certainly can move ever closer to it. "Sustainability is a goal, like liberty or equality: not a fixed endpoint to be reached but a direction that guides constructive change; the realist is as skeptical of claims concerning sustainability as she would be of a claim that perfect liberty had been attained" (Lee 1993b).

Sustainable development is certainly possible, and may be the best hope for conservation of global biodiversity. However, three things must change radically if this goal is to be achieved. First, the value systems that lie at the core of the human fabric and drive our collective behaviors need to change drastically (discussed in Chapter 19). In wealthy, developed countries, long-term global sustainability must replace short-term personal gain as the primary human motivation. People must learn to value the environmental services provided by natural ecosystems, to understand the relationship between ecosystem protection and their long-term economic security, to reduce excessive resource exploitation, and to appreciate their natural heritage. Second, the growth-oriented economic systems that drive human existence must be replaced by steady-state economic systems that accept natural limits to our artificial economies. Finally, human population growth must slow, stop, and eventually reverse; toward this goal, sustainable development projects must contain internal incentives to limit population growth. These topics are addressed more fully in the final chapter.

Questions for Discussion

1. Keeping in mind the difference between "growth" and "development," do you think global economies need to expand in order to maintain a state of sustainable development? If they continually expand, *is* it sustainable development?
2. Many claims of sustainability are, under the surface, false. What criteria might you use to judge sustainability?
3. Consider this scenario: A major U.S. building supply franchise contracts with a South American consortium to provide mahogany doors in a sustainable fashion. Mahogany trees are carefully managed in cooperatives so that relatively few are harvested annually, at or below the replacement rate, keeping the resource sustainable. The world market is then limited to the doors that can be made from this amount of mahogany and no more, keeping both price and demand high. Is this scenario in fact sustainable? How might a "cheater" external to the system prosper and thereby destroy the process?
4. Discuss some of the potential opportunities for and problems with possible ecotourism ventures near you. What issues would need to be addressed to ensure that ecotourism would be sustainable and not damaging to natural areas?
5. Some conservationists have proposed "extractive reserves" (i.e., non-timber harvest of forest products) as good models of economic and ecological sustainability. What are some potential extractive reserve products in your region? Discuss the limitations of extractive reserves. Under what circumstances might they be sustainable?
6. One of the keys to long-term sustainability is a stable or declining human population. However, declining populations do not simply change in numbers, but also in age structure and geographic distribution. What implications might these changes have for sustainable development? Think about issues such as taxes, trade, leisure time, health, resource demand, and tourism.

Suggestions for Further Reading

Daly, H. E. and J. B. Cobb, Jr. 1989. *For the Common Good: Redirecting the Economy toward Community, the Environment, and a Sustainable Future*. Beacon Press, Boston. Daly and Cobb identify the logical fallacies of economics as currently practiced, show how economics works against community and ecological sustainability, and provide excellent suggestions for the development of a new, ecologically and humanly more sensible, economics.

Goodland, R., H. Daly, and S. El Serafy (eds.). 1991. *Environmentally Sustainable Economic Development: Building on Brundtland*. Working paper, The World Bank, Washington, D.C. A critique of the principles laid out by *Our Common Future* (the Brundtland report). It helps to expose the fallacies of continued economic growth as the answer to sustainability.

Kirkby, J., P. O'Keefe, and L. Timberlake (eds.). 1995. *The Earthscan Reader in Sustainable Development*. Earthscan Publications, London. A collection of readings on various aspects of sustainable development, including environmental, economic, geographic, political, and social aspects.

Knight, R. L. and K. J. Gutzwiller (eds.). 1995. *Wildlife and Recreationists: Coexistence through Management and Research*. Island Press, Washington, D.C. Ecotourism offers great promise for sustainability, but has drawbacks, including the effects of people on wildlife and natural areas. This collection addresses the effects of recreationists on natural areas, including a series of case studies.

Korten, D. C. 1991–1992. Sustainable development. *World Policy Journal* 9:157–190. An outstanding analysis of sustainable development and the problems in economic institutions that promote unsustainability. Korten provides an astute perspective on traditional economics, global lending policies, and human attitudes, all of which need to be overhauled in order to move toward sustainability.

McNeely, J. A. (ed.). 1995. *Expanding Partnerships in Conservation*. Island Press, Washington, D.C. Forming partnerships, as demonstrated in the Applegate case study, is one way of garnering support for a sustainable existence. This collection offers principles and case studies of partnerships that can help to solve some of the problems raised in this chapter.

Western, D. and R. M. Wright (eds.). 1994. *Natural Connections: Perspectives in Community-Based Conservation*. Island Press, Washington, D.C. A collection of case studies and analyses of community-based conservation efforts, which provide a basis for truly sustainable development.

In addition, two collections of papers in academic journals discuss various aspects of sustainable development. *Ecological Applications*, Volume 3, number 4 (1993) is a forum on science and sustainability, with a large series of papers that address the role of scientists in these issues. *Annual Review of Ecology and Systematics*, Volume 26 (1995) also has a good series of papers that deal with a very different set of issues and concepts, especially the economic aspects of sustainability.

19

Meeting Conservation Challenges in an Uncertain Future

It is often said today that 'what we need are more facts.' Actually we already have more facts than we know how to interpret or how to use wisely. What we need most is the wisdom which facts ought to generate but often, unfortunately, do not.

Joseph Wood Krutch, 1962

We have now come a long way in our journey into the principles of conservation biology, but the most difficult task remains: the transduction of conservation knowledge into human lifestyle changes that are consistent with what we know about the natural world and our effects on it. The challenges facing the human species are legion, but none is greater than getting the majority of humanity to recognize the conservation problems facing the world, admit that they are serious problems, and commit to vastly changing the human condition in appropriate ways. As a species, we have barely begun that effort. Much of the necessary knowledge, ecological and otherwise, to accomplish the task is in place. What remains is a "buy-in" from *Homo sapiens* to live up to its moniker of "wise man." This is perhaps the greatest challenge in the history of humanity.

Momentous changes are needed in the way that humanity conducts its business and relates to the natural world if the principles of conservation biology are even to be given a chance to work. We discuss some of those necessary changes in this chapter, with the hope of clearly identifying areas in which we can make major and relatively rapid advances toward conservation of biodiversity. But the changes needed are not trivial, and resistance to them will be great. Thomas Berry (1988) stated this succinctly: "We must be clear concerning the *order of magnitude* of the changes that are needed. We are not concerned here with some minor adaptations, but with the most serious transformation of human–earth relations that has taken place at least since the classical civilizations were founded." Indeed, an entirely new way of thinking must be explored and adopted if biodiversity and the quality of human existence are to remain high. Such visions for a changing future are presented in Essay 19A, by Frederick Ferré, in his view of the "postmodern world."

In this concluding chapter we offer some guidance to help you find your way through the confusion, uncertainty, and challenges of the future. We

ESSAY 19A
The Postmodern World

Frederick Ferré, University of Georgia

If we think of the "modern" world as beginning in the 17th century, the period when a distinctly modern science was founded by Galileo, Descartes, and Newton, we can appreciate how rapidly we are leaving that world behind. The modern framework of ideas, despite nearly three centuries of triumph, has proved no longer adequate for our best scientific thinking, and the technological society shaped by these ideas is no longer satisfactory for life on this fragile planet.

We cannot be certain about what is coming next, once the current transition from the modern world's ideas, attitudes, technologies, and institutions is complete. For this reason we haltingly (and uninformatively) call the new era we are entering "postmodern." But if we look at the main ways in which modern ideas—both in the abstract and as incarnated in the structures of modern civilization—have failed us, and if we look along the vector of the new ideas that are gradually growing up to replace them, we may be able to speculate with some hope on the general character of the rising postmodern world.

The main features of modern scientific thinking were (1) its stress on quantities over qualities, (2) its tendency to break problems into ever smaller parts (reductionism), and (3) its firm rejection of explanations involving purpose (or mind) in nature.

First, all the founders of modern science were opponents of the ancient and medieval emphases on thinking qualitatively about things. Instead, they translated qualities like heat and color into attributes that could be measured and counted and turned into mathematical formulae. The process began in astronomy with Kepler's laws of motion, and in physics with Galileo's studies of falling bodies and Newton's experiments on the refraction of light. Only the numerable could be precisely known; therefore (it was too quickly concluded), only the quantitative could be "really real" or fundamentally important. This devotion to the quantifiable has resulted in rapid progress in all the fields in which qualities could be safely ignored, particularly in physics. But as the civilization built on these scientific attitudes grew rich and powerful—both quantitative measures—issues of quality seemed less and less to matter. The "bottom line" for the effective rulers of this civilization became a quantitative one. Quality, in personal lives, in environment, became a matter of "mere value judgments," and was relegated to the bottom of the priority list. But real human beings occupy a world of experienced qualities. Failure to nurture quality leads to the anger, despair, and violence all too familiar in the waning years of the modern world.

Second, typical modern thought rests on an assumption that problems are best solved by analysis: cutting them up into ever-smaller questions for individual solution. As modern science sought to give all its explanations in terms of littlest parts, it also encouraged specialization in smaller and smaller units of subject matter. Thus, modern civilization has at its foundations the assumption that reality is just a conglomeration of material particles and that ideal knowledge is more and more about less and less. When characteristically engineered modern technologies are introduced into the tangled web of causes and effects in nature, however, we find that "side effects" like climate change and ozone holes mock our compartmentalized ways of thinking and threaten us in potentially catastrophic ways.

Third, modern scientific thinking defined itself as determined to avoid ancient ways of explaining phenomena by including reference to real goals in nature. The modern way was to restrict explanation to quantified formulae dealing with prior causes only. Modern thinking, as a result, has had a hard time finding a place for itself in the real world. If there are no goals in nature, but humans have goals, then it seems that humans are not in nature. If there are no qualities except in our minds, where are our minds? The modern civilization that was built on these ideas has increasingly isolated and alienated humankind from the world of physics and even of biology. Hillsides became resources; animals turned into commodities.

In all these ways the modern worldview has fallen short. It has institutionalized the neglect of quality, the disregard for the subtler connectedness of things, and the alienation of humanity from nature. If we look, instead, at the direction in which new thinking is taking us, we find that in all these respects a postmodern consensus is developing. This is true not only for many disillusioned writers and artists but also for many scientists. The fact that some fields of science itself are becoming distinctly postmodern may encourage us to hope that whole new institutions and technologies grounded in new ways of thinking, now to be described, may be achieved in a postmodern world.

Although one could look to fundamental changes in physics, chemistry, and systems theory for postmodern elements, the science leading most obviously toward the postmodern reform is ecology. Ecology does not abandon quantitative, analytical tools, of course. It is not a premodern science, urging return to obscurity and imprecision; it is, rather, a new science incorporating, yet going beyond, the typical modern sciences. Although it uses modern quantitative analysis as a tool, it is rooted in the recognition of quality as a vital feature of the world it studies. Ecology can and must recognize the qualitative differences between healthy and damaged ecosystems. Its repertoire is wide, and includes "number crunching," but its "bottom line" is not numbers. Its postmodern goal is understanding life thriving in an environment.

Ecology also deals essentially in complexity and connection. Although it uses simplification (modeling) as a tool along the way, it recognizes that ecological systems are interconnected wholes made up of organisms that are themselves interconnected wholes. Reductive, overspecialized "tunnel vision" is ruled out by both the subject matter and the goals of ecology. In a world like ours, in which there are no "side effects" except those relative to our ignorance or neglect, ecology teaches us to look carefully on all sides before concluding that our technological interventions in nature are safe.

Ecology, if attended to, also overcomes the alienation of humanity from the rest of nature. Not only are we reminded of our connection to everything else, we are also shown to be part of a continuous, evolving organic world of interactive goals. Animals have interests, too; every species, not only *Homo sapiens*, has a good-of-its-kind. It is in the long-term interest of species to maintain the health of the complex whole in which thriving can be sustained.

The postmodern world is not yet here, but the modern world is visibly failing and new possibilities are coming to light. One possible future would be a world organized around the ideas and attitudes of ecology, the bellwether postmodern science. Such a world would nurture the human hunger for quality: for beauty, balance, creative advance. Its technologies and institutions would embody the recognition of the subtle, often surprising connections between disparate things, emphasizing the benefits of interdisciplinary thinking in education and the joys of cooperative pluralism in global culture. In such a world we would find methods of transportation and housing, heating and cooling, farming and manufacture, that respect the natural order, organic and inorganic. It would allow the human race to join the web of life as a significant participant rather than an exploiting tyrant. Such a postmodern world seems to be on its way; but it could use our help in being born.

---

emphasize two general approaches: tangible actions that can be taken to reduce uncertainty and risk in the short term, and major societal changes we should encourage that will provide the necessary conditions for conserving biodiversity in the long term. The fate of biodiversity depends on how well we, as a species, can adopt and incorporate these ideas.

The Nature and Centrality of Uncertainty

We live in a world characterized by many forms of uncertainty. Death, taxes, the final exam, and the sun rising and setting are examples of deterministic processes and events that we can count on with great certainty, but most of our decisions, either as citizens or as professional conservation biologists, are made in a climate of some uncertainty and risk. We know that we live in a probabilistic world where we must assess the odds of alternative conservation decisions, do the best we can, and try to minimize the adverse effects of consequences we did not intend. The success of this text will be measured somewhat by the extent to which you are now able to understand the complexity that characterizes much of conservation biology, determine and evaluate competing conservation decisions, and take actions to reduce the risk and consequences of failure.

The three great variables that influence uncertainty and risk are (1) the quality, depth, and breadth of information available; (2) the complexity and nonlinearity of the processes whose outcome we are trying to predict; and (3) how far into the future we wish to carry our predictions. It is critically important for the long-term prospects of conserving biodiversity that you come to terms with how you are going to make decisions now in order to improve the future. If you do not, if you become paralyzed by the seemingly overwhelming odds against success, then you have simply made a different kind of decision that will affect the future: a decision to do nothing.

Responding to Short-Term Economic Change

Nobody has a very clear idea of what the economies of the world will look like in a hundred years, although we can say with certainty that we will be closer to nature's finite limits and may have exceeded some, unless our appetite for consuming the world's natural resources substantially decreases. In the shorter run, say, over periods of several years to a decade, we can look at recent history as our best guide to the future. Thus, we can expect to see a global economy that is growing slowly, with some countries and regions doing better than others. The quality of life gap between poorer countries, such as many in Africa, and the richer industrialized countries will continue to expand. Within individual countries, frequent recessional periods will force the retrenchment of public programs, including those that support conservation of biodiversity. This is the uncertain economic environment of the future. Other trends that are likely to affect the conservation field in an uncertain future are offered by David Ehrenfeld in Essay 19B.

ESSAY 19B

Conservation Biology in the 21st Century

David Ehrenfeld, Cook College, Rutgers University

What will it be like to be a conservation biologist in the first decade of the 21st century? Writing in 1996, I choose this period because it is not so far off that prediction is indistinguishable from fantasy, yet it will be a critical time for the students who are reading this text. These are the years in which your careers will prosper or stagnate, the years when conservation biology will either grow to meet the enormous challenges that confront it, or decline to become just another ineffectual, self-congratulatory academic exercise. Time spent now in thinking about the probable condition of the world in which you will work is as important a part of your career preparation as learning about the determination of minimum viable population size or techniques for the assessment of habitat quality.

In a static world, there would be no need to follow this advice. If next year is going to be the same as the last, why bother to prepare to do anything differently from the way we have been doing it? But conservation biology is grounded in the perception of a rapidly changing world. Unlike the majority of economists, who act as if there is no environmental change that cannot be reversed by market forces, we know that human actions are causing momentous changes—some irreversible—in fundamental, global conditions and processes, changes that we cannot control and often cannot even understand. Conservation biologists recognize change and should not be taken by surprise when it occurs.

Many of the most important changes that are bound to affect us in the coming years will not be biological or physical: they will be social, political, and economic in nature. These are the changes that concern me here. My reading of the significant impending changes follows. Whether you accept it is not important; what matters is that you think about the future in a creative and open-minded way that lets you function effectively when it arrives.

It does not take a crystal ball to predict that the most striking difference between the 1980s, when conservation biology became a recognized discipline, and the first ten years of the 21st century will be the depletion of a variety of resources that have been an accepted part of our world since the end of the Second World War. Indeed, the decline is already well under way, and affects us strongly as at least four resources that are important to conservation biology fade away: money, social stability, general environmental awareness, and specialized knowledge of plants and animals.

Money. Conservation biology has never been a wealthy field like computer science or genetic engineering. We are not accustomed to having luxurious buildings and sumptuous grants showered upon us, nor are the "jobs available" pages of *Science* and *Nature* filled with dozens of advertisements in which academia and industry compete to attract promising recent graduates or senior conservation biologists. Nevertheless, we have benefited from the wealth that has been spent on the sciences in the past 50 years, and we will be seriously affected when it dries up. We have piggybacked conservation research onto grants for non-conservation projects; we have built conservation and restoration into the research agendas of established ecological granting panels and field stations; we have diverted government and university resources into conservation biology programs; we have received support from private foundations and conservation organizations.

How much of this support is likely to continue? In a world that is essentially broke, a world whose wealth and whose enormously complex administrative, corporate, and financial structures depend on readily available energy and other resources that are nearly exhausted, the flow of money that has sustained nonindustrial, nonmilitary "frills" such as conservation biology is being slowly turned off at the tap (Tainter 1988). When most of the grants and the fellowships disappear, when the field stations are closed, when the foundations see the inflation-adjusted market value of their corporate stock portfolios cut in half, and then cut in half again, what are you going to do?

Social Stability. The constant shifting of jobs from industrial nations to those with the lowest pay scales, the downsizing that comes with (and without) corporate mergers, the widening of the gap between rich and poor, the damaging of communities as mall-based superstores put local shops out of business, the perverting of the best parts of our culture by a mass media concerned only with commercial profits, and the resulting violence and social instability are all bound to affect conservation biologists. We cannot stand above these processes; they will plague us where we work and where we live (Goldsmith 1994; van Creveld 1991; Rifkin 1995; Sale 1995). How are you going to remain a conservation biologist in a society in angry turmoil?

Environmental Awareness. Conservation biology is ethically driven—it is a scientific response to a societally perceived crisis. The public is aware that many species are threatened with extinction and that many ecosystems are being degraded. More important, people *feel* a sense of impending or actual loss, and are willing to devote energy and resources to reducing the threat. This is not the case in many other academic areas. The branch of mathematics known as topology is an example; many factors determine the amount of support given to topology, but public opinion is not usually one of them. Conservation biology, however, depends ultimately on a deep public feeling of environmental loss, and this feeling comes only to those who have tasted enough of nature to miss the savor when it is gone.

The past ten years have seen a dramatic reduction in many people's day-to-day contact with nature, and a corresponding increase in the proportion of time spent in the human-created, electronic world of television, e-mail, the Internet, and other substitutes for direct experience of the sights, smells, touches, tastes, and sounds of the natural world in which we evolved (McKibben 1992). This reduced experience of nature in daily life is particularly noticeable in the young: this bodes ill for conservation biology. As Gary Nabhan and Stephen Trimble (1994) put it: "We are concerned about how few children now grow up incorporating plants, animals, and places into their sense of *home*." How can a public that does not know nature be expected to be passionately aroused—or even nostalgically uneasy—about its demise? When the crunch comes, how will you gain support for your work from a public that has experienced "nature" only while on vacation at a Disney theme park?

Specialized Knowledge. A preoccupation with the specific characterizes all of conservation biology. Most degraded places still have some kinds of plants and some kinds of animals living there. If the preservation of nature simply meant the maintenance of any sort of generic life form—"grass," "weeds," "trees," "insects," "vertebrates," without regard to species or to ecosystem associations—there would be no need for conservation biologists. Our purpose is to make sure that particular species in particular ecosystems continue to exist in the place where they evolved. But to do that, we have to know how to tell one species from another, and this is getting to be a problem.

Until now, conservation has been able to depend on a rich resource of plant and animal taxonomists, both professional and amateur, to identify species and define taxonomic relationships. During the late 1960s and 1970s, however, it became evident that biology departments would no longer support taxonomy and natural history: it was molecular biology that occupied the entire stage. Thirty years later, classic taxonomists are an aging lot; there are few graduate students who call themselves taxonomists or systematists; and natural history has all but vanished from the academic scene (Ehrenfeld 1993b). True, molecular systematics is thriving, but most of its practitioners are laboratory-based rather than field-based. The demise of classic taxonomy and natural history has left an enormous void. Today, there are many genera, even families, of organisms that have only one or no practicing taxonomists familiar with them. The situation is worsening, and is especially troublesome for tropical species (Parnell 1993). Will you still be able to be a conservation biologist if neither you nor anyone else knows exactly what it is you are trying to save?

The beginning of the 21st century is certain to be an unsettled and often dangerous time for the majority of people in both the industrial and nonindustrial worlds. There will be no magic formula to guarantee that a conservation biologist can work effectively under these conditions, although some individuals will be lucky. But I believe that there is a strategy that can help you cope with the resource problems I have described—a strategy that may, at the very least, tip the odds in your favor. This strategy has six elements; I list them without elaboration and in no particular order.

1. Minimize the cost and logistic complexity of your research.
2. Design your research to be flexible, so that your methods and even some of your objectives can be modified as changing circumstances warrant.
3. Take every opportunity that you can find to learn, in depth, the taxonomy of the groups you are studying and the natural history of all parts of your ecosystem.
4. Have a practical trade, skill, or alternative occupation that you can resort to if conservation biology cannot support you on a full-time basis. There are trades that are always in demand, regardless of circumstances. Pick one.
5. Whenever possible, design your research to include the participation and wisdom of the local community. Make it your goal that local people understand, approve of, participate in, and benefit from your work. Make a special effort to involve local schools and schoolchildren; work with the teachers and budget a modest amount of money to help them incorporate your project into their curricula.
6. Before the project ends, develop a mechanism to monitor the system and continue local participation after you are gone.

If you are not satisfied with this strategy, by all means invent one of your own. A diversity of strategies is bound to be more successful than a single one. What matters most is that the future finds you prepared to do your work, fully able to experience the joys and challenges of being a conservation biologist.

As conservation biologists, what are our options for securing resources to maintain critical conservation programs and advance the principles of conservation?

An analogy may help. Imagine that conservation biology is like a service industry, such as insurance sales, and the service we are selling is called "biodiversity protection." How do we simultaneously protect our industry, which we will call "BioPro, Inc.," from adverse economic events and encourage its development? We would probably pursue four general strategies (Figure 19.1). First, we would encourage people to value our service. Second, we would look for better ways to manage and develop our business. Third, we would look for the best investment of our income. And fourth, we would help to shape public policy so that our industry would receive incentives for continued growth and development. As you can imagine, this analogy would quickly break down if we followed it too far, but we simply ask, as conservationists, can we pursue similar strategies?

Increasing the Perceived Value of Conservation Biology

The most effective thing we can do is convince as many people as possible to share our conviction that conserving biodiversity is an important value and that, in various ways, public support will maintain this value. As individual professionals, we should make two commitments for strengthening public

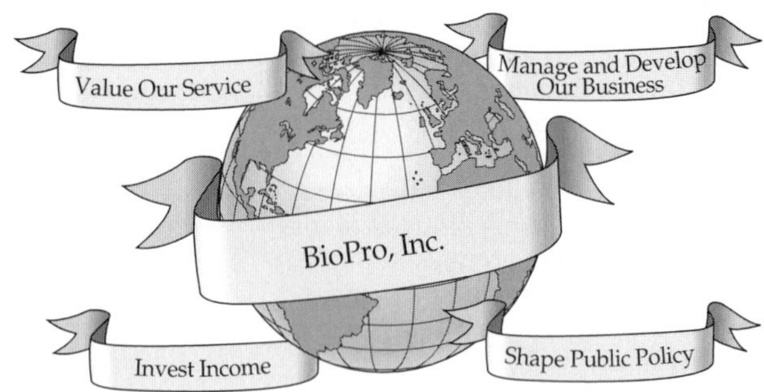

Figure 19.1 Our hypothetical corporation, "BioPro, Inc.," like any service industry, has four major concerns: we must get people to value our service, we must manage and develop our business, we must invest our income, and we must shape public policy to enhance our industry.

support: to formal and to informal environmental education. First, we should each find some means of actively contributing to environmental education in schools, especially at the elementary and secondary levels (Figure 19.2). If your reaction to this suggestion is, "I don't know anything about teaching children and adolescents, I'm a research scientist!," your protest is without merit. The potential range of contributions to environmental education is so large that even the most entrenched researcher can find something useful to offer. Probably the most generally useful contribution we can make is through helping teachers to develop curricular materials, such as case studies for teaching, photographic slides and films, simple experimental designs, or just by serving as resource contacts. More active involvement could include anything from leading an occasional field trip to visiting classrooms and telling students what conservation biologists do and why it is important.

Informal public education is also important, and the two best ways to communicate with the public are through popular "nature" articles and books, and through contact with print and broadcast journalists. Scientists, with some famous exceptions, tend to shy away from journalists, perhaps feeling that they will not understand what scientists do and therefore that the science will neither be appreciated nor correctly interpreted. Sometimes these concerns are valid, but because journalists are our bridge to the public, we can ill afford not to work with them. Besides, when communication has broken down, there is fault on both sides: the journalist may not understand what the

Figure 19.2 Educating children regarding nature and conservation is an easy and rewarding activity. The natural curiosity and open minds of children make them wonderful recipients for conservation education. Here, a member of the Savannah River Ecology Laboratory Environmental Outreach Program discusses snakes and their ecological roles with an eager group of elementary school students. (Photograph by David Scott.)

scientist is saying, and the scientist may have become too lazy or too preoccupied with his or her arcane work to communicate effectively to the public. The importance to conservation of communication with the public is elaborated further by Laura Tangley in Essay 19C.

ESSAY 19C
The Importance of Communicating with the Public

Laura Tangley, Conservation International

In the fall of 1992, the Brazilian journal *Goeldiana Zoologia* published a paper describing a new primate species, the Rio Maués marmoset (*Callithrix mauesi*). Like most reports in obscure scientific journals, this one would have gone virtually unnoticed if not for one thing: one of the three primatologists who described the new species, Russell Mittermeier, was president of a conservation organization.

On the day the report was published, the organization, Conservation International, sent out a press release on *Callithrix mauesi*. Within a few weeks, stories about the marmoset appeared in more than 500 magazines and newspapers, reaching an audience of at least 36 million worldwide.

More important, these 36 million people learned about the conservation significance of the finding. "The discovery of a new primate species attests to the vast diversity of life on earth that remains unknown to us," said Mittermeier in the press release. "It also shows how ignorant we still are of our fellow species—even fairly well-studied groups like our closest relatives, the primates." The release discussed the importance of biodiversity, the species extinction crisis, and the significance of the Amazon to protecting global biodiversity.

To Mittermeier, a conservation biologist, communicating the significance of this scientific discovery was at least as important as the discovery itself. After all, the conservation biologist is a new breed of scientist that cares deeply about saving, as well as studying, earth's plants, animals, and ecosystems. It was in fact biologists—including Mittermeier, E. O. Wilson of Harvard University, Peter Raven of the Missouri Botanical Garden, Paul Ehrlich of Stanford University, Norman Myers of Oxford University, and Daniel Janzen of the University of Pennsylvania, among many others—who first brought the biodiversity crisis to the attention of policymakers and the public.

Today, continued vigilance in science and conservation communication remains critical. Solving our most serious environmental problems, including pollution, overpopulation, deforestation, and species extinctions, will require that both the government and the private sector invest considerable amounts of time, effort, and money, something that is possible only if there is broad awareness and support by the public.

Similarly, public *mis*information can thwart conservation efforts. The best-known recent example has been the controversy surrounding the old-growth forests of the United States Pacific Northwest. This controversy, which has been depicted far too often as an issue of logging jobs versus the Spotted Owl, is in fact much more complicated. Although it is true that many jobs have been lost in the logging industry in recent years, the major causes—including increased automation and the practice of exporting raw logs as opposed to finished wood products—stem from economics, not conservation. An even more important point missed by the public throughout this controversy is that the forests themselves—not just the owl—are at stake. The primary forests of the United States, which once blanketed 385 million ha of the nation, have now been reduced to scattered remnants. The largest remaining blocks of old-growth forest are in the Pacific Northwest.

These ancient, complex ecosystems support hundreds of plant and animal species. Some of these species, including the Spotted Owl, live nowhere else on earth. Old-growth forests also ensure water quantity and quality, protect salmon fisheries and other economically important resources, and earn the region millions of dollars a year in tourism and recreation. So while important in its own right, the Spotted Owl is much more: the bird has become a symbol of the nation's last old-growth forests and the many services they provide.

Of course, mailing out a press release would have done little to prevent the misunderstanding surrounding the Spotted Owl, which was fueled in part by timber industry efforts to deliberately mislead the public. In addition, most biologists are in no position—or have no desire—to become so directly involved with the press. But this does not mean these scientists lack opportunities to communicate with the public.

Conservation biologists who care about the species and habitats they study should take advantage of every opportunity to share their knowledge and concern. When writing journal articles, for example, scientists should always explain the conservation implications of their work. If possible, they should include photographs or drawings of the species and ecosystems they study to bring their work to life. For those who like to write, submitting an article to a popular publication is an even better way to communicate with the public. Certainly it will experience broader readership than it would in a scientific journal.

In addition, conservation biologists should make themselves available to journalists who work on environmental stories for newspapers, magazines, radio, or television. Better still, they could offer to hold briefings for reporters who have access to large audiences, and keep those journalists up to date on new developments. Whenever possible, they should describe the species, ecosystems, and research involved in their projects in terms that the general public can understand.

Another good way to reach large audiences is to write editorials for newspapers and magazines. A particularly good time to do this is whenever the public's interest—and the interest of editors—has been piqued by some political or other kind of controversy.

Beyond these specific ideas, conservation biologists should simply be aware at all times of the importance of communicating with the public. Take every opportunity that arises to talk to students, friends, and family about conservation. Better still, invite people to visit your study site with you, or another natural area. As any biologist who cares about conservation knows, there is nothing better than direct experience in the field to awaken a lifelong love and concern for earth's biodiversity.

We must remember that the public supports the work of scientists through taxes, and it is simply unethical to deliberately keep the public ignorant of this work. The vast majority of the public may in fact be uninterested in what you do as a scientist, but they have a right to know, and we, as scientists, have an obligation to make an effort at communicating on their terms. This can only help in improving the value of our "product."

Improving Conservation Management and Development

A business that is operating under increased financial pressure cannot tolerate the luxury of inefficient operations and unnecessary management. The primary goal of conservation biology is the preservation of biodiversity, including the potential for adaptive responses to environmental change, over the long run. Therefore, the metric by which we should judge the institutions of conservation—including the management and effectiveness of their operations—is their contribution to the protection of biodiversity.

We can roughly divide conservation institutions into two classes, based on whether their mandate is direct protection, such as through land purchases and environmental law, or indirect protection, through research and education. Direct protection is the purview of individuals, private organizations, and some public agencies. Individuals may directly protect biodiversity through land protection and good stewardship, conservation easements, living bequests, and donations to other organizations. Private organizations may protect biodiversity through land purchases (e.g., The Nature Conservancy) or through support of conservation management (e.g., World Wildlife Fund). Public agencies, such as the nongame parts of natural resource agencies, may directly support biodiversity protection, and are also the instrument through which laws protecting biodiversity are implemented.

Indirect protection is usually the domain of educational institutions, and ranges from environmental education in the elementary grades through research and training at the university level. Increasingly, private stewardship organizations are supporting research (the Andrew W. Mellon Foundation has supported research in plant ecology) and training (the Jessie Smith Noyes Foundation has sponsored training programs for Latin American conservation biologists). Significant research and training is also conducted by public agencies; for example, the U.S. Fish and Wildlife Service, through its Western Hemisphere program, has supported research and training in Latin America.

How can we judge the effectiveness of such a multitude of programs? This broad question has to be divided into two smaller questions. First, do the goals of the programs really directly or indirectly improve the protection of biodiversity? Second, do the organizations have an effective program for achieving their goals? With regard to the first question, some institutions with conservation programs have goals only marginally related to the protection of biodiversity. Some examples include public agencies whose multiple-use mandates seriously compromise their ability to protect biodiversity. This is the central problem of protecting public resources as "commons," which we discuss in depth later in this chapter. Private stewardship organizations that are excessively focused on single-species protection may not represent the best allocation of scarce resources. Major lending agencies, such as large private banks, that compromise biodiversity protection in economic development projects may give little more than lip service to protection.

With regard to the second question, it is often difficult to gauge the effectiveness of conservation programs unless they have conducted programmatic evaluations, but it is possible to make some general observations. For example, other things being similar, a school that offers a few isolated units on environmental education is likely to be less effective than one that incorporates environmental education through all grade levels and courses. Public agencies that allocate large fractions of their budget and personnel to supporting game, recreational, and resource extraction interests, and only token support to biodiversity protection, are unlikely to be very effective protectors of biodiversity. Unfortunately, most U.S. natural resource agencies fall into this category, much to the frustration of the often excellent conservation biologists who work for them.

One way to evaluate the effectiveness of private stewardship organizations is to examine the proportion of their funds that are spent on programmatic activities versus administrative support or other fund-raising efforts. However, private stewardship organizations cannot be evaluated by the general formulas that might be applied to other "charitable" organizations. For example, the discovery that a charity associated with a particular religion has a low fund-raising cost in comparison with a secular conservation organization simply says that the religious charity has a "captive clientele" that requires relatively less effort for fund raising. It is more reasonable to compare similar conservation organizations with one another, comparing their public records of the ratio of programmatic funds to other overhead funds.

Improving Investment

We do not usually sell our conservation services for money, except as consultants, and so conservation biology as a service does not have investment income in the way other for-profit service industries do. However, because biodiversity protection has social value, we have access to funds from private donors, corporations, development banks, private foundations, international agencies, and governmental institutions. How can we best use those funds?

Most of the funds are made available only for restricted uses that match the interests of donors, or to meet the programmatic goals of foundations and public institutions. As conservation biologists, we have two options: either work actively to reshape the agendas of the donors and institutions so that they meet the most important needs of conservation biology, or try to find the best fit between our interests and the interests of those who support our work.

The latter approach is not necessarily as vulgarly opportunistic as it might appear. Perhaps because we have been doing an effective job of environmental education, the individuals and private and public agencies that support conservation biology are now far more knowledgeable and sophisticated about biodiversity protection than they were just a few years ago. Therefore, finding a match between an important conservation project and a source of potential support is not nearly as difficult now as it used to be.

It is also possible to reshape the agendas of the various donor and institutional sources supporting conservation programs. This is not an easy task because the setting of priorities for support is usually the product of considerable analysis and possibly some internal constraints. Consider first how a private foundation might set its priorities for supporting programs in conservation. A private foundation working from a restricted endowment or trust may be precluded from certain areas of activity, such as family planning and birth control, by the terms used to create the endowment or trust. Given the areas that are appropriate, the program directors of the foundation may consult with knowledgeable people outside the foundation to determine important areas that need support. With these priorities in mind, the program directors may look at what other foundations and public funding sources are doing and then choose to support some important kinds of programs that are currently underfunded. Usually, a board of directors of the foundation will then have to decide whether or not to approve the choices made by the program directors and what level of support should be made available. Still, by writing focused articles on the role of foundations and by cultivating interactions with program directors, it is possible to effect changes.

It is more difficult to reshape the agendas of public agencies because their priorities are usually compromises between what they should be, based on ecological reasoning, and what can receive political backing. During the Reagan and Bush administrations, for example, support for programs that encouraged family planning and birth control was actively discouraged and, in some cases, simply not allowed. The best avenues for reshaping the agendas of public agencies are through the public affairs offices or programs of professional societies such as the Society for Conservation Biology and the Ecological Society of America, and through NGOs such as the World Wildlife Fund and The Nature Conservancy.

While change may be slow and difficult to achieve, it is not impossible, and some recent successes can be cited. As recently as the late 1980s, support for biodiversity protection was nearly nonexistent in U.S. foreign assistance programs for developing nations. Now, biodiversity protection has become an active part of such programs to the extent that it is the norm for the U.S. Agency for International Development to include biodiversity support as part of each country's portfolio of programs. Similarly, the U.S. Endangered Species Act of 1973 and subsequent amendments to the Act have prohibited federal programs from jeopardizing threatened or endangered species and have authorized the federal departments of Commerce and Interior to protect and recover these vulnerable species. In large part, the improvement in federal program support for biodiversity protection is the result of collective efforts made by nongovernmental organizations and professional conservation societies.

Developing Policy Incentives

We need better ways for public policy to create economic incentives for biodiversity protection. Usually public policy influences biodiversity protection in two ways, both of which are negative: through punitive legislation that assesses fines or jail sentences when environmental laws are broken, and, usually inadvertently, by offering disincentives for protection. Examples of the latter include the mandate for multiple use of U.S. national forests—which places biodiversity protection on the same level as recreational use by off-road vehicles—and undervaluing grazing fees for cattle using public lands. Clearly, we need to eliminate such disincentives in public policy and find more innovative and flexible *positive* incentives for biodiversity protection.

One example of an innovative and positive economic incentive is the idea of a flexible environmental assurance bonding system (Costanza 1991). Such a system would encourage environmental technological innovation by incorporating environmental criteria and future uncertainty into the marketplace. Under this plan, development loans would require that the borrower take out a long-term bond against any environmental damage that might be caused by the project in the future. If damage occurred, then the bond and accrued interest could be used to repair the damage. If no damage occurred, then the value of the bond and some of the interest would return to the borrower. The hope is that the cost of the bond would encourage developers to be more cautious about projects and to pursue more environmentally benign forms of development. Obviously, the value of the bond must be high enough to provide the necessary economic incentive for borrowers to change their ways; also, the real cost of repairing any future damage must be accurately reflected by the face value and accrued interest of the bond.

Another example of a positive incentive is the "safe harbor" program being implemented by the U.S. Fish and Wildlife Service (Bean and Wilcove 1996). Under that program, private landowners are given strict assurances by the government that, if their good land stewardship results in colonization by endangered species, they will not lose flexibility in future land use. Thus, for example, if landowners in North Carolina retain longleaf pine trees to the age at which Red-cockaded Woodpeckers might nest in them, rather than clear-cutting before that happens, their present obligations under the Endangered Species Act will not increase. In other words, by volunteering to undertake a beneficial action or avoid a detrimental one, they will not be punished at a later date. This is a major step that allows landowners who would like to "do the right thing" to do so without fear of economic or legal constraints later on. It allows the possibility of real and tangible progress rather than assurances of destructive actions out of fear of the Endangered Species Act.

It is in innovative ways such as these that the conservation community—"BioPro, Inc."—must respond to short-term economic uncertainties and vagaries. It should be obvious that there is room for many more new perspectives and contributions in this area. Tom Lovejoy offers some innovative ideas for the enhancement of conservation actions in Essay 19D.

ESSAY 19D
Opportunities for Creative Conservation

Thomas E. Lovejoy, Smithsonian Institution

The scale and rate of environmental change sometimes seems so daunting as to be beyond addressing in any effective way. Yet, when challenged, the human mind is capable of considerable ingenuity, creativity, and new ways of problem solving. In many ways, the extinction crisis represents the ultimate challenge: to summon the creativity to prevent biotic impoverishment from permanently constraining what that very creativity might develop from biological diversity.

One answer lies in using biological diversity—the ultimate integrator of all environmental change—itself. In 1996, the dynamic octogenarian limnologist Ruth Patrick received the National Medal of Science for work that established an incontrovertible link between the so-called "brown" or pollution issues and the "green" or biodiversity conservation issues. Working on rivers, Dr. Patrick demonstrated that the numbers and kinds of species to be found provided a snapshot of a river's condition. So fundamental is this principle to environmental science and management that it now is taken as a basic assumption. Yet it is one that takes on renewed relevance today as society struggles with unprecedented pressures on land, waters, and their biota.

As discussed throughout much of this book, growing lists of endangered species make it increasingly apparent that biological diversity conservation can be most effectively dealt with at the ecosystem and landscape level rather than at the species level, and that some form of ecosystem management approach is in order. What is needed, therefore, is an innovative set of approaches so that large units of landscape with some degree of ecological cohesion can be managed in ways that provide flexibility, multiple options for human aspirations, and opportunities for creative solutions.

The best measure of whether an ecosystem is being managed sustainably draws directly from Ruth Patrick's work—namely, whether it maintains its characteristic biodiversity and ecosystem processes. Taken most simply, this means that the native species list for a particular ecosystem a hundred years or more hence should essentially be that which it has today, and that functions such as watershed protection, nutrient cycling, or pollination remain in good condition.

Achieving these goals will be no simple feat. It will require taking into account every factor (and the individual decisions that relate to each) *intrinsic* to the ecosystem, as well as every factor *extrinsic* to the ecosystem (even climate change)—which by definition are harder to control. And it will probably work only if there is substantial involvement of local people in the process of making decisions about the place in which they live.

In the absence of specific legislation, this means largely voluntary participation on the part of private landholders in collaboration with local, state, and federal agencies. In places like the five southern California counties that contain the California coastal sage scrub (and the California gnatcatcher), this voluntary engagement with land use planning seems to be working well. In such cases a landholder, in giving up a bit of the power to decide what to do with a piece of the overall mosaic, gains power to influence how other pieces of the mosaic will be managed in ways that can affect the single piece.

In the past, most environmental problems have arisen because of independent decisions, each seemingly reasonable or inconsequential by itself, but which in total create an undesirable condition. Such problems can be avoided or redressed by the aggregation of largely voluntary, consultative decision making. A number of such experiments are in progress around the nation.

In a way, what this new ecosystem approach represents is a fundamental change in how people view themselves with respect to nature. Instead of perceiving nature as something that exists as a fenced-off patch in the middle of a human-dominated landscape where people are totally free to do as they will, the new view is of people living and pursuing their activities and aspirations *within* nature.

Clearly, ecosystem management is no simple undertaking, and indeed, is a perpetual challenge, but its early results in various places seem quite promising. Clearly, there is still a great deal to be learned, but all of this is fundamental to sustainable development. As societies struggle to understand the term *sustainable development*, I believe that the two operational measures of sustainable ecosystem management mentioned above—characteristic biodiversity and ecosystem processes—offer a way to a sound definition of sustainable development. If those conditions are met—if an ecosystem is being sustainably managed—then surely if *all* the planets' ecosystems (however we might delineate them) were managed that way, the sum

$$\sum_{1}^{n} \begin{matrix}\text{Sustainable}\\ \text{Ecosystem}\\ \text{Management}\end{matrix} = \begin{matrix}\text{SUSTAINABLE}\\ \text{DEVELOPMENT}\end{matrix}$$

would be equivalent to sustainable development on a planetary basis.

It is one thing to identify operational measures of sustainable ecosystem management, but another to address its economic and social aspects. Economics, as practiced, tends to leave out environmental costs, treating them as "externalities" (see Chapter 15), and uses discount rates that virtually render long-term considerations valueless. By definition, these practices lead to environmentally destructive decision making. Indeed, most conservation biologists and environmentalists believe that the natural world and its contributions are vastly undervalued. As a consequence, numerous attempts at valuation of biodiversity are being made. Some believe that it is a mistake to try to put dollar values on nature, that only moral, aesthetic, and religious values should be used. I believe that it is a mistake not to use the best economic values we can obtain, and it seems likely that they are far higher than previously realized. A recent study by Costanza et al. estimates the global value of ecosystem services at $32 trillion (Costanza et al., unpublished data). In any case, using economic values should not preclude use of the other values.

Similarly, it is important to use innovative financial techniques such as debt-for-nature swaps to enhance conservation work. Born of my realization that international debt itself can create environmental problems, such swaps basically involve buying debt cheaply in hard currency from the original lender and redeeming (selling) it high, in local soft currency. Then the local partner, usually an NGO, applies the proceeds to conservation.

Most of the criticisms applied toward debt swaps have not been directed at the mechanism itself, but rather at the details of projects supported by it; this has happened less often as the novelty of debt swaps has worn off. Other criticisms involve alleged violations of national sovereignty. This is never an issue because a nation must participate voluntarily. Another criticism has been a potential inflationary effect, again largely illusory. New forms of debt-for-nature swaps have emerged, including the use of government-to-government debt.

Another interesting approach suitable for a flurry of creativity and innovation is known as "activities implemented jointly" under the Climate Change convention. The intent is to provide a mechanism to encourage economically efficient ways of curbing the growth of greenhouse gases, especially CO_2. Using this mechanism, a utility company planning a new fossil fuel plant might offset its CO_2 release by paying for energy-efficient conversion of an existing power plant or for protection of a forest or reforestation in another country. More complex arrangements might involve such a utility reducing the price of electric cars for use in another part of the world. I personally find the forest conservation option very attractive because it does not preclude other uses of the same piece of forest for non-CO_2 releasing activities such as ecotourism and extraction of minor forest products. In that way, there can be multiple income streams from the same tract of forest, making it far more valuable to conserve forests and their biodiversity than to clear-cut or convert them to other purposes.

There are important new ways in which the world of business can be helpful too. In fact, the private sector is so huge that without it, conservation problems will *not* be solved. Promising new approaches from the World Business Council for Sustainable Development include eco-efficiency—in which it pays to use less—and investing to promote change. For example, architect William McDonough brings the principle of deep design (Wann 1996) to bear on everything from molecules to buildings. He makes the point that often there are multiple ways to achieve a goal such as constructing office space or building a carpet factory and manufacturing carpet. With creativity, the office space can be built of sustainably produced materials and be energy efficient, the carpet can be toxic-free, and the effluent from the factory can be cleaner than good clean water standards.

These are just a few examples of new ways of thinking about solutions. In my own experience, a distinct stimulus is usually responsible for provoking new ideas. Such new ideas are unlikely to happen unless, with regularity, we lift our eyes to the horizon and confront the vast challenge of conserving the world's biodiversity. Such challenges require the best creativity that the human species can muster.

Responding to Long-Term Planetary Environmental Change

Any reading of either the long-term paleontological history of the earth or of its shorter-term history since the beginning of the Pleistocene must convey a sense of changing environments. In Chapter 4, we reviewed the most important of these environmental changes and showed how they influenced contemporary patterns of biodiversity, especially through the creation of centers of high endemism such as Madagascar. Other chapters have emphasized two related points. First, species distributions have changed markedly over the past 12,000 years or so, largely in response to changing climate. Second, community composition has not been constant, but rather, species have migrated largely independently of other species.

There is every reason to believe that the earth will continue to change in the future and that these changes will continue to influence biodiversity patterns and processes. However, as we have emphasized in our chapters on biodiversity losses, conservation reserves, and conservation management, there are two new factors that will profoundly affect our attempts to conserve biodiversity for future generations. The first is that human effects on the environment, primarily through habitat destruction and degradation, are accelerating the rate of extinction. The second is that increased fragmentation and isolation of natural habitat has greatly limited the possibilities for long-distance migration. Historically, species have responded to climate change by migrating, albeit over many generations, to more favorable regions. Fragmentation and isolation have largely foreclosed that option.

Of course we have no oracle to guide our conservation programs very far into the next millennium, but if we take the next hundred years as a reasonable time frame for conservation planning, there are some broad environmental changes that we can anticipate and whose effects we should be able to mitigate through careful planning now. There seems little doubt that global climate patterns are going to change significantly over the next hundred years. Our rampant industrialized economies continue to pollute the atmosphere to such an extent that ozone is being depleted over polar regions, and the heat balance of the globe is possibly being altered (Figure 19.3).

The engine for climate change is in place, but there are various degrees of uncertainty about different aspects of change, and great uncertainty over how the climate will change in any particular locality (Table 19.1). There are basically three options for conservation planning, given this degree of uncertainty. First, designs for reserves should include an array of climate refugia, such as permanent water sources should the climate become drier, or a greater altitudinal range should the temperature change. Second, there should be larger-scale planning for corridor connections that will allow animals and plants more opportunities to migrate, as has been discussed in several chapters and essays. Our third option is to plan for more active management of populations and reserves in order to minimize the effects of climate change. Such management programs might include anything from introducing new food sources, to maintaining high levels of heterozygosity and thereby preserving adaptability, to translocating populations to more favorable regions. It is up to individual conservation biologists and their agencies to develop locally workable ideas to mitigate the effects of an altered climate.

We should also realize that local climate change may not represent a drastic alteration from current patterns but may still be large enough to have some effect on population dynamics. How should we plan for uncertain change at this level? There are several general strategies worth considering. First, we may consider doing nothing beyond what is needed to deal with existing

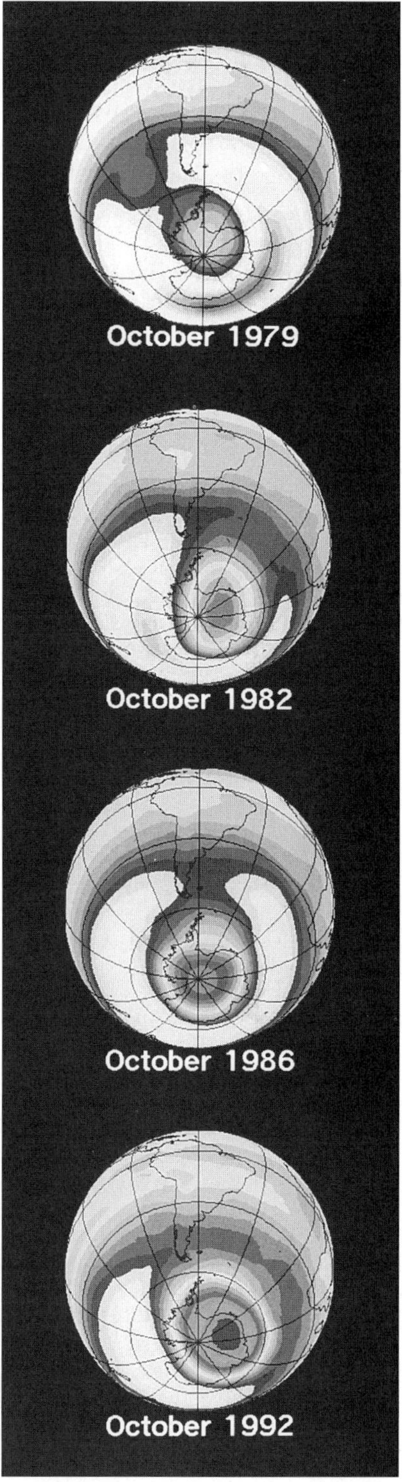

Figure 19.3 Although local patterns of atmospheric ozone depletion are difficult to predict, there is little doubt that ozone is being depleted to dangerously low levels over some parts of the earth. Note the changes in shape and size of the ozone hole over the South Pole over a 13-year period. (Courtesy of NASA.)

Table 19.1
Degrees of Consensus on Climate Change Issues

Issue	Consensus[a]			
	Virtually certain	Very probable	Probable	Uncertain
Basic characteristics				
Fundamental physics of the greenhouse effect	✓			
Added greenhouse gases add heat	✓			
Greenhouse gases are increasing because of human activity	✓			
Significant reduction of uncertainty will require a decade or more	✓			
Full recovery will require many centuries	✓			
Projected effects				
Extensive stratospheric cooling		✓		
Effects predicted for the mid-21st century				
Increase in global mean surface precipitation		✓		
Reduction of sea ice		✓		
Arctic winter surface warming		✓		
Rise in global sea level		✓		
Local details of climate change				✓
Tropical storm increases				✓
Details of next 25 years				✓

Data from World Resources Institute 1994.
[a]Virtually certain: a nearly unanimous agreement among scientists and no credible alternative view; Very probable: roughly a 9 out of 10 chance of occurring; Probable: roughly a 2 out of 3 chance of occurring; Uncertain: a hypothesized effect for which evidence is lacking.

problems. This approach would make sense if we had reason to believe that the system was likely to be resilient to moderate climate change—that is, that there might be some reshuffling of relative species abundances, but no species would be put at special risk of extinction. This neutral strategy might apply, for example, to communities whose member species are adapted to highly variable climates, such as those of the Great Plains of North America.

Second, in cases in which we think peripheral populations might suffer greater extinction rates, we should think of approaches that both decrease probabilities of local extinction and enhance recolonization following extinction. That is, our planning efforts should reflect the need to maintain sensitive populations well above their lower limits of viability, as well as considering source–sink dynamics and the "rescue effect" of metapopulation structure, as discussed in Chapter 7. Such a strategy might involve maintaining well-protected core habitat both as a source of migrants and as a hedge against stochastic sources of extinction, and satellite habitat both as a sink to absorb excess migrants and as a hedge against density-dependent sources of catastrophic mortality such as disease. The core–satellite model of reserve design may be the most cost-effective way to plan for moderate, but uncertain, climate change.

The other very predictable long-term environmental change is continued loss of natural areas and degradation of all habitat types. With the exception of some limited restoration activities, habitat destruction is a one-way street; we are destroying vast amounts of natural areas every year and creating no new ones to replace them (Figure 19.4). This pattern must be considered in all conservation planning. All protected areas become increasingly important as fewer such areas exist, and their management becomes more critical. Perhaps a good working rule is to remove from consideration any further destruction or degradation of any remaining natural areas, especially those with real wilderness characteristics.

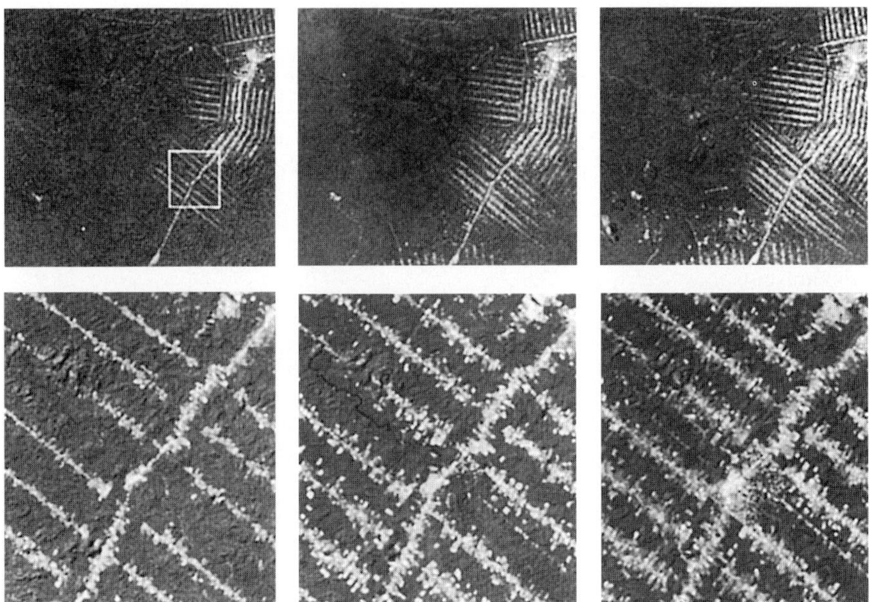

Figure 19.4 Progressive habitat loss is demonstrated by development in and destruction of the Amazon Basin in Brazil. These six Landsat satellite images of central Rondônia show progressive forest destruction in 1976 (left), 1978 (middle), and 1981 (right). In each case, a 185 × 185 km block is shown on the top, and an inset of 30 × 30 km is on the bottom. Uncut forest is dark, and cleared areas are light. Note the progressive deforestation in only five years. (Landsat images courtesy of Thomas A. Stone, Woods Hole Research Center.)

Responding to the Demographic Imperative

The first paragraph and first figure of this book focused on human population growth, and for good reason. The global human population is currently growing at about 1.7% per year (World Population Prospects 1990); if this growth rate continues, then today's population of about 5.7 billion will nearly double to 11 billion in about 41 years, an ominous threat. Several trends are masked by these aggregate statistics. The good news is that the growth rate of the world's population is expected to decline. Although the average growth rate was 1.73% in the late 1970s and 1.74% during the 1980s, the rate is expected to decline to 1.63% by the turn of the century (World Population Prospects 1990). Today's annual population growth rate is less than what it was only 10 years ago, and for the industrialized parts of the world at least, low growth rates may be a long-term demographic feature.

But the bad news is that, though global growth rates are slowing, they are still positive. Thus, each year during 1975–1980, about 74 million people were added to our finite globe, 88 million during each year of the late 1980s, and, even with a lower population growth rate, we will add at least 95 million people each year during the last half of the 1990s. To put that number in perspective, this means that *each year* through the turn of the century and beyond we will be adding to the planet more than one-third the existing population of the United States. At the current size of the human population, and with our destructive capabilities, *any* positive growth rate is cause for concern. Additionally, the countries that continue to experience high population growth rates are typically tropical or other developing countries, which are home to a large fraction of the world's biodiversity (Table 19.2). Of course, associated with this growth in population is an increase in demand for resources. Virtually any category of resource consumption one can measure continually increases as the human population expands (Table 19.3)

Fortunately, economies are generally improving in developing nations (with the exception of many African countries), and this is, of course, a welcome change from the debilitating poverty that has been their legacy. However, economies that are growing are also making increasing demands on nat-

Table 19.2
Countries with the Highest Fertility Rates (Average Number of Children per Woman)

Country	Total fertility rate	Population growth rate (%/yr)	Approx. doubling time (yrs)
Kenya	8.0	3.9	17.9
Afghanistan	7.6	2.6	26.9
Jordan	7.4	3.7	18.9
Tanzania	7.1	3.5	20.0
Zambia	7.0	3.5	20.0
Saudi Arabia	6.9	3.1	22.6
Ethiopia	6.7	2.3	30.4
Senegal	6.7	2.8	25.0
Nigeria	6.6	2.8	25.0
Pakistan	6.6	2.9	24.1
Sudan	6.5	2.8	25.0
Zimbabwe	6.5	3.5	20.0
Iran	6.3	3.2	21.8
Bangladesh	6.2	2.7	25.9
Zaire	6.1	3.1	22.6

Modified from Population Reference Bureau 1987.

ural resources. Because birth rates are inversely correlated with per capita gross national product, we would expect to see a country's birth rate decline as its economy improves. Indeed, the developing countries of Asia and Latin America have shown striking decreases in their population growth rates. If we compare the growth rates expected during 1995–2000 with the growth rates of the late 1980s, Colombia's growth rate will decline from 1.97% to 1.70%, and Malaysia's from 2.64% to 1.85%. For the regions as a whole, South America's rate will decrease from 2.01% to 1.71%, and Asia's from 1.87% to 1.68%, but Africa's will change imperceptibly, from 2.99% to 2.98% (World Resources Institute 1992).

By itself, population size is a misleading and simplistic index of concern for the human presence on earth. A more complete and realistic view of our effects must include not just our numbers, but our total impacts. The impact of

Table 19.3
Selected Indicators of Global Growth in Resource Consumption from 1950 to 1991

World indicator	1950	1991	% change
Grain production (million tons)	631	1696	270
Soybean production (million tons)	18	106	590
Meat production (million tons)	46	173	380
Fish catch (million tons)	22	97	440
Irrigated area (million hectares)	94	235	250
Fertilizer use (million tons)	14	136	970
Oil production (million barrels/day)	10.4	59	570
Natural gas production (trillion cubic feet)	6.7	77	1150
Automobile production (millions)	8	35	440

Data from Brown et al. 1994.

humanity on the earth and its resources is a function of at least its population size, times a measure of the average consumption of resources (an index of affluence), times a measure of the effects of the technologies used to attain that affluence. Ehrlich and Ehrlich (1990) refer to this as

$$I = P \times A \times T$$

in which overall impact (I) is a function of population size (P), times the per capita level of affluence (A), times the environmental disruptiveness of the technologies used (T).

The ***I* = *PAT*** approach indicates that we need to focus on more than population size. A large total impact may arise from many people, or a high consumptive standard of living, or damaging technologies, or combinations of all three. For example, a small, industrially based country could have a much greater global impact on the environment than a similar-sized country with a mixed, less resource-consumptive economy.

This relationship between population size, affluence, and technologies means that a developed country such as the United States, with the highest level of affluence in the world and many environmentally damaging technologies, cannot expand its population at all if it does not wish to increase its environmental impact, or if it wants to retain a high standard of living. Any expansion of such a population will have a larger environmental impact than an expansion in any other country. Conversely, there is little hope that a country like China, India, or many other developing nations will ever have a significantly higher standard of living for all its citizens unless it either reduces its population drastically or has huge and irreversible effects on the environment.

The $I = PAT$ perspective is critical because it more realistically balances the environmental influences of various cultures than does population size alone. The countries of Western Europe, for example, with stable populations, and the United States, with only a modestly expanding population, cannot simply point fingers at developing countries with high population growth rates and blame them for environmental damage when the overall impacts of the developed nations are probably much higher. According to Ehrlich and Ehrlich (1990), the total lifetime impact of a baby born in the United States is "twice that of one born in Sweden, 3 times one born in Italy, 13 times one born in Brazil, 35 times one in India, 140 times one in Bangladesh or Kenya, and 280 times one in Chad, Rwanda, Haiti, or Nepal." Thus, not only are decreased population growth rates desirable in developing nations, but population shrinkage and acceptance of limits to affluence are called for in the richer, developed nations.

Unfortunately, not everyone understands or accepts the population, affluence, and technology relationship. Hardin (1993) relates that "in 1984, ecologists were astounded at the official position taken by the United States [under the Reagan administration] at the U.N. conference on population and the environment in Mexico City; our spokesman said that 'population growth is neutral.' This was also the position taken by the Vatican. All other delegations supported the default position, $I = PAT$." It is incumbent upon all knowledgeable persons to educate humanity about the dangers inherent in such denialist views (Meffe et al. 1993).

What are we to make of population trends with regard to our long-term chances of protecting global biodiversity? On balance, we should recognize that 10 or 20 years ago we thought that the world's population picture today would be worse than it actually is. Some nations have been able to achieve drastic reductions in their population growth rates (Table 19.4). This change alone should provide some optimism that beneficial demographic shifts can happen rather quickly, and we should feel encouraged to participate in help-

Table 19.4
Countries with the Greatest Reductions in Fertility Rates (Average Number of Children per Woman) from 1960 to 1987

	Total fertility rate		
Country	1960	1987	% change
Singapore	6.3	1.6	−75
Taiwan	6.5	1.8	−72
South Korea	6.0	2.1	−65
Cuba	4.7	1.8	−62
China	5.5	2.4	−56
Chile	5.3	2.4	−55
Colombia	6.8	3.1	−54
Costa Rica	7.4	3.5	−53
Thailand	6.6	3.5	−47
Mexico	7.2	4.0	−44
Brazil	6.2	3.5	−44
Malaysia	6.9	3.9	−43
Indonesia	5.6	3.3	−41
Turkey	6.8	4.0	−41
Tunisia	7.3	4.5	−38
Sri Lanka	5.9	3.7	−37
India	6.2	4.3	−31
Philippines	6.6	4.7	−29
Peru	6.6	4.8	−27
Egypt	6.7	5.3	−21

From Brown et al. 1988.

ing to make further improvements. But this optimism may simply reflect our inability to develop accurate demographic models and predictions; perhaps the coming decades will have *higher* growth rates than predicted. Uncertainty looms large once again.

The effect of probable population and economic trends is likely to be a mixed bag: some trends may have positive effects on conservation, while others will be negative. For example, if a tropical country's economy is growing simply because it is selling more timber, then the consequences for biodiversity obviously are not improved. However, if the economy and the human condition are improving because the country is investing more in service industries or manufacturing—in the production of "value-added" goods—it is possible that less pressure may be put on forests as the primary source of foreign exchange. Furthermore, to the extent that economic advancement requires better-educated workers, there is a twofold effect on population growth. Family size is inversely related to level of education; as the level of education increases, average family size decreases (World Development Report 1992). Also, the process of acquiring education and training is a major commitment of time that tends to delay marriage and to increase the average age at first childbearing. These two factors, smaller family size and older parents, act as a powerful brake on population growth rates.

However, three assumptions must be met before a country's growing economy can lead to declining birth rates. First, the engine for economic growth must come from activities that require improved education and training rather than exploitation of natural capital. Second, the economic transformation must include both rural and urban sectors of the country. Third, and most important, women must fully participate in the transformation, both through educational opportunities and empowerment to make reproductive and other decisions.

Increasingly, conservation biologists are participants in international economic development projects. The protection of biodiversity now is frequently a requirement that countries must meet before they are eligible to receive development loans from multinational banks, such as the World Bank, or assistance from other countries. Thus, it is important that conservation biologists consider the probable human demographic consequences of economic development projects. It would be hypocritical to bring a conservation biologist into a development project to ensure biodiversity protection when the nature of the project encouraged local population growth. Unfortunately, some well-meaning economic development projects do just that.

Consider the following scenario. In the lowlands of a tropical country, a small farming and logging community receives foreign assistance targeted to meet two objectives: help farmers move away from dependence on chemicals in their farming practices, and improve the livelihood of loggers by building a small mill so they will receive more value for the trees they cut. These are worthy objectives, but unless the details are carefully thought through, success could backfire: short-term economic improvement could result in increased local population growth—either through higher reproductive rates or immigration from surrounding areas—that would undermine both long-term economic development and biodiversity protection.

In general, improving local economies can have adverse demographic consequences in two ways. Most obviously, migrants will be attracted from poorer areas (Figure 19.5). Less obviously, some types of development may offer incentives to have more children. Why would families opt to have more children? Very simply, the history of human demography in poor countries carries two powerful messages. First, parents have children as a form of insurance, because children are expected to provide for the needs of their parents

Figure 19.5 Positive changes in local economies can have critical demographic consequences. The illusion of economic success in cities can attract rural poor in search of a better life, but may instead result in suburban slums, such as this shantytown on the edge of Rio de Janeiro, Brazil. (Photograph by UPI/Bettmann.)

when aged. Second, parents tend to have children as long as each additional child is a positive economic asset to the family by increasing the family's labor pool (Figure 19.6).

This economic appraisal should not imply that parents in developing countries do not also love their children and make decisions for reasons other than economics. Whether parents limit the number of their children also will depend on their access to birth control materials and knowledge. Still, family economics is a powerful incentive that influences family size. For example, in rural Pakistan, each male child makes a positive economic contribution to the family. By the time a male child is 6 he is self-supporting, by age 12 he is a positive contributor to the family's economy, and by 22 he has already "paid back" the entire cost of his rearing and the cost of a sister of equal age (Murdoch 1980). Under these economic conditions, why would a family wish to limit its number of children?

Conservation biologists should look for socially acceptable disincentives to population growth as an integral part of the planning of any development process. In general, these brakes on population growth will involve gender equity (the full involvement of women in economic and social development), improved education and training of the participants, and improved livelihoods that do not require converting the family into a labor pool.

Clearly, population growth must be slowed, stopped, and eventually reversed. How quickly these changes can or should be made is the subject of considerable policy debate. If changes are forced through draconian population control programs, the result is more likely to be a political revolution than a demographic one, as Indian politicians discovered when citizens overwhelmingly rejected the austere population programs of Indira Gandhi and voted out the ruling party. Furthermore, it is not just increased numbers of people that are of concern, but their patterns of consumption as well. In these terms, the addition of one more North American has a far greater negative impact on the earth's resources than the birth of a child in rural India, Sudan, or any other developing country. As conservation biologists, we must look at the human demographic consequences of economic development projects; as responsible citizens, we must also take a global perspective of all develop-

Figure 19.6 These Honduran children contribute to the family economy by gathering fuelwood, weeding cotton fields, and tending the family's livestock and gardens. (Photograph by C. R. Carroll.)

ment. The problems of human population growth are further developed in Essay 19E by Paul Ehrlich.

ESSAY 19E

The Bottom Line

Human Population Control

Paul R. Ehrlich, Stanford University

As you learned in earlier chapters, humanity needs biodiversity as a source of foods, medicines, industrial products, and aesthetic pleasures. Even more important, microorganisms, plants, and animals are working parts of natural ecosystems that supply civilization with an array of critical services without which our economies would collapse. It is ironic, then, that human beings, in order to support themselves over the short term, are destroying natural ecosystems and the biodiversity they contain. We are paving ecosystems over, plowing them under, overgrazing, logging, flooding, draining, and poisoning them, and subjecting them to increased levels of ultraviolet-B radiation. In various ways we are changing their composition, structure, and extent so as to make them less hospitable to other organisms. In addition, anthropogenic modification of the atmospheric balance of gases is now raising the distinct possibility that climates will change at rates far in excess of the abilities of natural systems to adjust without massive extinctions of populations and species.

The large contribution to this destruction made by human population growth is easily demonstrated using the equation $I = P \times A \times T$. Unfortunately, there is no completely satisfactory statistic gathered by governments on per capita impact ($A \times T$). The best surrogate available as an index of each individual's destructive impact on ecosystems is per capita energy use, and therefore a society's impacts are best measured by its total energy use. Although it is an imperfect measure (among other things it tends to underestimate somewhat the impacts of the poorest societies), energy use so clearly is heavily involved in most environmentally damaging activities that employing it as a surrogate for them makes good sense.

Since 1850, worldwide energy use (and thus, roughly, I) has increased some 20-fold. In the same period, the human population (P) has increased about 5-fold, and per capita energy use ($A \times T$) about 4-fold. So population growth, by this measure, accounts for some 5/9 (about 55%) of the growth in environmental impact over the last 140 years.

Similar considerations show that, because of their very high per capita impacts, the rich nations account for roughly 70% of the environmental destruction now occurring. Nonetheless, continuing rapid population growth and substantial plans for development in poor nations indicate that their share of the blame may soon escalate. For example, if China and India should both choose to fuel future development with their abundant coal reserves, each could soon be adding more CO_2 to the atmosphere than the United States could remove by ceasing to use coal (now almost 25% of U.S. energy supply). That would happen, even under highly optimistic assumptions about success in controlling their population growth, before either China or India had achieved 15% of U.S. per capita energy consumption—just because of the gigantic size of those nations' populations.

Loss of biodiversity, however, may at first glance not seem as well indexed by energy statistics as is environmental deterioration overall. Because of the large-scale invasion of species-rich tropical forests by landless farmers, the greatest loss of *species* diversity is occurring in the poor nations. But energy-profligate rich nations bear indirect responsibility for their landlessness, and often contribute to other causes of tropical deforestation. Moreover, critical diversity of natural populations is being rapidly lost in the developed countries as habitats are altered and destroyed. Most important, rich nations are making the largest contribution to the massive threats to biodiversity posed by global warming and ozone depletion.

The growing human population also competes for resources very directly with populations of other animals. For instance, today the global human population of some 5.7 billion is collectively using, co-opting, or destroying about 40% of terrestrial net primary production—the basic food source of all land animals. That is not a cheering statistic when one realizes that 95 million people are added to the planet each year, 260,000 each day, 11,000 each hour.

One of the critical jobs for conservation biologists, then, is to press, wherever possible, for the halting and then reversing of population growth, reduction of wasteful consumption, and development and deployment of more benign technologies. In other words, conservation biologists must work to reduce all three components of I: P, A, and T. Properly inventorying biodiversity, designing and establishing appropriate reserves, enhancing non-reserve areas, and monitoring the results will fail to protect biodiversity in the long run unless the scale of the human enterprise is brought under control. To that end, conservation biologists should document as thoroughly as possible the ways in which P, A, and T promote the loss of biodiversity.

In overconsuming nations like the United States, it is critical to reduce birth rates to a level at which the population will soon stabilize and begin a slow decline. In rich nations that are still growing, probably all that is needed to get average family sizes well under two children is an intensive educational program explaining how large families hurt the chances for future generations to have decent lives. Italy and Spain are leading the way with average family sizes of 1.3 children.

In poor nations, the problems are more difficult to address, but a great deal is known about ways of reducing family sizes. One of the keys is education, human rights, equal opportunities, and adequate health care for women and their children. So conservation biologists would do well to support the liberation of women, something that would be socially desirable even if it did not produce a salutary reduction in family size.

Ways of reducing per capita consumption and ameliorating the effects of technologies are clear in principle but often rather difficult to achieve in practice. Many politicians and economists are under the impression that a continual increase in consumption is necessary to keep economic systems healthy. Fortunately, there is a new school of ecological economists who understand that goal to be physically impossible, and who are examining ways of designing economic systems not dependent on perpetual growth. Conservation biologists can work with these economists on such things as assigning monetary values to ecosystem services so that the importance of biodiversity can be better integrated into political decision making.

Ecological economists are also searching for ways to "get the prices right" so that, for example, the social and environmental costs of using fossil fuels (especially in internal combustion engines) are "internalized" in the price of the fuels. If that happened, relatively biodiversity-friendly technologies such as solar power would become economically attractive.

Dramatically reducing the *A* and *T* factors of the $I = PAT$ equation can be done in a decade or so. Humanely halting population growth and eventually reducing population size by lowering birth rates below death rates will take many decades. Considering the intense competition that already exists for space and energy between human populations and most other organisms, efforts to preserve biodiversity and natural ecosystems are doomed to fail in the end unless the growth and impact of the human population are brought under control.

The Tragedy of the Commons

Many, perhaps most, environmentally destructive practices come from misuse of common resource pools for private gain, what Garrett Hardin (1968) called "the tragedy of the commons." A tragedy of the commons can occur whenever a common, publicly "owned" resource (such as land, oceans, or clean air) is used for private gain without tight internal or external controls on that use, controls that are designed to ensure long-term sustainability. Often the resource is overused and may be destroyed. This pattern has also been termed "commonized costs, privatized profits" by Hardin (1993). That is, costs are shared publicly among many (commonized), while profits are realized by a few (privatized).

The classic example of the tragedy of the commons involves a publicly owned grazing land (a "commons") used by, say, 10 different herdsmen to graze their sheep. Suppose the land can support 100 sheep in a sustainable manner, but will be degraded over the long term if significantly more than 100 sheep graze. Also, more sheep mean less grass for each individual sheep, and thus a lower growth rate for all. If the system is uncontrolled, herdsman A may decide that he would like to graze 15 rather than 10 sheep. The costs associated with this action (commons degradation, and slightly less grass for each sheep because of those 5 extra grazers) are incurred by all 10 herdsmen (including A), but the profits from the extra sheep go only to herdsman A. Thus, it benefits A, at least in the short term, to "cheat" and graze extra sheep. Herdsman B then realizes this and decides to add 10 more of his sheep to the commons, thus also realizing a larger personal profit while spreading the costs among all 10 herdsmen. Herdsmen C, D, and E wake up to this, and—well, you get the picture. The land is terribly overgrazed, and eventually the grazing ecosystem collapses, but short-term profits increase for those who overexploit the system.

What are some tragedies of the commons occurring today? They are too numerous to enumerate, and occur virtually anywhere a publicly owned, unregulated resource exists. National forests, ocean fisheries, and grazing on rangelands are frequently cited as examples. Timber companies in the United States—often subsidized with taxpayer dollars through road building by the U.S. Forest Service and encouraged by public policies—clear-cut national forests, which are owned by all citizens, at high profits to the companies. The costs—such as lost opportunities to visit wilderness areas, lost ecosystem services, siltation of streams and loss of salmon fisheries, and subsidies paid through taxation—are commonized, or spread across all citizens, but collectively are high: the owners lose millions of hectares of primary forest and wilderness areas that will not return for several generations, if at all, and pay taxes to do it. The immediate (and privatized) profits to the timber companies are huge, but short-lived, because these forests are being rapidly depleted. The same pattern occurs with ocean fisheries ("owned" by everyone but exploited for profit by a few), which are easily overexploited, and on western U.S. public rangeland, where grazing fees are much lower than on privately owned lands, and overgrazing is consequently very common. Some of these ranges, incidentally, are used by large corporations, not struggling "cowboys" trying to make a living.

Regarding rangeland grazing, Hardin (1993) relates the following:

> A stockman in the western United States can raise his cattle either on private land or on government land managed by the Forest Service. In Idaho, as of 1990, the grazing fee on public land was only one-fifth what it was on private land. We can assume that a private land-owner sets his fee to cover the true cost of maintaining the carrying capacity of the land indefinitely. Obviously the government is not following this prudent rule. In direct costs, the Forest Service paid out $35 million for maintaining grazing lands, the costs being offset by only $11 million taken in as fees. Who paid the deficit? Taxpayers, of course. Costs were commonized while the profits (from the sale of beef) were privatized to the stockmen.

Other tragedies of the commons occur with respect to pollution and toxification of the environment. By releasing wastes into the air, rivers, or oceans (common resources "owned" by all citizens), the polluter profits by cheap or free disposal of wastes (Figure 19.7), while all citizens pay the costs, either of cleanup or of living in polluted areas. The same principle even applies to irresponsible automobile owners who do not fix "smoking" cars: The owners benefit (by saving repair bills) while spreading costs (more pollutants, possible illness) among the general population. As long as the costs of polluting are lower than the costs of responsible behavior toward the commons, heavy pollution will continue.

One solution is to eliminate the practice of free exploitation of publicly owned resources for private gain, and have all public costs paid by those who privately benefit. Not only does this seem eminently fair, but history bears out the recommendation. Hardin (1968) states that "the commons, if justifiable at all, is justifiable only under conditions of low-population density. As the human population has increased, the commons has had to be abandoned in

Figure 19.7 Air pollution, as seen in this view of Denver, Colorado, is an example of the tragedy of the commons. Clean air, a common resource, is destroyed by a few for profit, while many pay the health and economic costs. (Photograph by J. Robert Stottlemyer/Biological Photo Service.)

one aspect after another." Commons have become increasingly limited and protected throughout human history: we restricted food gathering by enclosing farms, and have restricted hunting and fishing to certain areas at certain times, within certain numerical limits. Restrictions on waste materials have increased throughout human history, resulting in more and stronger laws controlling pollution and treatment of wastes. However, some commons, such as rangeland and forests, have remained unregulated or poorly regulated, and that is of major concern to conservationists.

The full costs of exploitation must be transferred from the commons "owners" to the commons users. One way to accomplish this is to heavily tax users and fine abusers of common resources. Higher and unsubsidized grazing fees on rangelands, heavy taxes on and no subsidies for timber companies using publicly owned land, and severe fines for intentional or even accidental pollution are examples of necessary policy changes needed to reduce tragedies of commons use. Of course, such actions face stiff opposition from the users, who are used to receiving subsidies for their activities. In 1993, the Clinton/Gore administration attempted to raise grazing fees to more accurately represent the true public costs of grazing cattle on western rangeland in the United States; however, this move was vehemently resisted by powerful ranchers and their political representatives, and defeated. Likewise, restrictions on the cutting of old-growth forests are met with outcries from those personally benefiting from exploiting a common resource essentially free of charge, claiming themselves to be the real "endangered species." And polluting industries have always fought regulation of and fines for their activities. However, the true costs of use of common resources must be paid by the users if those resources are not to be overexploited for privatized, short-term gain at the price of commonized, long-term costs. Bobbi Low explores commons problems in greater depth in Essay 19F.

ESSAY 19F
"Commons" Problems in Conservation Biology

Bobbi S. Low, University of Michigan

A number of important environmental problems such as acid rain, global warming, or the endangerment of various species have the properties of "commons." Perhaps if we can understand better how commons function, we can solve some of the "conservation commons" problems.

When rights or property are not privately owned, they may be "open access"—owned by no one and accessed by all—or "commons"—owned by everyone in a specific group, but protected from outsiders. Open access resources typically disappear quickly, as everyone takes what they can, degrading the resource. Commons are more complex, and consist of two major types. The "Stiglerian commons" is the situation described by Garret Hardin (1968): benefits are concentrated, but costs are dispersed, as per the old English grazing commons, described in the main text. Cheating is highly profitable in such systems. "Olsonian commons," on the other hand, have dispersed benefits, but concentrated costs. Think of the problem of siting hazardous wastes: we all benefit when they are safely stored, but the small community where the wastes actually sit bears a concentrated cost. Thus the NIMBY ("Not In My Back Yard") response reflects a commons dilemma. Similarly, recent conflicts over Spotted Owl habitat management reflected a value held by the larger group (most of whom have never seen a Spotted Owl, but give value to knowing it exists), which imposed a perceived cost (loss of jobs in logging) on a local group.

Natural resources are frequently managed as commons. This has been true for a long time, and the problems of "collective action" (in which group members must agree on how to manage the resource) and cheating have been with us since humans first began to live in traditional hunter-gatherer societies (e.g., Hawkes 1993). Because cheating can be proftable in commons situations, there are a variety of proposed responses. One is to have local control of the resource; this has proven useful in many small-scale commons such as fisheries in developing countries (many successful examples in Ostrom 1990). Local control is clearly not a panacea, especially when profitable markets exist; local people may simply choose to destroy the resource for profit. Spotted Owl habitat would no longer exist had "local control" been the solution. Another option is for the larger group to make rules—government regulations. Oye and Maxwell (1995) note that in some modern Stiglerian commons, regulation can help narrow individual self-interest and broaden the good of the group (the Montreal Protocol on ozone-depleting gasses, for example). But regulations are expensive and not always maximally effective.

Private ownership is sometimes prescribed as a solution to foster long-term conservative strategies in the face of commons problems—but here, too, the strategy works only under specific conditions. It probably leads to good management when property is family-owned and not likely to be sold off, but may not lead to conservation management if an owner can make great profits, sell off, and leave—"get mine and get out." For example, oceanic whaling is a common pool resource: several nations hunt whales, and any nation that cheats, taking more than the agreed-upon catch, makes a larger profit, while the declining whale population hurts all the whalers. Would privatization solve the dilemma? Probably not, for as Colin Clark (1985) noted, money grows faster than whales. Thus, an economically rational whaler who owned all the world's whales would kill off as many as possible as quickly as possible, and bank the money!

So it makes sense to ask what makes successful commons work. A number of political, ecological, and social traits characterize successful common-pool regimes, ones that sustain their resources and last a long time. Socially, it seems to be true that most successful commons comprise small, tightly-knit and often kinship-based groups with highly stable membership. Ecologically, successful groups are typically dependent for subsistence on the continuance of the resource, and relatively isolated from high-stakes international markets. These conditions conspire to make cheating unlikely to be very profitable in terms of resources, and likely to be socially costly. "Get mine and get out" does not work well in such conditions.

Ostrom (1990) noted that successful commons are characterized by certain organizational conditions. They have clearly defined boundaries (and are thus able to keep outsiders from turning the situation into an open access free-for-all). They have collective-choice arrangements, so that the members all have some voice in decisions. Very importantly, they can monitor and catch individuals who cheat. They have graduated punishments, rather than Draconian sanctions for first offences. And they have conflict-resolution mechanisms. If the successful commons is embedded in a larger governmental structure, as most are today, the larger government recognizes the right of the commons to exist and make decisions.

Monitoring is crucial to a commons' success: if outsiders and within-group cheaters cannot be detected, it makes no sense for the commons members to exercise restraint, for any restraint simply becomes a cheater's profit. In many fisheries and wildlife examples (i.e., whales, ivory, and exotic fur trade), it is difficult to catch cheaters in the act of taking the resource. There is some suggestion that monitoring at the marketplace has potential, but wildlife poachers and collectors who seek exotic animals can easily avoid the open market.

Physical characteristics—the ecology of resource garnering—matter too. If the resources are widely dispersed, as are many open-sea fishes and whales, monitoring can be a serious problem, and it may be difficult to protect the resource from outsiders. When the resource fluctuates in an unpredictable way, agreements and monitoring can become difficult. Possible arrangements depend also on whether the resource is stationary in one group's territory (lakes, forest products) or moving (migratory fish and birds), and whether the resource can be stored, or must be immediately used or traded.

Thus, it is no surprise that the examples of successful commons that Ostrom and others review tend to be small and relatively isolated (e.g., mountain villages in Switzerland, villages in Japan, irrigation communities in the Phillippines). One of the largest is an irrigation system in Spain, which comprises a number of levels of governance. A telling comparative example comes from Nyaneba Nkrumah's (1995) work in Ghana. She identified two villages, each using the nearby savannah forest transition zone as a commons in similar ways, taking the same forest products. Because the villages are only 2 km apart and have the same major plant communities, assuming them to be ecologically similar is reasonable. Household sizes and total village populations are similar; people walk the same distance for firewood—they are entirely comparable in every measured way but one. The village of Adenya is inhabited by families who have lived there for a very long time, and most of the land is considered "lineage" land; Korkormu is largely comprised of immigrants (even the village chief is an immigrant) and more of the land is held as "crown" land. As you might predict, Adenya meets more of Ostrom's criteria of sustainable commons, and retains more plant productivity and species diversity. Korkormu villagers are having a negative impact on the biodiversity and biomass in their part of the forest.

No wonder the International Whaling Commission faces problems: negotiators change; negotiators must deal not only with the demands of other negotiators but with a variety of (non-identical) interests at home; monitoring is very difficult; getting agreement on sanctions can be very hard; the payoffs for overharvesting are great, and the costs (if caught) relatively small. Thus, none of the successful examples suggest that the easy "multiply up" solutions will work on very large-scale commons problems like whaling. Many organizational issues can be solved at large scales: we can become more sophisticated at monitoring, for example, and while it is difficult, it is seldom impossible to get reasonable collective-choice arrangements. But the less-studied aspects of the most successful commons may be crucial: at some level, social and monetary currencies seem to be traded off. That is, we are far less likely to cheat our family and old friends than to cheat strangers or remote acquaintances. In small scale commons, not only are the other actors family and friends, but the economic stakes are low; most are isolated, and there are few opportunities to turn cheating into high profit. In contrast, cheating by taking more whales results in high profits for the cheater, and hurts others not close to the cheater.

Communication and repeated interactions are critical to understanding how to solve larger-scale commons problems, and perhaps it is here that some hope lies. Ostrom et al. (1994), in exploring the dilemmas of cooperation versus defection in group decisions, structured a series of experiments in which they manipulated the payoffs for defecting, how much people were allowed to talk about the decisions, and how much they could discuss penalties for cheaters. "High-endowment" games, in which it paid handsomely to defect, had more defection. But even in high-endowment games, communication mattered: the more people could communicate, and the more they could sanction cheaters, the more they cooperated, and the better their payoff. Thus, while there are no easy answers to solving large-scale ecological "commons" problems, there are some clues, and some useful strategies to pursue.

Five Major Actions Needed to Conserve Biodiversity

The problems and challenges facing humanity with respect to conserving biological diversity can seem overwhelming, and consequently their solutions can appear diffuse and ineffective. However, we believe that concentration on five areas of effort could result in major advances toward conserving biodiversity and developing a sustainable human society, compatible with the natural world, at a reasonable standard of living. We identify the following five actions as most critical and most likely to have the greatest impact in the short term, and especially the long term. There are certainly other areas of endeavor that would also help in reversing the destructive trends evident today, but these five seem most pervasive and most likely to result in tangible progress.

1. First stabilize, then reverse human population growth. Our first and overriding major action must be a fundamental change in patterns of human population growth and impact if we are to avoid major and disastrous losses of biodiversity and increasing levels of human misery. Regardless of advances in any other areas, including scientific information or policy development, the human population juggernaut must be slowed and stopped. If not, it would appear that growth of this one species will continue to destroy, at an accelerating rate, natural habitats and ecosystem functions. We believe that, eventually, most conservation advances will be lost if the human population grows to the currently predicted levels of 12 to 15 billion by the end of the 21st century.

2. Protect tropical forests and other major centers of biodiversity. We know that the bulk of biological diversity occurs in tropical forests and a few other hot spots around the globe (see Chapter 5). Many of these are relatively small areas whose protection would conserve levels of biodiversity far out of proportion to their size. Even large regions such as the Amazon Basin represent only a small percentage of the total land area of the earth. Immediate protection of these areas and their biological treasures is necessary to save as many pieces as possible. This would not only keep millions of species in existence, but also would help to retain the ecosystem functions of these regions, as well as their role in controlling global climate patterns.

3. Develop a more global perspective of earth's resources, while solving problems locally wherever possible. Most humans have a tendency to think locally and in immediate time frames; that is, they discount things that are far away in time or space (Chapter 15). This is understandable; immediate needs such as food, shelter, and comfort dominate our senses, and they must be satisfied before we can contemplate larger temporal and spatial scales. However, we also have the ability as a species to think abstractly and understand patterns and trends over space and through time. We can understand and appreciate that global trends in resource use, natural habitat destruction, species loss, and so forth are ultimately detrimental to humanity and transcend political boundaries. Unfortunately for our long-term well-being, we often act as though political boundaries will protect us from the various forms of destruction now occurring, even though some problems, such as global warming, air and water pollution, and ozone depletion by definition are global.

The NIMBY ("Not In My Back Yard") phenomenon is a good example of this way of thinking; this is a common behavior wherein we tolerate some forms of destruction as long as they are far removed in time or space ("Put it somewhere, but not in *my* backyard"). But we need to overcome such time and space biases, look beyond local problems, and understand that destruction elsewhere or later may be just as bad as destruction here and now.

Globalization of problems, that is, accepting that on a finite planet, any problem, no matter where it occurs, should be of concern to all, is a key to reversing trends in environmental destruction. However, this does not mean that all problems should be *solved* globally. Hardin (1993) argues forcefully that any environmental or social problem that *can* be solved locally *should* be addressed that way, and not be approached in a global manner. Solutions to those problems that are truly global, of course, should be developed globally. He uses the analogy of potholes in roads. There are problems with potholes all over the world, but this does not argue for creation of a "Global Pothole Authority" to develop solutions. The solutions need to emerge locally, within the constraints and opportunities peculiar to each nation and each location. Likewise, solutions to many conservation problems, although they may be common through many parts of the world, should first be solved through local means whenever possible, with the participation of local people who best understand the problem and the potential solutions. But concern for all environmental problems must transcend political boundaries and become part of the operating consciousness of all humans. "Think globally, act locally" is more than just a catchy slogan for bumper stickers.

4. Develop ecological (steady-state) economics to replace growth economics. We cannot envision a bright future for humanity and the natural world if we retain an economy that requires continual and perpetual growth in order to sustain itself. Growth is a fundamental assumption of virtually all current political and economic systems, but expansion in size *in perpetuity* on a finite planet is logically unrealistic. As discussed in Chapter 15, continued expansion in size must eventually be abandoned and replaced by an equilibrium economy that functions in a steady-state environment (Daly 1991). Regardless of the rate, *any* positive economic expansion and increase in use of nonrenewable resources must eventually reach limits and exhaust supplies. High expansion rates incur limits sooner, slow rates later, but *limits will be reached*. This logical fact seems lost on most traditional economists, politicians, and laypeople, but that must change. The frenzied economic exploitation of our planet, what Ehrlich and Ehrlich (1990) call "The One-Time Bonanza," is destined to end eventually.

5. Modify human value systems to reflect ecological reality. Implicit in and necessary for all four of the above suggestions is a major change in human value systems (one perspective is elaborated by Eric Katz in Essay 19G). If fundamental changes do not take place in the way humans perceive their world and value natural systems, then we see little reason for optimism that biodiversity conservation will be effective or that humanity can live sustainably. Changes in value systems could be manifest in several ways.

ESSAY 19G

A New Vision

Humans and the Value of Nature

Eric Katz, New Jersey Institute of Technology

Many suggested answers to our environmental problems fall into two categories: innovations in science and technology, or changes in governmental, industrial, and social policies to deal with pollution and other environmental destruction. For philosophers, both kinds of choices—scientific development and implementation of policy—miss the real point. Neither an appeal to science nor adjustments in social policy go deep enough into the underlying cause of the environmental crisis: *an inappropriate set of values concerning the human relationship with the natural world.* Traditional values have failed. The solution to the environmental crisis is development of a new set of values, a new vision of the human relationship with nature. What is required is a radical reinterpretation of the human place in the natural world.

In analyzing the human relationship with the natural environment, the traditional perspective, at least in Western civilization, is that of an anthropocentric individualism. The entire natural world is evaluated in human terms. What is good for human beings, what human beings deserve—these are the primary considerations in the development of human knowledge and human society. Science is modeled after the vision of Francis Bacon to dominate and subdue the secrets of the natural world, to bend them to our will to make life more comfortable. And within the realm of social policy, the vision of the good society is based on the political philosophy of John Locke. Locke argued that man must cultivate the wild, untamed common land of the earth to claim it as private property and thus to improve it for the increase of human happiness and justice. The traditional value system results in an environmental policy that seeks to maximize human benefit. Nature is to be used wisely—conserved, preserved, and restored—so that humanity can reap the highest amount of good.

Is there anything wrong with the human race attempting to maximize its gain and increase its happiness? Is there a problem with the value system of anthropocentrism? Yes: it is possible to discern three fundamental mistakes in the traditional Western worldview.

The first mistake is the idea of anthropocentrism itself. The traditional value system considers human good to be the goal of all human activity. This perspective is clearly a remnant of pre-Copernican thought; it creates a value system based on an incorrect scientific notion of the geocentric universe. Since Copernicus, we know that the earth is not the center of the physical universe, but we have yet to understand the corollary moral point: humans are not the center of the moral universe. Our value system and worldview should not reflect a belief in our own centrality. Environmental policies need not focus on the exclusive and primary importance of humanity. The natural world exists independently from human beings, though not from our influence and power.

The second mistake is the notion of individualism, the belief that the world is a vast arena of interacting individuals. The 17th-century empiricists conceived of the world on the model of a billiard table, with billiard balls constantly moving, colliding, and interacting. Our notions of cause and effect relationships are derived from this picture of the collision of hard and discrete individual entities. Individualism is also the hallmark of the major Western political and ethical systems. We hold the rights of individual human beings to be fundamental, regardless of the form of government or the economic system.

But the belief in discrete individuals is actually a claim not supported by contemporary science. The world is actually a dynamic flow of process and change; it is not constituted by static individuals. The lessons of ecological science and conservation biology apply this insight to the interactions of humans and the natural world. The individual entity is not the central unit of concern; rather, the focus is on populations, habitats, and ecosystems. Our view of the world is holistic, not individualistic.

The third and final mistake is the most subtle, the most difficult to discern in our basic worldview: it is the idea of domination. Throughout our policies and activities, humans attempt to control the world. Our political and social systems attempt to control other humans; our science and technology attempt to dominate the natural world. If the purpose of science is to "predict and control" the natural world, then we try to make ourselves the masters of the universe. For pragmatic reasons alone, we ought to abandon this perspective, since we have done such a poor job. One way to view the contemporary environmental crisis is that it is the reaction to our inadequate attempts to predict and control—one meaning of David Ehrenfeld's (1981) "arrogance of humanism." But we ought to reject the idea of control for moral reasons as well—it is more ethical to permit all entities the freedom to flourish in their natural states. All beings are not tools for the satisfaction of human desires. Once we reject anthropocentrism, we reject domination also, and recognize that it is not the purpose of the natural world to be the victim of the human drive for power and domination.

An analysis of these three mistakes in the traditional Western value system suggests a new vision, a new perspective, on the human relationship with the natural world. By rejecting anthropocentrism, individualism, and domination, we can create a worldview that is nonanthropocentric, holistic, and liberating. This vision will be infused with a concern for an autonomous nonhuman natural world, a world that is unfolding and developing toward its own self-realization. The interrelated systems of the natural world will have meaning and value free of the domination and interests of humanity.

This new vision has enormous implications for practical environmental policy. It amounts to an almost magical change in the evaluation of nature's role in human life. At the very least, the natural world will be seen as an equal partner in the development of the good life. This new vision requires that we respect the processes and systems of nature, that we extend to them our basic understanding of moral obligations, that we develop a direct moral concern for the nonhuman world. In practical terms, it will require a much greater emphasis on the preservation of whole ecological systems and habitats.

Philosophy not only teaches us that our scientific descriptions of the world and our policies of action are shaped by our values; it also demonstrates that the world itself is determined by our concepts, our vision, our perspective on the fundamental nature of reality. Do we have the courage to admit the errors of the traditional worldview, to adopt a new vision, a new meaning of value, for the natural world? I believe that humanity must discover this courage. We have a moral obligation to recognize the value of a natural world freed of human domination.

First, the human species needs to accept limits—limits to growth, limits to personal wealth at public cost, and limits to planetary dominance. We as a species currently use some 40% of the primary production on the planet (Vitousek et al. 1986), with the figure rising as our numbers and technological prowess increase. Any system of logic indicates that there are natural limits to how much production we can co-opt, and how much energy we can produce,

Figure 19.8 Damage from the Mississippi River flood of 1993 is a consequence of our "conquer nature" mentality. Many communities that were developed in natural and expansive floodplains were supposed to be protected by huge levees and other engineering marvels designed to "control" the river's behavior. In this case they did not work, and nature won. The more important question now is whether we will have learned anything from this experience. (Photograph by Reuters/Bettmann.)

even apart from conservation concerns. Yet the prevailing approach to limits has been arrogance, an attitude that prevails through much of at least Western thought. This "techno-arrogance" (Meffe 1992), expressed as a frontier, "conquer nature" mentality, assumes that any challenges nature presents us can and should be overcome through our collective engineering abilities.

A rather astounding and illustrative example of this attitude concerns the 1991 and subsequent eruptions of Mt. Unzen in Japan. Rather than moving people and living within the natural constraints of volcanic activity, the Japanese government actually planned to reengineer the effects of volcanic eruptions with a series of dams, earth-retaining structures, and deep channels (Amato 1993). The same approach has guided the largely failed attempts in the United States to control river flows through dams and levees (McPhee 1989); that failure was evident in the Mississippi River floods of 1993 (Figure 19.8), which resulted in many billions of dollars of damage, to be paid by taxpayers (commonized costs) to individuals who have benefited from living in floodplains (privatized profits).

Second, we need to replace "bottom line," short-term thinking with a long-term perspective that includes concern for intergenerational equity. By continually eroding natural capital in the interests of current financial gain and increased standards of living, we may be condemning future generations to lifestyles constrained by extremely limited resources and highly degraded ecosystems.

Third, we need to replace narrow anthropocentrism with a broader world perspective. The present concept of the centrality and superiority of the human species automatically places the 5 to 100 million other species, plus their collective ecosystems, in a tenuous position at best. Whenever there is a question of human gain versus conservation of nature, the former is likely to prevail. Ironically, this ultimately runs counter to human benefit, because loss of these systems will be devastating to the rapidly increasing human population. A more inclusive perspective is, after all, in the best, and most selfish, interests of humanity.

Finally, we need to adopt and incorporate "ecological design principles" into all facets of human existence. As David Orr discussed in Essay 16A, we are at the dawn of a new way of thinking; we will by necessity have to replace our "control of nature" mentality with a "cooperate with nature" way of doing business. This must be done by replacing our industrial civilization—a "conquer nature" mentality—with an ecological design civilization—a "learn from and cooperate with nature" mentality. This transition is discussed in depth by Berry (1988).

Good ecological design, and the other changes in human value systems, must ultimately become part of the human psyche, and the accepted and common way of conducting the business of human existence on the planet (Wann 1996). A "business as usual" approach that continues the prevailing outlooks and methods of the past several centuries, while making modest alterations to placate environmentalists, is unlikely to last long in a world where natural resources are rapidly disappearing while the human population is rapidly expanding. There seems little choice here.

Good conservation for both humanity and nature comes down to nothing less than a revolution in human thought, on a par with the social changes wrought by the Industrial Revolution or struggles for racial equality. Such revolutions are not easy, quick, or painless, but they are necessary and inevitable. Human ethics and value systems are certain to evolve and become more sophisticated over time. Our values must evolve in the direction of sustainability and cooperation with, rather than conquest and destruction of, nature, if humankind is to continue to experience the rich rewards of living on a biologically complex and unique planet. Over 3 billion years of the history of life, and the future of conscious human thought and achievement, are at stake.

Summary

Transduction of the principles of conservation biology into actions that reflect our cumulative knowledge may be the greatest challenge in the history of humanity. Major changes are needed in the way that the human species interacts with the planet, which call for changes in human behavior as large as any in our history.

Conservation biology faces a number of challenges. It must operate within uncertainties of all kinds, including uncertain economic environments. To succeed, conservation biologists must convince the public that our science has value to all; we must improve the way that conservation biology is managed and developed; we must improve funding opportunities for conservation work; and we must influence policy development in positive ways. Conservation biologists also must work within certain long-term global environmental changes of uncertain magnitude and direction. The best we can do is plan for likely contingencies based on current knowledge.

The human "demographic imperative" is so overriding that all other success or failure may ultimately derive from it. Simply put, human population growth and increasing overall impact on the planet must be slowed, stopped, and reversed. Analysis of human impact must include not just population numbers, but effects from levels of affluence and consequences of technological development; total impact is thus a function of population size, affluence, and technology. Several countries have reversed disastrous population growth trends in little more than a decade, demonstrating that it can be done.

One of the major forms of destructive practice that has led to so much environmental degradation is the so-called "tragedy of the commons." Tragedies of the commons frequently occur when a commonly "owned" resource such as air, water, or wilderness is exploited for private gain at little to no expense to theuser, and is unregulated or poorly regulated. In these situations, the resources are typically overexploited to the benefit of a few, but the costs are spread among many. A solution is to have the costs of using these resources internalized to the users, rather than spread among public "owners."

We believe that five major actions on the part of humanity are needed to conserve biodiversity in the long term. First, the human population growth problem must be dealt with squarely and quickly. Second, tropical forests and other hot spots of biological diversity must be protected from further destruction. Third, we must develop a more global perspective on the earth's resources, but solve problems locally wherever possible. Fourth, we must replace growth-oriented economics with ecological, or steady-state, economics, which recognizes limits to natural resources and sinks. Finally, human value systems must change to reflect ecological realities. Humans need to accept limits, replace short-term, myopic thinking with long-term perspectives that include intergenerational equity, replace narrow anthropocentrism with a broader view, and incorporate ecological design principles as we move from an industrial age to an ecological age. Updated and appropriate value systems are, when all is said and done, the best hope for conservation of biological diversity.

Questions for Discussion

1. Consider these two positions: (A) The expected environmental effects of global change are so great that we must take extreme measures now to protect biodiversity in the future. (B) The uncertainty surrounding global climate change is so great that any measures we take now should be minimally intrusive and reversible. Compare these positions. Do you favor either one? Why?
2. Examine a series of development projects of the World Bank that have a component of biodiversity protection, with the following two questions in mind: What are the likely demographic consequences of each project? What set of demographic questions should be included as part of the general process of evaluating projects for support?
3. Professor Eugene P. Odum has commented that "poverty is no friend of the environment." In what ways does economic impoverishment lead to environmental degradation? Conversely, can economic wealth contribute to the same?
4. Select some important concept or issue in conservation biology that you believe the average citizen should understand. Develop a plan for introducing this concept or issue into elementary and secondary schools through curricular enhancement.
5. How would educating the general public about this issue differ from your plan in Question 4?
6. How about actually implementing the plan from Question 4? If you do not do it, who will?
7. The political reality is that the U.S. presidency changes hands every four to eight years, and national priorities for biodiversity protection also change; changes are prevalent in other governments as well. Discuss some creative ways to address major problems in conservation that require long-term solutions when the political support for policy implementation is ephemeral. We develop treaties and trade agreements with other countries, and these treaties survive elections; can we develop an analogue—domestic treaties—to protect our natural heritage? Are there existing models to work from?
8. Discuss the future of conservation biology. Where do you think the field is heading? Where do you see the largest advances? Where do you think you could make the best contributions, given your own talents, interests, and experiences?

Suggestions for Further Reading

Berry, T. 1988. *The Dream of the Earth.* Sierra Club Books, San Francisco. A visionary perspective on where humanity has been and where it is going with respect to the planet and the universe. Berry argues that we are moving into the fifth age of humanity, an ecological age, and are now in a very difficult transition period from the industrial age. Somewhat heavy reading, but a great mind expander.

Ehrenfeld, D. 1993. *Beginning Again. People and Nature in the New Millennium.* Oxford University Press, New York. An insightful collection of essays by the founding editor of *Conservation Biology*. Ehrenfeld first takes bearings on where we are at the end of the 20th century, illustrates how we are off course, and suggests some true headings. His essay on "The Overmanaged Society" is, by itself, worth the price of the book and should be read by every thinking human.

Hardin, G. 1993. *Living within Limits: Ecology, Economics, and Population Taboos*. Oxford University Press, New York. An outstanding update of Hardin's thoughts on human population growth and the human condition. Hardin exposes a number of myths and fallacies about the population problem in a frank and firm manner. He faces head-on a number of controversial and challenging topics such as immigration policy and the tragedy of the commons.

Orr, D. W. 1992. *Ecological Literacy: Education and the Transition to a Postmodern World*. State University of New York Press, Albany. An absolutely outstanding series of essays that will shape your own vision of the future. Orr argues persuasively that the core of human education should be ecology and our relationship with the natural world. He also has very perceptive insights into sustainability and the need for a transformation to a postmodern existence. A "must read."

Orr, D. W. 1994. *Earth in Mind. On Education and the Human Prospect*. Island Press, Washington, D.C. Another outstanding collection of essays from one of the most progressive and insightful thinkers of our time. Orr further explores the absolute necessity of a different focus in education, one that emphasizes life in a world with ecological limitations rather than narrow, disciplinary training geared primarily for exploitation. Don't miss it!

Tobin, R. 1990. *The Expendable Future*. Duke University Press, Durham, NC. An excellent critical analysis of United States policies on biodiversity protection and how priorities are developed to support (or thwart) implementation of those policies.

Wann, D. 1996. *Deep Design: Pathways to a Livable Future*. Island Press, Washington, D.C. Much of the design of human endeavors is flawed because it does not fully take into account inputs and outputs. Wann argues that design, whether of automobiles, communities, molecules, buildings, or anything else, should be sensitive to living systems and meet key criteria of renewability, recyclability, and nontoxicity. These "deep designs" are often based on nature and optimize goals while minimizing impact and effort. Good, stimulating reading

Glossary

LISTED AFTER EACH ENTRY IS THE CHAPTER NUMBER IN WHICH THE TERM IS HIGHLIGHTED AND DISCUSSED.

allele One of a pair of genes at a particular genetic locus. Chapters 4 and 6.

allopatric Describes two or more populations or species that occur in geographically separate areas. *See also* **sympatric**. Chapter 3.

allozyme One of several possible forms of an enzyme that is the product of a particular allele at a given gene locus. Chapter 6.

α-richness The number of species occurring within a given habitat. Chapter 4.

anthropocentrism Any human-oriented perspective of the environment, but usually used to emphasize a distinction between humans and nonhumans. For example, assessing a tropical forest in terms of its potential timber value would be an exclusively anthropocentric perspective. Chapters 1, 2.

area/perimeter ratio The ratio of internal area to edge habitat of a region. The area/perimeter ratio is an indication of the amount of interior habitat with respect to edge habitat, and may indicate potential success of a reserve in protecting interior species. Chapter 10.

background extinction rate Historical rates of extinction due to environmental causes not influenced by human activities, such as the rate of species going extinct because of long-term climate change. Chapter 1.

Bayesian statistics A branch of modern statistics that bases statistical inferences and decisions on a combination of information derived from observation or experiment and from prior knowledge or expert judgment. Contrast this approach with classical statistics, which regards only the data from observations or experiments as useful for estimation and inference. Chapter 11.

β-richness The change or turnover of species from one habitat to another. Chapter 4.

biocentrism A perception of the world that values the existence and diversity of all biological species, as opposed to a human-centered perspective (anthropocentrism). Chapter 2.

biodiversity The variety of living organisms considered at all levels of organization, including the genetic, species, and higher taxonomic levels, and the variety of habitats and ecosystems, as well as the processes occuring therein. Chapter 1.

biological species concept (BSC) A species concept based on reproductive isolation, which defines a species as groups of actually or potentially interbreeding populations, which are reproductively isolated from other such groups. Chapter 3.

biome A large, regional ecological unit, usually defined by some dominant vegetative pattern, such as the coniferous forest biome. Chapter 4.

biophilia A term coined by E. O. Wilson to describe humans' seemingly innate, positive attitudes about, and love for, nature and natural diversity. Chapters 1 and 10.

Biosphere Reserve A concept of reserve design in which a large tract of natural area is set aside, containing an inviolate core area for ecosystem protection, a surrounding buffer zone in which nondestructive human activities are permitted, and a transition zone in which human activities of greater impact are permitted. Three goals of a biosphere reserve are conservation, training (education), and sustainable human development compatible with conservation. Chapter 4.

buffer zone An area in a reserve surrounding the central core zone, in which nondestructive human activities such as ecotourism, traditional (low-intensity) agriculture, or extraction of renewable natural products, are permitted. Chapter 17.

cladistics A system of classification based on historical (chronological) sequences of divergence from a common ancestor. Chapter 3.

cladogram A diagram of cladistic relationships. An estimate or hypothesis of true genealogical relationships among species or other groupings. Chapter 3.

coadapted gene complex A concept in which particular gene combinations, presumably acting in concert through a long association, function particularly well together. Chapter 6.

cohesion species concept A species concept based on intrinsic cohesion mechanisms, such as gene flow and natural selection, that results in species cohesion (contrast with species isolation in the biological species concept). Chapter 3.

commons Originally referred to lands in medieval Europe that were owned by townships rather than by private individuals. Now used to include any exploitable resource that is not privately owned. Sometimes applied to so-called "open resources" that are neither privately owned nor regulated by a country or agency. Chapters 1, 19.

conservation biology An integrative approach to the protection and management of biodiversity that uses appropriate principles and experiences from basic biological fields such as genetics and ecology; from natural resource management fields such as fisheries and wildlife; and from social sciences such as anthropology, sociology, philosophy, and economics. Chapter 1.

critical habitat According to U.S. Federal law, the ecosystems upon which endangered and threatened species depend. Chapter 3.

cryptic species Distinct species that show little to no outward morphological differences, and thus are difficult to distinguish. Also called "sibling species." Chapter 3.

deep ecology An environmental philosophy that believes in the inherent rights of nature and a human existence that does minimal damage to natural systems. Chapter 2.

demand The aggregate desire for economic goods and services. The quantity of a good or service that consumers are willing to purchase at different prices. Demand involves the relationship between quantity and price. Chapter 15.

deme A randomly interbreeding (panmictic) local population. Chapter 6.

demographic bottleneck A significant, usually temporary, reduction in genetically effective population size, either from a population "crash" or a colonization event by a few founders. Chapter 6.

demographic uncertainty Chance populational events, such as sex ratios or the act of finding a mate, that influence survival in small populations. Chapter 7.

density-dependent factors Life history or population parameters that are a function of population density. Chapter 7.

density-independent factors Life history or population parameters that are independent of population density. Chapter 7.

dominance The condition when an allele exerts its full phenotypic effect despite the presence of another allele of the same gene. Chapter 6.

distancing An economic term that refers to the process of specialization that alienates people from each other, from the means of production of essential goods and services, and from the environment. Chapter 15.

distribution An economic term referring to the pattern of ownership of resources. The way in which natural resources and other assets are initially assigned among different owners. Chapter 15.

ecological release Habitat expansion or density increase of a species when one or more competing species are not present. Chapter 4.

ecological species concept (ESC) A species concept based on adaptive zones used by organisms. Chapter 3.

ecosystem management An approach to maintaining or restoring the composition, structure, and function of natural and modified ecosystems for the goal of long-term sustainability. It is based on a collaboratively developed vision of desired future conditions that integrates ecological, socioeconomic, and institutional perspectives, applied within a geographic framework defined primarily by natural ecological boundaries. Chapter 11.

edge effect (1) The negative influence of a habitat edge on interior conditions of a habitat, or on species that use interior habitat. (2) The effect of adjoining habitat types on populations in the edge ecotone, often resulting in more species in the edge than in either habitat alone. Chapter 9.

efficient allocation An economic term that refers to the market's ability to match resources with material ends. The apportionment of resources to the production of different goods and services. Chapter 15.

electrophoresis A process by which gene products of an individual organism are separated by an electrical field in a gel medium and then stained so that they may be identified and classified. Used to infer genotypes in populations. Chapter 6.

endangered species According to U.S. Federal law, a species in imminent danger of extinction throughout all or a significant portion of its range. Chapter 3.

endemic Any localized process or pattern, but usually applied to a highly localized or restrictive geographic distribution of a species. Chapter 4.

environmental modification Modification of the phenotype as a result of environmental influences on the genotype. Chapter 6.

environmental uncertainty Unpredictable sources of density-independent mortality, such as an early snowstorm, that jeopardize the survival of a small population by pushing it below its minimum viable population size. Chapter 7.

equilibrium A state reached when a population's birth and immigration rates are equal to its mortality and emigration rates. Also applied to species changes in a community or to any other ecological process in which the rate of increase equals the rate of decrease, resulting in a steady state. Chapter 1.

Evolutionarily Significant Unit (ESU) A population that is reproductively isolated from other conspecific population units, and which represents an important component in the evolutionary legacy of the species. Chapter 6.

evolutionary species concept (ESC) A species concept based on historical ties, and phenotypic cohesions and discontinuities. Chapter 3.

Evolutionary-Ecological Land Ethic A philosophical approach to conservation derived from the evolutionary and ecological perspective, first advanced by Aldo Leopold. Nature is seen not as a collection of independent parts, to be used as needed, but as an integrated system of interdependent processes and components, in which the disruption of some components may greatly affect others. This ethic is the philosophical foundation for modern conservation biology. Chapter 1.

extensive margin Refers to low-quality agricultural lands in which increased inputs do not produce greater net economic returns per unit land area; rather, economic returns are increased by increasing land area. Chapter 15.

externality A cost, usually in terms of environmental degradation, that results from an economic transaction, but which is not included as a debit against economic returns. Chapter 15.

feedback Refers to a system whose output modifies input to the system. Prices play this role in market systems. Chapter 15.

fencerow scale The connection of habitat patches by narrow rows of habitat to create corridors that areusually effective only for small, edge-tolerant species. Chapter 10.

fitness The relative contribution of an individual's genotype to the next generation in the context of the population's gene pool. Relative reproductive success. Chapters 4 and 6.

founder effect The principle that the founders of a new population carry only a random fraction of the genetic diversity found in the larger, parent population. Chapter 6.

founder model A rapid speciation scenario in which a small, isolated population, such as a few colonists on an island, undergoes rapid divergence from its parent population. Also called quantum speciation. Chapter 3.

fragmentation The disruption of extensive habitats into isolated and small patches. Fragmentation has two negative components for biota: loss of total habitat area, and the creation of smaller, more isolated, remaining habitat patches. Chapter 9.

Fundamental Theorem of Natural Selection The basic theorem of population genetics, which states that the rate of evolutionary change in a population is proportional to the amount of genetic diversity (specifically, additive genetic variance) available in the population. Chapter 6.

Gaia hypothesis A model of planetary dynamics postulating a tight interrelationship between life processes and the conditions on earth that support life. Feedback mechanisms are proposed by which biological processes modify the physical and chemical conditions that are appropriate for the biological processes. In the extreme viewpoint, the Gaia hypothesis holds that the earth is a superorganism. Now usually refers to the belief that biotic processes are the major regulators of physical processes. Chapter 2.

γ-richness The number of species found within a large region, which typically includes several habitats. Chapter 4.

GAP analysis The use of various remote sensing data sets to build overlaid sets of maps of various parameters (e.g., vegetation, soils, protected areas, species distributions) to identify spatial gaps in species protection and management programs. Chapter 12.

gene flow The uni- or bidirectional exchange of genes between populations due to migration of individuals and subsequent successful reproduction in the new population. Chapter 6.

gene locus The site on a chromosome occupied by a specific gene. Chapter 6.

gene pool The sum total of genes in a sexually reproducing population or deme. Chapter 6.

genetic drift Random gene frequency changes in a small population due to chance alone. Chapters 3, 6.

genetically effective population size (N_e) The size of an idealized population that would have the same rate of increase in inbreeding, or decrease in genetic diversity through drift, as the population in question. The functional size of a population, in a genetic sense, based on numbers of actual breeding individuals and the distribution of offspring among families. N_e is typically smaller than the census size of the population. Chapter 6.

genotype The entire genetic constitution of an organism, or the genetic composition at a specific gene locus or set of loci. Chapter 6.

geographic information system (GIS) A computerized system of organizing and analyzing any spatial array of data and information. Chapter 7.

geographic variation Change in a species' trait over distance or among different distinct populations. Measurable character divergence among geographically distinct populations that are often, though not necessarily, the result of local selection. Chapter 3.

gradual allopatric speciation The process of species formation by which a population is split into two or more subpopulations by a geographic barrier, followed by evolutionary divergence until one or more of the populations become distinct species. Chapter 3.

Hardy-Weinberg equilibrium The stability of gene frequencies expected in a sexual, diploid population when a number of assumptions are met, including random mating, a large population, and no migration, mutation or selection. Chapter 6.

heterozygosity A measure of the genetic diversity in a population, as measured by the number of heterozygous loci across individuals. Chapters 4 and 6.

heterozygous The condition in which an individual has two different alleles at a given gene locus. Chapter 6.

hierarchical gene diversity analysis An approach to defining population genetic structure for a species in nature that defines components of total genetic diversity in a spatially hierarchical fashion. Chapter 6.

homozygous The condition in which an individual has two of the same alleles at a given gene locus. Chapter 6.

hot spot A geographic location characterized by unusually high species richness, often of endemic species. Chapter 4.

$I = PAT$ An equation describing the total impact of humans on natural systems as a function of population size (P), level of affluence (A), and technological sophistication employed (T). Chapter 18.

inbreeding The mating of individuals who are more closely related than by chance alone. Chapter 6.

inbreeding depression A reduction in fitness and vigor of individuals as a result of increased homozygosity through inbreeding in a normally outbreeding population. Chapter 6.

incipient species A population or group of populations in the process of speciating. Also called semispecies. Chapter 3.

indicator species A species used as a gauge for the condition of a particular habitat, community, or ecosystem. A characteristic, or surrogate species for a community or ecosystem. Chapter 11.

inherent value *See* **intrinsic value**. Chapter 2.

instrumental value The worth of an entity as judged by its utility or usefulness to humans. Chapter 2.

intensive margin Refers to high-quality agricultural lands in which increased inputs produce greater net economic returns per unit land area. Chapter 15.

intermediate disturbance hypothesis An hypothesis (with good empirical support) that posits that maximum species richness in many systems occurs at an intermediate level (of intensity or frequency, or both) of natural disturbance. Chapter 10.

intrinsic value The worth of an entity independent from external circumstances or its value to humans; value judged on inherent qualities of an entity rather than value to other entities. Chapter 2.

keystone mutualist species Keystone species that perform a mutualistic function, such as plant species that are broadly used as pollen sources. Chapter 5

keystone species A species whose impacts on its community or ecosystem are large, and much larger than would be expected from its abundance. Chapters 5, 8.

land-bridge island Areas that are presently island habitats, but were formerly connected to the mainland during periods of lower ocean levels. Land-bridge islands tend to lose species over time in a process called "relaxation." Chapter 9.

landscape mosaic scale The connection of major landscape features using broad habitats (including interior habitat) as corridors. Chapter 10.

line corridor A simple, narrow corridor consisting of all edge habitat, usually connecting small habitat patches. Chapter 10.

locus *See* **gene locus**. Chapter 6.

mass extinction The extinction of large numbers of taxa during a relatively brief geologic time frame, such as the extinction of dinosaurs at the end of the Cretaceous Period. Chapter 5.

maximum sustained yield (MSY) The largest harvest level of a renewable resource that can be sustained over a period of many generations. Harvest of a natural population at the population size representing the maximum rate of recruitment into the population, based on a logistic growth curve. Chapter 12.

metapopulation A network of semi-isolated populations with some level of regular or intermittent migration and gene flow among them, in which individual populations may go extinct but can then be recolonized from other populations. Chapters 6 and 7.

minimum dynamic area The smallest area necessary for a reserve to have a complete, natural disturbance regime in which discrete habitat patches may be colonized from other patches within the reserve. Chapter 10.

minimum viable population (MVP) The smallest isolated population that has a specified statistical chance of remaining extant for a specified period of time in the face of foreseeable demographic, genetic, and environmental stochasticities, plus natural catastrophes. Chapter 6.

mobile link species Mobile keystone species who influence the survival or reproductive success of other species through their movement over a geographic area; e.g., highly specific pollinators. Chapter 5.

monetizing The process of placing monetary value on typically non-monetary goods and processes such as biological material or ecological processes. The process of converting values to economic units. Chapter 2.

monomorphic Description of a population in which nearly all individuals have the same genotype at a given locus. Chapter 6.

monophyletic Derivation of two or more taxa from a single, common ancestor. Chapter 3.

multiple use concept Refers to the simultaneous and compatible use of public land and water resources by different interest groups. For example, U.S. public law requires that national forests be open to recreational use, timber extraction, mining or other concessions, and biodiversity protection. In reality, the activities of the various interest groups generally conflict, and are often incompatible with biodiversity protection. Chapter 1.

multiple use module (MUM) A land protection model consisting of a central, protected core area surrounded by buffer zones of increasing human use further from the core. Chapter 10.

mutation A spontaneous change in the genotype of an organism at the genetic, chromosomal, or genomic level. "Mutation" usually refers to alterations to new allelic forms, and represents new material for evolutionary change. Chapter 6.

mutualism An interspecific relationship in which both organisms benefit; frequently a relationship of complete dependence. Examples include flower pollination and parasite cleaning. Chapter 8.

natural catastrophe A major environmental cause of mortality, such as a volcanic eruption, that can affect the probability of survival for both large and small populations. Chapter 7.

natural selection A process by which differential reproductive success of individuals in a population results from differences in one or more hereditary characteristics. Natural selection is a function of genetically based variation in a trait, fitness differences (differential reproductive success) among individuals possessing different forms of that trait, and inheritance of that trait by offspring. Chapter 6.

nested subset A pattern of species biogeographic distribution in which larger habitats contain the same subset of species in smaller habitats, plus new species found only in the larger habitat. Common species are found in all habitat sizes, but some species are found only in progressively larger habitats. Chapter 9.

network A reserve system connecting multiple nodes and corridors into a landscape that allows material and energy flow among the various components. Chapter 10.

node An area with unusually high conservation value that may serve as one center of a regional conservation network. Chapter 10.

nominalism A school of thought that questions the existence of species as real and natural groupings. Considers "species" to be a human-made concept. Chapter 3.

nonequilibrium A condition in which the rate of increase does not equal the rate of decrease. In nonequilibrial population growth, environmental stochasticity disrupts the equilibrium. Chapter 1.

option value An economic term that refers to assigning a value to some resource whose consumption is deferred to the future. Chapter 15.

overdominance The condition in which a heterozygote at a given locus has higher fitness than either homozygote. Also called heterozygote superiority. Chapter 6.

panmictic Exhibiting random breeding among individuals of a population. Chapter 6.

paradigm An established pattern of thinking. Often applied to a dominant ecological or evolutionary viewpoint; e.g., during earlier decades, the dominant paradigm in ecology held that communities were shaped by equilibrial processes. Chapter 1.

patch dynamics A conceptual approach to ecosystem and habitat analysis that emphasizes dynamics of heterogeneity within a system. Diverse patches of habitat created by natural disturbance regimes are seen as critical to maintenance of diversity. Chapter 10.

phenetic Pertaining to phenotypic similarities; e.g., a classification system based on phenotypic traits. Based on numerical measurements of individuals and mathematical analyses of morphological discontinuities. Chapter 3.

phenotype The physical expression (outward appearance) of a trait of an organism, which may be due to genetics, environment, or an interaction of the two. Chapter 6.

phylogenetic species concept (PSC) A species concept based on branching, or cladistic, relationships among species or higher taxa. The PSC hypothesizes the true genealogical relationship among species, based on the concept of shared, derived characteristics (synapomorphies). Chapter 3.

phylogeographic Evolutionary relationships among species populations based on geographic relationships and historical gene flow patterns. Chapter 6.

plasticity The condition of genetically based, environmentally induced variation in characteristics of an organism. Chapter 3.

plesiomorphic An evolutionarily primitive character shared by two or more taxa. *See* **synapomorphic**. Chapter 3.

pluralism A school of thought which holds that species concepts should vary with the taxon under consideration. Many different species definitions would be employed. Chapter 3.

point richness The number of species found at a single point in space. Chapter 4.

polymorphic Description of a population in which individuals have two or more genotypes at a given locus. Chapter 6.

polyploidy Possessing more than two complete sets of chromosomes. Chapter 3.

population viability analysis (PVA) A comprehensive analysis of the many environmental and demographic factors that affect survival of a population, usually applied to small populations at risk of extinction. Chapter 7.

populational view A philosophical perspective that embraces and recognizes variation in classes of objects. Objects, including species, are seen as belonging to a changing class of entity with inherent trait variation. Also called the evolutionary perspective. *Contrast with* **typological view**. Chapter 3.

quantitative genetics The study of phenotypic traits that are influenced by multiple genetic and environmental factors (polygenic traits). Chapter 6.

quantum speciation *See* **founder model**. Chapter 3.

recognition species concept A species concept based on reproductive mechanisms that facilitate gene exchange or a field for gene recombination. Chapter 3.

regional scale The largest scale of corridors in which major swaths of habitat connect regional networks of reserves. Chapter 10.

relaxation The loss of species on land-bridge islands following separation from the mainland or the loss of species during any process of habitat fragmentation and isolation. Chapter 9.

remote sensing Any technique for analyzing landscape patterns and trends using low altitude aerial photography or satellite imagery. Any environmental measurement that is done at a distance. Chapter 12.

rescue effect The recolonization of a habitat when a subpopulation of a metapopulation has gone locally extinct. Chapter 7.

residuals In restoration ecology, the remnants of natural systems that can provide the building blocks for system restoration or rehabilitation. Chapter 14.

Resource Conservation Ethic A philosophical approach to conservation derived from the views of forester Gifford Pinchot, based on the utilitarian philosophy of John Stuart Mill. Nature is seen as a collection of natural resources, to be used for "the greatest good of the greatest number for the longest time." Chapter 1.

restoration ecology The process of using ecological principles and experience to return a degraded ecological system to its former or original state. Chapter 14.

Romantic-Transcendental Conservation Ethic A philosophical approach to conservation derived from the writings of Emerson, Thoreau, and Muir, in which nature is seen in a quasi-religious sense, and as having uses other than human economic gain. This ethic strives to preserve nature in a wild and pristine state. Chapter 1.

scale The magnitude of a region or process. Refers to both spatial size—for example, a (relatively small-scale) patch or a (relatively large-scale) landscape—and temporal rate—for example, (relatively rapid) ecological succession or (relatively slow) evolutionary speciation. Chapter 2

secondary effects When the loss of or population change in a species affects other species, often through their trophic interactions. Chapter 5.

secondary extinctions Loss of a species as a direct or indirect result of the loss of another species. Chapter 8.

sentient Capable of feeling or perception. Refers to a state of self-awareness among organisms, usually applied only to vertebrates. Chapter 2.

sibling species *See* **cryptic species**. Chapter 3.

sink A habitat in which local mortality exceeds local reproductive success for a given species. Chapter 7.

sink population A population in a low-quality habitat in which the birth rate is generally lower than the death rate and population density is maintained by immigrants from source populations. Chapter 7.

SLOSS An acronym for "single large or several small," reflecting a debate that raged for several years asking whether, all else being equal, it was better to have one large reserve or several small reserves of the same total size. Chapter 10.

source A habitat in which local reproductive success exceeds local mortality for a given species. Chapter 7.

source and sink dynamics Spatial linkage of population dynamics such that high-quality habitats (sources) provide excess individuals that maintain population density, through migration, in low-quality habitats (sinks). Chapter 7.

source population A population in a high-quality habitat in which the birth rate greatly exceeds the death rate and the excess individuals leave as emigrants. Chapter 7.

spatially-explicit population model A population model, especially a simulation model, that takes space, differences in habitat quality, and inter-habitat movement into consideration. Chapter 7.

speciation Any of the processes by which new species form. Chapter 3.

species diversity Usually synonymous with "species richness," but may also include the proportional distribution of species. Chapter 4.

species problem The ambiguity of the species category and its definition. The "species problem"—what species definition(s) to use, and what constitutes species—has been with us for decades and is unlikely to be completely resolved in the near future. Chapter 3.

species richness. The number of species in a region, site, or sample. *See also* **α-**, **β-**, and **γ-richness**.

stewardship Management of natural resources that conserves them for future generations. Usually used to distinguish from short-term, utilitarian management objectives. Chapter 1.

stochastic Random; specifically refers to any random process, such as mortality due to weather extremes. Chapter 1.

strip corridor A broad corridor consisting of some interior habitat and intact and functioning communities. Chapter 10.

succession The natural, sequential change of species composition of a community in a given area. Chapter 8.

supply The aggregate amount of goods or services available to satisfy economic needs or wants. The quantity of a good or service which producers are willing to sell at different prices. Supply involves the relationship between quantity and price. Chapter 15.

sustainable development In general, the attempts to meet economic objectives in ways that do not degrade the underlying environmental support system. Note that there is considerable debate over the meaning of this term. In Chapter 18, we define it as "human activities conducted in a manner that respects the intrinsic value of the natural world, the role of the natural world in human well-being, and the need for humans to live on the income from nature's capital rather than the capital itself." Chapters 1 and 18.

sympatric A description of two or more populations or species that occur in the same geographic area. *See also* **allopatric**. Chapter 3.

synapomorphic An evolutionarily derived or advanced character, which is shared by two or more taxa. *See* **plesiomorphic**. Chapter 3.

synergistic interaction An interaction that has more than additive effects; e.g., when the joint toxicity of two compounds is greater than their combined, independent toxicities. Chapter 5.

threatened species According to U.S. Federal law, a species that is likely to become endangered in the foreseeable future. Chapter 3.

tragedy of the commons An idea (set forth primarily by Garrett Hardin) that unregulated use of a common, public resource for private, personal gain will result in overexploitation and destruction of the resource. Chapter 2.

typological view A philosophical perspective that embraces existence of a "type," or perfect form, of objects. Objects, including species, are seen as belonging to a relatively fixed class of entity in which individual variation is viewed as an imperfection. *Contrast with* **populational view**. Chapter 3.

utilitarian value *See* **instrumental value**. Chapter 2.

utilitarian view A philosophical term applied to any activity that produces a product useful to humans, typically in some economic sense. Also used to describe a system of values which is measured by its contribution to human well-being, usually in terms of health and economic standard of living. Chapter 1.

utility The "want-satisfying" power of goods; personal satisfaction received through an economic gain. Chapter 15.

vicariance The process of a continuously distributed biota becoming separated by an intervening geographic event (such as mountain uplift or river flow), or extinction of intervening populations, resulting in subsequent independent histories of the fragmented biotas, and possible speciation events. Chapter 4.

zoning An important component of reserve design that controls human activities within and adjacent to conservation reserves, so that reserve function may be protected while some human activities, including those supplying some economic benefit, may take place. Chapter 10.

Bibliography

Abel, N. and P. Blaikie. 1986. Elephants, people, parks and development: The case of the Luangwa Valley, Zambia. *Environ. Mgmt.* 10:735–751. [10]

Abele, L. G. and E. F. Connor. 1979. Application of island biogeographic theory to refuge design: Making the right decision for the wrong reasons. In R. M. Linn (ed.), *Proceedings of the First Conference on Scientific Research in the National Parks,* Vol. I. pp. 89–94. USDI National Park Service, Washington, D.C. [9]

Aber, J. D. 1987. Restored forests and the identification of critical factors in species-site interactions. In W. R. Jordan, III, M. E. Gilpin, and J. D. Aber (eds.), *Ecological Restoration as a Technique for Basic Research*, pp. 241–250. Cambridge University Press, Cambridge. [14]

Abugov, R. 1982. Species diversity and phasing of disturbance. *Ecology* 63:289–293. [4]

Adams, L. W. and A. D. Geis. 1983. Effects of roads on small mammals. *J. Appl. Ecol.* 20:403–415. [9]

Agee, J. K. and R. L. Edmonds. 1992. *Forest protection guidelines for the Northern Spotted Owl.* College of Forest Resources, University of Washington, Seattle, WA. Unpublished draft. [13]

Aiken, W. 1984. Ethical issues in agriculture. In T. Regan (ed.), *Earthbound: New Introductory Essays in Environmental Ethics,* pp. 247–288. Random House, New York. [2]

Allan, D. G. 1994. *Cranes and Farmers*. Endangered Wildlife Trust, Parkview, South Africa. [13]

Allee, W. C., A. E. Emerson, O. Park, T. Park and K. P. Schmidt. 1949. *Principles of Animal Ecology.* Saunders, Philadelphia. [7]

Allen, M. F. 1991. *The Ecology of Mycorrhizae.* Cambridge University Press, Cambridge. [14]

Allen, W. H. 1988. Biocultural restoration of a tropical forest. *BioScience* 38:156–161. [10]

Allendorf, F. W. 1983. Isolation, geneflow, and genetic differentiation among populations. In C. M. Schonewald-Cox, S. M. Chambers, B. MacBryde and L. Thomas (eds.), *Genetics and Conservation: A Reference for Managing Wild Animal and Plant Populations,* pp. 51–65. Benjamin/Cummings, Menlo Park, CA. [6]

Allendorf, F. W. and R. F. Leary. 1986. Heterozygosity and fitness in natural populations of animals. In M. E. Soulé (ed.), *Conservation Biology: The Science of Scarcity and Diversity,* pp. 57–76. Sinauer Associates, Sunderland, MA. [6]

Allendorf, F. W., R. B. Harris and L. H. Metzgar. 1991. Estimation of effective population size of grizzly bears by computer simulation. In *Proceedings of the Fourth International Congress of Systematics and Evolutionary Biology,* pp. 650–654. Fourth Dioscorides Press, Portland, OR. [6]

Alverson, D. L., M. H. Freeberg, S. A. Murawski and J. G. Pope. 1994. *A Global Assessment of Fisheries Bycatch and Discards.* FAO Technical Paper 339. Food and Agriculture Organization of the United Nations, Rome. 233 pp. [5]

Alverson, W. S., D. M. Waller and S. L. Solheim. 1988. Forests too deer: Edge effects in northern Wisconsin. *Conserv. Biol.* 2: 348–358. [9]

Amat, J. A. 1980. Biología y ecología de la comunidad de patos del Parque Nacional de Doñana. Ph.D. dissertation. University of Sevilla, Sevilla. [13]

Amato, I. 1993. Mt. Unzen be dammed! *Science* 261:827. [19]

Ames, R. T. 1992. Taoist ethics. In L. Becker (ed.), *Encyclopedia of Ethics,* pp. 1126–1230. Garland Press, New York. [2]

Andersen, A. N. 1983. Species diversity and temporal distribution of ants in the semiarid mallee region of northwestern Victoria. *Aust. J. Ecol.* 8:127–137. [4]

Andersen, R. A. 1992. Diversity of eukaryotic algae. *Biodiv. Conserv.* 1:267–292. [4]

Anderson, P. 1995. Ecological restoration and creation: A review. *Biol. J. Linn. Soc.* 56(*Suppl.*):187–211. [14]

Anderson, R. M. and R. M. May. 1986. The invasion, persistence and spread of infectious diseases within animal and plant communities. *Phil. Trans. R. Soc. Lond. B* 314:533–570. [8]

Anderson, R. M. and R. M. May. 1991. *Infectious Diseases of Humans: Dynamics and Control.* Oxford University Press, New York [8]

Anderson, S. H. and D. B. Inkley, (eds.). 1985. *Black-Footed Ferret Workshop Proceedings.* Wyoming Game and Fish Department, Cheyenne. [13]

Andren, H. and P. Angelstam. 1988. Elevated predation rates as an edge effect in habitat islands: Experimental evidence. *Ecology* 69:544–547. [9]

Andrewartha, H. G. and L. C. Birch. 1984. *The Ecological Web.* University of Chicago Press, Chicago. [7]

Angermeier, P. L. 1995. Ecological attributes of extinction-prone species: Loss of freshwater fishes of Virginia. *Conserv. Biol.* 9:143–158. [5]

Antonovics, J., A. D. Bradshaw and R. G. Turner. 1971. Heavy metal tolerance in plants. *Adv. Ecol. Res.* 7:1–85. [3]

Applegate Partnership. 1992. Applegate partnership vision statement. Applegate Partnership, Applegate, OR.

Arambarri, P. de, F. Cabrera and C. G. Toca. 1984. Estudio de la contaminacion del río Guadiamar y su zona de influencia (Marismas del Guadalquivir y Coto de Doñana) por residuos de industrias mineras y agrícolas. Consejo Superior de Investigaciones Científicas, Madrid. [13]

Archibald, G. W., Y. Shigeta, K. Matsumoto and K. Momose. 1981. Endangered cranes. In J. C. Lewis and H. Masatomi (eds.), *Crane Research Around the World,* pp. 1–12. International Crane Foundation, Baraboo, WI. [13]

Archie, M., L. Mann, and W. Smith. 1993. *Partners in Action: Environmental Social Marketing and Environmental Education.* Academy for Educational Development, Washington, D.C. [16]

Arnold, J. E. M., F. B. Armitage, W. L. Bender, N. V. L. Brokaw, H. Hilmi, J. R. Palmer and S. L. Pringle. 1989. *Executive Summary of the Draft Belize Tropical Forestry Action Plan.* Overseas Development Administration, London. Mimeographed. [15]

Arnold, S. F., D. M. Klotz, B. M. Collins, P. M. Vonier, L. J. Guillette, Jr. and J. A. McLachlan. 1996. Synergistic activation of estrogen receptor with combinations of environmental chemicals. *Science* 272:1489–1492. [5]

Aronson, J., S. Dhillion, and E. Le Floc'h. 1995. On the need to select an ecosystem of reference, however imperfect: A reply to Pickett and Parker. *Restor. Ecol.* 3:1–3. [14]

Arrhenius, O. 1921. Species and area. *J. Ecol.* 9:95–99. [4]

Arrow, K. J. and H. Raynaud. 1986. *Social Choice and Multicriterion Decision-Making.* MIT Press, Cambridge, MA. [15]

Arthington, A. H. and L. N. Lloyd. 1989. Introduced poeciliids in Australia and New Zealand. In G. K. Meffe and F. F. Snelson, Jr. (eds.), *Ecology and Evolution of Livebearing Fishes (Poeciliidae).* Prentice Hall, Englewood Cliffs, NJ. [8]

Ascher, W. 1993. *Political Economy and Problematic Forestry Policies in Indonesia: Obstacles to Incorporating Sound Economics and Science.* Center for International Development Research, Institution for Policy Sciences and Public Affairs, Duke University, Durham, NC. 37 pp. [17]

Ashley, M. V., D. J. Melnick and D. Western. 1990. Conservation genetics of the black rhinoceros (*Diceros bicornis*), I: Evidence from the mitochondrial DNA of three populations. *Conserv. Biol.* 4:71–77. [3]

Ashton, P. 1978. Crown characteristics of tropical trees. In P. B. Tomlinson and M. H. Zimmermann (eds.), *Tropical Trees as Living Systems.* pp. 591–615. Cambridge University Press, London. [18]

Ashworth, W. 1995. *The Economy of Nature: Rethinking the Connections Between Ecology and Economics.* Houghton Mifflin, New York. [16]

ASPRS/ACSM/RT 92. 1992. *The Third International Symposium on Advanced Technology in Natural Resource Management,* Washington, D.C. Vol. 5, *Resource Technology.* American Society for Photogrammetry and Remote Sensing and American Congress on Surveying and Mapping, Bethesda, MD [12]

Avise, J. C. 1989. A role for molecular genetics in the recognition and conservation of endangered species. *Trends Ecol. Evol.* 4:279–281. [3,6]

Avise, J. C. 1994. *Molecular Markers, Natural History and Evolution.* Chapman and Hall, New York. [6]

Avise, J. C. 1996. Introduction: The scope of conservation genetics. In J. C. Avise and J. L. Hamrick (eds.), *Conservation Genetics: Case Histories from Nature*, pp. 1–9. Chapman and Hall, New York. [6]

Avise, J. C. and seven others. 1987. Intraspecific phylogeography: The mitochondrial DNA bridge between population genetics and systematics. *Annu. Rev. Ecol. Syst.* 18:489–522. [6]

Avise, J. C. and R. M. Ball. 1990. Principles of genealogical concordance in species concepts and biological taxonomy. *Oxford Surv. Evol. Biol.* 7:45–67. [6]

Avise, J. C. and J. L. Hamrick (eds.). 1996. *Conservation Genetics: Case Histories from Nature.* Chapman and Hall, New York. [6]

Avise, J. C. and W. S. Nelson. 1989. Molecular genetic relationships of the extinct dusky seaside sparrow. *Science* 243:646–648. [6]

Bahm, A. J. 1971. Science is not value-free. *Policy Sci.* 2:391–396. [17]

Baker, A. J., and A. Moeed. 1987. Rapid genetic differentiation and founder effect in colonizing populations of common munas (*Acridotheres tristis*). *Evolution* 41:525–538. [6]

Baker, B. 1996. A reverent approach to the natural world. *BioScience* 46:475–478. [16]

Balick, M. J. and R. Mendelsohn. 1992. Assessing the economic value of traditional medicines from tropical rain forests. *Conserv. Biol.* 6:128–130. [15]

Ball, G. H. 1922. Variation in fresh-water mussels. *Ecology* 3:93–121. [3]

Balla, S. A. and K. F. Walker. 1991. Shape variation in the Australian freshwater mussel *Alathyria jacksoni* Iredale (Bivalvia, Hyriidae). *Hydrobiologica* 220:89–98. [3]

Ballard, W. B. and T. Spraker. 1979. Unit 13 wolf studies: Alaska Department of Fish and Game Projects W-17-9 and W-17-10 Progress Report. [10]

Bambach, R. K. 1986. Phanerozoic marine communities. In D. M. Raup and D. Jablonski (eds.), *Patterns and Processes in the History of Life*, pp. 407–428. Dahlem Konferenzen 1986. Springer-Verlag, Berlin. [8]

Bancroft, G. T. 1989. Status and conservation of wading birds in the Everglades. *Am. Birds* 43:1258–1265. [13]

Barbier, E. B., J. C. Burgess, T. M Swanson and D. W. Pearce. 1990. *Elephants, Economics, and Ivory.* Earthscan Publications, London. [18]

Barnes, A. M. 1982. Surveillance and control of bubonic plague in the United States. *Symp. Zool. Soc. Lond.* 50:237–270. [13]

Barnes, R. F. W. 1983. The elephant problem in Ruaha National Park, Tanzania. *Biol. Cons.* 26:127–148. [18]

Barnes, R. F. W. and E. B. Kapela. 1991. Found ivory records reveal changes in the Ruaha elephant population caused by poaching. *Afr. J. Ecol.* 29:289–294. [18]

Barr, J. 1972. Man and nature: The ecological controversy and the Old Testament. *Bull. John Rylands Library* 55:9–32. [2]

Barry, D. and M. Oelschlaeger. 1996. A science for survival: Values and conservation biology. *Conserv. Biol.* 10:905–911. [1]

Bart, J. 1995. Amount of suitable habitat and viability of Northern Spotted Owls. *Conserv. Biol.* 9:943–946. [7]

Bart, J. and E. D. Forsman. 1992. Dependence of Northern Spotted Owls on old-growth forests in the western USA. *Biol. Conserv.* 37:95–100. [13]

Bartlett, A. A. 1994. Reflections on sustainability, population growth, and the environment. *Pop. Environ.* 16:5–35. [18]

Barzen, J. 1994. ICF team discovers rare wildlife in Cambodia. *The ICF Bugle* 20(4):3–4. [13]

Baskin, Y. 1992. Africa's troubled waters. *BioScience* 42:476–481. [5]

Bass, A. L., D. A. Good, K. A. Bjorndal, J. I. Richardson, Z.-M. Hillis, J. A. Horrocks, and B. W. Bowen. 1996. Testing models of female migratory behavior and population structure in the Caribbean hawksbill turtle, *Eretmochelys imbricata*, with mtDNA control region sequences. *Mol. Ecol.* 5:321–328. [7]

Batisse, M. 1986. Developing and focusing the biosphere reserve concept. *Nature Res.* 22:1–10. [18]

Bator, F. 1957. The simple analytics of welfare maximization. *Am. Econ. Rev.* 47:22–59. [15]

Bauer, B. H., D. A. Etnier, and N. M. Burkhead. 1994. *Etheostoma (Ulocentra) scotti* (Osteichthyes: Percidae), a new darter from the Etowah River system in Georgia. *Bull. Ala. Mus. Nat. Hist.* 17:1–16. [9]

Bawa, K. S. 1990. Plant–pollinator interactions in tropical rain forests. *Annu. Rev. Ecol. Syst.* 21:399–422. [7]

Bean, M. J. and D. S. Wilcove. 1996. Ending the impasse. *Environ. Forum*, July/August: 22–28. [19]

Beaver, R. A. 1979. Host specificity of temperate and tropical animals. *Nature* 281:139–141. [4]

Bedward, M., R. L. Pressey, and D. A. Keith. 1992. A new approach for selecting fully representative reserve networks: Addressing efficiency, reserve design and land suitability with an iterative analysis. *Biol. Conserv.* 62:115–125. [12]

Beebee, T. J. C., R. J. Flower, A. C. Stevenson, S. T. Patrick, P. G. Appleby, C. Fletcher, C. Marsh, J. Natkanski, B. Rippey, and R. W. Battarbee. 1990. Decline of the natterjack toad *Bufo clamita* in Britain: Palaeoecological, documentary and experimental evidence for breeding site acidification. *Biol. Conserv.* 53:1–20. [5]

Beier, P. 1993. Determining minimum habitat areas and habitat corridors for cougars. *Conserv. Biol.* 7:94–108. [7]

Beier, P. 1995. Dispersal of juvenile cougars in fragmented habitat. *J. Wildl. Mgmt.* 59:228–237. [9]

Belden, R. C. and B. W. Hagedorn. 1993. Feasibility of translocating panthers into northern Florida. *J. Wildl. Mgmt.* 57: 388–397. [12]

Belemsobgo, U. 1995. Le modèle "Nazinga": Réussite technique et incertitudes sociales. *Le Flamboyant* 35: 22–27. [18]

Belize Tourist Board. 1992. *Visitor Statistics 1987–1991.* Immigration and Nationality Services of Belize. [18]

Bellah, R. N., R. Madsen, W. M. Sullivan, A. Swidler and S. M. Tipton. 1991. *The Good Society.* Alfred A. Knopf, New York. [15]

Belovsky, G. E. 1987. Extinction models and mammalian persistence. In M. E. Soulé (ed.), *Viable Populations for Conservation,* pp. 35–57. Cambridge University Press, Cambridge. [10]

Benke, A. C. 1990. A perspective on America's vanishing streams. *J. N. Am. Benthol. Soc.* 9:77–88. [9]

Bennitt, R., J. S. Dixon, V. H. Cahalane, W. W. Chase and W. L. McAtee. 1937. Statement of policy. *J. Wildl. Mgmt.* 1:1–2. [1]

Benstead, J. P., J. G. March, and C. M. Pringle. 1996. Effects of dams and associated water withdrawals on the migration of freshwater shrimps in a tropical river, Puerto Rico. (Abstract). *Bull. N. Am. Benthol. Soc.* 13:202. [9]

Bentham, H., J. A. Harris, P. Birch and K. C. Short. 1992. Habitat classification and soil restoration assessment using analysis of soil microbiological and physicochemical characteristics. *J. Appl. Ecol.* 29:711–718. [14]

Berg, R. Y. 1975. Myrmecochorus plants in Australia and their dispersal by ants. *Aust. J. Bot.* 23:475–508. [4]

Berger, P. L. and T. Luckman. 1987. *The Social Construction of Reality: A Treatise in the Sociology of Knowledge.* Penguin Books, New York. [17]

Berkes, F. (ed.). 1989. *Common Property Resources: Ecology and Community-Based Sustainable Development.* Bellhaven Press, London. [15]

Bernúes, M. 1990. Limnología de los ecosistemas acuáticos del Parque Nacional de Doñana. Ph.D. dissertation, Autonomous University of Madrid, Madrid, Spain. [13]

Berrill, M., S. Bertram, A. Wilson, S. Louis, D. Brigham, and C. Stromberg. 1993. Lethal and sublethal impacts of pyrethroid insecticides on amphibian embryos and tadpoles. *Environ. Toxicol. Chem.* 12:525–539. [5]

Berry, T. 1988. *The Dream of the Earth.* Sierra Club Books, San Francisco. [19]

Berry, W. 1977. *The Unsettling of America.* Sierra Club Books, San Francisco. [13]

Berry, W. 1989. The futility of global thinking. *Harper's Magazine,* September, 16–22. [16]

Berry, W. 1993. Decolonizing rural America. *Audubon Magazine,* March/April, 100–105. [16]

Bettenay, E. 1984. Origin and nature of the sandplains. In J. S. Pate and J. S. Beard (eds.), *Kwongan: Plant Life of the Sandplain,* pp. 51–68. University of Western Australia Press, Nedlands. [4]

Betz, R. F. and H. F. Lamp. 1992. Species compositions of old settler savanna and sand prairie cemeteries in northern Illinois and northwestern Indiana. In D. Smith and C. A. Jacobs (eds.), *Proceedings of the 12th North American Prairie Conference,* pp. 79–87. University of Northern Iowa, Cedar Falls. [14]

Bibby, C. J. and eight others. 1992. *Putting Biodiversity on the Map: Priority Areas for Global Conservation.* International Council for Bird Preservation, Cambridge. [5]

Bierregaard, R. O., T. E. Lovejoy, V. Kapos, A. A. dos Santos, and R. W. Hutchings. 1992. The biological dynamics of tropical rainforest fragments. *BioScience* 42:859–866. [9]

Biggins, D. E. and M. H. Schroeder. 1988. Historical and present status of the black-footed ferret. In *Proceedings of the Eighth Great Plains Wildlife Damage Control Workshop*, pp. 93–97. General Technical Report RM-154. USDA Forest Service, Fort Collins, CO. [13]

Biggins, D. E., M. H. Schroeder, S. C. Forrest, and L. Richardson. 1986. Activity of radio-tagged black-footed ferrets. *Great Basin Nat. Mem.* 8:135–140. [13]

Biggins, D. E., L. H. Hanebury, B. J. Miller and R. A. Powell. 1990. Release of Siberian polecats (*Mustela eversmanni*) on a prairie dog colony. (Abstract). 70th Annual Meeting of the American Society of Mammalogists. [13]

Biggins, D. E., J. Godbey, and A. Vargas. 1993. Influence of pre-release experience on reintroduced black-footed ferrets (*Mustela nigripes*). Unpublished report. National Biological Service, Midcontinent Ecological Science Center, Ft. Collins, CO. [13]

Bischof, L. L. 1992. Genetics and elephant conservation. *Endangered Species Update* 9:1–8. [6]

Bishop, R. C. 1978. Endangered species and uncertainty: The economics of a safe minimum standard. *Am. J. Agric. Econ.* 60:10–18. [2,15]

Bishop, R. C. 1993. Economic efficiency, sustainability, and biodiversity. *Ambio* 22:69–73. [15]

Bjorndal, K. A. 1982. *Biology and Conservation of Sea Turtles.* Smithsonian Institution Press, Washington, D.C. [13]

Blaikie, P. and H. Brookfield. 1987. *Land Degradation and Society.* Methuen, London. [15]

Blair, R. B. 1996. Land use and avian species diversity along an urban gradient. *Conserv. Biol.* 6:506–519. [9]

Blake, J. G. 1991. Nested subsets and the distribution of birds on isolated woodlots. *Conserv. Biol.* 5:58–66. [9]

Blake, J. G. and J. R. Karr. 1984. Species composition of bird communities and the conservation benefit of large versus small forests. *Biol. Conserv.* 30:173–187. [9]

Blake, N. M. 1980. Land Into Water—Water Into Land: A History of Water Management in Florida (Everglades). University Presses of Florida, Gainesville, FL. [13]

Blakesley, J. A., A. B. Franklin and R. J. Gutierrez. 1992. Spotted Owl roost and nest site selection in Northwestern California. *J. Wildl. Mgmt.* 56:388–392. [13]

Blanchard, K. A. 1995. Reversing population declines in seabirds on the north shore of the Gulf of St. Lawrence, Canada. In S. K. Jacobson (ed.), *Conserving Wildlife: International Education and Communication Approaches*, pp. 51–63. Columbia University Press, New York. [16]

Blaustein, A. R. 1994. Chicken Little or Nero's fiddle? A perspective on declining amphibian populations. *Herpetologica* 501:85–97. [5]

Blaustein, A. R., P. D. Hoffman, D. G. Hokit, J. M. Kiesecker, S. C. Walls, and J. B. Hays. 1994a. UV repair and resistance to solar UV-B in amphibian eggs: A link to population declines? *Proc. Natl. Acad. Sci. USA* 91:1791–1795. [5]

Blaustein, A. R., D. G. Hokit, R. K. O'Hara, and R. A. Holt. 1994b. Pathogenic fungus contributes to amphibian losses in the Pacific Northwest. *Biol. Conserv.* 67:251–254. [5]

Blaustein, A. R., D. B. Wake and W. P. Sousa. 1994c. Amphibian declines: Judging stability, persistence, and susceptibility of populations to local and global extinctions. *Conserv. Biol.* 8(1):60–71. [5]

Blaustein, A. R., B. Edmond, J. H. Kiesecker, J. J. Beatty and D. G. Hokit. 1995. Ambient ultraviolet radiation causes mortality in salamander eggs. *Ecol. Appl.* 5(3):740–743. [5]

Blaustein, A. R., J. M. Kiesecker, S. C. Walls, and D. G. Hokit. 1996. Field experiments, amphibian mortality, and UV radiation. *BioScience* 46(6):386–388. [5]

Blockstein, D. E. and H. B. Tordoff. 1985. Gone forever—a contemporary look at the extinction of the Passenger Pigeon. *Amer. Birds* 39:845–851. [7]

Blum, A. 1987. Students' knowledge and beliefs concerning environmental issues in four countries. *J. Environ. Educ.* 18(3): 7–14. [16]

Boateng, E. A. 1970. *A Geography of Ghana.* Cambridge University Press, Cambridge. [18]

Bockstael, N., R. Costanza, I. Strand, W. Boynton, K. Bell, and L.Wainger. 1995. Ecological economic modeling and valuation of ecosystems. *Ecol. Econ.* 14:143–159. [15]

Bodhi, B. 1987. Foreword. In *Buddhist Perspectives on the Ecocrisis,* pp. i–x. Buddhist Publication Society, Kandy, Sri Lanka. [2]

B.O.E. 1991. Real Decreto 16 Diciembre 1991 N° 1771/1991. Ministerio de Agricultura, Pesca y Alimentación. Parques Nacionales. Plan Rector de Uso y Gestión del de Doñana. *Boletín Oficial del Estado* N°301: 8401–8411. [13]

Boersma, P. D., D. L. Stokes and W. Conway. 1990. *Punta Tomba Management Plan.* New York Zoological Society, New York. [18]

Bok, D. 1990. *Universities and the Future of America.* Duke University Press, Durham, NC. [16]

Bond, W. 1983. On alpha-diversity and the richness of the Cape flora: A study in southern Cape fynbos. In F. J. Kruger, D. T. Mitchell and J. U. M. Jarvis (eds.), *Mediterranean-Type Ecosystems: The Role of Nutrients,* pp. 337–356. Springer-Verlag, Berlin. [4]

Bonfil, R. 1994. Overview of world elasmobranch fisheries. FAO Fisheries Technical Paper 341. Food and Agriculture Organization of the United Nations, Rome. 117 pp. [5]

Boo, E. 1990. *Ecotourism: The Potentials and Pitfalls.* World Wildlife Fund, Washington, D.C. [18]

Boone, J. L., J. Laerm and M. H. Smith. 1993. Taxonomic status of *Peromyscus gossypinus anastasae* (Anastasia Island cotton mouse). *J. Mammal.* 74:363–375. [6]

Bormann, F. H. and G. E. Likens. 1979. *Pattern and Process in a Forested Ecosystem.* Springer-Verlag, New York. [9]

Bos, E., M. T. Vu, A. Levin, and R. Bulatao. 1993. *World Population Projections.* 1992–93 edition. Johns Hopkins University Press, Baltimore. [18]

Botkin, D. B. 1990. *Discordant Harmonies: A New Ecology for the Twenty-First Century.* Oxford University Press, New York. [1,2]

Botkin, D. B. and M. J. Sobel. 1975. Stability in time-varying ecosystems. *Am. Nat.* 109:625–646. [10]

Bowen, B. W. 1995. Tracking marine turtles with genetic markers; Voyages of the ancient mariners. *BioScience* 45:528–534. [7]

Bowen, B. W. and J. C. Avise. 1995. Conservation genetics of marine turtles. In J. C. Avise and J. L. Hamrick (eds), *Conservation Genetics: Case Histories from Nature,* pp. 190–237. Chapman and Hall, New York. [7]

Bowen, B. W., A. B. Meylan and J. C. Avise. 1991. Evolutionary distinctiveness of the endangered Kemp's Ridley sea turtle. *Nature* 352:709–711. [3]

Bowen, B. W., A. B. Meylan, J. P. Ross, C. J. Limpus, G. H. Balazs and J. C. Avise. 1992. Global population structure and natural history of the green turtle (*Chelonia mydas*) in terms of matriarchal phylogeny. *Evolution* 46:865–881. [13]

Boyce, M. S. 1992a. Population viability analysis. *Annu. Rev. Ecol. Syst.* 23:481– 506. [7,10]

Boyce, M. S. 1992b. Wolf recovery for Yellowstone National Park: A simulation model. In D. R. McCullough and R. H. Barrett (eds.), *Wildlife 2001: Populations,* pp. 123–138. Elsevier Applied Science, London. [18]

Boyer, K. E. and J. B. Zedler. 1996. Damage to cordgrass by scale insects in a constructed salt marsh: Effects of nitrogen additions. *Estuaries* 19:1–12. [14]

Boyle, S. and F. Samson. 1985. Effects of nonconsumptive recreation on wildlife: A review. *Wildlife Soc. Bull.* 13:110–116. [18]

Bradford, D. F. 1989. Allotopic distribution of native frogs and introduced fishes in high Sierra Nevada lakes of California: Implication of the negative effect of fish introductions. *Copeia* 1989(3):775–778. [5]

Bradford, D. F. 1991. Mass mortality and extinction in a high-elevation population of *Rana muscosa. J. Herpetol.* 25(2):174–177. [5]

Bradford, D. F., F. Tabatabai and D. M. Graber. 1993. Isolation of remaining populations of the native frog, *Rana muscosa*, by introduced fishes in Sequoia and Kings Canyon National Parks, California. *Conserv. Biol.* 7(4):882–888. [5]

Bradford, D. F., D. M. Graber, and F. Tabatabai. 1994a. Population declines of the native frog, *Rana muscosa*, in Sequoia and Kings Canyon National Parks, California. *Southwestern Nat.* 39:323–327. [5]

Bradford, D. F., M. S. Gordon, D. F. Johnson, R. D. Andrews, and W. B. Jennings. 1994b. Acidic deposition as an unlikely cause for amphibian population declines in the Sierra Nevada, California. *Biol. Conserv.* 69:155–161. [5]

Bradshaw, A. D. 1983. The reconstruction of ecosystems. *J. Appl. Ecol.* 10:1–17. [14]

Bradshaw, A. D. 1984. Ecological principles and land reclamation practice. *Landscape Planning* 11:35–48. [14]

Bradshaw, A. D. 1995. Alternative endpoints for reclamation. In J. Cairns, Jr. (ed.), *Rehabilitating Damaged Ecosystems*, 2nd ed., pp. 165–185. CRC Press, Boca Raton, FL. [14]

Bradshaw, A. D. and M. J. Chadwick. 1980. *The Restoration of Land: The Ecology and Reclamation of Derelict and Degraded Land.* Blackwell Scientific Publications, Oxford. [14]

Braker, H. E. 1991. Natural history of a neotropical gap-inhabiting grasshopper. *Biotropica* 23:41–50. [18]

Brash, A. R. 1987. The history of avian extinction and forest conversion in Puerto Rico. *Biol. Conserv.* 39:97–111. [5]

Bratton, S. P. 1993. *Christianity, Wilderness and Wildlife: The Original Desert Solitaire.* University of Scranton Press, Scranton, PA. [2]

Brehm Fund for International Bird Conservation. 1987. Vietnam rediscovers rare cranes! *Flying Free* 5(2):1–3. [13]

Brenner, F. J. 1990. Mine reclamation: Opportunity for critical habitat development. In *Ecosystem Management: Rare Species and Significant Habitats*, pp. 235–238. New York State Museum Bulletin 471. [14]

Brewer, G. D. and P. deLeon. 1983. *The Foundations of Policy Analysis.* Dorsey Press, Homewood, IL. [17]

Briggs, J. C. 1996. *Global Biogeography.* Elsevier, Amsterdam. [4]

Brisbin, I. L. 1968. The Passenger Pigeon: A study in the ecology of extinction. *Modern Game Breeding* 4:13–20. [6]

Brisbin, I. L. 1995. Conservation of the wild ancestors of domestic animals. *Conserv. Biol.* 9:1327–1328. [5]

Brittingham, M. C. and S. A. Temple. 1983. Have cowbirds caused forest songbirds to decline? *BioScience* 33:31–35. [9]

Brocke, R. H., K. A. Gustafson and A. R. Major. 1990. Restoration of lynx in New York: Biopolitical lessons. *Trans. N. Am. Wildlife and Natural Resources Conference* 55:590–598. [12]

Brody, A. J. and M. P. Pelton. 1989. Effects of roads on black bear movements in western North Carolina. *Wildl. Soc. Bull.* 17:5–10. [9]

Brokaw, N. L. V. 1985. Treefalls, regrowth, and community structure in tropical forests. In S. T. A. Pickett and P. S. White (eds.), *The Ecology of Natural Disturbance and Patch Dynamics*, pp. 53–69. Academic Press, Orlando, FL. [18]

Brokaw, N. L. V. and T. Lloyd-Evans. 1987. *The Bladen Branch Wilderness.* Manomet Bird Observatory, Manomet, MA. [15]

Brothers, T. S. and A. Springarn. 1992. Forest fragmentation and alien plant invasion of central Indiana old-growth forests. *Conserv. Biol.* 6:91–100. [9]

Brower, L. P. 1995. Understanding and misunderstanding the migration of the monarch butterfly (Nymphalidae) in North America: 1857-1995. *J. Lepid. Soc. 49*: 304-385. [4]

Brower, L. P. and S. B. Malcolm. 1991. Animal migrations: Endangered phenomena. *Am. Zool.* 31:265–276. [4]

Brown, G. 1989. The viewing value of elephants. In S. Cobb (ed.), *The Ivory Trade and the Future of the African Elephant.* Ivory Trade Review Group, Oxford. [18]

Brown, G. and W. Henry. 1989. *The Economic Value of Elephants.* LEEC Paper 89–12, London. [18]

Brown, G. E., Jr. 1995. Mythmakers and soothsayers: The science and politics of global change. Presentation at NATO/Duke University School of the Environment, Workshop on Global Change Integrated Risk Assessment, October 15, Durham, NC. Unpublished manuscript. 7 pp. [17]

Brown, J. H. and A. Kodric-Brown. 1977. Turnover rates in insular biogeography: Effect of immigration on extinction. *Ecology* 58:445–449. [7,9]

Brown, J. H. and W. McDonald. 1995. Livestock grazing and conservation on southwestern rangelands. *Conserv. Biol.* 9:1644–1647. [9]

Brown, L. R. et al. 1994. *State of the World.* W. W. Norton, New York. [19]

Brown, L. R., C. Flavin and H. Kane. 1992. *Vital Signs.* W. W. Norton, New York. [18]

Brown, P., R. Wilson, R. Loyn and N. Murray. 1985. The Orange-Bellied Parrot—An RAOU conservation statement. RAOU Report Number 14. Royal Australian Ornithology Union, Moonee Ponds, Victoria. [6]

Browne, J. 1983. *The Secular Ark: Studies in the History of Biogeography.* Yale University Press, New Haven. [9]

Brubaker, L. B. 1988. Vegetation history and anticipating future vegetation change. In J. K. Agee and D. R. Johnson (eds.), *Ecosystem Management for Parks and Wilderness*, pp. 42–58. University of Washington Press, Seattle. [2,8]

Bruner, J. 1990. *Acts of Meaning*. Harvard University Press, Cambridge, MA. [17]

Brunner, R. D. 1995. Notes on basic concepts of the policy sciences. Center for Public Policy Research, University of Colorado, Boulder. 17 pp. [17]

Brunner, R. D. 1996a. A milestone in the policy sciences. *Policy Sci.* 29:45–68. [17]

Brunner, R. D. 1996b. Policy and global change research: A modest proposal. *Climate Change* 32:121–147. [17]

Brunner, R. D. and W. Ascher. 1992. Science and social responsibility. *Policy Sci.* 25: 295–331. [17]

Brunner, R. D. and T. W. Clark. 1997. A practice-based approach to ecosystem management. *Conserv. Biol.* 11:48–58. [17]

Bryant, B. (ed.). 1995. *Environmental Justice: Issues, Policies, and Solutions.* Island Press, Washington, D.C. [16]

Bryant, E. H., H. van Dijk, and W. van Delden. 1981. Genetic variability of the face fly, *Musca autumnalis* De Geer, in relation to a population bottleneck. *Evolution* 35:872–881. [6]

Buchanan, J. B. 1991. Spotted Owl nest site characteristics in mixed conifer forests of the eastern Cascade Mountains, Washington. M.S. Thesis, University of Washington, Seattle. [13]

Buchanan, J. M. 1954. Social choice, democracy, and free markets. *J. Pol. Econ.* 62:114–123. [15]

Buchmann, S. L. and G. P. Nabhan. 1996. *The Forgotten Pollinators.* Island Press, Washington, D.C. [2]

Buechner, M. 1987. Conservation in insular parks: Simulation models of factors affecting the movement of animals across park boundaries. *Biol. Conserv.* 41:57–76. [10]

Bull, A. T., M. Goodfellow and H. Slater. 1992. Biodiversity as a source of innovation in biotechnology. *Annu. Rev. Microbiol.* 46:219–252. [18]

Bullard, R. (ed.). 1993. *Confronting Environmental Racism: Voices from the Grassroots.* South End Press, Boston, MA. [16]

Bunt, J. S. 1975. Primary productivity of marine ecosystems. In H. Leith and R. H. Whittaker (eds.), *Primary Productivity of the Biosphere*, pp. 169–215. Springer-Verlag, New York. [4]

Burgess, H. 1986. The emergency condition of the Veddas. Letter to the directors, World Wildlife Fund, Washington, D.C. [10]

Burgess, R. L. and D. M. Sharpe (eds.). 1981. *Forest Island Dynamics in Man-Dominated Landscapes.* Springer-Verlag, New York. [9]

Burke, V. J. and J. W. Gibbons. 1995. Terrestrial buffer zones and wetland conservation: A case study of freshwater turtles in a Carolina bay. *Conserv. Biol.* 9:1365–1369. [10]

Burkey, T. V. 1989. Extinction in nature reserves: The effect of fragmentation and the importance of migration between reserve fragments. *Oikos* 55:75–81. [9]

Burkey, T. V. 1995. Extinction rates in archipelagoes: Implications for populations in fragmented habitats. *Conserv. Biol.* 9:527–541. [9]

Burrough, P. A. 1986. *Principles of Geographic Information Systems for Land Resources Assessment.* Oxford University Press, Oxford. [9]

Bush, M. B. 1994. Amazonian speciation: a necessarily complex model. *J. Biogeog.* 21:5–17. [4]

Bush, M. B. and P. A. Colinvaux. 1990. A pollen record of a complete glacial cycle from lowland Panama. *J. Veg. Sci.* 1:105–118 [4]

Butman, C. A. and J. T. Carlton (eds.). 1995. *Understanding Marine Biodiversity: A Research Agenda for the Nation.* National Academy Press, Washington D.C. [4, 7]

Butman, C. A., J. T. Carlton, and S. R. Palumbi. 1995. Whaling effects on deep-sea biodiversity. *Conserv. Biol.* 9:462–464. [7]

Buzas, M. A. and T. G. Gibson. 1969. Species diversity: benthic Foraminifera in western North Atlantic. *Science* 163:72–75. [4]

Byerly, R., Jr. 1989. The Policy Dynamics of Global Change, *Earthquest*, Spring, pp. 11–13, 24. [16]

Cabrera, F., M. Soldevilla, R. Cordón, and P. de Arambarri. 1987. Heavy metal pollution in the Guadiamar river and the Guadalquivir estuary (South West Spain). *Chemosphere* 16 (2/3):463–468. [13]

Cabrera, F., C. G. Toca, E. Díaz, and P. de Arambarri. 1984. Acid mine-water and agricultural pollution in a river skirting the Doñana National Park (Guadiamar river, South West Spain). *Water Res.* 18 (12):1469–1482. [13]

Caicco, S. L., J. M. Scott, B. Butterfield, and B. Csuti. 1995. A gap analysis of the management status of the vegetation of Idaho (U.S.A.). *Conserv. Biol.* 9:498–511. [12]

Cairns, J., Jr. (ed.). 1988. *Rehabilitating Damaged Ecosystems,* Vols. I and II. CRC Press, Boca Raton, FL. [14]

Cairns, J., Jr. (ed.). 1995. *Rehabilitating Damaged Ecosystems.* 2nd ed. CRC Press, Boca Raton, FL. [14]

Cairns, J., Jr. In press. Eco-societal restoration: Breaking down the barriers. In J. E. Williams, C. A. Wood, and M. P. Dombeck (eds.), *Watershed Restoration: Principles and Practices.* American Fisheries Society, Bethesda, MD. [11]

Callicott, J. B. 1986. On the intrinsic value of nonhuman species. In B. G. Norton (ed.), *The Preservation of Species: The Value of Biological Diversity,* pp. 138–172. Princeton University Press, Princeton, NJ. [2]

Callicott, J. B. 1987a. The conceptual foundations of the land ethic. In J. B. Callicott (ed.), *Companion to A Sand County Almanac: Interpretive and Critical Essays,* pp. 186–217. University of Wisconsin Press, Madison. [2]

Callicott, J. B. 1987b. The philosophical value of wildlife. In D. Decker and G. Goff (eds.), *Valuing Wildlife. Economic and Social Perspectives,* pp. 214–221. Westview Press, Boulder, CO. [2]

Callicott, J. B. 1989. *In Defense of the Land Ethic: Essays in Environmental Philosophy.* State University of New York Press, Albany. [2,12]

Callicott, J. B. 1990. Whither conservation ethics? *Conserv. Biol.* 4:15–20. [1]

Callicott, J. B. 1991. The wilderness idea revisited: the sustainable development alternative. *Envir. Prof.* 13:235–247. [2]

Callicott, J. B. 1992. Can a theory of moral sentiments support a genuinely normative environmental ethic? *Inquiry* 35:183–198. [2]

Callicott, J. B. 1994. *Earth's Insights. A Multicultural Survey of Ecological Wisdom.* University of California Press, Berkeley. [2]

Calvert, W. H. and L. P. Brower. 1986. The location of monarch butterfly (*Danaus plexippus* L.) overwintering colonies in Mexico in relation to topography and microclimate. *J. Lepid. Soc.* 40:164–187. [4]

Camhi, M. 1995a. Industrial fisheries threaten ecological integrity of the Galapagos Islands. *Conserv. Biol.* 9:715–724. [5]

Camhi, M. 1995b. Risk-prone management of the U.S. Atlantic shark fishery. *Shark News* 4:6–7. [5]

Camhi, M. 1996. Overfishing threatens sea's bounty. *Forum for Applied Research and Public Policy* 11:5–15. (See also related articles in special section, pp. 5–53.) [5]

Campbell, F. 1991. The appropriations history. In K. A. Kohm (ed.), *Balancing on the Brink of Extinction: The Endangered Species Act and Lessons for the Future,* pp. 134–146. Island Press, Washington, D.C. [3]

Campbell, N. A. 1987. *Biology.* Benjamin/Cummings, Menlo Park, CA. [3]

Cannon, J. R., J. M. Dietz, and L. A. Dietz. 1996. Training conservation biologists in human interaction skills. *Conserv. Biol.* 10:1277–1282. [1]

Canterbury, E. R. 1987. *The Making of Economics,* 3rd ed. Wadsworth, Belmont, CA. [15]

Carey, A. B., J. A. Reid and S. P. Horton. 1992. Northern Spotted Owls: Influence of prey base and landscape character. *Ecol. Monogr.* 62:223–250. [13]

Carey, C. 1993. Hypothesis concerning the causes of the disappearance of boreal toads from the mountains of Colorado. *Conserv. Biol.* 7(2):355–362. [5]

Cargill, S. M. and F. S. Chapin III. 1987. Application of successional theory to tundra restoration: A review. *Arct. Alp. Res.* 19:366–372. [14]

Carlson, A. and G. Aulen. 1992. Territorial dynamics of an isolated White-Backed Woodpecker (*Dendrocoposd leucotos*) population. *Conserv. Biol.* 6:450–458. [9]

Carlton, J. T. 1993. Neoextinctions of marine invertebrates. *Am. Zool.* 33:499–509. [4]

Carlton, J. T., G. J. Vermeij, D. R. Lindberg, D. A. Carlton and E. Dudley. 1991. The first historical extinction of a marine invertebrate in an ocean basin: The demise of the eelgrass limpet *Lottia alveus. Biol. Bull.* 180(1):72–80. [4, 7]

Caro, T. M. 1993. Behavioral solutions to breeding cheetahs in captivity: Insights from the wild. *Zoo. Biol.* 12:19–30. [6]

Caro, T. M. and M. K. Laurenson. 1994. Ecological and genetic factors in conservation: A cautionary tale. *Science* 263: 485–486. [6]

Carpenter, J. W., M. J. G. Appel, R. C. Erickson, and M. N. Novilla. 1976. Fatal vaccine-induced canine distemper virus infection in black-footed ferrets. *J. Am. Vet. Med. Assn.* 169:961–964. [13]

Carpenter, S. R. and J. F. Kitchell (eds.). 1993. *The Trophic Cascade in Lakes.* Cambridge University Press, Cambridge, England. [11]

Carr, A. 1967. *So Excellent a Fishe: A Natural History of Sea Turtles.* Scribner, New York. [7]

Carroll, C. R. 1990. The interface between natural areas and agroecosystems. In C. R. Carroll, J. H. Vandermeer and P. M. Rosset (eds.), *Agroecology,* pp. 365–384. Biological Resource Management Series. McGraw-Hill, New York. [1,10]

Carroll, C. R. 1992. Ecological management of sensitive natural areas. In P. L. Fiedler and S. Jain (eds.), *Conservation Biology: The Theory and Practice of Nature Conservation, Preservation and Management,* pp. 347–372. Chapman and Hall, New York. [12]

Carroll, C. R., J. H. Vandermeer, P. M. Rosset (eds.). 1990. *Agroecology.* Biological Resource Management Series. McGraw Hill, New York. [10]

Case, T. J. and M. L. Cody. 1987. Testing theories of island biogeography. *Am. Sci.* 75:402–411. [5]

Castells, M., J. Cruz, E. Custodio, F. García-Novo, J. P. Gaudemar, J. L. González Vallvé, V. Granados, A. Magraner, C. Román, M. Smart, and E. Van der Maarel. 1992. *Dictámen sobre estrategias para el desarrollo socioeconómico sostenible del entorno de Doñana.* Comisión Internacional de Expertos sobre el Desarrollo del Entorno de Doñana. Junta de Andalucía, Sevilla. [13]

Castroviejo, J. 1993. *Memoria. Mapa del Parque Nacional de Doñana.* Consejo Superior de Investigaciones Científicas. Agencia de Medio Ambiente, Junta de Andalucía. [13]

Caughley, G. 1976. The elephant problem: An alternative hypothesis. *East Afr. Wildl. J.* 14:265–283. [10]

Caughley, G. and A. Gunn. 1996. *Conservation Biology in Theory and Practice.* Blackwell Scientific, Cambridge, MA. [3]

Chambers, S. M. 1983. Genetic principles for managers. In C. M. Schonewald-Cox, S. M. Chambers, B. MacBryde and L. Thomas (eds.), *Genetics and Conservation: A Reference for Managing Wild Animal and Plant Populations,* pp. 15–46. Benjamin/Cummings, Menlo Park, CA. [6]

Chappel, C. 1990. Contemporary Jaina and Hindu responses to the ecological crisis. Paper presented at the 1990 meeting of the College Theological Society, Loyola University, New Orleans. [2]

Chargoff, E. 1980. Knowledge without wisdom. *Harper's Magazine,* May, 41–48. [16]

Charlesworth, B. 1980. *Evolution in Age Structured Populations.* Cambridge University Press, New York. [7]

Charlesworth, D. and B. Charlesworth. 1987. Inbreeding depression and its evolutionary consequences. *Annu. Rev. Ecol. Syst.* 18:237–268. [6]

Charnov, E. L. 1990. On evolution of age at maturity and adult life-span. *J. Evol. Biol.* 3:139–144. [7]

Chase, A. 1995. *In a Dark Wood.* Houghton Mifflin, NY. [11]

Chavis, B. F., Jr. and C. Lee. 1987. Toxic Wastes and Race in the United States: A National Report on the Racial and Socio-Economic Characteristics of Communities with Hazardous Waste Sites. Commission for Racial Justice, United Church of Christ, New York. [16]

Chen, J. and J. F. Franklin. 1990. Microclimatic pattern and basic biological responses at the clearcut edges of old-growth Douglas fir stands. *Northwest Environ. J.* 6: 424–425. [9]

Chen, J., J. F. Franklin and T. A. Spies. 1992. Vegetation responses to edge environments in old-growth Douglas fir forests. *Ecol. Applic.* 2:387–396. [9]

Chen, X. 1993. Comparison of inbreeding and outbreeding in hermaphroditic *Arianta arbustorum* (L.) (land snail). *Heredity* 71:456–461. [6]

Chesapeake Bay Program. 1995. The state of the Chesapeake Bay 1995. Chesapeake Bay Program, Annapolis, MD. [12]

Chesser, R. K. and M. H. Smith (eds.). 1996. *Population Dynamics in Ecological Space and Time,* University of Chicago Press, Chicago.

Chesser, R. K., O. E. Rhodes, Jr. and M. H. Smith. 1996. Gene conservation. In O. E. Rhodes, Jr., R. K. Chesser, and M. H. Smith (eds.), *Population Dynamics in Ecological Space and Time,* pp. 237–252. University of Chicago Press, Chicago. [6]

Chesser, R. K., O. E. Rhodes, Jr., D. W. Sugg and A. Schnabel. 1993. Effective sizes for subdivided populations. *Genetics* 135: 1221–1232. [6]

Christensen, N. L., A. Bartuska, J. Brown, S. Carpenter, C. D'Antonio, R. Francis, J. Franklin, J. MacMahon, R. Noss, D. Parsons, C. Peterson, M. Turner, and R. Woodmansee. 1996. The report of the Ecological Society of America Committee on the scientific basis for ecosystem management. *Ecol. Appl.* 6(3):665–691. [13]

Christensen, N. L. et al. 1989. Interpreting the Yellowstone fires of 1988. *BioScience* 39:678-685. [11]

Clark ,T. W., T. Donnay, P. Schuyler, P. Curlee, P. Cymerys, T. Sullivan, L. Sheeline, R. Reading, A. Marcer-Batlle, Y. DeFretes, and T. K. Kennedy, Jr. 1992. Conserving biodiversity in the real world: Professional practice using a policy orientation. *Endangered Species Update* 9 (5&6):5–8. [17]

Clark, C. 1985. *Bioeconomic Modeling and Fisheries Management.* Wiley Interscience, New York. [19]

Clark, C. W. 1973. Profit maximization and the extinction of animal species. *J. Polit. Econ.* 81:950–961. [2]

Clark, C. W. 1990. *Mathematical Bioeconomics.* John Wiley & Sons, New York. [12]

Clark, J. G. 1995. Economic development vs. sustainable societies: Reflections on the players in a crucial contest. *Annu. Rev. Ecol. Syst.* 26:225–248. [18]

Clark, T. W. 1989. Conservation Biology of the black-footed ferret, *Mustela nigripes.* Wildlife Preservation Trust Special Report no. 3, Philadelphia, Pennsylvania. [13]

Clark, T. W. 1993. Creating and using knowledge for species and ecosystem conservation: Science, organizations, and policy. *Perspect. Biol. Med.* 36:497–525. [17]

Clark, T. W. 1996. Learning as a strategy for improving endangered species conservation. *Endangered Species Update* 13 (1 and 2): 5–6 and 22–24. [13]

Clark, T. W. In press. *Averting Extinction: Restructuring Endangered Species Recovery.* Yale University Press, New Haven, CT. [13]

Clark, T. W. and J. R. Cragun. 1994. Organization and managerial guidelines for endangered species restoration programs and recovery teams. In M. L. Bowles and C. J. Whelan (eds.), *Restorations and Recovery of Endangered Species: Conceptual Issues, Planning and Implementation,* pp. 9–33. Cambridge University Press, London. [13]

Clark, T. W. and A. H. Harvey. 1988. Implementing endangered species recovery policy: Learning as we go? *Endangered Species Update* 5:35–42. [13]

Clark, T. W. and D. Zaunbrecher. 1987. The Greater Yellowstone Ecosystem: the ecosystem concept in natural resource policy and management. *Renew. Res. J.* 5(3):8-16. [11]

Clark, T. W., R. Crete, and J. Cada. 1989. Designing and managing successful endangered species recovery programs. *Environ. Mgmt.* 13:159–170. [13]

Clausen, J., D. D. Keck and W. M. Heisey. 1940. *Experimental Studies on the Nature of Species. I. Effects of Varied Environments on Western North American Plants.* Publication 520, Carnegie Institution of Washington, Washington, D.C. [3]

Clayton, C. and R. Mendelsohn. 1993. The value of watchable wildlife: A case study of McNeil River. *J. Environ. Mgmt.* 39: 101–106. [18]

Clebsch, E. E. C. and R. T. Busing. 1989. Secondary succession, gap dynamics, and community structure in a southern Appalachian cove forest. *Ecology* 70:728–735. [9]

Clegg, M., and 55 others. 1995. *Science and the Endangered Species Act.* National Academy Press, Washington, D.C. [3]

Clements, K. L. 1996. Beavers (*Castor canadensis*) on the upper coastal plain of South Carolina: Influences on avian community composition and landowner attitudes. M.S. thesis, University of Georgia, Athens. [8]

Clinebell II, R. R., O. L. Phillips, A. H. Gentry, N. Stark and H. Zuuring. 1995. Prediction of neotropical tree and liana species richness from soil and climatic data. *Biodiv. Conserv.* 4:56–90. [4]

Club of Earth. 1990. *Loss of Biodiversity Threatens Human Future.* Department of Biological Sciences, Stanford University, Stanford, CA. [5]

Cody, M. L. 1975. Towards a theory of continental species diversity: Bird distributions over Mediterranean habitat gradients. In M. L. Cody and J. M. Diamond (eds.), *Ecology and Evolution of Communities,* pp. 214–257. Belknap Press of Harvard University Press, Cambridge, MA. [4,10]

Cody, M. L. 1986. Structural niches in plant communities. In J. Diamond and T. J. Case (eds.), *Community Ecology,* pp. 381–405. Harper & Row, New York. [4]

Cogger, H. G. 1979. *Reptiles and Amphibians of Australia.* A. H. and A. W. Reed, Sydney. [8]

Colborn, T. 1995. Pesticides—how research has succeeded and failed to translate science into policy: Endocrinological effects on wildlife. *Environ. Health Perspect.* 103: 81–85. [17]

Colborn, T., D. Dumanoski and J. P. Myers. 1996. *Our Stolen Future.* Dutton, New York. [5,16]

Cole, J. 1996. The great eel rush: Maine's elvers under threat. *Audubon* July–August, 24, 26. [5]

Colinvaux, P. A., K.-B. Liu, P. DeOliveira, M. B. Bush, M. C. Miller and M. Steinitz Kannan. 1995. Temperature depression in the lowland tropics in glacial times. *Climate Change* 32:19–33. [4]

Colinvaux, P. A., M. Bush, M. K-Liu, P. E. De Oliveira, M. Riedinger and M. C. Miller. 1989. Amazonia without refugia: Vegetation and climate of the Amazon basin through a glacial cycle. Proceedings of the International Symposium on Global Changes in South America during the Quaternary. São Paulo, Brazil. [8]

Collins, B. S., K. P. Dunne and S. T. A. Pickett. 1985. Responses of forest herbs to canopy gaps. In S. T. A. Pickett and P. S. White (eds.), *The Ecology of Natural Disturbance and Patch Dynamics,* pp. 218–234. Academic Press, Orlando, FL. [6]

Colorado Department of Agriculture. 1996. What lies ahead for Colorado's ag lands? Colorado Department of Agriculture, Denver. [9]

Colwell, R. K. and G. C. Hurtt 1994. Nonbiological gradients in species richness and a spurious Rapoport effect. *Am. Nat.* 144: 570–595 [4]

Colwell, R. K. and J. A. Coddington. 1994. Estimating terrestrial biodiversity through extrapolation. *Phil. Trans. R. Soc. Lond. B* 345:101-118. [5]

Conant, R. 1975. *A Field Guide to Reptiles and Amphibians of Eastern and Central North America,* 2nd ed. Houghton Mifflin, Boston. [3]

Congdon, J. D., A. E. Dunham and R. C. van Loben Sels. 1993. Delayed sexual maturity and demographics of Blanding's turtles (*Emydoidea blandingi*): Implications for conservation and management of long-lived organisms. *Conserv. Biol.* 7:826–833. [7]

Connell, J. H. 1975. Some mechanisms producing structure in natural communities. In M. L. Cody and J. M. Diamond (eds.), *Ecology and Evolution of Communities,* pp. 460–490. Belknap Press of Harvard University Press, Cambridge, MA. [4]

Connell, J. H. 1978. Diversity in tropical rain forests and coral reefs. *Science* 199:1302–1310. [4,10]

Connell, J. H. 1983. On the prevalence and relative importance of interspecific competition: Evidence from field experiments. *Am. Nat.* 122:661–696. [4]

Connell, J. H. and E. Orias. 1964. The ecological regulation of species diversity. *Am. Nat.* 111:1119–1144. [4]

Connor, E. F. and E. D. McCoy. 1979. The statistics and biology of the species–area relationship. *Am. Nat.* 113:791–833. [9]

Cooke, G. D., E. B. Welch, S. A. Peterson and P. R. Newroth. 1986. *Lake and Reservoir Restoration.* Butterworth, Boston. [14]

Cooperrider, A. 1991. Reintegrating humans and nature: Introduction. In W. Hudson (ed.), *Landscape Linkages and Biodiversity,* pp. 141–148. Island Press, Washington, D.C. [11]

Corlett, R. T. 1992. The ecological transformation of Singapore, 1819–1990. *J. Biogeogr.* 19:411–420. [5]

Corn, P. S. and J. C. Fogleman. 1984. Extinction of montane populations of the northern leopard frog (*Rana pipiens*) in Colorado. *J. Herpetol.* 18(2):147–152. [5]

Corn, P. S. and F. A. Vertucci. 1992. Descriptive risk assessment of the effects of acidic deposition on Rocky Mountain amphibians. *J. Herpetol.* 26(4):361–369. [5]

Cornell, H. V. 1985. Species assemblages of cynipid gall wasps are not saturated. *Am. Nat.* 126:565–569.

Costanza, R. 1991. Assuring sustainability of ecological economic systems. In R. Costanza (ed.), *Ecological Economics,* pp. 331–343. Columbia University Press, New York. [18]

Costanza, R. (ed.). 1991. *Ecological Economics: The Science and Management of Sustainability.* Columbia University Press, New York. [15]

Costanza, R. and H. E. Daly. 1992. Natural capital and sustainable development. *Conserv. Biol.* 6:37–46. [15]

Costanza, R. and C. Folke. 1996. Valuing ecosystem services with efficiency, fairness and sustainability as goals. In G. Daily (ed.), *Nature's Services: Societal Dependence on Natural Ecosystems,* pp. 49–68. Island Press, Washington, D.C. [15]

Costanza, R. and C. Perrings. 1990. A flexible assurance bonding system for improved environmental management. *Ecol. Econ.* 2:57–76. [15]

Costanza, R., S. Farber and J. Maxwell. 1989. The valuation and management of wetland ecosystems. *Ecol. Econ.* 1:335–362. [15]

Costanza, R., H. E. Daly and J. A. Bartholomew. 1991. Goals, agenda, and policy recommendations for ecological economics. In R. Costanza (ed.), *Ecological Economics: The Science and Management of Sustainability,* pp. 1–21. Columbia University Press, New York. [15]

Costanza, R., O. Segura, and J. Martinez-Alier (eds.). 1996. *Getting Down to Earth: Practical Applications of Ecological Economics.* Island Press, Washington, D.C. [15]

Costanza, R., B. Norton and R. Bishop. 1997. The evolution of preferences: Why "sovereign" preferences may not lead to sustainable policies and what to do about it. *Ecol. Econ.* In press. [15]

Costanza, R., R. d'Arge, R. de Groot, S. Farber, M. Grasso, B. Hannon, S. Naeem, K. Limburg, J. Paruelo, R. V. O'Neill, R. Raskin, P. Sutton, and M. van den Belt. The total value of the world's ecosystem services and natural capital. *Nature.* In review.

Coston-Clements, L., L. R. Settle, E. E. Hoss and F. A. Cross. 1991. *Utilization of the Sargassum habitat by Marine Invertebrates and Vertebrates: A Review.* NOAA Technical Memorandum NMFS-SEFSC-296. [7]

Cottam, G. 1987. Community dynamics on an artificial prairie. In W. L. Jordan III, M. E. Gilpin and J. D. Aber (eds.), *Restoration Ecology,* pp. 257–270. Cambridge University Press, Cambridge. [14]

Coughenour, M. B. and F. J. Singer. 1996. Elk population processes in Yellowstone National Park under the policy of natural regulation. *Ecol. Appl.* 6:573–593. [7]

Courtenay, W. R., Jr. and G. K. Meffe. 1989. Small fishes in strange places: A review of introduced poeciliids. In G. K. Meffe and F. F. Snelson, Jr. (eds.), *Ecology and Evolution of Livebearing Fishes (Poeciliidae),* pp. 319–331. Prentice Hall, Englewood Cliffs, NJ. [8]

Cowling, R. M. (ed.). 1992. *The Ecology of Fynbos.* Oxford University Press, Cape Town [4]

Cowling, R. M., P. M. Holmes, and A. G. Rebelo. 1992. Plant diversity and endemism. In R. M. Cowling (ed.), *The Ecology of Fynbos,* pp. 62–112. Oxford University Press, Cape Town. [4]

Cox, G. W. and R. E. Ricklefs. 1977. Species diversity, ecological release, and community structuring in Caribbean land bird faunas. *Oikos* 29:60–66. [4]

Crabtree, A. F. (ed.). 1984. Proceedings of the Third International Symposium on Environmental Concerns in Rights-of-Way Management, Mississippi State University. [14]

Cracraft, J. 1983. Species concepts and speciation analysis. In R. F. Johnston (ed.), *Current Ornithology,* Vol. 1, pp. 159–187. Plenum Press, New York. [3]

Cracraft, J. 1992. The species of the birds-of-paradise (Paradisaeidae): Applying the phylogenetic species concept to a complex pattern of diversification. *Cladistics* 8:1–43. [3]

Craighead, F. C. 1971. *The Trees of South Florida.* University of Miami Press, Coral Gables, FL. [13]

Crance, C. and D. Draper. 1996. Socially cooperative choices: An approach to achieving resource sustainability in the coastal zone. *Environ. Mgmt.* 20:175–184. [12]

Creel, S. and N. Creel. 1996. Limitation of African wild dogs by competition with larger carnivores. *Conserv. Biol.* 10:526–538. [8]

Cromartie, J. 1994. Recent demographic and economic changes in the West. Economic Research Service, U.S. Department of Agriculture, Washington, D.C. [9]

Cronon, W. 1983. *Changes in the Land.* Hill and Wang, New York. [15]

Crouse, D., M. Donnelly, M. Bean, M. Sutton, and H. Upton. 1992. CITES and marine fishes: Report to the eighth meeting of the conference of the Parties, Kyoto (Japan), 2–13 March 1992. IUCN–World Conservation Union, Gland, Switzerland. [7]

Crouse, D. T., L. B. Crowder, and H. Caswell. 1987. A stage-based population model for loggerhead sea turtle (*Caretta caretta*) and implications for conservation. *Ecology* 68:1412–1423. [7, 13]

Crow, J. F. and M. Kimura. 1970. *An Introduction to Population Genetic Theory.* Harper & Row, New York. [6]

Crozier, R. H. 1992. Genetic diversity and the agony of choice. *Biol. Conserv.* 61:11–15. [3,6]

Crump, M. L., F. R. Hensley, and K. L. Clark. 1992. Apparent decline of the golden toad: Underground or extinct? *Copeia* 1992(2):413–420. [5]

Csuti, B., S. Polasky, P. H. Williams, R. L. Pressey, J. D. Camm, M. Kershaw, A. R. Kiester, B. Downs, R. Hamilton, M. Huso, and K. Sahr. 1997. A comparison of reserve selection algorithms using data on terrestrial vertebrates in Oregon. *Biol. Conserv.* 80:83–97. [12]

Culliton, T. J., M. A. Warren, and T. R. Goodspeed (eds.). 1990. 50 years of population change along the nation's coasts, 1960–2010. U.S. Dept. of Commerce, National Oceanic and Atmospheric Administration, Rockville, MD. 41 pp. [12]

Currie, D. J. and V. Paquin. 1987. Large-scale biogeographical patterns of species richness of trees. *Nature* 329:326–327. [4]

Curtis, J. T. 1956. The modification of midlatitude grasslands and forests by man. In W. L. Thomas (ed.), *Man's Role in Changing the Face of the Earth,* pp. 721–736. University of Chicago Press, Chicago. [9]

Cutler, A. 1991. Nested faunas and extinction in fragmented habitats. *Conserv. Biol.* 5:496–505. [9]

Cutlip, S. M. and A. H. Center. 1964. *Effective Public Relations.* 3rd ed. Prentice Hall, Englewood Cliffs, NJ. [13]

Czechura, G. V. and G. J. Ingram. 1990. *Taudactylus diurnus* and the case of the disappearing frogs. Memoirs of the Queensland Museum 29(2):361–365. [5]

Dahl, T. E. 1990. Wetland losses in the United States 1780's to 1980's. U.S. Department of Interior, Fish and Wildlife Service, Washington, D.C. [14]

Dahm, C. N. (ed.). 1995. Special Issue: Kissimmee River Restoration. *Restoration Ecology* 3(3):145-238. [14]

Daily, G. (ed.) 1997. *Ecosystem Services: Their Nature and Value.* Island Press, Washington, D.C. [1]

Daily, G. C. and P. R. Ehrlich. 1996. Preservation of Biodiversity in Small Rainforest Patches: Rapid Evaluations Using Butterfly Trapping. Unpublished data.

Daly, H. 1991. *Steady-State Economics,* 2nd ed. Island Press, Washington, D.C. [15,19]

Daly, H. E. 1992. Allocation, distribution, and scale: Towards an economics that is efficient, just, and sustainable. *Ecol. Econ.* 6:185–193. [15]

Dansereau, P. 1957. Description and recording of vegetation on a structural basis. *Ecology* 32:172–229. [4]

Darlington, P. J. 1957. *Zoogeography: The Geographical Distribution of Animals.* Wiley, New York. [5,9]

Darwin, C. R. 1859. *On The Origin of Species by Means of Natural Selection.* John Murray, London. [3,7]

Darwin, C. R. 1904. *The Descent of Man and Selection in Relation to Sex.* J. A. Hill and Company, New York. [2]
Dasmann, R. F. 1959. *Environmental Conservation.* John Wiley & Sons, New York. [1]
Dasmann, R. F. 1988. Biosphere reserves, buffers, and boundaries. *BioScience* 38: 487–489. [10]
Daugherty, C. H., A. Cree, J. M. Hay and M. B. Thompson. 1990. Neglected taxonomy and continuing extinctions of Tuatara (*Sphenodon*). *Nature* 347:177–179. [3,6]
Davidson, J. and H. G. Andrewartha. 1948a. Annual trends in a natural population of *Thrips imaginis* (Thysanoptera). *J. Anim. Ecol.* 17:193–199. [7]
Davidson, J. and H. G. Andrewartha. 1948b. The influence of rainfall, evaporation and atmospheric temperature on fluctuations in the size of a natural population of *Thrips imaginis* (Thysanoptera). *J. Anim. Ecol.* 17:200–222. [7]
Davidson, W. R. and V. F. Nettles. 1992. Relocation of wildlife: Identifying and evaluating disease risks. *Trans. N. Am. Wildlife and Natural Resources Conference* 57:466–473. [12]
Davies, S. 1987. *Tree of Life: Buddhism and Protection of Nature.* Buddhist Perception of Nature Project, Hong Kong. [2]
Davis, F. W., P. E. Stine, D. M. Stoms, M. I. Borchert, and A. D. Hollander. 1995. Gap analysis of the actual vegetation of California 1. The southwestern region. *Manrono* 42:40–78. [12]
Davis, G. M. and M. Mulvey. 1993. *Species status of Mill Creek.* Elliptio. SRO-NERP-22, Savannah River Site, Aiken, SC. [3]
Davis, M. B. 1981. Quaternary history and the stability of forest communities. In D. C. West, H. H. Shugart and D. B. Botkin (eds.), *Forest Succession: Concepts and Application,* pp. 132–153. Springer-Verlag, New York. [8,9]
Davis, M. B. 1986. Climatic instability, time lags, and community disequilibrium. In J. Diamond and T. J. Case (eds.), *Community Ecology,* pp. 269–284. Harper & Row, New York. [8]
Davis, S. M. 1991. Phosphorus inputs and vegetation sensitivity in an oligotrophic Everglades ecosystem. South Florida Water Management District. 37 pp. [13]
Davis, S. M. and J. C. Ogden (eds.), *Everglades, The Ecosystem and Its Restoration.* St. Lucie Press, Delray, FL. [13]
Davis, S. M., L. H. Gunderson, W. Park, J. Richardson, and J. Mattson. 1994. Landscape dimension, composition and function in a changing Everglades ecosystem. In S. M. Davis and J. C. Ogden (eds.), *Everglades, The Ecosystem and Its Restoration.* St. Lucie Press, Delray, FL. [13]
Davis, W. S. and T. P. Simon (eds.). 1995. Biological Assessment and Criteria: Tools for Water Resource Planning and Decision Making. Lewis, Boca Raton, FL. [14]
Dayton, P. K., S. F. Thrush, M. T. Agardy, and R. J. Hoffman. 1995. Environmental effects of marine fishing. *Aquatic Conservation: Marine and Freshwater Ecosystems* 5:205–232. [5]
de Boer, L. E. M. 1982. Karylogical problems in breeding owl monkeys, *Aotus trivirgatus. Int. Zoo Yearb.* 22:119–124. [6]
de Candolle, A. P. A. 1874. Constitution dans le règne végétal de groupes physiologiques applicables à la géographie ancienne et moderne. Archives des Sciences Physiques et Naturelles, Geneva, Switzerland. [4]
Deacon, J. E. and M. S. Deacon. 1979. Research on endangered fishes in national parks with special emphasis on the Devils Hole pupfish. In R. M. Lin (ed.), *Proceedings of the First Conference on Scientific Research in the National Parks,* pp. 9–19. U.S. National Park Service, Transactions and Proceedings, Series 5, Washington, D.C. [6]
Deacon, J. E. and C. D. Williams. 1991. Ash Meadows and the legacy of the Devils Hole pupfish. In W. L. Minckley and J. E. Deacon (eds.), *Battle against Extinction: Native Fish Management in the American West,* pp. 69–91. University of Arizona Press, Tucson. [10,12]
Delcourt, P. A. and H. R. Delcourt. 1987. *Long-Term Forest Dynamics of the Temperate Zone.* Springer-Verlag, New York. [8]
Del Tredici, P., H. Ling and G. Yang. 1992. The *Gingkos* of Tian Mu Shan. *Conserv. Biol.* 6(2):202–209. [2]
den Boer, P. J. 1970. On the significance of dispersal power for populations of carabid beetles (Coleoptera, Carabidae). *Oecologia* 4:1–28. [9]
Denniston, C. 1978. Small population size and genetic diversity: Implications for endangered species. In S. A. Temple (ed.), *Endangered Birds: Management Techniques for Preserving Threatened Species,* pp. 281–289. University of Wisconsin Press, Madison. [6]
Dery, D. 1984. *Problem Definition in Policy Analysis.* University Press of Kansas, Lawrence. [17]
Desert Fishes Council. *Proceedings of the Annual Symposium,* Vols. 1–24. Desert Fishes Council, Bishop, CA. [12]
Devall, B. and G. Sessions. 1985. *Deep Ecology: Living as if Nature Mattered.* Gibbs Smith, Salt Lake City, UT. [17]
DeVivo, J. C. 1996. Fish assemblages as indicators of water-quality within the Apalachicola–Chattahoochee–Flint (ACF) River Basin. Master's thesis, University of Georgia, Athens, GA. [9]
Diamond, J. 1989. Overview of recent extinctions. In M. Pearl and D. Western (eds.), *Conservation for the Twenty-First Century,* pp. 37–41. Oxford University Press, New York. [6]
Diamond, J. 1992. *The Third Chimpanzee: The Evolution and Future of the Human Animal.* Harper Perennial, New York. [1]
Diamond, J. M. 1972. Biogeographic kinetics: Estimation of relaxation times for avifaunas of Southwest Pacific islands. *Proc. Nat. Acad. Sci. U.S.A.* 69:3199–3203. [9]
Diamond, J. M. 1975. The island dilemma: Lessons of modern biogeographic studies for the design of natural preserves. *Biol. Conserv.* 7:129–146. [9]
Diamond, J. M. 1976. Island biogeography and conservation: Strategy and limitations. *Science* 193:1027–1029. [9]
Diamond, J. M. 1984a. Historic extinctions: A rosetta stone for understanding prehistoric extinctions. In P. S. Martin and R. G. Klein (eds.), *Quaternary Exinctions: A Prehistoric Revolution,* pp. 824–862. University of Arizona Press, Tucson. [8]
Diamond, J. M. 1984b. "Normal" extinctions of isolated populations. In M. H. Nitecki (ed.), *Extinctions,* pp. 191–246. University of Chicago Press, Chicago. [8]
Diamond, J. M. 1989. The present, past and future of human-caused extinctions. *Phil. Trans. R. Soc. Lond. B* 325:469–477. [5,8]
Diamond, J. M. 1996. A-bombs against amphibians. *Nature* 383:386–387. [8]
Diamond, J. M. and R. M. May. 1976. Island biogeography and the design of natural reserves. In R. M. May (ed.), *Theoretical Ecology: Principles and Applications,* pp. 163–186. W. B. Saunders, Philadelphia. [9]
Didham, R. K., J. Ghazoul, N. E. Stork, and A. J. Davis. 1996. Insects in fragmented forests: A functional approach. *Trends Ecol. Evol.* 11:255–260. [9]
Diefenbach, D. R. 1992. The reintroduction of bobcats to Cumberland Island, Georgia: Validation of the scent-station survey technique and analysis of population viability. Ph.D. dissertation, University of Georgia, Athens. [12]
Diefenbach, D. R., L. A. Baker, W. E. James, R. J. Warren, and M. J. Conroy. 1993. Reintroducing bobcats to Cumberland Island, Georgia. *Restor. Ecol.* 1:241–247. [12]
Diekelman, J. and R. Schuster. 1982. *Natural Landscaping: Designing with Native Plant Communities.* McGraw-Hill, New York. [14]
Dinerstein, E. and G. F. McCracken. 1990. Endangered greater one-horned rhinoceros carry high levels of genetic variation. *Conserv. Biol.* 7:39–52. [3]
Dinerstein, E. and E. Wikramanayake. 1993. Beyond "hotspots": How to prioritize investments in biodiversity in the Indo-Pacific region. *Conserv. Biol.* 7:53–65. [18]
Dixon, J. A. and M. M. Hufschmidt. 1990. *Economic Valuation Techniques for the Environment: A Case Study Workbook.* Johns Hopkins University Press, Baltimore. [15]
Doak, D. 1995. Source–sink models and the problem of habitat degradation: General models and applications to the Yellowstone grizzly. *Conserv. Biol.* 9:1370–1379. [7]
Doak, D., P. Kareiva, and B. Klepetka. 1994. Modeling population viability for the desert tortoise in the western Mohave Desert. *Ecol. Appl.* 4:446–460. [7]
Dobson, A. P. 1988. Restoring island ecosystems: The potential of parasites to control introduced mammals. *Conserv. Biol.* 2:31–39. [8]
Dobson, A. P. 1995. The ecology and epidemiology of rinderpest virus in Serengeti and Ngorongoro Crater conservation area. In A. R. E. Sinclair and P. Arcese (eds.), *Serengeti II: Dynamics, Management, and Conservation of an Ecosystem,* pp. 485–505. University of Chicago Press, Chicago. [8]
Dobson, A. P. and M. J. Crawley. 1994. Pathogens and the structure of plant communities. *Trends Ecol. Evol.* 9:393–398. [8]
Dobson, A. P. and P. J. Hudson. 1986. Parasites, disease and the structure of ecological communities. *Trends Ecol. Evol.* 1:11–15. [8]

Dobson, A. and M. Meagher. 1996. The population dynamics of brucellosis in the Yellowstone National Park. *Ecology* 77: 1026–1036. [7,8]

Dobzhansky, Th. 1970. *Genetics of the Evolutionary Process.* Columbia University Press, New York. [3]

Dodd, C. K. 1990. Effects of habitat fragmentation on a stream-dwelling species, the flattened musk turtle *Sternotherus depressus. Biol. Conserv.* 54:33–45. [9]

Dodson, C. H. and A. H. Gentry. 1991. Biological extinction in Western Ecuador. *Ann. Mo. Bot. Gard.* 78:273–295. [5]

Dold, C. 1995. Breeding plan helps black-footed ferrets in making comeback. *The New York Times*, Oct. 31, 1995, p. B6. [13]

Dominey, W. J. 1981. Anti-predator function of bluegill sunfish nesting colonies. *Nature* 290:586–588. [7]

Donoghue, M. J. 1985. A critique of the biological species concept and recommendation for a phylogenetic alternative. *The Bryologist* 88:172–181. [3]

Donovan, T. M., F. R. Thompson III, J. Faaborg, and J. R. Probst. 1995. Reproductive success of migratory birds in habitat sources and sinks. *Conserv. Biol.* 9:1380–1395. [9]

Doob, L. W. 1995. *Sustainers and Sustainability: Attitudes, Attributes, and Actions for Survival.* Praeger, Westport, CT. [17]

Dorf, E. 1976. Climate changes of the past and present. In C. A. Ross (ed.), *Paleobiogeography,* pp. 384–412. Benchmark Papers in Geology, 31. Dowden, Hutchinson and Ross, Stroudsburg, PA. [10]

Dowie, M. 1995. *Losing Ground: American Environmentalism at the Close of the Twentieth Century.* MIT Press, Cambridge, Mass. [16]

Drake, J. A., H. A. Mooney, F. di Castri, R. H. Groves, F. J. Kruger, M. Rejmanek and M. Williamson (eds.). 1989. *Biological Invasions: A Global Perspective.* John Wiley & Sons, New York. [8]

Drayton, B. and R. B. Primack. 1996. Plant species lost in an isolated conservation area in Metropolitan Boston from 1894 to 1993. *Conserv. Biol.* 10:30–39. [9]

Drobney, P. 1994. Iowa prairie rebirth. Rediscovering natural heritage at Walnut Creek National Wildlife Refuge. *Rest. Mgmt. Notes.* 12:16–22. [14]

Drost, C. A. and G. M. Fellers. 1996. Collapse of a regional frog fauna in the Yosemite area of the California Sierra Nevada, USA. *Conserv. Biol.* 10(2):414–425. [5]

Dryzek, J. S. 1990. *Discursive Democracy: Politics, Policy, and Political Science.* Cambridge University Press, New York. [17]

Dubinsky, Z. (ed.). 1990. *Coral Reefs.* Ecosystems of the World, Vol. 25. Elsevier, Amsterdam. [5]

Duda, M. D. 1991. A Bridge to the Future: The Wildlife Diversity Funding Initiative. A Needs Assessment for the Fish and Wildlife Conservation Act. Western Association of Fish and Wildlife Agencies. [14]

Dunning, J. B. and B. D. Watts. 1990. Regional differences in habitat occupancy by Bachman's Sparrow. *Auk* 107:463-472. [7]

Dunning, J. B., B. J. Danielson and H. R. Pulliam. 1992. Ecological processes that affect populations in complex landscapes. *Oikos* 65:169–175. [9]

Dunning, J. B., R. Borgella, K. Clements, and G. K. Meffe. 1995. Patch isolation, corridor effects, and colonization by a resident sparrow in a managed pine woodland. *Conserv. Biol.* 9:542–550. [7]

Dunwiddie, P. W. 1992. On setting goals: From snapshots to movies and beyond. *Rest. Mgmt. Notes.* 10(2):116–119. [14]

Dunwoody, S. 1986. The scientist as source. In S. Friedman, S. Dunwoody, and C. L. Rogers (eds.), *Scientists and Journalists,* pp. 3–16. The Free Press, New York. [16]

Durning, A. 1992. *How Much is Enough? The Consumer Society and the Future of the Earth,* W. W. Norton, New York. [16]

Dvorak, A. J. (tech. ed.). 1984. Ecological Studies of Disturbed Landscapes: A Compendium of the Results of Five Years of Research Aimed at the Restoration of Disturbed Ecosystems. U.S. Department of Energy, NTIS, Springfield, VA. [14]

Dworkin, R. 1994. *Life's Dominion.* Vintage, New York. [15]

Eagan, D. and D. Orr (eds.). 1992. *The Campus and Environmental Responsibility.* Jossey-Bass Publishers, San Francisco. [16]

Eagar, R. M. C. 1978. Shape and function of the shell: A comparison of some living and fossil bivalve molluscs. *Biol. Rev.* 53:169–210. [3]

East, R. 1981. Species–area curves and populations of large mammals in African savanna reserves. *Biol. Conserv.* 21:111–126. [10]

EBD (Estación Biológica de Doñana). 1991. Radio-rastreo y mortalidad del águila imperial y el lince en el Parque Nacional de Doñana y su entorno. Report. [13]

Ebenhard, T. 1988. Introduced birds and mammals and their ecological effects. *Swed. Wildl. Res.* 13:1–107. [8]

Echelle, A. A. 1991. Conservation genetics and genetic diversity in freshwater fishes of western North America. In W. L. Minckley and J. E. Deacon (eds.), *Battle Against Extinction: Native Fish Management in the American West,* pp. 141–153. University of Arizona Press, Tucson. [6]

Echelle, A. A., A. F. Echelle and D. R. Edds. 1987. Population structure of four pupfish species (Cyprinodontidae: Cyprinodon) from the Chihuahuan Desert region of New Mexico and Texas: Allozymic variation. *Copeia* 987(3):668–681. [6]

Echelle, A. F., A. A. Echelle and D. R. Edds. 1989. Conservation genetics of a spring-dwelling desert fish, the Pecos gambusia, *Gambusia nobilis* (Poeciliidae). *Conserv. Biol.* 3:159–169. [6]

Edmondson, W. T. 1991. *The Uses of Ecology: Lake Washington and Beyond.* University of Washington Press, Seattle and London. [14]

Edwards, R., S. Brechtel, R. Bromley, D. Hjertaas, B. Johns, E. Kuyt, J. Lewis, N. Manners, R. Stardom, and G. Tarry. 1994. *National Recovery Plan for the Whooping Crane.* Report Number 6. Recovery of Nationally Endangered Wildlife (RENEW) Committee, Ottawa. [13]

Edwards, T. C., C. G. Homer, S. D. Bassett, A. Falconer, R. D. Ramsy, and D. W. Wight. 1995. Utah Gap Analysis: An environmental information system. CD-ROM. Final project report 95-1. Utah Cooperative Fish and Wildlife Research Unit, Utah State University, Logan Utah. [12]

Edwards, T. C., Jr., E. T. Deshler, D. Foster, and G. G. Moisen. 1996. Adequacy of wildlife habitat relation models for estimating spatial distributions of terrestrial vertebrates. *Conserv. Biol.* 10:263–270. [12]

Ehrenfeld, D. W. 1970. *Biological Conservation.* Holt, Rinehart and Winston, New York. [1]

Ehrenfeld, D. W. 1976. The conservation of non-resources. *Am. Sci.* 64:660–668. [2]

Ehrenfeld, D. W. 1981. *The Arrogance of Humanism.* Oxford University Press, New York. [15,18,19]

Ehrenfeld, D. W. 1988. Why put a value on biodiversity? In E. O. Wilson and F. M. Peter (eds.), *Biodiversity,* pp. 212–216. National Academy Press, Washington, D.C. [2,15]

Ehrenfeld, D. W. 1991. The management of diversity: A conservation paradox. In F. H. Bormann and S. R. Kellert (eds.), *Ecology, Economics, Ethics: The Broken Circle,* pp. 26–39. Yale University Press, New Haven. [6,11]

Ehrenfeld, D. W. 1993a. *Beginning Again: People and Nature in the New Millennium.* Oxford University Press, Oxford. [16]

Ehrenfeld, D. W. 1993b. Forgetting. In *Beginning Again: People and Nature in the New Millennium*, pp. 65–72. Oxford University Press, New York. [19]

Ehrlich, P. R. 1961. Has the biological species concept outlived its usefulness? *Syst. Zool.* 10:167–176. [3]

Ehrlich, P. R. 1986. Extinction: What is happening now and what needs to be done. In D. K. Elliott (ed.), *Dynamics of Extinction,* pp. 157–164. John Wiley & Sons, New York. [3,4]

Ehrlich, P. R. and A. H. Ehrlich. 1981. *Extinction: The Causes and Consequences of the Disappearance of Species.* Random House, New York. [5]

Ehrlich, P. R. and A. H. Ehrlich. 1990. *The Population Explosion.* Simon & Schuster, New York. [19]

Ehrlich, P. R. and R. W. Holm. 1963. *The Process of Evolution.* McGraw-Hill, New York. [3]

Ehrlich, P. R. and D. D. Murphy. 1987. Conservation lessons from long-term studies of checkerspot butterflies. *Conserv. Biol.* 1:122–131. [6,7,10]

Ehrlich, P. R. and H. A. Mooney. 1983. Extinction, substitution, and ecosystem services. *BioScience* 33:248–254. [10]

Ehrlich, P. R., D. D. Murphy, M. C. Singer, C. B. Sherwood, R. R. White and I. L. Brown. 1980. Extinction, reduction, stability and increase: The responses of checkerspot butterfly (*Euphydryas*) populations to the California drought. *Oecologia* 46:101–105. [7]

Ehrlich, P. R., A. H. Ehrlich, and G. C. Daily, 1995. *The Stork and the Plow: The Equity Answer to the Human Dilemma*. Putnam, New York. [5]

Eldridge, N. (ed.). 1992. *Systematics, Ecology, and the Biodiversity Crisis*. Columbia University Press, New York. [3]

Elliot, R. 1992. Intrinsic value, environmental obligation and naturalness. *Monist* 75: 138–160. [2]

Ellis, A. J. 1975. Geothermal systems and power development. *Am. Sci.* 63(5):510–521. [12]

Ellis, D. H., G. F. Gee, and C. M. Mirande. 1996. *Cranes: Their Biology, Husbandry, and Conservation*. 2nd ed. Hancock House, Blaine, WA. [13]

Elton, C. S. 1946. Competition and the structure of ecological communities. *J. Anim. Ecol.* 15:54–68. [8]

Elton, C. S. 1949. Population interspersion: an essay on animal community patterns. *J. Ecol.* 37:1-23. [7]

Elton, C. S. 1973. The structure of invertebrate populations inside tropical rainforest. *J. Animal Ecol.* 42:55–104. [5]

Emberger, L., H. Gaussen, M. Kass, and A. de Phillips. 1976. *Carte Bioclimatique de la zone Mediterranenne*. UNESCO-FAO, Paris/Rome. [13]

Endler, J. A. 1973. Gene flow and population differentiation. *Science* 179:243–250. [6]

Endler, J. A. 1986. *Natural Selection in the Wild*. Princeton University Press, Princeton, NJ. [6]

Endler, J. A. 1989. Conceptual and other problems in speciation. In D. Otter and J. Endler (eds.), *Speciation and its Consequences*, pp. 625–648. Sinauer Associates, Sunderland, MA. [3]

Engels, T. M. and C. W. Sexton. 1994. Negative correlation of blue jays and golden-cheeked warblers near an urbanizing area. *Conserv. Biol.* 8:286–290. [9]

Environmental Protection Agency. 1994. Integrated Ecosystem Protection Research Program: A Conceptual Plan. Working draft, 89pp. [11]

Equipo 28. 1985. *El Río. El Bajo Guadalquivir*. Equipo 28, Sevilla. [13]

Erickson, R. C. 1973. Some black-footed ferret research needs. In R. L. Linder and C. N. Hillman (eds.), *Proceedings of the Black-footed Ferret and Prairie Dog Workshop*, pp. 153–164. South Dakota State University, Brookings, SD. [13]

Errington, P. L. and F. N. Hamerstrom, Jr. 1937. The evaluation of nesting losses and juvenile mortality of the ring-neck pheasant. *J. Wildl. Mgmt.* 1:3–20. [1]

Erwin, T. 1982. Tropical forests: Their richness in Coleoptera and other arthropod species. *Coleopt. Bull.* 36:74–82. [5]

Erwin, T. L. 1988. The tropical forest canopy: The heart of biotic diversity. In E. O. Wilson and F. M. Peter (eds.), *Biodiversity*, pp. 123–129. National Academy Press, Washington, D.C. [2,4]

Erwin, T. L. 1991. How many species are there?: Revisited. *Conserv. Biol.* 5:330–333. [5]

Eskey, C. R. and V. H. Haas. 1940. Plague in the western part of the U.S. *U.S. Public Health Bulletin* no. 254. [13]

Esser, G. 1995. Contribution of Monsoon Asia to the carbon budget of the biosphere, past and future. *Vegetatio* 121:175–188. [5]

Estes, J. A. and J. F. Palmisano. 1974. Sea otters: Their role in structuring nearshore communities. *Science* 185:1058–1060. [8]

Ewel, J. J. 1986. Invasibility: Lessons from South Florida. In H. A. Mooney and J. A. Drake (eds.), *Ecology of Biological Invasions of North America and Hawaii*, pp. 214–230. Springer-Verlag, New York. [8]

Faaborg, J. 1979. Qualitative patterns of avian extinction on Neotropical land-bridge islands: Lessons for conservation. *J. Appl. Ecol.* 16:99–107. [9]

Faeth, S. H. and E. F. Connor. 1979. Supersaturated and relaxing island faunas: A critique of the species–age relationship. *J. Biogeogr.* 6:311–316. [9]

Fahrig, L. 1996. Fragmentation and corridors: The misuse of theory in conservation biology. *Bull. Ecol. Soc. Am. (Suppl.)* 77(3):134. [9]

Fahrig, L. and G. Merriam. 1985. Habitat patch connectivity and population survival. *Ecology* 66:1762–1768. [9]

Fahrig, L. and G. Merriam. 1994. Conservation of fragmented populations. *Conserv. Biol.* 8:50–59. [9]

Fahrig, L., J. H. Pedlar, S. E. Pope, P. D. Taylor, and J. F. Wegner. 1995. Effects of road traffic on amphibian density. *Biol. Conserv.* 73:177–182. [9]

Faith, D. P. 1992. Conservation evaluation and phylogenetic diversity. *Biol. Conserv.* 61:1–10. [3,6]

Falconer, D. S. 1981. *Introduction to Quantitative Genetics*, 2nd ed. Longman, New York. [6]

Falk, D. A. and K. E. Holsinger, (eds.). 1991. *Genetics and Conservation of Rare Plants*. Oxford University Press, New York. [6]

FAO. 1981. Tropical Forest Resources Assessment Project. Food and Agricultural Organization of the United Nations, Rome. [5]

FAO. 1988. An Interim Report on the State of Forest Resources in Developing Countries. Food and Agricultural Organization of the United Nations, Rome. [5]

FAO. 1992. Marine fisheries and the law of the sea: A decade of change. Food and Agriculture Organization of the United Nations, Rome. [5]

FAO. 1993. Tropical Forest Resources Assessment. Food and Agricultural Organization of the United Nations, Rome. [5]

FAO. 1994. Review of the state of world marine fishery resources. Food and Agriculture Organization of the United Nations, Rome. 335 pp. [5]

FAO. 1995. The state of world fisheries and aquaculture. Food and Agriculture Organization of the United Nations, Rome. 57 pp. [5]

Farber, S. and R. Costanza. 1987. The Economic Value of Wetlands Systems. *J. Environ. Mgmt.* 24:41–51. [15]

Farnsworth, N. R. 1988. Screening plants for new medicines. In E. O. Wilson and F. M. Peter (eds.), *Biodiversity*, pp. 83–97. National Academy Press, Washington, D.C. [2]

Feder, H. M. 1966. Cleaning symbiosis in the marine environment. In S. M. Henry (ed.), *Symbiosis*, pp. 327–380. Academic Press, New York. [8]

Federal Agencies Committee. 1995. Data/GIS workgroup report on coordination, compatibility, and standardization of ecological resource inventories. Chesapeake Bay Program, Annapolis, MD. [12]

Feldmann, A. L. 1995. The effects of beaver (*Castor canadensis*) impoundment on plant diversity and community composition in the coastal plain of South Carolina. M.S. thesis, University of Georgia, Athens. [8]

Fellers, G. M. and C. A. Drost. 1993. Disappearance of the Cascades frog *Rana cascadae* at the southern end of its range, California, USA. *Biol. Conserv.* 65:177–181. [5]

FEMAT. 1993. Forest ecosystem management: An ecological, economic, and social assessment. Report of the Forest Ecosystem Management Assessment Team. USDA Forest Service, USDC National Marine Fisheries Service, USDI Bureau of Land Management, USDI Fish and Wildlife Service, USDI National Park Service, Environmental Protection Agency, Washington, D.C. [11]

Fenchel, T. 1975. Character displacement and coexistence in mud snails (Hydrobiidae). *Oecologia* 20:19–32. [8]

Fernández, J. A. 1982. *Guía de campo del Parque Nacional de Doñana*. Omega, Barcelona. [13]

Fernández-Delgado, C. 1987. Ictiofauna del estuario del Guadalquivir: su distribución y biología de las especies sedentarias. Ph.D. dissertation, University of Córdoba, Córdoba. [13]

Fernández-Delgado, C. 1996. La construcción de la presa de cierre en el Bajo Guadalquivir: una nueva amenaza para Doñana y su entorno. *Quercus* (127). In press. [13]

Fernández-Delgado, C., M. Herrera Arroyo; F. J. Sánchez-Polaina, and J. C. Ariza Vargas. 1994. *Inventario de las especies de peces del Parque Nacional de Doñana. Biología, Ecología y Conservación*. Convenio Instituto para la Conservación de la Naturaleza (ICONA), Universidad de Córdoba. 2 vols. Final report. [13]

Ferreras, P., J. J. Aldama, J. F. Beltran and M. Delibes. 1992. Rates and causes of mortality in a fragmented population of Iberian lynx *Felis pardina* Temminck, 1824. *Biol. Conserv.* 61:197–202. [9]

Finlayson, B. J. and K. M. Verrue. 1982. Toxicities of copper, zinc and cadmium mixtures to juvenile chinook salmon. *Trans. Amer. Fish. Soc.* 111:645–650. [11]

Fischer, M. and J. Stöcklin. 1997. Local extinctions of plants in remnants of extensively used calcareous grasslands 1950–1985. *Conserv. Biol.* 11:727–737. [9]

Fisher, A. C. and M. Hanemann. 1985. Endangered species: The economics of irreversible damage. In D. O. Hall, N. Myers and N. S. Margaris (eds.), *Economics of Ecosystem Management*, pp. 129–138. W. Junk, Dordrecht. [15]

Fisher, R. A. 1930. *The Genetical Theory of Natural Selection.* Clarendon Press, Oxford. [6]

Flader, S. L. and J. B. Callicott. 1991. *The River of the Mother of God and Other Essays by Aldo Leopold.* University of Wisconsin Press, Madison, WI. [9]

Flannery, T. 1994. *The Future Eaters.* Reed Books, Sydney, Australia. [17]

Fleming, D. M., W. F. Wolf and D. L. DeAngelis. 1994. Importance of landscape heterogeneity to Wood Storks in the Florida Eerglades. *Env. Mgmt.* 18:743– 757.

Font, I. 1983. *Climatología de España y Portugal.* Instituto Nacional de Meteorología, Madrid. [13]

Foose, T. J. 1983. The relevance of captive populations to the conservation of biotic diversity. In C. M. Schonewald-Cox, S. M. Chambers, B. MacBryde and L. Thomas (eds.), *Genetics and Conservation: A Reference for Managing Wild Animal and Plant Populations,* pp. 374–401. Benjamin/Cummings, Menlo Park, CA. [6]

Forcan, P. 1979. A world order for whales. In T. Wilkes (ed.), *Project Interspeak,* pp. 77–82. Graphic Arts Center, Portland, OR. [2]

Fore, L. S., J. R. Karr, and R. W. Wisseman. 1996. Assessing invertebrate responses to human activities: Evaluating alternative approaches. *J. N. Am. Benthol. Soc.* 15:212–231. [14]

Foreman, D., J. Davis, D. John, R. Noss and M. Soulé. 1992. The Wildlands Project Mission Statement. Special Issue. *Wild Earth:* 3–4. [3,10]

Forest Ecosystem Management Assessment Team. 1993. Forest Ecosystem Management: An Ecological, Economic, and Social Assessment. 1993-793-071. U.S. Government Printing Office, Washington, D. C. [11]

Forman, R. T. T. 1990. Ecologically sustainable landscapes: The role of spatial configuration. In I. S. Zonneveld and R. T. T. Forman (eds.), *Changing Landscapes: An Ecological Perspective,* pp. 173–198. Springer-Verlag, New York. [10]

Forman, R. T. T. 1992. Landscape corridors: From theoretical foundations to public policy. In D. A. Saunders and R. J. Hobbs, (eds.), *Nature Conservation 2: The Role of Corridors,* pp. 71–84. Surrey Beatty, Chipping Norton, Australia. [10]

Forman, R. T. T. 1993. *Landscape and Regional Ecology.* Cambridge University Press, Cambridge. [10]

Forman, R. T. T. 1995. *Land Mosaics: The Ecology of Landscapes and Regions.* Cambridge University Press, Cambridge. [10]

Forman, R. T. T. and S. K. Collinge. 1997. Nature conserved in changing landscapes with and without spatial planning. *Landscape and Urban Planning.* In press. [10]

Forman, R. T. T. and M. Godron. 1986. *Landscape Ecology.* John Wiley & Sons, New York. [7,9,10]

Forman, R. T. T. and P. N. Moore. 1991. Theoretical foundations for understanding boundaries in landscape mosaics. In A. J. Hansen and F. di Castri (eds.), *Landscape Boundaries: Consequences for Biodiversity and Ecological Flows,* pp. 236–258. Springer-Verlag, New York. [10]

Forman, R. T. T., A. E. Galli and C. F. Leck. 1976. Forest size and avian diversity in New Jersey woodlots with some land use implications. *Oecologia.* 26:1–8. [10]

Forrest, S. C., D. E. Biggins, L. Richardson, T. W. Clark, T. M. Campbell III, K. A. Fagerstone and E. T. Thorne. 1988. Population attributes for the black-footed ferret (*Mustela nigripes*) at Meeteetse, Wyoming, 1981–1985. *J. Mammal.* 69:261– 273. [13]

14th Dalai Lama (Tenzin Gyatso). 1992. A Tibetan Buddhist perspective on spirit in nature. In S. C. Rockefeller and J. C. Elder (eds.), *Spirit and Nature: Why the Environment is a Religious Issue,* pp. 109–123. Beacon Press, Boston. [2]

Fox, W. 1990. *Toward a Transpersonal Ecology. Developing New Directions for Environmentalism.* Shambala, Boston. [2]

Fox, W. 1993. What does the recognition of intrinsic value entail? *Trumpeter* 10:101. [2]

Frankel, O. H. 1983. The place of management in conservation. In C. M. Schonewald-Cox, S. M. Chambers, B. MacBryde and L. Thomas (eds.), *Genetics and Conservation: A Reference for Managing Wild Animal and Plant Populations,* pp. 1–14. Benjamin/ Cummings, Menlo Park, CA. [6]

Frankel, O. H. and M. E. Soulé. 1981. *Conservation and Evolution.* Cambridge University Press, Cambridge. [1,6,10]

Frankham, R. 1995. Inbreeding and extinction: A threshold effect. *Conserv. Biol.* 9:792–799. [6]

Franklin, I. R. 1980. Evolutionary change in small populations. In M. E. Soulé and B. A. Wilcox (eds.), *Conservation Biology: An Evolutionary-Ecological Perspective,* pp. 135–139. Sinauer Associates, Sunderland, MA. [6]

Franklin, J. F. and R. T. T. Forman. 1987. Creating landscape patterns by forest cutting: Ecological consequences and principles. *Landscape Ecol.* 1:5–18. [9,10]

Fraver, S. 1994. Vegetation responses along edge-to-interior gradients in the mixed hardwood forests of the Roanoke River Basin, North Carolina. *Conserv. Biol.* 8:822–832. [9]

Frazer, N. B. 1983. Survivorship of adult female loggerhead sea turtles, *Carretta caretta,* nesting on Little Cumberland Island, Georgia, USA. *Herpetologica* 39:436–447. [7]

Frazer, N. B. 1984. A model for assessing mean age-specific fecundity in sea turtle populations. *Herpetologica* 40:281–291. [7]

Frazer, N. B. 1992. Sea turtle conservation and halfway technology. *Conserv. Biol.* 6: 179–184. [7]

Frederick, P. C. and M. W. Collopy. 1989. Nesting success of five Ciconiiform species in relation to water conditions in the Florida Everglades. *Auk* 106:625–634. [13]

Freed, L. A., S. Conant and R. C. Fleischer. 1988. Evolutionary ecology and radiation of Hawaiian passerine birds. *Trends Ecol. Evol.* 2:196–202. [8]

Freeman, M. III. 1979. *The Benefits of Environmental Improvements.* Resources for the Future, Washington, D.C. [18]

Freemark, K. E. and H. G. Merriam. 1986. Importance of area and habitat heterogeneity to bird assemblages in temperate forest fragments. *Biol. Conserv.* 36:115–141. [9]

Freemuth, J. C. 1991. *Islands Under Siege: National Parks and the Politics of External Threats.* University Press of Kansas, Lawrence, KS. [10]

Friedel, M. H. 1991. Range condition assessment and the concept of thresholds: A viewpoint. *J. Range Mgmt.* 44:422–426. [14]

Friedman, S. M. 1983. Environmental reporting: Problem child of the media. *Environment* 25: 24–25. [16]

Friedman, S. M. 1986. The journalist's world. In S. Friedman, S. Dunwoody, and C. L. Rogers (eds.), *Scientists and Journalists,* pp. 17–41. The Free Press, New York. [16]

Friesen, L. E., P. F. J. Eagles, and R. J. MacKay. 1995. Effects of residential development on forest-dwelling neotropical migrant songbirds. *Conserv. Biol.* 9:1408–1414. [9]

Fritts, S. H. and L. N. Carbyn. 1995. Population viability, nature reserves, and the outlook for gray wolf conservation in North America. *Restor. Ecol.* 3:26–38. [12]

Fujita, R. M., M. S. Epstein, T. J. Goreau and K. Gjerde. 1992. *A Guide to Protecting Coral Reefs.* United Nations Environment Programme, Nairobi, Kenya. [5]

Funch, P. and R. M. Kristensen. 1995. Cycliophora is a new phylum with affinities to Entoprocta and Ectoprocta. *Nature* 378: 711–714. [4]

Funtowicz, S. O. and J. R. Ravetz. 1991. A New Scientific Methodology for Global Environmental Issues. In R. Costanza (ed.), *Ecological Economics: The Science and Management of Sustainability,* pp. 137–152. Columbia University Press, New York. [16]

Futuyma, D. J. 1986. *Evolutionary Biology,* 2nd ed. Sinauer Associates, Sunderland, MA. [3,4]

Gaines, S. D. and J. Lubchenco. 1982. A unified approach to marine plant-herbivore interactions. II. Biogeography. *Ann. Rev. Ecol. Syst.* 13:111–138. [4]

Gambradt, S. C. and L. B. Kats. 1996. Effect of introduced crayfish and mosquitofish on California newts. *Conserv. Biol.* 10: 1155–1162. [8]

Game, M. and G. F. Peterken. 1984. Nature reserve selection strategies in the woodlands of Central Lincolnshire, England. *Biol. Conserv.* 29:157–181. [10]

García, L., J. Calderón, and J. Castroviejo. 1989. *Las aves de Doñana y su entorno.* Estación Biológica de Doñana (CSIC)—Cooperativa Marismas del Rocío, Sevilla. [13]

García-Novo, F., L. Ramírez, and A. Martínez. 1976. El sistema de dunas de Doñana. *Naturalia Hispanica* N° 5. Publicaciones del Ministerio de Agricultura, Pesca y Alimentación. Secretaría General Técnica, Madrid. [13]

García-Novo, F., J. Merino Ortega, L. Ramírez, L. Rodenas, F. Sancho, A. Torres, F. González-Bernaldez, F. Díaz, C. Allier, V. Bresset, and A. Lacoste. 1977. *Doñana. Prospección e inventario de sus ecosistemas.* ICONA. Monografía N° 18. Publicaciones del Ministerio de Agricultura, Pesca y Alimentación. Secretaría General Técnica, Madrid [13]

Garland, T. and W. G. Bradley. 1984. Effects of a highway on Mojave Desert rodent populations. *Am. Midl. Nat.* 111:47–56. [9]

Garrott, R. A., P. J. White, and C. A. Vanderbilt White. 1993. Overabundance: An issue for conservation biologists? *Conserv. Biol.* 7:946–949. [8]

Gaston, K. J. 1991. The magnitude of global insect species richness. *Conserv. Biol.* 5: 283–296. [2]

Gates, D. M. 1993. *Climate Change and Its Biological Consequences.* Sinauer Associates, Sunderland, MA. [10]

Gates, J. E. and L. W. Gysel. 1978. Avian nest dispersion and fledgling success in field-forest ecotones. *Ecology* 59:871–883. [9]

Geist, V. 1971. *The Mountain Sheep.* University of Chicago Press, Chicago. [5]

Gentry, A. H. 1986. Endemism in tropical versus temperate plant communities. In M. E. Soulé (ed.), *Conservation Biology: The Science of Scarcity and Diversity*, pp. 153–181. Sinauer Associates, Sunderland, MA. [9]

Gentry, A. H. 1988. Changes in plant community diversity and floristic composition of environmental and geographical gradients. *Ann. M. Bot. Gar.* 75:1–34. [4]

Gentry, A. H. 1992. Tropical forest biodiversity: Distributional patterns and their conservational significance. *Oikos* 63:19–28. [5]

Georgiadis, N. and A. Balmford. 1992. The calculus of conserving biological diversity. *Trends Ecol. Evol.* 7:321–322. [3]

Gerrodette, T. and W. G. Gilmartin. 1990. Demographic consequences of changed pupping and hauling sites of the Hawaiian monk seal. *Conserv. Biol.* 4:423–430. [7]

Getz, W. M. and R. G. Haight. 1989. *Population Harvesting.* Monographs in Population Biology, no. 27. Princeton University Press, Princeton, NJ. [12]

Gibbs, J. P. and J. Faaborg. 1990. Estimating the viability of ovenbird and Kentucky warbler populations in forest fragments. *Conserv. Biol.* 4:193–196. [9]

Gibson, C. C. and S. A. Marks. 1995. Transforming rural hunters into conservationists: An assessment of community-based wildlife management programs in Africa. *World Devel.* 23: 941–957. [18]

Gilbert, L. E. 1980. Food web organization and conservation of neotropical diversity. In M. E. Soulé and B. A. Wilcox, (eds.), *Conservation Biology: An Evolutionary-Ecological Perspective*, pp. 11–34. Sinauer Associates, Sunderland, MA. [5]

Gilpin, M. and I. Hanski, (eds.). 1991. *Metapopulation Dynamics: Empirical and Theoretical Investigations.* Academic Press, San Diego. [11]

Gilpin, M. E. and M. E. Soulé. 1986. Minimum viable populations: Processes of species extinction. In M. E. Soulé (ed.), *Conservation Biology: The Science of Scarcity and Diversity*, pp. 19–34. Sinauer Associates, Sunderland, MA. [6,7]

Ginsburg, R. 1993. Quantitative Risk Assessment and the Illusion of Safety. *New Solutions*, Winter, 8–15. [16]

Given, D. R. 1994. *Principles and Practice of Plant Conservation.* Timber Press, Portland, OR. [15]

Glidden, C. and J. Goudet. 1994. The genetic structure of metapopulations and conservation biology. In V. Loeschcke, J. Tomiuk, and S. K. Jain (eds.), *Conservation Genetics*, pp. 107–114. Birkhauser Verlag, Basel, Switzerland. [6]

Gliessman, S. R. 1985. An agroecological approach for researching agroecosystems. In H. Vogtmann, E. Boehncke, and I. Fricke (eds.), *The Importance of Biological Agriculture in a World of Diminishing Resources*, pp. 184–199. Verlagsgruppe, Witzenhausen. [2]

Glynn, C. J. and A. R. Tims. 1982. Sensationalism in science issues: A case study. *Journalism Q.* 59:126–131. [16]

Goldschmidt, T., F. Witte and J. Wanink. 1993. Cascading effects of the introduced Nile perch on the detritivorous/phytoplanktivorous species in the sublittoral areas of Lake Victoria. *Conserv. Biol.* 7:686–700. [5]

Goldsmith, Sir J. 1994. *The Trap.* Carroll & Graf Publishers, New York. [19]

Goldstein, B. 1992. The struggle over ecosystem management at Yellowstone. *BioScience* 42: 183–187. [7]

Golley, F. B. 1994. Rebuilding a humane and ethical decision system for investing in natural capital. In A.-M. Jansson, M. Hammer, C. Folke, and R. Costanza (eds.), *Investing in Natural Capital: The Ecological Economics Approach to Sustainability*, pp. 169–178. Island Press, Washington, D.C. [15]

González, M. J., L. M. Hernández, M. C. Rico, and G. Baluja. 1984. Residues of organochlorine pesticides, polychlorinated biphenzis and heavy metals in the eggs of predatory birds from Doñana National Park (Spain), 1980–1983. *J. Environ. Sci. Health*, B19 (8,9): 759–772. [13]

Goodland, R. 1995. The concept of environmental sustainability. *Annu. Rev. Ecol. Syst.* 26:1–24. [18]

Goodman, R. 1980. Taoism and ecology. *Envir. Ethics* 2:73–80. [2]

Goodpaster, K. E. 1978. On being morally considerable. *J. Philos.* 75:308–325. [2]

Gordon, H. S. 1954. The economic theory of a common property resource. *J. Polit. Econ.* 62:124–142. [15]

Gore, A., Jr. 1992. *Earth in the Balance: Ecology and the Human Spirit.* Penguin Books, New York. [3]

Gore, A., Jr. 1993. *Reinventing Environmental Management.* Accompanying Report of the National Performance Review. U.S. Government Printing Office, Washington, D.C. [11]

Gore, J. A. (ed.). 1985. *The Restoration of Rivers and Streams: Theories and Experiences.* Butterworth, Boston. [14]

Gottlieb, R. 1993. *Forcing the Spring: The Transformation of the American Environmental Movement.* Island Press, Washington, DC. [16]

Gould, S. J. 1989. *Wonderful Life: The Burgess Shale and the Nature of History.* W. W. Norton, New York. [4]

Goulder, L. H. and D. Kennedy. 1996. Valuing ecosystem services: philosophical bases and empirical methods. In G. Daily (ed.), *Nature's Services: Societal Dependence on Natural Ecosystems*, pp. 23–47. Island Press, Washington, D.C. [15]

Goulding, M., N. J. H. Smith, and D. J. Mahar. 1996. *Floods of Fortune: Ecology and Economy along the Amazon.* Columbia University Press, New York. [9]

Gradwhol, J. and R. Greenberg 1988. *Saving the Tropical Forests.* Island Press, Washington, D.C. [2]

Graham, R. W. 1986. Response of mammalian communities to environmental changes during the late Quaternary. In J. Diamond and T. J. Case (eds.), *Community Ecology*, pp. 300–313. Harper & Row, New York. [8,10]

Graham, R. W., and 19 others. 1996. Spatial response of mammals to late Quaternary environmental fluctuations. *Science* 272: 1601–1606. [8]

Granados, M. 1987. Transformaciones históricas de los ecosistemas del Parque Nacional de Doñana. Ph.D. dissertation, University of Sevilla, Sevilla. [13]

Grant, V. 1957. The plant species in theory and practice. In E. Mayr (ed.), *The Species Problem.* pp. 39–80. AAAS Publication 50. [3]

Grassle, J. F. 1989. Species diversity in deep-sea communities. *Trends Ecol. Evol.* 4:12–15. [4]

Grassle, J. F. 1991. Deep-sea benthic biodiversity. *BioScience* 41:464–469. [4,5]

Grassle, J. F. and N. J. Maciolek. 1992. Deep-sea species richness: Regional and local diversity estimates from quantitative bottom samples. *Am. Nat.* 139:313–341. [4,5]

Grassle, J. F., P. Lasserre, A. D. MacIntyre and G. C. Ray. 1991. Marine biodiversity and ecosystem function: A proposal for an international research program. Biology International Special Issue no. 23. International Union for Biological Sciences, Paris, France. [5]

Greater Yellowstone Ecosystem. 1994. The natural and scenic values of rural private lands. In *Sustaining Greater Yellowstone, A Blueprint for the Future*, pp. 12–13. Greater Yellowstone Coalition, Bozeman, MT. [9]

Green, J. E. and R. E. Salter. 1987. *Methods for Reclamation of Wildlife Habitat in the Canadian Prairie Provinces.* Prepared for Environment Canada and Alberta Recreation, Parks and Wildlife Foundation by the Delta Environmental Management Group Ltd., Edmonton, Alberta. [14]

Greenberg, M. R., P. M. Sandman, D. B. Sachsman, and K. L. Salomone. 1989. Network television news coverage of environmental risks. *Environment* 31:16–44. [16]

Greenslade, P. J. M. and P. Greenslade. 1984. Soil surface insects of the Australian arid zone. In H. G. Cogger and E. E. Cameron (eds.), *Arid Australia*, pp. 153–176. Australian Museum, Sydney. [4]

Greenstone, M. H. 1984. Determinants of web spider species diversity: Vegetation structural diversity vs. prey availability. *Oecologia* 62:299–304. [4]

Greig, J. C. 1979. Principles of genetic conservation in relation to wildlife management in Southern Africa. *S. Afr. Tydskr. Naturnav.* 9:57–78. [6]

Grenfell, B. T. and A. P. Dobson (eds.). 1995. *Ecology of Infectious Diseases in Natural*

Populations. Cambridge University Press, Cambridge. [8]

Grier, N. M. 1920. Morphological features of certain mussel shells found in Lake Erie, compared with those of the corresponding species found in the drainage of the upper Ohio. *Ann. Carnegie Mus.* 13(2):145–182. [3]

Griffith, B., J. M. Scott, J. W. Carpenter and C. Reed. 1989. Translocation as a species conservation tool: Status and strategy. *Science* 245:477–480. [6]

Griffith, M. A. and T. T. Fendley. 1982. Pre- and post-dispersal movement behavior of subadult bobcats on the Savannah River Plant. In S. D. Miller and D. D. Everett (eds.), *Cats of the World,* pp. 277–289. National Wildlife Federation, Washington, D.C. [10]

Groom, M. J. and N. Schumaker. 1993. Evaluating landscape change: Patterns of worldwide deforestation and local fragmentation. In P. M. Kareiva, J. G. Kingsolver and R. B. Huey (eds.), *Biotic Interactions and Global Change,* pp. 24–44. Sinauer Associates, Sunderland, MA. [5]

Groombridge, B. (ed.). 1993. *1994 IUCN Red List of Threatened Animals.* IUCN, Gland, Switzerland, and Cambridge. [13]

Grover, H. D. 1990. Global climate change and planetary health. In *Proceedings of the Fourth National Environmental Health Conference,* pp. 93–108. San Antonio, Texas. [10]

Grumbine, R. E. 1990. Viable populations, reserve size, and federal lands management: A critique. *Conserv. Biol.* 4:127–134. [10]

Grumbine, R. E. 1992. *Ghost Bears: Exploring the Biodiversity Crisis.* Island Press, Washington, D.C. [1,3,18]

Grumbine, R. E. 1994. What is ecosystem management? *Conserv. Biol.* 8:27–38. [3]

Guha, R. 1989. *The Unquiet Woods: Ecological Change and Peasant Resistance in the Himalaya.* University of California Press, Berkeley. [2]

Guillette, L. J., D. A. Crain, A. A. Rooney, and D. B. Pickford. 1995. Organization versus activation: The role of endocrine-disrupting contaminants (EDCs) during embryonic development in wildlife. *Environ. Health Perspect.* 103:157–164. [5]

Guinon, M. 1987. No free lunch. *Rest. Mgmt. Notes* 7(2):56. [14]

Gunderson, L. H. 1992. Spatial and temporal hierarchies in the Everglades ecosystem. Ph.D. dissertation, University of Florida, Gainesville. [13]

Gunderson, L. H. 1994. Vegetation of the Everglades: Composition and determinants. In S. M. Davis and J. C. Ogden (eds.), *Everglades, The Ecosystem and Its Restoration.* St. Lucie Press, Delray Florida. [13]

Gunderson, L. H. and W. F. Loftus. 1993. The Everglades. In W. H. Martin, S. G. Boyce, and A. C. Echternacht (eds.), *Biodiversity of the Southeastern United States.* John Wiley and Sons, New York. [13]

Gunderson, L. H., C. S. Holling, and S. S. Light (eds.). 1995. *Barriers and Bridges to the Renewal of Ecosystems and Institutions.* Columbia University Press, New York. [3]

Gustafson, E. J., and G. R. Parker. 1992. Relationships between landcover proportion and indices of landscape spatial pattern. *Landscape Ecology* 7:101-110. [9]

Gutierrez, R. J. and eight others. 1992. In *The California Spotted Owl: A Technical Assessment of Its Current Status,* pp. 79–147. General Technical Report PSW-GTR-133. Albany, California: Pacific Southwest Research Station, Forest Service, U.S. Department of Agriculture. [13]

Haffer, J. 1969. Speciation in Amazonia forest birds. *Science* 165:131–137. [4]

Haffer, J. 1974. Avian speciation in tropical South America. *Publ. Nuttall Ornith. Club.*, no. 14. [4]

Hagan, J. M., W. M. Vander Haegen, and P. S. McKinley. 1996. The early development of forest fragmentation effects on birds. *Conserv. Biol.* 10:188–202. [9]

Haig, S. M., J. D. Ballou and S. R. Derrickson. 1990. Management options for preserving genetic diversity: Reintroduction of Guam rails to the wild. *Conserv. Biol.* 4:290–300. [6]

Haila, Y. 1990. Toward an ecological definition of an island: A northwest European perspective. *J. Biogeogr.* 17:561–568. [9]

Haila, Y., I. K. Hanski and S. Raivio. 1993. Turnover of breeding birds in small forest fragments: The "sampling" colonization hypothesis corroborated. *Ecology* 74:714–725. [9]

Hall, C. A. S. 1988. An assessment of several of the historically most influential theoretical models used in ecology and of the data provided in their support. *Ecological Modeling* 43:5–31. [12]

Hall, C. A. S., C. J. Cleveland and R. Kaufman. 1986. *Energy and Resource Quality: The Ecology of the Economic Process.* John Wiley & Sons, New York. [15]

Hall, P., S. Walker, and K. Bawa. 1996. Effect of forest fragmentation on genetic diversity and mating system in a tropical tree, *Pithecellobium elegans. Conserv. Biol.* 10:757–768. [9]

Halle, F. R., A. A. Oldemann and P. B. Tomlinson. 1978. *Tropical Trees and Forests: An Architectural Analysis.* Springer-Verlag, Berlin. [4]

Halliday, T. R. 1980. The extinction of the Passenger Pigeon, *Ectopistes migratorius,* and its relevance to contemporary conservation. *Biol. Conserv.* 17:157–162. [7]

Halvorson, C. H., J. T. Harris and S. M. Smirenski (eds.). 1995. *Cranes and Storks of the Amur River: The Proceedings of the International Workshop.* Arts Literature Publishers, Moscow, Russia. [13]

Hamilton, W. D. 1971. Geometry for the selfish herd. *J. Theor. Biol.* 31:295–311. [7]

Hammond, P.M. 1994. Practical approaches to the estimation of the extent of biodiversity in speciose groups. *Phil. Trans. R. Soc. Lond.* B 345:119-136. [5]

Hanemann, W. M. 1988. Economics and the preservation of biodiversity. In E. O. Wilson and F. M. Peter (eds.), *Biodiversity,* pp. 193–199. National Academy Press, Washington, D.C. [2,15]

Hansen, A. J., D. L. Urban and B. Marks. 1992. Avian community dynamics: The interplay of landscape trajectories and species life histories. In A. J. Hansen and F. di Castri (eds.), *Landscape Boundaries: Consequences for Biodiversity and Ecological Flows,* pp. 170–195. Springer-Verlag, New York. [10]

Hansen, A. J., S. L. Garman, J. F. Weigland, D. L. Urban, W. C. McComb, and M. G. Raphael. 1995. Alternative silvicultural regimes in the Pacific Northwest: Simulations of ecological and economic effects. *Ecol. Appl.* 5:535–554. [12]

Hanski, I. 1989. Metapopulation dynamics: Does it help to have more of the same? *Trends Ecol. Evol.* 4:113–114. [7]

Hanski, I. 1990. Density dependence, regulation and variability in animal populations. *Phil. Trans. R. Soc. Lond. B* 330: 141–150. [5]

Hanski, I., Moilanen, A., and Gyllenberg, M. 1996. Minimum viable metapopulation size. *Am. Nat.* 147:527–541. [7]

Hansson, L. 1991. Dispersal and connectivity in metapopulations. In M. E. Gilpin and I. Hanski (eds.), *Metapopulaton Dynamics: Empirical and Theoretical Investigations,* pp. 89–103. Linnaean Society of London and Academic Press, London. [9]

Harcourt, A. H. 1986. Gorilla conservation: Anatomy of a campaign. In K. Benirschke (ed.), *Primates: The Road to Self-Sustaining Populations*, pp. 31–46. Springer-Verlag, New York. [18]

Hardin, G. 1968. The tragedy of the commons. *Science* 162:1243–1248. [2,15,19]

Hardin, G. 1993. *Living Within Limits: Ecology, Economics, and Population Taboos.* Oxford University Press, New York. [18,19]

Hardt, R. A. and R. T. T. Forman. 1989. Boundary form effects on woody colonization of reclaimed surface mines. *Ecology* 70:1252–1260. [10]

Harley, J. L. and S. E. Smith. 1983. *Mycorrhizal Symbiosis.* Academic Press, New York. [8]

Harmon, D. 1987. Cultural diversity, human subsistence, and the national park ideal. *Environ. Ethics* 9:147–158. [18]

Harner, R. F. and K. T. Harper. 1976. The role of area, heterogeneity, and favorability in plant species diversity of pinyon-juniper ecosystems. *Ecology* 57:1254–1263. [9]

Harris, J. T. 1994. Cranes, people, and nature: Preserving the balance. In *The Future of Cranes and Wetlands*, pp. 1–14. Proceedings of the International Symposium, Wild Bird Society of Japan, Tokyo. [13]

Harris, L. D. 1984. *The Fragmented Forest: Island Biogeography Theory and the Preservation of Biotic Diversity.* University of Chicago Press, Chicago. [9,10]

Harris, L. D. and K. Atkins. 1991. Faunal movement corridors in Florida. In W. E. Hudson (ed.), *Landscape Linkages and Biodiversity,* pp. 117–134. Island Press, Washington, D.C. [10]

Harris, L. D. and P. B. Gallagher. 1989. New initiatives for wildlife conservation: The need for movement corridors. In G. MacKintosh (ed.), *Preserving Communities and Corridors,* pp. 11–34. Defenders of Wildlife, Washington, D.C. [9]

Harris, L. D. and G. Silva-Lopez. 1992. Forest fragmentation and the conservation of biological diversity. In P. L. Fiedler and S. K. Jain (eds.), *Conservation Biology: The*

Theory and Practice of Nature Conservation, Preservation, and Management, pp. 197–237. Chapman and Hall, New York. [9]

Harris, L. D. and R. D. Wallace. 1984. Breeding bird species in Florida forest fragments. *Proc. Annu. Conf. Southeastern Assoc. Fish Wildl. Agencies* 38:87–96. [9]

Harris, R. B. and F. W. Allendorf. 1989. Genetically effective population size of large mammals: Assessment of estimators. *Conserv. Biol.* 3:181-191. [6]

Harris, S. C., T. H. Martin, and K. W. Cummins. 1995. A model for aquatic invertebrate response to Kissimmee River restoration. *Restor. Ecol.* 3:181–194. [14]

Harrison, D. (ed.). 1992. *Tourism and the Less Developed Countries.* Bellhaven Press, London. [18]

Harrison, R. G., S. F. Wintermeyer, and T. M. Odell. 1983. Patterns of genetic variation within and among gypsy moth, *Lymantra dispar* (Lepidoptera: Lymantriidae), populations. *Ann. Entomol. Soc. Am.* 766:52–56. [6]

Harrison, R. L. 1992. Toward a theory of inter-refuge corridor design. *Conserv. Biol.* 6:293–295. [10]

Harrison, S. 1991. Local extinction in a metapopulation context: An empirical evaluation. *Biol. J. Linn. Soc.* 42:73–88. [7,9]

Harrison, S. 1994. Metapopulations and conservation. In P. J. Edwards, R. M. May, and N. R. Webb (eds.), *Large-Scale Ecology and Conservation Biology*, pp. 111–128. Blackwell Science, Oxford, UK. [9]

Harrison, S., D. D. Murphy and P. R. Ehrlich. 1988. Distribution of the Bay checkerspot butterfly, *Euphydryas editha bayensis:* Evidence for a metapopulation model. *Am. Nat.* 132:360–382. [6,9]

Harte, J. and E. Hoffman. 1989. Possible effects of acidic deposition on a Rocky Mountain population of the tiger salamander *Ambystoma tigrinum*. *Conserv. Biol.* 3(2):149–158. [5]

Hartl, D. L. and A. G. Clark. 1990. *Principles of Population Genetics.* 2nd ed. Sinauer Associates, Sunderland, MA. [6]

Hartley, D. 1995. Ruaha ecosystem management project: The first steps. In N. Leader-Williams, J. A. Kayera, and G. L. Overton (eds.), *Community-Based Conservation in Tanzania*, pp. 82–88. Wildlife Department, Dar-es-Salaam. [18]

Hartshorn, G. 1983. Plants. In D. H. Janzen (ed.), *Costa Rican Natural History*, pp. 118–183. University of Chicago Press, Chicago. [14]

Hartshorn, G., L. Nicolait, L. Hartshorn, G. Bevier, R. Brightman, J. Cal, A. Cawich, W. Davidson, R. Dubois, C. Dyer, J. Gibson, W. Hawley, J. Leonard, R. Nicolait, D. Weyer, H. White, and C. Wright. 1984. Belize: Country Environmental Profile: A Field Study. Robert Nicolait and Associates, Ltd., Belize City, Belize. [15]

Hartshorn, G. S. 1978. Tree falls and tropical forest dynamics. In P. B. Tomlinson and M. H. Zimmermann (eds.), *Tropical Trees as Living Systems*, pp. 617–638. Cambridge University Press, New York. [18]

Hartshorn, G. S. 1979. *Preliminary management plan for Sarapiquí.* Unpublished report to USAID/San José. Tropical Science Center, San José, Costa Rica. [18]

Hartshorn, G. S. 1980. Neotropical forest dynamics. *Biotropica* 12:23–30. [18]

Hartshorn, G. S. 1981. *Forestry potentials in the Palcazú Valley, Peru.* Unpublished report to USAID/Lima. JRB Association, McLean, VA. [18]

Hartshorn, G. S. 1988. *Natural regeneration of trees on the Palcazáu demonstration strips.* USDA Forest Service report, Washington, D.C. [18]

Hartshorn, G. S. 1989. Application of gap theory to tropical forest management: Natural regeneration on strip clear-cuts in the Peruvian Amazon. *Ecology* 70:567–569. [18]

Hartshorn, G. S. 1992. Forest loss and future options in Central America. In J. M. Hagan and D. W. Johnston (eds.), *Ecology and Conservation of Neotropical Migrant Landbirds*, pp. 13–19. Smithsonian Institution Press, Washington, D.C. [9]

Hartshorn, G. S. and W. Pariona A. 1993. Ecological forest management in the Peruvian Amazon: The Yánesha forestry cooperative in the Palcazú valley. In C. Potter and J. Cohen (eds.), *Perspectives on Biodiversity*, pp. 151–166. AAAS Press, Washington, D.C. [18]

Harwell, M. A., J. F. Long, A. M. Bartuska, J. H. Gentile, C. C. Harwell, V. Meyers, and J. C. Ogden. 1996. Ecosystem management to achieve ecological sustainability: The case of south Florida. *Environ. Mgmt.* 20:497–521. [12]

Haskell, D. G. 1995. A reevaluation of the effects of forest fragmentation on rates of bird-nest predation. *Conserv. Biol.* 9:1316–1318. [9]

Hassell, M. P. 1978. *The dynamics of arthropod predator-prey systems.* Monographs in Population Biology, no. 13. Princeton University Press, Princeton, NJ. [7]

Hawken, P. 1993. *The Ecology of Commerce.* Harper Collins, New York. [16]

Hawkes, K. 1993. Why hunter–gatherers work: An ancient version of the problem of public goods. *Curr. Anthropol.* 34(4):341–361. [19]

Hawksworth, D. L. 1991a. The fungal dimension of biodiversity: Magnitude, significance and conservation. *Mycol. Res.* 95:641–655. [4]

Hawksworth, D. L. (ed.). 1991b. *Improving the Stability of Names: Needs and Options.* Koeltz Scientific Books, Koenigstein. [4]

Hayes, M. P. and M. R. Jennings. 1986. Decline of ranid frog species in western North America: Are bullfrogs (*Rana catesbeiana*) responsible? *J. Herpetol.* 20(4): 490–509. [5]

Healy, R. G. and W. Ascher. 1995. Knowledge in the policy process: Incorporating new environmental information in natural resource policy making. *Policy Sci.* 28:1–19. [17]

Hecht, S. and A. Cockburn. 1989. *The Fate of the Forest: Developers, Destroyers, and Defenders of the Amazon.* Verso, New York. [2]

Hedrick, P. W. 1995. Gene flow and genetic restoration: The Florida panther as a case study. *Conserv. Biol.* 9:996–1007. [6]

Hedrick, P. W. and P. S. Miller. 1992. Conservation genetics: Techniques and fundamentals. *Ecol. Applic.* 2:30–46. [6]

Heesterbeek, J. A. P. and M. G. Roberts. 1995. Mathematical models for microparasites of wildlife. In B. T. Grenfell and A. P. Dobson (eds.), *Ecology of Infectious Diseases in Natural Populations.* Cambridge University Press, Cambridge. [8]

Heinselman, M. L. 1973. Fire in the virgin forests of the Boundary Waters Canoe Area, Minnesota. *Quat. Res.* 3:329–382. [10]

Hemley, G. (ed.). 1994. *International Wildlife Trade: A CITES Sourcebook.* World Wildlife Fund and Island Press, Washington, D.C. [3]

Henderson, C. 1984. Publicity strategies and techniques for Minnesota's nongame wildlife checkoff. *Transactions of the North American Wildlife and Natural Resource Conference* 49:181–189. [16]

Henderson, F. R., P. F. Springer and R. Adrian. 1969. *The black-footed ferret in South Dakota.* South Dakota Department of Game, Fish and Parks, Technical Bulletin 4. [13]

Henderson, M. T., G. Merriam and J. Wegner. 1985. Patchy environments and species survival: Chipmunks in an agricultural mosaic. *Biol. Conserv.* 31:95–105. [9]

Herkert, J. R. 1994. The effects of habitat fragmentation on midwestern grassland bird communities. *Ecol. Applic.* 4:461–471. [9]

Herliczek, J. 1996. Where is ecotourism going? *Amicus J.* 18:31–35 [18]

Herman, J. R., P. K. Bhartia, J. Ziemke, Z. Ahmad, and D. Larko. 1996. UV-B increases (1979–1992) from decreases in total ozone. *Geophys. Res. Lett.* 23(16):2117–2120. [5]

Hernández, L. M., M. J. González, M. C. Rico, M. A. Fernández, and A. Aranda. 1988. Organochlorine and heavy metal residues in falconiforme and ciconiforme eggs (Spain). *Bull. Environ. Contam. Toxicol.* 40: 86–91. [13]

Hernández, L. M., M. C. Rico, M. J. González, M. A. Hernán, and M. A. Fernández. 1986. Presence and time trends of organochlorine pollutants and heavy metals in eggs of predatory birds of Spain. *J. Field Ornithol.* 57(4):270–282. [13]

Heschel, M. S. and K. N. Paige. 1995. Inbreeding depression, environmental stress, and population size variation in scarlet gilia (*Ipomopsis aggregata*). *Conserv. Biol.* 9:126–133. [6]

Heyer, W. R., A. S. Rand, C. A. G. da Cruz, and O. L. Peixoto. 1988. Decimations, extinctions, and colonizations of frog populations in southeast Brazil and their evolutionary implications. *Biotropica* 20 (3):230–235. [5]

Hickey, L. J. 1984. Changes in the angiosperm flora across the Cretaceous-Tertiary boundary. In W. A. Bergren and J. A. van Couvering (eds.), *Catastrophes and Earth History*, pp. 279–313. Princeton University Press, Princeton, NJ. [5]

Hickey, R. J., M. A. Vincent, and S. I. Guttman. 1991. Genetic variation in running buffalo clover (*Trifolium stoloniferum*, Fabacae). *Conserv. Biol.* 5:309–316. [6]

Hillis, D. M., C. Moritz, and B. K. Mable (eds.). 1996. *Molecular Systematics.* 2nd ed. Sinauer Associates, Sunderland, MA. [6]

Hinegardner, R. 1976. Evolution of genome size. In F. J. Ayala (ed.), *Molecular Evolution,* pp. 179–199. Sinauer Associates, Sunderland, MA. [5]

Hines, J. M., H. R. Hungerford, and A. N. Tomera. 1986/1987. Analysis and synthesis of research on responsible environmental behavior: A meta-analysis. *J. Environ. Educ.* 18(2): 1–8. [16]

Hobbs, R. J. and D. A. Norton. 1996. Towards a conceptual framework for restoration ecology. *Restor. Ecol.* 4:93–110. [14]

Hobbs, R. J. and L. F. Huenneke. 1992. Disturbance, diversity, and invasion: Implications for conservation. *Conserv. Biol.* 6:324–337. [10]

Hoelzel, A. R., J. Halley, C. Campagna, T. Arnbom, B. LeBoeuf, S. J. O'Brien, K. Ralls, and G. A. Dover. 1993. Elephant seal genetic variation and the use of simulation models to investigate historical population bottlenecks. *J. Hered.* 84:443–449. [6]

Hof, J. G. and L. A. Joyce. 1992. Spatial optimization for wildlife and timber in managed forest ecosystems. *Forest Sci.* 38:489–508. [11]

Holdridge, L. R. 1967. *Life Zone Ecology.* Tropical Science Center, San José, Costa Rica. [4]

Holl, K. D. 1996. The effect of coal surface mine reclamation on diurnal lepidopteran conservation. *J. Appl. Ecol,* 33:225–236. [14]

Holling, C. S. 1973. Resilience and stability of ecological systems. *Annu. Rev. Ecol. Syst.* 4:1-23. [11]

Holling, C. S. 1978. *Adaptive Environmental Assessment and Management.* John Wiley and Sons, New York. [12]

Holling, C. S. 1986. Resilience of terrestrial ecosystems: local surprise and global change. In W. C. Clark and R. E. Munn (eds.), *Sustainable Development of the Biosphere,* pp. 292-317. Cambridge University Press, Cambridge. [11]

Holling, C. S. 1992. Cross-scale morphology, geometry, and dynamics of ecosystems. *Ecol. Monogr.* 62:447–502. [15]

Holling, C. S. 1995. What barriers? What bridges? In L. H. Gunderson, C. S. Holling and S. S. Light (eds.), *Barriers and Bridges to the Renewal of Ecosystems,* pp. 3-34. Columbia University Press, New York. [11]

Holling, C. S. and G. K. Meffe. 1996. Command and control and the pathology of natural resource management. *Conserv. Biol.* 10:328–337. [10]

Holling, C. S., C. J. Walters, S. M. Davis, J. C. Ogden, and L. H. Gunderson. 1994. The structure and dynamics of the Everglades system: Guidelines for ecosystem restoration. In S. Davis and J. Ogden (ed.), *Everglades, The Ecosystem and its Restoration.* St. Lucie Press, Delray, FL. [13]

Holling, C. S., D. W. Schindler, B. W. Walker, and J. Roughgarden. 1995. Biodiversity in the functioning of ecosystems: An ecological synthesis. In C. Perrings, K.-G. Mäler, C. Folke, C. S. Holling, and B.-O. Jansson (eds.), *Biodiversity Loss: Economic and Ecological Issues,* pp. 44–83. Cambridge University Press, New York. [15]

Holsinger, K. E. 1993. The evolutionary dynamics of fragmented plant populations. In P. M. Kareiva, J. G. Kingsolver, and R. B. Huey (eds.), *Biotic Interactions and Global Change,* pp. 198–216. Sinauer Associates, Sunderland, MA. [5]

Hopkins, R. A., M. J. Kutilek and G. L. Shreve. 1982. Density and home range characteristics of mountain lions in the Diablo Range of California. In S. D. Miller and D. D. Everett (eds.), *Cats of the World,* pp. 223–235. National Wildlife Federation, Washington, D.C. [10]

Hossner, L. R. (ed.). 1988. *Reclamation of Surface-Mined Lands,* Vols. I and II. CRC Press, Boca Raton, FL. [14]

Hotelling, H. 1931. The economics of exhaustible resources. *J. Polit. Econ.* 39: 137–175. [15]

Houde, E. D. and E. S. Rutherford. 1993. Recent trends in estuarine fisheries: Predictions of fish production and yield. *Estuaries* 16:161–176. [5]

Houghton, R. A., D. S. Lefkowitz and D. L. Skole. 1991. Changes in the landscape of Latin America between 1850 and 1985. I. Progressive loss of forests. *For. Ecol. Mgmt.* 38:143–172. [5]

Howard, D. J. 1993. Small populations, inbreeding, and speciation. In N. W. Thornhill (ed.), *The Natural History of Inbreeding and Outbreeding: Theoretical and Empirical Perspectives,* pp. 118–142. The University of Chicago Press, Chicago. [6]

Howard, L. O. and W. F. Fiske. 1911. The importation into the United States of the parasites of the gypsy moth and the brown-tailed moth. *Bull. U.S. Bur. Entomol.* no. 91. [7]

Howarth, F. G. 1985. Impacts of alien land arthropods and molluscs on native plants and animals in Hawaii. In C. P. Stone and J. M. Scott (eds.), *Hawaii's Terrestrial Ecosystems: Preservation and Management,* pp. 149–179. Cooperative National Park Resources Study Unit, University of Hawaii, Honolulu. [10]

Howarth, R. B. and R. B. Norgaard. 1992. Environmental valuation under sustainable development. *Am. Econ. Rev.* 82:473–477. [15]

Hughes, G. H. and T. M. Bonnicksen (eds.). 1990. *Restoration '89: The New Management Challenge.* Proceedings of the first annual meeting of the Society for Ecological Restoration. Society for Ecological Restoration, Madison, WI. [14]

Hummel, M. 1990. *A Conservation Strategy for Large Carnivores in Canada.* World Wildlife Fund Canada, Toronto. [10]

Hunter, M. L. 1990. *Wildlife, Forests, and Forestry: Principles of Managing Forests for Biodiversity.* Prentice Hall, Englewood Cliffs, NJ. [12]

Hunter, M. L., G. L. Jacobson and T. Webb. 1988. Paleoecology and the course-filter approach to maintaining biological diversity. *Conserv. Biol.* 2: 375–385. [10]

Hunter, M. L., Jr. 1996. *Fundamentals of Conservation Biology.* Blackwell Science, Cambridge, MA. [5]

Huston, M. A. 1980. Soil nutrients and tree species richness in Costa Rican forests. *J. Biogeogr.* 7:147–157. [4]

Huston, M. A. 1994. *Biological Diversity. The Coexistence of Species on Changing Landscapes.* Cambridge University Press, Cambridge. [4]

Hutchins, M. and W. Conway. 1995. Beyond Noah's Ark: The evolving role of modern zoological parks and aquariums in field conservation. *Int. Zoo Yrbk.* 34:117–130. [13]

Hutchinson, G. E. 1965. *The Ecological Theater and the Evolutionary Play.* Yale University Press, New Haven. [1]

Hutnik, R. J. and G. Davis (eds.). 1973. *Ecology and Reclamation of Devastated Land,* Vols. 1 and 2. Gordon and Breach, New York. [14]

Hvengaard, G. T., J. R. Butler and D. K. Krystofiak. 1989. Economic values of bird watching at Point Pelee National Park, Canada. *Wildl. Soc. Bull.* 17:526–531. [14]

ICCAT. 1995. Report of the standing committee on research and statistics. International Commission for the Conservation of Atlantic Tunas, Madrid, Spain. [5]

IEMTF. 1995. The Ecosystem Approach: Healthy Ecosystems *and* Sustainable Economies. Report of the Interagency Ecosystem Management Task Force, National Technical Information Service, U.S. Department of Commerce, Washington, D.C. [3]

Ingham, D. S. and M. J. Samways. 1996. Application of fragmentation and variegation models to epigaeic invertebrates in South Africa. *Conserv. Biol.* 10:1353–1358. [9]

Ingram, G. J. and K. R. McDonald. 1993. An update on the decline of Queensland's frogs. In D. Lunney and D. Ayers (eds.), *Herpetology in Australia: A Diverse Discipline,* pp. 297–303. Royal Zoological Society of New South Wales, Mosman, New South Wales, Australia. [5]

I.N.I.T.A.A. 1992. *Estudio sobre las mortalidades estivales de aves acuáticas del Parque Nacional de Doñana. Informe preliminar. Junio 1992.* Centro de Investigación y Tecnología del I.N.I.T.A.A. Ministerio de Agricultura, Pesca y Alimentación. Report [13]

Interagency Ecosystem Management Task Force. 1995. The ecosystem approach: Healthy ecosystems and sustainable economies. Vol. 1. Washington, D.C. [10]

Intergovernmental Panel on Climate Change (eds. J. T. Houghton, G. J. Jenkins and J. J. Ephramus). 1990. *Climate Change: The IPCC Scientific Assessment.* Cambridge University Press, Cambridge. [5,19]

Intergovernmental Panel on Climate Change (eds. J. T. Houghton, B. A. Callander and S. K. Barney). 1992. *Climate Change 1992: The Supplementary Report to the IPCC Scientific Assessment.* Cambridge University Press, New York. [5]

IUCN. 1991. *Protected Areas of the World: A Review of National Systems.* Vol. 3. Afrotropical. IUCN, Gland, Switzerland. [18]

IUCN. 1993. *World Conservation Strategy.* Gland, Switzerland. [18]

IUCN. 1994. *IUCN Red List Categories.* IUCN, Gland, Switzerland. [13]

IUCN. 1995. A global strategy for the conservation of marine turtles. International Union for the Conservation of Nature, Species Survival Commission, Marine Turtle Specialist Group, Gland, Switzerland. [13]

IUCN/UNEP/WWF. 1980. World Conservation Strategy: Living Resource Conservation for Sustainable Development. Gland, Switzerland. [18]

IUCN/UNEP/WWF. 1991. *Caring for the Earth: A Strategy for Sustainable Living.* Gland, Switzerland. [18]

Jablonski, D. 1986. Background and mass extinctions: The alteration of macroevolutionary regimes. *Science* 231:129–133. [5]

Jablonski, D. 1991. Extinctions: A palaeontological perspective. *Science* 253:754–757. [5]

Jablonski, D. 1994. Extinctions in the fossil record. *Phil. Trans. Royal Soc. Lond. B* 344:11–16. [5]

Jackson, L. L., N. Lopoukhine, and D. Hillyard. 1995. Ecological restoration: A definition and comments. *Restor. Ecol.* 3:71–75. [14]

Jackson, W. 1980. *New Roots for Agriculture.* University of Nebraska Press, Lincoln. [2]

Jackson, W. 1987. *Altars of Unhewn Stone: Science and the Earth.* North Point Press, San Francisco. [2]

Jacobson, S. and A. Lopez. 1994. Biological impacts of ecotourism: Tourism and nesting turtles in Totuguero National Park. *Wildlife Soc. Bull.* 22:414–416. [18]

Jacobson, S. J. 1995. Needs assessment techniques for environmental education. *Int. Res. Geogr. Environ. Educ.* 4(1): 125–133. [16]

Jacobson, S. J. and S. B. Marynowski. 1997. Public attitudes and knowledge about ecosystem management on Department of Defense land in Florida. *Conserv. Biol.* In press. [16]

Jacobson, S. K. 1990. Graduate education in conservation biology. *Conserv. Biol.* 4: 431–440. [1]

Janos, D. P. 1980. Mycorrhizae influence tropical succession. *Biotropica* (Suppl.) 12:56–64. [8]

Jansson, A. M., M. Hammer, C. Folke, and R. Costanza (eds.). 1994. *Investing in Natural Capital: The Ecological Economics Approach to Sustainability.* Island Press, Washington, D.C. [15]

Janzen, D. H. 1975. *Ecology of Plants in the Tropics.* Edward Arnold Publishers Ltd., London. [5]

Janzen, D. H. 1979. How to be a fig. *Annu. Rev. Ecol. Syst.* 10:13–51. [5]

Janzen, D. H. 1983a. No park is an island: Increase in interference from outside as park size decreases. *Oikos* 41:402–410. [9,10]

Janzen, D. H. (ed.). 1983b. *Costa Rican Natural History.* University of Chicago Press, Chicago. [16]

Janzen, D. H. 1986. The eternal external threat. In M. E. Soulé (ed.), *Conservation Biology: The Science of Scarcity and Diversity,* pp. 286–303. Sinauer Associates, Sunderland, MA. [9,10,11]

Jimenez, J. A., K. A. Hughes, G. Alaks, L. Graham, and R. C. Lacy. 1994. An experimental study of inbreeding depression in a natural habitat. *Science* 266:271–273. [6]

Joglar, R. L. and P. A. Burrowes. 1996. Declining amphibian populations in Puerto Rico. In R. Powell and R. W. Henderson (eds.), *Contributions to West Indian Herpetology: A Tribute to Albert Schwartz,* pp. 371–380. Society for the Study of Amphibians and Reptiles, Ithaca, NY. [5]

Johannes, R. E. and M. Riepen. 1995. Environmental, economic, and social implications of the live reef fish trade in Asia and the Western Pacific. The Nature Conservancy. 82 pp. [5]

Johns, A. D. 1985. Selective logging and wildlife conservation in tropical rain forest: Problems and recommendations. *Biol. Conserv.* 31:355–375. [5]

Johnsgard, P. A. 1983. *Cranes of the World.* Indiana University Press, Bloomington. [13]

Johnson, E. A. and S. L. Gutsell. 1994. Fire-frequency models, methods and interpretations. In M. Begon and A.H. Fitter (eds.), *Advances in Ecological Research,* Vol. 25, pp. 239-287. Academic Press, New York. [12]

Johnson, K. G. 1986. *Responses of Wildlife to Large Scale Even-Aged Silvicultural Practices.* Alabama Department of Conservation. Final report, Project no. W-35. [12]

Johnson, L. E. 1991. *A Morally Deep World. An Essay on Moral Significance and Environmental Ethics.* Cambridge University Press, Cambridge. [2]

Johnson, M. P. and P. H. Raven. 1973. Species number and endemism: The Galapagos Archipelago revisited. *Science* 179:893–895. [9]

Johnson, M. P. and D. S. Simberloff. 1974. Environmental determinants of island species numbers in the British Isles. *J. Biogeogr.* 1:149–154. [9]

Johnson, M. S. 1988. Founder effects and geographic variation in the land snail *Theba pisana. Heredity* 61:133–142. [6]

Johnson, M. S. and D. R. Chaffey. 1974. An Inventory of the Southern Coastal Plain Pine Forests, Belize. Land Resource Studyno. 15. Surrey: Ministry of Overseas Development. [15]

Johnson, M. S. and N. P. Woods. 1976. An Inventory of the Columbia River and Maya Mountains Forest Reserve. Draft mimeograph. Belize Forest Department. Belmopan, Belize. [15]

Johnson, N. K. 1975. Controls on number of bird species on montane islands in the Great Basin. *Evolution* 29:545–567. [9]

Johnson, R. G. and S. A. Temple. 1990. Nest predation and brood parasitism of tallgrass prairie birds. *J. Wildl. Mgmt.* 54: 106–111. [9]

Johnson, R. I. 1970. The systematics and zoogeography of the Unionidae (Mollusca: Bivalvia) of the southern Atlantic slope region. *Bull. Mus. Comp. Zool.* 140:263–450. [3]

Joint Appeal by Religion and Science for the Environment. 1992. *A Directory of Environmental Activities and Resources in the North American Religious Community.* National Religious Partership on the Environment, New York. [16]

Jones, C. G., J. H. Lawton and M. Shachak. 1994. Organisms as ecosystem engineers. *Oikos* 69:373–386. [8]

Jones, H. L. and J. Diamond. 1976. Short-term-base studies of turnover in breeding bird populations on the California Channel Islands. *Condor* 78:526–549. [7]

Jordan, C. F. 1986. Local effects of tropical deforestation. In M. E. Soulé (ed.), *Conservation Biology: The Science of Scarcity and Diversity,* pp. 410–426. Sinauer Associates, Sunderland, MA. [5]

Jordan, C. F. and E. G. Farnworth. 1982. Natural vs. plantation forests: A case study of land reclamation strategies for the humid tropics. *Environ. Mgmt.* 6:485–492. [14]

Jordan, W. R. III. 1987. Making a user-friendly national park for Costa Rica—A visit with Daniel Janzen. *Rest. Mgmt. Notes* 5(2):72–75. [14]

Jordan, W. R. III (ed.). 1990. Standards for restoration and management projects. In G. H. Hughes and T. M. Bonnicksen (eds.), *Restoration '89: The New Management Challenge,* Proceedings of the first annual meeting of the Society for Ecological Restoration, pp. 301–337. Society for Ecological Restoration, Madison, WI. [14]

Jurek, R. M. 1994. A bibliography of feral, stray, and free-roaming domestic cats in relation to wildlife conservation. California Fish and Game, Report no. 94–5, Sacramento, CA. [9]

Kadr, A. B. A. B. , A. L. T. E. S. A. Sabbagh, M. A. S. A. Glenid and M. Y. S. Izzidien. 1983. *Islamic Principles for the Conservation of the Natural Environment.* International Union for the Conservation of Nature and Natural Resources, Gland, Switzerland. [2]

Kale, H. W. 1983. Distribution, habitat, and status of breeding Seaside Sparrows in Florida. In T. L. Quay, J. B. Funderburg, Jr., D. S. Lee, E. F. Potter and C. S. Robbins (eds.), *The Seaside Sparrow, Its Biology and Management,* pp. 41–48. Occasional Papers of the North Carolina Biological Survey, North Carolina State Museum of Natural History, Raleigh, NC. [7]

Kant, I. 1959. *Foundations of the Metaphysics of Morals.* Library of Liberal Arts, New York. [2]

Kareiva, P. M., J. G. Kingsolver and R. B. Huey. (eds.). 1992. *Biotic Interactions and Global Change.* Sinauer Associates, Sunderland, MA. [10]

Karr, J. R. 1982a. Avian extinction on Barro Colorado Island, Panama: A reassessment. *Am. Nat.* 119:220–239. [5]

Karr, J. R. 1982b. Population variability and extinction in the avifauna of a tropical land bridge island. *Ecology* 63:1975–1978. [9]

Karr, J. R. 1990. Avian survival rates and the extinction process on Barro Colorado Island, Panama. *Conserv. Biol.* 4:391–397. [5]

Karr, J. R. 1991. Biological integrity: A long-neglected aspect of water resource management. *Ecol. Appl.* 1:66–84. [14]

Karr, J. R. 1996. Ecological integrity and ecological health are not the same. In P. C. Schulze (ed.), *Engineering within Ecological Constraints*, pp. 97–109. National Academy Press, Washington, D.C. [14]

Kattan, G. H., H. Alvarez-Lopez, and M. Giraldo. 1994. Forest fragmentation and bird extinctions: San Antonio eighty years later. *Conserv. Biol.* 8:138–146. [5]

Kauffman, E. G. and O. H. Walliser. (eds.). 1990. *Extinction Events in Earth History.* Springer-Verlag, New York. [5]

Kauffman, L. 1992. Catastrophic change in species-rich freshwater ecosystems: The lessons of Lake Victoria. *BioScience* 42(11):846–858. [5]

Keast, A. 1961. Bird speciation on the Australian continent. *Bull. Mus. Comp. Zool.* 123:305–495. [4]

Keeton, W. T. 1972. *Biological Science.* 2nd ed. W. W. Norton, New York. [3]

Keller, L. F., P. Arcese, J. N. M. Smith, W. M. Hochachka, and S. C. Stearns. 1994. Selection against inbred song sparrows during a natural population bottleneck. *Nature* 372:356–357. [6]

Kellert, S. R. 1984. Wildlife values and the private landowner. *Am. Forests* 90(11): 27–28, 60–61. [3]

Kempton, W., J. Boster, and J. Hartley. 1995. *Environmental Values in American Culture.* MIT Press, Cambridge, MA. [15]

Kennedy, E. D. and D. W. White. 1996. Interference competition from House Wrens as a factor in the decline of Bewick's Wrens. *Conserv. Biol.* 10:281–284. [7]

Kermack, W. O. and A. G. McKendrick. 1927. A contribution to the mathematical theory of epidemics. *Proc. R. Soc. Lond. A* 115:700–721. [8]

Keynes, J. M. 1936. *The General Theory of Employment, Interest, and Money.* Harcourt Brace, New York. [15]

Kieft, T. L. 1991. Soil microbiology in reclamation of arid and semiarid lands. In J. Skujins (ed.), *Semiarid Lands and Deserts: Soil Resource and Reclamation*, pp. 209–256. Marcel Dekker, New York. [14]

Kiesecker, J. M. and A. R. Blaustein. 1995. Synergism between UV-B radiation and a pathogen magnifies amphibian embryo mortality in nature. *Proc. Natl. Acad. Sci. USA* 92:11049–11052. [5]

Kiester, A. R., J. M. Scott, B. Csuti, R. F. Noss, B. Butterfield, K. Sahr, and D. White. 1996. Conservation prioritization using GAP data. *Conserv. Biol.* 10:1332–1342. [12]

Kilgore, B. M. 1976. Fire management in the national parks: an overview. In Proceedings of the Tall Timbers Fire Ecology Conference, p. 45–57 Florida State University Research Council, Tallahassee. [11]

King, C. 1935. *Mountaineering in the Sierra Nevada.* W. W. Norton, New York. [12]

King, R. B., I. C. Baillie, P. G. Bissett, R. J. Grimble, M. S. Johnson, and G. L. Silva. 1986. Land Resource Survey of Toledo District, Belize. Overseas Development Administration, Land Resources Development Centre, London. [15]

Kinne, O. (ed.). 1971. *Maine Ecology: A Comprehensive, Integrated Treatise on Life in Oceans and Coastal Waters.* Vol. I. Wiley Interscience. [4]

Kirk, D. 1975. *Biology Today,* 2nd ed. Random House, New York. [3]

Kirkpatrick, J. B. 1983. An iterative method for establishing priorities for the selection of nature reserves: An example from Tasmania. *Biol. Conserv.* 25:127–134. [12]

Klein, B. C. 1989. Effects of forest fragmentation on dung and carrion beetle communities in central Amazonia. *Ecology* 70:1715–1725. [9]

Kline, T. C., J. J. Goering, O. A. Mathisen and P. H. Poe. 1990. Recycling of elements transported upstream by runs of Pacific salmon: ^{15}N and ^{13}C evidence in Sashin Creek, southeastern Alaska. *Canad. J. Fish. Aquat. Sci.* 47:136–144. [9]

Kline, V. M. and E. A. Howell. 1987. Prairies. In W. R. Jordan III, M. E. Gilpin and J. D. Aber (eds.), *Restoration Ecology,* pp. 75–83. Cambridge University Press, Cambridge. [14]

Knapp, R. A. 1996. Non-native trout in the natural lakes of the Sierra Nevada: An analysis of their distribution and impacts on native aquatic biota. In *Sierra Nevada Ecosystem Project, Final Report to Congress*, Vol. 3, pp. 363–390. Center for Water and Wildland Resources, University of California, Davis. [5]

Knick, S. T. and J. T. Rotenberry. 1995. Landscape characteristics of fragmented shrubsteppe habitats and breeding passerine birds. *Conserv. Biol.* 9:1059–1071. [9]

Knight, R. and K. Gutzwiller (eds.). 1995. *Wildlife and Recreationists.* Island Press, Washington, D.C. [18]

Knight, R. L. and K. J. Gutzwiller (eds.). 1995. *Outdoor Recreation and Wildlife: Coexistence through Management and Research.* Island Press, Covelo, CA. [9]

Knight, R. L. and Peter B. Landres (eds.). 1997. *Stewardship across Boundaries.* Island Press, Covelo, CA. [10]

Knight, R. L., G. W. Wallace, and W. E. Riebsame. 1995. Ranching the view: Subdivisions versus agriculture. *Conserv. Biol.* 9:459–461. [9]

Knoll, A. H. 1984. Patterns of extinction in the fossil record of vascular plants. In M. H. Nitecki (ed.), *Extinctions,* pp. 21–68. University of Chicago Press, Chicago. [5]

Knoll, A. H. 1986. Patterns of change in plant communities through geological time. In J. Diamond and T. J. Case (eds.), *Community Ecology,* pp. 126–141. Harper & Row, New York. [8]

Koblentz-Mishke, O. J., V. V. Volkovinsky and J. G. Kabanova. 1970. Plankton primary productivity of the world ocean. In W. S. Wooster (ed.), *Scientific Exploration of the South Pacific,* pp. 183–193. National Academy of Sciences Press, Washington, D.C. [4]

Koebel, J. W., Jr. 1995. An historical perspective on the Kissimmee River restoration project. *Restor. Ecol.* 3:149–159. [14]

Koehn, R. K. and S. E. Shumway. 1982. A genetic/physiological explanation for differential growth rate among individuals of the American oyster, *Crassostrea virginica* (Gmelin). *Marine Biol. Lett.* 3:35–42. [6]

Koehn, R. K., W. J. Diehl and T. M. Scott. 1988. The differential contribution by individual enzymes of glycolysis and protein catabolism to the relationship between heterozygosity and growth rate in the coot clam *Mulinia lateralis. Genetics* 118:121–130. [6]

Koopowitz, H., A. D. Thornhill, and M. Andersen. 1994. A general stochastic model for the prediction of biodiversity losses based on habitat conversion. *Conserv. Biol.* 8:425–438. [5]

Köppen, W. 1884. Die Wärmezonen der Erde, nach Dauer der Heissen, Gemässigten und Kalten Zeit, und nach der Wirkung der Wärme auf die Organische Welt betrachtet. *Meterolog. Zeit.* 1:215–226. [4]

Korten, D. C. 1991–1992. Sustainable development. *World Policy J.* 9:157–190. [18]

Krebs, C. J. 1985. *Ecology: The Experimental Analysis of Distribution and Abundance.* 3rd ed. Harper & Row, New York. [8]

Krebs, C. J. 1988. *The Message of Ecology.* Harper & Row, New York. [8]

Kruger, F. J. 1981. Seasonal growth and flowering rhythms: South African heathlands. In R. L. Specht (ed.), *Heathlands and Related Shrublands,* pp. 1–4. (Ecosystems of the World, Vol. 9B). Elsevier, Amsterdam. [4]

Kruger, F. J. and H. C. Taylor. 1979. Plant species diversity in Cape fynbos: Gamma and delta diversity. *Vegetatio* 41:85–93. [4]

Krummel, J. R., R. H. Gardner, G. Sugihara, R. V. O'Neill, and P. R.Coleman. 1987. Landscape pattern in a disturbed environment. *Oikos* 48:321-324. [9]

Kuhn, T. S. 1972. *The Structure of Scientific Revolutions.* 2nd ed. University of Chicago Press, Chicago. [1]

Kupferberg, S. J. 1996. The ecology of native tadpoles (*Rana boylii* and *Hyla regilla*) and the impacts of invading bullfrogs (*Rana catesbeiana*) in a northern California river. Ph.D. dissertation. University of California, Berkeley. [5]

Kusler, J. A. and M. E. Kentula (eds.). 1990. *Wetland Creation and Restoration: The Status of the Science.* Island Press, Washington, D.C. [14]

Lack, D. 1947. *Darwin's Finches.* Cambridge University Press, Cambridge. [6,8]

Lack, D. 1976. *Island Biology: Illustrated by the Land Birds of Jamaica.* Blackwell Scientific Publications, Oxford. [9]

Lackey, R. T. 1997. Seven pillars of ecosystem management. *Landscape and Urban Planning.* In press. [11]

Laerm, J., J. C. Avise, J. C. Patton and R. A. Lansman. 1982. Genetic determination of the status of an endangered species of pocket gopher in Georgia. *J. Wildl. Mgmt.* 46:513–518. [6]

Lamberson, R. H., R. McKelvey, B. R. Noon and C. Voss. 1992. The effects of varying dispersal capabilities on the population dynamics of the Northern Spotted Owl. *Conserv. Biol.* 6:505–512. [13]

Lamberson, R. H., B. R. Noon, C. Voss and K. S. McKelvey. 1994. Reserve design for territorial species: The effects of patch size and spacing on the viability of the Northern Spotted Owl. *Conserv. Biol.* 8: 185-195. [13]

Lamont, B. B., A. J. M. Hopkins and R. J. Hnatiuk. 1984. The Flora—Composition, Diversity and Origins. In J. S. Pate and J. S. Berd (eds.), *Kwongan: Plant Life of the Sandplain,* pp. 27–50. University of Western Australia Press, Nedlands. [4]

Lande, R. 1987. Extinction thresholds in demographic models of territorial populations. *Am. Nat.* 130:624-635. [7,13]

Lande, R. 1988. Genetics and demography in biological conservation. *Science* 241: 1455–1460. [6,10]

Lande, R. 1995. Mutation and conservation. *Conserv. Biol.* 9:782–791. [6]

Langis, R., M. Zalejko, and J. B. Zedler. 1991. Nitrogen assessments in a constructed and a natural salt marsh of San Diego Bay, California. *Ecol. Applic.* 1:40–51. [14]

Larkin, P. A. 1977. An epitaph to the concept of maximum sustained yield. *Trans. Amer. Fish. Soc.* 106:1–11. [18]

Larmar, P. and R. Ring. 1994. Can planning rein in a stampede? *High Country News* 26:6–8. [9]

Laslett, P. and J. S. Fishkin (eds.). 1992. *Justice between Age Groups and Generations.* Yale University Press, New Haven. [15]

Lasswell, H. D. 1970. The emerging conception of the policy sciences. *Policy Sci.* 1:3–14. [17]

Lasswell, H. D. 1971. *Pre-view of the Policy Sciences.* Elsevier, New York. [17]

Lasswell, H. D. and A. Kaplan. 1950. *Power and Society: A Framework for Political Inquiry.* Yale University Press, New Haven, CT. [17]

Lasswell, H. D. and M. McDougal. 1992. *Jurisprudence for a Free Society: Studies in Law, Science, and Policy.* 2 vols. New Haven Press, New Haven, CT. [17]

Laurance, W. F. 1990. Comparative responses of five arboreal marsupials to tropical forest fragmentation. *J. Mammal.* 71:641–653. [9]

Laurance, W. F. 1991. Edge effects in tropical forest fragments: Application of a model for the design of nature reserves. *Biol. Conserv.* 57:205–219. [9]

Laurance, W. F., K. R. McDonald, and R. Speare. 1996. Epidemic disease and the catastrophic decline of Australian rain forest frogs. *Conserv. Biol.* 10(2):406–413. [5]

Lavelle, M. and M. Coyle. 1992. Unequal protection: The racial divide in environmental law. *Nat. Law J. Spec. Invest.,* September 21, s1–s12. [16]

Lawton, J. H. and K. C. Brown. 1986. The population and community ecology of invading insects. *Phil. Trans. R. Soc. Lond.* 314:607–617. [8]

Lawton, J. H. and V. K. Brown. 1993. Redundancy in ecosystems. In E.-D. Schulze and H. A. Mooney (eds.), *Biodiversity and Ecosystem Function,* pp. 255–270. Springer-Verlag, Berlin. [15]

Lea, I. 1827–1874. Observations on the genus *Unio.* Privately published, Philadelphia, PA. [3]

Leach, M. K. and T. J. Givnish. 1996. Ecological determinants of species loss in remnant prairies. *Science* 273:1555–1558. [5]

Leader-Williams, N. and S. D. Albon. 1988. Allocation of resources for conservation. *Nature* 336:533–535. [18]

Leary, R. F., F. W. Allendorf and K. L. Knudsen. 1983. Developmental stability and enzyme heterozygosity in rainbow trout. *Nature* 301:71–72. [6]

Leberg, P. L. 1991. Influence of fragmentation and bottlenecks on genetic divergence of wild turkey populations. *Conserv. Biol.* 5:522–530. [6,9]

Leck, C. F. 1979. Avian extinctions in an isolated tropical wet-forest preserve, Ecuador. *Auk* 96:343–352. [9]

Lee, K. N. 1993a. *Compass and Gyroscope: Integrating Science and Politics for the Environment.* Island Press, Washington, D.C. [11]

Lee, K. N. 1993b. Greed, scale mismatch, and learning. *Ecol. Applic.* 3:560–564. [18]

Lee, M. 1996. Elvers expressly. *Living Oceans News,* Spring, 1, 8. [5]

Lehman, J. T. 1986. Control of eutrophication in Lake Washington. In G. H. Orians et al. (eds.), *Ecological Knowledge and Environmental Problem-Solving,* pp. 301–312. National Academy Press, Washington, D.C. [14]

Lehmkuhl, J. F. and M. G. Raphael. 1993. Habitat pattern around Northern Spotted Owl locations on the Olympic Penisula, Washington. *J. Wildl. Mgmt.* 57:302–315. [13]

Leigh, E. G., Jr., R. T. Paine, J. F. Quinn, and T. H. Suchanek. 1986. Wave energy and intertidal productivity. *Proc. Natl. Acad. Sci., USA* 84:1314–1318. [4]

Lenat, D. R. 1988. Water quality assessment of streams using a qualitative collection method for benthic macroinvertebrates. *J. N. Am. Benthic Soc.* 7:222–233. [14]

Leonard, J. 1987. *Natural Resources and Economic Development in Central America.* International Institute for Environment and Development, Washington, D.C. [13]

Leopold, A. 1933. *Game Management.* Charles Scribner's Sons, New York. [11]

Leopold, A. 1938. Engineering and conservation. Lecture to the University of Wisconsin College of Engineering, 11 April 1938. [11]

Leopold, A. 1939. A biotic view of land. *J. Forestry* 37:727–730. [11]

Leopold, A. 1940. The state of the profession. *J. Wildl. Mgmt.* 4:343–346. [2]

Leopold, A. 1947. The ecological conscience. *Bulletin of the Garden Club of America,* September. [11]

Leopold, A. 1949. *A Sand County Almanac and Sketches Here and There.* Oxford University Press, New York. [1,2,8]

Leopold, A. 1953. *Round River. From the Journals of Aldo Leopold.* Oxford University Press, New York. [2]

Lesica, P. 1996. Using fire history models to estimate proportions of old growth forest in northwest Montana, USA. *Biol. Conserv.* 77: 33-39 [12]

Levin, D. A. 1979. The nature of plant species. *Science* 204:381–384. [3]

Levin, D. A. and W. L. Crepet. 1973. Genetic variation in *Lycopodium lucidulum:* A phylogenetic relic. *Evolution* 27:622–632. [6]

Levins, R. 1966. Strategy of model building in population biology. *Am. Sci.* 54:421-431. [7]

Levins, R. 1969. Some demographic and genetic consequences of environmental heterogeneity for biological control. *Bull. Entomol. Soc. Am.* 15:237-240. [7]

Levinton, A. and R. I. Bowman (eds.). 1981. *Patterns of Evolution in Galapágos Organisms.* Special Publication, AAAS, Pacific Division. [6]

Lewis, M. 1978. Acute toxicity of copper, zinc and managnese in single and mixed salt solutions to juvenile longfin dace, *Agosia chrysogaster. J. Fish. Biol.* 13:695–700. [11]

Licht, L. E. 1996. Amphibian decline still a puzzle. *BioScience* 46(3):172–173. [5]

Light, S. S., L. H. Gunderson, and C. S. Holling. 1995. The Everglades: Evolution of management in a turbulent environment. In L. H. Gunderson, C. S. Holling, and S. S. Light (eds.), *Barriers and Bridges to the Renewal of Ecosystems and Institutions.* Columbia University Press, New York. [13]

Limerick, P. N. 1988. *The Legacy of Conquest: The Unbroken Past of the American West.* W. W. Norton, New York. [9]

Limpus, C. and Reimer, D. 1994. The loggerhead turtle, *Caretta caretta,* in Queensland: A population in decline. In Proceedings of the Australian Marine Turtle Workshop, Sea World Nara Resort, Gold Coast, 1990, pp. 39–59. [13]

Limpus, C. J. 1993. Conservation of Marine Turtles in the Indo-Pacific Region. Queensland Department of Environment and Heritage. Unpublished report to the Australian Nature Conservation Agency. [13]

Limpus, C. J., and J. Miller. 1993. Family Cheloniidae. In C. J. Glasby, G. J. B. Ross, and P. L. Beesley (eds.), *Fauna of Australia,* Vol 2A: *Amphibia and Reptilia,* pp. 133–138. Australian Government Publishing Service, Canberra, Australia. [13]

Lindburg, D. G., B. S. Durrant, S. E. Millard and J. E. Oosterhuis. 1993. Fertility assessment of cheetah males with poor quality semen. *Zoo Biol.* 12:97–103. [6]

Lindenmayer, D. B. and H. A. Nix. 1993. Ecological principles for the design of wildlife corridors. *Conserv. Biol.* 7:627– 630. [10]

Liu, J. 1993. ECOLECON: An ECOLogical-ECONomic model for species conservation in complex forest landscapes. *Ecol. Modelling* 70:63–87.

Liu, J., F. W. Cubbage and H. R. Pulliam. 1994. Ecological and economic effects of forest landscape structure and rotation length: Simulation studies using ECOLECON. *Ecol. Econ.* 10:249–263. [12]

Liu, J., J. B. Dunning and H. R. Pulliam. 1995. Potential effects of a forest management plan on Bachman's Sparrows (*Aimophila aestivalis*): Linking a spatially explicit model with GIS. *Conserv. Biol.* 9:62–75.

Livingstone, D. A. 1975. Late quaternary climate change in Africa. *Annu. Rev. Ecol. Syst.* 6:249–280. [4]

Livingstone, D. A. and T. van der Hammen. 1978. Paleogeography and paleoclimatology. In *Tropical Forest Ecosystems*, pp. 61–90. UNESCO/UNEP/FAO. [4]

Llandres, C. and C. Urdiales. 1990. *Las aves de Doñana*. Lynx, Barcelona. [13]

Loar, J. M. 1985. *Application of habitat evaluation models in Southern Appalachian trout streams*. Publication 2383. Oak Ridge National Laboratory, Environmental Science Division. [12]

Lodge, D. M. 1993. Species invasions and deletions: community effects and responses to climate and habitat change. In P. M. Kareiva, J. G. Kingsolver and R. B. Huey (eds.), 1993. *Biotic Interactions and Global Change*, pp. 367–387. Sinauer Associates, Sunderland, MA. [8]

Loeschcke, V., J. Tomiuk, and S. K. Jain (eds.). 1994. *Conservation Genetics*. Birkhauser Verlag, Basel, Switzerland. [6]

Long, J. 1981. *Introduced Birds of the World*. David and Charles, London. [8]

Long, L. E., L. S. Saylor, and M. E. Soulé. 1995. A pH/UV-B synergism in amphibians. *Conserv. Biol.* 9:1301–1303. [5]

Lord, J. M. and D. A. Norton. 1990. Scale and the spatial concept of fragmentation. *Conserv. Biol.* 4:197–202. [9]

Lorimer, C. G. 1989. Relative effects of small and large disturbances on temperate forest structure. *Ecology* 70:565–567. [9]

Lovejoy, T. E. 1980. A projection of species extinctions. In Council on Environmental Quality, *The Global 2000 Report to the President: Entering the Twenty-First Century*, pp. 328–331. U.S. Government Printing Office, Washington, D.C. [5]

Lovejoy, T. E. and ten others. 1986. Edge and other effects of isolation on Amazon forest fragments. In M. E. Soulé (ed.), *Conservation Biology: The Science of Scarcity and Diversity*, pp. 257–285. Sinauer Associates, Sunderland, MA. [9,12]

Lovejoy, T. E. and H. O. R. Shubart. 1980. The ecology of Amazonian development. In F. Barbira-Scazzacchio (ed.), *Land, People and Planning in Contemporary Amazonia*, pp. 21–26. Cambridge University Press, Cambridge. [5]

Lovelock, J. 1988. *The Ages of Gaia. A Biography of Our Living Earth*. W. W. Norton, New York. [2]

Lovins, A. B. 1990. Four revolutions in electric efficiency. *Contemporary Policy Issues* 8:122–141. [15]

Low, B. and J. Heinen. 1993. Population, resources, and environment: Implications of human behavioral ecology for conservation. *Popul. Environ.* 15(1):7–41. [19]

Lowe-McConnell, M. 1993. Fish faunas of the African Great Lakes: Origins, diversity and vulnerability. *Conserv. Biol.* 7:634–643. [5]

Lubchenco, J. et al. 1991. The sustainable biosphere initiative: An ecological research agenda. *Ecology* 72:371–412. [18]

Ludwig, D. R. Hilborn and C. Walters. 1993. Uncertainty, resource exploitation, and conservation: Lessons from history. *Science* 260:17, 36. [16,18]

Lugo, A. E. 1988. Estimating reductions in the diversity of tropical forest species. In E. O. Wilson and F. M. Peter (eds.), *Biodiversity*, pp. 58–70. National Academy Press, Washington, D.C. [5]

Luken, J. O. 1990. *Directing Ecological Succession*. Chapman and Hall, London. [14]

Lydeard, C. and R. L. Mayden. 1995. A diverse and endangered aquatic ecosystem of the southeast United States. *Conserv. Biol.* 9:800–805. [5]

Lyons, J., S. Navarro-Perez, P. A. Cochran, E. Santana-C., and M. Guzman-Arroyo. 1995. Index of biotic integrity based on fish assemblages for the conservation of streams and rivers in westcentral Mexico. *Conserv. Biol.* 9:569–584. [14]

MacArthur, R. H. 1964. Environmental factors affecting bird species diversity. *Am. Nat.* 98:387–397. [4]

MacArthur, R. H. 1972. *Geographical Ecology: Patterns in the Distribution of Species*. Princeton University Press, Princeton, NJ. [4, 5, 7, 9]

MacArthur, R. H. and J. MacArthur. 1961. On bird species diversity. *Ecology* 42:594–598. [4,12]

MacArthur, R. H. and E. O. Wilson. 1963. An equilibrium theory of insular zoogeography. *Evolution* 17:373–387. [9]

MacArthur, R. H. and E. O. Wilson 1967. *The Theory of Island Biogeography*. Princeton University Press, Princeton, NJ. [4]

MacArthur, R. H., H. E. Recher and M. L. Cody. 1966. On the relation between habitat selection and species diversity. *Am. Nat.* 100:319–332. [4]

Mace, G. M. 1994. Classifying threatened species: Means and ends. *Phil. Trans. Royal Soc. Lond. B* 344:91–97. [5]

Mace, G. M. 1995. Classification of threatened species and its role in conservation planning. In J. H. Lawton and R. M. May (eds.), *Extinction Rates*, pp. 197–213. Oxford University Press, New York. [5]

Mace, G. M., N. Collar, and J. Cooke. 1992. The development of new criteria for listing species on the IUCN Red List. *Species* 19:16–22. [5]

MacKinnon, J. and K. MacKinnon. 1986a. *Review of the Protected Areas System in the Afrotropical Realm*. International Union for the Conservation of Nature and Natural Resources, Gland, Switzerland. [5]

MacKinnon, J. and K. MacKinnon. 1986b. *Review of the Protected Areas System in the Indo-Malayan Realm*. International Union for the Conservation of Nature and Natural Resources, Gland, Switzerland. [5]

MacMahon, J. A. 1979. North American deserts: Their floral and faunal components. In R. A. Perry and D. W. Goodall (eds.), *Arid Land Ecosystems: Structure, Functioning and Management*, Vol. 1. pp. 21–82. Cambridge University Press, Cambridge. [10]

MacMahon, J. A. 1981. Successional processes: Comparisons among biomes with special reference to probable roles of and influences on animals. In D. C. West, H. H. Shugart and D. B. Botkin (eds.), *Forest Succession: Concept and Application*, pp. 277–304. Springer-Verlag, New York. [14]

MacMahon, J. A. 1987. Disturbed lands and ecological theory: An essay about a mutualistic association. In W. R. Jordan III, M. E. Gilpin and J. D. Aber (eds.), *Restoration Ecology: A Synthetic Approach to Ecological Research*, pp. 221–237. Cambridge University Press, Cambridge. [14]

MacVicar, T. K. and S. S. T. Lin. 1984. Historical rainfall activity in central and southern Florida: Average, return period estimates and selected extremes. In P. J. Gleason (ed.), *Environments of South Florida: Present and Past II*. Miami Geological Society, Coral Gables, FL. [13]

Maddox, Bronwen. 1994. Fleets fight in overfished waters. *Financial Times*, 30 August, p 4. [5]

Mader, H. J. 1984. Animal habitat isolation by roads and agricultural fields. *Biol. Conserv.* 29:81–96. [9]

Mader, H. J., C. Schell and P. Kornacker. 1990. Linear barriers to movements in the landscape. *Biol. Conserv.* 54:209–222. [9]

Maille, P. and R. Mendelsohn. 1993. Valuing Ecotourism in Madagascar. *J. Environ. Mgmt.* 38:213–218. [18]

Majer, J. D. (ed.). 1989. *Animals in Primary Succession: The Role of Fauna in Reclaimed Lands*. Cambridge University Press, Cambridge. [14]

Malthus, T. 1963. *Principles of Population*. Reprint. Richard D. Irwin, Homewood, IL. [15]

March, J. G., J. P. Benstead, and C. M. Pringle. 1996. Migration of freshwater shrimp larvae: Elevational and diel patterns in two tropical river drainages, Puerto Rico [Abstract]. *Bull. N. Am. Benthol. Soc.* 13:161. [9]

Marglin, S. A. 1963. The social rate of discount and the optimal rate of investment. *Q. J. Econ.* 77:95–112. [15]

Margules, C. R. and M. P. Austin (eds.). 1992. *Nature Conservation: Cost Effective Biological Survey and Data Analysis*. CSIRO, Melbourne, Australia. [10]

Margules, C. R., A. J. Higgs and R. W. Rafe. 1982. Modern biogeographic theory: Are there any lessons for nature reserve design? *Biol. Conserv.* 24:115–128. [9]

Margules, C. R., A. O. Nicholls, and R. L. Pressey. 1988. Selecting networks of reserves to maximize biological diversity. *Biol. Conserv.* 43:663–676. [12]

Marks, G. C. and T. T. Kozlowski. 1973. *Ectomycorrhizae*. Academic Press, New York. [8]

Marks, S. A. 1984. *The Imperial Lion: Human Dimensions of Wildlife Management in Central Africa*. Westview Press, Boulder, CO. [18]

Marquis, R. L. and H. E. Braker. 1994. Plant-herbivore interactions: Diversity, specificity, and impact. In L. A. McDade, K. S. Bawa, H. A. Hespenheide and G. S. Hartshorn (eds.), *LaSelva: Ecology and Natural History of a Neotropical Rainforest*, pp. 261–281. University of Chicago Press, Chicago. [4]

Marsh, R. E. 1984. Ground squirrels, prairie dogs, and marmots as pests on rangeland. In Proceedings of the Conference for Organization and Practice of Vertebrate Pest Control, 30 August–3 September, 1982, Hampshire, U.K., pp. 195–208. ICI Plant Protection Division, Fernhurst, U.K. [13]

Martin, P. 1973. The discovery of America. *Science* 179:969–974. [1]

Martin, P. S. and R. G. Klein (eds.). 1984. *Quaternary Extinctions: A Prehistoric Revolution.* University of Arizona Press, Tucson. [1,5]

Martin, R. B. 1986. Communal area management plan for indigenous resources (Project CAMPFIRE). In R. H. V. Bell and E. McShane-Caluzi (eds.), *Conservation and Wildlife Management in Africa*, pp. 279–295. U.S. Peace Corps, Washington, D.C. [18]

Mary, F. and G. Michon. 1987. When agroforestry drives back natural forests: A socio-economic analysis of a rice-agroforest system in Sumatra. *Agroforestry Systems* 5:27–55. [1]

Master, L. 1990. The imperiled status of North American aquatic animals. *Biodiversity Network News* (The Nature Conservancy) 3:1–8. [9]

Mathisen, O. A. 1972. Biogenic enrichment of sockeye salmon lakes and stock productivity. *Verh. Int. Ver. Limnol.* 18:1089–1095. [9]

Maxson, L. R. and A. C. Wilson. 1974. Convergent morphological evolution detected by studying proteins of tree frogs in the *Hyla eximia* species group. *Science* 185:66–68. [6]

May, R. M. 1975. *Stability and Complexity in Model Ecosystems.* 2nd ed. Princeton University Press, Princeton, NJ. [4]

May, R. M. 1988. How many species are there on earth? *Science* 241:1441–1449. [4]

May, R. M. 1990. Taxonomy as destiny. *Nature* 347:129–130. [3]

May, R. M. 1992a. Bottoms up for the oceans. *Nature* 357:278–279. [5]

May, R. M. 1992b. How many species inhabit the Earth? *Sci. Am.* 267:42–48. [5]

May, R. M., J. H. Lawton, and N. E. Stork. 1995. Assessing extinction rates. In J. H. Lawton and R. M. May (eds.), *Extinction Rates*, pp. 1–24. Oxford University Press, New York. [5]

Mayr, E. 1942. *Systematics and the Origin of Species.* Columbia University Press, New York. [3]

Mayr, E. 1959. Darwin and the evolutionary theory in biology. In *Evolution and Anthropology: A Centennial Appraisal*, pp. 409–412. The Anthropological Society of Washington, Washington, D.C. [3]

Mayr, E. 1963. *Animal Species and Evolution.* Belknap Press of Harvard University Press, Cambridge, MA. [3]

Mayr, E. 1969. *Principles of Systematic Zoology.* McGraw-Hill, New York. [3]

Mayr, E. 1982. *The Growth of Biological Thought: Diversity, Evolution and Inheritance.* Harvard University Press, Cambridge, MA. [3,5]

McClenaghan, L. R., Jr. and T. J. O'Shea. 1988. Genetic variability in the Florida manatee (*Trichechus manatus*). *J. Mammal.* 69:481–488. [6]

McCorquodale, S. M. and R. F. DiGiacomo. 1985. The role of wild North American ungulates in the epidemiology of bovine brucellosis: A review. *J. Wildl. Dis.* 21: 351–357. [8]

McCoy, E. D. 1994. "Amphibian decline": A scientific dilemma in more ways than one. *Herpetologica* 50(1):98–103. [5]

McDade, L. A., K. S. Bawa, H. A. Hespenheide, and G. S. Hartshorn (eds.) 1994. *La Selva: Ecology and natural history of a Neotropical rain forest.* University of Chicago Press, Chicago. [16]

McDonald, K. A. and J. H. Brown. 1992. Using montane mammals to model extinctions due to global change. *Conserv. Biol.* 6:409–415. [10]

McDonald, K. R. 1990. *Rheobatrachus* Liem and *Taudactylus* Straughan & Lee (Anura: Leptodactylidae) in Eungella National Park, Queensland: Distribution and decline. *Trans. R. Soc. S. Aust.* 114(4):187–194. [5]

McDougal, M. S., W. M. Reisman, and A. R. Willard. 1988. The world community: A planetary social process. *University Calif. Davis Law Rev.* 21:807–972. [17]

McGarigal, K. and W. C. McComb. 1995. Relationships between landscape structure and breeding birds in the Oregon Coast Range. *Ecol. Monographs* 65:235–260. [9]

McIntyre, S. and G. W. Barrett. 1992. Habitat variegation, an alternative to fragmentation. *Conserv. Biol.* 6:146–147. [9]

McKelvey, K., B. R. Noon and R. H. Lamberson. 1993. Conservation planning for species occupying fragmented landscapes: The case of the Northern Spotted Owl. In P. M. Kareiva, J. G. Kingsolver and R. B. Huey (eds.), *Biotic Interactions and Global Change*, pp. 424–450. Sinauer Associates, Sunderland, MA. [7,9,11]

McKelvey, K. S. and J. D. Johnston. 1992. Historical perspectives on the forests of the Sierra Nevada and the Transverse Ranges of Southern California: Forest conditions at the turn of the century. In J. Verner et al., *The California Spotted Owl: A Technical Assessment of Its Current Status*, pp. 225–246. General Technical Report PSW-GTR-133. Albany, California: Pacific Southwest Research Station, Forest Service, U.S. Department of Agriculture. [13]

McKibben, B. 1989. *The End of Nature.* Anchor Books, New York. [1]

McKibben, B. 1992. *The Age of Missing Information.* Random House, New York. [19]

McKitrick, M. C. and R. M. Zink. 1988. Species concepts in ornithology. *Condor* 90:1–14. [3]

McLain, R.J. and R. G. Lee.1996. Adaptive management: promises and pitfalls. Environmental Management 20: 437-448. [12]

McNeely, J. A. 1988. *Economics and Biological Diversity: Developing and Using Economic Incentives to Conserve Biological Resources.* International Union for the Conservation of Nature and Natural Resources, Gland, Switzerland. [15]

McPhee, J. 1989. *The Control of Nature.* Farrar Straus Giroux, New York. [19]

McPheron, B. A., C. D. Jorgenson, and S. H. Berlocher. 1988. Low genetic variability in a Utah cherry-infesting population of the apple maggot, *Rhagoletis pomonella. Entomol. Exp. Appl.* 46:155–160. [6]

Meadows, D. H. 1990. Biodiversity: The key to saving life on earth. *Land Stewardship Letter* (Summer):4–5. [2]

Meagher, M. and M. E. Meyer. 1994. On the origin of brucellosis in bison of Yellowstone National Park: A review. *Conserv. Biol.* 8:645–653. [8]

Meffe, G. K. 1992. Techno-arrogance and halfway technologies: Salmon hatcheries on the Pacific coast of North America. *Conserv. Biol.* 6:350–354. [11,13,15,18,19]

Meffe, G. K. 1993. Sustainability, natural law, and the "real world." *The George Wright Forum* 10(4):48–52. [1]

Meffe, G. K. 1996. Conservation science—A creative tension. *Oryx* 30:226–228. [1,16]

Meffe, G. K. and A. L. Sheldon. 1988. The influence of habitat structure on fish assemblage composition in Southeastern blackwater streams. *Am. Midl. Nat.* 120: 225–240. [5]

Meffe, G. K. and R. C. Vrijenhoek. 1988. Conservation genetics in the management of desert fishes. *Conserv. Biol.* 2:157–169. [6]

Meffe, G. K., A. H. Ehrlich, and D. Ehrenfeld. 1993. Human population control: The missing agenda. *Conserv. Biol.* 7:1–3. [19]

Meine, C. 1992. Conservation biology and sustainable societies. In M. Oelschlaeger (ed.), *After Earth Day. Continuing the Conservation Effort*, pp. 37–65. University of North Texas Press, Denton, TX. [2,11]

Meine, C. and G. K. Meffe. 1996. Conservation values, conservation science: A healthy tension. *Conserv. Biol.* 10:916–917. [16]

Meine, C. D. 1995. The oldest task in human history. In R. L. Knight and S. F. Bates (eds.), *A New Century of Natural Resources Management*, pp. 7–35. Island Press, Washington, D.C. [13]

Meine, C. D. and G. W. Archibald. 1996. *The Cranes: Status Survey and Conservation Action Plan.* IUCN, Gland, Switzerland, and Cambridge, U.K. [13]

Menges, E. 1990. Population viability analysis for an endangered plant. *Conserv. Biol.* 4:52–62. [7]

Menges, E., D. M. Waller and S. C. Gawler. 1986. Seed set and seed predation in *Pedicularis furbishiae*, a rare endemic of the St. John River, Maine. *Am. J. Bot.* 73:1168–1177. [7]

Menges, E. S. 1992. Stochastic modeling of extinction in plant populations. In P. L. Fiedler and S. K. Jain (eds.), *Conservation Biology: The Theory and Practice of Nature Conservation Preservation and Management*, pp. 253–275. Chapman and Hall, New York. [18]

Menkhaus, S. and D. Lober. 1996. International ecotourism and the valuation of tropical rainforests in Costa Rica. *J. Environ. Mgmt* 47:1–10. [18]

Merola, M. 1994. A reassessment of homozygosity and the case for inbreeding depression in the cheetah, *Acinonyx jubatus*: Implications for conservation. *Conserv. Biol.* 8:961–971. [6]

Merriam, G. 1991. Corridors and connectivity: Animal populations in heterogeneous environments. In D. A. Saunders and R. J. Hobbs (eds.), *Nature Conservation 2: The Role of Corridors*, pp. 133–142. Surrey Beatty, Chipping Norton, Australia. [9]

Merriam, G., M. Kozakiewicz, E. Tsuchiya and K. Hawley. 1989. Barriers as boundaries for metapopulations and demes of *Peromyscus leucopus* in farm landscapes. *Landscape Ecol.* 2:227–235. [9]

Meyer, M. E. and M. Meagher. 1995. Brucellosis in free-ranging bison (*Bison bison*) in Yellowstone, Grand Teton, and Wood Buffalo National Parks: A review. *J. Wildl. Dis.* 31:579–598. [8]

Middleton, S. and D. Liittschwager. 1994. *Witness: Endangered Species of North America.* Chronicle Books, San Francisco. [9]

Milewski, A. V. and W. J. Bond. 1982. Convergence of myrmecochory in mediterranean Australia and South Africa. In R. C. Buckley (ed.), *Ant-Plant Interactions in Australia,* pp. 89–98. Junk, The Hague. [4]

Miller, A. 1985. Cognitive styles and environmental problem-solving. *Int. J. Environ. Stud.* 26:21–31. [17]

Miller, B., D. Biggins, L. Hanebury, and A. Vargas. 1993. Reintroduction of the black-footed ferret. In P. J. S. Olney, G. M. Mace, and A. T. C. Feister (eds.), *Creative Conservation: Interactive Management of Wild and Captive Animals*, pp. 455–463. Chapman and Hall, London. [13]

Miller, B., D. Biggins, C. Wemmer, R. Powell, L. Hanebury, D. Horn, and A. Vargas, 1990a. Development of survival skills in captive-raised Siberian polecats (*Mustela eversmanni*): I. Locating prey. *J. Ethol.* 8:89–94. [13]

Miller, B., C. Wemmer, D. Biggins, and R. Reading. 1990b. A proposal to conserve black-footed ferrets and the prairie dog ecosystem. *Environ. Mgmt.* 14:763–769. [13]

Miller, B., G. Ceballos, and R. Rading. 1994a. Prairie dogs, poison, and biotic diversity. *Conserv. Biol.* 8:677–681. [13]

Miller, B., R. Reading, C. Conway, J. A. Jackson, M. Hutchins, N. Snyder, S. Forrest, J. Frazier, and S. Derrickson. 1994b. Improving endangered species programs: Avoiding organizational pitfalls, tapping the resources, and adding accountability. *Environ. Mgmt.* 18:637–645. [13]

Miller, B., R. P. Reading, and S. Forrest. 1996. *Prairie Night.* Smithsonian Institution Press, Washington, D.C. [13]

Miller, R. R. 1961. Man and the changing fish fauna of the American Southwest. *Papers Mich. Acad. Sci. Arts Lett.* 46:365–404. [12]

Miller, R. R. and E. P. Pister. 1971. Management of the Owens pupfish, *Cyprinodon radiosus,* in Mono County, California. *Trans. Am. Fish. Soc.* 100:502–509. [12]

Miller, R. R., J. D. Williams and J. E. Williams. 1989. Extinctions of North American fishes during the past century. *Fisheries* 14(6):22–38. [5]

Miller, T. 1988. *Living in the Environment.* Preface. Wadsworth Biology Series. Wadsworth Publishing. Belmont, CA. [12]

Mills, L.C. 1995. Edge effects and isolation: Red-backed voles on forest remnants. *Conserv. Biol.* 9:395–403. [9]

Mills, L. S., M. E. Soulé and D. F. Doak. 1993. The keystone-species concept in ecology and conservation. *BioScience* 43:219–224. [8]

Minckley, W. L. 1983. Status of the razorback sucker, *Xyrauchen texanus* (Abbott), in the lower Colorado River. *Southwest. Nat.* 28:165–187.

Minckley, W. L. and J. E. Deacon (eds.). 1991. *Battle against Extinction: Native Fish Management in the American West.* University of Arizona Press, Tucson. [5,6,8]

Minckley, W. L., G. K. Meffe and D. L. Soltz. 1991. Conservation and management of short-lived fishes: The cyprinodontoids. In W. L. Minckley and J. E. Deacon (eds.), *Battle Against Extinction: Native Fish Management in the American West,* pp. 247–282. University of Arizona Press, Tucson. [10]

Mitchell, R. C. and R. T. Carson. 1989. *Using Surveys to Value Public Goods: The Contingent Valuation Method.* Resources for the Future, Washington, D.C. [15]

Mittermeier, R. A., T. Werner, J. C. Ayres and G. A. B. da Fonseca. 1992. O Pais da Megadiversidade. *Ciencia Hoje* 14:20–27. [19]

Mitton, J. B. and M. C. Grant. 1984. Associations among protein heterozygosity, growth rate, and developmental homeostasis. *Annu. Rev. Ecol. Syst.* 15:479–499. [6]

Mladenoff, D. J., M. A. White, J. Pastor and T. R. Crow. 1993. Comparing spatial pattern in unaltered old-growth and disturbed forest landscapes. *Ecol. Applic.* 3:294–306. [9]

Mladenoff, D. J., M. A. White, T. R. Crow, and J. Pastor. 1994. Applying principles of landscape design and management to integrate old-growth forest enhancement and commodity use. *Conserv. Biol.* 8:752–762. [9]

Mladenoff, D. J., T. A. Sickley, R. G. Haight, and A. P. Wydeven. 1995. A regional landscape analysis and prediction of favorable gray wolf habitat in the northern Great Lakes region. *Conserv. Biol.* 9:279–294. [9]

Mohsin, A. K. M. and M. A. Ambok. 1983. *Freshwater Fishes of Peninsular Malaysia.* University Pertanian Malaysia Press, Kuala Lumpur. [5]

Moldenke, A. R. and J. D. Lattin. 1990. Dispersal characteristics of old-growth soil arthropods: The potential for loss of diversity and biological function. *Northwest Environ. J.* 6:408–409. [9]

Monastersky, R. 1993. The deforestation debate. *Sci. News* 144:26–27. [5]

Montes, C., M. A. Bravo, A. Baltanás, P. J. Gutiérrez, G. Sancho, A. M. Marcos, J. R. Jordá, C. M. Duarte, P. Alcorlo, O. García, M. E. González, and M. Otero. 1993. *Bases ecológicas para la gestión integral del cangrejo rojo de la marisma (Procambarus clarkii) en el Parque Nacional de Doñana.* Convenio Instituto para la Conservación de la Naturaleza (ICONA)—Universidad Autónoma de Madrid. 2 vols. Final Report. [13]

Mooney, H. A. 1988. Lessons from Mediterranean-climate regions. In E. O. Wilson and F. M. Peter (eds.), *Biodiversity,* pp. 157–165. National Academy Press, Washington, D.C. [5]

Mooney, H. A. and J. A. Drake. (eds.). 1986. *Ecology of Biological Invasions of North America and Hawaii.* Springer-Verlag, New York. [8]

Moore, P. D. 1993. A helping hand in succession. *Nature* 364:14. [14]

Moritz, C. 1994. Defining "evolutionarily significant units" for conservation. *Trends Ecol. Evol.* 9:373–375. [6]

Morlan, J. C. and R. E. Frenkel. 1992. The Salmon River estuary. *Rest. Mgmt. Notes* 10(1):21–23. [14]

Morrison, P. H. 1990. *Ancient Forests in the Olympic National Forest: Analysis From a Historical and Landscape Perspective.* The Wilderness Society, Washington, D.C. [9]

Morrison, P. H. and F. J. Swanson. 1990. *Fire History and Pattern in a Cascade Range Landscape.* PNW-GTR-254. USDA Forest Service, Portland, OR. [9]

Moulton, M. P. 1985. Morphological similarity and the coexistence of congeners: An experimental test with introduced Hawaiian birds. *Oikos* 44:301–305. [8]

Moulton, M. P. 1993. The all-or-none pattern in introduced Hawaiian passeriforms: The role of competition sustained. *Am. Nat.* 141:105–119. [8]

Moulton, M. P. and S. L. Pimm. 1983. The introduced Hawaiian avifauna: Biogeographical evidence for competition. *Am. Nat.* 121:669–690. [8]

Moulton, M. P. and S. L. Pimm. 1985. The extent of competition in shaping an experimental avifauna. In J. Diamond and T. Case (eds.), *Community Ecology,* pp. 80–97. Harper & Row, New York. [8]

Moulton, M. P. and S. L. Pimm. 1986. Species introductions to Hawaii. In H. Mooney and J. A. Drake (eds.), *Ecology of Biological Invasions of North America and Hawaii,* pp. 231–249. Springer-Verlag, Berlin. [8]

Moulton, M. P. and S. L. Pimm. 1987. Morphological assortment in introduced Hawaiian passerines. *Evol. Ecol.* 1:113–124. [8]

Mountfort, G. 1958. *Portrait of a Wilderness: The Story of the Coto Doñana Expeditions.* Hutchinson & Co., Great Britain. [13]

Moyle, P. B. 1973. Effects of introduced bullfrogs, *Rana catesbeiana,* on the native frogs of the San Joaquin Valley, California. *Copeia* 1973(1):18–22. [5]

Moyle, P. B. and R. A. Leidy. 1992. Loss of biodiversity in aquatic ecosystems: Evidence from fish faunas. In P. L. Fiedler and S. K. Jain (eds.), *Conservation Biology: The Theory and Practice of Nature Conservation, Preservation, and Management,* pp. 127–169. Chapman and Hall, New York. [9]

Mueller-Dombois, D. 1987. Natural dieback in forests. *BioScience* 37:575–583. [9]

Muir, J. 1869. The unpublished journals of John Muir [27 July 1869]. [11]

Murcia, C. 1995. Edge effects in fragmented forests: Implications for conservation. *Trends Ecol. Evol.* 10:58–62. [9]

Murdoch, W. W. 1980. *The Poverty of Nations.* The Johns Hopkins University Press, Baltimore, MD. [19]

Murphy, D., and 10 others. 1994. On reauthorization of the Endangered Species Act. *Conserv. Biol.* 8:1–3. [3]

Murphy, D. D. 1991. Invertebrate conservation. In K. A. Kohm (ed.), *Balancing on the Brink of Extinction: The Endangered Species Act and Lessons for the Future,* pp. 181–198. Island Press, Washington, D.C. [3]

Murphy, D. D. and D. A. Duffus. 1996. Conservation biology and marine biodiversity. *Conserv. Biol.* 10(2):311–312. [4]

Murphy, D. D. and S. B. Weiss. 1988. Ecological studies and the conservation of the Bay checkerspot butterfly, *Euphydryas editha bayensis. Biol. Conserv.* 46:183–200. [9]

Murphy, D. D., K. E. Freas and S. B. Weiss. 1990. An environment-metapopulation approach to population viability analysis for a threatened invertebrate. *Conserv. Biol.* 4:41–51. [7,10]

Murrey, J. 1967. *The Elephant People.* Oxford University Press, New York. [10]

Musick, J. A., S. Branstetter, and J. A. Colvocoresses. 1993. Trends in shark abundance from 1974 to 1991 for the Chesapeake Bight region of the U.S. mid-Atlantic coast. In S. Branstetter (ed.), *Conservation Biology of Elasmobranchs*, pp 1–18. NOAA Tech. Rep. NMFS 115. [5]

Myers, N. 1979. *The Sinking Ark: A New Look at the Problem of Disappearing Species.* Pergamon Press, Oxford. [5]

Myers, N. 1981. A farewell to Africa. *Internat. Wildl.* 11 (Nov/Dec.): 36, 40, 44, 46. [2]

Myers, N. 1983. *A Wealth of Wild Species.* Westview Press, Boulder, CO. [2]

Myers, N. 1985. A look at the present extinction spasm. In R. J. Hoage (ed.), *Animal Extinctions: What Everyone Should Know,* pp. 47–57. Smithsonian Institution Press, Washington, D.C. [5]

Myers, N. 1986. Tackling mass extinction of species: A great creative challenge. The Horace M. Albright Lecture in Conservation, University of California, Berkeley. [5]

Myers, N. 1988. Threatened biotas: "Hot spots" in tropical forests. *The Environmentalist* 8:187–208. [4,5]

Myers, N. 1989. *Deforestation Rates in Tropical Countries and Their Climatic Implications.* Friends of the Earth, Washington, D.C. [5]

Myers, N. 1990a. The biodiversity challenge: Expanded hot-spots analysis. *The Environmentalist* 10(4):243–256. [4,5]

Myers, N. 1990b. Mass extinctions: What can the past tell us about the present and the future? *Global and Planetary Change* 82:175–185. [5]

Myers, N. 1992a. *Future Operational Monitoring of Tropical Forests: An Alert Strategy.* Joint Research Centre, Commission of the European Community, Ispra, Italy. [5]

Myers, N. 1992b. *The Primary Source.* W. W. Norton, New York. [5]

Myers, N. 1992c. Synergisms: Joint effects of climate change and other forms of habitat destruction. In R. L. Peters and T. E. Lovejoy (eds.), *Consequences of the Greenhouse Warming to Biodiversity,* pp. 344– 354. Yale University Press, New Haven. [5]

Myers, N. 1993. Questions of mass extinction. *Biodiv. Conserv.* 2:2–17. [5]

Myers, N. 1994. Population and biodiversity. In F. Graham-Smith (ed.), *Population: The Complex Reality,* pp. 117–136. North American Press/Fulcrum, Golden, CO. [5]

Myers, N. 1995. Population and Biodiversity. *Ambio* 24:56–57. [5]

Myers, N. 1996. The rich diversity of biodiversity issues. In Reaka-Kudla, M. L., D. W. Wilson and E. O. Wilson (eds.), *Biodiversity II: Understanding and Protecting Our Natural Resources,* pp. 125–138. National Academy Press, Washington, D.C. [5]

Myers, N. 1997. Consumption in relation to population, environment and development. *The Environmentalist.* In press. [5]

Myers, R. 1983. Site susceptibility to invasion by the exotic tree *Melaleuca quinquenervia* in south Florida. *J. Appl. Ecol.* 20:645–658. [13]

Nabhan, G. P. and S. Trimble. 1994. *The Geography of Childhood: Why Children Need Wild Places.* Beacon Press, Boston. [19]

Naeem, S., L. J. Thompson, S. P. Lawler, J. H. Lawton, and R. M. Woodfin. 1994. Declining biodiversity can alter the performance of ecosystems. *Nature* 368:734–737. [15]

Naess, A. 1989. *Ecology, Community, and Lifestyle.* Cambridge University Press, Cambridge. [2]

Naiman, R. J., J. M. Melillo and J. M. Hobbie. 1986. Ecosystem alteration of boreal forest streams by beaver (*Castor canadensis*). *Ecology* 67:1254–1269. [8]

Nantel, P., D. Gagnon, and A. Nault. 1996. Population viability analysis of American ginseng and wild leek harvested in stochastic environments. *Conserv. Biol.* 10:608–621. [7]

National Park Service and U.S. Fish and Wildlife Service. 1990. *Yellowstone wolf questions—A digest.* Extracts from *Wolves for Yellowstone? A report to the U.S. Congress.* YELL-560. Yellowstone National Park, WY. [12]

National Research Council. 1990. *Decline of the Sea Turtles: Causes and Prevention.* National Academy Press, Washington, D.C. [13]

National Research Council. 1992. *Restoration of Aquatic Ecosystems: Science, Technology, and Public Policy.* National Academy Press, Washington, D.C. [14]

National Research Council. *Statement to the Committee on Environmental Research,* January 15, 1992. [18]

National Research Council. 1993. *Sustainable Agriculture and the Environment in the Humid Tropics.* National Academy Press, Washington, D.C.

National Research Council. 1995. *Understanding Marine Biodiversity.* National Academy Press, Washington, D.C. 114 pp. [5]

National Research Council. 1996. *Upstream: Salmon and Society in the Pacific Northwest.* National Academy Press, Washington, D.C. 388 pp. [5]

National Research Council, Committee on Restoration of Aquatic Ecosystems. 1992. *Restoration of Aquatic Ecosystems: Science, Technology, and Public Policy.* National Academy Press, Washington, D.C. [14]

Nature Conservancy (UK). 1984. *Nature Conservation in Great Britain.* Nature Conservancy Council, Shrewsbury. [5]

Naumann, M. 1994. A water-use budget for the Caribbean National Forest of Puerto Rico. Special Report, USDA Forest Service, 53 pp.

Nehlsen, W., J. E. Williams, and J. A. Lichatowich. 1991. Pacific salmon at the crossroads: Stocks at risk from California, Oregon, Idaho, and Washington. *Fisheries* 16:4–21. [9, 11]

Nei, M. 1973. Analysis of gene diversity in subdivided populations. *Proc. Natl. Acad. Sci. U.S.A.* 70:3321–3323. [6]

Nei, M. 1975. *Molecular Population Genetics and Evolution.* North-Holland, Amsterdam. [6]

Nelson, H. L. 1987. Prairie restoration in the Chicago area. *Rest. Mgmt. Notes* 5(2):60–67. [14]

Nelson, M. E. and L. D. Mech. 1987. Demes within a northeastern Minnesota deer population. In B. D. Chepko-Sade and Z. T. Halpin (eds.), *Mammalian Dispersal Patterns,* pp. 27–40. University of Chicago Press, Chicago. [10]

Nelson, R. H. 1991. *Reaching for Heaven on Earth: The Theological Meaning of Economics.* Rowman and Littlefield, Savage, MD. [15]

Nelson, R. K. 1983. *Make Prayers to the Raven: A Koyukon View of the Northern Forest.* University of Chicago Press, Chicago. [2]

Nemecek, S. 1996. Return of the red wolf. *Sci. Am.* 274:31–32. [12]

Nevo, E. 1978. Genetic variation in natural populations: Patterns and theory. *Theor. Pop. Biol.* 13:121–177. [6]

Newmark, W. D. 1985. Legal and biotic boundaries of western North American national parks: A problem of congruence. *Biol. Conserv.* 33:197–208. [10]

Newmark, W. D. 1987. A land-bridge island perspective on mammalian extinctions in western North American parks. *Nature* 325:430–432. [10]

Newmark, W. D. 1991. Tropical forest fragmentation and the local extinction of understory birds in the eastern Usambara Mountains, Tanzania. *Conserv. Biol.* 5:67–78. [9]

Newmark, W. D. 1995. Extinction of mammal populations in western North American national parks. *Conserv. Biol.* 9:512–526. [9,10]

Nicholls, A. O., and C. R. Margules. 1993. An upgraded reserve selection algorithm. *Biol. Conserv.* 64:165–169. [12]

Nielsen, J. L. (ed.). 1995. Evolution and the Aquatic Ecosystem: Defining Unique Units in Population Conservation. American Fisheries Society Symposium 17, AFS, Bethesda, MD. [6]

Nilsson, S. G. 1986. Are bird communities in small biotope patches random samples from communities in large patches? *Biol. Conserv.* 38:179–204. [9]

Nimmo, D. and J. E. Combs. 1985. *Nightly Horrors: Crisis Coverage in Television Network News.* University of Tennessee Press, Knoxville. [16]

Nixon, K. C. and Q. D. Wheeler, 1992. Measures of phylogenetic diversity. In M. Novacek and Q. D. Wheeler (eds.), *Extinction and Phylogeny,* pp. 216–234. Columbia University Press, New York. [3]

Nkrumah, N. 1995. The Effects of Land and Tree Tenure Rights on Deforestation Patterns in the Forest Savannah Transition Zone, Ghana, West Africa. Master's Thesis, University of Michigan School of Natural Resources and Environment. [19]

NMFS. 1996. *Our Living Oceans: Report on the Status of U.S. Living Marine Resources, 1995.* U.S. Dept. Commerce, NOAA Tech. Memo. NMFS-F/SPO-19. 160 pp. [5]

NOAA. 1994. *Report of the 18th Northeast Regional Stock Assessment Workshop.* National Marine Fisheries Service, Woods Hole, MA. 71 pp. [5]

Noon, B. R., K. S. McKelvey, D. W. Lutz, W. S. LaHaye, R. J. Gutierrez and C. A. Moen. 1992. Estimates of demographic parameters and rates of population change. In J. Verner et al., *The California Spotted Owl: A Technical Assessment of Its Current Status,* pp. 175–186. General Technical Report PSW-GTR-133. Albany, California: Pacific Southwest Research Station, Forest Service, U.S. Department of Agriculture. [13]

Norgaard, R. B. 1989. The case for methodological pluralism. *Ecol. Econ.* 1:37–57. [15]

Norgaard, R. B. 1994. *Development Betrayed: The End of Progress and a Coevolutionary Visioning of the Future.* Routledge, London. [15]

Norris, R. 1992. Can ecotourism save natural areas? *National Parks* 66:30–35. [18]

Norse, E. A. (ed.) 1993. *Global Marine Biological Diversity: A Strategy for Building Conservation into Decision Making.* Island Press, Washington, D.C. [4]

Norse, E. A. 1996. A river that flows to the sea: The marine biological diversity movement. *Oceanography* 9(1):5–9. [4]

Norton, B. G. (ed.). 1986. *The Preservation of Species: The Value of Biological Diversity.* Princeton University Press, Princeton, NJ. [15]

Norton, B. G. 1987. *Why Preserve Natural Variety?* Princeton University Press, Princeton, NJ. [2]

Norton, B. G. 1991. *Toward Unity among Environmentalists.* Oxford University Press, New York. [2]

Norton, B. G. 1995. Ecological integrity and social values: At what scale? *Ecosystem Health* 1:228–241. [15]

Norton, D. A. 1991. *Trilepidea adamsii:* An obituary for a species. *Conserv. Biol.* 5:52–57. [7]

Norton, D. A., R. J. Hobbs, and L. Atkins. 1995. Fragmentation, disturbance, and plant distribution: Mistletoes in woodland remnants in the Western Australian Wheatbelt. *Conserv. Biol.* 9:426–438. [9]

Norway/U.N. Conference on Alien Species. 1996. Chairman's Report, The Trondheim Conferences on Biodiversity. [8]

Noss, R. F. 1981. The birds of Sugarcreek, an Ohio nature reserve. *Ohio J. Sci.* 81:29–40. [9]

Noss, R. F. 1983. A regional landscape approach to maintain diversity. *BioScience* 33:700–706. [7,9]

Noss, R. F. 1987. Corridors in real landscapes: A reply to Simberloff and Cox. *Conserv. Biol.* 1:159–164. [10]

Noss, R. F. 1990. Indicators for monitoring biodiversity: A hierarchical approach. *Conserv. Biol.* 4:355–364. [4,9]

Noss, R. F. 1991a. Effects of edge and internal patchiness on avian habitat use in an old-growth Florida hammock. *Natural Areas J.* 11:34–47. [9]

Noss, R. F. 1991b. Landscape connectivity: Different functions at different scales. In W. E. Hudson (ed.), *Landscape Linkages and Biodiversity,* pp. 27–39. Island Press, Washington, D.C. [10]

Noss, R. F. 1992. The wildlands project: Land conservation strategy. *Wild Earth* (Special Issue):10–25. [3,10]

Noss, R. F. and L. D. Harris. 1986. Nodes, networks, and MUMs: Preserving diversity at all scales. *Environ. Mgmt.* 10:299–309. [10]

Noss, R. F. and L. D. Harris. 1990. Habitat connectivity and the conservation of biological diversity: Florida as a case history. In *Proceedings of the 1989 Society of American Foresters National Convention,* Spokane, WA. pp. 131–135. Society of American Foresters, Bethesda, MD. [9]

Noss, R. F. and A. Cooperrider. 1994. *Saving Nature's Legacy: Protecting and Restoring Biodiversity.* Defenders of Wildlife and Island Press, Washington, D.C. [9]

Noss, R. F., E. T. LaRoe III, and J. M. Scott. 1995. Endangered ecosystems of the United States: A preliminary assessment of loss and degradation. Biological Report 28, National Biological Service, U.S. Department of the Interior, Washington, D.C. [12]

Noss, R. F., H. B. Quigley, M. G. Hornocker, T. Merrill and P. C. Paquet. 1996. Conservation biology and carnivore conservation in the Rocky Mountains. *Conserv. Biol.* 10:949–963. [9]

Noss, R. R. 1996. Conservation biology, values, and advocacy. *Conserv. Biol.* 10:904. [17]

Nowak, R. M. and J. L. Paradiso. 1983. *Walker's Mammals of the World.* 4th ed. Johns Hopkins University Press, Baltimore, MD. [10]

O'Brien, S. J. 1994. The cheetah's conservation controversy. *Conserv. Biol.* 8:1153–1155. [6]

O'Brien, S. J., D. E. Wildt, D. Goldman, C. R. Merril and M. Bush. 1983. The cheetah is depauperate in genetic variation. *Science* 221:459–462. [6]

O'Brien, S. J. and nine others. 1985. Genetic basis for species vulnerability in the cheetah. *Science* 227:1428–1434. [6]

Odum, E. P. 1953. *Fundamentals of Ecology.* W. B. Saunders, Philadelphia, PA. [2]

Odum, E. P. 1987. *The Georgia landscape: A changing resource.* Final report of the Kellogg Physical Resources Task Force, Institute of Ecology, University of Georgia, Athens, GA. [7]

Odum, E. P. 1988. *Kellogg Task Force, Physical Resources.* Institute of Ecology, University of Georgia. [12]

Odum, E. P. 1989. Input management of production systems. *Science* 243:177–182. [9]

Odum, E. P. 1993. *Ecology and Our Endangered Life-Support Systems.* 2nd ed. Sinauer Associates, Sunderland, MA. [1,5]

Odum, W. E., E. P. Odum and H. T. Odum. 1995. Nature's pulsing paradigm. *Estuaries* 18: 547–555. [11]

Ogden, J. C. 1978. Recent population trends of colonial wading birds on the Atlantic and Gulf Coastal plains. In A. Sprunt, J. C. Ogden and S. Winckler (eds.), *Wading Birds.* Research Report no. 7, pp. 137–153, National Audubon Society, NY [13]

Ogden, J. C. 1994. A comparison of wading bird nesting colony dynamics as an indication of ecosystem conditions in the southern Everglades. In S. M. Davis and J. C. Ogden (eds.), *Everglades, The Ecosystem and its Restoration.* St. Lucie Press, Delray, FL. [13]

Ogutu-Ohwayo, R. 1990. The decline of the native fishes of lakes Victoria and Kyoga (East Africa) and the impact of introduced species, especially the Nile Perch, *Lates niloticus* and the Nile Tilapia, *Oreochromis niloticus. Environ. Biol. Fishes* 27:81–96. [5]

Ohio Environmental Protection Agency. 1988. *Biological Criteria for the Protection of Aquatic Life.* Ohio EPA, Division of Water Quality Monitoring and Assessment, Surface Water Section, Columbus, OH. [14]

Oldeman, R. A. A. 1978. Architecture and energy exchange of dicotyledonous trees in the forest. In P. B. Tomlinson and M. H. Zimmermann (eds.), *Tropical Trees as Living Systems,* pp. 535–560. Cambridge University Press, London. [18]

O'Neill, R. V. and eleven others. 1988. Indices of landscape pattern. *Landscape Ecol.* 1:153–162. [9]

Opdam, P., D. van Dorp and C. J. F. ter Braak. 1984. The effect of isolation on the number of woodland birds in small woods in the Netherlands. *J. Biogeogr.* 11:473–478. [9]

Ophuls, W. 1977. *Ecology and the Politics of Scarcity.* W. H. Freeman, San Francisco. [16]

Opler, P. A. 1978. *Insects of American Chesnut: Possible Importance and Conservation Concern.*The American Chestnut Symposium. West Virginia University Press, Morgantown, WV. [8]

Orians, G. H. 1993. Endangered at what level? *Ecol. Appl.* 3:206–208. [12]

Orians, G. H. and W. E. Kunin. 1991. Ecological uniqueness and loss of species. In G. H. Orians, G. M. Brown, W. E. Kunin and J. E. Swierzbinski (eds.), *The Preservation and Valuation of Biological Resources,* pp. 146–184. University of Washington Press, Seattle. [4]

Orr, D. W. 1991. Politics, conservation, and public information. *Conserv. Biol.* 5:10–12. [16]

Orr, D. W. 1992. *Ecological Literacy: Education and the Transition to a Postmodern World.* State University of New York Press, Albany. [16]

Orr, D. W. 1994. The effective shape of our future. *Conserv. Biol.* 8:622–624. [9]

Ortmann, A. E. 1920. Correlation of shape and station in fresh water mussels (*Naiades*). *Proc. Am. Phil. Soc.* 59(4):269–312. [3]

Ostfeld, R. S. and C. D. Canham. 1993. Effects of meadow vole density on tree seedling survival in old fields. *Ecology* 74:1792–1801. [12]

Ostrom, E. 1990. *Governing the Commons.* Cambridge University Press, Cambridge. [19]

Ostrom, E., R. Gardner, and J. Walker. 1994. *Rules, Games, and Common-Pool Resources.* University of Michigan Press, Ann Arbor. [19]

O'Toole, R. 1991. Recreation fees and the Yellowstone forests. In R. B. Keiter and M. S. Boyce (eds.), *The Greater Yellowstone Ecosystem: Redefining America's Wilderness Heritage,* pp. 41–48. Yale University Press, New Haven. [18]

Otte, D. and J. A. Endler (eds.). 1989. *Speciation and Its Consequences.* Sinauer Associates, Sunderland, MA. [3]

Overbay, J. C. 1992. Ecosystem management. In *Proceedings of the National Workshop: Taking an Ecological Approach to Management,* pp. 3-15. USDA Forest Service Publication WO-WSA-3, Washington, DC. [11]

Oxley, D. J., M. B. Fenton and G. R. Carmody. 1974. The effects of roads on populations of small mammals. *J. Appl. Ecol.* 11:51–59. [9]

Oye, K. and J. Maxwell. 1995. Self-interest and environmental management. In R. O Keohane and E. Ostrom (eds.), *Local Commons and Global Interdependence,* pp. 191–222 . Sage Publications, London. [19]

Pace, F. 1991. The Klamath corridors: Preserving biodiversity in the Klamath National Forest. In W. E. Hudson (ed.), *Landscape Linkages and Biodiversity,* pp. 105–116. Island Press, Washington, D.C. [10]

Pacific Rivers Council. 1993. The decline of coho salmon and the need for protection under the Endangered Species Act. Report of the Pacific Rivers Council, P.O. Box 309, Eugene, OR. [9]

Packard, S. and C. F. Mutel (eds.). 1996. *The Tallgrass Restoration Handbook for Prairies, Savannas and Woodlands.* Island Press, Washington, D.C. [14]

Packard, S. and H. L. Nelson. (eds.). In press. *Prairie Restoration.* Island Press, Washington, D.C. [14]

Paine, R. T. 1966. Food web complexity and species diversity. *Am. Nat.* 100:65–75. [8]

Paine, R. T. 1969. The *Pisaster-Tegula* interaction: Prey patches, predator food preference, and intertidal community structure. *Ecology* 50:950–961. [8]

Paine, R. T. 1974. Intertidal community structure: Experimental studies on the relationship between a dominant competitor and its principal predator. *Oecologia* 15:93–120. [4]

Paine, R. T. 1995. A conversation on refining the concept of keystone species. *Conserv. Biol.* 9:962–964. [8]

Paine, R. T., J. T. Wootton and P. D. Boersma. 1990. Direct and indirect effects of Peregrine Falcon predation on seabird abundance. *Auk* 107:1–9. [8]

Panzer, R. 1984. *The Prairie Insect Fauna of the Chicago Region.* Sixth Illinois Prairie Workshop, pp. 1–6. [14]

Park, R., M. Trehan, P. Mausel, and R. Howe. 1989. The effects of sea level rise on U.S. coastal wetlands. In J. B. Smith and D. A. Tirpak (eds.), *The Potential Effects of Global Climate Change on the United States*: Appendix B: *Sea Level Rise*, pp. 1–55. U. S. Environmental Protection Agency, Washington, D.C. [14]

Parmenter, R. R. and J. A. MacMahon. 1983. Factors determining the abundance and distribution of rodents in a shrub-steppe ecosystem: The role of shrubs. *Oecologia* 59:145–156. [14]

Parmenter, R. R., J. A. MacMahon, M. E. Waaland, M. M. Stuebe, P. Landres and C. M. Crisafulli. 1985. Reclamation of surface coal mines in western Wyoming for wildlife habitat: A preliminary analysis. *Reclam. Reveg. Res.* 4:93–115. [14]

Parmenter, R. R., J. A. MacMahon and C. A. B. Gilbert. 1991. Early successional patterns of arthropod recolonization on reclaimed Wyoming strip mines: The grasshoppers (Orthoptera: Acrididae) and allied faunas (Orthoptera: Gryllacrididae, Tettigoniidae). *Environ. Entomol.* 20:135–142. [14]

Parnell, J. 1993. Plant taxonomic research, with special reference to the tropics: Problems and potential solutions. *Conserv. Biol.* 7(4): 809–814. [19]

Parsons, J. 1962. *The Green Turtle and Man.* University of Florida Press, Gainesville, FL. [7]

Partridge, E. (ed.). 1981. *Responsibility to Future Generations: Environmental Ethics.* Prometheus Books, Buffalo, NY. [15]

Pate, J. S. and J. S. Beard (eds.). 1984. *Kwongan. Plant Life of the Sandplain.* University of Western Australia Press, Nedlands, Australia. [4]

Paterson, H. E. H. 1985. The recognition concept of species. In E. S. Vrba (ed.), *Species and Speciation,* pp. 21–29. Transvaal Museum Monograph no. 4, Pretoria. [3]

Paton, P. W. C. 1994. The effect of edge on avian nest success: How strong is the evidence? *Conserv. Biol.* 8:17–26. [9]

Patten, D. T. 1991. Defining the Greater Yellowstone ecosystem. In R. B. Keiter and M. S. Boyce (eds.), *The Greater Yellowstone Ecosystem: Redefining America's Wilderness Heritage,* pp. 19–26. Yale University Press, New Haven. [18]

Patterson, B. D. 1987. The principle of nested subsets and its implications for biological conservation. *Conserv. Biol.* 1:323–334. [9]

Pauly, D. and V. Christensen. 1995. Primary production required to sustain global fisheries. *Nature* 374:255–257. [5]

Pearce, D. 1993. *Economic Values and the Natural World.* Earthscan, London. [15]

Pearson, S. M. 1993. The spatial extent and relative influence of landscape-level factors on wintering bird populations. *Landscape Ecol.* 8:3–18. [7]

Pearson, S. M., M. G. Turner, L. L. Wallace, and W. H. Romme. 1995. Winter habitat use by large ungulates following fire in northern Yellowstone National Park. *Ecol. Appl.* 5:744–755. [7]

Pechmann, J. H. K. and H. M. Wilbur. 1994. Putting declining amphibian populations in perspective: Natural fluctuations and human impacts. *Herpetologica* 50:65–84. [5]

Pechmann, J. H., D. E. Scott, R. D. Semlitsch, J. P. Caldwell, L. J. Vitt and J. W. Gibbons. 1991. Declining amphibian populations: The problem of separating human impacts from natural fluctuations. *Science* 253:892–895. [7,12]

Peet, J. 1992. *Energy and the Ecological Economics of Sustainability.* Island Press, Washington, D.C. [15]

Pelikan, J. 1992. *The Idea of the University: A Reexamination.* Yale University Press, New Haven. [16]

Perrings, C. 1995. The economic value of biodiversity. In V. H. Heywood (ed.), *Global Biodiversity Assessment*, pp. 823–914. Cambridge University Press, Cambridge. [15]

Perrings, C. A. 1994. Biotic diversity, sustainable development, and natural capital. In A.-M. Jansson, M. Hammer, C. Folke, and R. Costanza (eds.), *Investing in Natural Capital: The Ecological Economics Approach to Sustainability*, pp. 92–112. Island Press, Washington, D.C. [15]

Peters, C. M., A. H. Gentry and R. O. Mendelsohn. 1989. Valuation of an Amazonian rainforest. *Nature* 339:656–657. [2]

Peters, R. L. and J. D. S. Darling. 1985. The greenhouse effect and nature reserves. *BioScience* 35:707–717. [9,10]

Peters, R. L. and T. E. Lovejoy (eds.), 1992. *Global Warming and Biological Diversity.* Yale University Press, New Haven, CT. [9]

Peterson, G. L. and A. Randall (eds.). 1984. *Valuation of Wildland Benefits.* Westview Press, Boulder, CO. [2]

Petraitis, P. S. , R. E. Latham and R. A. Niesenbaum. 1989. The maintenance of species diversity by disturbance. *Q. Rev. Biol.* 64:418–464. [1,10]

Petterson, B. 1985. Extinction of an isolated population of the Middle Spotted Woodpecker *Dendrocopos medius* (L.) in Sweden and its relation to general theories on extinction. *Biol. Conserv.* 32:335–353. [9]

Pianka, E. R. 1966. Latitudinal gradients in species diversity: A review of concepts. *Am. Nat.* 100:33–46. [4]

Pianka, E. R. 1967. On lizard species diversity: North American flatland deserts. *Ecology* 48:333–351. [10]

Pianka, E. R. 1986. *Ecology and Natural History of Desert Lizards.* Princeton University Press, Princeton, NJ. [4]

Pickett, S. T. A. 1983. Differential adaptation of tropical tree species to canopy gaps and its role in community dynamics. *Trop. Ecol.* 24:68–84. [18]

Pickett, S. T. A. and R. S. Ostfeld. 1995. The shifting paradigm in ecology. In R. L. Knight and S. F. Bates (eds.), *A New Century for Natural Resources Management*, pp. 261–278. Island Press, Washington, D.C. [1,2,10]

Pickett, S. T. A. and J. N. Thompson. 1978. Patch dynamics and the design of nature reserves. *Biol. Conserv.* 13:27–37. [10]

Pickett, S. T. A. and P. S. White. 1985. *The Ecology of Natural Disturbance and Patch Dynamics.* Academic Press, San Diego, CA. [2]

Pickett, S. T. A. and V. T. Parker. 1994. Avoiding the old pitfalls: Opportunities in a new discipline. *Restor. Ecol.* 2:75–79. [14]

Pickett, S. T. A., V. T. Parker and P. L. Fiedler. 1992. The new paradigm in ecology: Implications for conservation biology above the species level. In P. L. Fiedler and S. K. Jain (eds.), *Conservation Biology:*

The Theory and Practice of Nature Conservation Preservation and Management, pp. 65–88. Chapman and Hall, New York. [1,10]

Picton, H. D. 1979. The application of insular biogeographic theory to the conservation of large mammals in the northern Rocky Mountains. *Biol. Conserv.* 15:73–79. [10]

Pillay, T. V. R. 1992. *Aquaculture and the Environment*. J. Wiley and Sons, New York. [5]

Pimentel, D. (ed.). 1988. *World Food, Pest Losses, and the Environment*. Westview Press, Boulder, CO. [15]

Pimentel, D. 1991. Diversification of biological control strategies in agriculture. *Crop Protection* 10:243–253. [5]

Pimm, S. L. 1991. *The Balance of Nature? Ecological Issues in the Conservation of Species and Communities*. University of Chicago Press, Chicago. [6,8,9]

Pimm, S. L. 1993. Life on an intermittent edge. *Trends Ecol. Evol.* 8:45–46. [9]

Pimm, S. L., H. L. Jones and J. Diamond. 1988. On the risk of extinction. *Am. Nat.* 132:757–785. [7,8,9]

Pinchot, G. 1947. *Breaking New Ground*. Harcourt, Brace and Co., New York. [1,2]

Piper, R. G., I. B. McElwain, L. E. Orme, J. P. McCraren, L. G. Fowler and J. R. Leonard. 1982. *Fish Hatchery Management*. U.S.D.I. Fish and Wildlife Service, Washington, D.C. [12]

Pister, E. P. 1991. Desert Fishes Council: Catalyst for change. In W. L. Minckley and J. E. Deacon (eds.), *Battle Against Extinction: Native Fish Management in the American West*, pp. 55–68. University of Arizona Press, Tucson. [12]

Pister, E. P. 1993. Species in a bucket. *Natural History* 102:14–19. [11]

Pitman, D. 1991. Wildlife as a crop. *Nature et Faune* 7(4): 20–26. [18]

Plotkin, M. J. 1988. The outlook for new agricultural and industrial products from the tropics. In E. O. Wilson and F. M. Peter (eds.), *Biodiversity*, pp. 106–116. National Academy Press, Washington, D.C. [2]

Plowright, W. 1982. The effects of rinderpest and rinderpest control on wildlife in Africa. *Symp. Zool. Soc. Lond.* 50:1–28. [8]

Poinar, G. O. 1983. *The Natural History of Nematodes*. Prentice-Hall, Englewood Cliffs, NJ. [4]

Population Reference Bureau. 1987. *World Population Data Sheet*. Population Reference Bureau, Washington, D.C. [19]

Pounds, J. A. and M. L. Crump. 1994. Amphibian declines and climate disturbance: The case of the golden toad and the harlequin frog. *Conserv. Biol.* 8(1):72–85. [5]

Pounds, J. A., and M. P. Fogden. 1996. Conservation of the golden toad: a brief history. *Bull. British Herpetological Society* (55):5-7. [5]

Powell, G. V. N. and R. Bjork. 1995. Implications of intratropical migration on reserve design: A case study using *Pharomachrus mocinno*. *Conserv. Biol.* 9:354–362. [9]

Power, D. M. 1972. Numbers of bird species on the California Islands. *Evolution* 26: 451–463. [9]

Power, M. E., et al. 1996. Challenges in the quest for keystones. *BioScience* 46:609-620. [8]

Power, M. E. and L. S. Mills. 1995. The keystone cops meet in Hilo. *Trends Ecol. Evol.* 10:182–184. [8]

Power, M. E. and W. J. Matthews. 1983. Algae-grazing minnows (*Campostoma anomalum*), piscivorous bass (*Micropterus* spp.), and the distribution of attached algae in a small prairie-margin stream. *Oecologia* 60:328–332. [8]

Power, M. E., W. J. Matthews and A. J. Stewart. 1985. Grazing minnows, piscivorous bass and stream algae: Dynamics of a strong interaction. *Ecology* 66:1448–1456. [8]

Power, T. M. 1996. *Lost Landscapes and Failed Economies:The Search for a Value of Place*. Island Press, Washington, D.C. [16]

Prendergast, J. R., R. M. Quinn, J. H. Lawton, B. C. Eversham, and D. W. Gibbons. 1993. Rare species, the coincidence of diversity hotspots and conservation strategies. *Nature* 365:335–337. [5]

Pressey, R. L. 1994. Ad hoc reservations: Forward or backward steps in developing representative reserve systems? *Conserv. Biol.* 8:662–668. [12]

Pressey, R. L., C. J. Humphries, C. R. Margules, R. I. Vane-Wright and P. H. Williams. 1993. Beyond opportunism: Key principles for systematic reserve selection. *Trends Ecol. Evol.* 8:124–128. [12]

Preston, F. W. 1960. Time and space and the variation of species. *Ecology* 41:611–627. [9]

Preston, F. W. 1962. The canonical distribution of commonness and rarity. *Ecology* 43:185–215, 410–432. [9]

Price, P. W. 1980. *Evolutionary Biology of Parasites*. Princeton University Press, Princeton, NJ. [8]

Primm, S. A. and T. W. Clark. 1996. Carnivore conservation in the Rocky Mountains: Making sense of the policy process. *Conserv. Biol.* 10:1036–1045. [17]

Prins, H. H. T. and H. P. van der Jeugd. 1993. Herbivore population crashes and woodland structure in East Africa. *J. Ecol.* 81:305–314. [8]

Pryor, L. D. and L. A. S. Johnson. 1971. *A Classification of the Eucalyptus*. Australian National University, Canberra. [4]

Pullan, R. A. 1984. The use of wildlife as a resource in the development of Zambia. In Ooi Jin Bee (ed.), *Natural Resources in Tropical Countries*, pp. 267–325. Singapore University Press, Singapore. [18]

Pulliam, H. R. 1983. Ecological community theory and the coexistence of sparrows. *Ecology* 64:45–52. [7]

Pulliam, H. R. 1988. Sources, sinks, and population regulation. *Am. Nat.* 132:652–661. [7,9]

Pulliam, H. R. 1992. Incorporating concepts from population and behavioral ecology into models of exposure to toxins and risk assessment. In R. Kendall and T. Lacher (eds.), *The Population Ecology and Wildlife Toxicology of Agricultural Pesticide Exposure*, pp. 13–26. Lewis Publishers, Chelsea, MI. [7]

Pulliam, H. R. 1996. Sources and sinks. Empirical evidence and population consequences. In O. E. Rhodes, R. K. Chesser and M. H. Smith (eds.), *Population Dynamics in Ecological Space and Time*, pp. 45–69. University of Chicago Press, Chicago. [7]

Pulliam, H. R. and B. J. Danielson. 1991. Sources, sinks, and habitat selection: a landscape perspective on population dynamics. *Am. Nat.* 137:S50–S66. [7]

Pulliam, H. R. and G. C. Millikan. 1982. Social organization in the nonreproductive season. *Avian Biol.* 6:169–193. [7]

Pulliam, H. R. and T. A. Parker. 1979. Population regulation of sparrows. *Fortschr. Zool.* 25:137–147. [7]

Pulliam, H. R., J. B. Dunning, Jr. and J. Liu. 1992. Population dynamics in a complex landscape: A case study. *Ecol. Applic.* 2:165-177. [7]

Pulliam, H. R., J. Liu, J. B. Dunning, D. J. Stewart, and T. D. Bishop. 1995. Modelling animal populations in changing landscapes. *Ibis* 137:S120–S126. [7]

Pusey, A. and M. Wolf. 1996. Inbreeding avoidance in animals. *Trends Ecol. Evol.* 11:201–206. [6]

Quintana-Ascencio, P. F. and E. S. Menges. 1996. Inferring metapopulation dynamics from patch-level incidence of Florida scrub plants. *Conserv. Biol.* 10:1210–1219. [9]

Rabinowitz, D., S. Cairns and T. Dillon. 1986. Seven forms of rarity and their frequency in the flora of the British Isles. In M. E. Soulé, (ed.), *Conservation Biology: The Science of Scarcity and Diversity*, pp. 182–204. Sinauer Associates, Sunderland, MA. [5,9]

Ralls, K. and J. Ballou. 1983. Extinction: Lessons from zoos. In C. M. Schonewald-Cox, S. M. Chambers, B. MacBryde and L. Thomas (eds.), *Genetics and Conservation: A Reference for Managing Wild Animal and Plant Populations*, pp. 164–184. Benjamin/Cummings, Menlo Park, CA. [6]

Ralls, K. and J. Ballou. 1986. Captive breeding programs for populations with a small number of founders. *Trends Ecol. Evol.* 1:19-22. [6]

Randall, A. 1986. Human preferences, economics, and the preservation of species. In B. G. Norton (ed.), *The Preservation of Species: The Value of Biological Diversity*, pp. 79–109. Princeton University Press, Princeton, NJ. [2]

Randall, A. 1988. What mainstream economists have to say about the value of biodiversity. In E. O. Wilson and F. M. Peter (eds)., *Biodiversity*, pp. 217–223. National Academy Press, Washington, D.C. [2,15]

Randall, A. 1991. The value of biodiversity. *Ambio* 20(2):64–68. [15]

Ranney, J. W., M. C. Bruner and J. B. Levenson. 1981. The importance of edge in the structure and dynamics of forest islands. In R. L. Burgess and D. M. Sharpe (eds.), *Forest Island Dynamics in Man-Dominated Landscapes*, pp. 67–95. Springer-Verlag, New York. [9]

Rapport, D. J. 1989. What constitutes ecosystem health? *Perspect. Biol. Med.* 33: 120–132. [14]

Rasmussen, E. M. 1985. El Niño and variations in climate. *Am. Sci.* 73:168–177. [13]

Ratti, J. T. and K. P. Reese. 1988. Preliminary test of the ecological trap hypothesis. *J. Wildl. Mgmt.* 52:484–491. [9]

Rau, J. R. 1987. *Ecología del zorro (*Vulpes vulpes*) en la Reserva Biológica de Doñana.* Ph.D. dissertation, University of Sevilla, Sevilla. [13]

Raunkaier, C. 1934. *The Life Forms of Plants and Statistical Plant Geography.* Clarendon Press, Oxford. [4]

Raup, D. M. 1988. Diversity crises in the geological past. In E. O. Wilson and F. M. Peter (eds.), *Biodiversity,* pp. 51–57. National Academy Press, Washington, D.C. [5]

Raup, D. M. 1991a. *Extinction: Bad Genes or Bad Luck?* W. W. Norton, New York. [5]

Raup, D. M. 1991b. A kill curve for Phanerozoic marine species. *Paleobiology* 17(1): 37–48. [5]

Raven, P., R. Norgaard, C. Padoch, T. Panayotou, A. Randall, M. Robinson and J. Rodman. 1992. *Conserving Biodiversity: A Research Agenda for Development Agencies.* National Academy Press, Washington, D.C. [2]

Raven, P. H. 1988. Our diminishing tropical forests. In E. O. Wilson and F. M. Peter (eds.), *Biodiversity,* pp. 119–122. National Academy Press, Washington, D.C. [2,5]

Raven, P. H. 1990. The politics of preserving biodiversity. *BioScience* 40(10):769–774. [5]

Raven, P. H., L. R. Berg and G. B. Johnson. 1993. *Environment.* Saunders College Publishing, New York. [5]

Rawls, J. 1971. *A Theory of Justice.* Oxford University Press, Oxford. [15]

Ray, G. C. and J. F. Grassle. 1991. Marine biological diversity. *BioScience* 41:453–457. [5]

Reading, R. P. 1993. Towards an endangered species reintroduction paradigm: A case study of the black-footed ferret. Ph.D. dissertation. [13]

Reading, R. P. and S. R. Kellert. 1993. Attitudes toward a proposed reintroduction of black-footed ferrets (*Mustela nigripes*). *Conserv. Biol.* 7:569–580. [13]

Reaka-Kudla, M. L., D. W. Wilson and E. O. Wilson, (eds.). 1996. *Biodiversity II: Understanding and Protecting Our Natural Resources.* National Academy Press, Washington, D.C. In press. [5]

Redclift, M. 1984. *Development and the Environmental Crisis: Red or Green Alternatives.* Methuen, London. [15]

Redente, E. F. and E. J. DePuit. 1988. Reclamation of drastically disturbed rangelands. In P. T. Tueller (ed.), *Vegetation Science Applications for Rangeland Analysis and Management,* pp. 559–584. Kluwer Academic Publishers, Dordrecht, The Netherlands. [14]

Redford, K. H. 1992. The empty forest. *BioScience* 42:412–422. [1]

Redford, K. H., A. Taber and J. A. Simonetti. 1990. There is more to biodiversity than the tropical rain forests. *Conserv. Biol.* 4: 328–330. [5]

Reffalt, W. 1991. The endangered species lists: Chronicles of extinction? In K. A. Kohm (ed.), *Balancing on the Brink of Extinction: The Endangered Species Act and Lessons for the Future,* pp. 77–85. Island Press, Washington, D.C. [3]

Regan, T. 1983. *The Case for Animal Rights.* University of California Press, Berkeley. [2]

Reh, W. and A. Seitz. 1990. The influence of land use on the genetic structure of populations of the common frog *Rana temporaria. Biol. Conserv.* 54:239–249. [9]

Reid, T. S. and D. D. Murphy. 1995. Providing a regional context for local conservation action. *BioScience* (Suppl.): 84–90. [12]

Reid, W. V. and K. R. Miller. 1989. *Keeping Options Alive: The Scientific Basis for Conserving Biodiversity.* World Resources Institute, Washington, D.C. [5]

Reisman, W. M. and A. M. Schreiber. 1987. Jurisprudence: Is it relevant? In W. M. Reisman and A. M. Schreiber (eds.), *Jurisprudence: Understanding and Shaping Law,* pp. 1–21. New Haven Press, New Haven, CT. [17]

Reith, C. C. and L. D. Potter. (eds.). 1986. *Principles and Methods of Reclamation Science.* University of New Mexico Press, Albuquerque. [14]

Repetto, R. 1992. Accounting for environmental assets. *Sci. Am.* 266:94–100. [18]

Reshetiloff, K. 1995. Chesapeake Bay: Introduction to an ecosystem. U.S. Environmental Protection Agency, Chesapeake Bay Program, Annapolis, MD. [12]

Rex, M. A. 1973. Deep-sea species diversity: decreased gastropod diversity at abyssal depths. *Science* 181: 1051–1053. [4]

Rex, M. A. 1983. Geographical patterns of species diversity in the deep-sea benthos. In G. T. Rowe (ed.), *The Sea, Volume 8,* pp. 453–472. John Wiley & Sons, New York. [4]

Rey-Benayas, J. M. and K. O. Pope. 1995. Landscape ecology and diversity patterns in the seasonal tropics from Landsat TM imagery. *Ecol. Appl.* 5:386–394. [5]

Reznick, D. N. and H. Bryga. 1987. Life-history evolution in guppies (*Poecilia reticulata*): 1. Phenotypic and genetic changes in an introduction experiment. *Evolution* 41:1370–1385. [3]

Reznick, D. N., H. Bryga and J. A. Endler. 1990. Experimentally induced life-history evolution in a natural population. *Nature* 346:357–359. [3]

Ricardo, D. 1926. *Principles of Political Economy and Taxation.* Reprint. Everyman, London. [15]

Rice, B. and M. Westoby. 1983. Species richness at tenth-hectare scale in Australian vegetation compared to other continents. *Vegetatio* 52:129–140. [4]

Rich, A. C., D. S. Dobkin, and L. J. Niles. 1994. Defining forest fragmentation by corridor width: The influence of narrow forest-dividing corridors on forest-nesting birds in southern New Jersey. *Conserv. Biol.* 8:1109–1121. [9]

Richards, S. J., K. R. McDonald, and R. A. Alford. 1993. Declines in populations of Australia's endemic tropical rainforest frogs. *Pacific Conserv. Biol.* 1:66–77. [5]

Ricklefs, R. 1987. Community diversity: Relative roles of local and regional processes. *Science* 235:167–171. [4]

Ricklefs, R. 1990. *Ecology,* 3rd. ed. W. H. Freeman, San Francisco. [5]

Ricklefs, R. and D. Schluter (eds.). 1993. *Species Diversity in Ecological Communities: Historical and Geographical Perspectives.* University of Chicago Press, Chicago.

Riemann, B. and E. Hoffmann. 1991. Ecological consequences of dredging and bottom trawling in the Limfjord, Denmark. *Mar. Ecol. Progr. Ser.* 69:171–178. [7]

Rifkin, J. 1995. *The End of Work: The Decline of the Global Labor Force and the Dawn of the Post-Market Era.* G. P. Putnam's Sons, New York. [19]

Riitters, K. H., R. V. O'Neill, C. T. Hunsaker, J. D. Wickham, D. H. Yankee, S. P. Timmins, K. B. Jones, and B. L. Jackson. 1995. A factor analysis of landscape pattern and structure metrics. *Landscape Ecol.* 10:23–40. [9]

Ripple, W. J., G. A. Bradshaw and T. A. Spies. 1991a. Measuring forest landscape patterns in the Cascade Range of Oregon, USA. *Biol. Conserv.* 57:73–88. [9]

Ripple, W. J., D. H. Johnson, K. T. Hershey and E. C. Meslow. 1991b. Old-growth and mature forests near Spotted Owl nests in western Oregon. *J. Wildl. Mgmt.* 55:316–318. [13]

Rivas-Martínez, S., M. Corta, S. Castroviejo, and E. Valdés. 1980. Vegetación de Doñana (Huelva, Espa–a). *Lazaroa* 2:5–189. [13]

Robbin, D. M. 1984. A new Holocene sea level curve for the upper Florida Keys and Florida Reef Tract. In P. J. Gleason (ed.), *Environments of South Florida: Present and Past II,* pp. 437–458. Miami Geological Society, Coral Gables, FL. [13]

Robbins, C. S., D. K. Dawson and B. A. Dowell. 1989. Habitat area requirements of breeding forest birds of the Middle Atlantic states. *Wildl. Monogr.* 103:1–34. [9]

Robbins, L. W., D. K. Tolliver and M. H. Smith. 1989. Nondestructive methods for obtaining genotypic data from fish. *Conserv. Biol.* 3:88–91. [6]

Robinson, J. G. 1993. The limits to caring: Sustainable living and the loss of biodiversity. *Conserv. Biol.* 7:20–28. [18]

Robinson, S. K. 1992a. *Effects of Forest Fragmentation on Migrant Songbirds in the Shawnee National Forest.* Report to Illinois Department of Energy and Natural Resources. Illinois Natural History Survey, Champaign, IL. [9]

Robinson, S. K. 1992b. Population dynamics of breeding Neotropical migrants in a fragmented Illinois landscape. In J. M. Hagan and D. W. Johnston (eds.), *Ecology and Conservation of Neotropical Migrant Landbirds,* pp. 408–418. Smithsonian Institution Press, Washington, D.C. [9]

Robinson, S. K., F. R. Thompson III, T. M. Donovan, D. R. Whitehead, and J. Faaborg. 1995. Regional forest fragmentation and the nesting success of migratory birds. *Science* 267:1987–1990. [9]

Rogers, L. L. 1987. Factors influencing dispersal in the black bear. In B. D. Chepko-Sade and Z. T. Halpin (eds.), *Mammalian*

Dispersal Patterns, pp. 75–84. University of Chicago Press, Chicago. [10]

Rojas, M. 1992. The species problem and conservation: What are we protecting? *Conserv. Biol.* 6:170–178. [3]

Rolston, H. 1988. *Environmental Ethics: Duties to and Values in the Natural World.* Temple University Press, Philadelphia, PA. [2]

Romme, W. H. and D. G. Despain. 1989. Historical perspectives on the Yellowstone fires, 1988. *BioScience* 39:695–699. [18]

Rood, J. P. 1987. Dispersal and intergroup transfer in the dwarf mongoose. In B. D. Chepko-Sade and Z. T. Halpin (eds.), *Mammalian Dispersal Patterns,* pp. 85–103. University of Chicago Press, Chicago. [10]

Root, T. 1988. Energy constraints on avian distributions and abundances. *Ecology* 69:330–339. [7]

Ropelewski, C. F. and M. S. Halpert. 1987. Global and regional scale precipitation patterns associated with the El Niño/Southern Oscillation. *Monthly Weather Rev.* 115:1606–1626. [13]

Rosenberg, A. A., M. J. Fogarty, M. P. Sissenwine, J. R. Beddington and J. G. Sheperd. 1993. Achieving sustainable use of renewable resources. *Science* 262:828–829. [18]

Rosenzweig, M. L. 1971. Paradox of enrichment: destabilization of exploitation ecosystems in ecological time. *Science* 171; 385–387 [4]

Rosenzweig, M. L. 1995. *Species Diversity in Space and Time.* Cambridge University Press, Cambridge. [4]

Roughgarden, J., S.W. Running, and P.A. Matson. 1991. What does remote sensing do for ecology? *Ecology* 72:1918-1922. [5]

Rubec, P. J. 1986. The effects of sodium cyanide on coral reefs and marine fish in the Philippines. In J. L. MacLean, L. B. Dizon, and L. V. Hosillos (eds.), *The First Asian Fisheries Forum,* pp. 297–302. Asian Fisheries Society, Manila, Philippines. [5]

Rudnicky, T. C. and M. L. Hunter. 1993. Avian nest predation in clearcuts, forests, and edges in a forest-dominated landscape. *J. of Wildl. Mgmt.* 57:358–364. [9]

Russell, H. S. 1976. *A Long Deep Furrow: Three Centuries of Farming in New England.* University Press of New England, Hanover, NH. [1,12]

Ryman, N. and F. Utter (eds.). 1987. *Population Genetics and Fishery Management.* University of Washington Press, Seattle. [6]

Sadovy, Y. 1993. The Nassau grouper, endangered or just unlucky? *Reef Encounter* 13:10–12. [5]

Safina, C. 1993a. Bluefin tuna in the West Atlantic: Negligent management and the making of an endangered species. *Conserv. Biol.* 7:229–234. [5]

Safina, C. 1993b. Pair trawling for tuna catches heat. *Fisheries* 18(4):4–5. [5]

Safina, C. 1994. Where have all the fishes gone? *Issues Sci. Tech.* 10:37–43. [5]

Safina, C. and S. Iudicello. 1995. Wise use below high tide. In R. Ebe and J. Echeverria (eds.), *Let the People Judge: Wise Use and the Private Property Rights Movement,* pp. 297–302. Island Press, Washington, D.C. [5]

Sagoff, M. 1980. On the preservation of species. *Columbia J. Environ. Law* 7:33–76. [2]

Sagoff, M. 1988. *The Economy of the Earth: Philosophy, Law, and the Environment.* Cambridge University Press, Cambridge. [2,15]

Sagoff, M. 1996. On the value of endangered and other species. *Environ. Mgmt.* 20(8): 897–911.

Sale, K. 1995. *Rebels Against the Future: The Luddites and Their War on the Industrial Revolution: Lessons for the Computer Age.* Addison-Wesley, Reading, MA. [19]

Salomone, K. L., M. R. Greenberg, P. M. Sandman, and D. B. Sachsman. 1990. A question of quality: How journalists and news sources evaluate coverage of environmental risk. *J. Communic.* 40:117–130. [16]

Sampson, F. B. and F. L. Knopf (eds.). 1996. *Ecosystem Management: Selected Readings.* Springer-Verlag, New York. [3]

Samson, F. B. 1983. Minimum viable populations—A review. *Nat. Areas J.* 3(3):15–23. [9]

Sanders, H. L. 1968. Marine benthic diversity: A comparative study. *Am. Nat.* 102:243–282. [4]

Sanders, H. L. and R. R. Hessler. 1969. Ecology of the deep-sea benthos. *Science* 163:1419–1424. [4]

Santiapillai, C. 1992. Asian rhino specialist group. *Species* 18:55. [3]

Santos, T. and J. L. Tellaria. 1992. Edge effects of nest predation in Mediterranean fragmented forests. *Biol. Conserv.* 61:1–5. [9]

Sarich, V. M. 1977. Rates, sample sizes, and the neutrality hypothesis for electrophoresis in evolutionary studies. *Nature* 265:24–28. [6]

Saunders, D. A. 1989. Changes in the avifauna of a region, district, and remnant as a result of fragmentation of native vegetation: The Wheatbelt of Western Australia. A case study. *Biol. Conserv.* 50:99–135. [9]

Saunders, D. A., R. J. Hobbs and C. R. Margules. 1991. Biological consequences of ecosystem fragmentation: A review. *Conserv. Biol.* 5:18–32. [9,10]

Savidge, J. A. 1987. Extinction of an island avifauna by an introduced snake. *Ecology* 68:660–668. [8]

Scatolini, S. R. and J. B. Zedler. 1996. Epibenthic invertebrates of natural and constructed marshes of San Diego Bay. *Wetlands* 16:24–37. [14]

Scheuer, J. H. 1993. Biodiversity: Beyond Noah's Ark. *Conserv. Biol.* 7:206–207. [3]

Schindler, D. W., P. J. Curtis, B. R. Parker, and M. P. Stainton. 1996. Consequences of climate warming and lake acidification for UV-B penetration in North American boreal lakes. *Nature* 379:705–708. [5]

Schmookler, A. B. 1993. *The Illusion of Choice: How the Market Economy Shapes Our Destiny.* State University of New York Press, Albany. [15]

Schneider, S. H. 1989. *Global Warming: Are We entering the Greenhouse Century.* Sierra Club Books, San Francisco, CA. [2]

Schneider, S. H. 1993. Scenarios of global warming. In P. M. Kareiva, J. G. Kingsolver and R. B. Huey (eds.), *Biotic Interactions and Global Change,* pp. 9–23. Sinauer Associates, Sunderland, MA. [5,19]

Schoener, T. W. 1983. Field experiments on interspecific competition. *Am. Nat.* 122:240–285. [4]

Schön, D. 1983. *The Reflective Practitioner: How Professionals Think in Action.* Basic Books, New York. [17]

Schön, D. and M. Rein. 1994. *Frame Reflection: Toward the Resolution of Intractable Policy Controversies.* Basic Books, New York. [17]

Schonewald-Cox, C. M. 1983. Conclusions: Guidelines to management: A beginning attempt. In C. M. Schonewald-Cox, S. M. Chambers, B. MacBryde and L. Thomas (eds.), *Genetics and Conservation: A Reference for Managing Wild Animal and Plant Populations,* pp. 414–445. Benjamin/Cummings, Menlo Park, CA. [10]

Schonewald-Cox, C. M. and J. W. Bayless. 1986. The boundary model: A geographical analysis of design and conservation of nature reserves. *Biol. Conserv.* 38:305–322. [10]

Schonewald-Cox, C. and M. Buechner. 1993. Park protection and public roads. In P. L. Fiedler and S. K. Jain (eds.), *Conservation Biology,* pp. 373–395. Chapman and Hall, New York. [9]

Schonewald-Cox, C. M., S. M. Chambers, B. MacBryde and L. Thomas (eds.). 1983. *Genetics and Conservation: A Reference for Managing Wild Animal and Plant Populations.* Benjamin/Cummings, Menlo Park, CA. [1,6]

Schowalter, T. D. 1988. Forest pest management: A synopsis. *Northwest Environ. J.* 4:313–318. [9]

Schroeder, M. H. and S. J. Martin. 1982. Search for the black-footed ferret succeeds. *Wyo. Wildl.* 46(7):8–9. [13]

Schuldt, J. A. and A. E. Hershey. 1995. Effect of salmon carcass decomposition on Lake Superior tributary streams. *J. N. Am. Benthol. Soc.* 14:259–268. [9]

Scott, A. and R. M. Scott. 1996. A conservation programme for the Blue Crane *Anthropoides paradiseus* in the Overberg, Southern Cape, South Africa. *Proceedings of the 1993 African Crane and Wetland Training Workshop,* pp. 395–401. International Crane Foundation, Baraboo, WI. [13]

Scott, J. M., S. Mountainspring, F. L. Ramsey and C. B. Kepler. 1986. *Forest Bird Communities on the Hawaiian Islands: Their Dynamics, Ecology and Conservation.* Cooper Ornithological Society, Berkeley, CA. [8]

Scott, J. M., B. Csuti, J. D. Jacobi and J. E. Estes. 1987. Species richness. *BioScience* 37:782–788. [12]

Scott, J. M., B. Csuti, and K. A. Smith. 1990. Playing Noah while paying the Devil. *Bull. Ecol. Soc. Am.* 71:156–159. [12]

Scott, J. M., T. Tear, and F. W. Davis. 1996. *Gap Analysis: A landscape Approach to Biodiversity Planning.* American Society of Photogrannetry and Remote Sensing. Bethesda, MD. 320 pp.

Scudder, G. G. E. 1974. Species concepts and speciation. *Can. J. Zool.* 52:1121–1134. [3]

Seal, U. S. 1985. The realities of preserving species in captivity. In R. J. Hoage (ed.), *Animal Extinctions: What Everyone Should Know,* pp. 71–95. Smithsonian Institution Press, Washington, D.C. [6]

Semlitsch, R. D., D. E. Scott, J. H. K. Pechmann, and J. W. Gibbons. 1996. Structure and dynamics of an amphibian community: Evidence from a 16-year study of a natural pond. In M. L. Cody and J. A. Smallwood (eds.), *Long-Term Studies of Vertebrate Communities*, pp. 217–248. Academic Press, San Diego, CA. [5]

Sen, A. 1995. Rationality and social choice. *Am. Econ. Rev.* 85:1–24. [15]

Sepkoski, J. J., Jr. 1982. Mass extinctions in the Phanerozoic oceans: A review. In L. T. Silver and P. H. Schultz (eds.), *Geological Implications of Impacts of Large Asteroids and Comets on the Earth*, pp. 283–289. Special Paper 190. The Geological Society of America, Boulder, CO. [5]

Sepkoski, J. J., Jr. 1984. A kinetic model of Phanerozoic taxonomic diversity. III. Post-Paleozoic families and mass extinctions. *Paleobiology* 10:246–267. [4]

Sepkoski, J. J., Jr. 1988. Alpha, beta, or gamma: Where does all the diversity go? *Paleobiology* 14:221–234. [5]

Sepkoski, J. J., Jr. and D. M. Raup. 1986. Periodicity in marine extinction events. In Elliott, D. K. (ed.) *Dynamics of Extinction*, pp. 3–36. John Wiley & Sons, New York. [4]

Servheen, C. 1985. The grizzly bear. In R. L. Di Silvestro (ed.), *Audubon Wildlife Report*, pp. 400–415. National Audubon Society, New York. [6]

Shabecoff, P. 1993. *A Fierce Green Fire: The American Environmental Movement.* Hill and Wang, NY. [16]

Shafer, C. L. 1991. *Nature Reserves: Island Theory and Conservation Practice.* Smithsonian Institution Press, Washington, D.C. [5]

Shafer, C. L. 1995. Values and shortcomings of small reserves. *BioScience* 45:80–88. [7]

Shaffer, M. L. 1981. Minimum population sizes for species conservation. *BioScience* 31:131–134. [7,9]

Shaffer, M. L. 1983. Determining minimum viable population sizes for the grizzly bear. *International Conference on Bear Research and Management* 5:133–139. [7]

Shaffer, M. L. 1987. Minimum viable populations: Coping with uncertainty. In M. E. Soulé (ed.), *Viable Populations for Conservation*, pp. 69–86. Cambridge University Press, Cambridge. [7]

Shaffer, M. L. 1990. Population viability analysis. *Conserv. Biol.* 4:39–40. [7]

Shaffer, M. L. and F. B. Sampson. 1985. Population size and extinction: A note on determining critical population sizes. *Am. Nat.* 125:144–152. [6]

Sheperd, R. G. 1981. Selectivity of sources: Reporting the marijuana controversy. *J. Communic.* 31:129–137. [16]

Sherman, C. K. and M. L. Morton. 1993. Population declines of Yosemite toads in the eastern Sierra Nevada of California. *J. Herpetol.* 27(2):186–198. [5]

Sherwin, W. B., N. D. Murray, J. A. M. Graves and P. R. Brown. 1991. Measurement of genetic variation in endangered populations: Bandicoots (Marsupialia: Peramelidae) as an example. *Conserv. Biol.* 5:103–108. [6]

Shiva, V. 1989. *Staying Alive: Women, Ecology and Development.* Zed Books, London. [2]

Sieving, K. E. 1992. Nest predation and differential insular extinction among selected forest birds of central Panama. *Ecology* 73:2310–2328. [5]

Sieving, K. E. and J. R. Karr. 1997. Avian extinction and persistence mechanisms in lowland Panama. In W. F. Laurance, R. O. Bierregaard, and C. Moritz (eds.), *Tropical Forest Remnants: Ecology, Management, and Conservation of Fragmented Communities.* University of Chicago Press, Chicago. In press. [5]

Signor, P. W. 1990. The geological history of diversity. *Annu. Rev. Ecol. Syst.* 21:509–539. [4,5]

Simberloff, D. 1981. Community effects of introduced species. In H. Nitecki (ed.), *Biotic Crises in Ecological and Evolutionary Time*, pp. 53–81. Academic Press, New York. [8]

Simberloff, D. 1986. Are we on the verge of a mass extinction in tropical rain forests? In D. K. Elliott (ed.), *Dynamics of Extinction*, pp.165–180. Wiley, New York. [5]

Simberloff, D. 1988. The contribution of population and community biology to conservation science. *Annu. Rev. Ecol. Syst.* 19:473–511. [9]

Simberloff, D. 1991. *Review of Theory Relevant to Acquiring Land.* Report to Florida Department of Natural Resources. Florida State University, Tallahassee. [9]

Simberloff, D. and L. G. Abele. 1976. Island biogeography theory and conservation practice. *Science* 191:285–286. [9]

Simberloff, D. and L. G. Abele. 1982. Refuge design and island biogeographic theory: Effects of fragmentation. *Am. Nat.* 120:41–50. [9]

Simberloff, D. and J. Cox. 1987. Consequences and costs of conservation corridors. *Conserv. Biol.* 1:63–71. [9]

Simberloff, D. and J. L. Martin. 1991. Nestedness of insular avifaunas: Simple summary statistics masking species patterns. *Ornis Fennica* 68:178–192. [9]

Simberloff, D., D. C. Schmitz, and T. C. Brown (eds.). 1997. *Strangers in Paradise: Impact and Management of Nonindigenous Species in Florida.* Island Press, Washington, D.C. [8]

Simberloff, D. S., J. A. Farr, J. Cox and D. W. Mehlman. 1992. Movement corridors: Conservation bargains or poor investments? *Conserv. Biol.* 6:493–504. [10]

Simon, J. L. 1981. *The Ultimate Resource.* Princeton University Press, Princeton, NJ. [15]

Simon, J. L. 1990. *Population Matters: People, Resources, Environment, and Immigration.* Transaction, New Brunswick, NJ. [18]

Simon, J. L. and H. Kahn (eds.). 1984. *The Resourceful Earth: A Response to Global 2000.* Blackwell, New York. [18]

Simon, N. 1962. *Between the Sunlight and the Thunder: The Wildlife of Kenya.* Collins, London. [8]

Simpson, B. B. and J. Haffer. 1978. Speciation patterns in the Amazonian forest biota. *Annu. Rev. Ecol. Syst.* 9:497–518. [4]

Simpson, G. G. 1961. *Principles of Animal Taxonomy.* Columbia University Press, New York. [3]

Sinclair, A. R. E. 1979. The eruption of the ruminants. In A. R. E. Sinclair and M. Norton-Griffiths (eds.), *Serengeti: Dynamics of an Ecosystem*, pp. 82–103. University of Chicago Press, Chicago. [8]

Singer, P. 1975. *Animal Liberation: A New Ethics for Our Treatment of Animals.* The New York Review, New York. [2]

Singhvi, L. M. n.d. *The Jain Declaration on Nature.* Federation of Jain Associations of North America, Cincinnati, OH. [2]

Sissenwine, M. P. and A. A. Rosenberg. 1993. Marine fisheries at a critical juncture. *Fisheries* 18:6–10. [5]

Skole, D. and C. Tucker. 1993. Tropical deforestation and habitat fragmentation in the Amazon: Satellite data from 1978–1988. *Science* 260:1905–1910. [5]

Slatkin, M. 1987. Gene flow and the geographic structure of natural populations. *Science* 236:787–792. [6]

Slobodkin, L. B. and D. E. Dykhuizen. 1991. Applied ecology, its practice and philosophy. In J. Cairns, Jr. and T. V. Crawford (eds.), *Integrated Environmental Management*, pp. 63–70. Lewis Publishers, Boca Raton, FL. [11]

Small, M. F. and M. L. Hunter. 1988. Forest fragmentation and avian nest predation in forested landscapes. *Oecologia* 76:62–64. [9]

Smith, A. T. and M. M. Peacock. 1990. Conspecific attraction and the determination of metapopulation colonization rates. *Conserv. Biol.* 4:320–327. [9]

Smith, F. D. M., R. M. May, R. Pellew, T. H. Johnson, and K. R. Walter. 1993a. How much do we know about the current extinction rate? *Trends Ecol. Evol.* 8:375–378. [5]

Smith, F. D. M., R. M. May, R. Pellew, T. Johnson, and K. Walter. 1993b. Estimating extinction rates. *Nature* 364:494–496. [5]

Smith, H. M. 1899. The mussel fishery and pearl-button industry of the Mississippi River. *Bull. U.S. Fish Comm.* 18:289–314. [3]

Smith, L. 1993. The land rush is on. *Greater Yellowstone Report* 10:1, 4–5. [9]

Smith, T. B. and R. K. Wayne. 1996. *Molecular Genetic Approaches in Conservation.* Oxford University Press, New York. [6]

Smyser, C. A. 1986. *Nature's Design: A Practical Guide to Natural Landscaping.* Rodale Press, Emmaus, PA. [14]

Snelson, F. F., Jr., S. H. Gruber, F. L. Murru and T. H. Schmid. 1990. Southern stingray, *Dasyatis americana:* Host for a symbiotic cleaner wrasse. *Copeia* 1990(4):961–965. [8]

Snodgrass, J. W. 1996. *The influence of beaver ponds on the temporal and spatial dynamics of southeastern stream fish assemblages.* Ph.D. dissertation, University of Georgia, Athens. [8]

Society for Ecological Restoration. 1990. *The Sistine Ceiling Debate.* Tape-recording of a symposium on the authenticity of restored ecosystems. Society for Ecological Restoration, Madison, WI. [14]

Society of American Foresters. 1993. *Sustaining long-term forest health and productivity.* Society of American Foresters, Bethesda, MD. [11]

Solis, D. M. and R. J. Gutierrez. 1990. Summer habitat ecology of Northern Spotted

Owls in northwestern California. *Condor* 92:739–784. [13]

Soulé, M. 1995. The social siege of nature. In M. Soulé and G. Lease (eds.), *Reinventing Nature? Responses to Postmodern Deconstruction*, pp. 137–170. Island Press, Washington, D.C. [15]

Soulé, M. E. 1980. Thresholds for survival: Maintaining fitness and evolutionary potential. In M. E. Soulé and B. A. Wilcox (eds.), *Conservation Biology: An Ecological-Evolutionary Perspective*, pp. 151–169. Sinauer Associates, Sunderland, MA. [6]

Soulé, M. E. 1985. What is conservation biology? *Bioscience* 35:727–734. [1,2]

Soulé, M. E. 1986a. Conservation biology and the "real world." In M. E. Soulé (ed.), *Conservation Biology: The Science of Scarcity and Diversity*, pp. 1–12. Sinauer Associates, Sunderland, MA. [1]

Soulé, M. E. (ed.). 1986b. *Conservation Biology: The Science of Scarcity and Diversity.* Sinauer Associates, Sunderland, MA. [6]

Soulé, M. E. (ed.). 1987. *Viable Populations for Conservation.* Cambridge University Press, New York. [5,7]

Soulé, M. E. 1991a. Conservation: Tactics for a constant crisis. *Science* 253:744–750. [5]

Soulé, M. E. 1991b. Theory and strategy. In W. E. Hudson (ed.), *Landscape Linkages and Biodiversity*, pp. 91–104. Island Press, Washington, D.C. [10]

Soulé, M. E. and K. Kohm (eds.). 1989. *Research Priorities for Conservation Biology.* Island Press, Washington, D.C. [8]

Soulé, M. E. and D. Simberloff. 1986. What do genetics and ecology tell us about the design of nature reserves? *Biol. Conserv.* 35:19–40. [10]

Soulé, M. E. and B. A. Wilcox (eds.). 1980a. *Conservation Biology: An Evolutionary-Ecological Perspective.* Sinauer Associates, Sunderland, MA. [1,7]

Soulé, M. E. and B. A. Wilcox. 1980b. Conservation biology: Its scope and its challenge. In M. E. Soulé and B. A. Wilcox (eds.), *Conservation Biology: An Evolutionary-Ecological Perspective*, pp. 1–8. Sinauer Associates, Sunderland, MA. [5]

Soulé, M. E., D. T. Bolger, A. C. Alberts, J. Wright, M. Sorice, and S. Hill. 1988. Reconstructed dynamics of rapid extinctions of chaparral-requiring birds in urban habitat islands. *Conserv. Biol.* 2:75–92. [9]

Sousa, W. P. 1984. The role of disturbance in natural communities. *Annu. Rev. Ecol. Syst.* 15:353–391. [10]

Specht, R. L. and E. J. Moll. 1983. Mediterranean-type heathlands and sclerophyllous shrublands of the world: An overview. In F. J. Kruger, D. T. Mitchell and J. U. M. Jarvis (eds.), *Mediterranean-Type Ecosystems: the Role of Nutrients*, pp. 41–65. (Ecological Studies no. 43). Springer-Verlag, Berlin. [4]

Spencer, C. N., B. R. McClelland, and J. A. Stanford. 1991. Shrimp stocking, salmon collapse and eagle displacement. *BioScience* 41:14–21. [9]

Sprent, J. F. A. 1992. Parasites lost? *Int. J. Parasitol.* 22:139–151. [8]

Sprugel, D. G. 1991. Disturbance, equilibrium, and environmental variability: What is "Natural" vegetation in a changing environment? *Biol. Conserv.* 58:1–18. [14]

Stacey, P. B. and M. Taper. 1992. Environmental variation and the persistence of small populations. *Ecol. Appl.* 2:18–29. [7]

Stangel, P. W., M. R. Lennartz and M. H. Smith. 1992. Genetic variation and population structure of Red-cockaded Woodpeckers. *Conserv. Biol.* 6:283–292. [6]

Stankey, G. 1994. Ecosystem Management: How to Institutionalize Inspiration? Discussion paper. Institutional Problem Analysis Workshop, The Applegate Partnership. [18]

Stanley, S. M. 1981. *The New Evolutionary Timetable.* Basic Books, New York. [5]

Stanley, T. R., Jr. 1995. Ecosystem management and the arrogance of humanism. *Conserv. Biol.* 9:255–262. [17]

Stapp, W. B., M. M. Cromwell, and A. Walls. 1995. The global rivers environmental education network. In S. K. Jacobson (ed.), *Conserving Wildlife: International Education and Communication Approaches,* pp.177–197. Columbia University Press, New York. [16]

Stebbins, R. C. and N. W. Cohen. 1995. *A Natural History of Amphibians.* Princeton University Press, Princeton,NJ. [5]

Stehli, F. G., R. G. Douglas and N. D. Newell. 1969. Generation and maintenance of gradients in taxonomic diversity. *Science* 164: 947–949. [4]

Stenseth, N. C. 1984. The tropics: Cradle or museum? *Oikos* 43:417–420. [5]

Stevens, G. C. 1989. The latitudinal gradient in geographical range: How so many species coexist in the tropics. *Am. Nat.* 133:240–256. [5,7]

Stevens, W. K. 1995. *Miracle Under the Oaks. The Revival of Nature in America.* Pocket Books, New York, NY. [14]

Stiassny, M. L. J. 1992. Phylogenetic analysis and the role of systematics in the biodiversity crisis. In N. Eldridge (ed.), *Systematics, Ecology, and the Biodiversity Crisis,* pp. 109–120. Columbia University Press, New York. [3]

Stiassny, M. L. J. 1996. An overview of freshwater biodiversity: with some lessons from African fishes. *Fisheries* 21(9):7–13. [5]

Stiassny, M. L. J. 1997. The medium is the message: Freshwater biodiversity in peril. In J. Cracraft and F. Grifo (eds.), *The Living Planet in Crisis.* Columbia University Press, New York. In press. [5]

Stiassny, M. L. J. and M. C. C. DePinna. 1994. Basal taxa and the role of cladistic patterns in the evaluation of conservation priorities: A view from freshwater. In P. L. Forey, C. J. Humphries, and R. I. Vane-Wright (eds.), *Systematics and Conservation Evaluation*, pp. 235–249. Systematics Association Special Volume Series. Clarendon Press, Oxford. [3]

St. Louis, V. L. and J. C. Barlow. 1988. Genetic differentiation among ancestral and introduced populations of the Eurasian tree sparrow (*Passer montanus*). *Evolution* 42:266–276. [6]

Stocks, A. and G. Hartshorn. 1993. The Palcazu project: Forest management and native Yanesha communities. *Journal of Sustainable Forestry* 1(1): 111-135. [18]

Stolarski, R., R. Bojkov, L. Bishop, C. Zerefos, J. Staehelin, and J. Zawodny. 1992. Measured trends in stratospheric ozone. *Science* 256:342–349. [5]

Stone, C. P. and J. M. Scott (eds.). 1985. *Hawaii's Terrestrial Ecosystems: Preservation and Management.* Cooperative National Park Resources Study Unit, University of Hawaii, Honolulu. [12]

Stone, D. E. 1988. The Organization for Tropical Studies (OTS): A success story in graduate training and research. In F. Almeda and C. M. Pringle (eds.), *Tropical rainforest diversity and conservation,* pp. 143–87. California Academy of Sciences and Pacific Division, AAAS, San Francisco. [16]

Stork, N. E. 1988. Insect diversity: Facts, fiction and speculation. *Biol. J. Linn. Soc.* 35:321–337.

Stouffer, P. C. and R. O. Bierregaard. 1995. Effects of forest fragmentation on understory hummingbirds in Amazonian Brazil. *Conserv. Biol.* 9:1085–1094. [9]

Stroud, R. (Ed.) 1992. *Stemming the Tide of Coastal Fish Habitat Loss.* National Coalition for Marine Conservation, Leesburg, VA. 258 pp. [5]

Sturt, G. 1923. *The Wheelwright's Shop.* Cambridge University Press, Cambridge. [16]

Sturtevant, V. and J. Lange. 1995. Applegate Partnership Case Study: Group Dynamics and Community Context. Departments of Sociology and Communication, Southern Oregon State College, Ashland. [18]

Sullivan, W. M. 1995. *Work and Integrity.* HarperBusiness, New York. [17]

Sutton, A. and M. Sutton. 1972. *Yellowstone: A Century of the Wilderness Idea.* Macmillan, New York. [18]

Svendsen, E., R. Mendelsohn and A. Davis. 1993. *The Ecotourism Value of Marine Diving Areas.* Yale School of Forestry and Environmental Studies, New Haven. [18]

Swanson, C., J. J. Cech, Jr., and R. H. Piedrahita. 1996. *Mosquitofish: Biology, Culture, and Use in Mosquito Control.* Mosqito Vector Control Association of California. [8]

Sward, S. 1990. Secretary Lujan and the squirrels: Interior chief calls Endangered Species Act "too tough." *San Francisco Chronicle,* May 12. [3]

Swihart, R. K. and N. A. Slade. 1984. Road crossing in *Sigmodon hispidus* and *Microtus ochrogaster. J. Mammal.* 65:357–360. [9]

Syme, G. F., C. Seligman, S. J. Kantola, and K. M. Duncan. 1987. Evaluating a television campaign to promote petrol conservation. *Environ. Behav.* 19:444–461. [16]

Tainter, J. A. 1988. *The Collapse of Complex Societies.* Cambridge University Press, Cambridge. [19]

Talbot, L. M. and M. H. Talbot. 1963. The wildebeest in western Maasailand. *Wildl. Monogr.* 12:1–88. [8]

Tangley, L. 1988. A new era for biosphere reserves. *BioScience* 38:148–155. [18]

Tangley, L. 1988. Beyond national parks. *BioScience* 38:146–147. [10]

Taylor, C. E. and G. C. Gorman. 1975. Population genetics of a "colonising" lizard: Natural selection for allozyme morphs in *Anolis grahami*. *Heredity* 35:241–247. [6]

Taylor, P. W. 1986. *Respect for Nature. A Theory of Environmental Ethics*. Princeton University Press, Princeton, NJ. [2]

Taylor, R. D. 1993. Elephant management in Nyaminyami district, Zimbabwe: Turning a liability into an asset. *Pachyderm* 17:19–29. [18]

Tellaria, J. L. and T. Santos. 1995. Effects of forest fragmentation on a guild of wintering passerines: The role of habitat selection. *Conserv. Biol.* 71:61–67. [9]

Temple, S. A. 1986. Predicting impacts of habitat fragmentation on forest birds: A comparison of two models. In J. Verner, M. L. Morrison and C. J. Ralph (eds.), *Wildlife 2000: Modeling Habitat Relationships of Terrestrial Vertebrates*, pp. 301–304. University of Wisconsin Press, Madison. [9]

Temple, S. A. and J. R. Cary. 1988. Modeling dynamics of habitat-interior bird populations in fragmented landscapes. *Conserv. Biol.* 2:340–347. [9]

Templeton, A. R. 1989. The meaning of species and speciation: A genetic perspective. In D. Otte and J. A. Endler (eds.), *Speciation and Its Consequences*, pp. 3–27. Sinauer Associates, Sunderland, MA. [3]

Templeton, A. R. 1990. The role of genetics in captive breeding and reintroduction for species conservation. *Endangered Species Update* 8:14–17. [11]

Templeton, A. R. 1994. Translocation in conservation. In R. C. Szaro and D. W. Johnston (eds.), *Biodiversity in Managed Landscapes: Theory and Practice*, pp. 315–325. Oxford University Press, New York. [6]

Templeton, A. R. and B. Read. 1984. Factors eliminating inbreeding depression in a captive herd of Speke's gazelle (*Gazella spekei*). *Zoo Biol.* 3:177–199. [6]

Tenner, E. 1996. *Why Things Bite Back: Technology and the Revenge of Unintended Consequences*. Knopf, New York. [18]

Terborgh, J. 1974. Preservation of natural diversity: The problem of extinction prone species. *BioScience* 24:715–722. [9]

Terborgh, J. 1986. Keystone plant resources in the tropical forest. In M. E. Soulé (ed.), *Conservation Biology: The Science of Scarcity and Diversity*, pp. 330–344. Sinauer Associates, Sunderland, MA. [5,8]

Terborgh, J. 1988. The big things that run the world: A sequel to E. O. Wilson. *Conserv. Biol.* 2:402–403. [5]

Terborgh, J. and B. Winter. 1980. Some causes of extinction. In M. E. Soulé and B. A. Wilcox (eds.), *Conservation Biology: An Evolutionary-Ecological Perspective*, pp. 119–134. Sinauer Associates, Sunderland, MA. [5,9]

Terborgh, J. and B. Winter. 1983. A method for siting parks and reserves with special reference to Columbia and Ecuador. *Biol. Conserv.* 27:45–58. [9]

The Conservation Foundation. 1988. *Protecting America's Wetlands: An Action Agenda*. The Conservation Foundation, Washington, D.C. [14]

Theobald, D. M. 1995. Landscape morphology and effects of mountain development in Colorado: A multi-scale analysis. Ph.D. dissertation, University of Colorado, Boulder. [9]

Thomas, C. D. 1990. What do real population dynamics tell us about minimum viable population sizes? *Conserv. Biol.* 4:324–327. [7]

Thomas, J. A. and M. G. Morris. 1995. Rates and patterns of extinction among British invertebrates. In J. H. Lawton and R. M. May (eds.), *Extinction Rates*, pp. 111–130. Oxford University Press, New York. [5]

Thomas, J. W. and J. Verner. 1992. Accomodation with socio-economic factors under the Endangered Species Act—More than meets the eye. *Trans. 57th North American Wildlife Natural Resources Conference*. 57:627–641. [13]

Thomas, J. W., E. D. Forsman, J. B. Lint, E. C. Meslow, B. R. Noon and J. Verner. 1990. *A Conservation Strategy for the Northern Spotted Owl*. U.S. Government Printing Office, Washington D.C. 1990-791-171/20026. [7,13]

Thompson, J. R. 1992. *Prairies, Forests, and Wetlands*. University of Iowa Press, Iowa City. [14]

Thornhill, N.W. 1993. (ed.). *The Natural History of Inbreeding and Outbreeding. Theoretical and Empirical Perspectives*. The University of Chicago Press, Chicago. [6]

Thorson, G. 1957. Bottom communities (sublittoral and shallow shelf). In H. Ladd (ed.), *Treatise of Marine Ecology and Paleoecology*. Geological Society of America Memoir 67. [4]

Tilman, D. 1982. *Resource Competition and Community Structure*. Princeton University Press, Princeton, NJ. [4]

Tilman, D. 1985. The resource ratio hypothesis of succession. *Am. Nat.* 125:827–852. [4]

Tilman, D. and J. A. Downing. 1994. Biodiversity and stability in grasslands. *Nature* 367:363–365. [15]

Tobias, D. and R. Mendelsohn. 1991. Valuing Ecotourism in a Tropical Rain-Forest Reserve. *Ambio* 20, 91–93. [18]

Todd, J. 1988. Solar aquatic wastewater treatment. *BioCycle* 29:38–40. [16]

Todd, J. 1991. Ecological engineering, living machines and the visionary landscape. In C. Etnier and B. Guterstam (eds.), *Ecological Engineering for Wastewater Treatment*, pp. 335–343. Bokskogen, Gothenburg, Sweden. [16]

Toft, C. A. 1991. An ecological perspective: The population and community consequences of parasitism. In C. A. Toft, A. Aeschilmann, and L. Bolis (eds.), *Parasite–Host Associations: Coexistence or Conflict?* pp. 319–343. Oxford University Press, Oxford. [8]

Toth, L. A. 1995. Principles and guidelines for restoration of river/floodplain ecosystems—Kissimmee River, Florida. In J. Cairns, Jr. (ed.), *Rehabilitating Damaged Ecosystems*, 2nd ed., pp. 49–73. CRC Press, Boca Raton, FL. [14]

Toth, L. A. 1995. Conceptual evaluation of factors potentially affecting restoration of habitat structure within the channelized Kissimmee River ecosystem. *Restor. Ecol.* 3:160–180. [14]

Traverse, A. 1988. Plant evolution dances to a different beat: Plant and animal evolutionary mechanisms compared. *Hist. Biol.* 1:277–301. [5]

Travis, J. 1994. Calibrating our expectations in studying amphibian populations. *Herpetologica* 50(1):104–108. [5]

Trexler, J. C. 1995. Restoration of the Kissimmee River: A conceptual model of past and present fish communities and its consequences for evaluating restoration success. *Restor. Ecol.* 3:195–210. [14]

Trexler, M. C. and L. H. Kosloff. 1991. International implementation: The longest arm of the law? In K. A. Kohm (ed.), *Balancing on the Brink of Extinction: The Endangered Species Act and Lessons for the Future*, pp. 114–133. Island Press, Washington, D.C. [3]

Triggs, S. J., R. G. Powlesland, and C. H. Daugherty. 1989. Genetic variation and conservation of kakapo (*Strigops habroptilus*: Psittaciformes). *Conserv. Biol.* 3:92–96. [6]

Truett, J. 1996. Bison and elk in the American Southwest: In search of the pristine. *Environ. Mgmt.* 20:195–206. [12]

Trüper, H. G. 1992. Prokaryotes: an overview with respect to biodiversity and environmental importance. *Biodiv. Conserv.* 1: 227–236. [4]

Tsonis, A.A. 1996. Widespread increase in low-frequency variability of precipitation over the past century. *Nature* 382: 700-702 [11]

Turgeon, D. D. and nine others. 1988. *Common and Scientific Names of Aquatic Invertebrates from the United States and Canada: Mollusks*. American Fisheries Society Special Publication 16. [3]

Turnbull, C. 1972. *The Mountain People*. Simon & Schuster, New York. [10]

Turner, I. M. 1996. Species loss in fragments of tropical rain forest: a review of the evidence. *J. Applied Ecol.* 33:200-209. [5]

Turner, I. M. and R. T. Corlett. 1996. The conservation value of small, isolated fragments of lowland tropical rain forest. *Trends Ecol. Evol.* 11:330–333. [9]

Turner, I. M., K. S. Chua, J. S. Y. Ong, B. C. Soong, and H. T. W. Tan. 1996. A century of plant species loss from an isolated fragment of lowland tropical rain forest. *Conserv. Biol.* 10:1229–1244. [9]

Turner, J. R. G. 1971. Two thousand generations of hybridisation in a *Heliconius* butterfly. *Evolution* 25:471–482. [3]

Turner, M. G. 1989. Landscape ecology: The effect of pattern on process. *Annu. Rev. Ecol. Syst.* 20:171–197. [7,9]

Turner, M. G. and R. H. Gardner, (eds.), 1991. *Quantitative Methods in Landscape Ecology*. Springer-Verlag, New York. [10]

Turner, M. G. and C. L. Ruscher. 1988. Changes in landscape patterns in Georgia, USA. *Landscape Ecol.* 1:241–251. [9]

Turner, M. G., V. H. Dale and R. H. Gardner. 1989. Predicting across scales: theory development and testing. *Landscape Ecol.* 3:245–252. [7]

Turner, M. G., Y. Wu, S. M. Pearson, W. H. Romme and L. L. Wallace. 1992. Landscape-level interactions among ungulates, vegetation, and large-scale fires in northern Yellowstone National Park. In G. E. Plumb and H. J. Harlow (eds.), *University of Wyoming National Park Service Research Center, 16th Annual Report,* pp. 206–211. Laramie, WY. [12]

Turner, M. G., Y. Wu, L. L. Wallace, W. H. Romme, and V. H. Brenkert. 1994. Simulating winter interactions among ungulates, vegetation, and fire in northern Yellowstone Park. *Ecol. Appl.* 4:472–496.

Turner, M. G., G. J. Arthaud, R. T. Engstrom, S. J. Hejl, and J. Liu. 1995. Usefulness of spatially explicit population models in land management. *Ecol. Appl.* 5:12–16. [7]

Turner, M. G., W. W. Hargrove, R. H. Gardner and W. H. Romme. Effects of fire on landscape heterogeneity in Yellowstone National Park, Wyoming. Unpublished manuscript. [7]

Twum-Barima, K. 1981. Forests of Ghana—A diminishing asset. In V. H. Sutlive, N. Altshuler, and M. D. Zamura (eds.), *Where Have All the Flowers Gone? Deforestation in the Third World.* Studies in Third World Societies, Pub. no. 13. College of William & Mary, Williamsburg, Virginia. [18]

Tyler, M. J. 1991. Declining amphibian populations—a global phenomenon? An Australian perspective. *Alytes* 9(2):43–50. [5]

Tyser, R. W. and C. A. Worley. 1992. Alien flora in grasslands adjacent to road and trail corridors in Glacier National Park (U.S.A.). *Conserv. Biol.* 6:253–262. [9]

U.S. Congress Office of Technology Assessment. 1993. *Harmful Non-Indigenous Species in the United States.* OTA-F-565. U.S. Government Printing Office, Washington, D.C. [17]

U.S. Department of the Interior. 1990. *Endangered and Threatened Species Recovery Programs.* U.S. Fish and Wildlife Service, Washington, D.C. [3]

U.S. Department of the Interior. 1992. *Recovery Plan for the Northern Spotted Owl.* Unpublished report. [13]

U.S. Fish and Wildlife Service. 1988. *Black-Footed Ferret Recovery Plan.* U.S. Fish and Wildlife Service, Denver, CO. [13]

U.S. Fish and Wildlife Service. 1988. *Endangered Species Act of 1973. As Amended Through the 100th Congress.* U.S. Department of the Interior, Washington, D.C. [3]

U.S. Fish and Wildlife Service. 1990. Experimental release of captive-raised black-footed ferrets—study plan. National Biological Service, Midcontinent Ecological Science Center, Ft. Collins, CO. 44 pages. [13]

U.S. Fish and Wildlife Service. 1992. National Survey of Fishing, Hunting, and Wildlife-Associated Recreation. U.S. Department of the Interior, Washington D.C. [18]

U.S. Fish and Wildlife Service. 1994. An Ecosystem Approach to Fish and Wildlife Conservation. Internal Working Draft, December 1994, US Fish and Wildlife Service, Washington, DC. [11]

U.S. Fish and Wildlife Service. 1994. *Whooping Crane Recovery Plan.* U.S. Fish and Wildlife Service, Albuquerque, NM. [13]

U.S. House of Representatives. 1973. Report no. 412, 93rd Congress, 1st Session. [3]

Uhl, C. and R. Buschbacher. 1985. A disturbing synergism between cattle ranch burning practices and selective tree harvesting in Eastern Amazon. *Biotropica* 17:265–268. [5]

Uhl, C., K. Clark, N. Dezzeo and P. Maquirino. 1988. Vegetation dynamics in Amazonian treefall gaps. *Ecology* 69:751–763. [18]

UNESCO. 1987. Makokou, Gabon, a research station in tropical forest ecology: Overview and publications (1962–1986). UNESCO, Paris. [18]

USDA Forest Service. 1982a. Golden Trout Wilderness Management Plan, Inyo and Sequoia National Forests. USDA Forest Service, San Francisco. [12]

USDA Forest Service. 1982b. Golden Trout Habitat and Wilderness Restoration on the Kern Plateau, Inyo National Forest. USDA Forest Service, San Francisco. [12]

USDI BLM. 1994a. Ecosystem management in the BLM: From concept to commitment. Washington, D.C. [11]

USDI BLM. 1994b. Blueprint for the future. Washington, D.C. [11]

Valverde, J. A. 1960. Vertebrados de las marismas del Guadalquivir (introducción a su estudio ecológico). *Arch. Inst. Aclim. Almería (C.S.I.C.),* N° 9:1–168. [13]

Valverde, J. A. 1967. *Estructura de una comunidad de vertebrados terrestres.* Monografías de Ciencia Moderna N/76. CSIC, Madrid. [13]

van Balen, B. and V. H. Gepak. 1994. The captive breeding and conservation programme of the Bali starling (*Leucopsar rothschildi*). In P. J. S. Olney, G. M. Mace, and A. T. C. Feistner (eds.), *Creative Conservation: Interactive Management of Wild and Captive Animals,* pp. 319–343. Chapman & Hall, London. [8]

van Creveld, M. 1991. *The Transformation of War.* The Free Press, New York. [19]

Van Den Avyle, M. J. and J. W. Evans. 1990. Temperature selection by striped bass in a Gulf of Mexico coastal river system. *N. Am. J. Fish. Mgmt.* 10:58–66. [9]

Van Devender, T. R. 1986. Climatic cadences and the composition of Chihuahuan Desert communities: The late Pleistocene packrat midden record. In J. Diamond and T. J. Case (eds.), *Community Ecology,* pp. 285–299. Harper & Row, New York. [8]

Van Dorp, D. and P. F. M. Opdam. 1987. Effects of patch size, isolation and regional abundance on forest bird communities. *Landscape Ecol.* 1:59–73. [9]

Van Riper, C. III and J. M. Scott. 1979. Observations on distribution, diet, and breeding of the Hawaiian thrush. *Condor* 81:65–71. [8]

Van Valen, L. 1976. Ecological species, multispecies, and oaks. *Taxon* 25:233–239. [3]

Vane-Wright, R. I., C. J. Humphries and P. H. Williams. 1991. What to protect? Systematics and the agony of choice. *Biol. Conserv.* 55:235–254. [3,6]

Vargas, A. 1994. Ontogeny of the black-footed ferret (*Mustela nigripes*) and effects of captive upbringing on predatory behavior and post release survival for reintroduction. Ph.D. dissertation, University of Wyoming, Laramie. [13]

Vaughan, C. 1981. Parque Nacional Corcovado: Plan de Manejo y Desarrollo. Editorial of the Universidad Nacional, Costa Rica. [13]

Vaughan, C. and L. Flormoe. 1995. Costa Rica's national system of conservation areas: Linking local human community sustainability with Neotropical biodiversity conservation. In D. Saunders, J. Craig, and L. Mattiske (eds.), *Nature Conservation: The Role of Networks,* pp. 467–473. Surrey Press, Sydney, Australia. [13]

Veit, R. R. and M. A. Lewis. 1996. Dispersal, population growth, and the Allee effect: Dynamics of the house finch invasion of eastern North America. *Am. Nat.* 148: 255–274. [7]

Veitayaki, J., V. Ram-Bidesi, E. Matthews, L. Gibson, and V. Vuki. 1995. Overview of destructive fishing practices in the Pacific Islands Region. South Pacific Regional Environment Programme, Apia, Western Samoa. 32 pp. [5]

Verner, J., K. S. McKelvey, B. R. Noon, R. J. Gutierrez, G. I. Gould, Jr. and T. W. Beck. 1992. *The California Spotted Owl: A Technical Assessment of Its Current Status.* U.S. Forest Service General Technical Report PSW-GTR-133. Pacific Southwest Research Station, Albany, CA. [7,13]

Vertucci, F. A. and P. S. Corn. 1996. Evaluation of episodic acidification and amphibian declines in the Rocky Mountains. *Ecol. Appl.* 6(2):449–457. [5]

Vickerman, K. 1992. The diversity and ecological significance of Protozoa. *Biodiv. Conserv.* 1:334–341. [4]

Vickery, P. D., M. L. Hunter, and S. M. Melvin. 1994. Effects of habitat area on the distribution of grassland birds in Maine. *Conserv. Biol.* 10:1087–1097. [9]

Viederman, S. 1991. Regulating technology for a sustainable future. *ISEE* (International Society for Ecological Economics) *Newsletter,* November. [16]

Viederman, S. 1992. Public Policy: Challenge to Ecological Economics. Unpublished manuscript. [18]

Viederman, S. 1996. Sustainable corporations: Isn't that an oxymoron? *Tomorrow: Global Environment Business,* VI, 4, July–August. [16]

Vietmeyer, N. 1986a. Exotic edibles are altering America's diet and agriculture. *Smithsonian* 16(9):34–43. [2]

Vietmeyer, N. 1986b. Lesser-known plants of potential use in agriculture and forestry. *Science* 232:1379–1384. [2]

Villard, M.-A., P. R. Martin, and C. G. Drummond. 1993. Habitat fragmentation and pairing success in the Ovenbird (*Seiurus aurocapillus*). *Auk* 110:759–768. [9]

Vitousek, P. M. and L. R. Walker. 1989. Biological invasion by *Myrica faya* in Hawaii: Plant demography, nitrogen fixation, ecosystem effects. *Ecol. Monogr.* 59:247–265. [8]

Vitousek, P. M., P. R. Ehrlich, A. H. Ehrlich and P. A. Matson. 1986. Human appropriation of the products of photosynthesis. *BioScience* 36:368–373. [19]

Vitt, L. J., J. P. Caldwell, H. M. Wilbur and D. C. Smith. 1990. Amphibians as harbingers of decay. *BioScience* 40: 418. [12]

Vogel, W. O. 1989. Response of deer to density and distribution of housing in Montana. *Wildl. Soc. Bull.* 17:406–413. [9]

Vogler, A. P. and R. DeSalle. 1994. Diagnosing units of conservation management. *Conserv. Biol.* 8:354–363. [6]

Vogt, K. and J. Gordon. 1996. *Ecosystems: Balancing Science and Management.* Springer-Verlag, New York. [3]

von Droste, B. 1988. The role of biosphere reserves at a time of increasing globalization. pp. 89–93 In V. Martin (ed.), For the Conservation of the Earth. Fulcrum, Golden, CO. [2]

von Humboldt, A. 1806. *The Physiognomy of Plants.* English ed., London, 1849. [4]

Vrijenhoek, R. C. 1989a. Genotypic diversity and coexistence among sexual and clonal lineages of *Poeciliopsis.* In D. Otte and J. A. Endler (eds.), *Speciation and Its Consequences,* pp. 386–400. Sinauer Associates, Sunderland, MA. [6]

Vrijenhoek, R. C. 1989b. Population genetics and conservation. In M. Pearl and D. Western (eds.), *Conservation for the Twenty-First Century,* pp. 89–98. Oxford University Press, New York. [6]

Vrijenhoek, R. C., M. E. Douglas and G. K. Meffe. 1985. Conservation genetics of endangered fish populations in Arizona. *Science* 229:400–402. [6]

Wagner, F. H. 1989. American wildlife management at the crossroads. *Wild. Soc. Bull.* 17:354–360. [11]

Wagner, F. H. and C. E. Kay. 1993. "Natural" or "healthy" ecosystems: Are U.S. national parks providing them? In M. J. McDonnell and S. T. A. Pickett (eds.), *Humans as Components of Ecosystems: The Ecology of Subtle Human Effects and Populated Areas,* pp. 257–270. Springer-Verlag, New York. [10]

Wake, D. B. and H. J. Morowitz. 1991. Declining amphibian populations—a global phenomenon? *Alytes* 9:33–42. [5]

Waldman, J. R. 1995. Sturgeons and paddlefishes: A convergence of biology, politics, and greed. *Fisheries* 20(9):20–21, 49. [5]

Wali, M. K. (ed.). 1979. *Ecology and Coal Resource Development.* Vols. 1 and 2. Pergamon Press, New York. [14]

Walker, B. H. 1992. Biological diversity and ecological redundancy. *Conserv. Biol.* 6:18–23.

Wallace, A. R. 1863. On the physical geology of the Malay archipelago. *J. R. Geogr. Soc.* 33:217–234. [2]

Wallace, A. R. 1878. *Tropical Nature and Other Essays.* Macmillan, London. [4]

Wallin, J. E. 1989. Bluehead chub (*Nocomis leptocephalus*) nests used by yellow fin shiners (*Notropis lutipinnis*). *Copeia* 1989 (4):1077–1080. [8]

Walters, C. J. 1986. *Adaptive Management of Renewable Resources.* McGraw Hill, New York. [12]

Walters, C. J. and L. H. Gunderson. 1994. Screening water policy alternatives for ecological restoration in the Everglades. In S. M. Davis and J. C. Ogden (eds.), *Everglades, The Ecosystem and its Restoration.* St. Lucie Press, Delray Florida. [13]

Walters, C. J., L. H. Gunderson, and C. S. Holling. 1992. Experimental policies for water management in the Everglades. *Ecol. Appl.* [13]

Wann, D. 1990. *Biologic: Environmental Protection by Design.* Johnson, Boulder, CO. [16]

Wann, D. 1996. *Deep Design: Pathways to a Livable Future.* Island Press, Washington, D.C. [19]

Wantrup, S. C. V. 1952. *Resource Conservation: Economics and Policies.* University of California Press, Berkeley, CA. [15]

Waples, R. S. 1991. Definition of "species" under the Endangered Species Act: Application to Pacific salmon. NOAA Technical Memorandum NMFS F/NWC-194. National Marine Fisheries Service, Seattle, WA. [3,6]

Ward, R.H., D.O.F. Skibinski, and M. Woodwark. 1992. Protein heterozygosity, protein structure, and taxonomic differentiation. *Evol. Biol.* 26:73-159. [6]

Warnock, G. J. 1971. *The Object of Morality.* Methuen, London. [2]

Warren, R. J., M. J. Conroy, W. E. James, L. A. Baker and D. R. Diefenbach. 1990. Reintroduction of bobcats on Cumberland Island, Georgia: A biopolitical lesson. *Trans. N. Am. Wild. and Nat. Res. Conf.* 55:580–589. [12]

Waterman, S. 1996. The great eel rush. *National Fisherman* 77, August, 16–17. [5]

Watt, A. S. 1947. Pattern and process in the plant community. *J. Ecol.* 35:12–22. [9]

Wayne, R. K., N. Lehman, D. Girman, P. J. P. Gogan, D. A. Gilbert, K. Hansen, R. O. Peterson, U. S. Seal, A. Eisenhawer, L. D. Mech, and R. J. Krumenaker. 1991. Conservation genetics of the endangered Isle Royale gray wolf. *Conserv. Biol.* 5:41–51. [6]

Weber, A. W. 1987. Socioecological factors in the conservation of afromontane forest reserves. In J. S. Marsh and R. A. Mittermeier (eds.), *Primate Conservation in Tropical Rain Forest,* pp. 205–229. Alan R. Liss, New York. [18]

Weber, P. 1993. Abandoned Seas: Reversing the Decline of the Oceans. Worldwatch Institute, Washington D.C. 66 pp. [5]

Weber, P. 1994. Net Loss: Fish, Jobs, and the Marine Environment. Worldwatch Institute, Washington, D.C. 76 pp. [5]

Weins, J. A. 1977. On competition and variable environments. *Am. Sci.* 65:590–597. [4]

Weiss, E. B. 1989. *In Fairness to Future Generations: International Law, Common Patrimony, and Intergenerational Equity.* Transnational Publishers, Ardsley-on-Hudson, NY. [15]

Weller, M. W. 1995. Use of two waterbed guilds as evaluation tools for the Kissimmee River restoration. *Restor. Ecol.* 3:211–224. [14]

Wennergren, U., M. Ruckelshaus, and P. Kareiva. 1995. The promise and limitations of spatial models in conservation biology. *Oikos* 74:349–356. [7]

Werner, E. E., G. G. Mittlebach, D. J. Hall and J. F. Gilliam. 1983. Experimental tests of optimal habitat use in fish: The role of relative habitat profitability. *Ecology* 64:1525–1539. [7]

West, D. C., H. H. Shugart and D. B. Botkin (eds.). 1981. *Forest Succession: Concept and Application.* Springer-Verlag, New York. [14]

West, N. E. 1983. Western intermountain sagebrush steppe. In N. E. West (ed.), *Ecosystems of the World,* Vol. 5. pp. 351–374. Elsevier, Amsterdam. [14]

Western, D. 1989a. Overview. In D. Western and M. C. Pearl (eds.), *Conservation for the Twenty-First Century,* pp. xi–xv. Oxford University Press, New York. [12]

Western, D. 1989b. Why manage nature? In D. Western and M. C. Pearl (eds.), *Conservation for the Twenty-First Century,* pp. 133–137. Oxford University Press, New York. [10]

Western, D. and W. R. Henry. 1979. Economics and conservation in Third World National parks. *BioScience* 29:414–418. [18]

Western, D. and M. C. Pearl (eds.). 1989. *Conservation for the Twenty-First Century.* Oxford University Press, New York. [5]

Western, D. and R. M. Wright (eds). 1994. *Natural Connections: Perspectives in Community-Based Conservation.* Island Press, Washington, D.C. [10]

Westman, W. E. 1990. Managing for biodiversity. *BioScience* 40:26–33. [12]

Westoby, M., K. French, L. Hughes, B. Rice and L. Rodgerson. 1991. Why do more plant species use ants for dispersal on infertile compared with fertile soils? *Aust. J. Ecol.* 16:445–455. [4]

Westrum, R. 1994. An organizational perspective: designing recovery teams from the inside out. In T. W. Clark, R. P. Reading, and A. L. Clarke (eds.), *Endangered Species Recovery. Finding the Lessons, Improving the Process,* pp. 327-349. Island Press, Washington, D.C. [11]

Weygoldt, P. 1989. Changes in the composition of mountain stream frog communities in the Atlantic Mountains of Brazil: Frogs as indicators of environmental deteriorations? *Stud. Neotrop. Fauna Environ.* 243(4):249–255. [5]

Wheelwright, N. T. 1983. Fruits and the ecology of resplendent quetzals. *Auk* 100: 286–301. [9]

Whitcomb, R. F., C. S. Robbins, J. F. Lynch, B. L. Whitcomb, M. K. Klimkiewicz and D. Bystrak. 1981. Effects of forest fragmentation on avifauna of the eastern deciduous forest. In R. L. Burgess and D. M. Sharpe (eds.), *Forest Island Dynamics in Man-Dominated Landscapes,* pp. 125–213. Springer-Verlag, New York. [9,10]

White, L. W. 1967. The historical roots of our ecologic crisis. *Science* 155:1203–1207. [2]

White, M. A. and D. J. Mladenoff. 1994. Old-growth forest landscape transitions from pre-European settlement to present. *Landscape Ecol.* 9:191–205. [9]

White, P. S. and S. T. A. Pickett. 1985. Natural disturbance and patch dynamics: an introduction. In S. T. A. Pickett and P. S. White (eds.), *The Ecology of Natural Disturbance and Patch Dynamics,* pp. 3–13. Academic Press, Orlando, FL. [10]

White, S. K. (ed.). 1995. *The Cambridge Companion to Habermas.* Cambridge University Press, New York. [17]

Whitmore, T. C. 1978. Gaps in the forest canopy. In P. B. Tomlinson and M. H. Zimmermann (eds.), *Tropical Trees as Living Systems,* pp. 639–655. Cambridge University Press, London. [18]

Whittaker, R. H. 1956. Vegetation of the Great Smoky Mountains. *Ecol. Monogr.* 26:1–80. [9]

Whittaker, R. H. 1970. *Communities and Ecosystems.* Macmillan, New York. [4]

Wiens, J. A. 1977. On competition and variable environments. *Am. Sci.* 65:590–597. [4]

Wiens, J. A. 1989. *The Ecology of Bird Communities.* Vol. 2. *Processes and Variations.* Cambridge University Press, New York. [9]

Wilcove, D. S. 1987. From fragmentation to extinction. *Nat. Areas J.* 7:23–29. [5]

Wilcove, D. S., C. H. McLellan and A. P. Dobson. 1986. Habitat fragmentation in the temperate zone. In M. E. Soulé (ed.), *Conservation Biology: The Science of Scarcity and Diversity,* pp. 237–256. Sinauer Associates, Sunderland MA. [9,10,12]

Wilcove, D. S., M. McMillan and K. C. Winston. 1993. What exactly is an endangered species? An analysis of the U.S. Endangered Species list: 1985–1991. *Conserv. Biol.* 7:87–93. [3]

Wilcox, B. A. 1980. Insular ecology and conservation. In M. E. Soulé and B. A. Wilcox (eds.), *Conservation Biology: An Ecological-Evolutionary Perspective,* pp. 95–117. Sinauer Associates, Sunderland, MA. [9]

Wilcox, B. A. and D. D. Murphy. 1985. Conservation strategy: The effects of fragmentation on extinction. *Am. Nat.* 125:879–887. [9,10]

Wildt, D. E., M. Bush, K. L. Goodrowe, C. Packer, A. E. Pusey, J. L. Brown, P. Joslin, and S. J. O'Brien. 1987. Reproductive and genetic consequences of founding isolated lion populations. *Nature* 329:328–331. [6]

Wiley, E. O. 1978. The evolutionary species concept reconsidered. *Syst. Zool* 27:17–26. [3]

Wilkinson, C. F. 1992. *Crossing the Next Meridian: Land, Water, and the Future of the West.* Island Press, Washington, D.C. [12]

Wille, C. 1991. Central America: Biodiversity at stake. In C. L. Cardieux (ed.), *Wildlife Extinction,* pp. 174–182. Stone Wall Press, Washington, D.C. [18]

Williams, C. B. 1943. Area and number of species. *Nature* 152:264–267. [9]

Williams, E. S., E. T. Thorne, M. J. G. Appel and D. W. Belitsky. 1988. Canine distemper in black-footed ferrets (*Mustela nigripes*) from Wyoming. *J. Wildl. Dis.* 24:385–398. [13]

Williams, G. C. 1966. *Adaptation and Natural Selection.* Princeton University Press, Princeton, NJ. [3]

Williams, J. D., M. L. Warren, K. S. Cummings, J. L. Harris and R.J. Neves. 1993. Conservation status of freshwater mussels of the United States and Canada. *Fisheries* 18(9):6–22. [3]

Williams, J. E. and J. N. Rinne. 1992. Biodiversity management on multiple-use federal lands: an opportunity whose time has come. *Fisheries* 17(3):4–5. [12]

Williams, J. E. and C. D. Williams. 1996. An ecosystem-based approach to management of salmon and steelhead habitat. Symposium on Pacific salmon and their ecosystems, Seattle, WA. In press. [11]

Williams, J. E., J. E. Johnson, D. A. Hendrickson, S. Contraras-Balderas, J. D. Williams, M. Navarro-Mendoza, D. E. McAllister and J. E. Deacon. 1989. Fishes of North America, endangered, threatened, or of special concern, 1989. *Fisheries* 14(6):2–38. [5]

Williams, P. H., C. J. Humphries and R. I. Vane-Wright. 1991. Measuring biodiversity: Taxonomic relatedness for conservation priorities. *Aust. Syst. Bot.* 4:665–679. [3]

Williamson, M. 1981. *Island Populations.* Oxford University Press, New York. [5]

Willis, C. K., R. M. Cowling, and A. T. Lombard. 1996. Patterns of endemism in the limestone flora of South African lowland fynbos. *Biodiv. Conserv.* 5:55–74. [4]

Willis, E. O. 1974. Populations and local extinctions of birds on Barro Colorado Island, Panama. *Ecol. Monogr.* 44:153–169. [9]

Wilson, E. O. 1971. *The Insect Societies.* Harvard University Press, Cambridge, MA. [5]

Wilson, E. O. 1984. *Biophilia.* Harvard University Press, Cambridge, MA. [1,2,10]

Wilson, E. O. 1985a. The biological diversity crisis. *BioScience* 35: 700–706. [2,5]

Wilson, E. O. 1985b. Time to revive systematics. *Science* 230:1227. [3,6]

Wilson, E. O. 1987. The little things that run the world (the importance and conservation of invertebrates). *Conserv. Biol.* 1:344–346. [3,8]

Wilson, E. O. 1988a. The current state of biological diversity. In E. O. Wilson and F. M. Peter (eds.), *Biodiversity,* pp. 3–18. National Academy Press, Washington, D.C. [3]

Wilson, E. O. 1988b. Conservation: The next hundred years. In D. Western and M. C. Pearl (eds.), *Conservation for the Twenty-First Century,* pp. 3–7. Oxford University Press, New York. [5]

Wilson, E. O. 1989. Threats to biodiversity. *Sci. Am.* 261:108–117. [5]

Wilson, E. O. 1992. *The Diversity of Life.* Belknap Press of Harvard University Press, Cambridge, MA. [3,4,5]

Wilson, E. O. 1994. *Naturalist.* Island Press, Washington, D.C. [16]

Wilson, E. O. and W. H. Bossert 1971. *A Primer of Population Biology.* Sinauer Associates, Sunderland, MA. [6]

Wilson, E. O. and F. M. Peter (eds.). 1988. *Biodiversity.* National Academy Press, Washington, D.C. [5]

Wilson, E. O. and E. O. Willis. 1975. Applied biogeography. In M. L. Cody and J. M. Diamond (eds.), *Ecology and Evolution of Communities,* pp. 522–534. Belknap Press of Harvard University Press, Cambridge, MA. [9]

Wissinger, S. A. and H. H. Whiteman. 1992. Fluctuation in a Rocky Mountain population of salamanders: Anthropogenic acidification or natural variation. *J. Herpetol.* 26(4):377–391. [5]

Witt, S. C. 1985. *Briefbook: Biotechnology and Genetic Diversity.* CSI, San Francisco. [5]

Wolfe, S. H., J. A. Reidenauer and D. B. Means. 1988. *An Ecological Characterization of the Florida Panhandle.* Biological Report 88(12). U.S. Fish and Wildlife Service, National Wetlands Research Center, Slidell, LA. [9]

Wondolleck, J. and S. Yaffee. 1994. Building Bridges Across Agency Boundaries: In Search of Excellence in the U.S. Forest Service. U.S.D.A. Forest Service. [10,18]

Wood, C. A. 1994. Ecosystem management: Achieving the new land ethic. *Renewable Res. J.* 12(1):6–11. [11]

Wood, S. L. (ed.). 1986. *The Black-footed Ferret.* Great Basin Naturalist Memoirs no. 8. Brigham Young University, Provo, UT. [13]

Woodruff, D. S. 1989. The problems of conserving genes and species. In M. Pearl and D. Western (eds.), *Conservation for the Twenty-First Century,* pp. 76–88. Oxford University Press, New York. [6]

Woodruff, D. S. 1992. *Biodiversity: Conservation and Genetics.* Proc. 2nd Princess Chulabhorn Congress of Scientific Technology, Bangkok. [6]

Woodruff, D. S. 1993. Non-invasive genotyping of primates. *Primates* 34:333–346. [6]

Wootton, T. J. and D. A. Bell. 1992. A metapopulation model of the Peregrine Falcon in California: Viability and management strategies. *Ecol. Applic.* 2:307– 321. [7,11]

World Commission on Environment and Development. 1987. *Our Common Future.* Oxford University Press, Oxford. [18]

World Commission on Environment and Development. 1992. *Our Common Future Reconvened.* Center for Our Common Future, Geneva. [18]

World Conservation and Monitoring Centre. 1992. *Global Biodiversity: State of the Earth's Living Resources.* Chapman & Hall, London. [4]

World Development Report. 1992. *Development and the Environment.* The World Bank. Oxford University Press, New York. [19]

World Population Prospects. 1990. United Nations Population Division, New York. [19]

World Resources Institute. 1991. *World Resources Report 1991–1992: A Guide to the Global Environment.* Oxford University Press, New York. [5]

World Resources Institute. 1994. *World Resources 1994–1995: A Guide to the Global Environment.* Oxford University Press, Oxford. [19]

World Resources Institute. 1995. *World Resources 1995–1996: A Guide to the Global Environment.* Oxford University Press, New York. [18]

Worster, D. 1979. *Nature's Economy. The Roots of Ecology.* Anchor Books, New York. [2]

Wotkyns, S. 1988. "Conserving the Bladen Rainforest." *Earth Island J.,* Summer, p. 9. [15]

Wright, A. C. S., D. H. Romney, R. H. Arbuckle, and V. E. Vial. 1959. Land in British Honduras: Report of the British Honduras Land Use Survey Team. Colonial Research Publication no. 24. Her Majesty's Stationery Office, London. [15]

Wright, S. 1922. Coefficients of inbreeding and relationship. *Am. Nat.* 56:330–338. [6]

Wright, S. 1965. The interpretation of population structure by F-statistics with special regard to systems of mating. *Evolution* 38:1358–1370. [6]

Wright, S. 1969. *Evolution and the Genetics of Populations.* Vol. 2, *The Theory of Gene Frequencies.* University of Chicago Press, Chicago. [6]

Wright, S. 1978. *Evolution and the Genetics of Populations.* Vol. 3. *Variability within and among Natural Populations.* University of Chicago Press, Chicago. [6]

Wu, J. and O. L. Loucks. 1995. From balance of nature to hierarchical patch dynamics: A paradigm shift in ecology. *Q. Rev. Biol.* 70:439–466. [14]

Wyant, J. G., R. A. Meganck, and S. H. Ham. 1995. A planning and decision-making framework for ecological restoration. *Environ. Mgmt.* 19:789–796. [14]

Yaffee, S. L., A. F. Phillips, I. C. Frentz, P. W. Hardy, S. M. Maleki, and B. E. Thorpe. 1996. *Ecosystem Management in the United States.* Island Press, Washington, D.C. [3]

Yan, N. D., W. Keller, N. M. Scully, D. R. S. Lean, and P. J. Dillon. 1996. Increased UV-B penetration in a lake owing to drought-induced acidification. *Nature* 381:141–143. [5]

Yeatman, C. W., D. Kafton and G. Wilkes (eds.). 1984. *Plant Genetic Resources: A Conservation Imperative.* AAAS, Washington, D.C. [5]

Yergin, D. 1992. *The Prize.* Simon and Schuster, New York. [15]

Yoakum, J. and W. P. Dasmann. 1971. Habitat manipulation practices. In R. H. Giles, (ed.), *Wildlife Management Techniques,* pp. 173–231. The Wildlife Society, Washington, D.C. [9]

Young, R. A. 1980. The relationship between information levels and environmental approval: The wilderness issue. *J. Environ. Educ.* 11:25–30. [16]

Zabik, J. M. and J. N. Seiber. 1993. Atmospheric transport of organophosphate pesticides from California's Central Valley to the Sierra Nevada mountains. *J. Environ. Qual.* 22:80–90. [5]

Zedler, J. B. 1993. Canopy architecture of natural and planted cordgrass marshes: Selecting habitat evaluation criteria. *Ecol. Appl.* 3:123–138. [14]

Zedler, J. B. and R. Langis. 1991. Comparisons of constructed and natural salt marshes of San Diego Bay. *Rest. Mgmt. Notes* 9(1):21–25. [14]

Zouros, E. and D. W. Foltz. 1987. The use of allelic isozyme variation for the study of heterosis. In M. C. Rattazzi, J. G. Scandalics and G. S. Whitt (eds.), *Isozymes,* pp. 1–59. *Current Topics in Biological and Medical Research* 13. Alan R. Liss, New York. [6]

Index

ABOUT THE BOOK

Editor: Andrew D. Sinauer
Project Editor: Kerry L. Falvey
Copy Editor: Norma Roche
Production Manager: Christopher Small
Book Production: Maggie Haddad
Art: Precision Graphics
Book Design: Christopher Small
Cover Design: Maggie Haddad
Cover Manufacturer: Henry N. Sawyer Company, Inc.
Book Manufacturer: Courier Westford, Inc.